Your Office
PREMIUM MEDIA SITE

D1449962

Improve your grade with hands-on tools and resources!

- Master *Key Terms* to expand your vocabulary.
- Prepare for exams by taking practice quizzes in the *Online Workshop Review*.
- Download *Student Data Files* for the applications projects in each chapter.

And for even more tools, you can access the following Premium Resources using your Access Code. Register now to get the most out of *Your Office!*

- *Blue Box Videos* are brief videos that accompany each active blue box in the workshop. These videos demonstrate the steps as well as the concepts to accomplish the individual skills of each workshop.*
- *Real World Interview Videos* feature real business professionals from a variety of backgrounds discussing how they use the skills and objectives of each workshop to be successful in their careers.*

*Access code required for these premium resources

Your Access Code is:

YOMEC-JEHAD-MOSSY-URBAN-DOLBY-TRIES

Note: If there is no silver foil covering the access code, it may already have been redeemed, and therefore may no longer be valid. In that case, you can purchase online access using a major credit card or PayPal account. To do so, go to **www.pearsonhighered.com/youroffice**, select your book cover, click on "Buy Access" and follow the on-screen instructions.

To Register:

- To start you will need a valid email address and this access code.
- Go to **www.pearsonhighered.com/youroffice** and scroll to find your text book.
- Once you've selected your text, on the Home Page, click the link to access the Student Premium Content.
- Click the Register button and follow the on-screen instructions.
- After you register, you can sign in any time via the log-in area on the same screen.

System Requirements

Windows 7 Ultimate Edition; IE 8
Windows Vista Ultimate Edition SP1; IE 8
Windows XP Professional SP3; IE 7
Windows XP Professional SP3; Firefox 3.6.4
Mac OS 10.5.7; Firefox 3.6.4
Mac OS 10.6; Safari 5

Technical Support

http://247pearsoned.custhelp.com

Your Office

Microsoft® Excel® 2013

COMPREHENSIVE

Amy Kinser

HAMMERLE | KINSER | MORIARITY
NIGHTINGALE | O'KEEFE

PEARSON

Boston Columbus Indianapolis New York San Francisco Upper Saddle River
Amsterdam Cape Town Dubai London Madrid Milan Munich Paris Montréal Toronto
Delhi Mexico City São Paulo Sydney Hong Kong Seoul Singapore Taipei Tokyo

Editor in Chief: Michael Payne
Acquisitions Editor: Samantha McAfee Lewis
Product Development Manager: Laura Burgess
Editorial Project Manager: Anne Garcia
Development Editor: Nancy Lamm
Editorial Assistant: Laura Karahalis
VP Director of Digital Strategy: Paul Gentile
Director of Digital Development: Taylor Ragan
Digital Media Editor: Eric Hakanson
Digital Content Producer: Jaimie Noy
Digital Project Manager: Zach Alexander
Production Media Project Manager: John Cassar

Director of Marketing: Maggie Moylan Leen
Marketing Manager: Brad Forrester
Marketing Coordinator: Susan Osterlitz
Marketing Assistant: Darshika Vyas
Managing Editor: Camille Trentacoste
Sr. Production Project Manager/IT Procurement Lead: Natacha Moore
Senior Art Director: Jonathan Boylan
Manager, Cover Visual Research & Permissions: Karen Sanatar
Manager of Rights & Permissions: Michelle McKenna
Cover and Interior Design: Jonathan Boylan
Composition: GEX Publishing Services
Full-Service Project Management: GEX Publishing Services

Credits and acknowledgments borrowed from other sources and reproduced, with permission, in this textbook appear on appropriate page within text.

Pearson Education Ltd., London
Pearson Education Singapore, Pte. Ltd
Pearson Education, Canada, Inc.
Pearson Education–Japan
Pearson Education Australia PTY, Limited

Pearson Education North Asia Ltd., Hong Kong
Pearson Educación de Mexico, S.A. de C.V.
Pearson Education Malaysia, Pte. Ltd.
Pearson Education, Upper Saddle River, New Jersey

Library of Congress Cataloging-in-Publication Data

Kinser, Amy.
  Microsoft Excel 2013 comprehensive / Amy Kinser.
      pages cm. — (Your Office)
  Includes bibliographical references and index.
  ISBN-13: 978-0-13-314322-5
  ISBN-10: 0-13-314322-8
  1. Microsoft Excel (Computer file) 2. Business—Computer programs.
  3. Electronic spreadsheets. I. Title.
  HF5548.4.M523K566 2014
  005.54 — dc23

                                                        2013011543
                                                        10 9 8 7 6 5 4 3 2 1
                                                        ISBN-13: 978-0-13-314322-5
                                                        ISBN-10: 0-13-314322-8

Dedications

I dedicate this series to my Kinser Boyz for their unwavering love, support, and patience; to my family; to my students for inspiring me; to Sam for believing in me; and to the instructors I hope this series will inspire!

Amy Kinser

I dedicate this book to my husband, John, and my two boys, Matthew and Adam. They provide me with all the support, love, and patience I could ever ask for—thank you boys!

Patti Hammerle

For my wife, Amy, and our two boys Matt and Aidan. I cannot thank them enough for their support, love, and endless inspiration.

J. Eric Kinser

I dedicate this book to my amazing wife, April. Without her support and understanding this would not have been possible.

Brant Moriarity

To my parents, who always believed in and encouraged me. To my husband and best friend, who gave me support, patience, and love. To my brother and my hero—may you be watching from Heaven with joy in your heart.

Jennifer Nightingale

This book is a product of the unselfish support and patience of my wife and daughters, Bonnie, Kelsie, and Maggie, and of the values instilled by my parents, Paul and Carol. They are the authors—I am just a writer.

Timothy O'Keefe

About the Authors

Amy S. Kinser, Esq., Series Editor

Amy holds a B.A. degree in Chemistry with a Business minor from Indiana University, and a J.D. from the Maurer School of Law, also at Indiana University. After working as an environmental chemist, starting her own technology consulting company, and practicing intellectual property law, she has spent the past 12 years teaching technology at the Kelley School of Business in Bloomington, Indiana—#1 ranked school for undergraduate program performance in the specialty of Information Systems according to 2012 Bloomberg Businessweek. Currently, she serves as the Director of Computer Skills and Senior Lecturer at the Kelley School of Business at Indiana University.

She also loves spending time with her two sons, Aidan and J. Matthew, and her husband J. Eric.

Patti Hammerle

Patti holds a bachelor's degree in Finance and a master's degree in Business from Indiana University Kelley School of Business. She is an adjunct professor at the Kelley School of Business in Indianapolis where she teaches The Computer in Business. In addition to teaching, she owns U-Can Computer Manuals, a company that writes and publishes computer manuals primarily for libraries to teach from. She has also written and edited other computer application textbooks.

When not teaching or writing, she enjoys spending time with family, reading, and running.

J. Eric Kinser

Eric Kinser received his B.S. degree in Biology from Indiana University and his M.S. in Counseling and Education from the Indiana School of Education. He has worked in the medical field and in higher education as a technology and decision support specialist. He is currently a lecturer in the Operations and Decision Technology department at the Kelley School of Business at Indiana University.

When not teaching he enjoys experimenting with new technologies, traveling, and hiking with his family.

Brant Moriarity

Brant Moriarity earned a B.A. in Religious Studies/Philosophy and an M.S. in Information Systems at Indiana University. He is a full-time lecturer at the Indiana University Kelley School of Business where he teaches The Computer in Business. In addition to teaching, he also builds and maintains websites, databases, and several web-based information systems. He is currently researching ways to utilize mobile technologies to enhance the classroom for both students and faculty.

Dr. Jennifer Paige Nightingale

Jennifer Nightingale, assistant professor at Duquesne University, has taught Information Systems Management since 2000. Before joining Duquesne University, she spent 15 years in industry with a focus in management and training. Her research expertise is in instructional technology, using technology as a teaching tool, and the impact of instructional technologies on student learning. She has earned numerous teaching and research honors and awards, holds an Ed.D. (instructional technology) and two M.S. degrees (information systems management and education) from Duquesne University, and a B.A. from the University of Pittsburgh.

Dr. Timothy P. O'Keefe

Tim is Professor of Information Systems and Chair of the Department of Information Systems and Business Communication at the University of North Dakota. He is an Information Technology consultant, co-founder of a successful Internet services company, and has taught in higher education for 30 years. Tim is married to his high school sweetheart, Bonnie; they have two beautiful daughters, Kelsie and Maggie. His life is greatly enriched by family, cherished friends and colleagues, and his dogs. In his spare time he enjoys traveling, cooking, and archery.

Brief Contents

Contents

EXCEL MODULE 4

EXCEL MODULE 5

APPENDIX

Acknowledgments

The *Your Office* team would like to thank the following reviewers who have invested time and energy to help shape this series from the very beginning, providing us with invaluable feedback through their comments, suggestions, and constructive criticism.

We'd like to especially thank our Focus Group attendees and User Diary Reviewers:

Heather Albinger
Waukesha County Technical College

Melody Alexander
Ball State University

Mazhar Anik
Owens Community College

David Antol
Hartford Community College

Cheryl Brown
Delgado Community College

Janet Campbell
Dixie State College

Kuan Chen
Purdue Calumet

Jennifer Day
Sinclair Community College

Joseph F. Domagala
Duquesne University

Christa Fairman
Arizona Western University

Denise Farley
Sussex County Community College

Drew Foster
Miami University of Ohio

Lorie Goodgine
Tennessee Technology Center in Paris

Jane L. Hammer
Valley City State University

Kay Johnson
Community College of Rhode Island

Susumu Kasai
Salt Lake Community College

Linda Kavanaugh
Robert Morris University

Jennifer Krou
Texas State University, San Marcos

Michelle Mallon
Ohio State University

Sandra McCormack
Monroe Community College

Melissa Nemeth
Indiana University–Purdue University Indianapolis

Janet Olfert
North Dakota State University

Patsy Ann Parker
Southwestern Oklahoma State University

Cheryl Reindl-Johnson
Sinclair Community College

Jennifer Robinson
Trident Technical College

Tony Rose
Miami University of Ohio

Cindi Smatt
North Georgia College & State University

Jenny Lee Svelund
University of Utah

William VanderClock
Bentley University

Jill Weiss
Florida International University

Lin Zhao
Purdue Calumet

We'd like to thank all of our conscientious reviewers, including those who contributed to our previous editions:

Sven Aelterman
Troy University

Nitin Aggarwal
San Jose State University

Angel Alexander
Piedmont Technical College

Melody Alexander
Ball State University

Karen Allen
Community College of Rhode Island

Maureen Allen
Elon University

Wilma Andrews
Virginia Commonwealth University

Mazhar Anik
Owens Community College

David Antol
Harford Community College

Kirk Atkinson
Western Kentucky University

Barbara Baker
Indiana Wesleyan University

Kristi Berg
Minot State University

Kavuri Bharath
Old Dominion University

Ann Blackman
Parkland College

Jeanann Boyce
Montgomery College

Lynn Brooks
Tyler Junior College

Cheryl Brown
Delgado Community College West Bank Campus

Bonnie Buchanan
Central Ohio Technical College

Peggy Burrus
Red Rocks Community College

Richard Cacace
Pensacola State College

Margo Chaney
Carroll Community College

Shanan Chappell
College of the Albemarle, North Carolina

Kuan Chen
Purdue Calumet

David Childress
Ashland Community and Technical College

Keh-Wen Chuang
Purdue University, North Central

Suzanne Clayton
Drake University

Amy Clubb
Portland Community College

Bruce Collins
Davenport University

Margaret Cooksey
Tallahassee Community College

Charmayne Cullom
University of Northern Colorado

Christy Culver
Marion Technical College

Juliana Cypert
Tarrant County College

Harold Davis
Southeastern Louisiana University

Jeff Davis
Jamestown Community College

Jennifer Day
Sinclair Community College

Anna Degtyareva
Mt. San Antonio College

Beth Deinert
Southeast Community College

Kathleen DeNisco
Erie Community College

Donald Dershem
Mountain View College

Bambi Edwards
Craven Community College

Elaine Emanuel
Mt. San Antonio College

Diane Endres
Ancilla College

Nancy Evans
Indiana University – Purdue University
Indianapolis

Christa Fairman
Arizona Western College

Marni Ferner
University of North Carolina, Wilmington

Paula Fisher
Central New Mexico Community College

Linda Fried
University of Colorado, Denver

Diana Friedman
Riverside Community College

Susan Fry
Boise State University

Virginia Fullwood
Texas A&M University, Commerce

Janos Fustos
Metropolitan State College of Denver

John Fyfe
University of Illinois at Chicago

Saiid Ganjalizadeh
The Catholic University of America

Randolph Garvin
Tyler Junior College

Diane Glowacki
Tarrant County College

Jerome Gonnella
Northern Kentucky University

Connie Grimes
Morehead State University

Debbie Gross
Ohio State University

Babita Gupta
California State University, Monterey Bay

Lewis Hall
Riverside City College

Jane Hammer
Valley City State University

Marie Hartlein
Montgomery County Community College

Darren Hayes
Pace University

Paul Hayes
Eastern New Mexico University

Mary Hedberg
Johnson County Community College

Lynda Henrie
LDS Business College

Deedee Herrera
Dodge City Community College

Marilyn Hibbert
Salt Lake Community College

Jan Hime
University of Nebraska, Lincoln

Cheryl Hinds
Norfolk State University

Mary Kay Hinkson
Fox Valley Technical College

Margaret Hohly
Cerritos College

Brian Holbert
Spring Hill College

Susan Holland
Southeast Community College

Anita Hollander
University of Tennessee, Knoxville

Emily Holliday
Campbell University

Stacy Hollins
St. Louis Community College Florissant Valley

Mike Horn
State University of New York, Geneseo

Christie Hovey
Lincoln Land Community College

Margaret Hvatum
St. Louis Community College Meramec

Jean Insinga
Middlesex Community College

Jon (Sean) Jasperson
Texas A&M University

Glen Jenewein
Kaplan University

Gina Jerry
Santa Monica College

Dana Johnson
North Dakota State University

Mary Johnson
Mt. San Antonio College

Linda Johnsonius
Murray State University

Carla Jones
Middle Tennessee State University

Susan Jones
Utah State University

Nenad Jukic
Loyola University, Chicago

Sali Kaceli
Philadelphia Biblical University

Sue Kanda
Baker College of Auburn Hills

Robert Kansa
Macomb Community College

Susumu Kasai
Salt Lake Community College

Linda Kavanaugh
Robert Morris University

Debby Keen
University of Kentucky

Mike Kelly
Community College of Rhode Island

Melody Kiang
California State University, Long Beach

Lori Kielty
College of Central Florida

Richard Kirk
Pensacola State College

Dawn Konicek
Blackhawk Tech

John Kucharczuk
Centennial College

David Largent
Ball State University

Frank Lee
Fairmont State University

Luis Leon
The University of Tennessee at Chattanooga

Freda Leonard
Delgado Community College

Julie Lewis
Baker College, Allen Park

Suhong Li
Bryant Unversity

Renee Lightner
Florida State College

John Lombardi
South University

Rhonda Lucas
Spring Hill College

Adriana Lumpkin
Midland College

Lynne Lyon
Durham College

Nicole Lytle
California State University,
San Bernardino

Donna Madsen
Kirkwood Community College

Susan Maggio
Community College of Baltimore County

Kim Manning
Tallahassee Community College

Paul Martin
Harrisburg Area Community College

Cheryl Martucci
Diablo Valley College

Sebena Masline
Florida State College of Jacksonville

Sherry Massoni
Harford Community College

Lee McClain
Western Washington University

Sandra McCormack
Monroe Community College

Sue McCrory
Missouri State University

Barbara Miller
University of Notre Dame

Michael O. Moorman
Saint Leo University

Kathleen Morris
University of Alabama

Alysse Morton
Westminster College

Elobaid Muna
University of Maryland Eastern Shore

Jackie Myers
Sinclair Community College

Russell Myers
El Paso Community College

Bernie Negrete
Cerritos College

Melissa Nemeth
Indiana University–Purdue University
Indianapolis

Kathie O'Brien
North Idaho College

Michael Ogawa
University of Hawaii

Rene Pack
Arizona Western College

Patsy Parker
Southwest Oklahoma State Unversity

Laurie Patterson
University of North Carolina, Wilmington

Alicia Pearlman
Baker College

Diane Perreault
Sierra College and California State University,
Sacramento

Theresa Phinney
Texas A&M University

Vickie Pickett
Midland College

Marcia Polanis
Forsyth Technical Community College

Rose Pollard
Southeast Community College

Stephen Pomeroy
Norwich University

Leonard Presby
William Paterson University

Donna Reavis
Delta Career Education

Eris Reddoch
Pensacola State College

James Reddoch
Pensacola State College

Michael Redmond
La Salle University

Terri Rentfro
John A. Logan College

Vicki Robertson
Southwest Tennessee Community
College

Dianne Ross
University of Louisiana at Lafayette

Ann Rowlette
Liberty University

Amy Rutledge
Oakland University

Candace Ryder
Colorado State University

Joann Segovia
Winona State University

Eileen Shifflett
James Madison University

Sandeep Shiva
Old Dominion University

Robert Sindt
Johnson County Community College

Cindi Smatt
Texas A&M University

Edward Souza
Hawaii Pacific University

Nora Spencer
Fullerton College

Alicia Stonesifer
La Salle University

Cheryl Sypniewski
Macomb Community College

Arta Szathmary
Bucks County Community College

Nasser Tadayon
Southern Utah University

Asela Thomason
California State University Long
Beach

Nicole Thompson
Carteret Community College

Terri Tiedema
Southeast Community College,
Nebraska

Lewis Todd
Belhaven University

Barb Tollinger
Sinclair Community College

Allen Truell
Ball State University

Erhan Uskup
Houston Community College

Lucia Vanderpool
Baptist College of Health Sciences

Michelle Vlaich-Lee
Greenville Technical College

Barry Walker
Monroe Community College

Rosalyn Warren
Enterprise State Community College

Sonia Washington
Prince George's Community College

Eric Weinstein
Suffolk County Community College

Jill Weiss
Florida International University

Lorna Wells
Salt Lake Community College

Rosalie Westerberg
Clover Park Technical College

Clemetee Whaley
Southwest Tennessee Community
College

Kenneth Whitten
Florida State College of Jacksonville

MaryLou Wilson
Piedmont Technical College

John Windsor
University of North Texas

Kathy Winters
University of Tennessee, Chattanooga

Nancy Woolridge
Fullerton College

Jensen Zhao
Ball State University

Molly Zimmer
University of Evansville

Mary Anne Zlotow
College of DuPage

Matthew Zullo
Wake Technical Community College

Additionally, we'd like to thank our MyITLab team for their review and collaboration with our text authors:

LeeAnn Bates

Jennifer Hurley

Ralph Moore

Jerri Williams

Jaimie Noy
Media Producer

Preface

The *Your Office* series focuses first and foremost on preparing students to use both technical and soft skills in the real world. Our goal is to provide this to both instructors and students through a modern approach to teaching and learning Microsoft Office applications, an approach that weaves in the technical content using a realistic business scenario and focuses on using Office as a decision-making tool.

The process of developing this unique series for you, the modern student or instructor, requires innovative ideas regarding the pedagogy and organization of the text. You learn best when doing—so you will be active from page 1. Your learning goes to the next level when you are challenged to do more with less—your hand will be held at first, but progressively the case exercises require more from you. Because you care about how things work in the real world—in your classes, your future jobs, your personal life—Real World Advice, Videos, and Success Stories are woven throughout the text. These innovative features will help you progress from a basic understanding of Office to mastery of each application, empowering you to perform with confidence in Windows 8, Word, Excel, Access, and PowerPoint, including on mobile devices.

No matter what career you may choose to pursue in life, this series will give you the foundation to succeed. *Your Office* uses cases that will enable you to be immersed in a realistic business as you learn Office in the context of a running business scenario—the Painted Paradise Resort and Spa. You will immediately delve into the many interesting, smaller businesses in this resort (golf course, spa, restaurants, hotel, etc.) to learn how a larger organization actually uses Office. You will learn how to make Office work for you now, as a student, and in your future career.

Today, the experience of working with Office is not isolated to working in a job in a cubicle. Your physical office is wherever you are with a laptop or a mobile device. Office has changed. It's modern. It's mobile. It's personal. And when you learn these valuable skills and master Office, you are able to make Office your own. The title of this series is a promise to you, the student: Our goal is to make Microsoft Office *Your Office*.

Key Features

- **Starting and Ending Files:** These appear before every case in the text. Starting Files identify exactly which Student Data Files are needed to complete each case. Ending Files are provided to show students the naming conventions they should use when saving their files. Each file icon is color coded by application.

- **Workshop Objectives List:** The learning objectives to be achieved as students work through the workshop. Page numbers are included for easy reference. These are revisited in the Concepts Check at the end of the workshop.

- **Real World Success:** A boxed feature in the workshop opener that shares an anecdote from a real former student, describing how knowledge of Office has helped him or her to get ahead or be successful in his or her life.

- **Active Text Box:** Represents the active portion of the workshop and is easily distinguishable from explanatory text by the blue shaded background. Active Text helps students quickly identify what steps they need to follow to complete the workshop Prepare Case.

- **Quick Reference Box:** A boxed feature in the workshop, summarizing generic or alternative instructions on how to accomplish a task. This feature enables students to quickly find important skills.

- **Real World Advice Box:** A boxed feature in the workshop, offering advice and best practices for general use of important Office skills. The goal is to advise students as a manager might in a future job.

- **Side Note:** A brief tip or piece of information aligned visually with a step in the workshop, quickly providing key information to students completing that particular step.

- **Consider This:** In-text critical thinking questions and topics for discussion, set apart as a boxed feature, allowing students to step back from the project and think about the application of what they are learning and how these concepts might be used in the future.

- **Concept Check:** Review questions appearing at the end of the workshop, which require students to demonstrate their understanding of the objectives in that workshop.

- **Visual Summary:** A visual review of the objectives learned in the workshop using images from the completed solution file, mapped to the workshop objectives using callouts and page references so students can easily find the section of text to refer to for a refresher.

- **Business Application Icons:** Appear with every case in the text and clearly identify which business application students are being exposed to, i.e., Finance, Marketing, Operations, etc.

- **MyITLab™ Icons:** Identify which cases from the book match those in MyITLab™.

- **Real World Interview Video Icon:** This icon appears with the Real World Success Story in the workshop opener and features an interview of a real business person discussing how he or she actually uses the skills in the workshop on a day-to-day basis.

- **Blue Box Video Icons:** These icons appear with each Active Text box and identify the brief video demonstrating how students should complete that portion of the Prepare Case.

- **Soft Skills Icons:** These appear with other boxed features and identify specific places where students are being exposed to lessons on soft skills.

Business Application Icons

Customer Service

Finance & Accounting

General Business

Human Resources

Information Technology

Production & Operations

Sales & Marketing

Research & Development

MyITLab Icons

MyITLab® MyITLab®
Grader

Video Icons

Real World Interview Videos

Workshop Videos

Soft Skills

Instructor Resources

The Instructor's Resource Center, available at www.pearsonhighered.com, includes the following:

- AACSB mapping that identifies which cases and exercises in the text prepare for AACSB certification.

- Business application mapping, which provides an easy-to-filter way of finding the cases and examples to help highlight whichever business application is of most interest.

- Annotated Solution Files with Scorecards assist with grading the Prepare, Practice, Problem Solve, and Perform Cases.

- Data and Solution Files

- Rubrics for Perform Cases in Microsoft Word format enable instructors to easily grade open-ended assignments with no definite solution.

- PowerPoint Presentations with notes for each chapter

- Audio PowerPoints which serve as great refreshers for students

- Instructor's Manual that provides detailed blueprints to achieve workshop learning objectives and outcomes and best use the unique structure of the modules.

- Complete Test Bank, also available in TestGen format

- Syllabus templates for 8-week, 12-week, and 16-week courses

- Additional Practice, Problem Solve, and Perform Cases to provide you with variety and choice in exercises both on the workshop and module levels.

- Scripted Lectures provide instructors with a lecture outline that mirrors the Workshop Prepare Case.

- Flexible, robust, and customizable content is available for all major online course platforms that include everything instructors need in one place. Please contact your sales representative for information on accessing course cartridges for WebCT or Blackboard.

Student Resources

- Student Data Files

- Blue Box videos walk students through each Blue Active Text box in the Workshop, showing and explaining the concepts and how to achieve the skills in the workshop. There is one video per Active Text box.

- Real World Interview videos introduce students to real professionals talking about how they use Microsoft Office on a daily basis in their work. These videos provide the relevance students seek while learning this material. There is one video per workshop.

- Soft Skills videos introduce students to important non-technical skills such as etiquette, managing priorities, proper interview preparation, etc.

Pearson's Companion Website

www.pearsonhighered.com/youroffice offers expanded IT resources and downloadable supplements. Students can find the following self-study tools for each workshop:

- Online Workshop Review
- Workshop Objectives
- Additional Cases
- Glossary
- MOS Certification Mapping

- Student Data Files
- Blue Box videos*
- Real World Interview videos*
- Soft Skills videos*

* Access code required for these premium resources

MyITLab for Office 2013 is a solution designed by professors for professors that allows easy delivery of Office courses with defensible assessment and outcomes-based training. The new **Your Office 2013** system will seamlessly integrate online assessment, training, and projects with My**IT**Lab for Microsoft Office 2013!

My**IT**Lab for Office 2013 features…

- **Assessment and training built to match Your Office 2013** instructional content so that My**IT**Lab works with Your Office to help students make Office their own.

- **Both project-based and skill-based assessment and training** allow instructors to test and train students on complete exercises or individual Office application skills.

Dear Students,

If you want an edge over the competition, make it personal. Whether you love sports, travel, the stock market, or ballet, your passion is personal to you. Capitalizing on your passion leads to success. You live in a global marketplace, and your competition is global. The honors students in China exceed the total number of students in North America. Skills can help set you apart, but passion will make you stand above. *Your Office* is the tool to harness your passion's true potential.

In prior generations, personalization in a professional setting was discouraged. You had a "work" life and a "home" life. As the Series Editor, I write to you about the vision for *Your Office* from my laptop, on my couch, in the middle of the night when inspiration strikes me. My classroom and living room are my office. Life has changed from generations before us.

So, let's get personal. My degrees are not in technology, but chemistry and law. I helped put myself through school by working full time in various jobs, including a successful technology consulting business that continues today. My generation did not grow up with computers, but I did. My father was a network administrator for the military. So, I was learning to program in Basic before anyone had played Nintendo's Duck Hunt or Tetris. Technology has always been one of my passions from a young age. In fact, I now tell my husband: don't buy me jewelry for my birthday, buy me the latest gadget on the market!

In my first law position, I was known as the Office guru to the extent that no one gave me a law assignment for the first two months. Once I submitted the assignment, my supervisor remarked, "Wow, you don't just know how to leverage technology, but you really know the law too." I can tell you novel-sized stories from countless prior students in countless industries who gained an edge from using Office as a tool. Bringing technology to your passion makes you well-rounded and a cut above the rest, no matter the industry or position.

I am most passionate about teaching, in particular teaching technology. I come from many generations of teachers, including my mother who is a kindergarten teacher. For over 12 years, I have found my dream job passing on my passion for teaching, technology, law, science, music, and life in general at the Kelley School of Business at Indiana University. I have tried to pass on the key to engaging passion to my students. I have helped them see what differentiates them from all the other bright students vying for the same jobs.

Microsoft Office is a tool. All of your competition will have learned Microsoft Office to some degree or another. Some will have learned it to an advanced level. Knowing Microsoft Office is important, but it is also fundamental. Without it, you will not be considered for a position.

Today, you step into your first of many future roles bringing Microsoft Office to your dream job working for Painted Paradise Resort and Spa. You will delve into the business side of the resort and learn how to use *Your Office* to maximum benefit.

Don't let the context of a business fool you. If you don't think of yourself as a business person, you have no need to worry. Whether you realize it or not, everything is business. If you want to be a nurse, you are entering the health care industry. If you want to be a football player in the NFL, you are entering the business of sports as entertainment. In fact, if you want to be a stay-at-home parent, you are entering the business of a family household where *Your Office* still gives you an advantage. For example, you will be able to prepare a budget in Excel and analyze what you need to do to afford a trip to Disney World!

At Painted Paradise Resort and Spa, you will learn how to make Office yours through four learning levels designed to maximize your understanding. You will Prepare, Practice, and Problem Solve your tasks. Then, you will astound when you Perform your new talents. You will be challenged through Consider This questions and gain insight through Real World Advice.

There is something more. You want success in what you are passionate about in your life. It is personal for you. In this position at Painted Paradise Resort and Spa, you will gain your personal competitive advantage that will stay with you for the rest of your life—*Your Office*.

Sincerely,

Amy Kinser
Series Editor

Painted Paradise
Red Bluff Golf Course & Pro Shop

Painted Paradise
Turquoise Oasis Spa

Painted Paradise
Painted Treasures Gift Shop

Painted Paradise
Silver Moon Lounge

Painted Paradise
Event Planning & Catering

Painted Paradise
Indigo5 Restaurant

Welcome to the Team!

Welcome to your new office at Painted Paradise Resort and Spa, where we specialize in painting perfect getaways. As the Chief Technology Officer, I am excited to have staff dedicated to the Microsoft Office integration between all the areas of the resort. Our team is passionate about our paradise, and I hope you find this to be your dream position here!

Painted Paradise is a resort and spa in New Mexico catering to business people, romantics, families, and anyone who just needs to get away. Inside our resort are many distinct areas. Many of these areas operate as businesses in their own right but must integrate with the other areas of the resort. The main areas of the resort are as follows.

- The **Hotel** is overseen by our Chief Executive Officer, William Mattingly, and is at the core of our business. The hotel offers a variety of accommodations, ranging from individual rooms to a grand villa suite. Further, the hotel offers packages including spa, golf, and special events.

  Room rates vary according to size, season, demand, and discount. The hotel has discounts for typical groups, such as AARP. The hotel also has a loyalty program where guests can earn free nights based on frequency of visits. Guests may charge anything from the resort to the room.

- **Red Bluff Golf Course** is a private world-class golf course and pro shop. The golf course has services such as golf lessons from the famous golf pro John Schilling and playing packages. Also, the golf course attracts local residents. This requires variety in pricing schemes to accommodate both local and hotel guests. The pro shop sells many retail items online.

  The golf course can also be reserved for special events and tournaments. These special events can be in conjunction with a wedding, conference, meetings, or other event covered by the event planning and catering area of the resort.

- **Turquoise Oasis Spa** is a full-service spa. Spa services include haircuts, pedicures, massages, facials, body wraps, waxing, and various other spa services—typical to exotic. Further, the spa offers private consultation, weight training (in the fitness center), a water bar, meditation areas, and steam rooms. Spa services are offered both in the spa and in the resort guest's room.

  Turquoise Oasis Spa uses top-of-the-line products and some house-brand products. The retail side offers products ranging from candles to age-defying home treatments. These products can also be purchased online. Many of the hotel guests who fall in love with the house-brand soaps, lotions, candles, and other items appreciate being able to buy more at any time.

  The spa offers a multitude of packages including special hotel room packages that include spa treatments. Local residents also use the spa. So, the spa guests are not limited to hotel guests. Thus, the packages also include pricing attractive to the local community.

- **Painted Treasures Gift Shop** has an array of items available for purchase, from toiletries to clothes to presents for loved ones back home including a healthy section of kids' toys for traveling business people. The gift shop sells a small sampling from the spa, golf course pro shop, and local New Mexico culture. The gift shop also has a small section of snacks and drinks. The gift shop has numerous part-time employees including students from the local college.

- **The Event Planning & Catering** area is central to attracting customers to the resort. From weddings to conferences, the resort is a popular destination. The resort has a substantial number of staff dedicated to planning, coordinating, setting up, catering, and maintaining these events. The resort has several facilities that can accommodate large groups. Packages and prices vary by size, room, and other services such as catering. Further, the Event Planning & Catering team works closely with local vendors for floral decorations, photography, and other event or wedding typical needs. However, all catering must go through the resort (no outside catering permitted). Lastly, the resort stocks several choices of decorations, table arrangements, and centerpieces. These range from professional, simple, themed, and luxurious.

- **Indigo5** and the **Silver Moon Lounge**, a world-class restaurant and lounge that is overseen by the well-known Chef Robin Sanchez. The cuisine is balanced and modern. From steaks to pasta to local southwestern meals, Indigo5 attracts local patrons in addition to resort guests. While the catering function is separate from the restaurant—though menu items may be shared—the restaurant does support all room service for the resort. The resort also has smaller food venues onsite such as the Terra Cotta Brew coffee shop in the lobby.

Currently, these areas are using Office to various degrees. In some areas, paper and pencil are still used for most business functions. Others have been lucky enough to have some technology savvy team members start Microsoft Office Solutions.

Using your skills, I am confident that you can help us integrate and use Microsoft Office on a whole new level! I hope you are excited to call Painted Paradise Resort and Spa *Your Office*.

Looking forward to working with you more closely!

Aidan Matthews

Aidan Matthews
Chief Technology Officer

Common Features of Microsoft Office 2013
Understanding the Common Features of Microsoft Office

OBJECTIVES

1. Understand Office applications and accounts   p. 4
2. Start Office programs and manipulate windows   p. 7
3. Use the Office Ribbon, contextual tools, and other menus   p. 14
4. Manage files in Office   p. 24
5. Get help   p. 30
6. Print and share files   p. 33
7. Use Windows SkyDrive   p. 35
8. Use touch mode, gestures, and Reading Mode   p. 38

Prepare Case

Painted Paradise Resort and Spa Employee Training Preparation

Sales & Marketing

The gift shop at the Painted Paradise Resort and Spa has an array of items available for purchase from toiletries to clothes to souvenirs for loved ones back home. There are numerous part-time employees including students from the local college. Frequently, the gift shop holds training luncheons for new employees. Your first assignment will be to start two documents for a meeting with your manager, Susan Brock—the beginning of meeting minutes and an Excel budget. To complete this task, you

DOC RABE Media / Fotolia

need to understand and work with the common features within the Microsoft Office Suite.

REAL WORLD SUCCESS

"I am a returning student and the thought of having to use a computer for anything other than e-mail and social networking scared me. It was not as bad as I anticipated by taking it one step at a time. Now, I feel comfortable typing a research paper and creating a budget on a spreadsheet. It is a welcoming feeling that all the Microsoft applications share the same look! Knowing the common elements gave me a jump-start for learning each additional Microsoft application."

- Esther, current student

Student data files needed for this workshop:

 Blank Word document

 Blank Excel workbook

 Blank Word document in SkyDrive

 cf01ws01Logo.jpg

You will save your files as:

 cf01ws01Minutes_LastFirst.docx

 cf01ws01Budget_LastFirst.docx

 cf01ws01Minutes_LastFirst.pdf

 cf01ws01SkyDrive_LastFirst.docx

Working with the Office Interface

When you walk into a grocery store, you usually know what you are going to find and that items will be in approximately the same location, regardless of which store you are visiting. The first items you usually see are the fresh fruit and vegetables while the frozen foods are near the end of the store. This similarity among stores creates a comfortable and welcoming experience for the shopper—even if the shopper has never been in that particular store. The brands may be different, but the food types are the same. That is, canned corn is canned corn.

Microsoft Office 2013 creates that same level of welcoming feeling and comfort with its Ribbons, features, and functions. Each application has a similar appearance or user interface. The interface for Microsoft Office 2013 is called Modern because of its sleek appearance. The new look is minimalist, mimicking the tiles on the Windows 8 Start screen. There is now a more two-dimensional appearance. There is no more shading or shadows and if you choose a background, there is only a hint of a watermark. In this section, you will learn to navigate and use the Microsoft Office interface.

Understand Office Applications and Accounts

Microsoft Word is a word-processing program. This application can be used to create, edit, and format **documents** such as letters, memos, reports, brochures, resumes, and flyers. Word also provides tools for creating **tables**, which organize information into rows and columns. Using Word, you can add **graphics**, which consist of pictures, online pictures, SmartArt, shapes, and charts that can enhance the look of your documents.

Microsoft Excel is a spreadsheet program. Excel is a two-dimensional grid that can be used to model quantitative data and perform accurate and rapid calculations with results ranging from simple budgets to financial and statistical analyses. Data entered into Excel can be used to generate a variety of charts such as pie charts, bar charts, line charts, or scatter charts, to name a few, to enhance spreadsheet data. Excel files are known as **workbooks**, which contain one or more worksheets. Excel makes it possible to analyze, manage, and share information, which can also help you make better and smarter decisions. New analysis and visualization tools help you track and highlight important data trends.

Microsoft PowerPoint is a presentation and slide program. This application can be used to create slide shows for a presentation, as part of a website, or as a stand-alone application on a computer kiosk. These presentations can also be printed as handouts.

Microsoft OneNote is a planner and note-taking program. OneNote can be used to collect information in one easy-to-find place. With OneNote, you can capture text and images, as well as video and audio. By sharing your notebooks, you can simultaneously take and edit notes with other people in other locations, or just keep everyone in sync and up to date. You can also take your OneNote notebooks with you and then view and edit your notes from virtually any computer with an Internet connection or your Windows 8 phone device.

Microsoft Outlook is an e-mail, contact, and information management program. Outlook allows you to stay connected to the world with the most up-to-date e-mail and calendaring tools. You can manage and print schedules, task lists, phone directories, and other documents. Outlook's ability to manage scheduled events and contact information is why Outlook is sometimes referred to as an **information management program**.

Microsoft Access is a relational database management program. Access is a three-dimensional database program that allows you to make the most of your data. Access is known as **relational database** software—or three-dimensional database software—because it is able to connect data in separate tables. Access connects the data through relationships formed from common fields that exist in both tables. For example, a business might have one table that lists all the employees—their employee ID, first name, last name, address, hire date, and job title. Another table might track data for each shift they are working—their employee ID, date, start time, and end time. Since the common field of employee ID is in both database tables, you could create a report of which employees are working on Thursday at noon along with their name and job title. Thus, Access is used primarily to compile, store, query, and report data. Best practice is to use Access to store data and Excel to model and analyze data by creating charts.

Microsoft Publisher is a desktop publishing program that offers professional tools and templates to help easily communicate a message in a variety of publication types, saving time and money while creating a more polished and finished look. Whether you are designing brochures, newsletters, postcards, greeting cards, or e-mail newsletters, Publisher aids in delivering high-quality results without the user having graphic design experience. Publisher helps you to create, personalize, and share a wide range of professional-quality publications and marketing materials with ease.

Microsoft Lync is a unified communication platform. With Lync, which is able to be fully integrated with Microsoft Office, users can keep track of their contacts' availability; send an instant message; start or join an audio, video, or web conference; or make a phone call—all through a consistent, familiar interface.

InfoPath is used to design sophisticated electronic forms, which enables you to gather information quickly and easily.

Understanding Versions of Microsoft Office 2013

Microsoft Office 2013 is a suite of productivity applications or programs. You can purchase the each application separately or as a package. The exact applications available depends on the package installed. Office 2013 is available in greater variety and flexibility than ever before.

People use different devices for different purposes. You may use your tablet for information consumption and entertainment. Likewise, you may prefer your desktop computer to write a paper. Office 2013 has embraced the concept of every device has its purpose with more flexible versions for platforms such as **Windows Phone** and **Windows Run Time (RT)** and a revised interface to better make use of a touch interface and ARM chip devices. Advanced RISC Machine (ARM) chips are designed for low energy embedded systems, such as in an iPad. The Windows Phone and Windows RT versions of Office 2013 contain substantively similar functionality for Word, PowerPoint, Excel, and OneNote as the Windows version of Office 2013. Visually, Windows RT even looks the same as the full Office 2013 for Windows. However, applications that run on Windows Phone and RT do not support some of the more sophisticated Office features or back-end Visual Basic programming. The advantage is that these versions are optimized for phones and tablets—Office for every device or purpose. This text is written to the full version of Office 2013 for Windows, not Windows Phone or RT.

Office 2013 will be available in two different ways. You can purchase Office 2013 the traditional way from a retailer for a one-time fee that can be installed on exactly one computer. In addition, Office 2013 can also be purchased on a subscription, cloud basis called Office 365. The **Office 365** version is the same product that comes with more frequent updates, the ability to install on more than one computer, more SkyDrive storage space, tight integration with SkyDrive, and several other additional perks. However, the subscription version requires a yearly fee instead of a one-time fee. At the time of this writing, the Office 365 version is competitively priced to be cheaper for many people despite the yearly fee. Furthermore, many different packages for Office 2013 exist from Home to Enterprise for both the traditional and Office 365 versions. Each package contains a different combination of the applications and options available in Office 2013. Ultimately, the decision on which version to purchase depends on your needs and personal situation. For the latest in pricing and options, you can visit **http://office.microsoft.com**.

Using Office 2013 on a Mac

Traditionally, Office is available in different suites for Macs and also came later in time than the PC version. For example, Office 2010 (PC version) was followed by Office 2011 (Mac version). Typically, Access has not been supported on Mac versions of Office. According to the Microsoft website at the time of writing this text, Microsoft stated that the Office 365 Home Premium version of Office will support a Mac installation when the full version is available. Importantly, the Office 365 Home Premium includes Access.

Two other popular options exist for using Office 2013 on a Mac—virtualization and dual boot. Virtualization of Office on a Mac is software that mimics Windows. Many different applications provide virtualization. In any major search engine, search for "PC virtualization on Mac" and you will find many software options for emulating a PC on a Mac. While many virtualization programs promise to mimic entirely, there can be some—usually minor—differences.

Dual boot is the ability to choose the operating system on startup. **Bootcamp** is the Mac software that allows the user to decide which operating system to launch on Intel chip-based Macs. The computer has both the Mac operating system and Windows installed. When the computer is turned on, the user is given the choice of operating system. Thus, the user can be running Windows. If Office is installed on the Windows partition, then Office can run the same as it does on any PC.

You should consult your instructor about the policy in your course. Policies on the usage of the Mac operating system and the Mac versions of Office vary greatly from course to course and school to school. Your instructor will be best able to advise you on what is acceptable for you.

Obtaining a Microsoft Account

Before you get started, Office 2013 requires users to sign in with a Microsoft account that comes with a free SkyDrive account, as shown in Figure 1. This typically will be an account for either the Microsoft Hotmail or Live domain. The Microsoft account gives you free e-mail and tracks your licenses for Microsoft applications. If you have used

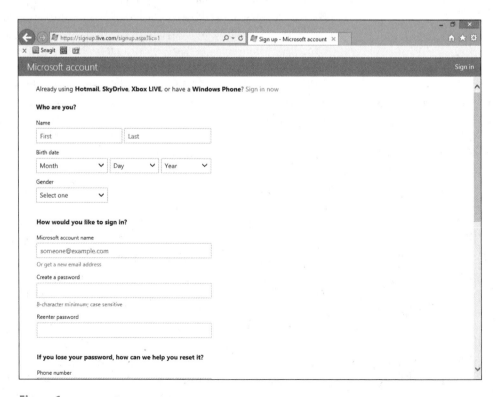

Figure 1   Microsoft account sign up page

Hotmail, SkyDrive, Xbox Live, or Windows phone in the past, you may already have a Microsoft account. The SkyDrive portion of the account is an online storage and collaboration cloud space. As of this writing, you are provided with 7+ GB of online cloud file storage on SkyDrive, additional storage is available for purchase. Microsoft has designed Office 2013 and SkyDrive to complement one another and is discussed in more detail later in this workshop.

If you are working in a computer lab or enterprise version of Windows 8, you may not need to sign into a Microsoft account to run Office or Windows 8. If you are running it on a personal computer, you will need to have a Microsoft account. You can create the account when you install Windows 8. If you install Office 2013 on an earlier version of Windows, you may need to sign up for an account. To sign up for an account, go to **https://signup.live.com** and follow the on-screen instructions. Your first name, last name, and profile image for your Microsoft account will appear in various screens of Windows and Microsoft Office.

Start Office Programs and Manipulate Windows

Office programs can start from the Windows 8 Start screen, as shown in Figure 2, or from search results. Windows 8 contains robust searching capabilities from the Search charm. The **Windows Start screen** is the main interface to launch applications, and it replaces the Windows 7 start button. The Windows **charms** are a specific and consistent set of buttons to users in every application: search, share, connect, settings, and start. Additionally, the procedure for opening an application via searching is the same no matter the configuration of the computer you are using. If you launch the application from the Windows 8 Start screen, the location of the application tile is dependent on the other applications installed on the computer and the applications pinned to the Start screen. On a personal computer you may prefer to use the Windows Start screen, but in a computer lab or unfamiliar computer the search method may be preferable.

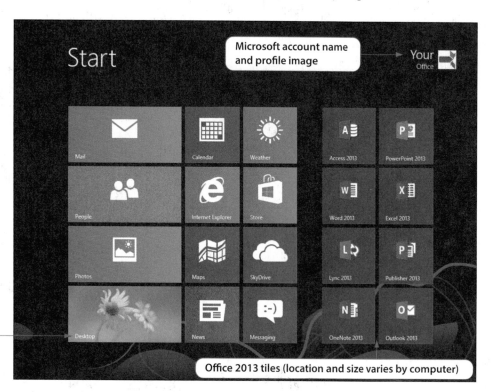

Figure 2 Windows Start screen

In addition to the Windows Start screen, each application has its own specific application Start screen, as shown in Figure 3. From the **Application Start screen**, you can select a blank document, workbook, presentation, database, or one of many application specific templates. Files that have already been created can also be opened from this screen. When existing files are double-clicked from a File Explorer window, the Start screen is not needed and does not open.

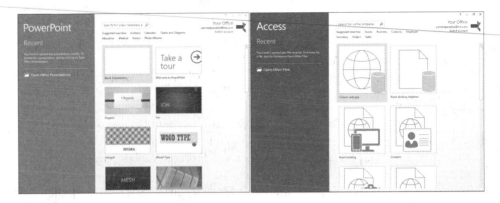

Figure 3 Application Start screens—PowerPoint and Access

Opening the Microsoft Word Start Screen

In the next exercise, you will use the search method to open the Word Start screen and start a new Word document. You will use this new document to start a template for meeting minutes with Susan Brock, the gift shop manager.

CF01.01

 To Open the Word Start Screen and Start a New Document

a. Click the **Start screen** or desktop, point to the **bottom-right corner** of the screen. The charms will be displayed on the right side of the screen.

b. Note the labels underneath each of the charms. Click the **Search** charm.

SIDE NOTE
Opening the Charms
Particularly useful when not using a touch screen, you can also open Windows Charms by pressing ⊞ + C.

SIDE NOTE
Alternate Method
Clicking a tile on the Windows Start screen will also open the application. Whereas, searching also finds unpinned applications.

Figure 4 Windows Start screen with Charms

c. Click the **Search** box at the top of the page. Type Word.

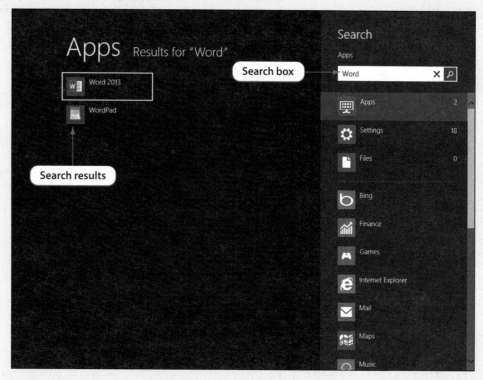

Figure 5 Windows Search screen

d. Click **Word 2013** in the search results. The Word Start screen is displayed when Word is launched.

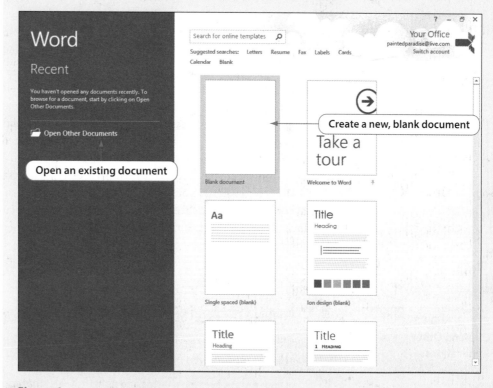

Figure 6 Word Start screen

e. Click **Blank document**.

Notice this opens a blank document—a blank piece of paper. The insertion point is at the first character of the first line.

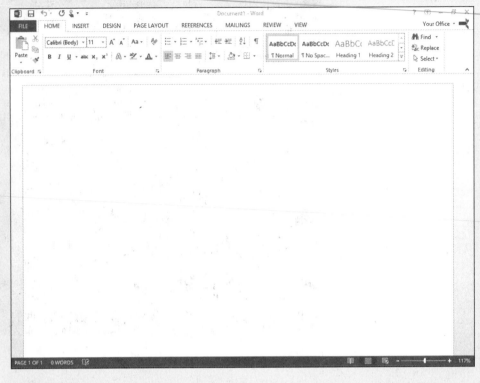

Figure 7   Blank Word document

Opening the Microsoft Excel Start Screen

Once you start working with these applications, you can have more than one application or more than one instance of the same application open at a time. Microsoft Excel is designed around the metaphor of a book. An Excel file is referred to as a workbook. Each Excel workbook can contain many different worksheets—pages in a book. Each sheet has rows represented by numbers. Further, each sheet has columns represented by letters of the alphabet. The intersection of any row and column is a cell. For example, cell B2 refers to the cell where column B and row 2 cross. The active cell is the currently selected cell. In a new worksheet, the active cell is the first cell of the first row, cell A1.

In the next exercise, you will use the search method to open the Excel Start screen and a new Excel spreadsheet. You will use this new document to start a budget for employee training lunches that you will finish in your meeting with Susan Brock, the gift shop manager.

CF01.02

 To Open the Excel Start Screen and Start a New Spreadsheet

a. Click the **Start screen** or desktop, point to the **bottom-right corner** of the screen. The charms will be displayed on the right side of the screen.

b. Point your mouse over the **charms** and note the labels that appear. Click the **Search** charm.

c. Click the **Search** box at the top of the page. Type **Excel**.

SIDE NOTE
Opening Other Applications
In Windows 8, you can open any of the other Office 2013 application with this search method.

d. Click **Excel 2013** in the search results.

Figure 8   Excel Start screen

e. Click **Blank workbook**.

Notice this opens a blank workbook with one worksheet named Sheet1. The active cell is A1.

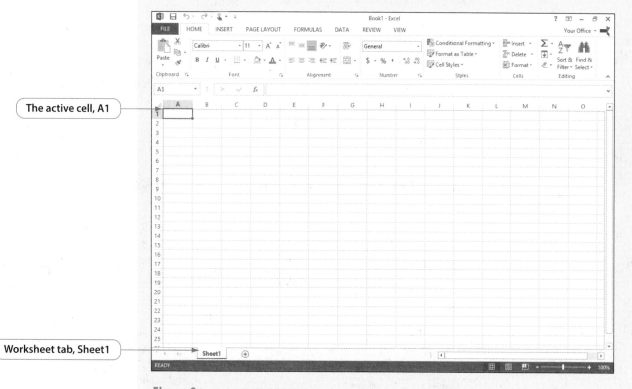

Figure 9   Blank Excel workbook

Switching Between Open Programs and Files

When two or more programs are running at the same time, you can also access them through the taskbar buttons. When moving your mouse pointer over a taskbar icon for an open program, a **thumbnail** or small picture of the open application file is displayed. This is a useful feature when two or more files are open for the same application. A thumbnail of each open file for that application is displayed, and you simply click the file thumbnail that you want to make the active application.

As an alternative to using the thumbnails, you can use the keyboard shortcut to move between applications by holding down [Alt] and pressing [Tab]. A small window appears in the center of the screen with thumbnails representing each of the open programs. There is also a thumbnail for the desktop. If you keep [Alt] pressed down, and then press [Tab] again, the active selection toggles and previews the selected open application. The program name at the top of the window indicates the program that will be active when you release [Alt]. This keyboard shortcut is particularly useful when giving presentations as it is one of the fastest ways to change the active application.

If you have a touch screen, you can also use a left bezel swipe to switch to the last application that you used. You can also show all open applications by swiping out from the left bezel a little, and then swipe back to the left bezel. Touch gestures are explained in more detail in the Windows 8 workshop.

In the next exercise, you will switch between the document and spreadsheet you are creating for the gift shop manager.

CF01.03

▶ To Switch Between Open Programs and Files

a. Press [Alt] + [Tab] at the same time. Notice the active application changes to Word.

b. On the taskbar, point to **Excel** , and then observe the thumbnail of the Excel file.

c. Click the **Book1 - Excel** thumbnail to make sure the Book1 workbook is the current active program.

d. Click cell **A6**, type Budget and then press [Tab].
    Later, you intend to add the gift shop logo. Thus, you left the first five rows blank and started in cell A6. Notice the active cell is now A7.

e. In cell **B6**, type 500, and then press [Enter].

Maximizing and Minimizing the Application Window

One feature common among all of the application's Ribbon is the five buttons that appear in the top-right corner of an application's title bar as shown in Table 1.

Button	Keyboard Shortcut	Action
Help [?]	[F1] (specific to active cursor location)	Opens Microsoft Help
Ribbon Display Options [⊞]	[Ctrl]+[F1] (toggles between collapsing and showing the Ribbon)	Auto-Hide Ribbon, Display Tabs, and Display Tabs and Commands
Minimize [—]	[Alt]+[Spacebar]	Hides a window so it is only visible on the taskbar
Restore Down [❐] and Maximize [▢]	[Alt]+[Spacebar]	When the window is at its maximum size, the button will restore the window to a previous, smaller size. When a window is in the Restore Down mode, the button expands the window to its full size.
Close [✖]	[Alt]+[F4]	Closes a file. Closes all files and **exits** the program if no other files are open for that program.

Table 1 Top-right Ribbon buttons

These buttons offer you the flexibility to size and arrange the windows to suit your purpose or to minimize a window and remove it from view. The largest workspace is when the window is maximized. If several applications are opened, the windows can be arranged using the Restore Down button so several windows can be viewed at the same time. If you are not working on an application and want to have it remain open, the Minimize button will hide the application on the taskbar.

In the next exercise, you will manipulate the sizing of the document and spreadsheet you are creating for the gift shop manager.

CF01.04

▶ To Minimize, Maximize, and Restore Down the Windows

a. On the **Excel** title bar, click **Minimize** ▭ to reduce the program window to an icon on the taskbar. The Word window will now be the active window in view.

b. On the **Word** title bar, click the **Restore Down** ⬓ button. Notice the window becomes smaller and can be resized by clicking and dragging at the corners.

c. Click **Maximize** ▢ to expand the Word program window to fill the screen.

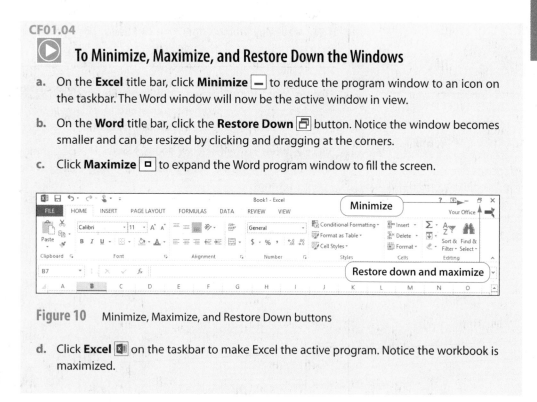

Figure 10   Minimize, Maximize, and Restore Down buttons

d. Click **Excel** 🗗 on the taskbar to make Excel the active program. Notice the workbook is maximized.

Zooming and Scrolling

To get a closer look at the content within the program, you can zoom in. Alternatively, if you would like to see more of the contents, you can zoom out. Keep in mind that the Zoom level only affects your view of the document on the monitor and does not affect the printed output of the document, similarly to using a magnifying glass to see something bigger—the print on the page is still the same size. Therefore, the zoom level should not be confused with how big the text will print—it only affects your view of the document on the screen.

On the right side of the status bar is a slide control that permits zooming in Word from 10% to 500%. The plus and minus propose an easy method, or you can drag the Zoom Slider ▭——┃——➕. In Excel and PowerPoint the zoom range is from 10% to 400%. When using zoom, sometimes text is shifted off the viewing screen. Depending on the program and the Zoom level, you might see the vertical or horizontal scroll bars, or both scroll bars, which can be used to adjust what is displayed in the window. The scroll bars have arrows that can be clicked to shift the workspace in small increments in a specific direction and a scroll box that can be dragged to move a workspace in larger increments. Lastly, touch screens allow you to zoom in and out using pinch and stretch gestures.

In the next exercise, you will zoom in and out on the document you are creating for the gift shop manager.

To Zoom and Scroll in Office Applications

a. On the taskbar, click **Word** [W]. On the Word title bar, if necessary, click **Maximize** [□] to expand the Word program window to fill the screen.

b. The insertion point should be at the beginning of the blank document and the cursor should be blinking. Type Painted Treasures.

> **Troubleshooting**
>
> If you made any typing errors, you can press [Backspace] to remove the typing errors and then retype the text.

SIDE NOTE
Methods for Zooming
Several ways exist to zoom Office applications: Zoom Slider, View tab in the Zoom group, [Ctrl] and a mouse wheel, and touch gestures.

c. On the Word status bar, drag the **Zoom Slider** [—————|————+] to the right until it reaches 500%. The document is enlarged to its largest size. This makes the text appear larger. Scroll to see the words **Painted Treasures**, if necessary.

d. On the Word status bar, click **500%**. Notice, this percentage is the Zoom level button that opens the Zoom dialog box. This dialog box provides options for custom and preset settings.

Painted Treasures

Figure 11 Zoom controls and dialog box

e. Click **Page width**, and then click **OK**.
   The Word document zooms to its page width. Notice that this zoom level will give you the maximum size without creating a horizontal scroll bar.

Use the Office Ribbon, Contextual Tools, and Other Menus

Office has a consistent design and layout that helps make it welcoming and comfortable to the user. Once you learn to use one Office 2013 program, you can use many of those skills when working with other Office programs. The **Ribbon** is the row of tabs with buttons across the top of the application. The Ribbon may be open as shown in Figure 12 or hidden. Your Ribbon may look different than as shown in Figure 12. The Ribbon will change based on the screen resolution of your monitor. This text shows all figures with a 1024 × 768 screen resolution.

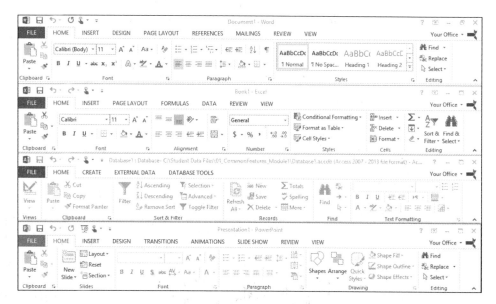

Figure 12 Ribbons of Word, Excel, Access, and PowerPoint

Each Office application's Ribbon has two tabs in common: the File tab and the Home tab. The File tab is the first tab on the Ribbon and is used for file management needs. When clicked, it opens a menu that provides access to the file-level features, such as saving a file, creating a new file, opening an existing file, printing a file, and closing a file, as well as program options. The Home tab is the second tab and contains the commands for the most frequently performed activities, including copying, cutting, and pasting; changing fonts and styles; and other various editing and formatting tools. The commands on these tabs may differ from program to program. Other tabs are program specific, such as the Formulas tab in Excel, the Design tab in PowerPoint, and the Database Tools tab in Access.

Using the Ribbon Tabs

You can enlarge your workspace by collapsing the Ribbon. The Ribbon Display Options button is located in the top-right corner of the window. In the next exercise, you will change the Ribbon display options and format the meeting minutes document using the Home tab.

CF01.06

▶ To Change Ribbon Display Options

a. In Word, click the **Ribbon Display Options** button 🔲, and then click **Show Tabs**. Notice that the Ribbon collapses, but the tabs are still visible.

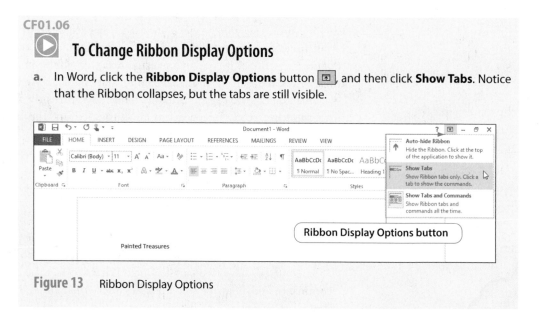

Figure 13 Ribbon Display Options

b. Click immediately after **Painted Treasures**, and then press ⌈Enter⌉. Type Meeting Minutes.

c. Point to the **INSERT** tab on the Ribbon. Notice that the INSERT tab is in a different color font but the current tab is still the active tab.

d. Click the **INSERT** tab.

The INSERT tab is now the active tab on the Ribbon. This tab provides easy access to insert different types of objects.

e. Click the **HOME** tab. The HOME tab is now the active tab on the Ribbon. If you click in the document again, notice that Ribbon commands toggle out of view again.

f. Click **Display Ribbon Options** ⌈⊞⌋, and then click **Show Tabs and Commands** to return the Ribbon options into constant view—or alternatively, double-click any of the tab names.

REAL WORLD ADVICE | **How Buttons and Groups Appear on the Ribbon**

If you noticed that your Ribbon appears differently from one computer to the next—the buttons and groups might seem condensed in size—there could be a few factors at play. The most common causes could be monitor size, lower screen resolution, or a reduced program window. Since the Ribbon changes to accommodate the size of the window or screen, buttons can appear as icons without labels and a group can be condensed into a button that must be clicked to display the group options. So, do not worry! All of the same features are on the Ribbon and in the same general area.

CONSIDER THIS | **Advantages of a Common Interface**

The Ribbon provides a common user interface. This common interface can help you learn additional applications quickly. What elements have you noticed that are common? What elements have you noticed that are different? Of the elements that are different, how are they still presented in a common way?

Using Buttons

Clicking a button will produce an action. For example, the Font group on the Home tab includes buttons for bold and italic. Clicking any of these buttons will produce an intended action. So, if you have selected text that you want to apply bold formatting to, simply click the Bold button and bold formatting is applied to the selected text.

Some buttons are **toggle buttons**—one click turns the feature on and a second click turns the feature off. When a feature is toggled on, the button remains highlighted. For example, in Word, on the Home tab in the Paragraph group, click the Show/Hide button. Notice paragraph marks appear in your document, and the button is highlighted to show that the feature is turned on. This feature displays characters that do not print. This allows you to see items in the document that can help to troubleshoot a document's formatting, such as when ⌈Tab⌋ is pressed an arrow is displayed, or when ⌈Spacebar⌋ is pressed dots appear between words. Click the Show/Hide button again, and the feature is turned off. The button is no longer highlighted, and the paragraph characters, as well as any other nonprinting characters, in the document are no longer displayed.

Some buttons have two parts: a button that accesses the most commonly used setting or command, and an arrow that opens a gallery menu of all related commands or options for that particular task or button. For example, on the Home tab in the Font group, the Font Color button ⌈A ⌄⌋ includes the different colors that are available for fonts. If you click the button, the default is to apply the last color used. Notice the last used color is also displayed on the icon. To access the gallery menu for other color options, click the arrow next to the Font Color button. Whenever you see an arrow next to a button, this is an indicator that more options are available.

The two buttons on your mouse operate in a similar fashion. The left mouse click performs an action. The right-click—or right mouse button—will never perform an action, but rather provides more options. The options that appear on the shortcut menu when you right-click change depending on the location of the mouse pointer.

In the next exercise, you will format the gift shop meeting minutes using bold and font color.

CF01.07

 To Use Buttons

a. In Word, click immediately before **Meeting Minutes** to position the insertion point to the left of the word **Meeting**, and then press and hold the left mouse button and drag to the right to select the words **Meeting Minutes**.

b. On the HOME tab, in the Font group, click **Bold** B. This will toggle on the Bold command. Notice that the bold button is now highlighted and the selected text is displayed in bold format.

SIDE NOTE

Text Selection

To select a single word, you can double-click the word to select it or triple-click for the entire paragraph. You can also use Shift and arrow keys to select text.

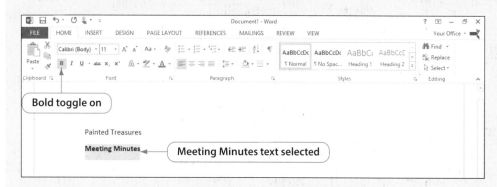

Figure 14   Bold toggled on with text highlighted

SIDE NOTE

Live Preview

Live Preview shows how formatting looks before you apply it. This feature is available for many of the gallery libraries.

c. With the text selected, on the HOME tab, in the Font group, click the **Font Color** arrow A. Under Standard Colors, point to, but do not click, **Dark Red**—under standard colors it is the first one. Notice the Live Preview feature that shows how the selected document text will change color. As the mouse pointer hovers over a color, a ScreenTip appears to show the color name.

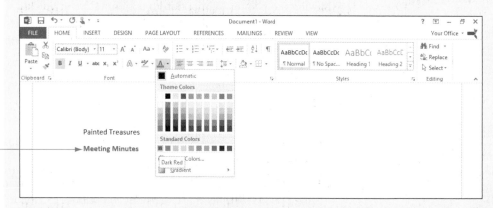

Figure 15   Live Preview of font color

d. Click **Dark Red**. The selected text should now be bold and dark red.

e. Click after **Meeting Minutes** to place your cursor after the end of the word **Minutes**. Notice that the Bold button is still highlighted and the Font Color button is shows Dark Red. Thus, any text you type right now will be bold and dark red.

f. In the Font group, click **Bold** [B] to toggle Bold off. Then, click the **Font Color** arrow [A ▾], and then select **Automatic**.

g. Press [Enter]. Type your first name and last name.

REAL WORLD ADVICE | **Using Keyboard Shortcuts and Key Tips**

Keyboard shortcuts are extremely useful, and some are universal to all Windows programs. They keep your hands on the keyboard instead of reaching for the mouse —increasing efficiency and saving time.

Pressing [Alt] will toggle the display of **key tips**—or **keyboard shortcuts**—for items on the Ribbon and Quick Access Toolbar. After displaying the key tips, you can press the letter or number corresponding to request the action from the keyboard.

For multiple key shortcuts, you hold down the first key listed and press the second key once. Some common keyboard shortcuts are listed below.

Press [Ctrl] and type C	Copy the selected item
Press [Ctrl] and type V	Paste a copied item
Press [Ctrl] and type A	Select all the items in a document or window
Press [Ctrl] and type B	Bold selected text
Press [Ctrl] and type Z	Undo an action
Press [Ctrl]+[Home]	Move to the top of the document
Press [Ctrl]+[End]	Move to the end of the document

Using Galleries and Live Preview

Live Preview lets you see the effects of menu selections on your document file or selected item before making a commitment to a particular menu choice. A **gallery** is a set of menu options that appear when you click the arrow next to a button which, in some cases, may be referred to as a More arrow [▾]. The menu or grid shows samples of the available options.

When you point to an option in a gallery, Live Preview shows the results that would occur in your file if you were to click that particular option. Using Live Preview, you can experiment with settings before making a final choice. When you point to a text style in the Styles gallery, the selected text or the paragraph in which the insertion point is located appears with that text style. Moving the pointer from option to option results in quickly seeing what your text will look like before making a final selection. To finalize a change to the selected option, click the style.

In the next exercise, you will format the gift shop meeting minutes using styles and add a list of topics for the meeting.

CF01.08

 To Use Styles and the Numbering Library

a. In Word, click immediately before **Painted Treasures** to position the insertion point to the left of the word **Painted**.

b. On the HOME tab, in the Styles group, click the **More** arrow [▾]. This will show all of the options for different styles. Point your mouse to **Title** to see the Live Preview. Then, select **Title** to change the words "Painted Treasures" to Title style. Notice that the style changed the whole line even though you did not select the text.

SIDE NOTE
Closing a Gallery
[Esc] will close a gallery without making a selection. Alternatively, you can click outside the gallery menu.

18 WORKSHOP 1 | Common Features of Microsoft Office 2013

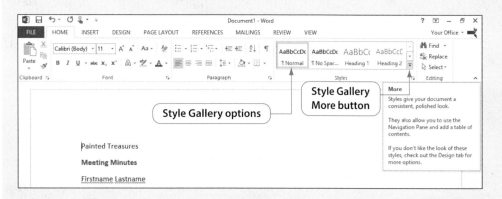

Figure 16   Styles gallery

c. Click immediately after your **last name**, press ⌈Enter⌉ twice, type Topics, and then press ⌈Enter⌉ one time.

d. On the HOME tab, in the Paragraph group, click the **Numbering** arrow ⌈☰ ▾⌉. The Numbering Library gallery opens. Point to, but do not click, the **third option** in the first row, the number one followed by a closing parenthesis.

e. Select the **Number Alignment: Left** style with **1)**—the third button in the first row.

Figure 17   Numbering Library

f. Type Training Lunch Budget - and then press ⌈Enter⌉. After the meeting, you intend to type the notes after the dash.

g. Type New Products - and then press ⌈Enter⌉ twice to end the numbered list.

Opening Dialog Boxes and Task Panes

Some Ribbon groups include a diagonal arrow in the bottom-right corner of the group section, called a **Dialog Box Launcher** ⌈◪⌉ that opens a corresponding dialog box or task pane. Hovering the mouse pointer over the Dialog Box Launcher will display a ScreenTip to indicate more information. Click the Dialog Box Launcher to open a **dialog box**, which is a window that provides more options or settings beyond those provided on the Ribbon. It often provides access to more precise or less frequently used commands along with the commands offered on the Ribbon; thus using a dialog box offers the ability to apply many related options at the same time and located in one place. As shown in Figure 18, many dialog boxes organize related information into tabs. In the Paragraph dialog box shown in the figure, the active Indents and Spacing tab shows options to change alignment, indentation, and spacing, with another tab that offers options and settings for Line and Page Breaks. A **task pane** is a smaller window pane that often appears to the side of the program window and offers options or helps you to navigate through completing a task or feature.

In the next exercise, you will use a dialog box to format some of the cells in the budget you are beginning for your manager, Susan Brock.

CF01.09

▶ To Open the Format Cells Dialog Box

a. On the taskbar, click **Excel** ▣ to make Excel the active program.

b. Click cell **B6**, the second cell in the sixth row.

c. On the HOME tab, in the Number group, click the **Number Dialog Box Launcher** ▣. The Format Cells dialog box opens with the Number tab displayed.

d. On the Number tab under Category, click **Currency**. Click in the **Decimal places** box, delete the 2, and then type 0.

SIDE NOTE
Check Box and Radio Options
Check boxes allow you to select more than one option in the group. Radio options only allow you to select one.

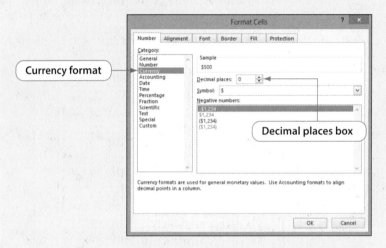

Figure 18   Format Cells Dialog Box

e. Click the **Alignment** tab, click the **Font** tab, and then click the **Border** tab to explore the available options.

f. Click the **Fill** tab. In the second row of colors, click the last **Light Green** color. The light green color will be shown in the Sample box.

g. Click **OK**. The format changes are made to the number, and the fill color is applied.

Inserting Images and Using Contextual Tools

In Word, Excel, PowerPoint, and Publisher, you can insert pictures from a file, a screen shot, or various online sources. The online options include inserting images within the Office Online Pictures collection, via a Bing search, or from your own SkyDrive. The Insert tab contains all of the options for using images in Word, PowerPoint, and Excel.

The term **contextual tools** refers to tools that only appear when needed for specific tasks. Some tabs, toolbars, and menus are displayed as you work and only appear if a particular object is selected. Because these tools become available only as you need them, the workspace remains less cluttered.

A **contextual tab** is a Ribbon tab that contains commands related to selected objects so you can manipulate, edit, and format the objects. Examples of objects that can be selected to produce contextual tabs include a table, a picture, a shape, or a chart. A contextual tab appears to the right of the standard Ribbon tabs. The contextual tab disappears when you click outside the target object—in the file—to deselect the object. In some instances, contextual tabs can also appear as you switch views.

In the next exercise, you will insert a Painted Treasures Gift Shop logo into the budget you are beginning for your manager, Susan Brock. This budget will become a part of Susan's larger budget that she must present to the CEO of Painted Paradise in an internal memo once a year. Logos are an excellent way to brand both internal and external communications.

CF01.10

 To Insert an Image

a. In **Excel**, click cell **A1**.

b. Click the **INSERT** tab, and then in the Illustrations group, click **Pictures**. The Insert Picture dialog box opens.

c. Navigate to your student data files, and then click **cf01ws01Logo**. Click the **Insert** button. The Painted Treasures Gift Shop logo is inserted on the worksheet and actively selected. Notice the logo is too large and covers the cells you created in row 6. Also, notice that the FORMAT contextual tab in the PICTURE TOOLS contextual tab group is now the active tab.

d. On the **FORMAT** tab, in the Size group, click in the **Shape Height** box. Delete **2.19**, type 1, and then press Enter. Notice the width automatically adjusts to keep the original image proportions.

The FORMAT contextual tab in the PICTURE TOOLS tab group

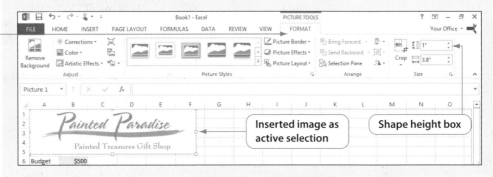

Figure 19   Picture Tools Format contextual tab and shape height

> **Troubleshooting**
> To see a contextual tab, the object relating to the tab must be selected. If you do not see it, click the image to reselect the image.

e. Click cell **A7**. Notice that the contextual tab disappears.

Accessing the Mini Toolbar

The **Mini toolbar** appears after text is selected and contains buttons for the most commonly used formatting commands, such as font, font size, font color, center alignment, bold, and italic. The Mini toolbar button commands vary for each Office program. The toolbar disappears if you move the pointer away from the toolbar, press a key, or click the workspace. All the commands on the Mini toolbar are available on the Ribbon; however, the Mini toolbar offers quicker access to common commands since you do not have to move the mouse pointer far away from the selected text for these commands.

In the next exercise, you will add some additional information to the budget you are beginning for your manager. You will also edit some of the cells with the Mini toolbar.

CF01.11

▶ To Access the Mini Toolbar

a. Click cell **A8**, the first cell in the eighth row of the worksheet. Type Expenses and then press Enter.

b. In cell **A9**, type Food and then press Enter.

c. In cell **A10**, type Drinks and then press Enter.

d. Click cell **B9**, type 450 and then press Enter. In cell **B10**, type 50.

e. Double-click cell **A8** to place the insertion point in the cell. Double-clicking a cell enables you to enter edit mode for the cell text.

f. Double-click cell **A8** again to select the text. The Mini toolbar appears and comes into view directly above the selected text. If you were to move the pointer off the cell, the Mini toolbar becomes transparent or disappears entirely. When you move the pointer back over the Mini toolbar it may become visible again or you may need to repeat the text selection.

> **Troubleshooting**
>
> If you are having a problem with the Mini toolbar disappearing, you may have inadvertently moved the mouse pointer to another part of the document. If you need to redisplay the Mini toolbar, right-click the selected text and the Mini toolbar will appear along with a shortcut menu. Once you select an option on the Mini toolbar, the shortcut menu will disappear and the Mini toolbar will remain while in use—or repeat the prior two steps, then make sure the pointer stays over the toolbar.

Figure 20   Mini toolbar

g. On the Mini toolbar, click **Italic** *I*.

h. Press Enter. Cell A9 is now selected.

The Mini toolbar is particularly helpful with the touch interface. When Office recognizes that you are using touch instead of a mouse or digitizer pen, it creates Mini toolbars that are larger and designed to work with fingers more easily. An example of a touch Mini toolbar in Excel touch mode is shown in Figure 21.

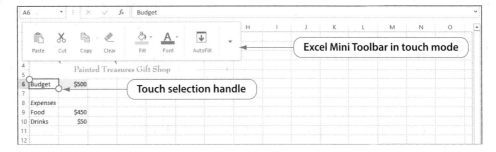

Figure 21   Excel Mini toolbar in touch mode

Using Shortcut Menus

Shortcut menus are also context sensitive and enable you to quickly access commands that are most likely needed in the context of the task being performed. A **shortcut menu** is a list of commands related to a selection that appears when you right-click—click the right mouse button. This means you can access popular commands without using the Ribbon. Included are commands that perform actions, commands that open dialog boxes, and galleries of options that provide Live Preview. As noted previously, the Mini toolbar opens when you click the right mouse button. If you click a button on the Mini toolbar, the shortcut menu closes, and the Mini toolbar remains open allowing you to continue formatting your selection.

In the next exercise, you will add some additional information to the budget you are beginning for your manager. You will also edit some of the cells with a shortcut menu.

CF01.12

 To Use the Shortcut Menu to Add Currency Formatting

a. Click cell **B9**, hold down your left mouse button, and then drag down to cell **B10** to select both B9 and B10. Right-click the selected range, **B9:B10**. A shortcut menu opens with commands related to common tasks you can perform in a cell, along with the Mini toolbar.

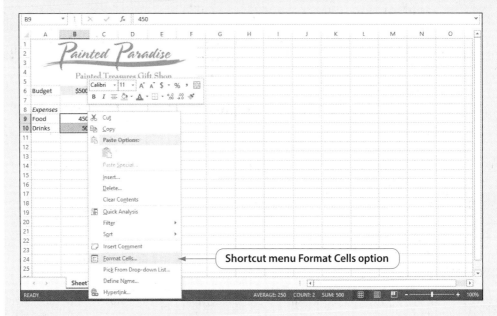

Figure 22   Shortcut menu with Mini toolbar

b. On the shortcut menu, select **Format Cells**. The shortcut menu closes, and then the Format Cells dialog box appears.

c. Click the **Number** tab, if necessary. Under Category, click **Currency**. Click in the **Decimal places** box, delete the 2, and then type 0. Click **OK**.

d. Click cell **A13**, type your first name and last name, and then press Enter.

Manipulating Files and Finding Help in Office

Creating, opening, saving, closing, troubleshooting, and printing files are common everyday tasks performed in any Office program. Most of these tasks can all be accessed from the File tab. These processes are basically the same for all the Office programs. When you start a program, you either have to create a new file or open an existing one. Since Office has a common interface, learning a new Office application is easy as long as you can find help when needed. In this section, you will use Office Help, making it easy to learn more.

Manage Files in Office

While working on an Office file, whether creating a new file or modifying an existing file, your work is stored in the temporary memory on your computer, not on the hard drive or your USB flash drive. Any work done will be lost if you were to exit the program, turn off the computer, or experience a power failure without saving your work or the program automatically saving your work. To prevent losing your work, you need to save your work and remember to save frequently—at least every 10 minutes or after adding several changes. That saves you from having to re-create any work you did prior to the last save.

You can save files to the hard drive, which is located inside the computer; to an external drive, such as a USB flash drive; to a network storage device; or to SkyDrive. Office has an **AutoRecovery** feature—previously called AutoSave—that will attempt to recover any changes made to a document if something goes wrong, but this should not be relied upon as a substitute for saving your work manually.

Using Office Backstage View

Office Backstage View has many options for managing your files in Office and is accessed via the File tab. Office Backstage View now includes a new area called Account. This enables you to log in to your Microsoft account or switch accounts. You can also see a list of connected services and add services, such as LinkedIn and SkyDrive. Save & Send has been replaced by Export and has been downsized. Table 2 lists the areas you can modify in Office Backstage View.

Area	Description
Info	File properties and protecting, inspecting, and managing versions of the file
New	Creating a new blank or template-based document
Open	Opening a file from your computer, recent documents list, or SkyDrive account
Save	Save your file to your computer or SkyDrive account
Save As	Save your file with a new name or format to your computer or SkyDrive account
Print	Preview your document for printing and print
Share	Share your file by invitation, e-mail, online presentation, or blog post
Export	Change the file type or create a PDF/XPS document
Close	Close the file
Account	User and Production information including connected services
Options	Launches the Application Options dialog box with many options including advanced options

Table 2 Office Backstage View

Saving a File

In addition to Office Backstage View, Office provides several ways to save a file. To quickly save a file, simply click Save 🔲 on the Quick Access Toolbar or use the keyboard shortcut of pressing Ctrl and then pressing S. The **Quick Access Toolbar** is the series of small icons in the top-left corner that can be customized to offer commonly used buttons. There are two different Save icons to show whether you are saving to your computer or to SkyDrive. When saving to SkyDrive, the Save icon looks more like a syncing icon.

The first time you save a new file, it behaves the same as the Save As command where the Save As dialog box opens. This allows you to specify the save options. In the Save As dialog box, you can name the file and specify the location to save it, similar to the first time you save a file. Once you save a file, the simple shortcut methods to save any changes to the file work fine to update the existing file. No dialog box will open to save after the first time—as long as you do not need to change the file name or location as with the Save As command.

A file name includes the name you specify and a **file extension** assigned by the Office program to indicate the file type. The file extension may or may not be visible depending on your computer settings. You can check your computer's setting in the File Explorer window under the View tab in the Show/hide group. The check box for File name extensions should be checked to see file extension as shown in Figure 23. Each Office program adds a period and a file extension after the file name to identify the program in which that file was created. Table 3 shows the common default file extensions for Office 2013.

Figure 23   File Explorer file extension setting

Application	Extension
Word 2013	.docx
Excel 2013	.xlsx
PowerPoint 2013	.pptx
Access 2013	.accdb

Table 3   Office 2013 default file extensions

REAL WORLD ADVICE   Sharing Files Between Office Versions

Different Office versions are not always compatible. The general rule is that files created in an older version can always be opened in a newer version, but not the other way around—a 2013 Office file is not easily opened in versions of Office prior to Office 2007. Sharing files with Office 2003 users is a concern because different file extensions were used. For example, .doc was used for Word files instead of docx, .xls instead of .xlsx for Excel, and so on.

It is still possible to save the Office 2013 files in a previous format version. To save in one of these formats, use the Save As command, and click the 97-2003 format option. If the file is already in the previous format, it will open in Office 2013 and be saved with the same format in which it was created. If a file is saved with a previous version's extension, it may not save all the new formatting features.

Name your file with a descriptive name that accurately reflects the content of the document, workbook, presentation, or database, such as "January 2014 Budget" or "012014 Minutes". The descriptive name can include uppercase and lowercase letters, numbers, hyphens, spaces, and some special characters—excluding ? "/ | < > * :—in any combination. File names can include a maximum of 255 characters including the extension—this includes the number of characters for the folder names to get to the file location known as the file path. Even though Windows 8 can handle a long file name, some systems cannot. Thus, shorter names can prevent complications when transferring files between different systems.

In the next exercise, you will name and save the files you have been creating for your meeting with your manager.

CF01.13

To Save a File

a. In Excel, click the **FILE** tab. Office Backstage View opens with command options and tabs for managing files, opening existing files, saving, printing, and exiting. Click **Save As**.

SIDE NOTE

Saving a File

The default save location is your SkyDrive account—you must be signed in. You can also save to Computer or Add a Place.

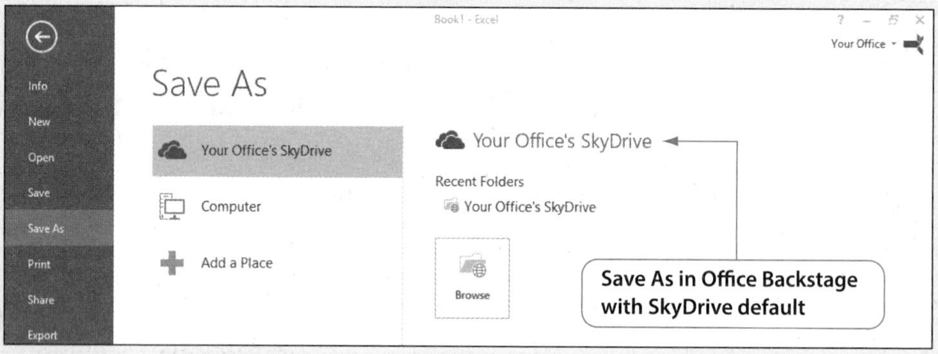

Figure 24 Save As with SkyDrive as default

b. Click **Computer**. Click **Browse**.

This will enable you to select the location on your computer where you are saving your files. The Save As dialog box opens. This provides the opportunity to enter a file-name and a storage location. The default storage location is the Documents folder and the suggested file name is the first few words of the first line of the document.

c. Click the **location** in the left pane, and then navigate through the folder structure to where your student data files are located. Click in the **File name** box, and then select the current suggested file name, if necessary. Navigate to where you are storing your files, and then type cf01ws01Budget_LastFirst using your last and first name in the File name box. Change the Save as type to **Excel Workbook**, if necessary.

This file name describes both the content of the file and the portion of this book that the file is associated. The "Budget" part describes the content. The "cf01ws01" describes Common Features workshop 1.

d. Click the **Save** button. The Save As dialog box closes, Excel returns to the HOME tab, and the name of your file appears in the Excel window title bar.

e. On the taskbar, click **Word** to make Word the active program. Repeat Steps b through d, and then save the file as cf01ws01Minutes_LastFirst using your last and first name.

Modifying Saved Files

Saved files only contain what was in the file the last time it was saved. Any changes made after the file was saved are only stored in the computer's memory and are not saved with the file. It is important to remember to save often—after making changes—so the file is updated to reflect its current contents. One of the most useful shortcuts is the keyboard shortcut for saving, which can be utilized by pressing Ctrl, and then pressing S.

Remember that it is not necessary to use the Save As dialog box once the file has been saved unless you want to save a copy of the file with a different name or you want to store it in a different location.

In the next exercise, you will modify and save the files that you have been creating for your meeting with your manager. You will save them to the same location you saved them to in the last exercise.

CF01.14

 To Modify and Save a File to the Previously Saved Location

a. In Word, click below the numbered list to make sure the insertion point is on the last line. Type today's date and then press Enter.

b. Press Ctrl+S. The changes you made to the document have just been saved to the file stored in the location you selected earlier. Recall that no dialog boxes will open for the Save after the first time the document has been saved.

REAL WORLD ADVICE | Saving Files

Most programs have an added safeguard or warning dialog box to remind you to save if you attempt to close a file without saving your changes first. Despite that warning, best practice dictates you save files before closing them or exiting a program. If you press the wrong answer on the warning by accident, you will lose work. Remembering to save before you close prevents this kind of accident.

Best practice also dictates saving often. The more often you save the less work you can lose in the event of an unexpected closing of the application. Pressing Ctrl and S only takes a few seconds. Train yourself now to use this keyboard shortcut regularly and often. If you do, it will become second nature and save you from losing work in the future!

Closing a File and Exiting an Application

When you are ready to close a file, you can click the Close command in Office Backstage View. If the file you close is the only file open for that particular program, the program window remains open with no file in the window. You can also close a file by using the Close button ✖ in the top-right corner of the window. However, if that is the only file open, the file and program will close when using that method of closing. If you exit the window, it will close both the file and the program. Exiting programs when you are finished with them helps save system resources and keeps your Windows desktop and taskbar uncluttered, as well as prevents data from being accidentally lost.

In the next exercise, you will modify, save, and close the Meeting Minutes document that you have been creating for your meeting with your manager. You are also finished with Excel. Thus, you will save and exit the budget you prepared.

To Modify and Close a Document

a. In Word, with the insertion point on the line under the date, type your course number and section and then press Enter. The text you typed should appear below the date.

b. Click the **FILE** tab, and then click **Close**. A warning dialog box opens, asking if you want to save the changes made to the document.

c. Click **Save**.

The document closes after saving changes, but the Word program window remains open. You are able to create new files or open previously saved files. If multiple Word documents are open, the document window of the file you just closed will remain open with the other documents that are currently still open in the window.

d. On the taskbar, click **Excel** to make Excel the active program.

e. Press Ctrl + S to save the file to the previous location. Click **Close** X in the top-right corner. Notice that the file closes and you exit the Excel application.

SIDE NOTE

Best Practice

Best practice is to save the file before closing instead of allowing the warning dialog box to prompt for the save.

Opening a File from the Recent Documents List

You create a new file when you open a blank document, workbook, presentation, or database. If you want to work on a previously created file, you must first open it. When you open a file, it copies the file from the file's storage location to the computer's temporary memory and displays it on the monitor's screen. When you save a file, it updates the storage location with the changes. Until then, the file only exists in your computer's memory. If you want to open a second file, while one is open, the keyboard shortcut of pressing Ctrl and then pressing O will open the Open tab of Office Backstage View. If you use the keyboard shortcut of Ctrl + F12 you will launch the Open dialog window without taking you to Office Backstage View.

In Office Backstage View, Office keeps a list of your most recently modified files— **Most Recently Used list**. As the list grows, older files are removed to make room for more recently modified files. You can also pin a frequently used file to always remain at the top of the list. To clear the recent files, right-click any file in the recent files list and select the option to clear unpinned files.

When opening files downloaded from the Internet, accessed from a shared network, or received as an attachment in e-mail, the file usually opens in a read-only format called **Protected View** in Reading Mode, as shown in Figure 25. In Protected View, the file contents can be seen and read, but you are not able to edit, save, or print the contents until you enable editing. If you see the information bar shown in Figure 25, and you trust the source of the file, simply click the Enable Editing button on the information bar.

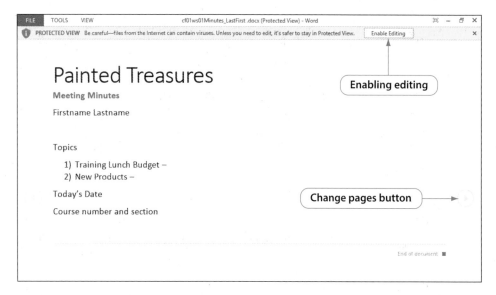

Figure 25   File opened in Protected View

CF01.16

To Reopen a Document from the Recent Documents List

a. In Word, click the **FILE** tab. Notice the Recent Documents list.

b. Point to **cf01ws01Minutes_LastFirst**. Notice the Pin icon . If you want the document to always remain at the top of this list, you would click the Pin icon.

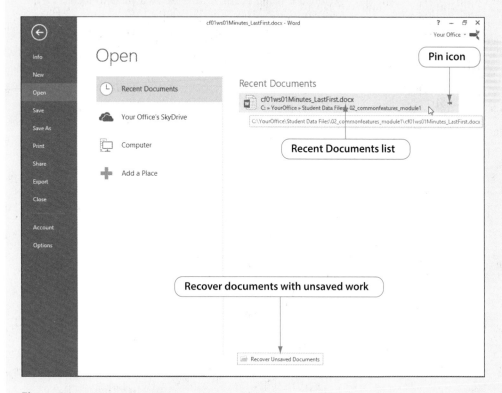

Figure 26   Recent Documents

c. Click **cf01ws01Minutes_LastFirst**. Word opens the file and exits Office Backstage View.

Get Help

Office 2013 Help can give you additional information about a feature or steps for how to perform a new task. Your ability to find and use help can greatly increase your Office repertoire and save you time from seeking outside help. Office has several levels of help from a searchable search window to more directed help such as ScreenTips.

Using the Help Window

The **Help** window provides detailed information on a multitude of topics, as well as access to templates, training videos installed on your computer, and content available on Office.com, the website maintained by Microsoft that provides access to the latest information and additional Help resources. To access the contents at Office.com you must have access to the Internet from the computer. If there is no Internet access, only the files installed on the computer will be displayed in the Help window.

Each program has its own Help window. From each program's Help window you can find information about the Office commands and features as well as step-by-step instructions for using them. There are two ways to locate Help topics—the search function and the Popular searches categories.

To search the Help system on a desired topic, type the topic in the search box and click the Search icon. Once a topic is located, you can click a link to open it. Explanations and step-by-step instructions for specific procedures will be presented. To access a subject or topic, click the subject links to display the subtopic links, and then click a subtopic link to display Help information for that topic.

In this exercise, you will learn how to insert a footer using Word help and then add a footer to the meeting minutes.

CF01.17

 To Search Help for Information about the Ribbon in Word

a. On the Word title bar, click **Microsoft Word Help** ？ . The Word Help window opens.

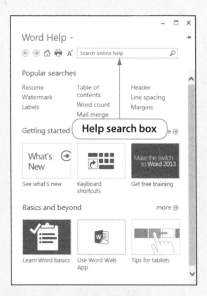

Figure 27 Word Help window

b. Click in the **Search** box or if you are online, the box will display **Search online help**. Type add a footer and then press Enter .

c. The Help window displays a list of the topics related to the keyword "footer". Scroll through the list to review the Help topics. Click the **Add a header or footer** from the list of results, and then read the information.

d. On the Help window title bar, click **Close** ✗ to close the window. Now that you know how to add a footer, you will add a footer to your Word document.

e. Click the **INSERT** tab, and then in the Header & Footer group, click **Footer**. Click **Blank**. Notice a footer is added at the bottom of your document.

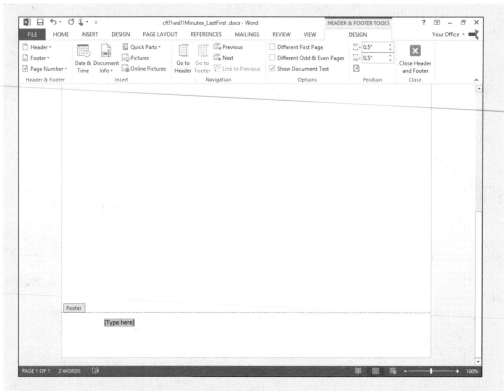

Figure 28 Document with blank footer inserted

f. On the HEADER & FOOTER TOOLS DESIGN tab, in the Insert group, click the **Document Info** button, and then select **File Name**. Notice Word inserts the name of the file.

g. On the HEADER & FOOTER DESIGN tab, in the Close group, click **Close Header and Footer**.

Using ScreenTips

ScreenTips are small windows that display descriptive text when you rest the mouse pointer over an object or button. You can point to a button or object in one of the Office applications to display its ScreenTip. In addition to the button's name, a ScreenTip might include the keyboard shortcut if one is available, a description of the command's function, and possibly more information.

In this exercise, you will use a ScreenTip to center the title of the meeting minutes.

CF01.18

▶ To Open ScreenTips and Topic-Specific Help

a. Press Ctrl + Home to place the insertion point right before **Painted Treasures**.

b. On the HOME tab, in the Paragraph group, hover the mouse over the **Center** button ☰. The ScreenTip is displayed with the button's name, its keyboard shortcut, and a brief description.

SIDE NOTE

ScreenTip and F1

If a topic for a ScreenTip does not exist in Help, the window will open to the starting search page.

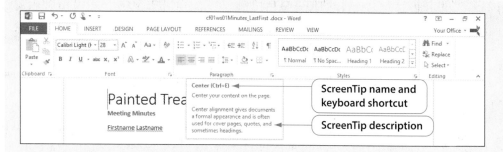

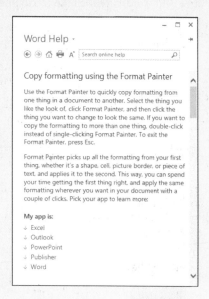

Figure 29   Center button Screen tip

c.   Click the **Center** button ≣ to center the Painted Treasures title.

d.   On the HOME tab, in the Clipboard group, point to the **Format Painter** to display the ScreenTip. With the mouse pointer still over the **Format Painter** and the ScreenTip showing, press F1 and notice that the Help window opens with information on how to use the Format Painter. Scroll down and read through the information.

Figure 30   Format Painter Word Help

e.   When you are finished reading, click the **Close** ✕ button in the top-right corner of the Word Help window. You do not need to use the Format Painter at this time.

f.   Press Ctrl + S to save the document.

Print and Share Files

In Office 2013, many ways exist for sharing files. There are times you will need a paper copy, also known as a hard copy, of an Office document, spreadsheet, or presentation. When a printed version is not needed, a digital copy will save paper and costs. Office 2013 provides many ways to share your document. You can use traditional ways of sharing by printing or exporting a PDF. You can also save it to SkyDrive, invite others to share the document, and specify whether others are allowed to edit the document. From inside of Office Backstage View, the document can be e-mailed to others, transformed into an online, browser-not-required presentation, or posted to a blog.

Printing a File

Before printing, carefully consider whether a paper copy is necessary. Even in the digital world, paper copies of documents make more sense in many situations. Always review and preview the file and adjust the print settings before sending the document to the printer. Many options are available to fit various printing needs, such as the number of copies to print, the printing device to use, and the portion of the file to print. The print settings vary slightly from program to program. Printers also have varied capabilities. It is advisable that you check the file's print preview to ensure the file will print as you intended. Doing a simple print preview will help to avoid having to reprint your document, workbook, or presentation, which requires additional paper, ink, and energy resources.

In this exercise, you will print the start of the meeting minutes document to handwrite notes on during the meeting.

CF01.19

 To Print a File

a. In Word, click the **FILE** tab to open Office Backstage View.

b. Click **Print**. The Print settings and Print Preview appear. Verify that the Copies box displays **1**.

c. Verify that the correct printer—as directed by your instructor—appears as the Printer. Choices may vary depending on the computer you are using. If the correct printer is not displayed, click the **Printer** button arrow, and then click to choose the correct or preferred printer from the list of available printers.

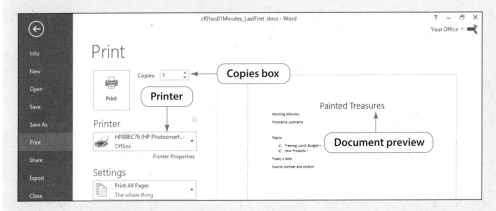

Figure 31 Printing settings

d. If your instructor asks you to print the document, click **Print**.

Exporting a PDF

When you want to give someone else a document, consider whether an electronic version of the file is better than a printed copy. A **portable document format—PDF—** is a type of document that ensures the document will look the same on someone else's computer. For example, different computers may have different fonts installed. A PDF maintains the font. Even if the computer viewing the file does not have the same fonts as the computer used to create the file, the viewer will see the correct font. Further, PDFs are a common file format used in business to share documents because of the readily available free readers.

In this exercise, you will export a PDF of the meeting minutes and e-mail a copy to a colleague who is also attending the meeting.

CF01.20

 To Export a PDF

a. Click the **FILE** tab to open Office Backstage View.

b. Click **Export**, and then click **Create PDF/XPS**.

c. Navigate to the location where your student files are stored. Verify the file name selected is **cf01ws01Minutes_LastFirst**. Notice settings in the Publish as PDF or XPS dialog box for optimizing for online verses printing publishing. Since your colleague will print this document, the default setting of Standard is appropriate.

d. Click **Publish**. Close the **PDF** file.

CONSIDER THIS | **Sending Files Electronically**

Sending an electronic file can be easier and cheaper than sending a printed copy to someone. What should you consider when deciding the type of file to send? When you send an application specific file, such as Word or Excel, what happens if the recipient does not have the application installed? When you send a PDF, how easy is it for a recipient to edit a document? How does the file type affect the quality of a recipient's printout?

Understanding the Cloud and Touch Integration

Over the past few years, cloud networks and touch screens started to proliferate the market. Thus, Office 2013 made many changes to allow Office to work better with these technologies. If you have never used any cloud technology, Office 2013 makes SkyDrive easy to use and provides some free storage space. If you do not have a touch screen, you can still take advantage of touch technology with a Windows 8 mouse that accepts touch gestures. Over the next several years, these technologies will become standard for most computers and devices. In this next section, you will learn about using SkyDrive and touch features.

Use Windows SkyDrive

When you use computing resources—either hardware or software—of another computer over a network, you are using **cloud computing**. The cloud uses economies of scale by combining the power of many computers. One example of cloud computing is online file storage and syncing—services such as SkyDrive, DropBox, or Box. Some services, such as SkyDrive, also allow you to edit the document online through a browser or to collaborate with simultaneous document editing. Specifically, **SkyDrive** is an online cloud computing technology that offers a certain amount of collaborative storage space free that is integrated with Office 2013.

Traditionally for file storage, files are saved locally on a hard drive or external storage device like a USB drive. A **USB drive** is a small and portable storage device—popular for moving files back and forth between a lab, office, and/or home computer. However, USBs are also easily lost. Further, file versions and backups are usually manually maintained causing versioning problems.

File storage cloud technologies are made possible through Apps that sync all the files for all of your devices. When you edit a file, your computer or device automatically updates the file in the online storage location. All of the other computers and devices check the online storage for changes and update as needed. Thus, when saving your file, you automatically place a copy online and in all of your synced computers. This creates an online backup if your computer crashes. Additionally, there is no USB drive to lose. File-versioning problems are also minimized. Once all applications are properly set up, you have your files everywhere you want them and shared with exactly who needs them without having copies of files around or e-mailing attachments.

REAL WORLD ADVICE | **Backing Up the Cloud**

Best practice still dictates bringing files to important meetings on a physical drive such as a USB drive as backup. Cloud technologies are dependent on an Internet connection. Nothing is worse than showing up for a presentation and you cannot get to your files because of a poor Internet connection.

The Save As option in Office Backstage View gives you direct access to SkyDrive, which you can access with the same Microsoft account discussed earlier in the workshop—except Access, which requires you to save locally. With SkyDrive Apps or SkyDrive Pro, you have a local folder directly accessible from the File Explorer that automatically syncs with SkyDrive. Thus, you can sync Access files in the local syncing SkyDrive folder.

Microsoft has designed Office 2013 and SkyDrive to complement one another. When Office 2013 is not available on the computer you are using, you can even view, download, upload, and perform some limited revision via a browser at SkyDrive.com.

Creating a Document on SkyDrive

To use SkyDrive, you need your Microsoft account. After you sign in, you can create new folders and save files into the folders. You will need to have Internet access to complete this exercise.

CF01.21

 To Create a New Document at SkyDrive

a. On the taskbar, click **Internet Explorer** to open Internet Explorer; or alternatively, from the search screen, search for Internet Explorer to open the program.

b. In the address bar type skydrive.live.com.

c. If prompted, log in with your Microsoft account created earlier in the workshop.

d. Click **Create**, and then click **Word document** to create a new document.

e. Type cf01ws01SkyDrive_LastFirst using your last and first name, and then click **Create**.

f. Type your first name and last name, and then press Enter.

g. Type List of New Gift Shop Products. You intend to edit the list and share it will all employees after the meeting.

h. Click the **FILE** tab, and then click **Save**.

i. To return to your SkyDrive folders, click **Exit** ⌷ x ⌷ in the top-right corner of the document.

j. Explore the SkyDrive browser interface. To add a file you previously saved, click **Upload**. To delete a file from the folder, select the check box in the top-right corner of the file's tile, click **Manage** from the menu across the top, and then click **Delete**. To share a file, select the check box in the top-right corner of the file's tile, and then click **Share**. Follow the prompts for sharing.

k. Click your **name or picture**—located in the top-right corner—and then click **Sign Out** to exit SkyDrive. Close Internet Explorer.

Roaming Settings

Office 2013's **roaming settings** are a group of settings that offer easy remotely synced user-specific data that affects the Office experience. Across logins these settings remain the same. When signing into Office 2013, the user will experience Office the same way, no matter whether they are on a desktop, a laptop, or a mobile device.

Office 2013 includes the following roaming settings: Most Recently Used List (MRU) Documents and Places, MRU Templates, Office Personalization, Custom Dictionary, List of Connected Services, Word Resume Reading Position, OneNote—custom name a notebook view, and in PowerPoint the Last Viewed Slide.

Word Resume reading appears when you reopen a document. You are given a choice to keep reading where you left off. Word remembers where you were—even when you reopen an online document from a different computer.

Inserting Apps for Office

To enhance the features of Office, Office 2013 is the first version of Office to allow you to install apps from Microsoft's Office Store—**Apps for Office**, as shown in Figures 32 and 33. These apps run in the side pane to provide extra features like web search, dictionary, and maps. You will have to create an account to take advantage of them. You must be running Office 2013, and you must be signed into Office with your Microsoft Account.

1. Open up any Office applications in which you want to use apps.
2. Go to the Insert tab, and then select Apps for Office. Select See All from the menu.
3. The Apps for Office window appears showing all the apps you have installed to your Microsoft account under My Apps. If you see the app you want, select the app, and then click Insert.
4. If you do not see the app you want, click the Find more apps at the Office Store link.
5. Search for the app you want, and then follow the steps online to install the app to your account. You may have to sign into your Microsoft account.
6. Once installed, return to the Office application and repeat steps 2 and 3.

Figure 32   Apps for Office window with one app installed

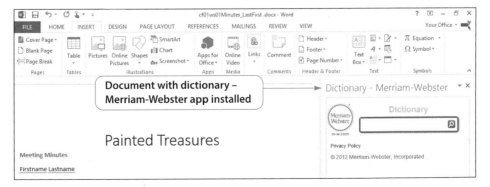

Figure 33   Dictionary - Merriam-Webster app

Use Touch Mode, Gestures, and Reading Mode

Office touch integration is based on the gestures underlying Windows 8 **touch gestures**. Microsoft provides an Office Touch Guide on the website and in Help by searching for Gesture Guide. The main gestures used are: tap, pinch, stretch, slide, and swipe. On a desktop with a touch-screen monitor, you can change this behavior back to the more traditional page navigation mode if you wish.

Using Touch Mode

Touch mode switches Office into a version that makes a touch screen easy to use. Click the Touch Mode button [icon] on the Quick Access Toolbar, and the Ribbon toolbar spreads its icons further apart for easier access to fingers. When you toggle this display mode, the on-screen controls space out a bit from each other to make them more accessible to users via touch. Figure 34 displays the normal Word 2013 Ribbon. Figure 35 displays the Ribbon in touch mode.

Figure 34   Normal Ribbon

Figure 35   Touch mode Ribbon

Using Touch Gestures

In addition to the main tap, pinch, stretch, slide, and swipe gestures, another common touch gesture is the bezel swipe gesture. **A bezel swipe gesture** is started on the bezel, which is the physical touch-insensitive frame that surrounds the display. The user swipes a finger from a part of the display edge into the display. Depending upon the device, a bezel swipe supports multiple object selection such as cutting, copying, pasting, and other operations on mobile touch-screen devices without conflicting with the panning and zooming gestures. Table 4 provides the Microsoft touch gestures guide.

Using Reading View

The new Reading View in Word 2013 is optimized for touch screens. By swiping your finger horizontally, you can navigate through the document. If you are reading, not writing or editing, **Read Mode** hides the writing tools and menus to leave more room for the pages themselves. Read Mode automatically fits the page layout to your device, using columns and larger font sizes, both of which you can adjust.

To	Gestures Steps
Enter full screen	1. Tap the Ribbon Display Options button in the top-right corner. 2. Tap Auto-hide Ribbon.
Enter standard view	1. Tap the Ribbon Display Options button. 2. Tap Show Tabs and Commands.
Show or hide touch keyboard	1. Tap the Touch Keyboard button to show. 2. Tap the Close button on the Touch keyboard to hide.
Scroll	1. Touch the document. 2. Move finger up and down while maintaining contact.
Zoom in and out	1. Stretch two fingers to zoom in. 2. Pinch two fingers to zoom out.
Place the cursor insertion point	1. Tap the location for the cursor.
Select and format text	1. Tap. 2. Drag the selection handle to desired selection. 3. Tap the selection to show and use the Mini toolbar.
Edit an Excel cell	1. Double-tap.
Change PowerPoint slides in Normal view	1. Make a quick vertical flick.

Table 4 Microsoft's Touch Gestures Guide

CF01.22

  To Use and Close Read Mode

SIDE NOTE
Alternative Method
On the status bar, click the Read Mode icon. Click Print Layout View to exit Read Mode.

a. Click the **VIEW** tab, and then in the Views group, click **Read Mode**. Notice this is the same view that protected documents are in when opened.

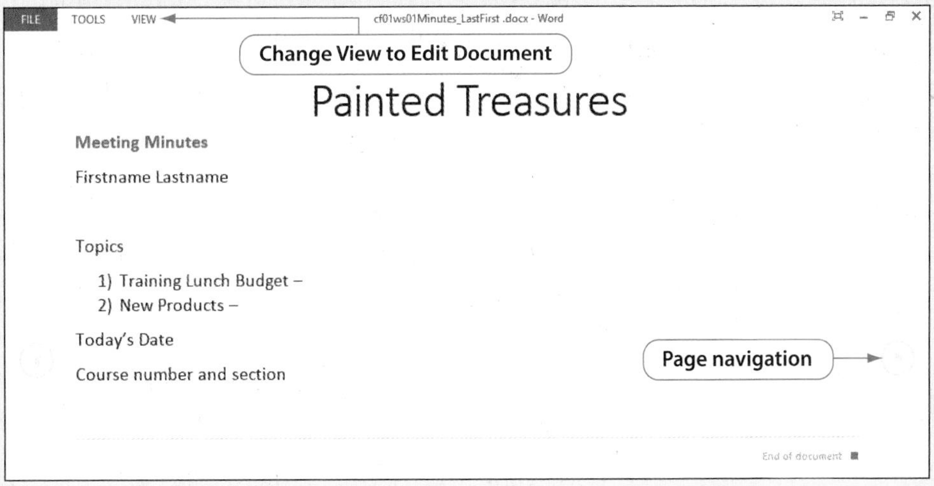

FILE   TOOLS   VIEW   cf01ws01Minutes_LastFirst .docx - Word

Change View to Edit Document

Painted Treasures

Meeting Minutes

Firstname Lastname

Topics
   1) Training Lunch Budget –
   2) New Products –

Today's Date

Course number and section

Page navigation

End of document ■

Figure 36 Meeting Minutes in Read Mode

b. Click the **VIEW** menu, and then select **Edit Document** to exit reading mode.

c. Press Ctrl+S. Then, click **Close** X in the top-right corner. Notice that the file closes and you exit the Word application.

Concept Check

1. What kind of Microsoft account and program do you need to create a budget? p. 4–6

2. What is the difference between the Windows and Word Start screens? p. 7–8

3. Which tab on the Ribbon would you use to change the margins in a Word document? p. 15

4. Explain the main purpose of Office Backstage View. p. 24

5. Describe ways to obtain help in Office 2013. p. 30–33

6. How could you share a newsletter with all the members of your business fraternity without printing? p. 33–35

7. What are the advantages of using SkyDrive instead of a USB flash drive? p. 35–36

8. What features in Office 2013 make using a touch screen easier? p. 38

Key Terms

Application Start screen   7
Apps for Office   37
AutoRecovery   24
Bezel swipe gesture   38
Bootcamp   6
Charms   7
Close   12
Cloud computing   35
Contextual tab   20
Contextual tools   20
Dialog box   19
Dialog Box Launcher   19
Document   4
Exit   12
File extension   25
Gallery   18
Graphic   4
Help   30

Information management
   program   4
Key tip   18
Keyboard shortcut   18
Live Preview   18
Maximize   12
Mini toolbar   21
Minimize   12
Most Recently Used list   28
Office 365   5
Office Backstage View   24
Portable document format
   (PDF)   34
Protected View   28
Quick Access Toolbar   25
Read Mode   38
Relational database   4
Restore Down   12

Ribbon   14
Ribbon display options   12
Roaming settings   37
ScreenTip   32
Shortcut menu   23
SkyDrive   35
Table   4
Task pane   20
Thumbnail   11
Toggle buttons   16
Touch gestures   38
Touch mode   38
USB drive   35
Windows Phone   5
Windows Run Time (RT)   5
Windows Start screen   7
Workbook   4

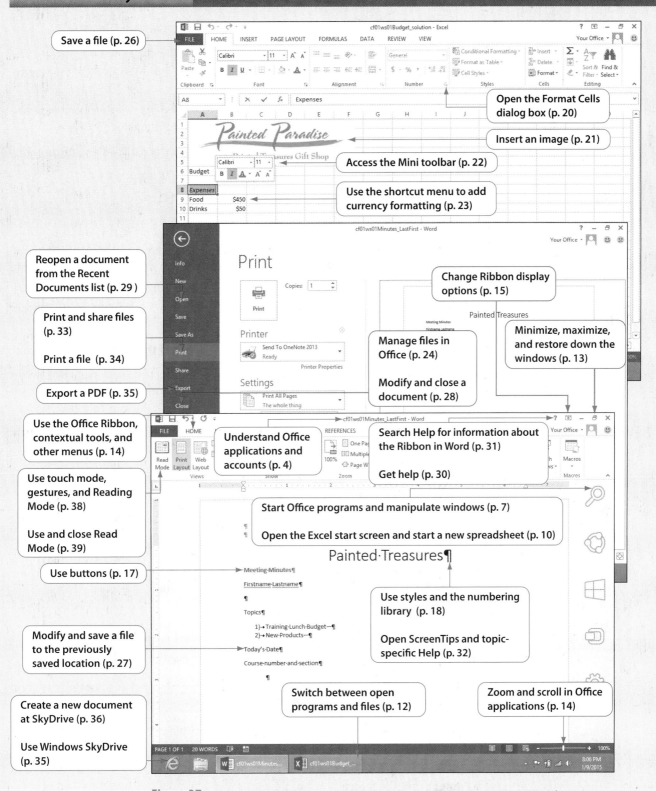

Save a file (p. 26)

Open the Format Cells dialog box (p. 20)

Insert an image (p. 21)

Access the Mini toolbar (p. 22)

Use the shortcut menu to add currency formatting (p. 23)

Reopen a document from the Recent Documents list (p. 29)

Print and share files (p. 33)

Print a file (p. 34)

Export a PDF (p. 35)

Use the Office Ribbon, contextual tools, and other menus (p. 14)

Use touch mode, gestures, and Reading Mode (p. 38)

Use and close Read Mode (p. 39)

Use buttons (p. 17)

Modify and save a file to the previously saved location (p. 27)

Create a new document at SkyDrive (p. 36)

Use Windows SkyDrive (p. 35)

Change Ribbon display options (p. 15)

Manage files in Office (p. 24)

Modify and close a document (p. 28)

Minimize, maximize, and restore down the windows (p. 13)

Understand Office applications and accounts (p. 4)

Search Help for information about the Ribbon in Word (p. 31)

Get help (p. 30)

Start Office programs and manipulate windows (p. 7)

Open the Excel start screen and start a new spreadsheet (p. 10)

Use styles and the numbering library (p. 18)

Open ScreenTips and topic-specific Help (p. 32)

Switch between open programs and files (p. 12)

Zoom and scroll in Office applications (p. 14)

Figure 37   Painted Paradise Resort and Spa Employee Training Preparation Complete

Student data file needed:

 Blank Word document

You will save your file as:

cf01ws01Agenda_LastFirst.docx

Creating an Agenda

Human Resources

Susan Brock, the manager of the gift shop, needs to write an agenda for the upcoming training session she will be holding. You will assist her by creating the agenda.

a.   Start **Microsoft Word 2013**, and then on the Word Start screen, click **Blank document**.

b.   On the HOME tab, in the Font group, click **Bold**.

c.   Type Training Agenda and then press Enter.

d.   Click **Bold** to toggle the feature off.

e.   Position the insertion point to the left of the word **Training**, press and hold the left mouse button, drag the cursor across the text to the end of the word **Agenda**, and then release the mouse button. All the text in the line should be highlighted.

f.   On the HOME tab, in the Font group, click the **Font Size** arrow. Select **20** to make the font size larger.

g.   In the Paragraph group, click the **Borders** arrow ⊞▾, and then select the first option, **Bottom Border**.

h.   Click the second line under the border you just inserted. Under Training Agenda, type today's date and then press Enter twice.

i.   In the Paragraph group, click the **Bullets** arrow. Under the Bullet Library, click the **circle** bullet—the third option in the gallery.

j.   Type Welcome trainees 2:00 pm and then press Enter.

k.   Type Using the Register and then press Enter.

l.   Type Customer Service Policies and then press Enter.

m.   Type Wrap-Up and then press Enter twice to turn off the bullet feature.

n.   Click the **FILE** tab to open Office Backstage View, and then click **Save As**.

o.   Click **Computer**, click **Browse**, and then Navigate to the location where you are saving your student data files.

p.   Type cf01ws01Agenda_LastFirst, using your last and first name.

q.   Click the **Save** button.

r.   Click the **INSERT** tab, and then in the Header & Footer group, click the **Footer** arrow, and then select the first option, **Blank**.

s.   On the HEADER & FOOTER TOOLS DESIGN tab, in the Insert group, click **Document Info**, and then select **File Name**.

t.   On the HEADER & FOOTER TOOLS DESIGN tab, in the Close group, click **Close Header and Footer** to exit the footer.

u.   Press Ctrl + S to save your changes.

v.   Close the cf01ws01Agenda_LastFirst document, and then exit Word.

w.   Submit your file as directed by your instructor.

Student data files needed:

 cf01ps1Expense.xlsx

cf01ps1Cookies.jpg

You will save your file as:

cf01ps1Expense_LastFirst.xlsx

Finance & Accounting

Formatting an Expense Report

Recently, you opened a business with a few partners called Midnight Sweetness. With the slogan "No more starving late-night studies," the business specializes in delivering freshly baked cookies, brownies, and other sweet treats to local college students. Midnight Sweetness has been a huge success. Currently, you rent a small building that includes major kitchen appliances. Now, you and your partners are looking for a bank loan to expand your business. You are responsible for putting together an expense report from last month to include in the bank application.

a. Open the **cf01ps1Expense** workbook. Save it as cf01ps1Expense_LastFirst. Click **Enable Content** if necessary.

b. Click cell **A1**, and then change the font to **bold**, **20** point, and the standard color **Blue**.

c. Click cell **A2**, and then change the font to **bold**.

d. Click cell **B3**, and then type your first and last name.

e. Click cell **A5**, and then right-align the text.

f. Click cell **A6**, and then right-align the text.

g. Click cell **A16**, and then right-align the text.

h. Click cell **A8**, and then change the font to italic.

i. Select the range **B9:B16**, and then format the cells as **Currency** with **0** decimals.

j. Click cell **B15**, and then add a **double bottom border**.

k. Click cell **D1**, insert the image **cf01ps1Cookies**, and then set the image height to **3.5**.

l. Save and close the cf01ps1Expense_LastFirst workbook, and then exit Excel.

m. Submit your file as directed by your instructor.

Student data file needed:

 Blank Excel workbook

You will save your file as:

cf01pf1OfficeTraining_LastFirst.xlsx

Information Technology

Creating a Training Schedule

One of the managers you work for at a local real estate company—Hope Properties—has asked you to create a training schedule in Excel for several of the trainings he is planning to schedule. The trainings include Windows 8, Word 2013, Excel 2013, and PowerPoint 2013. The trainings will be offered on Mondays: January 13, January 27, February 10, and February 24, 2014. Each training is three hours in length with one hour between sessions. The first session starts at 9:00 am. There are two trainings per day. You will create an attractive schedule using features you worked with in this workshop.

a. Start **Excel**. Using the features of Excel, create a training spreadsheet that is attractive and easy to read. Some suggestions include the following.

- Create column headings for the application and date of training.
- Enter the session times in the cells where the application and date meet.
- Format the date as a long date.
- Format the column headings.
- Format a title for the workbook.
- Use bold, italics, and colors.

b. Save and Close the cf01pf1OfficeTraining_LastFirst workbook, and then exit Excel.

c. Submit your file as directed by your instructor.

Perform 2: Perform in Your Life

Student data files needed:

 Blank Word document

 cf01pf2Vintage.docx

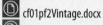 cf01pf2Dinner.xlsx

You will save your file as:

 cf01pf2Critique_LastFirst.docx

Improving the Appearance of Files

Finance & Accounting

Human Resources

Your boss at a local vintage clothing store has asked you to review a spreadsheet and a document—made by a prior employee—and make suggestions on what to do to improve the appearance of the document and spreadsheet. Examine the two files cf01pf2Vintage and cf01pf2Dinner. Answer the questions below.

a. Open a new blank document in Word, and then save the file as cf01pf2Critique_LastFirst.

b. List five items you would change in the document and why?

c. List five items you would change in the spreadsheet and why?

d. Exit Word, and then submit your file as directed by your instructor.

Additional Cases

Additional Workshop Cases are available on the companion website and in the instructor resources.

WORKSHOP 1 | NAVIGATE, MANIPULATE, AND PRINT WORKSHEETS

OBJECTIVES

1. Understand spreadsheet terminology and components   p. 46

2. Navigate within worksheets and workbooks, and navigate among worksheets   p. 49

3. Document your work   p. 52

4. Enter and edit data   p. 54

5. Manipulate cells and cell ranges   p. 58

6. Manipulate columns and rows   p. 65

7. Manipulate worksheets and workbooks   p. 72

8. Preview, export, and print worksheets   p. 78

Prepare Case

Red Bluff Golf Course and Pro Shop Golf Cart Purchase Analysis

Finance & Accounting

The Red Bluff Golf Course and Pro Shop makes golf carts available to its members for a fee. Recently, the resort has been running out of carts. The time has come for the club to add more golf carts to its fleet of 10. Club manager, Barry Cheney, wants to use Microsoft Excel to analyze the purchase of golf carts by model, price, and financing parameters.

Laura Gangi Pond / Shutterstock

REAL WORLD SUCCESS

"My family has operated the same farm for four generations. When I graduated from college I decided to become the first woman to run the family farm. I now track all of our production inputs and outputs using Excel. The quality information I produce with Excel has made our farm more efficient and more profitable. Farming is a business—a successful business requires intelligence in handling information as much, or more, than it requires intelligence in any other critical business activity."

- Leah, recent graduate

Student data file needed for this workshop:

 e01ws01GolfCarts.xlsx

You will save your files as:

 e01ws01GolfCarts_LastFirst.xlsx

 e01ws01GolfCartsP_LastFirst.pdf

 e01ws01Mowers_LastFirst.xlsx

Excel—What If Data and Information Could Speak?

Data play an integral part in supporting business. Without data, businesses are not able to determine their effectiveness in the market, let alone their profit or loss performance. In addition, as businesses grow and change, the types of data collected by a particular business is one of the few things that remain relatively static over time. Jobs change, products change, and businesses grow or evolve into different lines of business—even into different organizations—based on customer and market demands. However, the data gathered and analyzed is relatively constant. Data tracked typically only expand as new data is made available and deemed necessary for business purposes, or as new technologies easily capture data that was prohibitive to track in the past. Much of the same information is required about customers, vendors, products, services, materials, transactions, and so on regardless of the line, or type, of business. Many things may change, but the type of information remains the same.

The problem is that in all that data, there is so much information to decipher. Thus, data require processing—categorization, counting, averaging, summarization, statistical analysis, and formatting for effective communication—to reveal information that the data cannot tell you itself. With an application like Excel, it is possible to structure data and to process it in a manner that creates information for decision-making purposes. With the help of Excel, you give data a voice, a medium through which underlying trends, calculated values, predictions, decision recommendations, and other information can be revealed.

In this workshop, you will be introduced to spreadsheets, called worksheets in Excel. You will learn to create worksheets and to manipulate rows and columns, as well as to navigate in and among worksheets within a workbook. You will learn how to enter data—text, numbers, dates, and times—into a worksheet, and how to use a few powerful analysis features that enable you to give data a voice.

Understand Spreadsheet Terminology and Components

To learn the efficient and effective utilization of Excel, you must know the terminology and componentry of a spreadsheet. In this section, you will learn the basic terms that are used universally to reference spreadsheet components in Excel.

What Is a Spreadsheet?

A **spreadsheet** application is a computer program with a user interface that is made of a grid of rows and columns. The intersection of each row and column is called a **cell**. A **row** is a horizontal set of cells that encompasses all the columns in a worksheet and only one cell vertically. A **column** is a vertical set of cells that encompasses all the rows in a worksheet and only one cell horizontally. Each cell can contain text, numbers, formulas, and/or functions. A **formula** is an equation that produces a result and may contain numbers, operators, text, and/or functions. A **function** is a built-in program that performs a task such as calculating a sum or average. Both formulas and functions must always start with the equal sign (=). In Excel, each instance of a spreadsheet is referred to as a **worksheet**.

From balancing an accounting ledger to creating a financial report, many business documents use Excel spreadsheets. Excel spreadsheets are designed to support analyzing business data, representing data through charts, and modeling real-world situations.

Spreadsheets are also commonly used to perform **what-if analysis**. In what-if analysis, you change values in spreadsheet cells to investigate the effects on calculated values of interest.

Spreadsheets are used for much more than what-if analysis, however. A spreadsheet can be used as a basic collection of data where each row is a **record** and each column is a **field** in the record. Spreadsheets can be built to act as a simple accounting system. Businesses often use spreadsheets to analyze complex financial statements and information. Excel can calculate statistical values such as mean, variance, and standard deviation. Excel can even be used for advanced statistical models such as forecasting and regression analysis. Spreadsheet applications "excel" at calculations of most any kind.

What Is a Workbook?

A **workbook** is a file that contains at least one worksheet. In Microsoft Excel 2013, workbooks have a file extension of .xlsx. By default a new, blank workbook contains one worksheet, identified by a tab at the bottom of the Excel window titled Sheet1. As additional worksheets are added, they are given the default name Sheet*n* where "*n*" is an integer incremented by 1 for each new worksheet; for example, two new worksheets would be given the names Sheet2 and Sheet3. The active worksheet is denoted by a white tab with bold letters and a thick bottom border. Worksheets that are not active are denoted by gray tabs with normal letters. The number of worksheets that can be contained in a workbook is determined by the amount of available memory.

Once a workbook has been created, or opened, any changes to the workbook will need to be saved. Save and Save As accomplish the same task; however, Save As is useful for saving a copy of a file with a new name. It is also useful for creating a backup of a file or for creating a copy of a workbook when you want to use that workbook as the starting point for another workbook.

In the first exercise, you will learn how to start Excel, to open a workbook, and to save that workbook with a new name.

E01.00

 To Start Excel, and Open, Save, and Rename a Workbook

a. Point to the **bottom-right corner** of the Start screen or desktop.

   The Charms will appear on the right side of the screen. Move the pointer over the bottom charm. Note the labels underneath each of the charms.

b. Click **Search**.

c. Click inside the **Search** box at the top of the page, and then type Excel.

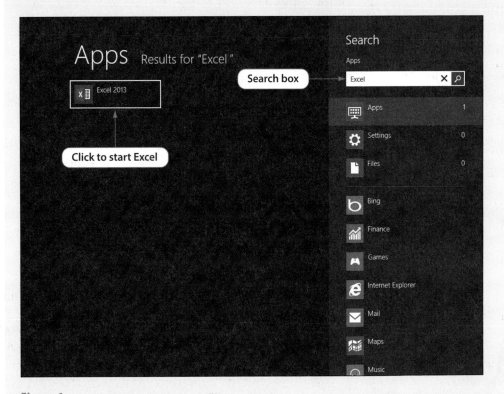

Figure 1 Starting Microsoft Excel 2013

d. Click **Excel 2013** in the search results.

e. In the lower-left corner of the Excel screen, click **Open Other Workbooks**.

f. In the **Open pane** under Places, click **Computer** and then click **Browse**.

g. Click the **disk drive** in the left pane where your student data files are located—you may have to double-click **Computer** to see the disk drive list, navigate through the folder structure, and then select **e01ws01GolfCarts**.

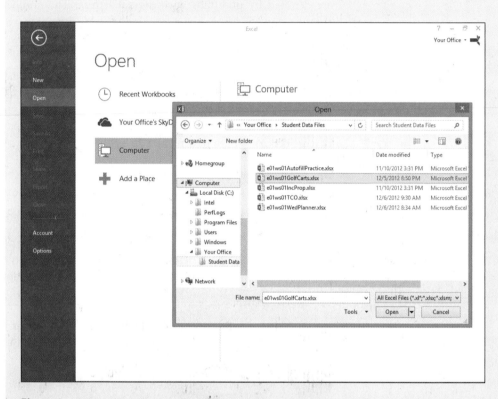

Figure 2   Open an existing workbook

h. Click **Open**.

i. Click the **FILE** tab to access Backstage view.

The Info pane is displayed. The Info pane displays document properties such as file size, create and modified dates, and author.

j. Click **Save As**, click **Browse**, and then in the Save As dialog box, navigate to the location where you are saving your files. Click in the **File name** box, type **e01ws01GolfCarts_LastFirst** using your last and first name. Click **Save**.

CONSIDER THIS | **Excel Can Store a Vast Amount of Data**

There are 1,048,576 rows x 16,384 columns = 17,179,869,184 cells in an Excel 2013 worksheet. With so much capacity, some are tempted to use Excel as a database. What other Office application would be better for storing vast amounts of data?

REAL WORLD ADVICE	AutoRecover and Quick Save—Outsmart Mr. Murphy!

Computers are not perfect. While life's imperfections often make things interesting, they are also an opportunity for Murphy's Law: Anything that can go wrong, will go wrong. However, never fear, AutoRecover and Quick Save are here!

Excel automatically saves your work every 10 minutes, but you can change that interval. Click in Backstage view under Options, and then click the Save tab. In the Excel Options dialog box, change the value in the Save AutoRecover information every box. The saved copies of your work are called AutoRecover files. If your computer shuts down unexpectedly, Office will recognize that the file you were working on was not closed properly and will give you the option of opening the most recent AutoRecover file.

The [Ctrl] + [S] shortcut quickly saves your file to the same location as the last save. Whenever you make a significant change to your file, save it right away using the "quick save" keyboard shortcut.

Navigate Within Worksheets and Workbooks

Workbooks often contain more than a single worksheet, and in order to effectively develop and use workbooks and worksheets you must be able to navigate between and among worksheets in a workbook and to navigate in the worksheets. In this section you will learn to navigate within a worksheet and to navigate between worksheets.

Navigate Among Worksheets

Workbooks often contain more than one worksheet. The workbook you have opened contains four worksheets. The worksheet tabs are located in the bottom-left corner of the Excel window. Each tab represents a single worksheet in the workbook.

The **active worksheet**, the worksheet that is visible, is readily identifiable because the background color of its worksheet tab is white and it has a thick bottom border. To make a different worksheet active, click its worksheet tab.

When you open a workbook that you have not worked with before, it is a good practice to spend some time familiarizing yourself with its worksheets. In the following exercise, you navigate among worksheets to familiarize yourself with the contents of the e01ws01GolfCarts_LastFirst workbook.

MyITLab®
Workshop 1 Training

E01.01

 To Change the Active Worksheet

a. Click the **May Golf Cart Usage Analysis** worksheet tab. This worksheet is an analysis of golf cart usage for the month of May that Barry Cheney built to assess whether the number of carts in the current fleet is optimal.

 Worksheet scroll arrows

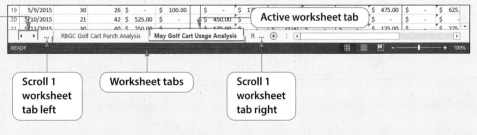

Scroll 1 worksheet tab left

Worksheet tabs

Scroll 1 worksheet tab right

Figure 3 Change the active worksheet

SIDE NOTE

Navigate Between Sheets Using Shortcuts

Ctrl + PageUp and Ctrl + PageDown move you one worksheet to the left and right respectively.

SIDE NOTE

Navigate Quickly Among Many Worksheets

Right-click the worksheet scroll arrows and select the worksheet you want to make active in the Activate dialog box.

b. Click the **RBGC Golf Cart Purch Analysis** worksheet tab in the bottom-left corner of the worksheet window. This worksheet is the start of a purchase analysis for replacement of the Red Bluff Golf Course fleet of golf carts.

c. Click the **Documentation** worksheet tab—you may need to scroll left using the worksheet scroll arrows to see the Documentation worksheet tab.

This worksheet is used to document the contents of the workbook. Documentation is an important component in a well-structured workbook.

> **Troubleshooting**
>
> All the figures in this text were taken at a monitor resolution of 1024 X 768. Higher or lower resolution will affect the way Excel displays Ribbon options.

Navigating Worksheets

Whether a worksheet is small or extremely large, navigation from one cell to another is necessary to enter, or to edit, numbers, formulas, functions, or text. Navigation requires an understanding of how Excel addresses rows, columns, and cells.

Each row is identified by a number in ascending sequence from top to bottom. Each column is identified by a letter in ascending sequence from left to right. The intersection of each row and column is called a cell. Each cell has a default name, called a **cell reference**—the combination of its column letter and row number. For example, the intersection of column A and row 1 has a cell reference of A1, and the intersection of column D and row 20 is cell D20.

Navigating in a small worksheet is simple—move the mouse pointer over a cell and click to make it the active cell. The **active cell** is the recipient of an action, such as a click, calculation, or paste. The border around the cell changes to a thick, green line. Any information you enter via the keyboard is placed into the active cell. **Worksheet navigation** is simply defined as moving the location of the active cell.

When part of a document—or in the case of Excel, a worksheet—is out of view because it is too large to be displayed in the visible application window, use the vertical and horizontal scroll bars to shift other parts of the document into view. The vertical scroll bar is on the right side of the application window, and the horizontal scroll bar is at the bottom right of the application window. It is important to note that scrolling does not move the active cell, only your view in the document.

For large worksheets, Go To allows rapid navigation. Although the worksheet you are currently working with is not large, knowledge of how to use the Go To dialog box to navigate directly to any cell in the worksheet by specifying a cell reference is a skill that you will find useful.

Keyboard shortcuts allow rapid navigation in a worksheet without having to usethe mouse. It is considered best practice to learn and use keyboard shortcuts whenever possible.

QUICK REFERENCE	Navigation with Keyboard Shortcuts

There are several keyboard shortcuts that may be used to navigate a worksheet and move the active cell:

Keyboard Shortcuts	Moves the Active Cell
Enter	Down one row
Shift + Enter	Up one row
→ ← ↓ ↑	One cell in the direction of the arrow key
Home	To column A of the current row
Ctrl + Home	To column A, row 1 (cell A1)
Ctrl + End	To the last cell, highest number row and far-right column, that contains information
End + → End + ← End + ↓ End + ↑	If the first cell in the direction of the arrow beyond the active cell contains data, to the last cell containing data in the arrow direction before an empty cell If the first cell in the direction of the arrow beyond the active cell is empty, to the next cell in the arrow direction that contains information
Page Up Page Down	Up one screen, down one screen
Alt + Page Up	Left one screen
Alt + Page Down	Right one screen
Ctrl + Page Up Ctrl + Page Down	One worksheet left One worksheet right
Tab Shift + Tab	One column right One column left

E01.02

 To Navigate Within a Worksheet

a. Click the **RBGC Golf Cart Purch Analysis** worksheet tab, and then press Ctrl + Home to make A1 the active cell. Press ↓ six times, and then press → four times. The active cell should be E7. Type 6495 and then press Ctrl + Enter to keep cell E7 active.

b. Press ←, and then press ↑ two times. The active cell should be D5. Type E-Z-GO and then press Enter.

   Notice that the active cell is now D6. Pressing Enter moved the active cell down one row.

c. On the HOME tab, in the Editing group, click **Find & Select**, and then click **Go To**. The Go To dialog box appears. Click in the **Reference** box, type D13, and then click **OK**. The active cell is now D13. On the HOME tab, in the Font group, click **Bold** B.

d. Press Home. This takes you to column A of the row with the active cell. The active cell should be A13. Type Total Interest Cost: and then press Ctrl + Enter.

e. Press Ctrl + Home to return the active cell to A1, and then click **Save** 🖫.

Touch Devices

If you have a device such as a tablet PC with a touch screen, you can control Excel 2013 using your finger. The commands on the Ribbon and in shortcut menus are the same, but Excel recognizes when you have touched the screen and enables touch mode. In **touch mode**, the Ribbon and shortcut menus are enlarged to make selecting commands with your fingertip easier. Figure 4 shows the Excel interface in touch mode.

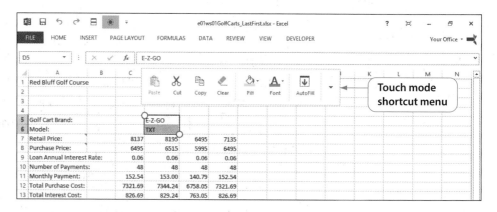

Figure 4   Touch mode in Excel 2013

Document Your Work

Worksheets are often used by people who did not develop them. Even if a worksheet will never be used by anyone other than its builder, best practice dictates that you document a workbook and its worksheets.

Documentation is vital to ensure that a worksheet remains usable. A well-documented worksheet is much easier to use and maintain, particularly for a user who did not develop the worksheet. You may use a worksheet on a regular basis, you may even have developed it, but over time you may forget how the worksheet actually operates.

Documentation takes several forms, such as descriptive file and worksheet names, worksheet titles, column and/or row titles, cell labels, cell comments, or a dedicated documentation worksheet. Many people do not take the time to document adequately because they do not feel it is time spent productively. Some do not feel it is necessary because they do not think anyone else will ever use the workbook. For a workbook to be useful, it must be accurate, easily understood, flexible, efficient, and documented. While accuracy is most important, an undocumented workbook can later create inaccurate data. Where documentation is concerned, less is not more—more is more.

Using Comments to Document a Workbook

Unlike documentation worksheets that generally include documentation for an entire workbook, comments are created specifically to add documentation to a worksheet and address individual fields, calculations, and so on and are included as content in an individual cell.

E01.03

To Document a Workbook Using Comments

a. Click the **RBGC Golf Cart Purch Analysis** worksheet tab. Notice that cell A7 has a red triangle in the upper-right corner. This indicates the existence of a comment. Point to cell **A7**. The comment that appears defines Retail Price.

b. Click cell **A9**. Click the **REVIEW** tab.

Figure 5   Insert a comment into a cell

c. In the Comments group, click **New Comment** to create a comment.

d. In the comment box, double-click the **user name** text that is automatically inserted into the comment. Press Delete to delete the user name. You may have to do this more than once if there are any spaces in the user name. Click the **HOME** tab. In the Font group, if Bold is turned off, then click **Bold** B to turn bold on. Click the **REVIEW** tab.

> **Troubleshooting**
>
> Double-clicking only selects a word. If your user name contains a space, repeat Step c until the user name is completely deleted before moving to Step d.

e. Type Annual Interest Rate, and then press Ctrl + B to turn off bold text. Press Enter, and then type Annual rate of interest in decimal or percentage format, e.g., 5% is entered as 0.05 or as 5%.

Cell A9 now has a red triangle in the top-right corner to indicate the presence of a comment.

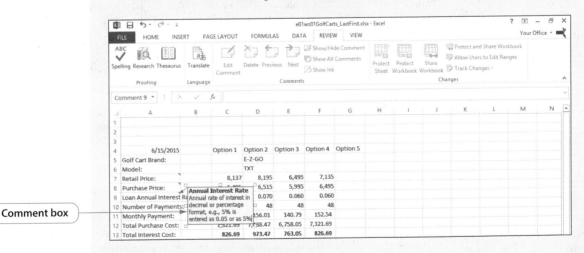

Figure 6   Documenting annual interest rate using a comment

f. Click cell **A10**, and then click **New Comment**.

g. In the comment box, double-click the **user name** text that is automatically inserted into the comment, and then press [Delete]. If necessary, repeat until the user name is completely removed. Click the **HOME** tab. In the Font group, if Bold is not turned on, click **Bold** [B].

h. Type # of Payments and then click **Bold** [B] to turn off bold text.

i. Press [Enter], type Total number of payments over the term of the loan and then press [Esc] two times to close the comment.

j. Click **Save** [⊞].

SIDE NOTE
Save Often

Murphy's Law for computers: The likelihood your computer will crash is proportional to the amount of time since you last saved.

Using a Worksheet for Documentation

A well-structured worksheet is self-documenting in that there are descriptive titles, column headings, and cell labels. However, a separate documentation worksheet includes information not generally specified in a worksheet, such as authorship, modification dates, and modification history.

SIDE NOTE
Shortcut to Insert the System Date

[Ctrl] + [;] is a keyboard shortcut that inserts the computer system date into the active cell.

E01.04

 To Document a Workbook Using a Documentation Worksheet

a. Click the **Documentation** worksheet tab—you may have to scroll left in the worksheet tabs. Click cell **A8**, and then type the current date in mm/dd/yyyy format.

b. Click cell **B8**, and then type your last name, first name.

c. Click cell **C8**, and then type Added comments to key headings.

d. Click **Save** [⊞].

S_S REAL WORLD ADVICE   Failing to Plan Is Planning to Fail

Winston Churchill said, "He who fails to plan, plans to fail." The first step in building a worksheet should be planning. There are several questions that should be considered before you begin actually entering information:

• What is the objective of the worksheet? Is it to solve a problem? Is it to analyze data and recommend a course of action? Is it to summarize data and present usable information? Is it to store information for use by another application?

• Do you have all of the data necessary to build this worksheet?

• What information does your worksheet need to generate?

• How should the information in your worksheet be presented? Who is the audience? What form will best present the worksheet information?

Plan your work before you begin—the time spent planning will be saved several times over, and the end result will be of higher quality.

Enter and Edit Data

In building and maintaining worksheets, the ability to enter, edit, and format data is fundamental. As data is entered via the keyboard, the data simultaneously appears in the active cell and in the formula bar. Figure 7 shows the result when a cell is double-clicked to place the insertion point into cell contents. If you click in the formula bar, the insertion point is displayed in the formula bar.

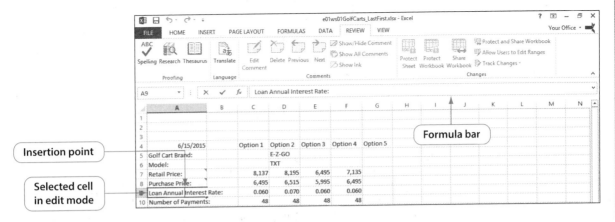

Insertion point

Selected cell in edit mode

Formula bar

Figure 7 Editing data in a cell

Using Text, Numbers, Dates, and Times

Text data consists of any combination of printable characters including letters, numbers, and special characters available on any standard keyboard.

Numeric data consists of numbers in any form not combined with letters and special characters such as the period (decimal) and/or hyphen (to indicate negativity). Technically, special characters such as the dollar sign ($) or comma (,) are not considered numeric. They are only displayed for contextual and readability purposes and are not stored as part of a numeric cell value.

In Excel, **date data** and **time data** are a special form of numeric data. Information entered in a recognized date and/or time format will be converted automatically to an Excel date and/or time value. Table 1 includes examples of valid dates and times that can be entered into Excel and how they will be displayed by default:

Enter	Excel Displays	Enter	Excel Displays
December 21, 2012	21-Dec-12	12/21/2012	12/21/2012
December 21, 2012 10 p	12/21/2012 22:00	2012/12/21	12/21/2012
Dec 21, 2012	21-Dec-12	13:00	13:00
21 Dec 2012 10:30	12/21/2012 10:30	1:00 p	1:00 PM

Table 1 Date entry and how Excel displays dates

If Excel recognizes a value as a date/time, it will right-align the entry. If you enter a date or time that is not recognized, Excel treats the information as text and left-aligns it in the cell. By default, Excel left-aligns text data and right-aligns numeric, date, and time data.

Storing Date and Time Data

Date and time information is automatically displayed in a format easily understood by the user, but Excel stores a date and time as a number where the digits to the left of the decimal place are the number of complete days since January 1, 1900, inclusive (1 = January 1, 1900) and the value to the right of the decimal place is the proportion of one day that represents a time value (1.1 = January 1, 1900 + 144 minutes = January 1, 1900 2:24 AM). The advantages of storing dates and times in what is commonly referred to as the 1900 date system are many:

- Sorting a list of dates and/or times is as simple as putting the list in ascending or descending numerical order.

- Since dates and times are real numbers, mathematical manipulation to add to, or to subtract from, dates and times is greatly simplified.
- Determining a time span is simply a function of subtracting one time from another—a single calculation.

The vast majority of applications and systems now store dates and times in this manner. The main difference among them is the base date. For example in DOS, Microsoft's precursor operating system to Windows, the base date is January 1, 1980.

REAL WORLD ADVICE   **Balance Cost with Consequences!**

The Y2K bug was the result of a widespread practice of storing the year as two digits—1999 was stored as 99; 2000 as 00. Most information systems sort information by date, and since 1999 is greater than 2000 when stored as a 2-digit year, as of 1/1/2000 many systems would have output incorrect information; it was feared that many systems would fail entirely.

Why store a 2-digit year? Unlike today, digital storage used to be very expensive—every character consumed expensive space.

The result was a massive worldwide effort in the late 1990s to eradicate the Y2K "bug" at a cost estimated by some to have exceeded $1 trillion—far more than was ever saved by storing 2-digit year values. The lesson for technology practitioners: Money saved by "cutting corners" today will cost you way more when you have to do it right later.

Do it right the first time, as much as is possible, and you will save a lot of time and resources in the long run.

SIDE NOTE
Undo Keyboard Shortcut
Ctrl + Z is a fast and efficient method of performing an Undo.

SIDE NOTE
Use Undo History
If you need to Undo a change but have made other changes since, click the Undo arrow to see the change history.

E01.05

To Enter Information into a Worksheet

a. Click the **RBGC Golf Cart Purch Analysis** worksheet tab, click cell **A2**, type Red Bluff Golf Course & Pro Shop and then press Enter.

b. In cell **A3**, type Golf Cart Purchase Analysis and then press Enter.

c. Notice the values in cells D11, D12, and D13. Click cell **D9**, type 0.06 and then press Enter. Notice the monthly payment in cell D11 changes to 153.00. The values in cells D11, D12, and D13 are automatically recalculated.

> **Troubleshooting**
> If the monthly payment is larger than it should be, you probably entered 0.6 or 006. That is actually 60% or 600% respectively for calculation purposes. You must enter the percentage, 6%, or enter 0.06—the decimal equivalent for 6%.

Wrapping Text and Line Breaks

Excel, by default, places all information in a single line in a cell. Text that is too long to fit in a cell is displayed over adjoining cells to the right, unless those cells contain information. If adjoining cells contain information, then lengthy text from cells to the left is not displayed.

Text truncation can be avoided by changing the alignment of a cell in order to wrap words or by placing hard returns into text to force wrapping at a particular location.

E01.06

▶ To Wrap Text in a Cell

a. Click the **Documentation** worksheet tab, click cell **C9**, and then type Entered a descriptive title for the cart purchase worksheet and updated the interest rate of the second golf cart. Press Ctrl + Enter.

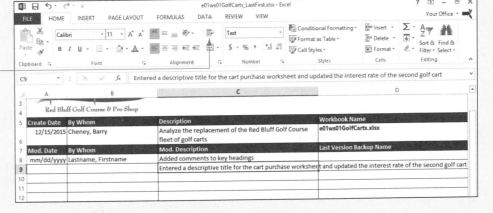

Figure 8 Wrap text

b. On the HOME tab, in the Alignment group, click **Wrap Text** . The vertical size of row 9 is increased to display all content within the boundaries of cell C9.

c. Click the **RBGC Golf Cart Purch Analysis** worksheet tab.

d. Double-click cell **A3**. If necessary, use either ← or → to move the insertion point, or click to position the insertion point, immediately after **Cart**. Press Delete to remove the space between Cart and Purchase, and then press Alt + Enter to insert a line break—often referred to as a hard return.

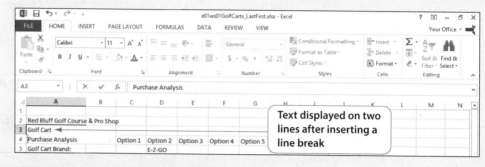

Figure 9   Insert a hard return to control text wrap location

e. Press Enter to complete the entry, and then click **Save** 🖫.

Manipulate Cells and Cell Ranges

Part of what makes a worksheet an efficient tool is the ability to perform actions that affect many cells at once. Knowing how to work with cells and cell ranges is an important part of maximizing your efficiency. **Cell range** refers to the cells in the worksheet that have been selected. A cell range can reference a single cell, several contiguous cells, or noncontiguous cells and cell ranges. A **contiguous cell range** consists of multiple selected cells, all directly adjacent to one another. A **noncontiguous cell range** consists of multiple selected cells, but at least one cell is not directly adjacent to other cells.

Cutting, Copying, and Pasting

Copy and paste copies everything in a cell, including formatting. Cut and paste moves everything in a cell, including formatting. However, through Paste Options 🗐 and Paste Special, you control exactly what is placed into the destination cells. A **destination cell** is the location into which the result of an operation, such as paste, is inserted. In the next exercise, you will learn to use Cut, Copy, and Paste in Excel. Later in this workshop, you will learn the advantages of Paste Options and Paste Special.

E01.07

  To Cut, Copy, and Paste Cells

a. Click the **RBGC Golf Cart Purch Analysis** worksheet tab, and then click cell **D5**. On the HOME tab, in the Clipboard group, notice that Paste 🗐 is not available—it is light gray in color.

b. In the Clipboard group, click **Cut** ✂.
   The solid border around cell D5 changes to a moving dashed border.
   Notice that once cell D5 has been cut to the Clipboard, Paste 🗐 is available.

c. Click cell **C5**.

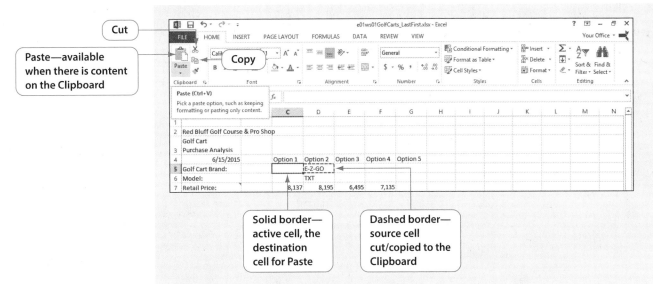

Figure 10   Cut, Copy, and Paste

d. In the Clipboard group, click **Paste**.

e. Click cell **D6**, and then in the Clipboard group, click **Copy** 📋. The solid border around cell D6 changes to a moving dashed border. Click cell **C6**, and then in the Clipboard group, click **Paste**.

f. Press Esc to clear the Clipboard and remove the dashed border from around cell D6. Notice that once the Clipboard is cleared, the Paste icon 📋 is again unavailable.

g. Click **Save** 💾.

Selecting Cell Ranges

Using the mouse, multiple cells can be selected simultaneously. Selected cells can be contiguous to each other or they can be noncontiguous. Once multiple cells are selected, they can be affected by actions such as clear, delete, copy, paste, formatting, and many other actions while offering the convenience of performing the desired task only once for the selected cells.

E01.08

▶ **To Select, Copy, and Paste to Contiguous and Noncontiguous Selections**

SIDE NOTE
Select a Range Using the Mouse
Click and hold on a cell and then drag the mouse pointer to select a cell range.

a. Click the **RBGC Golf Cart Purch Analysis** worksheet tab, and then click cell **C5**. Press Shift + ↓—the active cell border expands to include C5:C6, and the background color of selected cells also changes.

     Shift can be used in combination with other navigation keys and/or the mouse to select a contiguous range of cells.

b. Click the **HOME** tab, and then in the Clipboard group, click **Copy** 📋 to copy the selected cells to the Clipboard. Click cell **E5**, and then in the Clipboard group, click **Paste** to paste Clipboard contents to the selected cell.

c. Click cell **D5**, press and hold Ctrl, click cell **F5**, release Ctrl, and then press Shift + →.

     Ctrl is used in combination with other navigation keys and/or the mouse to select noncontiguous cell ranges.

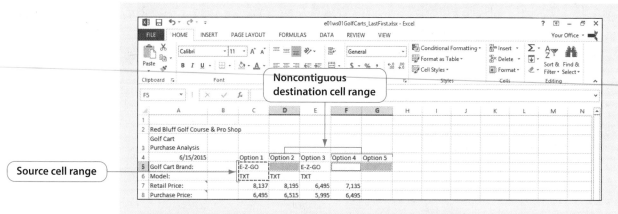

Source cell range

Noncontiguous destination cell range

Figure 11   Selecting a noncontiguous cell range

d. Click **Paste**, and then press Esc to clear the clipboard.

e. Click **Save** 🔲.

Dragging and Dropping

As worksheets are designed, built, and modified, it is often necessary to move information from one cell, or range of cells, to another. One of the most efficient ways to do this is called "drag and drop" and is accomplished with the mouse, as shown in the following exercise.

E01.09

 To Drag and Drop Cells

a. Click the **RBGC Golf Cart Purch Analysis** worksheet tab, and then click cell **A2**. Press and hold Shift, and then press ↓ two times. Cell range A2:A4 is selected. Point to the **border** of the selected range. The mouse pointer changes to a move pointer 🖟.

b. Click and hold the left mouse button, and then drag the selected cells up one row to cell range **A1:A3**. A ghost range, also referred to as a destination range, and destination range ScreenTip are displayed as the pointer is moved, to show exactly where the moved cells will be placed.

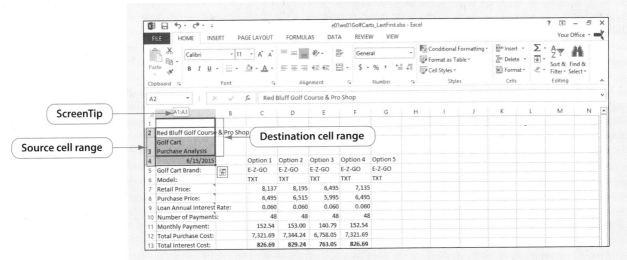

Figure 12   Drag and drop to move a cell range

c. Drop the dragged cells by releasing the mouse button.

d. Click cell **F13**. Press and hold `Shift`, press `End`, and then press `↑`. Cell range F4:F13 is selected. Press and hold `Shift`, and then press `↓` three times. Cell range F7:F13 is selected.

e. Move the mouse pointer until it is over the border of the selected range in column **F**. The mouse pointer changes to a move pointer. Press and hold `Ctrl`. The move pointer changes to a copy pointer. Drag the selected range until the ghost range is directly to the right of column F, over range **G7:G13**. Release the mouse button, and then release `Ctrl`.

   Cell range F7:F13 has been copied to cell range G7:G13.

f. Click **Save** .

Modifying Cell Information

Copying and pasting content from one range of cells to another range, or ranges, is a highly efficient way to reuse parts of a worksheet. The range you just copied into column G contains information that is calculated using formulas that you do not want to type more than once. However, once you have duplicated a cell or cell range, it is usually necessary to change some content.

   To edit the contents of cells, you double-click the cell to enter edit mode. The active cell will now contain an insertion point. If you want to change part of the content, use the arrow keys or click to position the insertion point at the desired location. If all the cell content is to be replaced, click the cell once to make it the active cell. All cell content will be replaced when you begin typing to enter the new content for the selected cell.

E01.10

▶ To Modify Worksheet Contents by Changing Copied Information

a. Click the **RBGC Golf Cart Purch Analysis** worksheet tab, click cell **D6**, type RXV, and then press `→`. Double-click cell **E6**, press `Home` to go to the left margin of the cell, type Freedom, and then press `Spacebar` once so the formula bar displays **Freedom TXT**. Press `Tab`, type Freedom RXV and then press `Tab`. Type The Drive and then press `Enter`.

b. In **G7**, type 6995 and then press `Enter`. In cell **G8**, type 6350 and then press `Ctrl` + `Enter`.
   Notice that when you changed the value in cell G8 that Monthly Payment, Total Purchase Cost, and Total Interest Cost are recalculated.

c. Click cell **G5**. Type Yamaha and then press Enter.

d. Click **Save** 🖫.

Inserting and Deleting Cells

It is often necessary to insert or remove cells in a worksheet. You may need to add or delete data or simply want to refine the white space in a worksheet to improve its readability.

You want to make the golf cart analysis worksheet easier to read and to use by refining the white space. **White space** refers to blank areas of a document that do not contain data or documentation. The blank space gives a document visual structure and creates a sense of order in the mind of the worksheet user. For example, white space above and below the titles "Loan Annual Interest Rate" and "Number of Payments" defines the area of information associated with financing the golf carts.

E01.11

 To Insert and Delete Cells and Cell Ranges in a Worksheet

a. Click the **RBGC Golf Cart Purch Analysis** worksheet tab, and then click cell **A4**. On the HOME tab, in the Cells group, click the **Insert** arrow.

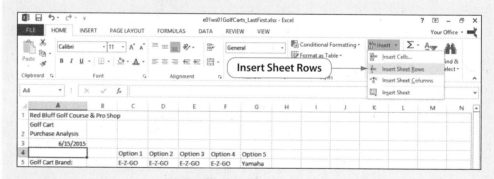

Figure 13 Home tab, Insert to insert sheet rows

SIDE NOTE
A Keyboard Shortcut to Insert
Ctrl + + will insert cells, rows, or columns depending on what is selected.

b. Click **Insert Sheet Rows**. Excel inserts a row above the active cell location and moves all cells in row 4 and below down.

c. Click cell **A8**, right-click cell **A8**, and then click **Insert** on the shortcut menu. In the Insert dialog box, click **Entire row**.

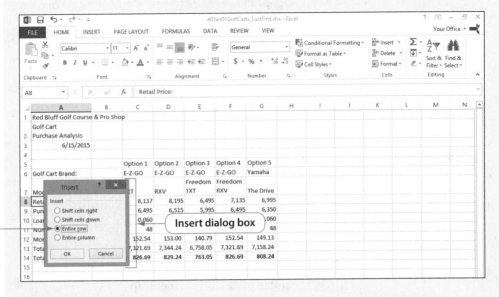

Insert Entire row

Insert dialog box

Figure 14 Insert dialog box

d. Click **OK**.

e. Click cell **A11**, and then press $\boxed{\text{Shift}}$ + $\boxed{\downarrow}$. Cell range A11:A12 is selected. In the Cells group, click the **Insert** arrow, and then click **Insert Sheet Rows**. Excel inserts a row for each row in the selected range.

f. Click cell **A15**, and then press $\boxed{\text{Shift}}$ + $\boxed{\downarrow}$. Right-click anywhere on the selected range, and then select **Insert** from the shortcut menu. Click **Entire row** in the Insert dialog box, and then click **OK**.

> **Troubleshooting**
>
> If you click the Insert button instead of the Insert arrow, Excel will default to inserting extra cells only, instead of a row. Press $\boxed{\text{Ctrl}}$ + $\boxed{\text{Z}}$ to undo the last change, and then repeat Step f.

g. Click cell **B5**, and then in the Cells group, click **Delete**.
   Notice that the Option headings in row 5 moved left.

> **Troubleshooting**
>
> Click the Delete icon, not the Delete arrow. Alternatively, you can click Delete Cells in the list.

h. Click cell **B6**, press and hold the mouse button, and then drag down until the active cell expands to select the range **B6:B19**. In the Cells group, click **Delete**. The remaining cell values in rows 6:19 moved left one cell.

   Inserting two rows above and below rows 13:14 appears to be too much. Often you cannot tell until you try, but the worksheet might look better if a couple of the rows of white space were removed.

i. Click a cell in row **11**, press $\boxed{\text{Ctrl}}$, and then click a cell in row **16**. In the Cells group, click the **Delete** arrow, and then click **Delete Sheet Rows**.

j. Click **Save** $\boxed{\square}$.

Merging and Centering vs. Centering Across

The titles in the golf cart analysis worksheet are in cells A1:A3. Although they contain the correct information to communicate the purpose of the golf cart analysis worksheet, they might better present that information with some formatting improvements. Titles that identify the general purpose of a worksheet are often at the top and centered above worksheet content.

Merge & Center ⊞▾ combines selected cells into a single cell and can be applied to horizontal or vertical cell ranges. Content in the left and/or top cell of the selected range is centered—all other data in the selected range is lost.

Center Across Selection removes the borders between cells such that a selected range looks like a single cell, but the original cells remain, the borders between them are hidden and the content is centered. Center Across Selection can only be applied horizontally. Additionally, Center Across Selection will never replace the data in the other cells.

E01.12

▶ **To Merge & Center Headings**

a. Click the **RBGC Golf Cart Purch Analysis** worksheet tab, and then press ⌈Ctrl⌋ + ⌈Home⌋. Press and hold ⌈Shift⌋, and then press ⌈→⌋ repeatedly until cell range **A1:F1** is selected. On the HOME tab, in the Alignment group, click **Merge & Center** ⊞▾.

b. Click cell **A2**. Press and hold ⌈Shift⌋, press ⌈↓⌋, and then press ⌈→⌋ repeatedly until cell range **A2:F3** is selected. In the Alignment group, click **Merge & Center** ⊞▾.

   Notice the warning message. If you Merge & Center data in more than one cell at a time, only the data in the upper-left cell of the selected range will be kept, the rest will be lost.

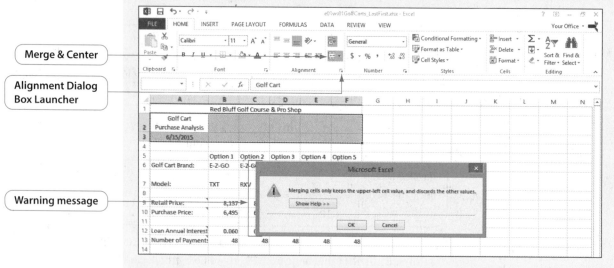

Figure 15 Merge and center a range containing multiple values and data

c. Click **Cancel**. You do not want to lose the data in cell A3.

> **Troubleshooting**
> You probably clicked OK instead of Cancel. Press ⌈Ctrl⌋ + ⌈Z⌋ to undo the last change and go back to Step b.

d. On the HOME tab, in the Alignment group, click the **Alignment Settings** Dialog Box Launcher. This opens the Format Cells dialog box. With the Alignment tab selected, click the **Horizontal** list, and then click **Center Across Selection**.

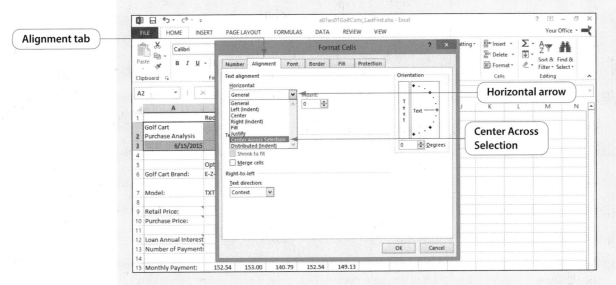

Figure 16 Center Across Selection

e. Click **OK**. Cell A2 content is centered across cell range A2:F2, and cell A3 content is centered across cell range A3:F3.

f. Click **Save**.

CONSIDER THIS | **Merge & Center and Cell Range Selection**

Try this: In the RBGC Golf Cart Purch Analysis worksheet, select cell range A1:D17. Try to select cell range A1:B9. Now select cell range A2:F16.

Merge & Center creates a single cell that can cause problems if you want to select a range of cells that includes only part of the merged cell range.

Some Excel experts feel Merge & Center should never be used. Do you agree?

Manipulate Columns and Rows

Any worksheet you create has default column widths and row heights. As you build, refine, and modify a worksheet, it is often necessary to add and/or delete columns and rows or to change column widths and/or row heights for formatting and content purposes. Fortunately, Excel makes these activities extremely easy to accomplish.

Selecting Contiguous and Noncontiguous Columns and Rows

To manipulate columns and rows, you must first indicate which of each you wish to affect by your actions. As with cells and cell ranges, you can select entire columns, rows, multiple columns, and multiple rows. You can select noncontiguous columns and rows, and even select multiple columns and multiple rows at the same time.

- To select a column or row click the header—the letter or number respectively—in the header.

- To select a range of contiguous columns or rows, point to and click the header at the start of the range you want to select. Hold down the mouse button, and then drag to select additional columns or rows, or click the header of the column or row at one end of the range you want to select, press and hold Shift, and then click the header of the column or row at the other end of the range.

- To select noncontiguous columns or rows, click the header of the first column or row you want to select. Press and hold Ctrl, and then click the headers of any additional columns and/or rows you want to select.

- To select all cells in a worksheet, point to the Select All ◿ button and when the pointer changes to ⊕, click the left mouse button. Click any cell to cancel the selection.

Inserting Columns and Rows

A selected range is defined as a contiguous set of cells, columns, or rows that are all part of a single contiguous selection. However, how you select cells, columns, and rows determines whether they are a single, contiguous range or are considered separate, individual selections.

If you click column C, press and hold Shift, and click column E, you have created a contiguous selection of columns C:E. All three columns are highlighted as a group. But, if you click column C, press and hold Ctrl, click column D, and then click column E, you have just selected three individual columns—three individual selections. In this situation, columns C, D, and E are treated by Excel as noncontiguous columns—there is a white border highlighted between the columns. Whether columns—or rows—are contiguous or are noncontiguous has an effect on how actions such as Insert are applied to a worksheet.

There is still a need to add some white space to the cart analysis worksheet—the columns of information for the different carts are too close together. One way to add white space is to insert a blank column between each column of cart information. Additionally, there is enough definitional difference between the Monthly Payment and the Purchase and Interest totals that some white space to separate them may be advisable. This can be accomplished by inserting a row in the appropriate locations.

SIDE NOTE
Select Several Rows or Columns Using Shift
Click the header of the first row or column, press Shift and then click the last row or column.

E01.13

▶ **To Insert a Column Between Each Column of Cart Data**

a. Click the **RBGC Golf Cart Purch Analysis** worksheet tab, and then click the header for column **C** to select column C. Click the **HOME** tab, and then in the Cells group, click **Insert**.

b. Click the header for column **E**, press and hold Ctrl, and then select column **F** and column **G** by clicking on each column header individually. Notice the white line between each column selection—this is not a selected range of columns, it is three individually selected columns.

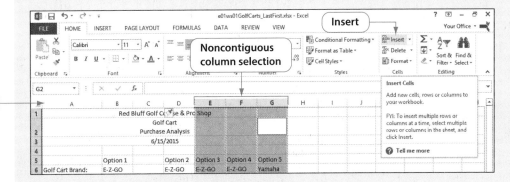

Figure 17   Use Ctrl to select individual columns, rows, cells, or ranges

Column headers

SIDE NOTE
Another Way to Insert/Delete

Select the cells or columns, right-click the selection, and then click Insert or Delete in the shortcut menu.

c. On the HOME tab, in the Cells group, click **Insert**.

A column has been inserted to the left of each selected column because columns E, F, and G were selected as noncontiguous individual columns. Had you selected columns E:G as a single contiguous selection, three columns would have been inserted to the left of column E.

> **Troubleshooting**
> If you now have three blank columns to the left of column H, you selected columns E:G as a contiguous selection. Press $\boxed{\text{Ctrl}}$ + $\boxed{\text{Z}}$ to Undo and repeat Steps b and c.

Notice also that the merged and centered cells in rows 1:3 expanded to include the inserted columns. This ensures that the content in rows 1:3 remains centered over the columns that were in the original merged range.

d. Click **Save** 🔲.

Adjusting Column Width and Row Height

You have inserted columns and rows to add additional white space, but there is still a need to refine the amount of white space in the worksheet. At this point there is too much—the information is spread too far apart.

Column width and row height often need to be adjusted for a couple of reasons. One reason is to reduce the amount of white space a blank column or row represents in a worksheet; the other is to allow the content of cells in a row or column to be displayed properly.

Column width is defined in characters. The default width is 8.43 characters. The maximum width of a column is 255 characters.

Row height is defined in points. A point is approximately 1/72 of an inch (0.035 cm). The default row height in Excel is 15 points, or approximately 1/6 of an inch (0.4 cm). A row can be up to 409 points in height (about 5.4 inches).

E01.14

To Manually Adjust Column Width and Row Height

a. Click the **RBGC Golf Cart Purch Analysis** worksheet tab, select column **C**, press and hold $\boxed{\text{Ctrl}}$, and then select columns **E**, **G**, and **I**.

b. In the Cells group, click **Format**. In the Cell Size list, click **Column Width**, and then in the **Column Width** dialog box, type **2**.

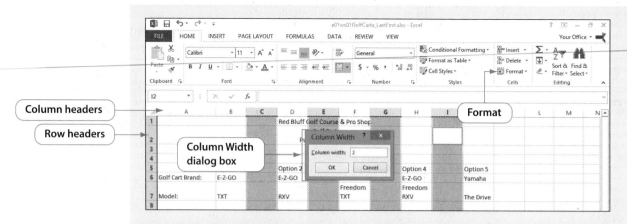

Column headers

Row headers

Column Width dialog box

Format

Figure 18 Column Width dialog box

c. Click **OK**.

d. Click the row **4** header, press and hold Ctrl, and then select row **8** and cells **A11** and **E14**.

e. In the Cells group, click **Format**, and then in the Cell Size list click **Row Height**. In the Row Height dialog box, type **7** and then click **OK**.

f. Click **Save** 💾.

Changing Column Widths Using AutoFit

Column width and row height can also be adjusted automatically based on the width and height of selected content using the AutoFit feature. AutoFit adjusts the width of columns—and the height of rows—to allow selected content to fit. Care is required in that data in unselected cells not be truncated or improperly displayed.

E01.15

 To Use AutoFit to Adjust Column Width

a. Click the **RBGC Golf Cart Purch Analysis** worksheet tab, click cell **A7**, press and hold Ctrl, and then select cells **B7**, **D7**, **F7**, **H7**, and **J7**.

b. Click the HOME tab, and then in the Cells group, click **Format**, and then click **AutoFit Column Width**.

Since AutoFit sizes columns to the selected content, columns B and D are too narrow to display most of their numeric information, so now the information is displayed as a series of number signs (#). Notice also that column A is too narrow to display the content of most of the cells in range A6:A17, so content is truncated on the right.

c. Select column **A** by clicking its header, press and hold Ctrl, and then select columns **B**, **D**, **F**, **H**, and **J**.

d. In the Cells group, click **Format**.

SIDE NOTE
AutoFit Row Height
AutoFit Row Height works in exactly the same manner as AutoFit Column Width.

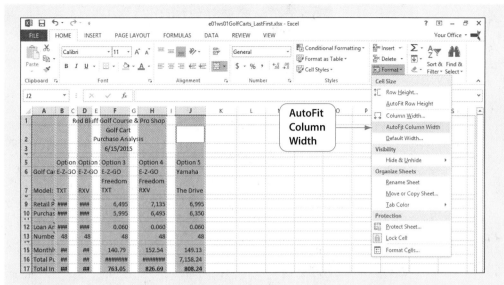

Figure 19 AutoFit Column Width results for selected cells

e. In the Cell Size menu, click **AutoFit Column Width**.

Since columns were selected instead of individual cells, the columns are automatically adjusted to the widest content in the column, resulting in no number signs.

Column width can also be set manually. Column A could be a little wider than set by AutoFit Column Width.

f. Click cell **A1** to deselect the columns. Point to the **border** between column A and column B. The pointer should change to ⊞. Click and hold the left mouse button. Drag the mouse to the right until column **A** is has a width of 26.00 (187 pixels). Notice the column width Screen Tip next to the ⊞ pointer.

Figure 20 Manually adjust column width

g. Release the left mouse button.

h. Click **Save** 🖫.

Deleting vs. Clearing

Worksheet data can be either cleared or deleted—there is a difference. Clearing contents from a cell does not change the location of other cells in the worksheet. Deleting a cell shifts surrounding cells in a direction determined from a prompt. When editing a string of characters in a cell, Delete works exactly as you would expect. When you are not in edit mode, pressing Delete clears content, but it does not delete the cell(s).

The golf cart analysis worksheet is formatted well, but Barry has decided that the E-Z-GO RXV, E-Z-GO Freedom TXT, and the E-Z-GO Freedom RXV are not options to be further considered so they are to be removed from the analysis. Barry also thinks the date in row 3 is not necessary, so you have been asked to delete that as well.

E01.16

To Delete Columns and Rows

a. Click the **RBGC Golf Cart Purch Analysis** worksheet tab. Click the header for column **C**, hold down the mouse button, and then drag right until columns **C** through **H** are selected.

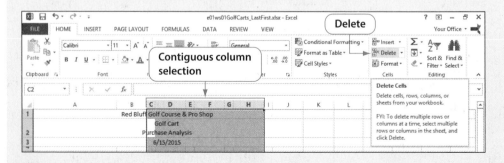

Figure 21 Contiguous columns selected for deletion

b. In the Cells group, click **Delete**.

c. Right-click cell **A3**, and then select **Delete**. In the Delete dialog box, select **Entire row**, and then click **OK**.

Now you need to fix the option headings since they are out of sequence.

d. Select cell **D4**, type **Option 2** and then press Ctrl + Enter.

e. Click **Save** 💾.

Inserting Columns That Contain Data

Barry has asked that the analysis include multiple payment schedules for 24, 36, and 48 months of interest for each of the two remaining golf carts in the analysis. The interest rate for 24-month financing is 5.0%, 36-month financing is 5.5%, and 48-month financing is 6.0%. Expanding the analysis to include additional payment schedules is easily accomplished by inserting new columns that have been copied to the Clipboard and then editing the newly inserted data.

E01.17

▶ To Expand the Analysis by Reusing and Editing Column Data

a. Click the **RBGC Golf Cart Purch Analysis** worksheet tab.

b. Right-click the header for column **B**, and then click **Copy**. Right-click the header for column **C**.

SIDE NOTE

Rows of Copied Data Can Be Inserted, Too

Rows can be copied and inserted, too. Simply select using row headers instead of column headers.

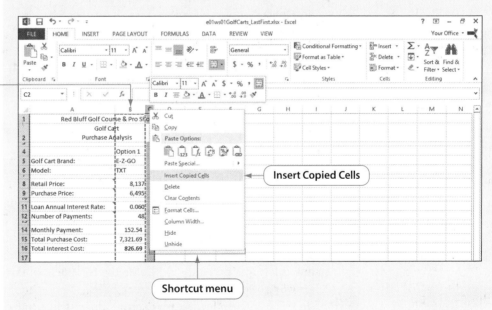

Figure 22 Insert columns that contain data

c. In the shortcut menu, select **Insert Copied Cells**.

d. Repeat Steps b–c one time. Press Esc to clear the Clipboard.

e. Click the header for column **F**. On the **HOME** tab, and then in the Clipboard group, click **Copy** 📋. Click and hold the column **F** header, drag the pointer to the right and select columns **F:G**, right-click anywhere in the selected columns, and then select **Insert Copied Cells**.

f. Press Esc to clear the Clipboard. The copied data now needs to be edited to generate the comparative loan terms Barry requested.

g. Click cell **B11**, type 0.05, press Tab, type 0.055, and then press Ctrl + Enter. Click cell **B12**, type 24, press Tab, type 36, and then press Ctrl + Enter.

h. Click cell **B11**, press and hold Shift, press ↓, and then press →. Press Ctrl + C to copy the selected range to the Clipboard. Click cell **F11**, and then press Ctrl + V. Press Esc to clear the Clipboard.

    Now you need to address some of the duplicate text data created when you inserted the copied columns.

i. Click cell **C4**, press and hold Shift, press →, and then press ↓ two times. Press Ctrl, click cell **G4**, press and hold Shift, press →, and then press ↓ two times. Press Delete.

j. Click cell **B4**, press and hold Shift, press ↓ two times, and then press → two times. Press Ctrl and then select cell **F4**. Press and hold Shift, press ↓ two times, and then press → two times. Click the **Alignment Settings** Dialog Box Launcher ⊡. In the **Horizontal** list, click **Center Across Selection**, and then click **OK**.

    The headings for Option 1 should be centered across columns B:D, and the headings for Option 2 should be centered across columns F:H.

k. Click the **Documentation** worksheet tab, click cell **C10**, and then type Added analysis for two additional loan terms.

l. Click the **RBGC Golf Cart Purch Analysis** worksheet tab, and then click **Save** ⊟.

Manipulating and Printing Workbooks and Worksheets

Worksheets must often be printed for discussion at meetings, for distribution in venues where paper is the most effective media, or to send digitally in a printed file format. Excel has a lot of built-in functionality that makes printed worksheets easy to read and understand. Further, as workbooks grow to include multiple worksheets and evolve to require maintenance, it is necessary to be able to create new worksheets, to copy worksheets, to delete worksheets, and to reorder worksheets.

In this section you will learn to create, copy, delete, and reorder worksheets in a workbook, and you will learn to use Excel's print functionality to ensure that your worksheets are usable when presented on paper.

Manipulate Worksheets and Workbooks

Worksheets can be added to a workbook, deleted from a workbook, moved/copied within a workbook, or moved/copied to other workbooks. Sheet names are displayed on each sheet's tab at the bottom of the application window, just above the status bar—see Figure 22. The white worksheet tab identifies the active worksheet. Gray worksheet tabs identify inactive worksheets.

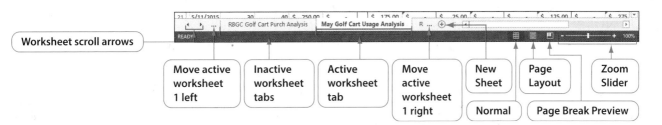

Worksheet scroll arrows	

Move active worksheet 1 left

Inactive worksheet tabs

Active worksheet tab

Move active worksheet 1 right

New Sheet

Page Layout

Zoom Slider

Normal

Page Break Preview

Figure 23 Worksheet tabs and controls

When a workbook contains a large number of worksheets or when worksheets have very long names, some worksheet tabs may not be visible in the application window. To bring tabs that are not visible into view, use the worksheet tab scrolling buttons to the left of the worksheet tabs.

Barry Cheney used the cart analysis to perform an analysis of lawn mowers he is considering for purchase. The RBGC Mower Purchase Analysis worksheet is located in the e01ws01GolfCarts_LastFirst workbook. Barry wants to present the mower analysis at an upcoming staff meeting. He asked you to create a separate workbook for the mower analysis. You will have to create a new workbook and move or copy the appropriate worksheets to the new workbook.

Creating a New Workbook

When you first open Excel, you can click Blank workbook to create a new, blank workbook. However, sometimes you may wish to create a blank workbook when Excel is already open. This can be accomplished in Backstage view.

E01.18

To Create a Blank Workbook

a. Click the **FILE** tab to access Backstage view.

b. Click **New**. Available templates will appear in the right pane.

c. Click **Blank workbook**. You will leave Backstage view and see the blank workbook.

d. Click the **FILE** tab, click **Save**, under **Save As**, click **Computer**, and then under Computer, click **Browse**. In the Save As dialog box, navigate to the location where you are saving your files. In the **File name** box, type **e01ws01Mowers_LastFirst** using your last and first name.

e. Click **Save**.

SIDE NOTE
Save As—Quickly
If a new workbook has not been saved, Ctrl + S takes you directly to the Save As dialog box.

Moving and Copying Worksheets Between Workbooks

Well-developed worksheets are often used as the starting point for new worksheets. Excel makes it easy to copy worksheets from one workbook to another. In the next exercise, you will copy the RBGC Mower Purchase Analysis and Documentation worksheets to the e01ws01Mowers_LastFirst workbook.

To Move or Copy a Worksheet to Another Workbook

a. Press `Ctrl` + `Tab` to make e01ws01GolfCarts_LastFirst the active workbook.

> **Troubleshooting**
>
> If `Ctrl` + `Tab` did not make e01ws01GolfCarts_LastFirst the active workbook, there are two possible explanations. One is that you have more than two workbooks open, so you need to press `Ctrl` + `Tab` more than once to cycle through open workbooks until e01ws01GolfCarts_LastFirst is active.
>
> The other possibility is that you closed e01ws01GolfCarts_LastFirst. In this case, you will need to open the file, at which time it will be the active workbook.

b. Right-click the **RBGC Mower Purchase Analysis** worksheet tab, and then select **Move or Copy** in the shortcut menu. In the Move or Copy dialog box, click the **To book** arrow, and then click **e01ws01Mowers_LastFirst**.

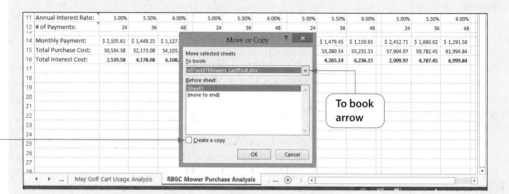

Figure 24   Move a worksheet to another workbook

c. Click **OK**.

The RBGC Mower Purchase Analysis worksheet is moved to the e01ws01Mowers_LastFirst workbook, which is now the active workbook.

d. Press `Ctrl` + `Tab` to make e01ws01GolfCarts_LastFirst the active workbook.

e. Right-click the **Documentation** worksheet tab, and then select **Move or Copy** in the shortcut menu. In the Move or Copy dialog box, click the **To book** arrow, and then click **e01ws01Mowers_LastFirst**. In the **Before sheet** box, click **Sheet1**, click the **Create a copy** check box, and then click **OK**.

The Documentation worksheet is copied to the e01ws01Mowers_LastFirst workbook, which is now the active workbook.

f. Press `Ctrl` + `Tab` to make e01ws01GolfCarts_LastFirst the active workbook. In the **Documentation** worksheet, select cell range **A22:D22**, press `Delete`, and then click **Save**.

g. Press `Ctrl` + `Tab` to make e01ws01Mowers_LastFirst the active workbook. In the **Documentation** worksheet, select cell range **A20:D21**. Press and hold `Ctrl`, select cell range **C8:C10**, and then press `Delete`.

h. Click the header for row **20**, and then press `Shift` + `↓`. On the HOME tab, in the Clipboard group, click **Cut** ✂. Right-click the header for row **23**, and then select **Insert Cut Cells**.

The documentation that had been in line 22 should now be in line 20.

i. Double-click cell **C6**. Position the insertion point after "carts". Press `Backspace` 19 times to delete **fleet of golf carts**. Type **fairway mower** and then press `Enter`.

j. Click **Save** 🖫.

Create a copy check box

To book arrow

Deleting, Inserting, and Renaming a Worksheet

Deleting a worksheet removes it from a workbook. This action cannot be undone. Unused worksheets are a form of clutter in a workbook and add unnecessary size to the stored workbook file.

Inserted worksheets are by default given a name such as "Sheet4" where the number is one larger than the last number used for a worksheet name. An inserted worksheet is automatically the active worksheet. To insert a worksheet, move to the right of the list of worksheet tabs and click New Sheet ⊕. In Excel 2013, new worksheets are always inserted to the right of the active worksheet.

The default worksheet names are not particularly descriptive and do nothing to help document the contents or purpose of a worksheet. Worksheets can be renamed by double-clicking the worksheet tab or by right-clicking the worksheet tab and clicking Rename on the shortcut menu. Worksheet names can be up to 31 characters long.

Now that you have created a separate workbook for the mower purchase analysis, Barry wants you to prepare a worksheet in the golf cart purchase analysis to extend the golf cart usage analysis to the month of June. He asked you to create a new worksheet and use the May usage analysis as a starting point. You just need to create the worksheet and get it ready for Barry to enter the data later. First, you should remove an unnecessary worksheet from the mower analysis workbook.

E01.20

 To Delete, Insert, and Rename a Worksheet

a. In the e01ws01Mowers workbook, right-click the **Sheet1** worksheet tab.

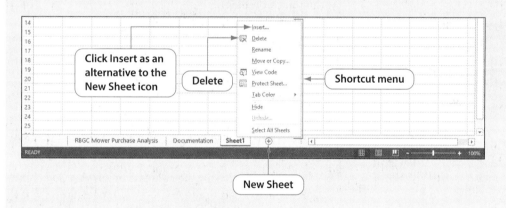

Figure 25   Delete or insert a worksheet

b. Select **Delete** in the shortcut menu. Click **Save** 🔲.
    Now prepare a new golf cart usage analysis worksheet for June.

c. Press ⌈Ctrl⌋ + ⌈Tab⌋ to make e01ws01GolfCarts_LastFirst the active workbook.

d. Click the **May Golf Cart Usage Analysis** worksheet tab.

e. Click **New Sheet** ⊕ to the right of the worksheet tabs. A new Sheet1 worksheet is inserted to the right of the May Golf Cart Usage Analysis worksheet.

f. To rename Sheet1, double-click the **Sheet1** worksheet tab, and then type June Golf Cart Usage Analysis to rename the new sheet.

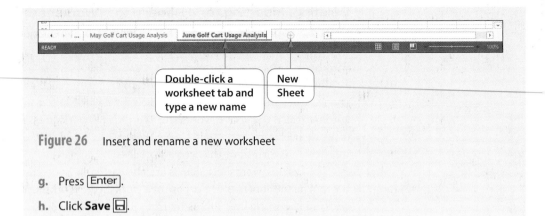

Double-click a worksheet tab and type a new name

New Sheet

Figure 26 Insert and rename a new worksheet

g. Press Enter.

h. Click **Save** 🖫.

Using Series (AutoFill)

The **AutoFill** feature is a powerful way to minimize the effort required to enter certain types of data. AutoFill copies information from one cell, or a series in contiguous cells, into contiguous cells in the direction the fill handle is dragged. AutoFill is a smart copy that will try to guess how you want values or formulas changed as you copy. Sometimes, AutoFill will save significant time by changing the contents correctly. Other times, AutoFill changes the contents in a way you did not intend—when that happens, Auto Fill Options 🖳 makes options available that may be helpful.

The fill handle is a small green square in the bottom-right corner of the active cell border. To engage the AutoFill feature, drag the fill handle in the direction you wish to expand the active cell. When you point to and drag the fill handle, the mouse pointer is a thin black plus sign.

To make the June Golf Cart Usage Analysis worksheet ready for data entry, you need to copy and then clear some of the May data, and generate date information for June.

E01.21

▶ To Quickly Generate Data Using AutoFill

a. In the e01ws01GolfCarts_LastFirst workbook, click the **May Golf Cart Usage Analysis** worksheet tab.

b. First you need to copy the contents of the May Golf Cart Usage Analysis worksheet to the June Golf Cart Usage Analysis worksheet. Press Ctrl + Home to make cell A1 the active cell, and then press Ctrl + A to select the entire worksheet.

c. On the HOME tab, in the Clipboard group, click **Copy** 🖹.

d. Click the **June Golf Cart Usage Analysis** worksheet tab, press Ctrl + Home to make A1 the active cell, and then click **Paste**.

e. Click cell **A11**. If necessary, scroll down until you can see cell A41. Press and hold Shift, and then click cell **A41**. Cell range A11:A41 should be selected. Press Delete.

f. Press Home. Cell A11 should be the active cell.

g. June contains one less day than May. You need to delete one row of the daily data. Right-click the header for row **12**, and then click **Delete** in the shortcut menu.

h. Click cell **A11**. Type 06/01/2015 and then press Ctrl + Enter.

i. Click and hold the **fill handle**, drag the fill handle down until the border around the cell range expands to include cells **A11:A40**, and then release the left mouse button.

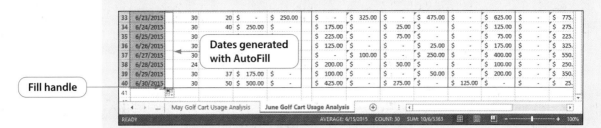

Figure 27 AutoFill dates for June Golf Cart Usage Analysis

Notice the date is incremented by one day in each cell from top to bottom.

j. Press Home to deselect the AutoFill range.

k. Click the **Documentation** worksheet tab, click cell **A22**, and then press Ctrl + : to insert today's date. Press Tab, type June Golf Cart Usage Analysis and then press Tab. Type your last name, first name, press Tab, and then type **G**. Since you entered text, Excel examines other contiguous cells that contain content in the same column and using the AutoComplete feature, completes the entry with other cell contents that begin with "G". Press Enter to accept the AutoComplete suggestion.

l. Click **Save** 💾.

REAL WORLD ADVICE **More on AutoFill, Anyone?**

You just met Aidan Matthews, the chief technology officer at Painted Paradise Resort and Spa. You explained to him the work you have been completing for Barry. He urged you to explore AutoFill further as it is very flexible and can assist you in many ways. As he reminisced on his time conducting Excel training sessions earlier in his career, he remembered a file he gave trainees to practice AutoFill. If you would like to try some more AutoFill activities, open Aidan's file e01ws01AutoFill, and follow the instructions provided in cell comments. Knowing in-depth how AutoFill behaves can save you time!

Moving or Copying a Worksheet

The order of worksheets in a workbook can be changed by reordering the worksheet tabs. To move a worksheet, make the target worksheet the active worksheet by clicking on its tab. Click and hold on the worksheet tab, drag the worksheet tab to its new location, and drop it by releasing the mouse button. As a worksheet is dragged, a small black triangle ▼ will appear between worksheet tabs. This indicates the location where the worksheet will be inserted if the mouse button is released.

To copy a worksheet within a workbook, after clicking on the worksheet tab, press and hold Ctrl and drag a copy of the worksheet to a new location.

In the e01ws01GolfCarts_LastFirst workbook, the Documentation worksheet is the first—on the far left—worksheet. Painted Paradise Resort & Spa standards require the Documentation worksheet must be the far-right worksheet in a workbook. You must move the Documentation worksheet.

E01.22

 To Move and Copy a Worksheet

a. In the e01ws01GolfCarts_LastFirst workbook, click and hold the **Documentation** worksheet tab. The mouse pointer will change to the move worksheet pointer 🔖. Move the mouse to the right until ▼ appears to the right of the June Golf Cart Usage Analysis worksheet tab.

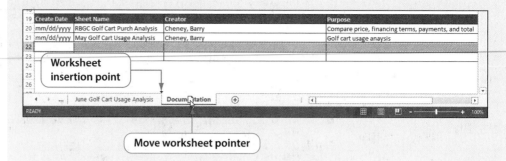

19	Create Date	Sheet Name	Creator	Purpose
20	mm/dd/yyyy	RBGC Golf Cart Purch Analysis	Cheney, Barry	Compare price, financing terms, payments, and total
21	mm/dd/yyyy	May Golf Cart Usage Analysis	Cheney, Barry	Golf cart usage anaysis
22				
23				
24				
25				
26				

Worksheet insertion point

June Golf Cart Usage Analysis   Documentation   ⊕

READY   100%

Move worksheet pointer

Figure 28   Move a worksheet

b. Release the mouse button to move the Documentation worksheet to the location of the ▼.

   Barry has decided he wants the most recent golf cart usage analysis to be first (left) in the sequence of worksheets. You need to move the June Golf Cart Usage Analysis to the left of the May Golf Cart Usage Analysis.

c. Click and hold the **June Golf Cart Usage Analysis** worksheet tab. Move the ▼ pointer to the left until it is between the RBGC Golf Cart Purch Analysis and May Golf Cart Usage Analysis worksheets. Release the mouse button.

   Barry also wants you to create a July Golf Cart Usage Analysis worksheet. He feels three months of usage data will help him better determine the number of carts to purchase. Rather than create a new worksheet and then copy a range of cells from another worksheet, this time copy the May Golf Cart Usage Analysis worksheet in its entirety to a new worksheet.

d. Click and hold the **May Golf Cart Usage Analysis** worksheet tab, and then press and hold Ctrl. The mouse pointer will change from ▨ to the Copy Worksheet pointer ▨. Move the mouse to the left until ▼ appears to the left of the June Golf Cart Usage Analysis worksheet tab. Release the mouse button.

   A copy of the May Golf Cart Usage Analysis worksheet has been created called "May Golf Cart Usage Analysi (2."

e. Double-click the **May Golf Cart Usage Analysi (2** worksheet tab, type July Golf Cart Usage Analysis and then press Enter.

f. Click cell **A11**. Type 07/01/2015 and then press Ctrl + Enter.

g. Click and hold the **fill handle**, drag the fill handle down until the border around the cell range expands to include cells **A11:A41**, and then release the mouse button.

h. Press Ctrl + Home to deselect the Auto Fill range.

i. Click the **Documentation** worksheet tab, click cell **A23**, and then press Ctrl + ; to insert today's date. Press Tab, type July Golf Cart Usage Analysis and then press Tab. Type your last name, first name; press Tab; and then type G and press Enter.

j. Click the **July Golf Cart Usage Analysis** worksheet tab.

k. Click **Save** 💾.

Preview, Export, and Print Worksheets

Excel has a great deal of flexibility built into its printing functionality. To appropriately present your work in printed form, it is important that you understand how to take advantage of Excel's print features.

Barry Cheney is very pleased with the e01ws01Mowers_LastFirst workbook you created for him. He wants the workbook printed for the staff meeting. This will require that the analysis be printed on paper with appropriate headings and titles, and be exported to PDF for distribution via e-mail. In this section of the workshop, you will learn the different print features in Excel so your work can be most effectively presented on the printed page.

Exporting a Workbook to PDF

PDF is an acronym for Portable Document Format. It is a document representation standard developed by Adobe Systems and was made an open standard in 2008. One way to distribute a worksheet in a manner that allows it to be read—but not altered—by anyone with a free PDF reader application is to export it to a PDF.

Barry wants you to export the e01ws01GolfCarts_LastFirst workbook to PDF.

E01.23

 To Export a Workbook to PDF

a. In the e01ws01GolfCarts_LastFirst workbook, click the **FILE** tab, and then click **Export**.

b. In the far-right pane, under Create a PDF/XPS Document, click **Create PDF/XPS**.

c. In the Publish as PDF or XPS dialog box, click **Options**. In the Options dialog box, under Publish what, click **Entire workbook**.

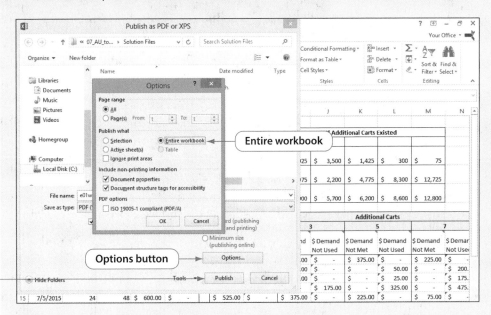

Figure 29 Export Options dialog box

d. Click **OK**. Be sure **Open file after publishing** is checked.

e. Navigate to where you are saving your Excel files, edit the filename listed in the File name box to display **e01ws01GolfCartsP_LastFirst**, and then click **Publish**.

Once the PDF file is created, it is opened in Modern Reader, the built-in Windows 8 PDF document viewer.

> **Troubleshooting**
> Your pdf file may not open in Modern Reader if a different pdf reader, such as Adobe Reader is installed as the default pdf file reader. If the pdf file dislpays in a different reader, close the reader and skip to Step h.

f. Right-click anywhere on the screen and a menu bar will appear at the bottom of the screen. Click **More**.

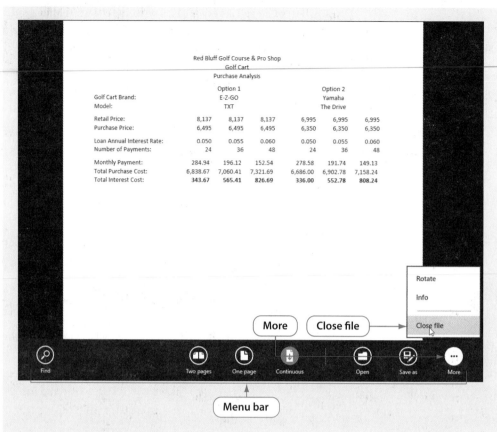

		Option 1			Option 2		
Golf Cart Brand:		E-Z-GO			Yamaha		
Model:		TXT			The Drive		
Retail Price:	8,137	8,137	8,137	6,995	6,995	6,995
Purchase Price:	6,495	6,495	6,495	6,350	6,350	6,350
Loan Annual Interest Rate:	0.050	0.055	0.060	0.050	0.055	0.060
Number of Payments:	24	36	48	24	36	48
Monthly Payment:	284.94	196.12	152.54	278.58	191.74	149.13
Total Purchase Cost:	6,838.67	7,060.41	7,321.69	6,686.00	6,902.78	7,158.24
Total Interest Cost:	343.67	565.41	826.69	336.00	552.78	808.24

Rotate

Info

Close file

(More)   (Close file) ———▶

Find   Two pages   One page   Continuous   Open   Save as   More

▲
(Menu bar)

Figure 30   Modern Reader in Windows 8

g. Click **Close file**. Move the mouse pointer to the top edge of the screen. The pointer will change to a hand 🖐. Click and hold the left mouse button until the mouse pointer changes to ✋, and then swipe to the bottom of the screen. This will close Modern Reader. Click the **Desktop** tile.

h. Click **Close** ✗ to close the e01ws01GolfCarts_LastFirst workbook. Submit the e01ws01GolfCartsP_LastFirst file as directed by your instructor.

Using Worksheet Views

In the bottom-right corner of the application window are three icons that control the worksheet view. Normal view ⊞ is what you use most of the time when building and editing a worksheet. Only the cells in the worksheet are visible; print specific features such as margins, headers, footers, and page breaks are not displayed.

Page Layout view 🗐 shows page margins, print headers and footers, and page breaks. It presents you with a reasonable preview of how a worksheet will print on paper.

Page Break Preview 🗐 does not show page margins, headers or footers, but it allows you to manually adjust the location of page breaks. This is particularly helpful when you would like to force a page break after a set of summary values and/or between data categories and force part of a worksheet to print on a new page.

To Switch Among Worksheet Views and Adjust Page Breaks

a. In the e01ws01Mowers_LastFirst workbook, click the **RBGC Mower Purchase Analysis** worksheet tab.

b. Click the **FILE** tab, and then click **Print**.

   Notice that the worksheet does not print on a single page nor does information break across pages correctly.

c. Press Esc to leave Backstage view, and then click **Page Break Preview** 📖 on the status bar.

   Only the part of the worksheet that will print is displayed. A dashed blue border indicates where printing will break from one page to another.

d. Use the **Zoom Slider** to adjust the zoom level to make the pages as large as possible without hiding any data off the visible application window.

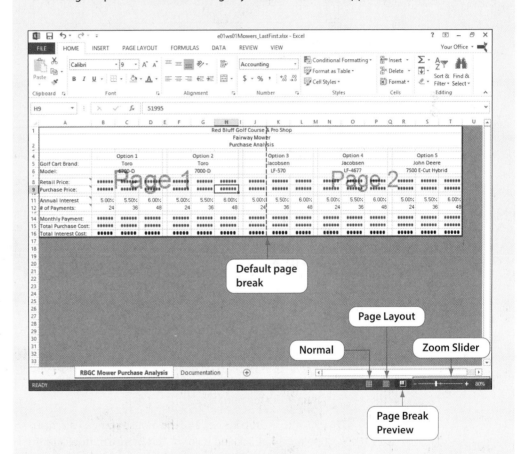

Figure 31 Page Break Preview

Now move the default page break since it divides Option 3 between two pages.

e. Move the pointer over the vertical dashed line between columns **J** and **K** to display the Vertical Page Break pointer ↔. Click and move the page break between columns **I** and **J**.

Notice the page break changes to a solid blue line. By moving the page break, you changed it from a default break to a hard page break. A **default page break** is placed by Excel wherever it is necessary to split content between pages. If the size of content changes, the location of a default break can change. A **hard page break** remains in its defined location until you move it. Changes in content size have no effect on the location of a hard page break.

Now you need to insert a new page break so that Option 5 will print on a separate page.

SIDE NOTE

Why Not Just Select R1?
You cannot select cell R1. Merge & Center is applied to cell range A1:T1.

f. Click the **PAGE LAYOUT** tab on the Ribbon—not Page Layout on the status bar.

Select cell **R2**. In the Page Setup group, click **Breaks**, and then click **Insert Page Break**.

Two page breaks are inserted, a horizontal page break above the active cell, and a vertical page break to the left of the active cell. You only want the vertical page break between columns Q and R.

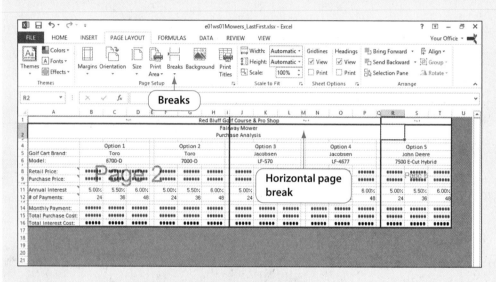

Figure 32   Insert horizontal and vertical page breaks in Page Break Preview

g. Point to the horizontal page break, and the mouse pointer will change to ⬍. Drag the **horizontal page break** off the bottom—or top—of the print area to remove it. There should now be page breaks after column I and after column Q.

Notice that the titles in rows 1:2 are split between two pages. You need to remove them from the print area.

h. Point to the top border, and the mouse pointer will change to the Horizontal Page Break pointer ⬍. Click and hold the left mouse button, and then move the top border down until it is between rows **2** and **3**.

i. Click **Page Layout** 🗒 on the status bar, and then press Ctrl + Home. Page Layout view displays the worksheet with print margins. A thin border shows which part(s) of the worksheet will be printed on a page and also shows the location of the header.

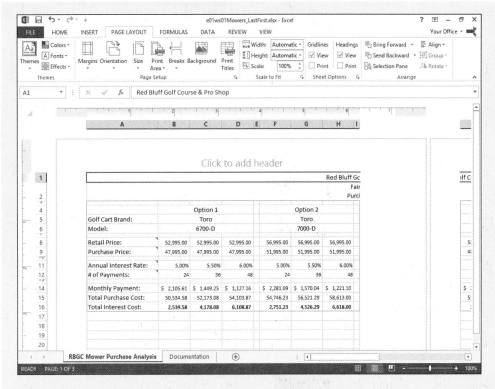

Figure 33 Page Layout view

j. Click **Normal** ⊞ on the status bar. The thin lines between rows 2 and 3, rows 16 and 17, columns I and J, and columns Q and R show the print area and the locations of page breaks.

k. Click **Save** 🔲.

| QUICK REFERENCE | Switching Among Worksheet Views |

On the right side of the status bar do the following:

1. Click ⊞ for Normal view.
2. Click 🔳 for Page Layout view.
3. Click 🔲 for Page Break Preview.

Using Print Preview and Printer Selection

Print Preview presents a view of your document as it will appear when printed. You can use the scroll bar on the right or the page navigation arrows on the bottom to view additional pages if your worksheet requires more than one page to print.

Often, a computer is connected to a local area network, or LAN. More than one print device can be made available to a computer via a LAN. You must be sure to select the printer/device you want to use. The default printer is selected automatically and is usually acceptable. When a different printer is required, click the Printer Status arrow to see a list of available devices.

Printing a worksheet is as simple as clicking the Print button on the Print tab in Backstage view. If more than one copy is desired, change the number in the Copies box to the right of the Print button. The copy count can be increased or decreased by clicking the arrows or by clicking in the Copies box and entering the number of copies from the keyboard.

To Print Preview

a. Click the **FILE** tab, and then click **Print**. If your computer has access to a printer, the Printer box displays the default printer. Click the **Printer Status** arrow to determine what print devices are available on your network. The right pane displays a preview of what will print.

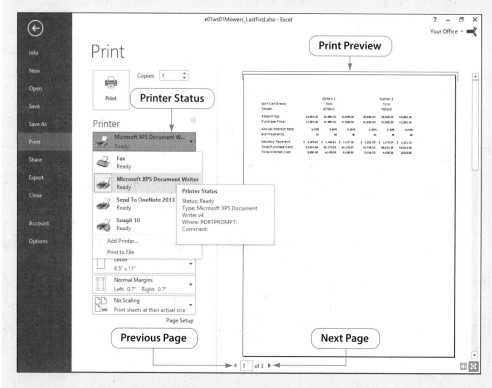

Figure 34   Print Preview and the Printer list

Troubleshooting

The list of devices displayed in the Printer list is determined by your installation, so the list of available printers will not match those shown in Figure 34.

---

b. Click **Next Page** to view page 2, and then click **Next Page** to view page 3.

Notice that pages 2 and 3 do not have any row headings. None of the pages have a page title. There is more to be done before this worksheet is ready for printing.

c. Press Esc to leave Backstage view.

Using Print Titles

When a worksheet is too large to print on a single page, it is often difficult to keep track of what information is being viewed from one page to another. Headers, such as those in column A of the golf cart analysis, are only printed on the first page.

Print titles can be included on each printed page so every column and/or row is labeled and easily identified from one page to another. Since you set page breaks between cart categories, you should print at least one column on each page that identifies cell contents in each row.

E01.26

 To Specify Print Titles

a. Click the **PAGE LAYOUT** tab, and then in the Page Setup group, click **Print Titles**. The Page Setup dialog box will appear.

b. On the Sheet tab of the Page Setup dialog box, under Print titles, in the Columns to repeat at left box, type **A:A**.

The Print Titles feature requires the specification of a range, even when only a single column will be printed, thus the need to enter column A as A:A.

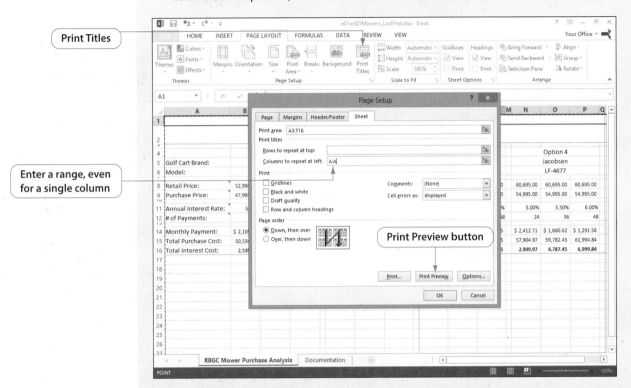

Figure 35 Sheet tab in the Page Setup dialog box for creating print titles

c. Click **Print Preview**. In the Print Preview pane, click **Next Page** to view page 2, and then click **Next Page** to view page 3.

Notice that pages 2 and 3 now have row headings.

d. Click **Save** 🔲.

Adding Headers and Footers

There are often items of information that should be included on a printed document that are not necessary in a worksheet. These items might include the following:

- Print date
- Print time
- Company name
- Page number
- Total number of pages
- Filename and location

Headers place information at the top of each printed page. Footers place information at the bottom of each printed page. The header and footer are divided into three sections: left, center, and right—information can be placed in any combination of the sections. You may include information in either or both the header and footer as deemed necessary.

E01.27

 To Add a Header and Footer

a. Click the **RBGC Mower Purchase Analysis** worksheet tab, and then press [Ctrl] + [Home] to make A1 the active cell.

b. Click **Page Layout** 📖 on the status bar. If necessary, use the **Zoom Slider** ━━━━━━ to adjust zoom to 100%.

c. Select **Click to add header** in the top margin of Page Layout view. The DESIGN tab for HEADER & FOOTER TOOLS will appear on the Ribbon.

d. Click the **left section** of the print header, and then in the Header & Footer Elements group, click **Current Date**.

e. Click the **center section** of the print header, type Red Bluff Golf Course && Pro Shop without entering a space between the two "&"s, press [Enter], and then type Mower Purchase Analysis.

   The ampersand (&) performs a special function in headers and footers. It indicates the start of a field name. For example "&[Page]" is the field name for "page number." To display "&" in the print header, it must be entered twice, and it will then be displayed as a single character.

f. Select the **right section** of the print header. In the Header & Footer Elements group, click **Page Number**, press [Spacebar] to add a space, and then type of. Press [Spacebar] to add a space again, and then in the Header & Footer Elements group, click **Number of Pages**.

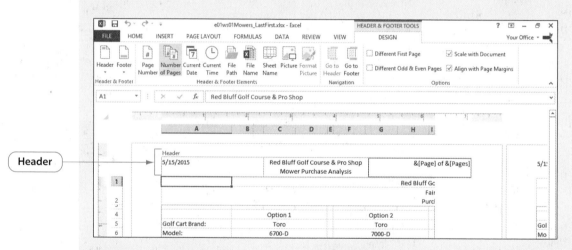

Figure 36   Page Layout view—Add information to the page header

g. In the Navigation group, click **Go to Footer**.

h. Click the **left section** of the print footer, and then in the Header & Footer Elements group, click **File Name**. Select any cell in the worksheet, press [Ctrl] + [Home], and then on the status bar, click **Normal** ▦.

i. Click the **FILE** tab, and then click **Print**. In the Print Preview pane, click **Next Page** to view page 2, and then click **Next Page** to view page 3.

   Notice the header and footer are added to every page.

j. If your computer is attached to a printer, the Printer Status control displays the default printer. If you want to print to a different printer, click the **Printer Status** arrow next to the printer name, and then select the desired printer from the list. Click **Print** or submit your workbook file as directed by your instructor.

k. Click **Save** 💾.

Changing Page Margins and Scaling

Page margins are the white space at the edges of the printed page. Normal margins for Excel are 0.7 inches on the left and right sides of the page, 0.75 inches on the top and bottom of the page, and 0.3 inches for the header and footer, if included.

Margins can be changed to suit conventions or standards for an organization, to better locate information on the page, or to avoid a page break at the last column or line of a worksheet.

It is not uncommon for worksheets to be too large to print on a single page, or to be so small that they appear lost in the top-left corner of the page. Scaling changes the size of the print font to allow more of a worksheet to be printed on a page or for a worksheet to be printed larger and use more page space. A printed worksheet that has been scaled to fit a sheet of paper generally looks more professional and is easier to read and understand than a worksheet that is printed on two pages that uses only a small part of the second page.

Barry Cheney looked at the printout you just produced and decided he wants to see the entire worksheet on a single page. Adjusting page margins and/or the print scaling can be used to print more of a worksheet on a single page.

E01.28

 To Change Page Margins and Scaling

a. Click the **RBGC Mower Purchase Analysis** worksheet tab, click the **FILE** tab, and then click **Print**.

b. Under Settings, click the **Scaling** arrow—the last setting.

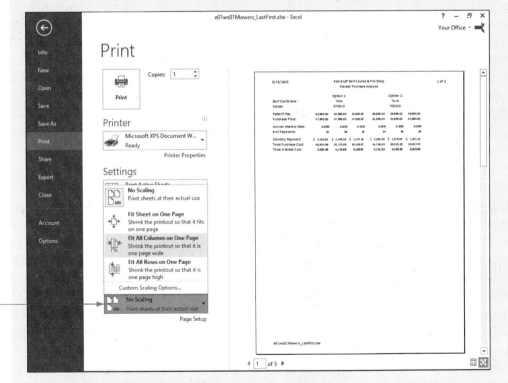

Figure 37   Print—Scaling control in Backstage view

c. Click **Fit All Columns on One Page**.

d. Click the **Margins** arrow, just above the Scaling setting, and then in the Margins list, select **Narrow**.

e. Click **Save** 🔲.

Changing Page Orientation and Print Range

Worksheets can be oriented to print on paper in one of two ways: **portrait**—the vertical dimension of the paper is longer, or **landscape**—the horizontal dimension of the paper is longer. Landscape orientation is generally used when a worksheet has too many columns to print well on a single page in portrait orientation. Scaling the worksheet to fit all columns on a single page can work in portrait orientation, but if scaling makes the data too small to be readable, landscape orientation is an option.

Print range defines what part of a workbook will be printed. The default is Print Active Sheets. This is often adequate, but you can also choose to print only a selected range of cells, or to print the entire workbook.

Barry Cheney does not like the last printout you produced either, the print is too small. He suggests changing the page orientation to landscape.

E01.29

 To Change Page Orientation and Print Range

a. Click the **RBGC Mower Purchase Analysis** worksheet tab, click the **FILE** tab, and then click **Print**.

b. Click **Orientation**—fourth from the bottom under Settings—and then click **Landscape Orientation**. Narrow margins probably are not necessary at this point, so you should set them back to Normal.

c. Click the **Margins** control, and then select **Normal**.

d. Click the **Print Range** arrow—the first setting under Settings, and then click **Print Entire Workbook**.

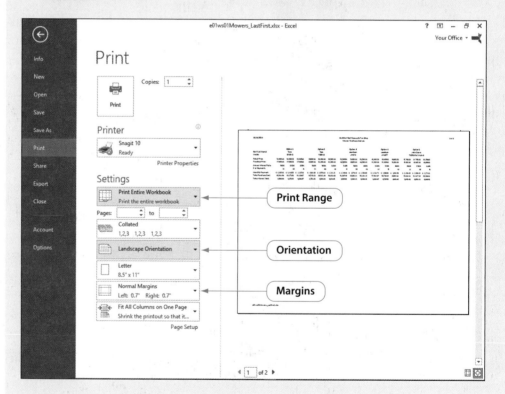

Figure 38   Page Orientation and Print Range

e. Click **Print** or submit your workbook file as directed by your instructor.

f. Click **Save** 🖫.

g. Click **Close** ☒ to close this workbook.

Concept Check

1. Explain the following terms for a reader who is not familiar with Excel:
   - Worksheet p. 46
   - Workbook p. 47
   - Cell p. 46
   - Row p. 46
   - Column p. 46
   - Spreadsheet p. 46

2. How do you quickly navigate to the last row in a worksheet that contains data? What happens when you press [End] in Excel? How do you move from one worksheet to another in Excel? What purpose does the Go To dialog box serve? How do you access the Go To dialog box? p. 49

3. Why is documentation important? Why do many people not properly document their workbooks? What are the possible costs associated with inadequate documentation? p. 52

4. What happens if you select a cell that contains important data, type "Jabberwocky" and then press [Enter]? How does the outcome change if you first double-click a cell that contains important data, type "Jabberwocky" and then press [Enter]? p. 55

5. How do you select noncontiguous cells? Is the ability to select noncontiguous cells important to the effective use of Excel? If yes, why? If no, why make use of noncontiguous cell selection? p. 58

6. Describe two ways in which columns and rows can be inserted and deleted. p. 66

7. How do you reorder worksheets in a workbook? p. 72

8. Explain the purpose of print titles, page headers, and page footers, and when you would use them. What are page orientation and scaling, and how can they be used in tandem to allow you to efficiently print a professional-looking worksheet? p. 78

Key Terms

Active cell   50
Active worksheet   49
AutoFill   76
Cell   46
Cell range   58
Cell reference   50
Column   46
Contiguous cell range   58
Date data   55
Destination cell   58
Field   46

Formula   46
Function   46
Keyboard shortcut   50
Landscape   88
Noncontiguous cell range   58
Numeric data   55
PDF   79
Portrait   88
Print Preview   83
Record   46
Row   46

Spreadsheet   46
Text data   55
Time data   55
Touch mode   52
What-if analysis   46
White space   62
Workbook   47
Worksheet   46
Worksheet navigation   50

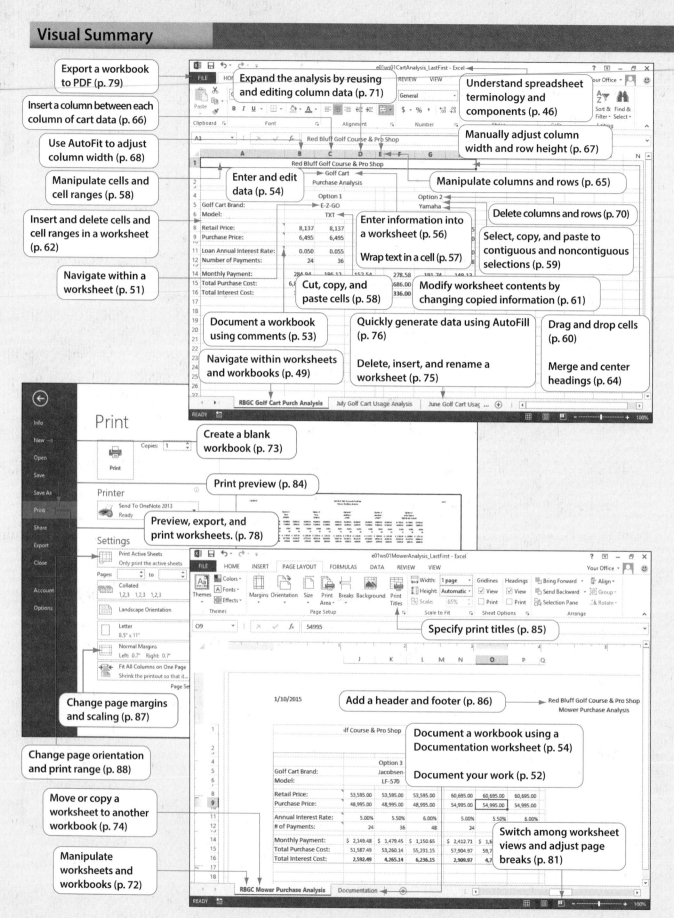

Figure 39 Red Bluff Golf Course and Pro Shop Golf Cart Purchase Analysis Final Document

Student data file needed:

 e01ws01WedPlan.xlsx

You will save your file as:

 e01ws01WedPlan_LastFirst.xlsx

e01ws01WedPlan_LastFirst.pdf

Red Bluff Resort Wedding Planning Worksheet

Sales & Marketing

Weddings are becoming an important part of the resort's business. Thus, Patti Rochelle started a worksheet to improve the wedding planning process for her staff. Last year, on average, the resort hosted three weddings per week and has done as many as six in a weekend. The worksheet Patti wants you to finish will allow for changes in pricing to be immediately reflected in the planning process.

You have been given a workbook that includes product/service categories, prices, and an initial worksheet structure in order to help standardize the process and pricing of weddings. You will build a worksheet that calculates the price of a wedding and doubles as a checklist to use as weddings are set up to ensure subcontractors, such as DJs, are reserved in a timely fashion and that all contracted services are delivered.

a. Start **Excel**, click **Open Other Workbooks**, and then double-click **Computer**. Click the disk drive in the left pane where your student data files are located, navigate through the folder structure, and then double-click **e01ws01WedPlan**. Click the **FILE** tab, click **Save As**, and then double-click **Computer**. In the Save As dialog box, navigate to the location where you are saving your files. In the File name box, type e01ws01WedPlan_LastFirst using your last and first name, and then click **Save**.

b. Double-click the **Sheet3** worksheet tab, type Wedding Planner and then press Enter. Double-click the **Sheet1** worksheet tab, and then type Documentation as the new name for the worksheet. Press Enter, click cell **B20**, and then type Wedding Planner. Press Ctrl + Home.

c. Right-click the **Sheet2** worksheet tab, and then select **Delete**.

d. Click the **Wedding Planner** worksheet tab.

e. Type the information into the indicated cells as follows.

Data Item	Cell	Value
Wedding Date	B2	6/18/2015
Start Time	D2	4:00 PM
End Time	D3	5:00 PM
Reception Start Time	G2	6:00 PM
Reception End Time	G3	12:00 AM
Total Hours	B5	8
Reception Hours	D5	6
Estimated Guests	B7	300
Piano Player (Hours)	C28	1
String Quartet (Hours)	C29	2
DJ (Hours)	C32	4
Discount	H33	-0.05

f. Click cell **E2**. Point to the border of the active cell, and when the mouse pointer changes, click and hold the left mouse button, drag cell **E2** to cell **G7**, and then release the mouse button.

g. Select cell range **F2:G3**, press Ctrl + X, click cell **H7**, and then press Ctrl + V. Select cell range **C2:D3**, press Ctrl + X, click cell **H4**, and then press Ctrl + V.

h. Select cell range **A2:B2**, press Ctrl + X, and then click cell **G3** to make it the active cell. Press Ctrl + V, and then select columns **G:H**. On the HOME tab, in the Cells group, click the **Format** arrow, and then click **AutoFit Column Width**.

i. Select columns **B:C**, and in the Cells group, click **Format**, and then click **Column Width**. Type 17 in the Column Width box, and then click **OK**. Click the header for column **E**, and then right-click and select **Delete** from the shortcut menu. In the Cells group, click the **Format** arrow, and then click **Column Width**. Type 2 in the Column Width box, and then click **OK**.

j. Press Ctrl + Home. Point to the border of the active cell, and when the mouse pointer changes to the move pointer, click and hold the left mouse button, and then drag cell **A1** to cell **F1**.

k. Select cell range **B9:C9**, press Ctrl and then select cell range **B34:C34**. In the Alignment group, click **Merge & Center**.

l. Click cell **A27**, and then in the Cells group, click the **Insert** arrow, and then click **Insert Sheet Rows**.

m. Click **Page Layout** on the status bar, scroll to the bottom of the worksheet, and then click **Click to add footer**. Click in the left section of the Footer. If necessary, under HEADER & FOOTER TOOLS, click the **DESIGN** tab. In the Header & Footer Elements group, click **File Name**, and then click a cell in the worksheet. Press Ctrl + Home, and then click **Normal** on the status bar.

n. Click the **Documentation** worksheet tab. Repeat Step m.

o. Click cell **A8**, and then type today's date in mm/dd/yyyy format. Click cell **B8**, and then type your last name, first name. Click cell **C8**, type Completed Ms. Rochelle's initial work - reorganized worksheet to function better as a checklist, and then press Ctrl + Home.

p. Click and hold the **Documentation** worksheet tab, and then move the **Documentation** worksheet to the right of the Wedding Planner worksheet.

q. Click the **Wedding Planner** worksheet tab, select cell range **F1:H35**, click the **FILE** tab, and then click **Print**. Under Settings, click the **Print Range** arrow, and then click **Print Selection**. If necessary, click the **Printer Status** arrow, select your printer, and then click **Print**. Press Ctrl + Home.

r. Click the **FILE** tab. Click **Print**. Click the **Scaling** arrow, and then select **Fit All Columns on One Page**. Press Esc. Click the **Documentation** worksheet tab. Click the **FILE** tab, and then click **Print**. Click the **Orientation** arrow, and then select **Landscape Orientation**. Click the **Scaling** arrow, and then select **Fit All Columns on One Page**.

s. Click **Export**, and then click **Create PDF/XPS**. Be sure **Open file after publishing** is not checked. Click **Options**. In the Options dialog box, under Publish what, click **Entire workbook**, and then click **OK**. Navigate to the folder where you are saving your files. In the File name box, type e01ws01WedPlan_LastFirst using your last and first name. Click **Publish**. Save and close the workbook.

t. Submit your file as directed by your instructor.

Problem Solve 1

MyITLab®
Grader
Homework 1

Student data file needed:
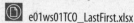 e01ws01TCO.xlsx

You will save your file as:
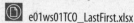 e01ws01TCO_LastFirst.xlsx

Finance &
Accounting

Automobile Total Cost of Ownership

Most people own, or will at some time own, an automobile. Few actually take the time to calculate what owning an automobile actually costs—called "Total Cost of Ownership." This is an important calculation for both individuals and for businesses. In this Problem Solve, you will complete the development of an automobile total cost of ownership worksheet for your supervisor, Jan Bossy, CFO at your place of employment.

a. Start **Excel**, and then open **e01ws01TCO**. Save the workbook as e01ws01TCO_LastFirst using your last and first name.

b. Double-click the **Sheet1** worksheet tab, and then rename Sheet1 Documentation. Double-click the **Sheet2** worksheet tab, and then rename Sheet2 Auto TCO.

c. Type the Value information into the indicated cells as follows.

Data Item	Cell	Value
Model	B3	Scion TC
Purchase Price	B4	19547
Annual Interest Rate	B6	4.75%
Miles Driven / Year	E4	15000
Fuel Cost / Gallon	E5	3.90
MPG	E6	26

d. Merge and center the worksheet heading across cell range **A1:F1**.

e. Select cell range **C16:C22**, and then press ⌨Ctrl + ⌨C to copy the selected range to the Clipboard. Select cell range **D16:F16**, and press ⌨Ctrl + ⌨V to paste the Clipboard contents into the selected range.

f. Select cell range **B15:C15**. Use the AutoFill handle to expand the selected range to select **B15:F15**.

g. Select row **15** by clicking on the header, and then in the Cells group, click **Insert**.

h. Click cell **B15**, type 5-year Total Cost of Ownership Analysis and then select cell range **B15:F15**. In the Alignment group, apply **Center Across Selection**.

i. On the status bar, click **Page Layout**. Scroll to the bottom of the worksheet, and then click **Click to add footer**. In the Header & Footer Elements group, click **File Name**. Click a cell in the worksheet. Press ⌨Ctrl + ⌨Home. Click **Normal** on the status bar.

j. Click the **Documentation** worksheet tab, and then repeat Step i.

k. Click cell **A4**, and then enter today's date in mm/dd/yyyy format. Click cell **B4**, and then type your last name, first name. Click cell **C4**, and then type Completed Ms. Bossy's Automobile Total Cost of Ownership worksheet. Press ⌨Ctrl + ⌨Enter. Apply **Wrap Text** to cell C4. Click cell **B16**, type Auto TCO and then press ⌨Ctrl + ⌨Home.

l. Click the **Auto TCO** worksheet tab. Apply **AutoFit Column Width** to column **A**. Select columns **B:F**. On the HOME tab, in the Cells group, click the **Format** arrow, and then set **Column Width** to 12.

m. Right-click the **Sheet3** worksheet tab, and then select **Delete**.

n. Click and hold the **Auto TCO** worksheet tab. Move the Auto TCO worksheet to the left of the Documentation worksheet.

o. Click the **FILE** tab, and then click **Print**. Under Settings, click the **Orientation** arrow, select **Landscape Orientation**, and then press ⌨Esc. Click the **Documentation** worksheet tab. Click the **FILE** tab, and then click the **Print** tab. Click the **Orientation** arrow, and then select **Landscape Orientation**. Click the **Scaling** arrow, and then select **Fit All Columns to One Page**. Click the **Print Range** arrow, select **Print Entire Workbook**, and then click **Print**. Save and close the workbook.

p. Submit your file as directed by your instructor.

Perform 1: Perform in Your Career

Student data file needed:

 e01ws01IncProp.xlsx

You will save your file as:

e01ws01IncProp_LastFirst.xlsx

Finance & Accounting

Property Investment Analysis

You were recently hired by O'Miller Property Investment for an internship. A determining factor in Kelsie O'Miller's decision to give you this opportunity was your ability to work with Microsoft Excel. Ms. O'Miller just started a workbook that she wants to use to compare properties under consideration for acquisition.

She has asked you to finish the worksheet by doing a little formatting and expanding the worksheet to allow the side-by-side comparison of six properties.

a. Start **Excel**, and then open **e01ws01IncProp**. Save the workbook as e01ws01IncProp_ LastFirst.

b. Rename the Sheet3 worksheet Property Analysis and then rename the Sheet1 worksheet Documentation. Delete the **Sheet2** worksheet, and then click the **Property Analysis** worksheet tab.

c. Set the width of column A so that no portion of any row heading is hidden, and then delete column B.

d. Insert new rows into the worksheet above Loan APR, Income, Interest Paid Year 1, and Net Carrying Costs.

e. Copy all of the information for a loan and paste two more loan columns on the right. Use the AutoFit feature to adjust the column width of the new loan columns if necessary. Use the AutoFill handle to number the loans.

f. Type the following information into the indicated columns:

Data Item	G	H
Purchase Price	750000	499000
Down Payment	100000	100000
Loan APR	0.06	0.055
Income	97500	75000
Property Taxes	-6500	-5250
Repairs	-12000	-10000
Insurance	-5000	-4300
Advertising	-800	-550

g. Center the worksheet titles—the top two lines—across all columns that contain headings and data. Adjust row height where necessary so that titles are entirely visible.

h. Insert a column between the columns that contain loan information. For any column to the left of a column that contains loan data, set the column width to 3.

i. Move the values for Depreciation Years and Income Tax Rate one column to the right.

j. Add comments to the headings of Net Price, Interest Paid Year 1, Annual Depreciation, Net Carrying Costs, and Net Cash Flow that define each term.

k. In the Documentation worksheet, insert today's date into cell A4. Type your last name, first name into cell B4, and then type into cell C4 an appropriate description of your activities in this workbook. Change any other necessary information in the Documentation worksheet.

l. Add the File Name to the page footer in both worksheets.

m. Move a worksheet so that the worksheets are in the following order from left to right: Property Analysis, Documentation.

n. For printing the Property Analysis worksheet, set its orientation to Landscape. For the Documentation worksheet, set its orientation to Landscape, and then set scaling to Fit All Columns on One Page. Set Print Range to Print Entire Workbook.

o. Submit your file as directed by your instructor.

Additional
Cases

Additional Workshop Cases are available on the companion website and in the instructor resources

WORKSHOP 2 | FORMAT, FUNCTIONS, AND FORMULAS

OBJECTIVES

1. Format cells, cell ranges, and worksheets   p. 96

2. Create information with functions   p. 112

3. Calculate totals in a table   p. 117

4. Create information with formulas   p. 120

5. Use conditional formatting to assist decision making   p. 123

6. Hide information in a worksheet   p. 129

7. Document functions and formulas   p. 131

Prepare Case

Red Bluff Golf Course & Pro Shop Sales Analysis

Finance & Accounting

The Red Bluff Golf Course & Pro Shop sells products ranging from golf clubs and accessories to clothing displaying the club logo. In addition, the Pro Shop collects fees for rounds of golf and services such as lessons from golf pro John Schilling.

Manager Aleeta Herriott needs to track Pro Shop sales by category on a day-by-day basis. Sales, at least to some extent, are a reflection of traffic in the Pro Shop and can be used to help determine staffing requirements on different days of the week.

Samot / Shutterstock

In addition, summary sales data can be compared to inventory investments to determine if product mix is optimal, given the demands of clientele.

Each item or service at the time of sale is recorded in the Pro Shop point-of-sale (POS) system. At the end of each day, the POS system produces a cash register report with categorized sales for the day. This is the data source of each day's sales for the worksheet. Aleeta has created an initial layout for a sales analysis workbook, but she needs you to finish it.

REAL WORLD SUCCESS

"I worked in an insurance agency while I was in college. Part of my job was to administer marketing strategies. Every month we received data from our parent company that identified prospective clients. I used Excel to calculate a ranking so I could contact prospects with the highest potential value first. Agency performance was significantly improved as a result, and I received a regional award for efficiency improvement."

- Mike, alumnus and insurance agent

Student data files needed for this workshop:

 e01ws02WeekSales.xlsx

 e01ws02red_bluff.jpg

You will save your file as:

 e01ws02WeekSales_LastFirst.xlsx

 e01ws02WSFormulas_LastFirst.pdf

Worksheet Formatting

To be of value, information must be effectively communicated. Effective communication of information generally requires that the information is formatted in a manner that aids in proper interpretation and understanding.

Some of the most revolutionary ideas in history have been initially recorded on a handy scrap of paper, a yellow legal pad, a tape recorder—even on a paper napkin. Communication of those ideas generally required they be presented in a different medium and that they be formatted in a manner that aided others' understanding. The content may not have changed, but the format of the presentation is important. People are more receptive to well-formatted information because it is easier to understand and to absorb. While accuracy of information is of utmost importance, what use is misunderstood accurate data? In this section, you will manipulate a worksheet by formatting numbers, aligning and rotating text, changing cell fill color and borders, using built-in cell and table styles, and applying workbook themes.

Format Cells, Cell Ranges, and Worksheets

There are several ways to present information. If different technologies, mediums, and audiences are considered, a list of more than 50 ways to present information would be easy to produce—the list could include such varied communication methods as books, speeches, websites, tweets, RSS feeds, and bumper stickers. An analysis of such a list however, would reveal a short list of generic communication methodologies:

- Oral
- Written narrative
- Tabular
- Graphical

Excel is an application specifically designed to present information in tabular and graphical formats. **Tabular format** is the presentation of text and numbers in tables—essentially organized in labeled columns and numbered rows. **Graphical format** is the presentation of information in charts, graphs, and pictures. Excel facilitates the graphical presentation of information via charts and graphs based on the tabular information in worksheets. This workshop is focused on formatting information for tabular presentation.

E02.00

 To Get Started

a. Start **Excel**, and then open the student file **e01ws02WeekSales**.

b. Click the **FILE** tab, click **Save As**, double-click **Computer**, and then in the Save As dialog box, navigate to the location where you are saving your files. In the **File name** box type e01ws02WeekSales_LastFirst using your last and first name.

c. Click **Save** ⊟.

Number Formatting

Through number formatting, context can be given to numbers that can reduce the need for text labeling, such as for date and/or time values. Most of the world's currencies can be represented in Excel through number formatting. Financial numbers, scientific numbers, percentages, dates, times, and so on all have special formatting requirements and can be properly displayed in a worksheet. The ability to manipulate and properly display many different types of numeric information is a feature that makes Excel an incredibly powerful and ubiquitously popular application.

Numbers can be formatted in many ways in Excel, as shown in Table 1.

Format Name	Ribbon	Format List	Keyboard Shortcut	Example
Accounting	$ ▾	🖼		$ (1,234.00)
Comma[1]	,		Ctrl+Shift+!	(1,234.00)
Currency		🖼		-$1,234.00
			Ctrl+Shift+$	($1,234.00)
General	ABC 123		Ctrl+Shift+~	-1234
Number		General ▾		-1234.00
Percentage	%		Ctrl+Shift+%	7%
		%		-7.00%
Short Date		🖼		6/28/2015
			Ctrl+Shift+#	28-Jun-15
Time		🕐		6:00:00 PM
			Ctrl+Shift+@	6:00 PM

[1] Comma format is Accounting format without a currency symbol.

Table 1 Common number formats

SIDE NOTE
More about the Comma Style
Comma Style is simply the Accounting Number Format without a monetary symbol.

E02.01

▶ To Format Numbers

a. Click the **Weekly Sales** worksheet tab.

b. Select cell range **B6:H6**. Click the **HOME** tab, and then in the Number group, click **Accounting Number Format** $ ▾. The top row of numbers is often formatted with a currency symbol to indicate that subsequent values are currency as well.

> **Troubleshooting**
>
> If any of the cells you just formatted display number signs (#), select the cell(s), and in the Cells group, click Format, then on the Cell Size menu, click AutoFit Column Width.

c. Select cell range **B7:H8**, and then in the Number group, click **Comma Style** .

d. Select cell range **C29:C30**, press and hold Ctrl, click cell **C33**, and then select **C36:C38**. In the Number group, click **Percent Style** %, and then in the Number group, click **Increase Decimal** once.

e. Click cell **C31**, press Ctrl, and then click **C34**. In the Number group, click the **Number Format** General arrow, and then click **More Number Formats**. The Format Cells dialog box is displayed. Under Category, select **Currency**.

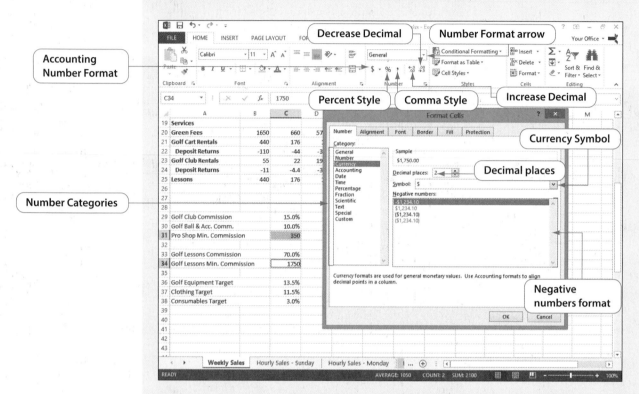

Figure 1 Number Format options

f. Double-click the **Decimal places** box, type **0** and then click **OK**.

g. Click **Save**.

REAL WORLD ADVICE Accounting Number Format vs. Currency Number Format

The Accounting and Currency number formats are both intended for monetary values. The Accounting format has the following characteristics:

- Negative numbers are surrounded in parentheses.
- The currency symbol is aligned to the left side of the cell.
- Zero values are displayed as a long dash (—) aligned at the decimal position.
- The decimal place is aligned.

The Currency format has the following characteristics:

- Negative numbers can be identified with a dash (–), parentheses, or displayed in red. The red color option can be combined with parentheses as well.
- The currency symbol is placed directly left of the value.
- Zero values are displayed as 0 with zeroes in each decimal place.

  It is important to understand the differences so you can make intelligent formatting decisions.

Displaying Negative Values and Color

Negative numbers often require more than parentheses or a hyphen to call attention to the fact that a value is less than zero. The phrase "in the red" is often used to describe financial values that are less than zero, so, not surprisingly, Excel makes it very easy to display negative numbers in a red font color.

E02.02

To Display Negative Numbers in Red

a. Click the **Weekly Sales** worksheet tab.

b. Select cell range **B20:H22** (not B20:H25; you will format B23:H25 later). On the HOME tab, in the Number group, click the **Number Format** arrow General ⌄ , and then click **More Number Formats**.

c. Under Category, click **Number**. If necessary, enter **2** in the **Decimal places** box. Make sure **Use 1000 Separator (,)** is checked. Under Negative numbers, select the red negative number format **(1,234.10)**, and then click **OK**.

> **Troubleshooting**
> If the negative numbers in B22:H22 are not displayed in black, you didn't select the correct negative number format. Press Ctrl+Z and repeat Steps b–c.

d. Click **Save** 🖫.

SIDE NOTE
Accounting Format in Red?
Conditional formatting, covered later in this workshop, can be used to display Accounting formatted numbers in red.

Approximately 8–12% of men of European descent are color blind. This does not mean they cannot see any color, but for about 99% of them, it means they have trouble distinguishing between reds and greens. How should this information affect the way you format your worksheets?

Formatting Date and Time

Excel stores a date and time as a number where the digits to the left of the decimal place are the number of complete days since January 1, 1900, inclusive. The right side of the decimal place is the decimal portion of the current day, which represents the current time. This date system allows Excel to use dates in calculations. For example, if you add 7 to today's date, the result is the date one week in the future.

While useful for computer systems and applications like Excel, people have not been taught to interpret time in this manner, so unformatted date and time values—those displayed in General format—mean little or nothing to us. Date and time formatting allows Excel date and time values to be displayed in a fashion that allows human interpretation. A heading that identifies a column as date values gives context to the information, but in the case of date information, without proper formatting, it is for the most part unusable by the reader.

E02.03

 To Format a Cell or Cell Range as a Date or Time

a. Click the **Weekly Sales** worksheet tab.

b. Click cell **B4**; this is an unformatted date in Excel. On the HOME tab, in the Number group, click the **Number Format** arrow `General ▾`, and then click **Short Date**. Click and hold down the left mouse button on the **fill handle**, and drag the **fill handle** right until the border around the active cell expands to include cells **B4:H4**, and then release the left mouse button. The date in cell B4 has been incremented by one day in each of the cells in C4:H4.

c. Notice the number signs in F4:H4. In the Cells group, click **Format**, and then click **AutoFit Column Width**.

d. Click the **Hourly Sales - Sunday** worksheet tab. Select cell range **A6:A7**. In the Number group, click the **Number Format** arrow `General ▾`.

Notice the Time format includes hours, minutes, and seconds. You have no need to display seconds, so you need to use the Format Cells dialog box to access additional time formats.

e. Click **More Number Formats**. Under Category, select **Time**. In the Type box, select **1:30 PM**.

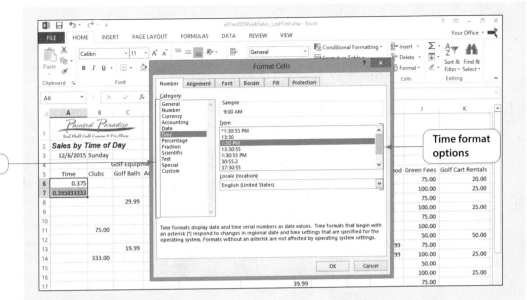

Number Categories

Time format options

Figure 2 Time Formatting options

f. Click **OK**.

g. Click and hold the **fill handle**, and then drag the fill handle down to encompass cells **A6:A28**.

   The series in cell range A6:A7 has been expanded through cell A28. Note that each cell is incremented by 30 minutes from the cell above. The 30-minute increment was determined by the time difference between cells A6 and A7. That is why you selected two cells before using Auto Fill in cell range A6:A28.

h. Click **Save** .

S S CONSIDER THIS | **Excel stores time values as decimal portions of one day as follows:**

- 1 = 1 day = 1,440 minutes
- .1 = 144 minutes = 2:24 AM
- .01 = 14.4 minutes = 12:14:24 AM

For this system to work in conjunction with date values, 0 and 1 are displayed as equivalent time values: 12:00:00 AM. However, in reality once a time value increases to 1, the date increments by 1 day and time reverts to 0. Would you be able to adapt if your digital watch or cell phone showed time the way Excel stores it? Would there be any advantages if time were actually displayed and handled in this format? What about date values?

Aligning Cell Content

Cell alignment allows cell content to be left-aligned, centered, and right-aligned horizontally, as well as top-aligned, middle-aligned, and bottom-aligned vertically. Certain cell formats align left or right by default. Number formats align right, including date and time formats. Text formatting aligns left by default, and for the most part, horizontal alignment changes will be made to alphabetic content such as titles, headings, and labels.

E02.04

 To Align Text

a. Click the **Weekly Sales** worksheet tab, select cell range **A5:A25**, and then in the Alignment group, click **Align Right** ▤.

b. Click cell **A5**, press and hold ⌈Ctrl⌉, and then select cells **A10**, **A15**, and **A19**. In the Alignment group, click **Align Left** ▤, and then in the Alignment group, click **Increase Indent** ▤.

c. Select cell range **I4:J4**, and then click **Align Right** ▤. The content in J4 is truncated, so the width of column J needs to be increased. Point to the border between the headers for columns **J** and **K**. The mouse pointer will change to ⊞. Double-click to apply AutoFit to the width of column J.

d. Select cell range **B4:J4**, and then in the Alignment group, click **Bottom Align** ▤. In the next exercise, you will rotate the dates in cell range B4:H4. Applying Bottom Align ensures the contents of cell range I4:J4 will align at the bottom of the cell once the dates are rotated.

e. Click **Save** 🖫.

Setting Content Orientation

Sometimes, it is helpful to display information at an angle or even vertically rather than the standard horizontal left to right. This is particularly true for tabular information. When formatting charts and graphs, rotating textual content can be very helpful in presenting information in a space-efficient, yet readable manner.

E02.05

 To Rotate Text

a. Click the **Weekly Sales** worksheet tab.

b. Select cell range **B4:H4**.

c. In the Alignment group, click **Orientation** ▧.

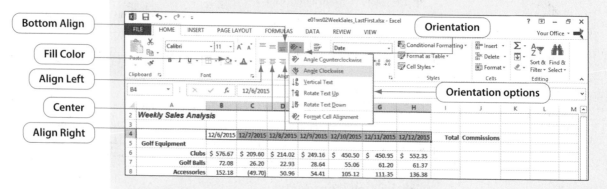

Figure 3 Orientation list

d. Select **Angle Clockwise**, and then in the Alignment group, click **Center** ▤.

e. In the **Font** group, click **Bold** Ⓑ.

f. Click **Save** 🖫.

Changing Fill Color

Fill color refers to the background color of a cell. It can be used to categorize information, to band rows or columns as a means of assisting the reader to follow information across or down a worksheet, or to highlight values.

It is generally a best practice to use muted or pastel fill colors. Bright colors are difficult to view for long periods of time and often make reading difficult. Bright background colors should only be used sparingly to highlight a value that requires attention, such as a value outside normal operating parameters.

E02.06

 To Change Cell Background Color

a. Click the **Weekly Sales** worksheet tab.

b. Select the cell range **B4:H4**.

c. Press Ctrl, and then select cell range **A5:A25**. In the Font group, click the **Fill Color** arrow to display the color palette. Under Theme Colors, point to any color in the palette and a ScreenTip will appear identifying the color name. Select **Tan, Background 2, Darker 10%** (third column, second row).

d. Click cell **A4**, press Ctrl, and then select cell range **I4:J4**. Click the **Fill Color** arrow. Under Theme Colors, click **Tan, Background 2, Darker 25%**.

e. Click cell **A9**, press Ctrl, and then select cells **A14** and **A18**. In the Font group, click the **Fill Color** arrow, and then click **No Fill**. Click cell **A1**.

f. Click **Save**.

Adding Cell Borders

In the previous exercise, you changed the background color in a range of cells. When the background color is changed for a range of contiguous cells, cell borders are no longer visible. If it would be preferable to have visible cell borders, cell borders can be formatted to make them visible.

E02.07

 To Format Cell Borders

a. Select cell range **B4:J4**, press Ctrl, and then select cell range **A5:A25**.

b. In the Font group, click the **Borders** arrow.

> **Troubleshooting**
> The Borders button may look different in your Excel application window than it does when referenced in this text; this is because the Borders button in the Font group of the Home tab displays the last border setting applied.

Borders arrow

Borders menu

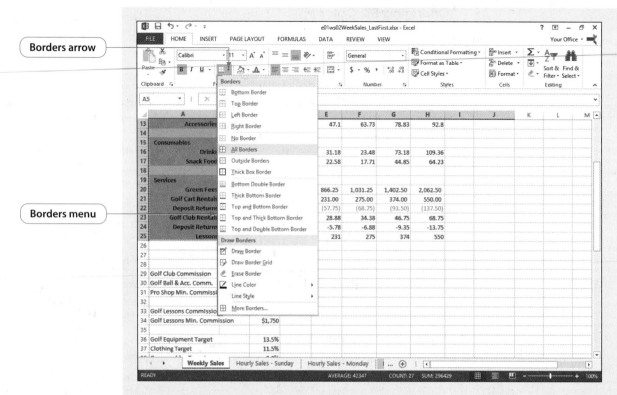

Figure 4 Borders list

SIDE NOTE

Hide the Ribbon to See More of Your Worksheet
Double-click the Home tab to hide the Ribbon. Double-click the Home tab again to unhide it.

c. In the Borders list, select **All Borders**.

d. Click cell **A5**, press Ctrl, and then select cells **A10**, **A15**, and **A19**. In the Font group, click the **Borders** arrow, and then in the Borders list, select **Thick Bottom Border**.

e. Click cell **J9**, click the **Borders** arrow, and then click **Top and Double Bottom Border**.

f. Select cell range **B9:I9**, press Ctrl, and then select cell ranges **B14:I14**, **B18:I18**, and **B26:I26**. Click the **Borders** arrow, and then click **Top and Bottom Border**.

g. Select cell range **B27:I27**, click the **Borders** arrow, and then click **Bottom Double Border**.

h. Click **Save**.

Too much formatting results in a worksheet that is difficult to look at, that is difficult to read, and that conveys a sense that the designer lacked a plan. Here are some formatting guidelines:

- Format for a reason, not just for appearances.
- Use at most three fonts in a worksheet. Use each font for a purpose, such as to differentiate titles.
- Only use color to assist in readability, categorization, or identification purposes. For example, use organization colors for titles, bright colors to highlight small details, and background colors for categorization.
- Background colors should be pale, pastel colors. Bright background colors are tiring for the reader and can become painful to look at after a while.
- Special characters such as the ($) should be applied only as necessary. A $ sign in the first value of a column of numbers is often sufficient to identify its values as monetary. Then format subtotals and totals with a $ to differentiate them.

Copying Formats

Formatting a cell can consist of several steps involving fonts, colors, sizes, borders, alignment, and so on. You gain a significant efficiency advantage by reusing your work. Once a cell is formatted properly, you can apply the formatting properties to other cells. Copying formats from one cell to another saves a great deal of time.

Format Painter is a tool that facilitates rapid application of formats from one cell to other cells. To use the Format Painter, simply select the cell that is the source of the format you want to copy, click the Format Painter in the Clipboard group on the Home tab, and then select the cell or range of cells you want to "paint" with the source cell's formatting.

E02.08

▶ To Use the Format Painter to Copy Formats

a. Click the **Weekly Sales** worksheet tab.

b. Click cell **B21**, and then in the Clipboard group, click **Format Painter**. The mouse pointer will change to ⬚. Select cell range **B23:H25**.

c. Click cell **B6**, double-click **Format Painter**, and then select cell range **B11:H11**. Select cell range **B16:H16**, select cell range **B20:H20**, and then click **Format Painter** to toggle it off. Cell B20 is not displayed properly after formatting. Point to the border between the headers for columns **B** and **C**. Double-click to apply AutoFit to the width of column B.

d. Click **Save**.

SIDE NOTE
How to Use the Format Painter Multiple Times
Double-click Format Painter, and it will remain active until you click it again, or press Esc.

Paste Options/Paste Special

When a cell is copied to the Clipboard, there is much more than a simple value ready to be pasted to another location. Formats, formulas, and values are all copied and can be selectively pasted to other locations in a workbook.

Different paste options are shown in Table 2. Although there are a large number of paste options, most worksheet activities require only a few of these options. Paste, Paste Formatting, and Paste Values will accomplish most of what you will need to do. The various paste options are also additive, in that you can first paste a value to a copied cell and then paste the format from the copied cell, after which you could paste the formula from the copied cell.

Button	Function	Pastes
	Paste	All content from the Clipboard to a cell
	Formatting	Only the formatting from the Clipboard to a cell
	Values	Only the value from the Clipboard to a cell
	Formulas	Only the formula from the Clipboard to a cell
	Paste Link	A link (e.g., =A25) to the source cell from the Clipboard to a cell
	Transpose	A range of cells to a new range of cells with columns and rows switched

Table 2   Paste options

E02.09

▶ To Use Paste Options to Copy Formats

a. Click the **Weekly Sales** worksheet tab.

b. Click cell **B7**. In the Clipboard group, click **Copy** 📋 to copy cell B7 to the Clipboard. Select cell range **B12:H13**, press Ctrl, and then select cell range **B17:H17**.

c. Right-click the **selected range**. The shortcut menu is displayed, which includes options that are determined by the context of the object that is the focus of the right-click.

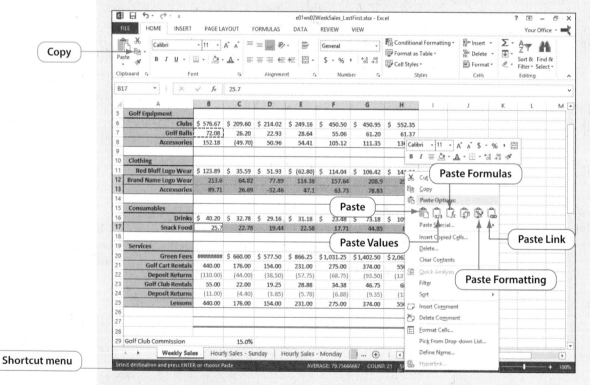

Figure 5   Paste Options menu

d. Point to each button on the Paste Options menu and notice what happens in the selected cell range.

e. On the Paste Options menu, click **Formatting** 🖌, and then press Esc to clear the Clipboard.

f. Click **Save** 💾.

Using Built-In Cell Styles

Built-in cell styles are predefined and named combinations of cell- and content-formatting properties that can be applied to a cell or range of cells to define several formatting properties at once. A built-in cell style can set the font, font size and color, number format, background color, borders, and alignment with just a few clicks of the mouse. Built-in cell styles allow for rapid and accurate changes to the appearance of a workbook with very little effort.

E02.10

 To Apply Built-In Cell Styles

a. Click the **Hourly Sales - Sunday** worksheet tab.

b. Click cell **B4**, press Ctrl, and then select cell **H4**. In the Styles group, click **Cell Styles**. The Cell Styles gallery appears.

Cell Styles gallery

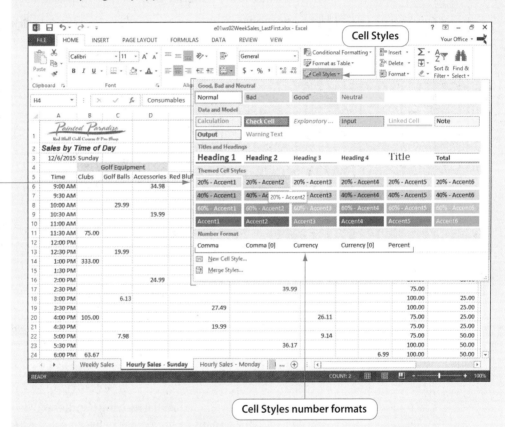

Cell Styles number formats

Figure 6 Cell Styles gallery

c. Under Themed Cell Styles, select **20% - Accent2**.

d. Click cell **E4**, press Ctrl, and then select cell **J4**. In the Styles group, click **Cell Styles**, and then select **40% - Accent2**.

e. Select cell range **A3:B3**, press Ctrl, and then select cell ranges **B4:P5** and **A5:A33**.

f. Click **Cell Styles**, and then under Titles and Headings, select **Heading 4**.
   Notice that in cell range B4:O4, the Accent2 cell background colors have not changed.

g. Select cell range **B29:P29**, and then in the Styles group, click **Cell Styles**, and then under Titles and Headings, select **Total**.

h. Click **Save** 🖫.

SIDE NOTE

Multiple Styles Can Be Applied to One Cell

How the cell is ultimately formatted is determined by the order in which styles are applied.

Inserting a Picture

Painted Paradise Resort & Spa has logos for each of its core businesses. All documents must include the appropriate logo whenever possible. Excel allows images, such as logos, to be inserted into a worksheet. Images are not contained in a cell, like data, but can be sized to fit cell borders using the Snap to Grid feature. In the next exercise, you will insert the Red Bluff Golf Course & Pro Shop image into the Weekly Sales worksheet.

E02.11

To Insert an Image into a Worksheet

a. Click the **Weekly Sales** worksheet tab.

b. Click cell **A1**. Click the **INSERT** tab, and then in the Illustrations group, click **Pictures**. In the Insert Picture dialog box, navigate to the location where your student data files are stored, click the **e01ws02red_bluff** file, and then click **Insert**.

c. Click the **FORMAT** tab, and then in the Arrange group, click **Align Objects** [icon]. If Snap to Grid is not selected—it does not have a border around it as shown around View Gridlines—then click **Snap to Grid** to select.

Figure 7   Insert a picture and toggle on Snap to Grid

d. Click and hold the right horizontal **resizing handle**, and then drag the edge of the **logo** to the left until it snaps to the border between columns **A** and **B**. Click and hold the bottom vertical **resizing handle**, and then drag the bottom edge of the **logo** up until it snaps to the border between rows **1** and **2**. Click cell **B6** to deselect the picture.

e. Click **Save** [icon].

Applying Table Styles

A **table** is a powerful tabular data-formatting tool that facilitates data sorting, filtering, and calculations. Once a collection of data has been defined as a table by the application of a table style, it has special table properties not available to data simply entered into rows and columns of cells.

A **table style** is a predefined set of formatting properties that determine the appearance of a table. One of the useful features of a table style is the ability to "band" rows and columns. **Banding** is alternating the background color of rows and/or columns to assist in visually tracking information. Banding can be accomplished manually by changing the background color of a range of cells—a row for example—and then pasting the formatting into every other row. Manually banding a table is a tedious process at best. By applying a table style to a selected range of rows and columns, banding is accomplished in a couple of clicks. Most importantly, table banding is dynamic. If a row or column is inserted into—or deleted from—the worksheet, the banding is automatically updated. If banding is done manually, insertions and deletions require the banding to be manually updated as well.

Tables also allow for calculations in a total row such as summations, averages, or counts for each column in the table. These calculations are possible without table formatting; however, a table simplifies them.

E02.12

 To Apply a Table Style to a Cell Range

a. Click the **Hourly Sales - Monday** worksheet tab.

b. Select the cell range **A5:P28**. Click the **HOME** tab, and then in the Styles group, click **Format as Table**. The Table Styles gallery appears.

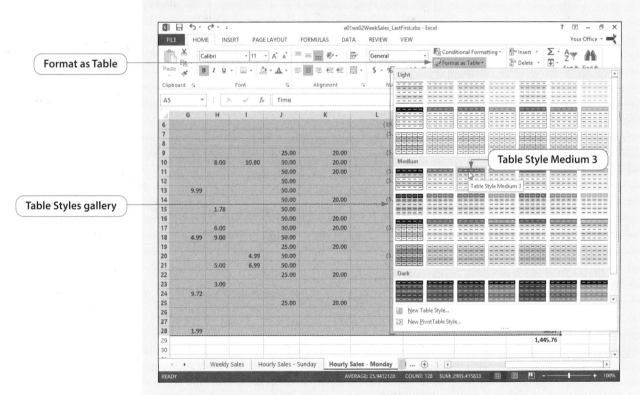

Figure 8 Table Style gallery

c. Under Medium table styles, select **Table Style Medium 3**. The Format As Table dialog box appears.

d. Since row 5 contains column headings, be sure **My table has headers** is checked, and then click **OK**. The TABLE TOOLS DESIGN tab is displayed.

Notice the rows of table data are in descending order by time. The arrow next to each column heading in the table in row 5 allows you to sort or filter the entire table by the information in each column.

e. Click cell **A6**, and then click the **Filter** arrow ▾ for the Time column (cell **A5**).

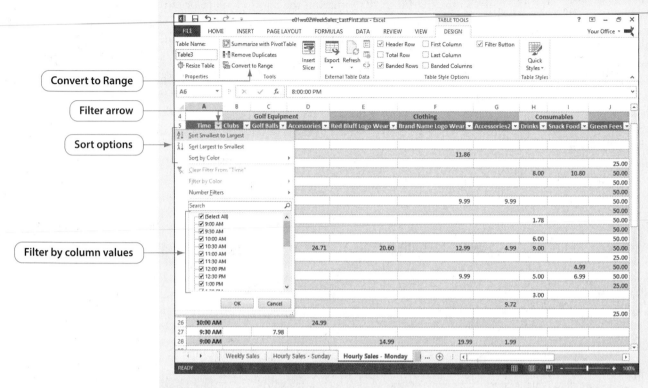

Figure 9 Table Tools Design tab and Table filter menu

f. On the displayed list, click **Sort Smallest to Largest**.

> **Troubleshooting**
>
> Is the Table Tools Design tab not available when you want to select it? Check to make sure the active cell is somewhere in the table you formatted. A worksheet can contain many tables. Excel only makes the Table Tools Design tab available when the active cell is part of a formatted table.

g. Scroll down until row 5 disappears at the top of the window.

Notice what happens to the column headers. If the active cell is inside a table, when you scroll table column headings off the visible application window, table column headings replace worksheet column headings.

h. Click the **Hourly Sales - Sunday** worksheet tab. Select cell range **A5:P28**. In the Styles group, click **Format as Table**. Under Medium table styles, select **Table Style Medium 10**. The Format As Table dialog box appears. Be sure **My table has headers** is checked, and then click **OK**.

i. Click the **DESIGN** tab, and then in the Tools group, click **Convert to Range**. In the alert box that appears, click **Yes**.

Convert to Range removes all table functionality, but leaves in place the headers and cell formatting of the selected table design. This is a great way to quickly format a range with a theme and row banding, but if you do not want the data filtering and other table features, you can keep the visual formatting.

j. Click cell **B6**, and then click **Save** 🖫.

Changing Themes

A **theme** is a collection of fonts, styles, colors, and effects associated with a theme name. The **default** theme, the theme that is automatically applied unless you specify otherwise, is the Office theme. Changing the assigned theme is a way to very quickly change the appearance of the worksheets in your workbook. When a different workbook theme is applied, the built-in cell styles in the Styles group on the Home tab change to reflect the new workbook theme. Applying a workbook theme assures a consistent, well-designed look throughout your workbook.

E02.13

 To Change the Theme

a. Click the **Hourly Sales - Sunday** worksheet tab.

b. Click the **PAGE LAYOUT** tab, and then in the Themes group, click **Themes**. The Themes gallery is displayed.

c. Click the **Parallax** built-in theme. Note that any cell that was assigned a cell style now reflects the corresponding cell style in the Parallax theme and that the default font has changed to Corbel.

d. Click the **Hourly Sales - Monday** worksheet tab. In the Themes group, click **Themes**, and then click the **Metropolitan** theme.

   The table styles applied to these worksheets reveal the extent to which a change in theme can change the appearance of a worksheet. Note also that themes affect the entire workbook. A theme cannot be selectively applied to individual worksheets in a workbook.

e. Click the **Weekly Sales** worksheet tab. Click the **HOME** tab.

   Notice that the background colors that were set using cell formatting are also affected by the new workbook theme. Also notice that for any cell where a font was not explicitly set, the font has changed to Calibri Light.

f. Click **Save** 🖫.

REAL WORLD ADVICE | **Formatting Does Not Change the Data Value, But Formatting Can Make Information More Valuable**

Formatting affects how information is displayed and understood. It does not change the value stored in a cell. Special formatting characters such as the dollar sign ($) and comma (,) are not stored with values, but they make financial values easier to read and to understand. Formatting helps turn data into information.

The next time you are adding formatting to a worksheet, ask "Does this formatting make my worksheet easier to understand?" or "Does this formatting add value in other ways?" such as confirming your organizational identity or its look and feel. If the answer to both questions is "No," maybe you should reconsider.

Remember, formatting does not change a data value, but it certainly can add information value. If formatting does not add value, it is likely unnecessary and may detract from the overall value of your worksheet. Consider your formatting decisions carefully.

Creating Information for Decision Making

In Excel, new information is most often produced through the use of functions or formulas to make calculations against data in the workbook.

Often, the objective is to improve decision making by providing additional information. In this section, you will manipulate data using functions and formulas and add information using conditional formatting to highlight or categorize information based on problem-specific parameters.

Create Information with Functions

Functions are one of Excel's most powerful features. A **function** is a program that performs operations on data. Function syntax takes the following form:

function name (argument 1,…, argument n)

where "function name" is the name of the function, and **arguments** inside the parentheses are the values the function requires. Different functions require different arguments. Arguments can be entered as letters, numbers, cell references, cell ranges, or other functions. Some functions do not require any arguments at all. There are more than 400 functions built into Excel that can be categorized as financial, statistical, mathematical, date and time, text, and several others—collectively these are referred to, not surprisingly, as **built-in functions**.

Part of what makes functions so useful is the use of cell references as arguments. Cell references enable you to use information from a particular cell or cell range in a function. Recall that a **cell reference** is the combination of a cell's column and row addresses. When a function that includes a cell reference as an argument is copied, the cell reference is changed to reflect the copied location relative to the original location. For example, say a function in cell B26 calculates the sum of cells B1:B25; if you copy the function from cell B26 to cell C26, the function in cell C26 will automatically be changed to summate C1:C25—the copied function will be relatively adjusted one column to the right.

Using the SUM, COUNT, AVERAGE, MIN, and MAX Functions

Of the more than 400 functions built into Excel, commonly used functions such as SUM, COUNT, AVERAGE, MIN, and MAX are readily available via the AutoSum $\boxed{\Sigma \text{ AutoSum } \cdot}$ button in the Function Library group on the Formulas tab, or in the Editing group on the Home tab. There are two ways to use AutoSum functions. You either select the **destination cell**, the cell that is to contain the function, or the "destination" of the AutoSum operation; you can also select the **source cell(s)**, the cell(s) that contain the data supplied to the function.

When you invoke AutoSum with the destination cell(s) selected, Excel inspects your worksheet and automatically includes a range adjacent to the active cell. Adjacent cells above the active cell are used by default. If there are no adjacent cells above, then adjacent cells to the left are used for the range. Excel does not inspect cell ranges to the right or below the active cell.

If a column of source cells is selected, if the cell at the bottom of the selected range does not contain data, the bottom cell is treated as the destination cell. If a row of source cells is selected, if the far-right cell in the selected range does not contain data, the far-right cell is treated as the destination cell. If the bottom or far-right cell contains data, the next open cell is used as the destination cell. Table 3 contains examples of the different ways in which data can be included in a function.

Type of Data	Function
Numbers	=SUM(1,3,5,7,11,13)
Cell range	=AVERAGE(B3:B25)
List of noncontiguous cells	=COUNT(B3,B9,C5,D14)
Column or columns	=SUM(J:J) or =AVERAGE(J:L)
Row or rows	=MIN(9:9) or =MAX(9:11)
Combination	=MIN(B3,B9:B15,C12/100,D:E)

Table 3 Function variations

Using the SUM Function by Selecting Destination Cells

The SUM function produces a sum of all numeric information in a specified range, list of numbers, list of cells, or any combination. In the next exercise you will generate new information in the Weekly Sales worksheet by selecting destination cells and inserting the SUM function.

E02.14

▶ To Use the SUM Function by Selecting Destination Cells

a. Click the **Weekly Sales** worksheet tab.

b. Click cell **B9**. On the HOME tab, in the Editing group, click **AutoSum** [Σ AutoSum ▾]. Excel inspects the cells above B9 and suggests that you want to sum range B6:B8 by surrounding it with a dashed, moving border. Since the suggested range is correct, press [Enter].

c. Select cell range **C9:H9**, press and hold [Ctrl], and then select cell ranges **B14:H14, B18:H18, B26: H26, I6:I9, I11:I14, I16:I18**, and **I20:I26**. Click **AutoSum** [Σ AutoSum ▾].

SIDE NOTE
Double-Click AutoSum
If you are sure Excel will predict the correct range, just double-click AutoSum.

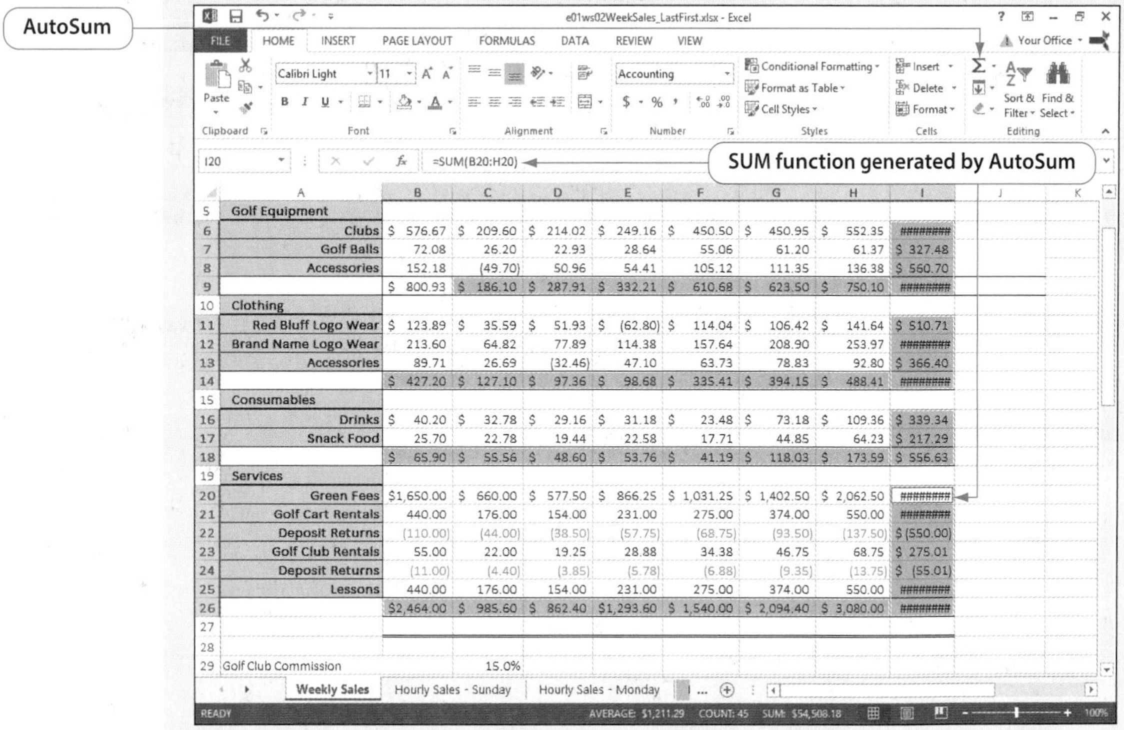

Figure 10 SUM function

d. In the Cells group, click **Format**, and then click **AutoFit Column Width**.

AutoSum will operate on noncontiguous cell ranges as well, but it must be handled a little differently. To calculate the total sales for each day, you must sum the category totals.

e. Click cell **B27**, and then click **AutoSum** Σ AutoSum ▾. AutoSum recognizes that cell B26 contains a SUM function and only selects B26 as the predicted range. Press and hold [Ctrl], select cells **B18**, **B14**, and **B9**, and then click **AutoSum** Σ AutoSum ▾ again.

f. Drag the **fill handle** and expand the active cell to encompass cell range **B27:I27**. If any of the cells display number signs, in the Cells group, click **Format**, and then click **AutoFit Column Width**.

g. Click **Save** 💾.

SIDE NOTE
SUM Shortcut

SUM can be quickly invoked by pressing [Alt]+[=].

Using the SUM Function by Selecting Source Cells

Inserting a function using AutoSum after selecting source cells works particularly well when the source range does not contain contiguous data, as in the Hourly Sales - Sunday worksheet. In the next exercise, you will generate new information in the Hourly Sales - Sunday worksheet by selecting source cells and inserting a SUM function using the AutoSum button.

E02.15

▶ **To Use the SUM Function by Selecting Source Cells**

a. Click the **Hourly Sales - Sunday** worksheet tab. Double-click the **HOME** tab to hide the Ribbon and make more of the worksheet visible.

b. Select cell range **B29:B6**. If you start your selection with the cell where you wish to insert the SUM(), then when the function is inserted you will see it in the formula bar. Press [Alt]+[=] to insert a SUM function.

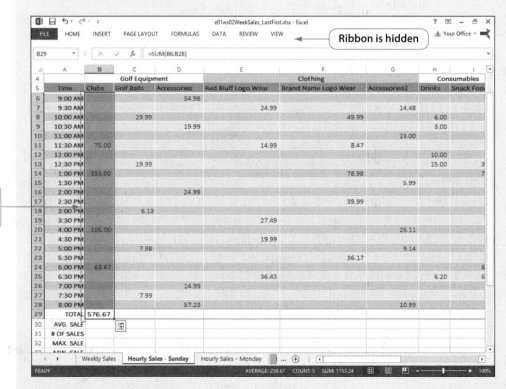

Figure 11 Inserting a SUM function with source cells selected

Since the bottom cell in the selected range did not contain data, the SUM function is placed into cell B29.

c. Select cell range **B6:O6**, and then press Alt+=.

Since the far-right cell in the selected range contained data, the SUM function is placed into cell P6, the next open cell to the right. Now you could use Auto Fill to complete the summations for columns C:P and rows 7:28, but there is a way to use AutoSum to insert all of the formulas at once.

d. Select cell range **B6:P29**. You have included a row of empty cells below your destination range and a column of empty cells to the right of your destination range. In this case, you are actually selecting both the source and destination cells. Press Alt+=. You may have to scroll to the right to see column P.

e. Double-click the **HOME** tab to unhide the Ribbon, press Ctrl+Home to deselect the selected range and select cell **A1**. Click **Save** 🖫.

Using COUNT and AVERAGE

The **COUNT function** returns the number of cells in a cell range that contain numbers. It can be used to generate information such as the number of sales in a period by counting invoice numbers, the number of people in a group by counting Social Security numbers, and so on.

The **AVERAGE function** returns a weighted average from a specified range of cells. The sum of all numeric values in the range is calculated and then divided by the count of numbers in the range. Essentially the AVERAGE function is SUM/COUNT.

COUNT and AVERAGE can be inserted in any manner by which the SUM function can be inserted. In the next exercise, you will calculate averages and counts for the Hourly Sales - Sunday worksheet and take advantage of AutoSum's feature that places results in the first open cell following a selected destination range.

E02.16

▶ To Use the COUNT and AVERAGE Functions

a. Click the **Hourly Sales - Sunday** worksheet.

b. Select cell range **B6:P28**. In the Editing group, click the **AutoSum** arrow .

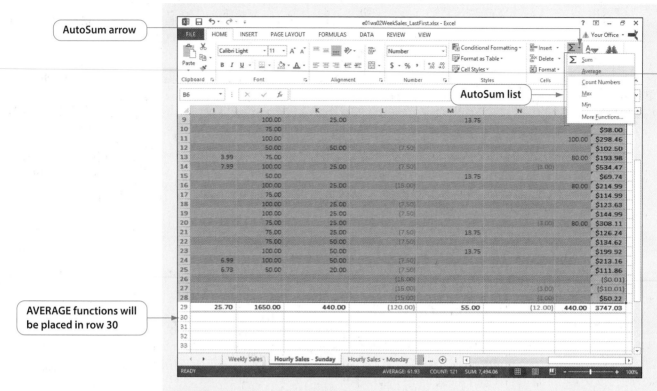

AutoSum arrow

Figure 12 AutoSum AVERAGE function

Select **Average**. Click cell **P30**.

Notice that Excel expanded the selected range to include row 29, but inserted the AVERAGE functions into row 30, the first available empty cells below the selected destination range. Also notice that the AVERAGE function in cell P30 does not include row 29; it includes the rows specified in the originally selected range.

c. Select cell range **B6:O28**, click the **AutoSum** arrow, and then select **Count Numbers**. You do not select column P for this calculation because a count of the number of half-hour periods in the sales day, which is what a count of the numbers in column P would represent, would not be of any value.

Once again, AutoSum expanded the selected range to include row 29, but this time inserted the COUNT functions into row 31, the first available empty cells below the selected destination range.

d. Click **Save**.

SIDE NOTE

Shift + ↑

Use this key combination to decrease the selected range by 1 row rather than reselect the entire range.

Using MIN and MAX

An average gives you an incomplete picture. If your instructor stated that the average on the exam is 75%, you do not have any information about the actual score distribution. Everyone in the class may have gotten a C with the low of 71% and high of 79%. Conversely, no one may have gotten a C with half the class getting an A and half getting an F. Both situations could have a 75% average but are very different distributions. The average should never be relied on without looking at additional statistics that help complete the picture. While many statistics exist to do this, the minimum and the maximum value provide at least a little more insight into the distribution of data by defining the extremes. The **MIN function** and **MAX function** examine all numeric values in a specified range and return the minimum value and the maximum value, respectively.

▶ To Use the MIN and MAX Functions

a. Click the **Hourly Sales - Sunday** worksheet tab.

b. Select cell range **B6:P28**, click the **AutoSum** arrow $\boxed{\Sigma\ \text{AutoSum} \cdot}$, and then select **Max**.

 The MAX functions were inserted into row 32, the first available empty row below the selected destination range.

c. Rather than select cell range **B6:P28** over again, press $\boxed{\text{Shift}}$+$\boxed{\uparrow}$ to remove row 29 from the selected range. Cell range B6:P28 should now be selected. Click the **AutoSum** arrow $\boxed{\Sigma\ \text{AutoSum} \cdot}$, and then select **Min**.

 The MIN functions were inserted into row 33, the first available empty row below the selected destination range. The functions inserted into the Hourly Sales - Sunday worksheet can be used to calculate the same values in the Hourly Sales - Monday worksheet. They simply need to be copied between worksheets.

d. Click the header for row **29**, press and hold $\boxed{\text{Shift}}$, and then click the header for row **33**. In the Clipboard group, click **Copy** 🗐.

e. Click the **Hourly Sales - Monday** worksheet tab, click cell **A29**, and then in the Clipboard group, click **Paste**.

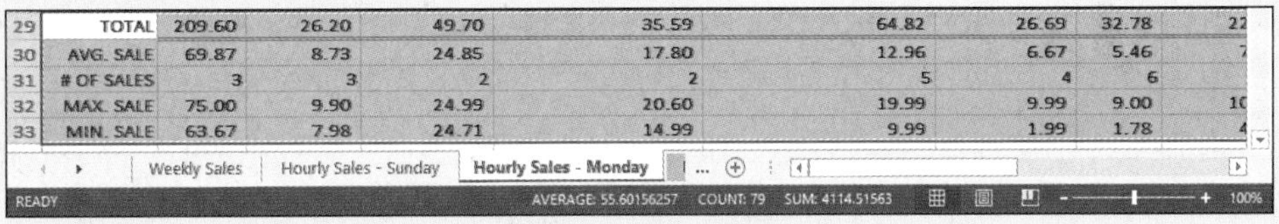

29	TOTAL	209.60	26.20	49.70	35.59	64.82	26.69	32.78	22
30	AVG. SALE	69.87	8.73	24.85	17.80	12.96	6.67	5.46	7
31	# OF SALES	3	3	2	2	5	4	6	
32	MAX. SALE	75.00	9.90	24.99	20.60	19.99	9.99	9.00	10
33	MIN. SALE	63.67	7.98	24.71	14.99	9.99	1.99	1.78	4

| ◂ ▸ | Weekly Sales | Hourly Sales - Sunday | **Hourly Sales - Monday** | ... ⊕ | ◂ | | ▸ |

READY   AVERAGE: 55.60156257   COUNT: 79   SUM: 4114.51563   ⊞ ▦ ▦   – —▬—— + 100%

Figure 13 AVERAGE, COUNT, MAX, and MIN functions

 The functions in rows 29:33 in the Hourly Sales - Sunday worksheet have been copied to the same locations in the Hourly Sales - Monday worksheet.

f. Click **Save** 🖫.

Calculate Totals in a Table

When a range is formatted as a table, the range is structured such that every column is assigned a name, either by the user or automatically by Excel. Data in a table can be easily sorted and/or filtered by the values in each column. When you filter data, you choose which data are visible and which data are not. Visible data are included in table calculations and hidden data are not.

Using Tables and the Total Row

An Excel table can include a total row that allows you to calculate a number of different statistics for each column in the table. The Hourly Sales - Monday worksheet has been formatted as a table. In the next exercise, you will add a total row and use the total row to sum each column in the table.

 To generate a statistic such as the sum, average, or standard deviation in a total row, you click the filter arrow and select from the menu. A table total row uses the SUBTOTAL function to generate values. The **SUBTOTAL function** calculates results based on only data that is visible in a table, so you can filter table data and the SUBTOTAL values will automatically recalculate.

Further, when calculating values from a table, you can reference data in the table using structured references. An extensive discussion of structured references is outside the scope of this workshop, but since a table is a data structure defined by its column titles, you can perform calculations by referencing the column titles—the structure identifiers—in the table.

E02.18

 To Use Sum in a Table Total Row and Filter the Results

a. Click the **Hourly Sales - Monday** worksheet tab.

b. Click cell **B28** to place the active cell inside the table range. The TABLE TOOLS DESIGN tab is displayed. Click the **DESIGN** tab, and then in the Table Style Options group, click the **Total Row** check box.

   This adds a special total row that works with the table format to total each column as you specify. Notice that the formulas you copied into this worksheet in the previous exercise have been moved down one row.

c. Click cell **B29**, and then click the **function list** arrow ▾ next to cell B29.

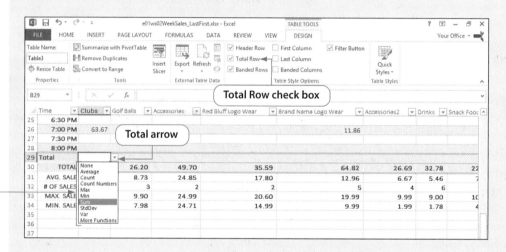

Figure 14   Calculating the sum in a table total row

d. Select **Sum**.

   Excel does not need to predict the summed range for a table. It automatically sums all the visible rows in the table column. Notice the formula bar. Even though you selected Sum from the Table Totals menu, Excel uses a SUBTOTAL function in a table total row. The **SUBTOTAL function** can return any of 11 different values including all of the AutoSum functions, the product, standard deviation, and variance.

e. Drag the **fill handle** to copy cell B29 to cell range **C29:P29**. If the table range is scrolled off the top of the window, expand the cell range to include the column titled **Total**. If any cells in the total row contain # signs, select those cells. Click the **HOME** tab, and then in the Cells group, click **Format**, and then select **AutoFit Column Width**.

f. Press Ctrl+Home, and then click the **filter** arrow in cell **A5**. Since this is the Time column, you can filter the table data by selecting—or deselecting—values in the time column. Click **(Select All)** to deselect all time values in the table. Then click **9:00, 9:30, 10:00, 10:30, 11:00** and **11:30**. This will filter the table to display only sales in the morning hours.

SIDE NOTE
What Is the SUBTOTAL Function?
To learn more about the SUBTOTAL function, press F1, type SUBTOTAL into Search Help, and then press Enter.

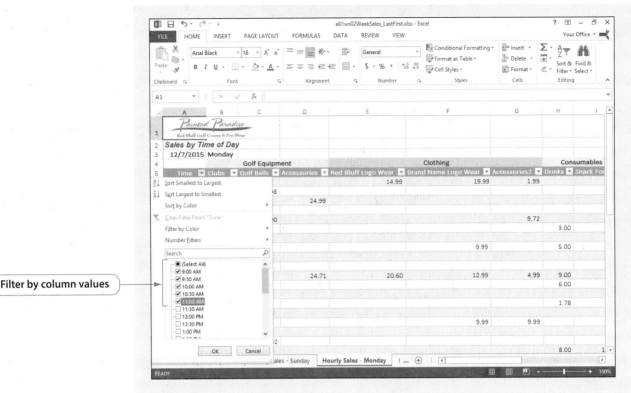

Figure 15 Table filter menu

g. Click **OK**, and then click cell **B29**.

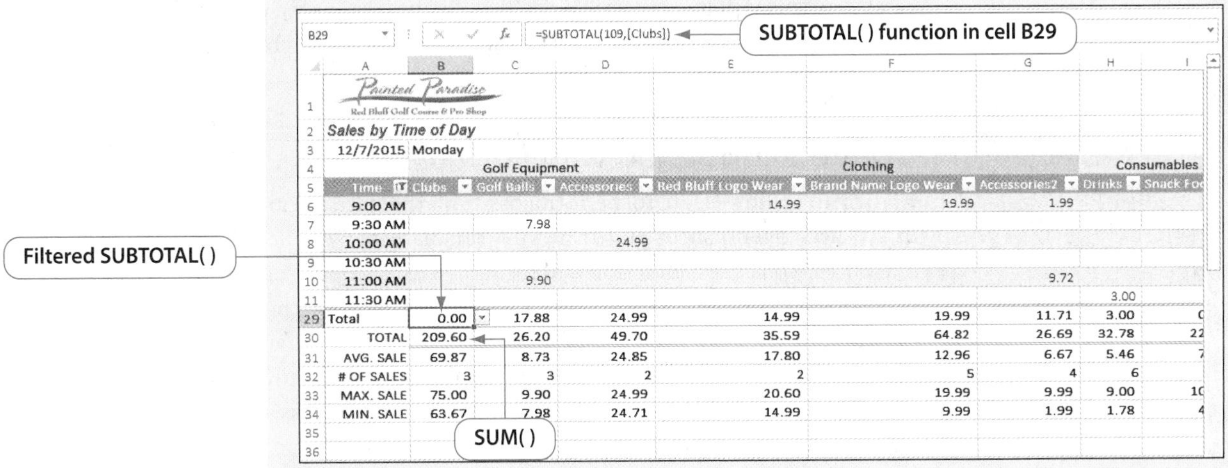

Figure 16 Filtered table total row

Notice in Figure 16 that the Total values in row 29 no longer equal the TOTAL values in row 30. The SUBTOTAL function used to calculate the sums in row 29 only include the visible data. You filtered the table to exclude all hours 12:00 PM or later, notice that rows 12:28 are hidden—rows 12:28 are not included in the SUBTOTAL calculations in row 29.

In Figure 16, notice the formula bar displays the function in cell B29: =SUBTOTAL(109,[Clubs]). This formula uses a structured reference that is unique to tables in Excel. It is the equivalent of =SUBTOTAL(109,B6:B28), but it uses the column name in the table to identify the range against which the function is to act. The number "109" indicates that the SUBTOTAL function is to calculate a sum. The following Quick Reference lists the values for different SUBTOTAL statistics.

h. Click **Save** 🖫.

The first argument listed in the SUBTOTAL function identifies the statistic to be calculated. 1–11 return values that include all values in the specified range. 101–111 return values that include only the visible values in the specified range.

Function # All values	Function # Visible values	Statistic
1	101	AVERAGE
2	102	COUNT
3	103	COUNTA
4	104	MAX
5	105	MIN
6	106	PRODUCT
7	107	STDEV
8	108	STDEVP
9	109	SUM
10	110	VAR
11	111	VARP

One quirk associated with the SUBTOTAL function is that when it is used to calculate statistics against a table, the function number visibility is irrelevant. For example, if you specify function number 9, and then filter the table data such that only part of the table data is visible, only visible data will be included in the calculation. Value visibility is only a factor in SUBTOTAL function calculations for data not included in a table.

Create Information with Formulas

A **formula** allows you to perform basic mathematical calculations using information in the active worksheet and others to calculate new values; formulas can contain cell references, constants, functions, and mathematical operators. Formulas in Excel have a very specific syntax. In Excel, formulas always begin with an equal sign (=). Formulas can contain references to specific cells that contain information; a **constant**, which is a number that never changes, such as the value for π (pi); **mathematical operators** such as $+, -, *, /, \wedge$; and functions. Cells that contain formulas can be treated like any other worksheet cell. They can be referenced, edited, formatted, copied, and pasted.

If a formula contains a cell reference, when copied and then pasted into a new location, the cell reference in the formula changes. The new cell reference reflects a new location relative to the old location. This is called a **relative cell reference**. For example, as shown in Figure 17, when the formula in the left column is copied one column to the right and two rows down, the cell references in the formula change to reflect the destination cell relative to the original cell. Consequently, columns A and J are changed to B and K respectively—one column right, and rows 3 and 12 are changed to 5 and 14, two rows down. Note that the column and row numbers of the cells that contain the formulas are not shown in Figure 17. The active cell address does not matter in relative addressing. All that matters is the relative shift in columns and rows from source to destination, and the cell references in the formula.

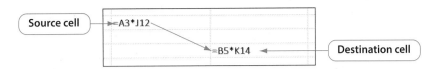

Figure 17 Relative referencing when copying from a source cell to a destination cell

Relative cell references allow you to reuse formulas in a well-designed worksheet. You can enter a formula once and use it many times without having to reenter it in each location and change the cell references. Simply copy and paste it to a new location.

Further, relative references adjust formulas to ensure correctness when the structure of the worksheet changes. If a column is inserted to the left of a cell referenced in a formula, or a row is inserted above a cell referenced in a formula, the cells referenced by the formula will be adjusted to ensure the formula still references the same relative locations.

Using Operators

Excel formulas are constructed using basic mathematical operators very similar to those used in a mathematics and exactly the same as used in most programming languages. Table 4 contains the mathematical operators recognized in Excel.

Operation	Operator	Example	Formula Entered in Current Cell
Addition	+	=B4+B5	Assign the sum of B4 and B5 to the current cell.
Subtraction	-	=B5-B4	Assign the difference of B4 and B5 to the current cell.
Multiplication	*	=B5*3.14	Assign B5 multiplied by 3.14 to the current cell.
Division	/	=B5/B4	Assign the result of dividing B5 by B4 to the current cell.
Exponentiation	^	=B4^2	Assign the square of B4 to the current cell.

Table 4 Mathematical operators in Excel

SIDE NOTE

Copy a Formula and Not Change Relative References

Select the formula in the formula bar, click 🖺, press Esc, and then Paste.

SIDE NOTE

How to Remember Order of Operations

P arentheses
E xponentiation
D ivision and/or
M ultiplication
A ddition and/or
S ubtraction.

Applying Order of Operations

Order of operations is the order in which Excel processes calculations in a formula that contains more than one operator. Mathematical operations execute in a specific order:

1. Parentheses
2. Exponentiation
3. Multiplication and division
4. Addition and subtraction

Excel scans a formula from left to right while performing calculations using the above order of operation rules. Thus you can control which part of a calculation is performed first by enclosing parts of a formula in parentheses. Portions of a formula enclosed in parentheses are evaluated first, following the previously listed order. Table 5 contains some examples of the effect of order of operations on formula results.

Formula	Result	Formula	Result
=4-2*5^2	-46	=(5+5)*4/2-3*6	2
=(4-2)*5^2	50	=(5+5)*4/(2-3)*6	-240
=5+5*4/2-3*6	-3	=(5+5)*4/(2-3*6)	-2.5

Table 5 Order of operations

Golf pro John Schilling is paid a commission of sales. He receives 70% of all lesson fees received by the Pro Shop. Pro Shop manager Aleeta Herriott is in charge of all golf club sales. She receives a 15% commission on all sales of clubs and a 10% commission on golf balls and accessories. You need to add commission calculations to the worksheet.

E02.19

 To Calculate Commissions Using Formulas

a. Click the **Weekly Sales** worksheet tab.

b. Select cell **J25**. In this cell, you will calculate the commissions John Schilling earned on golf lessons. The total revenue from golf lessons for the week is in cell I25, and the commission paid for golf lessons is in cell C33. Type =I25*C33.

<aside>
SIDE NOTE
Enter Formulas with the Mouse

To enter the formula in J25 without typing cell references, type =, click cell I25, type *, click cell C33, and press Enter
</aside>

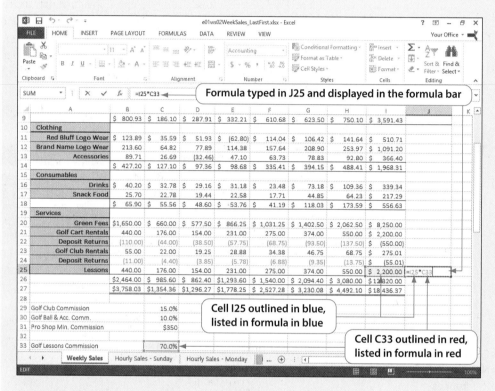

Figure 18 Entering a formula into a cell

c. Press Enter,

d. Click cell **J6**. In this cell, you need to calculate the commissions that Aleeta Herriott earned selling golf clubs in the Pro Shop. To multiply the total golf club sales for the week by the commission percentage on golf club sales, type =I6*C29 and then press Enter.

e. In cell **J7**, calculate the commission earned on Pro Shop accessories. To multiply the sum of golf ball and accessory sales for the week by the appropriate commission, type =(I7+I8)*C30 and then press Enter.

<aside>
SIDE NOTE
A Faster Way to Sum Commissions

In cell J9, double-click AutoSum Σ and you will generate the same result without typing the formula.
</aside>

f. In cell **J9**, sum Aleeta Herriott's commissions. Type =SUM(J6:J7), and then press Enter.

g. Click **Save** 💾.

> **Troubleshooting**
>
> Excel allows you to copy formulas from one location to another and adjusts cell references to ensure calculation accuracy. This is not necessarily true when a formula is moved from one location to another, however. If you move a formula by dragging it from one location to another, cell references do not change. Be sure you double-check a formula after you move it to ensure it is still producing a correct result.

REAL WORLD ADVICE | An Alternative to Typing Cell References

An alternative, and more accurate, method to typing cell references into a formula is to type only the operators and then select the cells from the worksheet. The steps to enter the daily sales total in the Weekly Sales worksheet would be as follows:

1. Select cell B27.

2. Type =.

3. Click cell B9, and then type +.

4. Click cell B14, and then type +.

5. Click cell B18, and then type +.

6. Click cell B26, and then press Enter.

This method of building formulas is much less error prone than typing cell references. Learning this methodology would be worth your effort.

Use Conditional Formatting to Assist Decision Making

As discussed previously, one of the primary purposes of information analysis in Excel worksheets is to assist in decision making. People are often influenced by the format by which information is presented. Worksheets can be huge—thousands of rows and dozens of columns of information. The number of calculated items can be daunting to analyze, digest, and interpret. To the extent Excel can be used to assist the decision maker in understanding information, decision making speed and quality should improve.

Conditional formatting is one way Excel can aid the decision maker by changing the way information is displayed based on rules specific to the problem the worksheet is designed to address.

Highlighting Values in a Range with Conditional Formatting

Conditional formatting allows the specification of rules that apply formatting to a cell as determined by the rule outcome. It is a way to dynamically change the visual presentation of information in a manner that adds information to the worksheet.

Conditional formatting can be used to highlight information by changing cell fill color, font color, font style, font size, border, number format, and by adding visual cues like scales and icons. In the next exercise, you will apply conditional formatting to highlight the sales figures in each category that are above average for each day's sales.

E02.20

▶ To Highlight High and Low Category Sales and to Display Negative Accounting Number Formatted Cells in Red

a. Click the **Weekly Sales** worksheet tab.

b. Select cell range **B9:H9**. Click the **HOME** tab, and then in the Styles group, click **Conditional Formatting**. Point to **Top/Bottom Rules**, and then select **Top 10 Items**. In the Top 10 Items dialog box, in the Format cells that rank in the TOP box, double-click **10**, and then type **1**. Click the **with** arrow.

Conditional Formatting

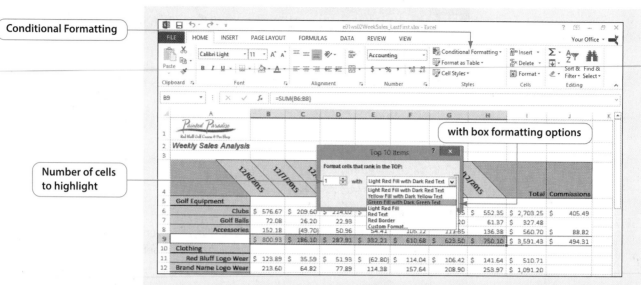

with box formatting options

Number of cells
to highlight

Figure 19 Top 10 Items dialog box

c. Select **Green Fill with Dark Green Text**, and then click **OK**.

d. In the Styles group, click **Conditional Formatting**, point to **Top/Bottom Rules**, and then select **Bottom 10 Items**. In the Bottom 10 Items dialog box, in the Format cells that rank in the BOTTOM box, double-click **10**, and then type **1**. Click **OK**.

Now you can copy the formatting you just added to B9:H9 to the other category totals and to the overall totals in the Weekly Sales worksheet.

e. With cell range **B9:H9** still selected, in the Clipboard group, double-click **Format Painter** ☝. Select cell ranges **B14:H14**. Select cell range **B18:H18**. Select cell range **B26:H26**. Select cell range **B27:H27**. Click **Format Painter** ☝ to turn off the Format Painter.

Recall that Accounting Number Format does not include the option to display negative numbers in red—notice cell C8. This can be accomplished with conditional formatting.

f. Select cell range **B6:I27**. In the Styles group, click **Conditional Formatting**, point to **Highlight Cells Rules**, and then click **Less Than**. In the Format cells that are LESS THAN box, type **0**. Click the **with** box arrow, and then select **Red Text**. Click **OK**.

g. Click **Save** 🖫.

> **Troubleshooting**
>
> Be sure to double-check the results of any copy-and-paste activity when conditional formatting is involved. A row of cells that contain conditional formatting was copied to the Clipboard. The row must be pasted from the Clipboard, using Paste Formatting 🔖 one row at a time, or the conditional formatting rules will be broken.

Applying Conditional Formatting to Assess Benchmarks Using Icon Sets

Conditional formatting can also be used to highlight whether or not a value satisfies a particular criteria such as a benchmark. The staff in the Pro Shop is guaranteed a minimum commission amount—stored in cells C31 and C34. It is much preferable that a staff member's commissions exceed the minimum. You can use conditional formatting to clearly identify whether or not Aleeta Herriott's commissions in the Pro Shop and John Schilling's commissions for lessons exceed the contractual minimum.

E02.21

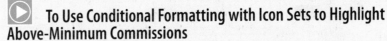 **To Use Conditional Formatting with Icon Sets to Highlight Above-Minimum Commissions**

a. Click cell **J9**. In the Styles group, click **Conditional Formatting**, point to **Icon Sets**, and then click **More Rules**. In the New Formatting Rule dialog box, under Select a Rule Type, make sure **Format all cells based on their values** is selected.

b. Under Edit the Rule Description, click the **Icon Style** arrow, and then click the first item in the list, **3 Arrows (Colored)**—you will have to scroll up.

c. Under **Icon**, click the **arrow** ⊡ next to the yellow arrow, and then select the **red down arrow** for the middle Icon box—the Icon Style box will change to Custom. In the bottom Icon box, select **No Cell Icon**, and then select **Number** in both Type boxes.

d. Double-click in the top **Value** box and then press ⌂Delete⌂. Click **Collapse dialog box** 🔢 in the top Value box, select cell **C31**—the minimum commission for the Pro Shop manager, and then click the **Expand dialog box** icon 🔢.

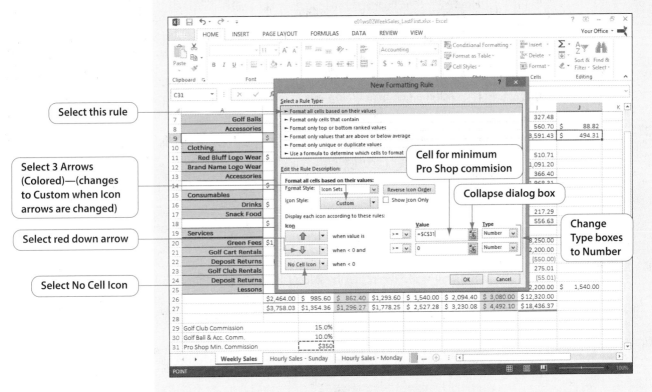

Figure 20 Conditional formatting using icon sets

e. Click **OK**. Now you can use the conditional format you just created for the golf lessons commission in cell J25.

f. With cell **J9** selected, click **Format Painter** 🖌, and then click cell **J25** to paste formatting, including conditional formatting.

g. In the Styles group, click **Conditional Formatting**, and then select **Manage Rules**. The Conditional Formatting Rules Manager dialog box is displayed.

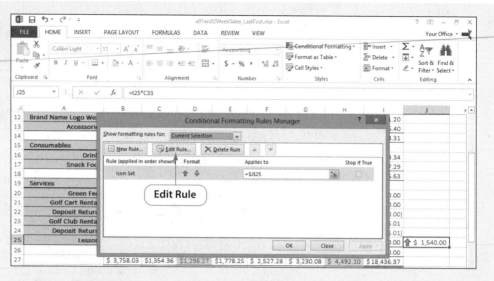

Figure 21 Conditional Formatting Rules Manager dialog box

h. In the Conditional Formatting Rules Manager dialog box, click **Edit Rule**. In the **Edit Formatting Rule** dialog box, under Display each icon according to these rules, double-click the top **Value** box.

i. Click the **Collapse dialog box** icon in the top Value box. Click cell **C34**—the minimum commission for the RBGC golf pro, and then click the **Expand dialog box**.

j. Click **OK**, and then click **OK**.

k. Click **Save**.

Using Conditional Formatting to Assess Benchmarks Using Font Formatting

In the previous exercise, you used arrow icons to indicate whether or not commission minimums had been met by Aleeta Herriott and John Schilling. Any of the conditional formatting features can be used to visually highlight benchmark satisfaction. Aleeta has used historical sales data to identify a proportion of weekly sales that is a minimum goal (benchmark) for each product category. In the next exercise, you will format weekly sales totals to be displayed in a bold and green font if they meet or exceed benchmarks.

E02.22

To Highlight Sales that Meet or Exceed Benchmarks

a. Click cell **I9**. In the Styles group, click **Conditional Formatting**. Point to **Highlight Cells Rules**, and then select **More Rules**. In the New Formatting Rule dialog box, under Select a Rule Type, click **Use a formula to determine which cells to format**.

b. In the **Format values where this formula is true** box, type =I9/I27>=C36 (golf equipment percentage of total sales compared to the golf equipment benchmark percentage of sales). Click **Format**. On the Font tab, in the Font style box, click **Bold**. Click the **Color** arrow.

Figure 22 Conditional formatting using a formula

c. Under Standard Colors, click **Green**. Click **OK** two times. In the Cells group, click **Format**, and then select **AutoFit Column Width**. Now copy formatting from cell **I9** to the cells that contain the week's total sales for **Clothing** and **Consumables**.

d. With **I9** selected, double-click **Format Painter** . Click cell **I14**, and then click cell **I18**. Click **Format Painter** to turn it off. Copying formatting will have made some incorrect relative changes to the cell references in the formula you entered in Step b so you need to edit the copied rules.

e. Click cell **I14**, and then in the Styles group, click **Conditional Formatting**, and then select **Manage Rules**. Click the **Formula: = I14/I32>=C41** rule, and then click **Edit Rule**.
   The source formula: =I9/I27>=C36 was adjusted relatively to =I14/I32>=C41. I32 is not the correct cell reference for the total sales weekly total, and C41 is not the correct cell reference for the benchmark percentage for Clothing.

f. In the **Format values where this formula is true** box, double-click **I32**, type **I27**, and then double-click **C41**.

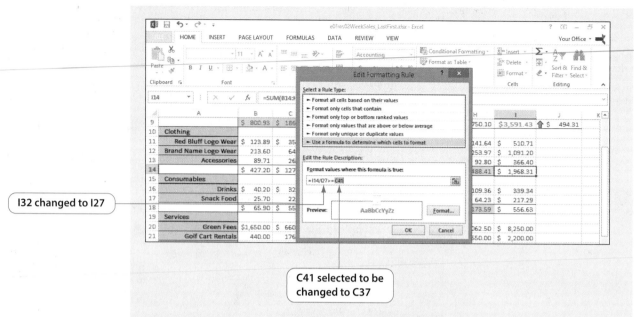

132 changed to I27

C41 selected to be changed to C37

Figure 23   Edit conditional formatting using the Rules Manager

g. Type **C37**, click **OK**, and then click **OK**.

h. Click cell **I18**, and then in the Styles group, click **Conditional Formatting**, and then select **Manage Rules**. Click the **Formula: = I18/I36>=C45** rule, and then click **Edit Rule**.

i. In the **Format values where this formula is true** box, double-click **I36**, and then type **I27**. Double-click **C45**, type **C38**, click **OK**, and then click **OK**.

j. Click **Save** .

Removing Conditional Formatting

Once conditional formatting has been applied to a cell or range of cells, it may be necessary to remove the conditional formatting without affecting other cell formatting or cell contents. Conditional formatting can be removed from a selected cell or cell range, and it can be removed from the entire sheet, depending upon which option is chosen.

When you applied the conditional formatting to cell range B6:I27 that displayed negative numbers in red regardless of the number format, several cells that did not contain data were also conditionally formatted. Although applying conditional formatting to a large range of cells all at once is efficient, applying it to cells that do not contain data in the current design may cause unforeseen problems as the worksheet is modified in the future. You need to remove the conditional formatting in the empty cells.

S₂ CONSIDER THIS | **How Might You Use Conditional Formatting?**

Can you think of ways you could use conditional formatting in worksheets to aid personal decisions? Could you use conditional formatting as an aid in tracking your stock portfolio? Monthly budget and expenses? Checking account?

SIDE NOTE

View More of the Worksheet

Click the View tab, and in the Show group, uncheck Formula Bar. Double-click any Ribbon tab to hide the Ribbon.

E02.23

To Remove Conditional Formatting from a Range of Cells

a. Select cell range **B10:I10**, press Ctrl, and then select cell ranges **B15:I15** and **B19:I19**.

b. In the Styles group, click **Conditional Formatting**, and then click **Manage Rules**. Click the **Show formatting rules for** arrow, and then select **Current Selection**. The Conditional Formatting Rules Manger will display the rules applied in the currently selected cells. Click the **Cell Value < 0** rule.

Notice the Cell Value < 0 rule that was applied to the selected ranges even though the ranges do not contain any data.

Show formatting rules for arrow

Cell Value < 0 rule

SIDE NOTE

Another Way to Remove Conditional Formatting

Click Conditional Formatting, point to Clear Rules, and then select Clear Rules from Selected Cells.

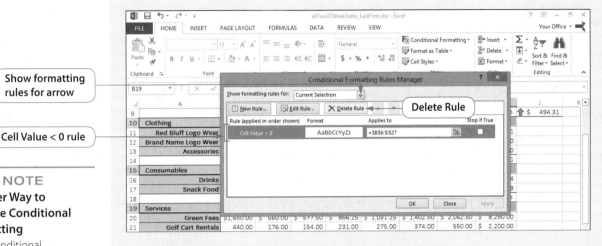

Figure 24 How to remove conditional formatting

c. Click **Delete Rule**, and then click **OK**.

d. Click **Save**.

Hide Information in a Worksheet

A worksheet can contain information that may not be necessary, or even desirable, to display. This is often true of a list of parameters. A **parameter** is a term generally used to describe a value included for calculation or comparison purposes that is stored in a single location such as a worksheet cell so that it can be used many times but be edited in a single location. Another example of hidden information would be hiding detailed information used to calculate totals until such time that the person using the worksheet would like to see it.

Hiding information in a worksheet is relatively simple. Entire worksheet rows and columns can be hidden. Simply select the rows and/or columns to be hidden by clicking on the row or column heading. Right-click with the mouse pointer over the heading or in the selected row(s) or column(s), and click Hide on the shortcut menu that appears.

Gridlines are very helpful in visualizing and navigating a workbook during development, but some feel they clutter a worksheet. Gridlines can be "hidden" simply by unchecking the Gridlines box in the Show group of the View tab.

Hiding Worksheet Rows

In the Weekly Sales worksheet, rows 29:38 contain parameters that are used to calculate commissions, to identify minimum commission levels, and to specify sales percentage benchmarks for golf equipment, clothing, and consumables. Once the Weekly Sales worksheet has been fully developed, there is little need to have this data visible. In fact, having this kind of data visible can be problematic in that a user could inadvertently, or intentionally, change the data and cause the worksheet to display incorrect information. In the next exercise you will hide rows 29:38 from view in the Weekly Sales worksheet.

E02.24

To Hide Rows in a Worksheet

a. Click the heading for row **29** in the **Weekly Sales** worksheet, press and hold [Shift], and then click the **heading** for row **38**.

b. Right-click anywhere in the selected rows.

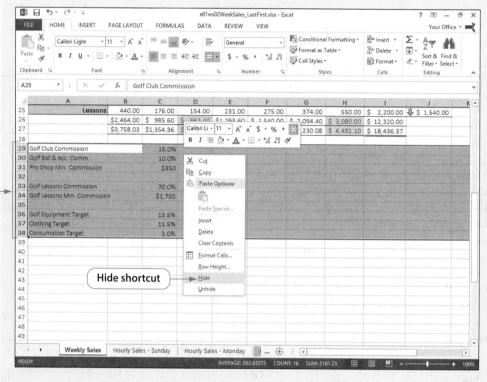

Figure 25 Hide rows using the shortcut menu

c. Select **Hide** on the shortcut menu.

d. Press [Ctrl]+[Home], then click **Save** .

Hiding Worksheet Gridlines

Gridlines assist in identifying cells when manipulating a worksheet. Once a worksheet is complete, some people feel gridlines detract from a worksheet's professional appearance. In the next exercise, you will turn off, or hide, gridlines in the Weekly Sales worksheet.

E02.25

To Hide Gridlines in a Worksheet

a. Click the **VIEW** tab, and then in the Show group, click **Gridlines** to toggle gridlines off. Notice that the worksheet now has a white background. To many users, this is much more visually appealing than a worksheet where gridlines are visible.

b. Click **Save** .

Document Functions and Formulas

An important part of building a good worksheet is documentation. Ms. Herriott included the standard documentation worksheet in the e01ws01WeeklySales workbook and updated it to reflect what she had accomplished prior to assigning completion of the workbook to you.

Showing Functions and Formulas

What is displayed in a cell that contains a function or a formula is the calculated result. The function or formula that generated the displayed value is only visible one cell at a time by selecting a cell and then looking at the formula bar. When Show Formulas is on, the calculated results are hidden, and functions and formulas are shown in the cells instead, whenever applicable.

Show Formulas is very helpful in understanding how a worksheet is structured. It is an essential aid when correcting errors or updating the function of a worksheet. A worksheet that has Show Formulas turned on can be printed and/or exported for documentation purposes.

E02.26

 To View Worksheet Formulas and Export to PDF

a. Click the **Weekly Sales** worksheet tab.

b. Click the **FORMULAS** tab, and then in the Formula Auditing group, click **Show Formulas** .

   Cells now display formulas rather than values. Notice that Show Formulas also displays cell data without formatting.

c. Use the **Zoom Slider** on the status bar to move the zoom level so you can view the entire worksheet on the monitor.

Show Formulas (turned on)

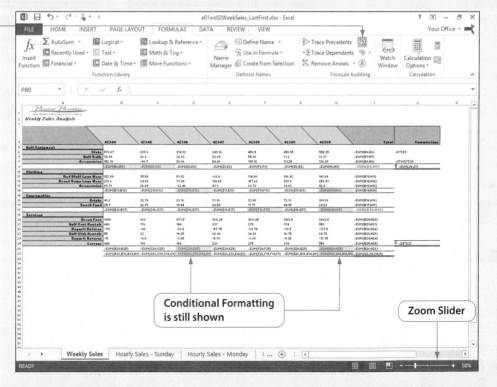

Figure 26 Show Formulas

d. Click the **PAGE LAYOUT** tab, and then in the Scale to Fit group, click the **Width** arrow, and then click **1 page**. This will scale your worksheet to print in the width of a single page.

e. In the Scale to Fit group, click the **Height** arrow, and then click **1 page**. This will scale your document to print in the height of a single page.

f. In the Page Setup group, click **Orientation** and then select **Landscape**.

g. Click the **FILE** tab to enter Backstage view, and then click **Export**. Under Create a PDF/XPS Document, click **Create PDF/XPS**. In the Publish as PDF or XPS dialog box, double-click the **File name** box, and then type **e01ws02WSFormulas_LastFirst**, using your last and first name. Make sure **Open file after publishing** is checked. Click **Publish**.

h. The Weekly Sales worksheet with Show Formulas turned on is displayed as a PDF document in Modern Reader. Move the pointer to the top of the screen. Click and hold the left mouse button and swipe to the bottom of the screen to close Modern Reader. Click the **Desktop** tile to return to Excel.

i. Click the **FORMULAS** tab, and then click **Show Formulas** 🗺 to toggle Show Formulas off and return to the default Normal view.

j. Use the **Zoom Slider** ⊟————│————⊞ on the status bar to set the zoom to **100%**.

k. Click **Save** 🔲.

SIDE NOTE

Shortcut to Toggle Show Formulas

Press Ctrl + ~ to toggle Show Formulas on and off.

REAL WORLD ADVICE | **Print Formula View for Documentation**

You need to document your workbooks. As the worksheets you develop become more complex—use more functions and formulas—the need for documentation increases. Once your worksheet is complete, one vital documentation step is to print a Formula view of your worksheet. If anything ever goes wrong with your worksheet in the future, a Formula view printout may be the fastest way to fix it. Remember, an environmentally friendly documentation option can be to print to PDF. **Portable Document Format (PDF)** was developed by Adobe Systems in 1993 and is a file format that has become a standard for storing files. PDF preserves exactly the original "look and feel" of a document but allows its viewing in many different applications. Exporting to PDF is a great way to document your worksheets.

Updating Existing Documentation

You have made some significant and very important improvements to the e01ws02WeekSales_LastFirst workbook. You must document those updates that require identification or explanation.

E02.27

 To Update Existing Documentation

a. Click the **Documentation** worksheet tab.

b. Complete the following:
   - Click cell **A8**, type today's date in mm/dd/yyyy format, and then press Enter.
   - Click cell **B8**, type your name in Lastname, Firstname format, and then press Enter.
   - Click cell **C8**, type Green background - high sales for the week, and then press Enter.
   - In cell **C9**, type Red background - low sales for the week, and then press Enter.
   - In cell **C10**, type Bold and green week total - sales proportion benchmark met, and then press Enter.
   - In cell **C11**, type Commission - green arrow - minimum met, and then press Enter.
   - In cell **C12**, type Commission - red arrow - minimum not met, and then press Enter.

c. Click the **Weekly Sales** worksheet tab.

d. Click the **FILE** tab, and then click **Print**. Under Settings, click the **Print Active Sheets** arrow, and then click **Print Entire Workbook**. Submit your work as directed by your instructor.

e. Click **Save** 🖫.

f. Close ❌ **Excel**.

REAL WORLD ADVICE | The Power and Risk of "Machine Decision Making"

Never forget that tools like Excel are decision-making aids, not decision makers. Certainly there are highly structured decisions that can be programmed into a worksheet in Excel such that the result is the decision, such as a product mix problem. Excel is often used for the analysis of information in less highly structured problems. In addition, generally not all factors in a decision can be quantified and programmed into a worksheet.

Computers make calculations; people make decisions.

Concept Check

1. Why should you format data in Excel? How might you format data for a person who is color blind? p. 96–100

2. What are the different functions made available via the AutoSum button? What does each function calculate? p. 112

3. What are the advantages of calculating totals in a table total row? p. 117–118

4. What operator begins all formulas and functions in Excel? What purpose do parentheses serve in Excel formulas? p. 120–121

5. What is conditional formatting? How can conditional formatting assist in decision making? p. 123

6. List two reasons why it may be necessary to hide rows or columns of information in a worksheet. p. 129

7. Why is the PDF file format good for saving documentation? p. 132

Key Terms

Argument   112
AVERAGE function   115
Banding   109
Built-in cell style   107
Built-in function   112
Cell alignment   101
Cell reference   112
Conditional formatting   123
Constant   120
COUNT function   115

Default   111
Destination cell   112
Fill color   103
Format Painter   105
Formula   120
Function   112
Graphical format   96
Mathematical operator   120
MAX function   116
MIN function   116

Order of operations   121
Parameter   129
Portable Document Format (PDF)   132
Relative cell reference   120
Source cells   112
SUBTOTAL function   117
Table   108
Table style   109
Tabular format   96
Theme   111

View worksheet formulas and export to PDF (p. 131)

Insert an image into a worksheet (p. 108)

Use conditional formatting to assist decision making (p. 123)

Remove conditional formatting from a range of cells (p. 129)

Align text (p. 102)

Change cell background color (p. 103)

Hide gridlines in a worksheet (p. 130)

Update existing documentation (p. 133)

Use the SUM function by selecting destination cells (p. 113)

Calculate commissions using formulas (p. 122)

Use conditional formatting with icon sets to highlight above-minimum commissions (p. 125)

Format cell borders (p. 103)

Format a cell or cell range as a date or time (p. 100)

Rotate text (p. 102)

Highlight sales that meet or exceed benchmarks (p. 126)

Format numbers (p. 97)

Use paste options to copy formats (p. 106)

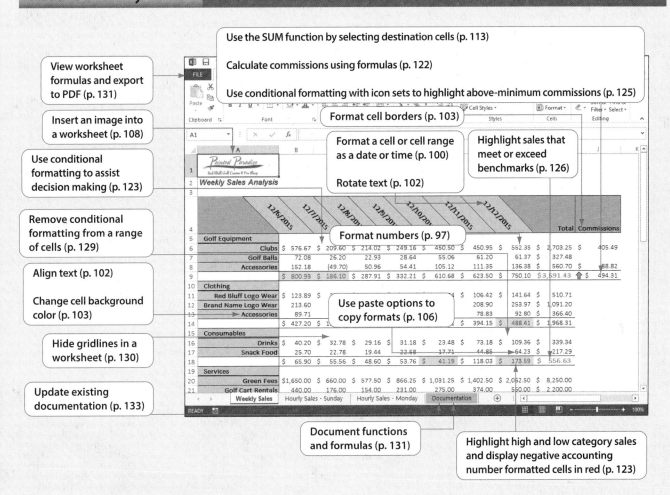

Document functions and formulas (p. 131)

Highlight high and low category sales and display negative accounting number formatted cells in red (p. 123)

Display negative numbers in red (p. 99)

Hide information in a worksheet (p. 129)

Hide rows in a worksheet (p. 130)

Format cells, cell ranges, and worksheets (p. 96)

Use the Format Painter to copy formats (p. 105)

Create information with formulas (p. 120)

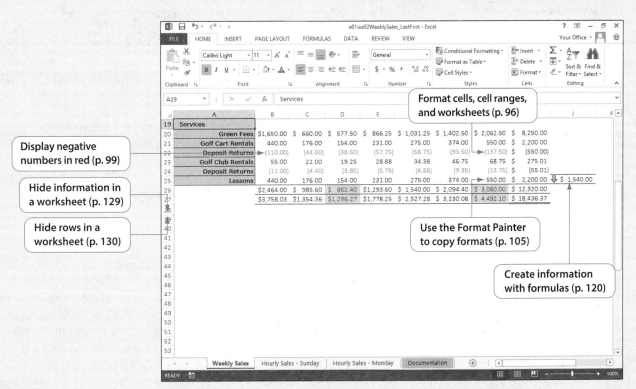

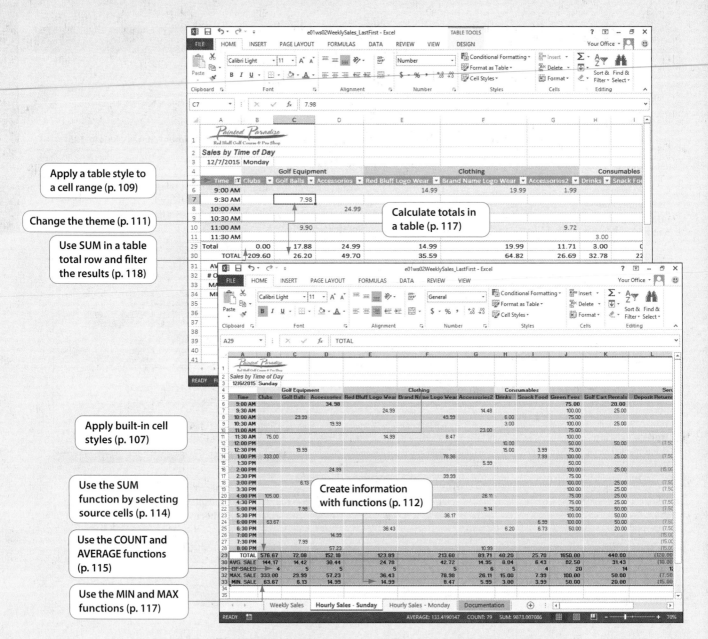

Apply a table style to a cell range (p. 109)

Change the theme (p. 111)

Use SUM in a table total row and filter the results (p. 118)

Calculate totals in a table (p. 117)

Apply built-in cell styles (p. 107)

Use the SUM function by selecting source cells (p. 114)

Create information with functions (p. 112)

Use the COUNT and AVERAGE functions (p. 115)

Use the MIN and MAX functions (p. 117)

Figure 27 Red Bluff Golf Course & Pro Shop Sales Analysis Final

Practice 1

Student data files needed:
e01ws02SpaSchd.xlsx
turquoise_oasis.jpg

You will save your files as:
e01ws02SpaSchd_LastFirst.xlsx
e01ws02SpaSchdPrt_LastFirst.pdf

Spa Schedule

Production & Operations

Irene Kai, another manager of the Turquoise Oasis Spa, has exported sales data from a database program into an Excel spreadsheet to facilitate the analysis of services received by a client during a visit to the spa. This spreadsheet is in the initial development stages, but the intention is to keep track of the treatments performed on an individual client during their stay at the resort, the consultant that performed each service, and the treatments that seem most popular. This will allow the staff to review spa usage in a visually appealing layout, notice trends in treatment choices, and improve the scheduling of therapists. In the future, it might lead to the mailing of special promotions to regular or repeat customers, a reevaluation of pricing, or the addition or deletion of treatments based on popularity.

Irene has imported the data and created a workbook that will consist of three worksheets. One worksheet contains the clients' names, a list of the dates of service, type of treatment administered, the cost of the treatment, and the consultant that performed that service. A second worksheet has a list of spa therapists and the days of the week and times that each is available.

a. Start **Excel**, click **Open Other Workbooks**, double-click **Computer**, navigate to where your student data files are located, and then open **e01ws02SpaSchd**. Click the **FILE** tab, click **Save As**, and then double-click **Computer**. In the Save As dialog box, navigate to the location where you are saving your files. In the **File name** box, type e01ws02SpaSchd_LastFirst using your last and first name, and then click **Save**.

b. Click the **Documentation** worksheet tab, click cell **A8**, and then press [Ctrl]+[;] to enter the current date. Press [Tab]. In cell **B8**, type your name in Lastname, Firstname format.

c. Click the **Schedule by Date** worksheet tab. Click the **PAGE LAYOUT** tab, and then in the Themes group, click **Themes**, and then select **Organic** from the gallery.

d. Click cell **A1**. Click the **HOME** tab, and then in the Cells group, click **Format**, and then click **Row Height**. Type 50 in the **Row height** box, and then click **OK**.

e. Click cell **D1**. Click the **INSERT** tab, and then in the Illustrations group, click **Pictures**. Navigate to the location where your student data files are stored, click **turquoise_oasis**, and then click **Insert**. Click the **FORMAT** tab, and then in the Arrange group, click **Align**, and then if Snap to Grid is not selected, click **Snap to Grid**. Click the right horizontal **resizing handle** and snap the right **edge** of the logo to the border between columns **F** and **G**. Click the bottom vertical **resizing handle**, and snap the bottom edge of the logo to the border between rows **1** and **2**.

f. Select the cell range **A2:J2**. Click the **HOME** tab, and then in the Alignment group, click **Merge & Center**. In the Style group, click **Cell Styles**, and then select **Heading 4** in the gallery.

g. Select cell range **A4:J4**, click **Cell Styles**, and then select **Heading 3** in the gallery.

h. Click cell **A2**, and then in the Clipboard group, click **Copy**. Select cell range **A26:A30**, right-click cell **A26**, and then in the Paste Options shortcut menu, select **Formatting**. In the Alignment group, click **Align Left**.

i. Click cell **A6**. In the Clipboard group, click **Format Painter**, and then select cell range **A7:A23**.

j. Select cell range **I6:I23**. In the Number group, click the **Number Format** arrow, and then select **Currency**. In the Number group, click **Decrease Decimal** two times.

k. Select cell range **C6:C23**. Click the **Number Format** arrow, and then click **More Number Formats**. In the **Type** box, select **1:30 PM**, and then click **OK**.

l. Select cell **J10**, press [Alt]+[=], select the cell range **I6:I9**, and then press [Enter]. Select cell **J13**, press [Alt]+[=], select cell range **I11:I12**, and then press [Enter]. Select cell **J18**, press [Alt]+[=], select cell range **I14:I17**, and then press [Enter]. Select cell **J21**, press [Alt]+[=], select cell range **I19:I20**, and then press [Enter]. Select cell **J24**, press [Alt]+[=], select cell range **I22:I23**, and then press [Enter].

m. Select cell **C28**, and then type =MAX(J6:J24). Press [Ctrl]+[Enter], click cell **J24**, click the **Format Painter**, and then click cell **C28**.

n. Right-click the **column H** header, and then select **Hide** from the shortcut menu.

o. Select cell range **A4:J24**. In the Styles group, click **Format as Table**, and then select **Table Style Medium 2** from the gallery menu. In the Format as Table dialog box, check **My table has headers**, and then click **OK**. In the Table Style Options group, click **Total Row**. Click the **HOME** tab, click cell **J10**, click the **Format Painter**, and then click cell **J25**.

p. In the Editing group, click **Sort & Filter**, and then click **Filter** to turn off column filters.

q. Select cell **J10**, press and hold Ctrl, and then select cells **J13**, **J18**, **J21**, and **J24**. In the Styles group, click **Conditional Formatting**, point to **Highlight Cells Rules**, and then select **Greater Than**. Type =C$31 in the **Format cells that are GREATER THAN** box. Click the **with** arrow, and then select **Custom Format**. In the Format Cells dialog box, on the Font tab, in the Font style box, click **Bold**. Click the **Color** arrow, and select **Green, Accent1** from the palette. Click **OK**, and then click **OK** again.

r. Click the **Therapist Schedule** worksheet tab. Select cell **C8**, type Monday, and then press Ctrl+Enter. Click and hold the **fill handle**, and then expand the active cell to encompass cell range **C8:C14**. Press Ctrl+C. Click cell **C16**, press and hold Ctrl, and then click cell **C24**. Press Ctrl+V.

s. Select cell range **A6:D6**. In the Styles group, click **Cell Styles**, and then select **40% - Accent5** from the gallery menu. In the Font group, click **Bold**.

t. Select cell range **A8:A14**. Press Ctrl, and then select cell ranges **B8:B14**, **A16:A22**, **B16:B22**, **A24:A30**, and **B24:B30**. In the Alignment group, click **Merge & Center**. In the Alignment group, click **Orientation**, and then select **Vertical Text**. In the Alignment group, click **Middle Align**. In the Font group, click **Bold**. Select columns **A:B**. In the Cells group, click **Format**, and select **AutoFit Column Width**.

u. Right-click the **header** for row **5**, and then click **Delete**.

v. Click the **Documentation** worksheet tab. Click cell **C8**, and then type Calculated daily totals. Press Enter. Type Determined maximum day's sales. Press Enter. Type Formatted daily sales totals that met target as green and bold. Press Enter. Type Finished and formatted the Therapist Schedule worksheet. Press Ctrl+Home.

w. Click the **Schedule by Date** worksheet tab. Click the **PAGE LAYOUT** tab, and then in the Page Setup group, click **Orientation**, and then select **Landscape**. In the Scale to Fit group, click the **Width** arrow, and then click **1 page**.

x. Click the **FORMULAS** tab, and then in the Formula Auditing group, click **Show Formulas**. Click the **FILE** tab, click **Export**, and then under Create a PDF/XPS Document, click **Create PDF/XPS**. Be sure **Open file after publishing** is not checked. Click **Options**. In the Options dialog box, under Publish what, click **Entire workbook**, and then click **OK**. Navigate to the folder where you are saving your files. In the File name box, type e01ws02SpaSchdPrt_LastFirst using your last and first name, and then click **Save**.

y. Submit your files as directed by your instructor.

Problem Solve 1

Finance & Accounting

Student data file needed:
e01ws02Portfolio.xlsx

You will save your file as:
e01ws02Portfolio_LastFirst.xlsx

Stock Portfolio Monthly Dividend Income

One method that is used by retirees to provide income during their retirement years is investing in dividend-paying stocks. The dividends allow the investor to make withdrawals from their retirement account without having to reduce their invested principal. Michael Money, president and chief investment officer of your new employer, Excellent Wealth Management, has developed a worksheet to show how a portfolio of stocks can create an additional income stream for his clients. You are asked to determine how much income the current portfolio is generating in order to assist with future investment decisions, in the form of adding to current investments, or diversifying and adding other dividend-paying investments.

a. Start **Excel**, and then open **e01ws02Portfolio**. Save the workbook as e01ws02Portfolio_LastFirst replacing Last and First with your name.

b.   Center and bold cell range **B2:F3**.

c.   Merge and center cell range **A1:N1**. Apply the **Title** cell style, and then **Bold** the range.

d.   Select cell range **N12:N16**, and then calculate row totals using the AutoSum SUM function.

e.   Calculate the average of Total Dividends Received in cell **G8**.

f.   Apply cell style **Heading 3** to cells **G7**, **B10**, and **B18**.

g.   Apply the **Currency** format to cell ranges **B4:F4**, **B6:G4**, **B8:G8**, **B12:N16**, and **B20:N25**.

h.   In cell **B7**, calculate the yield of Prime Steel—the annual dividends per share divided by the price per share. Copy the formula to cell range **C7:F7**. Format the yield figures as **Percent Style** with 2 decimal places.

i.   Hide rows **10:17**.

j.   Format cell range **A19:N24** as a table with headers and a total row. Apply **Table Style Light 11**. Sort by STOCK from A-Z, and then turn off Filters.

k.   Select cell range **B20:N25**. Use the AutoSum SUM function to calculate row and column totals.

l.   Apply a top border to cell range **A25:N25** and a left border to cell range **N19:N25**.

m.   Apply cell style **20% - Accent3** to cell ranges **A20:A25**, **B25:N25**, and **N20:N24**.

n.   Apply **Conditional Formatting** to cell range **B20:M24**. Display the **Top 10 Items** as **Green Fill with Dark Green Text**.

o.   Apply **Conditional Formatting** to cell range **B25:M25**. Display the **Above Average** values with a **Double** underline.

p.   Apply **Conditional Formatting** to cell range **N20:N24**. Display the **Above Average** values with a **Double** underline.

q.   Turn off gridlines in the **Dividend Portfolio** worksheet.

r.   In the **Documentation** worksheet, enter today's date in mm/dd/yyyy format into cells **A4** and **A16**. Type your name in Lastname, Firstname format into cell **B4**. In cell **C4**, type Completed Mr. Money's Monthly Dividend Income worksheet. In cell **B16**, type Dividend Portfolio. Make cell **A1** the active cell.

s.   For the **Dividend Portfolio** worksheet, set Orientation to **Landscape**, and then set Scaling to **Fit All Columns on One Page**. Change print settings to **Print Entire Workbook**. Print and/or submit your workbook file as directed by your instructor.

t.   Save and close the workbook.

Perform 1: Perform in Your Life

Student data file needed:

 e01ws02PriceChngs.xlsx

You will save your file as:

e01ws02PriceChngs_LastFirst.xlsx

Tracking Stock Price Movements

Finance & Accounting

Excel can be used to track changes in stock prices over time. Not only can you record the actual prices, but by using formulas and some formatting you can easily calculate the percentage changes in price and pick out the winners and losers in your portfolio.

After demonstrating your Excel skills for Mr. Money, he would like you to work with some real data for a client (your instructor). The client may decide to modify the specifications given below. Because customer service is of the utmost importance to Excellent Wealth Management, be sure to follow any client requests very carefully.

a.   Start **Excel**, and then open **e01ws02PriceChngs**. Save the workbook as e01ws02PriceChngs_LastFirst replacing Last and First with your name.

Use a website that provides access to historic stock price data for Steps b–d. Options include, but are not limited to, finance.yahoo.com or google.com/finance.

b. Select five (5) companies that are publicly traded. Enter the company name in each cell, starting with B3:F3. In the cell immediately below each company name, enter the ticker symbol—the abbreviation that the company's stock uses.

c. Enter the eight (8) most recent dates that denote the first trading day of a quarter starting in cell A5:A12. For example, the first trading day of 1Q2011 was 1/3/2011. The first trading day of 2Q was 4/2/2011. Format the dates entered as Long Date. Adjust the widths of columns A:F to fit the data you entered.

d. Look up the historic closing prices for each stock for the dates entered in Step d, and then enter these values into the corresponding cells.

e. Under the first company's historic closing price data, calculate the minimum price that was observed. Copy the formula to the cells under each of the other companies' historic price data.

f. Under the minimum price that was calculated, determine the maximum closing price that was observed. Copy the formula to the appropriate cell for each of the other companies.

g. For each company, calculate the Current Gross Margin as the closing price at the end of the most recent quarter—the closing price at the end of the first quarter.

h. Format the historic price data, the minimum and maximum closing prices, and the current gross margin with an appropriate format.

i. Select the range that contains the historic closing prices for the first company. Apply conditional formatting to the range using the Gradient Fill Green Data Bar.

j. Apply the same conditional formatting to each of the other companies using the Format Painter.

k. Use conditional formatting to highlight the largest Maximum, smallest Minimum, largest Current Gross Margin, and smallest Current Gross Margin calculated in Steps e–g.

l. Right align the text of the headings in cells A3:A15. Center the company names and tickers for each range. Merge and center **Price Performance** across the respective data ranges. Merge and center **Excellent Wealth Management** across all of the columns used in the worksheet, and then apply the Heading1 cell style. Make sure all of the data is visible in each of the cells.

m. Apply the Heading4 cell style to all row and column headings, and then apply the Output cell style to the ticker symbols.

n. Apply an appropriate workbook theme, and then adjust the widths of columns A:F if necessary.

o. Copy the worksheet to a new worksheet named Auditing. Show the formulas in this worksheet, and then adjust the column widths of columns A:F to fit the displayed content.

p. Update the Documentation worksheet to reflect the changes that have been made to the workbook.

q. Click the **Stocks** worksheet tab, and then adjust print settings to ensure a usable printed worksheet and to print all worksheets in the workbook. Submit your file as directed by your instructor.

Additional
Cases

Additional Workshop Cases are available on the companion website and in the instructor resources.

MODULE CAPSTONE

More Practice 1

Student data files needed:
- e01mpBvgSales.xlsx
- e01mpIndigo5.jpg

You will save your file as:
- e01mpBvgSales_LastFirst.xlsx

Beverage Sales and Inventory Analysis

Finance & Accounting   Production & Operations

The Painted Paradise Resort and Spa offers a wide assortment of beverages through the Indigo5 restaurant and bar. The resort must track the inventory levels of these beverages as well as the sales and costs associated with each item. Analyze the inventory and sales data found in the worksheet. There are four categories of beverages: Beer, Wine, Soda, and Water. You also have three inventory figures: Starting, Delivered, and Ending. Resort management wants you to generate an analysis of beverage sales in which you identify units sold of each beverage, cost of goods sold, revenue, profit, profit margin, and appropriate totals and averages.

a. Start **Excel**, and then open **e01mpBvgSales**. Save the file with the name e01mpBvgSales_LastFirst, using your first and last name.

b. Click the **Documentation** worksheet tab, click cell **A6**, press Ctrl, and then select cells **A8** and **A20**. Press Ctrl+; and then press Ctrl+Enter to enter today's date. Click cell **B6**, press Ctrl, and then select cells **B8** and **C20**. Type your Last name, First name, and then press Ctrl+Enter. Click cell **C6**, type Formatting Beverage Sales worksheet and then press Enter. In cell **B20**, type Beverage Sales. In cell **D20**, type Weekly beverage sales analysis.

c. Click the **Beverage Sales** worksheet tab, select cell range **D2:J2**, and then click **Merge & Center** for the selected range. Apply the **Title** cell style to the selected range.

d. Select cell range **D3:J3**, and then click **Merge & Center** for the selected range. Apply the **Heading 4** cell style to the selected range.

e. Insert a **hard return** at the specified locations in the following cells—be sure to remove any spaces between the words, and then press Alt+Enter to insert the hard return.
- Between **Starting** and **Inventory** in **C6**
- Between **Inventory** and **Delivered** in **D6**
- Between **Ending** and **Inventory** in **E6**

f. Make the following formatting changes.
- Format the height of row 6 to 30.
- Select cell range **A6:K29**, and then apply **AutoFit Column Width**.
- Select cell range **C6:K6** along with cells **B13**, **B19**, **B26**, **B30**, and **B31**. Apply **Align Right**.
- Select cell ranges **C13:K13**, **C19:K19**, **C26:K26**, and **C30:K30**. Add a **Top and Bottom Border** to the selected cell ranges. Select cell range **C31:K31**, and then add a **Bottom Double Border** to the selected range.

g. Select cell range **C7:F31**. Format the selected range as **Number** with a comma separator and zero decimal places. Select cell range **G7:J31**, and then format the selected range as **Number** with a comma separator and two decimal places.

h. Make the following calculations.

- Click cell **F7**. Calculate Units Sold by adding Starting Inventory to Inventory Delivered and then subtracting Ending Inventory. Type =C7+D7-E7, and then copy cell **F7** to cell ranges **F8:F12**, **F15:F18**, **F21:F25**, and **F28:F29**. If any cells contain pound signs (#), select the column, and then apply **AutoFit Column Width**.

- Click cell **H7**. Calculate Cost of Goods Sold as Units Sold multiplied by Cost Per Unit. Type =F7*G7, and then copy cell **H7** to cell ranges **H8:H12**, **H15:H18**, **H21:H25**, and **H28:H29**. If any cells contain a string of pound signs (#), select the column, and then apply **AutoFit Column Width**.

- Click cell **J7**. Calculate Revenue as Units Sold multiplied by Sale Price Per Unit. Type =F7*I7, and then copy cell **J7** to cell ranges **J8:J12**, **J15:J18**, **J21:J25**, and **J28:J29**. If any cells contain a string of pound signs (#), select the column, and then apply **AutoFit Column Width**.

- Click cell **K7**. Calculate Profit Margin as (Revenue - Cost of Goods Sold)/Revenue. Type =(J7-H7)/J7. Copy cell **K7** to cell ranges **K8:K12**, **K15:K18**, **K21:K25**, and **K28:K29**.

i. Select cell ranges **C13:F13**, **C19:F19**, **C26:F26**, **C30:F30** and cells **H13**, **J13**, **H19**, **J19**, **H26**, **J26**, **H30** and **J30**. Click **AutoSum**. If any cells contain a string of number signs (#), select the cells, and then apply **AutoFit Column Width**.

j. Click cell **C31**. Calculate the total number of items in Starting Inventory for all categories combined by using the SUM() function. Type =SUM(C13,C19,C26,C30) and then copy cell **C31** to cell range **D31:F31** as well as cells **H31** and **J31**. If any cells contain a string of number signs (#), select the cells, and then apply **AutoFit Column Width**.

k. Copy cell **K12**, and then from **Paste Options**, paste **Formulas** into cells **K13**, **K19**, **K26**, **K30**, and **K31**. Select cell range **K7:K31**. Format the selected range as **Percentage** with one decimal place. If any cells contain a string of pound signs (#), select the cells, and then apply **AutoFit Column Width**.

l. Select cells **H13**, **J13**, **H19**, **J19**, **H26**, **J26**, **H30**, **J30**, **H31**, and **J31**. Format the selected cells as **Currency**. If any cells contain a string of pound signs (#), select the cells, and then apply **AutoFit Column Width**.

m. Select cell range **F7:F12**. Use conditional formatting to highlight the beer with the highest number of units sold for the week as **Green Fill with Dark Green Text**. Use **Top 10 Items** in Top/Bottom Rules, and then change the number of ranked items to **1**.

n. Copy cell **F12**. Select cell range **J7:J12**. Right-click the selected cell range, and then under Paste Options, click **Paste Formatting**. Continue pasting conditional formatting as follows.

- Select cell range **F15:F18**, and then click **Paste Formatting**.
- Select cell range **J15:J18**, and then click **Paste Formatting**.
- Select cell range **F21:F25**, and then click **Paste Formatting**.
- Select cell range **J21:J25**, and then click **Paste Formatting**.
- Select cell range **F28:F29**, and then click **Paste Formatting**.
- Select cell range **J28:J29**, and then click **Paste Formatting**.

o. Select cell range **J7:J12**, press Ctrl, and then select cell ranges **J15:J18**, **J21:J25**, and **J28:J29**. Click **Increase Decimal** two times.

p. Select cell range **A6:K6**, press Ctrl, and then click cells **A14**, **A20**, and **A27**. In the Themed Cell Styles group, apply **Accent6** to the selected cells. With the cells still selected, press Ctrl, and then select cell ranges **B13:K13**, **B19:K19**, **B26:K26** and **B30:K31**. Click **Bold**.

q. Delete row 4.

r. Press Ctrl+Home. Click the **INSERT** tab, and then in the Illustrations group, click **Pictures**. Navigate to the location of your student data files, and then click

e01mpIndigo5. Click **Insert**. Under PICTURE TOOLS, on the FORMAT tab, in the Arrange group, click **Align**, and then click **Snap to Grid**. Drag the square resizing handle on the right side of the logo left until the right border is between columns **B** and **C**. Drag the square resizing handle on the bottom of the logo and up until the bottom border is between rows **4** and **5**.

s. Click the **PAGE LAYOUT** tab, and then in the Themes group, click Themes, and then click **Wood Type** to change the workbook theme. Apply **AutoFit Column Width** to columns **A:K**. Set Page Orientation to **Landscape**, set the Width to **1 page**, and then press Ctrl+Home.

t. Click the **Documentation** worksheet tab. Click cell **C8**, and then enter a descriptive sentence or two that accurately reflects the activities in this exercise. Press Ctrl+Home. Click the **Beverage Sales** worksheet tab.

u. Click **Save**. Close Excel. Submit your file as directed by your instructor.

Problem Solve 1

MyITLab® Grader

Homework 1

Student data files needed:

 e01ps1HotelDisc.xlsx

e01ps1PaintedPar.jpg

You will save your file as:

 e01ps1HotelDisc_LastFirst.xlsx

Analysis of Hotel Sales Discounts

Finance & Accounting   Production & Operations

The Painted Paradise Resort and Spa has 700 rooms. The Painted Paradise Resort and Spa gives discounts to guests who meet certain conditions. First, the Paradise Club discount, a 9% discount applicable to all products and services at the resort, is offered to guests who opt into the resort's rewards program. Another 10% discount, good on hotel rooms and services, is offered to groups who book a large block of rooms. Finally, at the discretion of the resort management, rooms may be charged at a complimentary rate. The resort's management would like to get an idea of how much revenue is lost to discounts on Friday and Saturday nights, the busiest nights of the week.

a. Start **Excel**, and then open **e01ps1HotelDisc**. Save the file with the name e01ps1HotelDisc_LastFirst, using your first and last name.

b. Click the **Documentation** worksheet tab, click cell **A6**, press Ctrl, and then select cells **A8** and **A20**. Press Ctrl+: and then press Ctrl+Enter to enter today's date. Click cell **B6**, press Ctrl, and then select cells **B8** and **C20**. Type your Last name, First name and then press Ctrl+Enter. Click cell **C6**, type Formatting Hotel Discounts worksheet and then press Enter. Click cell **B20**, and then type Hotel Discounts. Click cell **D20**, and then type Analysis of weekend hotel room discounts by room type.

c. Click the **Hotel Discounts** worksheet tab. Set the height of row **1** to **40**. Click cell **C1**. Click the **INSERT** tab, and then in the Illustrations group, click **Pictures**. Navigate to the location of your student data files, and then click the **e01ps1PaintedPar** file. Click **Insert**. Click the **FORMAT** tab, and then in the Arrange group, click **Align**. Make sure **Snap to Grid** is selected. Drag the resizing handle on the right side of the logo to the left until the right border is between columns **F** and **G**. Drag the resizing handle on the bottom of the logo up until the bottom border is between rows **1** and **2**.

d. Apply the **Heading 4** cell style to cells **A2**, **A12**, **A24**, and **A41**.

e. Apply the **Heading 3** cell style to cells **A3:G3** and **A7:G7**.

f. Change the font color in cells **A4:A5** and **A8:A10** to **Dark Blue, Text 2**, and then apply **Bold**.

g. Format the range **B8:G10** as **Percent Style** with one decimal place.

h. Apply Table Styles as follows.

- Format cells **A13:G17** as **Table Style Light 9** with the option **My table has headers** checked. Under TABLE TOOLS, on the DESIGN tab, in the Table Style Options group, check **First Column**, in the Tools group, click **Convert to Range**, and then click **Yes**.
- Format cells **A18:G22** as **Table Style Light 9** with **My table has headers** checked. Check **First Column**, click **Convert to Range**, and then click **Yes**.
- Format cells **A25:H31** as **Table Style Medium 2** with **My table has headers** checked. Check **First Column** and **Last Column**, click **Convert to Range**, and then click **Yes**.
- Format cells **A33:H39** as **Table Style Medium 2** with **My table has headers** checked. Check **First Column** and **Last Column**, click **Convert to Range**, and then click **Yes**.
- Format cells **A42:H46** as **Table Style Medium 2** with **My table has headers** checked. Check **First Column** and **Last Column**, click **Convert to Range**, and then click **Yes**.

i. Apply number formatting as follows:

- Format cells **B26:G29**, **B34:G37**, and **B43:G45** as **Number**. Negative numbers should not be displayed in red. Make sure to display **2 decimal places** and that **Use 1000 Separator (,)** is checked.
- Format cells **B30:H31**, **H26:H29**, **B38:H39**, **H34:H37**, **B46:H46**, and **H43:H45** as **Accounting**.

j. Calculate the following:

- In cell **B26**, enter a formula to multiply the total number of One Double rooms rented on Friday by the Standard Rate for a One Double room. Click **AutoSum**, and then select the cell range **B14:B17**. Edit the formula to multiply the SUM() function by the Standard Rate for a One Double room in cell **B5**.
- In cell **B27**, calculate the discount total for the Paradise Club for One Double rooms for Friday night. Enter a formula to multiply the number of Paradise Club One Double rooms rented on Friday by the Standard Rate for a One Double room by the Paradise Club discount. The result of the formula will be a negative number to reflect the discount total.
- In cell **B28**, calculate the Group discount total. Multiply the Standard Rate for a One Double room by the number of Group Discount rooms sold for Friday night by the Group Discount.
- In cell **B29**, calculate the Comp discount total. Multiply the Standard Rate for a One Double room by the number of Comp Discount rooms sold for Friday night by the Comp Discount.

k. Select cell range **B26:B29**. Click and hold the **fill** handle, and then expand the selection to include **B26:G29**.

l. Calculate the following:

- In cell **B34**, Gross Sales for One Double rooms for Saturday night. Multiply the Standard Rate for each room type by the number of rooms rented of that type for Saturday night (sum all four types of sales).
- In cell **B35**, Paradise Club discount total for One Double rooms for Saturday night. Multiply the number of Paradise Club rooms sold Saturday night by the Standard Rate by the Paradise Club Discount.
- In cell **B36**, Group discount total for One Double rooms for Saturday night. Multiply the Standard Rate by the number of Group One Double rooms sold Saturday night by the Group Discount.
- In cell **B37**, comp discount total for One Double rooms for Saturday night. Multiply the Standard Rate by the number of Comp One Double rooms sold Saturday night by the Comp Discount.

m. Select cell range **B34:B37**. Click and hold the **fill** handle, and then expand the selection to include **B34:G37**.

- In cell **B43**, calculate the Paradise Club discounts for Friday and Saturday night for One Double rooms. Add the Friday Paradise Club discounts to the Saturday Paradise Club discounts.
- Use the **fill** handle to copy cell **B43** to cell range **B44:B45**. In the Auto Fill Options menu, select **Fill Without Formatting**.

n. Copy cell range **B43:B45** to cell range **C43:G45**.

o. Calculate the Net Sales for each room type on each night, the total sales and discounts for all room types on each night, the Total Discounts for each room type for both nights, and the Total of each discount type for the weekend.

- Select cell ranges **B30:G30**, **H26:H30**, **B38:G38**, **H34:H38**, **B46:G46** and **H43:H46**. Click **AutoSum**.

p. In cell **B31**, calculate Total Discounts for Friday for One Double rooms by subtracting Gross Sales from Net Sales. Copy the formula to cell range **C31:H31**.

q. Copy the formulas in cell range **B31:H31** to cell range **B39:H39**.

r. Apply **Bold** to cell ranges **B31:H31**, **B39:H39**, and **B46:G46**. Apply **AutoFit Column Width** for columns **A:H**. Use the resizing handles to reposition the right side of the logo in row 1 between columns **F** and **G**, and then click cell **A1**.

s. On the PAGE LAYOUT tab, set Orientation to **Landscape**, and then set Width to **1 page**.

t. In the **Documentation** worksheet, in cell **C8**, enter a descriptive sentence or two that accurately reflects the activities in this exercise. Press [Ctrl]+[Home]. Click the **Hotel Discounts** worksheet tab.

u. Click **Save**, and then close Excel, submit your file as directed by your instructor.

Problem Solve 2

MyITLab®
Grader
Homework 2

Production & Operations

Human Resources

Student data file needed:

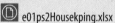 e01ps2Housekping.xlsx

You will save your file as:

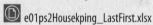 e01ps2Housekping_LastFirst.xlsx

Housekeeping Staff Performance

The Painted Paradise Resort and Spa takes great pride in the efficiency of its housekeeping staff. The housekeeping staff at the Painted Paradise Resort and Spa is expected to properly clean a hotel room in an average of 25 minutes and never more than 30 minutes. Management is interested in how long it takes to actually begin cleaning rooms after guests check out. This is referred to as lag time—time when a room cannot be rented. The Painted Paradise Resort and Spa wants guests to be able to check in early at no charge as long as there is a room available. By keeping lag time to a minimum, room availability is maximized.

a. Start **Excel**, and then open **e01ps2Housekping**. Save the file as e01ps2Housekping_LastFirst, using your first and last name.

b. Click the **Documentation** worksheet tab, and then select cells **A6**, **A8**, and **A20**. Press [Ctrl]+[;] and then press [Ctrl]+[Enter] to enter today's date. Select cells **B6**, **B8**, and **C20**. Type your Last name, First name and then press [Ctrl]+[Enter]. Click cell **C6**, and then type Completed the Housekeeping Analysis worksheet. In cell **B20**, type Housekeeping Analysis. In cell **D20**, type Analyze housekeeping efficiency.

c. Click the **Housekeeping Analysis** worksheet tab. In cell range **C8:F8**, replace hyphens and any surrounding spaces with a **hard return**. In cell **B8**, replace the space between **Checkout** and **Time** with a **hard return**.

d. Apply formatting as follows.

- **Merge** cell ranges **A24:B24**, **A25:B25**, **A26:B26**, **A27:B27**, and **A29:B29**.
- Apply **Merge & Center** to cell ranges **B7:D7**, **C22:D22**, and **E22:F22**.
- Apply **AutoFit Column Width** in columns **A:H**.
- Apply **Align Right** to cell ranges **A3:A5**, **E3:E4**, **A24:A29**, **C23:F23**, and cells **A8**, **C3**, and **H8**.
- **Center** align the cell range **B8:F8**.
- Apply the **40% - Accent2** cell style to cells **A2**, **B7**, and **C22**. Apply the **60% - Accent2** cell style to cell **E22**.
- Apply the **Heading 2** cell style to cell **A2**.
- Apply the **Heading 3** cell style to cell range **A8:H8** and cells **B7**, **C22**, and **E22**.
- Apply the **Heading 4** cell style to cell ranges **A3:A5**, **E3:E4**, **A24:A29**, **C23:F23**, and cell **C3**.

e. Adjust the column width for the following columns.

- Column **A** to **18**
- Columns **B:F** to **12**
- Column **H** to **10**

f. Calculate the following.

- Room Clean Lag Time in cell **E9** by subtracting the Checkout Time from the Room Clean Start Time. Copy the formula you just created to cell range **E10:E20**.

  Notice the cells that contain formulas that subtract one time value from another time value are automatically formatted as time values.
- Room Clean Duration in cell **F9** by subtracting the Room Clean Start Time from the Room Clean End Time. Copy the **formula** you just created to cell range **F10:F20**.
- Total Room Cleaning Time—Lag in cell **D24** by summing all individual Room Clean Lag Time.
- Total Room Cleaning Time—Duration in cell **F24** by summing all individual Room Clean Duration.
- Average Room Cleaning Time—Lag and Duration in cells **D25** and **F25**, respectively.
- Minimum Room Cleaning Time—Lag and Duration in cells **D26** and **F26**, respectively.
- Maximum Room Cleaning Time—Lag and Duration in cells **D27** and **F27**, respectively.
- Calculate the number of Maintenance Issues Reported in cell **C29**. Format cell **C29** as **Number** with zero decimal places.
- Apply **Conditional Formatting** to the cell range **E9:E20** so Room Clean Lag Times that are greater than the Allowed Average Room Cleaning Time Lag display cell values in **Red Text**.

  Apply **Conditional Formatting** to the cell range **F9:F20** so Room Clean Durations that are greater than the Allowed Average Room Cleaning Time Duration displays cell values in **Red Text**.

  Apply **Conditional Formatting** to cell **D24** to change the font color to **Red Text** if the value in D24 is greater than the value in cell C24: under Format cells that are GREATER THAN:, in the far-left box, type =C24. Copy formatting from cell D24 to cell ranges **D25:D27** and **F24:F27**.

g. Format the cell ranges **E9:F20**, **D24:D27** and **F24:F27** with the standard color Green font color.

h. Apply the **Retrospect** workbook theme.

i. Turn off the worksheet gridlines.

j. On the PAGE LAYOUT tab, set Width to **1 page**.

k. In the **Documentation** worksheet, in cell **C8**, enter a descriptive sentence or two that accurately reflects the activities in this exercise. Press Ctrl + Home.

l. Click the **Housekeeping Analysis** worksheet tab, and then press Ctrl + Home.

m. Click **Save**, and then close Excel. Submit your file as directed by your instructor.

Perform 1: Perform in Your Life

Student data file needed:	You will save your file as:
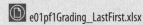 Blank Excel workbook	e01pf1Grading_LastFirst.xlsx

Grade Analysis

Information Technology

Most students are concerned about grades and want to have some means of easily tracking grades, analyzing performance, and calculating the current grade (as much as is possible) in every class.

a. Start **Excel**, and then open a blank workbook. Save the file as e01pf1Grading_LastFirst using your first and last name. Rename Sheet1 with a name appropriate for this exercise.

b. Enter the standard 90-80-70-60 grading scale into your worksheet. Build the scale in descending order with letter grades in the cell to the right of the point score.

c. Look in your syllabus for a list of assignments, exams, and other point-earning activities. Enter the assignments into Excel. For completed assignments, enter the points possible and your score. Be sure to label all data items.

d. Include the following calculations:

- Calculate the percentage score for each point-earning activity, and then use conditional formatting to indicate whether you received an "A," "B," "C," or below a "C" on each assignment.

- Calculate the possible points earned to date and total points earned to date in the class.

- Calculate the current overall percentage earned in the class.

- Calculate the percentage you need to earn on the final examination to achieve an "A," "B," and "C" given the points possible to date and points earned to date.

e. Conditionally format the percentage required to achieve an "A" in the course to visually indicate how hard you may have to study for the final examination.

For example, if you will have to score at least an 80% on the final examination to achieve an "A" in this course, color the cell that contains the points required to achieve an "A" red to show that you have to study pretty hard for the final examination. Use other colors to indicate whether or not you must score less than 80% or less than 70% on the final examination to achieve an "A" in the course. Use parameters to identify the cutoff values for "A," "B," and "C."

f. Repeat Step h for the percentage required to achieve a "B" in the course.

g. Repeat Step h for the percentage required to achieve a "C" in the course.

h. Apply the following conditional formatting:

- Add conditional formatting to visually indicate if an "A" is not possible because the percentage required on the final examination to achieve an "A" exceeds 100%.

- Add conditional formatting to visually indicate if an "B" is not possible because the percentage required on the final examination to achieve an "B" exceeds 100%.

- Add conditional formatting to visually indicate if an "C" is not possible because the percentage required on the final examination to achieve an "C" exceeds 100%.

i. Ask your instructor whether to include any other courses you are currently taking.

j. Include a completed and well-structured Documentation worksheet.

k. Insert the File Name in the left footer of all worksheets.

l. Modify any page settings to ensure your worksheets each will print on a single page. Specify portrait or landscape orientation as is appropriate to maximize readability.

m. Save your file, and then close Excel. Submit your file as directed by your instructor.

Perform 2: Perform in Your Career

Student data file needed:

Blank Excel workbook

You will save your file as:

e01pf2TimeTrack_LastFirst.xlsx

Personal Time Tracking

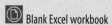

Finance & Accounting

Human Resources

You have started working as a computer programmer with BetaWerks Software Corporation. The company requires you to track the time that you spend doing different things during the day each week. This helps the company determine how many of your hours are billable to customers. You have several different projects to work on as well as a few training sessions throughout the week. The company pays for one 15-minute coffee break and a one-hour lunch each day. Any additional time is considered personal time.

a. Start **Excel**, and then open a blank workbook. Save the file as **e01pf2TimeTrack_LastFirst** using your first and last name. Rename Sheet1 with a name appropriate to this exercise.

b. Create a worksheet to track your time for the company this week. The following requirements must be met:
   - The worksheet should identify the first day of the workweek with a title such as: Week of mm/dd/yyyy.
   - Your time must be broken down by project/client and weekdays.
   - Time not billable to a project should be classified as Unbillable.
   - Unbillable time should be broken into at least two categories: Breaks and Work.

c. Set up your worksheet so you can easily calculate the amount of time you spent working on each account, in meetings, in training, and on breaks according to the information below:
   - Monday, you spent two hours in a meeting with your development team. This is billable to the BetaWerks Software company as unbillable hours. Following the meeting, you took a 20-minute coffee break. After your break, you spent two hours and 15 minutes working on your project for the Garske Advising. After a one-hour lunch, you attended a two-hour training and development meeting. Before heading home for the day, you spent two hours working on the ISBC Distributing project.
   - Tuesday morning you spent four hours on the Klemisch Kompany project. To help break up the morning, you took a 20-minute coffee break at 10:00. You only had time for a 30-minute lunch because you had to get back to the office for a team-building activity. The activity lasted 40 minutes. To finish the day, you spent four hours working on the Garske Advising assignment.
   - Wednesday morning, you spent two hours each on the Garske Advising and Klemisch Kompany projects. Lunch was a quick 30 minutes because you had a conference call with Mr. Atkinson from ISBC at 1 p.m. The conference call took one hour, and then you spent an additional three hours working on the project.
   - Thursday, the day started with a 30-minute update with your supervisor. Following the meeting, you were able to spend two hours on the ISBC project. After a 15-minute coffee break, you started on a new project for K&M Worldwide for 90 minutes.

You took a 45-minute lunch break, and then spent two and a half hours on the Klemisch Kompany project and two hours on your work for L&H United.

- Friday started with a two-hour training and development session about a new software package that BetaWerks is starting to implement, followed by a 15-minute coffee break. After your coffee break, you were able to squeeze in two more hours for L&H United before taking a one-hour lunch. After lunch, you put in four hours on the Klemisch Kompany project before finally going home for the week.

d. BetaWerks bills your time spent on each account according to the following rates:

Klemisch Kompany	$275
Garske Advising	$250
ISBC Distributing	$225
K&M Worldwide	$175
L&H United	$200

e. Your salary is $100,000/year with benefits. Given two weeks of vacation, you cost BetaWerks $2,000 in salary and benefits per week.

f. Include in your worksheet a calculation of your profit/loss to BetaWerks for the week.

g. Be sure to document your worksheet using a separate Documentation worksheet, comments, and instructions.

h. Modify any page settings to ensure your worksheets each will print on a single page. Specify portrait or landscape orientation as is appropriate to maximize readability.

i. Insert the **File Name** in the left footer of all worksheets.

j. Save your file, and then close Excel. Submit your file as directed by your instructor.

Perform 3: Perform in Your Team

Student data file needed:

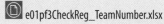 Blank Excel workbook

You will save your file as:

e01pf3CheckReg_TeamNumber.xlsx

Check Register

Finance & Accounting

You volunteer your time with a local nonprofit, the Mayville Community Theatre. Because of your business background, the board of directors has asked you to serve as the new treasurer and to track all of the monetary transactions for the group.

a. Select one team member to set up the document by completing Steps b through e. Then continue with Step d.

b. Open your browser, and then navigate to either **https://www.skydrive.live.com**, **https://www.drive.google.com**, or any other instructor assigned location. Be sure all members of the team have an account on the chosen system—a Microsoft or Google account.

c. Create a new workbook, and then name it e01pf3CheckReg_TeamNumber. Replace Number with the number assigned to your team by your instructor.

d. Rename Sheet1 as Check Register - Team #. Replace # with the number of your team.

e. Share the worksheet with the other members of your team. Make sure that each team member has the appropriate permission to edit the document.

f. Hold a team meeting, and make a plan. Layout the worksheet you are going to build on paper, discuss the requirements of each of the remaining steps, and then divide the remaining steps (g–n) among team members. Note that the steps should be completed in order, so as each team member completes his or her steps, he or she should notify the entire team, not just the team member responsible for the next step.

g. Create the Check Register worksheet to track receipts and expenditures that should be assigned to one of the following categories: Costumes, Marketing, Operating and Maintenance, Scripts and Royalties, and Set Construction. Also track the following for each receipt or expenditure: the date, amount of payment, check/reference number, recipient, and item description.

h. Enter the following receipts and expenditures under the appropriate category.

Date	Item	Paid To	Check or Ref. #	Amount
11/1/2015	Starting Balance	N/A		$1793.08
11/2/2015	Royalties for "The Cubicle"	Office Publishing Company	9520	-$300.00
11/2/2015	Scripts for "The Cubicle"	Office Publishing Company	9521	-$200.00
11/5/2015	Building Maintenance—Ticket Office	Fix It Palace	9522	⁻$187.92
11/8/2015	Patron Donation	N/A	53339	$1,000.00
11/12/2015	Costumes for "The Cubicle"	Jane's Fabrics	9523	⁻$300.00
11/22/2015	Building Materials for set construction of "The Cubicle"	Fix It Palace	9524	⁻$430.00
11/30/2015	TV and Radio ads for "The Cubicle"	AdSpace	9525	⁻$229.18
11/30/2015	General Theater Operating Expenses—November	The Electric Co-op, City Water Works	9526	-$149.98
12/15/2015	Ticket Revenue from "The Cubicle"	N/A	59431	$1,115.50
12/30/2015	General Theater Operating Expenses—December	The Electric Co-op, City Water Works	9527	-$195.13

i. Periodically, money is deposited into the checking account. Include a way to track deposits.

j. Finally, include a running balance. This should be updated any time money is deposited or withdrawn from the account.

k. If the running account balance drops below $1,000, there should be a conditional formatting alert for any balance figure below the threshold.

l. Document the check register using a separate Documentation worksheet, explicit instructions, and comments where helpful.

m. Modify any page settings to ensure your worksheets each will print on a single page. Specify portrait or landscape orientation as is appropriate to maximize readability.

n. Insert the File Name in the left footer on all worksheets in the workbook. Include a list of the names of the students in your team in the right section of the footer.

o. Press Ctrl+Home, save your file, and then close Excel. Submit your file as directed by your instructor.

Student data file needed:

 e01pf4ProjBill.xlsx

You will save your file as:

 e01pf4ProjBill_LastFirst.xlsx

Project Management Billing

Finance & Accounting

John Smith works with you at the Excellent Consulting Company. Each week, consultants are required to track how much time they spend on each project. A worksheet is used to track the date, start time, end time, project code, a description of work performed, and the number of billable hours completed. At the bottom of the worksheet, the hours spent on each project are summarized so clients can be billed. In your role as an internal auditor, you have been asked to double-check a tracking sheet each week. By random selection, Mr. Smith's tracking worksheet needs to be checked this week. Make sure his numbers are accurate, and ensure that his worksheet is set up to minimize errors. His worksheet is also badly in need of some formatting for appearance and clarity.

a. Start **Excel**, and then open **e01pf4ProjBill**. Save the file as e01pf4ProjBill_LastFirst replacing LastFirst with your own name.

b. Make sure all calculated figures are correct. If you subtract Start Time from End Time and multiply the difference by 24, the result is the number of hours between the two times.

c. Examine client totals, and then correct any problems with formulas.

d. Apply formatting such as cell styles, bold, a theme, and so on to improve the appearance of the worksheet.

e. Apply any data formatting that will make the data easier to interpret.

f. Add documentation.

g. Insert the File Name in the left footer on all worksheets in the workbook.

h. Modify any page settings to ensure the worksheets each will print on a single page. Specify portrait or landscape orientation as is appropriate to maximize readability.

i. Save your file, and then close Excel. Submit your file as directed by your instructor.

WORKSHOP 3 | CELL REFERENCES, NAMED RANGES, AND FUNCTIONS

OBJECTIVES

1. Understand the types of cell references   p. 154

2. Create named ranges   p. 162

3. Create and structure functions   p. 166

4. Use and understand math and statistical functions   p. 168

5. Use and understand date and time functions   p. 174

6. Use and understand text functions   p. 177

7. Use financial and lookup functions   p. 181

8. Use logical functions and troubleshoot functions   p. 186

Prepare Case

Painted Paradise Resort and Spa Wedding Planning

Sales & Marketing

Finance & Accounting

Clint Keller and Addison Ryan just booked a wedding at Painted Paradise Resort and Spa. When requested by a happy couple, the Turquoise Oasis Spa coordinates a variety of events including spa visits, golf massages, and gift baskets made up of various spa products. Given the frequency of wedding events at the Turquoise Oasis Spa, Meda Rodate has asked for your assistance in designing an Excel workbook that can be used and reused to plan these events in the future.

Vladimir Voronin / Fotolia

REAL WORLD SUCCESS

"The skills I have learned through Excel have become incredibly valuable in my everyday life. I recently worked at a private golf course, and was asked to create an inventory workbook to track Beverage Cart sales. This would allow the golf course to forecast demand and predict the amount of starting inventory we needed to maintain. In addition, we needed to use functions that would be user-friendly for the beverage cart employees. At the end of the day, the beverage cart employees would count to see how many items from the set amount of inventory were missing, input the numbers into the Excel workbook, and Excel would compute the amount of sales the beverage cart employee would need to turn in. The remaining amount would equal the tips the employee had earned. The use of Excel functions not only helped the Golf Course track its inventory, but also its profits."

- Kristen, alumnus

Referencing Cells and Named Ranges

The value of Excel expands as you move from using the spreadsheet for displaying data to analyzing data in order to make informed decisions. As the complexity of a spreadsheet increases, techniques that promote effective and efficient development of the spreadsheet become of utmost importance. Integrating cell references within formulas and working with functions are common methods used in developing effective spreadsheets. These skills will become the foundation for more advanced skills.

A **cell reference** is used in a formula or function to address a cell or range of cells. A cell reference contains two parts, a column reference—the alphabetic portion that comes first, and a row reference—the numeric portion that comes last. For example, cell reference B4 refers to the intersection of column B and row 4. When a formula is created, you can simply use values, like =5*5. However, writing a formula without cell references is limiting. Formulas with cell references are substantially more powerful. For example, the formula =B4*C4, where cells B4 and C4 contain values to be used in the calculation, allows the formula to reference a cell (or cell range) rather than a value (or values). This means that when data changes in an individual cell, any formulas that reference the cell are automatically recalculated. In this section you will use cell referencing and named ranges to build a worksheet model for planning events at the Turquoise Oasis Spa.

Understand the Types of Cell References

There are three different types of cell referencing: relative, absolute, and mixed. A **relative cell reference** changes when the formula or function is copied to another location. The change in the cell reference will reflect the number of rows and/or columns that the cell was copied from, relative to its original location. An **absolute cell reference** does not change if a formula or function is copied to another location. An absolute reference is specified by placing a dollar sign ($) in front of both the column letter(s) and row number. For example, to make B4 an absolute reference you would specify $B$4. A **mixed cell reference** is essentially a combination of relative and absolute cell references. In a mixed cell reference, the column or row portion of the reference is absolute and the corresponding row or column is relative. For example, $B4 is a mixed reference where the column is absolute and the row is relative. B$4 is a mixed reference where the column is relative and the row is absolute. In essence, the dollar sign ($) sign locks down the letter or number it precedes so it will not change when copied.

QUICK REFERENCE	Types of Cell Referencing

Below are examples of the three types of cell referencing for cell A4:

1. Relative cell referencing: =A5+B5
2. Absolute cell referencing: =$A$5+B5
3. Mixed cell referencing: =$A5+B5

Cell referencing is a useful feature when formulas need to be copied across ranges in a spreadsheet. When creating a spreadsheet and developing a formula that will not be copied elsewhere, relative and absolute cell referencing is not necessary. However, data arranged in a table may require a formula to perform calculations on each row, or record. Excel allows this process to be completed quickly and easily by using cell referencing. The formula can be constructed once and then quickly copied across a range of cells.

REAL WORLD ADVICE | Creating Dynamic Workbooks

The use of cell references in formulas helps make spreadsheets in Excel extremely powerful. By using a cell reference to refer to a value in a formula you can make your spreadsheet flexible. In other words, using cell references makes your spreadsheet easier to use and more efficient. If something about your business changes and requires an update to a value in your spreadsheet, you need only make the update in one place.

Open the Starting File

Meda Rodate would like for the Turquoise Oasis Spa to become more efficient in planning for wedding events. She has asked for your help in designing an Excel workbook to accomplish this goal. You will begin by opening the wedding planning workbook and organizing the number and pricing of spa gift baskets by constructing common Excel functions using various types of cell referencing.

E03.00

 To Open the Excel Workbook

a. Start **Excel**, click **Open Other Workbooks**, double-click **Computer**, and then browse to your student data files. Locate and select **e02ws03Wedding**, and then click **Open**.

b. Click the **FILE** tab, click **Save As**, and then Browse to your student files. In the File name box, type e02ws03Wedding_LastFirst using your last and first name, and then click **Save**.

c. Click the **INSERT** tab, and then in the Text group, click **Header & Footer**.

d. On the HEADER & FOOTER TOOLS DESIGN tab, in the Navigation group, click **Go to Footer**. If necessary, click the left section of the footer, and then click File Name in the Header & Footer Elements group.

e. Click any cell on the spreadsheet to move out of the footer, press [Ctrl]+[Home], click the **VIEW** tab, and then in the Workbook Views group, click **Normal**, and then click the **HOME** tab.

Using Relative Cell Referencing

Relative cell referencing (as shown in Figure 1) is the default reference type when constructing formulas in Excel. Remember that relative cell referencing changes the cells in a formula if it is copied or otherwise moved to another location. This includes the use of copy and paste or the AutoFill feature to copy a formula to another location. If a formula is copied to the right or left, the column references will change in the formula. If a formula is copied up or down, the row references will change in the formula.

Relative cell referencing is useful in situations where the same calculation is needed in multiple cells but the location of the data needed for the calculation changes relative to the position of the calculation cell. The GiftBaskets worksheet contains a list of individual items that are included in the different types of gift baskets offered at the Turquoise Oasis Spa. The worksheet contains the prices for individual items in the baskets, the number of each item in the basket, and the prices of each basket.

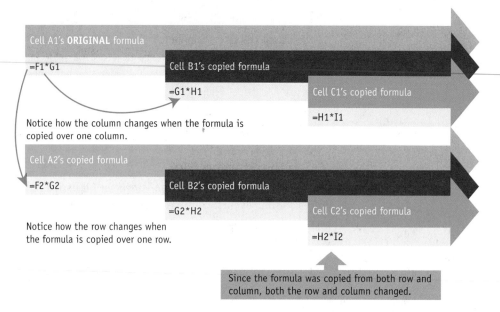

Cell A1's **ORIGINAL** formula

=F1*G1

Cell B1's copied formula

=G1*H1

Cell C1's copied formula

=H1*I1

Notice how the column changes when the formula is copied over one column.

Cell A2's copied formula

=F2*G2

Cell B2's copied formula

=G2*H2

Cell C2's copied formula

=H2*I2

Notice how the row changes when the formula is copied over one row.

Since the formula was copied from both row and column, both the row and column changed.

Figure 1   Understanding relative cell referencing

The Turquoise Oasis Spa allows wedding parties to specify up to three different kinds of custom gift baskets. Each gift basket can contains up to four different items in each basket. The workbook has been set up such that cells with a blue fill need to be changed from one event to another. In this exercise you will use relative cell referencing to display the total number of items in each type of gift basket.

SIDE NOTE

Alternate Method

You can also use AutoFill with a formula in a horizontal range by selecting the range and pressing ⌈Ctrl⌉ and typing R.

E03.01

To Use Relative Cell Referencing

a. Click the **GiftBaskets** worksheet, and then click cell **F9**.

b. Type =SUM(B9:E9) and then press ⌈Ctrl⌉+⌈Enter⌉.

c. Click the **AutoFill handle** on the bottom-right corner of cell **F9**, and then drag down to copy the formula to cell **F11**.

Notice that the formula in cell F11 refers to cells B11:E11. Since the formula copied down, the row reference changed from 9 to 10 and finally to 11.

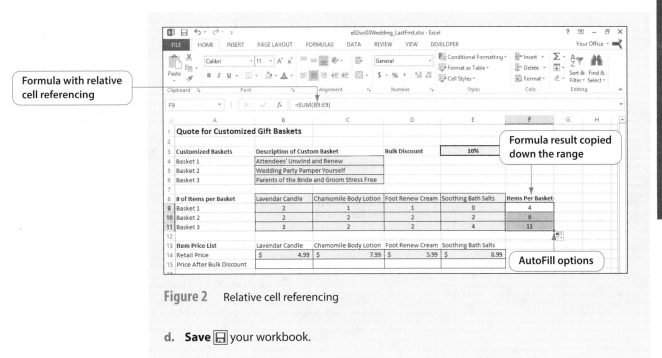

Figure 2 Relative cell referencing

d. **Save** 🔲 your workbook.

Using Absolute Cell Referencing

Absolute cell referencing (as shown in Figure 3) is useful when a formula needs to be copied and the reference to one or more cells within the formula must not change as the formula is copied. Thus, the column and row address of a referenced cell remains constant regardless of the position of the cell when the formula is copied to other cells.

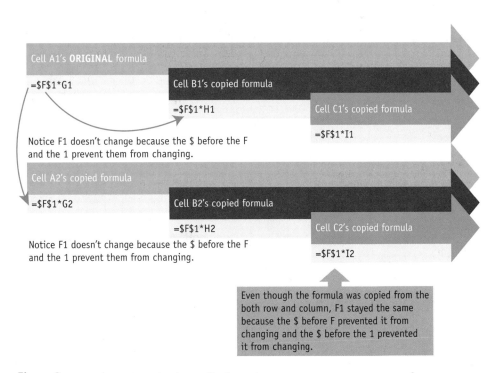

Cell A1's **ORIGINAL** formula

=$F$1*G1

Cell B1's copied formula

=$F$1*H1

Cell C1's copied formula

=$F$1*I1

Notice F1 doesn't change because the $ before the F and the 1 prevent them from changing.

Cell A2's copied formula

=$F$1*G2

Cell B2's copied formula

=$F$1*H2

Cell C2's copied formula

=$F$1*I2

Notice F1 doesn't change because the $ before the F and the 1 prevent them from changing.

Even though the formula was copied from the both row and column, F1 stayed the same because the $ before F prevented it from changing and the $ before the 1 prevented it from changing.

Figure 3 Understanding absolute cell referencing

Meda has decided to offer a bulk percentage discount on all gift baskets purchased for this event due to the large number of baskets being ordered. In this exercise you will modify the formulas in cells B15:E22 of the GiftBaskets worksheet using absolute cell referencing to include this discount.

E03.02

 To Use Absolute Referencing to a Formula

a. Click the **GiftBaskets** worksheet, and then click cell **B15**.

b. Type =B14-(B14*$E$3) and then press Ctrl+Enter.

c. Click the **AutoFill handle** ⊞ on cell **B15**, and then drag to the right to copy the formula to cell **E15**.

   Notice that the formula in cell E15 now refers to cell E3. The dollar sign in front of the column and row headings force Excel to keep the same cell reference as the formula is copied. Notice the formula in cell E15 also refers to cell E3.

   Also, notice that the $ sign before row 3 is not required since the formula was not copied to a different row. However, no matter where this formula is copied to on the worksheet the calculation should always use cell E3. Thus, common practice is to put a $ sign before the column and row making the cell reference absolute.

SIDE NOTE
Using F4

An alternative to typing the $ signs is to press F4 after typing or selecting the cell reference.

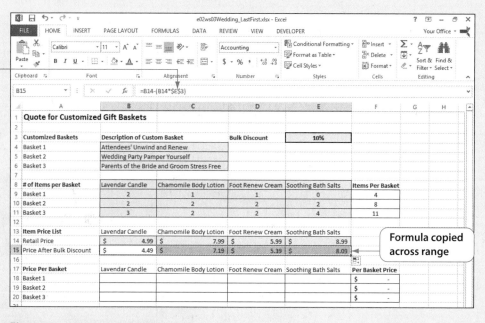

Figure 4   Absolute cell referencing

d. **Save** 💾 your workbook.

Using Mixed Cell Referencing

Mixed cell references can be very useful in the development of spreadsheets. Mixed cell references refer to referencing a cell within the formula where part of the cell address is preceded by a dollar sign to lock—either the column letter or the row value—as absolute reference. This will leave the other part of the cell as relatively referenced when the formula is copied to new cells. Figure 5 shows a representation of how mixed cell referencing works.

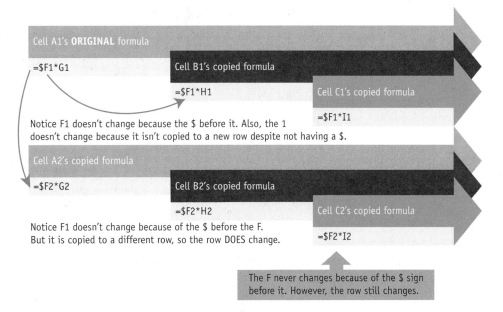

Figure 5 Understanding mixed cell referencing

REAL WORLD ADVICE | **Layout of a Spreadsheet Model**

Think of a spreadsheet model as an interactive report. Some of the data is static and may not change often, if ever. Some of the data, as in the Wedding Planning workbook, will need to change with each use of the spreadsheet. It can be helpful to color-code cells so anyone using the spreadsheet can easily see which cells require a change and which should be left alone. For example, in the Wedding Planning workbook cells with a blue fill are cells that need to be updated from one event to another.

If you need to verify that the formula has the correct relative and absolute referencing after it has been copied or moved into other cells within the spreadsheet, a quick and easy verification is to examine one of the cells in edit mode. Best practice dictates following these steps:

1. Double-click a cell containing the formula to enter edit mode.
2. In edit mode, notice the color-coded borders around cells match the cell address references in the formula. Using the color-coding as a guide, verify that the cell(s) are referenced correctly.
3. If the referencing is incorrect, notice which cells are not referenced correctly.
4. Exit out of edit mode by pressing Esc and returning to the original formula.
5. Edit the cell references, and then copy the corrected formula again.
6. Always recheck the formula again to see if your correction worked when copied into other cells or cell ranges.

Repeat this process as needed. Instead of typing the dollar signs within your cell references, F4 can be used to change the type of cell referencing. If the insertion point is placed within a cell reference in your formula, press F4 one time and Excel will insert dollar signs in front of both the row reference and column reference. If you press F4 again, Excel places a dollar sign in front of the row number only. If you press F4 a third time, Excel places a dollar sign in front of the column reference and removes the dollar sign from the row reference. Pressing F4 a fourth time returns the cell to a relative reference.

In this exercise you will update the range B18:E20 to include formulas that calculate the price of individual items included in each basket type using mixed cell referencing.

E03.03

 To Use Mixed Cell Referencing

a. Click the **GiftBaskets** worksheet, and then click cell **B18**.

b. Type =B9*B$15 and then press Ctrl+Enter.

c. Click the **AutoFill handle** + on cell **B18**, and then drag down to copy the formula to cell **B20**.

   Notice that the formula in cell B20 still refers to cell B15. The dollar sign in front of the row heading forces Excel to use row 15 as the referenced row no matter where the formula is copied to. However, the column will change as the formula is copied to the left or right in the worksheet.

d. With range **B18:B20** still selected, click the **AutoFill handle** + on cell **B20**, and then drag to the right to copy the formulas to the range **E18:E20**. Notice that as the formulas are copied column B changes while the row reference to row 15 remains unchanged as the formula is copied to the range.

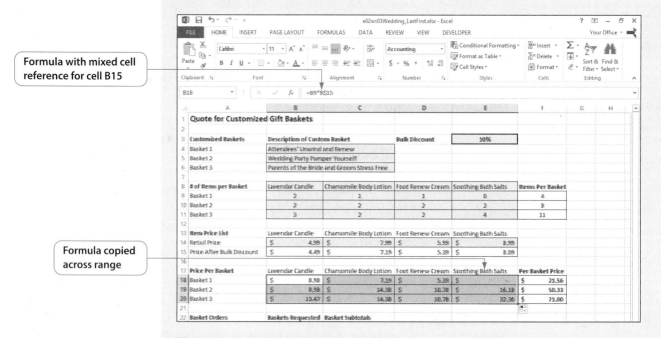

Formula with mixed cell reference for cell B15

Formula copied across range

Figure 6   Mixed cell referencing

e. Click cell **E14**, type 11.99 and then press ⬚Enter⬚.

   Notice that the values in cells E19:E20 have been updated. For reference, E20 previously displayed $32.36; now it displays $43.16.

f. **Save** 🖫 your workbook.

CONSIDER THIS | **Cell Referencing**

In cell B18 of the GiftBaskets worksheet the formula uses mixed cell referencing by referring to cell B$15. Would there have been a different result if absolute referencing would have been used? Would there have been a different result if relative referencing had been used? Why would these options be incorrect?

REAL WORLD ADVICE **Building for Scalability**

When you develop a spreadsheet you should consider the potential for the model to expand. A good spreadsheet model allows the user to add more data as needed. Instead of assuming current conditions will never change, your spreadsheet should be built to accommodate growth. While developing the model, you may consider using hypothetical data so you can see how the model will look when it has real data.

QUICK REFERENCE **Understanding Referencing Based on Copy Destination**

Cell references in a formula can change when copied. To understand where to put a $ sign, you must understand how the cell references will change when copied. Excel determines what to change by the original location and the copy destination. Remember, the $ locks down the letter or number it precedes so it will not change.

Original Location	Copy Destination	Column Becomes	Row Becomes	Considerations
A1	Formula will not be copied.	N/A	N/A	Cell referencing is irrelevant.
A1	A5	The column references will not change.	The row references will change by 4 rows.	Adding a $ sign before the column is irrelevant. Add a $ before the row if the row should not change.
A1	C1	The column references will change by 2 columns.	The row references will not change.	Add a $ before the column if the column should not change. Adding a $ before the row is irrelevant.

(Continued)

Original Location	Copy Destination	Column Becomes	Row Becomes	Considerations
A1	C5	The column references will change by 2.	The row references will change by 4.	Since both the column and row references will change, add a $ before any references that should not change.

Create Named Ranges

Once you are comfortable working with formulas and cells there is a natural progression to using named ranges and functions. A **named range** is a group of cells that have been given a name that can then be used within a formula or function. Named ranges are an extension of cell references and provide a quick alternative for commonly used cell references or ranges.

Spreadsheet formulas that use cell references such as =C5*C6 may be easy to interpret when simple. However, as the size and complexity of the workbook increases, so does the difficulty and time needed to incorporate cell references in formulas. This is especially the case with workbooks that use multiple worksheets. The use of named ranges enables a developer to quickly develop formulas that make sense. It also increases the legibility of formulas to other individuals using the same workbook. For example, the formula =SUM(BasketSubtotals) is much easier to interpret than =SUM(C23:C25). You can quickly understand the formula if it is written with assigned names you designate.

Creating Named Ranges Using the Name Box

Named ranges are easy to create as you develop a spreadsheet. A named range can be either a single cell or a group of cells. Most named ranges are groups of cells used within multiple formulas. A simple way to name a range is to select the range and use the Name Box to create the name. This allows for a custom name to be given to the range. When naming ranges, a descriptive name should be used for the range being named. Named ranges do have some restrictions for the types of characters that can be used. Named ranges cannot start with a number, cannot contain spaces, and the name cannot resemble a cell reference.

QUICK REFERENCE | **Conventions for Naming Ranges**

Below is a list of conditions that must be meet when creating named ranges.

1. Names for ranges must start with a letter, an underscore (_), or a backslash (\ ).

2. Create names that provide specific meaning to the range being named.

3. Spaces cannot be used while created a named range. Instead use an underscore, a hyphen character, or capitalize the first letter of each word. For example, HairStyles.

4. Do not use combinations of letters and numbers that resemble cell references.

In this exercise you will create a named range using the Name box. This named range can then be used in future calculations as an absolute cell reference.

E03.04

 To Create a Named Range Using the Name Box

a. Click the **GiftBaskets** worksheet, and then select the range **C23:C25**.

b. Click in the **Name** box to select the existing text. Type BasketSubtotals and then press Enter to create a new named range. Notice that when the range C23:C25 is selected the text BasketSubtotals will be displayed in the Name box.

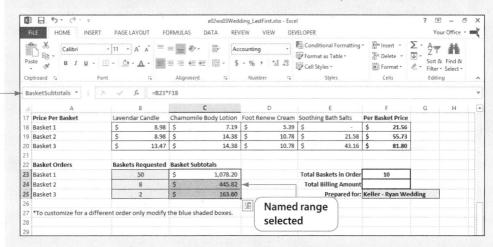

Figure 7 Name range applied to C23:C25

> **Troubleshooting**
> If you click outside of the Name Box before pressing Enter, the named range will not be created.

c. **Save** 🖫 your workbook.

Modifying Named Ranges

If a named range has been created incorrectly it can be redefined by selecting the correct data and naming the range again. Alternatively, the Name Manager can be used to modify an existing range or to view a list of already defined ranges. The **Name Manager** can be used to create, edit, delete, or troubleshoot named ranges in a workbook.

Currently the range BasketsRequested only includes gift basket option 2 and 3. In this exercise you will modify a named range that was previously created in the workbook.

E03.05

 To Modify a Named Range

a. Click the **GiftBaskets** worksheet, click the **Name** box arrow, and then click **BasketsRequested**.

Notice that the range selected is B24:B26. This is the incorrect range. The correct range is B23:B25.

b. Click the **FORMULAS** tab, and then in the Defined Names group, click **Name Manager**.

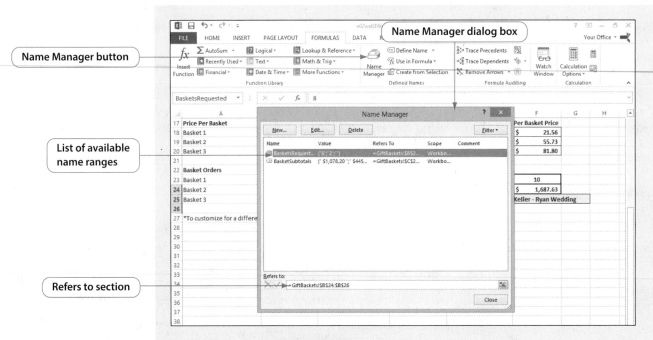

Figure 8 Name Manager

c. From the displayed list of names, click **BasketsRequested**, and then in the Refers to box, select the text **$B$24:$B$26**.

d. Type **$B$23:$B$25**, click **Close**, and then click **Yes** to accept the changes to the named range.

e. Click the **Name** box arrow, and then click **BasketsRequested**.
Notice that the correct range, B23:B25, is now selected.

f. **Save** 🖫 your workbook.

Using Named Ranges

Using named ranges in place of cell references is a simple process. Instead of typing the cells that you want to use in a formula, you can type the range name you have created. Excel will begin to recognize the name you are typing and offer to automatically complete the name for you. Another method of using named ranges is to use the Paste Name feature in Excel. While typing a formula you can press F3 to view a list of named ranges in the workbook and then insert it into the formula you are constructing.

Meda has requested that the worksheet display the total amount that the wedding party is to be billed for the gift baskets being made. In this exercise you will use a named range to create a calculation to display the total price of the requested gift baskets in the worksheet.

E03.06

 To Use Named Ranges in a Formula

a. Click the **GiftBaskets** worksheet, and then click cell **F24**.

b. Type **=SUM(B** and then notice that a list of functions and named ranges beginning with the letter "B" appear in a list.
The named ranges appear with a 🗐 next to the name of the range. The functions have 𝑓𝑥 to the left of the function name.

c. Type **ask**, press ⬇, and then press ⎡Tab⎤ to select the **BasketSubtotals** named range. Press ⎡Ctrl⎤+⎡Enter⎤ to complete the formula.

d. **Save** 🖫 your workbook.

Creating Named Ranges from Selections

At times your worksheet's data will be organized in such a way that the names for your ranges exist in a cell in the form of a heading, either for each row or each column in the data set. Rather than selecting each row or column separately in a time-consuming process, you can use the Create from Selection method.

The Create from Selection method is a process that produces multiple named ranges from the headings in rows, columns, or both, from the data set. The key element is to realize that the names for the ranges need to exist in a cell adjacent to the data range. Most commonly, these names are column headers that make for very convenient names for each column of data.

In this exercise you will create named ranges for the item subtotals for each type of gift basket. You will then apply the named ranges to the formulas in cells F18:F20.

E03.07

 To Created Named Ranges and Apply the Names to Formulas

a. Click the **GiftBaskets** worksheet, and then select the range **A18:E20**.

b. On the FORMULAS tab, in the Defined Names group, click **Create from Selection**.

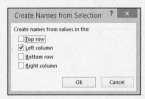

Figure 9   Create from Selection dialog box

c. Confirm that the **Left column** check box is selected, and then click **OK**.

d. Select the range **B18:E18**.

Notice that the Name box displays the name **Basket_1**. In creating the named range Excel substituted all space characters in the name with underscore characters. Ranges B19:E19 and B20:E20 will appear similarly.

e. Select the range **F18:F20**, and then in the Defined Names group, click the **Define Name** arrow, and then click **Apply Names**. Notice that Excel has detected three potential named ranges that can be substituted into the formulas in the selected range.

Apply Names dialog box

Names detected in selected cells

Figure 10   Apply Names dialog box

f. Click **OK**. Notice that the formula in cell F18 now reads =SUM(Basket_1).

g. **Save** 🖫 your workbook.

Understanding Functions

A **function** is a named calculation where Excel calculates the output based on the input provided. These can be fairly simple such as using the SUM function that adds any cell address range as input. Conversely, functions can be more complex. For example, calculating a monthly loan payment is accomplished by indicating various arguments—the loan amount, number of payments, and interest rate. **Arguments** are any inputs used by a function to compute the solution. As long as you have the correct inputs, Excel will perform the calculation for the function. In this section, you will use common business functions to continue building the worksheet module used for planning events at the Turquoise Oasis Spa.

Create and Structure Functions

Functions are composed of several elements and need to be structured in a particular order. When discussing functions, you need to be aware of the syntax of an Excel function. The **syntax** is the structure and order of the function and the arguments needed for Excel to perform the calculation. If you understand the syntax of a function, you can easily learn how to use new functions quickly. The syntax for a function is represented in Figure 11.

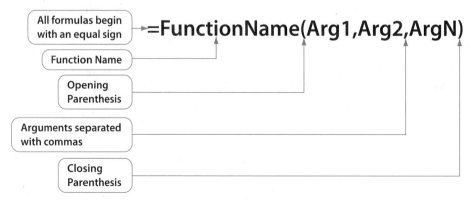

Figure 11   Syntax of a function

The FunctionName is any function that is in the Excel library. Examples are SUM, COUNT, and TODAY. With all functions, a pair of parentheses () are required after the FunctionName that may contain arguments associated with the function. Functions such as SUM() have one or more arguments that are required. If the required argument(s) are not supplied an error will occur. Some functions, like TODAY() do not have any arguments. These functions do not need any inputs to be able to generate output. The TODAY() function simply uses the clock on the computer to return the current date. Even though there are no arguments needed, the () parentheses are always included, which helps Excel understand that a function is being used.

Arguments can either be required or optional. The required arguments always come before any optional arguments. All arguments are separated with commas. Optional arguments are identified with square brackets [] around the argument name. You never type the square brackets into the actual construction of the function. They are only used to inform you that the argument is optional.

For example, the syntax for the SUM function is:

=SUM(number1, [number2], …)

The first argument is required; the SUM function must have a number, cell, or range to begin the calculation. The second argument—a second cell or range—is optional. Notice that the second argument uses square brackets to identify that it is optional. The periods following the second argument indicate that one or more arguments can be added as needed. The SUM function can hold up to 255 arguments.

Arguments, like variables in a math equation, need to be appropriate values that are suitable for the function. With Excel, the acceptable values can take six common forms, including other functions, as shown in Table 1.

Form of Input	Example	Explanation
Numeric value	5	Type the value
Cell reference	C5	Type the cell or range of cells
Named range	SALES	Type the name of the range
Text string	"Bonus"	Type the text with quotes " " so Excel will recognize it as a text string rather than a named range
Function	SUM(C5:C19)	Type a function following the correct syntax of the function name, pair of parentheses, and any arguments
Formula	(C5+D5)/100	Type the formula following correct mathematical formula structure

Table 1 Function argument formats

Functions are typically categorized for easy access. The primary categories are shown in Table 2. Functions can be found in the Formulas tab under these categorical names. They can also be searched to find the usage and syntax of functions that are unfamiliar.

Category	Description
Compatibility	A set of functions that are compatible with older versions of Excel
Cube	Working with data and filtering, similar to pivot tables
Database	Performing calculations in Excel on data that meets specific criteria
Date & Time	Working with serial date and time values
Engineering	Working with engineering formulas and calculations
Financial	Working with common financial formulas
Information	Providing data about cell content within a worksheet
Logical	Evaluating expressions or conditions as being either true or false
Lookup & Reference	Working with indexing and retrieving information from data sets
Math & Trig	Working with mathematics
Text	Working with text strings
Statistical	Working with common statistical calculations
User Defined	Working with functions created by the user or by third-party add-ins
Web	Working with URL, XML, and web services connections

Table 2   Function categories

Use and Understand Math and Statistical Functions

At the most fundamental level, spreadsheets are used to perform calculations. These calculations may result in loan payments, GPA calculations, profit margins, or even age calculations. Excel has a large array of functions available for simple and complex mathematical functions. There are functions available to sum, count, perform algebra or trigonometry, and create a wide range of statistical calculations.

Using Math and Trig Functions

The math and trigonometry functions are useful for various numerical manipulations. For example, there are several functions that round data in a cell or calculation. The **ABS function**, for example, returns the absolute value of the number analyzed by the function. A cell or calculation resulting in the number –4 would be returned as 4 by the ABS function. The **INT function** rounds down any decimal values associated with a number to the nearest whole number. The **ROUND function** is important when you want to round a number to a specific number of digits. The ROUND function can round values to the left or right of the decimal in a number. For example, using the ROUND function you could change the number 115.89 to 116 by rounding to the ones place. You could also display 120 by rounding to the integer value to the tens place. While ROUND will round to the nearest digit, ROUNDDOWN and ROUNDUP can be used to force the rounding in a particular direction. Commonly used math functions are shown in Table 3.

When a function is used to round data, the result of that function is used in future calculations. This is different from formatting a cell to a specific number of decimal places as formatting does not change the underlying data.

Function	Usage
ABS(Number)	Returns the absolute value of a number
INT(Number)	Rounds a number down to the nearest integer
RAND( )	Returns a random number from 0 to less than 1
RANDBETWEEN(Bottom,Top)	Returns a random integer between the numbers you specify
ROUND(Number,Num_digits)	Rounds a number to a specified number of digits
ROUNDDOWN(Number,Num_digits)	Rounds a number down to a specified number of digits
ROUNDUP(Number,Num_digits")	Rounds a number up to a specified number of digits

Table 3   Commonly used math functions

There are two common methods for creating functions: by using the Function Arguments dialog box and by typing the function in the cell. The **Function Arguments** dialog box provides additional information and previews results of the formula being constructed. When first developing the skills for using functions in Excel, the Function Arguments dialog box can be very valuable. As more experience with functions are gained, the Function Arguments dialog box may become less useful, particularly when nesting multiple functions together.

Meda has received some historical data on wedding events that she would like to have summarized. When planning new events, this historical data will be helpful to refer to. The data contains four items of interest:

1. The number of days spent by wedding parties at the Painted Paradise Resort and Spa—the value was previously calculated used decimals based on check-in and checkout times. Meda would like this data to be in integers or whole number of days. Since wedding parties receive a late checkout time, these values would need to be rounded down to the nearest whole number.

2. The price of merchandise that was returned after the wedding took place—the price in the column represents the money refunded to customers for the merchandise. The system used at the spa erroneously allowed employees to enter some of this data as a negative value or as a positive value. This data must be displayed as positive values.

3. Data displaying the amount spent in total by each wedding party at the Turquoise Oasis Spa—the average of this column has been calculated in the WeddingSummary worksheet cell C2. Currently, the average is formatted to display too many decimal places. However, the actual value of the cell has many more than two decimals. Meda plans to use this average in subsequent calculations. Formatting the cell to two decimals will not change the value of the cell. Thus, the value needs rounded to two decimals.

4. Data indicating whether the bridal party from the wedding is a member of the spa—the system used by the spa indicates a 1 for spa members and a null value for nonmembers. When this data was imported into Excel the result for nonmembers was the text "Null".

To Use the INT and ABS Functions

SIDE NOTE
Alternate Method
Instead of typing B9 in the Function Arguments dialog box, you can click cell B9. The cell reference will be supplied automatically.

a. Click the **WeddingSummary** worksheet, and then click cell **C9**.

b. To the left of the formula bar, click **Insert Function** 𝑓𝑥. Click the **Or select a category** arrow, and then select **Math & Trig**.

c. In the **Select a function** box, scroll down, click **INT**, and then click **OK**.

d. Type **B9** and notice that to the right of the dialog box, you see the value currently in cell B9. Under the current value you will see a preview of the result of the INT function.

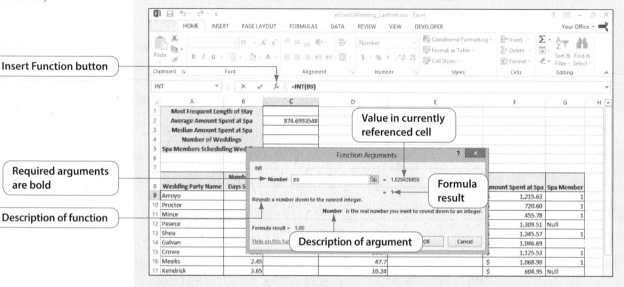

Insert Function button

Required arguments are bold

Description of function

Value in currently referenced cell

Formula result

Description of argument

Figure 12   Function Arguments dialog box

e. Click **OK**, and then double-click the **AutoFill handle** ➕ to copy cell **C9** down to **C39**.
   Notice the values in column B have now been rounded down to the nearest whole number. Illustratively, the value of cell C24 is 4.00 even though the value in cell B24 is 4.50. Since all of the values are now whole days without a decimal value, the format for C9:C39 needs to have decimals decreased to zero decimals.

f. With the range **C9:C39** selected, click the **HOME** tab, and then in the Number group, click **Decrease Decimal** twice.

g. Click cell **E9**, and then click **Insert Function** 𝑓𝑥. If necessary, click the **Or select a category** arrow, and then select **Math & Trig**.

h. In the Select a function box, click **ABS**, and then click **OK**.

i. In the Function Arguments dialog box, in the Number box, type **D9** and then click **OK**. Double-click the **AutoFill handle** ➕ to copy cell **E9** down to **E39**. All values in column D now appear as positive numbers.

j. **Save** 💾 your workbook.

SIDE NOTE
Function Help
Click the Help on this function link in the lower left of the Function Arguments dialog box to open Excel Help for the function being used.

Inserting a Function Using Formula AutoComplete

Functions can also be constructed without using the Function Arguments dialog box. This is accomplished by typing the equal sign and typing the function name directly into the cell. Excel will still provide guidance using this method. Additionally, as needed, you can always enter the Function Arguments dialog box to get more assistance.

When you initially type in the beginning of a function name, the Formula AutoComplete listing of functions will be shown from which you can select the appropriate function. Formula AutoComplete will provide a list of functions and named ranges that match the text following the equal sign. The list will automatically reflect changes as you type in more letters. Excel will even display a short description of the function when the function name is highlighted. As the function names appear you can use ⬇, ⬆, ➡, ⬅, or your mouse to move through the listing. To select a function, press Tab or double-click the selected function.

Once the function is selected, the arguments will be listed in a movable tag, called a ScreenTip, to provide guidance in completing the function. The argument you are currently editing will be displayed in bold. If you have entered some of the arguments, you can click the argument in the ScreenTip, and Excel will relocate the insertion point to that argument. In this exercise you will insert the ROUND function using Formula AutoComplete.

E03.09

 To Insert a Function Using Formula AutoComplete

a. Click the **WeddingSummary** worksheet, and then double-click cell **C2** to begin editing the function.

b. Click after the **equal sign** to place the insertion point before the AVERAGE function. Type ROUND(to begin the new function.

   Notice how the Formula AutoComplete suggested possible functions while you typed "round". Also, notice that the number argument is shown in bold font to indicate that this is the argument being edited.

c. Point to the **left edge** of the ScreenTip box, and then drag the ScreenTip to the right of cell **C2**.

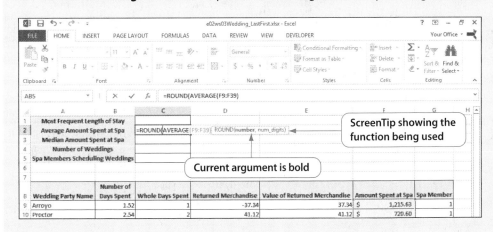

Figure 13   ScreenTip showing the ROUND function

d. Click after the **ending parenthesis** for the AVERAGE function, type , and then notice the num_digits argument of the ROUND function is in bold.

e. Type 2) to complete the num_digits argument. This will round the result of the AVERAGE function to two decimal places.

f. Press Ctrl + Enter.

Notice that the value in cell C2 is now $874.70, or rounded to two decimal places. Importantly, if you had formatted cell C2 to display only two decimal places, the cell would also show $874.70 on the screen. However, formatting does not change the value. So, even though the cell would show $874.70, the cell value used in subsequent mathematical calculations would still be $874.699355. If you increase the number of decimals for cell C2 after using the ROUND function, you will see the cell value is changed to $874.700000.

g. **Save** 💾 your workbook.

REAL WORLD ADVICE	Rounding vs. Formatting

Formatting text as currency will only give the appearance of true rounding. Any calculations using a cell formatted as currency but containing extra decimal places will include all decimal places in the calculation. Using the ROUND function will eliminate extra decimal places. Thus, future calculations will use the value displayed as a result of the ROUND function.

Using Statistical Functions

Similar to mathematical functions, statistical functions, as shown in Table 4, handle common statistical calculations such as averages, minimums, and maximums. Statistical functions are extremely useful for business analysis as they aggregate and compare data. Common descriptive statistics are used to describe the data. The average, median, and mode are common descriptive statistics that help describe the nature of a data set. They help understand and predict future data.

Statistical Functions	Usage
AVERAGE(Number1,[Number2],...)	Returns the mean from a set of numbers
COUNT(Value1,[Value2],...)	Counts the number of cells in a range that contain numbers
COUNTA(Value1,[Value2],...)	Counts the number of cells in a range that are not empty
COUNTBLANK(Range)	Counts the number of empty cells in a range
MEDIAN(Number1,[Number2],...)	Returns the number in the middle of a set of numbers
MAX(Number1,[Number2],...)	Returns the largest number from a set of numbers
MIN(Number1,[Number2],...)	Returns the smallest number from a set of numbers
MODE.SNGL(Number1,[Number2],...)	Returns the value that occurs most often within a set

Table 4 Commonly used statistical functions

The **MEDIAN function** is used to measure the central tendency or the location of the middle of a set of data. For example, in a range from 1 to 3, 2 would be the middle of the data or the median. Another measure commonly used to locate data in a range is mode. There are three methods for calculating the mode of a range of data in Excel 2013. The **MODE.SNGL function** returns the most frequently occurring value in a range of data. If more than one number occurs multiple times in a range of data, the **MODE.MULT function** can be used to return a vertical array, or list, of the most frequently occurring values in a range of data.

The **MODE function**, like MODE.SNGL, returns the most frequently occurring value in a range of data. It is important to note that in Excel 2010 this function was replaced by MODE.SNGL and MODE.MULT. The MODE function is still available in Excel 2010 and 2013 to provide backwards compatibility with earlier versions of Excel. Because of this, the function will appear in the Formula AutoComplete menu with a warning icon next to it.

The **COUNTA function** is useful for counting the number of cells within a range that contain any type of data. This is distinct from the **COUNT function** that only counts cells in a given range that contain numeric data. Using COUNTA is a great method to count the number of records in a data set. On the WeddingSummary worksheet column G contains a list of whether or not the bridal party was a member of the spa. When the data was imported into Excel the system used by the spa marked members with the number one. Nonmembers were marked with the text "Null".

E03.10

▶ To Use Statistical Functions

a. Click the **WeddingSummary** worksheet, and then click cell **C1**.

b. Type =MODE.SNGL(C9:C39) and then press `Ctrl`+`Enter`.
   Cell C1 now displays the most frequently occurring number of days stayed by a wedding party, 4.

c. Click cell **C3**, type =MEDIAN(F9:F39) and then press `Enter`.
   Cell C3 now displays the median amount spent by wedding parties at the spa, $899.77, representing the middle value as compared to the data for the average amount spent at the spa.

d. Click cell **C4**, type =COUNTA(A9:A39) and then press `Enter`.
   The COUNTA function counts all of the cells in the range A9:A39 to display the 31 wedding parties represented in the data.

e. Click cell **C5**, type =COUNT(G9:G39) and then press `Ctrl`+`Enter`.
   The COUNT function counts the numbers occurring in column G. Notice that since the only values in column G are numbers, COUNTA would also work in this instance.

f. **Save** 🖬 your workbook.

Use and Understand Date and Time Functions

Date and time functions are useful for entering the current day and time into a worksheet as well as calculating the intervals between dates. This category of functions is based on a serial date system where each day is represented sequentially from a starting point. In Microsoft applications, that standard is 1/1/1900, which has a serial number of 1. Thus, dates prior to that will not be recognized by the system. Interestingly, when Apple initially made its starting point, it began in 1904. Excel settings can be changed to use the Apple starting point, but it is generally accepted practice to keep the default setting of 1/1/1900 as the starting point. Using two different starting points for dates in Excel spreadsheets can cause significant problems. Common date and time functions are shown in Table 5.

Function	Usage
DATE(Year,Month,Day)	Returns the number that represents the date in Microsoft Excel date-time code
DATEDIF(Date1,Date2,Interval)	Returns the time unit specified between two dates, including the two dates (inclusive)
DAY(Serial_number)	Returns the day of the month, a number from 1 to 31
MONTH(Serial_number)	Returns the month, a number from 1 to 12
NETWORKDAYS(Start_date,End_date,[Holidays])	Returns the number of whole workdays between two dates, inclusive; does not count weekends and can skip holidays that are listed
TODAY( )	Returns the computer system date
WEEKDAY(Serial_number,[return_number],[Return_type])	Returns a number from 1 to 7 representing the day of the week. Can be set to return 0–6 or 1–7
WEEKNUM(Serial_number, [Return_type])	Returns the week number in the year, which week of the year the date occurs
YEAR(Serial_number)	Returns the year of a date, an integer in the range 1900–9999

Table 5 Common date functions

CONSIDER THIS | **Dates in Microsoft Applications**

Do you suppose the same Microsoft employees developed Access, Excel, Word, and PowerPoint? Is it possible that even within a company, there may have been differences in the starting date? Does Access use the same 1/1/1900 for its date starting point? See if you can find out.

Using Date and Time Functions

Excel tracks time by the number of days that have occurred since 1/1/1900. Time is represented by the decimal portion of this number. The decimal is based on the number of minutes in a day (24*60=1440). Thus, a 0.1 decimal is equal to 144 minutes. A full date and time value—such as 5/14/2015 8:35 AM—would appear as 42138.35804. There are 42138 days between 1/1/1900 and 5/14/2015. The time of 8:35 AM is represented by the .35804 portion of the number.

The TODAY and NOW functions are two common functions for inserting the current date into a spreadsheet. There is a slight—but significant—difference between the TODAY and NOW functions. The key difference is that the **TODAY function** simply puts in the current date while the **NOW function** puts in the current date and time. If you think about it, the TODAY function only works with integer representation of days while the NOW function uses decimals to include the time in addition to the day. Both functions can be formatted to show just the date, and you can work with time calculations that mix the two functions. Common time functions are listed in Table 6.

Function	Usage
HOUR(Serial_number)	Returns the hour in a time value, from 0 to 23
MINUTE(Serial_number)	Returns the minute in a time value, from 0 to 59
MONTH(Serial_number)	Returns the month, a number from 1 to 12
SECOND(Serial_Number)	Returns the number of seconds in a time value, from 0 to 59
NOW( )	Returns the computer system date and time

Table 6 Common time functions

REAL WORLD ADVICE **NOW vs. TODAY**

Be careful using NOW versus TODAY, especially when doing date calculations. Both functions use a serial number, counting from 1/1/1900. But, the NOW function also includes decimals for the time of day while TODAY works with integer serial numbers. At noon, on 5/1/2015 the NOW function has the value of 42125.5 while the TODAY function has a value of 42125.0. If you are using these date functions inside another function this could change the result if you are comparing a date the user provided. It is suggested to use the TODAY function if a user will be inserting the date into Excel by hand so the hand-typed value will be compared or used in a calculation with the function, eliminating the decimal issue.

DATEDIF is a useful date function because it enables you to calculate the time between two dates. The function can return the time unit as days, months, or years. However, while all the other functions are listed and can be found in Excel, Help and the Function Library do not offer any information about the DATEDIF function. You will not find any information on the DATEDIF function unless you search the Microsoft site. Since no information exists on it within Excel, this is one function that you must hand type and do the research to understand the syntax. Nonetheless, DATEDIF is one of the more useful date functions.

The syntax of the function is as follows:

=DATEDIF(Date1, Date2, Interval)

The first argument is the starting date in time—the older date—while the second argument is the ending date in time—the newer, more recent date. It may be helpful to remember that time lines are usually depicted as moving left to right, just as they would be listed in the DATEDIF function. The third argument is the interval that should be used, like the number of months or days between the two dates. The unit is expressed as a text value and therefore must be surrounded by quotes for correct syntax. The viable unit value options are shown in Table 7.

Unit Value	Description
"D"	Returns the number of complete days between the dates
"M"	Returns the number of complete months between the dates
"Y"	Returns the number of complete years between the dates
"MD"	Returns the difference between days in two dates, ignoring months and years
"YM"	Returns the difference between months in two dates, ignoring days and years
"YD"	Returns the difference between days in two dates, ignoring years

Table 7   Unit value options for DATEDIF

The options "D", "M", and "Y" are commonly used to calculate differences between dates. For example, using "Y" for the Interval argument is common practice for calculating an age. The options "YM", "YD", and "MD" are not as commonly used because they ignore certain aspects of the date structure. For example, using "YM" for the Interval argument with the dates 7/1/2014 and 9/12/2015 will result in a value of 2. This is because the "YM" unit value ignores the years in the two dates and only calculates the number of whole months between July (7) and September (9). Using "M" in the Interval argument will result in the value 14, the more commonly expected result.

Meda has asked for your help in completing an analysis of customers in the Keller-Ryan wedding party that have requested spa services. As part of the spreadsheet model she would like the current date to appear in cell B1 and the current age of customers to appear in column C. In this exercise you will use common date functions to complete the analysis.

E03.11

To Use Date and Time Functions

a. Click the **SpaServices** worksheet tab, and then click cell **B1**.

b. Type =TODAY() and then press Ctrl + Enter.
    Notice that cell B1 now displays the current date. Each time the worksheet is opened, or when a cell is edited, the current date will be updated and displayed in cell B1. Since the time of day is not relevant here, the TODAY function is preferred over the NOW function.

c. Click cell **C5**, type =DATEDIF(B5,TODAY(),"Y") and then press Ctrl + Enter.
    The TODAY function is nested inside of the DATEDIF function. Since the interval is set to year, using "Y", the result is that the age of the guest is always current in this calculation.

> **Troubleshooting**
> No ScreenTip help will appear when typing the DATEDIF function. If the DATEDIF function returns a #NUM! error the most likely problem is mixing up the order of the two dates within the function. The first date should be the earliest date and the second date the most recent one. The other common error is actually typing in a date as the argument. Typing 12/3/2015 will be interpreted as division instead of a date. The value must either be in serial date format or typed inside of quotation marks.

d. Double-click the **AutoFill handle** + to copy cell **C5** down to **C22**. The current ages of all guests are now displayed in column C.

e. **Save** 🖫 your workbook.

Use and Understand Text Functions

Excel is frequently used to bring data together from multiple different locations and/ or systems, including text data. Many times, the data is inconsistent from one source to another. For example, one workbook could list First Name Last Name—Olivia Stone— and the next may list names Last Name, First Name—Stone, Olivia. In situations like this, knowing how to alter text data is extremely valuable and time saving.

There are a multitude of reasons why text data in a cell may need to be altered. Names in a cell may need to be separated or combined. Several pieces of data may be stored in a single cell but need to be separated into many columns of data for easier analysis. Excel contains a wide array of functions and features that allow for the manipulation of text data. Some newer features in Excel are optimized for touch-screen devices. This makes it easier to manipulate data when using Excel on a mobile device such as a tablet computer.

Text functions can be used to change the appearance of data, such as displaying text in all lowercase letters. Text functions can also be used to cleanse text. Cleansing text involves removing unwanted characters, rearranging data in a cell, or correcting erroneous data.

Using Text Functions

Text functions help manage, manipulate, and format text data. Data stored as text is commonly referred to as a string. Text functions can change the way data is viewed, cut a string of text into multiple pieces, or combine multiple pieces of text together into one string of text. While most text functions can be used individually, they become increasingly powerful when nested together to transform text. A list of common text functions are listed in Table 8.

The **LEFT function** returns a set number of characters from the left side of a cell. The number of characters the LEFT function will return is defined in the num_chars argument. This number can be simply typed in, or it can be more dynamically calculated using other functions. The **FIND function** searches for a specified string of text in a larger string of text and returns the position number where the specified text begins. By using the FIND function in the num_chars argument of the LEFT function, a dynamic formula can be constructed to separate a portion of text from one cell into another.

Function	Usage
CONCATENATE(text1,text2,...)	Joins text1, text2,...,textn together in order into a single string value
FIND(find_text,within_text,[start_num])	Finds find_text in within_text. The search begins at start_num (start_num defaults to 1) and is case sensitive. The starting position of find_text is returned. If the find_text is not present an error will be returned.
LEFT(text,[num_chars])	Returns a string num_chars long from the left side of text
LEN(text)	Returns a number that represents the number of characters
MID(text,start_num,num_chars)	Returns a string extracted from text beginning in position start_num that is num_chars long
RIGHT(text,[num_chars])	Returns a string num_chars long from the right side of text
TRIM(text)	Returns text with any leading, trailing, or extra spaces between words removed
UPPER(text)	Returns text with all characters in uppercase
PROPER(text)	Returns text with only the first letter in uppercase, all other letters will return in lowercase
SEARCH(find_text,within_text,[start_num])	Finds find_text in within_text. The search begins at start_num (start_num defaults to 1) and is case insensitive. The starting position of find_text is returned. If the find_text is not present an error will be returned.
TEXT(value,format_text)	Returns a number value as a string with the format specified in format_text

Table 8   Common text functions

Meda has asked that you rearrange some of the data on the SpaServices worksheet. Column A contains a list of guests first and last names. To provide better customer service Meda would like the first names of the guests in a separate column that can be used later. The names in column A are arranged in a consistent format. The text in the cell begins with the guest's first name followed by a single space character. After the space character is the guest's last name. Given this format, the space character can be used by text functions to separate the first name from the last name. You will use the FIND and LEFT functions to display only the first name of the guest in column D.

E03.12

 To Nest the FIND and LEFT Functions

a. Click the **SpaServices** worksheet, and then click cell **D5**.

b. Type =LEFT(A5, to begin the text function. The LEFT function will begin at the left side of cell A5 and return all characters from position 1 until the number specified by the num_chars argument.

c. Type FIND(" ",A5)) and then press ⌈Ctrl⌉+⌈Enter⌉ to complete the function.

   Notice the name Olivia appears in cell D5. To separate the first name, you take advantage of the text pattern of the space. To separate text, you must identify the text pattern. The pattern must be consistent in some way to use text functions. Here the FIND function looks for the space character that separates the first and last names. For cell A5, the FIND function returns a 7 because the name Olivia contains six characters and the space after the name is the seventh character. Since you will not want to include the space character, the TRIM function can be used to remove it.

d. Double-click cell **D5** to begin editing the function. Click after the **equal sign** to place the insertion point before the LEFT function. Type Trim(to begin the TRIM function.

e. Click after the last closing parenthesis. Type) and then press Ctrl + Enter to complete the TRIM function. The number of characters in cell D5 is now 6 as the trailing space character has been removed.

f. Double-click the **AutoFill handle** ➕ to copy cell **D5** down to **D22**. The first names of all guests are now displayed in column D.

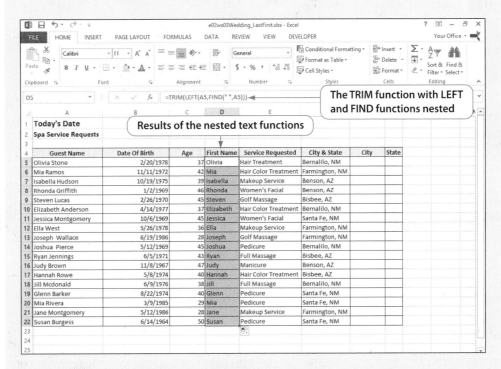

Figure 14 Result of nesting the FIND function

g. **Save** 💾 your workbook.

Using the Flash Fill

The Flash Fill feature in Excel 2013 makes data cleansing easier and faster than using traditional text functions. **Flash Fill** recognizes patterns in data as you type and automatically fills in values for text and numeric data. Flash Fill involves less typing than text functions, which makes it easier to use on mobile or touch-screen devices.

To work correctly Flash Fill must be completed in a column adjacent to the data being manipulated. There are two ways to use the Flash Fill. Providing two suggested values will initiate the automatic Flash Fill to a suggestion for cleansing your data. This suggestion will preview along the column adjacent to the data. Pressing Enter will accept the suggestion and populate the column of cells. Flash Fill can also be initiated on the Data tab. This is useful for cleansing data in cells that are not directly adjacent to the data or for numeric data. Flash Fill will not automatically suggest values for numeric data.

The SpaServices worksheet includes a list of the city and state of origin for each guest attending the wedding. Separating these values into individual columns will be helpful for future tasks such as counting the number of guests from each state. In this exercise you will use the Flash Fill feature to separate the guest's city and state of origin into individual columns.

E03.13

 To Use Flash Fill

a. Click the **SpaServices** worksheet, and then click cell **G5**.

b. Type Bernalilo and then press Enter to move to cell G6.

c. Type Farmington and notice the Flash Fill suggestion appears down the column of data. Press Enter to accept the suggestion.

   Notice column G now contains only the city names from the list of cities and states in column F.

> **Troubleshooting**
>
> The Flash Fill feature requires two suggested values before it will offer a suggestion for the column of data you are in. These two suggested values must be typed in consecutive actions. If you clicked in another cell or pressed another key on the keyboard between typing "Bernalilo" and "Farmington"—Flash Fill will not offer a suggestion.

d. Select cell **H5**, type NM and then press Ctrl+Enter.

   Since the State column is not next to the column with the city and state text, typing a suggested value for Flash Fill will not work. Using the Flash Fill button from the DATA tab will accomplish the task of isolating the state from column F.

e. Click the **DATA** tab, and then in the Data Tools group, click **Flash Fill**.

   Notice column H now contains only the state abbreviations from the list of cities and states in column F. Importantly, notice that Flash Fill inserts static data. Thus, if the values in column F change, columns G and H will not be automatically updated. If you needed them to be automatically updated, you would need to use text functions.

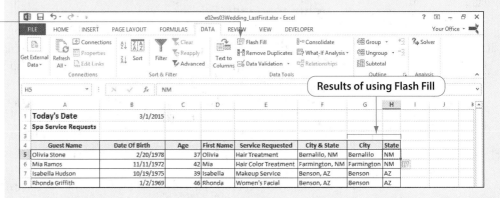

Figure 15   City names and state abbreviations separated with Flash Fill

f. **Save** your workbook.

REAL WORLD ADVICE | Flash Fill vs. Text Functions

The Flash Fill feature of Excel 2013 is a quick, powerful, and touch-screen friendly way to work with text and numeric data. It is easy to use, but the data you insert using Flash Fill is not automatically updated if the underlying data changes. Flash Fill will not update prior values if new data is added or if the existing data changes. Text functions will update their results if underlying data changes, and they can be easily copied to accommodate new data. If data will be added or changed in your workbooks on a regular basis, use text functions!

Use Financial and Lookup Functions

Excel has many functions available to help businesses make decisions. These decisions may include calculating payments on a loan or returning data from a table based upon a specific value in a worksheet. The ability to combine these processes in more complex tasks is even more powerful. For example, a lookup function can retrieve an interest rate from a table of data to be used in a subsequent loan calculation. As with other functions, lookup and reference functions when combined with financial functions can be an effective combination.

Using Lookup and Reference Functions

Lookup and reference functions look up matching values in a table of data. Lookup and reference functions can be used for simple matches or complex retrieval tasks. This can be as simple as retrieving a value from a vertical or horizontal list, or as complex as finding the value of a cell within a table of data at a given row and column intersection. Common lookup and reference functions can be found in Table 9.

Function	Usage
HLOOKUP(lookup_value,table_array, row_index_num,[range_lookup])	Finds lookup_value in the top row of table_array and returns a value from row_index
INDEX (array,row_num,[column_num])	Returns a value from array by indexes specified as row_num and column_num
MATCH(lookup_value,lookup_array, [match_type])	Finds lookup_value in lookup_array
VLOOKUP(lookup_value,table_array, col_index_num,[range_lookup])	Finds lookup_value in the first column of table_array and returns a value from column_index

Table 9   Common lookup and reference functions

The **VLOOKUP function** matches a provided value in a table of data and returns a value from a subsequent column similar to looking up a phone number in a phone book. The "V" signifies that the function matches the provided value vertically, in the first column of the table of data. The syntax of a VLOOKUP is as follows:

=VLOOKUP(lookup_value, table_array, col_index_number, [range_lookup])

The lookup_value argument can be any text, number, or a reference to a cell that contains data. The table_array argument is a range in a spreadsheet. The range can be a single column of cells or multiple columns of cells. The VLOOKUP function will match the lookup_value on the first column of the supplied table_array. The col_index_number is the column number of the corresponding value that will be returned. The optional range_lookup argument allows the VLOOKUP to perform an approximate or exact match.

The range_lookup argument is TRUE for an approximate match. An approximate match allows the VLOOKUP to return the first value less than the range_lookup on the first column of the table_array. For example, looking up the value 50 on a range containing 45 and 55 would return 45. The range_lookup argument is FALSE for an exact match. An exact match will force the VLOOKUP to find the same value supplied in the lookup_value in the first column of the table_array. If the value cannot be found, the function will return an error.

The Turquoise Oasis Spa has recently partnered with a local bank to offer financing to customers that are booking large, costly events. Booking spa services usually is one of the last things guests will book. Thus, some guests will book less than they desire due to budget concerns. The spa is hoping that offering a financing package and discounts for large events will increase spa revenue.

As part of the workbook you are building for the spa, Meda has asked that you finish the WeddingFinancing worksheet that she started. This worksheet contains cells for guests to enter information about the wedding being planned. The worksheet already has cells prepared for entering the cost of the event, the down payment supplied by the guest, the annual interest rate, and the term of the loan in years. You have been asked to complete this worksheet so that when a wedding is scheduled, the guest will have an understanding of the basic elements of the financing plan. In this exercise you will use a lookup function to return the discount that the spa will provide based on the total cost of the wedding event being planned.

E03.14

 To Use the VLOOKUP function

a. Click the **WeddingFinancing** worksheet tab, and then click cell **B7**.

b. Type **=VLOOKUP(B3,** to begin the VLOOKUP function.
   This will use the value in B3 as the lookup value to match on the list of discounts.

c. Type **E4:F8,2,TRUE)** and then press [Enter] to complete the VLOOKUP function.
   The VLOOKUP matches the value in B3 on the range E4:E8. When a match is found, the corresponding row value from column F will be returned. By placing TRUE as the range_lookup argument the VLOOKUP will perform an approximate match. This means an event costing $37,000 will returns a 5.0% discount.

> **Troubleshooting**
> If the VLOOKUP function returns a #N/A error, check to make sure the range_lookup argument is TRUE. Using FALSE for the argument will force the VLOOKUP into an exact match. Since $37,000 is not listed in E4:E8, an error will be returned.

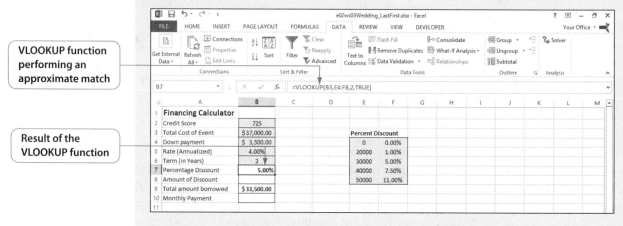

Figure 16 WeddingFinancing worksheet using the VLOOKUP function

d. Click cell **B8**, type =B3*B7 and then press Ctrl+Enter.

This will apply the 5.0% discount to the $37,000 event cost resulting in a discount of $1,850.

e. **Save** 🖫 your workbook.

If the range_lookup argument is left blank it will default to TRUE for an approximate match. If the range_lookup should be FALSE, but is mistakenly left blank an incorrect result will be returned. Best practice dictates that you should always specify the range_lookup even though it is optional.

Using Financial Functions

A foundation for a successful business is generating revenue—any income brought into the business, prior to paying any expenses out—and hopefully yielding net profits. This also applies to personal finances where individuals generate income with the main goal of covering their expenses as they go through life with a net profit to spare. Having a foundational knowledge of financial terms is thus an important element of succeeding in both your personal and professional life. Some common financial terms that you will see and hear or possibly make use of in an Excel spreadsheet are shown in Table 10.

Financial Term	Definition
APR	The annual percentage rate; an interest rate expressed in an annual equivalent
Compounding interest	A process of charging interest on both the principal and the interest that accumulates on a loan
Interest payment	The amount of a payment that goes toward paying the interest accrued
NPV	The net present value of future investments
Period	The time period of payments, such as making payments monthly
Principal payment	The amount of a payment that goes toward reducing the principal amount
Principal value	The original amount borrowed or loaned
PV	Present value—the total amount that a series of future payments is worth now
Rate (and APR)	The interest rate per period of a loan or an investment
Simple interest	The interest charged on the principal amount of a loan only
Term	The total time of a loan, typically expressed in years or months
Time value of money	Recognizing that earning one dollar today is worth more than earning one dollar in the future

Table 10   Financial terminology

Financial functions are a set of predefined functions that can be used for calculating interest rates, payments, and analyzing loans. Some common financial functions are listed in Table 11.

Financial Functions	Usage
PMT(rate,nper,pv,[fv],[type])	Calculates periodic payment for a loan based on a constant interest rate and constant payment amounts
IPMT	Calculates periodic interest payment for a loan based on a constant interest rate and constant payment amounts
PPMT	Calculates periodic principal payment for a loan based on a constant interest rate and constant payment amounts
NPV	Calculates the net present value based on a discount interest rate, a series of future payments, and future income

Table 11   Common financial functions

A common and useful financial function in Excel is the PMT function. The **PMT function** determines the periodic payment for a loan based upon constant payments and interest rate. The PMT function by default returns a negative value. The function is really calculating an outflow of cash, a payment to be made. Within the financial and accounting industry, an outflow of cash is considered a negative value. In other words, this function assumes you are actually making a payment—taking money out of your pocket to give to someone else, or a negative value. Since some people may be confused seeing the value as negative, the value can be made positive by simply inserting a negative sign prior to the function or placing the absolute value function—ABS() —around the PMT function.

The syntax of the PMT function is as follows:

=PMT(rate,nper,pv,[fv],[type])

The first argument is the rate, which is the periodic interest rate. Importantly, the interest rate must be for each period. Most loans are discussed in terms of annual percentage rate (APR), while the period would be a shorter time period such as quarterly or monthly. The APR would need to be divided by 12 to get an equivalent monthly interest rate.

The second argument is nper, which is the number of periods or total number of payments that will be made for the loan. Again, many loans are discussed in years while the payments would be monthly. Thus, you will often need to determine the total number of periodic payments with a calculation.

The third required argument is PV, which is the present value of an investment or loan—the amount borrowed that needs to be paid back. The last two arguments are optional. The FV argument is the future value attained after the last payment is made. If this argument is left blank, the PMT function assumes FV to be zero. The Type argument indicates when a payment is due. If left blank, the PMT function assumes payments are due at the end of a period, if a one is supplied then payments are assumed due at the beginning of a period.

In this exercise, you will calculate the monthly payment for the customer for the event being planned using the PMT function.

E03.15

 To Use the PMT Function

a. Click the **WeddingFinancing** worksheet, and then click cell **B10**.

b. Type **=-PMT(** to begin the PMT function.

   As previously mentioned the PMT function is calculated by default as a negative value. The negative sign before the PMT function will display the final result as a positive number.

c. Type **B5/12,** to complete the rate argument. Because the interest rate in cell B5 is annual, you need to divide by 12 to get the interest rate per payment—in this case monthly.

d. Type **B6*12,** to complete the number of periods argument. Because the term of the loan is in years, you will need to multiply the term by 12 to get the total number of payments—in this case months—in the loan.

e. Type **B9)** and then press ⌃**Ctrl**+**Enter** to supply the present value of the loan and complete the PMT function.

   The original loan amount was $37,000. Cell B9 takes the original amount in B3, subtracts the down payment supplied in cell B4, and subtracts the amount of the discount in cell B8.

SIDE NOTE
Unit Conversions
Be careful when converting the arguments of the PMT function. Monthly payments are converted using 12, quarterly are converted using 4.

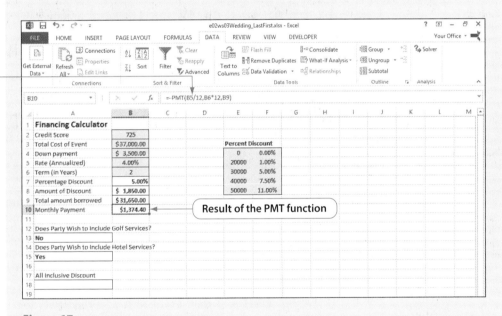

PMT function calculating a monthly payment

Result of the PMT function

Figure 17   PMT function used to calculate a monthly payment

f. **Save** 💾 your workbook.

Use Logical Functions and Troubleshoot Functions

When constructing a spreadsheet the need will often arise to evaluate criteria in a range of cells and make a decision based on those criteria. Excel contains functions that can evaluate a wide range of criteria and return customized results. For example, a comparison of two cells to see if their values are the same may result in a cell displaying TRUE, a customized text response, or even performing another calculation. As the formulas in a spreadsheet become more complicated errors may occur in the spreadsheet. Understanding some basic spreadsheet troubleshooting techniques can easily correct these errors.

Using Logical Functions

Logical functions evaluate statements, or declarations, as being either true or false. For example, the statement "the sky is blue" is a declaration that can be evaluated as true. If the statement was "Is the sky blue?" the response would be a yes/no instead of true/false. So, all logical functions are structured around the concept of declaring a position or statement that Excel will evaluate and return as True or False.

The best way to think of a declaration is to think of using comparison symbols like the =, >, <, or >= symbols as shown in Table 12. When you set up a statement of X>Y, Excel can evaluate that comparison as true or false.

Comparison Operator Symbol	Example	Declarative Clause
<	A < B	A is less than B
>	A > B	A is greater than B
=	A = B	A is equal to B
<=	A <= B	A is less than or equal to B
>=	A >= B	A is greater than or equal to B
<>	A <> B	A does not equal B

Table 12 Comparison operators

The most common logical function to learn is the IF function. The **IF function** will return one of two values depending upon whether the supplied logical test being evaluated is true or false. The syntax of the IF function is as follows:

=IF(logical_test,[value_if_true],[value_if_false])

The first argument is the logical_test, the statement you want to evaluate as TRUE or FALSE. Excel will then evaluate it as either true or false. The second argument is the result you want returned in the cell if the expression is evaluated as true. The third argument is the result you want in the cell if the expression is evaluated as false.

Notice that only the logical_test argument is required. The last two arguments are optional. If you leave them out, Excel will automatically return TRUE or FALSE as the result of the function. However, it is much more common and expected that you will supply something for all three arguments. If you consider the context, logical statement, and results of the IF function, the structure begins to fall into place.

It is possible to create intricate logical statements using the AND and the OR functions. These functions allow you to evaluate multiple logical statements within a single IF function. The **AND function** returns TRUE if all logical tests supplied are true; otherwise, it returns FALSE. The **OR function** returns TRUE if any one logical test supplied is true; otherwise, it returns FALSE. The components can incorporate values, cells, named ranges, and even other functions. Common logical functions and their usage are listed in Table 13.

Logical Functions	Usage
IF(logical_test,[value_if_true],[value_if_false])	Returns one of two values, depending upon whether the logical statement is evaluated as being true or false
IFERROR(value,value_if_error)	Returns a specified value if a function or formula returns an error; otherwise, it returns the value of the function or formula
AND(logical1,logical2,...)	Returns true if logical1, logical2,…logicaln all return true
OR(logical1,logical2,...)	Returns true if any one of logical1, logical2,…logicaln return true

Table 13 Common logical functions

CONSIDER THIS | **Variations in Constructing Formulas**

In Excel, there can be many ways that a formula can be written. Some are more efficient than others. At a minimum, every IF statement can be written two ways. Why? Provide an example with both ways.

To encourage couples getting married to use the resort for all of their wedding services, the Painted Paradise Resort and Spa is offering an all-inclusive discount of $500.00. The availability of the discount to the guests must be evaluated in two steps. First, the discount can only be offered if the guest's credit score is at least 650. Secondly, the wedding party must use both the golf course and hotel as part of their event. Common logical functions can be used to evaluate if a wedding party is eligible for the all-inclusive discount. If the wedding party is eligible, they will receive a $500 discount. If they are not eligible, the cell should display a zero.

E03.16

 To Use the IF and the AND functions

a. Click the **WeddingFinancing** worksheet, and then click cell **C10**.

b. Type =IF(to begin the IF function and enter the logical_test argument.
   The credit score of the guest is located in cell B2. The IF function will need to test for a value in this cell of greater than or equal to 650.

c. Type B2>=650, to complete the logical_test argument and enter the value_if_true argument.
   The IF function should return the text "Sufficient Credit Score" if the value in B2 is 650 or greater. If the value is less than 650 the text "Insufficient Credit Score" should be returned.

d. Type "Sufficient Credit Score", "Insufficient Credit Score") and then press [Ctrl]+[Enter] to complete the IF function. If necessary, use the AutoFit feature on column C.
   Notice that since the value in B2 is 725, the text "Sufficient Credit Score" is returned by the IF function.

e. Click cell **A18**, and then type =IF(to begin the IF function and enter the logical_test argument. Since the discount requires both golf services and hotel services to be used by the wedding party, the AND function will be used in the logical test of the IF function to evaluate this criteria.

SIDE NOTE
Using Quotes
Quotation marks must be used in an IF function to return text values. To return numeric data do not use quotation marks.

f. Type AND(A13="Yes",A15="Yes"), to insert the AND function into the IF function and complete the logical_test argument.

The AND function will now return TRUE if cells A13 and A15 both contain the text "Yes". Otherwise it will return FALSE to the IF function.

g. Type 500, to complete the value_if_true argument.

If the AND function returns TRUE, the number 500 will be displayed in cell A18. This will give a $500 discount to the wedding party.

h. Type 0) to complete the value_if_false argument and complete the IF function.

If the AND function returns FALSE, the number 0 will be displayed in cell A18 and no discount will be given. Notice that no discount is currently given as cell A13 displays No.

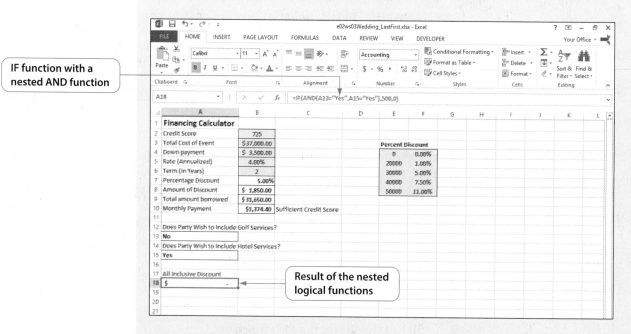

Figure 18 IF function with a nested AND function

i. Click cell **A13**, type Yes and then press Ctrl+Enter.

Cell A18 now displays a discount as both cells A13 and A15 display Yes.

j. Save 🖫 your workbook.

IF functions can range from simple tests of a statement to complex, nested formulas. Table 14 shows four examples of IF functions with varying levels of complexity.

Context: Display the word "Good" if the exam score in J10 is better than or equal to the target goal of 80, which is in cell B2. If it is worse than 80, display the word "Bad".

Example: =IF(J10>=$B$2,"Good", "Bad")

Interpretation: If the value of cell J10 is greater than or equal to the value in B2, the text "Good" is displayed. Otherwise, the text "Bad" is displayed.

Context: Display the status of an employee meeting his or her goal of getting a number of transactions, where transactions are listed in the range of A2:A30 and the target number of transactions are in cell C3.

Example: =IF(COUNT(A2:A30)>=C3,"Met Goal", "")

Interpretation: If the count of transactions that are listed in range A2:A30 is greater than or equal to the value in C3 (the target goal for the employee), then the employee met his or her goal and the text "Met Goal" should be displayed. Otherwise, the goal was not met and no value should be displayed. This can be accomplished by supplying two quotation marks with no characters typed between them.

Context: For tracking any projects that have not been completed, check the text in H20, and if it does not say "Complete", assume the project is not complete and calculate how many months are left when A3 has today's date and A4 has the targeted completion date.

Example: =IF(H20<>"Complete", DATEDIF(A3,A4,"M"),0)

Interpretation: If H20 does not say "Complete" to represent a completed project, calculate the number of months left, based on dates in cells A3 and A4. Otherwise, show a zero.

Context: Determine salary by checking if the employee generated less revenue than their goal, listed in B2. If so, they simply get their base pay. If they do meet their goal or generate more revenue than their goal, they get a bonus, which is a percent of sales added to their base pay. Since this may result in a value that has more than two decimals, the result needs to be rounded to two decimals.

Example: =ROUND(IF(SUM(Sales<B2,Base,Base+BonusPercent*(Sum(Sales))),2)

Interpretation: The ROUND( ) function will round the result to two decimals. Inside the ROUND function, the SUM(Sales) functions will sum the range named Sales to give the total sales. The IF statement then indicates that IF the total Sales is less than the value in B2 (the sales goal), provide the value that is in the range called Base (Base pay). Otherwise, the total Sales must be greater than B2 and the pay would be calculated as the Base (Base pay) plus the value in the named range, BonusPercent times the total Sales.

Table 14   Examples of IF functions

CONSIDER THIS | **What IF There Are Three Options?**

An IF statement can handle just two results: true and false. Are most real-world situations that simple? How could you use an IF statement if there are more than two results? It is possible!

Troubleshooting Functions

Logical functions dramatically increase the value of a spreadsheet. However, on the path to learning how to use functions, and even as an experienced spreadsheet user, you will still make typing errors during the development of functions. Excel does an excellent job of incorporating cues to help you determine where you have gone astray with a function.

When you make a mistake with a function that prevents Excel from returning a viable result, Excel will provide an error message. While these may seem cryptic initially, they actually can be interpreted. Typically an error message will be prefaced with a number symbol (#). Examples would be #VALUE!, #N/A, #NAME?, or #REF!. Over time you will learn to recognize common issues that would cause these error messages.

QUICK REFERENCE	Common Error Messages

1. **#NAME?**—This error indicates that text in a formula is not recognized. Excel treats unrecognized text as a named range that does not exist. This is often due to missing quotes around a text string or mistyping the function or range name.

2. **#REF!**—This error indicates a reference that Excel cannot find. This is often due to changes like a deleted worksheet, column, row, or cell.

3. **#N/A**—This error indicates that a value is not available in one or more cells specified. Common causes occur in functions that try to find a value in a list but the value does not exist. Rather than returning an empty set—no value—Excel returns this error instead.

4. **#VALUE!**—This error occurs when the wrong type of argument or operand is being used, such as entering a text value when the formula requires a number. Common causes can be the wrong cell reference that contains a text value rather than a numeric value.

5. **#DIV/0!**—This is a division by 0 error and occurs when a number is divided by zero or by a cell that contains no value. While it can occur due to an actual error in the design of a formula, it also may occur simply due to the current conditions within the spreadsheet data. In other words, this is common when a spreadsheet model is still in the creation process and data has not yet been entered into the necessary cells. Once proper numeric data does exist, the error disappears.

There are numerous ways to troubleshoot erroneous functions in Excel. When you encounter an error, you can quickly check the cell references and arguments of the function by double-clicking the cell to edit the function. This is beneficial since, while a function is being edited, Excel will outline any cells or ranges included in the function and display the ScreenTip for the function.

On the Commission worksheet, Meda has set up a quick analysis that rewards the employee scheduling the event with a commission of the total cost of the event. The commission earned is then added to the base event pay for the employee. The base event pay is contingent upon the employee level. After setting up the worksheet, she noticed an error in one of the cells. Additionally, the table located in the Commission worksheet states that managers have a base event pay of $1,250. However, the value shown for the manager in the worksheet is only $750.

E03.17

 To Troubleshoot a Function

a. Click the **Commission** worksheet tab, and then click cell **B4**.

   Notice the #N/A error being returned by the VLOOKUP function in the cell. Recall that this error commonly occurs because a value cannot be found on a list.

b. Click the **Error Message** button ◈ ▾ next to cell B4. Notice that the error message states a value is not available.

c. Double-click cell **B4** to edit the formula.

   Notice the outlines around the cells that are part of the VLOOKUP function. From this view you can verify that cell B3 is correctly referenced as the lookup value. Cells E4:F8 are correctly referenced as the table array. The column index number will return a value from column F if a value is found in column E.

   Notice the range_lookup argument is set to FALSE. This means the lookup is performing an exact match. Since $17,000 does not occur in the range E3:E7, the VLOOKUP will return a #N/A error.

d. Place the insertion point at the end of the **range_lookup** argument, and then delete the text **FALSE**. Type TRUE and then press Ctrl+Enter to fix the formula. Notice that the value 5% now appears in cell B4.

e. Double-click cell **B8** to edit the formula.

   Notice the range_lookup argument is set to TRUE. This means the lookup is performing an approximate match and is returning the incorrect base event pay rate.

f. Place the insertion point at the end of the **range_lookup** argument, and then delete the text **TRUE**. Type FALSE and then press Ctrl+Enter to fix the formula. Notice that the value $1,250 now appears in cell B8.

g. Complete the Documentation worksheet, **save** 🖫 your workbook, and then **close** ✕ Excel. Submit your work as directed by your instructor.

REAL WORLD ADVICE   Function Construction Guidelines

As you develop a spreadsheet, follow these guidelines for creating formulas and functions:

1. Use parentheses for grouping operations in calculations in order to get the correct order. However, do not overuse parentheses as it quickly adds to the complexity of the formula. For example, use =SUM(Sales) instead of =(SUM(Sales)).

2. When inserting numbers into a function, use formatting such as 10000. Do not enter 10,000 using a comma. The comma is a formatting element, and in Excel it is used to separate arguments. Best practice for functions and formulas dictates entering the 10,000 value in a cell and then using the cell address in the formula.

3. Insert currency as 4.34 instead of $4.34 as this will get confusing with relative and absolute cell referencing. Then, format the cell that will contain the result as Accounting or Currency. Best practice for functions and formulas dictates entering the 4.34 value in a cell and then using the cell address in the formula.

4. Enter percentages as decimals, such as .04. Then, format the number as a percentage.

5. Logical conditions have three parts—two components to compare and the comparison sign. Do not type ">5" when there is no value to evaluate as being greater than 5.

6. Use the negative sign, such as –333 to indicate negative numbers in formulas as opposed to (333).

7. Always put quotes around text unless it is a named range. Numeric values do not require quotes unless the number will be used in a textual context and not for a mathematical equation, such as displaying a zip code or telephone number.

8. Avoid unneeded spaces in formulas. Excel will allow a function such as = SUM(A2:A10). Best practice dictates typing the function as =SUM(A2:A10) with no extra spaces.

Concept Check

1. Explain the three different types of cell referencing. p. 154

2. Why are named ranges useful? What limitations are there in creating the names for ranges? p. 162

3. Why is the syntax of an Excel function important? How can you distinguish between required and optional portions of a function? p. 167–168

4. In the math and statistical functions, what are the differences between the ROUND function and the INT function? Give a business example of when you would use each. p. 168–169

5. What is the difference between the TODAY() and NOW() functions? Why is this difference important? p. 175

6. What are common uses for text functions? Why is the Flash Fill feature useful on mobile devices? p. 177, 179

7. Explain the difference between the TRUE and FALSE parameters for the range_lookup argument of a VLOOKUP function. Give a business example of how you would use a VLOOKUP with a PMT function. p. 182

8. Give a business example where an IF function would be useful. How would using the AND or OR functions in the logical_test argument change the way the IF function works? p. 187

Key Terms

ABS function   168
Absolute cell reference   154
AND function   186
Argument   166
Cell reference   154
COUNT function   173
COUNTA function   173
Date and time functions   174
DATEDIF function   175
Financial functions   184
FIND function   177
Flash Fill   179

Function   166
Function arguments   169
IF function   186
INT function   168
LEFT function   177
Logical functions   186
Lookup and reference functions   181
MEDIAN function   173
Mixed cell reference   154
MODE function   173
MODE.MULT function   173
MODE.SNGL function   173

Name Manager   163
Named range   162
NOW function   175
OR function   186
PMT function   184
Relative cell reference   154
ROUND function   168
Syntax   166
Text functions   177
TODAY function   175
VLOOKUP function   181

Insert a function using formula AutoComplete (p. 171)

Use statistical functions (p. 173)

Create and structure functions (p. 166)

Use the INT and ABS functions (p. 170)

Use and understand date and time functions (p. 174)

Use and understand text functions (p. 177)

Use date and time functions (p. 176)

Nest the FIND and LEFT functions (p. 178)

Use and understand math and statistical functions (p. 168)

Use Flash Fill (p. 180)

Use the VLOOKUP function (p. 182)

Use the PMT function (p. 185)

Use financial and lookup functions (p. 181)

Use the IF and the AND functions (p. 187)

Use logical functions and troubleshoot functions (p. 186)

Troubleshoot a function (p. 190)

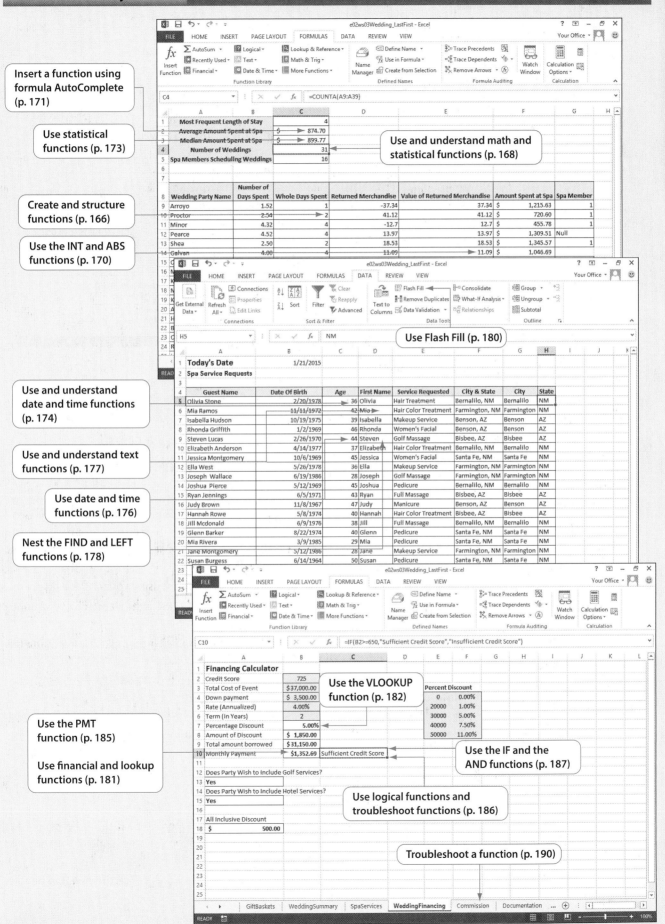

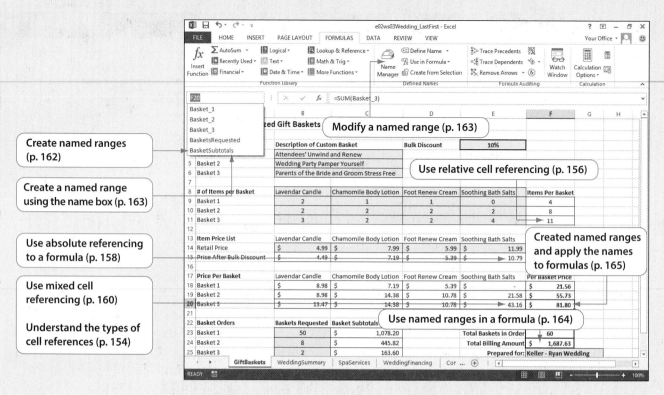

Figure 19   Painted Paradise Resort and Spa Wedding Planning Complete

Callouts in figure:

Create named ranges (p. 162)

Create a named range using the name box (p. 163)

Use absolute referencing to a formula (p. 158)

Use mixed cell referencing (p. 160)

Understand the types of cell references (p. 154)

Modify a named range (p. 163)

Use relative cell referencing (p. 156)

Created named ranges and apply the names to formulas (p. 165)

Use named ranges in a formula (p. 164)

Practice 1

Student data file needed:

 e02ws03Bonus.xlsx

You will save your file as:

e02ws03Bonus_LastFirst.xlsx

Massage Therapist Bonus Workbook

Human Resources

Meda Rodate has been constructing a workbook that would enable her to analyze the goals for massage therapists and calculate their pay. The massage therapists have a base pay and earn commission on massages along with a bonus. Meda has asked that you make some modifications to the workbook that she began to facilitate her analysis.

a. Open **e02ws03Bonus**. Save it as **e02ws03Bonus_LastFirst** using your last and first name.

b. Click the **Bonus** worksheet tab, and then click cell **J17**. Click in the **Name** box, type Bonus and then press Enter.

c. Click the **FORMULAS** tab, and then in the Defined Names group, click **Name Manager**. Click **Christy** in the list of named ranges in the workbook.

d. In the Refers to box, delete the existing range, and then type =Bonus!$B$12:$K$12. Click **Close**, and then click **Yes** to save changes.

e. Click cell **B4**. Type =B3, and then press F4 twice to create the mixed cell reference B$3. Type *A4 and then press F4 three times to create the mixed cell reference $A4. Press Ctrl+Enter.

f. Click the **AutoFill** handle, and then drag down to copy the formula to cell **B8**. With the range B4:B8 still selected, click the **AutoFill** handle, and then drag to the right to copy the formulas to the range **B4:K8**.

g. Click cell **F19**, type =SUM(Christy), and then press Enter. Repeat this process for cells F20:F22, replacing the named range in the SUM function with the name of the therapist in cells A20:A22 respectively.

h. Click cell **D25**, type =C19*C25, and then press Ctrl+Enter. Click the **AutoFill** handle, and then drag down to copy the formula to cell **D28**.

A bonus is earned if the therapist attains two goals. First, if the generated actual revenue for a therapist is greater than the goal for that therapist. Second, if the actual number of massages completed for a therapist was greater than or equal to the goal of that therapists. If the goal is met, cells D19:D22 and G19:G22 should display a 1; otherwise, they should display a 0.

i. Click cell **D19**, type =IF(C19>B19,1,0) and then press [Ctrl]+[Enter]. Click the **AutoFill** handle, and then drag down to copy the formula to cell **D22**.

j. Click cell **G19**, type =IF(F19>=E19,1,0) and then press [Ctrl]+[Enter]. Click the **AutoFill** handle, and then drag down to copy the formula to cell **G22**. If both goals are met, cells E25:E28 should display the bonus amount in cell J17; otherwise, they should display 0.

k. Click cell **E25**, type =IF(AND(D19=1,G19=1),Bonus,0) and then press [Ctrl]+[Enter]. Click the **AutoFill** handle, and then drag down to copy the formula to cell **E28**.

l. Click cell **F25**, type =B25+D25+E25, and then press [Ctrl]+[Enter]. Click the **AutoFill** handle, and then drag down to copy the formula to cell **F28**.

m. On the **INSERT** tab, in the Text group, click **Header & Footer**. On the HEADER & FOOTER TOOLS DESIGN tab, in the Navigation group, click **Go to Footer**. Click in the **left footer** section, and then in the Header & Footer Elements group, click **File Name**.

n. Click any **cell** on the spreadsheet to move out of the footer, and then press [Ctrl]+[Home]. On the **VIEW** tab, in the Workbook Views group, click **Normal**.

o. Click the Documentation worksheet. Click cell **A6**, and then type in today's date. Click cell **B6**, and then type in your first and last name. Complete the remainder of the Documentation worksheet according to your instructor's direction.

p. Click **Save**, close Excel, and then submit your files as directed by your instructor.

Problem Solve 1

MyITLab® Grader
Homework 1

Production & Operations

Student data file needed:

 e02ws03CarRental.xlsx

You will save your file as:

e02ws03CarRental_LastFirst.xlsx

Express Car Rental

Jason Easton is a member of the support/decision team for the San Diego branch of Express Car Rental. He created a worksheet to keep track of weekly rentals in an attempt to identify trends in choices of rental vehicles, length of rental, and payment method. This spreadsheet is designed only for Jason and his supervisor to try and find weekly trends and possibly use this information when marketing and forecasting the type of cars needed on site. The data for the dates of rental, daily rates, payment method, and gas option have already been entered.

a. Open **e02ws03CarRental**, and then save the file as e02ws03CarRental_LastFirst using your last and first name.

b. On the RentalData worksheet, in cell **E6**, enter a date formula to determine the length of rental in days. Copy this formula to the range **E7:E32**.

c. Name the range **A37:B40** RentalRates.

d. In cell **G6**, use the appropriate lookup and reference function to retrieve the rental rate from the named range **RentalRates**. The function should look for an exact matching value from column A in the data. Copy the function down the column to cell **G32**.

e. Name the range **B42** Discount and then name the range **B44** GasCost.

f. In cell **H6**, enter a formula to determine any discount that should be applied. If the payment method was Express Miles or Rewards, the customer should receive the discount shown in B42. If no discount should be applied, the formula should return a zero. Use the named range for cell **B42**, not the cell address, in this formula. Copy the function down the column to cell **H32**.

g. In cell **J6**, enter the correct formula to determine the cost of gas if the customer chose that option as indicated in column I. Use the named range for cell **B44** in this formula. Copy the function down the column to cell **J32**.

h. In cell **K6**, enter the correct formula to determine the total cost of the rental by based on the daily rate, the number of days rented, the cost of gas, and any discount given to the customer. Copy the function down the column to cell **K32**.

i. In cell **B46**, use the appropriate function to calculate the Median length of rental in days.

j. In cell **B47**, use the appropriate function to count the number of rentals in the data.

k. Complete the Documentation worksheet according to your instructor's direction. Insert the **filename** in the left custom footer section of the Header/Footer tab in the Page Setup dialog box on all worksheets in the workbook.

j. Click Save, close Excel, and then submit your files as directed by your instructor.

Perform 1: Perform in Your Life

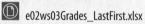

Student data file needed:

e02ws03Grades.xlsx

You will save your file as:

e02ws03Grades_LastFirst.xlsx

Calculate Your Grade

Information Technology

Using the e02ws03Grades workbook construct an evaluation of your grades in a class you are currently taking. The workbook provided has an example grading scale, though this can be modified to meet the requirements of the course you are taking.

a. Open **e02ws03Grades**, and then save the file as e02ws03Grades_LastFirst.

b. Create a basic structure for entering the names of assignments, the points possible on an assignment, and the current percentage grade of an assignment. Enter your assignments and respective grades in the worksheet.

c. Create named ranges for the points possible, points earned, and the grading scale ranges. Use these named ranges in calculations as appropriate.

d. In an adjacent column calculate your percentage grade on each assignment. Use the appropriate function to round the resulting percentage to two decimal places.

e. In an adjacent column use the appropriate function to look up the letter grade on the assignment using the grading scale provided.

f. Summarize the total points possible and your total points earned. Calculate your course grade as a percentage of the total points possible. Use the appropriate function to round the resulting percentage to two decimal places.

g. Calculate your letter grade for the course using the appropriate function.

h. Some courses provide extra credit. Create a cell that displays Yes if your course offers extra credit or No if it does not. Create another cell that displays the number of credits you have earned.

i. Construct an IF function that adds the extra credit points earned into your course grade if extra credit for the course is available and the extra credit points earned is greater than zero.

j. Complete the Documentation worksheet according to your instructor's direction. Insert the **filename** in the left custom footer section of the Header/Footer tab in the Page Setup dialog box on all worksheets in the workbook.

k. Click Save, close Excel, and then submit your files as directed by your instructor.

Additional Cases

Additional Workshop Cases are available on the companion website and in the instructor resources

WORKSHOP 4 | EFFECTIVE CHARTS

OBJECTIVES

1. Explore chart types, layouts, and styles p. 198

2. Explore the positioning of charts p. 202

3. Understand different chart types p. 205

4. Change chart data and styles for presentations p. 214

5. Edit and format charts to add emphasis p. 223

6. Use sparklines and data bars to emphasize data p. 227

7. Recognize and correct confusing charts p. 230

Prepare Case

Turquoise Oasis Spa Sales Reports

The Turquoise Oasis Spa managers, Irene Kai and Meda Rodate, are pleased with your work and would like to see you continue to improve the spa spreadsheets. They want to use charts to learn more about the spa. To do this, Meda has given you a spreadsheet with some data, and she would like you to develop some charts. Visualizing the data with charts will provide knowledge about the spa for decision-making purposes.

Sales & Marketing

PhotoSG / Fotolia

REAL WORLD SUCCESS

"In my internship, I used a combo chart to analyze inventory trends over time, presenting inventory buildup or shrinkage on one axis and production levels on another. I was able to use this visual representation to better understand supply chain coordination throughout a quarter, providing my superiors with data to improve our operating efficiency. By combining these charts with charts presenting demand variance, our company was able to pinpoint sources of inventory buildup and higher operating costs."

- Steven, alumnus

Student data files needed for this workshop:

 e02ws04SpaSales.xlsx

 e02ws04TurquoiseOasis.jpg

You will save your file as:

 e02ws04SpaSales_LastFirst.xlsx

Designing a Chart

With Excel you can organize data so it has context and meaning, converting data into meaningful information. **Data visualization** is the graphical presentation of data with a focus upon qualitative understanding. It is central to finding trends and supporting business decisions. Modern data visualization can include beautiful and elegant charts that include movement and convey information in real time. Even basic charts are at the heart of data visualization. Charts enlighten you as you compare, contrast, and examine how data changes over time. Learning how to work with charts means not only knowing how to create them but also realizing that different knowledge can be discovered or emphasized by each type of chart.

While it may seem simple to create a pie chart or bar chart, there are many considerations in creating your charts. Charts, as with pictures, are worth a thousand words. However, people interpret charts differently if the chart is not well developed. A well-developed chart should provide context for the information, without overshadowing key points. Finally, it is easy to confuse people with the choice and layout of a chart. You should create charts that use accurate, complete data, and your objective should be to provide a focused, clear message. In today's data-rich world, many interpretations or messages can be extracted from the data. There are three primary objectives businesses have in charting: data exploration, hypothesis testing, and argumentation.

Using the **data exploration objective**, you simply manipulate the data, and try to evaluate and prioritize all the interpretations or messages. There may be a need to create multiple charts, using a variety of data sources, layouts, and designs as you interpret the data. In this case, examine the data and let the charts tell a story.

Using the **hypothesis testing objective**, you may have some ideas or hypotheses about the data. Maybe you believe that a certain salesperson performs better than the others. Or maybe you believe that certain types of massages are more popular with particular types of customers. Charts can visually support or refute a hypothesis.

Using the **argumentation objective**, you have a position you want the data to visually support. You will need to select a specific and appropriate chart layout, use the necessary data, and design a chart that conveys your message clearly and unambiguously. Further, you have an ethical obligation to accurately represent the data. Misrepresenting data can result in lawsuits, loss of your job, or even cost lives.

Regardless of the objective, just a small set of data allows you to create a variety of charts, each offering a different understanding of the data. In this workshop, you will start with understanding the concepts for creating a chart in Excel, and understand which type of chart will depict the information in the best and most efficient manner.

Explore Chart Types, Layouts, and Styles

When you decide to represent data visually, you need to make some initial decisions about the basic design of the chart. These initial decisions include the location of the chart, the type of chart, the general layout and style, and what data you will be using. These elements can be set initially and modified later. Best practice dictates that you first consider and develop the basic design of the chart.

Regardless of the location or type of chart, the process of creating a chart starts with the organization of the data on the spreadsheet. The typical structure is to have labels across the top of the data, along the left side of the data, or both. While the labels do not have to be directly next to the data, it helps when selecting data and making your chart. The data may have been brought in from an external data source, like Access. The data may need to be filtered, calculated, or reorganized prior to creating a chart.

When you are ready to create a chart, select the cells that contain both the label headings and the data. People rarely create a perfect chart the first time. Initially, you may start a chart, work with it for a while, and then realize a different chart type would better convey the information. Fortunately, Excel provides ample flexibility when designing charts. Thus, if you change your mind, you can modify the chart or simply start over.

Opening the Starting File

A chart in Excel is an object that sits above the worksheet. Clicking on the chart will allow you to modify aspects of the chart or even change the type of chart. You have been asked to review a pie chart that displays the use of portable massage tables by different therapists.

E04.00

 To Open the SpaSales Worksheet

a. Start **Excel**, click **Open Other Workbooks**, and browse to your student data files. Locate and select **e02ws04SpaSales**, and then click **Open**.

b. Click the **FILE** tab, and then click **Save As**. Browse to the location where you are saving your files. In the File name box, type **e02ws04SpaSales_LastFirst**, using your last and first name, and then click **Save**.

c. On the **INSERT** tab, in the **Text** group, click **Header & Footer**.

d. On the **HEADER & FOOTER TOOLS DESIGN** tab, in the Navigation group, click **Go to Footer**. If necessary, click the **left section** of the footer, and then in the Header & Footer Elements group, click **File Name**.

e. Click any **cell** on the worksheet to move out of the footer, press Ctrl + Home, and then on the status bar, click **Normal**.

Modifying an Existing Chart

When you click an existing chart, you are activating the chart area. It will be highlighted on the border while the middle of the sides and the corners will have selection handles used to resize the chart. The chart border can also be used to move the entire chart to a new location within the spreadsheet. The Chart Tools contextual tab will appear on the Ribbon, and to the right of the chart three buttons will appear that provide quick access to common functions such as modifying chart elements, changing the chart layout, or filtering the chart data.

When a chart is selected, the data used in creating the chart will be highlighted in the worksheet, offering a visual clue of the associated data. In the TableUse worksheet you will see a pie chart describing the use of massage tables by individual therapists at the spa. A purple border surrounds the data that represents the legend labels. The range with a blue border is the data that represents the data series for the pie slices. A **data series** is a group of related data values to be charted. A **data point** is an individual data value in a data series. A chart may contain multiple data series or a single data series.

Subcomponents of the chart can also be selected, such as the background, various text elements, and even the individual chart elements themselves. Click components to make them active, and adjust specific items through either the Ribbon options or by right-clicking to display the shortcut menu to see available options. In this exercise, you will modify an existing pie chart on the TableUse worksheet.

REAL WORLD ADVICE First Impressions

First impressions are important with charts. You want the audience to receive the correct message during the initial moments. If the audience is distracted by the look and feel of the chart, they may stop looking for the message in the chart or extend the chaotic personality of the chart to the presenter. Thus, the chart can become a reflection upon you and your company.

MyITLab® Workshop 4 Training

SIDE NOTE
Alternate Method
Any action completed in the Chart Formatting Control can be completed through the Chart Tools contextual tab on the Ribbon.

E04.01

To Modify an Existing Chart

a. Click the **TableUse** worksheet tab. Notice the pie chart located below the data on this worksheet.

b. Click the **chart border** of the chart to select the chart and display the CHART TOOLS contextual tabs.

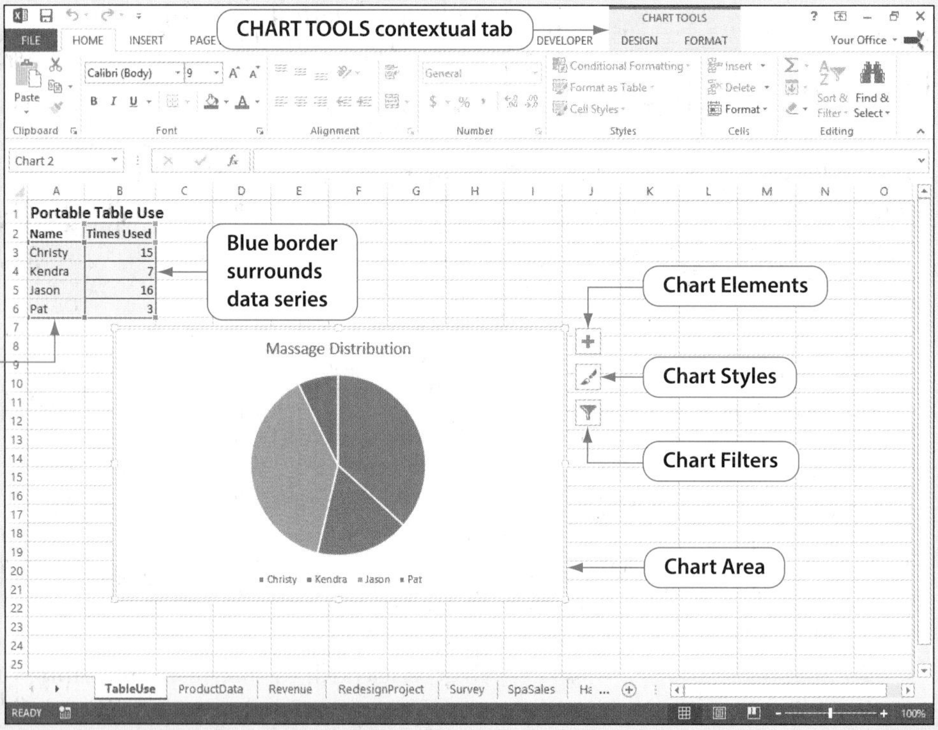

Figure 1 Selected pie chart

c. To the right of the chart, click **Chart Elements** [+], and then click **Data Labels**. This will display the number of times each therapist used a portable massage table in the corresponding slice of the pie chart.

d. Click the **Data Labels** arrow, and then select **More Options**. This will open the Format Data Labels task pane.

e. Under the **LABEL OPTIONS** group, click to deselect **Value**, and then click **Percentage**.

SIDE NOTE

Hover to See Icon Information

When presented with a set of icons, hover the mouse over an icon, and a ScreenTip will appear offering descriptive information.

f. Click the **chart border** of the chart, click **Chart Styles** 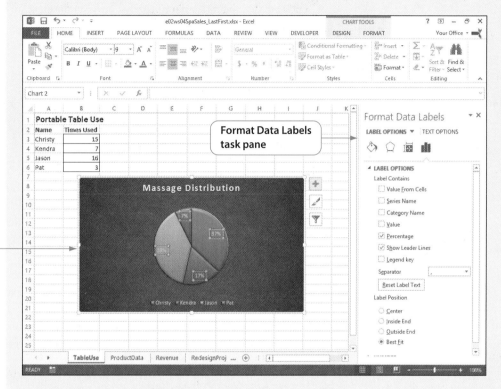, and then scroll down and point to **Style 7**. Notice the chart changes to display a live preview of the style. Click **Style 7**, and then click **Chart Styles** to close the control. This chart now displays the percent of portable table usage for each massage therapist at the spa.

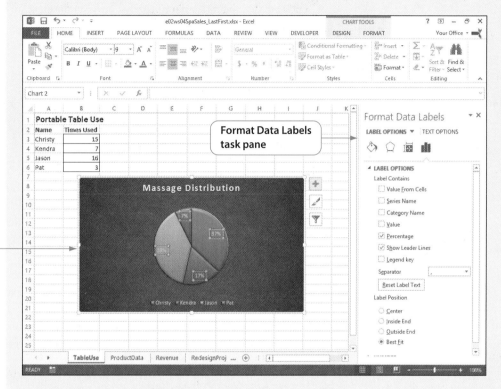

Format Data Labels task pane

Pie chart with new style and data labels

Figure 2 Modified chart

g. Close the Format Data Labels task pane, and then click **Save**.

CONSIDER THIS | **Misleading Charts**

Charts are supposed to frame information. But, have you ever seen a chart in a newspaper, online article, or magazine that would lead the viewer to an incorrect assumption or conclusion? Look for a chart that is misleading, discuss the context and possible incorrect conclusions that could be made, and consider the ethical aspect for the creator of the chart.

It is possible to navigate through a chart using some of these guidelines:

- Click the chart border to activate the Chart Tools contextual tabs.
- Click chart objects to select individual chart components.
- Click outside a chart object or press Esc to deselect an object.
- Under the Chart Tools contextual tabs, on the Format tab, in the Current Selection group, use the Chart Elements box to select specific chart objects.
- Use border corner handles to resize selected objects.
- Click the chart border, and drag to move a chart object.

Explore the Positioning of Charts

When developing a chart, consider the chart location, as this might affect the flexibility of moving and resizing your chart components. There are two general locations for a chart—either within an existing worksheet or on a separate worksheet, referred to as a chart sheet. A **chart sheet** is a special worksheet that is dedicated to displaying chart objects. Excel 2013 has several new features that allow you to quickly analyze data. Two of these are the Quick Analysis tool and the Recommended Charts feature. The **Quick Analysis** tool is a contextual tool that appears when you select data in a worksheet and offers single-click access to formatting, charts, formulas, PivotTables, and sparklines. The Recommended Charts feature is located on the Insert tab on the Ribbon. The **Recommended Charts** feature quickly analyzes a selection in a worksheet and recommends chart types that best fit your data. The Recommend Charts option also appears in the Quick Analysis tool under the Chart heading.

Creating Charts in an Existing Worksheet

Placing a chart within a worksheet can be very helpful, allowing you to display the chart beside the associated data source. When comparing charts side by side, placing the charts on the same worksheet can also be handy. Additionally, placing a chart within the worksheet may offer easy access to chart components when copying and pasting components into other applications.

Your manager, Irene, would like you to work with some data. Irene would like the data organized and presented in an effective graphical manner to aid in the analysis of the data so it is more informative. Specifically she would like to compare the total number of massages given over an eight-week period of time.

E04.02

 To Create a Chart in an Existing Worksheet

a. Click the **ProductData** worksheet tab, and then select the range **A2:B12** as the data to use for creating a chart. Notice that once the data is selected, the Quick Analysis tool is displayed below and to the right of cell B12.

b. Click **Quick Analysis** 🔲 , and then click **CHARTS**.

c. Point to the **Clustered Column** chart suggestion. Notice that a live preview of the chart is displayed.

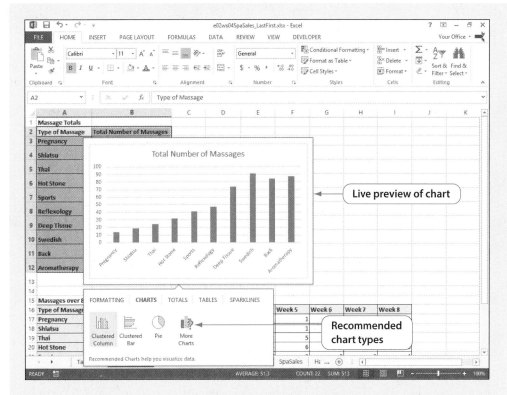

Figure 3 Quick Analysis tool with a suggested chart

d. Click **Clustered Column** to insert the chart into the worksheet.

Notice the chart appears on the currently active worksheet and shows colored borders surrounding the associated data linked to the chart. This chart displays the total number of each type of massage offered by the Spa.

e. Click the **chart border** when the pointer appears as a four-way arrow ⬚. Be careful not to click the corners or middle areas of the border that are designated by small handles and used for resizing the chart. Drag the **border** to move the chart to the right of the data so the top-left chart corner is approximately in cell **D2**.

f. Click **Save** 💾.

Modifying a Chart's Position Properties

Charts created within the worksheet will appear as objects that "float" on top of the worksheet. The default property settings resize the chart shape if any of the underlying rows or columns are changed or adjusted. Therefore if the width of a column that lies behind the chart is increased, the chart width will increase accordingly. It is possible to change this setting, locking the size and position of the chart so it does not resize or move when columns or rows are resized, inserted, or deleted.

For example, additional data may be added to the ProductData worksheet. This data may require underlying columns to be widened or new columns inserted. Without adjusting the default settings on the chart, it could become distorted when changes are made to the worksheet.

To Modify the Chart Position on a Worksheet

a. On the **ProductData** worksheet, right-click the **chart border**, and then click **Format Chart Area**. This will open the Format Chart Area task pane.

b. In the Format Chart Area task pane, click **Size & Properties** 🗔, and then click the **PROPERTIES** arrow to expand the PROPERTIES group.

c. Click **Move but don't size with cells**.

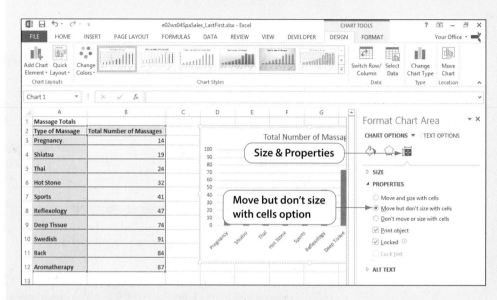

Figure 4 Format Chart Area task pane

d. Close ☒ the Format Chart Area task pane, and then click **Save** 🖫.

The chart size will not be resized if the width or height of the columns or rows underneath are changed or adjusted, but the chart will move along with the cells that it is sitting over. From here, you can easily move the chart by dragging the border, or you can resize the chart by clicking and dragging the corners.

Placing Charts on a Chart Sheet

As previously defined, a chart sheet is a worksheet that only contains chart objects. The familiar cell grid is replaced with the actual chart. Having the chart on a separate chart sheet can make it easier to isolate and print on a page. Chart sheets are also useful when you want to create a set of charts and easily navigate between them by worksheet names rather than looking for them on various worksheets. Due to the nature of chart sheets, the data associated with the chart will be on a different worksheet.

Irene has mentioned that she would like to use this chart in future presentations and would like to be able to easily isolate and print the chart. To facilitate this you will move the chart to a chart sheet.

E04.04

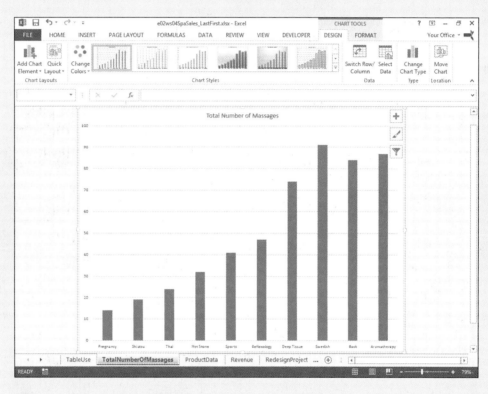

To Move a Chart to a Chart Sheet

a. On the **ProductData** worksheet, select the **clustered column chart**.

b. On the **CHART TOOLS DESIGN** tab, in the **Location** group, click **Move Chart**. The Move Chart dialog box is displayed.

c. In the Move Chart dialog box, click the **New sheet** option. In the New sheet box, clear the **existing name**, and then type TotalNumberOfMassages. Click **OK**. Notice that you now have a new chart sheet tab in your workbook file. This chart sheet is exclusively for the chart and will not have the normal worksheet appearance.

d. Applying a color to the worksheet tab will allow the chart sheet to be easily distinguished from the rest of the worksheets in the workbook. Right-click the **TotalNumberOfMassages** worksheet tab. Point to **Tab Color**, and then click **Blue, Accent 1** in the first row, fifth column as the tab color.

Figure 5   TotalNumberOfMassages chart sheet

e. Click **Save**.

Understand Different Chart Types

When creating a chart it is important to choose the correct type of chart to use. Each chart type conveys information differently. The chart type sets the tone for the basic format of the data and what kind of data is included. Thus, it helps to become familiar with the types of charts that are commonly used for business decision making and for presentations. Always consider which type is appropriate for the message you are trying to convey.

Creating Pie Charts

Pie charts are commonly used for depicting the relationships of the parts to the whole such as comparing staff performance within a department or comparing the number of transactions of each product category within a time period.

For a pie chart you need two data series—the labels and a set of corresponding values. This is similar to the data selection made in the TableUse sheet to indicate the percentage of times each person used the portable massage table. Note that the data can be described as a percentage of the whole as in the chart.

The questions you have will influence what textual data you will include in any chart. If you are exploring a use fee, then having the percentage would indicate which therapist would be contributing the most fees, and the actual numbers may not be a crucial element. When you create a chart, examine it to see if it answers your questions.

In this exercise, you will create a simple pie chart that shows the proportion of revenue each of four different massage types earned for the spa in the month of June.

E04.05

To Create a Pie Chart

a. Click the **Revenue** worksheet tab, and then select the range **A1:E2**.

b. Click **Quick Analysis** [image], click **CHARTS**, and then click **Pie**.

c. Click the **chart border**, and then drag to move the chart to the upper left corner of cell **G4**. This will place the chart to the right of the data set.

d. Point to the **bottom-right corner** of the chart until the pointer changes to [image], and then drag to resize the chart so the bottom-right corner is over cell **M17**. This chart displays the proportion of revenue generated by each massage type.

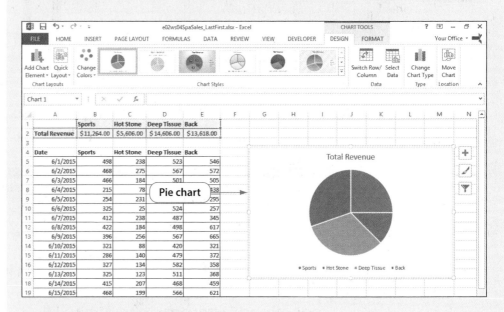

Figure 6   Total Revenue pie chart

e. Click **Save** [image].

Even though all the data is used to show every massage type, you do not have to use all the data. If the goal is to examine the data and extract a portion of the information, like the fact that several massage types have low or high average ratings, it may be better to only show a few massage types rather than include too much information. Showing a subset of massage types may help to emphasize particular ratings.

In determining how to proceed once the data has been initially examined, start developing hypotheses and questions. For example, it may be that hot stone massages are very new and need to be marketed more as they currently represent a small portion of revenues. Develop questions, and then use the data to determine the validity of the questions and make strategic decisions.

Creating Line Charts

Line charts help convey change over a period of time. They are great for exploring how data in a business, such as sales or production, changes over time. Line charts help people to interpret why the data is changing and to make decisions about how to proceed. For example, when a doctor examines a heart rate on an electrocardiogram, he or she is looking at data over time to see what has been happening. The doctor wants to determine if there are issues, and then make decisions whether the patient should go home, be given medications, or have surgery.

To create a line chart you need to have at least one set of labels and at least one set of corresponding data. It is possible to have multiple data series, each series representing a line on the chart. You have been provided with data listing revenue generated by four different types of massages. The data is organized by day throughout the month of June. In this exercise, you will create a line chart displaying daily revenue by massage type in June. Each day will appear as a point on the line that is created. Each massage type would be a separate line on the chart.

E04.06

 To Create a Line Chart

a. On the **Revenue** worksheet, select cell **A4**, press Ctrl, and then press A to select the entire data set, including the labels.

b. Click **Quick Analysis** , click **CHARTS**, and then click **Line**.

c. On the **CHART TOOLS FORMAT** tab, in the Current Selection group, click the **Chart Elements** arrow, and then click **Chart Title**. Type Revenue by Massage Type for June and then press Enter.

d. Click the **chart border**, and then drag to move the chart to place the top-left corner in cell **G20**. This will place the chart to the right of the data set.

e. Point to the **bottom-right corner** of the chart until the pointer changes to , and then drag to resize the chart so the bottom-right corner is over cell **M33**. This chart displays the revenue generated by each type of massage through the month of June.

SIDE NOTE

Inserting a Chart

Charts can also be inserted by clicking the Insert tab, and then in the Charts group, clicking Recommended Charts.

Figure 7 Revenue by Massage Type for June line chart

Troubleshooting

If you end up with a chart that looks dramatically different than what you would expect, check the colored borders around the linked data set. It is very common to select all the data in a table when the intention was to select just part of the data. If too much data was selected, you can delete the selected chart by pressing Delete. Alternatively, you could select the corner of a colored link data border and drag the border to adjust the set of data. The blue-border data is displayed in the chart. When that border is adjusted, the associated label data is automatically adjusted accordingly. The chart is also automatically adjusted so changes can be immediately seen.

---

f.   Click **Save** 🖫.

Creating Column Charts

Column charts are useful for comparing data sets that are categorized, like departments, product categories, or survey results. Column charts are also useful for showing categories over time where each column represents a unit of time. Column charts are good for comparisons both individually, in groups, or stacked. Column chart data can easily allow for grouping of data so comparisons of the groups can occur.

In the TotalNumberOfMassages chart it is easy to interpret that pregnancy massages represent a small portion of the total massages provided. On the other hand, Swedish, aromatherapy, back, and deep tissue massages represent a large portion of the data.

Creating Bar Charts

Bar charts are useful for working with categorical data. Bar charts are similar to column charts except the bars are horizontal representations of the data rather than vertical. Like column charts, bar charts can depict a single piece of data, can be grouped data series, and can be stacked.

Because bar charts typically use groups and sum data, stacked bar charts can be useful when you want to see how the individual parts add up to create the entire length of each bar. For example, with the data on the ProductData worksheet, you may want to compare each type of massage, summing revenue or counting sales for each type of massage.

The x-axis would be number of massages or revenue. While it is the same data as used for the line chart, it conveys information about an output without the emphasis on time that is inherent with the line chart.

While bar charts are often viewed as simply being column charts turned on their sides, there is a particular bar chart that does use time values on the x-axis. It is a **Gantt chart**, which shows a project schedule where each bar represents a component or task within the project. The breakdown of tasks is useful for scheduling. Gantt charts are commonly used with project management. Gantt charts can be complex showing start times, end times, sequence of tasks, and people assigned to each task. A basic Gantt chart can be created that is informative and helps a team successfully complete a project. You have been asked to create a Gantt chart that will assist Irene and Meda visualize the timeline of a project to redesign the massage therapy rooms.

E04.07

 To Create a Bar Chart

a. Click the **RedesignProject** worksheet tab, and then select the range **A3:D8**.

b. Click **Quick Analysis**, click **CHARTS**, and then click **More Charts**.

c. In the Insert Chart dialog box, click the **All Charts** tab, and then click **Bar** from the list of chart types. Click **Stacked Bar**, and then click **OK**.

d. Click the **Chart Title**, type Project Schedule and then press Enter.

e. Click the **blue data bar** within the chart corresponding with the Series "Start Date" to select the data series. **Right-click** a blue data bar, and then select **Format Data Series**. In the Format Data Series task pane, click **Fill & Line**.

f. Click the **FILL** arrow to expand the FILL group, and then click **No Fill**.

g. Click the **BORDER** arrow to expand the BORDER group, and then click **No Line**.

h. Click the **Vertical (category) Axis** corresponding to the project tasks. In the Format Axis task pane, click **Axis Options**, and then select **Categories in reverse order**.

i. Click the **Horizontal (value) Axis** corresponding to the start dates above the plot area. In the Format Axis task pane, click **TEXT OPTIONS**, and then click **Textbox**. Click in the box for **Custom angle**, if necessary delete the existing value, and then type 45. Press Enter.

j. Click the **chart border**, and then drag so the top-left corner is over cell **A11**. This chart visually displays both the number of days completed and the number of days remaining for each project listed in the worksheet.

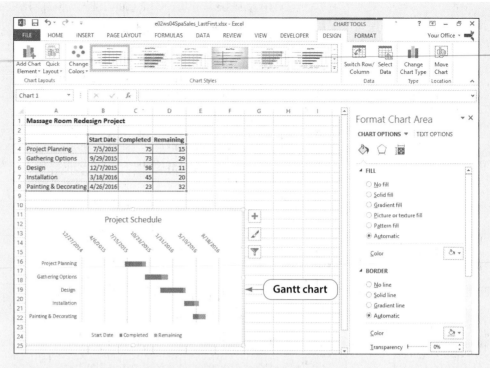

Figure 8   Completed Gantt chart

k.   Close ⌧ the Format Chart Area task pane, and then click **Save** 💾.

The resulting Gantt chart depicts the time for each task in the project. For each bar, the task is set up with the amount completed and the amount that is remaining. The tasks are staggered to show the relation of each task to the other.

Creating Scatter Charts

Scatter charts, also called scatter plots, are a particular type of chart that conveys the relationship between two numeric variables. This type of chart is very common as a statistical tool depicting the correlation between the two variables. The standard format is to have the x-axis data on the far-left column and the y-axis data in a column on the right side.

Irene and Meda have data from a survey showing the requested temperature of the room used for massages and the age of the customer. This data may reveal important information as to what temperature is typically requested by different age groups. They have asked you to create a scatter chart of the requested temperatures of rooms and ages of customers.

E04.08

 To Create a Scatter Chart

a. Click the **Survey** worksheet tab, and then select the range **A2:B53**. This will include the data and labels for Age and Temp.

b. Click **Quick Analysis** 📊, click **CHARTS**, and then select **Scatter**.

c. Click the **chart border**, and then drag to move it to the right of the data so the top-left corner is over cell **E2**.

   The default scale of the chart does not bring out any trends to the data. Adjusting the scaling of the y-axis will help display any trends in the data.

d. Double-click the **Vertical (Value) Axis** corresponding to the temperature requested. In the Format Axis task pane, click **Axis Options** ▼, click the **AXIS OPTIONS** arrow to expand the AXIS OPTIONS group, and then click in the box for **Minimum**.

e. Select the existing number, type 65 and then press ⏎Enter.

   Notice the resulting scatter plot has a slight upward trend as the age of the customer increases. This knowledge may lead to decisions that help provide better customer service.

f. Click the **Chart Title**, type Relationship Between Age and Temperature, and then press ⏎Enter. This chart shows the relationship between increasing age and temperatures requested for massages.

g. Close ✖ the Format Chart Title task pane, and then click **Save** 💾.

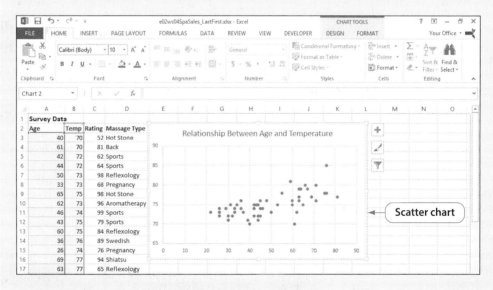

Figure 9   Scatter chart of temperature requested and age

Creating Area Charts

An **area chart** is a variation of a stacked line chart that emphasizes the magnitude of change over time and visually depicts a trend. The area chart stacks a set of data series and colors each area that is created. This type of chart has a nice visual characteristic because each colored layer changes, growing or shrinking, as it moves across time periods. Thus, with an area chart, the x-axis is typically a time sequence. The area chart could also use categories instead of time on the x-axis where each layer again is showing the individual contribution to the area; thus, it is a quantitative chart that shows growth or change in totals.

Irene has asked you to create a chart to further understand the differences in the types of massages given over the past eight weeks at the spa. You will create an area chart for this purpose.

E04.09

 To Create an Area Chart

a. Click the **ProductData** worksheet tab, and then select the range **A16:I26**.

b. Click **Quick Analysis** 📧, click **CHARTS**, and then select **Stacked Area**.

c. Click the **Chart Title**, type Massage Types Over Past 8 Weeks and then press Enter.

d. Click the **chart border**, and then drag to move the chart so the top-left corner is over cell **D3**. This chart shows the total number of massages offered for each of the past eight weeks with emphasis placed on the different massage types.

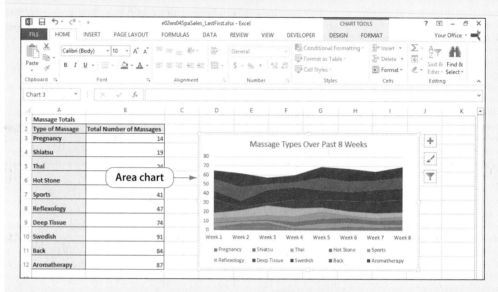

Figure 10   Area chart of massage types over past 8 weeks

e. Click **Save** 🔲.

QUICK REFERENCE	Chart Selection Guidelines

The common types of charts and their usage are listed below:

- Pie—Used for comparing the relationship of parts to a whole
- Line—Shows changes within a data series; often used with time on the x-axis
- Column—Compares data vertically; can incorporate a time element and groups
- Bar—Compares data horizontally; stacked bar can show progress, growth
- Scatter—Used for correlations, exploring the relationship between two variables
- Area—Used to highlight areas showing growth over time or for categories; a variation of a line chart list

Creating Combination Charts

A **combination chart** displays two different types of data by using multiple chart types in a single chart object. Combination charts can enhance the understanding of data when the scale of data needing to be charted varies greatly. For example, consider monitoring the number of items sold in the spa to customers over a 12-month span of time. To fully comprehend the data it would be helpful to explore both the number of items sold and the profit from items sold. However, a single item may cost hundreds of dollars. This makes creating a chart to compare these two pieces of data difficult. In prior versions of Excel, creating a combination chart was a difficult and time-consuming process. In Excel 2013, combination charts are a standard chart type.

Meda has asked that you analyze the quantities of spa products sold from the prior year's sales and compare that to the profits over the same time span. Currently, only data from January to November is available. Meda has asked that you proceed with creating a chart and add the December data when it becomes available.

E04.10

 To Create a Combination Chart

a. Click the **SpaSales** worksheet tab, and then select the range **A1:C12**.

b. Click **Quick Analysis** , click **CHARTS**, and then select **More Charts**.

c. In the Insert Chart dialog box, click the **All Charts** tab. From the list of charts, click **Combo**.

   Before you insert the chart, you will have an opportunity to customize how the data will look. The default chart shows the month on the x-axis while using a line chart for profit—in red, and a clustered column chart for quantity sold—in blue.

d. Next to **Profit**, click to select the **Secondary Axis** check box. This scales the line chart for profit on a separate axis from quantity, allowing the trend over time between the two to be compared. Click **OK**.

e. Click the **Chart Title**, type Quantity Sold and Profit and then press Enter.

f. Click the **chart border**, and then drag to move the chart so the top-left corner is over cell **E2**.

   This chart compares the number of spa products sold and the profit from products sold in the same chart. Notice that in January the profit for items sold is lower than might be expected by the quantity sold.

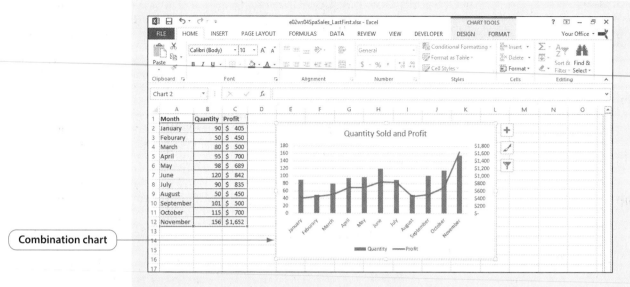

Combination chart

Figure 11   Combination chart of quantity sold and profit

g.   Click **Save** 🖫.

Exploring Chart Layouts

As you have seen, a chart can help answer questions and may even generate more questions. This helps move toward the understanding of information, which can also lead to better decision making. Creating these initial charts to explore data is quick and efficient and informs the user.

When presenting a chart to others, the context of the chart is of utmost importance. Without context, your audience will try to guess the context. You need to provide meaning.

Providing context means providing textual guidance to the audience. The audience will see the pie chart, but you need to inform them more about the data. Thus, labels are another crucial element needed to provide context in charts. The labels include the chart title and axes titles, the legend, and the labels for the data. All these elements should work cohesively to convey a complete picture of what the chart is trying to convey to the audience. In this section, you will change the appearance of charts by altering their layout and color patterns. You will also add chart titles and modify the titles of the chart axis.

Change Chart Data and Styles for Presentations

While the default chart settings are pleasant visually, you can still improve the look and feel of the chart. The chart layouts are available under the Chart Tools contextual tabs, on the Design tab, in the Chart Layouts group. Excel provides many options for arranging the components on a chart. This includes placement of the titles and legend as well as the display of information such as the data point values.

Chart styles are a variation of chart layouts. Where chart layouts focus on location of components, styles focus more on the color coordination and effects of the components. Chart styles are located on the Chart Tools Design tab, in the Chart Styles group. For easier access, Excel 2013 displays the Chart Styles icon to the right side of any chart when it is selected. The choices mix color options with shadows and 3-D effects to create a variety of templates. You can also start with a template, and then adapt it to suit your tastes.

Chart data is the underlying data for the chart and labels. There can be many reasons for modifying data, and it can be accomplished through various methods. For example, if the data needs to be swapped between the data points and the axis data, you can use the Data group to switch rows and columns or select new data for a chart.

Changing the Appearance of a Chart

Because charts in Excel are connected to data on the worksheet, changes to the data are automatically reflected in the chart. This is extremely useful if you have a model that is using some calculations that are then used in a chart. You can do what-if analysis by changing data in a worksheet; the corresponding changes will appear on the chart.

Charts may need to be modified when the amount of data being charted needs to be changed. For example, a chart might have too much information included, making it difficult to get a clear picture. Conversely, a chart may need to be modified as new data becomes available. If the new data is adjacent to the existing data, it is a simple process to expand the existing data series. This is achieved by resizing the borders around the data series after activating the chart. Irene has just provided you with the December data for quantity and profit for the spa. You need to add this data to the SpaSales worksheet and adjust the combination chart accordingly. Additionally you will modify the appearance of the chart.

E04.11

 To Modify the Layout and Data in an Existing Chart

a. On the **SpaSales** worksheet, click cell **A13** to select it.

b. Type December and then press ⎡Tab⎤. Type 165 and then press ⎡Tab⎤. Type 1701 and then press ⎡Ctrl⎤ + ⎡Enter⎤.

c. Click the **chart area** portion of the chart. Click the **sizing handle** on the lower edge between cells **A12** and **B12**, and then drag the sizing handle down one row so that the range **A2:C13** is now being charted. The chart will now display the quantity sold and profits for the month of December.

d. On the **CHART TOOLS DESIGN** tab, in the Type group, click **Change Chart Type**.

e. Near the bottom of the Change Chart Type dialog box, next to the Profit series, click the **Chart Type** arrow. Select **Area**, and then click **OK**.

f. To the right of the chart, click **Chart Styles** ⟋, scroll down, and then click **Style 6**. Click **Chart Styles** ⟋ to close the style gallery.

g. On the **CHART TOOLS DESIGN** tab, in the Chart Layouts group, click **Quick Layout**. In the displayed gallery, click **Layout 9**. Notice that the new layout added labels for the x- and y-axis on the chart. These axis titles will be revised at a later point.

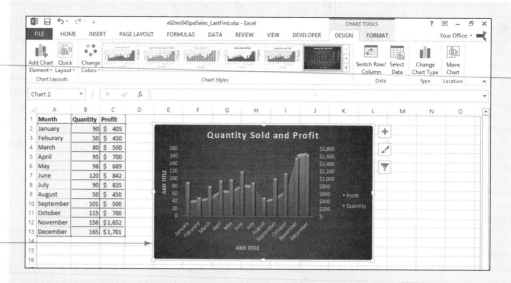

Combination chart with modified style and labels

Figure 12 Modified combination chart

h. Click **Save** .

Inserting Objects

If you work for a company, it would be useful to insert the company logo into any chart that is used outside the company. After all, marketing occurs everywhere. It may also be useful to use images to help convey the tone of the presentation. This can be accomplished with an image inserted into the chart. Irene mentioned she would be using the chart sheet in the workbook in a variety of presentations. Given this, you will modify the appearance of the chart by inserting the Turquoise Oasis Spa logo and a shape object containing the title of the chart.

E04.12

▶ **To Insert Objects into a Chart**

a. Click the **TotalNumberOfMassages** chart worksheet tab, and then select the **chart**, if necessary.

b. Click the **INSERT** tab, and then in the Illustrations group, click **Pictures**. In the left pane of the Insert Picture dialog box, navigate to the location where you store your student data files, and then click **e02ws04TurquoiseOasis**. Click **Insert**.

c. On the **PICTURE TOOLS FORMAT** tab, in the Size group, click the **Shape Height** 📏 box. Clear any existing text, type 0.9 and then press Enter.

d. Click in the **Chart Area**. On the **CHART TOOLS DESIGN** tab, in the **Chart Layouts** group, click **Quick Layout**. In the gallery that appears, click **Layout 4**. Notice that the new layout added labels for the x-axis on the chart.

e. Click any of the **columns** in the chart. On the **CHART TOOLS FORMAT** tab, in the **Shape Styles** group, click the **More** arrow, and then click **Subtle Effect - Orange, Accent 6** in the fourth row, seventh column.

f. Click the **INSERT** tab, and then in the Illustrations group, click **Shapes**. In the displayed gallery, in the Rectangles group, click **Rounded Rectangle**—the second option. Click to place the **rectangle** below the Turquoise Oasis Spa logo.

g. Type **Number of Massage Services by Type**. On the **DRAWING TOOLS FORMAT** tab, in the Size group, click the **Shape Height** ⬚ box, type **0.8** and then press Enter. In the **Shape Width** ⬚ box, type **2.2** and then press Enter.

h. In the Shape Styles group, click the **More** arrow, and then select **Subtle Effect - Orange, Accent 6** in the fourth row, seventh column.

i. Click the **HOME** tab, and then in the Font group, click the **Font Size** arrow, and then select **16**.

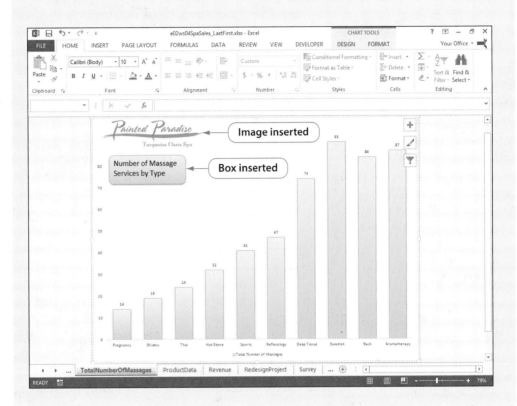

Figure 13   Picture and shape inserted into a chart

j. Click **Save** 🖫.

Exploring Titles for the Chart and Axes

Chart and axes titles are added easily under the Chart Tools Format tab or with the Chart Elements button that appears on the right side of charts in Excel 2013. Chart titles can be added within the chart or they can reference cells on the spreadsheet for easy updating. You have been asked by Meda to alter the title of the Gantt chart on the RedesignProject worksheet to match the text in cell A1. She has also asked you to clarify the horizontal and vertical axis labels on the combination chart in the SpaSales worksheet.

To Modify Chart Titles and Axis Labels

a. Click the **RedesignProject** worksheet tab, and then click the **chart border** of the Gantt chart.

b. Click the **chart title** at the top of the chart, and then click the **formula bar**. Type = and then click cell **A1**.

c. Press [Enter].

   Notice the title of the chart now matches the contents of cell A1. If the text in cell A1 is changed, the chart title will be updated automatically.

d. Click the **SpaSales** worksheet tab, and then click the **chart border** of the combination chart. Click the **Horizontal (Category) Axis Title** box, and then press [Delete].

e. Click the **Vertical (Value) Axis Title**, type Quantity and then press [Enter].

f. On the **CHART TOOLS DESIGN** tab, in the Chart Layouts group, click **Add Chart Element**.

g. Point to **Axis Titles**, and then select **Secondary Vertical**. Type Profit and then press [Enter].

h. Click **Save** 🖫.

CONSIDER THIS | **The Unit of Analysis**

You are presented with a chart titled "2013 Sales Report" and the x-axis is showing 20, 30, 40, and so on for the scale. What is this report depicting? Is it the number of sales transactions—number sold—or the revenue for 2013? Are the 20, 30, and 40 the actual numbers or in hundreds or thousands? What context should there be to make certain the audience knows the meaning of the chart?

Working with the Legend and Labeling the Data

The legend is an index within a chart that provides information about the data. With some charts the legend is added automatically. With other charts, such as pie charts, it is possible to incorporate the same information beside each pie slice as labels.

When the parts are labeled on the chart, the legend is not needed and can be removed. Labels can also be added alongside the data on the chart. This is quite informative as it moves the information from a legend to the data. This can be a visually useful addition.

The data labels can be added, moved, or removed through the Chart Elements button that appears to the right of a selected chart or through the Chart Tools Design tab.

E04.14

 To Work with Legends and Data Labels

a. Click the **Revenue** worksheet tab, and then click the **chart border** of the line chart.

b. To the right of the chart, click **Chart Elements** ⊞, move the pointer over Legend and click the **Legend** arrow, and then click **Right**.

c. Click the **chart border** of the pie chart. To the right of the chart, click **Chart Elements** ⊞, and then click to select the **Data Labels** check box. Click the arrow next to **Data Labels**, and then select **Data Callout**.

d. Click **Legend** to clear the check box. This will remove the legend from the pie chart.

e. Click **Chart Elements** ⊞ again to close it, and then click **Save** 🖫.

Troubleshooting

Adding and removing chart elements may alter the position of other elements of your chart. You may need to reposition existing or new elements in the chart to clarify the meaning of the chart.

Modifying Axes

The x-axis and y-axis scales are automatically created through a mathematical algorithm within Excel. However, sometimes the scale needs to be modified as you have already seen. For example, when the scale of numbers is large, a significant gap can exist from 0 to the first data point. In this case, you can modify the scale to start at a more appropriate number instead of 0—the standard minimum value for Excel. When you need to compare two or more charts, the scales must be consistent. Any time you put charts side by side, you need to also make sure your x-axis and y-axis scales are the same. Your audience may not realize otherwise and make incorrect assumptions or decisions. The axis data may also be too crowded, making it difficult to read. In this situation, you would be able to modify the layout of the scale by adjusting the alignment of the data. The data on the axis can be vertical, horizontal, or even placed at an angle.

The Format Axis task pane is used to manually set the axis options for consistency between a set of charts. Under the Axis Options, the default Excel scale minimum and maximums are set automatically based on data. This setting can be changed to allow for customized minimum and maximum values to be applied to the chart. If the source data for the chart is changed, the scale will remain fixed and will not automatically be updated; therefore, any fixed values may also need to be reevaluated as source data changes.

E04.15

 To Modify a Chart Axis

a. Click the **RedesignProject** worksheet tab, and then click the **chart border** of the Gantt Chart.

b. Double-click **Horizontal (Value) Axis** at the top of the chart. This will open the Format Axis task pane to the Axis Options group. Click the **Minimum** box. The value displayed is the Excel serial number for the date 12/27/2014.

c. Delete the existing value, type **7/1/2015** and then press ⌈Enter⌉. Excel will recognize that you have typed a date into the field and translate this into the serial number 42186.

d. Close ⌈**x**⌋ the Format Axis task pane.

> **Troubleshooting**
> If the value you type in any of the Axis Options boxes does not work for your chart, click the Reset button to the right of the box to change the value back to the chart default.

> **SIDE NOTE**
> **Format Task Pane**
> If the Formatting task pane is open, click an element within the chart to activate the corresponding options within the pane.

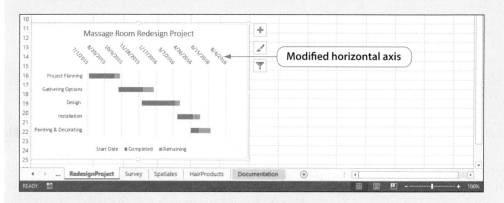

Figure 14   Gantt chart with a modified axis

e. Click **Save** 🖫.

Changing Gridlines

Gridlines are the lines that go across charts to help gauge the size of the bars, columns, or data lines. In Excel, the default is to display the major gridlines—the gridlines at the designated label values, and not to display the minor gridlines—the gridlines between the label values. If the chart is a line or column chart it puts in the horizontal major gridlines while the bar chart puts in vertical major gridlines. The default is a good starting point, but personal preferences can dictate which lines to display. The Format Major Gridlines task pane allows for the customization of gridlines in a chart.

E04.16

 To Modify Gridlines on a Chart

a. Click the **Revenue** worksheet tab, and then click the **chart border** of the line chart.

b. To the right of the chart, click **Chart Elements** +, move the pointer over Gridlines and click the **Gridlines** arrow, and then select **Primary Major Vertical**.

c. Click **Chart Elements** + again to close it.

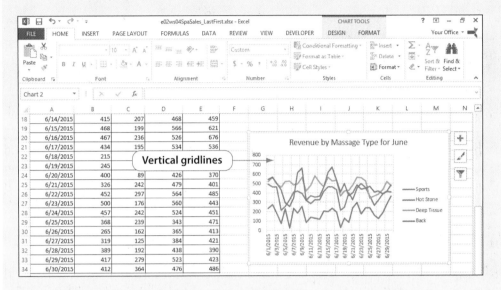

Figure 15   Vertical gridlines added to a line chart

d. Click **Save** 🖫.

Analyzing with Trendlines

A common analysis tool to use within a chart is the trendline. A **trendline** is a line that uses current data to show a trend or general direction of the data. Data, however, can have a variety of patterns. For scatter plots that explore how two variables interact, a linear trend may be seen. If data fluctuates or varies a great deal, it may be more desirable to use a moving average trendline. Instead of creating a straight line based on all the current data, the moving average trendline uses the average of small subsets of data to set short trend segments over time. The moving average trendline will curve and adjust as the data moves up or down.

The trend or pattern of the data may suggest or predict what will happen in the future. For linear trends, the predicted data can be charted using a linear trendline added to a scatter chart and the current trend of the data.

Adding a trendline for the scatter chart on the Survey worksheet data may help confirm the hypothesis that older customers desire a warmer room than younger customers. This may lead the staff to adjust the room temperature prior to a customer arriving. The staff could predict the desired temperature based on the age of the customer. This could help improve customer satisfaction. Again, you may want to consider other demographics— characteristics—of the customers that allow for providing a customized and personalized service that will build customer loyalty and repeat business. It is easier to retain existing customers than find new customers.

For example, the scatter chart on the Survey worksheet shows that as the age of the customer increases so does the temperature of the room they request. Adding a trendline to this chart will further illustrate this relationship.

E04.17

To Insert a Trendline

a. Click the **Survey** worksheet tab, and then click the **chart border** of the scatter chart.

b. To the right of the chart, click **Chart Elements** ⊞, and then click **Trendline**.

c. Click the **Trendline** arrow, and then click **More Options**. In the Format Trendline task pane, click **Fill & Line** ◇.

d. Click the **Dash type** arrow, and then click **Solid** (the first option). Close ⊠ the Format Trendline task pane.

SIDE NOTE
Types of Trendlines
Different types of trendlines can be added to a chart using the Chart Elements button.

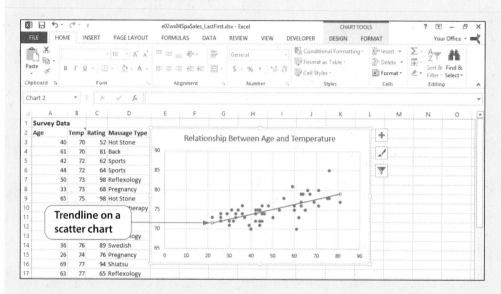

Trendline on a scatter chart

Figure 16 Scatter chart of age and temperature

e. Click **Save** 🖫.

QUICK REFERENCE	Chart Trendlines

The following is a listing of the types of trendlines available within Excel:

- Linear trendline—Adds/sets a linear trendline for the selected chart series

- Exponential trendline—Adds/sets an exponential trendline for the selected chart series

- Linear Forecast trendline—Adds/sets a linear trendline with a two-period forecast for the selected chart series

- Two-Period Moving Average trendline—Adds/sets a two-period moving average trendline for the selected chart series

Trends show patterns over time. When looking at hourly sales at a restaurant, it becomes important to look at more than one day's worth of hourly sales to obtain a better understanding of the trend. Charting multiple days reveals any trends and consistent patterns. For example, maybe it is discovered that on Friday and Saturday, hourly sales are consistently higher than other days of the week. This would suggest a need for scheduling more people to work on those days. If only one day had been charted, or even just one week, the overall weekly trends may have been missed or interpreted incorrectly.

Edit and Format Charts to Add Emphasis

When formatting a chart, it is important to have a plan in mind as to the overall layout and look and feel. With a well-thought-out plan, it will be easy to apply the desired adjustments to the components with regard to position, color, and emphasis. Typically, you can either create a unique layout or modify one of Excel's many layouts. Either way, being able to make formatting changes is easy and a very useful and powerful way to convey information. In this section, you will explore various ways to format a chart.

Adding Color to Chart Objects

Working some color into charts can be helpful from a marketing perspective. Excel offers options that allow changing the interior color as well as the border color. Chart colors can be added to match a company's color scheme or to highlight certain important aspects of the data. Remember, while it is possible to add value to charts with color, it is also possible to overdo it. Irene has mentioned to you that she will be using the pie chart on the Revenue worksheet in a presentation. She would like for you to enhance the visual appeal of the chart before her presentation.

E04.18

 To Change the Coloring of a Chart

a. Click the **Revenue** worksheet tab, and then click the **chart border** of the pie chart.

b. On the **CHART TOOLS DESIGN** tab, in the Chart Styles group, click **Change Colors**, and then in the gallery that appears, select **Color 4** (the fourth option).

c. On the **CHART TOOLS FORMAT** tab, in the Shape Styles group, click **Shape Fill**, and then select **Orange, Accent 6, Lighter 40%**.

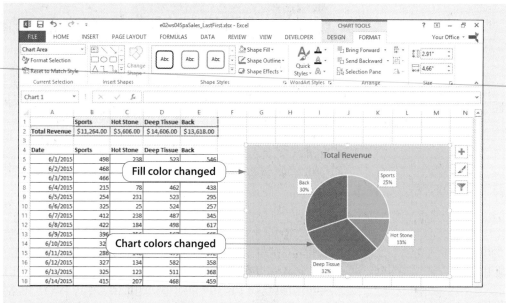

Figure 17 Pie chart with added color

d. Click **Save** 💾.

Working with Text

Whether the text is in a box, title, legend, or axis scale, you can change the formatting of text and the backgrounds of the text objects in charts. The text can be formatted as WordArt, and shapes can be modified to common Shape Styles. The pie chart that was modified with a new color scheme now has a title that is difficult to read. Increasing the font size and bolding the font in the chart title box will address this problem.

E04.19

 To Format Text Within a Chart

a. On the **Revenue** worksheet, if necessary click the **chart border** of the pie chart.

b. Click the **Chart Title**, and then on the **HOME** tab, in the Font group, click **Bold** B. In the Font group, click the **Font Size** `11 ▾` arrow, and then select **16**.

c. Click **Save** 💾.

Exploding Pie Charts

The traditional pie chart is a pie with all the slices together. Preset options offer a pie chart with a slice pulled slightly away from the main pie, or you can manually move a slice outward creating an exploded pie chart. This technique allows for highlighting a particular piece of the pie. As part of her presentation, Irene wants to emphasize the hot stone massage type as it represents the least amount of revenue in the data series. Visual emphasis on this point can be easily created by exploding the slice of the pie chart representing the revenue percentage of hot stone massages.

E04.20

 To Create an Exploding Pie Chart

a. On the **Revenue** worksheet, if necessary click the **chart border** of the pie chart.

b. Click the **plot area**. Notice that the entire pie is selected.

c. Click the **Hot Stone** slice of the pie, and then drag the **slice** slightly to the right.

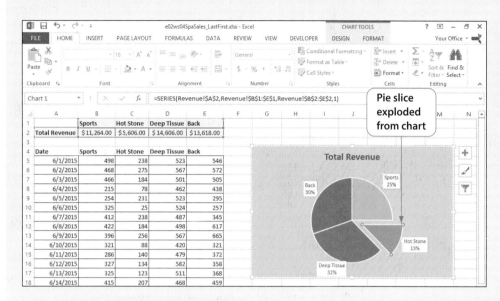

Figure 18   Exploded pie chart

d. Click **Save** 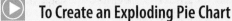.

Changing 3-D Charts and Rotation of Charts

The 3-D effect and rotation of charts is something that should be used conservatively. The effect can be done well, or it can be overused, resulting in a chart that goes overboard and distracts from the intended message. You can choose the 3-D effect when starting to develop a chart. Additionally, options are available to rotate the 3-D effect, giving the chart a crisp distinctive look. The 3-D format can be applied to a variety of objects. The 3-D Rotation setting is intended for the chart area only. The pie chart showing the total revenue by massage type can be enhanced with 3-D effects and rotation.

E04.21

 To Change the Chart Type to 3-D

a. On the **Revenue** worksheet, if necessary click the **chart border** of the pie chart.

b. On the **CHART TOOLS DESIGN** tab, in the Type group, click **Change Chart Type**.

c. In the Change Chart Type dialog box, click the **All Charts** tab, click **3-D Pie**, and then click **OK**.

d. Double-click the **chart area** to open the Format Chart Area task pane. Click **Effects** ⬠, and then click the **3-D ROTATION** arrow to expand the 3-D ROTATION group.

e. Click in the box for **Y Rotation**, delete the existing value, and then type 50. Click in the box for **Perspective**, delete the existing value, and then type 30.

f. Click the **3-D FORMAT** arrow to expand the 3-D FORMAT group. Click the **Top Bevel** arrow, and then select **Cool Slant** in the first row, fourth column. Close [×] the Format Chart Area task pane.

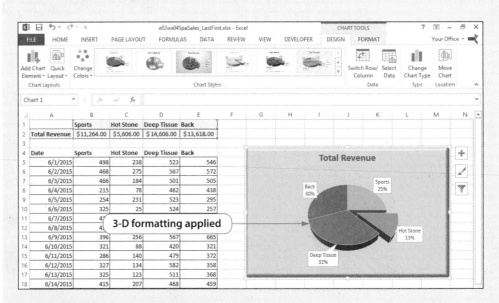

Figure 19 Pie chart with 3-D formatting applied

g. Click **Save** [💾].

| **QUICK REFERENCE** | **Formatting Options for Chart Objects** |

Below are format options for charts and their descriptions:

- Number—Format data as currency, date, time, and so on.
- Fill—Fill the background of a component with a color, picture, or pattern.
- Border Color—Set the color of the border for a component.
- Border Styles—Set the thickness and type of border for a component.
- Shadow—Add shadowing effect to a component.
- Glow and Soft Edges—Add glow and edge effects to a component.
- 3-D Format—Add 3-D effects to component.
- Alignment—Align text direction for a component, such as left, top, vertical, or horizontal.

Effectively Using Charts

The effectiveness of a chart is dependent on the chart type, the layout, and the formatting of the data. Charts should provide clarity and expand the understanding of the data. Charts used in a presentation should support the ideas you want to convey. The charts should highlight key components about an issue or topic being addressed in the presentation. Providing too much information on a chart can confuse or hide the issue being discussed. It can be difficult to get a point across if the chart is confusing, cluttered, or packed with too much information. In this section, you will use sparklines and data bars to emphasize data. You will also recognize and correct confusing charts.

Use Sparklines and Data Bars to Emphasize Data

The same data can be viewed through various perspectives, emphasizing different parts of information. Charts typically do three things:

- Support or refute assertions
- Clarify information
- Help the audience understand trends

Sparklines and data bars are tools in Excel that can accomplish these three goals.

Emphasizing Data

As with any set of data, you can reasonably expect to find multiple ideas that could be emphasized in a chart. Typically within a business, one to three key issues might be chosen for discussion. The idea is to eliminate any extraneous data from the chart that does not pertain to the issues being emphasized. Common methods can be employed to emphasize the idea in the chart. When using a single chart, highlight a particular data set within the chart to help focus attention to a key point. Depending on the chart type, the emphasis may be depicted differently as shown in Table 1.

Single Chart Types	Common Emphasis Methods
Pie chart	Explode a pie slice
Bar/Column	Use an emphasizing color on the bar/column
Line	Line color, weight, and marker size
Scatter	Adding a trendline

Table 1 Emphasis methods for single chart types

Exploring Sparklines

Sparklines are small charts that are embedded into the cells in a worksheet, usually beside the data, to facilitate quick analysis of trends. A sparkline can be used within a worksheet to give an immediate visual trend analysis, and it adjusts as the source data changes. The sparkline can graphically depict the data over time through either a line chart or a bar chart that accumulates the data. Sparklines can also depict data points in the series as a win/loss chart. The default setting is for values above 0 to be a win, while values below 0 are a loss. This value can be modified under the Format tab using the Sparkline Axis button.

Irene and Meda would like to better examine sales of hair products at the spa. They have collected some data for you to analyze from the last eight weeks. Adding sparklines adjacent to the data will emphasize the trend in products over time.

E04.22

 To Insert Sparklines

a. Click the **HairProducts** worksheet tab, and then select the range **A3:A7**.

b. Click the **INSERT** tab, in the Sparklines group, click **Line**. In the Create Sparklines dialog box, in the **Data Range** box, type **C3:N7** and then click **OK**.

c. On the **SPARKLINE TOOLS DESIGN** tab, in the Style group, click the **More** arrow, and then select **Sparkline Style Accent 2, Darker 50%** (first row, second column). The sparklines show the changes in hair products sold over the 12 months represented by the data.

d. Click cell **A1** to deselect the sparklines.

Sparklines inserted into the worksheet

Figure 20   Sparklines applied to hair products data

e. Click **Save** 🖫.

The sparklines show the trend in units of hair products sold over a 12-month time frame by type of product. For example, notice that the sales of the For Men products were steady until Month 7 when they spiked, came back down in month 9, and then spiked again in Month 11. This is very easy to visualize with sparklines next to the data.

QUICK REFERENCE	Working with Sparklines

Using the following process will help in the development of sparklines:

- Select any cell within the added sparklines to display the Sparkline Tools contextual tabs.
- Ungroup sparklines using the Ungroup button on the Sparkline Tools Design tab.
- Group sparklines again using the Group button on the Design tab.
- Change colors and styles using the options available in the Style group.
- Choose to show high or low points using the options in the Show group.

Inserting Data Bars

Data bars are graphic components that are overlaid onto data in worksheet cells. The graphic component is added to a cell and interprets a set of data in a range adjusting the bar and, if necessary, the bar color to help a spreadsheet user gain a quick understanding of the data. Data bars can be applied as a one-color solid fill or a gradient fill from left to right as the numerical value gets bigger.

Data bars are components of the Conditional Formatting feature. This technique can be employed with scores, ratings, or other data where the user would want to do a visual inspection to see a relative scale on the data. Irene and Meda have requested one more enhancement to the hair products analysis you have already begun. They would like a small visual cue added to a list of profits by hair product type. Adding data bars to the profits of all hair products sold at the spa over the past 12 months will provide emphasis on which products were and were not profitable.

E04.23

To Insert Data Bars

a. On the **HairProducts** worksheet, select the range **C10:C14**.

b. Click the **HOME** tab, and then in the Styles group, click **Conditional Formatting**, and then point to **Data Bars**.

c. Under Gradient Fill, select **Green Data Bar** (row one, second option). The inserted data bars clearly show that Conditioner is the highest grossing product while For Men is the lowest grossing product.

d. Click cell **A1** to deselect the data bars.

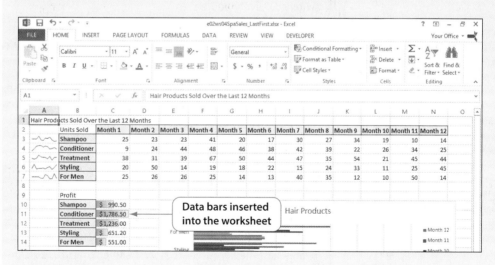

Figure 21   Data bars inserted

e. Click **Save** 💾.

Recognize and Correct Confusing Charts

The process of working with and creating visually appealing charts with clear messages involves recognizing when you have a confusing chart. It is possible to have too much information or ambiguous information. This could include missing labels or legends, or textual information on a chart that is not clear. Additionally, a commonly made error is to use the incorrect chart type when analyzing data.

Correcting a Confusing Chart

Irene has pointed out that on the HairProducts sheet, a clustered bar chart was created that is difficult to interpret. The chart is based on the same data from which you created sparklines. Irene would like to be able to use the chart to compare different lines of product. The chart that was created shows the number of units sold as the bars, with each product having a different bar for each month in the data.

E04.24

To Correct a Confusing Chart

a. On the **HairProducts** worksheet, click the **chart border** of the clustered column chart.

b. On the **CHART TOOLS DESIGN** tab, in the Type group, click **Change Chart Type**. In the Change Chart Type dialog box, on the **All Charts** tab, click **Line**, and then click **OK**.

c. In the **Data** group, click **Switch Row/Column**. Since the data being charted is time sensitive, the time element should be shown on the x-axis.

> **Troubleshooting**
>
> Depending on your data, Excel may suggest a chart with the x- and y-axis already switched, saving you a step.

d. Double-click the **Horizontal (Category) Axis** to open the Format Axis task pane. Click **TEXT OPTIONS**, and then click **Textbox** 🔠.

e. Click in the **Custom angle** box, if necessary delete the existing value, and type 45. Close ✕ the Format Axis task pane.

f. Click the **Chart Title**, click the **formula bar**, and then type =. Click cell **A1**, and then press Enter.

g. To the right of the chart, click **Chart Filters** ▼, and then under SERIES, click **Select All** to deselect all of the product options. Then click only the check boxes for **Shampoo** and **Conditioner**.

> **Troubleshooting**
>
> If the Chart Elements, Chart Styles, and Chart Filter buttons do not automatically appear to the right of the selected chart, use the horizontal scroll bar to create more space to the right of the selected chart. The buttons will only appear if there is enough space beside the chart.

h. Click **Apply**, and then click **Chart Filters** ▼ again to close it. Notice that the lines for these two products do not show similar trends as might be expected.

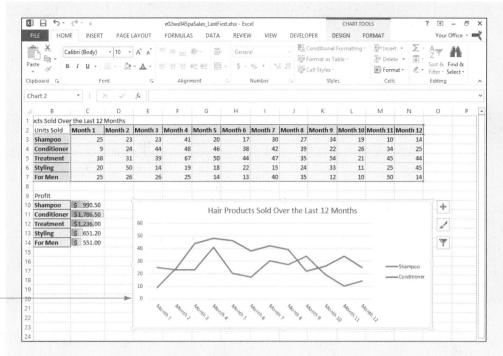

Hair products chart after changes

Figure 22 Corrected line chart

Troubleshooting

If you click the chart to see the source data associated with the chart and only see some of the data selected with a blue border, a chart component might have been clicked by mistake instead of the full chart area. To get the data set associated with the entire chart, under Chart Tools, click the Format tab. In the Current Selection group, change the Chart Element to Chart Area. Data associated with the selected component will be highlighted with a colored border.

---

i. Click **Save** 🖫.

Preparing to Print a Chart

Printing charts uses essentially the same process as printing a worksheet. When printing a chart sheet, select the chart sheet, go through the normal printing process, and adjust print options as you would for a worksheet. The chart will be a full-page display. If the chart is on a regular worksheet, it will be printed if you choose to print everything on the worksheet. In this case, the chart will be the size you developed on the worksheet. This is convenient when you want to print some tables or other data along with the chart. Finally, if you want to print just the chart on the worksheet, select the chart first, then choose the Print Selected Chart print option to print only the current chart.

Another useful technique when exploring data through charts is the ability to create static copies of the chart that can be used to compare with later versions. You can, in essence, take a picture of a chart that will not retain the underlying data. In this manner, subsequent versions of the chart can be made into images for comparisons. The process of creating a picture of the chart is to select the chart, copy it, then use the Paste Special option and paste it as a picture. When pasting as a picture, there are multiple picture format options such as a PNG, JPEG, or GIF files.

These are common issues you should try to avoid in the development of charts.

- Not enough context; users do not understand the chart.
  - Add titles to horizontal and vertical axis.
  - Add a chart title that conveys context of time and scope.
  - Add data labels to show percentages or values of chart elements.
- Too much information is on the chart.
  - Use a subset of the data, rather than all the data.
  - Summarize the data so it is consolidated.
- Incorrect chart type is used.
  - Choose a type more appropriate, such as a line chart for trends.
- Chart has issues with readability.
  - Check the color scheme to ensure text is readable.
  - Check font characteristics such as font type or font size.
  - Move data labels, and remove excess information.
  - Resize the overall chart to provide more area to work.
  - Check the color scheme and formatting so it is professional and does not hide chart information or text.
- Information or labeling is misleading.
  - Check the scaling to ensure it is appropriate and labeled for the correct units.
  - Consider the following wording: Does "Sales" mean the number of transactions or the total revenue?

E04.25

 To Print a Chart

a. On the **HairProducts** worksheet, click the **chart border** of the line chart.

b. On the **FILE** tab, click **Print**. Notice that under Settings, the option for Print Selected Chart is selected by default.

c. Verify that the selected chart fits within the orientation of the page. If necessary, change the orientation of the page to **Landscape Orientation**.

d. Verify that the correct printer—as directed by your instructor—appears on the Printer button. Choices may vary depending on the computer you are using. If the correct printer is not displayed, click the **Printer** button arrow, and then click to choose the correct or preferred printer from the list of available printers. If your instructor asks you to print the document, click the **Print** button.

e. Complete the Documentation worksheet and submit your workbook as directed by your instructor. Click **Save** 🗗, and then close ✖ Excel.

Concept Check

1. What are some important items to consider when choosing the design and layout of a chart? p. 198

2. What are the two possible locations for a chart in Excel? Why would you choose one over the other? p. 202

3. Compare the purpose of a column chart and a pie chart. Give an example scenario for using the two different types of charts. p. 205–208

4. Why is it important to add elements and styles to charts such as titles, legends, and labels? p. 214

5. List two possible ways to add emphasis to an existing chart. p. 223

6. How are sparklines and data bars different from other chart objects in Excel? What are they commonly used for? p. 227–229

7. What are common mistakes that can be made when designing charts? Why is it important to correct these mistakes in existing charts? p. 230

Key Terms

Area chart   211
Argumentation objective   198
Bar chart   208
Chart sheet   202
Column chart   208
Combination chart   213
Data bars   229

Data exploration objective   198
Data point   199
Data series   199
Data visualization   198
Gantt chart   209
Hypothesis testing objective   198
Line chart   207

Pie chart   206
Quick Analysis   202
Recommended Charts   202
Scatter chart   210
Sparkline   227
Trendline   221

Visual Summary

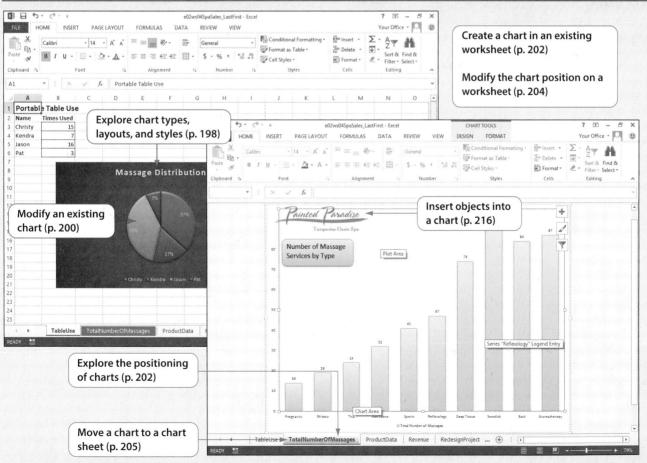

Create a chart in an existing worksheet (p. 202)

Modify the chart position on a worksheet (p. 204)

Explore chart types, layouts, and styles (p. 198)

Modify an existing chart (p. 200)

Insert objects into a chart (p. 216)

Explore the positioning of charts (p. 202)

Move a chart to a chart sheet (p. 205)

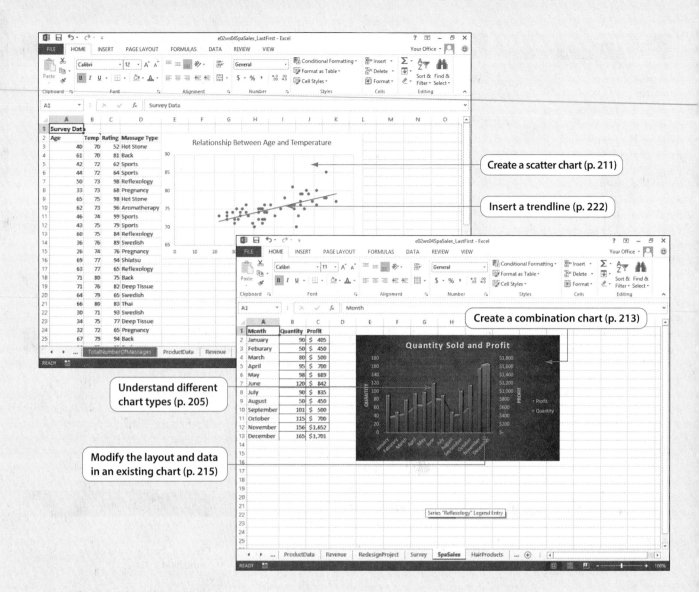

Create a scatter chart (p. 211)

Insert a trendline (p. 222)

Create a combination chart (p. 213)

Understand different chart types (p. 205)

Modify the layout and data in an existing chart (p. 215)

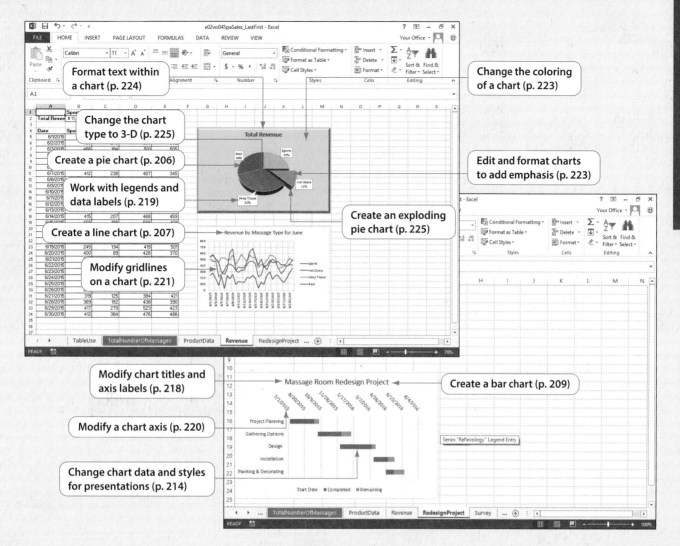

Format text within a chart (p. 224)

Change the coloring of a chart (p. 223)

Change the chart type to 3-D (p. 225)

Create a pie chart (p. 206)

Edit and format charts to add emphasis (p. 223)

Work with legends and data labels (p. 219)

Create a line chart (p. 207)

Create an exploding pie chart (p. 225)

Modify gridlines on a chart (p. 221)

Modify chart titles and axis labels (p. 218)

Create a bar chart (p. 209)

Modify a chart axis (p. 220)

Change chart data and styles for presentations (p. 214)

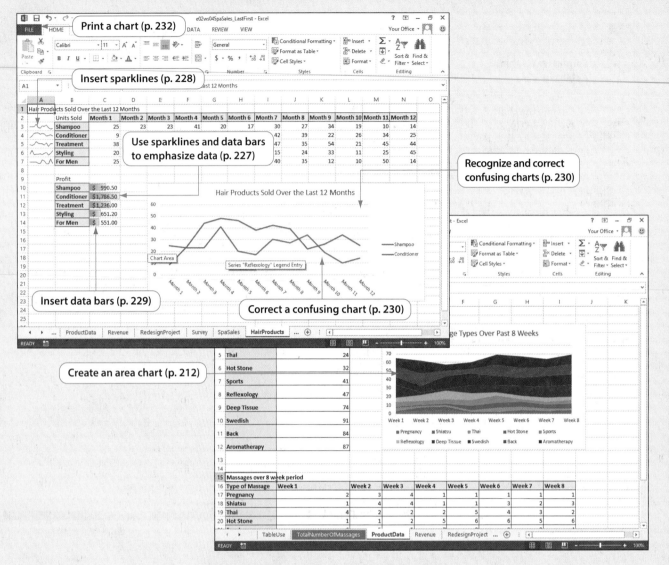

Figure 23   Turquoise Oasis Spa Sales Reports Final Document

Practice 1

Student data file needed:

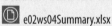 e02ws04Summary.xlsx

You will save your file as:

e02ws04Summary_LastFirst.xlsx

Product Sales Report

Sales & Marketing

Irene Kai and Meda Rodate have pulled together data pertaining to sales by the spa's massage therapists. In addition to massages, the therapists should also promote skin care, health care, and other products. With the monthly data, the managers want a few charts developed that will enable them to look at trends, compare sales, and provide feedback to the therapists. You are to help them create the charts.

a. Open the **e02ws04Summary** workbook. Save its as e02ws04Summary_LastFirst using your last and first.

b. Click the **Projections** worksheet tab, and then select the range **A4:B12**. Click **Quick Analysis**, click **CHARTS**, and then click **Clustered Column**. Click the **chart border**, and position the chart so that the top-left corner is over cell **D4**.

c. Click the **Chart Title**, and then click in the **formula bar**. Type = Projections!$A$1 and then press Enter.

d. To the right of the chart, click **Chart Styles**, and then select **Style 6** from the list. Click Chart Styles again to close the gallery.

e. Double-click the **Vertical (Value) Axis** to open the Format Axis task pane. Click in the **Minimum** box, clear the existing text, and then type 100. Close the Format Axis task pane.

f. Click the **Transactions** worksheet tab. Select the range **B5:J5**, press and hold Ctrl, and then select the range **B10:J10**. On the **INSERT** tab, in the **Charts** group, click the **Insert Pie or Doughnut Chart** arrow. Click **Pie**, the first option under 2-D Pie. Click the **chart border** of the chart, and position the chart so that the top-left corner is over cell **C12**.

g. Click the **Chart Title**, type Total Transactions by Therapist, and then press Enter.

h. To the right of the chart, click **Chart Elements**. Click the **Data Labels** arrow, and then click **More Options**. In the Format Data Labels task pane, under LABEL OPTIONS, under Label Contains, select **Percentage**. Under Label Position, select **Outside End**. Close the Format Data Labels task pane.

i. To the right of the chart, click **Chart Elements**. Click the **Legend** arrow, and then click **Right**.

j. Click the **Pie**—be careful not to click the label text. Click once again on the **red pie slice** for Meda that has the associated label 15, 6%. Drag the slice slightly **to the right** so it is exploded from the rest of the pie.

k. Click the **Revenue** worksheet tab, and then select the range **B10:J10**. Click the **INSERT** tab, and then in the Sparklines group, click **Line** to add sparklines to the worksheet. In the **Data Range** box, type B6:J9 and then click **OK**. Click any **cell** outside of the sparklines to deselect the sparklines.

l. On the INSERT tab, in the Text group, click **Header & Footer**. Under **HEADER & FOOTER TOOLS**, on the **DESIGN** tab, in the **Navigation** group, click **Go to Footer**. Click in the **left footer section**, and then in the **Header & Footer Elements** group, click **File Name**.

m. Click any **cell** on the worksheet to move out of the footer, and then press Ctrl + Home. On the status bar, click **Normal**.

n. Click the **Documentation** worksheet. Click cell **A6**, and then type in today's date. Click cell **B6**, and then type in your first and last name. Complete the remainder of the **Documentation** worksheet according to your instructor's direction.

o. Click **Save**, close Excel, and then submit your file as directed by your instructor.

Problem Solve 1

Homework 1

Research & Development

Student data file needed: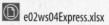

e02ws04Express.xlsx

You will save your file as:

e02ws04Express_LastFirst.xlsx

Express Car Rental

Thomas Reynolds is the corporate buyer for vehicles put into service by Express Car Rental. Tom has the option to buy several lots of vehicles from another rental agency that is downsizing. He wants to get a better idea of the number of rentals nationwide by vehicle type. The corporate accountant has forwarded Tom a worksheet containing rental data for last year. Tom wants to use this summarized data but feels that embedding charts will provide a quicker analysis in a more visual manner for the chief financial officer at their meeting next week.

a. Open **e02ws04Express**, and then save the file as e02ws04Express_LastFirst. Replace LastFirst with your actual name.

b. Use the data on the **AnnualData** worksheet, and create a **3-D Pie** chart of the number of annual rentals for the six car types. Reposition the chart below the monthly data.

c. On the 3-D pie chart, change the title to Annual Rentals. Change the font of the title to **Arial Black**, **16** pt, and **bold**. Adjust the data labels on the pie chart to include the **category name** and **percentage** only. Position the label information outside of the chart. Change the font size of the labels to **8** and apply **bold**. Delete the legend.

d. On the pie chart, explode the slice of the chart that represents the auto type with the **lowest percentage of annual rentals**.

e. Increase the data used in the column chart to include the months of **July**, **August**, and **September**.

f. Select the **clustered column** chart located below the monthly data. Change the chart type to **Line with Markers**. Switch the row and column data so that the months **July to December** are represented on the x-axis.

g. Change the chart style to **Style 6**. On the line chart, add **primary major vertical grid lines**. Change the chart title to Rentals by Auto Type for July to December.

h. Create a **3-D clustered column** chart using the data for the **Semi-Annual Totals** for all auto types on the AnnualData worksheet. The primary horizontal axis should be the auto types.

i. Move the 3-D column chart from the AnnualData worksheet to a chart sheet, and then name that sheet SemiAnnualReport. If necessary, add the chart title Semi-Annual Total to the chart. Adjust the 3-D Rotation of the chart to the following.
- X Rotation of **20**
- Y Rotation of **15**
- Perspective of **15**

j. Reposition the **SemiAnnualReport** worksheet after the AnnualData worksheet.

k. Complete the **Documentation** worksheet according to your instructor's direction. Insert the **filename** in the left custom footer section of the Header/Footer tab in the Page Setup dialog box on all worksheets in the workbook.

l. Click Save, close Excel, and then submit the file as directed by your instructor.

Perform 1: Perform in Your Career

Student data file needed:

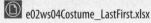 e02ws04Costume.xlsx

You will save your file as:

e02ws04Costume_LastFirst.xlsx

Costume Sales

Sales & Marketing

You work for a costume store. The store has recently compiled a summary of units sold and profit over the past year. Adding some charts to the worksheet would help them to better understand their customer demands and sales trends. The store would like you to visually represent the monthly units sold and the profit so the managers can visually identify any instances where units sold and profit do not correspond.

a. Open **e02ws04Costume**, and then save the file as e02ws04Costume_LastFirst. Replace LastFirst with your actual name.

b. Create a combination chart to the right of the monthly sales data. Represent the number of costumes sold as a column chart and profit as a line chart. Plot the profit data on a secondary axis.

c. Apply a **style** to the chart, and then add an appropriate chart title. Include a legend to describe the data being charted.

d. Adjust the primary vertical axis to have a minimum of 170 and the secondary vertical axis to have a minimum of 3000.

e. Create an appropriate chart under the combination chart that visually depicts the percentage of the number of costumes sold by each costume type. Apply **3-D** formatting to the chart and label appropriately.

f. Superhero costumes should be the largest percentage of sales in the data. Emphasize this in the chart by changing the presentation of the chart item that represents Superhero costumes sold.

g. Apply data bars to the Profit data for Costume Type to visualize the profit by costume type. Choose any gradient fill color.

h. Complete the **Documentation** worksheet according to your instructor's direction. Insert the **filename** in the left custom footer section of the Header/Footer tab in the Page Setup dialog box on all worksheets in the workbook.

i. Click Save, close Excel, and then submit the file as directed by your instructor.

Additional
Cases

Additional Workshop Cases are available on the companion website and in the instructor resources.

MODULE CAPSTONE

More Practice 1

Student data file needed:

 e02mpSales.xlsx

You will save your file as:

e02mpSales_LastFirst.xlsx

Restaurant Marketing Analysis

Sales & Marketing

The accounting system at the Indigo5 Restaurant tracks data on a daily basis that can be used for analysis to gauge its performance and determine needed changes. The restaurant is considering entering into a long-term agreement with a poultry company and getting a new refrigeration unit to store the chicken. If Indigo5 enters the agreement, the poultry company agrees to give Indigo5 a substantial discount for a specified period of time. Management would like to stimulate sales for the lowest revenue producing chicken item and any chicken items not meeting a sale performance threshold. Thus, some of this savings will be passed to the guests by placing these chicken items on sale.

a. Start **Excel**, and then open **e02mpSales**.

b. Save the file as e02mpSales_LastFirst, using your last and first name.

c. Click the **Indigo5ChickenSales** worksheet, and then click cell **D2**. Type =TODAY() and then press Enter.

   Notice the data on the worksheet. The range A13:E18 contains four months of actual sales quantities for each menu item. Whereas, the range A22:E27 contains the sales projections that Indigo5 made for the same four months prior to the start of each month.

d. Click cell **B4**, type =SUM(B22:E22) and then press Ctrl+Enter. In cell **B4**, double-click the **AutoFill** handle to automatically fill cell range **B4:B9**. The range now returns the total quantity projection over the four months for each item.

e. Click cell **C4**, type =SUM(B13:E13) and then press Ctrl+Enter. In cell **C4**, double-click the **AutoFill** handle to automatically fill cell range **C4:C9**. The range now returns the total quantity of actual sales over the four months for each item.

f. Click cell **D4**, type =AVERAGE(B13:E13) and then press Ctrl+Enter. In cell **D4**, double-click the **AutoFill** handle to automatically fill cell range **D4:D9**. The range now returns the average monthly quantity for actual sales over the four months for each item.

g. Now you need to determine the price for each item to use in revenue calculations. Notice a list of menu prices is in cells A30:B44. Select the range **A30:B44**. Click the **Name** box, type Prices and then press Enter. The price listing is now named Prices to use in later calculations.

h. Click cell **E4**, type =VLOOKUP(A4,Prices,2,FALSE) and then press Ctrl+Enter. In cell **E4**, double-click the **AutoFill** handle to automatically fill the cell range **E4:E9**. The range now returns the price of each item by looking up the item and exactly matching the item name in the Prices list.

i. Click cell **F4**, type =E4*C4 and then press Ctrl+Enter. In cell **F4**, double-click the **AutoFill** handle to automatically fill cell range **F4:F9**. The range now returns the total revenue for each item.

j. Now you need to determine whether the item fell short or exceeded the sales projection.

Click cell **G4**, type =ROUND(C4/B4,2) and then press Ctrl+Enter. In cell **G4**, double-click the **AutoFill** handle to automatically fill cell range **G4:G9**. The range now returns a projection percentage. An item that fell short of the sales projection will be under 100%. An item that exceeded the sales projection will be over 100%.

k. Now you need to determine what item has the highest revenue. Click cell **H4**, type =IF(F4=MAX($F$4:$F$9),"Best Item","") and then press Ctrl+Enter. In cell **H4**, double-click the **AutoFill** handle to automatically fill cell range **H4:H9**. The range now returns a blank for all items except the one with the highest sales revenue—which returns Best Item.

l. Now you need to determine which items to put on sale to stimulate sales. An item should be put on sale if its % of Projection is less than the Sale Threshold in cell L4. An item should also be put on sale if its sales revenue is the lowest. Click cell **I4**, type =IF(OR (G4<$L$4,G4=MIN($F$4:$F$9)),"Put on Sale","") and then press Ctrl+Enter. In cell **I4**, double-click the **AutoFill** handle to automatically fill cell range **I4:I9**.

   The range now returns Put on Sale for two items—the item with the lowest sales revenue and two items with a % of Projection less than 95%. All other items return a blank.

m. Now you need to how many days the sale will last based on dates given by the poultry company. Click cell **L7**, type =DATEDIF(L5,L6,"d") and then press Ctrl+Enter.

n. Select the range **B13:E18**. Click the **INSERT** tab, and then in the Sparklines group, click **Line**. Select the location range **F13:F18**, and then click **OK**. Click the **DESIGN** tab, and then in the Show group, click the **Markers** check box.

o. Now you need to create a chart comparing the percentage of all sales each item represents.
   Select the range **A3:A9**. Press and hold Ctrl, and then select the range **F3:F9**.

   • Click the **INSERT** tab, and then in the Charts group, click the **arrow** next to the Insert Pie or Doughnut Chart button. Select the first option for a **Pie Chart**.

   • Click the **chart border**, and then drag to move the chart so the top-left corner is over the top-left corner of cell **G10**. Click on the **right resizing handle**, and then drag the right chart border to the border between columns **L** and **M**. Click the **bottom resizing handle**, and then move the bottom of the chart to the border between rows **22** and **23**.

   • On the DESIGN tab, in the Chart Styles group, select **Style 3**.

   • Click the chart title, **Total Revenue**. Click a second time on **Total Revenue** to place your cursor into the title. Erase "Total Revenue", and then type Chicken Sales Revenue by Menu Item.

p. Now you need to look at loan options for the new refrigeration unit. Click the **Poultry Loan** worksheet tab.

q. You need to look at a quarterly payment as it varies for different numbers of payments—or terms in years—and the annual interest rate. Indigo5 would like to make quarterly payments—four payments per year. Click cell **C12**, and type =-PMT($B12/4,C$11*4,$C$6) and then press Ctrl+Enter. In cell **C12**, double-click the **AutoFill** handle to automatically fill cell range **C12:C14**. With C12:C14 selected, drag the **AutoFill** handle to column **E** to fill the range **C12:E14**.

   Notice that the mixed cell addressing of the $ before the B will make the B stay the same and not change when copied—same for the $ before the 11. Notice that when copied, the formula will always contain $C$6 since it has an absolute reference of a $ before both the column and the row.

r. Indigo5 would like to use the option that keeps the payment under $2,000, has the shortest term, and the lowest interest rate. Click cell **D12**, and then click the **Bold** button to indicate that option as the best.

s. Click the **Indigo5ChickenSales** worksheet tab. Click the **PAGE LAYOUT** tab, and then in the Page Setup group, click the **Page Setup Dialog Box Launcher**. Click the **Header/Footer** tab. Click **Custom** Footer, then click the **Insert File Name** button to place the file name in the left section of the footer. Click **OK** twice. Repeat this step for the **PoultryLoan** worksheet.

t. Click the **Documentation** worksheet. Click cell **A6**, and then type in today's date. Click cell **B6**, and then type in your first and last name. Complete the remainder of the **Documentation** worksheet according to your instructor's direction.

u. Click **Save**, close Excel, and then submit your file as directed by your instructor.

Problem Solve 1

Human Resources

MyITLab®
Grader
Homework 1

Student data file needed:
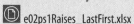 e02ps1Raises.xlsx

You will save your file as:
e02ps1Raises_LastFirst.xlsx

Employee Raise Evaluation

Painted Paradise Resort & Spa evaluates employee performance yearly and determines raises. You have been asked to assist with compiling and analyzing the data. Upper management also started the workbook. You are to finish the document and keep the data confidential.

a. Start **Excel**, and then open **e02ps1Raises**. Save the file as e02ps1Raises_LastFirst.

b. The **Addresses** worksheet includes data from the payroll database. You need to cleanse the data so this worksheet can be used in a mail merge to create salary notice letters. Add the following.

- In column **E**, extra spaces and a dash were left in the data by the database in case the zip code had an extension. In cells **F7:F14**, enter a LEFT function to return the ZipCode without the unnecessary "–".

- In column **G**, the database did not export the formatting for the phone numbers. In cells **H7:H14**, use Flash Fill to add formatting back to the phone number. If done correctly, cell H7 will return **(505) 555-1812**. Hint: There is only one space between the ")" and the 5.

c. The **Evaluations** worksheet includes evaluation data collated from various managers. Managers rated employees both quantitatively—numerically—and qualitatively—written notes. The number scores and notes support the raise recommendation made by the manager. Add the following.

- In cells **I3:I10**, calculate the average numerical ratings for each employee. Only managers get evaluated by the Leadership rank in column **H**. Column **C** indicates whether the employee is a manager. Thus, the average calculation should only include the values in column **H** if the employee is a manager. Even if a rating is given to a non-manager employee in column **H**, that number should not be included in the average in column **I**. Hint: This calculation requires the use of an IF statement.

- In cells **B13:B20**, exported data from the rating system combines the manager's raise recommendation of High, Standard, or Low followed by the manager's notes. In cells **J3:J10**, use a combination of text functions to return just the manager's raise recommendation—High, Standard, or Low. The values returned should not have extra spaces before or after the word. Hint: The names in A3:A10 are in the same order as A13:A20. Also, notice the text pattern is always the recommendation followed by a space.

- For use later, give the range **A3:J10** the name evaluations.

d. On the **Payroll** worksheet, there is an analysis for raises you need to finish. First, you need to get all the applicable data to making the raise determination on this worksheet. Add the following.

- In cell **F1**, enter a formula to always return the current date.
- In cells **E6:E13**, add a DATEDIF function that will calculate the years employed based on today's date in cell F1 and the HireDate in column **B**.
- In cells **F6:F13**, add a VLOOKUP function that returns the raise recommendation— High, Standard, or Low—for each employee by exactly matching the Name in column **A** in the range you named **evaluations**.
- In cells **G6:G13**, add a VLOOKUP function that returns the starting raise percentage based on the ranges in the Standard Raise table in cells **A16:B19** and the number of years employed in column **E**.

e. On the **Payroll** worksheet, you now need to begin determining the employee's final raise. Add the following.

- In cells **H6:H13**, add an IF function that will award anyone with a Raise Recommend of High an extra bonus listed in cell **F2**. All other employees get zero bonus.
- In cells **I6:I13**, add an IF function that will give anyone with a Raise Recommend of Low a deduction listed in cell **F3**. All other employees get zero deduction.
- In cells **J6:J13**, add a calculation that returns the final raise amount with the value— not just formatted—rounded to the hundreds position. For example, a final raise of $1,625 rounded to the hundreds returns a value of $1,600. The final raise amount is the salary multiplied by the Standard Raise % and then adding any bonus and subtracting any deduction. Hint: The num_digits argument will need to be negative.
- In cells **K6:K13**, add a calculation that returns the Final % Increase. The final increase is determined by dividing the Raise Amt by the Salary.
- In cells **L6:L13**, add a calculation that returns the New Salary by adding the Salary and Raise Amt.

f. On the **Payroll** worksheet, you now need to add a few summary measures for upper management. Add the following.

- In cell **J1**, add a function that calculates the Net Payroll Increase based on the Raise Amt in cells **J6:J13**.
- In cell **J2**, add a function that calculates the Average Raise % based on the Final % Increase in cells **K6:K13**.
- Based on the data in cells **A5:A13** and **K5:K13**, add a **3-D Clustered Column**. Hint: Use Ctrl to select noncontiguous ranges for the chart.
- Under chart styles, set the chart to **Style 3**. Change the vertical axis to start at a lower bound of 0.01—for 1%. Then, change the title to read Final % Increase Comparison.
- Move and resize the chart so the upper-left corner is in cell **F14** and the lower-right corner is in cell **L22**. Set the chart title to **11** pt font. Set the vertical and horizontal axis labels to **9** pt font.

g. Complete the **Documentation** worksheet according to your instructor's direction. Insert the filename in the left custom footer section of the Header/Footer tab in the Page Setup dialog box on all worksheets in the workbook.

h. Click Save, close Excel, and then submit the file as directed by your instructor.

Student data file needed:

 e02ps2Advertising.xlsx

You will save your file as:

e02ps2Advertising_LastFirst.xlsx

MyITLab®
Grader
Homework 2

Sales &
Marketing

Advertising Review

The Painted Paradise Resort & Spa has been investing in advertising using different advertising media. When guests check in, the employee asks the guest how they heard about Painted Paradise Resort & Spa. Based on the customer's response, the employee then notes in the system either magazine, radio, television, Internet, word of mouth, or other. Since almost every guest is asked, the number surveyed represents a significant portion of the actual guests. The past year's data is located on the GuestData worksheet. Every time a guest answers an advertising source—such as a magazine—as how he or she heard about the resort, it is considered a guest result. Ideally, the resort wants to purchase advertising at a low cost but then see as many guest results as possible.

Every year, upper management sets the advertising budget before the beginning of the fiscal year—July 1 start. For this next year, upper management gave you more television budget because of a new video marketing campaign. Also, the advertising contracts get negotiated every year, as the media vendors require a one-year commitment. The contracts are negotiated after the budget is set. You will develop charts for an upcoming presentation that will discuss a marketing strategy, potential changes to the budget given the new media prices, anticipated monthly guest results, and prospects of hiring a marketing consulting company with a high retainer that would require a loan.

a. Start Excel, and then open **e02ps2Advertise**. Save the file as e02ps2Advertise_LastFirst.

b. On the **GuestData** worksheet in the cells **A6:J17**, the data indicates the number of guests responding that he or she heard of the resort from the listed method—Guest Results. Add the following.

- In cell **H2**, add a COUNTA function to determine the number of months listed in cells A6:A17.

- In cell **J2**, add a DATEDIF to calculate the survey duration in years using the 2014 Fiscal Start date and 2015 Fiscal Start date.

- In cells **B6:B17**, use Flash Fill to return the three character code for the month—JUL for July.

- Select cells **L6:M17**, and then name the range season.

- In cells **C6:C17**, add a VLOOKUP that will exactly match the month in column **B** to return the correct season—Low, Mid, or High—based off the named range **season**.

- In cells **D19:J19**, calculate the averages for each column with a rounded value—not just formatted—to zero decimal places.

- For later use, create the following named ranges.

Cell	Name
D19	AvgMagazine
E19	AvgRadio
F19	AvgTelevision
G19	AvgInternet

c. On the **AdvertisingPlan** worksheet, an analysis of past Guest Results and the new budget has been started. First, you need to finish out the past year analysis. Add the following.

- In cell **F2**, enter a function that will return the current date.

- Set the following cells to these formulas.

Cell	Name
D6	=AvgMagazine
D7	=AvgRadio
D8	=AvgTelevision
D9	=AvgInternet

* Note that these are monthly averages. Thus all calculations on this worksheet are estimates based on the monthly average.

- In cells **E6:E9**, calculate the Amount Spent—this is a monthly figure—by multiplying the Cost Per Ad and the Ads Placed.
- In cells **F6:F9**, calculate the Cost per Guest Result by dividing the Amount Spent by the Past Guest Results.
- In cells **C10:F10**, calculate the appropriate totals for each column.

d. On the **AdvertisingPlan** worksheet, you need to finish out the new budget year analysis. Add the following.

- In cells **I6:I9**, calculate the Number of Ads that can be purchased based off the New Budget and the New Cost Per Ad in columns **G** and **H**. Hint: A partial ad cannot be purchased. Further, $324 would not be enough to purchase one radio ad since the cost per ad is $325.
- In cells **J6:J9**, calculate the Amount to Spend—this is a monthly figure—by multiplying the New Cost Per Ad and the Ads to Place.
- In cells **G10** and **I10:J10**, calculate the appropriate totals for each column. If necessary, change the format for cell I10 to general.
- In cell **H11**, calculate the amount of the budget remaining by subtracting the Amount to Spend total from the New Budget total. Note, the totals are in row 10. A negative number indicates the new plan is over budget. A positive number indicates the new plan is under budget and has excess spendable funds.
- In cells **K6:K9**, add a formula that will return Increase? if the Ads to Place is equal to zero or if the New Cost Per Ad is less than or equal to the Budget +/- in cell H11. Any others should return Decrease?. This column now indicates the media types for which the resort may want to consider an increase or decrease to the Ads to Place—along with any necessary budget adjustment.
- In cells **L6:L9**, calculate the Anticipated Guest Results by dividing the Amount to Spend by the Cost per Guest Result—column F. The resulting value—not the just the format—should be rounded to zero decimals.
- In cell **L10** calculate the appropriate total for Anticipated Guest Results.
- In cell **L11**, calculate the amount of anticipated guest results compared to the past by subtracting the Past Guest Results total from the Anticipated Guest Results total. Note, the totals are in row 10. A negative number indicates an anticipated decrease in Guest Results. A positive number indicates an anticipated increase in Guest Results.
- Evaluate the statements in cells **H15:L18**. Bold any false statements.

e. Starting on the **AdvertisingPlan** worksheet, you need to make two charts for your presentation. Create the following two charts.

- Based on the data in cells **A5:A9**, **D5:D9**, and **L5:L9**, add a **3-D Clustered Column** chart. Hint: Use Ctrl to select noncontiguous ranges for the chart.
- Under chart styles, set the chart to **Style 6**. Then, change the title to read PAST V. ANTICIPATED MONTHLY GUEST RESULTS.
- Move and resize the chart so the upper-left corner is in cell **A11** and the lower-right corner is in cell **F22**. Set the chart title to **12** pt font.

- Based on the data in cells **A5:A9**, **D5:D9**, and **E5:E9**, add a **Clustered Column - Line on Secondary Axis Combo Chart**. Hint: Use ⎡Ctrl⎤ to select noncontiguous ranges for the chart. Make this chart appear on its own worksheet—chart sheet—named GuestResultsBySpending.

- Under chart styles, set the chart to **Style 6**. Then, change the title to read Past Advertising Amount Spent compared to # of Guest Results Experienced, monthly.

- Set the chart title to **16** pt font, set all axis data labels to **18** pt font, and then set all legend text to **12** pt font.

f. On the **MarketingConsultants** worksheet, a monthly loan payment analysis has been started. The resort is considering hiring marketing consultants. However, they require a large up-front retainer fee. The resort would need to take out a loan to cover the cost. The resort needs an analysis of the loan payment by varying interest rate and down payment amount. Add the following.

- In cells **D10:H13**, add a **PMT** function to calculate the monthly payment. Enter one formula that can be entered in cell **D10** and filled to the remaining cells. Hint: Think carefully about where $ signs are needed for mixed and absolute cell addressing. Also, the down payment can be subtracted from the Retainer—or Principal—Amount in the third argument of the PMT function.

g. Complete the **Documentation** worksheet according to your instructor's direction. Insert the **filename** in the left custom footer section of the Header/Footer tab in the Page Setup dialog box on all worksheets in the workbook.

h. Click Save, close Excel, and then submit the file as directed by your instructor.

Perform 1: Perform in Your Life

Student data file needed:

 Blank Excel workbook

You will save your file as:

e02pf1Ideal_LastFirst.xlsx

Your Ideal Career Start

Human Resources

Even if this is your first semester, you have probably already begun to think about the type of job or career you want. Further, when you are studying long hours, it can be fun to imagine the new car you might buy at your ideal career start after graduation. For this project, pretend—if you need to—that you are graduating this semester. In this project, you need to find currently available jobs and establish criteria to help you pick your most desired position. Then, you will find the ideal new car to purchase, but your new position's salary must be able to afford the monthly payment.

a. Open a blank Excel workbook. Save the workbook as e02pf1Ideal_LastFirst. Apply a **Theme**, and then use cell styles where appropriate. Keep the workbook professional, but feel free to optionally add elements such as a picture of your ideal career start or new car.

b. Create a worksheet named JobData. Go to the Internet, and then find five or more jobs that interest you. You can grab positions from multiple websites or just one website— from the same website will be easiest. Copy and paste that data into the **JobData**. On the JobData worksheet, accomplish the following.

- The goal is to get separate columns of data listed below by copying from the Internet and separating—or cleaning—the data using Excel's Flash Fill feature and/or text functions. Depending on how you copy and paste from the web, this will be harder or easier. You can gather more data than listed below if it is relevant for you to picking the ideal job. At a minimum, you must have the following.

Data (no extra characters in or around the data)	Description
Company Name	Full name as you would address a letter to the company
Job Title	Full job title and needs to be descriptive of the position. For example, "Entry Level" is not a sufficient title. "Application Support Analyst— Entry Level" is a sufficient title.
State	State position is located in. State should be in a column by itself, not in combination with the city or address.
Pay or Pay Range	Salary or hourly rate. If a pay range is provided, separate out the low and high end of the range separately. Hint: Try not to mix pay types. For example, if you are looking for a salary position, choose all salary positions.

Table 1 Required minimum job position data

- Add headers, comments, and/or notes to make clear to your instructor what Excel steps you took to get to the final job data. Leave all formulas you create in the worksheet— show your work, and don't delete it. Indicate where Flash Fill was used. Keep your work organized.
- Indicate on the worksheet the website you used to find the job posting, for example Monster.com or CareerBuilder.com. Also, indicate the date and your full name on the worksheet somewhere.

c. Create another worksheet called JobAnalysis. In an organized fashion, copy onto the worksheet only the clean copies of data that you intend to use. Add the following elements to this worksheet.

- Use an IF statement in combination with any other Excel formulas/functions to indicate whether a job is in a state you find desirable. You should indicate a minimum of two states as desirable.
- Create a table that establishes pay range categories for Below Expected, Expected, and Above Expected based on your personal job expectations. Use this table in a VLOOKUP to determine which category for each of the positions you are evaluating.
- Add any other additional formulas and functions to help you determine the most desirable position.
- The worksheet must ultimately indicate one final Most Desired job position.

d. Create another worksheet called MyNewCar. Add the following elements to this worksheet.

- Cells that indicate the following information about the car you would like: Manufacturer, Model, Year, Price, and URL to a webpage that provides this information. You may pick a preowned car if you indicate that on the worksheet.
- A loan analysis for a monthly payment. Your monthly payment will vary by the price of the car, down payment, term or number of payments, and annual interest rate. Research realistic current interest rates for the type of car you wish to purchase. Your analysis should evaluate various options for two of the following: interest rate, term, or down payment.
- Somewhere on the worksheet, calculate or input the monthly income from your Most Desired job on the JobAnalysis worksheet.
- You need to be able to afford the car you pick. The amount you will be able to afford will vary greatly on individual circumstances—such as marital status, credit card debt, and homeowner status. For the purposes of this project, the car you pick cannot have a monthly payment greater than 10% of your gross—pretaxes or deductions—salary for your Most Desired job. Create an analysis of the percentage your loan payment represents of your monthly salary. Bold or otherwise indicate feasible loan options. If none of the loan options are under 10%, you will have to do one or a combination of the following: pick a new car, increase your down payment, extend your term, or find a lower interest rate.

e. Build at least one meaningful chart on either the JobAnalysis or MyNewCar worksheet. Include at least a one-sentence explanation near the chart explaining the chart's significance.

f. Complete the **Documentation** worksheet according to your instructor's direction. Insert the **filename** in the left custom footer section of the Header/Footer tab in the Page Setup dialog box on all worksheets in the workbook.

g. Save your work, and then close Excel. Submit the file as directed by your instructor.

Perform 2: Perform in Your Career

Student data file needed:

e02pf2Investment.xlsx

You will save your file as:

e02pf2Investment_LastFirst.xlsx

Investment Portfolios

Finance & Accounting

You have started working as an investment intern for a financial company that helps clients invest in the stock market. Your manager gives you a spreadsheet detailing some periodic investments in Nobel Energy, Inc. (NBL) made by one of the clients. The client would like a report and charts on the NBL investment and the stock's performance. Your manager has asked you to finish this report.

a. Open workbook **e02pf2Investment**. Save the workbook as **e02pf2Investment_LastFirst**. Apply a **theme**, and then use cell styles where appropriate for a professional looking spreadsheet.

b. On the NBLInvestment worksheet, add the following calculations.

- In column **F**, a formula to calculate total value was already entered by your manager. Update the formula to return a value of only two decimals. Hint: The cell value needs to change, which is different than merely formatting to two decimals.

- In column G, starting in the second row—cell **G22**—enter a formula to sum up the quarterly investments as of the date in column A to provide a cumulative total. For example, cell G22 should return the sum of the Quarterly investments on 1/2/2013 and 4/1/2013. Next, cell G23 should return the sum of the Quarterly investments on 1/2/2013, 4/1/2013, and 7/1/2013. Thus, column G returns a running total of investments so that the last cell—G33—reflects the total of all investments from 1/2/2013 thru 1/3/2016.

- In column **H**, calculate the total growth. If total value is more than 0, then total growth is total value – total investment. Otherwise, the total growth is either 0 or a negative value. A negative value means that the investment shrunk instead of grew.

- In column **I**, calculate the total growth %: if total value is more than 0, then total growth % is total growth / total investment; otherwise, the total growth % is 0.

- In column **J**, calculate the quarterly growth: if total value is more than 0, then quarterly growth is total growth—total growth from the previous quarter; otherwise, quarterly growth is 0.

- In column **K**, calculate quarterly growth %: if total value is more than 0, then quarterly growth % is quarterly growth / total investment; otherwise, quarterly growth % is 0.

c. Create a **combo chart** for Total Portfolio Performance that displays the Total Value, Total Investment and Total Growth % over time. Hint: You will need to show a secondary axis for Total Growth %.

d. Create a **combo chart** for Quarterly Performance that displays the Quarterly Growth and the Quarterly Growth % over time. Hint: You will need to show a secondary axis for Quarterly Total Growth %.

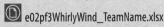

e. Complete the **Documentation** worksheet according to your instructor's direction. Insert the **filename** in the left custom footer section of the Header/Footer tab in the Page Setup dialog box on all worksheets in the workbook.

f. Save your work, and then close Excel. Submit the file as directed by your instructor.

Perform 3: Perform in Your Team

Student data file needed:

 e02pf3WhirlyWind.xlsx

You will save your file as:

e02pf3WhirlyWind_TeamName.xlsx

Theme Park Expansion

Production & Operations

You work for Whirly Wind Theme Park—a preeminent amusement park next to a large lake. Whirly Wind is primarily a thrill and roller-coaster park. While Whirly Wind has a water section in the park, it is small and outdated. Your manager assigned you to a team to help with the analysis for an expansion of the park's water area and overall capacity. Your manager needs help looking at past sales, sales trends, loan options, and project management. Your manager has provided you with a starting workbook that needs work and elaboration.

a. Select one team member to set up the document by completing Steps b–d.

b. Open your browser and navigate to either **https://www.skydrive.live.com**, **https://www.drive.google.com**, or any other instructor assigned location. Be sure all members of the team have an account on the chosen system—such as a Microsoft or Google account.

c. Open **e02pf3WhirlyWind**, and then save the file as e02pf3WhirlyWind_TeamName replacing TeamName with the name assigned to your team by your instructor.

d. Share the spreadsheet with the other members of your team. Make sure that each team member has the appropriate permission to edit the document.

e. Hold a team meeting and discuss the requirements of the remaining steps. Make an action and communication plan. Consider which steps can be done independently and which steps require completion of prior steps before starting.

f. On the **RevenueHistory** worksheet, you will find data about past revenue—earned income before any costs. Whirly Wind is only open from the first of April until the end of October every year. Whirly Wind is located in the Midwest of the United States with typical Midwest weather. Whirly Wind offers discounted season passes during the month of April and October every year. Below is a description of the provided data.

Data	Description
Month	The first day of the month for the data in that row.
Monthly Revenue	All revenue from all sources for that month—April through October.
Attendance	The number of guests that entered the park that month. The guests may have been paid guests or season pass/comp guests who did not have to pay. Attendance is not reflective of time spent in the park. If a guest leaves and comes back into the park, the guest is still only counted once. The Max Monthly Capacity is also listed in cell J4.
Ticket Sales (Any Kind)	All ticket sales that month. This includes single day, multiple day, and all variations of a season pass. If a guest buys a season pass in April, the revenue is accounted for in April. However, the guest can still enter the park from May to October of that year without adding any money to the monthly ticket sales.
Food & Merch Sales	All other revenue besides ticket sales. This is primarily food and merchandise. However, it also includes a few other things such as parking.
Avg Temp (Degrees)	The average temperature for the park that particular month.

Table 2 Whirly Wind revenue data

g. The data on the **RevenueHistory** worksheet could be analyzed in several ways. At a minimum, add the following to the worksheet.
- Calculations for appropriate averages, mode for attendance, and average ticket cost per guest in attendance that month.
- Each team member should independently create 1–2 charts about the data on this worksheet.
- The team should meet and decide which charts to include in the final file. The final file should have a minimum of four charts and a maximum of six charts. The team should pick the charts that provide insight into the sales trends of the park.

h. On the **Loan** worksheet, you will find the basic information about three loan options to finance Whirly Wind's expansion. Make the following updates to the loan worksheet.
- In column **F**, calculate the loan—or funding—needed to do the expansion.
- In column **G**, calculate the cost per extra capacity—or amount per extra guest attendance based off the total cost in column **D**.
- In column **H**, research and provide current interest rates applicable to these three loan options.
- Below row **7**, add a loan analysis to provide the monthly payment amount for the three loan options. Whirly Wind is considering a term of 2, 3, or 5 years only.
- Below row **7**, add an analysis indicating which loan options are Ideal or Not Preferred. If the loan meets Whirly Wind's Preferences in columns J:L, the loan is Ideal. Any loan not meeting all of those preferences is Not Preferred.
- Add any other calculations your team feels is relevant to determining the best loan for Whirly Wind.

i. On the TimeLine worksheet, you will see the applicable dates and project days needed to complete each state of the expansion project. On this worksheet, add the following.
- In column **E**, add a calculation to determine the number of Total Needed days based on the Start Date and Projected End Date.
- In column **D**, add a calculation to determine the number of days remaining based on the Total Needed and Completed.
- On the worksheet somewhere, calculate the total project duration in months.
- On the worksheet somewhere, calculate the current project date with the TODAY function.
- Add a Gantt chart for the project timeline.

j. Apply a **Theme**, and then use **cell styles** where appropriate and to make professional.

k. As a team, answer the questions on the TeamComments worksheet.

l. Complete the **Documentation** worksheet according to your instructor's direction. Minimally, include enough detail to identify which parts of the worksheets/workbook each team member completed.

m. Insert the **filename** in the left custom footer section of the Header/Footer tab in the Page Setup dialog box on all worksheets in the workbook. In a custom header section, include the **names** of the students in your team—spread the names evenly across each of the three header sections: left section, center section, and right section.

n. Save your work, and then close Excel. Submit the file as directed by your instructor.

Student data file needed:

 e02pf4Fit.xlsx

You will save your file as:

e02pf4Fit_LastFirst.xlsx

BMI Health Analysis

Research & Development

A state health agency wants to examine health data on college students starting with the body mass index (BMI). You recently started as an intern to the school's grant-funded initiative, Fit School. Fit School works with the state health agency and counsels student clients on improving health. The agency gave your manager this file with historical data from 1952 through 2011, current data from your school, and a health counselor's tool to help analyze a client's health condition. Your manager thought the file was confusing and had errors. Your manager asked you to look at the data, correct the errors, and create some new components on the spreadsheet.

You calculate BMI using a person's height (in inches) and weight (in pounds). The formula for BMI is as follows:

Weight/Height^2 * 703 (the notation in Excel to square height is Height^2)

For example, if a client weighs 120 pounds and is 5 feet 6 inches tall, their BMI is as follows:

120/66^2 * 703=19.37

The BMI has categories as follows.

- Underweight: less than 18.5
- Normal: 18.5 or greater and less than 25
- Overweight: 25 or greater and less than 30
- Obese: 30 or greater

a. Start Excel, and then open **e02pf4Fit**. Save the file as e02pf4Fit_LastFirst.

b. Throughout the workbook, **cell styles** should be applied to appropriate headings and titles using an appropriate **theme**. Also, BMI calculations do not have many decimals. Change BMI values—not just the format—to be rounded to two decimals except those on the Historical worksheet.

c. The **Historical** worksheet shows average BMI numbers for males and females from 1952 to 2011. The agency wants to see the trend of average BMI index numbers for males and females over the entire time period. The current chart is confusing. Update the chart as follows.

- The chart should be a more appropriate chart type.
- The chart should have a more descriptive title and clean, understandable x-axis and y-axis labels.
- The chart should have a professional, business look so it can be used by the state agency in a presentation.
- Adjust the scales and create gridlines that help convey the context as appropriate.

d. The **CurrentData** worksheet has data for students at your school. This worksheet has errors and needs some additions. Update this worksheet as follows.

- The Weight Category in column F looks up the BMI Category from a table located on the BMICategories worksheet with the range named BMICategory. This calculation is not working correctly and produces erroneous #N/A errors. Fix errors in this workbook that cause this formula to not work correctly. Hint: Look carefully at the construction of the BMICategory look up table values and name range definition.

- The Female and Male BMIs are being separated in columns G and F. This separation will allow separate averages for male and female to be calculated. The formulas are returning male results for females and female results for males. Update the formulas so the correct values are showing.
- Add averages appropriately to the bottom of the data set.

e. The **HealthAnalysis** worksheet is a tool for counselors to help clients assess their current health and set goals. This worksheet has errors and needs additions. Update this worksheet as follows.

- The BMI Calculation in cell B6 will return an error if height—B4—and weight—B5—are blank. Modify cell **B6** to return a blank value if either height or weight is blank.
- In the prior step, you fixed the BMI category lookup on the CurrentData worksheet to work correctly. Cell B7 uses the same name range for the table—BMICategory. Cell B7 contains a different error causing it to work incorrectly. Find and fix the error. Then, modify cell B7 to return a blank value if cell B6 is blank.
- Cell C7 contains a formula that should return the words "At Risk BMI" for Overweight and Obese clients. For all other clients, cell C7 should return a blank. Even after fixing cell B7, this formula returns incorrect results. Find and fix the error.
- Cell B11 should calculate the client's age. This formula is returning an error. Find and fix the error. Then, modify cell **B11** to return a blank value if cell B10 is blank.
- The worksheet coloring should be professional and help indicate to the counselor which cells should be modified or changed when meeting with a client.

f. The **BMIEstimateTable** is for counselors to print out and give to clients for future estimation of BMI as the client's weight changes. This worksheet is not working properly. Update this worksheet as follows.

- The formulas in cells **C4:Q21** are not returning the correct results. Fix the formulas.
- The worksheet does not print well. Update the **settings** and **coloring** to look professional when printed in black and white ink.

g. Insert the **filename** in the left custom footer section of the Header/Footer tab in the Page Setup dialog box on all worksheets in the workbook. Complete the **Documentation** worksheet according to your instructor's direction.

h. Save your work, and then close Excel. Submit the file as directed by your instructor.

WORKSHOP 5 | COMPLEX CONDITIONAL AND RETRIEVAL FUNCTIONS

OBJECTIVES

1. Preview the data and use IF functions p. 254, 257

2. Build nested IF functions p. 261

3. Integrate conjunction functions into IF functions p. 267

4. Use conditional statistical functions p. 274

5. Use conditional math functions p. 278

6. Construct database functions p. 280

7. Explore LOOKUP functions p. 283

8. Retrieve data using MATCH, INDEX, and INDIRECT p. 288

9. Handle errors with the IFERROR function p. 294

Prepare Case

Red Bluff Golf Course & Pro Shop Sales Analysis

The Red Bluff Golf Course & Pro Shop generates revenue through its golfers, golfer services, and pro shop sales. Barry Cheney, the manager, receives revenue data on a monthly basis. He would like to have some reports developed that will help track sales as well as analyze his profit margins. He has a worksheet started with some sample data and wants you to continue developing some reports. These reports will help Barry make educated decisions about the business, such as which items to place on sale or discontinue.

Finance & Accounting   Production & Operations

Gualberto Becerra / Shutterstock

REAL WORLD SUCCESS

"During the summer following my sophomore year, I obtained an internship with a top technology consulting firm. Several students from other local colleges also worked with me. One day, three of the interns, including me, were assigned to work on a project. Our manager asked us if anyone knew how to create a VLOOKUP in Excel. I was the only one who did!"

- Sahiba, current student

Student data file needed for this workshop:

 e03ws05GolfSales.xlsx

You will save your file as:

 e03ws05GolfSales_LastFirst.xlsx

Integrating Logical Functions

Making decisions, regardless if they are personal or business driven, involves evaluation and choices. Golfers use logic as they play, evaluating the scenario—distance to the green; wind speed and direction; obstacles such as water features, sand traps, or trees; and terrain including grass height and elevation—as it changes with every shot. For instance, if a golfer is 300 yards away from the green and has an unobstructed shot, a driver or a 1-iron might be chosen. If he or she is in a sand trap and 20 feet from the hole—pin—a sand wedge would be chosen. Likewise, a business succeeds based upon the ability to choose whether to buy or lease, build or buy from a supplier, or advertise in a magazine or on the radio. Being able to evaluate conditions and apply logic in choosing the best option is the foundation of logical functions. A **logical function** is a function that returns a result, or output, based upon evaluating whether a logical test is true or false. Logical functions enable evaluation and choices to be integrated into a worksheet. The most common logical functions include IF, AND, OR, and NOT. Another logical function, IFERROR, is a special function that is included at the end of the workshop.

The foundation of logical functions is a logical expression or logical test. A **logical test** is an equation that involves logical operators that can be evaluated as being either true or false. The evaluation of the logical test determines the outcome or result. For example, the logical expression "the distance to the green is more than 300 yards" compares the actual distance to 300 yards. The test—compare whether the ball is lying more than or less than 300 yards away—will help determine the result of which club will be chosen. **Logical operators**, as listed in Table 1, are used to create logical tests. In this section, you will create IF and nested IF functions along with creating formulas that include conjunction functions, such as AND and OR.

Operator	Description	TRUE	FALSE
<	Less than	5 < 7	10 < 3
>	Greater than	10 > 3	3 > 10
<=	Less than or equal to	5 <= 5	5 <= 4
>=	Greater than or equal to	5 >= 4	3 >= 10
<>	Not equal to	2 <> 4	2 <> 2

Table 1 Logical operators

Preview the Data

Barry Cheney, the Red Bluff Golf Course & Pro Shop manager, has asked you to develop a worksheet to assist him with decision making. Another staff member had developed the worksheet and populated it with some sample data. When Barry realized the person was simply entering values for the calculated fields rather than using formulas, he decided to turn the project over to you. He entered additional data to demonstrate how he would like it to look; however, the manually entered calculations need to be replaced with formulas.

The Data Inputs worksheet has been created to store the data that will be used in formulas. Keeping the supporting data on a separate sheet makes it easier to streamline the printed report. Additionally, the worksheet needs to be formatted to analyze different amounts of data. For example, there could be 113 transactions in one time period and 154 in another. Barry believes that having enough room for 200 transactions will be sufficient for managing the business.

Within the workbook, named ranges have been created for most, but not all, of the data. Using named ranges makes creating formulas easier because you do not need to worry about adding absolute and mixed cell references.

The data on the Transactions worksheet is created with two sections. The first section contains data that Barry will receive on a monthly basis from the IT staff. It contains the transaction data listed in Table 2.

Data Field	Description
Trans_ID	Transaction number
Trans_Time	Time of the transaction
SKU	Product ID number
Pay_Type	Method of payment
Trans_Qty	Purchase quantity
Coupon_Num	Coupon number, if used
Emp_ID	Employee that completed the transaction
Cust_Cat	Customer category

Table 2 Sales data descriptions

The second section of data contains fields that need to be calculated. Currently the data has been manually calculated—as **static data**—and then typed into the worksheet, a very inefficient practice. You will replace the static data in this section with calculations. The fields' descriptions are briefly detailed in Table 3.

Data Field	Description for Calculated Fields
SKU_Cat	Product category
Emp_Position	Employee position
Shift	Time period when the transaction occurred
Coupon_Target	Type of customer targeted for the coupon
Coupon_Hit	Whether the coupon was submitted by the correct customer type
Coupon_Amt	Percentage off for the coupon
Retail	Retail price of the product
Line_Item_Total	Total revenue (price × qty – coupon)
Card_Charge	Whether the transaction used a credit card
Trans_Group	Category of transaction based on the amount of the transaction
Big_Ticket_Item	Category of nonaccessory items
Sales_Point1	Incentive points calculation for sales team
Sales_Point2	Additional incentive points calculation for sales team

Table 3 Calculated fields' descriptions

Opening the Starting File

To create complex conditional and retrieval functions, you first need to open the Golf Sales workbook.

To Save the Golf Sales Workbook

a. Start **Excel**, and then open the file **e03ws05GolfSales**.

b. Click the **FILE** tab, click **Save As**, and save the file as an **Excel workbook** in the folder or location designated by your instructor with the name e03ws05GolfSales_LastFirst using your last and first name. If necessary, click **Enable Content** in the Security Warning.

Barry would like you to analyze the monthly Red Bluff Golf Course & Pro Shop sales data to transform the data into information that he can use to make sound business decisions. Being able to address the following questions may provide insight into how he can increase sales, decrease expenses, or provide better customer service.

- What types of products sell well? What types do not sell well?
- What percent of the transactions come from credit card sales?
- What is the average transaction amount?
- Who purchases more in terms of quantity or dollar amount: hotel guests or local customers?
- Which sales team members sell the most? Which sell the least?

CONSIDER THIS | **How Would These Questions Help Any Business?**

The questions that Barry will address are not unique to the Red Bluff Golf Course & Pro Shop. Any business that is concerned with generating revenue would ask the same types of questions. Based on the analysis, Barry might decide to create a marketing strategy that will help increase the average sales to local customers or ask the human resource department to provide sales training to all employees. How would these answers help management make decisions? What might management surmise from the answers to the questions that Barry needs to consider?

Exploring the data, finding the answers to questions, and developing knowledge from the Red Bluff Golf Course & Pro Shop information will help management gain and maintain a competitive advantage. A **competitive advantage** is the strategic advantage that a business has over its competition. Attaining a competitive advantage strengthens and positions a business better within the business environment. Barry is hopeful that developing the worksheets properly will help with decision making.

CONSIDER THIS | **Can You Identify a Business That Has a Competitive Advantage?**

Think about the businesses you walk or drive by on a regular basis. Or think about the commercials you see when you watch television. When you watch or visit McDonald's, do you think about their competition? What makes you choose McDonald's over Burger King or Wendy's, or do you? Based on 2011 sales, Wendy's became the second most popular fast-food hamburger restaurant, surpassing Burger King, which held that position for 40 years. Why? How did Wendy's surpass Burger King? How does McDonald's maintain its first place position? How much money do these companies spend to maintain or gain a competitive advantage?

Use IF Functions

The **IF function** is the most common logical function, and it evaluates a logical test. The logical test evaluates a logical condition, or statement, as being either true or false and can involve either values or other functions. The IF function has three arguments—where two are optional:

$$=IF(logical\_test, [value\_if\_true], [value\_if\_false])$$

Suppose you want a list of all golf club members who have a handicap—a method used to level the playing field for golfers of different skill levels—at or below 0. A golfer who has a handicap of 0 or below is known as a scratch golfer. An IF function could be created that would check the handicap and return the words "Scratch Golfer" if the handicap is less than or equal to 0. You could then establish an initial IF statement that starts as:

$$=IF(C5<=0)$$

Since the [value_if_true] argument is not defined, and if cell C5 contains a value that is less than or equal to 0, Excel will return the word TRUE in the cell that has the function. Since the [value_if_false] argument is not defined, and if cell C5 contains a value that is greater than 0, Excel will return the word FALSE. However, simply returning TRUE or FALSE is not valuable for a manager and is not usually best practice or the desired result. Instead, you would want to provide specific values for Excel to display. It is more valuable to use:

$$=IF(C5<=0,"Scratch Golfer","Handicapped Golfer")$$

This way, instead of a generic TRUE or FALSE response, the user would see "Scratch Golfer" if the value in C5 is less than or equal to 0. Otherwise, "Handicapped Golfer" would be displayed. The IF function is exclusive because it only has two outcomes: one when the logical test is true and one when the logical test is false.

CONSIDER THIS | **Why Is It Better to Display Specific Values?**

The IF function can be written to include only one argument, and the results will either be TRUE or FALSE if the optional arguments are not defined. Why is it better to provide specific values for Excel to display? How can this help the user analyze the results?

One of the easiest ways to begin working with IF functions is to use a decision tree. A **decision tree** allows you to break down potential decisions in a logical, structured format. By using the decision tree, you can take a problem or decision and break down the potential possibilities. Consider the previous example. If the formula =IF(C5<=0,"Scratch Golfer","Handicapped Golfer") was inserted into a decision tree, it would be diagrammed with three labeled branches—in black, the values for each argument—in blue, and then finished with the IF function syntax—in red as shown in Figure 1.

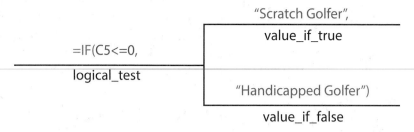

$$=IF(C5<=0,$$

logical_test

"Scratch Golfer",
value_if_true

"Handicapped Golfer")
value_if_false

Figure 1 Decision tree

| QUICK REFERENCE | Diagramming a Decision Tree |

A decision tree helps keep your thoughts organized as you work through writing your formula. Complete the following steps to create your decision tree.
1. Draw and label the three branches.
2. Determine and write the logical test argument.
3. Determine and write the [value_if_true] argument.
4. Determine and write the [value_if_false] argument.
5. Fill in the IF function syntax.
6. Type your formula into Excel.

Constructing an IF Statement

The credit card company charges a fee to process each transaction. Barry would like to track credit card usage versus other types of transactions—cash and check. In the worksheet, he needs a column to indicate whether a customer used a credit card to pay for their items. If the customer did, he wants Excel to display the word "Charge". Otherwise, he does not want anything to appear in the cell.

SIDE NOTE
Pasting Named Range Lists
When using multiple named ranges in a workbook, especially one that you did not create, it is easier to paste a list and refer back to it as needed.

E05.01

 To Create an IF Function

a. Click the **Data Inputs** worksheet tab. Click cell **I48**, press F3, and then click **Paste List** so the current ranges with the names are listed.

b. Click the **Transactions** worksheet tab, click cell **Q9**, type =IF(D9="Ccard","Charge","") and then press Ctrl+Enter.
   This checks if the Pay_Type value in D9 is equal to "Ccard". If that is true, the word "Charge" will be returned. Otherwise, an empty set, indicated with double quotes with nothing between, will be returned.

c. With cell Q9 selected, click the **AutoFill** handle in the bottom-right corner of the cell, and then drag it down to copy the formula down to cell **Q208** to overwrite the static values.
   Rows where there are no records will be evaluated as FALSE and return an empty set.

d. Click cell **M9**. The coupon is a match when the Cust_Cat is the same as the Coupon_Target. When they are different, it is not a match. Type =IF(H9<>L9,"No Match","Coupon Match") and then press Ctrl+Enter.

The logical test is stating that H9 is not equal to L9. Thus, when they are equal, the test returns a value of FALSE, and it is a Coupon Match.

> **Troubleshooting**
>
> If you see an error after pressing Ctrl+Enter, ensure that you entered all necessary quotation marks. Additionally, ensure that you typed quotation marks and did not type two apostrophes.

e. With cell **M9** selected, click the **AutoFill** handle in the bottom-right corner of the cell, and then drag down to copy the formula down to cell **M208** to overwrite the static values. While the formula is not giving an error message, the result is not correct in the rows where there are no records. This is a modeling issue that you will address later in this workshop.

f. Click **Save** 🔲.

Using Different Elements in an IF Statement

As previously mentioned, the [value_if_true] and [value_if_false] arguments are both optional and could be omitted from the function. In this case, the values TRUE and FALSE are returned when the function is evaluated. While this may be intuitive, it is not user friendly. You can use a variety of elements, including numerical values, text strings, cell references, named ranges, and other functions for the arguments in an IF function. Figure 2 provides an example.

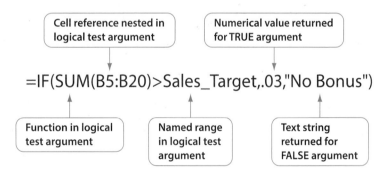

Figure 2 Function argument example

In this example, .03 is a numerical value. "No Bonus" is a text string and should have quotes around the string. Quotes—shown as a **double prime symbol**, not the curly double quotation marks you use when writing papers—let Excel know that the element is a text string and not a numeric value, cell reference, or named range. Sales_Target is a named range. This may look like a text string, but because it does not have curly double quotes, Excel will look for a range with that named range. If a Sales_Target named range does not exist, Excel will return the #NAME? error message, which occurs when Excel does not recognize text in a formula. Finally, SUM(B5:B20) is a function that is part of the logical test. Excel will automatically recognize function names.

E05.02

 To Use Different Elements in an IF Statement

a. Click the **Revenue Report** worksheet tab, and then click cell **E21**.

Barry wants to evaluate the number of items being sold. If the total number of items sold is more than 50, then the current goal is met. If that is true, he wants to have "Goal Met" displayed; otherwise, he wants "Under Goal" displayed.

b. Type =IF(SUM(and then press F3 to open the Paste Name dialog box. Scroll down as needed, click to select **Trans_Qty**, and then click **OK**. Type)>50,"Goal Met","Under Goal") and then press Ctrl + Enter.

This will evaluate whether the sum of the quantity sold is greater than 50. However, Excel uses a static value—50—in the logical test. If the goal changes, the function will no longer be valid.

c. With cell **E21** selected, press F2 to enter edit mode. Select **50** within the formula, and then type E20. Press Ctrl + Enter, and then click **Save** 🖫.

Notice that as E20 was typed in the formula, Excel recognized it as a valid cell reference and changed the font within the formula to blue and then placed a blue border around E20. By using a cell reference rather than a numeric value, when the goal value in cell E20 changes, the Qty Sold Status formula will still calculate the correct result.

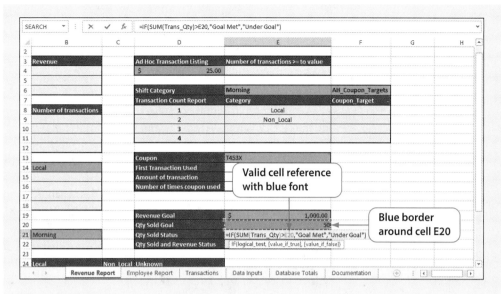

Figure 3 IF function

Build Nested IF Functions

The function =IF(SUM(Trans_Qty)>E20,"Goal Met","Under Goal") is a **complex function**, a function that combines multiple functions into one formula because the logical test involved evaluating a function. A special type of complex function is a nested IF function. A single IF statement provides two outcomes for a single logical test. But what happens if you have more than two options or possible outcomes? A **nested IF function** uses IF functions as arguments within another IF function and increases the logical outcomes that can be expressed.

Building Nested IF Functions

The purchase price is included in the sales data, and Barry would like to categorize the transactions as Low, Medium, High, or Ultra depending on the purchase price amount. The business requirements for each category are provided in Table 4.

	Greater than or equal to	Less than
Low	$0	$25
Medium	$25	$100
High	$100	$250
Ultra	$250	

Table 4 Transaction ratings

Creating a number line of the business requirements similar to the one shown in Figure 4 can be helpful in visualizing the logic. When looking at the number line and breaking it up based on the $25 and $100 amounts, you can see that there are four possible categories or alternatives. Since one IF function cannot handle four outcomes, a nested IF function is needed.

Figure 4 Nested IF number line

Working from left to right across a number line, an initial logical test will check for the far-left range—0 to 25. The initial logical statement starts with

$$=\text{IF}(P9<25,\text{"Low"},\text{"everything else"})$$

Excel checks whether the value in P9 is less than $25, and will categorize the type of transaction. If the logical test is true, the value of "Low" will be returned as the outcome. If false, Excel will return "everything else", which for now replaces the Medium, High and Ultra categories. This is similar to assuming there are only two options—Low if the test is true; everything else if the test is false as shown in Figure 5, Part 1. Parts 2 and 3 will be discussed in a later section.

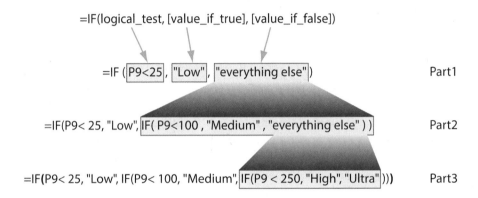

Figure 5 Nested IF logic

E05.03

 To Begin Writing a Nested IF Formula

a. Click the **Transactions** worksheet tab. Click cell **R9**, type =IF(P9<'Data Inputs'!$K$20,'Data Inputs'!$I$20,"everything else") and then press Ctrl+Enter. Notice that you are checking to see if Line_Item_Total is less than $25, and the cells you are referencing on the Data Inputs worksheet are the different transactions groups, outlined in Table 4.

b. With cell **R9** selected, click the **AutoFill** handle, drag down to copy the formula down to cell **R208** to overwrite the static values, and then click **Save** 🖫.

   Notice that "Low" shows up for Purchase Prices less than $25 and "everything else" is displayed for all other values. Also, note that when there is no price in the column P cell references—no value—the IF statement is returning a result of Low. This will be explored in a later exercise.

Working with IF Function Ranges

In the real world, it helps to work with real numbers, like 25, 100, and 250, when developing the logic of the formula. However, it is hazardous to use the numbers in the formula when they may change. It is much better to build the worksheet for flexibility. It is easier to change a worksheet cell value than it is to search formulas to find the number you need to update. Whenever possible, use a cell reference in a formula instead of a number.

Adding Another Outcome

The initial function works well when there are two outcomes, such as "Low" and "everything else". However, when the value is greater than $25, you have established that it is not a low transaction, but you still do not know if it is Medium, High, or Ultra. Thus, you need a second logical statement for the [value_if_false] argument replacing the "everything else" as depicted in Figure 5, Part 2. The values below $25 have been eliminated by the first IF function and do not need to be checked again. The second IF function should check for values below $100. If the outcome is true, you want Excel to display "Medium". If the outcome is false, you will not need to write a third IF function. Since there are three possible outcomes, and the first two are false, the outcome cannot be anything other than High or Ultra—replaced by "everything else". Development of the function would continue as:

$$=IF(P9<25,"Low",IF(P9<100,"Medium","everything else"))$$

Easy Tricks for a Nested IF Function

Two important items to note when writing nested IF functions.
- First, consider the number of outcomes. The number of IF functions needed is always one less than the number of outcomes. For example, if you had five possible outcomes of Very Cold, Cold, Warm, Hot, and Very Hot, you immediately know that you will need to nest four IF functions, three of which are nested inside the main IF function.
- Second, the number of parentheses needed to close your functions at the end of your formula is always the same number as the amount of IF functions you used. In the previous example where you would use four IF functions, you know immediately that you will need four closing parentheses at the end of your formula. Keep in mind that this would not include any parentheses that may be needed in the final [value_if_false] argument.

▶ To Nest an IF Function

a. Click the **Transactions** worksheet tab. Click cell **R9**, and then press F2 to enter edit mode. Select **"everything else"** including the quotes, replace it by typing IF(P9<'Data Inputs'!$K$21,'Data Inputs'!$I$21,'Data Inputs'!$I$22) and then press Ctrl+Enter so R9 remains the active cell.

> **Troubleshooting**
>
> If you receive an error after typing your formula, ensure that you enclosed Data Inputs inside apostrophes. These are needed when referencing another worksheet that has a space in the name, like 'Data Inputs'.

b. Click the **AutoFill** handle, drag down to copy the formula down to cell **R208**, and then click **Save** 🔲.

  Notice that "Low" is displayed when the Line_Item_Total price is less than $25, and "Medium" is displayed when the Line_Item_Total price is less than $100, but greater than or equal to $25. "High" is displayed for all other values unless the price column cell is empty.

If the Line_Item_Total price is not Low—not less than $25, the second nested IF function will check whether it is less than $100. If it is, then the text "Medium" will be displayed. The possibility of the price being less than $25 was eliminated with the first logical test. This is why best practice dictates working left to right—low to high—with the number line. It allows you to take advantage of the process of elimination without having to nest additional functions—such as AND—within the nested IF function. The function checks for the far-left range first—$0 to $25, and if the first logical test evaluates to TRUE, then Excel knows it is in that range, knows the outcome, and ends—the other nested IF functions will not be evaluated. However, if the first logical test is FALSE, indicating that the price is $25 or greater, you need a second IF function to determine whether the outcome is Medium (if the second test returns TRUE) or High (if the second test returns FALSE).

> **CONSIDER THIS** | **Left or Right When Working with Nested IFs**
>
> Consider the process of working with the ranges on a number line in a left-to-right fashion. Would it be possible to start on the right side and work to the left? Do you suppose it would be possible to start with any range and construct the logic of the options in any order?

Completing the Nested IF Function

What if you decided to add another category? Perhaps you would like to categorize any Line_Item_Total price that is greater than or equal to $250 as Ultra. This would require adding one more IF function in the [value_if_false] at the end of the second IF function, as shown in Figure 5, Part 3. The nested function would be expanded to be:

=IF(P9<25,"Low",IF(P9<100,"Medium",IF(P9<250,"High","Ultra")))

To Nest a Third IF Function

a. Click the **Transactions** worksheet tab, Click cell **R9**, and then press F2 to enter edit mode. Select **'Data Inputs'!$I$22**, replace it by typing IF(P9<'Data Inputs'!$K$22,'Data Inputs'!$I$22,'Data Inputs'!$I$23) and then press Ctrl + Enter so R9 remains the active cell.

b. With cell **R9** selected, click the **AutoFill** handle, drag down to copy the formula down to cell **R208**, and then click **Save** 💾.

Recall that "Low" is still displayed for empty price cells and will be addressed in a later section. Notice the cells that contain data have one of four outcomes returned appropriately for each Line_Item_Total price. There are three parentheses at the far right of the formula, one for each IF function. The options are exhaustive because any number that is provided for the Line_Item_Total price will fall into one of the four groups.

SIDE NOTE

Pairing Parentheses

Each function needs a pair of parentheses. Excel color codes each parenthesis to indicate which parentheses are paired.

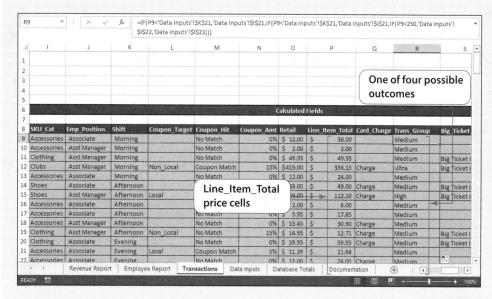

Figure 6 Nesting a third IF function

Nested IF functions can be challenging to write. One way to simplify the development process is to use a decision tree as shown in Figure 7. Begin by drawing and labeling the first three branches. You can then begin to construct the first IF function—also called the first level of the formula—using the first two possible outcomes by completing the logical test and [value_if_true] arguments. Because Excel stops evaluating an IF function once the [value_if_true] argument is reached, the additional branches will always "grow" off of the [value_if_false] branch. If the result is not "Low", then it has to be either "Medium", "High", or "Ultra". Thus, the [value_if_false] branch becomes another logical test, and another level in the formula—the second level. As you add possible outcomes, such as Ultra, you can continue adding branches to the [value_if_false] branches. Not only does this assist with keeping your thoughts organized, it also helps you understand the logic of what you are doing.

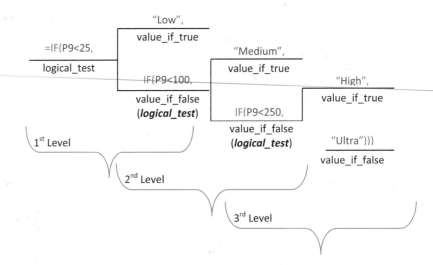

Figure 7 Nested IF decision tree

QUICK REFERENCE	Diagramming Decision Trees for a Nested IF Function

Since IF functions can have up to 64 levels, writing nested IF functions can be challenging if you just begin by typing the function directly into Excel. To ease the process, begin by drawing and labeling the first three branches and then complete the following steps to create your decision tree.

1. Determine and write the logical test argument.
2. Determine and write the [value_if_true] argument.
3. Determine and write the [value_if_false] argument, which will serve as the next IF function.
4. Continue steps 1–3 until all levels have been written.
5. Fill in the IF function syntax.
6. Type the formula into Excel.

In addition to the decision tree, realizing that nested IF statements are a process of elimination can also help you write them. In this example, the function can return one of four outcomes—Low, Medium, High, or Ultra. Also, notice you only had to use three IF statements. The very last outcome—Ultra—is returned only if the other three possibilities are eliminated by the three logical tests for Low, Medium, and High. Thus, you need one less IF statement than outcomes. Knowing this rule of thumb can help you figure out the syntax given that the number of IF statements needed will vary from problem to problem. Figure 8 shows the syntax for a nested IF statement and shows the location of the outcome determined by the process of elimination.

Last value_if_false determined
by a process of elimination.

=IF(logical_test,value_if_true,IF(logical_test,value_if_true,IF(logical_test,value_if_true,value_if_false)))

=IF(P9<25,"Low",   )

IF(P9<100,"Medium",   )

IF(P9<250,"High","Ultra"   )

OR

=IF(P9<25,"Low",IF(P9<100,"Medium",IF(P9<250,"High","Ultra")))

Figure 8   Nested IF syntax

REAL WORLD ADVICE | **Working with IF Function Ranges**

You will want to consider whether your ranges go to the left or right of infinity or if you have actual lower and upper bounds. If a value should never be negative, then it may be necessary to incorporate a starting point for the far-left range. The same would apply for the right side. For some values, such as the credit limit, you may want to check that the value is not above $50,000. While data validation can be used to limit the values, if you actually have a lower or upper limit, you will need to consider whether to test for this in the IF statements.

Integrate Conjunction Functions into IF Functions

While nesting IF functions allows handling more than two outcomes, conjunction functions allow evaluation of multiple logical tests and enable linking or joining of functions or formulas. The conjunction functions within Excel are AND, OR, and NOT. The **AND function** is used when the logical tests must all be true, whereas the **OR function** is used when any combination of logical tests has at least one TRUE outcome. The **NOT function** is appropriate when there are many options that do fit the desired criteria and only one option that does not fit the criteria. It is important to realize the syntax for these functions is similar to any other function—the arguments are parenthetical following the function name. A user might think the syntax would be something like:

X AND Y

Whereas the correct syntax is:

AND(logical1,[logical2],…)
OR(logical1,[logical2],…)
NOT(logical1)

Using the AND Function

At least one logical test must be included, and additional logical test arguments are optional for the AND function. For example, students wanting to be eligible for a university scholarship must have an ACT score of 30 or more AND a high school GPA of 3.5 or better. Using named ranges, to evaluate whether or not a student achieved these goals, the AND function would be written as:

$$AND(ACT>=30,GPA>=3.5)$$

Both conditions must be met, in order to display TRUE. Just like the IF function, the outcomes of either TRUE or FALSE are not valuable to a manager. Generally, conjunction functions are nested within other functions, such as an IF function. An AND function could be used in an IF statement:

$$IF(AND(ACT>=30,GPA>=3.5),"Eligible","Not Eligible")$$

In this case, the ACT>=30 is the first logical argument, and the GPA>=3.5 is the second logical argument. The logic for evaluating an AND function with two logical tests—AND(Logical Test 'A',Logical Test 'B')— is shown in Table 5 in a logical truth table. When the AND function is nested in the logical test argument of an IF function, both logical tests need to be evaluated as TRUE for the [value_if_true] argument to be returned. If either evaluates to FALSE, then the AND function will return a FALSE for the logical test. Of the four outcomes, only one would return a value of TRUE.

Logical Test 'A'	Logical Test 'B'	AND Function Result
TRUE	TRUE	TRUE
TRUE	FALSE	FALSE
FALSE	TRUE	FALSE
FALSE	FALSE	FALSE

Table 5 AND logical truth table

Barry wants to evaluate the status of employees. If an employee is an assistant manager and the Percent of Goal is greater than 25%, then he wants to have the status be "On Target". Otherwise, it should return a result of "Increase Sales". Because there are two conditions that lead to the results and they both must be true, an AND function can be used within the logical test for the IF function.

E05.06

 To Use the AND Function Within an IF Function

a. Click the **Employee Report** worksheet tab, and then click cell **B17**.

b. Type =IF(AND(B4="Asst Manager",B9>0.25),"On Target","Increase Sales"), press Enter, and then click **Save** 🖫.

   Both logical tests in the AND function must be evaluated to TRUE for the AND to return a TRUE. When this happens, the [value_if_true] argument executes.

Using the OR Function

The OR function works in the same way as an AND function, except the logical evaluation of the arguments is different. Where the AND function requires all arguments to be TRUE, the OR function requires only one of the arguments to be evaluated as TRUE. Thus, the OR function with two logical tests—OR(Logical Test 'A', Logical Test 'B')—as depicted in the logical truth table in Table 6, shows that three of the four combinations would return a result of TRUE.

Logical Test 'A'	Logical Test 'B'	OR Function Result
TRUE	TRUE	TRUE
TRUE	FALSE	TRUE
FALSE	TRUE	TRUE
FALSE	FALSE	FALSE

Table 6 OR logical truth table

Because there are two Non_Local coupons listed in the Coupons table on the Data Inputs worksheet tab, the Coupon_Num value on the Transactions worksheet can be either coupon; thus, an OR function can be used in conjunction with an IF statement to convert the data. Once the target for the coupon is known, it is possible to determine whether a nonlocal customer used a nonlocal coupon, which is the desired use. Management would like to know whether local customers are using local coupons.

E05.07

 To Use the OR Function Within an IF Function

a. Click the **Transactions** worksheet tab, and then click cell **L9**.

b. Type =IF(OR(F9=, click the **Data Inputs** worksheet tab, click cell **I5**, press F4, then type ,F9=. Click cell **I7**, press F4, type),"Non_Local","Local") and then press Ctrl+Enter. If either one of the logical tests in the OR evaluates to TRUE, then the logical test for the IF function will be TRUE and "Non_Local" is displayed.

c. Click the **AutoFill** handle, and then drag down to copy the formula down to cell **L208** to overwrite the static values. Click **Save** 🖫.

   Notice that this provides a "Local" result for rows where there is no data. This will be explored and changed in a later section.

Using the NOT Function

The NOT function allows creation of logical statements in which it creates the opposite or reverse result. This is particularly useful when there are many values that would result in a TRUE and only one that would return a FALSE. For example, if you wanted to charge state tax to all states except Texas, you could use NOT(State="Texas") so if the value were Texas, that is TRUE and the result of the NOT function would be FALSE. If the state was Ohio, then Ohio=Texas is FALSE, and NOT FALSE is TRUE. So, all other states would return the same result.

Barry recognizes that the accessories items do not cost a lot or take up much space. All of the other categories of products found in the SKU_Cat column are big ticket items where there is a larger margin or possibility or making a higher profit. The shop makes a larger profit from selling the big ticket items, so Barry may want some analyses on just those items. He would like a column that distinguishes the big-ticket items, regardless of the category. You can accomplish this task in one logical test using the NOT function.

E05.08

To Use the NOT Function Within an IF Function

a. Click the **Transactions** worksheet tab. Click cell **S9**, type =IF(NOT(I9="Accessories"),"Big Ticket Item","") and then press `Ctrl`+`Enter`.

   If the category is Accessories, the logical expression in the NOT function will evaluate to TRUE, but the NOT function will reverse it to be NOT TRUE, or FALSE. When FALSE, the result will be nothing—an empty text string, indicated by typing double quotes.

b. With cell **S9** selected, click the **AutoFill** handle, and then drag down to copy the formula down to cell **S208** to overwrite the static values. Click **Save** 🖫.

   Notice that this provides a "Big Ticket Item" result for rows where there is no data. The formula should check whether there is a transaction. This will be evaluated and changed later.

Combining an OR Function in an AND Function

There are more complex situations where it is necessary to combine the OR with the AND function. This can be challenging because you need to determine whether to put the AND inside the OR, or vice versa. A lot depends on the situation and, just like in math, you need to be careful with grouping.

Barry wants to give motivational points to the sales team for certain transactions. Sales_Point1 will look for Trans_Group results of High or Ultra transactions that occur in the morning or afternoon shift and will award one point. Otherwise it will return zero points. The logic for this is illustrated in Figure 9. The formula requires both an OR function and AND function within the IF statement. The initial step is to think through the situation and organize the conditions using pseudo code. **Pseudo code** is using the structure of the functions, but with wording that is written for understanding the function's structure logically. Here, there are four conditions to evaluate. The first two are Shift is Morning or Shift is Afternoon. They cannot be joined with an AND, since they are exclusive, only one can be true. So, you need to use an OR function. The same applies to the Trans_Group because a transaction cannot be both High and Ultra. The requirement mentions the High transactions have to occur in one of the two shifts, so an AND needs to be used to combine the High transaction with either of the shifts. Thus, the AND is the outer function with two OR functions inside.

Logic:

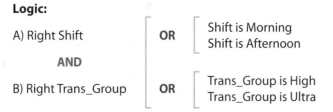

A) Right Shift   **OR** [Shift is Morning
Shift is Afternoon

         AND

B) Right Trans_Group   **OR** [Trans_Group is High
Trans_Group is Ultra

Pseudo code:

IF(**AND**(Right Shift, Right Trans_Group), earn a point, no points)

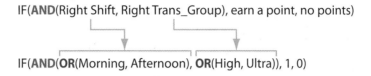

IF(**AND**(**OR**(Morning, Afternoon), **OR**(High, Ultra)), 1, 0)

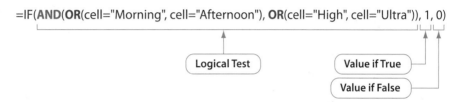

=IF(**AND**(**OR**(cell="Morning", cell="Afternoon"), **OR**(cell="High", cell="Ultra")), 1, 0)

(Logical Test)   (Value if True)

(Value if False)

Figure 9   Logic of nesting OR in AND functions

E05.09

To Use the OR Function Nested Within an AND Function

a. Click the **Transactions** worksheet tab. Click cell **T9**, type
=IF(AND(OR(K9="Morning",K9="Afternoon"),OR(R9="High",R9="Ultra")),1,0) and
then press [Ctrl]+[Enter].

b. With cell **T9** selected, click the **AutoFill** handle, drag down to copy the formula down
to cell **T208** to overwrite the static values, and then click **Save** 🖫.

This shows a point will be awarded when the shift is Morning or Afternoon, and
has the added condition that the Trans_Group results display either High or Ultra. The
second OR needs to be added, and the two OR functions will be combined with an AND
function, requiring each to return a TRUE result.

REAL WORLD ADVICE   **Working with Complex AND and OR Conditions**

In the real world, you will want to confirm complex conditions. For example, the
statement "All employees in division X or division Y with more than three years
of experience receive training" can be interpreted as all employees from the two
divisions that have more than three years of experience get training. Or, it could
mean that all employees from division X get training and all employees from
division Y with more than three years experience get training. If you are unsure of
the conditions being requested, get clarification before proceeding.

Combining an AND Function in an OR Function

For the second set of motivational points, Barry wants to give points to encourage the sales team to increase the purchasing of both the local and out-of-town—nonlocal—customers. He believes nonlocal customers tend to purchase more than the local customers, so the transaction amount for them is set higher than for the local customers. Ultimately, he would like to see the average transactions increase for all customers. He may change the transaction amounts that determine the points, so these have been included in the workbook. For a point to be earned, the transaction needs to be either a local customer with more than $50 spent or a nonlocal customer that spent more than $100. The structure of this logical statement is shown in Figure 10 with pseudo code. It shows there are two ways to earn the points, and either will work; thus, an OR function is the outer function. The two ways of earning points both require an AND function. The AND functions combine the Line_Item_Total condition with the Cust_Cat condition, requiring both to be evaluated as TRUE.

Logic:

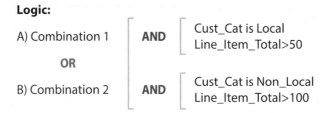

Pseudo code:

IF(**OR**(Combination1, Combination 2), earn a point, no points)

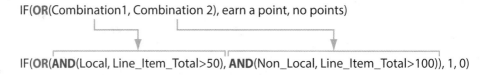

IF(**OR**(**AND**(Local, Line_Item_Total>50), **AND**(Non_Local, Line_Item_Total>100)), 1, 0)

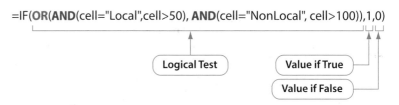

=IF(**OR**(**AND**(cell="Local",cell>50), **AND**(cell="NonLocal", cell>100)),1,0)

Logical Test

Value if True

Value if False

Figure 10   Logic of nesting AND in OR functions

E05.10

▶ To Use the AND Function Nested Within an OR Function

a. Click the **Transactions** worksheet tab. Click cell **U9**, type =IF(AND(H9=, click the **Data Inputs** worksheet tab, click **I14**, and then press F4. Type ,P9>, click **J14**, press F4, type),1,0), and then press Ctrl + Enter.

b. Click the **AutoFill** handle, and drag to copy the formula down to cell **U208** to overwrite the static values.

   This will show that transactions from local customers spending more than $50 will get 1 point, but no others will get a point. The second inside logical AND condition to test for non_local customers spending more than $100 needs to be added with the OR as the outside joining function.

c. Click cell **U9**, press ⎡F2⎤, and then position the cursor to the right of the **IF(**. Type OR(AND(H9='Data Inputs'!$I$13,P9>'Data Inputs'!$J$13),. Place the cursor to the right of **$J$14)**, and then type) so there is a closing parenthesis for the OR function that was just added. Press ⎡Ctrl⎤+⎡Enter⎤.

d. Click the **AutoFill** handle, and then drag to copy the formula down to cell **U208**. Click **Save** 🖫. Now, if either of the AND logical statements evaluate to TRUE, a point will be given.

Using Conditional Aggregate Functions

It is quite common to run a calculation, like adding or averaging sales, and then evaluating whether the average or total met a specific goal or benchmark. This incorporates both a calculation and a logical decision into one equation. This is possible to handle by nesting the SUM or AVERAGE function within the IF function. However, these functions will calculate the entire range selected. With a workbook that includes more sophisticated decision-making models, it is often desirable to perform calculations on some of the data in the range, based upon some criteria. For example, in a data set of sales transactions, it may be useful to sum all of the credit card sales, ignoring the cash or check sales.

The addition of conditional aggregate functions in Excel makes this task manageable. **Conditional aggregate functions** are functions that consolidate or summarize a subset of data that has been filtered based upon one or more criteria. This is different from the traditional functions that calculate using all cells that are in a specified range. If SUM(A1:C10) is used, it adds all the values in all the cells in that range. With an aggregate function, a range would still be provided, but the aggregation would only use cells that meet a given criteria. The criteria can be on the data that is being aggregated or on associated data.

The criteria for determining which subset of data is chosen can be constructed in a variety of ways, as defined in Table 7. Quotes are needed with the logical operators. The ampersand is used for combining the logical operator with another component. Elements such as named ranges and cell references cannot go inside quotes because Excel would interpret them as text strings rather than named ranges or cell references. For example, "> B4" would check for values greater than the string >B4 instead of a value that is in cell B4. This applies to all the functions discussed here.

In this section, conditional functions and database functions will be developed using this foundation. The functions will provide analysis of a data set for the purpose of gaining knowledge from the information.

Criteria	Action
B4	Selects if the value equals the value in B4
">10"	Selects if the value is greater than 10
">="&Goal	Selects if the value is greater than or equal to the value in the named range 'Goal'
"><"&B5	Selects if the value is not equal to the value in B5

Table 7 Criteria options

Use Conditional Statistical Functions

Excel recognizes the need for having statistical functions that would calculate a subset of data that meets the specified criteria. There is a set of common functions that have been merged with the logical functions, including the COUNT and AVERAGE functions. They have been set to handle both a single criterion and multiple criteria for filtering.

Using the COUNTIF Function

The **COUNTIF function** counts the number of cells that meet the specified criteria. This differs from the SUMIF and SUMIFS functions, which sum the data in the cells that meet the given criteria. For example, a COUNTIF function that uses a range with 12 cells would return a value between 1 and 12 because the cells are counted. If the same range was used with a SUMIF, the result is determined by the sum of the values within the cells, not the number of cells. The COUNTIF function has two arguments, range and criteria. The syntax for the COUNTIF function is:

$$=COUNTIF(range, criteria)$$

The range is the cells that will be counted, and the criteria is the logical statement that will determine which cells to count within the formula cell range. For example, if there was a range of data in which the cells contained the data "Handicapped Golfer" or "Scratch Golfer" and the criteria was "Scratch Golfer", the function would count every occurrence in the cell range where the cell data content (criteria) equals "Scratch Golfer".

Barry wants to count the transactions based upon the transaction amount. You can accomplish this using the Trans_Group data range that has been classified as Low, Medium, High, and Ultra. Counting each of those will give the number by each classification. Additionally, Barry would like to count the number of times a specific coupon is used and the number of transactions greater than or equal to a specific value.

SIDE NOTE
Without Formatting
It is recommended that you copy the formula down without formatting so you do not need to fix your border styles.

SIDE NOTE
Using the Ampersand
The ampersand (&) is a symbol that adds—concatenates—the text in the quotes with the value in the cell reference.

SIDE NOTE
Using Logical Symbols
Logical symbols like > or < are alphanumeric and are placed within quotes. Because D4 is a cell reference, quotes are not used.

E05.11

 To Create a COUNTIF Function

a. Click the **Revenue Report** worksheet tab. Click cell **B9**, type =COUNTIF(Trans_Group,'Data Inputs'!I20) and then press Ctrl + Enter .

b. With cell **B9** selected, double-click the **AutoFill** handle to copy the formula down without formatting to cell **B12**.

   Notice the 190 value seems unusually high compared to the remaining values. This is because the formula returns a value of "Low" in any remaining cells on the Transactions sheet where reference cells in the formula are blank. This is an example of why a formula needs to account for all possibilities when validating the information. This will be addressed later in the workshop.

c. Click cell **E16**, type =COUNTIF(Coupon_Num,E13) and then press Enter .

   This will count the times the coupon listed in E13 was used in the Coupon_Num range found on the Transactions worksheet.

d. Click cell **E4**, type =COUNTIF(Line_Item_Total,">="&D4) and then press Enter . Click **Save** 💾. This is different because the criteria uses the value in D4 instead of looking for the string "D4".

In the real world, you would check for errors as you develop a workbook, looking for numbers that do not make sense or seem out of line. Try testing data to ensure formulas work the way you expect them to. It may be that an issue is caused by cells being referenced in a formula rather than the formula itself. Develop techniques, such as using formula auditing and testing a range of data, to ensure calculations are correct.

Using the COUNTIFS Function

The **COUNTIFS function** allows for multiple criteria in multiple ranges to be evaluated and counted. The syntax for the COUNTIFS function is:

=COUNTIFS(criteria_range1, criteria1, [criteria_range2, criteria2],…)

There is no distinction between a criteria_range argument found in COUNTIFS and a range argument used in COUNTIF. When counting, it simply counts the cells that meet the criteria; thus, the range of cells to count and the criteria_range are the same range.

However, when using multiple criteria, all criteria ranges must have exactly the same shape—the same number of rows and same number of columns. Then, the cells within the multiple ranges are compared and all criteria have to evaluate to TRUE to be counted. In Figure 11, the first set of cells will be TRUE if the value is 392. Cells A1 and B3 would be TRUE. In the second range, the cells would be evaluated as TRUE if they have a value of 28. Cells F1, F2, and G3 meet that second criteria. However, cells in the same relative position within the two ranges must both be TRUE to be counted. Thus the pairs A1 and F1 and B3 and G3 both are TRUE so the COUNTIF would return a value of 2 for this COUNTIFS example. The criterion is met for the cell in F2, the first column, second row, for the second range, but it is not met for cell A2 in row 2, column 1, for the first criteria range, so that set is not counted. Thus, the number of cells in one range determines the maximum count that can be obtained.

COUNTIFS(A1:B3, "=392", F1:G3, "=28")

	A	B			F	G
1	**392**	439		1	**28**	83
2	439	375		2	28	37
3	827	**392**		3	48	**28**

Figure 11   COUNTIFS calculation

Barry wants to count the number of transactions, grouped by the coupon target and shift. The table on the Transactions worksheet has been set up to show the coupon targets and the current shift desired. The shift may change, so it needs to be referenced. Two criteria must match for a count to occur. The two ranges checked will be the Shift and the Coupon_Target and since both are the same shape, the first cell in both ranges will be evaluated. If both are true for their criteria, that pair will be counted, continuing for the remaining cells in the two ranges.

E05.12

To Create a COUNTIFS Function

a. Click the **Revenue Report** worksheet tab. Click cell **F8**, type
=COUNTIFS(Shift,$E$6,Coupon_Target,E8) and then press `Ctrl`+`Enter`.
This formula checks for the Shift category of "Morning" and for "Local" coupon targets. When both occur, the set is counted.

b. With cell **F8** selected, double-click its **AutoFill** handle to copy the formula without formatting down to cell **F11**, and then click **Save** 🖫.

Using the AVERAGEIF Function

The **AVERAGEIF function** averages the number of cells that meet the specified criteria. This differs from the AVERAGE function, which averages the data in the selected cells. The AVERAGEIF function has three arguments, two required and one optional. The syntax for the AVERAGEIF function is:

$$=AVERAGEIF(range, criteria, [average\_range])$$

If the [average_range] argument is omitted, Excel assumes the same range specified in the range argument will be used for filtering the data and for averaging. For example, if Barry wanted to find the average for only the scratch golfers, he would average the handicaps for people that have a handicap greater than 0. This would filter the data based on the handicap and would average the same range.

With the AVERAGEIF function, the third argument is only required if one range of data is being averaged based on criteria of a second range.

For the Revenue Report, the average sales will be calculated for local customers. Additionally, an average will be calculated for the type of transaction used for the local customers. Thus, it will retrieve the local customers that used cash and average the line item total for those records. The same thing will be done for the checks and credit card transactions for the local customer transactions.

E05.13

To Create an AVERAGEIF Function

a. Click the **Revenue Report** worksheet tab. Click cell **B15**, type
=AVERAGEIF(Cust_Cat,B14,Line_Item_Total) and then press `Enter`.

b. Click **Save** 🖫.

Using the AVERAGEIFS Function

The **AVERAGEIFS function** averages a range of data, selecting data to average based on the criteria specified. The AVERAGEIFS function expands on the AVERAGEIF function, allowing multiple criteria to determine the subset of data. However, it is important to note that the order of the arguments changes. The syntax for the AVERAGIFS function is:

$$=AVERAGEIFS(average\_range, criteria\_range1, criteria1, [criteria\_range2, criteria2], ...)$$

The average range is moved to become the first argument on the assumption that different ranges would be used for determining the filtered subset of data. After the average range, there are pairs of criteria ranges and criteria. In this fashion multiple criteria can be used to filter the data to be averaged. Similar to the COUNTIFS function, the two ranges must be the same shape, having the same number of rows and columns. With the AVERAGEIFS function, all ranges must be the same size, although they do not have to be adjacent nor even on the same worksheet as shown in Figure 12.

Barry wants to find the average Line_Item_Total based on the Cust_Cat and the Pay_Type. He would like flexibility so cells will need to be referenced in the formula.

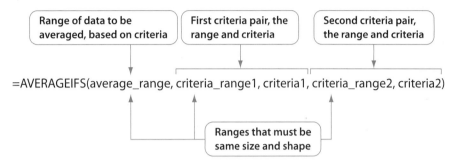

Figure 12   AVERAGEIFS function

E05.14

To Create an AVERAGEIFS Function

a. Click the **Revenue Report** worksheet tab. Click cell **B16**, if necessary, and then type =AVERAGEIFS(Li. Double-click **Line_Item_Total** when it appears in the AutoComplete list.

b. Type ,Cu and then double-click **Cust_Cat** when it appears in the AutoComplete list.

c. Type ,$B$14,P and then double-click **Pay_Type** when it appears in the AutoComplete list.

d. Type ,A16) and then press Ctrl+Enter. Now the Customer Type can be changed in B14, and the Average will automatically adjust.

e. Click cell **B16**, double-click the **AutoFill** handle to copy the formula without formatting down through **B18**, and then click **Save**.

f. Click cell **B14**, and then type Non_Local to test your formulas. Notice that your numbers will be updated because you changed the criteria that the AVERAGEIFS function is referencing.

g. Press Ctrl+Z to change the value in B14 back to "Local".

Use Conditional Math Functions

Conditional math functions work in a similar fashion as the statistical functions just covered. The conditional math functions include the SUMIF and SUMIFS functions.

Using the SUMIF Function

The **SUMIF function** selects values from a range of data based on criteria and then adds those values together. The SUMIF function sums data based on one criterion. The syntax for the SUMIF function is:

$$=\text{SUMIF(range, criteria, [sum\_range])}$$

For the SUMIF function, because there is only one criterion allowed, the first argument is the range associated with the criterion. The second argument is the criterion itself, which will determine which values are summed. The third argument, [sum_range], is optional because you can set the criterion on the actual sum range. If the [sum_range] argument is omitted, the default is to assume the range and the sum_range are the same. However, a great feature with this function is that the criteria can be set on one range, like the payment type, while summing a second range, like the payment amount.

E05.15

 To Create a SUMIF Function

a. Click the **Revenue Report** worksheet tab. Click cell **B22**, type =SUMIF(Shift,B21,Line_Item_Total) and then press Enter. This will select those transactions that occurred during the morning shift and sum the Line_Item_Total values.

b. Click cell **B4**, type =SUMIF(Cust_Cat,A4,Line_Item_Total) and then press Ctrl + Enter. This will total the revenue for each customer type.

c. In cell **B4**, double-click the **AutoFill** handle to copy the formula without formatting down through cell **B6**, and then click **Save** ⊟. Now each subset of line item totals has been summed and then grouped by the customer type.

Using the SUMIFS Function

With the **SUMIFS function**, it is assumed that multiple criteria would be set, thus having a sum_range different from at least one criteria_range. Thus, the order is changed to have the sum_range first, then add a criteria_range and criteria for each constraint or filter. For example, you could indicate the sales range to sum and have a criterion of only summing transactions that were made online and were set up as gifts. The syntax for the SUMIFS function is:

$$=\text{SUMIFS(sum\_range, criteria\_range1, criteria1, [criteria\_range2, criteria2],...)}$$

The structure for the arguments is the same as with the AVERAGEIFS function. The criteria ranges have to match the sum_range in shape. If there are multiple criteria, the cells are evaluated for each criterion with a result of TRUE to be used in the subset of data, as shown in Figure 13.

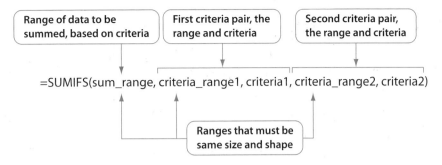

| Range of data to be summed, based on criteria | First criteria pair, the range and criteria | Second criteria pair, the range and criteria |

=SUMIFS(sum_range, criteria_range1, criteria1, criteria_range2, criteria2)

Ranges that must be same size and shape

Figure 13   SUMIFS calculation

The report has been set up to sum the Line_Item_Total range filtered by the SKU_Cat and the Cust_Cat. This way, the report will show a grid indicating revenue from Local or Non_Local, grouped by the Product Categories of Clothing, Clubs, Accessories, and Shoes.

E05.16

 To Create a SUMIFS Function

a. Click the **Revenue Report** worksheet tab. Click cell **B25**, type =SUMIFS(Line_Item_Total,SKU_Cat,$A25,Cust_Cat,B$24) and then press Ctrl + Enter. The mixed cell referencing is used so the formula can be copied to the other cells within the grid.

b. In cell **B25**, double-click the **AutoFill** handle to copy the formula without formatting down to cell **B28**.

c. With the range **B25:B28** still selected, click the **AutoFill** handle on the lower-right corner of the range, and then drag to the right to cell **D28** to copy the formula without formatting over to cell range B25:D28. Press Home.

d. Click the **Employee Report** worksheet tab, and then click cell **B6**.

The Employee Sales Report also needs some conditional sums. The Total Sales Revenue for the sales staff needs to be calculated. The current Sales Staff is an Asst Manager named Hample who has a Staff ID Number of 15, which will be used as the conditional filter.

e. Type =SUMIF(Emp_ID,A6,Line_Item_Total) and then press Enter.

f. Click cell **B13**.

The staff has a goal for each product category. Currently, Clothing is listed in B11, and the associated goal for Hample is also provided. The percentage of that goal is Hample's sales for clothing divided by the goal.

g. Type =SUMIFS(Line_Item_Total,SKU_Cat,B11,Emp_ID,A6)/B12 and then press Enter.

This will sum the records if both the SKU category is clothing and the employee ID is 15. Referencing the cells allow the category and sales staff to be changed, incorporating flexibility.

h. Click cell **B15**, type =SUMIF(Emp_ID,A6,Sales_Point1)+SUMIF(Emp_ID,A6,Sales_Point2) and then press Enter.

The incentive points need to be added up for the staff person listed. This has to be done by adding two SUMIF functions. It cannot be done in one SUMIFS function as that sums on multiple criteria, and the only criteria in this case is the Emp_ID. The sales point columns cannot be combined into one sum range as the Sales_Point1 and Sales_Point2 data would not match up in the same cells for the same range shape, thus they need to be tallied separately and then combined.

i. Click **Save**.

Construct Database Functions

Excel's worksheet structure of rows and columns allows the use of certain kinds of simple databases, and database functions are specifically designed to work with this type of data. An **Excel database** is a way of storing data that is made up of **records** (rows) and **fields** (columns). Different types of data can be organized in this manner, including common information as a contact list or a catalog of your smartphone applications. In a database, each record is one unit of data—such as an application in your collection, and each field is a specific piece of information—such as the application's name. An important aspect of databases is that each record contains the same fields. Thus, each application record will contain a title field, a rating field, a price field, a developer field, and so on. Furthermore, Excel databases must include field names that are always listed in the first row.

Database functions execute common calculations such as sum, average, and count and are designed specifically for use with an Excel database. The power of database functions lies in the fact that they permit you to identify which records to include in the calculation. Consider the smartphone application database example. The database functions let you calculate things such as the following:

- The total number of applications in your collection created by Rovio

- The highest-rated application in your collection

- The most expensive application in your collection

All database functions are named using the format DXXX() where XXX is the name of the corresponding nondatabase Excel function. For example, in the DSUM function, the D indicates that the function is a database function, and SUM is the name of the corresponding nondatabase Excel function. Additionally, all database functions include the same three arguments. Using the DMAX() function as an example, the syntax is:

$$=DMAX(database, field, criteria)$$

For the DMAX function, because the function is using data included in an Excel database, the database argument specifies the range containing the database, including the field names in the first row. The second argument, field, is the name of the database field that the calculation will use. The third argument, criteria, is the range containing the criteria that tell the function which records to use in the calculation and is a two-cell range that is one column wide and two rows high. The upper cell contains the field name that the criterion applies to; the lower cell contains the value that you want to match. For example, you could use the DMAX function to find the Line_Item_Total that contains the highest price within the filter criteria listed in range L1:U2, as shown in Figure 14.

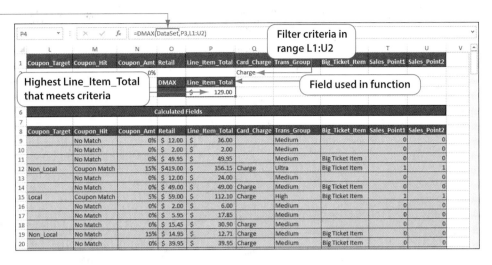

Figure 14 DMAX function

Using the DSUM Function

The **DSUM function**—similar to the SUMIFS function—is a database function that is ideal for setting up a criteria range and then calculating the sum based on the filters within that criteria range. An advantage of using the DSUM function is that you can see the criteria on the worksheet and understand the calculation much easier. Secondly, the criteria can be modified on the worksheet and the result is updated automatically. Thus, instead of editing a SUMIFS function, the DSUM criteria are changed in cells on the worksheet and there is no need to actually alter the function. The syntax of the DSUM function is

$$=DSUM(database, field, criteria)$$

The database argument is a range of cells that make up the data set, such as transaction data, which includes records and fields. The field is the field label of the column to be summed, such as Line_Item_Total. The criteria is a range of cells that contains the conditions you specify. The criteria range includes a column field label or list of field labels on the top row and one or more cell rows below the field label(s) for the criteria condition. Criteria can be put onto multiple fields at the same time. When this is done, all the criteria must be evaluated to TRUE for the record to be included in the summation of the fields. Common database functions are described in Table 8.

Database Function	Description
DAVERAGE	Averages the values in the field (column) of records in a list or database that match conditions you specify
DCOUNT	Counts the cells that contain numbers in a field (column) of records in the database that match the conditions you specify
DCOUNTA	Counts nonblank cells in the field (column) of records in the database that match the conditions you specify
DGET	Extracts a single value from a field (column) of a database that matches the conditions you specify
DMAX	Returns the largest number in the field (column) of records in the database that match the conditions you specify
DMIN	Returns the smallest number in the field (column) of records in the database that match the conditions you specify
DPRODUCT	Multiplies the values in the field (column) of records in the database that match the conditions you specify
DSTDEV	Estimates the standard deviation based on a sample by using numbers in a field (column) of records in a database that match conditions you specify
DSTDEVP	Calculates the standard deviation based on the entire population by using numbers in a field (column) of records in a database that match conditions you specify
DSUM	Adds the numbers in a field (column) of records in the database that match conditions you specify
DVAR	Estimates the variance based on a sample by using the numbers in a field (column) of records in a database that match conditions you specify
DVARP	Calculates the variance based on the entire population by using the numbers in a field (column) of records in a database that match conditions you specify

Table 8   Database functions

E05.17

 To Create a DSUM Function

a. Click the **Database Totals** worksheet tab. Click cell **G2**, type Non_Local and then press Enter.

   This value is the constraint for filtering the records. Only records that are nonlocal customers will be used in the DSUM function.

b. Click cell **B5**, type =DSUM(DataSet,B4,A1:K2) and then press Enter.

   The DataSet is the transaction database data found on the Transactions worksheet. B4 is the field that will be summed. A1:K2 is the two rows of information that is the criteria.

c. Press Home, and then click **Save** 🖫.

d. Click cell **A2**, type Check and then press Enter.

   This changes the value reflected in B5 immediately, and once again, flexibility has been integrated into the formula. B4 is the field to be summed. If Barry wants to sum the line item total or the transaction quantity, he simply puts the field name into B4. The formula will automatically be updated. The field chosen for B4 should be a numerical field like the Line_Item_Total or the Trans_Qty.

e. Press Home, and then click **Save** 🖫.

Retrieving Data Using LOOKUP and Reference Functions

With sets of data, it is also useful to be able to look for and retrieve specific data. For example, you may have exam scores and you need to convert the numerical score into a letter grade. Within a business, you may need to convert a coupon number into a percentage number so the amount of the discount can be calculated. In both cases, you want to search for, or look up a value, and then retrieve some corresponding information. You need to refer to or retrieve specific information. A variety of functions exist for this type of data analysis. In this section, you will create functions that will look up information based on the initial data set. Then you will work to evaluate and eliminate errors within the worksheet model.

Explore LOOKUP Functions

There are two LOOKUP functions—VLOOKUP and HLOOKUP—you can use to look up a value and then, using that value as a reference, return data that is associated with that value. LOOKUP functions are extremely valuable when working with tables where the data is in rows or columns.

Using the VLOOKUP Function with an Approximate Match

The **VLOOKUP function** is the more commonly used LOOKUP function. It has four arguments, three of which are required; the other is optional. The syntax for the VLOOKUP function is:

=VLOOKUP(lookup_value, table_array, col_index_number, [range_lookup])

The "V" in VLOOKUP stands for vertical and is used when your comparison values are located in a column—vertically—to the left of the data that you want to find. For example, a teacher could use a VLOOKUP to look up an exam score and retrieve the corresponding letter grade. The setup for the VLOOKUP function shown in Figure 15 uses a TRUE value for the optional [range_lookup] argument. It should be noted that if this optional argument is omitted, Excel defaults to the TRUE argument, which will find the next lower value for a specified value. Because a TRUE argument will not search for an exact match and will return the next lower match that it finds, it should also be noted that the far-left lookup_value column must be sorted in ascending order to ensure the appropriate value is returned. In Figure 15, the lookup_value is 72, and when Excel encounters the value of 80, Excel will assume the closest value in this example will be approximate to the lower 70 score value. A score of 79 will also drop down to the closest match less than that value, so 79 would also return the 70 value result.

VLOOKUP(B1, table, 2, TRUE)

Cell A1	Cell B1		1	2
C	72		SCORE	GRADE
			0	F
			60	D
			70	C
			80	B
			90	A

Figure 15 VLOOKUP function

For the Employee Report, Barry wants to give incentives to staff that do well in selling products. He is awarding points for certain transactions, and a set of rewards has been set up for redeeming points earned during the time period. The more points earned, the better the rewards. He will adjust the awards and point levels needed to attain the various choices. On the Employee Report worksheet, the incentive points have been added. The point value needs to be converted to show their reward level. There are four reward levels, and no reward is an additional possibility. As Figure 15 illustrates, a VLOOKUP can be used to find the approximate match and return the appropriate result to the points attained.

Using the VLOOKUP Function with an Exact Match

The other optional argument for a VLOOKUP searches for an exact match. You search for an exact match daily in a contact list when looking for a phone number associated with a name. You search for a name and from the name obtain the phone number or other data that has been stored in the little table such as the one shown in Figure 16 that demonstrates the process and components of a phone contact list within the structure of a VLOOKUP. Each row contains the information for a person. The value you look up is the name. The information returned is in the adjacent columns to the right of the name. The lookup_value is the value Excel will look for in the far-left column of the table array. For a phone number, an exact match is needed. This is achieved with the optional [range-lookup] argument set to FALSE or a 0. If the VLOOKUP does not find an exact match in the left column of the table_array, it will return a #N/A error—not available. If the fourth argument is assigned a FALSE, or 0 value, the VLOOKUP will return an exact match, and it will not be necessary to sort the lookup_value column in ascending order.

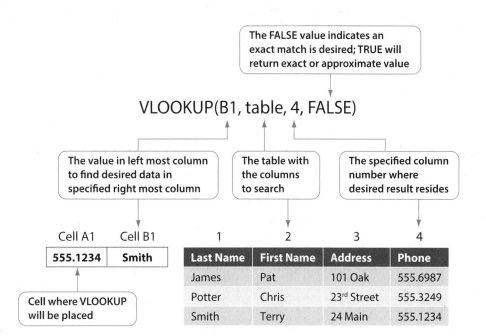

| | | 1 | 2 | 3 | 4 |

The FALSE value indicates an exact match is desired; TRUE will return exact or approximate value

VLOOKUP(B1, table, 4, FALSE)

The value in left most column to find desired data in specified right most column

The table with the columns to search

The specified column number where desired result resides

Cell A1 | Cell B1

555.1234 | Smith

Cell where VLOOKUP will be placed

Last Name	First Name	Address	Phone
James	Pat	101 Oak	555.6987
Potter	Chris	23rd Street	555.3249
Smith	Terry	24 Main	555.1234

Figure 16 Exact match VLOOKUP for phone number

The SKU_Cat will be included with the data brought into the Transactions worksheet, but the retail purchase price will not be included. This data, however, can be found by referencing a SKU_List table that is maintained on the Data Inputs worksheet. The Item ID will need to be found in the SKU_List table, and the corresponding Retail_Price can then be included. This means the first column of the range where the search will occur must contain the Item ID. Because an exact match must be found, the table does not have to be sorted.

E05.19

To Find an Exact Match in VLOOKUP

a. Click the **Transactions** worksheet tab. Click cell **O9**, type =VLOOKUP(C9,SKU_List,6,FALSE) and then press Ctrl + Enter.

The SKU_List on the Data Inputs worksheet has the list and is a named range. The Item ID in cell reference C9 is also located in the first column of the table. The corresponding Retail Price is pulled from the sixth column, counting from left to right within the SKU_List table.

b. With cell **O9** selected, click the **AutoFill** handle, and then drag to copy the formula down to cell **O208** to overwrite the static values. The formula will display a #N/A error for any cells referencing a blank cell in column C, but this will be corrected in a later exercise when the worksheet is checked and updated for errors.

c. Click cell **N9**.

The coupon percentage needs to be determined from the coupon number provided in column F. The Coupons table is set up on the Data Inputs worksheet and is a range named Coupons.

d. Type =VLOOKUP(F9,Coupons,2,FALSE) and then press Ctrl + Enter.

Note the #N/A error that appears. Because no coupon was used in the column F cell reference, Excel cannot find an exact match and returns an error message that means it is not applicable or not available.

e. With cell **N9** selected, click the **AutoFill** handle, and then drag to copy the formula down to cell **N208** to overwrite the static values.

Note the error messages occur for all the transactions that do not have a Coupon_Num entry listed in the column F cell. This can be corrected when the worksheet is checked and updated for errors.

f. Click cell **I9**, type =VLOOKUP(C9,SKU_List,3,FALSE) and then press [Ctrl]+[Enter].

The SKU_Cat needs to be determined by looking at the SKU in column C. The SKU_List on the Data Inputs worksheet has the Item ID on the left side so it can be searched. Looking at the SKU_List table, the Category is listed in the third column. The search needs to find an exact match, not approximate. From that, the VLOOKUP can be created.

g. In cell **I9**, click the **AutoFill** handle, and then drag to copy the formula down to cell **I208** to overwrite the static values.

The formula will display a #N/A error for any cells referencing a blank cell in column C, but this will be corrected in a later exercise when the worksheet is checked and updated for errors.

h. Click **Save** 🖫.

REAL WORLD ADVICE   **The VLOOKUP Function in Business**

Businesses use LOOKUP functions on a regular basis because they have a tremendous amount of data stored in multiple workbooks. Employers will expect you to be comfortable with LOOKUP functions when you seek employment. An interviewer may even ask you if you know how to work with them.

Using the HLOOKUP Function

The **HLOOKUP function** works in the same manner as the VLOOKUP function except the lookup_value is checked horizontally in the top row of the table_array. As seen in Figure 17, the HLOOKUP wants a row_index_number indicating which row below the lookup row the target value can be found. By comparison, the VLOOKUP used a col_index_num. All the remaining arguments are the same and operate in a similar manner. The HLOOKUP also uses the optional [range_lookup] argument with the same approximate or exact match options.

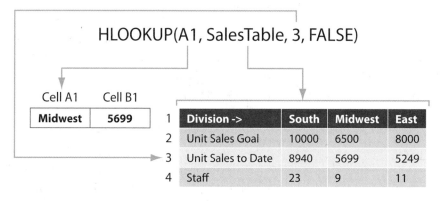

Figure 17   HLOOKUP function

For the report, a section is set up to analyze individual staff. With an individual listed, formulas will be created to retrieve information pertaining to that person, such as each employee's revenue goal.

Barry would also like to be able to retrieve data about the Transaction Groups, the Shifts, or the Coupons that have been established on the Data Inputs worksheet. Because the worksheet needs to be flexible, he wants to be able to choose one of those options and have the categories appear for that option, and then calculate the sum when it can be applied to appropriate categories on the Transactions worksheet. But first, an adjustment to the Revenue Report worksheet will be developed.

E05.20

 To Create an HLOOKUP Function

a. Click the **Data Inputs** worksheet tab, and then select range **B12:G17**.

   This is the data and headings for the HLOOKUP function. It will be used to search in the first row for the different reporting groups as needed.

b. Click the **FORMULAS** tab, and then in the Defined Names group, click **Define Name**.

c. In the New Name dialog box, replace **AH_Shifts** by typing AH_ReportTable in the Name box, and then click **OK**. Now the table can be referenced easily in formulas.

d. On the FORMULAS tab, in the Defined Names group, click **Create from Selection**. Uncheck the **Left column** check box, and then click **OK**. Now, each report group has also been named so they can easily be referenced.

e. Click the **Revenue Report** worksheet tab, click cell **E8**, type =HLOOKUP($F$6,AH_ReportTable,D8+1,FALSE) replacing the text that is in the cell, and then press Ctrl+Enter.

   This will look for the Ad Hoc Report Name listed in F6 within the AH_ReportTable range on the Data Inputs worksheet. Once that data is found, Excel will retrieve the category item. Because the function has FALSE as the last argument, Excel will look for an exact match to the value in F6.

f. Click cell **E8**, and then click the **AutoFill** handle and drag to copy the formula down through **E11**.

   Using the numbers in column D allows the formula to be copied without having to edit the row_index_num within each formula. If it had been hard-coded into the formula, it could not have been copied to the other cells without editing them.

g. Click the **Transactions** worksheet tab, and then click cell **K9**.

   The Shift needs to be determined from the time of the transaction. The Shifts named range has been created on the Data Inputs worksheet for range B20:D21. The times fall within time ranges. Thus, searching for an exact match would rarely succeed. Instead, an approximate match is needed.

h. Type =HLOOKUP(B9,Shifts,2,TRUE) and then press Ctrl+Enter. This will find an approximate match, and then pull the corresponding result from the second row in the table.

i. Click cell **K9**, click the **AutoFill** handle, and then drag to copy the formula down to cell **K208** to overwrite the static values. Ignore the #N/A errors, which will be corrected later.

j. Click the **Employee Report** worksheet tab, and then click cell **B8**.

   The overall goal for the staff, currently Hample, needs to be retrieved. The staff's goals are listed on the Data Inputs worksheet. The data can be pulled from the table and can be flexible so it will be updated when the staff member listed in A4 changes.

k. Type =HLOOKUP(A4,'Data Inputs'!B4:F9,6,FALSE) and then press Enter.

l. Click cell **B9**, type =B6/B8 and then press Enter so the percent of goal is now determined.

m. Click **Save** 🔲.

CONSIDER THIS | **Using VLOOKUP or Nested IF**

Take the situation of converting an exam score to a letter grade. Could you create an IF function statement that would accomplish the same task? What logical issues would lead you to use a VLOOKUP versus a nested IF? Which one would be more efficient?

Retrieve Data Using MATCH, INDEX, and INDIRECT

VLOOKUP and HLOOKUP search the first column or row of data and "look" to the right or down to retrieve a value. What if you wanted to find the name of the person with the phone number (412) 555-8767 in the phone book? Would that be easy to do? Unfortunately, the task becomes more difficult because a traditional phone book is organized by name, not by phone number.

To overcome this limitation in the VLOOKUP and HLOOKUP functions, the MATCH and INDEX functions work to accomplish the same type of process. The primary difference is that these two functions together overcome the limitation of data arrangement. With the MATCH and INDEX functions, you have the added flexibility of multiple data ranges that can be located throughout the worksheet. The ability to use MATCH and INDEX together is a powerful capability within Excel.

Using the MATCH Function

The **MATCH function** looks for a value within a range and returns the position of that value within the range. The position is a relative location starting from the top row of the table array. The syntax for the MATCH function is:

$$=MATCH(lookup\_value, lookup\_array, [match\_type])$$

The optional [match_type] argument uses a value of −1, 0, or 1. The default value of 1 is assumed if it is omitted. A [match_type] value of 0 is used for an exact match, a 1 returns a match for the largest value that is less than or equal to the lookup_value, and a −1 finds the smallest value that is greater than or equal to the lookup_value. The exact match will return the row where the first occurrence of the match resides. This means that if there are multiple occurrences of a value, Excel will return the first one it finds, from the top, and will not find subsequent values. The 1 will find the location of the value that is closest to the value, but not greater than the value. The −1 value will return the position of the value that is closest to the lookup_value, but not less than the lookup_value. Thus, by being able to return either the next lowest or next higher value, the match has a little more flexibility than the VLOOKUP function. In either the 1 or −1 options, the data has to be sorted in ascending order or descending order, respectively, or the match process will not work correctly.

The MATCH function returns a number that indicates the position, or row, in which the match was found. This value will be relative to the top row of the range. While the function indicates the lookup_array is one range, the range must be one continuous range that is only in one column. If you try to use a range that includes more than one column, the MATCH function will not work.

For the Revenue Report, Barry wants to be able to check the transactions and see when the first transaction that used a coupon occurred. Using the MATCH function will enable him to determine the transaction number of the first occurrence.

E05.21

 To Create a MATCH Function

a. Click the **Revenue Report** worksheet tab. Click cell **E14**, type =MATCH(E13,Coupon_Num,0) and then press ⏎.

The coupon listed in E13 will be searched in the Coupon_Num field as the lookup_array within the Transactions worksheet. The third argument in the function is 0, indicating the search should be for an exact match.

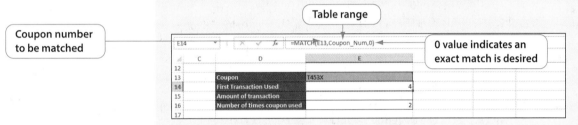

Figure 18 MATCH function

b. Click **Save** 💾.

If the coupon listed in E13 is not used in any of the transactions, it will return the #N/A error, which indicates it could not find the coupon listed. If the coupon listed was typed incorrectly, this would also return a #N/A error. It would not be easy to determine whether a #N/A error indicates if the discount coupon typed in was simply not used or if it was not a valid coupon.

REAL WORLD ADVICE | **Handling Typing Errors**

With a short list of options, like coupon numbers, using a comment to list the coupon codes is a reasonable solution. But, it is still possible to make typing errors. To minimize typing errors, you will typically create a drop-down list of the options. This eliminates typing errors and is a more efficient method. Learning to incorporate drop-down lists in a cell is handled in another workshop. It is a valuable tool to use in validating data.

Using the Index Function

The **INDEX function** works in conjunction with the MATCH function. The INDEX function returns the value of an element in a table or array selected by the row and column number indexes and has two argument lists to select. The first list of arguments uses an array and returns a value from a specified cell or range. The second list of arguments uses a reference and returns a reference to specified cells. The more common set of arguments, which will be discussed here, is with the array that returns a value. The value gets returned from a range based on the row and column indicated. The indexing starts from the top-left corner of the table. Thus, the left column, first row, of the table would be row 1 and column 1. The index is relative based on the top-left corner of the array. The syntax for the INDEX function is:

$$=\text{INDEX(array, row\_number, [column\_number])}$$

The array is the range of data; the row_number is the row in which the value will be found; and if the [column_number] is provided, it will be the column number, starting from the left of the range from which the result will be retrieved. The INDEX function works with the MATCH function extremely well because the MATCH function indicates the row where a match was found, and then the INDEX can go to that row and another column to retrieve associated data.

E05.22

 To Create an INDEX Function

a. Click the **Revenue Report** worksheet tab, and then click cell **E15**.

Knowing when the first transaction occurred, the amount of the transaction prior to the discount could be pulled from the transaction data using the INDEX function. The transaction total would be price*quantity for that transaction, which is in row 4 of the data.

b. Type **=INDEX(Trans_Qty,E14)*INDEX(Retail,E14)** and then press ⏎ Enter.

This goes to the fourth record in the Trans_Qty field found on the Transactions worksheet, retrieves the value, then retrieves the value from the fourth record in the Retail field range, and multiplies the two values to compute the total amount of the transaction.

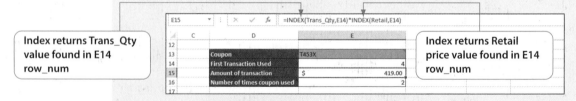

Figure 19 INDEX function

c. Press ⎈ Ctrl + ⌂ Home.

d. Click the **Employee Report** worksheet tab, and then click cell **B20**.

Barry wants to be able to list the rewards for the different levels so it is available as he talks with his staff. Currently, it shows Level_1 in B19. He wants the three Level_1 rewards to be listed below. He can use the INDEX function and the numbers in column A to retrieve the information.

e. Type **=INDEX(Level_1,A20)** and then press ⎈ Ctrl + ⏎ Enter.

f. In cell **B20**, use the **AutoFill** handle to copy the formula without formatting down to **B22**.

   The items available for Level_1 are now listed. However, the formulas would need to be changed if a different level was desired. In a later section, this will be modified to automatically be updated when cell B19 is modified.

g. Click cell **B4**.

   The position for the staff member, currently listed as Hample, needs to be retrieved. However, in the table, Hample is not the first column. It could still be searched, but using a VLOOKUP would not work because the position field is to the left of the Last Name field in the table on the Data Inputs worksheet. The MATCH function can locate the row where Hample exists, and then go to the same row for the positions and retrieve his position.

h. Type =MATCH(A4,'Data Inputs'!L27:L31) and then press Ctrl+Enter. This will show the row where Hample is located—in row 1.

i. Press F2 to edit cell **B4**. Click in the **Formula Bar** to position the insertion point to the right of the = sign, and then type INDEX('Data Inputs'!I27:I31,. Position the cursor at the end of the formula, type) and then press Enter. The formula is now set to retrieve Hample's position value using the nested MATCH function to determine the row_num argument.

j. Click the **Transactions** worksheet tab, and then click cell **J9**. The employee position for all the transactions needs to be retrieved and accomplished in a similar manner as retrieving Hample's position.

k. Type =INDEX('Data Inputs'!$I$27:$I$31,MATCH(G9,'Data Inputs'!$J$27:$J$31,0)) and then press Ctrl+Enter. The dollar signs, which make the references absolute, are necessary because the ranges need to stay in place as the formula is copied down the column.

l. Click the **AutoFill** handle, and then copy the formula down to cell **J208** to overwrite the static values. The errors will be fixed later when the sheet is error checked.

m. Click the **Employee Report** worksheet tab, and then click cell **B12**.

   Currently the value is $200 for the clothing goal for Hample. But, for flexibility, Barry wants this number to be updated if the staff member changes and if the product category changes. Fortunately, the Sales Goals table found on the Data Inputs worksheet has all the goal values listed for each category for each staff member, and the named range has been saved as Goals.

n. Click the **Name** box, and then choose **Goals** from the list of named ranges.

   You will see it selects the data associated with the staff and the goals for each category. If the row and column within the table is known, the INDEX function can be used to pull the value for the appropriate goal value. By using the MATCH functions within the INDEX function, the goal can be retrieved. Building it a piece at a time will help with the development by testing the subcomponents.

o. Click the **Employee Report** worksheet tab. Click cell **D12**, type =MATCH(B11,'Data Inputs'!A5:A9,0) and then press Ctrl+Enter. This will be deleted once you create the entire formula piece by piece.

   This is the first piece and shows the row where the lookup_value from B11—Clothing—is found in the Goals range. The last argument, with 0, indicates an exact match should be found.

p. Click cell **D13**, type =MATCH(A4,'Data Inputs'!B4:F4,0) and then press Ctrl+Enter.

   This will be deleted once you create the entire formula piece by piece. The formula returns the column where the staff member is located in the Goals named range on the Data Inputs worksheet.

SIDE NOTE
Viewing Named Ranges
To navigate to the Goals named range, you can also press F5 to open the Go To dialog box, select Goals, and then click OK.

q. Click cell **B12**. Knowing the MATCH functions work, the complex function can be constructed.

r. Type =INDEX(Goals,MATCH(B11,'Data Inputs'!A5:A9,0),MATCH(A4,'Data Inputs'!B4:F4,0)) and then press Enter.

The Goals range on the Data Inputs worksheet array is used. The first MATCH function is the row within the table, and the second MATCH function is the column within the range. Using those coordinates, the INDEX function returns the correct goal value.

s. Select cells **D12:D13**, press Delete to remove the test functions, and then click **Save** 🖫.

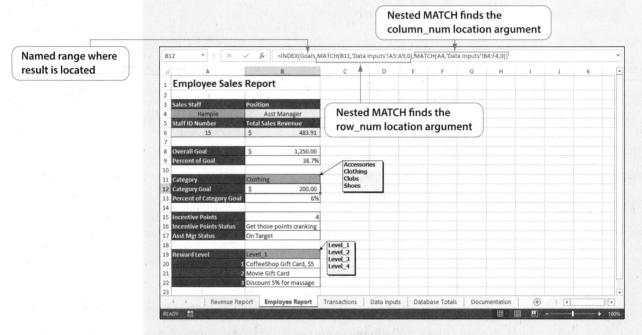

Figure 20   INDEX function with nested MATCH functions

Using the INDIRECT Function

The **INDIRECT function** is another reference function that can be used to add flexibility to a worksheet. The INDIRECT function is valuable because it can change a text string within a cell to a cell reference. The syntax for the INDIRECT function is:

$$=INDIRECT(ref\_text, [a1])$$

The argument typically is a cell reference or a text string, and within that cell you can enter in another cell, range, or named range. The function tells Excel to interpret the cell's value as a reference rather than a text string. In other words, the cell referenced in the INDIRECT function reroutes to a new reference. In Figure 21, the formula in cell A1 does not use a specific named range. The AVERAGE function does not go directly to the named range. It goes indirectly, to B1, which redirects the function to use the range listed in B1. The INDIRECT function pulls the value in B1, the range named "Pat" as a range to be averaged. Instead of changing the named range in the formula, the name can be changed in cell B1 from "Pat" to "Chris" and it would give the average for Chris. This adds flexibility to choose which named range to average.

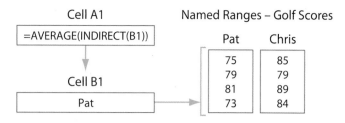

Cell A1	Named Ranges – Golf Scores	
=AVERAGE(INDIRECT(B1))	Pat	Chris
	75	85
Cell B1	79	79
	81	89
Pat	73	84

Figure 21   INDIRECT function logic

The optional INDIRECT argument will not be a concern for the average user. The function defaults to the **A1 reference method** if the A1 argument is omitted, which merely refers to the A1 reference method for cell references. If letters appear for the column headings, the reference style for Excel is currently A1. In this mode, cells are referenced using a letter for the column and a number for the row.

The alternative method is referred to as the **R1C1 reference style**. If numbers appear for the column headings, the reference style for Excel is currently R1C1. For example, if a value is in the third row and fourth column, the cell reference would be R3C4. Excel allows you to set the R1C1 reference style check box as a default option under Formulas within the Excel Options dialog box.

Whichever reference style mode Excel is in, all cell references typed in formulas must be in that reference style form—A1 or R1C1. If not, an error will be produced. The A1 reference style is the easiest to use in Excel and the default method.

On the Employee Report worksheet, if Barry wants to look at the different rewards in the different levels, the formulas would need to be changed again. Preferably, the value in B19 could show the level that is to be displayed. And, since it is the name of the range that holds the list of rewards, it could be used in the three formulas. Using the INDIRECT function would allow the value in cell B19 to change, and the reward list would automatically be updated.

E05.23

 To Create an INDIRECT Function

a. Click the **Employee Report** worksheet, and then click cell **B20**.

b. Click in the **Formula Bar**. Select the **Level_1** text, type INDIRECT($B$19) and then press ⌈Ctrl⌉+⌈Enter⌉.

c. Double-click the **AutoFill** handle to copy the formula without formatting down to **B22**, press ⌈Ctrl⌉+⌈Home⌉, and then click **Save** 🔲.

> **Troubleshooting**
> If your borders change once you copy the formula down, you click the Auto Fill Options button and then select Fill Without Formatting.

The complete formula in B20 should now appear as =INDEX(INDIRECT($B$19),A20). Now, instead of hard-coding the named range, the formula goes to A20 and pulls the value in A20 to use as the range, indirectly, by going first to B19, and B19 is directing the formula to use the Level_1 value contained in the cell as the named cell range.

Handle Errors with the IFERROR Function

Because logical functions are used in decision-making scenarios where flexibility and scalability are desirable, there are times in the development of the formulas when the functions may return error messages. Because there could be multiple users of varying skills, it is important to minimize the occurrence of error messages within the workbook. Error messages tend to make users uncomfortable because they believe they did something wrong. Additionally, if the error message is legitimate, and other calculations reference those cells, the errors will carry forward into the next formulas, compounding the problem.

The solution is to be aware of when errors may occur—such as a dividing by 0 or because you are referencing an empty cell—and create functions in a way that eliminates the error message from being viewed. During development, it is possible to anticipate and handle errors within the formula if you consider the values being used and the possible answers.

REAL WORLD ADVICE   Using a Blank or a Zero to Hide an Error

Does it matter what you put in for a result or outcome for an IF statement? What are the implications when you use "" versus a 0? This is not an easy decision if the cell will be used in another formula. When a calculation refers to a cell where you have used a blank, created with the double quotes, the result will be a #VALUE! error or #DIV/0! error. The calculation will not be able to compute the blank as a numerical value. Conversely, if you enter a 0 for a value so it is numerical, then that number would be used in aggregate functions. This could potentially miscalculate an average. Because of this, you have to be careful when you decide to leave the cell blank or enter a 0. Consider how the result will be used. If it is not going to be used in later calculations, then using the blank is a viable solution. Otherwise, you may need to enter a 0. An alternative to consider when cells in a range contain a 0 is to use a calculation formula that allows you to filter data based on certain criteria. For example, if you need to average your results that contain cells with a 0, you can use the AVERAGEIF and only average the numbers that are greater than 0.

Using the IFERROR Function

The **IFERROR function** is a useful tool for detecting an error and displaying something more user-friendly than the error message. With the IFERROR function, it is possible to evaluate if an error will occur and replace one of Excel's default error messages with another value that you specify; otherwise, the formula result will be returned. The syntax for the IFERROR function is:

$$=IFERROR(value, value\_if\_error)$$

The first argument, value, is the formula that is going to be checked for existing errors. If the value works and a valid output exists, that formula result will be returned. However, if the value returns any error message, such as #N/A or #DIV/0!, then the value_if_error value will be returned.

When examining the Transactions worksheet, you will see there are error messages showing up within the range in two different contexts. First, when there are not any transaction records, error messages exist throughout. Secondly, in a few columns, error messages occur even when there are transactions. The #N/A is not only distracting, it is confusing to users because they may believe there are calculation errors when in actuality the errors are valid errors.

In the process of checking the values and eliminating errors, it is best to start with formulas that are simple and do not reference other cells that have formulas. For example, if an error exists in a formula in cell A1, that error will create an error in any other formula that references A1. For the Transactions data, it also makes sense to first correct fields where the error message occurs only where data does not exist. Checking the formulas, it appears that fields such as SKU_Cat, Emp_Position, and Shift have errors only when cells are empty. A simple way to eliminate this type of error is to leave the cell blank if an error message occurs.

E05.24

 To Eliminate Errors

a. Click the **Transactions** worksheet tab, and then click cell **I9**. Click in the **Formula Bar**, place the insertion point to the right of the equal sign, and then type IFERROR(.

b. Reposition the cursor at the end of the formula, type ,"") and then press Ctrl+Enter.

c. In cell **I9**, double-click the **AutoFill** handle to automatically update the entire column of formulas. This will update any error cells with a blank cell whenever there is no record for the formula cell references in those fields.

d. Click cell **J9**, click in the **Formula Bar** to place the insertion point to the right of the equal sign, and then type IFERROR(. Click to place the insertion point at the end of the formula, type ,"") and then press Ctrl+Enter.

e. Click cell **K9**, click in the **Formula Bar** to place the insertion point to the right of the equal sign, and then type IFERROR(. Click to place the insertion point at the end of the formula, type ,"") and then press Ctrl+Enter.

f. Select range **J9:K9**, and then double-click the **AutoFill** handle in the bottom-right corner of the range to copy the formula down to **J208:K208** and overwrite the existing formulas.

g. Click cell **L9**.

With this column, there are no error messages. However, "Local" is displayed whenever there is not a value in the Coupon_Num field. Evaluating any calculations on the formula results, such as a COUNT formula, would be erroneous because of the incorrect "Local" values. The formula needs to show nothing when there is no coupon. An IF function that checks if the Coupon_Num field is empty will eliminate the issue.

h. Click in the **Formula Bar** to place the insertion point to the right of the equal sign, type IF(F9<>"", and then click to reposition the insertion point at the end of the formula. Type ,"") and then press Ctrl+Enter.

This will check F9 using <> "" to see if I5 or I7 on the Data Inputs worksheet contain values. If either does, it will check for the type of coupon and return the corresponding value. If it does not contain a value, the cell will remain blank.

i. Double-click the **AutoFill** handle to copy the formula down to **L208** and overwrite the existing formulas.

j. Click cell **M9**. Click in the **Formula Bar** to place the insertion point to the right of the equal sign, type IF(H9<>"", and then click to reposition the insertion point at the end of the formula. Type ,"") and then press Ctrl+Enter.

This column has the same issue as the Coupon_Target column. This will check H9 using <> "" to see if L9 on the Data Inputs worksheet contain values. If either does, it will check for the type of coupon and return the corresponding value. If it does not contain a value, the cell will remain blank.

k. Click cell **M9**, and then double-click the **AutoFill** handle to copy the formula down to **M208**.

l. Click cell **N9**.

This cell has the #N/A error because the formula cannot locate an exact VLOOKUP value to match a blank cell found in the Coupon_Num field. The IFERROR function will correct this issue.

m. Click in the **Formula Bar** to place the insertion point to the right of the equal sign, and then type IFERROR(. Click to reposition the insertion point at the end of the formula, type ,0) and then press Ctrl+Enter. Double-click the **AutoFill** handle to copy the formula down to **N208**.

n. Click cell **O9**, click in the **Formula Bar** to place the insertion point to the right of the equal sign, and then type IFERROR(. Click to reposition the insertion point at the end of the formula, type ,0) and then press Ctrl+Enter. Double-click the **AutoFill** handle to copy the formula down to **O208**.

o. Click cell **P9**, and then type =ROUND(O9*E9-(O9*E9*N9),2). This function will round the calculation to take Retail price times Trans_Qty and then subtract the discount calculations.

p. Press Ctrl+Enter. Click the **AutoFill** handle, and then copy the formula down to **P208**. Click **Save** 🖫. Because column P still contained hard-coded values, this formula will display the correct calculation for the Line_Item_Total.

Eliminating Errors

Earlier you used the IFERROR function to correct the values in column N (Coupon_Amt) by placing a zero for any error references. What if you had used a blank cell correction instead? When a 0 or "" is placed in a formula, the worksheet should be checked to ensure that the 0 or blank does not interfere with formulas that reference those cells. For example, a 0 would affect the AVERAGE function. If there is a 0 where there is no record, this would miscalculate the average.

E05.25

 To Evaluate and Eliminate Errors

a. Click the **Transactions** worksheet tab, and then click cell **N9**. Click in the **Formula Bar**, select the **0** at the end located before the last closing parenthesis, and then type "" to replace the zero with an empty text string. Press Ctrl+Enter. Notice the #VALUE! error is displayed in cells P9, R9, T9, and U9.

b. Double-click the **AutoFill** handle to copy the formula down to **N208**. Notice the #VALUE! errors that appear in numerous cells for the affected columns.

c. Press Ctrl+Z to undo the AutoFill. Press Ctrl+Z again to undo the formula change to cell N9. The worksheet should return to normal without the errors.

d. Click cell **R9**.

The formula in column R returns a value of Low for records that have no transactions.

e. Click the **Revenue Report** worksheet tab, and then click cell **B9**.

Recall that B9 counts the number of Low values on the Transaction worksheet for the Trans_Group column; thus, the 190 is correct for the current amount of Low values, but the count is not valid or accurate. This supports the need to carefully evaluate the formulas throughout the entire worksheet.

SIDE NOTE

Expand the Formula Bar

If you cannot see the end of your formula, expand the Formula Bar. Place your cursor between the Formula Bar and column headings until it changes into a double arrow. Drag your cursor down until you see the entire formula.

f. Click the **Transactions** worksheet tab, and then if necessary, click cell **R9**. Click in the **Formula Bar** to place the insertion point to the right of the equal sign, type IF(A9<>"", and then click to reposition the cursor at the end of the formula. Type ,"") and then press Ctrl + Enter.

This checks if there is a transaction ID in Trans_ID. If there is a transaction ID, the formula does the calculation; otherwise, it leaves the cell blank. Using the "" is appropriate as the field is a text-oriented field.

g. Double-click the **AutoFill** handle to copy the formula down to **R208**.

h. Click cell **S9**. Click in the **Formula Bar** to place the insertion point to the right of the equal sign, type IF(A9<>"" and then click to reposition the cursor at the end of the formula. Type ,"") and then press Ctrl + Enter.

This column has the same issue of values for the nonexistent transactions. Setting it up like column R will correct this issue. If there is a transaction, the formula calculation continues; otherwise, the cell remains blank. Using the "" is appropriate as the field is a text-oriented field.

i. Click cell **S9**, and then double-click the **AutoFill** handle to copy the formula down to **S208**.

j. Complete the Documentation worksheet and submit your file as directed by your instructor. **Close** ☒ Excel.

Concept Check

1. Describe three types of data inputs that can be used for arguments within an IF function. p. 257

2. Explain how a decision tree can help you write a nested IF function. p. 257

3. Construct pseudo code for the following situation: The result "Loan" is displayed for an applicant that has either salary greater than $100,000 and a credit score of at least 700, or a salary greater than $50,000 and a credit score of at least 750. Otherwise, the result displayed is "No Loan". p. 270

4. Describe three conditional statistical functions. p. 274

5. Describe two conditional math functions. p. 278

6. What is an Excel database? Explain how database functions differ. p. 280

7. Provide examples of when you would use the TRUE/FALSE options for the fourth argument in a VLOOKUP. p. 283

8. What is the primary advantage of using the MATCH and INDEX combination versus a VLOOKUP function? p. 288

9. What benefit is there to using the IFERROR function when it increases the complexity of the formulas? p. 294

Key Terms

Visual Summary

Begin writing a nested IF formula (p. 262)

Nest an IF function (p. 264)

Nest a third IF function (p. 265)

Evaluate and eliminate errors (p. 296)

Build nested IF functions (p. 261)

Eliminate errors (p. 295)

Handle errors with the IFERROR funtion (p. 294)

Use the OR function within an IF function (p. 269)

Create an IF function (p. 258)

Eliminate errors (p. 295)

Find an exact match in VLOOKUP (p. 285)

Use the NOT function within an IF function (p. 270)

Use the OR function nested within an AND function (p. 271)

Integrate conjunction functions into IF functions (p. 267)

Use the AND function nested within an OR function (p. 272)

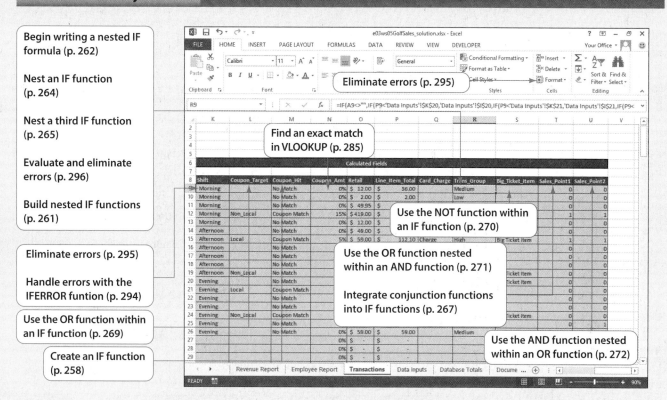

Create an AVERAGEIF function (p. 276)

Create an AVERAGEIFS function (p. 277)

Use conditional statistical functions (p. 274)

Create a SUMIF function (p. 278)

Create a SUMIFS function (p. 279)

Use conditional math functions (p. 278)

Create a COUNTIF function (p. 274)

Create a COUNTIFS function (p. 276)

Create an HLOOKUP function (p. 287)

Explore LOOKUP functions (p. 283)

Create an INDEX function (p. 290)

Create a MATCH function (p. 289)

Retrieve data using MATCH, INDEX, and INDIRECT (p. 288)

Use different elements in an IF statement (p. 260)

Preview the data and use IF functions (p. 254, 257)

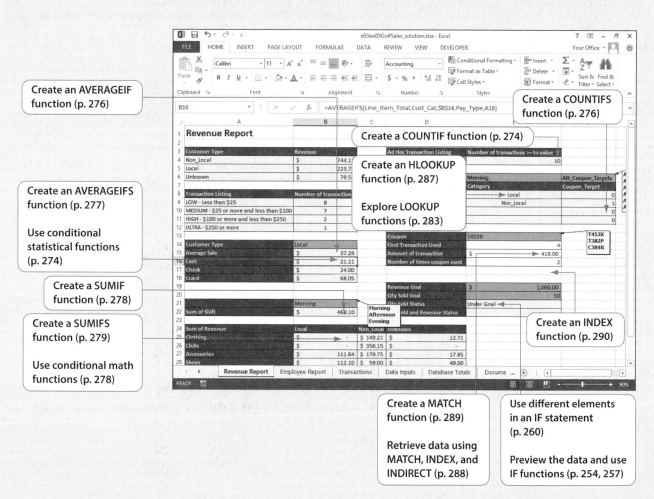

MODULE 3

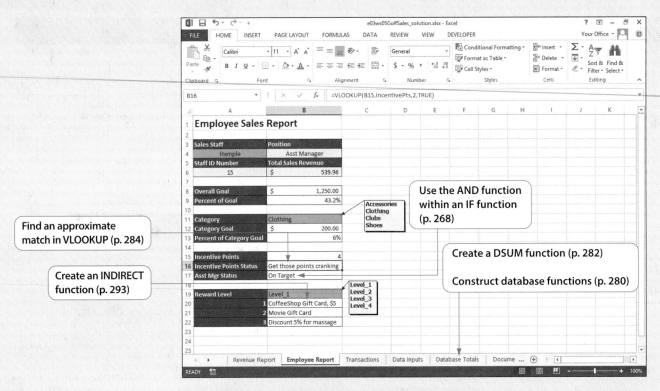

Find an approximate match in VLOOKUP (p. 284)

Create an INDIRECT function (p. 293)

Use the AND function within an IF function (p. 268)

Create a DSUM function (p. 282)

Construct database functions (p. 280)

Figure 22 Red Bluff Golf Course & Pro Shop Sales Analysis Final Workbook

Practice 1

Student data file needed:

e03ws05Scramble.xlsx

You will save your file as:

e03ws05Scramble_LastFirst.xlsx

Managing Golf Scramble Registrations

Production & Operations

The Red Bluff Golf Club is getting ready for another charity golf scramble tournament. Because it holds charity events on a regular basis, Barry Cheney, the manager, would like a workbook developed that will track information about the registrations such as foursomes, registrations, t-shirts, and fees. You have been asked to continue the development of reports to support decision making for the tournament.

a. Open the **e03ws05Scramble** workbook. Save it as **e03ws05Scramble_LastFirst** using your last and first name. Click **Enable Content** if necessary.

b. Create named ranges that will help with the development of the formulas.

   • Click the **Registrations** worksheet tab, click cell **B8**, and then press Ctrl+A to select the range of data.

   • Click the **FORMULAS** tab, and then in the Defined Names group, click **Define Name**. Type ScrambleData in the Name box, and then press Enter.

   • On the FORMULAS tab, in the Defined Names group, click **Create from Selection**. In the Create Names from Selection dialog box, verify the **Top row** check box is checked, and then click **OK**.

   • Click the **Data Inputs** worksheet tab, and then select range **B24:E27**. On the FORMULAS tab, in the Defined Names group, click **Create from Selection**. In the Create Names from Selection dialog box, verify the **Top row** check box is checked, and then click **OK**.

- Select range **B13:D15**, click in the **Name** box to the left of the formula bar, type **Sponsor_Fees** and then press Enter.

- Select cell **B2**, click in the **Name** box, type **Mulligan_Fee** and then press Enter.

c. Click the **Registrations** worksheet tab, and then click cell **M8**. To create a level playing field, there is a maximum score per hole based on a player's handicap. Type =IF(E8<>"",VLOOKUP(H8,'Data Inputs'!$A$6:$C$10,3),"") and then press Ctrl+Enter. Double-click the **AutoFill** handle to copy the formula down to **M79**. The Max Hole score will only be calculated if there is a player name.

d. Click **E2**, type **Hole in One** and then press Enter. In cell **F5**, type =DSUM(ScrambleData,F4,E1:M2) and then press Enter. This will create a DSUM function that will use the filtering in range E1:M2 for the criteria and the field listed in F4 for the summation field.

e. Determine each player within a particular foursome.

- Click the **Report** worksheet tab, click cell **C12**, and then type =MATCH(E2,Foursome_Name,0) to determine the position of the first player in the foursome, located on the Registrations worksheet. Press Enter.

- In cell **C13**, type =C12+1 and then press Enter. Click cell **C13**, and then click the **AutoFill** handle to copy the formula down to **C15**. This will find the row position for the other players in the foursome within the Registration data set.

- Click cell **B12**, type =INDEX(Sponsor_Level,C12) and then press Enter. This will determine the sponsor level, if applicable.

- Click cell **A12**, type =INDEX(Early_Bird,C12) and then press Enter. This will retrieve the early bird information for each of the players in the foursome.

- Select range **A12:B12**, and then use the **AutoFill** handle to copy the formula down through range **A15:B15**.

f. To complete the information for each player, his or her data can be retrieved from the Registration data based on the row where the player's data exists. The row was determined in column C. Each person was listed for their team, but he or she still needs to register and submit a shirt size and other information. If the player has not registered, he or she will need to be reminded to register.

- Click cell **E12**, type =IF(INDEX(Shirt_Size,C12)= "","No","Yes") and then press Tab. This will look to see if a shirt size has been inputted, indicating the player has registered.

- Click cell **F12**, type =INDEX('Registrations'!$D$8:$D$79,C12) and then press Tab. This will display the first name of the person.

- Click cell **G12**, type =INDEX('Registrations'!$E$8:$E$79,C12) and then press Tab. This will display the last name of the person.

- Click cell **H12**, type =IF(INDEX('Registrations'!$I$8:$I$79,C12)="","Missing", INDEX('Registrations'!$I$8:$I$79,C12)) and then press Tab. This will return "Missing" if the person did not sign up for any Mulligans. If he or she did, it will return how many were purchased.

- Click cell **I12**, type =IF(INDEX(Captain,C12)= "Y", "Yes","") and press Tab. This will check the record to see if the person was designated in column C on the Registration worksheet as the captain. If so, it will return "Yes". Otherwise, it will remain blank.

- Click cell **J12**, type =IF(OR(COUNTIF($H$12:$H$15,"Missing")>0,SUM($H$12:$H$15)<5),"Contact captain about mulligans","") and then press Enter. This provides a note indicating that the captain should be notified and encouraged to purchase Mulligans. The note will be given if any registrations are missing or if the total number of Mulligans is less than five total for the team.

- Select range **E12:J12**, and then use the **AutoFill** handle to copy the formulas without formatting down through range **E12:J15**.

g. Compile data about the foursome listed in E2.

- Click cell **E3**, type =AVERAGEIF(Foursome_Name,E2,Handicap) and then press Enter.
- Click cell **E4**, type =IF(I12="Yes",B12,IF(I13="Yes", B13,IF(I14="Yes",B14,B15))) and then press Enter.
- In **E5**, type =IF(I12="Yes",A12,IF(I13="Yes",A13,IF(I14="Yes",A14,A15))) and then press Enter.
- In cell **E6** type =IF(E3<'Data Inputs'!A19,'Data Inputs'!B19,IF(E3<'Data Inputs'!A20,'Data Inputs'!B20,'Data Inputs'!B21)) and then press Enter.
- Click cell **E7**, type =SUM(H12:H15) and then press Enter.
- Click cell **E8**, type =IF(OR(SUM(H12:H15)>=8,AND(E5="Yes",SUM(H12:H15)>=6)),2,0)+VLOOKUP (E4,'Data Inputs'!E6:F9,2,FALSE) and then press Enter.

h. Click cell **E18**. The listing of team names needs to be retrieved from the registration table. Type =IFERROR(INDEX(Foursome_Name,MATCH(D18,Registration_Number,0)),"") and then press Enter. Click cell **E18**, and then click the **AutoFill** handle to copy the formula down through **E35**.

i. Click cell **F18**, type =SUMIF(Foursome_Name,E18,Mulligans) and then press Ctrl+Enter. Double-click the **AutoFill** handle to copy the formula down to cell **F35**.

j. Click cell **H3**, type =HLOOKUP(E4,Sponsor_Fees,IF('Report'!E5="Yes",2,3),FALSE) and then press Enter.

k. In cell **H4**, type =SUMIF(Foursome_Name,E2,Mulligans)*Mulligan_Fee and then press Enter.

l. In cell **H5**, type =SUM(H3:H4) and then press Enter.

m. Click cell **K4**, type =COUNTIF(Shirt_Size,J3) and then press Enter.

n. In cell **K5**, type =INDEX('Data Inputs'!B25:E27,MATCH(K4,'Data Inputs'!A25:A27,1),MATCH(J3,'Data Inputs'!B24:E24,0)) and then press Enter.

o. Select columns **A:C**, right-click, and then click **Hide** to hide the columns from the user.

p. Click the **Documentation** worksheet. Click cell **A6**, and then type in today's date. Click cell **B6**, and then type in your first and last name. Complete the remainder of the **Documentation** worksheet according to your instructor's direction.

q. Click **Save**, close Excel, and then submit your file as directed by your instructor.

Problem Solve 1

MyITLab®
Grader
Homework 1

Finance & Accounting

Student data file needed:	**You will save your file as:**
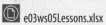 e03ws05Lessons.xlsx	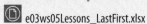 e03ws05Lessons_LastFirst.xlsx

Managing Students at a Local Music Studio

A local music studio, Fiddlers, has a large client base who take lessons on a regular basis. Additionally, some students are members of Fiddlers' competition band, which travels throughout the country and competes with some of the best musicians in the world. The owners need to be able to calculate the revenue generated through lessons and specific students. Additionally, they need to be able to calculate how much each member of the competition band will need to pay toward the next trip. The owners also need to be able to keep track of the cost of competition band uniforms, permission slips, and attendees. Furthermore, the teachers want to be able to track how many students they have and also give a free lesson to students for every five paid lessons, with a maximum of two free lessons. You have been asked to help construct a workbook that the owners can use to help manage their data.

a. Open the **e03ws05Lessons** workbook. Save it as *e03ws05Lessons_LastFirst* using your last and first name. Enable the content if necessary.

b. Create named ranges that will help with the development of the formulas.

- On the **Student Data** worksheet, select range **A7:K94**, and then name the range Student_Data. Create a named range for each column in the Student_Data named range using the top row as the range values.
- On the **Data Inputs** worksheet, select range **A3:B3**, and then create a named range using the left column as the name.
- Select range **A6:E10**, and then create a named range using Lesson_Pricing as the name.
- Select range **A13:E17**, and then create a named range using Trans_Fees as the name.
- Select range **A20:G24**, and then create a named range using Uniform_Fees as the name.
- Select range **H6:J7**, and then create a named range using Entry_Fee as the name.

c. On the Student Data worksheet, in cell **E5**, add a **COUNTIF** function to count the Teacher field in the Student_Data table that meets the filter criteria in cell **E4**. Copy the formula over to cell **I5**.

d. In cell **K5**, add a **DCOUNTA** function to count the StudentID field in the Student_Data table that meet the filter criteria in the range **D1:K2**.

e. In cell **K8**, add a **VLOOKUP** function nested in an **IFERROR** function to retrieve the price per hour located in column C in the Lesson_Pricing named range for each student based on the student's skill level located in the Skill level field. The value should be looking for an exact match. To prevent an error from being displayed when the skill level is not known, use the IFERROR function to leave the cell blank. Copy the formula down to **K94**.

f. On the Lesson Data worksheet, in cell **F3**, add a **MATCH** function nested in an **INDEX** function to retrieve the skill level of each student listed in column B. To prevent zeros from displaying when the skill level is not known, nest the INDEX and MATCH functions in an IF function to leave the cell blank when the skill level equals 0. Copy the formula down to **F121**.

g. In cell **G3**, add a **MATCH** function nested in an **INDEX** function to retrieve the total fee located in the Lesson_Pricing table on the Data Inputs worksheet for each student listed in column B. To prevent an error from being displayed when the skill level is not known, nest the INDEX and MATCH functions inside an IFERROR function and display the default total fee of **$50**. Copy the formula down to **G121**.

h. On the Report worksheet, in cell **B3**, add a **VLOOKUP** function to look up the teacher's name in the Student_Data table for the student listed in cell B2. The value should be looking for an exact match.

i. In cell **B4**, add an **AVERAGEIF** function to calculate the teacher's average fee in the Price_Per_Hour field for the teacher listed in cell B3.

j. In cell **B5**, add a **VLOOKUP** function to look up the student's skill level in the Student_Data table for the student listed in cell B2. The value should be looking for an exact match.

k. In cell **B6**, add a **COUNTIF** function to count the StudentID field on the Lesson Data worksheet that meets the filter criteria in cell B2.

l. In cell **B7**, add a **SUMIF** function to sum the Total Fee field on the Lesson Data worksheet that meets the filter criteria in cell B2.

m. In cell **B8**, add a nested **IF** function to determine how many free lessons the student has earned. If the student has had less than 5 total lessons, display **0 earned**. If the student has had between 5 and 10 lessons, display **1 earned**; otherwise, display **2 earned**.

n. In cell **E5**, add a **VLOOKUP** function to look up the student's uniform size in the Student_Data table for the student listed in cell B2. The value should be looking for an exact match.

o. In cell **E7**, add a **HLOOKUP** function to retrieve the student's registration fee in the Entry_Fee named range for the registration type in cell E3. The value should be looking for an exact match.

p. In cell **I13**, add a **COUNTIF** function to count the number of uniforms in the Student_Data table that meet the filter criteria in cell H12.

q. In cell **I14**, add a **MATCH** function nested in an **INDEX** function to retrieve the uniform fee located in the Uniform_Fee table on the Data Inputs worksheet that meets the filter criteria in cells H12 and I13. To prevent an error from displaying when no uniforms of the size located in H12 are needed, nest the INDEX and MATCH functions inside an **IFERROR** function to leave the cell blank.

r. Create the following formulas to complete the Performance Report.
- In cell **B12**, add a **VLOOKUP** function to retrieve the student's first name in the Student_Data table that meets the filter criteria in cell A12. The value should be looking for an exact match. Copy the formula down to **B38**.
- In cell **C12**, add a **VLOOKUP** function to retrieve the student's last name in the Student_Data table that meets the filter criteria in cell A12. The value should be looking for an exact match. Copy the formula down to **C38**.
- In cell **D12**, add a **VLOOKUP** function to retrieve whether or not the student has a permission slip on file in the Student_Data table that meets the filter criteria in cell A12. The value should be looking for an exact match. Copy the formula down to **D38**.
- In cell **E12**, add a **VLOOKUP** function nested in an IF function to retrieve the student's uniform size. To prevent zeros from being displayed when the uniform size is not known, nest the VLOOKUP function in an IF function to leave the cell blank when the skill level equals 0. The value should be looking for an exact match. Copy the formula down to **E38**.
- In cell **F12**, add an **AND** function nested in an **IF** function to determine if the student has a permission slip and a uniform. If the student has a permission slip and the uniform size is not blank, then display **Yes** in the field; otherwise, display **No**. Copy the formula down to **F38**.

s. In cell **F39**, add a **COUNTIF** function to determine how many students are currently traveling to the competition as indicated by "Yes" in cell range **F12:F38**.

t. In cell **E8**, add a **MATCH** function nested in an **INDEX** function to retrieve the transportation fee located in the Trans_Fee table on the Data Inputs worksheet that meets the filter criteria in cell E4 and F39.

u. Complete the **Documentation** worksheet according to your instructor's direction. Insert the **filename** in the left custom footer section of the Header/Footer tab in the Page Setup dialog box on all worksheets in the workbook.

v. Click **Save**, close Excel, and then submit the file as directed by your instructor.

Student data file needed:

 e03ws05Training.xlsx

You will save your file as:

 e03ws05Training_LastFirst.xlsx

Building a Police Training Tracker

Human Resources

One of the first tasks you have been assigned as a new recruit with the local police department is to build a workbook that will be used to track various training activities offered on a regular basis. This will keep all officers updated on preparedness. Training activity data has been entered into a workbook. For some training, a score and certification process is in effect to ensure all officers are performing at or above the level of expectations set forth by the commanding officer. Other activities, such as exercise or weightlifting, do not require scoring or certification. You have been asked to help construct a workbook that your fellow officers and commanding officer can use to help manage departmental data.

a. Open the **e03ws05Training** workbook, and then save it as e03ws05Training_LastFirst.

b. On the Data Inputs worksheet, create named ranges using the top row as field names for the range A2:C19.

c. On the Training Data worksheet, select cell range A9:J91, create a named range for the entire table, and then create named ranges for all fields using the top row as the field names.

d. In cell G10, add an IF function that will evaluate the value in the Class_Name field. When the value in C10 is equal to Combat, Weightlifting, or Exercise, the formula will return Physical; otherwise, the formula should return Class.

e. In cell H10, add a lookup function nested in an IF function that will determine the level of reimbursement as noted on the Data Inputs worksheet. The lookup value will be based on the Score field, but the reimbursement schedule is different for Physical training versus Class training.

f. In cell I10, add a lookup function nested in an IF function that will determine whether or not certification was achieved. If the score is greater than zero, the function will return the value in the second column of the certification table on the Data Inputs worksheet—cell range F9:G11. If the score is not greater than zero, the cell should remain blank.

g. In cell J10, add a formula that divides the Time field value by 30 and then multiplies this result by the points earned, retrieved from the ClassInfo named range by using an HLOOKUP function.

h. Select range G10:J10 and then double-click the AutoFill handle to copy the formulas down to row 91. Adjust column widths as needed.

i. In cell H5, add a function that will count the PID_Entry field in the Training_Data table that meets the filter criteria in the range A2:J3.

j. In cell H6, add a function that will average the Cost field in the Training_Data table that meets the filter criteria in the range A2:J3.

k. In cell B6, add a function that will count the Class_Name in B5 in the Training_Data table.

l. Click the Report worksheet tab, select cell C4, and then add a complex function that returns the PID function for the Last Name value in cell C3. Ensure that you nest your complex function inside a third function to ensure that no errors will appear if cell C3 is blank. Display No PID in lieu of an error message.

m. In cell B8, add a function that will count the number of PID_Entry training sessions for the officer listed in cell A8.

n. In cell C8, add a function that will average the scores obtained by the PID_Entry officer listed in cell A8.

o. In cell D8, add a function that will count the number of times an "Honors" rating for the Result field was obtained for the PID_Entry officer listed in cell A8.

p. In cell E8, add a function that returns the value "Gold" if the value in the Courses field is greater than 4 and the number of courses equals the number of Honors earned in all courses taken. Gold status should be returned if both conditions are met; otherwise, leave the cell blank.

q. In cell F8, add a function that will sum the points obtained by the PID_Entry officer listed in cell A8.

r. In cell G8, add a complex logical function that will evaluate the training and return an Improvement Plan or Okay status. Two OR conditions must be met to return the Okay status. If the police officer has Points greater than 7 and an Average Score greater than 72, "Okay" status will display. Or, if the Courses completed are greater than 3 and an Average Score is greater than 78, "Okay" status will display; otherwise, "Improvement Plan" will display.

s. Select range B8:G8 and then copy the formulas down to row 24. Adjust column widths as needed.

t. Complete the **Documentation** worksheet according to your instructor's direction. Insert the **filename** in the left custom footer section of the Header/Footer tab in the Page Setup dialog box on all worksheets in the workbook.

u. Click **Save**, close Excel, and then submit the file as directed by your instructor.

Additional
Cases

Additional Workshop Cases are available on the companion website and in the instructor resources.

WORKSHOP 6 | ANALYZE DATA USING TABLES

OBJECTIVES

1. Work with data and information in data tables   p. 308

2. Use the SUBTOTAL function and filters in data tables   p. 322

3. Develop and customize PivotTables   p. 326

4. Develop and customize PivotCharts   p. 341

Prepare Case

Golf Course Marketing Strategies

Sales & Marketing

The manager of the Red Bluff Golf Course & Pro Shop would like to develop marketing strategies for increasing golf course patronage. Aleeta Herriott, the manager, has requested data about the golf course's activity over the past years. She needs to be able to work with the data to understand the current patronage, such as where the patrons were from, how many patrons were on each transaction, the tee time, and so forth. Exploring the data is key in determining the marketing strategy because it helps her learn about customer preferences. After analyzing the data, Aleeta will present her ideas to the board of directors.

tawan / Shutterstock

REAL WORLD SUCCESS

"My instructor taught my class how to work with large amounts of data and explained that we would need to use these skills when we enter the work force. I never imagined that as a marketing analyst I would be working with so much data and that I would have to use the skills my instructor taught. PivotTables have become a way of life for me. I could never have been able to make sense of all the data I collect had it not been for PivotTables and PivotCharts. Thank goodness I learned how to work with these data analysis tools!"

- Stephanie, recent graduate

Student data file needed for this workshop:

 e03ws06GolfMktg.xlsx

You will save your file as:

 e03ws06GolfMktg_LastFirst.xlsx

Organizing Data with Tables

While Excel can analyze large amounts of data, users can sometimes be overwhelmed with the volume of data that needs to be evaluated. Information overload can quickly set in as it becomes difficult to track the data across many rows and columns. However, using tools contained in Excel can help you understand the data more easily. For example, viewing data in tables allows you to examine the data in an organized manner. By organizing data, you can easily make decisions based on your analysis. In this section, you will work with data and information in data tables.

Work with Data and Information

The Red Bluff Golf Course & Pro Shop's manager, Aleeta, wants to analyze data collected over the years. Daily transactions from the past 10 years exist within the Red Bluff Golf Course & Pro Shop's database, but there is too much data to import into Excel—there are over one million rows of data! Rather, she has requested a random sample of data for her initial analysis. The database administrator was able to run a query on the database and provide a set of data to explore.

Opening the Starting File

To work with data tables, you first need to open the Golf Marketing workbook.

E06.00

 To Save the Golf Marketing Workbook

a. Start **Excel**, and then open **e03ws06GolfMktg**.

b. Click the **FILE** tab, click **Save As**, and save the file as an Excel workbook in the folder or location designated by your instructor with the name e03ws06GolfMktg_LastFirst using your last and first name. If necessary, click **Enable Content** in the Security Warning.

CONSIDER THIS | **Is Data Really That Important?**

Data is one of the most valuable assets within an organization, and without data, managers would have an extremely difficult time making decisions. Think about the daily decisions you make. For example, think about the last time you went out to lunch. You may consider location, menu, and price—all of which is data. What else might you consider before choosing where to eat lunch? What data do you use to make other decisions throughout the day?

Work with Data and Information in Data Tables

Regardless of the career you choose, the need to work with data is common. **Raw data** are considered to be elements or raw facts—numeric or text—that may or may not have meaning or relevance. For example, data such as "blue" or "brown" are raw data without context, and thus of minimal value to anyone. **Information**, however, is data that has context, meaning, and relevance, and therefore it is valuable to a user. The value is determined by the user and may vary between users. Thus information is created by users when they organize, interpret, and present data in a meaningful context.

Data sets are named collections of related sets of information that are composed of separate elements—the data. If a set of data is not organized, it is difficult to determine the context and transform the data into information. The user is informed by understanding the method in which the data has been gathered and organized. For example, the raw data, "blue" and "brown", by themselves may not have any significance. By transforming this raw data into the context of studying the eye color of men and women, and knowing the data were collected from a set of subjects allows information to be created. By having information, a user can determine whether one eye color is more prevalent in males. Excel is an excellent tool for manipulating data. Because of this, the user can transform the data into information, which can lead to good decision making. Organizing the data using an Excel table is a good first step toward creating and evaluating information effectively.

Organizing Data Sets

With data, care should be taken to protect its integrity. This includes keeping a backup of the original data so if errors occur it is possible to return to the original data and start over. Whenever possible, check your data for completeness and accuracy. Also, strive to organize data within the workbook in a meaningful and efficient manner that allows for new data to be added as needed. Finally, it is best to keep sets of data separated. Avoid using cells immediately surrounding the sets of data. This will minimize the possibility of mistakenly assuming the content in the adjacent cells is part of the main data set. When possible, keep related data on one worksheet while reporting and analyzing the data on another worksheet.

MyITLab®
Workshop 6 Training

E06.01

 To Prepare a Backup Copy of Data

a. Right-click the **Golf Data** worksheet tab, and then select **Move or Copy**. The Move or Copy dialog box opens.

b. In the Before sheet box, click **(move to end)**, click the **Create a copy** check box, and then click **OK**. A new worksheet is displayed with the name **Golf Data (2)**.

c. Right-click the **Golf Data (2)** worksheet tab, and then select **Rename**. Replace **2** with backup and then press [Enter] to rename the worksheet.

d. Click the **Golf Data** worksheet tab to return to the worksheet that will be modified.

e. On the Golf Data worksheet, select **rows 1 through 10**. Click the **HOME** tab, and then in the Cells group, click **Insert**. This will insert 10 rows and move the data set down to row 11 starting with the field headings.

f. Click **Save** 💾.

CONSIDER THIS | **Placement of Calculations and Analysis**

You could place the data and subsequent analysis anywhere within a spreadsheet. Why place the analysis at the top of the data set? Why not place it at the bottom of the data set? What are the advantages and disadvantages of either? How about placing the analysis on another worksheet?

Organizing a Data Set Within a Table

While the data may already be arranged in a spreadsheet, an Excel table establishes the data as more than a simple collection or range of raw facts presented in rows and columns. An Excel table can help provide context to the user by organizing the data in a meaningful way. Data can be converted to an Excel table that offers additional capability allowing the user to manipulate the data and to generate information and value for a variety of needs. The data table has both flexibility and scalability. New columns and rows can be added, and the table will extend to include them automatically. Formatting and formula references automatically adjust as well.

E06.02

 To Create a Data Table in Excel

a. Click the **Golf Data** worksheet tab, and then click cell **D15**.

b. Click the **INSERT** tab, and then in the Tables group, click **Table**. The Create Table dialog box opens.

c. In the Where is the data for your table box, verify that the range **$A$11:$H$211** is selected, and then verify the **My table has headers** check box is checked.

> **Troubleshooting**
> If Excel fails to guess the correct range selection, you can either adjust the range by typing in the correct range or drag to select the correct range.

d. Click **OK**.

An Excel table will be created with banded coloring. Additionally, the TABLE TOOLS DESIGN contextual tab will appear, containing all the options available for working with a table.

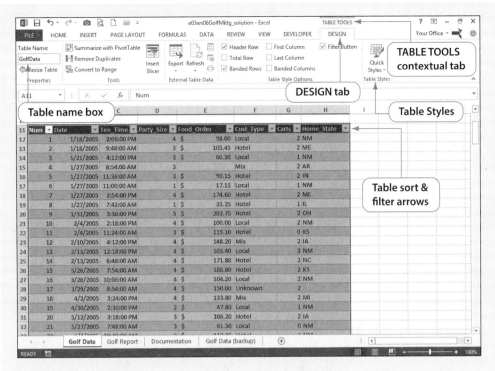

Figure 1 Excel data table

SIDE NOTE
Table Names
Because of the way that Excel is configured, table names cannot include spaces.

SIDE NOTE
Changing Table Styles
Access the Style gallery to change the look of the table to one of a variety of styles that offer different color schemes.

SIDE NOTE
Reference Tax Rates
Tax rates change. Keep these input values on a worksheet so they can be easily updated as needed and referenced in formulas.

e. Under the TABLE TOOLS tab, click the **DESIGN** tab. In the Properties group, click in the **Table Name** box. Replace **Table1** with **GolfData** and then press Enter. This will name the table GolfData and create a named range for the entire data set, excluding the field headings.

f. Select cells **A11:H212**. Click the **FORMULAS** tab, and then in the Defined Names group, click **Create from Selection**. Verify that the **Top row** check box is selected, click the check box next to **Right column** to deselect it if necessary, and then click **OK**. The named ranges will be used in your formulas.

g. Click the **FORMULAS** tab, and then in the Defined Names group, click **Name Manager**. In the Name Manager dialog box, click the **GolfData** named range in the list if necessary, and then notice at the bottom of the dialog box that the Refers to range is displayed as ='GolfData'!$A$12:$H$211.

   The tag beside the GolfData range is a small table, indicating it is associated with the table. The option to delete this range is not available since it is associated with the Excel table. You also can see all the other named ranges that you created.

h. Click **Close**.

i. Click cell **I11**, type Tax and then press Enter.

   Notice Excel automatically applied the formatting color to the newly added table cells to match the rest of the table. Excel also adjusts the named ranges that are associated with the table to include the new records.

j. In cell I12, type ='Golf Report'!$B$3*, click cell **E12**, and then press Enter. Select range **$I$11:$I$211**. Click the **HOME** tab, and then in the Number group, click **Accounting Number Format**.

   Notice [@[Food_Order]] is inserted at the end of the formula. Excel uses a structured reference rather than a regular cell reference. It inserted [@[Food_Order]] instead of E12 because it automatically sets ranges within the table that will adjust as columns or rows are added or deleted. The table also automatically copies the formula down the entire column similar to applying Auto Fill.

> **Troubleshooting**
> If your table did not automatically update, Excel may be configured to not update data tables automatically. Click the Formulas tab, and then in the Calculation group, click the Calculation Options arrow, and then select Automatic.

k. Scroll down until cell A212 is visible. Notice the field heading in row 11 replaces the column lettering when you scroll. Click cell **A212** to add a new record to the data.

  The field headings again disappear and are replaced with column letters when you click in cell A212 because this cell is outside the table range. However, the field headings reappear after you type the data for the first cell in the new row.

l. Using the following data, add a new record in row 212, pressing Tab after each entry. Notice that the banded color formatting appears as soon as data are initially entered and that the Tax field is copied down automatically because it is a calculation. On the HOME tab, in the Number group, click **Accounting Number Format**.

Field	Data
Num	201
Date	12/31/2011
Tee_Time	8:30:00 AM
Party_Size	4
Food_Order	104.80
Cust_Type	Hotel
Carts	2
Home_State	LA

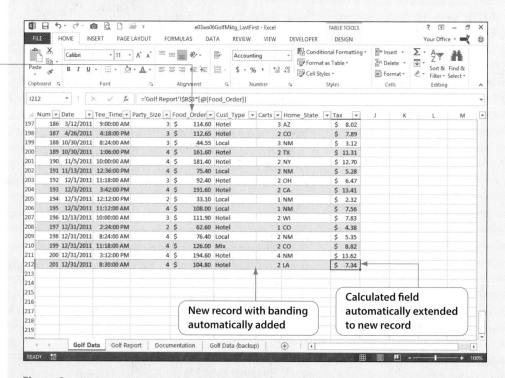

Figure 2   Adding a new record to an Excel table

m. Click the **FORMULAS** tab, and then in the Defined Names group, click **Name Manager**. The Name Manager dialog box opens. In the list, click the **GolfData** named range, and then notice the range is now **$A$12:$I$212**. The range has changed to include the newly created column and row. Click **Close**.

n. Click Ctrl + Home to return to cell A1.

o. Click **Save** 🖫.

A table defaults to a table style that has banded rows, making it easier to read data across rows. There are options to change the applied style for banded rows—and/or columns—with alternating colors. As new rows of data are added, the table range expands, including the table formatting. Similar to rows, new columns are also automatically formatted and added to the table. The new column added in the previous exercise is included in the GolfData named range.

When a formula is created in a cell of a new column, it will automatically copy it to the rest of that column in the table. In the previous exercise, a cell reference was added by clicking cell E12. Excel substituted the table field heading reference for the cell name. However, E12 could have been typed into the formula and the result would have been the same.

It is also possible to remove the Excel table structure as well as the extra functionality. When the table is converted back to a range of data using the **Convert to Range** option—located on the Design tab, in the Tools group—the formatting remains, but the functionality of tables, such as adding new columns or rows, will no longer automatically be added or updated to the named ranges, and formulas would need to be manually copied down a column.

Filtering Data Sets

The data sets used in business may be large and contain numerous fields. It is useful to gain an understanding of the data by looking at subsets of data rather than the entire set at one time. Filtering data sets is useful and makes it possible to view specific data. Filtering is also useful for selecting and copying a subset of data to move to a new worksheet. **Filtering** is a process of hiding records that do not meet specified criteria in a data set. It enables a user to examine and analyze, if desired, a subset of records.

Filters can be established on either a range of data or on an Excel table. For a range of data, a filter can be set by clicking the Filter button in the Sort & Filter group on the Data tab. When applying a filter to a data range, be sure the active cell is within the range to help ensure the correct data range is selected. However, if an Excel table has been created, the range will be established based upon the initial creation process, decreasing the chance for error. Additionally, the filter is a standard part of the Excel table, eliminating the need to apply a filter feature to the data set.

The filter feature adds arrow buttons for each field heading, which offer menus with filtering options to select the criteria for each field. By selecting criteria for a certain field heading, any records that do not meet the criteria will be hidden until the filter criterion is removed. The filters can be added, modified, and cleared as needed. Additionally, various filtering criteria can be applied using multiple fields. Thus, it would be possible to filter for a specific party size and on the number of golf carts used within the GolfData table.

Filtering data allows for the exploration of the data. For example, Red Bluff Golf Course & Pro Shop's manager, Aleeta, may want to determine how many instances of two-person golf parties spend more than $75 on food. For this example, Aleeta would filter for parties containing two people, which would exclude any parties that contained a number other than two. Then, the data would be explored further by filtering the records based on the total each two-person party spent on food. The two-person golf parties that spent more than $75 are then displayed and available for easy analysis.

To Filter Data in a Data Table

a. Click the **Golf Data** worksheet tab. Click the **Party_Size filter** arrow ▾, and then click **(Select All)** to deselect it. Click the **2** check box, and then click **OK**. All the other options will be hidden or filtered, showing only the records that meet the checked criteria.

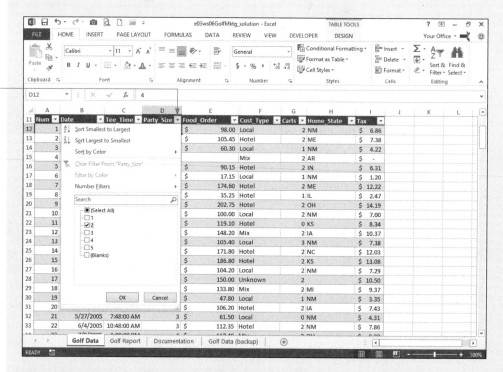

Figure 3   Filter list

b. Click the **Food_Order filter** arrow ▾, point to **Number Filters**, and then select **Greater Than**.

c. In the Custom AutoFilter dialog box, click in the **box** on the top-right side of the dialog box. Type **75** and then click **OK**.

Notice the Filter icon is displayed on the filter button as a visual cue that the field heading has a filter applied. Examine the row numbers and notice the visible row numbers start at 81 and jump to 88, 108, 110, and 159. The other rows of data are still there, but are hidden. The data still exists, and it can be redisplayed.

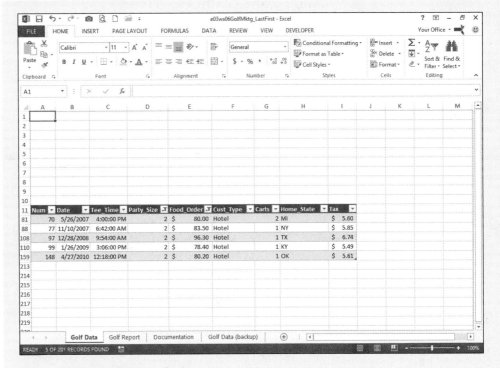

Figure 4 Filtered data

d. Click **Save** 🖫.

Filtering hides the rows of data that do not fit the selected criteria. In this case, both criteria must be true for the rows to be displayed. It is easy to remove, or clear, filters and apply other filters. The **standard filter** displays the values in the field that can be toggled on and off through the use of check boxes. If the check boxes are not able to provide a filter for the desired criteria, there are options above the check boxes that are specific for the type of data contained in the field. For example, the options available for fields with numeric values will differ from the options available if the field data contains date or text values.

REAL WORLD ADVICE | **Developing Questions for Data Analysis**

It is vital to have an understanding of the company data so relevant questions can be explored. The managers could find the average size of the golf parties, but this does not provide much value. However, it may be useful to know whether larger groups tend to order more food per person than smaller groups. Based on the answer, a marketing strategy could be developed and implemented. Always consider the value of the question.

Clearing and Changing Filters

There are times when you have several filters to apply or that the current filter is not providing the output needed to answer your question. Thus, clearing and changing the filters becomes an important task.

E06.04

▶ To Clear and Change Filters

a. Click the **Golf Data** worksheet tab. Click the **Party_Size filter** arrow ▼ in cell D11, and then select **Clear Filter from "Party_Size"**.

b. Click the **Date filter** arrow ▼ in cell B11.

Notice it has a listing of years with plus signs. Click the **plus sign** beside 2009. It will expand to months, and if needed, individual days could be shown and selected.

c. Point to **Date Filters** and notice the list of options are specific for dates. Select **Between** to display the Custom AutoFilter dialog box.

d. Click in the box to the right of the box displaying **is after or equal to**, type 1/1/2009 and then in the box to the right of the box displaying **is before or equal to**, type 12/31/2009. Click **OK**. The results will display food orders over $75 that occurred in 2009.

e. Point to the **Date filter** arrow ▼ for cell B11 to display a ScreenTip indicating the details of the filter. The filter arrow button will also have a smaller triangle next to a filter icon, which indicates that the field has a filter applied.

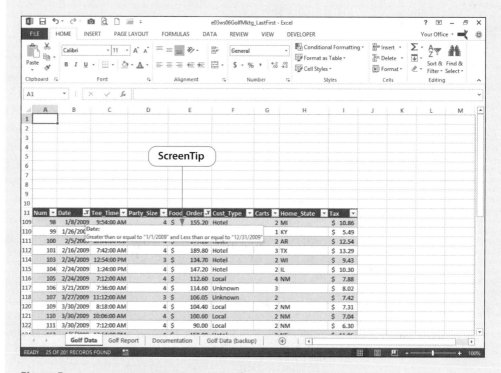

Figure 5   Display filter information

f. Select the filtered range **A109:I144**, and then press Ctrl + C.

g. Click **New Sheet** ⊕. This will create a new worksheet with cell A1 being the active cell. Press Ctrl + V. The subset of data will be pasted into the new worksheet. Press Esc.

Having data filtered can be useful, especially when there is a complete data set and someone else needs to examine some, but not all of the data. The filtered data can be copied and pasted to a new worksheet so it can be analyzed separately.

h. Right-click the **Sheet2** worksheet tab, and then select **Rename**. Type 2009 Data, and then press Enter. Verify columns **A:I** are selected. Click the **HOME** tab if necessary, and then in the Cells group, click **Format**. Select **AutoFit Column Width** so the columns are wide enough to view all the data. Press Ctrl+Home.

i. Click **Save** 🖫.

Using the Advanced Filter Feature

While the filtering feature is great for ad hoc and spur-of-the-moment exploration of data, the filtering mechanism makes it difficult to easily see what filters exist. A user would need to hover over or click the displayed filter arrows to evaluate which filters are applied. With the **Advanced Filter** feature, the filtering criteria live on the spreadsheet. The filtering criteria must be set up in a specific format. A top row with field headings that are identical to the data set must be established. Then, criteria can be set up in one or more cells below the field names. Once the criteria area has been set up, the Advanced Filter can be applied. It will hide records in the same manner as the filters on the data set. Only records matching the criteria will be displayed.

E06.05

To Create an Advanced Filter

a. Click the **Golf Data** worksheet tab. Select range **A11:I11**, press Ctrl+C, select cell **A1**, and then press Ctrl+V. Press Esc.

b. Click cell **A11**. Click the **DATA** tab, and then in the Sort & Filter group, click **Clear** to clear all current filters that have been applied to the data set.

c. Click cell **F2**, type Hotel and then press Ctrl+Enter.
   The range B1:I2 will be the data criteria area. The first row contains the field names that could potentially be used for setting constraints or criteria. The second row and below could be used for the criteria for particular fields. In this case, there is only one criterion set, the customer type of Hotel. With this arrangement, the advanced filter is ready to be created and will find the records that meet the criteria entered in the data criteria area.

d. On the DATA tab, in the Sort & Filter group, click **Advanced** to display the Advanced Filter dialog box.

e. Click in the **List range** box if necessary, and then delete any range references currently listed.

f. Click the **Collapse Dialog** button 🔢. Select the cell range **A11:I212**. The List range will change to display **GolfData[#All]**, recognizing the data range of the table. Click the **Expand Dialog** button 🔢.

g. Click in the **Criteria range** box, click the **Collapse Dialog** button 🔢, and then select **B1:I2**. Click the **Expand Dialog** button 🔢. Verify **Filter the list, in-place** is selected, and then click **OK**.

The data in the table is filtered to show only the Hotel Cust_Type transactions as shown in Figure 6. It is possible to add additional criteria. All criteria have to be met for the record to be shown. If only Hotel customers from Texas with food orders over $100 were shown, all three of those constraints must be true for the record to be displayed. The three constraints are thus joined with an AND clause. If Cust_Type equals Hotel AND Home_State equals TX AND Food_Order is greater than $100, the record will be displayed. By listing all three constraints on one row, Excel will know to have all three arguments set to true for the record to be included in the results.

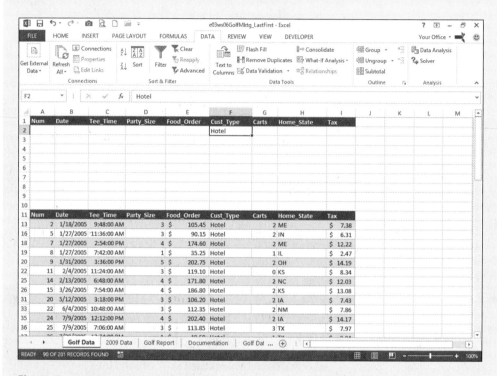

Figure 6   Advanced filter with Hotel Cust_Type

h. Click cell **E2**, type **>100** and then press ⏎Enter. Click cell **H2**, type **TX** and then press ⏎Enter.

i. On the DATA tab, in the Sort & Filter group, click **Advanced**. Verify that the range in the List range box is **$A$11:$I$212** and the range in the Criteria range box is **$B$1:$I$2**. Click **OK**.

The settings in the Advanced Filter will remain from the previous time, thus the List range and Criteria range are the same as the first time the advanced filter was run. The data set should adjust to show Hotel customers from Texas, with food orders greater than 100. To add additional criteria, add it to the criteria range. For example, to also include all records that have a Party_Size of 1 with customer type of Local, a second row would be used. Criteria on an individual row must all be true as mentioned. Each row of criteria acts like an OR, joining the two sets of filtering criteria. Records meeting either the first row of criteria or the second row of criteria will be displayed.

j. Click cell **D3**, type **1** and then press ⏎Enter. Click cell **F3**, type **Local** and then press ⏎Enter.

k. On the DATA tab, and then in the Sort & Filter group, click **Advanced**. Click to place your insertion point at the end of the text in the Criteria range box, press ⏎Backspace to delete the **2**, and then type **3** so the Criteria range displays **$B$1:$I$3**. Click **OK**.

SIDE NOTE

Empty Rows of Criteria

If the criteria range for the Advanced Filter includes a row with no criteria, the entire record set will be returned because nothing is constraining the records.

When adding a second row of criteria as shown in Figure 7, the criteria in the Advanced Filter must also be adjusted. The same would apply if the additional row of criteria were removed from the Advanced Filter. The results will show records for food orders greater than $100 from Texas Hotel customers and all parties of 1 for Local customers. The constraints on one row will not impact the constraints on another row. Thus there are parties of 1 that did not spend more than $100.

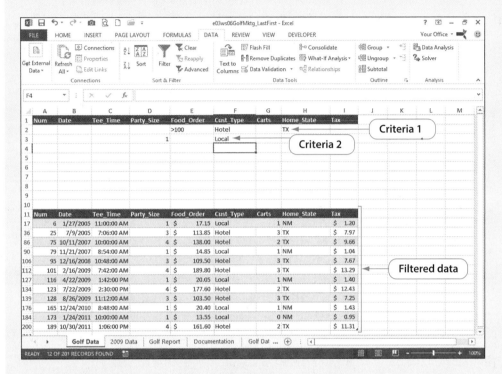

Figure 7   Filtered data using multiple criteria

l.   Click **Save** 🖫.

CONSIDER THIS | **Using the Right Rows of Criteria**

What would happen if you forget to adjust the criteria range? What would happen if you do not extend the range to include a new row of criteria? What would happen if you delete a row of criteria, but leave that row in your criteria range? Do you think you would return the same filter results? How would it affect your decision making?

Using Slicers to Filter Data

Slicers were introduced in Excel 2010 as an interactive way to filter PivotTable data. In Excel 2013, slicers can now also be used to filter data in Excel tables, query tables, and other data tables. One of the benefits to using slicers is that they are easy to generate and use. Additionally, slicers indicate the current filter so you will know exactly what data you are viewing.

E06.06

 To Create a Filter Using a Slicer

a. Click cell **F17**. Click the **INSERT** tab, and then in the Filters group, click **Slicer**. The Insert Slicers dialog box opens.

b. Click the **Cust_Type** check box, and then click **OK**. Notice the filter you applied earlier is removed and the Cust_Type slicer is displayed.

c. Drag the **Cust_Type** slicer so its top-left corner is in the top-left corner of **K2**. Click **Unknown** in the slicer. The table displays only the Unknown customer type.

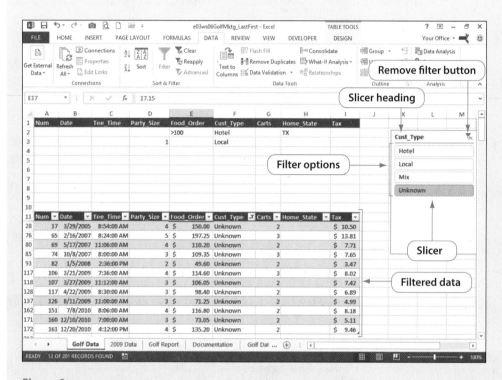

Figure 8 Filtered data using a slicer

d. Press [Ctrl], and then click **Local** in the slicer. Notice once you release [Ctrl] that the table displays both the Unknown and Local customer types.

e. Click **Clear Filter** in the top-right corner of the slicer to remove the filter.

f. Drag the **bottom edge** of the Cust_Type slicer to adjust the height so that the extra white space is no longer visible. Do not drag it too far that you see a scroll bar on the right side.

g. Click cell **D12**. Click the **INSERT** tab, and then in the Filters group, click **Slicer**. Click the **Home_State** check box, and then click **OK**. The Home_State slicer is displayed.

h. Drag the **Home_State** slicer so its top-left corner is in the top-left corner of **K11**. Click **Unknown** in the Cust_Type slicer. The table displays only the Unknown customer type.

i. Right-click the **Home_State** slicer, and then select **Slicer Settings**. The Slicer Settings dialog box opens.

SIDE NOTE

Selecting Multiple Criteria

Pressing [Ctrl] allows you to select multiple criteria on a slicer.

SIDE NOTE

Inserting Slicers

You must have a cell selected in your data table in order to insert a slicer.

SIDE NOTE

Renaming Slicer Headings

You can also double-click the heading, and then type a new name in the formula bar.

j. Under the Header section, replace **Home_State** with Home State in the Caption box, and then click **OK**.

k. Right-click the **Home State** slicer, and then select **Size and Properties**. The Format Slicer pane opens.

l. Click the **POSITION AND LAYOUT** arrow, and then under Layout, change the number of columns to **3**. **Close** ☒ the Format Slicer pane. Notice that the states are much easier to see.

m. Right-click the **Cust_Type** slicer, and then select **Slicer Settings**. The Slicer Settings dialog box opens.

n. Under the Header section, replace **Cust_Type** with Customer Type in the Caption box, and then click **OK**.

o. In the Customer Type slicer, click **Mix**. Notice that the Home State slicer automatically filters the states where the Mix customer type live.

p. In the Home State slicer, click **AZ**. Press Ctrl, click **CA**, and then click **TX**. You may need to scroll up to find the states.

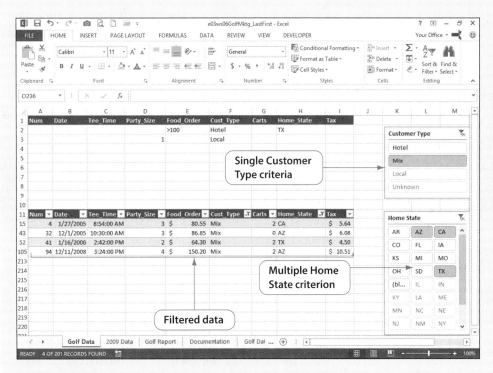

Figure 9 Filtered data using multiple slicers

q. To further customize your slicers, click the **Customer Type** slicer. Under the SLICER TOOLS contextual tab, click the **OPTIONS** tab. In the Slicer Styles group, click the **More** arrow. Under Dark, click **Slicer Style Dark 2**.

r. Click the **Home State** slicer. Under the SLICER TOOLS contextual tab, click the **OPTIONS** tab. In the Slicer Styles group, click the **More** arrow. Under Dark, click **Slicer Style Dark 2**. Click cell **A1**.

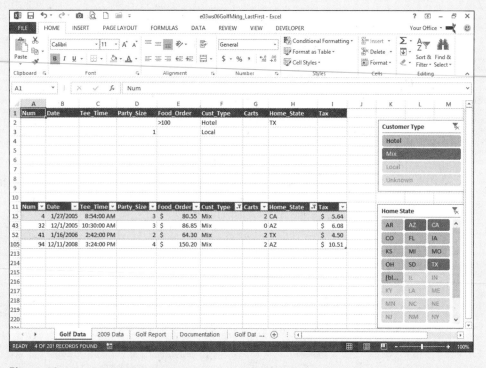

Figure 10 Customized slicers

s. Click **Save** 🔲.

Use the SUBTOTAL Function and Filters in Data Tables

To **aggregate** data means to consolidate or summarize the data, similar to the way an executive summary consolidates and summarizes a project or a report. Functions like SUM or AVERAGE aggregate an entire set of data. However, when a set of data is filtered to show a subset of the entire data set, it would be useful to be able to aggregate the subset of data instead of the entire set of data. This is impossible to conduct with standard functions as they will run calculations on the data regardless of whether the records—or rows—are hidden or displayed. Thus, the applied data filters have no impact on standard functions.

While the subset of data could be copied to another worksheet and then aggregated, it would be an inefficient method of analyzing data. By copying the subset of data, it duplicates the data and complicates the analysis. It would be more efficient to have the flexibility of adjusting the filter and having the aggregation of the subset of data also adjust. It is possible to accomplish this using the SUBTOTAL function.

The **SUBTOTAL function** is specific to the filtering mechanism and will only run calculations on the data that is in the subset when a filter is applied. Any records that are on hidden rows will not be used in the calculation of the SUBTOTAL function. The SUBTOTAL function has two arguments. The first argument requires a function number to indicate which aggregate function to apply, such as SUM, AVERAGE, or COUNT. The second argument is one or more ranges to be aggregated. The syntax of the SUBTOTAL function is as follows.

=SUBTOTAL(function_num, ref1, [ref2],…)

The function_num argument informs Excel which function to use on the subset of records. When typing this function, a list will appear to help if you are not familiar with which argument number to use. There are two sets of function numbers, 1–11 and 101–111, as shown in Table 1. The first set, 1–11, will return result values for rows that are visible and rows that have been hidden using the Hide Rows command. The second set, 101–111, will ignore rows that have been formatted to be hidden, again using the Hide Rows command, thus returning a value of visible rows only. Keep in mind that the SUBTOTAL function ignores any rows not included when a filter is applied, no matter which function_num value you use. Thus, the difference between these two sets of argument values only comes into importance when using the Hide Rows command, and it is of no importance when applied to filtered data.

Function_Num (includes hidden values)	Function_Num (ignores hidden values)	Function
1	101	AVERAGE
2	102	COUNT
3	103	COUNTA
4	104	MAX
5	105	MIN
6	106	PRODUCT
7	107	STDEV.S
8	108	STDEV.P
9	109	SUM
10	110	VAR.S
11	111	VAR.P

Table 1 Subtotal function list

CONSIDER THIS | **Selecting a Function Number from the List**

The purpose of analyzing data is to aid in decision making. Perhaps you wanted to use all the data including the hidden rows. What would happen if you chose a function number—function_num—that does not include hidden values? How would it affect your decision making?

REAL WORLD ADVICE | **Hiding Rows and Filtering**

It is unusual to use the Hide Rows feature when filtering, and is not a recommended practice. Any time filters are removed, any hidden rows will become unhidden. It becomes complicated to try and work with both filtering data and hiding rows. It is recommended that all records be visible when filtering. Any records that should not be used in the SUBTOTAL calculations should be excluded using the filtering process.

Summarizing a Data Set

Filters can provide answers to many questions, but they may not give you all the results you need to make sound decisions. Functions such as SUBTOTAL, AVERAGE, and AVERAGEIF functions can help summarize the data in the data set.

E06.07

To Summarize a Data Set

a. Click the **Golf Data** worksheet tab. Click cell **B5**, type Average and then press Enter. In cell **B6**, type Overall and then press Enter. In cell **B7**, type Filter and then press Enter. In cell **B8**, type By State and then press Enter. In cell **B9**, type Customer Type and then press Enter.

b. Click cell **D8**, type NM and then press Enter. In cell **D9**, type Local. Click cell **E8**, type Number of Records and then press Enter. In cell **E9**, type Sum of Food Order and then press Enter.

c. Select columns **B:E**, and then double-click the **border margin** between column B and column C to automatically fit the text in columns B through E.

d. Select range **B5:B9**, press and hold Ctrl, and then select range **E5:E9**. Press Ctrl, and then type **B** to bold the text.

e. Click cell **C5**, type =AVERAGE(Food_Order) and then press Enter.

The overall average uses the named range and will calculate the average using every record. The AVERAGE function uses all data even if it is hidden.

f. In cell **C6**, type =SUBTOTAL(. Notice that a listing for the function number will appear with the available choices for the function that will be used on the filtered records.

g. Double-click **1 - AVERAGE** from the list.

SIDE NOTE

Named Ranges

To edit or view existing named ranges, click the Name Manager button on the Formulas tab.

SIDE NOTE

Editing Named Ranges

When creating named ranges on a table using Create from Selection, the named range will expand as additional rows of data are added.

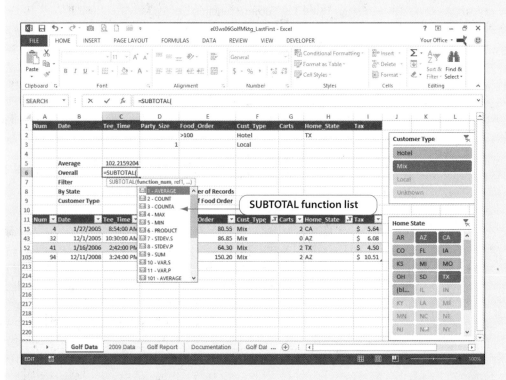

Figure 11 SUBTOTAL function

h. Type , Food_Order) and then press Enter. The SUBTOTAL function ignores any data that is hidden because of the filter you previously applied.

i. In cell **C7**, type =AVERAGEIF(Home_State,D8,Food_Order) and then press Enter. The AVERAGEIF function will include hidden records, just like the AVERAGE function.

j. In cell **C8**, type =AVERAGEIF(Cust_Type,D9,Food_Order) and then press Enter.

k. Click cell **F8**, type =SUBTOTAL(2,Num) and then press Enter. This will count the number of records that are visible and would be included in any subtotal calculation.

l. In cell **F9**, type =SUBTOTAL(9,Food_Order) and then press Enter. This will sum the values in any record or row that are visible within the data set.

m. Select range **C5:C8**, press and hold Ctrl, and then select cell **F9**. Click the **HOME** tab, and then in the Number group, click **Accounting Number Format**.

n. Click **Save** 🔲.

Because you have entered several different formulas, it is now possible to see the variance within the different averages that have been calculated. Notice that only the SUBTOTAL function ignores hidden records and only uses visible filtered records to calculate the average. The other functions provide results based on all the records, without regard to visible and hidden records.

Organizing and Analyzing with PivotTables and PivotCharts

It is possible to accomplish a great deal through the use of tables and filters—the SUBTOTAL function and other aggregate functions like SUMIF or AVERAGEIF. However, what if there is a need to really dig deep and explore a data set so you have the ability to answer all kinds of questions? What if those initial questions drive subsequent questions?

PivotTables provide a more expanded solution for exploring data—they are especially useful when you are looking at a huge table of data that can become overwhelming. A **PivotTable** is an interactive table that extracts, organizes, and summarizes data. PivotTables are used for data analysis and looking for trends and patterns for decision-making purposes. Among other functions, a PivotTable can automatically sort, count, total, or give an average of the data stored in one table or spreadsheet. Excel then displays the results in a separate table, called a PivotTable. Here are some examples of questions PivotTables can help to answer:

- How often are clubs rented for a round of golf?
- How many customers came from each state last year?
- Has the mix between hotel and local customers changed over time?
- How much revenue has each employee generated over the last 12 months?

These questions can easily be answered with a PivotTable report because PivotTables can easily group the time period to years, quarters, months, or all three. The flexibility comes from using an interface that allows the table to be built without having to create formulas and functions to do the grouping, summarizing, or calculating. And, because PivotTables are interactive, they can be adjusted with a few clicks, rearranged by dragging fields, or cleared to start the process over if the layout becomes too muddled. In this section, you will develop skills needed for working with PivotTables and PivotCharts.

Develop and Customize PivotTables

An understanding of the general process is helpful when working with PivotTables. First, it is important to make sure the data set is well organized. A PivotTable can be created on an existing worksheet or a new worksheet. When it is created, a link or connection is established to a source range of data. After determining the data source and where to insert the blank PivotTable, the interactive part begins. The PivotTable is blank or clear to begin with, but it can be developed by considering what data to group and what data to summarize. The final step is to explore and work with the options within the PivotTable to fine-tune the layout to fit your specific needs. If needed, it is possible to create PivotCharts, covered later, with chart data based on PivotTable adjustments, thus offering charted data based on extracted subsets of data analysis.

Creating PivotTables

The creation of a PivotTable is a two-step process: selecting the data set and location where the PivotTable will be created, and working with the data fields to group and summarize the selected data. When creating a PivotTable, ensure the source data are arranged in an area with column headings representing each field and the rows representing each record, preferably with no other information or content in cells that are adjacent to the data set just like with a data table. In addition, there should be clear, concise field headings in the top cell for each column of data. Excel will use these as the labels within the PivotTable. Finally, if there are automatic subtotals or other summary functions at the bottom of the data, be sure to remove these. They will cause confusion if they are incorporated into a PivotTable.

REAL WORLD ADVICE | **Consider the Fields Needed for the PivotTable**

You should consider if you are going to add data and want to name the data set range so you can add data to the named range. Add any calculated fields to the data initially. For example, with quantity and price, there may be a need to add a new column named Revenue that is the price times the quantity. Or, if there is a field that has both the city and state, you might want to separate the data into two columns so it is possible to group by city or by state. If there are potential changes, working with a table is optimal as it makes adding fields easy, and those new fields can be incorporated into PivotTables simply by refreshing the data.

There are only two options with regard to the location of a PivotTable. A PivotTable can be created on a new worksheet or the worksheet where your data lives. PivotTables automatically expand and contract on a worksheet as variables are added, removed, and rearranged. Creating a PivotTable on a new worksheet will set it apart and reduce the chance of the PivotTable interfering with or disturbing other data. If a PivotTable is placed on an existing worksheet with other data, it is best to choose a location where it is below or to the right of any existing data. This allows the PivotTable room to expand to the right or down as needed, without interfering with the existing data. While it is possible to create multiple PivotTables from the same data set, only one PivotTable is permitted per worksheet.

REAL WORLD ADVICE | PivotTables Add to File Size

PivotTables, while valuable, quickly add to the size of an Excel file. It is better to use PivotTables for multiple purposes than to create a set of separate PivotTables. As the file size increases, there is added risk of corrupting your file. Thus it becomes important to remember to back up and maintain your backup files.

CONSIDER THIS | PivotTables and Hidden Data

A filter applied to the data set will not affect the PivotTable creation process. The PivotTable will ignore the filter and use all the data—including the hidden data. Why is this important when using the data for decision making?

Similar to creating an Excel table, when creating a PivotTable from a data set, one cell within the data set should be the active cell. Excel will automatically detect the range in the process of setting up the initial PivotTable area. It is possible to adjust the data range used if Excel mistakenly includes other information that is not needed in the PivotTable data range. If the data has been established as a table, the creation of a PivotTable is based upon the current range for the table.

E06.08

 To Create a PivotTable from an Excel Table

a. Click the **Golf Data** worksheet tab, and then click cell **H11**.

Troubleshooting
If you have a few cells selected in a data set when you begin creating a PivotTable, you may end up creating a PivotTable that only has the subset selection as the range. It is best to only have one cell selected in your data set when you create the PivotTable.

b. Click the **DESIGN** tab, and then in the Tools group, click **Summarize with PivotTable**. The Create PivotTable dialog box opens.

Troubleshooting
If the data you are using is not in a table, click the Insert tab, and then in the Tables group, click PivotTable.

c. Verify that the **GolfData** Table/Range is selected. Verify that **New Worksheet** is selected, and then click **OK**. The PivotTable is inserted on a new sheet named **Sheet3**.

d. Double-click the **Sheet3** worksheet tab, replace **Sheet3** with Pivot Analysis and then press Enter.

e. Click cell **A1**. Notice that the PIVOTTABLE TOOLS contextual tabs disappear and only a blank PivotTable area is showing below cell A1.

f. Click cell **A3**.
   The PivotTable Fields pane will reappear on the right side of the screen. The PIVOTTABLE TOOLS contextual tabs are now available.

g. Click **Save** 🖫.

SIDE NOTE
Selecting Cells
You can select any cell within the PivotTable to redisplay the PivotTable Fields pane and PivotTable Tolls contextual tabs.

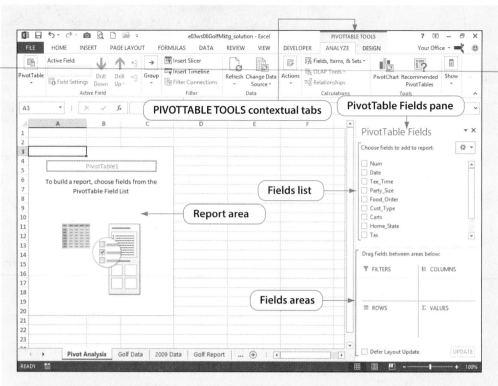

Figure 12   PivotTable layout

> **Troubleshooting**
>
> If you close the PivotTable Fields pane and need to display it again, first select a cell in the PivotTable. Under the PivotTable Tools contextual tab, click the Analyze tab. In the Show group, click the Show arrow if necessary, and then select Field List.

Building a PivotTable

Once the worksheet is set up for constructing the PivotTable, the interactive part of the process begins. The focus is to construct a table that will group and summarize subsets of the data in a useful and meaningful manner. There are a few guidelines for choosing how to arrange the fields.

It helps to distinguish fields as either grouping variables or summary variables, because these two types get placed in different areas within the PivotTable. **Grouping variables** can be thought of as any fields within the data set that could be used to categorize or group for comparison. For example, gender is a common variable used to group and analyze data. It may be necessary to compare the salaries between females and males. Dates are also great for grouping into months, quarters, and years to explore trends over time. Conversely, **summary variables** are data that are not categorical in nature and can be aggregated by summing, counting, or averaging, such as gross revenue, quantity, or price.

Grouping variables are placed along the top or the left side of the PivotTable. The aggregation of data occurs when records in the data are grouped by selected variables. The results would be placed in the bottom-right areas of the aggregate summary. This layout is shown in Figure 12.

The grouping variables are positioned in the COLUMNS or ROWS areas at the bottom of the PivotTable Fields pane. The summary variables are positioned in the VALUES area below the PivotTable Fields list. Fields can be chosen from the PivotTable Fields list. Fields can be dragged and dropped from the PivotTable Fields list to any of the four quadrant areas at the bottom of the PivotTable Fields pane. Alternatively, you can check the check box beside the field names to select the field. When the check box beside a field is checked, Excel will try to guess where that field should be placed based on the data values contained in the field. If it is text or dates, it will default to the ROWS area. If it is numerical data, it may be considered a summary variable and placed into the VALUES area—the calculations area of the PivotTable. Additionally, you can place fields into the FILTER area, which will allow you to filter data based on the field or fields placed in that area. For example, if you choose to place a Days field into the FILTER area, you could simply display data for the weekend—Saturday and Sunday. If Excel puts the field into the wrong area, it can be dragged from one area to another, or you can click the field name in the applicable area's box to access a list of options for the field, which include options to move the field's location. If a field is not needed, its check box can be unchecked to remove it from the PivotTable design. It is possible to have multiple fields in any of the PivotTable areas.

E06.09

 To Set Up a PivotTable

a. Click the **Pivot Analysis** worksheet tab. Under Choose fields to add to report in the PivotTable Fields area, click the **Cust_Type** field check box.

It appears in the PivotTable and displays all the customer types under the Row Labels heading. Additionally, Cust_Type is also displayed under the ROWS area on the PivotTable Fields pane.

b. Click the **Home_State** field check box.

Excel will add both fields to the Row Labels area. The Home_State is displayed for each Cust_Type, which you can view if you scroll down the worksheet. If you prefer that each Home_State be listed with the Cust_Type grouped for each state, then the order of the grouping can be switched.

c. In the ROWS area, click the **Home_State** field arrow, and then select **Move Up**. This will change the order of the groups for the two fields within the ROWS area.

d. In the PivotTable Fields list, click the **Food_Order** check box, and then click cell **B5**.

Excel, detecting numerical data, puts this into the VALUES area and defaults to summing the values. Notice the label in B3 indicates the field being aggregated and what calculation is being applied—in this case, Sum. Cell B5 displays the sum of the golf parties that stayed at the hotel with a home state of Arkansas. The value is calculated, but there is no formula within the cell.

e. Click the **Golf Data** worksheet tab. Click cell **H15**, type AR and then press `Enter`. Click cell **E15**, and then press `Delete`. Select **D43:F43**, and then press `Delete`.

f. Click the **DATA** tab, and then in the Sort & Filter group, click **Clear**. On the Customer Type slicer, click **Hotel**. On the Home State slicer, click **AR**. Notice the Sum of Food Order in cell F9 is now $545.20.

g. Click the **Pivot Analysis** worksheet tab.

Notice the Sum of Food Order in cell B5 is the same as in cell F9 on the Golf Data worksheet. While it is possible to use formulas and filtering to obtain an answer, the PivotTable generates the answers for all the groups with less effort involved. Thus, PivotTables facilitate comparing summary data more efficiently.

h. Drag the **Cust_Type** field in the ROWS area to the **COLUMNS** area.

Previously, the table had consisted of many rows that extended down the worksheet. Now, the number of rows and columns are more evenly distributed, thus making the PivotTable more readable.

The columns in the PivotTable should now show the different types of customers. Cell B5 now displays the sum of the food purchased by the hotel golf parties that are from Arkansas. In cell A33, the value indicates blanks—the records where there is no home state indicated. Finally, notice how the PivotTable expands both in rows and columns as the fields are added and removed. This is the interactive attribute of a PivotTable and also why it is best to have a PivotTable on a worksheet by itself.

i. In the PivotTable Fields list, click the **Home_State** check box to remove the field from the PivotTable, and then click the **Date** check box. **Date** will now be in the ROWS area. Most of the time it will group within each unique date, so it would be helpful if the dates could be aggregated.

j. Right-click **A9**, and then select **Group**. The Grouping dialog box opens with **Months** highlighted in the By list.

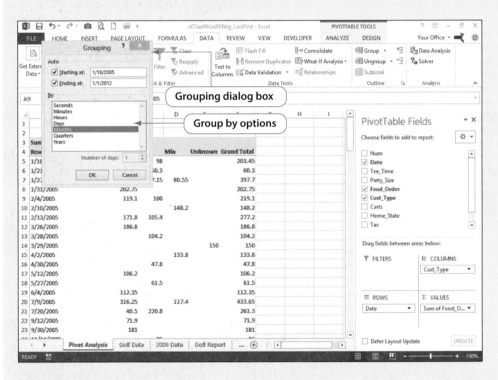

Figure 13 Grouping by dates

SIDE NOTE
Grouping with Missing Data

When grouping dates, the PivotTable will not know how to group blank data. A date must exist for every record before grouping data.

k. Click **Months** to remove the blue highlighting. Click **Quarters** to select it as a grouping level, click **Years** to select it as a grouping level, and then click **OK**.

The dates will now be grouped by year, and within each year all four quarters within the year will be listed. On the PivotTable Fields list, a Years field is now displayed. In the ROWS area, notice the first grouping is Years. Within each Year, the subgroup is Date, which is the Quarters. If the grouping needs to be changed, you can right-click one of the cells in column A and select Group again to change the grouping options. Or, select Ungroup and the individual dates will reappear.

l. Click **Save** 🖫.

CONSIDER THIS | **Group on Rows or Columns**

The fields for grouping could be all in the ROWS area, all in the COLUMNS area, or a mixture. What issues may arise if you have all the grouping fields as row labels or all as column labels? What would you use as a rule of thumb for the number of groups within each area?

REAL WORLD ADVICE **Which Fields Are Better for Row Labels?**

While it is possible to choose any grouping field on either the ROWS or COLUMNS, there are some guidelines. Typically you want your PivotTable to go down more than across. People are more accustomed to scrolling up or down in a document rather than left or right. So, if you have a lot of groups within a field, it is better to put those fields along the row side of the PivotTable instead of across the top in columns. It is better to have the user scroll up or down instead of across.

Configuring PivotTable Options

With PivotTables there are two contextual tabs available to aid in the control of PivotTable elements: Analyze and Design. The Analyze tab has all the options for fine-tuning the PivotTable. Many of these options can also be accessed by right-clicking any cell within the PivotTable. Some are very useful in creating the structure of the PivotTable.

The Design tab focuses on formatting and on the appearance of designing the PivotTable. Options include choosing from a variety of styles, and whether or not to display band row and/or column colors, report layouts, and so forth. Additionally, formatting can always be done through the traditional Format Cells dialog box found by right-clicking any cell in the PivotTable. This is not recommended, though, as it will only format the selected cell. Data formatted through the Value Field Settings dialog box applies to all other cells within the same field. This eliminates the need to select a range of data and for being concerned with how the formatting will change as the PivotTable changes shape or is restructured.

Additionally, new fields can be added. Remember that when data are in an Excel table, it is possible to add a new field that is automatically included. If, while working with the PivotTable, a new calculation is needed, it is possible to add a calculated field directly to the PivotTable without changing the original data set. You also can return to the underlying data, add the new fields, and then use the Refresh button on the Analyze tab to update the PivotTable data for any changes made to the source data.

Finally, it is possible to change the layout, adding totals, grand totals, and labels within the PivotTable to enhance the look and feel of the PivotTable. This is useful in creating a structure that will be used in a presentation.

To Work with PivotTable Options

a. Click the **Pivot Analysis** worksheet tab. Click cell **B6**, which displays the data for the Sum of Food_Order in the first quarter of 2005 for all parties staying at the hotel.

b. Under the PIVOTTABLES TOOLS contextual tab, click the **ANALYZE** tab. In the Active Field group, click **Field Settings**. The Value Field Settings dialog box opens.

c. Click **Number Format**. The Format Cells dialog box opens. Click **Currency** in the Category list. Click **OK**, and then click **OK** in the Value Field Settings dialog box. Notice that all values within the Values section have now changed to Currency format.

d. Mouse over cell **B6**. A ScreenTip appears, informing you about the data within that cell.

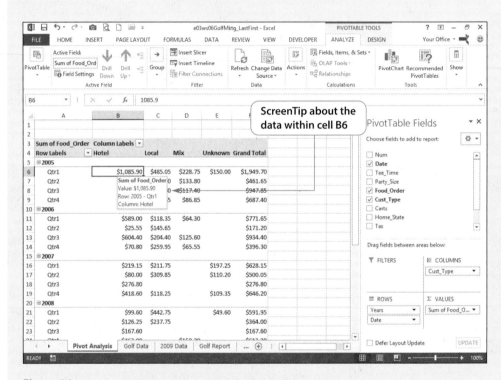

Figure 14 Currency format in PivotTable

e. Right-click cell **B6**, point to **Summarize Values By**, and then select **Average**.

It may be useful to compare the values. For example, it may be important to know how the hotel average sales compares to the overall average of the Painted Paradise Resort and Spa within each time period.

SIDE NOTE

PivotTable Formatting

It is not recommended to use the standard formatting techniques found on the Home tab with PivotTables. The PivotTable is dynamic, and the regular formatting techniques will not make use of the dynamic attributes.

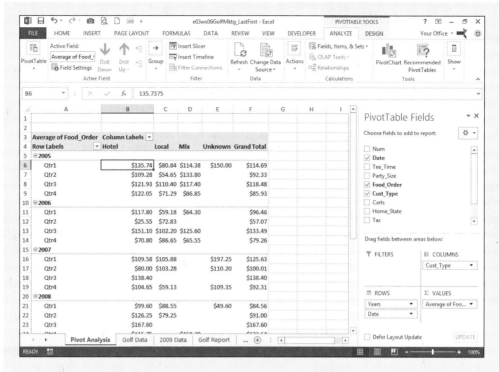

Figure 15 Summarize by average

f. Right-click cell **B6**, point to **Summarize Values By**, and then select **Sum**. Right-click cell **B6**, point to **Show Values As**, and then select **% of Row Total**.

Because the values are sums, the Grand Total row average is 100%. So, in Qtr 1 of 2006, the three percentages—Hotel, Local, and Mix—add up to the 100%.

Keep in mind that this average is based on the average Food_Order purchases for each Cust_Type golfing party. However, golfing parties have anywhere from one to five people, so if the average purchases per person was desired, the PivotTable would need to be adjusted to calculate an average by dividing the Food_Order by Party_Size.

g. In the PivotTable Fields list, uncheck the **Food_Order** field.

h. On the ANALYZE tab, in the Calculations group, click **Fields, Items, & Sets**. Select **Calculated Field**. The Insert Calculated Field dialog box opens.

i. In the Name box, type Food Per Person and then press Tab. In the Formula box replace =0 with =Food_Order/Party_Size. Click **Add**, and then click **OK**.

The average food cost per person is now displayed. For example, B6 is the total food order for all hotel parties during Qtr 1 of 2005 divided by the sum of all the party sizes during that same time period. Notice there are some #DIV/0! errors in the table. This is because those are cells where there was no activity, so Excel is trying to divide by 0. Because this error message is a valid error that could reasonably be expected, it can also be hidden.

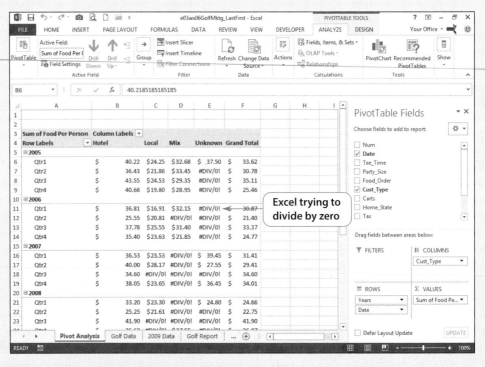

Figure 16 Calculated field

j. Click cell **B6** if necessary. On the ANALYZE tab, in the PivotTable group, click **Options**. The PivotTable Options dialog box opens.

SIDE NOTE

Retaining Labels

When you change a label in a PivotTable, the new label will be retained. If a field is removed and added again, the new label will still be retained.

k. Click the **Layout & Format** tab if necessary, and then under the Format section, click the **For error values show** check box. Because you want nothing to be displayed when there is an error, leave the box blank, and then click **OK**.

Notice the error messages are now replaced with a blank cell. Now the data from 2005 through 2011 should be showing, by quarter. However, if the analysis were to focus on just a couple of years, the data could be filtered even more.

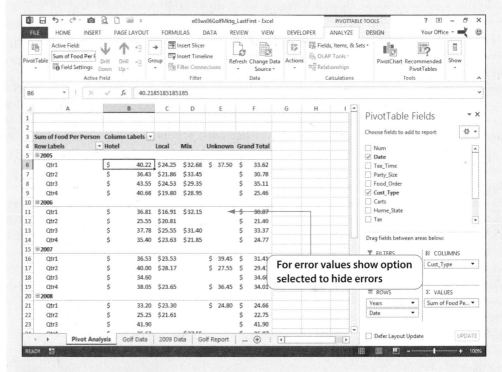

Figure 17 PivotTable options

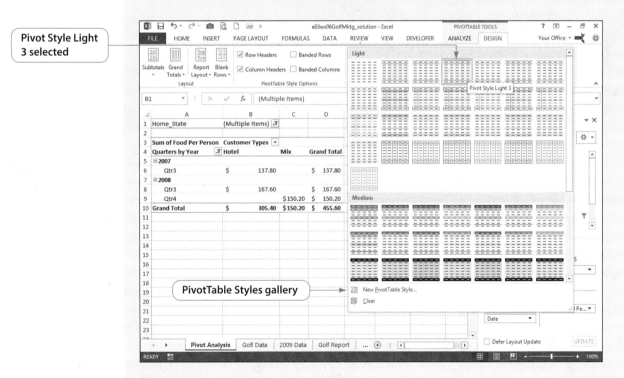

l. In cell A4, click the **Row Labels** arrow. The Filter menu opens. Click the **(Select All)** check box to toggle all the options off. Click the **2006**, **2007**, and **2008** check boxes, and then click **OK**.

This allows quick filtering of the records. The updated results are displayed. Only those three filter years will be displayed for the Row Labels. Notice in cell A4 there is now a filter icon to the right of the Row Labels label indicating a filter has been applied. If another level of grouping is required, the Report Filter can be used. It allows an overarching level of grouping to be added. Fields where there are minimal options with many records, such as Year, Party_Size, or Carts, make good selections for the Report Filter.

m. Click cell **B3**, type Customer Types and then press ⌷Enter⌷. Click cell **A4**, type Quarters by Year and then press ⌷Enter⌷. This will make the names more informative to the users.

n. In the PivotTable Fields list, click the **Home_State** check box. Drag the **Home_State** field listed in the ROWS area to the **FILTERS** area located above the ROWS area. You may have to scroll down in the ROWS area. Home_State will now appear in cells A1:B1.

o. Click cell **B1**, click the **Filter** arrow, and then click the **Select Multiple Items** check box. Click the **(All)** check box to clear all the check boxes, and then click the **AR** and **AZ** check boxes to display the Arizona and Arkansas data. Click **OK**.

p. Under the PIVOTTABLES TOOLS contextual tab, click the **DESIGN** tab. In the PivotTable Styles group, click the **More** arrow. Under Light, click **Pivot Style Light 3**.

q. Click **Save** 🔲.

Figure 18 Report filter with customization

Adding a Slicer to the PivotTable

Finally, more options can be added using a slicer to create yet another layer of slicing to the data. A **slicer** is a visual mechanism for quickly filtering data in a PivotTable. A slicer is an object that sits or floats on top of the spreadsheet that lists the data options of a field. The user can quickly select one or more of the list items to filter on the fly.

E06.11

To Insert and Customize a Slicer

SIDE NOTE
Moving the Slicer
The slicer will not move as the PivotTable changes shape. Point to the border of the slicer, and then when the Move pointer appears, drag the border edge to a new location.

a. Click the **Pivot Analysis** worksheet tab. Click the **ANALYZE** tab. In the Actions group, click the **Clear** arrow, and then select **Clear Filters**. In cell **A4**, click the **Quarters by Year** arrow. The Filter menu opens. Click the **(Select All)** check box to toggle all the options off. Click the **2006**, **2007**, and **2008** check boxes, and then click **OK**.

b. Click the **INSERT** tab, and then in the Filters group, click **Slicer**. The Insert Slicer dialog box opens. Click the **Tee_Time** check box, and then click **OK**. Click the **9:18:00 AM** time slot in the Tee_Time slicer. Press and hold Shift, scroll down, and then click the **12:00:00 PM** time slot. The data for those time slots will be incorporated into the PivotTable.

The slicer floats on the spreadsheet with all available Tee_Times. The PivotTable will reflect the filters applied to the slicer. Shift can be used to select a range of options, or you can use Ctrl to pick and choose options to include in the PivotTable. With the Tee_Time slicer, there are three times listed at the top that are displayed as bolder text compared to the rest of the times, which are listed as gray text. This is because within the Arizona and Arkansas data there are only records that have the bolder tee times. There are no records in the subset of data that have other tee times.

c. Right-click the **Tee_Time** slicer, and then select **Slicer Settings**. The Slicer Settings dialog box opens.

d. Under the Header section, replace **Tee_Time** with Tee Times in the Caption box, and then click **OK**.

e. Right-click the **Tee Times** slicer, and then select **Size and Properties**. The Format Slicer pane opens.

SIDE NOTE
Customizing Slicers
Customizing slicers can make them more visually appealing and easier to use.

f. Click the **POSITION AND LAYOUT** arrow, and then under Layout, change the number of columns to **3**. **Close** ✕ the Format Slicer pane. Notice that the tee times are much easier to see.

g. Drag the **Tee Times** slicer so its top-left corner is in the top-left corner of **G2**.

h. Drag the **bottom-right corner** of the Tee Times slicer until all three columns are visible.

i. To further customize your slicers, click the **Tee Times** slicer if necessary. Under the SLICER TOOLS contextual tab, click the **OPTIONS** tab. In the Slicer Styles group, click the **More** arrow. Under Dark, click **Slicer Style Dark 2**.

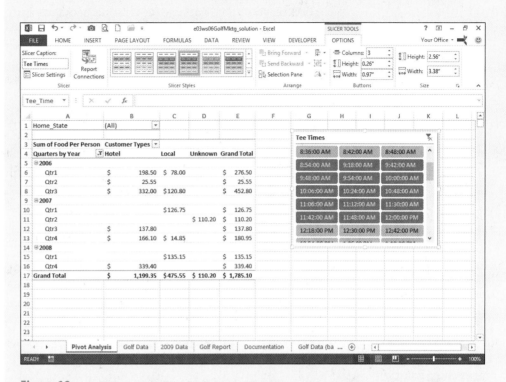

Figure 19 PivotTable and slicer with customization

j. Click **Save** 🔲.

Working with PivotTable Totals

Design options on the PivotTable Tools Design tab focus on the look and feel of the PivotTables. The options available include layout and styles. To get a perspective of the design options, it will be useful to clear the filters from the current PivotTable and begin with a basic structure. An important piece of data within a PivotTable can be totaled or summed numbers.

E06.12

 To Modify the Design and Work with Totals

a. Click the **Pivot Analysis** worksheet tab. Right-click the **Tee Times** slicer border, and then select **Remove "Tee Times"**.

b. Click cell **A5**. In the PivotTable Fields list, uncheck **Date**, **Cust_Type**, **Home_State**, **Years**, and **Food Per Person**.

This returns the PivotTable back to the starting point. Notice there will be filter icons to the right of field names in the PivotTable Fields list. These indicate the filter is still available with the previous settings and can be brought back into the PivotTable by checking the check box.

c. In the PivotTable Fields list, click the check boxes to select **Date**, **Cust_Type**, **Food_Order**, and **Years**. The years are grouped within each quarter, so in the ROWS area, click the **Years** field arrow, and then select **Move to Beginning** so the quarters are subgroups within each year. Notice the filter is still only showing 2006 through 2008.

> **Troubleshooting**
>
> You may need to scroll down in the ROWS area to find the Years field.

d. In the ROWS area, drag the **Cust_Type** field to the **COLUMNS** area. In the ROWS area, drag the **Food_Order** field to the **VALUES** area. The field changes to Count of Food_Order. Click the **Count of Food_Order** arrow, and then select **Value Field Settings**. Under Summarize value field by, select **Sum**, and then click **OK**.

e. Right-click cell **A4**, and then select **Group**. Verify that **Quarters** and **Years** are selected, and then click **OK**.

f. Under the PIVOTTABLES TOOLS contextual tab, click the **DESIGN** tab. In the Layout group, click the **Subtotals** arrow. Select **Show all Subtotals at Bottom of Group**.

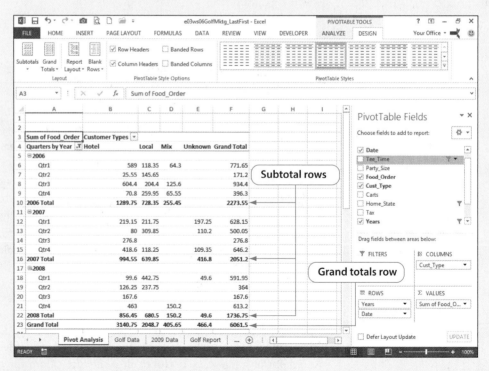

Figure 20 PivotTable subtotals

g. On the DESIGN tab, in the PivotTable Style Options group, click the **Banded Rows** check box.

This will put alternating colors on the rows. A PivotTable style, which consists of templates, can also be selected if desired.

h. Right-click cell **B6**, and then select **Number Format**. Under Category, click **Currency**, and then click **OK**.

i. On the DESIGN tab, in the Layout group, click **Report Layout**. Select **Show in Tabular Form**.

SIDE NOTE
Customizing Reports
It is best practice to customize your PivotTable report so your audience understands what you are trying to communicate.

j. Click cell **A3**, and then type Food Order Totals. Press Tab two times. In cell **C3**, type Customer Type and then press Enter. Click cell **B4**, and then type Quarters. Press Enter.

k. Select columns **B:C**. Click the **HOME** tab, and then in the Cells group, click **Format**. Select **AutoFit Column Width** so the columns are wide enough to view all the data. Press Ctrl+Home.

l. Click **Save**.

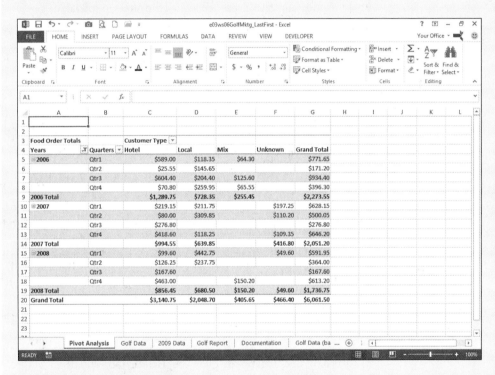

Figure 21   Stylized PivotTable

Updating and Sharing Data in PivotTables

There are many options for organizing and summarizing data. What happens if the data changes? What are the options for giving a subset of data to another person? These capabilities are available in PivotTables. If adding data to a PivotTable is necessary, the data source and range of data can be changed. After making changes to the source data set, the PivotTable data should be refreshed so the changes are updated in the PivotTable as well.

With a technique called "drilling down," it is also possible to give a subset of data to people without having to provide data they do not need or should not have in the first place. **Drilling down** is a method for accessing the detailed records that were used in a PivotTable to get to the aggregated data. It allows a user to select an individual piece of data in the PivotTable and then create a copy of individual records that were used to get that summary data on another worksheet.

E06.13

 To Update, Refresh, and Drill Down

a. Click the **Golf Data** worksheet tab. Click the **DATA** tab, and then in the Sort & Filter group, click **Clear** to clear all the filters in the table.

b. Drag the **Customer Type** slicer so its top-left corner is in the top-left corner of **L2**. Drag the **Home State** slicer so its top-left corner is in the top-left corner of **L11**.

c. Click cell **J11**, type Region and then press Enter. In cell **J12**, type =IF(OR(H12="NM",H12="TX",H12="AZ"),"Tri_State","") and then press Enter. Notice the formula will automatically fill in the new column.

d. Click the **Pivot Analysis** worksheet tab. Click cell **A6**, and then click the **ANALYZE** tab. In the Data group, click **Refresh**. Notice the new field for Region now appears in the PivotTable Fields list and could be integrated into the PivotTable as needed.

e. Click cell **C5**.

This is the food order revenue from customers during the first quarter of 2006. The underlying records that were used in generating the $589.00 total need to be retrieved.

f. Double-click cell **C5**. The action of double-clicking any cell within the PivotTable initiates the drill-down process where Excel will copy and paste the records that are associated with that value to another worksheet.

g. Double-click the **Sheet4** worksheet tab, replace **Sheet4** with 2006 Local and then press Enter.

h. Click column **B**. Click the **HOME** tab, and then in the Cells group, click **Format**. Select **AutoFit Column Width** to see the dates.

i. On the 2006 Local worksheet, click cell **E7**. Type =SUM(E2:E6) and then press Ctrl+Enter. Notice the sum is 589, which corresponds to the data in the PivotTable.

j. Click **Save** 🖫.

SIDE NOTE

Cell vs. Table References

When adding the new field "Region," you typed the cell references. If you click cell H12, Excel will insert [@[Home_State]] into the formula instead of H12. Either method will yield the same result.

Develop and Customize PivotCharts

The visual representation of data through charts can be powerful. **PivotCharts** are charts that are tied to the data within a PivotTable. When the PivotTable data are rearranged, they are automatically updated in the PivotChart. Conversely, when making changes to the PivotChart the corresponding changes are seen in the PivotTable.

PivotCharts have an added component of filtering. The chart has drop-down elements with filtering options. Multiple PivotCharts can be associated with one PivotTable; however, because they are all tied together, best practice dictates having only one PivotChart associated with one PivotTable. Additionally, be careful when making use of a PivotChart in a presentation so that no changes occur accidentally within the PivotTable that could yield unwanted changes to the chart. Once a PivotChart is created, all formatting elements from a regular chart are available.

Adding a PivotChart

PivotCharts provide a visual representation of the data in a PivotTable. It is easier to see a trend by looking at a "picture" of the data as opposed to viewing the data in table format. For example, by looking at a PivotChart that displays the spa's revenue over the past 12 months, you can easily see the movement of the trends without even thinking about it. By viewing data in a PivotTable, you would need to think about whether the numbers are higher or lower than the one you previously viewed. Once you view the data in a PivotChart, it is easy to read details such as month and total revenue for each month.

E06.14

To Add a PivotChart

a. Click the **Pivot Analysis** worksheet tab, and then click cell **A6**. Under the PIVOTTABLES TOOLS contextual tab, click the **ANALYZE** tab.

b. In the Tools group, click **PivotChart**. The Insert Chart dialog box opens. Click the **Clustered Column** chart in the first position if necessary, and then click **OK**.

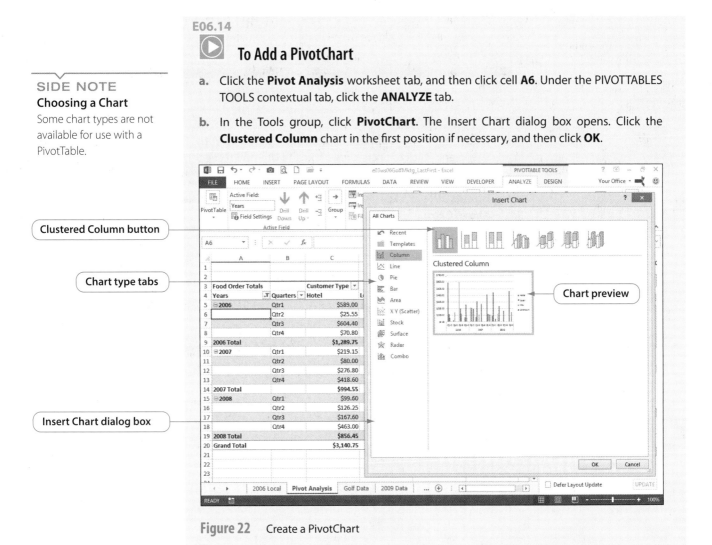

Figure 22 Create a PivotChart

c. With the chart selected, under the PIVOTCHART TOOLS contextual tab, click the **DESIGN** tab. In the Location group, click **Move Chart**. The Move Chart dialog box opens. Select **New sheet** if necessary, and then in the New sheet box, replace **Chart1** with PivotChart. Click **OK**. There will be filtering options on the chart that allow you to change the filters within the chart.

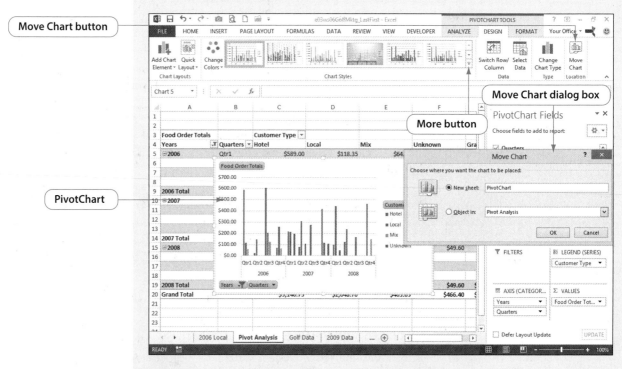

Figure 23 Move Chart dialog box

d. On the PivotChart worksheet, click the **Customer Type** filter button to display the filter menu. Click to uncheck the **Mix** and **Unknown** check boxes, and then click **OK**.

e. Under the PIVOTTABLES TOOLS contextual tab, click the **DESIGN** tab. In the Chart Layouts group, click **Add Chart Element**, point to **Chart Title**, and then select **Above Chart**.

f. Double-click the **Chart Title** box, replace **Chart Title** with Food Purchases by Customer Type, 2006-2008 and then press Esc.

g. On the DESIGN tab, in the Chart Styles group, click the **More** arrow. Select **Style 6**.

h. In the Chart Layouts group, click **Add Chart Element**, point to **Axis Titles**, and then select **Primary Vertical**.

i. Double-click the **Axis Title** box. Replace **Axis Title** with Revenue and then press Esc.

j. On the DESIGN tab, in the Chart Styles group, click **Change Colors**. Under Monochromatic, select **Color 6**.

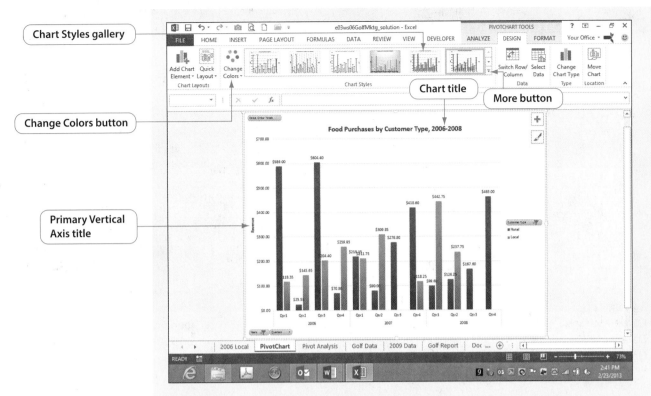

Figure 24 Customized PivotChart

k. Complete the Documentation worksheet and submit your file as directed by your instructor. **Save** 🔲 the workbook, and then **close** ❌ Excel.

QUICK REFERENCE | **PivotTable and PivotChart Best Practices**

When creating a PivotTable or PivotChart, remember the following.

- Once you have selected your data, ensure the source data are arranged in an area with column headings representing each field and the rows representing each record.

- Distinguish fields as either grouping variables or summary variables.

- Format the PivotTable or PivotChart so it is easy to read and your audience understands what it is you are trying to communicate.

- Know who your audience is prior to developing your PivotTable or PivotChart. It could make a difference in how much detail you display.

1. You have a batch of data in a spreadsheet that you are going to analyze. What are some tips for working with the data set to help prevent and correct errors? p. 310

2. You are chatting with a colleague who mentions that the SUBTOTAL function performs sum, average, count, or other functions, and questions why a person would use that function when the SUM, AVERAGE, and COUNT functions already exist. What is the difference when using the SUBTOTAL to sum data versus the SUM function? p. 322

3. What type of data would work well for the row and column labels within a PivotTable? What are some examples? p. 326

4. Describe two benefits of using an Excel PivotChart over an Excel PivotTable. p. 341

Key Terms

Advanced filter   317
Aggregate   322
Convert to range   313
Data set   309
Drilling down   339

Filtering   313
Grouping variable   328
Information   308
PivotChart   341
PivotTable   325

Raw data   308
Slicer   336
Standard filter   315
SUBTOTAL function   322
Summary variable   328

Visual Summary

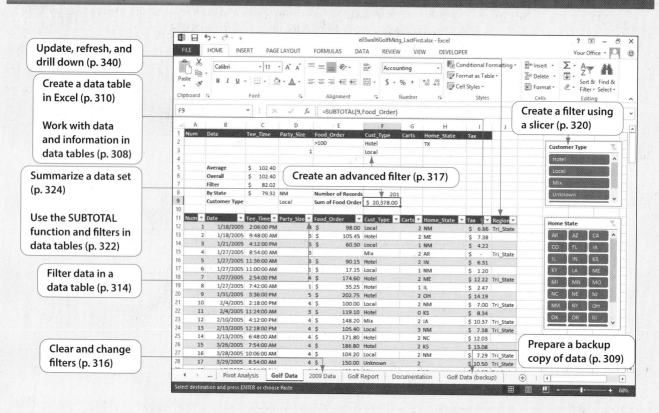

Update, refresh, and drill down (p. 340)

Create a data table in Excel (p. 310)

Work with data and information in data tables (p. 308)

Summarize a data set (p. 324)

Use the SUBTOTAL function and filters in data tables (p. 322)

Filter data in a data table (p. 314)

Clear and change filters (p. 316)

Create a filter using a slicer (p. 320)

Create an advanced filter (p. 317)

Prepare a backup copy of data (p. 309)

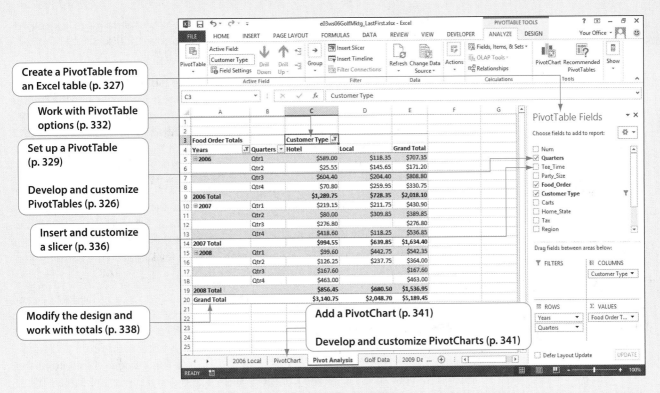

Annotations pointing to the figure:
- Create a PivotTable from an Excel table (p. 327)
- Work with PivotTable options (p. 332)
- Set up a PivotTable (p. 329)
- Develop and customize PivotTables (p. 326)
- Insert and customize a slicer (p. 336)
- Modify the design and work with totals (p. 338)
- Add a PivotChart (p. 341)
- Develop and customize PivotCharts (p. 341)

Figure 25   Golf Course Marketing Strategies Final Workbook

Practice 1

Student data file needed:

 e03ws06EmpSales.xlsx

You will save your file as:

e03ws06EmpSales_LastFirst.xlsx

New Employee Sales Analysis

Sales & Marketing

The management team has requested data from the information systems team on new golf shop employees. The data are from the sales database and only includes sales for three employees over the period of a week. With that data they would like you to set up some analyses they can review. In addition, they have some questions they would like answered. These questions are representative of the type of analysis they will use with the data. You must set up PivotTables that will help them understand the data.

a. Start **Excel**, and then open **e03ws06EmpSales**. Click the **FILE** tab, and then click **Save As**. In the Save As dialog box, navigate to the location where you are saving your files. In the File name box, type e03ws06EmpSales_LastFirst using your last and first name, and then click **Save**.

b. Right-click the **Golf Shop Data** worksheet tab, and then select **Move or Copy** to display the Move or Copy dialog box. Click to select **(move to end)**, click to check the **Create a copy** check box, and then click **OK**. A new worksheet will appear that is named Golf Shop Data (2). Right-click the **Golf Shop Data (2)** worksheet tab, and then click **Rename**. Replace the **2** with backup and then press [Enter].

c. Click the **Golf Shop Data** worksheet tab. Click cell **C20**, click the **INSERT** tab, and then in the Tables group, click **Table**. Verify the table range box displays **$A$20:$K$90** and the **My table has headers** check box is checked, and then click **OK**. With the data still selected, click the **FORMULAS** tab, and then in the Defined Names group, click **Create from Selection**. Verify that only the **Top row** check box is checked, uncheck the Left column if necessary, and then click **OK**.

d. Select range **A20:K20**, press ⌈Ctrl⌋, and then type C to copy the range. Click cell **A1**, press ⌈Ctrl⌋, and then type V to paste the field labels in row 1. Click cell **C2**, and then type Accessories. Click cell **K2**, type Friday and then press ⌈Enter⌋.

e. Click cell **G20**, press ⌈Ctrl⌋, and then type A to select the table. Click the **DATA** tab, and then in the Sort & Filter group, click **Advanced**. If a message asking to include the column labels in the selection to allow the Filter command to work properly appears, click **Yes**. In the Advanced Filter dialog box, click in the **Criteria range** box, and then select **A1:K2**. Verify that **Filter the list, in-place** is selected. Ensure that Excel automatically made the criteria range an absolute reference, and then click **OK**.

f. Select **A20:K72**, press ⌈Ctrl⌋, and then type C to copy the filtered data. Click **New sheet** to insert a new worksheet. Select cell **A1** if necessary, press ⌈Ctrl⌋, and then type V to paste the subset of data. Press ⌈Esc⌋, select columns **A:K**, and then click the **HOME** tab. In the Cells group, click **Format**, and then select **AutoFit Column Width**. Right-click the **Sheet2** worksheet tab, and then select **Rename**. Type Friday Filter and then press ⌈Enter⌋. Press ⌈Ctrl⌋+⌈Home⌋.

g. Click the **Golf Shop Data** worksheet tab, and then click cell **C20**. Click the **INSERT** tab, and then in the Filters group, click **Slicer**. Click the **Category** check box, and then click **OK**. Drag the **Category** slicer so its top-left corner is in the top-left corner of **L2**. In the slicer, click **Accessories**, press ⌈Ctrl⌋, and then click **Clothing**. Drag the **bottom edge** of the Category slicer to adjust the height so that the extra white space is no longer visible. To further customize your slicers, click the **Category** slicer if necessary. Under the SLICER TOOLS contextual tab, click the **OPTIONS** tab. In the Slicer Styles group, click the **More** arrow. Under Light, click **Slicer Style Other 1** in the first row, seventh column.

h. On the Golf Shop Data worksheet, click cell **C20**. Click the **INSERT** tab, and then in the Tables group, click **PivotTable**. Select **Existing Worksheet**, and then click in the **Location** box. If necessary, clear any existing text. Click the **Golf Report** worksheet tab, click cell **A10**, and then click **OK**.

i. In the PivotTable Fields pane, in the PivotTable Fields list, click the **Category**, **QTY**, and **Emp_ID** check boxes.

j. In the VALUES area, click **Sum of Emp_ID**, and then click **Move to Column Labels**.

k. The Employee IDs are not informative, so they should be changed to the employee's first names.
   - Click cell **B11**, and then type Chuck.
   - Click cell **C11**, and then type Jennifer.
   - Click cell **D11**, and then type Allie.
   - Select columns **B:D**, and then click the **HOME** tab. In the Cells group, click **Format**, and then select **AutoFit Column Width** so the employee names can be seen.
   - Apply **Pivot Style Light 17** to the PivotTable.
   - Select range **B12:C12**. Right-click the **range**, and then select **Value Field Settings**. Click **Number Format**, and then select **Currency**. Click **OK**, and then click **OK**.

l. View the data in the PivotTable to answer questions 1 and 2 on the Golf Report worksheet. You will answer question 3 later in this project.
   - View the data in the PivotTable to answer question 1. By looking at the Grand Total column, you notice that the total units of clothing sold is 26. Click cell **A2**, and then type 26.
   - View the data in the PivotTable to answer question 2. By looking at the Clothing row, you notice that Allie sold the most clothing with 10 units. Click **A4**, and then type Allie. Click **B4**, and then type 10.

m. Click any cell in the PivotTable, and then uncheck the **Category**, **QTY**, and **Emp_ID** fields.

n. Click cell **A10**. Click the **ANALYZE** tab, and then in the Calculations group, click **Fields, Items, & Sets**. Select **Calculated Field**.
   - In the Name box, type Subtotal and then press Tab.
   - Click **Retail** in the Fields list, and then click **Insert Field**.
   - Type *.
   - Click **QTY** in the Fields list, and then click **Insert Field**.
   - Click **OK**.

o. Click the **Golf Shop Data** worksheet tab, and then select cell **K20**. Click the **DATA** tab, and then in the Sort & Filter group, click **Clear**. Click cell **L20**, type Subtotal and then press Enter. Type =. Click cell **F21**, type * and then click cell **G21**. Press Enter to calculate the subtotal for each line item.

p. Click the **Golf Report** worksheet tab, and then click cell **A10**.
   - Click the **ANALYZE** tab, and then in the Calculations group, click **Fields, Items, & Sets**, and then select **Calculated Field**.
   - In the Name box, type Tax and then press Tab.
   - Click **Subtotal** in the Fields list, and then click **Insert Field**.
   - Type *.07 and then click **OK**.

q. In the PivotTable Fields list, click **Product ID**, **Category**, and **Day**. Verify the **Subtotal** and **Tax** fields are checked.
   - Drag the **Day** field from the ROWS area to the **FILTERS** area.
   - Drag the **Product ID** in the ROWS area below the **Category** field.
   - Click cell **B12**. Click the **ANALYZE** tab, and then in the Active Field group, click **Field Settings**. Click the **Show Values As** tab, and then click **Number Format**. Click **Currency**, click **OK**, and then click **OK**.
   - Click cell **C12**. On the ANALYZE tab, in the Active Field group, click **Field Settings**. Click the **Show Values As** tab, and then click **Number Format**. Click **Currency**, click **OK**, and then click **OK**.

r. On the ANALYZE tab, in the Filter group, click **Insert Slicer**. Click the **Emp_ID** check box, and then click **OK**. Click **Allie** in the Emp_ID slicer. Drag the **Emp_ID** slicer so its top-left corner is in the top-left corner of **E10**. Drag the **bottom edge** of the Emp_ID slicer to adjust the height so that the extra white space is no longer visible. Right-click the **Emp_ID** slicer, and then select **Slicer Settings**. In the Caption box, replace **Emp_ID** with Employee and then click **OK**. To further customize your slicer, click the **Employee** slicer if necessary. Under the SLICER TOOLS contextual tab, click the **OPTIONS** tab. In the Slicer Styles group, click the **More** arrow. Under Light, click **Slicer Style Other 1** in the first row, seventh column.

s. In cell **B8**, click the **Filter** arrow. Click the **Select Multiple Items** check box. Uncheck the **(All)** check box, click the **Friday** and **Saturday** check boxes, and then click **OK**.

t. Click cell **B10**. Click the **DESIGN** tab, and then in the Layout group, click the **Subtotals** arrow. Select **Show all Subtotals at Bottom of Group**.

u. View the data in the PivotTable to answer question 3. By looking at the Sum of Subtotal column and the Clubs Total row, you notice that the total clubs revenue Allie generated is $419. Click cell **A6**, type $419 and then press Enter.

    v. Complete the following to create a PivotChart.

- On the Golf Report worksheet tab, click **Clear Filter** on the slicer, and then close the PivotTable Fields pane. Click cell **A10**, type Categories, and then press `Tab`. In cell **B10**, type Pre-tax Total and then press `Tab`. In cell **C10**, type Tax Total and then press `Tab`.

- Click cell **A12**. Under the PIVOTTABLES TOOLS contextual tab, click the **ANALYZE** tab. In the Tools group, click **PivotChart**. Click the **Line** tab, and then click **Line with Markers** in the fourth position. Click **OK**.

- With the chart selected, under the PIVOTCHART TOOLS contextual tab, click the **DESIGN** tab. In the Location group, click **Move Chart**. Select **New sheet** if necessary, and then in the New sheet box, replace **Chart1** with PivotChart Analysis. Click **OK**.

- Under the PIVOTTABLES TOOLS contextual tab, click the **DESIGN** tab. In the Chart Layouts group, click **Add Chart Element**, point to **Chart Title**, and then select **Above Chart**. Double-click the **Chart Title** box, and then replace **Chart Title** with Total Sales and Tax by Category. Press `Esc`.

- In the Chart Layouts group, click **Add Chart Element**, point to **Axis Titles**, and then select **Primary Horizontal**. Double-click the **Axis Title** box, replace **Axis Title** with Category and then press `Esc`.

- On the DESIGN tab, in the Chart Styles group, click the **More** arrow. Select **Style 8**, in the first row, eighth column.

w. Click the **Documentation** worksheet. Click cell **A8**, and then type in today's date. Click cell **B8**, and then type in your first and last name. Complete the remainder of the **Documentation** worksheet according to your instructor's direction.

x. Click **Save**, close Excel, and then submit your file as directed by your instructor.

Problem Solve 1

MyITLab® Grader
Homework 1

Finance & Accounting

Student data file needed:

📄 e03ws06Tutor.xlsx

You will save your file as:

📄 e03ws06Tutor_LastFirst.xlsx

Analyzing the Learning Center's Data

The Learning Center at your school has been tracking the students, including you, who attend tutoring sessions. Because you have been doing well in your Excel sessions, they have asked you to analyze the data that has been collected over the past two semesters.

a. Start **Excel**, and then open **e03ws06Tutor**. Save the file as e03ws06Tutor_LastFirst using your last and first name.

b. Create a copy of the Student Data worksheet, and then place it at the end of the workbook. Rename the Student Data (2) worksheet as Student Data (backup).

c. On the Student Data worksheet, insert a table with headers that uses the range $A$11:$G$211. With the data table selected, create named ranges using the top row as the names.

d. Copy range **A11:G11**, and then paste the range in cell **A1**. In cell **C2**, type Sophomore. In cell **D2**, type Microsoft Office.

e. Create an advanced filter using the data in range **A1:G2**. Filter the list in-place to display the filtered data on the Student Data worksheet. Copy the filtered data, and then paste it in cell **A1** on the Filter worksheet. Resize the columns so all the data is visible.

f. On the Student Data worksheet, in cell **H11**, type TotalDue. In cell **H12**, enter a formula that multiplies TotalSessions and Rate. Format the TotalDue column as **Currency** with **0** decimal places. Create a named range for the TotalDue column that uses the column heading as the name.

g. Insert a slicer for the Subject field. Click **Science** and **Math** in the Subject slicer. Drag the **Subject** slicer so the top-left corner is in the top-left corner of J1. Drag the **bottom edge** of the Subject slicer to adjust the height so that the extra white space is no longer visible. Apply **Slicer Style Dark 5** to the slicer.

h. Use the SUBTOTAL function to complete the following.
   - In cell **F6**, insert a formula that counts the number of cells in the LastName field that are not empty.
   - In cell **F7**, insert a formula that averages the cells in the Rate field.
   - In cell **F8**, insert a formula that sums the cells in the TotalDue field.

i. Using the range **$A$11:$H$211**, insert a PivotTable in cell **A10** on the Analysis worksheet.

j. Configure the PivotTable using the following:
   - Add **Subject**, **LastName**, and **TotalSessions** to the PivotTable.
   - Move **Subject** to the COLUMNS area.
   - Right-click cell **H12**, point to **Sort**, and then sort the data in descending order.
   - Apply **Pivot Style Dark 6** to the PivotTable.
   - Change the color of the table to **Color 16**.
   - View the data in the PivotTable to answer question 1. Enter the student's last name who attended the most tutoring sessions in cell A2, and then enter the student's last name with the second highest number in cell B2.

k. Remove **LastName** and **TotalSessions** from the PivotTable, and then modify the PivotTable so you can answer the second question.
   - Add the **TotalDue**, **Date**, and **ClassStanding** fields to the PivotTable.
   - Move **Subject** to the **ROWS** area.
   - Move **ClassStanding** to the **FILTERS** area.
   - Format column B in the PivotTable as **Currency** with **0** decimal places.
   - On the ANALYZE tab, modify the dates to be displayed by month.
   - On the DESIGN tab, modify the subtotals so they are displayed at the bottom of the group.
   - In cell **A10**, use the Filter arrow to display data for **Aug**, **Sep**, **Oct**, **Nov**, and **Dec**.
   - View the data in the PivotTable to answer question 2. Enter the amount of revenue that was generated during the fall semester (August 25, 2014-December 31, 2014) in cell A4.

l. Modify the PivotTable so you can answer the third question.
   - Add the **FirstName** field to the PivotTable.
   - Move **FirstName** to the **VALUES** area.
   - In cell **B8**, use the Filter arrow to display data for **Sophomore**.
   - View the data in the PivotTable to answer question 3. Enter the total sophomores that used the Learning Center's services in cell A6.

m. Modify the PivotTable to prepare for creating a PivotChart.
   - Remove the **FirstName** field from the PivotTable.
   - Remove the **ClassStanding** filter, and then move ClassStanding to the **COLUMNS** area.
   - Move the **Date** field as the filter.
   - In cell **A10**, type Amount Due. In cell **A11**, type Subject by Month.

n. Using the data in the PivotTable, insert a Clustered Column PivotChart. Format the PivotChart as follows.
   - Move the PivotChart to a new sheet named Revenue Chart.
   - Add an Above Chart title. Replace **Title** with Revenue Generated by Class and Subject.
   - Apply **Style 8** to the PivotChart, and then change the color to **Color 16**.

o. Complete the **Documentation** worksheet according to your instructor's direction. Insert the **filename** in the left custom footer section of the Header/Footer tab in the Page Setup dialog box on all worksheets in the workbook.

p. Click **Save**, close Excel, and then submit the file as directed by your instructor.

Perform 1: How Others Perform

Student data file needed:
 e03ws06Charity.xlsx

You will save your file as:
 e03ws06Charity_LastFirst.xlsx

Raising Money for a Good Cause

Finance & Accounting

As an individual who volunteers for a local nonprofit organization that helps raise money for worthy causes, you are working with an organization that has been tracking donations collected for several charities. You were asked to analyze the financial data to see how they are performing.

a. Open **e03ws06Charity**. Save the file as e03ws06Charity_LastFirst using your last and first name.

b. On the Contributors worksheet, insert a table using range **$A$11:$L$111**. Create named ranges for all columns in the table.

c. Create an advanced filter for all contributors on the mailing list who donated to the **Dunk-a Prof** event. Filter the data on the same worksheet.

d. In range **K4:K8**, use the **SUBTOTAL** function to calculate the total transactions, the largest and smallest donation amounts, the average donation, and the total donations.

e. Using the data on the **Contributors** worksheet, insert a **PivotTable** in cell **A10** on the Data Analysis worksheet. Configure the PivotTable so you are able to answer questions 1, 2, and 3. Format the PivotTable with appropriate headings and cell formats. Show subtotals at the bottom of the group. Ensure that you are able to filter the PivotTable using the Mailing List field. Resize the fields as needed. Change the color of the PivotTable to match the colors in the workbook.

f. Insert two slicers that include appropriate headings and formats. Move the slicers so they do not cover any data. Create a filter using both slicers. Ensure that one slicer has multiple criteria selected. Change the color of the slicers to match the colors in the workbook.

g. Insert a PivotChart on a new sheet. Format the PivotChart with an appropriate title. Apply an appropriate style to the PivotChart. Change the color of the PivotChart to match the colors in the workbook.

h. Complete the **Documentation** worksheet according to your instructor's direction. Insert the **filename** in the left custom footer section of the Header/Footer tab in the Page Setup dialog box on all worksheets in the workbook.

i. Click **Save**, close Excel, and then submit the file as directed by your instructor.

Additional
Cases

Additional Workshop Cases are available on the companion website and in the instructor resources.

MODULE CAPSTONE

More Practice 1	

Student data file needed:

 e03mpDesserts.xlsx

You will save your file as:

e03mpDesserts_LastFirst.xlsx

Indigo5 Dessert Analysis

Sales & Marketing

Robin Sanchez, the chef at Indigo5, was discussing dessert sales with the restaurant manager, Alberto Dimas. They want to examine the production levels and the sales of their signature desserts. To do so, they have collected data from last week's sales and included it in a workbook so you can analyze the data. Once the analysis is completed, you will present it to Chef Sanchez and Mr. Dimas so they can make marketing decisions about the restaurant's dessert menu.

a. Start **Excel**, and then open **e03mpDesserts**. Click the **FILE** tab, and then click **Save As**. In the Save As dialog box, navigate to the location where you are saving your files. In the File name box, type e03mpDesserts_LastFirst using your last and first name, and then click **Save**.

b. Right-click the **Dessert Sales** worksheet tab, and then select **Move or Copy** to display the Move or Copy dialog box. Click to select **(move to end)**, click to check the **Create a copy** check box, and then click **OK**. A new worksheet will appear that is named Dessert Sales (2). Right-click the **Dessert Sales (2)** worksheet tab, and then click **Rename**. Replace the **2** with backup and then press Enter.

c. Click the **Input Data** worksheet tab. You will create named ranges to use in formulas.
    - Select **A3:D9**. Click in the **Name** box, type Dessert_List and then press Enter.
    - Select **A12:B19**. Click in the **Name** box, type Employee_List and then press Enter.
    - Select **G3:M4**. Click in the **Name** box, type Daily_Goal and then press Enter.
    - Select **F12:G15**. Click in the **Name** box, type Goal_Grade and then press Enter. Press Ctrl+Home.

d. Click the **Dessert Sales** worksheet tab, and then click cell **B10**. Click the **INSERT** tab, and then in the Tables group, click **Table**. Verify the range is =$A$10:$D$210 and that the **My table has headers** check box is checked. Click **OK**.

e. To begin your analysis, create the following fields and formulas.
    - Click cell **E10**. Type Dessert and then press Tab. In cell **F10**, type Day and then press Tab. In cell **G10**, type Category and then press Tab. In cell **H10**, type Emp Name and then press Tab. In cell **I10**, type Revenue and then press Enter.
    - Click cell **E11**, type =VLOOKUP(B11,Dessert_List,2,FALSE) and then press Tab. The VLOOKUP will look up the Dessert ID from the Dessert_List named range and return the name of the dessert. FALSE indicates an exact match will be needed.
    - In cell **F11**, type =INDEX(Daily_Goal,1,WEEKDAY(C11,1)) and then press Tab. This will pull the value from the Daily_Goal named range, looking in Row 1. The WEEKDAY function will pull the day of the week, returning a number from 1 to 7, which will translate to the column field name within the Daily_Goal table.
    - In cell **G11**, Crème Brulee and Dutch Apple Pie are the two desserts that are prepared just prior to serving and are served warm. Thus, if the dessert is either of

those, the category should be "Warm". Otherwise, it should be "Cool." In cell **G11**, type =IF(OR(E11="Creme Brulee",E11="Dutch Apple Pie"),"Warm","Cool") and then press [Tab].

- In cell **H11**, type =VLOOKUP(A11,Employee_List,2,FALSE) and then press [Tab]. The VLOOKUP will look up Emp ID in the Employee_List named range and retrieve the employee's name from the second column of the named range. FALSE indicates an exact match will be needed.

- In cell **I11**, type =VLOOKUP(B11,Dessert_List,4,FALSE)*D11 and then press [Enter]. This will look up the Dessert ID in the Dessert_List named range and retrieve the selling price. Then, the selling price is multiplied by the quantity sold to calculate the total dessert revenue generated.

f. Select range **I11:I210**. Click the **HOME** tab, and then in the Number group, click **Accounting Number Format**. Highlight columns **G:I**. On the HOME tab, in the Cells group, click **Format**, and then select **AutoFit Column Width**.

g. On the Dessert Sales worksheet, create the following named ranges.

- Click cell **E10**, press [Ctrl]+[A] to select the entire table. Click in the **Name** box, type Dessert_All and then press [Enter].

- Click the **FORMULAS** tab, and then in the Defined Names group, click **Create from Selection**. Verify that only the **Top row** check box is selected, and then click **OK**.

h. Select **A10:I10**, and then press [Ctrl]+[C] to copy the header information. Click cell **A1**, and then press [Ctrl]+[V] to paste the headers. Press [Esc] to deselect range A10:I10.

i. Click cell **F2**, and then type Tuesday. Press [Tab], and then type Cool under Category.

j. Click cell **C10**. Click the **DATA** tab, and then in the Sort & Filter group, click **Advanced**. Confirm **$A$10:$G$210** is displayed in the List range input box, and if necessary, edit the range as specified to select the entire table. Click in the **Criteria range** input box, select range **A1:I2**, and then click **OK** to filter the data.

k. Calculate the following subtotals.

- Click cell **C5**, and then type =SUBTOTAL(1,Revenue) to calculate the average dessert check. Press [Enter]. The "1" indicates to average the filtered records on the Revenue field for records currently displayed in the table.

- In cell **C6**, type =SUBTOTAL(3,Dessert_ID) to count the number of desserts. Press [Enter]. The "3" indicates to count the nonblank cells in the Dessert_ID field for records currently displayed in the table.

- In cell **C7**, type =SUBTOTAL(9,Qty) to sum the number of desserts sold. Press [Enter]. The "9" indicates to sum the numbers in the Qty field for records currently displayed in the table.

l. Click cell **G10**. Click the **INSERT** tab, and then in the Filters group, click **Slicer**. In the Insert Slicers dialog box, click the **Dessert** and **Emp Name** check boxes. Click **OK**. Format the slicers as follows.

- Drag the **Emp Name** slicer so its top-left corner is in the top-left corner of cell **K1**. Right-click the **Emp Name** slicer, and then select **Slicer Settings**. In the Caption box, replace **Emp Name** with Employee. Click **OK**.

- To further customize your slicer, click the **Employee** slicer if necessary. Under the SLICER TOOLS tab, click the **OPTIONS** tab. In the Slicer Styles group, click the **More** arrow. Under Dark, click **Slicer Style Dark 4** in the second row, fourth column.

- Right-click the **Employee** slicer, and then in the Format Slicer pane select **Size and Properties**. Click the **POSITION AND LAYOUT** arrow, and then change the **1** in Number of columns to **2**. Close the **Format Slicer** pane. Drag the **bottom edge** of the slicer to adjust the height so that the extra white space is no longer visible.

- Drag the **Dessert** slicer so its top-left corner is in the top-left corner of cell **K10**. Drag the **bottom right corner** of the slicer to adjust the height and width so that the extra white space is no longer visible and all dessert names are visible.

- To further customize your slicer, click the **Dessert** slicer if necessary. Under the SLICER TOOLS contextual tab, click the **OPTIONS** tab. In the Slicer Styles group, click the **More** arrow. Under Dark, click **Slicer Style Dark 4** in the second row, fourth column.

- In the Employee slicer, click **Joe**, press Ctrl, and then click **Wayne**. In the Desserts slicer, click **Carrot Cake**, press Ctrl, click **Double Chocolate Delight**, press Ctrl, and then click **New York Cheesecake**.

m. Click the **Report** worksheet tab, click cell **B3**, and then create the following formulas.

- Type =SUMIF(Dessert,A3,Qty) and then press Ctrl+Enter. Double-click the **AutoFill** handle to copy this formula down through **B8**.

- Click cell **B11**, type =SUMIFS(Qty,Dessert,$A11,Day,B$10) and then press Ctrl+Enter. Double-click the **AutoFill** handle to copy this formula down though **B16**, and then drag the **AutoFill** handle to copy across to **H16** so the formula is copied to the range **B11:H16**. This sums the Qty field where both the dessert and day criteria are true.

- Click cell **B18**, type =SUM(B11:B16)/HLOOKUP(B10,Daily_Goal,2,FALSE) and then press Enter. This sums the day's quantity sold and divides this value by the day's goal. The goal is found using the HLOOKUP in the Daily_Goal named range.

- In cell **B19**, type =VLOOKUP(B18,Goal_Grade,2) and then press Enter.

- Select **B18:B19**, and then drag the **AutoFill** handle to copy the formulas to fill the range **C18:H19**.

- Click cell **B23**, type =IF(B21="Employee","Emp_Name","Dessert") and then press Enter. This determines which data named range is associated with the category that is in cell B21. It will then be used in other formulas to select that named range.

- In cell **B24**, type =SUMIF(INDIRECT(B23),B22,Qty) and then press Enter. This uses the named range in B23 as the criteria range and sums the Qty field.

- In cell **B25**, type =AVERAGEIF(INDIRECT(B23),B22,Qty) and then press Enter. This averages the Qty field, using the named range listed in B23 as the criteria field.

- Click cell **F3**. The End Level is either Low or Okay. If the Bake Time is Day Bake and has an ending quantity lower than the Day Bake level listed in G6 on the Input Data worksheet, the formula will return Low. The formula also returns Low if the Bake Time is Fresh Bake, and the ending quantity for the Fresh Bake item is less than the Fresh Bake value listed in cell G7 on the Input Data worksheet. In cell F3, type =IF(OR(AND(E3="Day Bake",C3<'Input Data'!$G$6),AND(E3="Fresh Bake",C3<'Input Data'!$G$7)),"Low","Okay") and then press Ctrl+Enter.

- Double-click the **AutoFill** handle to copy the formula down to cell **F8**.

- The Adjust column checks if either of two situations is true. If either are true, the chef will need to produce more; otherwise, the cell can remain blank. If requests are more than 5, indicating that the item sold out, more need to be produced. Or, if the end level is low and the bake time is Day Bake, then more need to be produced. Click cell **G3**, type =IF(OR(D3>5,AND(F3="Low",E3="Day Bake")),"Produce More","") and then press Ctrl+Enter. Double-click the **AutoFill** handle to copy the formula down to cell **G8**. Press Ctrl+Home.

n. Click the **Dessert Sales** worksheet tab, and then click cell **B10**. Click the **INSERT** tab, and then in the Tables group, click **PivotTable**. Select the **New Worksheet** option, and then click **OK**. Double-click the **Sheet2** worksheet tab, replace **Sheet2** with PivotTable Analysis and then press Enter to rename the worksheet.

o. Complete the following to create your PivotTable.

- In the PivotTable Fields List, check the **Qty**, **Dessert**, **Day**, and **Category** check boxes.

- Drag the **Dessert** field to the **COLUMNS** area, and then drag the **Dessert** field to the **FILTERS** area.

- In cell **B3**, select the **Column Labels** filter button, and then click **(Select All)** to deselect all the items. Click the **Crème Brulee**, **Dutch Apple Pie**, and **New York Cheesecake** check boxes, and then click **OK**.

- Under the PIVOTTABLE TOOLS contextual tab, click the **DESIGN** tab. In the PivotTable Styles group, click the **More** arrow. Under Medium, select **Pivot Style Medium 5**. In the PivotTable Style Options group, click the **Banded Rows** check box.

- Click cell **A3**, type Total Quantity and then press Tab. In cell **B3**, type Desserts and then press Enter. In cell **A4**, type Day and Dessert Type and then press Enter. Select columns **A:B**. Click the **HOME** tab. In the Cells group, click **Format**, and then select **AutoFit Column Width**.

- Under the PIVOTTABLE TOOLS contextual tab, click the **DESIGN** tab. In the Layout group, click **Subtotals**, and then select **Show all Subtotals at Bottom of Group**.

- Click cell **A5**. Under the PIVOTTABLE TOOLS contextual tab, click the **ANALYZE** tab. In the Tools group, click **PivotChart**. Click **Line**, click **Stacked Line**, the second option, and then click **OK**. Close the PivotChart Fields pane.

- Click the **DESIGN** tab, and then in the Location group, click **Move Chart**.

- In the Move Chart dialog box, select **New sheet**. Click in the **New Sheet** box, replace **Chart1** with PivotChart Analysis and then click **OK**.

- Under the PIVOTCHART TOOLS contextual tab, click the **DESIGN** tab. In the Chart Layouts group, click **Add Chart Element**, point to **Chart Title**, and then select **Above Chart**. Double-click in the **Chart Title** box, replace **Chart Title** with Total Quantity Sold by Day and Dessert Type and then click Esc.

- In the Chart Styles group, click **Change Colors**, and then select **Color 4**. In the Chart Styles group, click the **More** arrow. Select **Style 13**.

p. Click the **Documentation** worksheet. Click cell **A8**, and then type in today's date. Click cell **B8**, and then type in your first and last name. Complete the remainder of the **Documentation** worksheet according to your instructor's direction.

q. Click **Save**, close Excel, and then submit your file as directed by your instructor.

Problem Solve 1

MyITLab® Grader
Homework 1

Sales & Marketing

Student data file needed:

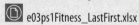 e03ps1Fitness.xlsx

You will save your file as:

e03ps1Fitness_LastFirst.xlsx

Managing the Hotel Exercise Classes

The hotel has started facilitating fitness classes for hotel guests. Guests can register for classes prior to their arrival or when they arrive to the hotel. Several instructors lead the classes, and each instructor has multiple skills. The fitness center manager would like to have a spreadsheet developed that will track class enrollment. The spreadsheet will provide an overview of guest enrollment with some analysis, which will be used for better decision-making.

a. Start **Excel**, and then open **e03ps1Fitness**. Save the file as e03ps1Fitness_LastFirst using your last and first name.

b. Copy the **Enrollment** worksheet to the end of the workbook to make a backup copy of the data. Rename the worksheet Enrollment (backup).

c. On the **Input Data** worksheet, select range **B11:H14**. Create named ranges using the top row as the name for your named ranges. Each range is the list of instructors that can teach individual classes. Select range **B4:H8**. Create named ranges using the top row as the name for your named ranges. Each range includes fitness class details.

d. On the **Enrollment** worksheet, in cell **A14**, insert a table using range **A13:D106** and the top row as the headers.

e. In cell **D14**, enter a HLOOKUP function that will look up the class number in cell B14 and use the ClassInfo table to return the Fee from the fifth row of the table with an exact match. Copy the formula down to cell D106 if necessary.

f. In cell **E13**, create a new column header named Class Name. In cell **E14**, enter a HLOOKUP function that will look up the class number in cell B14 and use the ClassInfo table to return the Class Category name from the second row of the table with an exact match. Copy the formula down to cell E106 if necessary.

g. Select **A13:E106**, and then name the entire range **Enrollment**. Create named ranges using the top row as the name for your named ranges. Copy range **A13:E13**, and then paste in range **A1:E1** to set up the advanced filter criteria area. Enter the following filter criteria.

- In cell **C2**, type F.
- In cell **E2**, type Yoga.

h. Create the following formulas on the Enrollment worksheet.

- In cell **B6**, create a DCOUNTA function to count the Student_ID field in the Enrollment table that meet the filter criteria specified in range A1:E2.

- In cell **B7**, create a DAVERAGE function to average the Fee field in the Enrollment table that meet the filter criteria specified in range A1:C2. This will average all fees collected from females.

- In cell **B8**, create a DSUM function to sum the Fee field in the Enrollment table that meet the filter criteria specified in range A1:E2. This will total all yoga fees collected from females.

i. On the **Report** worksheet, create calculations that will help hotel employees manage the fitness class enrollments. The user will put an "x" in range E4:E10, indicating which class to report upon and an "x" in range H4:H5 if employees want a report on a specific gender.

- In cell **A4**, use a MATCH function nested in an INDEX function to retrieve the Class that was selected in E4:E10. The MATCH should find the row where the "x" is located and would be used within the INDEX to pull the associated Class value from the same row within range F4:F10.

- In cell **B4**, use a MATCH nested in an INDEX function to retrieve the Gender that was selected in H4:H5, looking at the "x" in column H and returning the "F" or "M" for the Gender criteria. Using a MATCH nested in an INDEX function, retrieve the gender that was selected in H4:H5. Nest the MATCH and INDEX formula inside of the IFERROR function, in case the user does not select a specific gender. The IFERROR should leave the cell blank, using "", if a gender is not selected.

- In cell **C4**, create a COUNTIF formula that counts the enrollment for the named range Class that has the class number listed in A4. The range criteria should reference the Class named range.

- In cell **B7**, create an HLOOKUP formula that will look up the Class in A4 within the ClassInfo named range and return the maximum enrollment, which is in the third row of that table. The value should be looking for an exact match.

- In cell **B8**, create an HLOOKUP formula that will use the Class in A4 and retrieve the Class Category type from the ClassInfo named range in row 2, also looking for an exact match.

- In cell **B11**, create an IF function to indicate the availability of reservations. If the number enrolled in C4 is greater than or equal to the maximum enrollment in B7, then FULL OR OVERBOOKED should be displayed. Otherwise, Spots Available should be displayed.

- The instructors for each class are listed on the Input Data worksheet in range B12:H14. The instructors for the Aerobics class need to be counted. In cell **B12**, create a complex function that will determine the number of instructors for the class listed in A4. Use the COUNTA, INDIRECT, INDEX, and MATCH functions.

- Click cell **B13**. Using an HLOOKUP function nested in an AND function nested in an IF function, return either Split Class or Can't Split based on business options. Two conditions are needed to determine if a class can be split. Using the ClassInfo table, one row shows if a class can be split. That condition can be determined with a HLOOKUP. The second is if there is more than one instructor, as shown in cell B12. If both conditions are met, the class can be split. Otherwise, the class cannot be split.

j. Insert a PivotTable using the Enrollment named range on the Enrollment worksheet. Insert the PivotTable on a new worksheet named Pivot Analysis. Complete the following to create your PivotTable.

- Add the **Student_ID**, **Gender**, and **Class Name** fields to the PivotTable.
- Move **Gender** to the **COLUMNS** area. Move **Student_ID** to the **VALUES** area.
- In cell **B3**, replace **Column Labels** with Gender. In cell **B4**, replace **F** with Female. In cell **C4**, replace **M** with Male. In cell **A3**, replace **Count of Student_ID** with Total Students. In cell **A4**, replace **Row Labels** with Classes. Resize the column widths as needed.
- Apply **Pivot Style Light 10** to the PivotTable.

k. Insert a Clustered Column PivotChart on the Pivot Analysis worksheet. Customize the PivotChart as follows.

- Reposition the **PivotChart** so its top-left corner is in the top-left corner of cell **F3**. Drag the **bottom-right corner** so the PivotChart fills column **N**.
- Change the color of the PivotChart to **Color 13**.
- Apply **Style 8** to the PivotChart.
- Add a chart title above the chart. Replace **Chart Title** with Enrollment by Class and Gender.

l. Complete the **Documentation** worksheet according to your instructor's direction. Insert the **filename** in the left custom footer section of the Header/Footer tab in the Page Setup dialog box on all worksheets in the workbook.

m. Click **Save**, close Excel, and then submit the file as directed by your instructor.

Problem Solve 2

MyITLab® Grader
Homework 2

Sales & Marketing

Human Resources

Student data file needed:

e03ps2MarketRep.xlsx

You will save your file as:

e03ps2MarketRep_LastFirst.xlsx

Analyzing the Hotel Marketing Efforts

You have been assigned to conduct market analysis for the Painted Paradise Resort and Spa marketing representatives. Data pertaining to guests has been compiled for a 30-day period. Using the initial data, tables, and information, the marketing manager wants you to analyze the data so it can be used for decision-making purposes, such as which representative is performing at or above expectations.

a. Start **Excel**, and then open **e03ps2MarketRep**. Save the file as e03ps2MarketRep_LastFirst using your last and first name.

b. Copy the **Sales Data** worksheet to the end of the workbook to make a backup copy of the data. Rename the worksheet Sales Data (backup).

c. On the **Input Data** worksheet, create the following named ranges. Name the range F3:J4 Reps. Name the range A8:B14 Events.

d. Modify the Sales Data worksheet to prepare for and perform data analysis.

- In cell **K10**, type Rep Name. In cell **K11**, create an HLOOKUP function that looks up the marketing representative's number in column J and retrieves the corresponding name from the Reps named range. Resize the column so all the data is visible if necessary. AutoFill to cell **K167**.

- In cell **L10**, Add a new field label named Coupon. Resize the column so the header is visible if necessary.

- Copy range A10:K10, and then paste it in cell A1. In cell **B2**, type >6/10/2015, and then in cell **K2**, type Unassigned.

- In cell **L11**, use IF functions with nested AND and OR functions to create a formula that determines whether or not a customer has earned a promotional coupon. This coupon will be given to customers based on the pseudo-code information on the Input Data worksheet in F8:I17. There are two ways for a coupon to be earned. First, if the customer stays three or more days and has five or more in his party, then a coupon is given. Secondly, if the sum of their activities, such as enjoying the spa, playing golf, and dining, is greater than two—based on the data in columns F:H in the Sales Data worksheet table—and there are two or more in the party, a coupon is given. Since these values may change, the cells in the Input Data worksheet should be referenced. AutoFill to cell **L167**.

- Insert a table using **A10:L167** as the range. Create named ranges for each column in the table using the column headers as the names.

- Create an advanced filter using the criteria in range **A1:K2**.

- In cell **D6**, use the SUBTOTAL function to calculate the average length of stay using the Days named range. Format the cell with **2** decimal places.

- In cell **D7**, use the SUBTOTAL function to calculate the maximum stay using the Days named range.

- In cell **D8**, use the SUBTOTAL function to calculate the total number of stays—rows—displayed in the filtered data.

e. On the **Monthly Report** worksheet, create functions using the Sales Data worksheet that will help management understand business trends.

- In cell **B4**, create a function that will count the number of guests who participated in the activity listed in range A4. Copy the formula down to **B6**.

- In cell **B9**, create a function that will sum the activities in the event range listed in cell A9. Copy this formula down to cell **B14**.

- In cell **F4**, create a function that will look up the rep ID in the Reps named range and find the name of the rep. Copy the formula down to cell **F8**.

- In cell **G4**, create a function that will sum the range listed in G3 for the Rep listed in E4. Use appropriate cell referencing. Copy the formula over range **G4:I8**.

- In cell **J4**, create a formula that sums the range G4:I4. Copy the formula down to cell **J8**.

- In cell **F14**, create a function that will find the Cust_ID in the row number located in **E13**.

- In cell **B18**, create a function that will use the criteria in range A20:J21 to sum the category listed in **B17**.

- In cell **F17**, create a function that will find the longest—maximum—number of days spent at the resort.

- In cell **F18**, create a function that will find the Cust_ID who stayed at the resort for the longest time period located in F17.

f. Complete the **Documentation** worksheet according to your instructor's direction. Insert the **filename** in the left custom footer section of the Header/Footer tab in the Page Setup dialog box on all worksheets in the workbook.

g. Click **Save**, close Excel, and then submit the file as directed by your instructor.

Student data file needed:

 e03pf1Volunteer.xlsx

You will save your file as:

 e03pf1Volunteer_LastFirst.xlsx

Student Club Volunteer Report

Production & Operations

Your student club wants to set up a spreadsheet to track club members' volunteer activities. This will allow them to set goals, show they are helping the community, track how members are performing, and assess their efforts. Using the sample data provided, you will analyze data for tracking and monitoring volunteer activities.

a. Open **e03pf1Volunteer**, and then save your file as e03pf1Volunteer_LastFirst.

b. Create the following named ranges.

- On the Input Data worksheet, create named ranges for the columns in range A2:L12, including the Goal list of jobs in column A. Create a named range for the Goals for the range B3:L12. Create a named range for the GoalStatus table in A18:B21.

- On the Volunteer Work worksheet, create a table with the Volunteer Work data set. Create named ranges for each column in the data set. Create a named range for the entire data set, including the field labels.

c. Create an advanced filter on the Volunteer Work worksheet. Set up the criteria field headings and criteria in rows 1 and 2. In cell A5, use a function to calculate the number of donations made within the filtered data. In cell B5, use a function to calculate the total donations made within the filtered data. Insert two slicers, and then use it to filter the data. Customize the slicers with appropriate columns, colors, and headings if necessary. Resize and move the slicers so they do not overlap data.

d. On the Volunteer Report worksheet, create a report for the individual section in range B4:B9.

- In cell B4, create a function that will pull the goal for the member listed in B2 for the category listed in B3.

- In cell B5, create a function that will determine the actual time the member listed in B2 has actually logged for the category listed in B3.

- In cell B6, based on the Goal Status table in A18:B21 on the Input Data worksheet, create a formula that provides status feedback for the member listed in B2.

- In cell B7, create a formula that will add up the overall goal of the member in B2 for all categories.

- In cell B8, create a formula that will calculate the total time logged for the member in B2 for all categories.

- In cell B9, create a formula that will determine how much has been raised by the member listed in B2.

e. On the Volunteer Report worksheet, create a report for all members in range B14:D24.

- In cells B14:B24, create a function for each cell that totals the entire Time of the Student range using criteria listed in column A.

- For C14:C24, create a function for the Donation sum range for each cell that will find the Student in column A volunteering for the job listed in the Work Category range specified in C13. When that job changes, the totals should change for C14:C24 accordingly.

- For D14:D24, create an INDEX function for the Goals array with two nested MATCH functions. Nest the formula in a function that will leave the cell blank if an error occurs.

f.   In range E2:E5, create the following.

- In cell E3, create a function that will find the amount of the top donation. From that value find the other information in range E2:E5 associated with that donation.
- In cell E2, create a function to find the first Student that received that donation (use a nested MATCH to find row number argument).
- In cell E4, create a function to find the Work_Category activity that person did for the donation (use a nested MATCH to find row number argument).
- In cell E5, use a function to count the number of people who received the Top Donation amount.

g.   Create a graphical representation, similar to a thermometer, to show the progress toward the overall donation goal of $10,000. In range H5:H24, create an IF function that will sum Donation and test if it is greater than G5. If true, it will return "XXXX"; otherwise, the function will return a blank cell. Apply a conditional formatting that fills the cells in and does not show "XXXX". Choose a color that matches the workbook colors.

h.   Type criteria in any cells in the range A27:E27, and then perform the following.

- In cell B31, use a database function for the table located on the Volunteer Work worksheet to determine the total Time donated based on the criteria range A26:E27.
- In cell B32, create a database function for the table located on the Volunteer Work worksheet to determine the maximum donation based on the criteria range A26:E27.

i.   Use the data on the Volunteer Work worksheet to create a PivotTable and correlating PivotChart, each on a new worksheet. Format both with appropriate headings, titles, colors, and other formatting as you deem necessary. Name each new worksheet appropriately.

j.   Complete the **Documentation** worksheet according to your instructor's direction. Insert the **filename** in the left custom footer section of the Header/Footer tab in the Page Setup dialog box on all worksheets in the workbook.

k.   Click Save, close Excel, and then submit the file as directed by your instructor.

Perform 2: Perform in Your Career

Student data file needed:

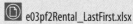 e03pf2Rental.xlsx

You will save your file as:

e03pf2Rental_LastFirst.xlsx

Student Car Rental Service

Production & Operations

A new business has started that keeps cars close to campus and rents them to students by the hour. They have GPS and can be reserved online. Students can use their university ID as a means for reserving and renting the cars. This makes it easy for students without cars to run errands or take a weekend trip. As a new hire, you have been asked to work with the data and complete an analysis model for the management team. Your success with this project may lead to a quick promotion!

a.   Open **e03pf2Rental**, and then save your file as e03pf2Rental_LastFirst.

b.   On the Input Data worksheet, create a range name for checkup miles in range G5:J6. Create named ranges for the range L4:M7 using the top row as the range names.

c.   On the Rental Data worksheet, prepare the worksheet and then complete the following data analysis.

- Add a new field label in K11 named Checkup.
- Add a new field label in L11 named Model.

- In cell K12, create a logical function that will return Y if the Note column equals either Damage or Repair; otherwise, the function will return N.
- In cell L12, create a function that will look up the CarID in the Input Data worksheet table A5:C33 and return the Model of the car.
- Insert a table, and then name it Rental_ALL.
- Create named ranges from the selection for each column.
- Create an advanced filter using the column headings and two rows of criteria. In range A5:A7, type Total Miles, Average Price, and Total Rentals. In range B5:B7, create three formulas that calculate the total miles driven, the average rental price, and the total number of rentals in the filtered data set. Format range A5:B7 appropriately.
- Insert a slicer with an appropriate format. Resize and move as needed. Apply a new filter using the slicer.
- Use the data to create a PivotTable and correlating PivotChart, each on a new worksheet. Format both with appropriate headings, titles, colors, and other formatting as you deem necessary. Name each new worksheet appropriately.

d. On the Report worksheet, begin creating a rental report.
- In cell B4, create a formula that will sum the CarID range based on A4 criteria for the miles used by each car.
- In cell C4, create a formula that will count the times each CarID has made a trip based on A4 criteria.
- In cell D4, create a formula that will count the number of times each CarID based on A4 criteria needed to have a checkup indicated by a "Y" in the Checkup column range within the Rental Data.
- In cell E4, create a logical function that will return the result "YES" if the car needs to be pulled for a more thorough checkup; otherwise, a "NO" should be returned. Pseudo-code can be found on the Input Data worksheet in cells F14:I21. A car should be pulled in three different situations as outlined in the pseudo-code on the Input Data worksheet. First, a car should be pulled if it has more than 2,000 miles. Secondly, a car should be pulled if it has more than five trips. Third, a car should be pulled if it has both more than 2,000 miles and has had more than three trips. The logical test arguments within the formula should reference the pseudo-code cells on the Input Data worksheet to allow for flexibility if the conditional values should be later adjusted.
- In cell H4, create a formula that will count the number of trips in the Miles range that have mileage greater than in H3.
- Apply appropriate formats as needed.

e. The range G7:J11 on the Report worksheet will determine the number of rentals that had damage or a repair note. It is set up to input the Make in I7, currently listed as "Honda", and all the associated models will be listed in cell range H9:H11. Then, the number of damage and repair notices will be counted for each model.
- In cell H9, create a function that will pull the first model from the range that is associated with the make that is listed in I7.
- In cell I9, create a formula that will count the number of records that have Damage— as defined in cell I8—for the model that is listed in cell H9. In cell J9, apply a similar formula, but replace the damage criteria with the repair criteria found in cell J8.

f. Complete the **Documentation** worksheet according to your instructor's direction. Insert the **filename** in the left custom footer section of the Header/Footer tab in the Page Setup dialog box on all worksheets in the workbook.

g. Click Save, close Excel, and then submit the file as directed by your instructor.

Student data file needed:

 e03pf3Roadhouse.xlsx

You will save your file as:

 e03pf3Roadhouse_TeamName.xlsx

Managing Inventory at the Roadhouse Bar and Grill

Production & Operations

You and your team manage the Roadhouse Bar and Grill, a local restaurant that specializes in home-cooked meals for breakfast, lunch, and dinner. The owner has given you a scaled-down version of the data with one days' worth of transactions. Your team needs to manage the inventory of beverage items to ensure you have enough beverages for each day you are open for business. You decided to create a shared folder in the "cloud" so you can share the workbook with your management team. All members of the management team will be responsible for updating portions of the database and sharing the updated database via the shared cloud folder.

a. Select one team member to set up the document by completing Steps b–d.

b. Open your browser and navigate to either **https://www.skydrive.live.com**, **https://www.drive.google.com**, or any other instructor assigned location. Be sure all members of the team have an account on the chosen system—such as a Microsoft or Google account.

c. Open **e03pf3Roadhouse**, and then save the file as e03pf3Roadhouse_TeamName replacing TeamName with the name assigned to your team by your instructor.

d. Share the spreadsheet with the other members of your team. Make sure that each team member has the appropriate permission to edit the document.

e. Hold a team meeting and discuss the requirements of the remaining steps. Make an action and communication plan. Consider which steps can be done independently and which steps require completion of prior steps before starting.

f. In Excel, your team members will need to complete the following. Apply formatting such as resizing fields, and use absolute cell references and relative cell references as deemed necessary.

- On the General Report worksheet, create named ranges for the Servings List and Employee List. On the Beverage Data worksheet, create named ranges for the beverage data list.

- On the Transactions worksheet, use functions to complete columns F, G, and I. Create a formula in column J to calculate the total spent on beverages based on the quantity sold and price.

- Using the data in range A10:J210, insert a table and then create appropriate named ranges. Enter two rows of filter criteria in rows 2 and 3 that will be used to create an advanced filter and then apply the filter. In range B6:B8, create appropriate database functions based on the specifications listed in range A6:A8. Clear the advanced filter. In range G6:G8, create appropriate subtotal functions based on the specifications listed in range F6:F8.

- Create a PivotTable for the data in your table, and insert it on the PivotTable Analysis worksheet. Insert a customized slicer. Format the PivotTable with appropriate headings, titles, colors, and other formatting as you deem necessary. Use the PivotTable to answer the three questions at the top of the worksheet.

- Create a PivotChart on a new worksheet. Format it with appropriate headings, titles, colors, and other formatting as you deem necessary. Name the new worksheet appropriately.

- On the Beverage Data worksheet, insert a function in column G that retrieves the serving type from the Servings List on the General Report worksheet.

- On the General Report worksheet, insert a function to calculate the number of transactions in range C3:C5 based on the criteria in range A3:A5 and in the table. Insert a function to calculate the shift analysis in range F3:F5 based on the criteria in range D3:D5.

- In row 22, enter filter criteria and then use functions to calculate the values in range E25:E27.

g. Complete the **Documentation** worksheet according to your instructor's direction. Minimally, include enough detail to identify which parts of the worksheets/workbook each team member completed.

h. Insert the **filename** in the left custom footer section of the Header/Footer tab in the Page Setup dialog box on all worksheets in the workbook. In a custom header section, include the **names** of the students in your team—spread the names evenly across each of the three header sections: left section, center section, and right section.

i. Save your work, and then close Excel. Submit the file as directed by your instructor.

Perform 4: How Others Perform

Student data file needed:

 e03pf4Shipping.xlsx

You will save your file as:

 e03pf4Shipping_LastFirst.xlsx

Shipping at ABC Distributor

Production & Operations

ABC Distributor ships to its retail companies across the United States. Shipments are typically in quantities of 20 to 500 units. The company examines shipping data to evaluate and adjust the shipments of items and reduce shipping expenses. In the spreadsheet provided, data with some analysis has been started. The company knows there are issues and would like help getting things straightened out along with setting up and customizing additional information.

a. Open **e03pf4Shipping**, and then save your file as e03pf4Shipping_LastFirst.

b. On the Shipping Data worksheet, a table has been set up and a calculated field was added, but the formulas need to be developed and possibly corrected.

- In cell H16, the function that will retrieve the weight from the ProductWeights named range was set up, but it seems to be giving an error message in some cells. Check the formula and make sure it will retrieve the weight correctly.

- In cell I16, create a function that will retrieve the Category in the second row of the Size_Category_List array, using the Weight field as the lookup value.

- In cell J16, create a formula that will find the shipping Unit_Cost by dividing ShipCost by Qty shipped.

c. On the Shipping Data worksheet, create an advanced filter.

d. Set up calculations on the filtered data based on one of three data fields specified in cell B5.

- In cell B6, create a function that will find the average of the filtered data based upon the field name listed in B5.

- In cell B7, create a function that will find the sum of the filtered data based upon the field name listed in B5.

e. On the Shipping Report worksheet, database statistics need to be created or corrected.

- Set up a criteria range starting in cell A3.

- In cell E4, type CA as criterion for the State.

- In cell B7, create a function that will average the field listed in B6 for the ShipData_All database using the criteria range A3:J4.

- In cell B8, create a function that will find the minimum of the field listed in B6 for the ShipData_All database using the criteria range A3:J4.
- In cell B9, create a function that will find the maximum of the field listed in B6 for the ShipData_All database using the criteria range A3:J4.
- In cell B10, create a function that will find the sum of the field listed in B6 for the ShipData_All database using the criteria range A3:J4.
- In cell G6, find the largest ShipCost from the ShipData.
- In cell G7, knowing the largest shipping cost value in G6, create a function to find the City location in conjunction with the row number for the largest shipping cost value in G6.
- In cell G9, find the largest Qty shipped from the ShipData.
- In cell G10, similar to the function developed in cell G7, find the City location for the row number that had the largest shipment quantity value in G9.

f. Summary data was partially created and needs to be completed for the cities where shipments have been fulfilled.

- In cell B14, use a function to find the average ShipCost of shipments to the City range listed in A14.
- In cell E14, use a function to find the total number of shipments to the City listed in A14.
- In cell F14, an IF function with a nested AND function has been created that should evaluate the shipments and return "Evaluate" if the record meets the criteria indicating that the shipment should be reviewed; otherwise, a blank cell is returned. The Input Data worksheet offers pseudo-code for Evaluation 1 in cells D3:G7. The function will check if the number of Times_Rushed divided by Shipments to the city is greater than 0.25 (reflected in cell G5 on the Input Data worksheet), and if the average unit weight (Ave_Wt) is equal to LG in the Size_Category_List array, then the shipment will be evaluated. But, it appears that something may not have been set up correctly. Check the formula cell references to determine if it makes logical sense. Correct the formula so it works correctly.
- In cell G14, create an IF function that will evaluate the shipments a second time and return "Evaluate" if the shipment meets the criteria; otherwise, the formula should return a blank cell. For this second evaluation, two OR conditions should return an Evaluation result. First, if the Ave_Cost is greater than 300, or secondly, when the Ave_Cost is greater than 200 and the Times_Rushed have been three or more. The Input Data worksheet offers pseudo-code for Evaluation 2 in cells D9:G14.

g. On the Shipping Data worksheet, create a PivotTable that is on a new worksheet named PivotTable Analysis. Insert a slicer. Format with appropriate heading, colors, and other formatting as you deem necessary.

h. Create a Line with Markers PivotChart. Format with appropriate headings, titles, colors, and other formatting as you deem necessary. Name the new worksheet appropriately.

i. Complete the **Documentation** worksheet according to your instructor's direction. Insert the **filename** in the left custom footer section of the Header/Footer tab in the Page Setup dialog box on all worksheets in the workbook.

j. Click Save, close Excel, and then submit the file as directed by your instructor.

WORKSHOP 7 | MULTIPLE WORKSHEETS, WORKBOOKS, AND TEMPLATES

OBJECTIVES

1. Group worksheets
   p. 368

2. Create summary
   worksheets   p. 375

3. Work with multiple
   workbooks   p. 385

4. Collaborate using
   multiple workbooks
   p. 390

5. Use existing
   templates   p. 398

6. Create templates from
   an existing workbook
   p. 402

Prepare Case

Human Resources

Turquoise Oasis Spa Therapist Sales and Service Analysis

The Turquoise Oasis Spa serves resort guests with a full range of services from traditional and alternative massage to aroma and detoxification therapy. The spa is open seven days a week. Meda Rodate, the spa manager, would like a workbook that allows her to summarize and compare the sales of each therapist and service for each day the spa is open.

A worksheet created from the salon and spa point-of-sales system each week can be used for the source of spa sales data. Each sale is listed by location, date, time, product, and therapist.

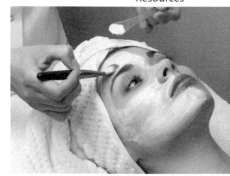

Serghei Starus / Shutterstock

REAL WORLD SUCCESS

"During my internship I worked in the sales department, and one of my jobs was to summarize weekly reports sent in from the various sales people. Everyone sent their information to me in different formats, and it took a long time to pull it all together—sometimes a day or more! I finally remembered that Excel can consolidate data, so I sent a template to the sales people asking them to fill it in each week. Now I could open their files, consolidate the data, and in a few hours have what used to take me days to complete! They really liked how easy the template was to use, and my boss was totally impressed with my ingenuity and said she will use the method with the next intern."

- Rebecca, recent graduate

Student data files needed for this workshop:

 e04ws07Spa.xlsx

 e04ws07SpaSales.xlsx

 e04ws07SpaLogo.jpg

 e04ws07SpaLink.xlsx

 e04ws07SpaPrices.xlsx

You will save your files as:

 e04ws07Spa_LastFirst.xlsx

 e04ws07SpaKia_LastFirst.xlsx

 e04ws07SpaPrices_LastFirst.xlsx

 e04ws07SpaToDo_LastFirst.xlsx

 e04ws07SpaLink_LastFirst.xlsx

 e04ws07SpaRodate_LastFirst.xlsx

 e04ws07SpaTemp_LastFirst.xltx

 e04ws07SpaCal_LastFirst.xlsx

Working with Multiple Worksheets

An Excel workbook can contain many, potentially hundreds, of worksheets. A single worksheet is a two-dimensional object: the rows are one dimension, and columns represent a second dimension. When a workbook contains more than one worksheet, the multiple worksheets can represent the third dimension as long as the worksheets share an identical layout. Data from multiple worksheets can be referenced to generate new data via formulas, functions, and consolidation. Data can be copied and pasted from one worksheet to another and can be filled from one worksheet to many worksheets. Multiple worksheets can be selected at the same time, called **grouping**, and actions such as data entry and formatting can affect all the worksheets in the group at once, greatly increasing efficiency.

Data can be accessed between worksheets using 3-D references, and even named ranges can include cells from multiple worksheets—these are called, not surprisingly, 3-D named ranges.

In this section you will work with the Spa workbook, which contains multiple worksheets. There are three sheets—one for each therapist—that need additional information added as well as two additional worksheets with schedule and price information about their services. You will complete the therapists' worksheets and then add additional worksheets to come up with summary information for the three therapists.

Group Worksheets

Grouping worksheets allows you to perform certain tasks once and have those tasks affect the same cells for all worksheets in the group. There are multiple ways to group worksheets. You can click the tab of a worksheet, hold down Ctrl, and then click the worksheet tab of additional worksheets you want to include in the group. The tabs of each worksheet included in the group will be highlighted with a white—or light—background color as a visual indicator. The file name in the title bar of the window will also show [Group] to remind you that you have worksheets grouped. Alternatively, if all of the worksheets you would like to group are contiguous to one another, you can click the worksheet tab of a worksheet on one end, hold down Shift, and then click the worksheet tab on the other end of the contiguous worksheets.

Ungrouping worksheets is accomplished by either right-clicking a grouped worksheet tab and selecting Ungroup Sheets from the shortcut menu, or by clicking the tab of a worksheet that is not grouped.

Opening the Starting File

A workbook has already been started by Meda Rodate, the spa manager. She included data for product pricing in the PriceList worksheet and sales for December 16, 2015, in the SpaSales worksheet. She also created three additional worksheets, one for each of the spa therapists: Christy Istas; Kendra Mault; and Jason Niese. You will work with the existing worksheets to add formatting and formulas to make the workbook more useful.

E07.00

 To Open the Spa Analysis Workbook

a. Start **Excel**, and then open the student data file **e04ws07Spa**.

b. Click the **FILE** tab, and then click **Save As**. Save the file as an **Excel Workbook** in the folder where you are saving your files, with the name e04ws07Spa_LastFirst replacing LastFirst with your actual name. If necessary, click **Enable Content**.

Grouping Worksheets

When worksheets are grouped, what you do to one worksheet happens to the other worksheets in the group. For example, you can enter data, add formatting, insert and delete rows or columns, and delete or clear cells on all the worksheets in the group. While grouping worksheets is often the most efficient way to modify a workbook, there are some Excel features that are not available for grouped worksheets; for example, conditional formatting cannot be directly applied to grouped worksheets. In that case, conditional formatting would have to be applied to each worksheet individually.

In the Spa workbook, you will group the worksheets for each of the therapists and change the tab color for all the worksheets so they are easy to identify. You will do the same for the PriceList and SpaSales worksheets. The PriceList and SpaSales worksheets contain source data, whereas the IstasChristy, MaultKendra, and NieseJason worksheets contain the analysis. By coloring their respective worksheet tabs differently, you will create a visual differentiation between the two types of worksheets in the workbook.

E07.01

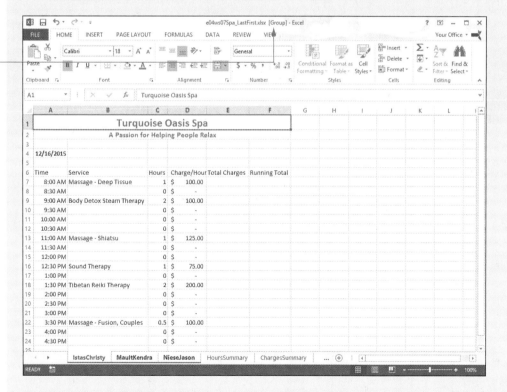

To Group Worksheets and Change the Tab Color

MyITLab®

Workshop 7 Training

a. Click the **IstasChristy** worksheet tab.

b. Press and hold ⌷Shift⌷, and then click the **NieseJason** worksheet tab.

The IstasChristy, MaultKendra, and NieseJason worksheets are now grouped. Notice the [Group] tag next to the filename in the title bar that indicates you are in grouped worksheet mode.

[Group] tag on the title bar indicates that worksheets are grouped together

SIDE NOTE

Alternative Way to Group

To select all the worksheets in a workbook, right-click any worksheet tab, and then click Select All Sheets in the shortcut menu.

SIDE NOTE

Alternative Way to Ungroup

You can also ungroup worksheets by clicking on the worksheet tab of a worksheet that is not in the group.

Figure 1 Worksheets grouped

c. Right-click the **IstasChristy** worksheet tab, point to **Tab Color**, and then select **Dark Blue, Text 2, Lighter 60%**.

d. Right-click the **IstasChristy** worksheet tab, and then click **Ungroup Sheets**.

e. Click **Save** 🖫.

Entering Data

Grouping worksheets can save a lot of data entry time. Grouped worksheets make the entry of worksheet structural elements like titles, column headings, and row labels fast and efficient. Be careful though—errors made, such as misspellings or misplacement of a heading, are compounded across all grouped worksheets.

In the Spa workbook, you will group the therapist's worksheets again and enter information that will pertain to all the therapists. By grouping, the therapist's worksheets will all have the same structure, be visually consistent, and make data entry in the future much more efficient.

E07.02

 To Enter Data into Grouped Worksheets

a. Click the **IstasChristy** worksheet tab, press and hold Shift, and then click the **NieseJason** worksheet tab.

b. Click cell **A25**, type Total and then press Ctrl+Enter.

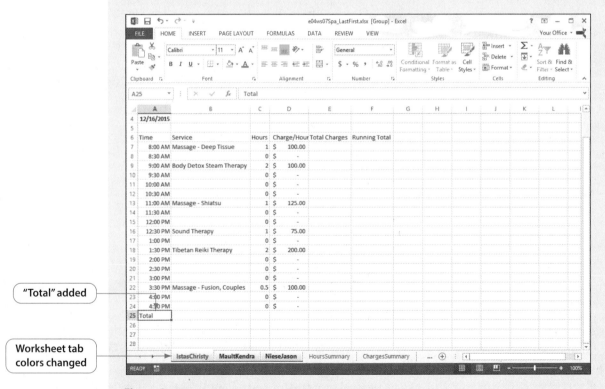

"Total" added

Worksheet tab colors changed

Figure 2   Data entered on IstasChristy worksheet

c. Click the **MaultKendra** worksheet tab. Notice that the text entered into the IstasChristy worksheet tab is also in the MaultKendra worksheet. Click the **NieseJason** worksheet tab, and you will see the same result.

d. Right-click the **IstasChristy** worksheet tab, and then select **Ungroup Sheets**.

e. Click **Save** 🖫.

Entering Formulas

Entering formulas into grouped worksheets is a very efficient way to simultaneously create new data in multiple worksheets and is no different than entering data in grouped worksheets. Occasionally, while a formula may appear to work on multiple grouped worksheets, the data may appear too similar on the worksheets or even incorrect. It is very important to carefully check the results of your formulas to ensure they show the intended results.

In the Spa workbook, part of the therapist's worksheets have been added, but two columns have no data. You will add formulas to these columns to calculate both the Total Charges for each therapist and the Running Total for each therapist.

E07.03

 ## To Enter Formulas and Functions into Multiple Worksheets

a. Click the **IstasChristy** worksheet tab, press and hold ⎇Shift⎵, and then click the **NieseJason** worksheet tab.

b. Click cell **E7**, type =C7*D7 and then press ⎇Ctrl⎵+⎇Enter⎵. Use the **fill handle** to copy the formula to cell range **E8:E24**.

This formula multiples the Charge/Hour by the number of hours to get the total charge for each service listed. Dashes appear in place of zeroes because the Accounting Number Format is applied to this range of cells on the IstasChristy worksheet.

c. Click cell **F7**, type =E7 and then press ⎇Enter⎵. In cell **F8**, type =F7+E8 and then press ⎇Ctrl⎵+⎇Enter⎵. Use the **fill handle** to copy the formula in cell **F8** to cell range **F9:F24**.

The Running Total should be the cumulative total for services performed. The first service will simply be the amount of that service, but all services after the first one will be the cumulative amount for the day, so each service in column E will be added to the previous service total charges in column F.

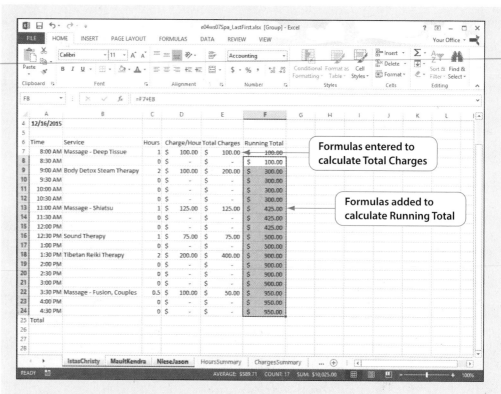

	A	B	C	D	E	F
4	12/16/2015					
5						
6	Time	Service	Hours	Charge/Hour	Total Charges	Running Total
7	8:00 AM	Massage - Deep Tissue	1	$ 100.00	$ 100.00	100.00
8	8:30 AM		0	$ -	$ -	$ 100.00
9	9:00 AM	Body Detox Steam Therapy	2	$ 100.00	$ 200.00	$ 300.00
10	9:30 AM		0	$ -	$ -	$ 300.00
11	10:00 AM		0	$ -	$ -	$ 300.00
12	10:30 AM		0	$ -	$ -	$ 300.00
13	11:00 AM	Massage - Shiatsu	1	$ 125.00	$ 125.00	$ 425.00
14	11:30 AM		0	$ -	$ -	$ 425.00
15	12:00 PM		0	$ -	$ -	$ 425.00
16	12:30 PM	Sound Therapy	1	$ 75.00	$ 75.00	$ 500.00
17	1:00 PM		0	$ -	$ -	$ 500.00
18	1:30 PM	Tibetan Reiki Therapy	2	$ 200.00	$ 400.00	$ 900.00
19	2:00 PM		0	$ -	$ -	$ 900.00
20	2:30 PM		0	$ -	$ -	$ 900.00
21	3:00 PM		0	$ -	$ -	$ 900.00
22	3:30 PM	Massage - Fusion, Couples	0.5	$ 100.00	$ 50.00	$ 950.00
23	4:00 PM		0	$ -	$ -	$ 950.00
24	4:30 PM		0	$ -	$ -	$ 950.00
25	Total					

Formulas entered to calculate Total Charges

Formulas added to calculate Running Total

Figure 3   Formulas entered to calculate Total Charges and Running Total

d. Click the **HoursSummary** worksheet tab to ungroup the worksheets.

e. Click **Save** 🖫.

Filling Contents Across Worksheets

Fill Across Worksheets is a command that can be used to copy cell contents, formats, or both contents and formats to worksheets in a group. The source and destination worksheets must all be included in the group. Unlike copy and paste, where cells can be copied from one location in a worksheet to a different location in the same worksheet or a different worksheet, Fill Across Worksheets will only fill to the same location in different worksheets; for example, cell A5 in Sheet1 can only be filled to cell A5 in other worksheets.

When using Fill Across Worksheets, the decision of whether to fill All, Contents, or Formats is dependent on what exactly you need to copy. Choose Contents when the target worksheets are already formatted or will be formatted differently than the source worksheet.

In the Spa workbook, you will complete the IstasChristy worksheet and then apply the content and format to the other therapists' worksheets.

To Fill Contents Across Worksheets

a. Click the **IstasChristy** worksheet tab. Select cells **C25:E25**, on the **HOME** tab, in the **Editing** group, click **AutoSum** Σ AutoSum ▾.

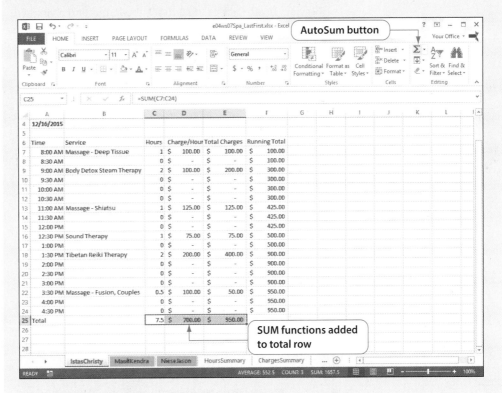

Figure 4 Formulas added to IstasChristy worksheet

b. With the range C25:E25 still selected on the **IstasChristy** worksheet tab, press and hold Shift, and then click the **NieseJason** worksheet tab. On the **HOME** tab, in the **Editing** group, click **Fill** ⬇, select **Across Worksheets**, click **Contents**, and then click **OK**.

The SUM functions in cells C25:E25 on the IstasChristy worksheet should be copied to both the MaultKendra and NieseJason worksheets.

c. Click the **HoursSummary** worksheet tab to ungroup the sheets, and then click **Save** 🖫.

Formatting Cells

By grouping worksheets, you can apply cell formatting to multiple worksheets at once. For example, any of the formatting tools in the Font, Alignment, and Number groups on the Home tab can be applied to grouped worksheets. Any Ribbon tools that are not available when worksheets are grouped will be grayed out. Note that table formatting cannot be applied to grouped worksheets, nor can any modifications to cell formats—or cell contents—inside a table be applied when worksheets are grouped.

To Format Cells on Grouped Worksheets

a. Click the **IstasChristy** worksheet tab, press and hold Shift, and then click the **NieseJason** worksheet tab. Select cells **A6:F6**, and on the **HOME** tab, in the **Styles** group, click **Cell Styles**, and then select **Accent5**. Select cells **A25:E25**, click **Cell Styles**, and then select **Total**. Click cell **F25** to see the formatting changes.

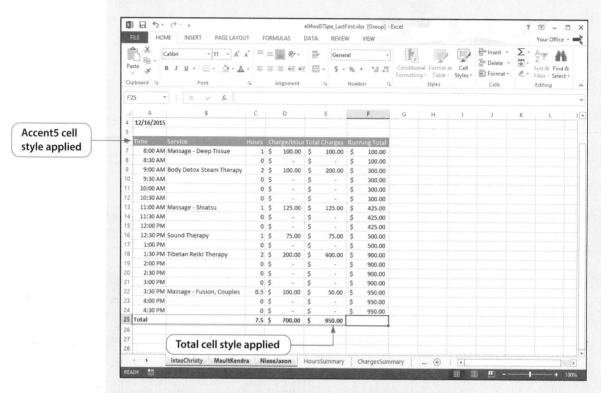

Figure 5 Cells formatted

b. Right-click the **MaultKendra** worksheet tab, and select **Ungroup Sheets**. Click **Save** 💾.

REAL WORLD ADVICE | **Copying and Pasting Data in Grouped Worksheets**

Data can be copied from a single worksheet into grouped worksheets. Data can be copied from one set of grouped worksheets and then pasted into the same or a different set of grouped sheets. The criteria that determines whether or not Clipboard data can be pasted into a new location are as follows:

- The new location must have room available such that the pasted range has exactly the same shape as the copied range.
- When multiple worksheets are grouped, the pasted range cannot overlap the copied range in any dimension; for example, copied cells from group Sheet1:Sheet2 cannot then be copied to a paste range in group Sheet2:Sheet3, but they could be pasted to Sheet1:Sheet2 as long as the rows and columns of the copied range and the paste range do not overlap.

Filling Formats Across Worksheets

Filling formats across worksheets is similar to filling content across worksheets, but in this case, only the formatting is applied. By using the Fill Across Worksheets command, you can copy formatting without affecting formulas and other data. You will fill the formatting from columns E and F in the IstasChristy worksheet to the MaultKendra and NieseJason worksheets. Since the content of each therapist's worksheet is unique, using Fill Across Worksheets for the formats will create identical formatting without affecting therapist-specific content.

E07.06

 To Fill Formats Across Worksheets

a. Click the **IstasChristy** worksheet tab, and then select cells **E7:F24**.

b. Press and hold Shift, and then click the **NieseJason** worksheet tab. On the **HOME** tab, in the **Editing** group, click **Fill** ⬇, and then select **Across Worksheets**. Click **Formats**, and then click **OK**.

c. Right-click the **IstasChristy** worksheet tab, select **Ungroup Sheets**, and then click **Save** 🖫. Verify that all three worksheets have matching formatting.

REAL WORLD ADVICE | **Some Things Are Different When Worksheets Are Grouped**

- You can use worksheet grouping to reorder your worksheets, but remember that the group will move as one in the reordering process. If you want to reorder the placement of worksheets within a group, the worksheets need to be ungrouped and the reorder placement done manually.

- Be careful when printing—if you print when worksheets are grouped, every worksheet in the group is available for print, not just the active worksheet. The Print Preview navigation information will display the available pages for printing from the group. If you only want one worksheet to print, either specify which pages to print in the print options, or ungroup and select the target worksheet.

- Many of Excel's commands and features are not available when worksheets are grouped, for example the entire Data tab, table features and formatting, conditional formatting, shapes, charts, and sparklines.

Create Summary Worksheets

If your workbook contains multiple worksheets, you may want to summarize—or consolidate—the data on the multiple worksheets onto one summary worksheet. This can be useful when the worksheets represent different months' worth of data and you want to come up with a year-end summary. Or, in the case of the spa, you have multiple therapists and want to combine all their individual data onto one summary worksheet.

One of Excel's more powerful features is the ability to reference data between worksheets. If you think of a worksheet as a two-dimensional array, then multiple worksheets in a workbook can be thought of as a three-dimensional array. Multiple worksheets represent a third dimension; therefore, references that address data across multiple worksheets are called 3-D references and 3-D named ranges. By using a 3-D formula with 3-D references, you can easily create a summary worksheet from multiple worksheets that are updated automatically as the source data is updated.

Another option, if your multiple worksheets contain either an identical structure, or data with identical row and/or column labels, is to create a summary worksheet using the Consolidate feature. Consolidated data can be generated with or without links to the original source data. Summary data created using the Consolidate feature that is not linked is not automatically updated when the source data are changed, but if you create a summary and link the consolidated data back to source data, then changes to source data are automatically reflected in the linked consolidation.

There are two ways data can be consolidated—by position and by category. **Consolidate by position** aggregates data in the same position in multiple worksheets. **Consolidate by category** aggregates data in cells with matching row and/or column labels; the labels do not need to be in the same row/column in each worksheet, there can be a different number of labels among the worksheets, and there can be a different mix of labels among the worksheets.

QUICK REFERENCE | **When and How to Consolidate**

If you want to summarize data from multiple places (worksheets or workbooks), you have several options. The option you choose will depend on where the data is located and how it is organized.

- **Consolidate by position**—Use this method if you want to arrange the data in all the worksheets in identical order and location.

- **Consolidate by category**—Use this method if you want to organize the data differently than how it is presented in the separate worksheets, but use the same row and column labels so the consolidated worksheet matches the data.

- **Consolidate by formula**—Use this method if you want to use formulas with cell references or 3-D references to the other worksheets that you are combining because you do not have a consistent position or category of data to use.

- **PivotTable report**—Use this method if you want to use a PivotTable instead of a consolidation.

Creating a 3-D Reference

Three-dimensional references, or **3-D references**, allow formulas and functions to use data from cells and cell ranges across worksheets.

A 3-D reference has the following structure: =**worksheet name!cell reference**. For example, the 3-D reference to cell C25 in worksheet Sheet3 is Sheet3!C25. Individual cells in multiple worksheets can be referenced using a range of worksheets as well. For example, to reference cell C25 in Sheet1, Sheet2, and Sheet 3—assuming all three sheets are in that order and contiguous—the reference is specified as Sheet1:Sheet3!C25. Lastly, a range of cells can be referenced across several worksheets—the cell range C3:C25 in worksheets Sheet1 through Sheet3 is specified as Sheet1:Sheet3!C3:C25.

In the Spa workbook, you will delete the date entered in cell A4 of the three therapist's worksheets and change it so the date is entered on the IstasChristy worksheet and the other two worksheets have a 3-D reference to it.

E07.07

 To Create a 3-D Reference

a. Click the **MaultKendra** worksheet tab, press and hold Shift, and then click the **NieseJason** worksheet tab. Click cell **A4**, and then press Delete.

b. In cell **A4**, type = and then click the **IstasChristy** worksheet tab. Click cell **A4**, and then press Ctrl+Enter. This should insert a reference to cell A4 from the IstasChristy worksheet tab in cell A4 on both the MaultKendra and NieseJason worksheet tabs.

c. Click the **IstasChristy** worksheet tab to ungroup the sheets, and then click **Save** 🖫.

Naming a 3-D Reference

A **3-D named range** references the same cell, or range of cells, across multiple worksheets in a workbook. A 3-D named range cannot be defined in the Name box; you must click Define Name in the Defined Names group on the Formulas tab.

In the Spa workbook, you will name ranges of cells so you can refer to them at a later time by the name and not the cell reference.

E07.08

 To Create a 3-D Name

a. Click the **IstasChristy** worksheet tab, and then click cell **E25**.

b. Click the **FORMULAS** tab, and in the **Defined Names** group, click **Name Manager**.

There is already one named range in the workbook, ProductTable. This name refers to cells A2:D26 on the PriceList worksheet and is used in the VLOOKUP function in cells D7:D24. The VLOOKUP in cell D7 is used to look up the Charge/Hour for the service entered in cell B7. The Charge/Hour is found in the table called ProductTable.

c. Click **New** in the Name Manager dialog box, and then type TotalCharges3D in the Name box. To the right of the **Refers to** box, click the **Collapse Dialog** button . Press and hold Shift, click the **NieseJason** worksheet tab, and then click the **Expand Dialog** button 🖼. The Refers to box should now show **='IstasChristy:NieseJason'!$E$25**.

This reference is to cell E25 on the IstasChristy worksheet, the MaultKendra worksheet, and the NieseJason worksheet, in that order.

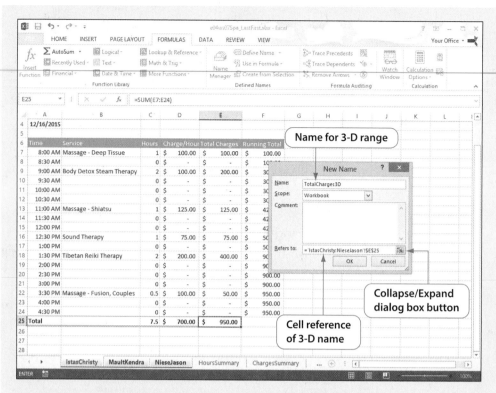

Figure 6 3-D named range added to worksheet

d. Click **OK**, notice that **TotalCharges3D** is listed in the Name Manager now, and then click **Close**.

e. Click **Save** 🖫.

REAL WORLD ADVICE | **Order Matters When Working with Grouped Worksheets**

When you assign a name to a range of cells, the first cell reference and the last cell reference are recognized, and all the cells in between are included in the range. For example, a range of cells A1:C25 named "Profits" will always use the values in cells A1:C25, no matter how you move the cells around.

Naming ranges that span multiple worksheets works the same way. The difference is that if you start with a range of worksheets, as in the case example that looks like IstasChristy:NieseJason, when you rearrange the worksheets, the range will no longer be accurate. For example, if you decide to move the MaultKendra tab to the right of the NieseJason worksheet, it would no longer be included in the named range IstasChristy:NieseJason. You therefore have to be extremely careful when you have named ranges and want to rearrange the worksheets. One option is to name a blank worksheet "Begin" to use for the first worksheet in the named range and another blank worksheet named "End" to use as the last worksheet in the range. This way, you are always reminded to keep the actual worksheets with data between the Begin and End worksheets.

Creating a 3-D Formula

When you have data on multiple worksheets and want to consolidate that data into a summary worksheet, you can use a **3-D formula**. A 3-D formula references the same cell, or range of cells, across multiple worksheets in a workbook. Creating a 3-D formula is very similar to creating any other formula, but instead of typing the formula, it is generally easier to point to and click the cells. That way you can avoid spelling errors that may make the formula incorrect.

In the Spa workbook, you will summarize the number of hours and total charges for all three therapists on a new summary worksheet. The formula for hours will be a simple 3-D formula, and the total charges will be a 3-D SUM function.

E07.09

 To Create a 3-D Formula

a. Click the **HoursSummary** worksheet tab, click cell **B7**, and then type =. Click the **IstasChristy** worksheet tab, click **C7**, and then type +. Click the **MaultKendra** worksheet tab, click **C7**, and then type +. Click the **NieseJason** worksheet tab, click **C7**, and then press Ctrl+Enter. The formula you should see is =IstasChristy!C7+MaultKendra!C7+ NieseJason!C7.

This formula adds the values in cell C7 on all three worksheets.

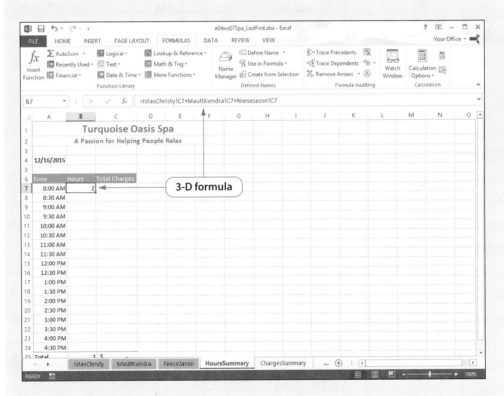

Figure 7 3-D formula added to worksheet

b. Use the **fill handle** to copy this formula to cells **B8:B24**.

c. Click cell **C7**, and then type =SUM(. Click the **IstasChristy** worksheet tab, click **E7**, press and hold Shift, click the **NieseJason** worksheet tab, type), and then press Ctrl+Enter. The formula you should see is =SUM(IstasChristy:NieseJason!E7).

This formula sums the values in cell E7 on sheets IstasChristy through NieseJason.

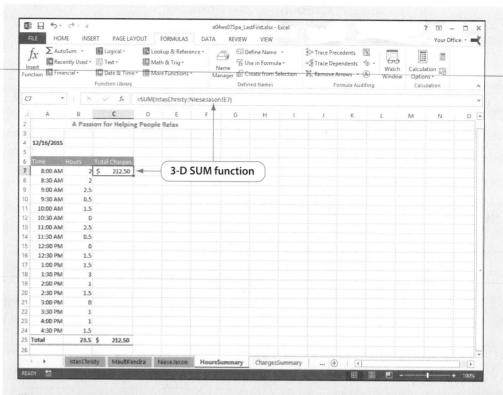

Figure 8   3-D SUM function added to worksheet

d.   Use the **fill handle** to copy this formula to cells **C8:C24**.

e.   Click **Save** 💾.

Consolidating Data by Position

Consolidate by position can be used to create a summary worksheet when the source worksheets all have an identical structure, such that the same location in each worksheet contains the same relative data—if cell A5 contains sales discounts for bulk sales in the January worksheet, cells A5 in worksheets February through December also contain sales discounts for bulk sales. The range selected in each worksheet must include the exact same number of rows and columns in each worksheet that is part of the consolidation.

In the Spa workbook, you will consolidate data by position to summarize the total charges and running totals by appointment time.

E07.10

 To Consolidate Data by Position

SIDE NOTE
Only One per Worksheet

A worksheet can store only one consolidation. If you want to create more than one consolidation, they should be placed into different worksheets.

a.   Click the **ChargesSummary** worksheet tab, and then click cell **B7**. Click the **DATA** tab, and then in the **Data Tools** group, click **Consolidate**. In the Consolidate dialog box, make sure **Sum** is selected in the Function box. Click the **Reference** box, click the **IstasChristy** worksheet tab, and then select cell range **E7:F24**. If necessary, scroll to the left of the worksheet tabs and move the Consolidate dialog box to make the selection.

b. Click **Add** in the Consolidate dialog box.

c. Click the **MaultKendra** worksheet tab, and notice range **E7:F24** is still selected. Click **Add** in the Consolidate dialog box.

d. Click the **NieseJason** worksheet tab, and notice range **E7:F24** is still selected. Click **Add** in the Consolidate dialog box.

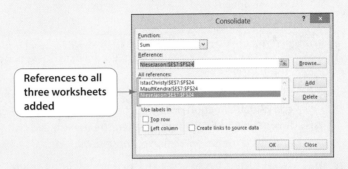

References to all three worksheets added

Figure 9　Ranges added to Consolidate dialog box

e. Click **OK** in the Consolidate dialog box.

f. Click **Save** .

Consolidating Data by Category

Consolidating by category is more flexible than consolidating by position. When consolidating by category, Excel examines row and/or column headings to determine which cells should contribute to a given calculation. Data does not need to be in the same relative position between and among worksheets; they simply need to share the same row and/or column labels. Labels can even be repeated multiple times in a single worksheet.

In this exercise you will consolidate therapists' sales by service, rather than by time. Because there is no way of knowing ahead of time where specific services will be located in the source worksheets, consolidation by category is the only realistic option.

E07.11

▶ To Consolidate Data by Category

a. Click the **ServiceSummary** worksheet tab, and then click cell **A6**. Click the **DATA** tab, and then in the **Data Tools** group, click **Consolidate**. In the Consolidate dialog box, make sure **Sum** is selected in the Function box, and then click the **Reference** box.

b. Click the **IstasChristy** worksheet tab, and then select cell range **B6:E24**. Note that you do not include the Running Total because a sum of Running Total by category would be a meaningless number. Click **Add**.

c. Click the **MaultKendra** worksheet tab, verify cells **B6:E24** are selected, and then click **Add**. Click the **NieseJason** worksheet tab, verify cells **B6:E24** are selected, and then click **Add**. Check the **Top row** box under the Use labels in section, and then check the **Left column** box under the Use labels in section.

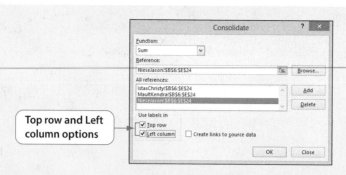

Top row and Left column options

Figure 10 Consolidate dialog box options

d. Click **OK** in the Consolidate dialog box. Click cell **A6**, and then type Service. The consolidate function does not copy the title of the far-left column. Press [Ctrl]+[Enter]. Row 10 will be blank because there are rows in each worksheet for times that are blank and this is the consolidation of those rows.

e. Select cells **A6:D20**. Click the **HOME** tab, in the **Cells** group, click **Format**, and then select **AutoFit Column Width**.

f. Click cell **D20**, type =SUM(TotalCharges3D), and then press [Ctrl]+[Enter]. This SUM function uses the 3-D named range created in an earlier exercise.

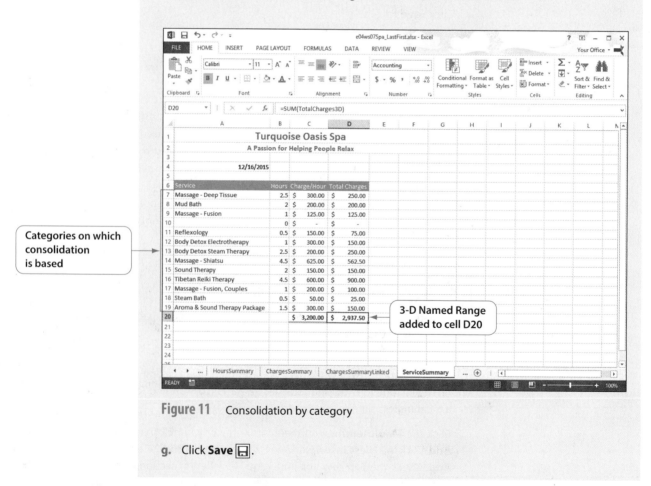

Categories on which consolidation is based

3-D Named Range added to cell D20

Figure 11 Consolidation by category

g. Click **Save** 🔒.

Creating Links to Source Data in a Consolidation

A data consolidation may contain links to source data that will include the cell references from other worksheets that contributed to the consolidated data result. The source cell reference details are placed into hidden rows that can be viewed if necessary.

A consolidation that includes links to source data must be placed into a worksheet separate from all source data. The Consolidate feature cannot create links to the worksheet that contains the consolidation.

Be aware that if you create links to source data—which you will not in this exercise—then you will not be able to edit the data in the consolidation. If the source data has changed, you will have to re-create the consolidation a second time.

In Spa workbook, you will create a linked consolidation of sales by appointment time.

REAL WORLD ADVICE | Considerations for Including Links to Source Data

When data is consolidated and links to the source data are included, the consolidation will not be automatically updated when changes are made to the source data.

In such a case, the entire data consolidation must be deleted and then regenerated. Some would recommend you avoid linking to source data in situations where a consolidation by category will need to be occasionally updated unless consolidation by position could be used as well.

E07.12

 To Consolidate with Links to Source Data

a. Click the **ChargesSummaryLinked** worksheet tab, and then click cell **A6**. Click the **DATA** tab, and in the **Data Tools** group, click **Consolidate**. In the Consolidate dialog box, make sure **Sum** is selected in the Function box, and then if necessary, click the **Reference** box.

b. Click the **IstasChristy** worksheet tab, select cell range **A6:F24**, and then click **Add** in the Consolidate dialog box. Click the **MaultKendra** worksheet tab, verify cells **A6:F24** are selected, and then click **Add**. Click the **NieseJason** worksheet tab, verify cells **A6:F24** are selected, and then click **Add**.

c. Check the **Top row** box under the Use labels in section, check the **Left column** box under the Use labels in section, and then check the **Create links to source data** box. Click **OK**.

d. Select columns **A:G**. Click the **HOME** tab, and on the **HOME** tab, in the **Cells** group, click **Format**, and then select **AutoFit Column Width**.

e. Select cell range **A10:A78**. The hidden rows include the links to the consolidated data. On the **HOME** tab, in the **Number** group, click the **Number Format** arrow, and then select **More Number Formats**. Click **Time** in the Category box, and then click **1:30 PM** in the Type box. Click **OK**.

f. Click the **Expand Outline** button ⊞ next to row 14.

Rows 11:13, which were previously hidden, are revealed. Notice the filename for your workbook is shown in column B. Consolidate can be used among multiple workbooks, and column B identifies the source workbook for each item of data. Because you are consolidating sheets in a single workbook, column B is irrelevant.

Notice that column C is empty. Service names are text and cannot be summated, so column C does not contain any information. Further, Charge/Hour in column E is not particularly informative. A sum of Charge/Hour is not a meaningful number—its inclusion, while necessary for consolidation, is not meaningful.

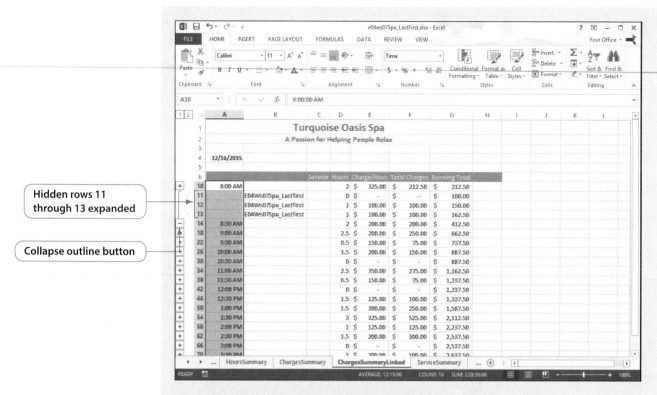

Figure 12 Hidden rows in consolidated summary

g. Click the **Level 2 outline** button ☐2☐ just to the left of the Select All button ◢. The source data that contributes to each of the subtotals for a category—time in this case—is expanded.

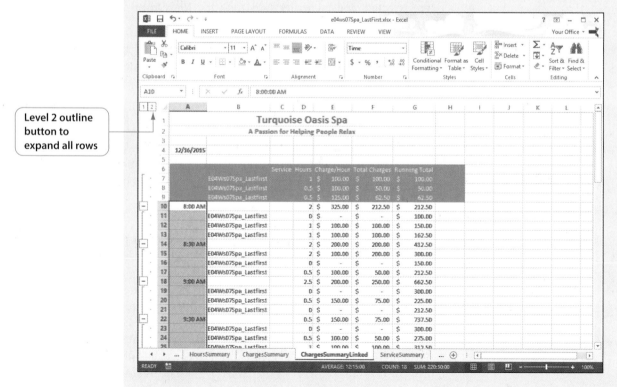

Figure 13 Level 2 outline in consolidated summary

h. Click cell **G8**.

Notice the contents in the formula bar. The 50.00 in cell G8 came from source data in the MaultKendra worksheet, in cell F7. Because a linked consolidation keeps track of the locations of source data, any changes to source data are automatically reflected in the consolidation.

i. Click **Save** 🖫 . Click the **IstasChristy** worksheet tab and keep the Spa workbook open.

REAL WORLD ADVICE | **Consolidating Between Different Workbooks**

Not only can you consolidate worksheets, but also workbooks. The easiest way is to have all the source workbooks open, start defining the consolidation, and then navigate to each workbook, select the source range with the mouse, and add the reference to the consolidation. This type of consolidation is useful if you have staff members using similar structured workbooks and need to combine the data for a summary. If you know you are going to need this kind of summary information, it may be useful to provide your staff or group members with templates to work from or some other standard worksheet, so when it comes time to collaborate it will be quick and easy for one person to do.

Using Multiple Workbooks

Excel can access data in other workbooks using external references in formulas and functions. A primary advantage of the ability to reference data in multiple workbooks is that you can access data at its source—in its original location. You do not need to copy the data to your workbook and then be concerned about keeping the copied data up to date when the original data changes.

In this section, you will work with multiple workbooks at a time. You will create a copy of the Spa workbook and link it to the SpaPrices workbook. Then you will create copies of the SpaPrices workbook in order to collaborate using two source workbooks and one master workbook. You will change data in the two source workbooks, and then merge the changes into the master workbook.

Work with Multiple Workbooks

Working with multiple workbooks is very similar to working with multiple worksheets. Excel 2013 opens each workbook in an individual window, so you can use multiple monitors to view different workbooks, or you can arrange the windows on one monitor to see multiple workbooks at one time.

Data can be referenced between workbooks using 3-D ranges and formulas, so when the source workbook is updated, the changes flow through to the summary workbook. You can also choose whether or not to link workbooks to make the updating automatic or not.

Viewing Multiple Workbooks at One Time

When you want to view multiple workbooks on one screen, you can choose how they are arranged. Once you have all the workbooks open on your desktop, you can choose to arrange them in four different ways: Tiled, Horizontal, Vertical, or Cascade. How you choose to view them will be determined by how you want to work with them and your personal preference.

In this exercise, you will open another workbook along with the Spa workbook already open, and then you will view the two workbooks in different views.

E07.13

 To View Multiple Workbooks at One Time

a. Click the **FILE** tab, and then click **Open**. Navigate to where your student data files are located, click **e04ws07SpaPrices**, and then click **Open**. The two workbook windows will cascade, one in front of the other.

> **Troubleshooting**
>
> Do you have more than two workbooks open? All open workbooks will be included in this arrangement, so if you do not want to see a particular workbook, be sure and close it and arrange the workbooks again.

b. Click the **VIEW** tab, and in the **Window** group, click **Arrange All**, click the **Tiled** option, and then click **OK**. Notice the workbooks are resized to fit on one screen. To edit a workbook, click the workbook to make it active, and then make your changes.

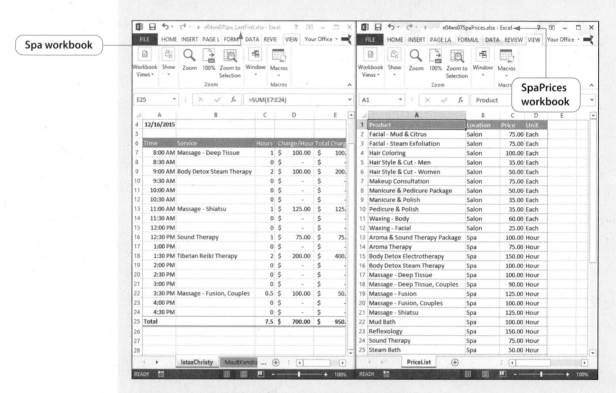

Figure 14 Workbooks arranged with the Tiled option

c. On either of the workbooks, click **Arrange All** again, click the **Horizontal** option, and then click **OK**. Notice the workbooks are resized to fit the width of the screen, one above the other.

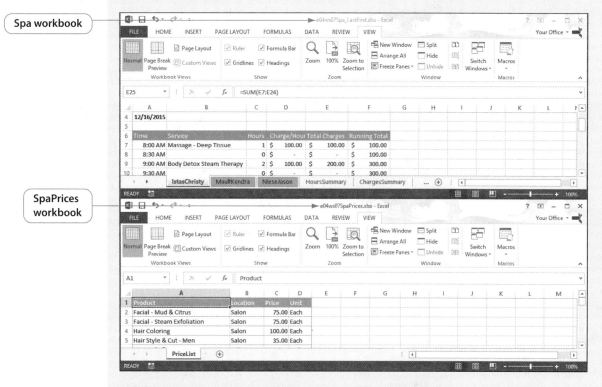

Figure 15 Workbooks arranged with the Horizontal option

d. Close **e04ws07Spa_LastFirst**, but keep **e04ws07SpaPrices** open for use in the next exercise.

Linking Workbooks

When you need data from a different workbook, the advantage to referencing that data at its source rather than copying it into your workbook is that when the source data is changed, your workbook can also be changed to reflect the most current data.

Excel recognizes when a workbook is linked to another workbook, or workbooks, through external references and will prompt you when the workbook is opened and ask whether or not you want to update links. Which option you choose will depend on whether you want the workbook to be updated or not.

Linking to other workbooks does create some potential problems, however. Links to workbooks are easily broken, especially if files are moved or deleted. Excel tries to prevent this from happening by using relative addresses. In a relative link, the address of a linked workbook is defined by its location in relation to the location of the destination workbook. If either workbook is moved when the destination workbook is closed, the links will be broken. If possible, it is considered good practice to store all workbooks in a linked relationship together in the same folder.

When you use a relative link, the reference will include the file name in brackets, the sheet name, an exclamation point, and the following cell reference:

='[filename.xlsx]worksheet name'!cell reference

In this exercise, you will use a copy of the Spa workbook that excludes the PriceList worksheet, and then link to the SpaPrices workbook to use the pricing data from there. By linking to the SpaPrices workbook, you will correct the errors that appear when you first open the SpaLink workbook.

E07.14

To Link Data in Different Workbooks

a. Click the **FILE** tab, and then click **Open**. Navigate to where your student data files are located, click **e04ws07SpaLink**, and then click **Open**.

b. Click the **FILE** tab, and then click **Save As**. Navigate to where you are saving your files, click the **File name** box, and then type **e04ws07SpaLink_LastFirst** replacing LastFirst with your actual name. Click **Save**.

c. Click the **VIEW** tab, in the **Window** group, click **Arrange All**, and then select **Horizontal**. Click **OK**.

d. In the **e04ws07SpaLink_LastFirst** workbook, click the **IstasChristy** worksheet tab, press and hold Shift, click the **NieseJason** worksheet tab, and then click cell **D7**. In the formula bar, highlight **#REF!** in the VLOOKUP function.

Notice all the formulas in columns D:F return a #REF! error now. Because the PriceList worksheet was removed, all the formulas that referenced that worksheet have a cell reference error. You will replace that missing reference with a reference to the SpaSalonPrices workbook.

VLOOKUP formula with #REF! error that occurred because PriceList worksheet was deleted

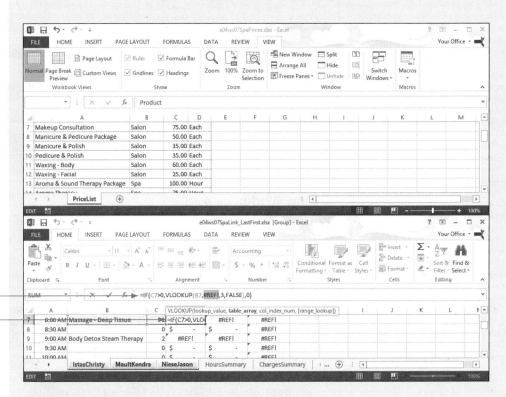

Figure 16   #REF! error in the formula

e. Click the **e04ws07SpaPrices** workbook, and then select cells **A2:D26**. This becomes the new lookup range for the VLOOKUP function. The formula bar should show =IF(C7>0,VLOOKUP(B7,[e04ws07SpaPrices.xlsx]PriceList!$A$2:$D$26,3,FALSE),0).

> **Troubleshooting**
> Remember that the #REF! error in Excel ends with an exclamation point! Be sure to highlight all of #REF! in the above step, or the correction to the formula will not work.

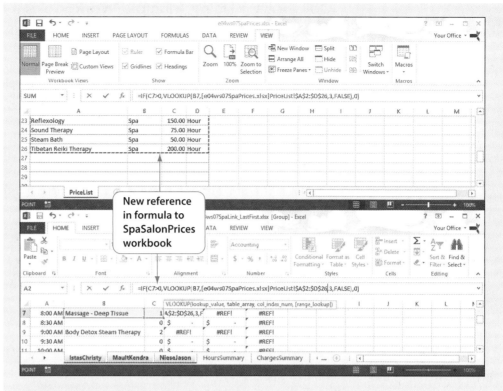

Figure 17   New reference to a workbook

f. Press Ctrl+Enter. Use the **fill handle** to copy **D7** to cells **D8:D24**. This will eliminate all the #REF! errors on the worksheet.

g. Click the **ChargesSummary** worksheet tab to ungroup the worksheets, and then click **Save** 🖫. Keep the two workbooks open for the next exercise.

REAL WORLD ADVICE   **Planning Linked Workbooks**

- **Make your links easy to track**—Consider changing the formatting of a linked cell to something identifiable so you can easily identify cells with a linked formula.

- **Avoid circular links**—Workbooks should not have links to each other. The links should be one-way from one workbook to another. A circular link will slow down opening and updating the workbooks.

- **Turn on Automatic Calculation**—Source workbooks that you link to should have automatic calculation turned on to make updating quicker and error free. This is the automatic default setting, but it can be verified under Options on the File tab by opening the Options dialog box and scrolling to the Formulas section.

- **Consider where you will store your files**—If one file is stored on a network drive, and the other linked file is stored on your computer's hard drive, someone opening the file on the network drive will not have access to the linked file on your hard drive. This means links will not be updated.

Collaborate Using Multiple Workbooks

Collaboration allows workbooks to be shared among different users and then merged together for a final product. Excel allows users to collaborate in the creation of a workbook; however, it is more common for users to collaborate in keeping data in a workbook up to date once the workbook has been developed. When a workbook is shared, you can save additional copies of your workbook for distribution to other users. The shared copies can be changed by other users and the changes merged back into the master workbook.

Some things to consider when you are sharing workbooks and editing shared workbooks:

- Not all features are available. For example, merged cells, conditional formats, data validation, charts, pictures, drawings, hyperlinks, scenarios, outlines, subtotals, data tables, PivotTable reports, worksheet and workbook protection, and macros all cannot be changed once the workbook is shared.

- Whenever you save a shared workbook, it will be updated with changes other users have made since the last time you saved it. If you want to monitor these changes, you can keep the workbook open and have Excel update it with changes automatically or at specified time intervals.

- If you are changing a cell while another user is changing the same cell, you will be prompted with a conflict resolution dialog box that will allow you to choose whose changes to keep.

- Each user has their own settings, or custom view, saved of the workbook that allows you to save print settings and any filters you may have created.

The spa and salon have updated prices for a few of their services, and the price changes are not currently reflected in the e04ws07SpaPrices workbook. Rather than obtaining the updated prices from Meda Rodate and Irene Kia and entering them into the worksheet yourself, it is better to have Meda and Irene update copies of the workbook directly to avoid any errors.

In this exercise, you will play three roles:

1. Yourself, as you create copies of a workbook for collaboration and later merge updated data from the copies back into the master workbook.
2. Meda Rodate, as you update prices for spa services in a collaboration copy of the e04ws07SpaPrices workbook created for Meda.
3. Irene Kia, as you update prices for salon services in a collaboration copy of the e04ws07SpaPrices workbook created for Irene.

Sharing a Workbook

You will need to share the e04ws07SpaPrices workbook with Meda Rodate and Irene Kia and then merge their updated data into your master copy. Merging workbooks is not a functionality that is available by default on the Ribbon or the Quick Access Toolbar, so you need to customize the Quick Access Toolbar to include the Compare and Merge Workbooks icon.

E07.15

 To Share a Workbook for Collaborative Work

SIDE NOTE
Shortcut to Switching Windows
If your windows are no longer arranged neatly, you can use the Switch Windows button on the View tab to switch from one workbook to the other.

SIDE NOTE
Sharing a Linked Workbook
If A is linked to B, then A must be closed when shared copies of B are created; if not, the references in A will be automatically changed to reference the new files.

a. Make **e04ws07SpaPrices** the active workbook, and then click **Maximize** ▢. Press `Ctrl`+`Home` to return to cell **A1**. Click the **FILE** tab, click **Save As**, and then in the Save As dialog box, navigate to the folder where you are saving your files. In the **File name** box, type e04ws07SpaPrices_LastFirst replacing LastFirst with your actual name, and then click **Save**.

Because e04ws07SpaLink is open and is linked to e04ws07SpaPrices, saving e04ws07SpaPrices with a new name will automatically update the links in e04ws07SpaLink_LastFirst.

b. Make **e04ws07SpaLink_LastFirst** the active workbook. Click **Save** ▢, and then click **Close** ☒. The e04ws07SpaPrices_LastFirst workbook should be the only workbook open.

c. Above the HOME tab, click the **Customize Quick Access Toolbar** button ▾, and then select **More Commands** from the menu. You must do this before sharing the workbook because customizing the Quick Access Toolbar is not allowed in shared workbooks.

Quick Access Toolbar options

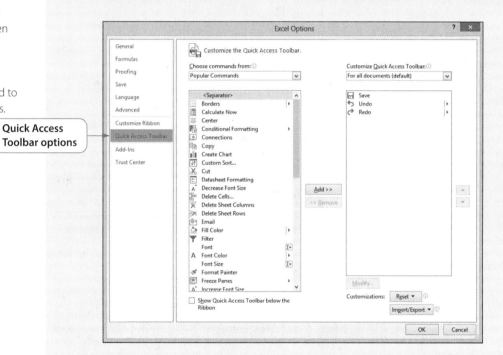

Figure 18   Customize the Quick Access Toolbar

d. Click the **Choose commands from** arrow, and then select **All Commands**. Scroll through the list of Commands, click **Compare and Merge Workbooks**, and then click **Add**.

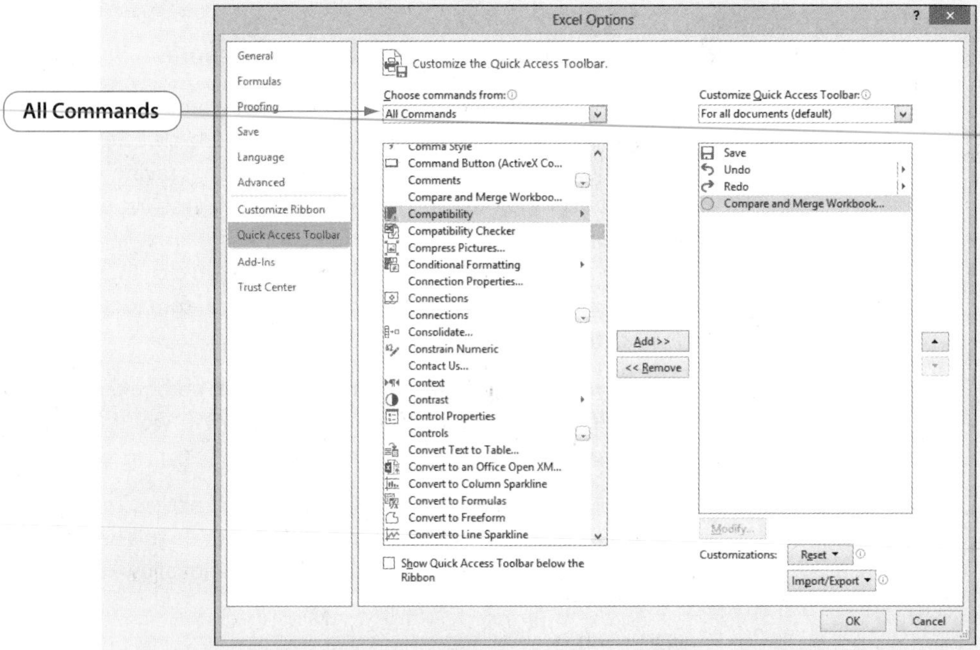

All Commands

Figure 19 Compare and Merge Workbooks button on the Quick Access Toolbar

e. Click **OK**. Compare and Merge Workbooks ⊚ now appears on the Quick Access Toolbar.

f. Click the **REVIEW** tab, and in the **Changes** group, click **Share Workbook**. If necessary, click the **Editing** tab in the Share Workbook dialog box, check the **Allow changes by more than one user at the same time** box, and then click **OK**.

g. Click **OK** in the alert box that says **This action will now save the workbook**. Notice that once a workbook is shared, the Compare and Merge Workbooks icon changes to a green color.

You will now make copies of the workbook so you can play the role of Rodate and Kia and make changes to each of their copies of the workbook.

h. Click the **FILE** tab, and then click **Save As**. Navigate to where you are saving your files. In the **File name** box, type e04ws07SpaRodate_LastFirst replacing LastFirst with your actual name, and then click **Save**.

i. Click the **FILE** tab, and then click **Open**. Under **Recent Workbooks** select **e04ws07SpaPrices_LastFirst**. All copies of a shared workbook should be made from the original shared workbook and not copies of the shared workbook.

j. Click the **FILE** tab, and then click **Save As**. Navigate to where you are saving your files. In the **File name** box, type e04ws07SpaKia_LastFirst replacing LastFirst with your actual name, and then click **Save**.

k. In the **e04ws07SpaKia_LastFirst** workbook, make the following changes in the Price column for the listed products:

Service	Cell	New Price
Facial – Mud & Citrus	C2	100
Makeup Consultation	C7	100
Manicure & Pedicure Package	C8	70
Manicure & Polish	C9	45
Pedicure & Polish	C10	45
Waxing – Body	C11	75

l. Click **Save** 🖫, click the **FILE** tab, and then select **Close** to close the workbook.

> **Troubleshooting**
> If you close Excel along with the file by mistake, just restart Excel and continue with the next step.

m. In the **e04ws07SpaRodate_LastFirst** workbook, make the following changes in the Price column for the listed products:

Service	Cell	New Price
Massage – Deep Tissue	C17	125
Massage – Deep Tissue, Couples	C18	112.50
Massage – Fusion	C19	150
Massage – Fusion, Couples	C20	137.50
Massage – Shiatsu	C21	150
Steam Bath	C25	75
Tibetan Reiki Therapy	C26	225

n. Click **Save** 🖫, click the **FILE** tab, and then select **Close** to close the workbook. Keep Excel open for the next exercise.

Merging Shared Workbooks

The **Compare and Merge Workbooks** command will compare the changes made in each shared workbook and then provide you with the option to update the workbook with those changes. Some things to consider when you are comparing and merging shared workbooks:

- You can only merge a shared workbook with copies of that workbook that were made from the same shared workbook.
- You cannot merge workbooks that are not shared.
- The shared workbooks must have unique file names different from the original workbook.
- All copies of the shared workbooks should be saved in the same folder as the shared workbook.

Now that the changes have been made to the individual workbooks, you will merge the changes back into the original workbook, e04ws07SpaPrices_LastFirst.

E07.16

 To Compare and Merge Workbooks

a. Click the **FILE** tab, and then in the Recent Workbooks list, click **e04ws07SpaPrices_LastFirst**. Notice that the title bar of the window displays [Shared] after the file name. This is to remind you that the workbook is shared.

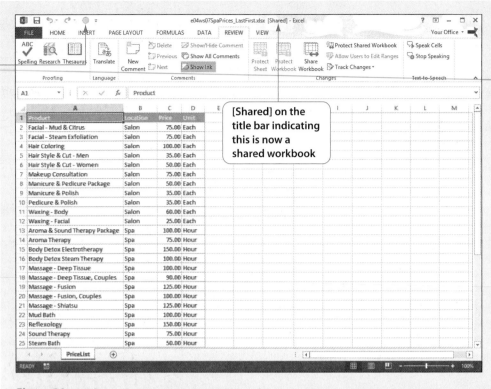

Figure 20   Shared workbook

b. On the Quick Access Toolbar, click **Compare and Merge Workbooks** 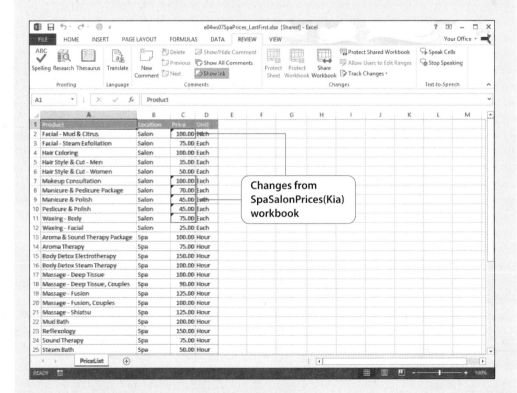. If necessary, navigate to the location where you saved your files, select **e04ws07SpaKia_LastFirst**, and then click **OK**.

Any cell values that are changed as a result of the merge are highlighted.

Changes from
SpaSalonPrices(Kia)
workbook

Figure 21   Changes showing on merged workbook

c. On the Quick Access Toolbar, click **Compare and Merge Workbooks** , and then if prompted, click **OK** to save the workbook. Select **e04ws07SpaRodate_LastFirst**, and then click **OK**.

d. Click **Save** 🖫.

Keeping Track of Changes

As long as workbooks are shared, you can view the changes made and continue making changes to the shared workbooks. This **change history** is information that is maintained about all changes made in past editing sessions to the shared workbooks. The information includes who made the change, when the change was made, and what data was changed. When you save the workbook, the History worksheet will be hidden and you will have to use the Track Changes options to add the History worksheet again. However, once you stop sharing the workbook, the change history will be deleted and no longer be available.

For this exercise, you will not stop sharing the workbook so the change history will be saved to review in the future.

REAL WORLD ADVICE | **Keeping Track of Changes**

When you share a workbook, Excel creates a change history log so you can keep track of changes made to the workbook from the other shared workbooks. Once you stop sharing the workbook though, Excel assumes you have accepted all the changes and therefore have no need to keep the history. If you want to view the history after you turn off sharing, you should copy and paste the history data to another worksheet—or workbook. Your other option would be to not stop sharing the workbook so the History worksheet is not deleted.

E07.17

▶ **To Save the Change History**

a. Click the **REVIEW** tab. In the **Changes** group, click **Track Changes**, and then click **Highlight Changes**.

b. Click the **When** arrow, and then select **All**. Check the **List changes on a new sheet** box.

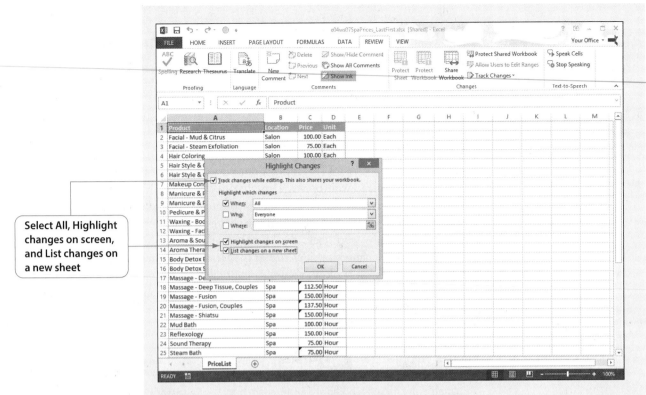

Figure 22 Highlight Changes dialog box options

c. Click **OK**. A new worksheet named **History** will be added to the workbook that shows all the details about the changes made.

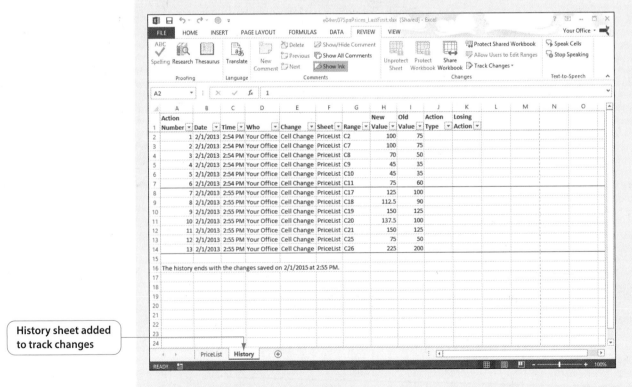

Figure 23 New History sheet

d. Click **Save** 🖫, click the **FILE** tab, and then select **Close** to close the workbook.

e. Click the **FILE** tab, and then in the Recent Workbooks list, click **e04ws07SpaLink_LastFirst**. Click **Enable Content** to update all the links with the new data.

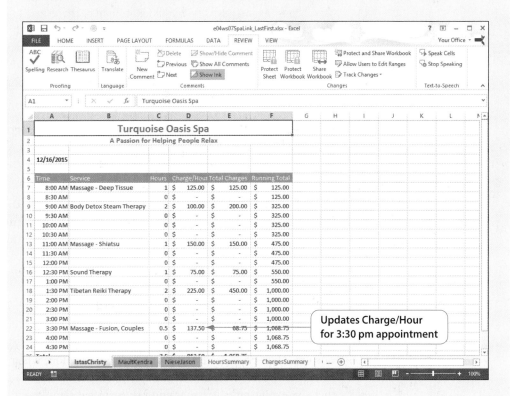

Figure 24   New data from shared and merged workbooks

Notice that, for example, on the IstasChristy worksheet, the Charge/Hour for the 3:30 appointment for Massage – Fusion, Couples is now $137.50.

f. Click **Save** 🖫, click the **FILE** tab, and select **Close** to close the workbook. Keep Excel open for the next exercise.

QUICK REFERENCE	To Stop Sharing a Workbook

When you are done tracking changes in a shared workbook, it is good practice to stop sharing it so changes are not made by mistake.

1. Click the **REVIEW** tab, and in the **Changes** group, click **Share Workbook**.

2. In the Share Workbook dialog box, uncheck Allow changes by more than one user at the same time, click **OK**, and then click **Yes** in the alert that appears.

Using and Creating Templates

In its simplest form, an Excel **template** is a workbook that provides a starting point for building other similar workbooks. In its intended form, a template is a worksheet framework—a worksheet that contains cell formats, structural data such as column headings and data labels, and formulas necessary to achieve the template's purpose, such as totaling invoice line items, calculating sales tax, or tracking and totaling the time spent on a project.

In reality, a template is just a workbook saved with a different file extension—the .xltx extension. Templates, if stored in the default location, do have one special differentiator that may make their creation advantageous: they are readily available via the File tab when creating a new workbook. In addition, when opening templates from the default template location, the file will default to saving as a normal Excel workbook with the .xlsx extension, thereby leaving the original template file in its original form—ready to use again for future development needs.

Templates, by default, are saved to the system drive in the Users\User name\AppData\Roaming\Microsoft\Templates folder. Any templates added to that folder are available from the File tab.

Any workbook can be used as a template for another workbook. Simply open a workbook and save it with the template extension and a new file name.

In this section, for the spa, you will use a local template for a to-do list, then you will search online for a template to use for a group calendar. Finally, you will use the SpaSales workbook to create a template that the managers can use for each of the staff.

Use Existing Templates

Microsoft Excel has a number of local templates. **Local templates** are stored in the Program Files\Microsoft Office\Templates\1033 folder. The number 1033 is the language ID number for English (US). This folder will change depending upon which language version of Office you have installed. Templates for all the Office applications are stored in this folder.

Local templates are accessed from the File tab. You can add your own templates to the built-in templates folder by saving, or moving, your templates to that folder.

Using Local Templates

Local templates are the templates you see when you click the File tab. They are commonly used, have formatting and other features already applied, and are ready for you to enter your personal data. Any data that appears in the template is there as an example, so be sure and delete that sample data before you save your workbook.

You will choose the Project tracker from the local templates to create a project list for the spa employees.

E07.18

▶ To Find, Open, and Use a Local Template

a. Click the **FILE** tab, click **New**, and then click **Project tracker** in the list of templates.

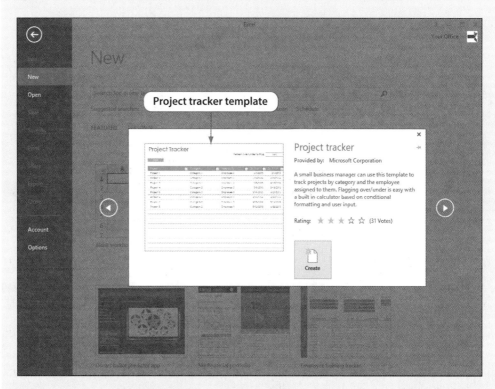

Figure 25   List of local templates on File tab

b. Click **Create** to start using the template. Click the **FILE** tab, and then click **Save As**. Navigate to the folder where you are storing your files, type e04ws07SpaToDo_LastFirst replacing LastFirst with your actual name, and then click **Save**.

c. Click the **Setup** worksheet tab, and then enter the following categories and employees.

Category	Employee
Supplies	Istas
Inventory	Niese
Subscriptions	Kendra

d. Click the **Project Tracker** worksheet tab. Enter the following data for the Spa in **rows 6 and 7**, replacing the sample data already there. Notice the lists available when you click certain cells. You have the option to make a selection from the list or to type in your value.

Project	Category	Assigned To	Est. Start	Est. Finish	Est. Work
Order supplies	Supplies	Kendra	5/7/15	5/9/15	2
Purge inventory	Inventory	Istas	4/3/15	4/10/15	7

e. Select cells **B8:G13**, and then press ⌈Delete⌋ to delete the contents of the cells. This will delete only the content and none of the formatting in these cells.

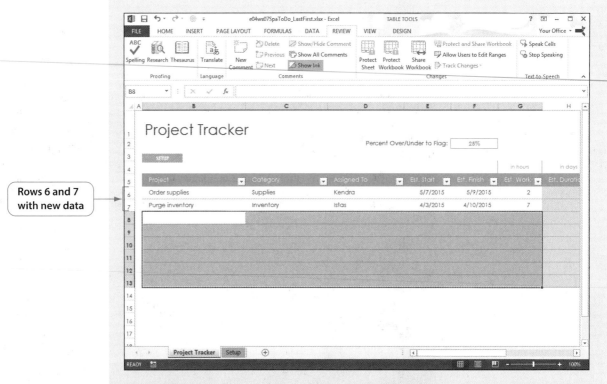

Rows 6 and 7 with new data

Figure 26 Example data replaced with actual data

f. Click **Save** 🖫, click the **FILE** tab, and then click **Close**. Keep Excel open for the next exercise.

CONSIDER THIS | **How Could Excel Facilitate Work as a Team?**

So far in this workshop, you have learned how to group worksheets, consolidate worksheets, merge data from individual worksheets into a master worksheet, and build and use templates. Think about a couple of group or team projects you have been involved with in your educational career, and consider how the Excel capabilities listed above might have aided your efforts with the following:

- Tracking team member contributions to a project
- Tracking project progress toward completion
- Bringing the work of team members together into one coherent final product
- Supporting a team member that is struggling with a part of the project by facilitating the involvement of other team members' assistance

How else might Excel facilitate team work in your education? How about in your career?

Using Online Templates

Online templates are templates stored online that can be downloaded to your computer. There are literally hundreds of Excel templates available online. Microsoft, through its template site at Office.com, fosters a community of Office users who download templates posted by other users. Users can rate templates on a scale of 1 to 5 stars. User ratings are averaged, and the average is posted next to each template.

Some people are very good at generating data through formulas and functions; others are experts at presenting information graphically or at formatting tabular content attractively. Office users can post their templates to Office.com so others can benefit from their expertise.

In this exercise, you will download a template from Office.com and use it to create an event calendar for the spa to provide to their customers.

E07.19

▶ To Find, Open, and Use an Online Template

a. Click the **FILE** tab, and then click **New**.

b. In the **Search online templates** box at the top of the window, type calendar.

c. Click **Start searching** 🔍. Scroll down, and then click the full page yearly calendar called **Small business calendar (any year Mon-Sun)**. The whole title is visible when you point to the icon for the template. Click **Create**. If necessary, click **Enable Editing** in the Protected View bar at the top of the window.

d. Click the **FILE** tab, click **Save As**, and then navigate to where you are saving your files. In the **File name** box, type e04ws07SpaCal_LastFirst replacing LastFirst with your actual name, and then click **Save**.

e. In the top left corner of the workbook, click the spinner **arrow** ⬍ next to the year, and then change the year to **2015**.

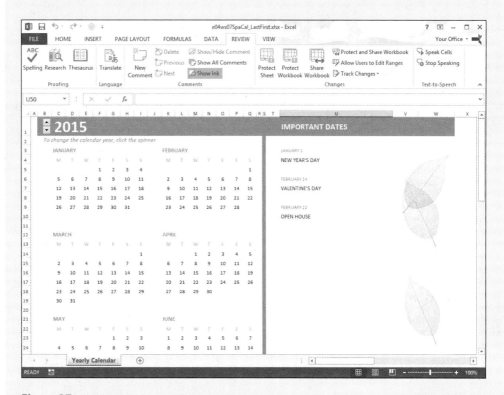

Figure 27 Changed year on template

f. Click cell **U44** and change it to 3356 Hemmingway Circle. Change cell **U45** to Santa Fe, NM 87594. Change cell **U47** to 505.555.1564. Change cell **U48** to kmasters@paintedparadise.com. Change cell **U49** to www.paintedparadiseresort.com.

g. Right-click the **image** below the resort's website address and select **Change Picture**. In the Insert Pictures dialog box, click **Browse** next to **From a file**. Navigate to your student files, select **e04ws07SpaLogo**, and then click **Insert**.

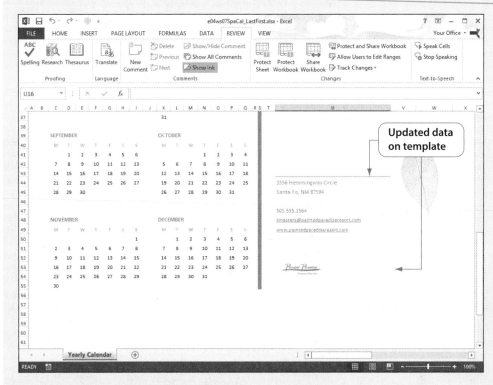

Figure 28 Updated workbook template

h. Click the **FILE** tab, and then click **Close** to close the workbook. Keep Excel open for the next exercise.

Create Templates from an Existing Workbook

Creating templates is really no different than creating workbooks—you simply remove any specific data and save the workbook as a template.

You can create templates from your own workbooks, or you can create them by modifying a template to better fit your needs.

Creating a Template from a Workbook

The Spa Sales Daily workbook has the time slots and schedules for one particular day: December 16, 2015. This is a good format to use for other dates, especially since the Spa workbook uses this format to summarize the data. You will delete the date, service, and duration details, but leave the appointment times and therapist names so each day can be updated easily. You will also change the tab name to something less specific.

E07.20

 To Create a Template from a Workbook

a. Click the **FILE** tab, click **Open**, navigate to your student files, and then click **e04ws07SpaSales**. Click **Open**.

b. Select cells **A2:A55**, and then press Delete to delete the dates.

c. Select cells **D2:E55**, and then press Delete to delete the service descriptions and hours.

d. Right-click the **MondaySales** worksheet tab, select **Rename**, type DailySales and press Enter.

e. Click the **FILE** tab, click **Save As** and in the **File name** box, type e04ws07SpaTemp_LastFirst replacing LastFirst with your actual name. Click **Excel Workbook** in the **Save as type** list, and then select **Excel Template**. Navigate to the location where you are saving your files and click **Save**.

f. Click the **FILE** tab, click **Close** to close the workbook, and then close Excel.

CONSIDER THIS | **Should Templates Contain External References?**

Templates generally are used to create worksheets or workbooks with consistent structure and format. While templates can, and often do, contain formulas, consider carefully before creating a template that includes external references to other workbooks. For such a template to be used, the linked workbook must be available in the proper location. The probability of breaking external links in a template is quite high, even if the template is well documented. It would be very easy for a user to copy the template to a new folder, open it to create a new workbook, and consequently break the external references (links).

If you were creating a template and had to reference data in another workbook, what steps could you take to minimize the probability that the external links would get broken by someone using the template?

Concept Check

1. The ability to group worksheets creates an opportunity for you to greatly increase the efficiency of your work. List three ways in which grouping worksheets can increase your efficiency.   p. 368

2. What are the three ways you can consolidate data across worksheets? When would you use each of the three different ways?   p. 376

3. What are the different ways you can see multiple workbooks on one screen at the same time? When might you want to do this?   p. 385

4. What is the advantage to sharing a workbook? How can you keep track of all the changes made?   pp. 390–395

5. What are the suggested search categories for online templates? With so many templates available, how do you know which ones might be better than others?   pp. 398–400

6. How do you create a custom template? Once you do, how do you make sure it shows on the File tab?   p. 402

Key Terms

3-D formula   379
3-D reference   376
3-D named range   377
Change history   395
Collaboration   390

Compare and Merge Workbooks   393
Consolidate by category   376
Consolidate by position   376
Fill Across Worksheets   372
Grouping   368

Local templates   398
Online templates   400
Template   398

Visual Summary

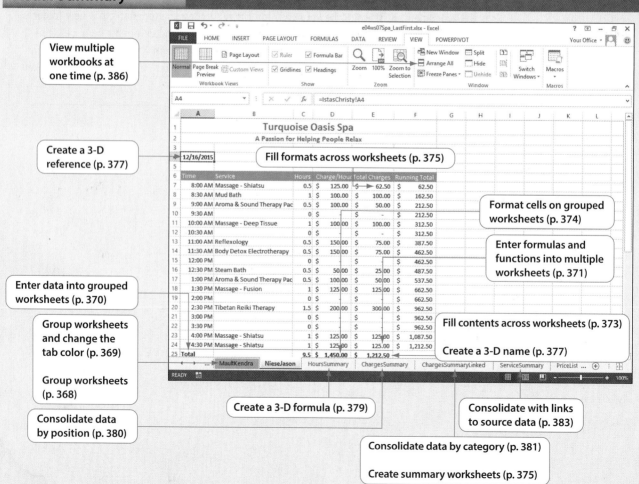

View multiple workbooks at one time (p. 386)

Create a 3-D reference (p. 377)

Fill formats across worksheets (p. 375)

Format cells on grouped worksheets (p. 374)

Enter formulas and functions into multiple worksheets (p. 371)

Enter data into grouped worksheets (p. 370)

Group worksheets and change the tab color (p. 369)

Group worksheets (p. 368)

Consolidate data by position (p. 380)

Fill contents across worksheets (p. 373)

Create a 3-D name (p. 377)

Create a 3-D formula (p. 379)

Consolidate with links to source data (p. 383)

Consolidate data by category (p. 381)

Create summary worksheets (p. 375)

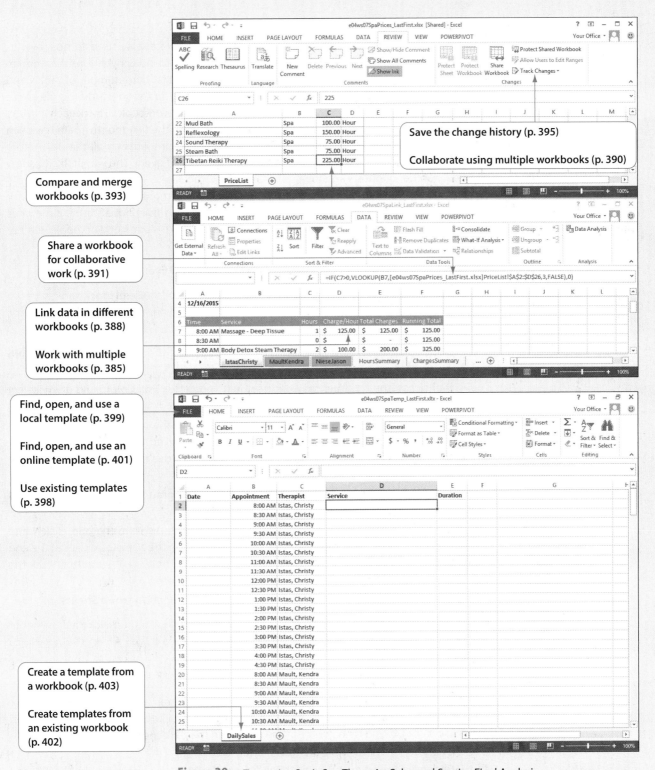

The callout boxes in the figure read:

Compare and merge workbooks (p. 393)

Share a workbook for collaborative work (p. 391)

Link data in different workbooks (p. 388)

Work with multiple workbooks (p. 385)

Find, open, and use a local template (p. 399)

Find, open, and use an online template (p. 401)

Use existing templates (p. 398)

Create a template from a workbook (p. 403)

Create templates from an existing workbook (p. 402)

Save the change history (p. 395)

Collaborate using multiple workbooks (p. 390)

Figure 29 Turquoise Oasis Spa Therapist Sales and Service Final Analysis

Practice 1

Student data files needed:

- e04ws07Event.xlsx
- e04ws07EventLink.xlsx
- e04ws07EventRooms.xlsx

You will save your files as:

- e04ws07Event_LastFirst.xlsx
- e04ws07EventTemp_LastFirst.xltx
- e04ws07EventRooms_LastFirst.xlsx
- e04ws07EventRoom2_LastFirst.xlsx
- e04ws07EventLink_LastFirst.xlsx

Corporate Event Planning at the Resort

Production & Operations

The Painted Paradise Resort and Spa has several rooms that can be used to host events. Corporate events generally include small meetings, seminars, and conventions that require tables, seating, and often a meal. Room setup, as well as a standard number of tables and chairs are included in the daily room rate, as are refreshments for the guests during the event.

Patti Rochelle, the corporate event planner, has started a workbook to track each months' daily events in each of the three rooms they have available. The first month's data has been entered, but she needs help finishing the workbook and consolidating all the data into a monthly report. For each day of the month and each type of event, she would like to show the total number of guests and the total charges incurred.

She would also like to create a template to use every month, and she would like for the daily rate to link to the external workbook that contains this information, so if the rates change, her workbook will be updated. She would also like to share her workbook with her staff so they can make changes where necessary.

a. Start **Excel**, and then open the student data file **e04ws07Event**.

b. Click the **FILE** tab, and then click **Save As**. Save the file as an **Excel Workbook** with the name e04ws07Event_LastFirst replacing LastFirst with your actual name. If necessary, click **Enable Content**.

c. Click the **JanMusica** worksheet tab, press and hold Shift, and then click the **JanPueblo** worksheet tab.

- Right-click the **JanMusica** worksheet tab, point to **Tab Color**, and then select **Olive Green, Accent 3**.

- Click cell **E8**, and then enter a formula to calculate the total charges. The formula should multiply the **# Days** and the **Room Rate**, using an absolute reference for the Room Rate. The formula will look like =D8*$C$5. Use the **fill handle** to copy the formula to cell range **E9:E38**.

- Select cells **A7:E39**. On the **HOME** tab, in the **Editing** group, click **Fill**, click **Fill Across Worksheets**, select **Formats** and then click **OK**.

- Click cell **E39**, click the **FORMULAS** tab, and in the **Defined Names** group, click **Name Manager**. Click **New**, and then type TotalCharges3D in the Name box. Click at the end of the **cell reference** in the Refers to box, press and hold Shift, and then click the **JanPueblo** worksheet tab. Click **OK**, and then click **Close**.

- Right-click the **JanMusica** worksheet tab, and then select **Ungroup Sheets**.

d. Click the **JanEldorado** worksheet tab, press and hold Shift, and then click the **JanPueblo** worksheet tab. Click cell **A3**, and then create a reference to cell A3 on the JanMusica worksheet. The reference should look like =JanMusica!A3.

e. Click the **GuestSummary** worksheet tab.

- Click cell **B8**, type =, click the **JanMusica** worksheet tab, click **C8**, and then type +. Click the **JanEldorado** worksheet tab, click **C8**, type +, click the **JanPueblo** worksheet tab, click **C8**, and then press Ctrl+Enter. Use the **fill handle** to copy this formula to cells **B9:B38** on the GuestSummary worksheet.

- Click cell **C8**, and then type =SUM(. Click the **JanMusica** worksheet tab, click **E8**, and then press and hold Shift. Click the **JanPueblo** worksheet tab, type) and then press Ctrl+Enter. Use the **fill handle** to copy this formula to cells **C9:C38**.

f. Click the **RoomSummary** worksheet tab.

- Click cell **B8**, click the **DATA** tab, and then in the **Data Tools** group, click **Consolidate**.

- In the Consolidate dialog box, make sure **Sum** is selected in the Function box. Click the **Reference** box, click the **JanMusica** worksheet tab, and then select cell range **C8:E38**. Click **Add**.

- Click the **JanEldorado** worksheet tab, verify cells **C8:E38** are selected, and then click **Add**.

- Click the **JanPueblo** worksheet tab, verify cells **C8:E38** are selected, and then click **Add**. Click **OK**.
- Click cell **D39**, type =SUM(TotalCharges3D) and then press Enter.

g. Click the **EventSummary** worksheet tab.

- Click cell **A7**, on the **DATA** tab, in the **Data Tools** group, click **Consolidate**. In the Consolidate dialog box, make sure **Sum** is selected in the Function box, and then click the **Reference** box.
- Click the **JanMusica** worksheet tab, and then select cell range **B7:E38**. Click **Add**.
- Click the **JanEldorado** worksheet tab, verify the cell range **B7:E38** is selected, and then click **Add**.
- Click the **JanPueblo** worksheet tab, verify the cell range **B7:E38** is selected, and then click **Add**.
- Check the **Top row** box.
- Click **OK**. Click cell **A7**, and then type Event.

h. Click the **EventSummaryLinked** worksheet tab.

- Click cell **A7**, and then on the **DATA** tab, in the **Data Tools** group, click **Consolidate**. In the Consolidate dialog box, make sure **Sum** is selected in the Function box, and then click the **Reference** box.
- Click the **JanMusica** worksheet tab, select cell range **A7:E38**, and then click **Add**. Click the **JanEldorado** worksheet tab, and then click **Add**. Click the **JanPueblo** worksheet tab, and then click **Add**.
- Check the **Top row** box, and then check the **Create links to source data** box. Click **OK**.
- Select columns **A:F** and on the **HOME** tab, in the **Cells** group, click **Format**, and then select **AutoFit Column Width**.
- Select cells **A11:A131**, on the **HOME** tab, in the **Number** group, click the **Number Format** arrow, and then select **Short Date**.
- Save and close the workbook, but keep Excel open.

i. Click the **FILE** tab, and then open **e04ws07EventLink**. Save the file as an **Excel Workbook** with the name e04ws07EventLink_LastFirst replacing LastFirst with your actual name. If necessary, click **Enable Content**.

j. Click the **FILE** tab, and then open **e04ws07EventRooms**. Click the **VIEW** tab, in the **Window** group, click **Arrange All**, click the **Tiled** option, and then click **OK**.

k. In the **e04ws07EventLink_LastFirst** workbook, the RoomRates worksheet has been deleted, so the reference to that worksheet shows an error.

- Click the **JanMusica** worksheet tab, click cell **C5**, and then replace the reference with a new reference to cell **B8** in the **e04ws07EventRooms** workbook by typing = and then clicking on cell **B8** in **e04ws07EventRooms**.
- Click the **JanEldorado** worksheet tab, click cell **C5**, and then replace the reference with a new reference to cell **B7** in the **e04ws07EventRooms** workbook.
- Click the **JanPueblo** worksheet tab, click cell **C5**, and then replace the reference with a new reference to cell **B6** in the **e04ws07EventRooms** workbook.
- Save, and then close the **e04ws07EventLink_LastFirst** workbook.

l. Make **e04ws07EventRooms** the active workbook, and then save it as e04ws07EventRooms_LastFirst replacing LastFirst with your actual name.

- If necessary, click the **Customize Quick Access Toolbar** button, and then select **More Commands** from the menu. Click the **Choose commands from** arrow, select **All Commands**, select **Compare and Merge Workbooks**, and then click **Add**. Click **OK**.

- Click the **REVIEW** tab, and in the **Changes** group, click **Share Workbook**. Check the **Allow changes by more than one user at the same time** box, and then click **OK**. Click **OK** again.

m. Click the **FILE** tab, and then click **Save As**. Navigate to where you are saving your files. In the **File name** box, type e04ws07EventRoom2_LastFirst replacing LastFirst with your actual name, and then click **Save**.

- Change the **Daily Rate** for **Pueblo** to $825, and then change the **Daily Rate** for **Eldorado** to $1,750.
- Save and close the workbook but keep Excel open.

n. Open **e04ws07EventRooms_LastFirst**. On the Quick Access Toolbar, click **Compare and Merge Workbooks.** Navigate to the location where you are saving your files, select **e04ws07EventRoom2_LastFirst**, and then click **OK**.

- On the **REVIEW** tab, click **Track Changes**, and then click **Highlight Changes**. In the **When** list, select **All**. Check the **List changes on a new sheet** box, and then click **OK**.
- Save and close the workbook but keep Excel open.

o. Open **e04ws07Event_LastFirst**. Click the **JanMusica** worksheet tab, press and hold Shift, and then click the **JanPueblo** worksheet tab.

- Select cells **B8:D38**, and then clear the **Contents** from the cells. Ungroup the worksheets.
- Change the name of the **JanMusica** worksheet tab to Musica. Change the name of the **JanEldorado** tab to Eldorado, and then change the name of the **JanPueblo** tab to Pueblo.
- Save the workbook in your student folder as a template called e04ws07EventTemp_LastFirst replacing LastFirst with your actual name.

p. Click the **Documentation** worksheet. Click cell **A6**, and then type in today's date. Click cell **B6**, and then type in your first and last name. Complete the remainder of the **Documentation** worksheet according to your instructor's direction.

q. Click **Save**, close Excel, and then submit your file as directed by your instructor.

Problem Solve 1

Student data files needed:

 e04ws07Parks.xlsx

 e04ws07ParkRates.xlsx

You will save your files as:

 e04ws07Parks_LastFirst.xlsx

 e04ws07ParkRates_LastFirst.xlsx

 e04ws07ParksLink_LastFirst.xlsx

 e04ws07ParksTemp_LastFirst.xltx

 e04ws07ParkRate2_LastFirst.xlsx

Park Management LLC

Finance & Accounting

As the newest staff member for Park Management LLC, you have been asked to consolidate information that has been collected for each of the company's locations. Park Management LLC manages museums and parks in three states: Indiana, Ohio, and Kentucky. Each state has a workbook with quarterly data, and the management would like to see this data consolidated into one report. On each workbook there is also a sheet for Rate information, but this is not always current, so you will need to link the workbooks to the master Rate workbook that another staff member updates.

a. Open **e04ws07Parks**, and then save it as e04ws07Parks_LastFirst.

b. Group worksheets **Quarter1** through **Quarter4**. Create formulas in the cell range **D6:E10** to calculate the admission collected from both adult and children visitors for each location using the appropriate rates in the **Rates** worksheet.

c. In cells **B11:E11**, calculate the total adults and children visitors as well as the adult and child admission collected. Format cells **D11:E11** with the **Accounting Number Format**. Format the number of visitors with the **Comma Style** and no decimals. **AutoFit** columns **A:E**. Add a bottom border to cells **B10:E10**, and then type Total in cell **A11**.

d. On the **Summary** worksheet enter a **3-D SUM** function in cells **B6:E10** to calculate the total visitors and admissions for each category and location from Quarter1 through Quarter4.

e. Use **Fill Across Worksheets** to copy the formatting for cells **B6:E10** from the Quarter4 worksheet to the Summary worksheet. Use **Fill Across Worksheets** to copy the content and formatting from cells **A11:E11** on the Quarter4 worksheet to the Summary worksheet. AutoFit columns **B:E** in the Summary worksheet.

f. On the **LinkedSummary** worksheet, in cell **A5**, create a linked consolidation using cells **A5:E11** from each of the quarter worksheets. Select **Top Row**, and **Create links to source data** in the Consolidate dialog box.

g. Change the column width of column **A** to **20**, hide column **B**, and use the **AutoFit** feature for columns **C:F**. Save the workbook.

h. Save **e04ws07Parks_LastFirst** as e04ws07ParksLink_LastFirst. Delete the **Rates** worksheet. Open **e04ws07Parks_LastFirst**. Arrange the two workbooks so you can see them side by side.

i. On **e04ws07ParksLink_LastFirst**, group the **Quarter1** through **Quarter4** worksheets. Click cell **D6**, and then in the formula bar replace the **#REF!B6** with a link to cell **B6** on the **Rates** worksheet on **e04ws07Parks_LastFirst**. Change the cell reference **$B$6** to a relative reference—to remove the absolute reference, and then copy the formula to cell **E6** and cells **D7:E10**. Ungroup the sheets. Save and close the workbooks, but leave Excel open.

j. Open **e04ws07ParkRates**, save it as e04ws07ParkRates_LastFirst and then add the **Compare and Merge Workbooks** button to the Quick Access Toolbar.

k. Share the workbook and allow changes to be made. Save **e04ws07ParkRates_LastFirst** as e04ws07ParkRate2_LastFirst.

l. On **e04ws07ParkRate2_LastFirst**, change the Indiana History Museum rates for an Adult to $8.00 and for a Child to $5.00. Save the changes, and then close the workbook.

m. Open **e04ws07ParkRates_LastFirst**, and then compare and merge the workbook with **e04ws07ParkRate2_LastFirst**. Track all the changes in a new **History** worksheet. Do not stop sharing the workbook. Save and close the workbook.

n. Create a template from **e04ws07Parks_LastFirst** to use for the other states with the same parks. Group the **Quarter1** through **Quarter4** worksheets, and then clear the contents from cells **B6:C10**. Delete **Indiana** from cell A2. Save the template as e04ws07ParksTemp_LastFirst.

o. Complete the **Documentation** worksheet according to your instructor's direction. Insert the **filename** in the left custom footer section of the Header/Footer tab in the Page Setup dialog box on all worksheets in the workbook.

p. Click Save, close Excel, and then submit the file as directed by your instructor.

Student data file needed:

 Blank Excel workbook

You will save your files as:

e04ws07Popcorn_LastFirst.xlsx

e04ws07Troop467_LastFirst.xlsx

e04ws07TroopLink_LastFirst.xlsx

e04ws07TroopSales_LastFirst.xlsx

e04ws07TroopTemp_LastFirst.xltx

Volunteering as the Kernel Master

Finance & Accounting

You recently signed up to be the Kernel Master for your local Boy Scout council. Your job is to track the popcorn sales for each troop in the council and create a summary report. You will have to share the workbook with the troop leaders so they can update their sales data on a regular basis. You will also create a template for them to work with to make the sharing easier.

a. Create a workbook with four worksheets: the first three worksheets will be for the three troops you have to track and the fourth worksheet will be for a summary of the three troops. Name the workbook e04ws07TroopSales_LastFirst.

- Insert the filename in the left section of the footer for all the worksheets.
- All four worksheets should be formatted the same way and include at least five rows with different popcorn flavors, a column for units sold, a column for cost per unit, and a column for total sales.
- Units sold and total sales should be totaled and formatted appropriately.
- The summary worksheet should use a 3-D formula to add together sales from all three troop worksheets.

b. Insert a fifth worksheet to consolidate the three troop worksheets and show the links from the consolidation. Use the AutoFit feature on the remaining columns, and then save the changes.

c. Save **e04ws07TroopSales_LastFirst** as e04ws07TroopLink_LastFirst.

d. Create a second workbook named e04ws07Popcorn_LastFirst that will be the master list of all flavors of popcorn, the unit size, and the cost. Insert the filename in the left section of the footer. Link **e04ws07TroopLink_LastFirst** to the master list by changing the numbers in the cost per unit to cell references that link to the workbook.

e. Create a template from the **e04ws07TroopLink_LastFirst** workbook, and then name it e04ws07TroopTemp_LastFirst. Clear the contents of any cells that are not necessary to include in the template.

f. If necessary, add the **Compare and Merge Workbooks** button to the Quick Access Toolbar. Share the **e04ws07TroopSales_LastFirst** worksheet, and then name the shared file e04ws07Troop467_LastFirst. Change the sales for troop 467, and then compare and merge the two workbooks. Create a new sheet with the change history. Do not stop sharing the workbook.

g. Complete the **Documentation** worksheet according to your instructor's direction. Insert the **filename** in the left custom footer section of the Header/Footer tab in the Page Setup dialog box on all worksheets in the workbook.

h. Click Save, close Excel, and then submit the file as directed by your instructor.

Additional Cases

Additional Workshop Cases are available on the companion website and in the instructor resources.

WORKSHOP 8 | REFINE AN EXCEL APPLICATION

OBJECTIVES

1. View formula precedents and dependents   p. 412

2. Evaluate formulas   p. 414

3. Correct circular references   p. 414

4. Use the Watch Window   p. 416

5. Control data entry with data validation   p. 418

6. Create and use macros   p. 430

7. Change how to navigate a workbook   p. 436

8. Protect workbooks and worksheets   p. 441

Prepare Case

Turquoise Oasis Spa Application

Finance & Accounting

Meda Rodate, manager for the Turquoise Oasis Spa, wants to improve the layout of the existing spa invoice and automate the invoice process as much as possible to ensure data accuracy and consistency. The invoice currently has formulas in the Charge/Hour and Amount columns, but they often get deleted by mistake. The Therapist name is often misspelled, the room number is often wrong, and Meda even thinks the subtotal amount may not be calculating correctly. Another problem arises when the description of the service is not entered correctly, and then the charge/hour cannot be found in the lookup table.

Olga Lyubkina / Shutterstock

In this workshop you will modify an invoice application for the Turquoise Oasis Spa. Meda Rodate has started the application, but since she is unable to finish it, you will assist her. The invoice application has several requirements she cannot satisfy:

- Data validation to minimize data entry errors
- Automatically generated invoice number
- Automated data cleanup using macros
- Protection of the application to stop users from mistakenly changing application content and structure

REAL WORLD SUCCESS

"As an intern, one of my jobs was to do a lot of data entry each week. I was given a workbook from the last intern to use, and had to delete the data from the previous week, then save the workbook with a different name, and then enter the new weekly data. It often took me more time to set up the workbook each week than it did to enter the data. I finally created a macro to clear the data for me, so with the click of a button I had the worksheet cleared and was ready to enter the new data. After that, I set up macros for all the repetitive tasks I had to do in Excel. Not only did it make my job easier, but it gave me more time to be creative, which definitely got the attention of my boss!"

— Jarrett, intern

Student data file needed for this workshop:

 e04ws08Spa.xlsx

You will save your files as:

 e04ws08Spa_LastFirst.xlsx

 e04ws08SpaMacro_LastFirst.xlsm

 e04ws08Spa2_LastFirst.xlsx

Auditing Formulas

Formula-auditing tools show you which cells are used in a formula and how they are used. Whether you are working with a worksheet you developed or one developed by someone else, being able to see all the cells that are part of a formula makes evaluating the accuracy and relevance of the formula easier. Excel's formula-auditing tools include Trace Precedents, Trace Dependents, and Evaluate Formula.

Both tracing a formula and evaluating a formula are useful in understanding how a worksheet is structured, and they are particularly useful if a complex formula is not producing a correct result. In this section, you will use formula-auditing tools to gain a clearer understanding of how the invoice worksheet is structured and to correct an error in an invoice formula.

View Formula Precedents and Dependents

Tracing formulas draws lines from a formula to cells that supply source data (precedents) and to formulas that use the result of a formula (dependents). A **precedent cell** is a cell that supplies a value to the formula in the active cell, and a **dependent cell** is a cell whose value depends on the value in the active cell for its result. When you select to trace precedents, Excel finds and marks with arrows all the cells that supply values to the active cell. When you select to trace dependents, Excel shows you with an arrow all the cells that depend on the value in the active cell. This is helpful to see which cells will be affected by a change to the active cell.

Opening the Starting File

Since you did not create the Spa workbook, you will audit the worksheet before you start making changes to it. This will allow you to better understand how the invoice is set up and to check for any possible errors in the formulas.

E08.00

To Open the Spa Workbook

a. Start **Excel**, and then open the student data file **e04ws08Spa**.

b. Click the **FILE** tab, and save the file as an **Excel Workbook** in the folder where you are saving your student files with the name e04ws08Spa_LastFirst, using your first and last name.

Auditing Formulas with Trace Dependents and Trace Precedents

Every formula has precedents, and some may also have dependents. While you can always click a cell to see the cell references included in a formula, sometimes a visual cue is helpful to see how the formula works. When you choose to **trace dependents** and **trace precedents**, Excel puts arrows on the workbook to show you how the formula in the cell is constructed. These arrows make it easier to find errors than just looking at the cell references in the formula.

In the Spa workbook, you will look at the formulas to make sure they are constructed properly and work the way they are supposed to work. If not, you will make changes to fix the formulas.

E08.01

 To Trace Precedents and Trace Dependents

a. Click the **Invoice** worksheet, select cell **F31**, and then on the **FORMULAS** tab, in the **Formula Auditing** group, click **Trace Precedents**.

A blue arrow is displayed that begins with a blue dot in cell F16 and ends with an arrow in cell F31. The cell range F16:F30 is outlined in blue. This outlined range is a precedent to the calculation in cell F31. Notice that the precedent range F16:F30 is determining the subtotal, and is missing cell F15, the first row of the invoice.

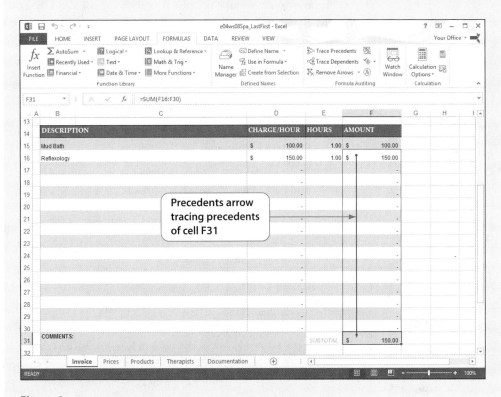

Figure 1   Trace Precedents arrow

b. In the Formula Auditing group, click **Trace Dependents**.

An arrow is displayed from cell F31 to F33 and from F33 to F35. The formula in cell F33 is a dependent cell to the formula in F31, and the formula in cell F35 is a dependent cell to the formula in F33. This means the value in F33 will depend on the value in F31, and the value in F35 will depend on the value in F33.

c. In the Formula Auditing group, click **Remove Arrows**.

d. If necessary, select cell **F31**, and in the formula bar, change F16 to F15 to correct the SUM function so it includes all the rows of the invoice. Press Ctrl + Enter.

e. Click **Save** 🖫.

Evaluate Formulas

Evaluating a formula walks you through the steps taken in calculating the result of a formula. The **Evaluate Formula** dialog box breaks down the formula into its individual pieces and evaluates each part separately so you can see how the formula works. It is similar to using trace precedents and trace dependents, but without the arrows filling up the screen.

Using the Evaluate Formula Tool

In the Spa workbook, there is a problem with the calculation of the Sales Tax and the Total invoice amount because it is showing a #VALUE! error instead of a result. You will use Evaluate Formula to determine what is wrong with the formula in cell F33.

E08.02

 To Evaluate Formulas

a. Select cell **F33**, and then on the **FORMULAS** tab, in the **Formulas Auditing** group, click **Evaluate Formula** ⓕ.

b. The formula =F31*E33 is displayed in the Evaluation box. Click **Evaluate**. It shows the value of F31 as 250, which is correct.

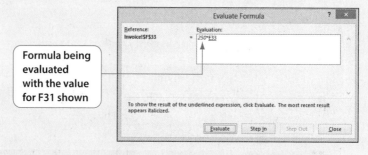

Formula being evaluated with the value for F31 shown

Figure 2 Evaluate Formula dialog box

c. Click **Step In**. This shows that the value of E33 is the text **SALES TAX**, which is not correct. Click **Step Out** to view the cell references replaced by the values in the formula.

The value should be the sales tax rate, or 6.50%, not the text "SALES TAX." This is what is causing the #VALUE! error in the cell.

d. Click **Close**. You cannot edit a formula in evaluation mode. Click in the **formula bar**, and then change E33 to D33. Press Ctrl+Enter.

e. Click **OK** in the circular reference warning dialog box. You will correct this problem in the next exercise.

f. Click **Save** 🖫.

SIDE NOTE
Select All Cells That Contain a Formula
Press Ctrl and type **G**, click Special, and then select Formulas. Notice the categories of formulas you can select. Click OK.

Correct Circular References

Excel uses the term **circular reference** to describe a single formula that references itself or multiple formulas that reference each other. Technically, the formulas are precedents and dependents of one another. A circular reference is a problem for Excel because it means action A requires action B to complete before it can execute, but action B requires action A to complete before it can execute.

Finding and Correcting Circular References

In the Spa workbook, when you corrected the formula referencing the Sales Tax value in the preceding exercise, you saw a circular reference warning dialog box. This means there is a circular reference somewhere in the worksheet. The message in the status bar indicates the circular reference is in cell F35, so you will have to correct it in order to calculate the total correctly.

E08.03

 To Identify and Correct Circular References

a. Select cell **F35**, and then on the **FORMULAS** tab, in the **Formula Auditing** group, click **Trace Precedents**.

The arrow is red, indicating an error. Notice that the SUM function in cell F35 includes a cell reference to cell F35, which is causing the circular reference.

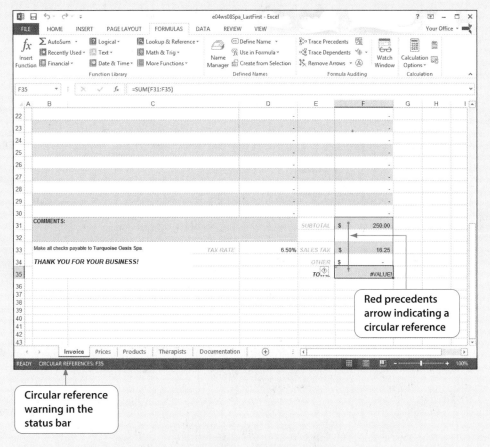

Figure 3   Circular reference as shown by Trace Precedents arrow

b. Click in the **formula bar**, and change F35 to **F34**. Press Ctrl+Enter. This removes the trace arrow and corrects the formula.

c. Click **Save**.

Use the Watch Window

The **Watch Window** is an Excel feature that makes it possible to monitor cells the user considers important in a separate window. The Watch Window is particularly useful when you are making changes in one worksheet or workbook and you want to monitor the effect of your changes to values in several other worksheets or workbooks.

To include a cell in the Watch Window, the workbook that contains the cell must be open and must remain open. As soon as the workbook is closed, any cells in that workbook that are being watched are removed from the Watch Window.

Opening and Using the Watch Window

In the Spa workbook, you will set up a Watch Window to watch the subtotal, sales tax, and total cells. This way, as rows are being added to the invoice, there will be no need to scroll to the bottom to see the total.

E08.04

 To Track Changes Using the Watch Window

a. Click the **FORMULAS** tab, in the **Formula Auditing** group, click **Watch Window**. This will open the Watch Window, which will be empty.

b. If necessary, move the Watch Window out of the way, press and hold Ctrl, and then select cells **F31**, **F33**, and **F35**. In the Watch Window, click **Add Watch**. Click **Add** to confirm the cells you selected.

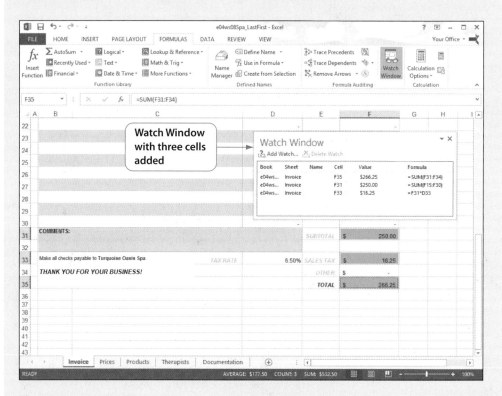

Figure 4   Watch Window

c. Drag the **title bar** of the Watch Window to the top of the worksheet window.

   The Watch Window will dock below the Ribbon and stay there. You can also dock the Watch Window on the bottom, left, or right of the worksheet window. To undock the Watch Window, simply drag the title bar toward the middle of the application window.

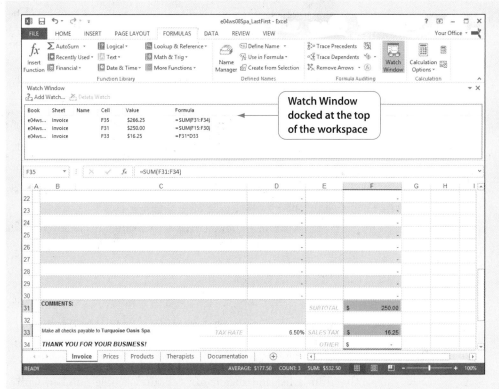

Figure 5 Watch Window docked

d. Select cell **E15**, type **2**, and then press `Ctrl`+`Enter`.
   Notice that all the cells in the Watch Window changed.

e. In the Formula Auditing group, click **Watch Window** to close the Watch Window. The Watch Window also closes when you close the workbook so each time you open the workbook you will have to open the Watch Window to use it; however, you will not have to add the cells again since they will be saved.

f. Click **Save** 💾.

Creating Data Validation Rules

Probably the greatest single source of errors in a workbook is human error. While it is impossible to completely eliminate human error while editing a workbook, Excel provides data validation tools that can help ensure data entry errors are kept to a minimum. **Data validation** includes rules that determine what can and cannot be entered in specific cells. **Validation criteria** are constraints that limit what users are allowed to enter into a particular cell. In this section, you will create various data validation rules for different cells throughout the workbook.

- **Any value**—Does not validate data, but does allow the use of an input message to give data entry instructions.

- **Whole number**—Limits the data value in a cell to a specified range of integers.

- **Decimal**—Limits the number of decimal places that can be used in a cell.

- **List**—Requires the user to select a value from a list of predefined values.

- **Date**—Requires that data entered into a cell represent a valid date.

- **Time**—Requires that data entered into a cell represent a valid time.

- **Text length**—Places a limit on the number of text characters that can be entered into a cell.

- **Custom**—Allows the user to create custom criteria by specifying a formula that data entered into a cell must satisfy to be considered valid.

Control Data Entry with Data Validation

In its simplest form, data validation restricts a single validation criteria per cell. For example, with a simple validation rule you cannot specify that a cell can contain an item from a list and that it can contain a whole number. Custom validation can be used to apply multiple validation criteria to a cell, but the formulas required tend to be much more complex.

Each of the validation criteria can be specified with an Input Message and/or an Error Alert. The Input Message and Error Alert are tools to assist you in communicating data validation constraints to the user. The **Input Message** appears when a user makes a validated cell active and prompts a user before data is entered with information about data constraints; the **Error Message** informs a user when entered data violates validation constraints.

Setting Up a List Validation

List validation presents the user with a list of data values that the user can choose from. Data for the list must be included as part of the workbook; it cannot be in an external workbook.

The Spa workbook has one validation rule created for the Description lines of the invoice. You will add more data validation rules to limit what can be entered in other cells and cell ranges.

In the Spa workbook, the Therapist field will use a list value to choose from a list of therapists that can be found on the Therapists worksheet.

To Create and Use a List Validation

a. Select cell **E10**. Click the **DATA** tab, in the **Data Tools** group, click **Data Validation**. Click the **Settings** tab, click the **Allow** box arrow, and then select **List**. Verify that **In-cell dropdown** and **Ignore blank** options are checked.

b. Click the **Source** box, click the **Therapists** worksheet tab, and then select cells **A2:A4**. The Source box should show =Therapists!$A$2:$A$4. Click the **Source** box again to return to the whole Data Validation dialog box.

SIDE NOTE

Why Check Ignore Blank?

If you do not check Ignore blank, Excel will return an error from the validated cell if you delete its value.

SIDE NOTE

Named Ranges

Use named ranges to identify source data for list validation. They can make your worksheet easier to interpret and understand.

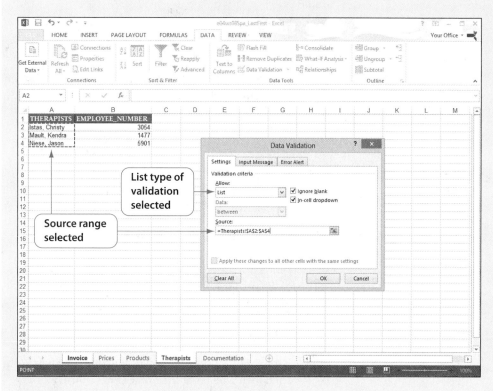

Figure 6   List validation rule

c. Click the **Input Message** tab. In the Title box type Select a therapist, and then in the Input message box type Select the therapist who delivered the services listed. Click the **Error Alert** tab, click the **Title** box, and then type Not a valid name. Click the **Error message** box, type The name you entered is not a valid name. Please select a name from the list. and then click **OK**.

d. Click the **filter** arrow ▼ next to cell **E10**, and then select **Istas, Christy**.

e. Click **Save** 🔲.

Specifying a Decimal Validation

Decimal validation restricts users to enter only data that contains digits and a decimal place. Validation of this type may require a minimum or maximum value depending on the criteria chosen, such as equal to, between, not equal to, not between, greater than, or less than.

In the Spa workbook, the number of hours for any service needs to be restricted to 2 hours or less, which is the spa policy.

E08.06

 To Specify a Decimal Validation Rule

a. Select cells **E15:E30**. Click the **DATA** tab, in the **Data Tools** group, click **Data Validation**.

b. Click the **Settings** tab, click the **Allow** box arrow, and then select **Decimal**. Verify that **Ignore blank** is checked. Click the **Data** box, select **less than or equal to**, and then in the **Maximum** box, type **2**.

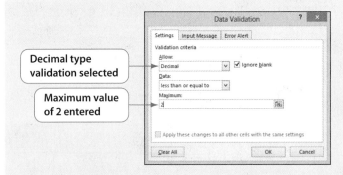

Decimal type validation selected

Maximum value of 2 entered

Figure 7   Decimal validation rule

c. Click the **Input Message** tab, click the **Title** box, type Hours, click the **Input message** box, and then type Enter the number of service hours.

d. Click the **Error Alert** tab, click the **Style** box arrow, and then select **Warning**. Click the **Title** box, and then type Invalid value. Click the **Error message** box, type The hours you entered exceed the maximum recommended and then click **OK**.

e. Click **Save** 🔲.

Specifying a Date Validation

Date validation works very similar to decimal validation except the value entered must be a date that satisfies the specified criteria. Date criteria values can be explicitly entered, referenced by a cell address, or derived from a formula.

In the Spa workbook, the date entered in cell E6 should be restricted to the current date or earlier. This way, invoices may not be dated with a future date. The TODAY function will be used for the date criteria so the date entered will always be compared to the current date based on the function.

To Limit Data Entry to a Date

a. Select cell **E6**. Click the **DATA** tab, in the **Data Tools** group, click **Data Validation**. Click the **Settings** tab, click the **Allow** box arrow, and then select **Date**. Verify that **Ignore blank** is checked.

b. Click the **Data** box arrow, and then select **less than or equal to**.

c. Click in the **End date** box, and then type =TODAY(). This function represents the current date, which means the invoice cannot have a date later than the current date.

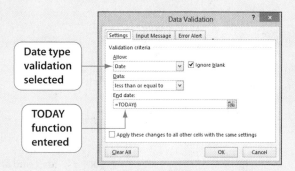

Figure 8   Date validation rule

d. Click the **Input Message** tab, click the **Title** box, and then type Invoice Date. Click in the **Input message** box, and then type Enter the date in the following format: MM/DD/YYYY.

e. Click the **Error Alert** tab, click in the **Title** box, and then type Error. Click the **Error message** box, type Future dates are not allowed and then click **OK**.

f. Select cell **E6**, type =TODAY() to enter the current date, and then press ⌈Ctrl⌉+⌈Enter⌉. If you wanted to enter a date manually, that is, not using the TODAY function, as long as the date is in the correct format (MM/DD/YYYY) and is on or before the current date, it would be allowed.

g. Click **Save** 🖫.

Specifying a Time Validation

Time validation is similar to date validation with the only difference that data entered must be a time value.

In the Spa workbook, you will add validation criteria to cell E8 to ensure only a time value between 8:00 AM and 4:30 PM, the spa hours, can be entered.

E08.08

 To Limit Data Entry to a Time Value

a. Select cell **E8**. Click the **DATA** tab, in the **Data Tools** group, click **Data Validation**. Click the **Settings** tab, click the **Allow** box arrow, and then select **Time**. Verify that **Ignore blank** is checked.

b. Click the **Start time** box, and then type 8:00 AM. Click the **End time** box, and then type 4:30 PM.

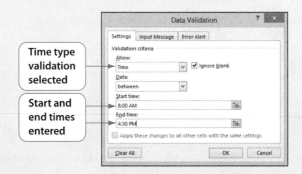

Figure 9   Start and end time validation

c. Click the **Input Message** tab, click the **Title** box, and then type Appointment Time. Click in the **Input message** box, and then type Enter the appointment time as HH:MM AM/PM.

d. Click the **Error Alert** tab, click the **Title** box, and then type Error. Click the **Error message** box, type The time must be between 8:00 AM and 4:30 PM, and then click **OK**.

e. Select cell **E8**, type 2:30 PM, and press Ctrl + Enter.

f. Click **Save** 🖫.

Using Whole Number Validation

Whole number validation is similar to decimal validation with the exception that only integer values are valid and no decimals. A valid range or a minimum or maximum value may also be specified.

In the Spa workbook, you will set the range of numbers allowed in cell E12 to be between 1001 and 5140. These refer to the highest and lowest guest room numbers in the resort.

E08.09

 To Limit Data Entry to a Whole Number with a Minimum and Maximum Value

a. Select cell **E12**. Click the **DATA** tab, in the **Data Tools** group, click **Data Validation**. Click the **Settings** tab, click the **Allow** box arrow, and then select **Whole number**. Verify that **Ignore blank** is checked.

b. Click the **Minimum** box, and then type 1001. Click the **Maximum** box, and then type 5140.

SIDE NOTE

Messages Not Required

The Input Message and Error Message for a data validation rule are helpful but not required when creating the rule.

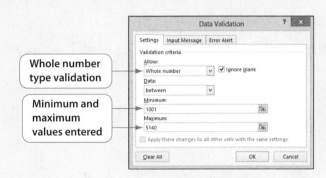

Whole number type validation

Minimum and maximum values entered

Figure 10   Whole number validation rule

c. Click **OK**. Select cell **E12**, type 1001, and then press ⌈Ctrl⌉+⌈Enter⌉.

d. Click **Save** 🖫.

Setting Up Text Length Validation

Text length validation is used to limit the number of characters that can be entered into a cell. Data from workbooks is often imported into databases that have fixed field lengths. Using text length validation on a cell that will be imported into a database can help prevent the data from being truncated, or cut off, when it is imported. Text length validation can also prevent cells from becoming too long, which may prevent a range from printing on one page, which is often a requirement for an invoice or other worksheet.

In the Spa workbook, you will restrict the comments section, cell C31, to 180 characters.

To Limit the Length of Text Entered in a Cell

a. Select cell **C31**. On the **DATA** tab, in the **Data Tools** group, click **Data Validation**. If necessary, click the **Settings** tab, click the **Allow** box arrow, and then select **Text Length**. Verify that **Ignore blank** is checked.

b. Click the **Data** box arrow, and select **less than or equal to**. Click the **Maximum** box, and then type 180.

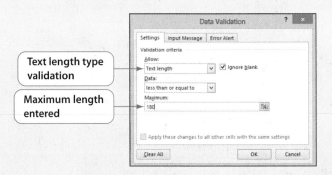

> Text length type validation
>
> Maximum length entered

Figure 11   Maximum length of text value rule

c. Click the **Input Message** tab, click the **Title** box, and then type Comments. Click the **Input message** box, type Comments may not be more than 180 characters and then click **OK**.

d. Click **Save** 🖫.

Using Any Value Validation

Any value validation is a way to use the Input Message option of data validation to convey instructions to a user about a particular cell. The moment an Any Value validated cell is made active, the Input Message is displayed as a prompt to the user. There are no criteria, data restrictions, or error messages set up with an Any Value validation.

In the Spa workbook, you will create a prompt so when the user clicks on the Tax Rate in cell D33, a prompt appears with more information about the tax rate. There will be no value associated with the data validation and no error message, just the input message to provide information.

 To Use Data Validation to Display Data Entry Prompts

a. Select cell **D33**. Click the **DATA** tab, in the **Data Tools** group, click **Data Validation**.

b. If necessary, click the **Input Message** tab. Click the **Title** box, and then type Tax Rate. Click in the **Input message** box, type All items and services require the 6.50% sales tax and then click **OK**. Since you are not restricting data in this cell, changes to the Settings tab and Error Alert tab should not be made.

c. Click **Save** 🖫.

Creating a Custom Data Validation

Custom validation allows you to specify more complex criteria than allowed with the other validation types. Using custom validation, you can apply multiple criteria simultaneously—for example, you can specify a valid range of whole numbers if a number is entered and limit the length of a text value if a text value is entered.

The Painted Paradise Resort and Spa has 700 hotel rooms—140 rooms on each of five floors. Rooms are numbered using a codified data value. A **codified data value** is formed following a system of rules where the position of information is tied to its context. Turquoise Oasis room numbers are codified values: the first digit is the floor the room is located on and the next three digits are the room number on that floor. For example, the 79th room on floor 3 is room 3079. The lowest room number is 1001 and the highest room number is 5140.

In the previous exercise you used whole number validation to limit the value entered for room number to a range of numbers bounded by the lowest and highest room number values in the hotel. The problem is that there are many invalid values within that range. Each floor has 140 rooms. On floor 3, room numbers range from 3001 to 3140. There are no valid room numbers from 3141 to 3999; so the majority of values allowed by whole number validation criteria used in the previous exercise are invalid.

In the Spa workbook, you will change the data validation for the room number that only specifies a minimum and maximum value and create a custom validation rule that will allow only the following numbers to be entered in cell E12 for the room number: 1001–1140, 2001–2140, 3001–3140, 4001–4140, and 5001–5140. You will save this invoice as a new invoice to distinguish the two different data validation rules you have entered for this particular cell.

E08.12

 To Create a Custom Validation Rule for Room Numbers

a. Click the **FILE** tab, and save the file in the folder where you are saving your student files with the name e04ws08Spa2_LastFirst, using your first and last name.

b. Select cell **E12**. Click the **DATA** tab, in the **Data Tools** group, click **Data Validation**.

c. Click the **Settings** tab, in the **Allow** box, select **Custom**, select the existing text in the **Formula** box, and then replace it with =AND(LEFT(E12,1)<="5",LEFT(E12,1)>="1", RIGHT(E12,3)>="001",RIGHT(E12,3)<="140").

> **Troubleshooting**
> If you have trouble entering the data validation formula without making an error, type the formula into a blank cell on the Invoice worksheet. If there is no error, then copy and paste from the formula bar into the Data Validation dialog box.

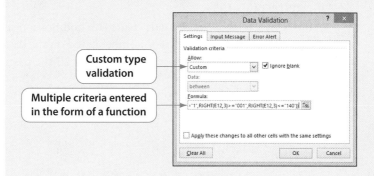

Figure 12 Custom validation rule

By starting with an AND function, all the criteria in the function must be true for there not to be an error. So Excel will check the number entered in cell E12 and as long as it meets ALL of the following criteria the room number will be accepted. Otherwise, the Alert Message will appear.

- The LEFT(E12,1)<="5" tests to make sure that the first digit (the digit on the left) of the room number in cell E12 is less than or equal to 5, since there are only 5 floors to the resort.
- The LEFT(E12,1)>="1" tests to make sure that the first digit of the room number is greater than or equal to 1. So together with the criteria above, the first digit must be between 1 and 5.
- The RIGHT(E12,3)>="001" tests to make sure that the 3 digits to the right must be greater than or equal to "001" since the room numbers on each floor start with 1.
- The RIGHT(E12,3)<="140" tests to make sure that the 3 digits to the right must be less than or equal to 140 since the highest room number on each floor is 140.

d. Click **OK**. Type 3120, and then press Ctrl + Enter.

e. Click **Save** 🖫.

CONSIDER THIS | **When Data Validation Might Not Be the Best Option**

Data validation is an excellent tool to use in workbooks where you want to restrict data entry to certain values or ranges of values. There may be times when a list of data is required and data validation can require the use of that list for choosing a value.

However, there may be times when data validation rules can hinder data entry rather than enhance it. Can you think of a time when data validation might hinder a user who is trying to enter data in a workbook? In what types of situations might that occur? Can you think of any other options available other than data validation?

Using Formulas to Generate a Value

Codification schemes consist of rules that combine data values in specific formats and locations to generate a new data value. A codification scheme is not entered through data validation, but rather as a formula in the cell. The spa would like to use a codification scheme to automatically generate invoice numbers.

The invoice number will be the combination of the appointment date in "yyyymmdd" format, appointment time in "hhmm" format, and employee number, all separated by single spaces. For example, an appointment with Christy Istas, whose employee ID is 3054, on 5/14/2014 at 2:30 PM would have an invoice number of "20140514 1430 3054."

In the Spa workbook, you will create this codification scheme in a formula that will automatically generate the invoice number based on the data entered in the invoice. You will build the formula one piece at a time until all the pieces of the codification scheme are included.

To Create a Codification Scheme for the Invoice Number

a. Select cell **E4**, type =IF(E6>0,TEXT(E6,"YYYYMMDD"),""), and then press Ctrl+Enter. This formats the invoice number so the date is the first part of the invoice number in the format YYYYMMDD, but it displays nothing if cell E6—the date—is empty.

b. Click in the **formula bar**. Place the insertion point at the end of the formula, type &" "&IF(E8>0,TEXT(E8,"HHMM"),""), and then press Ctrl+Enter.

There should be a space between the quotes that are between the & symbols so there will be a space between the time of the appointment in HHMM format and the invoice number. There should be no space between the quotation marks at the end of the IF function so that the result displays nothing for the time portion if cell E8 (the time) is empty.

c. Click in the **formula bar**. Place the insertion point at the end of the formula, type &" "&IF(E10>0,VLOOKUP(E10,Therapists,2),""), and then press Ctrl+Enter.

There should be a space between the quotes that are between the & symbols so there will be a space between the employee number of the therapist selected and the end of the invoice number, but there should be no space between the quotation marks at the end of the IF function so it displays nothing for the therapist's employee number if cell E10 is empty. The therapist's employee number comes from the named range Therapists on the Therapists worksheet and is found using the VLOOKUP function. The final invoice number in cell E4 should be YYYYMMDD 1430 3054 where YYYY is the 4-digit year, MM is the 2-digit month, and DD is the 2-digit day of the current date entered in the invoice.

Codification scheme formula entered

Result of formula

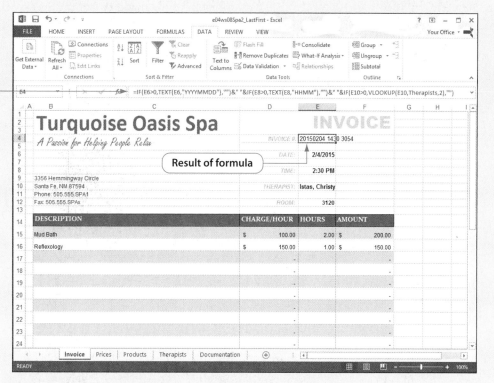

Figure 13   Codification scheme for invoice number

d. Click **Save** 💾.

Validating with Text-to-Speech Manually

Excel includes a **text-to-speech** feature that can assist you in manually validating data. This feature requires speakers or headphones. To use the text-to-speech feature, you have to add at least one text-to-speech button to the Ribbon. There are five buttons available to choose from, described in the following Quick Reference.

QUICK REFERENCE	Text-to-Speech Options

There are a number of text-to-speech buttons you can add to the Ribbon. The buttons you choose will determine how you can use text-to-speech.

- **Speak Cells**—Click to hear the contents of the selected cell and adjacent cells.
- **Speak Cells - Stop Speaking Cells**—Click to stop hearing the cell contents read.
- **Speak Cells by Columns**—Click to hear the cell contents read in the column selected.
- **Speak Cells by Rows**—Click to hear the cell contents read in the row selected.
- **Speak Cells on Enter**—Click to hear the cell contents read when you press `Enter`.

This type of editing allows you to hear what you entered as well as see what you entered and can help you find mistakes you might otherwise overlook. This feature has replaced the speech recognition feature in earlier versions of Excel; however, speech recognition is still available in the different versions of Windows.

In the Spa workbook, you will add two of the Speak Cells buttons to a new group on the Review tab and use it to have the contents of a cell read to you.

E08.14

 To Use Text-to-Speech for Data Proofing

a. Click the **FILE** tab, click **Options**, and then in the Excel Options dialog box, click **Customize Ribbon**.

b. Click the **Choose commands from** arrow, and then select **Commands Not in the Ribbon**.

c. In the **Main Tabs** list, right-click **Review**, and then select **Add New Group** from the shortcut menu. Right-click **New Group (Custom)**, and then select **Rename** from the shortcut menu. Type Text-to-Speech in the Display name box.

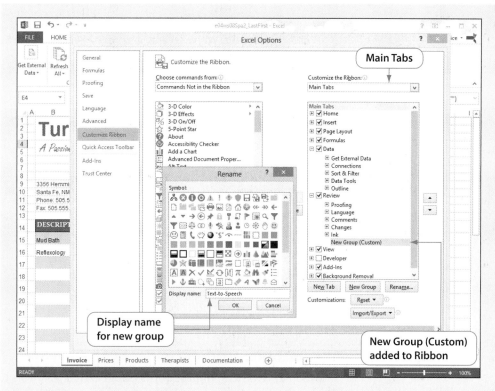

Figure 14   New group for Ribbon

d. Click **OK**, and then click **Text-to-Speech (Custom)** in the Main Tabs list box.

e. In the Commands list, scroll down and select **Speak Cells**, and then click **Add**. Select **Speak Cells - Stop Speaking**, and then click **Add**.

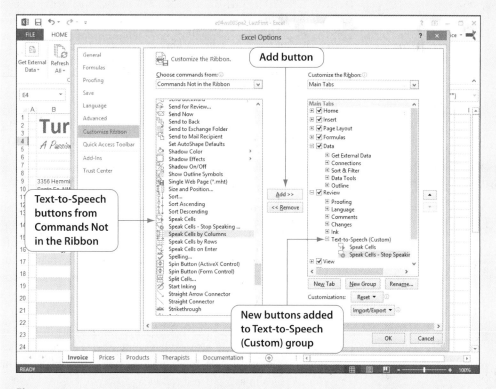

Figure 15   Text-to-speech buttons to add to Ribbon

Developing User-Friendly Excel Applications

There are many characteristics that can be listed to describe a user-friendly application, whether an Excel application or an application developed in a different technology:

- Easy-to-understand user interface
- User-entered data is validated as much as is possible.
- Easy, guided navigation
- Unnecessary functionality is hidden or disabled.
- Offers protection from users inadvertently changing data that would break the application
- Only essential content is visible.
- Good documentation exists.

So far, in developing the invoice application, the workbook is easy to understand—it is modeled after a standard invoice design and layout, and data validation has been applied to ensure correct data entry as much as possible.

In this section, you will modify the invoice workbook to make it an even better application by implementing macros, hiding unnecessary workbook parts like scroll bars and gridlines, and protecting the cells that should not be changed by a user.

Create and Use Macros

Visual Basic for Applications (VBA) is a computer programming language. A **macro** is a Visual Basic program in Excel that automates activities such as mouse movements and clicks, menu selections, and data entry. If a task is performed repeatedly in a worksheet, it is probably a candidate to be recorded as a macro, particularly if incorrectly performing the task could damage the worksheet.

In the Spa workbook, you will create two different macros. One macro will clear the data from the invoice, and the other will automatically apply formatting to a range of cells. First, you will set up a Trusted Location for your macro-enabled workbook so when you open it, the macros will not be blocked.

Creating a Trusted Location

When you save a workbook with a macro, Excel recognizes it as a potential threat, primarily because macros can contain legitimate commands as well as viruses. A **Trusted Location** is a folder that has been identified in the Microsoft Office Trust Center as a safe location for opening files that contain active code that includes macros. If a workbook in a Trusted Location is opened, macros contained in the document will be automatically enabled; if the location where the file is stored is not a Trusted Location, the Trust Center will block any macros and other items that could contain malicious code, and you will have to manually enable the content when you open it.

By default, Excel already has some Trusted Locations set up for templates and other start files. For the Spa Invoice workbook, you will add the folder you are saving your student files in as a trusted folder.

E08.15

 To Create a Trusted Location

a. Click the **FILE** tab, click **Options**, click **Trust Center**, and then click **Trust Center Settings**.

b. Click **Trusted Locations**, click **Add new location**, click **Browse**, navigate to the folder where you save your student files, and then select that **folder**.

c. Click **OK,** click **OK** again, and then verify your folder has been added to the list of **User Locations**. Click **OK**, and then click **OK** again.

d. Click **Save** 🔲.

Adding the Developer Tab to the Ribbon

Recording macros is generally considered an activity for worksheet developers. The **Developer tab** is not visible by default in Excel, so in order to record a macro, the Developer tab needs to be added to the Ribbon.

You will add the Developer tab to the Ribbon so you can access the buttons necessary to create macros for the Spa workbook.

E08.16

 To Add the Developer Tab to the Ribbon

a. Click the **FILE** tab, click **Options**, and then click **Customize Ribbon**.

b. In the **Main Tabs** list, click the **Developer** check box, and then click **OK**.

c. Click **Save** 🔲.

Creating an Absolute Macro Reference

As with cell references in formulas, cell references in macros can be absolute or relative. **Absolute macro references** affect exactly the same cell address every time the macro is run. Absolute macro references are set when the macro is recorded. The location of the active cell when the macro is run is irrelevant. Macros are recorded with absolute references by default.

In the Spa workbook, you will record a macro to clear the current data but leave all the formulas necessary for the invoice to calculate correctly.

E08.17

 To Record an Absolute Macro

a. Click the **Invoice** worksheet, on the **DEVELOPER** tab, in the **Code** group, click **Record Macro**.

b. In the **Macro Name** box, type ClearCells. In the **Shortcut key** box**,** type c. In the **Description** box, type To clear contents from cells.

Record Macro on Developer tab

Macro name

Macro shortcut key

Macro description

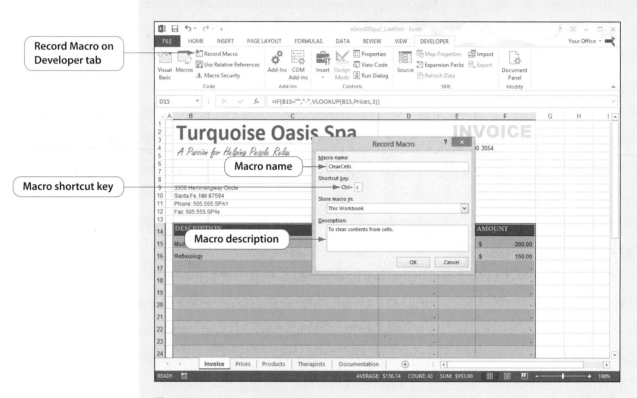

Figure 16 Macro dialog box

c. Click **OK**. Select cell **E6**, press and hold Ctrl, and then select cells **E8**, **E10**, **E12**, **C31**, **B15:B30**, and **E15:E30**.

d. On the **HOME** tab, in the **Editing** group, click **Clear**, and then select **Clear Contents**. Press Ctrl+Home.

e. On the **DEVELOPER** tab, in the **Code** group, click **Stop Recording**.

f. Click the **FILE** tab, click **Save**, and then click **No**. To save the macro, you will have to save the workbook as a macro-enabled workbook.

g. In the Save As dialog box, in the **File name** box, type e04ws08SpaMacro_LastFirst, using your first and last name. Click the **Save as type** box, and then select **Excel Macro-Enabled Workbook**. Click **Save**.

You should always test your macro to make sure it works. You can add data to the invoice, then run the macro to see if it works correctly.

REAL WORLD ADVICE | A Macro Cannot Be Undone

The effects of a macro cannot be reversed using the Undo feature. In fact, running a macro in Excel deletes the entire Undo history. If the macro is relatively simple, the easiest way to "fix" it is to delete it and start over again! The other option, discussed in the "Working with Relative Macro References" section that follows, is to modify the program in the VBA editor. This requires some knowledge of programming, so for most users, deleting the macro and starting over is generally the simplest option.

Working with Relative Macro References

Relative macro references identify cells relative to the location of the active cell when the macro was recorded. Whereas an absolute macro reference will always make changes to the same cells whenever the macro is run, a relative macro reference will make changes to the cells relative to where the active cell is located.

For example, if you want to change the formatting of the cell you are on and the cell to the right of the cell you are on, then you would record a relative macro. This way, regardless of which cell is active, the macro will affect that cell and the cell to the right of it.

When a customer is charged a special price, the spa likes to highlight that invoice item. In the Spa workbook, you will create a macro to highlight a row in the invoice.

C3, B29, A7:A26, C7:I26

E08.18

 To Record a Relative Macro

a. Select cell **B15**, click the **selection** arrow, and choose **Facial – Mud & Citrus**. Select cell **E15**, type **1**, and then press Ctrl+Enter.

b. Select cell **B15**. Click the **DEVELOPER** tab, in the **Code** group, click **Use Relative References**. This will toggle the Use Relative References button on, which is evident by the color the button changes to.

c. Click **Record Macro**, type HighlightItem for the macro name, and then assign h for the shortcut key. In the macro description, type To highlight an invoice special. and then click **OK**.

d. Select cells **B15:F15**, on the **HOME** tab, in the **Font** group, click **Bold** B, click the **Font Size** arrow, and then select **14**.

e. Click the **DEVELOPER** tab, in the **Code** group, click **Stop Recording**.
    You should always test your macro to make sure it works. You can add data to cells B16:F16 and run the macro to see if it makes the range of cells bold and a larger font size.

f. Click **Save** 🖫.

Adding a Macro to a Button

Macros can be run using the keyboard shortcuts you apply when first creating the macro, from the Developer tab, or even from a button that you can add to a worksheet. A button makes it easy for a user to run a macro with little or no knowledge about how a macro works.

In the Spa workbook, you will create a macro button to run the ClearCells macro.

To Create a Macro Button

SIDE NOTE
Running a Macro from the Ribbon

To run a macro from the Ribbon, on the Developer tab, in the Code group, click Macros, select the macro name, and click Run.

a. Click the **DEVELOPER** tab, in the **Controls** group, click **Insert**, and then select **Button (Form Control)** 🔲. Click in the top-left corner of cell **G2**, and then drag to the bottom-right corner of cell **H3** to draw the button.

b. Under Macro name, click **ClearCells**.

> **Troubleshooting**
> Be very careful once you create a button to run a macro. Even when editing the button and its properties, if you left-click the button the macro will run.

c. Click **OK**. Right-click the button, select **Edit Text**, delete the text, and type Clear Invoice. Right-click the button, and then select **Exit Edit Text**.

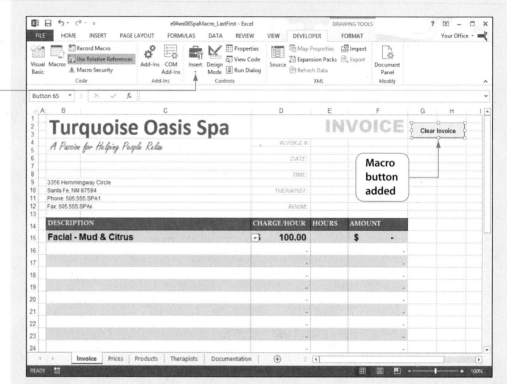

Figure 17   Macro button on the worksheet

d. Select cell **G5** to deselect the button. Click the button to run the macro, and verify the data in the invoice, for cells B15 and E15, is cleared.

The clear cells macro in this example clears the contents of the cells, but not the formatting, so the special formatting you applied with the HighlightItem macro is still applied to cells B15:F15. You will modify the macro in the next section to format the cells back to Arial font size 9 without bold formatting.

e. Click **Save** 💾.

Modifying a Macro

If you make a mistake when recording a macro, you can delete the macro and record a new one, or if you know VBA you can edit a macro and change the VBA that Excel produced.

In the Spa workbook, you will edit the ClearCells macro to format the invoice area as Arial font size 9 without bold, in order to delete the special formatting you added with the HighlightItem macro. Without knowing the VBA language, you will record a new macro with the steps to change the formatting and then copy and paste the new macro steps into the existing ClearCells macro.

E08.20

 To Modify a Macro Using VBA

a. Click the **DEVELOPER** tab, in the **Code** group, click **Record Macro**. Name the macro ClearFormatting, and then assign a lowercase k to the shortcut key. For the description type To clear special highlighting from invoice and then click **OK**.

b. Select cells **B15:F30**. Click the **HOME** tab, in the **Font** group, click **Bold**. In the **Font** group, click the **Font Size** arrow, and then select **9**.

c. Click the **DEVELOPER** tab, in the **Code** group, click **Stop Recording**.

d. In the **Code** group, click **Macros**. Select **ClearCells**, and then click Edit.

A new VBA window opens with the actual code for the macro you recorded. Each macro you recorded will show in the window separated by a horizontal line.

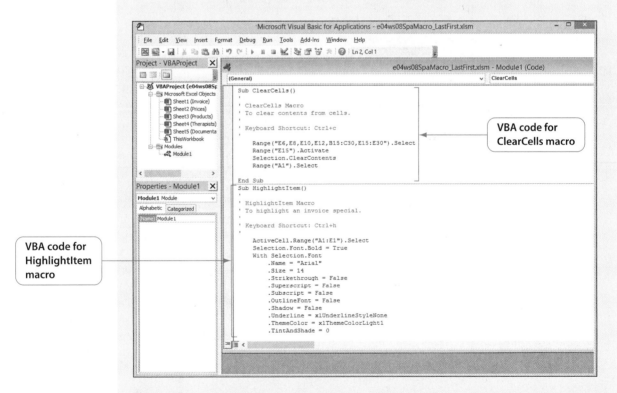

Figure 18 VBA window

e. Scroll to the bottom to see the ClearFormatting macro. Select the text that starts with **Range** and ends with **Selection.Font.Bold=False**, right-click, and then select **Copy**.

f. Scroll to the top to see the code for the ClearCells macro. Place your insertion point after the lines **Range ("A1").Select**, right-click, and then select **Paste**.

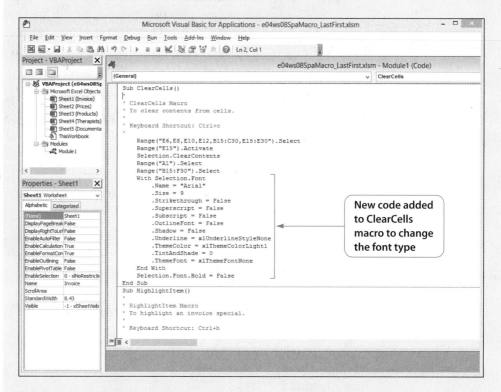

Figure 19   Edited VBA code

g. On the menu, click **File**, and then select **Close and Return to Microsoft Excel**. Your changes will be saved automatically and the VBA window will close.

   You can test your macros by selecting cell B15 and running the HighlightItem macro. Then click the Clear Invoice button to run the ClearCells macro and make sure that not only the cells were cleared but also that the font was changed back to its original formatting.

h. Click **Save** 🖫.

Change How to Navigate a Workbook

Workbook navigation is defined as moving from one cell to another in a worksheet and moving between worksheets. Assisting workbook users by adding navigational aids to a workbook and by hiding worksheets and features that are not needed by the user makes that workbook much more usable and easier to understand, and it makes its appearance much cleaner and less intimidating.

In the Spa workbook, you will add a hyperlink to navigate to a different worksheet, then hide unnecessary worksheets, worksheet tabs, scroll bars, row and column headings, and gridlines. This will give the invoice a cleaner look and make it look less like an Excel workbook.

Navigating with Hyperlinks

A **hyperlink** is a link that opens another page or file when you click it. In Excel, a hyperlink can open a worksheet, another workbook, a file, a picture, an e-mail address, a photo, a webpage, or another program. The hyperlink can be text or a picture and makes it easy for a user to get additional information that is in another location.

In the Spa workbook, there are multiple worksheets with information about the prices, products, and therapists. Since the charge/hour is automatically filled in based on the description the user chooses, you will add a hyperlink to that heading so the user can find more information about the charge/hour.

E08.21

 To Add Hyperlinks to the Workbook

a. Select cell **D14**, click the **INSERT** tab, in the **Links** group, click **Hyperlink**.

b. In the **Link to** box, select **Place in This Document**.

c. In the **Or select a place in this document** box, click **Prices**.

> **Troubleshooting**
> Click and hold on a cell that contains a hyperlink until the mouse pointer changes to ⊕, then the cell will be selected without accessing the hyperlink.

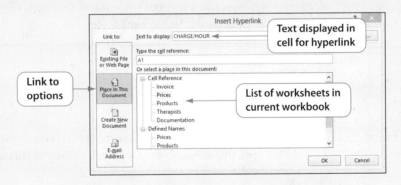

Figure 20   Inserting a hyperlink

d. Click **OK**.

The font color of the text in cell D14 will change to the default font color for a hyperlink. The text will also be underlined. If you click the text, Excel will display the Prices worksheet.

e. Click **Save** 🖫.

SIDE NOTE

Editing a Hyperlink
Right-click the hyperlink, and then select Edit Hyperlink.

Hiding Worksheets

A workbook with data stored in multiple worksheets can seem cluttered and difficult to navigate. There may be times when you would rather users not see data or have access to background calculations and code that has been placed in another worksheet. Since this data is often required for formulas, functions, and other calculations in a workbook, the worksheets can be hidden so a user cannot easily access them.

In the Spa workbook, you will hide the Therapists worksheet since the employee number is listed, which could be considered confidential information.

E08.22

 To Hide a Worksheet

a. Right-click the **Therapists** worksheet tab, and then click **Hide** from the shortcut menu. This will hide the worksheet so it can no longer be accessed by a worksheet tab.

b. Click **Save** 🖫.

SIDE NOTE
Unhide a Worksheet
Right-click any worksheet tab, select Unhide, select the name of the hidden worksheet, and click OK.

Hiding Worksheet Tabs

When you hide a worksheet, any hyperlinks to that worksheet will no longer work. Excel assumes if you want the data on the worksheet hidden, then you would not want access to the data through a hyperlink. However, if you do want to access the data on a worksheet through a hyperlink, but not through the worksheet tab, you can hide the worksheet tabs instead. Hiding worksheet tabs will affect the whole workbook and hide either all the worksheet tabs or none of the worksheet tabs. Once you hide the tabs, you have to show them again to continue navigating to individual worksheets, especially if you do not have hyperlinks set up to each worksheet.

In the Spa workbook, you will hide the worksheet tabs so the Charge/Hour link you created will still be functional but the tabs will not be visible. Because navigating back to the Invoice worksheet will be impossible if you click the Charge/Hour link, you will first add a hyperlink on the Prices worksheet to get back to the Invoice worksheet.

E08.23

 To Hide Worksheet Tabs

a. Click the **Prices** worksheet tab, select cell **F1**, click the **INSERT** tab, in the **Links** group, and then click **Hyperlink**. In the **Or select a place in this document** box, select **Invoice**, and then click **OK**.

b. Click the **Invoice** worksheet tab. Click the **FILE** tab, click **Options**, and then click **Advanced**. Scroll down until the **Display options for this workbook** group is visible.

SIDE NOTE
Show Worksheet Tabs
On the File tab, click Options, click Advanced, scroll down, and check Show sheet tabs. Click OK.

> **Troubleshooting**
> If the Invoice worksheet is not the active worksheet when you hide the worksheet tabs, you will have no way to get back to that worksheet if you do not have any hyperlinks set up. If this happens, repeat the steps to hide the worksheet tabs, check Show sheet tabs, and click OK.

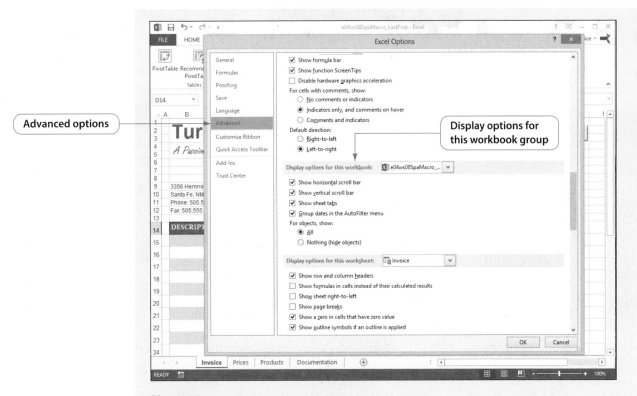

Advanced options

Display options for this workbook group

Figure 21 Display options for this workbook

c. Click **Show sheet tabs** to uncheck the option, and then click **OK**.

Notice that the sheet tabs at the bottom of the window are no longer visible.

d. Click **Save** 📄.

Hiding Scroll Bars

Depending on the size of the worksheet and the resolution of your monitor, vertical and/or horizontal scroll bars may or may not be necessary. You can choose to hide the scroll bars but should only do so if all cells will be visible on one screen, regardless of the screen size. This option will affect the whole workbook, not just one worksheet.

The Spa workbook does require some scrolling, but you will hide, and then unhide, the scroll bars as practice. You will be able to use your mouse to scroll or the keyboard arrows to scroll if necessary, but those will be your only ways to scroll with the scroll bars hidden.

E08.24

 To Hide Scroll Bars

a. Click the **FILE** tab, click **Options**, and then click **Advanced**. Scroll down until the **Display options for this workbook** group is visible. Click **Show horizontal scroll bar**, click **Show vertical scroll** bar to uncheck the options, and then click **OK**.

Notice that both scroll bars are gone from the application window, but you can still scroll with your mouse or the arrow keys on the keyboard. Assuming the invoice width fits and just the length is too long for the window, you will unhide the vertical scroll bar.

b. Click the **FILE** tab, click **Options**, and then click **Advanced**. Scroll down until the **Display options for this workbook** group is visible. Click **Show vertical scroll bar**, and then click **OK**.

c. Click **Save** 📄.

Some navigation options are for the whole workbook while some are for individual worksheets. When you are thinking about changing these options, you should carefully consider what each worksheet looks like and how the option will affect each worksheet. Hiding the scroll bars for one worksheet might be fine, but if another worksheet needs them to navigate, then you should probably not hide them. On the other hand, when you hide row and column headings, this is an option for each worksheet, so one worksheet can have them hidden while another worksheet can have them showing.

Hiding Row and Column Headings

Row and column headings are helpful when you are building a formula or even a workbook, but once the workbook is complete and ready to use for data entry, many times the row and column headings become unnecessary. This option is available for individual worksheets, so hiding them on one worksheet will not hide them on all the worksheets.

Data entry into the Spa workbook will not rely on cell references since the cells are well labeled. You will hide the row and column headings that will make the workbook look more like an invoice than an Excel workbook.

E08.25

▶ To Hide Row and Column Headings

SIDE NOTE

Display Row and Column Headings

Repeat Step a, and then in the Display options for this worksheet group, click Show row and column headers.

a. Click the **FILE** tab, click **Options**, and then click **Advanced**. Scroll down until the **Display options for this worksheet** group is visible, and then click **Show row and column headers** to uncheck the options.

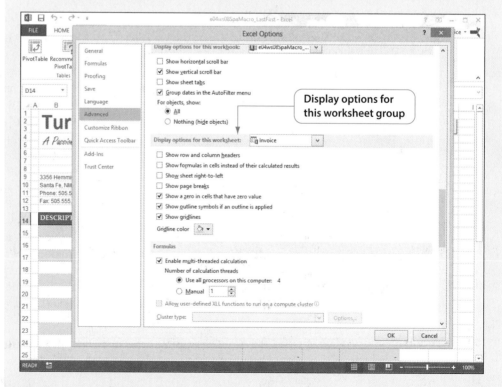

Figure 22 Display options for this worksheet

b. Click **OK**.

Notice that the column headers—A, B, C—and row numbers—1, 2, 3—are no longer showing.

c. Click **Save** 💾.

Hiding Gridlines

Gridlines are the vertical and horizontal lines on a worksheet that help define a cell's boundaries. Gridlines are helpful while you are creating a workbook, but they are not always necessary to use in a workbook. The gridlines you see when creating the workbook are not printed unless you select the print option to actually print the gridlines. This print option is still available even if the gridlines are hidden on the workbook.

The Spa workbook has little need for gridlines since most of the areas for data entry are clearly marked, therefore you will hide the gridlines.

E08.26

 To Hide Gridlines

a. Click the **VIEW** tab, in the **Show** group, click **Gridlines** to deselect this option.

b. Click **Save** 💾.

SIDE NOTE

How to Display Gridlines

On the View tab, in the Show group, click Gridlines.

Protect Workbooks and Worksheets

Once a workbook or worksheet has been developed and tested, but before you give it to other users, you may want to protect parts of the workbook that users should not be able to change. If a user clicks on a cell that contains a formula and inadvertently presses Delete, a critical part of the application could be erased. Unless the user thinks quickly enough to undo the mistake, the Excel application could be broken.

Excel allows for protection of applications in two layers: the workbook level to control who has access to the workbook, and the worksheet level to protect worksheets from alteration. Ideally, only users who are authorized to use a workbook can access it, and only those who are authorized can change the contents of cells or change worksheet structures where appropriate.

At the worksheet level, there are many options available to customize the type of editing that will be allowed on the worksheet. These options are described in the following Quick Reference.

When an option in the Protect Sheet dialog box is checked, that option will be allowed when the worksheet is protected. By default, only the first two options listed here are allowed when the worksheet is protected. The Protect Sheet dialog box lists the following options.

- **Select locked cells**—This is selected by default and allows the user to select cells with the Locked check box selected in the Format Cells dialog box.

- **Select unlocked cells**—This is also selected by default and allows the user to select cells with the Locked check box cleared in the Format Cells dialog box.

- **Format cells**—Enables all items in the Format cells dialog box, as well as conditional formatting. However, the Protection tab and Merge Cells command remain unavailable.

- **Format columns**—Enables every item in the Column submenu of the Format menu.

- **Format rows**—Enables every item in the Row submenu of the Format menu.

- **Insert columns**—Allows a user to insert columns.

- **Insert rows**—Allows a user to insert rows.

- **Insert hyperlinks**—Allows a user to insert hyperlinks.

- **Delete columns**—Allows a user to delete any column that does not contain a locked cell.

- **Delete rows**—Allows a user to delete any row that does not contain a locked cell.

- **Sort**—Enables the Sort option on the Data tab for data in a range that does not contain a locked cell.

- **Use AutoFilter**—Allows a user to change filter criteria for an existing filter, but not add or delete a filter.

- **Use PivotTable & PivotChart**—Allows a user to make changes to an existing PivotTable or PivotChart.

- **Edit objects**—Removes any protection from an object except any related to the object's properties.

- **Edit scenarios**—Removes protection from scenarios.

Protection at the workbook level is not nearly as flexible as is protection at the worksheet level. Worksheet protection allows many options for protection at the individual cell level, whereas workbook protection only allows you to require a password to open a worksheet, to lock down the structure of the workbook—prohibiting adding, deleting, or moving worksheets, and to mark a workbook as Final, which tells users the worksheet they are using is the final version intended for their use.

Any user can turn the worksheet or workbook protection on or off. This means, you may want to use a password when you turn on protection. Passwords are case sensitive, can be up to 256 characters in length, and can contain letters, numbers, and symbols such as #,$,!—basically any character than can be entered via the keyboard.

However, there is no way to retrieve this password if you forget what it is. This means, if you forget the password, you will not be able to turn the protection off and edit your worksheet or workbook again!

Unlocking Cells

By default, all cells in a worksheet are locked. This does not affect your worksheet until you turn on worksheet protection. Once Protect Sheet is turned on, locked cells cannot be edited. To allow editing, the cells must be unlocked before the protection is turned on.

The Spa workbook has some cells that should be locked and protected, and it has some cells that the user will need to enter data into. You will unlock the cells that require data entry and then protect the worksheet, but without a password. First you will show the row and column headers to make your navigation of the worksheet easier.

E08.27

To Unlock Cells and Protect a Sheet

a. Click the **FILE** tab, select **Options**, and then click **Advanced**. Scroll down to **Display options for this worksheet**, click **Show row and column headers**, and then click **OK**.

b. Select cell **E6**, press and hold Ctrl, and then select cells **E8**, **E10**, **E12**, **D14**, **C31**, and **F34** and cell ranges **B15:B30** and **E15:E30**. On the **HOME** tab, in the **Cells** group, click **Format**, and then select **Lock Cell**. This unlocks the selected cells.

For the hyperlink in cell D14 to work, the cell must be unlocked.

(handwritten: C3, B29, A1:A26, C7:I26)

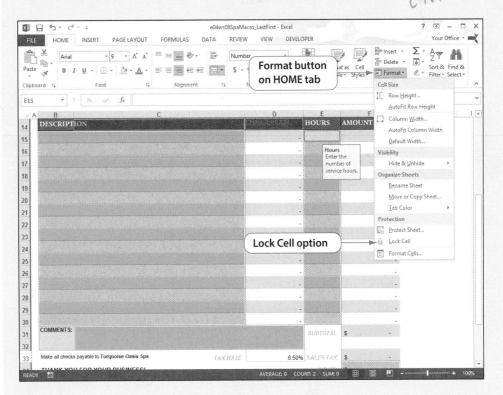

Figure 23 Lock cell option on the Format button

c. In the Cells group, click **Format**, and then select **Protect Sheet**. Uncheck the **Select locked cells** check box.

Select locked cells option unchecked

Figure 24 Select locked cells option

d. Click **OK**, click cell **B20**, and then press [Home].

Notice that the function of [Home] changes when the sheet is protected. Rather than move the active cell to column A of the current row, it moves the active cell to the top-most and left-most unlocked cell in the worksheet, in this case, cell E6.

e. Click **Save** [💾].

Hiding Formulas

When a worksheet is protected, if cells with formulas are locked, then they cannot be selected. Therefore, if they contain a formula, that formula cannot be viewed in the formula bar. However, a user could still use the Show Formulas button on the Formulas tab to view the formula in a locked cell.

To completely hide formulas in a worksheet is a three-step process:

1. Select all cells in which you want to hide formulas.
2. Hide the formulas.
3. Leave all cells that contain formulas locked, and then protect the worksheet with Select locked cells unchecked.

These three steps must be performed in this order, since once Protect Sheet is toggled on, the Format button on the Home tab will not be available.

In the Spa workbook, you will have to unprotect the worksheet to make any changes. Then you will hide all the cells in the workbook rather than selecting individual cells with formulas since there are so many. Then you will protect the worksheet again.

E08.28

 To Hide Formulas

a. Click the **HOME** tab, in the **Cells** group, click **Format**, and then select **Unprotect Sheet**.

b. Click the **FILE** tab, click **Options**, click **Advanced**, scroll down, and then under **Display options for this workbook** click **Show horizontal scroll bar**. Click **OK**.

c. On the **FORMULAS** tab, in the **Formula Auditing** group, click **Show Formulas** [🔢]. Scroll to the right to see the cells with formulas.

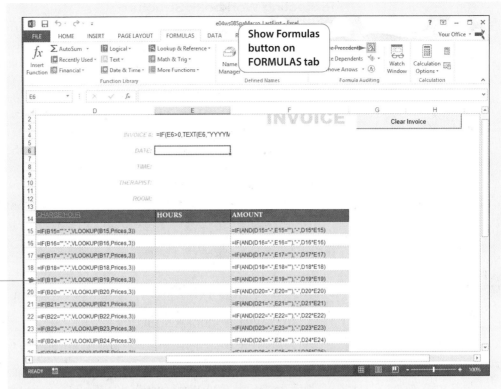

Show Formulas button on FORMULAS tab

Formulas showing in worksheet

Figure 25 Worksheet with formulas showing

Hide
B7:B26, J7:J27,
C27: 128

d. Select cell **E4**, press and hold ⌃Ctrl⌄ and select cells **D15:D30**, **F15:F30**, **F31**, **F33**, and **F35**. Click the **HOME** tab, in the Cells group, click **Format**, and then select **Format Cells**.

e. Click the **Protection** tab, and then click **Hidden**. Click **OK**.

f. In the Cells group, click **Format**, click **Protect Sheet**, and then click **OK**.
   Notice that formulas are no longer displayed. All cells that contain formulas are locked, so viewing formulas in the formula bar is not possible. The Show Formulas button will toggle on, but the formulas still will not be visible.

g. Click the **FORMULAS** tab, in the **Formula Auditing** group, click **Show Formulas**. This will resize the columns to their normal width when the formulas are not showing.

h. Click the **FILE** tab, click **Options**, and then click **Advanced**. Scroll down to the **Display options for this worksheet**, and then click the **Show horizontal scroll bar** check box. Scroll down, click the **Show row and column headers** check box, and then click **OK**.

i. Click **Save** 🖫.

CONSIDER THIS | **Changing Navigation Tools and Other Features**

By hiding areas of the workbook, including gridlines, row and column headings, and scroll bars, as well as hiding, protecting, and locking cells certainly makes your workbook more secure. Users who are not familiar with Excel may appreciate these enhancements because it makes navigating and using the workbook simpler and often less intimidating. When you are deciding which features to hide and lock, take into consideration your end user. If your user is more advanced in Excel, could you see any frustrations they may encounter when working with a protected and locked workbook? What features might be more helpful to them and which would be less helpful?

Protecting Workbook Structure

Protecting the workbook structure stops users from inserting, deleting, hiding, unhiding, and moving worksheets in a workbook. If a user accidentally deletes a formula from a cell, and if the user recognizes the error, Undo can be used to fix the problem. But Undo cannot undelete a worksheet that has been deleted.

Further, if a user decides to rename a worksheet, any unopened workbook that accesses data in the renamed worksheet will have its 3D references broken, and Undo will not fix it. If a worksheet in your workbook is accessed by other workbooks and you want to ensure that a user cannot delete or rename a critical worksheet, using Protect Workbook Structure will secure the worksheets and their names.

Protecting the workbook structure has an optional password. Like the worksheet protection password, if the password is lost, then the protection cannot be turned off. Use passwords with caution.

In the Spa workbook, even though the worksheet tabs are hidden, you will protect the workbook structure.

E08.29

 To Protect Workbook Structure

a. Click the **REVIEW** tab, in the **Changes** group, click **Protect Workbook**.

b. Verify that **Structure** is checked, and then click **OK**. You will not add a password for this exercise. On the REVIEW tab, notice that the Protect Workbook button is now toggled on—it is a different color.

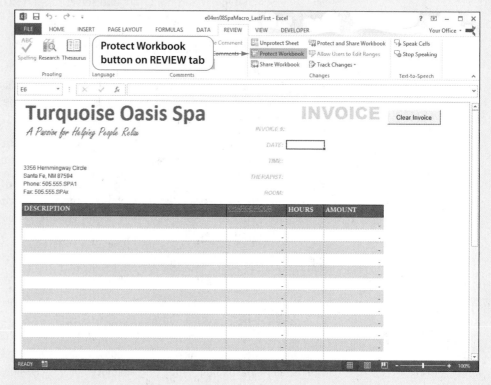

Figure 26   Protect Workbook button

c. Click **Save** 🖫.

SIDE NOTE
Turn Off Workbook Protection
To turn off workbook protection, on the Review tab, in the Changes group, click Protect Workbook.

Encrypting a Workbook

The highest level of protection is to encrypt the workbook with a password; this prevents the workbook from being opened without the password. When a password is entered into the Encrypt Document dialog box, the workbook is encrypted when it is saved. **Encryption** uses a password to create code that is used to translate the saved Excel workbook into a stream of uninterpretable characters that can only be translated back using the password. For the user, the net result is that after a workbook has been saved with an encryption password, the password is required to open the workbook again.

Again, use caution when assigning passwords. If a password is lost, the workbook cannot be opened.

For the Spa workbook, you will encrypt the workbook with a password and then remove it.

E08.30

 To Encrypt a Workbook

a. Click the **FILE** tab, click **Protect Workbook**, and then select **Encrypt with Password**.

b. In the Encrypt Document dialog box, type spainvoice in the Password box. In Excel, passwords are case sensitive, so type very carefully.

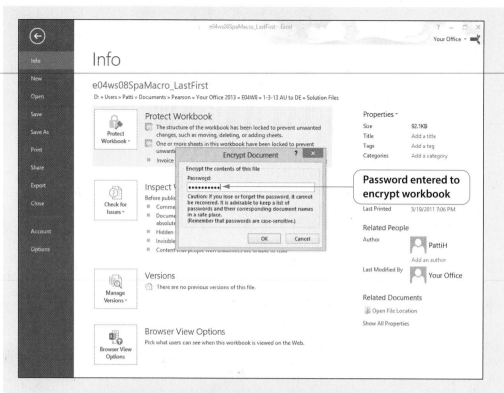

Figure 27 Encrypt a workbook with a password

c. Click **OK**, and then type spainvoice again. Click **OK**. When you close and open the workbook, you will be prompted for the password.

d. Click **Save** 💾.

Marking a Workbook as a Final Draft

When you are creating a workbook for someone else to use and have the final version complete, it is helpful to use the Mark as Final option to indicate the workbook is complete and ready for use. Mark as Final is a very weak form of protection, however. Even though a workbook has been marked as final, users are given the option to Edit Anyway. Mark as Final really represents a means of communicating the development status of a workbook. A workbook that has been marked as final will display the Marked as Final ✎ icon on the status bar.

Once a workbook has been marked as final, other workbook protection functionality cannot be changed until the Mark as Final is turned off.

As the final step to creating the Spa workbook, you will mark this version as final.

E08.31

 To Mark a Workbook as Final

a. Click the **FILE** tab, click **Protect Workbook**, and then select **Mark as Final**. Click **OK** in the alert box, and then click **OK** in the next alert box.

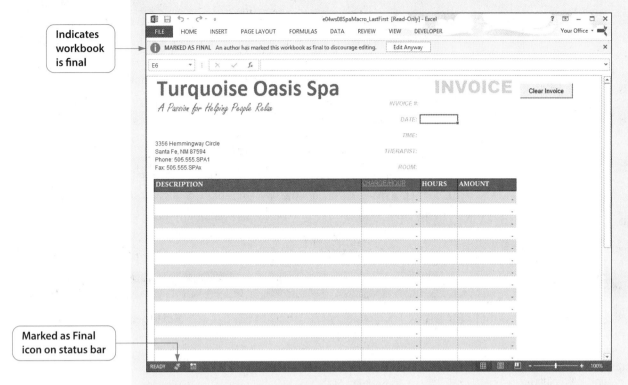

Figure 28 Mark workbook as final copy

b. Click the **FILE** tab, and then notice that the description under Protect Workbook says the workbook is marked as final.

Figure 29 Workbook marked as final

c. Click **Close** ⊠ to close the workbook, and then close Excel.

1. What are precedents and dependents, and why is it important to be able to trace them? p. 412

2. When would you use the Evaluate Formulas tool? What does the tool do? p. 414

3. What is a circular reference? How do you know if your workbook has a circular reference? p. 414

4. What is the Watch Window? When would it be beneficial to have a Watch Window open? p. 416

5. How does data validation work? Why would you use it? p. 417

6. What is a macro? What are the two kinds of macros, and how are they different? p. 430

7. Why would you want to turn off the navigational features of a workbook? p. 436

8. What is the difference between protecting a workbook structure and protecting a worksheet? p. 441

Key Terms

Absolute macro reference 431
Any value validation 424
Circular reference 414
Codification scheme 426
Codified data value 425
Custom validation 425
Data validation 417
Date validation 420
Decimal validation 420
Dependent cell 412
Developer tab 431

Encryption 447
Error Message 418
Evaluate Formula 414
Gridlines 441
Hyperlink 437
Input Message 418
List validation 418
Macro 430
Precedent cell 412
Relative macro reference 433
Text length validation 423

Text-to-speech 428
Time validation 421
Trace dependents 412
Trace precedents 412
Trusted Location 430
Validation criteria 417
Visual Basic for Applications (VBA) 430
Watch Window 416
Whole number validation 422

Visual Summary

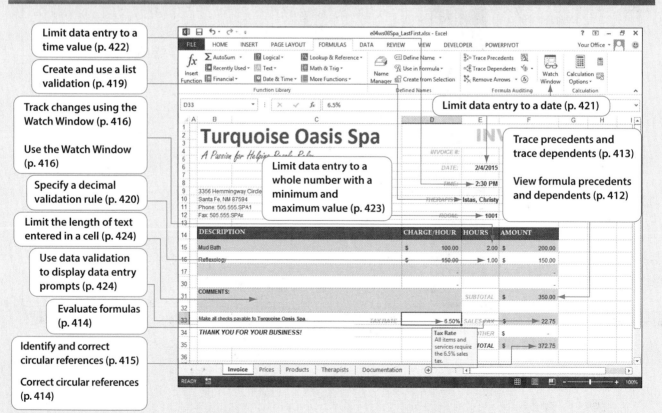

Limit data entry to a time value (p. 422)

Create and use a list validation (p. 419)

Track changes using the Watch Window (p. 416)

Use the Watch Window (p. 416)

Specify a decimal validation rule (p. 420)

Limit the length of text entered in a cell (p. 424)

Use data validation to display data entry prompts (p. 424)

Evaluate formulas (p. 414)

Identify and correct circular references (p. 415)

Correct circular references (p. 414)

Limit data entry to a date (p. 421)

Trace precedents and trace dependents (p. 413)

View formula precedents and dependents (p. 412)

Limit data entry to a whole number with a minimum and maximum value (p. 423)

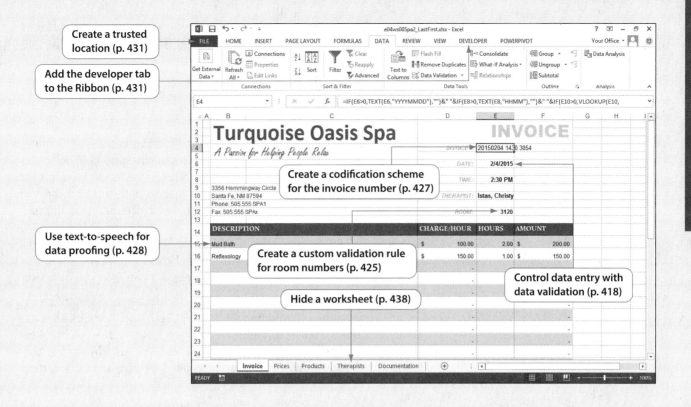

Create a trusted location (p. 431)

Add the developer tab to the Ribbon (p. 431)

Create a codification scheme for the invoice number (p. 427)

Use text-to-speech for data proofing (p. 428)

Create a custom validation rule for room numbers (p. 425)

Control data entry with data validation (p. 418)

Hide a worksheet (p. 438)

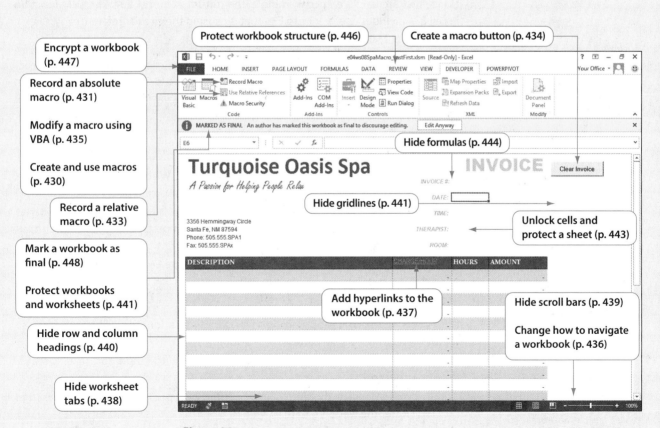

Protect workbook structure (p. 446)

Create a macro button (p. 434)

Encrypt a workbook (p. 447)

Record an absolute macro (p. 431)

Modify a macro using VBA (p. 435)

Create and use macros (p. 430)

Record a relative macro (p. 433)

Mark a workbook as final (p. 448)

Protect workbooks and worksheets (p. 441)

Hide row and column headings (p. 440)

Hide worksheet tabs (p. 438)

Hide formulas (p. 444)

Hide gridlines (p. 441)

Unlock cells and protect a sheet (p. 443)

Add hyperlinks to the workbook (p. 437)

Hide scroll bars (p. 439)

Change how to navigate a workbook (p. 436)

Figure 30   Turquoise Oasis Spa Application Final

Practice 1

Student data file needed:

e04ws08Wedding.xlsx

You will save your file as: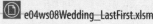

e04ws08Wedding_LastFirst.xlsm

Painted Paradise Resort Wedding Planner

Finance & Accounting

Painted Paradise Resort has a wedding chapel and reception facilities capable of handling 300 people. Wedding guests stay in the hotel, dine in the restaurant, play golf, go to the spa, shop in the gift shop—often use a wedding as an opportunity to stay at the resort for a weekend. The resort is becoming a popular wedding destination, and Patti Rochelle, the events manager, has been trying to update a workbook she uses to generate wedding cost estimates for prospective clients.

She has an attractive and functional design developed. The calculations are pretty much handled; however, her worksheet still requires a lot of manual data entry, and she would like a macro to clear data from the wedding planner after an estimate has been generated and printed.

a. Start **Excel**, and then open **e04ws08Wedding**. Click the **FILE** tab, and then click **Save As**. In the Save As dialog box, navigate to the location where you are saving your files, and then in the File name box, type e04ws08Wedding_LastFirst, using your first and last name. Select **Excel Macro-Enabled Workbook** in the Save as type box, and then click **Save**.

b. Select the estimated cost total in cell **E34**. On the **FORMULAS** tab, in the **Formula Auditing** group, click **Trace Precedents**.

  • Notice the Circular Reference warning in the status bar for cell E34. The SUM function in cell E34 includes a reference to E34 that is causing the circular reference.

  • Click in the **formula bar**, and then change **E34** to E32.

c. On the **FORMULAS** tab, in the **Formula Auditing** group, click **Watch Window**. Select cells **E16**, **E21**, **E25**, **E28**, **E32**, and **E34**, and then click **Add Watch**. In the Add Watch dialog box, click **Add**. Verify the cells were added to the Watch Window, and then close the Watch Window.

d. Select cell **C8**. On the **DATA** tab, in the **Data Tools** group, click **Data Validation**. You will create a rule so the number entered is between 25 and 300.

  • Click the **Settings** tab, and in the **Allow** box, select **Whole number**. In the **Data** box, verify that **between** is selected. In the **Minimum** box, type 25 and then in the **Maximum** box type 300.

  • Click the **Input Message** tab, and then in the **Title** box type Guests. In the **Input message** box, type Enter the estimated number of guests.

  • Click the **Error Alert** tab, and then in the **Title** box type Error. In the **Error message** box, type The number of guests is not valid. and then click **OK**.

  • In cell **C8** type 150.

e. Select cell **C10**. In the Data Tools group, click **Data Validation**. You will create a rule so the date entered must be the current date or later.

  • Click the **Settings** tab. In the **Allow** box, select **Date**. In the **Data** box, select **greater than or equal to**. In the **Start date** box type =TODAY().

  • Click the **Input Message** tab, and then in the Title box type Date. In the **Input message** box, type Enter the wedding date.

  • Click the **Error Alert** tab, and then in the **Title** box, type Error. In the **Error message** box, type The wedding date must be today or later. and then click **OK**.

  • In cell **C10**, type =TODAY().

f. Select cell **C11**. In the Data Tools group, click **Data Validation**. You will create a rule so the time entered must be between 10:00 AM and 8:00 PM.

- Click the **Settings** tab, and then in the **Allow** box select **Time**. In the **Data** box, select **between**. In the **Start time** box, type 10:00 AM and then in the **End time** box, type 8:00 PM.
- Click the **Input Message** tab, and then in the **Title** box, type Time. In the **Input message** box, type Enter the wedding start time.
- Click the **Error Alert** tab, and then in the **Title** box, type Error. In the **Error message** box, type The start time must be between 10:00 am and 8:00 pm. and then click **OK**.
- In cell **C11**, type 2:00 PM.

g. Select cells **C20:C21**. In the Data Tools group, click **Data Validation**. You will create a rule so the data entered must come from a list of cells on the Parameters worksheet.

- Click the **Settings** tab, and then in the **Allow** box, select **List**. Click the **Source** box, click the **Parameters** worksheet tab, and then select cells **A9:A10**.
- Click the **Input Message** tab, and then in the **Title** box, type Amenities. In the **Input message** box, type Select an option from the list. and then click **OK**.
- In cell **C20**, click the arrow, and then select **Standard**.
- In cell **C21**, click the arrow, and then select **Deluxe**.

h. Select cell **F10**. In the Data Tools group, click **Data Validation**. You will create a custom rule so the room number entered must have two digits, start with the number 1 or 2, and end with a number less than 7; the room numbers available are 10–16 and 20–26.

- Click the **Settings** tab. In the **Allow** box, select **Custom**. Click the **Formula** box, then type =AND(LEFT(F10,1)<="2",LEFT(F10,1)>="1",RIGHT(F10,2)<="7").
- You will not add an Input message for this cell. Click the **Error Alert** tab. In the **Title** box, type Room #. In the **Error message** box, type Invalid room number. Click **OK**.
- In cell **F10**, type 15.

i. If necessary, add the DEVELOPER tab to the Ribbon.

- Click the **FILE** tab, click **Options**, click **Customize Ribbon**, and then under **Customize the Ribbon**, check **Developer**. Click **OK**.

j. Assign the folder where you save your student files as a trusted location.

- Click the **FILE** tab, click **Options**, click **Trust Center**, click **Trust Center Settings**, and then click **Trusted Locations**.
- Click **Add new location**, browse to the folder where you save your student files, and then click **OK**. Click **OK** again, and then click **OK** again.

k. On the **DEVELOPER** tab, in the **Code** group, click **Record Macro**.

- In the **Macro name** box type ClearContents. In the **Shortcut key** box, type c. In the **Description**, type Delete all user-entered data from the worksheet. and then click **OK**.
- Select cells **C5:C6**, press and hold Ctrl, and then select cells **C8**, **C10:C11**, **C20:C21**, **C24:C25**, ,**C28**, and **F10**. Press Delete.
- Select cell **C5**. On the **DEVELOPER** tab, in the Code group, click **Stop Recording**.

l. Click **Undo** to undo the changes you made recording the macro.

m. On the **DEVELOPER** tab, in the **Controls** group, click **Insert**, and then select **Button (Form Control)**.

- Click in the top-left corner of cell **E5** next to the Bride's name, and then drag to the bottom-right corner of cell **F6** to size and add the button.
- Select **ClearContents**, and then click **OK**.
- Right-click the button, and then select **Edit Text**. Delete the current text, and then type Clear Cells. Right-click the button, and then select **Exit Edit Text**.

n. Select cell **B19**. On the **INSERT** tab, in the **Links** group, click **Hyperlink**.

- Select **Place in This Document**, and then select **Parameters**. Click **OK**.
- Click the **Parameters** worksheet. Select cell **D15**, and then insert a **Hyperlink** back to the **Wedding_Planner** worksheet.

o. Click the **Documentation** worksheet. Click cell **A6**, and then type in today's date. Click cell **B6**, and then type in your first and last name. Complete the remainder of the Documentation worksheet according to your instructor's direction. Right-click the **Documentation** worksheet tab, and then select **Hide**.

p. On the Wedding Planner worksheet, select cells **C5:C6**, **C8**, **C10:C11**, **F10**, **C20:C21**, **C24:C25**, and **C28**—the cells are all formatted with gray where the data is entered. On the **HOME** tab, in the **Cells** group, click **Format**, and then select **Lock Cell**.

q. Click the **FILE** tab, click **Options**, click **Advanced**, and do the following:

- Scroll down to **Display options for this workbook**, and then click **Show horizontal scroll bar**.
- Scroll down to **Display options for this worksheet**, and then click **Show row and column headers**. Click **OK**.

r. On the **VIEW** tab, in the **Show** group, click **Gridlines**.

s. On the **FORMULAS** tab, in the **Formula Auditing** group, click **Show Formulas**.

- Select all the **cells** that show a formula.
- On the **HOME** tab, in the **Cells** group, click **Format**, select **Format Cells**, click the **Protection** tab, and then click **Hidden**. Click **OK**.
- On the **FORMULAS** tab, in the **Formula Auditing** group, click **Show Formulas**.

t. On the **HOME** tab, in the **Cells** group, click **Format**, and then select **Protect Sheet**. Click **Select locked cells** to uncheck the option, and then click **OK**.

u. On the **REVIEW** tab, in the **Changes** group, click **Protect Workbook**, verify **Structure** is selected, and then click **OK**.

v. Click the **FILE** tab, click **Protect Workbook**, and then select **Mark as Final**. Click **OK** to save the workbook, click **OK** again, and then close Excel. Submit your file as directed by your instructor.

Problem Solve 1

Finance & Accounting

Student data file needed:

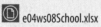 e04ws08School.xlsx

You will save your file as:

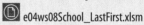 e04ws08School_LastFirst.xlsm

School Athletic Budget

The athletic director at the local high school has been given a worksheet to track revenue and expenses on a trial basis for the next six months. He is not at all computer literate and is terrified to use the workbook on a regular basis, so he has asked you to help modify the workbook so he knows exactly what to enter and the chances of deleting important formulas is minimized as much as possible.

You will create a Watch Window, validation rules, and macros to make data entry as simple as possible. Then you will protect the worksheet and the workbook structure, as well as hide all the formulas, so the chance of deleting critical cells is minimized. Finally you will mark the workbook as final so when you send it to the athletic director, he knows it is the version he should be using.

a. Start **Excel**, and then open **e04ws08School**. Save the workbook as a Macro-Enabled Workbook named e04ws08School_LastFirst. Click **OK** at the circular error message; you will correct this in Step b.

b. Use **Trace Precedents** to illustrate the circular reference error in cell **E33**. Correct the formula in cell E33 by entering the correct cell range; the SUM function should add cells E6:E32.

c. Create a **Watch Window** to view cells **E33**, **F33**, **G33**, and **H33**.

d. Add data validation to cell **G1** that allows values from a list with the source data from cells **B15:B19** on the **List Data** worksheet. The Input Message should have a title Reported By and a message that says Choose a name from the list. The Error Alert should have a title that says Error and an Error message that says Please choose a name from the list.

e. Add data validation to cell **G2** that only allows today's date or earlier. Use the function =TODAY(). There will be no input message, but the Error Alert should have a title Incorrect Date, and the Error message should say Date must be today or earlier.

f. Add data validation to cell **G3** with only an Input Message that says Please enter a time in the flowing format: HH:MM AM/PM.

g. Add data validation to cell **C34** to limit the length of the text to 200 characters. Only include an Error message that says Comments cannot exceed 200 characters.

h. Add a formula to cell **G4** that creates a Report ID from the date and the ID number on the List Data worksheet of the person who made the report. The formula will include an IF function, the TEXT function, and a VLOOKUP function.

i. Insert a hyperlink in cell **D3** on the **Budget Data Entry** worksheet that links to the **List Data** worksheet. Insert a hyperlink in cell **E1** on the **List Data** worksheet that links to the **Budget Data Entry** worksheet.

j. Click the **FILE** tab, add a **Text-to-Speech** group to the **REVIEW** tab, and then include the **Speak Cells** and **Stop Speaking** buttons.

k. If necessary, add the **DEVELOPER** tab to the Ribbon. Create an absolute macro that will clear the contents of all cells that data is entered into by the user. This includes cells **G1:G3**, **B6:D32**, **F6:F32**, and **C34**. Make sure the cursor is back at the top right of the worksheet when the macro is run. Name the macro ClearContents and assign the letter c as the shortcut key.

l. Create a relative macro that will bold the font in a row of the report. The **Use Relative References** button should be toggled on before the macro is recorded. Name the macro BoldRow and then assign the letter b as the shortcut key.

m. Add a button in cell **H1** that will run the macro **BoldRow**. Change the text on the button to read Bold Row and then resize the button as necessary to read all the text.

n. In the **Format Cells** dialog box, unlock cells **G1:G3**, **B6:D32**, **D3**, **F6:F32**, and **C34**. In the Format Cells dialog box, hide all cells that have formulas: **G45**, **E6:E32**, **G6:H32**.

o. In the **Excel Options** dialog box, hide the **horizontal scroll bar**, the **row and column headers**, and the **sheet tabs**. On the **VIEW** tab, hide the gridlines. Protect the worksheet.

p. Enter the following data in the report:

    REPORTED BY: Jamie
    DATE ENTERED: =TODAY()
    TIME ENTERED: 2:00 PM

EXPENSE DATE	ITEM TYPE	EXPENSE ITEM	ACTUAL COST
1/3/2014	Revenue	Donations	2700
1/4/2014	Expense	Field Supplies	450
1/7/2014	Expense	Coach clinic/travel	275

q. Click the **Documentation** worksheet. Click cell **A6**, and then type in today's date. Click cell **B6**, and then type in your first and last name. Complete the remainder of the Documentation worksheet according to your instructor's direction. Mark the workbook as final, close Excel, and then submit your file as directed by your instructor.

Information
Technology

Student data file needed:

 e04ws08Running.xlsx

You will save your file as:

e04ws08Running_LastFirst.xlsm

Running Ahead

You have just started running with a new running group at your school. You want to track your progress, so your friend gives you an Excel workbook that she has created. Your friend is not comfortable with Excel and asks you to modify the workbook so they can only enter data in the appropriate cells, and they want to add consistent data. You take the workbook and make those changes so you can share the workbook with your friend as well as the whole group, even those not familiar with Excel.

a. Start **Excel**, and then open **e04ws08Running**. Save it as a macro-enabled workbook with the name **e04ws08Running_LastFirst**. Click **OK** at the error message; you will correct this in Step b.

b. Find and correct the circular reference in the worksheet. Hint: Use other formulas in the worksheet to determine what the correct formula should be.

c. In the **Log** worksheet, enter data validation rules in cells **A5:A10**, **B5:B10**, **E5:E10**, **F5:F10**, and **G5:G10**. Use the data on the **Data worksheet** tab for list values where appropriate.

d. Enter at least 5 rows of data to test your validation rules.

e. Enter at least one hyperlink on the **Log** worksheet to go to the **Data** worksheet, and then add another hyperlink on the **Data** worksheet to go to the **Log** worksheet. Use either existing text or add new text.

f. If necessary, add the **DEVELOPER** tab to the Ribbon. Create a relative **macro** to insert a new row in the table. Add a **button** to the **Log** worksheet to run the macro. Make sure all formulas are copied to any new rows where necessary.

g. Create an absolute macro to clear data from cells that do not contain formulas. Undo the changes you made while recording the macro so your data will still be recorded. Add a **button** to the **Log** worksheet to run the macro.

h. Remove all unnecessary navigation tools from the workbook.

i. Hide all formulas from view, protect the worksheet but allow users to enter data in appropriate fields, protect the structure of the workbook, and then mark the workbook as final. Do not add passwords. Make sure you can still use the hyperlinks to move from one worksheet to another (Hint: Unlock any cells with hyperlinks).

j. Save and close the workbook.

k. Complete the **Documentation** worksheet according to your instructor's direction. Insert the **filename** in the left custom footer section of the Header/Footer tab in the Page Setup dialog box on all worksheets in the workbook.

l. Click Save, close Excel, and then submit the file as directed by your instructor.

Additional
Cases

Additional Workshop Cases are available on the companion website and in the instructor resources.

MODULE CAPSTONE

Student data file needed:

 e04mpIndigo5.xlsx

You will save your file as:

 e04mpIndigo5_LastFirst.xlsm

Indigo5 Meal and Menu Tracking

Production & Operations

To help plan the menu at the Indigo5 restaurant, Alberto Dimas, the restaurant manager, would like to be able to see how many meals in each category are being sold each season. He has created a spreadsheet that has the meals broken down by season with the average price, average cost, and dishes sold for each category, but he is having trouble consolidating and summarizing the data. He would also like to include a form to fill out for estimates for special events. When guests plan a special event, they can pick up to four food categories. Based on the average prices of each category, Alberto would like an estimated cost for the event.

a. Start **Excel**, and then open the student data file **e04mpIndigo5.xlsx**. Click **OK** for the Circular Reference warning dialog box.

b. Click the **FILE** tab, and then save the file as an **Excel Macro-Enabled Workbook** in the location where you are saving your files with the name e04mpIndigo5_LastFirst using your first and last name.

c. Click the **Winter** worksheet tab, press and hold [Shift], and then click the **Fall** worksheet tab.

  - Right-click the **Winter** worksheet tab, point to **Tab Color**, and then select the standard color **Purple**.
  - On the **Winter** worksheet tab, click cell **A20**, and then type Total.
  - Select cell **D20**, and then type =SUM(D5:D19).
  - Select cells **A20:D20**, on the **HOME** tab, in the **Styles** group, click **Cell Styles**, and then select **Total**.
  - Right-click the **Winter** worksheet tab, and then select **Ungroup Sheets**.

d. Click the **YearSummary** worksheet tab. Click cell **D5**, type =SUM(, click the **Winter** worksheet tab, click **D5**, press and hold [Shift], click the **Fall** worksheet tab, type), and then press [Ctrl]+[Enter]. Use the **fill handle** to copy this formula to cells **D6:D19**.

  - Click the **Fall** worksheet tab, press and hold [Shift], and then click the **YearSummary** worksheet tab. In the Fall worksheet, select cells **D5:D19**, on the HOME tab, in the **Editing** group, click **Fill**, select **Across Worksheets**, click **Formats**, and then click **OK**.
  - On the **Fall** worksheet, select cells **A20:D20**, on the HOME tab, in the **Editing** group, click **Fill**, select **Across Worksheets**, verify **All** is selected, and then click **OK**.

e. Click the **YearSummaryLinked** worksheet tab.

  - Click cell **A5**, and then on the **DATA** tab, in the **Data Tools** group, click **Consolidate**. In the Consolidate dialog box, make sure **Sum** is selected in the Function box, and then click in the **Reference** box.
  - Click the **Winter** worksheet tab, select cell range **A4:D19**, and then click **Add**. Click the **Spring** worksheet tab, and then click **Add**. Click the **Summer** worksheet tab, and then click **Add**. Click the **Fall** worksheet tab, and then click **Add**.
  - Check the **Top row** box, check the **Left column** box, and then check the **Create links to source data box**. Click **OK**.

- Use the AutoFit feature on columns **A:E**, select cell **A5**, and then type Category.
- Select column **B**, on the **HOME** tab, in the **Cells** group, click **Format**, point to **Hide & Unhide**, and then select **Hide Columns**.

f. Click the **SpecialEvents** worksheet tab. Select cell **D15** (the estimated total). On the **FORMULAS** tab, in the **Formula Auditing** group, click **Trace Precedents**.
   - Notice the Circular Reference warning in the status bar for cell D15. The SUM function in cell D15 includes a reference to D15 which is causing the circular reference.
   - Click in the **formula bar**, and then change **D15** to D14.

g. On the **FORMULAS** tab, in the **Formula Auditing** group, click **Watch Window**. Select cells **B6**, **B8**, and **D15**, and then click **Add Watch**. Click **Add**, and then close the Watch Window.

h. Select cell **B8**. On the **DATA** tab, in the **Data Tools** group, click **Data Validation.** You will set a rule so the number entered is a whole number between 10 and 100.
   - Click the **Settings** tab, and in the **Allow** box, select **Whole number**. In the **Data** box, verify that **between** is selected. In the **Minimum** box, type 10 and then in the **Maximum** box type 100.
   - Click the **Input Message** tab. In the **Title** box type Guests and then in the **Input message** box type Enter the estimated number of guests.
   - Click the **Error Alert** tab. In the **Title** box type Error and then in the **Input message** box type The number of guests is not valid. Click **OK**.
   - In cell **B8** type 90.

i. Select cell **B6**. On the DATA tab, in the Data Tools group, click **Data Validation**. You will set a rule so the date entered must be after the current date.
   - Click the **Settings** tab. In the **Allow** box, select **Date**. In the **Data** box, select **greater than**. In the **Start date** box type =TODAY().
   - Click the **Input Message** tab. In the **Title** box, type Date. In the **Input message** box, type Enter event date.
   - Click the **Error Alert** tab. In the **Title** box, type Error. In the Error message box, type The date must be later than today. Click **OK**.
   - In cell **B6**, type =TODAY() +1. This will enter tomorrow's date.

j. Select cells **B11:B14**. On the DATA tab, in the **Data Tools** group, click **Data Validation**. You will set a rule so the data entered must come from a list of cells on the **YearSummary** worksheet.
   - Click the **Settings** tab. In the **Allow** box, select **List**. Click the **Source** box, click the **YearSummary** worksheet tab, and then select cells **A5:A19**.
   - Click the **Input Message** tab. In the **Title** box, type Category. In the **Input message** box, type Select an option from the list. Click **OK**.
   - Select cell **B11**, click the **arrow**, and then select **Appetizer**.
   - Select cell **B12**, click the **arrow**, and then select **Fish**.
   - Select cell **B13**, click the **arrow**, and then select **Poultry**.
   - Select cell **B14**, click the **arrow**, and then select **Desserts**.

k. You will enter a formula to create the Estimate No. based on the event date and season.
   - Select cell **E6**, and then type =IF(B6>0,TEXT(B6,"YYYYMMDD"),"")&B7. This will convert the date into text based on the format YYYYMMDD and add the text value entered in B7 to the end of it.
   - In cell **B7** select **Winter**.

l. Save your workbook.

m. If necessary, add the **DEVELOPER** tab to the Ribbon.

- Click the **FILE** tab, click **Options**, click **Customize Ribbon**, and then under **Customize the Ribbon**, click **Developer**. Click **OK**.

n. If necessary, save the folder where you save your student files as a trusted location.

- Click the **FILE** tab, click **Options**, click **Trust Center**, click **Trust Center Settings**, and then click **Trusted Locations**.
- Click **Add new location**, browse to the folder where you save your student files, and then click **OK**. Click **OK** again, click **OK** again, and then click **OK** again.

o. On the **DEVELOPER** tab, in the **Code** group, click **Record Macro**.

- In the **Macro name** box, type ClearContents. In the **Shortcut key** box, type c. In the **Description** box, type Delete all user-entered data from the worksheet. Click **OK**.
- Select cells **B3:B4,** press and hold Ctrl, and then select cells **B6:B8** and cells **B11:B14**. Press Delete.
- Select cell **B3**. On the **DEVELOPER** tab, in the CODE group, click **Stop Recording**.

p. Click **Undo** to undo the changes you made recording the macro.

q. On the **DEVELOPER** tab, in the **Controls** group, click **Insert**, and then select **Button (Form Control)**.

- Click in the top-left corner of cell **G1**, and then drag to the bottom-right corner of cell **H2** to size and add the button.
- Select **ClearContents**, and then click **OK**.
- Right-click the button, and then select **Edit Text**. Delete the current text, and then type Clear Form. Click cell **G4** to deselect the button.

r. Select cell **A10**. On the **INSERT** tab, in the **Links** group, click **Hyperlink**.

- Select **Place in This Document**, select **YearSummary**, and then click **OK**.
- Click the **YearSummary** worksheet. Select cell **H2**, type Back to Special Events and then insert a **hyperlink** to the **SpecialEvents** worksheet.

s. Right-click the **Documentation** worksheet tab, and then select **Hide**.

t. Click the **SpecialEvents** worksheet tab. Select cells **B3:B4, B6:B8** and cells **B11:B14**. On the **HOME** tab, in the **Cells** group, click **Format**, and then select **Lock Cell**.

u. Click the **FILE** tab, click **Options**, click **Advanced**, and then scroll down to the Display options for this workbook section.

- Click **Show horizontal scroll bar** and **Show vertical scroll bar**. This will turn off all the scroll bars for the workbook.
- In the Display options for this worksheet section, click **Show row and column headers**. This will turn off the row and column headers for the SpecialEvents worksheet. Click **OK**.

v. On the **VIEW** tab, in the **Show** group, click **Gridlines**. This will turn off the gridlines for the SpecialEvents worksheet.

w. On the **FORMULAS** tab, in the **Formula Auditing** group, click **Show Formulas**.

- Select all the cells that show a formula EXCEPT for the Event date, which is entered by the user.
- On the **HOME** tab, in the **Cells** group, click **Format**, select **Format Cells**, click the **Protection** tab, and then click **Hidden**. Click **OK**.
- On the **FORMULAS** tab, in the Formula auditing group, click **Show Formulas**.

x. On the **HOME** tab, in the **Cells** group, click **Format**, and then select **Protect Sheet**. Click **Select locked cells** to uncheck the option, and then click **OK**.

y. On the **REVIEW** tab, in the Changes group, click **Protect Workbook**, verify **Structure** is selected, and then click **OK**.

z. Click the **Documentation** worksheet. Click cell **A6**, and then type in today's date. Click cell **B6**, and then type in your first and last name. Complete the remainder of the **Documentation** worksheet according to your instructor's direction.

aa. Click the **FILE** tab, click **Protect Workbook**, and then select **Mark as Final**. Click **OK** to save the workbook, click **OK** again, and then close Excel. Submit your file as directed by your instructor.

Problem Solve 1

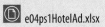

Student data file needed: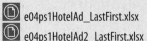
e04ps1HotelAd.xlsx

You will save your files as:
e04ps1HotelAd_LastFirst.xlsx
e04ps1HotelAd2_LastFirst.xlsx

Finance & Accounting

Hotel Advertising

The Painted Paradise Golf Resort and Spa tends to attract local residents for weekend getaways and special events, so the management has an aggressive marketing strategy that includes many different mediums for its advertising. In April, William Mattingly, CEO, would like to present a summary of the advertising costs to the board of trustees. The report to the board will include the budgeted amount for each month as well as the actual amount spent, along with a consolidated summary of the quarter.

To make it easier and more consistent for different areas of the resort to advertise, he would also like an advertising request form created so the managers understand what their options for advertising are.

a. Open **e04ps1HotelAd.xlsx**, and then save it in the location where you are saving your files as e04ps1HotelAd_LastFirst, using your last and first name.

b. With **JanAds**, **FebAds**, and **MarAds** worksheets grouped, select cell **A13**, and then type Total. Enter a formula in cells **B13:C13** to calculate the sum of each column. Enter a formula in cells **D5:D13** that calculates the difference between the Actual and Budget amounts (B5-C5). Format cells **A13:C13** with the **Total** style. Ungroup the worksheets.

c. On the **Q1Summary** worksheet tab, enter a 3D formula in cells **B5:B12** to sum the Actual advertising amounts. Enter a 3D formula in cells **C5:C12** to sum the Budget advertising amounts.

d. With the **MarAds** and **Q1Summary** worksheets grouped, select cells **D5:D12** and fill **All** across the worksheets. Select cells **A13:D13** and fill **All** across the worksheets. Select cells **B5:C12** and fill **Formats** across the worksheets.

e. On the **Q1Averages** worksheet tab, create a consolidated summary based on position. The summary should find the average actual and budget amounts for each type of advertising for January through March using cells **A5:C12**. (*Hint:* Select Left column only, and do not link to the data.)

f. On the **Q1Averages** worksheet tab, calculate the difference (Over/Under) in cells **D5:D12**. In cell **A13**, type Total. Enter a formula in cells **B13:D13** to calculate the totals. Format cells **A13:D13** with the **Total** style.

g. On the **AdRequest** worksheet tab, create a list validation rule in cell **C9** with the source data from cells **A3:A10** on the **AdOptions** worksheet. The **Input message** should say Choose type from list and the **Error message** should say Invalid type. In **C9** select **Television**.

h. On the **AdRequest** worksheet tab, create a date validation rule in cell **C11** so the date must be greater than today's date. (*Hint:* Use the TODAY function. Do not enter any messages. In **C11** type =TODAY()+1.)

i. On the **AdRequest** worksheet tab, create a date validation rule in cell **C12** so the date must be greater than the date in cell C11. (*Hint*: The source will be =C11.) In **C12** enter =TODAY()+2. Select cell **C14**, and then type 400. Select cell **C15**, and then type 3.

j. On the **AdRequest** worksheet tab, create a text length validation rule in cell **C18** to limit the comment to 200 or fewer characters. The **Input Message** should say Comment must be less than or equal to 200 characters. In cell **C18** type Television ad for three mornings during the news.

k. On the **AdRequest** worksheet, add a hyperlink in cell **A9** to go to the **AdOptions** worksheet. On the **AdOptions** worksheet, add a hyperlink in cell **A2** to go to the **AdRequest** worksheet.

l. Customize the Ribbon to add the **Speak Cells** and **Stop Speaking Cells** buttons in a new group on the **REVIEW** tab called **Text-to-Speech**.

m. If necessary, add the **Compare and Merge Workbooks** button to the Quick Access Toolbar. Share the workbook, and save a copy as e04ps1HotelAd2_LastFirst, using your last and first name.

n. In **e04ps1HotelAd2_LastFirst**, on the **JanAds** worksheet tab, select cell **B5**, and then change it to 4520. Select cell **B12**, and then change it to 610. Save and close the workbook, but leave Excel open.

o. Open **e04ps1HotelAd_LastFirst**. Compare and merge the workbook with **e04ps1HotelAd2_LastFirst**, and then track and save all changes on a new sheet. Do not stop sharing the workbook.

p. Hide the **vertical** and **horizontal scroll bars** for the workbook. Hide the **row and column headers** for the AdRequest worksheet.

q. Hide the **gridlines** on the AdRequest worksheet. On the AdRequest worksheet, unlock cells **C9**, **C11:C12**, **C14:C15**, and **C18**.

r. Complete the **Documentation** worksheet according to your instructor's direction. Insert the **filename** in the left custom footer section of the Header/Footer tab in the Page Setup dialog box on all worksheets in the workbook.

s. Click Save, close Excel, and then submit the file as directed by your instructor.

Problem Solve 2

MyITLab®
Grader
Homework 2

Student data files needed:

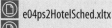 e04ps2HotelSched.xltx

e04ps2HotelEmp.xlsx

You will save your file as:

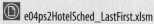 e04ps2HotelSched_LastFirst.xlsm

Hotel Scheduling

Human Resources

The hotel at the Painted Paradise Golf Resort and Spa needs a better way to track employee hours. Ideally, each department will use an Excel spreadsheet to track the hours, and that way data is easily accessible and can be shared. A former employee created a template to use, but it still needs work before it can be handed over to the managers to use. You will save the template as a workbook and make changes to it so it will be complete.

a. Open **e04ps2HotelSched.xltx**, click **OK** in the circular reference warning box, and then save it in the location where you are saving your files as an **Excel Macro-Enabled Workbook** named e04ps2HotelSched_LastFirst, using your last and first name.

b. On the **Schedule** worksheet, create a list validation rule in cells **A7:A26** with the source data from cells **A3:A12** on the **Employees** worksheet. The **Input message** should say Choose a name from the list. and the **Error message** should say Invalid name. In cell **A7**, select **Eric Mosley**.

c. In cells **C7:I26** create a list validation rule with the source data from cells **A3:A9** on the **Shifts** worksheet. Leave the messages blank.

d. In cell **C3**, create an any value validation rule with an **Input message** that says Enter the starting date for the week. Select cell **C3**, and then type =TODAY().

e. Select cell **J27**, and then correct the formula so there is no longer a circular reference.

f. Click the **Employees** worksheet tab, and then delete column B. This will cause a #REF! error on the Schedule worksheet. Click the **Schedule** worksheet tab, and then modify the table array reference in the VLOOKUP formulas in cells **B7:B26** to reference cells **A6:B15** (named Employee) on the **e04ps2HotelEmp.xlsx** workbook. If necessary, close e04ps2HotelEmp.

g. On the **Schedule** worksheet, select cell **A6**, and then insert a hyperlink to go to the **Employees** worksheet. On the **Employees** worksheet, select cell **D2**, and then insert a hyperlink to go to the **Schedule** worksheet.

h. If necessary, add the **DEVELOPER** tab to the Ribbon. On the **Schedule** worksheet, create a new macro to clear cells **C3**, **B29**, **A7:A26**, and **C7:I26**. Name the macro NewWeek with a keyboard shortcut of n and the description Clears cells for new week. End the macro on cell **C3**. Undo the changes the macro made. Insert a button in cells **A32:A33** to run the NewWeek macro. Change the button text to New Week.

i. Create a second macro using relative references to add **bold** and a **dark red font color** to an employee's name and ID number. Name the macro ChangeFont with a keyboard shortcut of f and the description Change the font of an employee's name and ID. Insert a button in cells **B32:C33** to run the ChangeFont macro, and then change the button text to Change Font.

j. Unlock the cells required for data entry (**C3**, **A7:A26**, **C7:I26**, and **B29**). Hide the **gridlines** on the Schedule worksheet.

k. On the **Schedule** worksheet, hide columns **K:R**. Hide all formulas in cells **J7:J27** and **C27:I28**. Hide row and column headers, protect the Schedule worksheet (do not use a password), and then mark the workbook as final.

l. Complete the **Documentation** worksheet according to your instructor's direction. Insert the **filename** in the left custom footer section of the Header/Footer tab in the Page Setup dialog box on all worksheets in the workbook.

m. Click Save, close Excel, and then submit the file as directed by your instructor.

Perform 1: Perform in Your Life

Student data file needed:

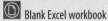 Blank Excel workbook

You will save your files as:

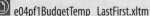 e04pf1Budget_LastFirst.xlsm

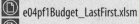 e04pf1BudgetTemp_LastFirst.xltm

College Expense Budgeting

Finance & Accounting

Very few students keep track of what it actually costs to attend a college or university. The costs are usually higher than a person realizes and often cross a staggering array of categories. For an example see the list below, which is not nearly inclusive. It may be very helpful to have this type of information readily available for student aid applications, for decision-making associated with extending your education by a semester or two, to add a major or minor, for seeking financing for a different car from a local bank, or maybe to help you decide whether or not you can really afford a different car.

You will create a workbook that contains four worksheets. Two of the worksheets will be monthly budgets for the two upcoming semesters. The third worksheet will consolidate the two semesters of data, and the fourth worksheet will be a form to track your expenses. At a minimum, your worksheets should address the following expenses:

- Tuition
- Fees
- Books
- Room and board
- Entertainment
- Clothing
- Utilities
- Groceries
- Transportation

a. Start **Excel**. Save the blank workbook as e04pf1Budget_LastFirst using your last and first name. The file should be saved as an **Excel Macro-Enabled Workbook**.

b. Create three worksheets: one for the fall semester, one for the spring semester, and one for a summary sheet.
  - All three worksheets should have the categories listed in column A, the months as column headings, and a total column and total row.
  - The summary worksheet should be created using a consolidation method for all months in both the fall and spring semesters.

c. Create a fourth worksheet that will be a form for you to use to track your expenses. Create at least 10 lines on the form, and make sure the form includes the following:
  - One column should be for the category of expense and should have a list validation rule to choose from one of the categories listed on your Summary worksheet.
  - One column should be to enter a more detailed description of your expense. Enter a validation rule to limit the text length to 75 characters.
  - One column should be to enter the actual amount of the expense.
  - One column should be a running total of your expenses.

d. Create a macro to clear the data from all the cells on the form you created that are not formulas. Add a button to run the macro.
  - Enter at least three lines on your form, and run your macro to test it.

e. Create another macro to highlight any unusual expenses you might add to the form. Add a button to run the macro.
  - Enter at least one line on your form to test the macro.

f. On the worksheet with the form, modify any navigational options that would make it look more like a form and less like an Excel workbook.

g. Format all tables and cells appropriately, add headings where appropriate, and then name worksheets appropriately. Set up any protection necessary to protect your formulas, and then save all your changes.

h. Save the workbook as a macro-enabled template to share with your friends. Name it e04pf1BudgetTemp_LastFirst.

i. Insert the **filename** in the left custom footer section of the Header/Footer tab in the Page Setup dialog box on all worksheets in the workbook.

j. Click Save, close Excel, and then submit the file as directed by your instructor.

Student data file needed:

 Blank Excel workbook

You will save your files as:

 e04pf2Time_LastFirst.xlsx

e04pf2Time2_LastFirst.xlsx

Finance & Accounting

Production & Operations

Law Firm Time Billing Summary

Professionals often generate revenue by billing clients for their time. This is certainly true of attorneys. Attorneys need to keep an accurate log of the time they spend working on each client's account or case.

Assume you are an attorney working in an intellectual property firm and your specialty is patents, trademarks, and copyrights. You will create a workbook that contains billing information for two weeks of your time, and then you will compile a quick summary of the billable hours dedicated to each client.

You also want to send this out to colleagues with whom you share some of these clients so your colleagues can update the hours if necessary.

Assume the clients you are currently working with include the following:

Acme Corp
Carryss Candies
Incom Corporation
Mammoth Pictures
Mooby Corp
Omni Consumer Products
Powell Motors
Primatech
QWERTY Logistics
Wernham Hogg Enterprises

a. Start **Excel**, and then create a workbook called **e04pf2Time_LastFirst** using your last and first name.

b. Create a worksheet for the list of client names.

c. Create two worksheets for tracking billable hours for week 1 and week 2.
   - On each sheet, include the following columns: client/project, date, billable hours, and description.
   - On each sheet, below the column headings, add a list data validation rule to the next 10 rows to look up the client's name from the client worksheet. On each sheet, enter data in the 10 rows after the column headings. Make sure you have a variety of dates (one week's worth) and clients on each worksheet.
   - On each sheet, add a total row to add the billable hours for the week.
   - Format both worksheets appropriately so their formatting matches.

d. Create a summary of billable hours by client/project by using consolidation by category. The summary should consolidate based on client and total client hours for the two weeks. Format the summary worksheet to match the week 1 and week 2 worksheets. Hide any columns that when consolidated are not necessary. Include a total row.

e. Add the **Text-to-speech** group on the **REVIEW** tab to include the **Speak Cells** and **Stop Speaking Cells** buttons.

f. If necessary, add the Compare and Merge Workbooks button to the Quick Access Toolbar.

- Make a copy of the worksheet called e04pf2Time2_LastFirst. Share the workbook, make changes to the billable hours for week 1 in **e04pf2Time2_LastFirst**, and then compare and merge the workbooks.

- Create a history tracking sheet to keep track of the changes made. Do not stop sharing the file.

g. Insert the **filename** in the left custom footer section of the Header/Footer tab in the Page Setup dialog box on all worksheets in the workbook.

h. Click Save, close Excel, and then submit the file as directed by your instructor.

Perform 3: Perform in Your Team

Student data file needed:

Blank Excel workbook

You will save your file as:

e04pf3Expenses_TeamName.xlsx

Team Expense Reimbursement with Summary

Finance & Accounting

The organization you work for has used paper forms for years, but now that so many employees have smart phones, tablet computers, laptops, or other such devices, they would like to create electronic forms. In the past, team members have submitted their expenses individually, and it was up to the payroll manager to consolidate the information to be able to create a team summary of expenses for a project.

You have been asked by your supervisor to create a workbook that can be used by teams of employees to track expenses for a project. The workbook should contain one worksheet for each team member as well as a worksheet to summarize team expenses.

a. Select one team member to set up the document by completing Steps b through e.

b. Open your browser and navigate to either **https://www.skydrive.live.com**, **https://www. drive.google.com**, or any other instructor assigned location. Be sure all members of the team have an account on the chosen system—such as a Microsoft or Google account.

c. Create a new workbook, and then name it e04pf3Expenses_TeamName using the team name assigned to your team by your instructor.

d. Share the spreadsheet with the other members of your team. Make sure that each team member has the appropriate permission to edit the document.

e. Hold a team meeting and discuss the requirements of the remaining steps. Make an action and communication plan. Consider which steps can be done independently and which steps require completion of prior steps before starting.

Team member 1 should complete the following:

f. Create a worksheet with a table to track expenses. Include the following columns: Date, Description, Hotel, Transportation, Meals, Phone, Mileage, Other, and Total. Format at least 20 rows as a table.

g. Create data validation rules in the Date column to accept only dates less than or equal to today.

h. Create data validation in the expense columns to restrict the values to decimals, between $2.00 and $999.

i. Create three more copies of the worksheet just created, one for each team member. Name the worksheets with each team member's first name.

j. Enter at least five lines of expenses on the worksheet for team member 1.

Team member 2 should complete the following after team member 1 has uploaded the workbook.

k. On the worksheet for team member 2, enter at least five lines of expenses.

l. For all four worksheets (one for each member), do the following.
- Insert a **formula** in the **Total** column to add the columns **Hotel** through **Other**.
- Add a total line to total expenses by each column.

Team member 3 should complete the following after team member 2 has uploaded the workbook.

m. On the worksheet for team member 3, enter at least five lines of expenses.

n. Insert a new worksheet, call it TeamSummary and then move it after the team member 4 worksheet.

o. Add a title to the worksheet.

Team member 4 should complete the following after team member 3 has uploaded the workbook.

p. On the worksheet for team member 4, enter at least five lines of expenses.

q. On the TeamSummary worksheet, consolidate all four team members' expense reports by Description. Format the results as appropriate. (*Hint*: Do not include the date column in the consolidation.)

r. Insert the **filename** in the left custom footer section of the Header/Footer tab in the Page Setup dialog box on all worksheets in the workbook. In a custom header section, include the **names** of the students in your team—spread the names evenly across each of the three header sections: left section, center section, and right section.

s. Save your work, and then close Excel. Submit the file as directed by your instructor.

t. Create a new Word document in the assignment folder in SkyDrive, and then name it a05pf3Expenses_TeamName using the name assigned to your team by your instructor.

u. In the Word document, each team member must list his or her first and last name as well as a summary of their planned contributions. As work is completed on the database, this document should be updated with the specifics of each team member's contributions.

Perform 4: How Others Perform

Student data file needed:
 e04pf4College.xlsm

You will save your files as:
 e04pf4College_LastFirst.xlsm
 e04pf4College_LastFirst.docx

Education Costs Worksheet

Finance & Accounting

A fellow student has created a workbook to track his expenses for the next two semesters of school. You like the idea of being able to do this and have asked him for the workbook so you could use it as well. You are a little confused about how it works, and since he did not leave any instructions, you have to figure out what he has done on your own. You will use the Formula Auditing tools, as well as what you know about macros, data validation, and 3-D formulas to understand how this workbook is set up. You will also find and correct the circular reference somewhere in the workbook.

a. Open **e04pf4College.xlsm**, and then save it as a macro-enabled workbook called e04pf4College_LastFirst, using your last and first name. Click **OK** in the circular warning dialog box.

b. Locate and correct the circular reference.

c. Open a Word document, save it as e04pf4College_LastFirst, and type the answers to the following questions in the Word document:

- Click the **TotalCosts** worksheet tab. In cells B5:B7, B10:B12, and B15:B18, what kind of formula is used? If you did not use this particular formula, what other formula would also work in these cells to get the same result?

- Click the **Winter2014** worksheet tab. Look at the cells with the comments (they have red triangles in the top-right corner). What does this comment refer to? Edit the macro in the workbook. What is the description of the macro, and what does it do? What kind of macro is it?

- Select cell **B5** on the Winter2014 worksheet. Use **Trace Precedents** and **Trace Dependents** to determine the cells precedents and dependents, and then list all the cell references for each.

- Is there any data validation on any of the worksheets? Is data validation appropriate for any of the cells? Why or why not?

- Click the **TotalCosts** worksheet tab. If appropriate, unlock any cells for data entry and protect the rest of the worksheet. Is protecting the Winter2014 and Spring2015 worksheets appropriate? Why or why not? (*Hint*: Try it to see what happens and check to see if you lose any functionality.) How could you change the workbook to be able to protect the expense summary sections for each semester?

WORKSHOP 9 | ORGANIZE, IMPORT, EXPORT, AND CLEANSE DATA SETS

OBJECTIVES

1. Understand the importance of external data sets   p. 470

2. Understand and import XML data   p. 475

3. Connect to an Access database   p. 482

4. Clean imported data   p. 487

5. Use Flash Fill to cleanse data   p. 496

6. Separate data using text functions and wizards   p. 498

7. Clean date-related data   p. 504

Prepare Case

Red Bluff Golf Course & Pro Shop Data Integration

Sales & Marketing

The Red Bluff Golf Course & Pro Shop manager, Aleeta Herriott, has asked you to create a report that analyzes costs and revenues from tournaments hosted over the past year. In the past, her staff had to manually reenter data from different sources in order to create this report because no one at the resort knew how to import the data. As a result, they rarely completed the report. Aleeta worries about the accuracy of the reports that were compiled because of the manual data entry. However, she did keep all the original files. Recently, a new Golf database was created to track sales and allow for easy export to Excel for analysis. However, Aleeta wants you to design a spreadsheet that will help them automate the process of gathering and standardizing the data from the past for analysis.

Chad McDermott / Shutterstock

REAL WORLD SUCCESS

"Recently I was asked to develop a series of reports on enrollments at the university I work for. The data on students enrolling at the university was made available to us using an Access database. By importing the data into Excel from Access, I was able to create a broad range of statistics, graphs, and reports spanning several years of data. The result was a comprehensive view of our data that provided unique insights for our university."

- Dave, alumnus

Student data files needed for this workshop:

 e05ws09TournamentData.xlsx

 e05ws09Customers.csv

 e05ws09TournamentReport.xlsx

 e05ws09Golf.accdb

 e05ws09MenuOptions.xml

You will save your files as:

 e05ws09TournamentData_LastFirst.xlsx

e05ws09TournamentReport_LastFirst.xlsx

Working with Data Sets

One reason that spreadsheets are so popular is because of their ability to combine data and information from a wide variety of sources. Once you have advanced beyond the novice level to become a more advanced user, you will very likely need to integrate data from multiple sources. Most organizations have their data spread throughout the organization in a wide variety of devices and formats. Your organization may collect data on websites or in word-processing programs, databases, network servers, or even in paper reports. In this section, you will learn about external data sets and how to connect to them. You will also work with web queries and import data.

Understand the Importance of External Data Sets

Anything that is not stored in an Excel format (.xls or .xlsx) or not stored locally is considered to be **external data**. Spreadsheet applications such as Excel offer a wide variety of tools to help the user extract external data and integrate it into reports so that it can be actively used to make better decisions. By using the import tools, you can avoid a lot of extra typing. Microsoft has continued to expand the file types that can be easily imported, and this feature has improved considerably in recent years. Common file formats that you can import include HTML, XML, text, and .accdb files from Microsoft Access.

One of the reasons that spreadsheets are such powerful tools is that they have evolved into the de facto means of consolidating diverse types of data. For example, someone may want you to work on an analysis or report, but they are not able to grant you access to their databases. In this case, one solution would be for them to export their data to a text format, which you can then easily import into Excel.

QUICK REFERENCE	Common Data Sources for Excel
Source	**Description**
Microsoft Access (.mdb, .accdb)	Import data from relational database tables created in Access (.mdb, .accdb) formats.
HTML (.html)	Link to data stored in tabular form on websites.
Comma separated (.csv)	Convert data stored in a comma-delimited format—.csv files. Even though this is a separate file type, you cannot choose it when importing data into Excel. Excel will automatically open a .csv file.
XML (.xml)	Import data stored in .xml format.
Text (.txt)	Exchange data between mainframes and other systems using the .txt format.
dBASE (.dbf)	Data stored in a popular PC database program; converts from .dbf files
SQL Server	A popular relational database server for corporate web servers
Analysis Services	Designed to import data formatted as a data cube in SQL Server Analysis Services
Microsoft Query	A query wizard to help in importing data from less common or unlisted sources using ODBC (standard data conversion drivers)
Data Connection Wizard	Another query wizard for creating and maintaining connections with unlisted data sources; uses OLEDB drivers

Opening the Starting File

Data can be easily shared online between companies, within companies, and between companies and their customers. While this data can be placed into a workbook by copying from the website and pasting into a workbook, linking to a web page is the more efficient process. By linking the web page to a workbook, the data can be updated without having to visit the web page and performing a copy-and-paste process every time the data is updated. You have been asked by Aleeta Herriott to import data from a web page that lists online transactions related to golf tournaments through the Painted Paradise website.

E09.00

 To Open the Starting File

a. Start **Excel**, click **Open Other Workbooks**, and then browse to your student data files. Locate and select **e05ws09TournamentData**, and then click **Open**.

b. Click the **FILE** tab, and then click **Save As**. Browse to the location where you are saving your files. In the File name box, type e05ws09TournamentData_LastFirst, using your first and last name, and then click **Save**.

c. To insert your filename as a footer, on the INSERT tab, in the Text group, click **Header & Footer**.

d. On the DESIGN tab, in the Navigation group, click **Go to Footer**. If necessary, click the **left section** of the footer, and then click **File Name** in the Header & Footer Elements group.

e. Click any cell on the spreadsheet to move out of the footer, press Ctrl+Home, on the VIEW tab, in the Workbook Views group, click **Normal** ▦. Click the **HOME** tab.

Using a Web Query

One popular way to integrate information from web pages is to use a web query. A **query** is a question that you would ask a database such as Access. Access allows users to formulate queries in a variety of tools or languages to search for information in the database. You might think of a web query as something you could type into a search engine such as Google or Bing in order to search the web. However, in Excel, a **web query** is a way of importing data into a spreadsheet directly from a web page. This could be stock prices from a financial website such as **http://money.msn.com**, or it could be sales data from a company web server.

More and more, companies are using websites to make their data available to users. Financial, governmental, and even college-related data is uploaded and refreshed daily. By linking this data to a spreadsheet via a web query, users can automatically update the data for use in their spreadsheet applications. Web queries are tied to specific URLs; when the URL changes, the web query will no longer be able to access the data. This makes it important to have the exact URL address when importing data.

E09.01

To Import Web Data

a. Click the **Suppliers** worksheet tab.

b. On the DATA tab, in the Get External Data group, click **From Web**.

c. In the New Web Query dialog box, click in the **Address** box, and then delete any text. Type the following URL: http://www.paintedparadiseresort.com/Red_Bluff_Web.htm. If you get a security warning message, select **No**, and continue.

d. Click **Go**.

The New Web Query window now displays the target website. The black selection arrows indicate data that Excel can easily import into a spreadsheet.

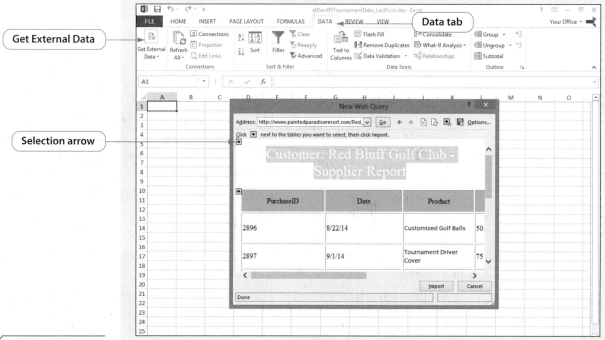

Figure 1   Creating a web query

e. Click the second black **Selection** arrow to select the table.

f. Click **Import**, accept the default location of cell **A1**, and then click **OK**. The data from the website is now located in the Suppliers worksheet.

g. **Save** 💾 the file.

Editing a Web Query

You may have noticed that the data you pulled into your spreadsheet from the web page with your original web query retained some, but not all, of the web page formatting. For example, the column widths remained as they were in the web page, the data in the Date column is formatted as Date, and the data in the Amount column is formatted as Currency. Web queries can be modified so that they are set to retain all the formatting from the target HTML tables. Excel gives you several options for formatting your web query. The default None option retrieves the text with some basic formatting. The Rich Text Formatting only option retains most of the text formatting. The Full HTML formatting option allows you to import more advanced features, like tables and hyperlinks. If this data is used in meetings or reports, the formatting from the website would make the data more presentable.

SIDE NOTE
Alternate Method
If you copy and paste data from a website, you will be given the option to convert the data into a Refreshable Web Query.

SIDE NOTE
Connection Speed
Because of the variable speed of connections and the amount of data being downloaded from a website, it may take several minutes for the data to download.

E09.02

 To Modify Web Queries

a. Click the **DATA** tab, and then in the Connections group, click **Connections**.

b. In the Workbook Connections dialog box, click **Properties**.

c. Accept the default Connection name in the Connection name box, and in the Description box, type Supplier report for tournaments. Click to check the **Refresh data when opening the file** check box, if necessary.

d. Click the **Definition** tab, and then click **Edit Query** in the bottom-left corner of the dialog box.

e. Click the **Options** button in the top-right corner of the window. Click the **Full HTML formatting** option, and then click **OK**.

f. Click **Import**, click **OK**, and then click **Close**. The data will not update until the web query is refreshed. In the Connections group, click **Refresh All**. You should see that the data has now changed to include the blue colors in the table field headers and borders to divide each cell.

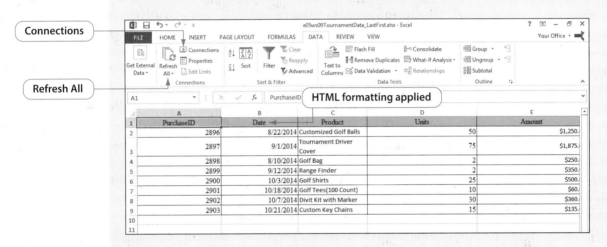

Figure 2　Modified web query

g. **Save** 🖫 the file.

CONSIDER THIS | **Beyond Spreadsheets**

The amount of data in the business world is growing rapidly—faster, in fact, than at any time in history. Companies and governments store massive amounts of data. Facebook alone stores over 40 billion photos. What kinds of data could a company like Facebook be collecting that you might not have considered, and how could the information be used—both positively and negatively?

Data privacy is a very important topic. One of the primary means of breaching customer data is through the loss of a file that contains private data. An available option in the Connection Properties is to Remove data from the external data range before saving the workbook. If checked, this option will remove any data stored from the data query when the workbook is closed. Removing this data is one means of securing your workbook.

Saving a Web Query

At times, you will want to share your completed web query with other users. By saving a copy of your web query, you create a permanent file that contains a connection to the data. This file can then be used in any Microsoft Office application, including Microsoft Word.

E09.03

 To Save a Web Query

a. Click the **DATA** tab, and then in the Connections group, click **Connections**.

b. In the Workbook Connections dialog box, click **Properties** for the Connection web query you just created.

c. In the Connection Properties dialog box, click the **Definition** tab, and then click **Edit Query**. The same web page you saw before is displayed.

d. Click the **Save Query** 🔲 button, located next to the Options button. The Save Workspace dialog box defaults to a special Queries folder that is displayed as the default location for saving queries.

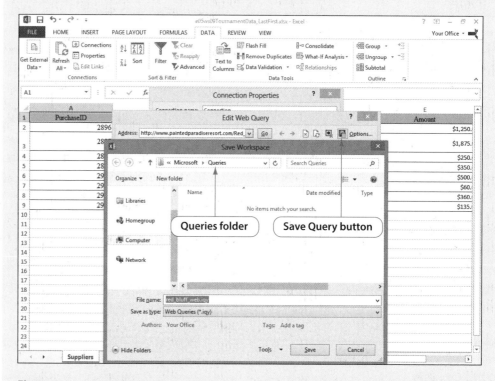

Figure 3   Saving a web query

e. Navigate to where you stored your student data files, accept the default file name, click **Save**, and then click **Cancel** twice. Click **Close** to exit the remaining dialog boxes.

f. **Save** 🖫 the file.

How Is Connecting to Web Data Different from Copying and Pasting?

It may seem simpler to just copy the web data and then paste it into your worksheet. In fact, you can copy and paste for the occasional import of web data. With a newer browser, you can right-click a web table and copy it to Excel with the Export to Microsoft Excel option. However, when you use the copy-and-paste method, you will have to spend time reformatting the data to use it in your formulas in Excel. More importantly, web queries provide a great advantage when you are creating an application that needs to be updated frequently. The web query will create a connection to the web page and automatically update the data in your Excel file.

Working with XML Data and Text Files

Two of the most common data formats for importing data into Excel are XML data and text files. In the following section, you will learn how to import data in these two formats into Excel.

Understand and Import XML Data

XML, or Extensible Markup Language, is an increasingly popular tool working behind the scenes in Excel. A little knowledge of how it is used shows that you are well beyond the usual beginner's knowledge of spreadsheets. In an earlier exercise, you imported data that was stored in a table on a web page. This made it easier to import the data into Excel without reformatting it. However, in some cases, data on web pages is not stored in an organized manner. That is to say, the data may not be in a table that is easily accessible with Excel. **XML** was created to help give structure to web page data so that it can be searched and processed more efficiently. XML allows users to define their own tags in order to define the content of the document.

Most web pages are programmed in **HTML** or Hypertext Markup Language. Both XML and HTML are examples of markup languages. **Markup languages** use special sequences of characters or "markups" inserted in the document to indicate how the document should look when it is displayed or printed. The markup indicators are often called "tags" and are enclosed in angle brackets (< >). These tags tell the processor of the document what to do with it. HTML is used to format and display the web data, whereas XML was developed to help convert web data into a tabular structure so it could be easily stored and transported. Unlike HTML, the tags in XML actually describe the content of the data between the tags. So, HTML uses tags such as <H1></H1> to help describe the formatting of the document. XML uses tags to describe the actual content between the tags <revenue></revenue>. Because of this, XML capabilities were soon extended to databases, spreadsheets, and word processors and became the de facto standard for transmitting data between systems and different applications.

One of the most powerful aspects of XML is that you can define custom tags for content specific to a particular industry. In HTML, all the tags are predetermined so the browser knows how to interpret them. XML is different in that as long as the rules for creating XML tags and documents are followed, you can define the tags any way you like.

The goal of XML is to allow users to automate the storage, transmission, and processing of content. To accomplish this, XML separates the content from the format and structure of the document. To understand how to process an XML document, it is crucial to understand its structure. The structure of an XML document is described in the XML schema or data map. The **XML schema** describes the structure of an XML document in terms of what XML elements it will contain and their sequence. In Excel, the term **XML map** is synonymous with XML schema. An **XML element** includes the start and stop tags and everything in between, such as <revenue>$345,678</revenue>. The document structure is separate from the actual content of the document itself and uses a completely separate file with an .xsd extension. It is similar in concept to the idea of a mail merge. The content is contained in the .xml file, the formatting is described in an .xsl file, and the structure of all the data elements is laid out in the schema or .xsd file. All of these files are merged in the resulting XML document, just as a list of names and addresses is merged with a form letter in Word, as illustrated in Figure 4.

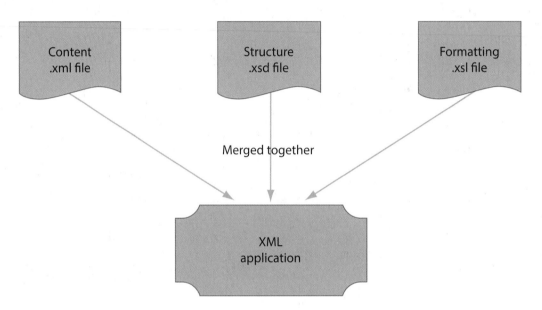

Figure 4   XML document files

Determining the structure of any document may not be obvious. If you were to look at a book index or a table of contents, you would know just by glancing at them what these two different documents were. This is because over the years, publishers have defined what the structure of an index or table of contents should look like. It is the same way with schemas. You can define the structure of a sales order document to contain the customer number, name, date, productID, cost, and total cost. All of these would be represented as elements within the XML schema. So when Excel processes an XML file, it looks for an existing XML schema to check whether it has received a valid XML document. This way, it can automate the processing of XML files since it knows what to expect because it is defined by the schema.

Adding the Developer Tab to the Ribbon

To import XML data into an Excel document, you first need to activate the Developer tab. The Developer tab provides access to many useful Excel features such as macros, Visual Basic, and form control tools.

To Add the Developer Tab to the Ribbon

a. Click the **FILE** tab, and then click **Options**.

b. From the list on the left, click **Customize Ribbon**. In the list of tabs on the right, select **Developer**.

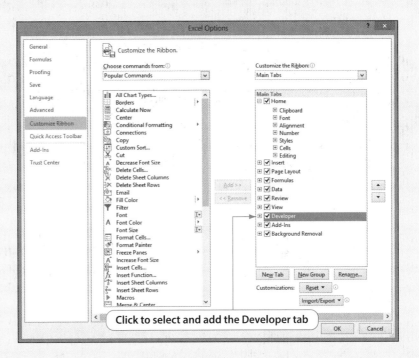

Figure 5 Adding the Developer tab

c. Click **OK**. Click the **DEVELOPER** tab to view it on the Ribbon.

Importing XML Data

In this exercise, you will be working with an XML file in which no schema has been specified. This XML file replicates a maintenance list for the Red Bluff Golf Course & Pro Shop. By saving the data in this XML document, it can be electronically transmitted, queried, and stored. When Excel imports the maintenance list data into a worksheet, it automatically creates an XML schema, or XML map as it is called in Excel. When viewing an XML file in Internet Explorer (IE) 6.0 and above, you can also export an XML file into Excel by right-clicking anywhere in the browser window, selecting Export to Microsoft Excel, and following the directions. Both methods give the same results. Figure 6 shows the XML file used in this exercise as viewed in IE.

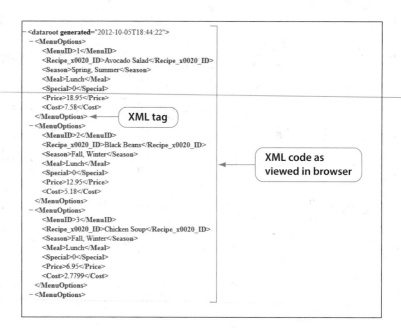

```
<dataroot generated="2012-10-05T18:44:22">
  - <MenuOptions>
        <MenuID>1</MenuID>
        <Recipe_x0020_ID>Avocado Salad</Recipe_x0020_ID>
        <Season>Spring, Summer</Season>
        <Meal>Lunch</Meal>
        <Special>0</Special>
        <Price>18.95</Price>
        <Cost>7.58</Cost>
    </MenuOptions>        XML tag
  - <MenuOptions>
        <MenuID>2</MenuID>
        <Recipe_x0020_ID>Black Beans</Recipe_x0020_ID>
        <Season>Fall, Winter</Season>
        <Meal>Lunch</Meal>                    XML code as
        <Special>0</Special>                  viewed in browser
        <Price>12.95</Price>
        <Cost>5.18</Cost>
    </MenuOptions>
  - <MenuOptions>
        <MenuID>3</MenuID>
        <Recipe_x0020_ID>Chicken Soup</Recipe_x0020_ID>
        <Season>Fall, Winter</Season>
        <Meal>Lunch</Meal>
        <Special>0</Special>
        <Price>6.95</Price>
        <Cost>2.7799</Cost>
    </MenuOptions>
  - <MenuOptions>
```

Figure 6   XML viewed in IE

When you drag the XML elements from the XML Source pane into your spreadsheet, you are binding your data to the cell in which you placed the element. So, whenever you refresh the data by clicking on the Refresh button, it should automatically connect to the source to import the changes and update the data on your worksheet.

The Red Bluff Golf Course & Pro Shop uses the Indigo5 restaurant to cater food and drinks for many of its hosted tournaments. A list of current menu options and pricing has been sent to you as an XML file.

E09.05

 To Import XML Data

a.   Click the **MenuOptions** worksheet tab.

b.   On the DEVELOPER tab, in the XML group, click **Source**. The XML Source pane is displayed on the right side of your worksheet.

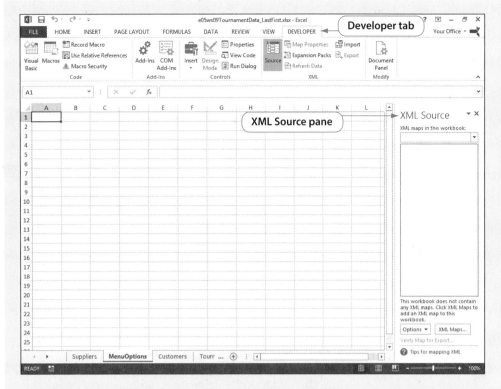

Figure 7 The Developer Tab and XML Source pane

c. Click **XML Maps** in the bottom-right corner of the XML Source pane. A list of XML maps attached to the current workbook is displayed. In this instance, no maps are attached yet, so you will not see any displayed in the pane.

d. In the XML Maps dialog box, click **Add**. In the Select XML Source dialog box, navigate to where your student data files are stored, click **e05ws09MenuOptions**, and then click **Open**. A dialog box opens stating that no schema exists for this file. Click **OK** two times to close the dialog boxes.

e. Drag the **MenuOptions** element with all of its child elements from the XML Source pane to cell **A1**. Only the data headers from the XML file will initially appear. The XML data will be imported as an Excel table.

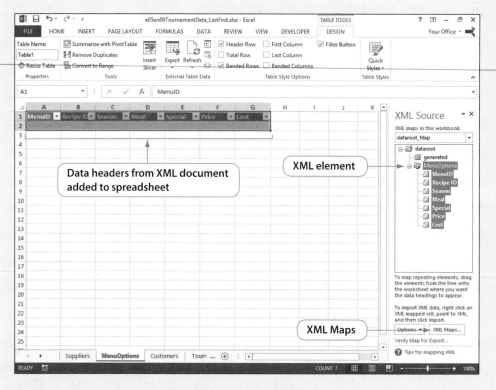

Figure 8 XML document imported into Excel

f. In the External Table Data group, click **Refresh**.

g. **Close** [x] the XML Source pane, and then **Save** [💾] your work.

REAL WORLD ADVICE | **Editing an XML File**

Data in an XML file may not always be formatted exactly the way you will need it. If you need to modify an XML file, a simple text editor such as Notepad or WordPad can open and save changes to an XML file.

Importing Text Files

Text data files used to be called flat files because they were structured as simple lines of data separated by delimiters. **Text data** consists of any grouping of characters, numbers, or dates. A **text file** is just a simple container of text data that is structured by the use of delimiters. A **delimiter** is just a way of indicating the beginning and end of a text data segment. As a container of data, a text file can transmit virtually any kind of data. They are simple to understand and transmit but are not as efficient as binary files because they take up more space in memory. Many different computer systems share data by transmitting text files back and forth. For that reason, text files are one of the most commonly used computer file formats. Text files—also called ASCII files—have no metadata associated with them, so they are not used for transmitting graphics, formulas, or any special formatting. In this context, **metadata** is simply data about data. For digital graphics, metadata could include when the image was created, source information, key words, format instructions, and captions.

Like XML and HTML files, you can import text files two different ways: one file at a time by opening the file in Excel, or by creating a live connection that is maintained between the file source and the target workbook. If you are going to use the application often and the external data will change frequently, you will want to maintain a live connection. Otherwise, you can just import the text files as needed. Both methods are similar and easy to accomplish in Excel.

Text files are known as plain text because they contain just text, without any formatting. There are no special fonts, images, or hyperlinks allowed. What makes the text understandable is the use of delimiters to separate the data. The use of the delimiter tells the receiving computer when the next data value begins. The most common file types that use delimiters are .csv, .txt, and .prn as shown in Table 1.

File Type	Sample			
.csv—comma separated	ProductNum,ProductName,DateShipped,Quantity Shipped			
	59313,XL Golf Shirts,3/15/13,35			
	72316,Men's Shoe,2/5/13,10			
	47423,Head covers,3/6/13,20			
.txt—tab delimited	PNum	PName	Shipped	Quantity
	59313	XL Golf Shirts	3/15/13	35
	72316	Men's Shoe	2/5/13	10
	47423	Head covers	3/6/13	20
.prn—space delimited	PNum PName Shipped Quantity			
	59313 XL_Golf_Shirts 3_15_13 35			
	72316 Mens_Shoe 2_5_13 10			
	47423 Head_covers 3_6_/13 20			

Table 1 Common delimited text file formats

You can import a text file by simply clicking the File tab to open Backstage view and clicking Open. Navigate to the file, and then click Open. This is a quick way to view the data, and it often works well enough for your immediate needs. However, if you want to take advantage of all the text import features, you can use the Text Import Wizard that can be initiated by clicking the From Text button on the Data tab in Excel.

REAL WORLD ADVICE | **More Advanced Features of the Text Import Wizard**

If you do not want to include all the headings or if there is a comment at the beginning of the file, you can tell Excel to start in any row below a target row so it will omit extraneous text. Sometimes Excel will incorrectly identify the language used in the text file, and this may throw off the Text Import Wizard. You can manually change this by clicking the File tab, clicking Options, and then clicking Language. Also, occasionally you will get a text file that is too big to import into Excel. By previewing the data in the Text Import Wizard, you can see exactly how much it will import and then split the file into two or more files using one of the free file-splitting utilities, such as GSplit.

Red Bluff's web developer has exported some customer data from the new Red Bluff website and saved it as a text file. The customers in this list have indicated they are interested in attending future golf tournaments.

E09.06

▶ To Import Text Data

a. Click the **Customers** worksheet tab. On the DATA tab, in the Get External Data group, click **From Text**.

b. In the Import Text File dialog box, navigate to the folder where your student data files are stored, and select **e05ws09Customers**.

c. Click **Import**. The Text Import Wizard recognizes that the file is delimited and has this option selected. Since the first line in the text file contains headings for the data, select **My data has headers**, and then click **Next**.

d. Notice the sample data from the file is separated by commas. Under Delimiters, select the **Comma** option, and then click as needed to deselect any other options that may be selected already. Excel shows you a preview of how the data will be separated into cells when imported. Click **Next**.

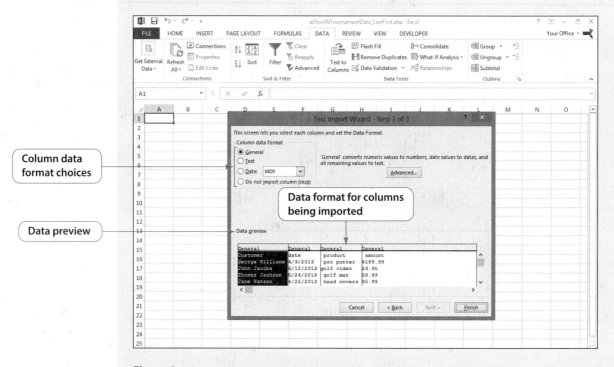

Figure 9 Importing a comma-delimited file

e. Click **Finish**, and then in the Import Data dialog box, click **OK** to accept cell A1 as the location to import the data.

f. **Save** 🖫 your work.

Connect to an Access Database

Data may be collected and stored in a database such as Access and then imported into Excel. This process leverages Excel's powerful charting and analysis features. It also protects the data in the Access database as Excel will import only a copy of the data, leaving the original data safely in the Access database. Over the years, Excel has evolved, making it easier to move data back and forth between Access and Excel. In this section, you will learn how to connect your Excel spreadsheet to the data in an Access database.

Connecting to an Access Database

At the most basic level, you can copy and paste data from an Access table into a blank Excel worksheet. Within Access, users also have the option of exporting tabular data into an Excel format. For longer-term projects, one can also create a permanent connection between an Access database and the Excel application by using the Access Import feature. This live data can be imported as a simple table, or even a PivotTable report or PivotChart.

To understand how to import data from an Access database into Excel, it is important to review how the data is stored in Access. As a tool for using relational databases, Access stores data as a set of one or more tables. By definition, a **relational database** is a collection of tables linked together by shared fields. Each table consists of rows and columns, with each row being uniquely identified by a primary key field. The **primary key** functions as a unique identifier for each row or record. Fields such as Customer_Number or Part_Number are commonly used as primary keys. Multiple tables are designed to be linked by joining a common field. In some cases, the primary key field of one table is connected to match a common field of another table in which the field for the other table is not a primary key. This field is then known as a **foreign key** field when linked to a primary key field in another table.

With a little background, you can quickly understand the basics of relational databases like Access. Figure 10 shows the tblPayments table from the Red Bluff Golf Course & Pro Shop database that tracks payments for upcoming tournaments. Across the top you can see all the field labels, and each row represents a single payment record. The PaymentID field is the unique identifier for each payment, and this field functions as the primary key field. The primary key is automatically generated by Access. Important data for the golf course and the pro shop is kept in other tables for employees, members, and member lessons. Information in each of these different tables is linked through the primary key in one table being shared as the foreign key in another table.

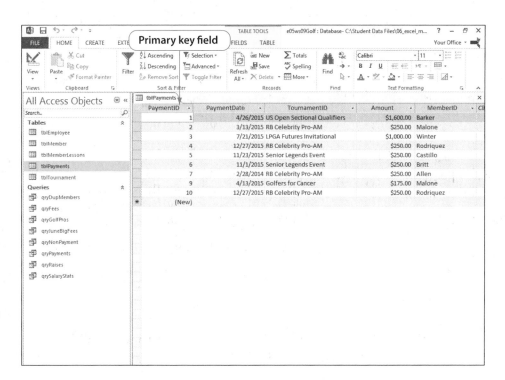

Figure 10   Payment table in Access for the Red Bluff Golf Course & Pro Shop

You have been asked to import the qryPayments query from the Golf database. This query organizes various data from the database concerning the tournaments that Red Bluff members have paid entry fees to attend. After the data is imported into Excel, it can be further analyzed.

E09.07

To Connect to an Access Database

a. Click the **Tournaments** worksheet tab.

b. On the DATA tab, in the Get External Data group, click **From Access**. This will display the Select Data Source dialog box. Navigate to the folder where your student data files are stored, select **e05ws09Golf.accdb**, and then click **Open**.

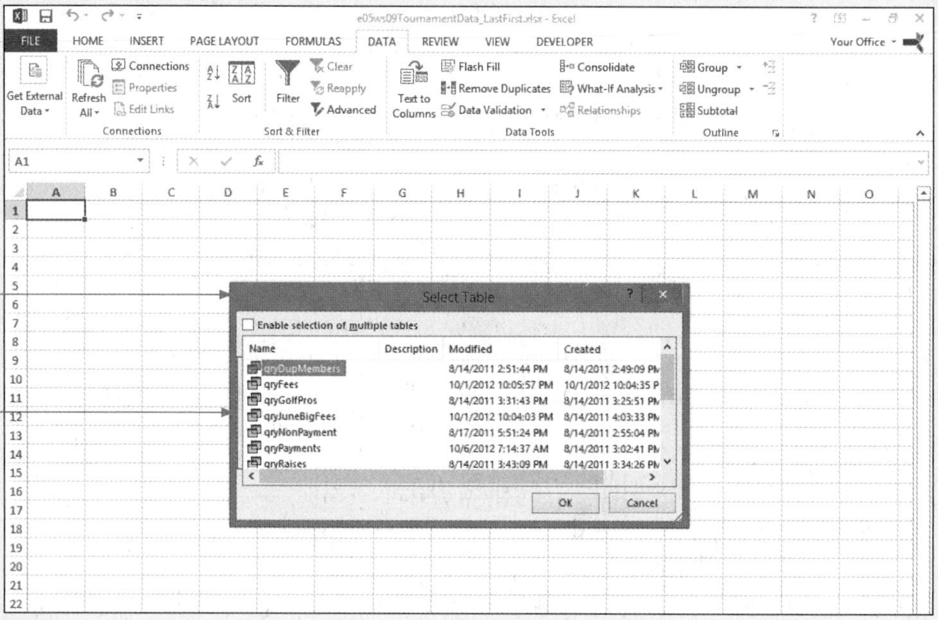

SIDE NOTE

Drag Access Data into Excel

You can import tables and queries from Access by dragging the object from the Navigation Pane and dropping it into the desired starting cell.

Figure 11 Connecting to an Access database

c. In the Select Table dialog box, click the **qryPayments** query, and then click **OK**.

d. The Import Data dialog box provides the option to import this data as a table, PivotTable report, or PivotChart. Make sure the default option **Table** is selected, and then verify the **Existing worksheet** option is selected and the input box displays **=$A$1** to indicate the data will be imported into cell A1.

e. Click **OK**, and then click **Save** 🖫.

SIDE NOTE

Importing Zip Codes

Leading zeros in zip codes often get removed. Avoid this by formatting your cells as General or Text, or use the Special cell formatting category Zip Code.

Using Microsoft Query to Query an Access Database

Sometimes, instead of importing a complete table into an Excel worksheet from Access, users prefer to pick and choose specific fields. Perhaps you want to create a PivotTable report showing sales by region and country. **Microsoft Query** is a special tool to help users import individual data fields into their Excel applications. Excel has a query wizard built into its Microsoft Query function that can be a very powerful aid for linking a worksheet to an Access database.

It is very common for business users to use Excel to routinely access a wide variety of data sources in the course of their work. By using Microsoft Query to access external data, users do not have to redo the query; they can simply refresh their connection to the source data so the Excel application reflects any changes.

Red Bluff members often sign up for lessons in advance of tournaments they have signed up to attend. To better understand this consumer behavior, you have been asked to query the golf course's database concerning member lessons.

E09.08

 To Import Data from an Access Database Using Microsoft Query

a. Click the **Lessons** worksheet tab.

b. On the DATA tab, in the Get External Data group, click **From Other Sources**, and then click **From Microsoft Query** in the gallery.

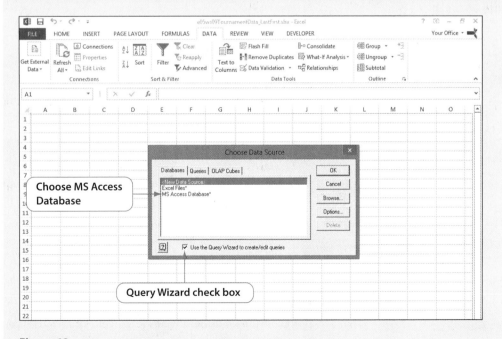

Figure 12 Connecting to an Access database with Microsoft Query

c. In the Choose Data Source dialog box, click **MS Access Database**, ensure **Use the Query Wizard to create/edit queries** is checked, and then click **OK**.

d. In the Select Database dialog box, under Directories, double-click the **folder** where your student data files are stored, and then under Database Name, select **e05ws09Golf**. Click **OK**.

e. In the Query Wizard - Choose Columns dialog box, scroll through the list of tables and columns until you see the **qryFees** query, and then click the **Expand Outline** button ⊞ to see the available fields.

f. Double-click to select and move **LastName** to the Columns in your query box. Using the same technique, double-click the **FirstName**, **ScheduledDate**, and **Fee** fields to move them into the Columns in your query list.

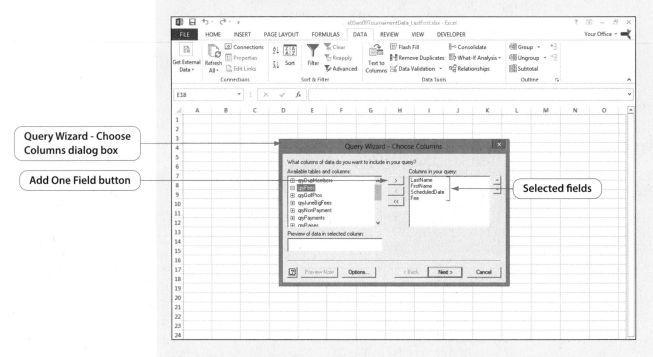

Figure 13   Selecting fields for Microsoft Query

g. Click **Next**, click to select the **ScheduledDate** field, click the first **Filter** arrow, and then click **is greater than or equal to**. In the input box to the right, type 6/1/2015.

h. Ensure the **And** operator is selected, click the next **Filter** arrow, and then click **is less than or equal to**. In the input box to the right, type 6/30/2015.

i. Click **Fee**, click the first **Filter** arrow, and then click **is greater than or equal to**. In the input box to the right, type 150.

j. Click **Next**, click the **Sort by** arrow, click **LastName**, and then accept the default Ascending order. Click in the input box under **Then by**, click **FirstName**, and then keep the Ascending option. Click **Next**.

k. Click **Finish**, verify **Existing worksheet** is selected and the input box displays =$A$1, and then click **OK**. The Access data is imported and displayed starting in cell A1.

l. Complete the **Documentation** worksheet as directed by your instructor.

m. **Save** 🖫 your work, print or submit your workbook as directed by your instructor, and then close ✖ the file.

Making Data Useful

Once data is imported into Excel, it may require manipulation to fit your needs, such as formatting it differently and cleaning the data before it can be used for decision-making purposes. Sometimes this is straightforward and entails simply using the spelling checker or using the Find and Replace feature. Other times it may require extensive reformatting or reorganization of multiple columns.

This can be a major problem for corporations. The cost to businesses in man-hours to correct and find bad data is estimated to be billions of dollars each year. Of course, the impact of bad data can also cost companies unnecessary problems in bad decisions based on the data. In this section you will learn some efficient methods to save time when cleaning data so it is ready to be used in your Excel applications.

Clean Imported Data

Data cleansing is the process of fixing obvious errors in the data and converting the data into a useful format. **Data verification** is the process of validating that the data is correct and accurate. Importantly, data cleansing is not data verification. For example, if you were to clean phone numbers, you would fix or mark as questionable a record with a four-digit phone number. If you were to verify a phone number, you would call the phone number and verify that it dialed the person it purported to call. Data verification is very costly both in time and money. Thus, for the majority of data, most companies will only conduct data cleansing and not necessarily data verification.

Using Text Functions to Clean Data

Previously, you imported text data into Excel with some of the built-in tools. Recall that text data refers to strings of characters. Do not be confused by this term since it can include special characters, spaces, and numbers as well. Text is a very generic data type. Often, data from external sources might easily be cleaned up with proper formatting, for example, formatting number values into currency values. Excel offers a range of **text functions** that help manage text data. Excel text functions help to manipulate and standardize data and can offer additional tools to automate the process.

QUICK REFERENCE	Common Text Functions	
Function Name	**Description**	**Example**
CLEAN(text)	Removes any nonprinting characters from a text string. The CLEAN function removes the first 32 nonprinting character codes, but it does not remove nonprinting character codes for higher values.	If cell A2 contains =CHAR(6)&"text", =CLEAN(A2) will leave only "text".
LOWER(text)	Converts a text string to all lowercase characters	=LOWER(Apt. 4B) will result in "apt.4b"
PROPER(text)	Capitalizes only the first letter in each word of a text string with the remaining characters in lowercase	Given cell A2 contains the string "this is a TITLE", =PROPER(A2) returns "This Is A Title".

(Continued)

Function Name	Description	Example
TRIM(text)	Removes all spaces from text except for single spaces between words; this includes extra spaces at the beginning or at the end of the string.	Given cell A2 contains the string "profit margin", =TRIM(A2) would remove the extra spaces to yield "profit margin".
UPPER(text)	Converts all the characters in a text string to uppercase	=UPPER("total") will result in the word "TOTAL".

CONSIDER THIS | **Why Should You Care About Bad Data?**

Have you ever received mail in which your name or address was misspelled? This is one example of how bad data is propagated. At some point, your name was entered into a database incorrectly, and then that list of names was sold to others. Studies indicate that the total cost to businesses from bad data is well into the billions of dollars. How else does bad data get into the system? What are some basic steps you could take to prevent or minimize the problem?

Text functions help users extract and standardize their data in ways that make life easier; a little knowledge of these advanced functions can reap big rewards. One of the golf club manufacturers is sponsoring a hole-in-one prize for an upcoming tournament. If one of the tournament participants gets a hole in one on hole 9, he or she will receive a free set of golf clubs. To be eligible for the prize, customers filled out entry cards and the information was entered into a database. You have been asked to clean up this data in the spreadsheet shown in Figure 14.

The formulas you use in other spreadsheet applications will malfunction when they encounter the irregular spacing found in the Name column of the spreadsheet you have been given. Consider the contents of cell A2, "ANDERSON RACHEL S.". The text is typed in all capital letters. Only the first letter of each string of text should be capitalized. There is also an extra space between the "RACHEL" and the "S" that needs to be removed.

Three helpful functions can change the case of characters in a string of text. **LOWER** can be used to change uppercase characters to lowercase, and the **UPPER** function can be used to change all characters in a cell to uppercase. The **PROPER** function will capitalize only the first letter of each word in the text string while changing the other characters to lowercase. The **TRIM** function will remove extra spaces from a string of text. The **CLEAN** function removes nonprintable characters, such as line breaks, but will leave other characters.

E09.09

 To Clean Your Data File

a. If necessary, start **Excel**, click **Open Other Workbooks**, and then browse to your student data files. Locate and select **e05ws09TournamentReport**, and then click **Open**.

b. Click the **FILE** tab, and then click **Save As**. Browse to the location where you are saving your files. In the File name box, type e05ws09TournamentReport_LastFirst, using your first and last name, and then click **Save**.

c. To insert your filename as a footer, on the INSERT tab, in the Text group, click **Header & Footer**.

d. On the DESIGN tab, in the Navigation group, click **Go to Footer**. If necessary, click the **left section** of the footer, and then click **File Name** in the Header & Footer Elements group.

e. Click any cell on the spreadsheet to move out of the footer, press Ctrl+Home, on the VIEW tab, in the Workbook Views group, click **Normal** ⊞, and then click the **HOME** tab.

f. On the CustNames worksheet, click cell **B2**, type =PROPER(A2) and then press Ctrl+Enter. Double-click the **AutoFill** handle to copy cell **B2** down to cell **B26**. Resize the columns to show all the names if necessary. This function will capitalize the first letter of each name and leave the rest in lowercase.

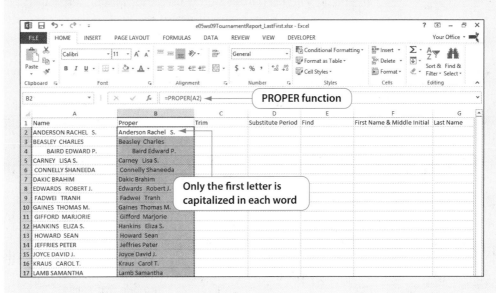

Figure 14   Using the PROPER function

> **Troubleshooting**
> It is not necessary to type these text functions in uppercase in order for them to work.

SIDE NOTE
Alternate Method
You can nest text functions to achieve more efficiency. Typing =PROPER(TRIM(A3)) will provide the same result.

g. Click cell **C2**, type =TRIM(B2) and then press Ctrl+Enter. The TRIM function will remove any extra spaces before or after the names as well as extra spaces between names.

h. Double-click the **AutoFill** handle on cell **C2** to copy the TRIM function down to cell **C26**. Resize the columns to show all the names if necessary.

i. **Save** 🖫 your work.

Cleaning extra spaces is only half the problem. Many times there are nonprinting characters that are not easily visible—such as a hard return or other unseen characters that are often transferred from Internet data. This can be quite frustrating when performing a logical test on that data or when using one of the LOOKUP functions. If you do not have clean data with all the extra spaces or unprintable characters removed, you will get an error message.

Using Text Functions to Separate String Data

In the CustNames worksheet example, the goal is to manipulate the content within each of the cells to move the first and last names to their own separate cells. Be observant when analyzing the data. Notice any patterns that help to define the best functions to use when preparing the text for the company's specific needs.

Consider the contents of cell C2, "Anderson Rachel S.". For tasks such as mail merges, breaking the name into first, middle, and last columns would be useful. This can be accomplished in many ways. One of which would be to find the space character between the last name and first name in the string of text. Once located, everything in front of that space could be removed, leaving only the first name and middle initial.

The **FIND** function is useful for finding a specific string of text in a larger string. The FIND function will return the first position number of the text that was searched for. There are two common functions for replacing specific strings of text in a second text string. The **REPLACE** function will replace strings of text in a second string of text based upon a starting position and number of characters to replace. The **SUBSTITUTE** function replaces one string of text for another string based upon the number of instances of the search string. The **LEFT** function can be used to extract a specific number of characters from a string of text beginning at the left side of the string.

Below are some additional text functions to consider along with a description of what each does.

Function Name	Description	Example
CONCATENATE(Text1, [Text2], ...Textn)	This function is used to join up to 255 text strings into one text string.	=CONCATENATE(A1," ",B1) will return the value of A1, a space, and the value of B1 in one text string.
FIND(find_text, within_text, [start_num])	Locates a particular string of data within a second text string, and returns the number of the starting position of the first text string from the starting position of the second text string. The "start_num" is an optional parameter giving a position within the string of where to start the search. If omitted, the position is assumed to be 1.	=FIND(" ","ABC corp.") will return the value of 4 since the space is the fourth character.

Function Name	Description	Example
REPLACE(old_text, start_num, num_chars, new_text)	Replaces part of a text string, based on the number of characters you specify, with a different text string. Old_text is the original string, start_num is the position to start replacing text, num_chars the number of characters to replace, and new_text is what string to replace in that position.	If cell A2 contains "2012", then =REPLACE(A2,3,2,"15") results in "2015" by starting at the third position and replacing two characters with "15".
SEARCH(find_text, within_text, [start_num])	Locates one text string within a second text string, and returns the number of the starting position of the first text string from the starting character of the second text string. This function is not case sensitive.	Given cell A2 contains the string "revenue", =SEARCH("e",A2,6) returns "7" as the position of the next "e" after the starting position of six characters. If the start_num argument value of 6 is omitted, the formula would return 2.
SUBSTITUTE(text, old_text, new_text, [instance_num]).	Similar to REPLACE. This function substitutes new_text for old_text in a text string. "Text" is the text string or the cell reference to text data.	If cell A2 contains "sales data", then =SUBSTITUTE (A2,"sales","cost") results in "cost data".
LEFT(text,[num_chars])	This function returns the characters in a text string based on the number of characters you specify starting with the far-left character in the string. The text argument is a string of text or a cell reference to text data, and the num_chars argument specifies the characters to extract.	If cell A2 contains the text string "sale price", then =LEFT(A2,4) will return the word "sale".
LEN(text)	This function returns the number of characters, including spaces, in a text string.	If cell A2 contains the string "Excel 2013", then =LEN(A2) will return the number "10".

(Continued)

QUICK REFERENCE	Additional Text Functions *(Continued)*

Function Name	Description	Example
MID(text,start_num,num_chars)	This function returns a specific number of characters from a text string starting at the position you specify and based on the number of characters you specify.	If cell A2 contains the string "purchase price", then =MID(A2,10,10) yields "price". It takes ten characters starting at the tenth position. If num_chars exceed the remaining string length, MID returns to the end of the string.
RIGHT(text, [num_chars])	Returns the characters in a text string based on the number of characters you specify starting from the far-right character position.	If cell A2 contains the string "item price", then =RIGHT(A2,5) will result in "price".

E09.10

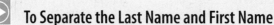

To Separate the Last Name and First Name

a. Click the **CustNames** worksheet tab, click cell **D2**, type =SUBSTITUTE(C2,".","",1) and then press Ctrl+Enter. Double-click the **AutoFill** handle to copy cell **D2** down to cell **D26**. Resize the columns to show all the names if necessary.

The SUBSTITUTE function searches cell D2 for a period character—the first set of double quotes. The new_text argument replaces the period—in this case with a blank, as is found in the second set of double quotes—since you do not want a period to be found in the name field. The last argument is instance_num of 1, which signals to only do this substitution for the first period encountered, but not for any remaining period characters.

b. Click cell **E2**, type =FIND(" ",D2) and then press Ctrl+Enter. The Find function returns the position number of the first space character in cell D2. Double-click the **AutoFill** handle for cell **E2** to copy the function down to cell **E26**.

> **Troubleshooting**
>
> In Step b of this exercise be careful to put a space between the double quotes to indicate the character to search for is a space character. This function will return a number telling you how many characters there are before encountering the character specified as the first function argument—in this case—a space. As can be expected, the number of characters the function will return will vary for the names in each cell.

SIDE NOTE
The SUBSTITUTE Function
If the SUBSTITUTE function does not find the string supplied for the old_text argument, it will not return an error.

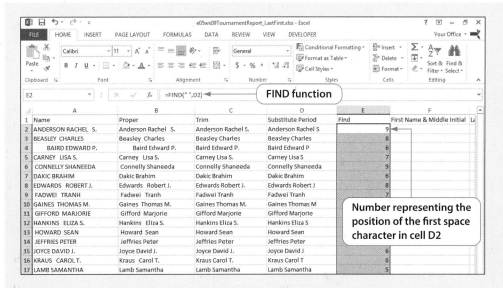

Figure 15   Using the FIND function

c. Click cell **F2**, type =REPLACE(D2,1,E2,"") and then press Ctrl + Enter. Double-click the **AutoFill** handle to copy cell **F2** down to cell **F26**. Resize the columns to show all the names if necessary.

    The REPLACE function examines the text in cell D2. The 1 in the second argument of the function tells the Replace function to begin at the first position of the cell. REPLACE then uses the value in E2, a nine, to move nine characters into cell D2 and replace any text before and including the ninth position with a null value—the last argument in the function.

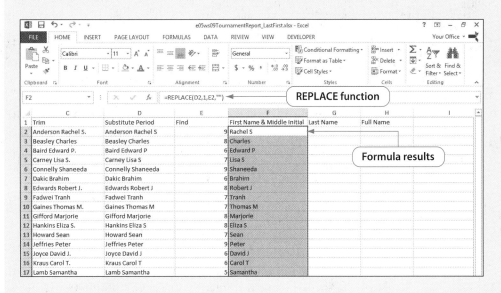

Figure 16   Results of using REPLACE

SIDE NOTE
Using TRIM

Instead of removing extra spaces from a text function by subtracting position numbers, the TRIM function could be used.

d. Click cell **G2**, type =LEFT(D2,E2-1) and then press Ctrl + Enter. Double-click the **AutoFill** handle to copy cell **G2** down to cell **G26**, and then resize the column if necessary.

The LEFT function examines the text in cell D2. The second argument tells the LEFT function how many characters to return. Consider the last name in cell D2, "Anderson". This name is eight characters long. Since the space found in D2 occurs at the ninth position, you can subtract one from E2 to return the first eight characters.

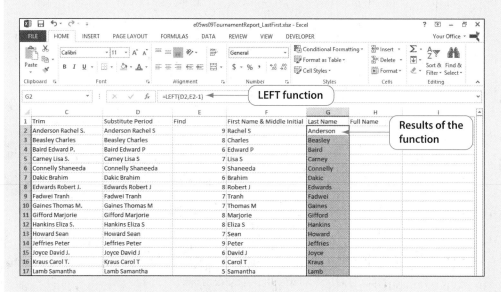

Figure 17   Results of using the LEFT function

e. **Save** 🖫 your work.

Concatenating Data

Concatenating data refers to combining or joining multiple strings of data to form a single string. Using the current worksheet data example, the goal is to change the name order from the original version of last name, first name, and middle initial to a result of first name, middle initial, followed by last name. It would be useful to show it all together in a single field. The previous exercise separated the name data; all that is needed is to string it together in the desired order. There are a variety of ways to accomplish this in Excel. You could manually string together data using the ampersand (&), or you can use the CONCATENATE function to string together data to join into one cell.

CONCATENATE is a text function used to join up to 255 text strings into one text string. One of the advantages of using this function is that it also allows users to do some formatting of the data at the same time if needed, such as nesting the function in combination with the PROPER function to have the first character in each word capitalized.

In the data provided, the first name plus middle initial appears in column F and the last name is stored in column G. Column H will be used to join the data using the ampersand. The ampersand will accomplish the same task as the CONCATENATE function, only with less typing. Keep in mind that spaces (entered between a set of double quotes) will need to be added at the appropriate points when joining strings of text together.

▶ To Join Strings of Text

a. Click cell **H2**, and then type **=F2&" "&G2**. Press Ctrl+Enter, and then double-click the **AutoFill** handle to copy the formula down to cell **H26**. Resize the column if necessary. Cell H2 now displays "Rachel S Anderson", combining the results of F2 and G2 with a space character between them.

> **Troubleshooting**
>
> Are spaces missing between the names in the final result? Check to see if a space was typed between the double quotes in the formula. Recall that in addition to text from a cell reference, quotes can be used to string together additional characters—in this case a space between the words.

Ampersand used to join cells and text string

Result of joining cells and text string

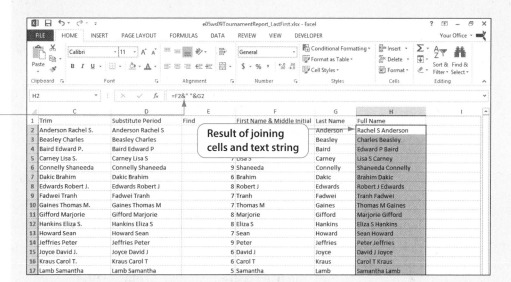

Figure 18   Using the ampersand to join columns

b. **Save** 💾 your work.

REAL WORLD ADVICE | **Recognizing Data Patterns Is Important!**

The secret to understanding how to clean your data is realizing that there are character patterns in the data. Delimiters like commas and spaces in between words can become crucial signposts that the resourceful Excel user can exploit with text functions. When you see a character pattern in your data, you can use the FIND operator to find just about anything, especially commas and spaces. Once you start looking for character patterns, you will be amazed at how many there are.

Use Flash Fill to Cleanse Data

Excel 2013 has a new feature call Flash Fill that can make data cleansing easier and faster than using traditional text functions. **Flash Fill** recognizes patterns in data as you type and automatically fills in values for text and numeric data. Because Flash Fill involves less typing than traditional text functions, it can be easier to use on touch-enabled devices.

Using Flash Fill to Cleanse Text Data

Flash Fill works by examining the pattern of data in the cell next to where you are typing. If a pattern can be detected, a suggested fill will be displayed in the column you are typing in. Before you use the Flash Fill feature, there are a couple of key points to keep in mind. For Flash Fill to work, you must type in an adjoining column or row to your existing data. There cannot be a blank column or row between the data and where you are typing. You will need to make two edits to the RegistrationData worksheet before Flash Fill will be activated. The first names and middle initials of the customers from the tournament golf club giveaway are still in a single column. For letters to be prepared to send to the entrants, the first name needs be to extracted to a single column.

E09.12

 To Use Flash Fill on Text Strings

a. Click the **RegistrationData** worksheet tab, and then click cell **B2**.

b. Type Rachel and then press Enter to move to cell B3.

c. Type Charl and then press Enter.

   Notice that as you type, Flash Fill will recognize the pattern you are trying to complete. A list of all of the first names from column A will appear as suggestions in column B.

> **Troubleshooting**
> Flash Fill relies on consecutive actions in order to offer a suggestion. If you clicked on another cell or pressed a button on the keyboard between typing "Rachel," pressing Enter, and typing "Charles"—Flash Fill will not offer a suggestion.

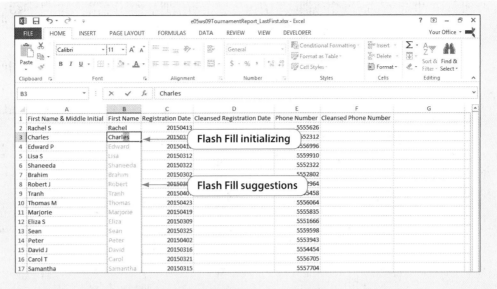

Figure 19   Using Flash Fill to cleanse first names

d. **Save** your work.

Using Flash Fill to Cleanse Numeric Data

Flash Fill is disabled by default on numeric data. When using the Flash Fill feature on numeric data, you may need to provide an additional example of how the data should be arranged. The Flash Fill feature can then be used through the Data tab in the Ribbon.

The registration dates that were provided are in numeric format, but not in a format that Excel recognizes as a date. The dates provided are in YYYYMMDD format, or for cell C2—20150413. Flash Fill can be used in this situation to reorganize the date into the MM/DD/YYYY or 4/13/2015 format. Additionally, the phone number in cell E2 was provided as 5555626 and needs to be displayed as 555-5626.

In this exercise, the registration date and entrant phone numbers will be properly formatted using Flash Fill.

E09.13

▶ To Reformat Numeric Data with Flash Fill

a. Click cell **D2**, type 4/13/2015 and then press Enter.

b. In cell **D3**, type 3/18/2015 and then press Enter.
   Notice that no suggestions from Flash Fill appear.

c. On the DATA tab, in the Data Tools group, click **Flash Fill**. Flash Fill will complete the list of dates through cell D26.

d. Click cell **F2**, type 555-5626 and then press Enter.

e. Type 555-2312 and then notice the suggestions that appear from Flash Fill. Since you are mixing text in with the phone numbers, Flash Fill will make suggestions. Press Enter to accept the suggestions.

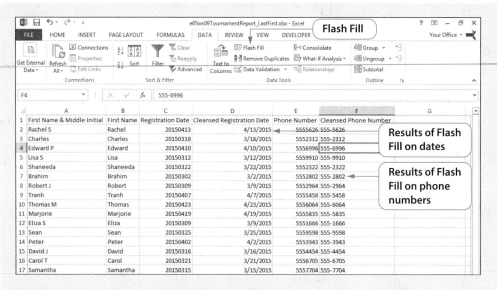

Figure 20 Using Flash Fill to cleanse numeric data

f. **Save** 🔲 your work.

Separate Data Using Text Functions and Wizards

Imported data can often contain strings of text that need to be separated in addition to being cleansed or to be useful in a spreadsheet analysis. The text functions in Excel can be used to separate strings of text or to reorganize strings of text so they can be better used. There are also wizards, such as the Convert Text to Columns Wizard, that can be useful in separating and reorganizing strings of text.

Using the LEN and the MID Functions to Separate Data

The **LEN** function is a useful way to calculate the length of a specified string of values. The basic syntax contains only one argument, the string of text you wish to view the length of. So if you typed =LEN("Red Bluff") the function would return the result of 9, which includes counting the space character. This can help when you want to tell Excel how to find the data you want to extract. However, beware of spaces at the front or end of a cell entry, as LEN will count these, and you may not even know it! To avoid this problem, you can always nest the TRIM function or apply TRIM before applying the LEN function to your data.

You have been provided with a list of addresses for members who have registered for an upcoming tournament. By separating these addresses from a single address column into three final columns—Street Address, City, and State, the golf course can further analyze where their members are located. To accomplish this task, you will use the text functions LEN, RIGHT, and MID in conjunction with other text functions. The **RIGHT** function tells Excel to start counting from the right side of the string. The **MID** function works in a similar fashion to the LEFT function in that it returns characters from a cell from left to right. The difference is that the second argument of the function allows you to direct MID to begin returning characters from the middle of a cell.

E09.14

 To Extract the Customer's First Name from the List of Names

a. Click the **Address** worksheet tab, and then click cell **E2**.

Column C already contains a FIND function that locates the comma in cell B2. Column D already contains a LEFT function that has extracted the street address in B2.

b. Type =LEN(D2) and then press Ctrl+Enter. The length of the street address in cell D2 is 14 characters. Double-click the **AutoFill** handle to copy the formula down to cell **E17**.

c. Click cell **F2**, type =MID(B2,C2+2,LEN(B2)-E2) and then press Ctrl+Enter.

This extracts the combination of city name and state from cell B2. The MID function begins extracting text in cell B2 at the 17th position. This position is used because the comma position in C2 is 15 and the street address begins after an additional comma and space character. The third argument of the MID function dictates how many characters to extract from cell B2. Taking the length of B2, 27 characters, and subtracting the length of the street address, 14, results in the MID function taking 13 characters out of B2.

d. Double-click the **AutoFill** handle on cell **F2** to copy the formula down to cell **F17**.

e. Click cell **G2**, type =RIGHT(F2,2) and then press Ctrl+Enter. Double-click the **AutoFill** handle to copy the formula down to cell **G17**. This will extract the first two characters from the right of the text string in cell F2.

> **SIDE NOTE**
> **Flash Fill**
> Since this data is consistent, you could use Flash Fill to extract the city and state text from column B.

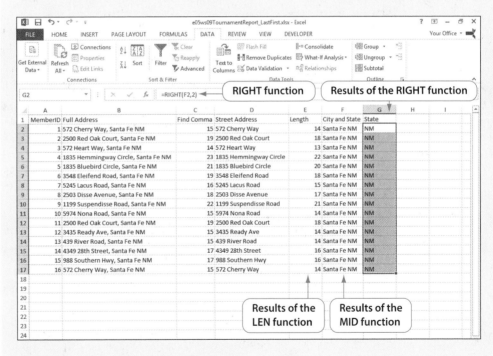

Figure 21   Results of the LEN, MID, and RIGHT functions

f. **Save** 🖫 your work.

MODULE 5

So how do you know which of these three formulas to use if they all work in a similar manner?

1. If the desired text starts on the left side of the cell, use the LEFT function.
2. If the desired text starts from the right side of the cell, and is consistently located relative to the right side of the cell, use the RIGHT function.
3. And if the desired text is in the middle of a text string, use the MID function.

Using Wizards for Separating Data

You have already separated data using the REPLACE and FIND functions. However, Excel provides a special wizard called the **Convert Text to Columns Wizard** for separating simple data cell content. This wizard can often provide another option to consider whenever it can be applicable. This is a very handy Excel feature because it walks you through the whole process of separating your data and gives you control over a variety of formatting options.

You have been provided with a list of names of golf course members who have registered for tournaments but who have not yet purchased anything at the pro shop. The pro shop would like to target them in a new promotion to offer them a 10% discount. To help accomplish this, your boss would like you to separate the name data into two separate fields.

E09.15

 To Separate Name Data

a. Click the **Members** worksheet tab, and then select cells **A2:A14**.

b. On the DATA tab, in the Data Tools group, click **Text to Columns**.

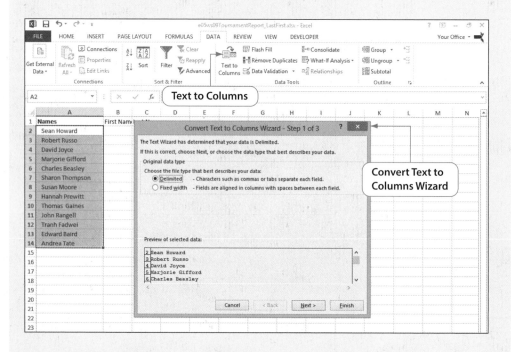

Figure 22 Using Convert Text to Columns to separate name data

c. In the Convert Text to Columns Wizard, under Choose the file type that best describes your data, make sure **Delimited** is selected, and then click **Next**.

d. Under Delimiters, click to check the check box next to **Space**, click to uncheck the check box next to **Tab**, and then click **Next**.

e. Click in the **Destination** box, change the destination cell reference to **$B$2**, and then click **Finish**.

Troubleshooting

By default, the Convert Text to Columns Wizard will begin the output of the data in the first cell you selected. The result will be to paste the separated data over the original data. It is best practice to change the destination cell to begin to the right of your original data if possible.

---

f. **Save** 🖫 your work.

REAL WORLD ADVICE   Wizard vs. Manual vs. Flash Fill?

There are many tools in Excel to cleanse and reorganize data. The main goal is always to reach for the tool that fulfills the needs at hand in the most efficient manner. So now that you have seen how to separate data with text functions, Flash Fill, and the Convert Text to Columns Wizard, when do you know which one to choose over the other?

- The Convert Text to Columns Wizard is designed for simple cell content, so if you are separating text data rarely, and the data fits the requirements of the wizard, the Convert Text to Columns Wizard will be the easiest and most efficient to use.

- If you will be converting data repetitively, or the data consistently comes from an external source and needs to be cleaned up, text functions are the best option.

- Flash Fill works well with consistently organized data and is optimized for working on touch-enabled devices.

Removing Duplicates

It is easy to enter a customer contact more than once or to have multiple customer entries when merging customer data from multiple sources. This is one of the most common data entry errors. Even when steps are taken to minimize redundant data, there is a chance that duplicate entries will still result.

Excel provides an easy tool for removing duplicate entries—the **Remove Duplicates** button found on the Data tab in the Data Tools group. In the Remove Duplicates dialog box, you specify which columns you want the wizard to check. Excel searches whichever columns you have selected and prompts you to remove any duplicates that it finds. However, use this tool with caution, since it will not show what Excel is about to delete. Click OK to delete the duplicates.

You have been asked to examine data that was manually entered concerning golf lessons attended by members of the golf club prior to a tournament in the past year. Since each member can only attend one lesson per day, any duplicate values should be removed. The record contains the member's last name, date of the lesson, and fee.

E09.16

  To Remove Duplicates

a. Click the **Lessons** worksheet tab, and then select the names in cells **A1:C18**.

b. On the DATA tab, in the Data Tools group, click **Remove Duplicates**.

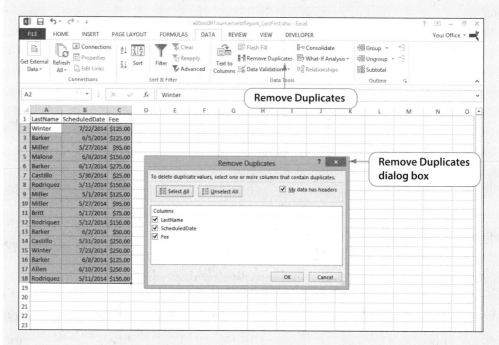

Figure 23   Removing duplicates

c. Make sure that the **My data has headers** box is checked in the top-right corner of the Remove Duplicates dialog box. Ensure that all three columns are selected to check for duplicates, and then click **OK**.

d. Excel returns a message saying **2 duplicate values found and removed; 15 unique values remain**. Click **OK**.

e. **Save** your work.

REAL WORLD ADVICE | **Identifying Duplicate Data**

Identifying duplicate data can be a time-consuming and challenging task. While the best practice is to use a unique identifier or primary key for each record, duplicate data can still be created. Before removing data from a data set, be sure to thoroughly investigate the records to ensure they are true duplicates.

Using Conditional Formatting to Identify Duplicates

In the previous methods for removing duplicates, Excel automatically deletes the records once it finds them and you click OK, without specifying which records were deleted. You can identify duplicates by using conditional formatting if it is necessary to examine the records first. Prior to Excel 2007, you had to write a complex logical test formula with conditional formatting to achieve the same result. Recent versions of Excel have made this concept much easier to perform. With the Conditional Formatting feature, Excel now has a special predefined rule for identifying duplicate values.

The accounts manager at the Red Bluff Golf Course & Pro Shop has asked you to go through a list of invoices for items related to several past tournaments in order to identify if there are any duplicates among them. You will not be deleting any of the data, rather you will only highlight duplicate records for further investigation. In viewing the long list of numbers, it is apparent that the most efficient and simplest method would be to create a conditional formatting rule in Excel to highlight any duplicate invoices.

E09.17

 To Find and Highlight Duplicates Using Conditional Formatting

a. Click the **Invoices** worksheet tab, and then select **A1:A277**.

b. On the HOME tab, in the Styles group, click **Conditional Formatting**.

c. In the gallery that appears, point to **Highlight Cells Rules**, and then click **Duplicate Values**.

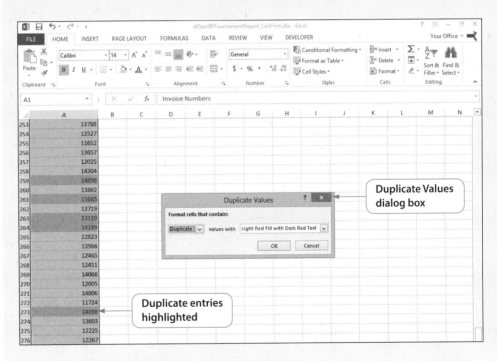

Figure 24   Using Conditional Formatting to identify duplicates

d. Accept the default entries in the Duplicate Values dialog box, click **OK**, and then press Ctrl + Home. The duplicate values are now highlighted.

e. In the Editing group, click **Sort & Filter**, and then click **Sort A to Z**. This will allow for easier viewing of the duplicate records.

f. **Save** 🖫 your work.

Clean Date-Related Data

One of the biggest problems in combining data from a variety of sources is coming up with a standard date format. Some users include a full, four-digit year, whereas others use two digits. Some include a zero with single-digit months, whereas others do not. In fact, different countries change the order of the date components around completely.

Another problem with dates is that sometimes when you import web data into Excel or you paste it in as text from an external source, the default format for the dates is a text format. These text dates are usually left-aligned instead of right-aligned, and they may also be marked with an error indicator icon (if error checking is turned on). This creates problems when the date field is used in other calculations, such as when you create a PivotTable and want to group the data by date. The **DATEVALUE** function converts a date in a text format into a serial value. In Excel, a date is actually a real number where the value is calculated as the number of days since December 31, 1899. So January 1, 1900, is equivalent to a value of 1 in this system. Converting dates into serial values is what allows you to use dates in mathematical calculations.

You have been asked to convert the dates on a list of invoices related to purchases made for the next Seniors Golf tournament at the Red Bluff Golf Course & Pro Shop. Once cleansed, these dates can be used in PivotTables or other means of analysis.

E09.18

 To Convert Text Using DATEVALUE

a. Click the **SalesCommission** worksheet tab.

b. Click cell **D2**, type =DATEVALUE(B2) and then press Ctrl+Enter. In the Number group, click the **Number Format** arrow, and then select **Short Date** as the format for the cell.

c. Double-click the **AutoFill** handle to copy the formula down to cell **D11**.

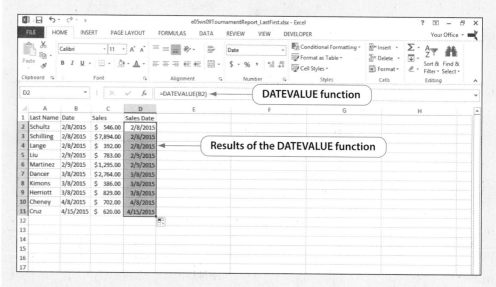

Figure 25   Results of the DATEVALUE function

d. **Save** your work.

Reconstructing Dates Using Text to Columns

Because there are many different date formats, working with dates can be very tricky. For example, the standard European format for dates is DD/MM/YY, whereas in the United States the standard is MM/DD/YY. Excel contains several date functions that make working with dates and converting dates much easier.

The date data received from the RB Celebrity Pro-Am Tournament, concerning purchases made at the pro shop prior to the 3/14/2015 tournament, is in DD/MM/YYYY format. You will use the Convert Text to Columns Wizard to change the date format on a list of purchases.

E09.19

 ### To Convert a European Date to a U.S. Standard

a. Click the **Purchases** worksheet tab, and then select cells **B2:B11**.

b. On the DATA tab, in the Data Tools group, click **Text to Columns**.

c. In the Convert Text to Columns Wizard, under Choose the file type that best describes your data, select **Fixed Width**, and then click **Next**.

> **Troubleshooting**
> Before attempting to rearrange dates by using the LEFT, RIGHT, and MID text functions, keep in mind that Excel stores dates as a serial number, and it is the cell formatting that displays this serial number in a date format. The LEFT function extracts a specified number of characters from a text string starting from the far-left character. The RIGHT function does the same starting from the far-right character. And the MID function extracts characters starting in the middle of the text string. So applying the LEFT function to a date will only return the specified numbers beginning on the left of the serial number for that date. You can extract the day, month, and year from a date field by using Convert Text to Columns or applying the DAY, MONTH, YEAR functions.

d. There are no column breaks to add, remove, or move, so click **Next**.

e. Under Column data format, click **Date**, click the **Date** arrow, and then click **DMY**. Click the **Destination** box, and then adjust the cell reference by typing **$C$2**. Click **Finish**. Resize the columns if necessary to show all the dates.

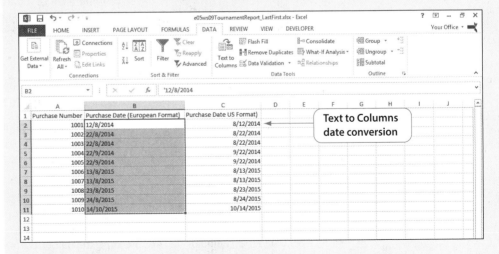

Figure 26   Converting a European date to a U.S. date

f. **Save** 🖫 your work.

Creating Dates with Date Functions

There are many features in Excel to help you process date-related data. It might seem that working with dates in Excel is a confusing process. But any business person can tell you that doing calculations with dates and manipulating them is something that you are sure to encounter. Knowing how to apply some of the more sophisticated functions will heighten your value to any company.

Aleeta Herriott has been so impressed with your work that she has asked for help in sorting out some data from customer transactions that occurred just after the RB Celebrity Pro-Am tournament on 3/14/2015. The data has already been imported from the .csv file for a summary sales report and converted into an Excel format. But it still has some strange looking date fields that are preventing Aleeta from running her own Excel formulas. When the raw data was first imported, it looked as if the source system put the name of the day (such as Tuesday) in front of the standard date format for the Ord_Date field. In addition, the data imported the standard date format into Excel as three separate fields with the headings Ord_Year, Ord_Day, and Ord_Month. Technically, there is nothing wrong with the data itself, but with several hundred thousand transactions in the report, it makes doing any date-related calculations challenging.

The **DATE** function returns the sequential serial number that represents a particular date. Making use of the DATE function allows a quick conversion of the data in the three separate fields since you can find the serial date with the following arguments:

=DATE(year, month, day)

QUICK REFERENCE	Common Date Functions in Excel
Function Name	**Description**
DATE(year, month, day)	Returns the sequential serial number that represents a particular date
DATEVALUE(date_text)	Returns the serial number of the date represented by date_text. Use DATEVALUE to convert a date represented by text to a serial number.
DAY(serial_number)	Returns the day of the month from a date entry. The serial_number argument has to be a serial date or cell reference to a date formatted cell. The DATE function can be used to determine the serial number if needed.
MONTH(serial_number)	Returns the month (i.e., 1–12) of the date entry
YEAR(serial_number)	Returns the year corresponding to a date. This works for years from 1900 to 9999.
WORKDAY(start_date, days, [holidays])	Returns the corresponding date that is the number of days from the start_date, minus weekends and holidays. The start_date must be in serial or date format.
NETWORKDAYS(start_date, end_date, [holidays])	Returns the number of whole working days between two given dates
WEEKDAY(serial_number, [return_type])	Returns the day of the week corresponding to a date (1–7). The optional return_type argument allows you to change how days are counted.

E09.20

 To Combine Multicolumn Dates into a Single Column

a. Click the **CustomerTransactions** worksheet tab, and then right-click **column E**.

b. Click **Insert**. Click cell **E1**, type Complete_Date and then press Enter. Resize column E to fit if necessary.

c. In cell **E2** type =DATE(B2,D2,C2). Press Ctrl+Enter. On the HOME tab, in the Number group, click the **Number Format** arrow, and then click **Short Date** to format the column data as a date. Double-click the **AutoFill** handle to copy down to cell **E15**.

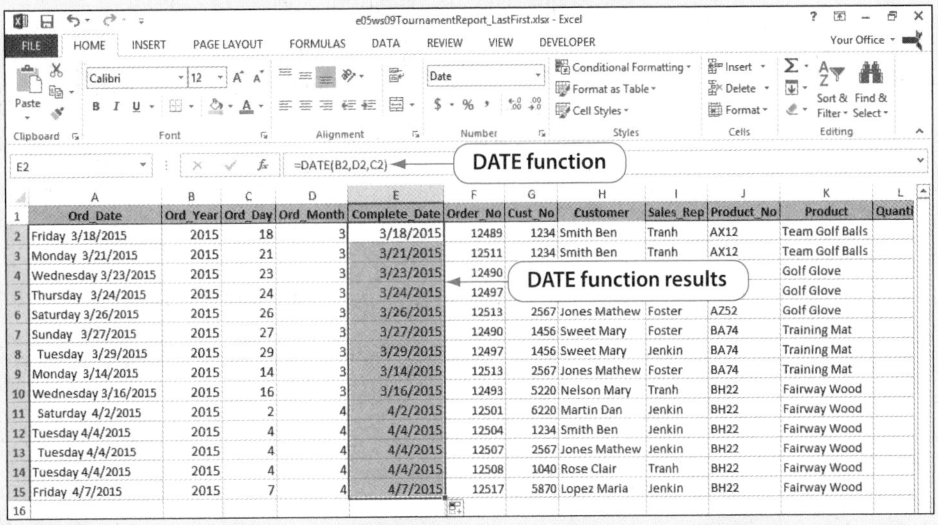

Figure 27 Combining data to make a complete date

d. **Save** 💾 your work.

Using the NETWORKDAYS Function

Because the Red Bluff Golf Course is famous for its competitive layout and challenging greens, it is often asked to host golf tournaments. It currently hosts several major and minor tournaments. The most popular event is the Senior Legends tournament, which occurs in December. Golf tournaments have to be scheduled years in advance, and members have to be alerted about them so they learn to expect times when the course is unavailable to them. It is also important for the maintenance staff to schedule enough workdays to keep everything looking nice and for the inventory in the pro shop to be restocked in time for each event.

With this in mind, Barry Chaney, the Red Bluff Golf Course manager, has asked you to help him build a long-term tournament schedule report. In talking with him, you learned that he would really like to keep track of the number of working days he has between events so he can give members and staff plenty of notice prior to an event. With a little research, you discovered a function called **NETWORKDAYS** that can be used to calculate the number of available work days between two given dates. Its syntax looks like this: =NETWORKDAYS(start_date, end_date, [holidays]).

The optional holidays argument at the end allows users to factor in how specific holidays might reduce the number of available work days. Additional research shows that the TEXT function can be used to display the name of the day by using the dddd format as one of the arguments. The **TEXT** function allows you to display numeric data as text in addition to using special formatting strings to display the text.

▶ To Calculate the Available Workdays Using NETWORKDAYS

a. Click the **TSchedule** worksheet tab. Click cell **G5**.

b. Type =NETWORKDAYS(F5,E6,$I$5:$I$12), press Ctrl+Enter, and then double-click the **AutoFill** handle to copy down to cell **G9**.

Notice that cell G9 shows a negative number. This is because the formula in G9 does not refer to the correct end date for the next golf tournament.

c. To correct the error, click cell **G9**, and then click the **formula bar** to edit the E10 cell reference. Select the text **E10**, type E13 and then press Enter. The negative number should change to a positive 60.

d. Click cell **G13**, and then type =NETWORKDAYS(F13,E14,$J$5:$J$12) to do the same for the 2016 Season tournament schedule. Press Ctrl+Enter, click the **AutoFill** handle, and then drag to copy down to cell **G16**.

Notice you do not need to copy down to G17. For the 2016 season, the end date for the first 2017 event is unavailable. Thus you cannot calculate the available workdays between the 2016 Senior Legends event and the next event since the schedule for 2017 is unknown at this time.

e. Click cell **H5**, type =TEXT(E5,"dddd") and then press Ctrl+Enter. Click the **AutoFill** handle, and then drag down to cell **H9**. This allows you to determine the day of the week each event will start.

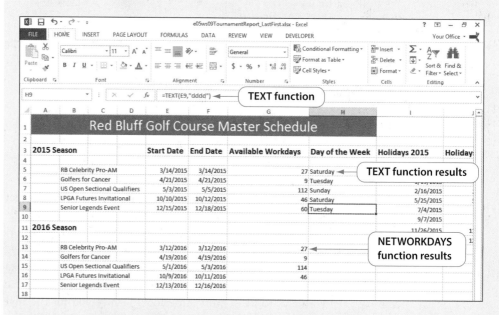

Figure 28 Calculating the number of workdays with NETWORKDAYS

f. Click cell **H5**, press Ctrl, and then type C to copy the formula in H5. Select the range **H13:H17**, press Ctrl, and then type V to paste the formula into the range.

g. **Save** 🖫 your work and then **close** ❌ Excel.

h. Complete the Documentation worksheet and submit your file as directed by your instructor.

Concept Check

1. What is a web query? How is it used to import data into Excel? p. 471–472

2. What is a markup language? Give two examples, and describe how they are useful. p. 475–476

3. What are the benefits of importing data from an Access database into Excel? p. 482

4. How are character patterns in data used to help clean and manipulate data within a cell? p. 487

5. What does the Flash Fill feature do in Excel? How does Flash Fill handle text and numeric data differently? p. 496

6. What are text functions? How are they used for cleaning data? p. 498

7. Why is it important to clean date-related data? p. 504

Key Terms

CLEAN 488
CONCATENATE 494
Convert Text to Columns Wizard 500
Data cleansing 487
Data verification 487
DATE 506
DATEVALUE 504
Delimiter 480
External data 470
FIND 490
Flash Fill 496
Foreign key 483
HTML 475
LEFT 490

LEN 498
LOWER 488
Markup language 475
Metadata 480
Microsoft Query 484
MID 498
NETWORKDAYS 507
Primary key 483
PROPER 488
Query 471
Relational database 483
Remove Duplicates 501
REPLACE 490
RIGHT 498

SUBSTITUTE 490
TEXT 507
Text data 480
Text file 480
Text functions 487
TRIM 488
UPPER 488
Web query 471
XML 475
XML element 476
XML map 476
XML schema 476

Visual Summary

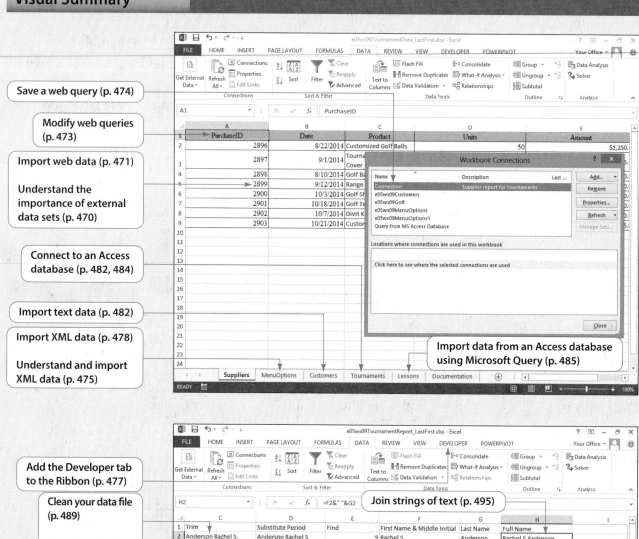

- Save a web query (p. 474)
- Modify web queries (p. 473)
- Import web data (p. 471)
- Understand the importance of external data sets (p. 470)
- Connect to an Access database (p. 482, 484)
- Import text data (p. 482)
- Import XML data (p. 478)
- Understand and import XML data (p. 475)
- Import data from an Access database using Microsoft Query (p. 485)

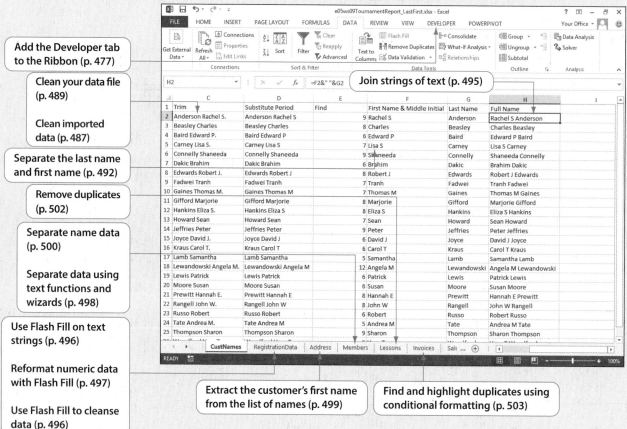

- Add the Developer tab to the Ribbon (p. 477)
- Clean your data file (p. 489)
- Clean imported data (p. 487)
- Separate the last name and first name (p. 492)
- Remove duplicates (p. 502)
- Separate name data (p. 500)
- Separate data using text functions and wizards (p. 498)
- Use Flash Fill on text strings (p. 496)
- Reformat numeric data with Flash Fill (p. 497)
- Use Flash Fill to cleanse data (p. 496)
- Join strings of text (p. 495)
- Extract the customer's first name from the list of names (p. 499)
- Find and highlight duplicates using conditional formatting (p. 503)

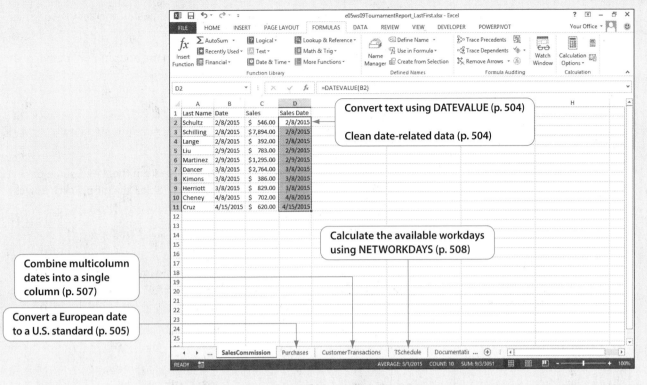

Figure 29 Red Bluff Golf Course & Pro Shop Final Data Integration

---

Practice 1

Student data files needed:

e05ws09Newsletter.xlsx

e05ws09Customer.xml

e05ws09ProShop.accdb

You will save your file as:

e05ws09Newsletter_LastFirst.xlsx

Red Bluff Golf Course & Pro Shop Special Promotions Spreadsheets

Sales & Marketing

The Red Bluff Golf Course & Pro Shop regularly runs special promotions to sell golf equipment and clothing. When customers visit the pro shop website, they can opt to receive electronic copies of the pro shop newsletter via e-mail. The website administrator then e-mails the pro shop an XML file containing the customer information at the end of every week. Customers who walk into the pro shop can also opt to receive the newsletter by writing their name and e-mail address on a sign-up sheet. At the end of each day, these names are then entered into an Access database. You have been asked to take the XML file of the website customer data and integrate it with the customer data from the Access database. All that combined data then needs to be sorted and cleaned so it can be used to send out e-mail versions of the pro shop newsletter.

a. Open the **e05ws09Newsletter** workbook. Save it as e05ws09Newsletter_LastFirst, using your first and last name. Click **Enable Content** if necessary.

b. Click the **WebNewsletter** worksheet tab. To insert a file name footer, on the INSERT tab, in the Text group, click **Header & Footer**. On the DESIGN tab, in the Header & Footer Elements group, click **Go to Footer**. If necessary, click the **left section** of the footer, and then click **File Name**.

c. Click any cell on the spreadsheet to move out of the footer, press Ctrl+Home, on the VIEW tab, click **Normal**, and then click the **HOME** tab.

d. If necessary, click the **WebNewsletter** worksheet tab to make it the active worksheet, and then click cell **A3**.

e. On the DEVELOPER tab, in the XML group, click **Source**. In the bottom-right corner of the window click **XML Maps**.

f. In the XML Maps dialog box, click **Add**, navigate to where your student data files are stored, and then click to select **e05ws09Customer.xml**. Click **Open**, and then click **OK** if you get a warning message stating there is no XML schema for this file. In the XML Maps dialog box, click **OK**.

g. Drag the **customer** element with all of its child elements from the XML Source pane to cell **A1**. On the TABLE TOOLS DESIGN tab, in the External Table Data group, click **Refresh**.

h. Click the **InStoreNewsletter** worksheet tab. On the DATA tab, in the Get External Data group, click **From Access**.

i. In the Select Data Source dialog box, navigate to where your student data files are stored, click **e05ws09ProShop.accdb**, and then click **Open**. In the Import Data dialog box, verify the location in the **Existing worksheet** box is set to =$A$1 so the import starts at cell A1, and then click **OK**.

j. Select the cell range **A2:B9**, press Ctrl, and then type C to copy the range. Click the **WebNewsletter** worksheet tab, click cell **A9**, press Ctrl, and then type V to paste the range. Resize the columns as needed to fit the contents.

k. Click cell **C1**, type Cleansed Names and then press Enter. In cell **C2** type =CLEAN(A2) and then press Enter. This will copy the formula down to C16. Resize column C to show the whole name if needed.

l. Click cell **D1**, type Trimmed Names and then press Enter. In cell **D2**, type =TRIM(C2) and then press Enter. This will copy the formula down to D16. Resize the column to show the whole name.

m. Click cell **E1**, type Proper Names and then press Enter. In cell **E2**, type =PROPER(D2) and then press Enter. This will copy the formula down to E16. Resize the column to show the whole name.

n. Click cell **F1**, type Last Names and then press Tab. In cell **G1**, type First Names and then press Enter.

o. Click cell **F2**, type =LEFT(E2,FIND(",",E2)-1) and then press Enter. Resize the column to show the whole name.

p. Click cell **G2**, type =MID(E2,FIND(",",E2)+2,LEN(E2)-LEN(F2)) and then press Enter. Resize the column to show the whole name.

q. Click the **Documentation** worksheet. Click cell **A6**, and then type in today's date. Click cell **B6**, and then type in your first and last name. Complete the remainder of the **Documentation** worksheet according to your instructor's direction.

r. Click **Save**, close Excel, and then submit your file as directed by your instructor.

Production &
Operations

Student data file needed:

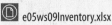 e05ws09Inventory.xlsx

You will save your file as:

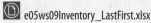 e05ws09Inventory_LastFirst.xlsx

Cleansing Inventory Data

You currently work part-time in an automotive parts store. Because word of your knowledge of Excel has spread, you have been contacted by the district manager. The database used for keeping track of inventory has been corrupted, causing some issues with the inventory data. You have been asked to use your expertise of Excel to clean the inventory data.

a. Open **e05ws09Inventory**, and then save the file as e05ws09Inventory_LastFirst, using your first and last name. Click **Enable Content** if necessary.

b. Click the **Inventory** worksheet tab, and then insert the **file name** in the left section of the footer.

c. Remove any duplicates that exist in the Inventory worksheet. Duplicate records are any records with the same InventoryCode and ItemNumber.

d. The word "paint" was misspelled as "piant" throughout the Category/Manufacturer column. In column G, create a heading called Step 1. In this new column, replace all spellings of "PIANT" with "PAINT" from column C.

e. The data in the Category/Manufacturer column has nonprintable characters before and after the data contained in each cell. There are several spaces before and after the data that need to be removed. Using the data in column G, cleanse the Category/Manufacturer data with the following steps.

- In **H1**, type Step 2 as the column heading. Use the appropriate function to remove any nonprintable characters from column G.

- In **H2**, type Step 3 as the column heading. Use the appropriate function to remove any extra spaces in the data from column H.

- The category and manufacturer should be in two separate columns to the right of the Category/Manufacturer column. Display the corrected values in their own columns. Use the label Category in column J and Manufacturer in column K.

- Use Flash Fill to place the category data in proper case in column J.

- Use Flash Fill to place the Manufacturer data in column K. Owing to the nature of the data, Flash Fill will need to be invoked from the **DATA** tab.

f. In cell **L1**, type InvCode. Use the appropriate function to display the inventory code as all uppercase letters.

g. In cell **M1,** type ItemCode as the column heading. The ItemCode is a combination the inventory code in all uppercase letters, with the item number appended to it. For example, the first ItemCode should be RLXF920569. Use the appropriate function in column M to create this new ItemCode for all items in the data.

h. Resize columns as needed and then save the workbook. Print or submit your file as directed by your instructor.

i. Complete the **Documentation** worksheet according to your instructor's direction. Insert the **filename** in the left custom footer section of the Header/Footer tab in the Page Setup dialog box on all worksheets in the workbook.

j. Click **Save**, close Excel, and then submit the file as directed by your instructor.

Student data files needed:

 e05ws09Stocks.xlsx

 e05ws09Stocks.txt

You will save your file as:

e05ws09Stocks_LastFirst.xlsx

Stock Portfolios

Finance & Accounting

Suzie Fredrickson is an investment advisor. One of the interns who recently left had been monitoring three customers for the office. He had saved the information on the three customers in a text file. Suzie wants the data in a spreadsheet with some additional functionality added to make tracking the portfolios easier. She has asked you to handle the spreadsheet work.

a. Open **e05ws09Stocks**, save the file as **e05ws09Stocks_LastFirst**, using your first and last name. Click **Enable Content** if necessary.

b. Click the **CustomerImport** worksheet tab, and insert the **file name** in the left section of the footer.

c. Import the text file **e05ws09Stocks.txt** into the CustomerImport worksheet.

Each customer in the imported data owns two different stocks. The imported data must be separated into columns such that the stock names and corresponding number of shares are in their own columns. The numbers of shares owned are 4 characters in length.

d. Cleanse the data using the following guidelines:

- The names of each customer should be arranged with the last name first, followed by a comma and a single space character, and ending with the first name. The names should be formatted with uppercase first letters and the remaining letters in lowercase.

- The stock symbols should be displayed as all uppercase letters.

- The number of shares of each stock owned by a customer should be displayed as a number.

e. Use the three portfolio worksheets to construct a summary of the stocks, number of shares, and portfolio value for each customer. Each worksheet must contain the following:

- Copy the cleansed data for each customer to one of the portfolio worksheets.

- Use a web query to import the two stocks owned by that customer below the customer data. You may import the data in any format you wish. For example, you can import historical prices (as long as the most recent prices are included), or only the most recent prices. You may use the financial site of your choice. Some options include **http://money.msn.com/** and **http://www.google.com/finance**.

- In the worksheet, enter a formula that will calculate the total value of the customer's portfolio based on the number of shares of each stock owned and the closing price of the stocks from the prior day. Format the number as Accounting. Create an appropriate heading for the cell

f. On each of the portfolio worksheets, format the headings for the cells containing the customer name, stocks, and number of shares with an appropriate style.

g. Complete the **Documentation** worksheet according to your instructor's direction. Insert the **filename** in the left custom footer section of the Header/Footer tab in the Page Setup dialog box on all worksheets in the workbook.

h. Click **Save**, close Excel, and then submit the file as directed by your instructor.

Additional Cases

Additional Workshop Cases are available on the companion website and in the instructor resources.

WORKSHOP 10 | DATA TABLES, SCENARIO MANAGER, AND SOLVER

OBJECTIVES

1. Perform break-even analysis   p. 516

2. Analyze variables in formulas through the use of data tables   p. 523

3. Use Goal Seek   p. 529

4. Use the Scenario Manager to create scenarios   p. 532

5. Create scenario reports p. 535

6. Understand the use of the Solver add-in p. 538

7. Solve complex problems using Solver   p. 539

8. Generate and interpret Solver answer reports p. 545

Prepare Case

The Red Bluff Golf Course & Pro Shop Business Planning Analysis

Production & Operations

The Red Bluff Golf Course & Pro Shop manager Barry Cheney has been considering expanding the club house to accommodate a steady increase in business. This expansion could include more space for the pro shop and more guest accommodations. He will need to provide a detailed analysis of past sales along with sales forecasts to ensure Mr. Mattingly, the resort's CEO, that the money spent on the improvements

Steve Cukrov / Shutterstock

and expansion will have positive financial benefits for Red Bluff. To increase management's understanding of the current capacities, Barry has collected data about traffic, sales, and product mix. He has asked you to analyze this data using Excel's What-If Analysis tools.

REAL WORLD SUCCESS

"I recently created a workbook detailing changes to several products our company manufactures. In the workbook I used a data table to analyze the changes in profits resulting from different cost and demand combinations. The use of form controls and conditional formatting made the worksheet intuitive and easy to use."

- Carter, alumnus

Student data file needed for this workshop:

 e05ws10GolfWhatIf.xlsx

You will save your file as:

 e05ws10GolfWhatIf_LastFirst.xlsx

Examining Cost-Volume-Profit Relationships

Managers need to analyze business data in order to help them plan and monitor the organization's day-to-day operations. **Cost-volume-profit (CVP) analysis** is the study of how cost and volume are related and the effect their relationship has on profit—if you manufacture products. Management relies on the accounting department to provide the data needed to perform CVP analysis. This data allows management to not only perform CVP analysis but also examine operational risks as a suitable cost structure is chosen.

Consider the Red Bluff Golf Course & Pro Shop. Organizations such as this do not simply decide to renovate or expand operations based on an impulse. Nor do they decide to acquire an existing business or open a new location this way either. Managers spend a great deal of time analyzing past sales data along with future or projected sales data to determine if every strategy from beginning to end has the desired results in mind—increased profit or greater market share.

For example, if Red Bluff does expand or renovate its business, in what ways will it expand or renovate? Will the expansion include more space for the pro shop, an indoor golf simulator, or areas for guests to relax? Will it be for housing more of the retail products sold? Or will Red Bluff simply upgrade existing facilities? Management needs to know what the most popular services are before making any decisions about the types of areas to add. What about revenue? If a loan is taken out and its costs rise because of the interest on the loan, what sales volume or revenue does Red Bluff need to generate in order to afford the increased costs? CVP analysis is a way of evaluating the relationships among the fixed and variable costs, the sales volume—either in terms of units or dollars—and the profits. In this section, you will create a break-even analysis, work with conditional and custom formatting, use Goal Seek, and create data tables to analyze data.

Perform Break-Even Analysis

CVP analysis is used to help understand how changing volumes of sales or revenue affect profits. One of the main CVP analysis tools is break-even analysis, which can help managers understand the relationships among cost, volume, and profit. Managers can use **break-even analysis** to calculate the break-even point in sales volume or dollars, estimate profit or loss at any level of sales volume, and help in setting prices. The **break-even point** is the sales level at which revenue equals total costs—there is neither a profit nor a loss. Understanding how profit of an item or service is affected by other variables requires an analysis of the costs. This analysis helps identify the items or services that change as sales volume changes and those that do not.

When calculating the break-even point, you need to consider the fixed, variable, and mixed costs. **Fixed costs** are expenses that never change regardless of how much product is sold or how many services are rendered. For example, when the golf course is open for business, they have to pay management salaries, insurance, depreciation of building and equipment, and so on, regardless of how many customers they have during the day. **Variable costs**, however, do change based on how many products are sold or services are rendered. For example, with every new golf course membership, Red Bluff provides three personalized golf balls to the new member. The cost of ordering the customized golf balls depends on how many memberships are sold in a given day. Thus, the cost of the supplies used varies depending on the services rendered. **Mixed costs** are costs that contain a variable component and a fixed component. Consider utilities such as electricity and water. Utility companies charge a specific amount—electric companies charge per kilowatt hour used and water companies charge a base fee and then per gallon used, but the bill will vary depending on the usage per billing cycle.

To determine the break-even point, the golf course would need to consider all costs before it can determine its profit. For example, consider the Red Bluff Golf Course & Pro Shop golf polo shirts. The manufacturer charges $22.79—a variable cost—to produce one shirt. The total variable cost would be the variable cost per polo shirt multiplied by the number of polo shirts ordered. The manufacturer charges $15,000 per production run—a fixed cost—regardless of how many shirts are manufactured. This fee covers the costs that the manufacturer incurs to set up the production line. Red Bluff sells the golf polo shirts for $49.99 and would need to sell approximately 552 to break-even. A graph displaying this analysis is shown in Figure 1.

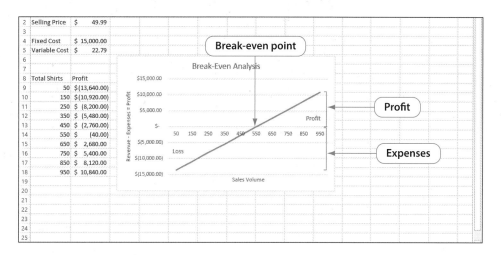

Figure 1 Break-even analysis chart

Opening the Starting File

Barry Cheney is considering raising the current price of golf lessons. He has given you a workbook that includes information for some of the business activities such as costs, prices, revenues, and profits as provided by the accounting department.

E10.00

To Open the Starting File

a. Start **Excel**, click **Open Other Workbooks**, and browse to your student data files. Locate and select **e05ws10GolfWhatIf**, and then click **Open**.

b. Click the **FILE** tab, and then click **Save As**. Browse to the location where you are saving your files. In the File name box, type e05ws10GolfWhatIf_LastFirst, using your first and last name, and then click **Save**.

c. To insert the filename as a footer, on the INSERT tab, in the Text group, click **Header & Footer**.

d. On the DESIGN tab, in the Navigation group, click **Go to Footer**. If necessary, click the **left section** of the footer, and then click **File Name** in the Header & Footer Elements group.

e. Click any cell on the spreadsheet to move out of the footer, press Ctrl+Home, on the VIEW tab, and then in the Workbook Views group, click **Normal**. Click the **HOME** tab.

Performing Break-Even Analysis

The prices for golf lessons are dependent on client demand. Barry would like for you to determine the break-even point for the price of golf lessons depending on these customer demands.

E10.01

To Create a Break-Even Analysis

a. If necessary, click the **Break-Even Analysis** worksheet tab. Click cell **D6**, type =D4*D5 and then press Enter to calculate the gross revenue—the amount of money generated by servicing clients.

b. Click cell **D13**, type =SUM(D9:D12) and then press Ctrl+Enter to calculate the total fixed costs.

c. Click cell **D15**, type =D6*C15 and then press Enter to calculate the total commission the golf instructors will earn.

d. In cell **D16**, type =C16*D4 and then press Enter to calculate the cost of supplies.

e. In cell **D17**, type =D15+D16 and then press Enter to calculate the total variable costs.

f. In cell **D18**, type =D13+D17 and then press Enter to calculate the total expenses.

g. In cell **D19**, type =D6-D18 and then press Ctrl+Enter to calculate the net income—how much profit the golf course will generate.

h. Click cell **D4**, type 50 and then press Ctrl+Enter to try and find the break-even point. Notice that your net income is still negative (–$1,418.50).

i. In cell **D4**, type 60 and then press Ctrl+Enter to try and find the break-even point. Notice that your net income is still negative (–$393.00). However, you are getting closer to finding the break-even point.

j. In cell **D4**, type 64 and then press Ctrl+Enter. Notice that your net income finally has become positive—$17.20. Thus, the golf instructors would have to service 64 clients before making a profit. All clients above and beyond 64 will continue to generate a profit.

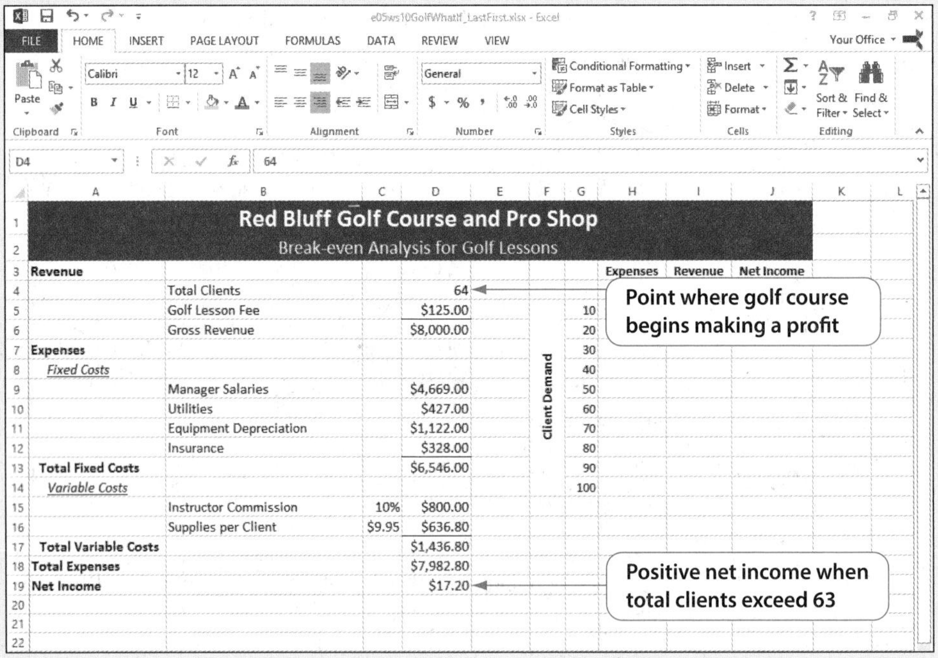

SIDE NOTE

No Value Displays in Cell D6

You are setting up the spreadsheet to perform a break-even analysis. Once you enter a value in D4, all the zeros will be replaced with values.

Figure 2 Working with a break-even analysis

k. **Save** 💾 your work.

Using the Scroll Bar to Perform Break-Even Analysis

Managers use break-even analysis to determine the minimum volume the business needs to make and sell if it is a manufacturer, or buy and sell if it is a retail business, to be sustainable. Once you know a variable cost per unit and total fixed costs, you can calculate the break-even point. By knowing the break-even point, you can set sales goals, prices, and employee hours. When you entered various numbers in the previous exercise, you were performing what-if analysis. **What-if analysis** is the use of several different values in one or more formulas to explore all the various results. These different values are called variables. A **variable** is a value that you can change to see how the change affects other values. Throughout your career, your day will consist of what-if questions. For example, "What if you sell more golf lessons at a lower price? Would you generate more net revenue than if you sold fewer at a higher price?"

REAL WORLD ADVICE | The Operative Word Is "Tools"

The operative word in what-if analysis tools is "tools." It is important to understand that these tools help managers analyze data so the manager can make the best decision based on the information he or she has. Analyzing data is only one component of decision making. Managers make decisions through exploring different options as well as reviewing documents, personal knowledge, or business models to identify and solve problems and make decisions. The fact is that these tools support organizational decision-making activities and are a method of analyzing and interpreting data.

Another way you can determine the break-even point is by using a scroll bar. The **scroll bar** is a form control that allows you to change a number in a target cell location in single-unit increments. The scroll bar is a type of **scenario tool** because of the ability to calculate numerous outputs in other cells by referencing the target cell in formulas and functions. When you use scenario tools to aid in decision making, you are performing what-if analysis. For example, Red Bluff managers can use the scroll bar to change the number of clients and price of each golf lesson to determine when the business will meet and exceed its goal. This can be a challenge to determine if you were to perform this analysis manually—by entering random numbers into cells—because it is extremely time consuming and you do not want users to make physical changes to your spreadsheet model. Additionally, in many cases, when the price increases, the total number of items that can be sold will decrease. In this example, the higher the price of a golf lesson, the fewer clients Red Bluff will have booking the service.

E10.02

 To Create a Break-Even Analysis Using a Scroll Bar

a. Click the **DEVELOPER** tab, and then in the Controls group, click **Insert**.

b. Click **Scroll Bar (Form Control)** , and then draw the scroll bar in the area of cells **E4** through **E17**. Be careful not to select the ActiveX Scroll Bar from the Insert menu.

Figure 3 Break-even analysis using the scroll bar

c. On the DEVELOPER tab, in the Controls group, click **Properties**. In the Format Control dialog box, click the **Control** tab, if necessary. Because you want to analyze the net income from 60 clients to 100 clients, you need to type the following criteria in the Format Control dialog box.

Current value: type 64

Minimum value: type 60

Maximum value: Leave at the default value of **100**

Incremental change: Leave at the default value of **1**

Page change: Leave at the default value of **10**

Cell link: type $D$4

SIDE NOTE

Right-Click Works Too

You can also right-click the scroll bar, and then click Format Control to enter the scroll bar properties.

Scroll bar properties

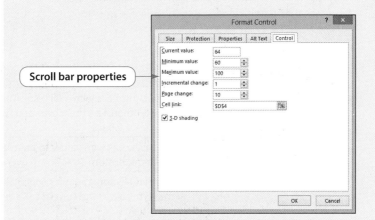

Figure 4 Format Control dialog box

d. Click **OK**, click a cell away from the scroll bar to deactivate the scroll bar, and then click the **up** arrow ⌃ on the scroll bar.

You will notice that the value decreases. Analyze the net income for 60 to 100 clients.

e. Scroll down to the maximum value of 100 by clicking the **down** arrow ⌄ on the scroll bar. Notice that with 100 clients, the golf course would make a profit of $3,709.

f. Scroll up until you have a net income that is at the break-even point. Notice that the golf course would have to service 64 clients in order to make a profit.

g. **Save** 🖫 your work.

SIDE NOTE

Squares Around the Edge

The squares around the edge mean the control is active. To deactivate the control, click a blank area away from it.

SIDE NOTE

Select an Existing Control

To select an existing control object, press Ctrl, and then click the control.

CONSIDER THIS | **How Would You Use the Scroll Bar?**

Using the scroll bar can be a quick-and-easy method to find the break-even point once the spreadsheet is formulated. How could you find the break-even point if you wanted higher pricing? Would it be easier to type values into the price and clients cells? Would you rather change the data on the worksheet with a scroll bar? Which would be more efficient?

Using Conditional Formatting

When you format fonts, borders, alignment, fill colors, and so on, you are making the spreadsheet easier for you to use and read. The same is true about conditional formatting. **Conditional formatting** applies custom formatting to highlight or emphasize values that meet specific criteria, as seen in Table 1. This kind of formatting is called conditional because the formatting occurs when a particular condition is met. For example, a manager may want to highlight cells for employees who exceeded monthly sales quotas or products that are selling below cost.

QUICK REFERENCE	Conditional Formatting Options
Conditional formatting makes the data easier to read and understand because it adds a visual or graphical element to the cells or values.	

Conditional Formatting	Description
Highlight Cells Rules	Highlights cells with a fill color, font color, or border if values are greater than, less than, between two values, equal to a value, or duplicate values
Top/Bottom Rules	Formats cells with values in the top 10 items, top 10%, bottom 10 items, bottom 10%, above average, or below average
Data Bars	Applies a color gradient or solid fill bar; the width of a solid fill bar symbolizes the current cell's value as compared to other cells' values
Color Scales	Formats different cells with different colors; one color is assigned to the lowest group of values, another color is assigned to the highest group of values, and gradient colors are assigned to other values
Icon Sets	Inserts an icon from the icon palette in each cell to point out values as compared to each other

Table 1   Conditional formatting options

E10.03

 To Create Conditional Formatting

a. Click cell **D19**, on the HOME tab, in the Styles group, click **Conditional Formatting**, point to **Highlight Cells Rules**, and then click **Less Than** to open the Less Than dialog box.

b. Click the **Format cells that are LESS THAN** box, and then type **0**. Click the **with** arrow on the right side of the dialog box, click to select the **Red Text** option, and then click **OK**.

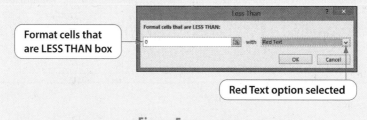

Figure 5   Less Than dialog box

c. In the Styles group, click **Conditional Formatting**, point to **Highlight Cells Rules**, and then click **Greater Than** to open the Greater Than dialog box. Type 0.

d. Click the **with** arrow on the right side of the dialog box, click to select the **Green Fill with Dark Green Text** option, and then click **OK**.

e. Click the **up** arrow ⌃ on the scroll bar.
Notice when the net income becomes a negative number that the font changes to red. This makes it easier for users to identify when the golf course has not reached the break-even point.

f. **Save** 🖫 your work.

Analyze Variables in Formulas Through the Use of Data Tables

Excel contains three types of what-if analysis tools—Goal Seek, Data Tables, and Scenario Manager. A **data table** takes sets of input values, determines possible results, and displays all the results in one table on one worksheet. Because data tables only focus on one or two variables, the results are easy to read and share in tabular form. Although it is limited to only one or two variables, a data table can include as many different variable values as needed.

Using One-Variable Data Tables

A one-variable data table has input values that are listed either down a column—referred to as column-oriented—or across a row—referred to as row-oriented. A **one-variable data table** can help you analyze how different values of one variable in one or more formulas will change the results of those formulas. The formulas that are used in a one-variable data table must refer to only one input cell. For example, you can use a one-variable data table to see how different interest rates affect a monthly car payment by using the PMT function. In this case, the interest rate cell would be the input cell of the one-variable data table. The results display all possible interest rates provided in a data table after Excel performs a what-if analysis on these variables, as shown in Figure 6.

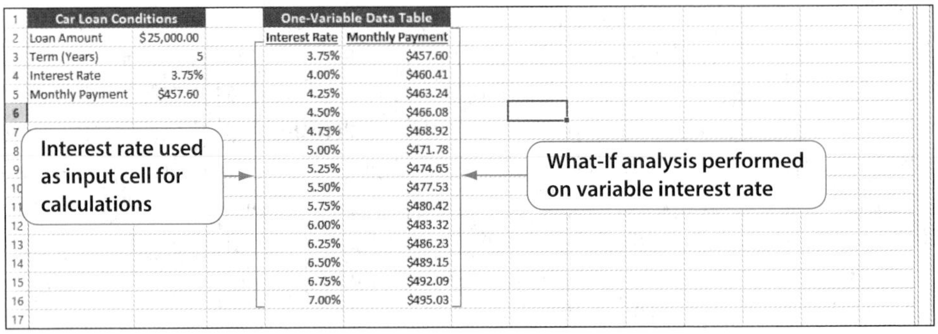

Figure 6　Analyzing data with a one-variable data table

The Red Bluff manager would like you to determine how much the monthly payment on a loan would be based on varying interest rates. On the Break-Even Analysis worksheet, he also wants to avoid a loss of net income and know when the target profit is greater than $2,000. Applying custom formatting will make the data easier to read. Finally, he would like you to build a traditional cost-volume-profit chart off the one-variable data table that will further analyze the break-even point for golf lesson pricing.

E10.04

▶ To Create a One-Variable Data Table

a. Click the **LoanConditions** worksheet tab, click cell **D3**, and then type 4. Press [Enter], in cell D4 type 5, and then press [Ctrl]+[Enter]. Select the range **D3:D4**, and then drag the AutoFill handle down to cell **D9**. Click cell **E2**, type =B6, and then press [Ctrl]+[Enter].

b. Right-click cell **E2**, and then click **Format Cells**. In the Format Cells dialog box, if necessary, click the **Number** tab. Under Category, click **Custom**, and then click the **Type** box. Delete any existing text, and then type "Monthly Payment" to hide the results of the formula and display the typed text as a column heading. Click **OK**, and then select the range **D2:E9** to select the data for your data table.

c. On the DATA tab, in the Data Tools group, click **What-If Analysis**, and then click **Data Table** to open the Data Table dialog box.

d. Press [Tab] to move the insertion point to the Column input cell box, type $B$4 and then click **OK**. Notice that Excel calculated the monthly payment for each interest rate.

e. Select the range **E3:E9**, on the **HOME** tab, in the **Styles** group, click **Conditional Formatting**, point to **Data Bars**, and then under Gradient Fill, click **Green Data Bar**.

SIDE NOTE

Typing $B$4 into the Column Input Cell

The interest rates being used are listed in a column. This is why you entered the interest rate cell—$B$4—into the column input cell box.

Red Bluff Loan Conditions		One-Variable Data Table	
Loan Amount	$200,000		Monthly Payment
Term (Years)	10	4%	$1,772
Interest Rate	6.00%	5%	$1,856
Down Payment	$25,000	6%	$1,943
Monthly Payment	$1,942.86	7%	$2,032
		8%	$2,123
		9%	$2,217
		10%	$2,313

What-If analysis performed on interest rate variables

Gradient Fill Green Data Bar option applied

Figure 7   One-variable data table with conditional formatting

SIDE NOTE

Data Tables Automatically Update

If you change the formula used as a row or column input cell, the data table will be automatically updated as you update your data.

f. Click the **Break-Even Analysis** worksheet tab, click cell **H4**, and then type =D18. Press Tab. Type =D6 and then press Tab. In cell **J4**, type =D19 and then press Enter.

g. Select the range **H4:J4**, right-click any of the selected cells, and then click **Format Cells**. On the **Number** tab, under Category, click **Custom**, and then click the **Type** box. Delete any existing text, and then type ;;; to hide the results of the formulas. Click **OK**.

h. Select the range **G4:J14** to select the data for your data table. On the **DATA** tab, in the **Data Tools** group, click **What-If Analysis**, and then click **Data Table** to open the Data Table dialog box.

i. Press Tab to move the insertion point to the Column input cell box, type **$D$4** and then click **OK**. Notice that Excel calculated the expenses, revenue, and profit based on client demand.

j. Select the range **J5:J14**, and then on the HOME tab, in the styles group, click **Conditional Formatting**. In the **Styles** group, point to **Highlight Cells Rules**, and then click **Less Than** to open the Less Than dialog box. Click the **Format cells that are LESS THAN** box, type **0**, click the **with** arrow in the box to the right, and then if necessary, click the **Light Red Fill with Dark Red Text** option. Click **OK**.

k. Click **Conditional Formatting** again, point to **Highlight Cells Rules**, and then click **Greater Than** to open the Greater Than dialog box. Click the **Format cells that are GREATER THAN** box, type **2000**, click the **with** arrow in the box to the right, and then click the **Green Fill with Dark Green Text** option. Click **OK**.

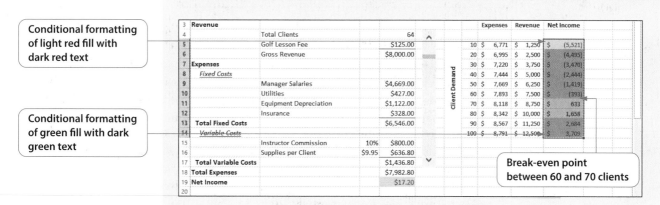

Conditional formatting of light red fill with dark red text

Conditional formatting of green fill with dark green text

Break-even point between 60 and 70 clients

Figure 8   One-variable data table of break-even analysis

l. Select the range **G3:I3**, hold down Ctrl, and then select the range **G5:I14**. On the INSERT tab, in the Charts group, click **Line**, and then select **Line** in the 2-D Line category. Click the **border edge** of the Line chart, and then drag to move it until the upper-left corner is in cell **F16**.

m. Click **Chart Elements** ⊞, click the **arrow** to the right of Axis Titles, and then select the check box for **Primary Horizontal**.

n. Click the **horizontal axis title** text box, type ~~Client Demand~~ and then press Enter. Click the **Chart Title** text box, type Cost-Volume-Profit and then press Enter.

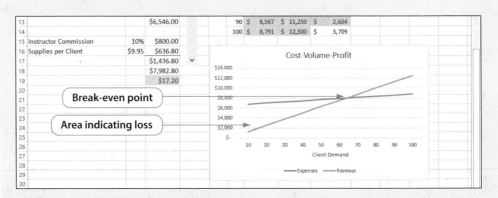

Figure 9 Traditional cost-volume-profit chart

o. Click any cell outside the chart to deselect it. Press Ctrl + Home.

p. **Save** 🖫 your work.

CONSIDER THIS | **What Does the Chart Tell You?**

Have you ever heard that a picture is worth a thousand words? Look at the chart you just created. Can you tell where the break-even point is? Is it easier to look at the chart and tell instantly, or is it easier to look at the data table?

Using Two-Variable Data Tables

A two-variable data table has input values that are listed both down a column and across a row. A **two-variable data table** can help you analyze how different values of two variables in one or more formulas change the results of those formulas. For example, you can use a two-variable data table to see how different interest rates and loan amounts affect a monthly car payment by using the PMT function. In this case, the interest rate and loan amount cells would be the input cells. The results display all possible payment variations in a data table after Excel performs a what-if analysis using the interest rate cell as one variable—the row input cell—and loan amounts as the other variable—the column input cell—in calculating the payment variations See Figure 10.

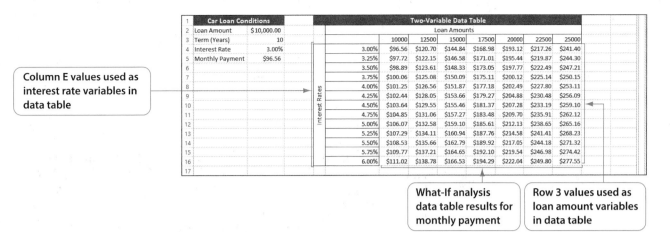

Column E values used as interest rate variables in data table

Car Loan Conditions	
Loan Amount	$10,000.00
Term (Years)	10
Interest Rate	3.00%
Monthly Payment	$96.56

Two-Variable Data Table	Loan Amounts						
Interest Rates	10000	12500	15000	17500	20000	22500	25000
3.00%	$96.56	$120.70	$144.84	$168.98	$193.12	$217.26	$241.40
3.25%	$97.72	$122.15	$146.58	$171.01	$195.44	$219.87	$244.30
3.50%	$98.89	$123.61	$148.33	$173.05	$197.77	$222.49	$247.21
3.75%	$100.06	$125.08	$150.09	$175.11	$200.12	$225.14	$250.15
4.00%	$101.25	$126.56	$151.87	$177.18	$202.49	$227.80	$253.11
4.25%	$102.44	$128.05	$153.66	$179.27	$204.88	$230.48	$256.09
4.50%	$103.64	$129.55	$155.46	$181.37	$207.28	$233.19	$259.10
4.75%	$104.85	$131.06	$157.27	$183.48	$209.70	$235.91	$262.12
5.00%	$106.07	$132.58	$159.10	$185.61	$212.13	$238.65	$265.16
5.25%	$107.29	$134.11	$160.94	$187.76	$214.58	$241.41	$268.23
5.50%	$108.53	$135.66	$162.79	$189.92	$217.05	$244.18	$271.32
5.75%	$109.77	$137.21	$164.65	$192.10	$219.54	$246.98	$274.42
6.00%	$111.02	$138.78	$166.53	$194.29	$222.04	$249.80	$277.55

What-If analysis data table results for monthly payment

Row 3 values used as loan amount variables in data table

Figure 10 Two-variable data table for car loan

One way that a two-variable data table can be useful is when you want to analyze the relationships among cost, sales volume, and profit. When doing so, you need to consider how demand affects the price of a product or service. The analyses you have performed thus far have assisted in determining the break-even point for products and services. Additionally, you have considered the quantity of products that may be sold or the number of clients that may be serviced. The bottom line is that these analyses have clearly indicated how this relationship between the price and revenue affects demand.

A product or service is **elastic**—or responsive to change—if a small change in price is accompanied by a large change in the quantity demanded. The opposite is also true. A product is **inelastic**—or not responsive to change—if a large change in price is accompanied by a small amount of change in demand. This effect is known as the price elasticity of demand and can be calculated by dividing the change in quantity demanded by the change in price. When calculating the elasticity as shown in Figure 11, some assumptions do need to be made about your business and how any changes in price will affect demand. The quotient is conveyed as an absolute value because it is assumed that demand will never increase when prices increase.

Elasticity = [% change in quantity demanded / % change in price]

Figure 11 Elasticity formula

For example, the Red Bluff manager may assume that if he increases the price of golf lessons by 15% that demand will decrease by 20%. When calculating the elasticity, you are calculating the price elasticity of demand. Thus, if Mr. Cheney wanted to calculate the elasticity of demand, the equation would be as shown in Figure 12.

Elasticity = [-20% / 15%] = -1.33

Figure 12 Elasticity calculation of price increase for golf lessons

In this formula, a decrease in price of 20% divided by a 15% increase in demand equals -1.33. Elasticity calculations can be evaluated as absolute values. Here the elasticity value is 1.33. However, instead of having to calculate and interpret elasticity, you can use a two-way data table to view how the price of a product or service responds to change. The golf course manager would like you to determine how much net income would be generated for golf lessons based on varying prices and client demand.

REAL WORLD ADVICE	A Two-Variable Data Table Is NOT Calculating Elasticity

The two-variable data table you are creating does not actually tell you about the elasticity of price versus demand. It calculates the outcomes of varying prices of golf lessons and client demand. When determining selling prices or financing a project, the risk is that the yield will not generate adequate revenue to cover operating costs and to repay debt obligations. A two-variable data table gives you another way of assessing the risk associated with pricing a product or service at a certain level or anticipating a specific level of demand.

E10.05

 ### To Create a Two-Variable Data Table

a. Click the **FeesAndDemand** worksheet tab, click cell **E3**, type =B7 to reference the Net Income formula that Excel will use to calculate your data table, and then press Ctrl+Enter.

b. Right-click cell **E3**, and then click **Format Cells**. On the Number tab, under Category, click **Custom**, click the **Type** box, delete any text, and then type ;;;. Click **OK**.

c. Select the range **E3:L16** to select the data for your data table. On the DATA tab, in the Data Tools group, click **What-If Analysis**, and then select **Data Table** to open the Data Table dialog box.

d. With the insertion point in the **Row input cell** box, type $B$3 and then press Tab to move to the Column input cell box. Type $B$2 and then click **OK**. Notice that Excel calculated the net income for the combination of client demand and golf lesson pricing.

e. Select the range **F4:L16**, and then on the HOME tab, in the Number group, click the **Number Format** arrow General , and then click **Currency**.

f. On the HOME tab, in the Styles group, click **Conditional Formatting**, point to **Highlight Cells Rules**, and then click **Less Than** to open the Less Than dialog box. Click the **Format cells that are LESS THAN** box, and then type 0. If necessary, click the **with** arrow, click to select the **Light Red Fill with Dark Red Text** option, and then click **OK**.

g. Click **Conditional Formatting** again, point to **Highlight Cells Rules**, and then click **Greater Than** to open the Greater Than dialog box. Type 3500 in the Format cells that are GREATER THAN box, click the **with** arrow, click to select the **Green Fill with Dark Green Text** option, and then click **OK**. Press Ctrl+Home.

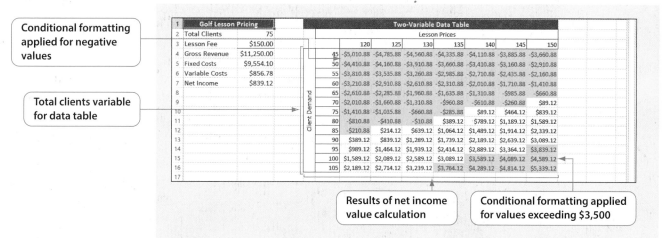

Conditional formatting applied for negative values

Total clients variable for data table

Results of net income value calculation

Conditional formatting applied for values exceeding $3,500

Figure 13 Two-variable data table of lesson fees and client demand

h. **Save** 💾 your work.

Products and services are often evaluated by their elasticity. When interpreting elasticity, consider the following:

- Relatively elastic: If the elasticity is greater than one, demand is very responsive to changes in price.

- Relatively inelastic: If the elasticity is less than one, large changes in price will cause small changes in demand.

- Perfectly elastic: For high elasticity values, any change in price causes a vast change in demand.

- Perfectly inelastic: For elasticity values of zero, a change in price has no influence on demand.

- Unit elastic: For elasticity values of one, any change in price results in an equal and opposite change in demand.

Use Goal Seek

Goal Seek is another scenario tool that maximizes Excel's cell-referencing capabilities and enables you to find the input values needed to achieve a goal or objective. To use Goal Seek, you select the cell—variable cell—containing the formula that will return the result you are seeking. Once you have selected the cell, indicate the target value you want the formula to return. Then, finally, select the location of the input value that Excel can change to reach the target. In simpler terms, when you perform Goal Seek, Excel is manipulating the data much like you would in an algebraic equation that requires you to solve for x.

Through a process called **iteration**, Goal Seek repeatedly enters new values in the variable cell to find a solution to the problem. Iteration continues until Excel has run the problem 100 times or has found an answer within .001 of the target value you specified. Because Goal Seek calculates so quickly, you save significant time and effort. Without Goal Seek, you would have to manually type one number after another in the formula or a related cell to attempt to find the solution.

Using Goal Seek

You will use the data given to you by the Red Bluff manager to forecast quantities and prices of the less-popular selling items. This will ensure that the management and employees are striving to meet the sales goals for the items that currently are not selling very well.

E10.06

 To Forecast Using Goal Seek

a. Click the **SalesForecast** worksheet tab, and then click cell **E5**.

b. On the DATA tab, in the Data Tools group, click **What-If Analysis**, and then click **Goal Seek** to open the Goal Seek dialog box. Excel automatically selects the active cell as the Set cell value; in this case, cell E5.

c. Red Bluff wants to set a sales goal of $25,000 for stock golf balls. Because you know the selling price and target goal of the stock golf balls, you can calculate the quantity needed to sell to meet the sales goal. Click the **To value** box, type **25000**, press Tab, and then in the By changing cell box, type **$C$5**.

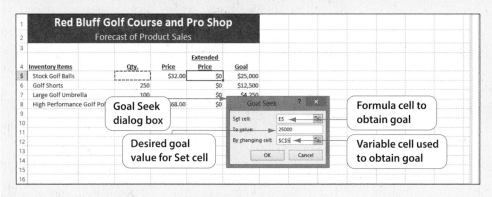

Figure 14   What-if analysis using Goal Seek

d. Click **OK** twice to run Goal Seek and close the Goal Seek Status dialog box. Notice that in order to reach its $25,000 sales goal for stock golf balls, Red Bluff would need to sell 78.25 packages of golf balls. Click cell **C5**. On the HOME tab, in the Number group, click the **Number Format** arrow General ▾, click **Number**, and then click the **Decrease Decimal** button twice to format with no decimal places because the pro shop cannot sell part of a package of golf balls.

Troubleshooting

If Excel displays in the Goal Seek Status dialog box that it could not find a viable solution, click Cancel, and then ensure that you have entered the correct values in the Goal Seek dialog box. Some rules to keep in mind: Verify the Set cell box contains a formula, the To value box contains the result desired for the formula, and the By changing cell box contains a reference to the cell that can be adjusted to achieve the goal.

e. On the DATA tab, in the Data Tools group, click **What-If Analysis**, and then click **Goal Seek** to open the Goal Seek dialog box.

f. Red Bluff wants to set a sales goal of $12,500 for golf shorts. Because you know the quantity and target goal, you can calculate the price needed to charge to meet the sales goal. In the **Set cell** box, replace any text by typing $E$6, press Tab, and then in the **To value** box, type 12500. Press Tab, and then in the **By changing cell** box, type $D$6.

g. Click **OK** twice to run Goal Seek and close the Goal Seek Status dialog box.
   Notice that Red Bluff should charge $50 to meet its sales goal volume of 250 pairs of golf shorts. Additionally, if 250 pairs are sold, the sales revenue goal of $12,500 would be met.

h. On the DATA tab, in the Data Tools group, click **What-If Analysis**, and then click **Goal Seek** to open the Goal Seek dialog box.

i. Red Bluff wants to set a sales goal of $4,250 for large golf umbrellas. Because you know the quantity and target goal, you can calculate the price needed to charge to meet the sales goal. In the **Set cell** box, type $E$7 to replace the text, press Tab, and then in the **To value** box, type 4250. Press Tab, and then in the **By changing cell** box, type $D$7.

j. Click **OK** twice to run Goal Seek and close the Goal Seek Status dialog box.
   Notice that Red Bluff should charge $42.50 to meet its sales goal volume of 100 large golf umbrellas. Additionally, if 100 umbrellas are sold, the sales revenue goal of $4,250 would be met.

k. On the DATA tab, in the Data Tools group, click **What-If Analysis**, and then click **Goal Seek** to open the Goal Seek dialog box.

l. Red Bluff wants to set a sales goal of $18,675 for high-performance golf polos. You can calculate the quantity the pro shop needs to sell to meet the sales goal. In the **Set cell** box, type $E$8 to replace any text, press Tab, and then in the **To value** box, type 18675. Press Tab, and then in the **By changing cell** box, type $C$8.

m. Click **OK** twice to run Goal Seek and close the Goal Seek Status dialog box.
   Notice that if 275 golf polos are sold, the sales revenue goal of $18,675 would be met.

n. Click cell **C5**. On the HOME tab, in the Clipboard group, click **Format Painter** , and then select the cell range **C6:C8** to copy the Number format settings to these cells. Press Ctrl+Home.

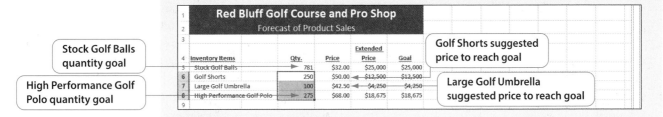

Figure 15 Results of Goal Seek analysis

o. **Save** your work.

Using the Scenario Manager

A **scenario** allows you to build a what-if analysis model that includes variable cells linked by one or more formulas or functions. By running the scenarios, you have the ability to compare multiple variables and their combined effects on the various calculated outcomes. Managers can use scenarios to view best-case, worst-case, and most-likely scenarios in order to make decisions and solve problems. For example, the Red Bluff Golf Course & Pro Shop manager might want to compare best-case, most-likely, and worst-case scenarios for sales based on sales volumes at the pro shop in a week.

Scenarios can be most beneficial because they can use multiple variables. Through the use of Goal Seek and data tables, you learned that you could use what-if analysis tools when you want to analyze the effects on various calculations when inputting one or two variables. Scenarios can evaluate one, two, or many variables. For example, the Red Bluff manager may want to view best-case, worst-case, and most-likely scenarios of the pro shop's total net income based on variable costs, fixed costs, and gross revenue of both retail products and golf lessons. In this section, you will learn how to use the **Scenario Manager**, the third type of what-if analysis tool, to manage scenarios by adding, deleting, editing, and viewing scenarios, and to create scenario reports.

Use the Scenario Manager to Create Scenarios

You can use scenarios to predict the outcome of different situations in your spreadsheet. Before creating a scenario, you need to design your worksheet to contain at least one formula or function. This formula or function will rely on other cells and can have different values inserted into it. The significant step in creating the various scenarios is identifying the various data cells whose values can differ in each scenario. You can then select these cells—known as **changing cells**—in the worksheet before you open the Scenario Manager dialog box. Once the Scenario Manager dialog box is open, you can enter and define the different scenarios. Each scenario includes a scenario name, input or changing cells, and the values for each input cell.

Designing a Scenario

Barry Cheney would like you to determine how much net income—profit—the Red Bluff Golf Course & Pro Shop is forecasted to generate based on varying retail sales, revenue from services rendered, and variable costs. You have been given the forecasted amounts and need to enter the formulas that will help calculate each scenario.

E10.07

 To Design a Worksheet Used for Scenarios

a. Click the **ProfitForecast** worksheet tab.

b. Click cell **D6**, type =SUM(D4:D5) to calculate the forecasted total or gross revenue, and then press [Enter].

c. Click cell **D13**, type =SUM(D9:D12) to calculate the total forecasted fixed costs, and then press [Enter].

d. Click cell **D15**, type =D6*C15 to calculate the forecasted employee commissions, and then press [Enter].

e. In cell **D16**, type =D13+D15 to calculate the forecasted total expenses, and then press [Enter].

f. In cell **D17**, type =D6-D16 to calculate the forecasted net income, and then press [Ctrl]+[Enter].

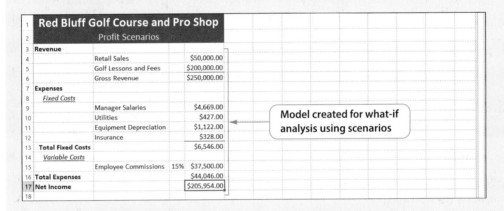

Figure 16 Forecasting model

g. **Save** 🖫 your work.

Adding, Deleting, and Editing Scenarios

Once you identify the changing cells—which can be anywhere on your worksheet—you can then select these cells in the worksheet before you open the Scenario Manager dialog box, or you can enter the target cells directly into the Scenario Manager dialog box as well as enter and define the different scenarios. Each scenario represents different what-if conditions to evaluate the spreadsheet model. Once scenarios are added, they are stored under the name you assigned to them. The number of scenarios you can create is limitless.

To Add, Delete, and Edit Scenarios

a. In the ProfitForecast worksheet, select the range **D4:D5**. These will be your changing cells.

b. On the DATA tab, in the Data Tools group, click **What-If Analysis**, and then click **Scenario Manager** to open the Scenario Manager dialog box.

c. In the Scenario Manager dialog box, click **Add** to begin creating your first scenario. In the Add Scenario dialog box, type Most Likely Scenario in the Scenario name box.

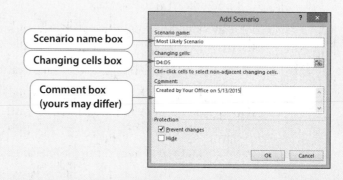

Figure 17   Add Scenario dialog box

d. Click **OK**. The values that are entered in cells D4 and D5 are the most likely scenario values. Click **OK**.

e. In the Scenario Manager dialog box, click **Add** to begin creating your second scenario. In the Add Scenario dialog box, type Best-case Scenario in the Scenario name box, and then click **OK**. The Scenario Values dialog box will open.

f. The Red Bluff manager believes that the best-case scenario would result in revenue of $100,000 in Retail sales and $325,000 in golf lessons and fees. Type 100000 in the $D$4 box, and then type 325000 in the $D$5 box.

Figure 18   Scenario Values dialog box

g. Click **OK**, and then in the Scenario Manager dialog box, click **Add**.

h. In the Add Scenario dialog box, type Worst-case Scenario in the Scenario name box, and then click **OK**. The Scenario Values dialog box will open.

i. The Red Bluff manager believes that the worst-case scenario would result in revenue of $25,000 in retail sales and $75,000 in golf lessons and fees. Type 25000 in the $D$4 box, type 75000 in the $D$5 box, and then click **OK**.

j. Because the Red Bluff manager already created a forecast with the most likely scenario values entered, he decided that he does not need this scenario and e-mails you to let you know. In the Scenario Manager dialog box, click to select **Most Likely Scenario** under Scenarios, and then click **Delete** to delete the Most Likely Scenario.

k. The Red Bluff manager also informed you that the worst-case scenario would have retail sales forecasted at $20,000. In the Scenario Manager dialog box, click to select **Worst-case Scenario** under Scenarios, click **Edit**, and in the Edit Scenario dialog box, click **OK**.

l. In the $D$4 box of the Scenario Values dialog box, change 25000 to 20000, and then click **OK**.

Viewing Scenarios

After you create the scenarios, you can view the results by using the Show button at the bottom of the Scenario Manager dialog box. This is helpful to double-check whether the values entered in each scenario are accurate. Excel will replace the existing values in your spreadsheet with those entered into each scenario.

E10.09

 To View Scenarios

a. In the Scenario Manager dialog box, click to select **Best-case Scenario** under Scenarios, and then click **Show**.
  Notice how Excel automatically replaces the existing values in D4 and D5 with $100,000 for Retail sales and $325,000 for Golf Lessons and Fees. The Net Income result is $354,704.

b. Click to select the **Worst-case Scenario** under Scenarios, and then click **Show**.
  Notice how Excel automatically replaces the existing values in D4 and D5 with $20,000 for Retail sales and $75,000 for Golf Lessons and Fees. The Net Income result is $74,204.

Create Scenario Reports

Although you can view your scenarios while the Scenario Manager dialog box is open, you will probably want to view them side by side to compare the results. Additionally, it is not possible to print and distribute them very easily this way. You can create a **Scenario Summary report** automatically by clicking the Summary button in the Scenario Manager dialog box. The Summary button opens the Scenario Summary dialog box where you can choose the type of report you would like to create.

Generating a Scenario Summary Report

By selecting the Scenario Summary option, you can create a worksheet that includes subtotals and the results of the scenarios. Barry Cheney would like to be able to view the current scenario modeled in the worksheet along with the best-case and most-likely scenarios.

E10.10

 To Generate a Scenario Summary Report

a. In the Scenario Manager dialog box, click **Summary** to open the Scenario Summary dialog box.

b. Leave the Report type at the default selection of Scenario summary, verify the Result cell is **D17**, and then click **OK**. Notice that Excel adds a new worksheet named Scenario Summary to your workbook.

c. Format the Scenario Summary report so it is easier to read. On the HOME tab, in the Alignment group, select cells **B6:C6**, click **Merge & Center**, and then replace the **$D$4** text by typing Retail Sales. Press Enter.

d. Select cells **B7:C7**, click **Merge & Center**, and replace the **$D$5** text by typing Lessons and Fees. Press Ctrl+Enter. Adjust the **width** of column B so that the text can be read.

e. Select cells **B9:C9**, click **Merge & Center**, and replace the **$D$17** text by typing Net Income. Press Ctrl+Home.

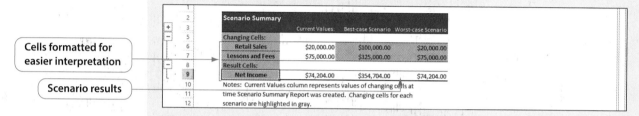

Cells formatted for easier interpretation

Scenario results

		Current Values:	Best-case Scenario	Worst-case Scenario
Scenario Summary				
Changing Cells:				
Retail Sales		$20,000.00	$100,000.00	$20,000.00
Lessons and Fees		$75,000.00	$325,000.00	$75,000.00
Result Cells:				
Net Income		$74,204.00	$354,704.00	$74,204.00

Notes: Current Values column represents values of changing cells at time Scenario Summary Report was created. Changing cells for each scenario are highlighted in gray.

Figure 19 Scenario summary report

f. **Save** 💾 your work.

Generating a Scenario PivotTable Report

A scenario PivotTable report can also be created automatically by clicking the Summary button in the Scenario Manager dialog box. The Summary button opens the Scenario Summary dialog box where you can choose the **Scenario PivotTable report** option. You can create a worksheet that includes a summary of the scenarios in PivotTable format. PivotTables allow even more manipulation of data because of the two-dimensional view they provide.

E10.11

 To Generate a Scenario PivotTable Report

a. Click the **ProfitForecast** worksheet tab.

b. On the DATA tab, in the Data Tools group, click **What-If Analysis**, and then click **Scenario Manager** to open the Scenario Manager dialog box.

c. In the Scenario Manager dialog box, click to select the **Best-case Scenario**, and then click **Edit**.

d. Barry Cheney wants to see if the Red Bluff Golf Course & Pro Shop could still be profitable if the employees earn different commissions based on sales. In the Edit Scenario dialog box, click the **Changing cells** box to place the insertion point after the range D4:D5, and then type ,C15. Click **OK**.

e. In the Scenario Values dialog box, in the $C$15 box, verify the value displays 0.15 to reflect the commission of 15%, and then click **OK**.

f. In the Scenario Manager dialog box, click to select **Worst-case Scenario**, and then click **Edit**.

g. In the Edit Scenario dialog box, click the **Changing cells** box to place the insertion point after the range D4:D5, and then type ,C15. Click **OK**.

h. In the Scenario Values dialog box, click the row 3 **$C$15** box, delete the 0.15 value, type .075 to change the commission to 7.5%, and then click **OK**.

i. Barry also wants you to re-create the most-likely scenario. In the Scenario Manager dialog box, click **Add**, type Most-likely Scenario in the Scenario name box, and then click **OK**. Your D4:D5, C15 changing cells will automatically be entered into the Changing cells box.

j. Type the following values for each changing cell in each box of the Scenario Values dialog box. Type 25000 in box 1, type 162500 in box 2, and then type 0.10 in box 3.

k. Click **OK**, and then click **Summary** in the Scenario Manager dialog box to open the Scenario Summary dialog box.

l. Barry wants to view the ending values for gross revenue, commission, and net income. Click to change the Report type to **Scenario PivotTable report**, click the **Result cells** box, delete any existing text, type =D6,C15,D17 and then click **OK**. Notice that Excel added a new worksheet named Scenario PivotTable to your workbook.

m. Format your PivotTable report so it is easier to read the data. Click cell **A1**, replace the existing **$D$4:$D$5,$C$15** text by typing Retail Sales and Golf Lessons and Fees and then press Ctrl+Enter. On the **HOME** tab, in the **Cells** group, click **Format**, and then click **Column Width**. In the Column width box, set the width of column A to **34**. Click **OK**.

n. Click cell **A2**, type Scenario PivotTable Report, press Ctrl+Enter, select the range **A2:D2**, and then click **Merge & Center**. Click the **Bold** button, click the **Font Size** arrow, and then click **16**.

o. Click cell **A3**, type Scenarios and then press Tab.

p. Add headings to your data. Click cell **B3**, type Gross Revenue and then press Tab. In cell **C3**, type Commission and then press Tab. In cell **D3**, type Net Income and then press Ctrl+Enter.

q. Select the range **B3:D3**, and then in the Alignment group, click **Center**, and then click **Format**. Click **Column Width**, in the Column width box type 14, and then click **OK**.

r. Select the range **B4:B6**, hold down Ctrl, select the range **D4:D6**, click the **Number Format** arrow, and then click **Currency**. Click the **Decrease Decimal** button two times to format with no decimal places.

s. Select the range **C4:C6**, click the **Number Format** arrow, and then click **Percentage**. Click the **Decrease Decimal** button once to format with one decimal place, and then press Ctrl+Home.

1	Retail Sales and Golf Lessons and Fees (All)			
2	Scenario PivotTable Report			
3	Scenarios	Gross Revenue	Commission	Net Income
4	Best-case Scenario	$425,000	15.0%	$354,704
5	Most-likely Scenario	$187,500	10.0%	$162,204
6	Worst-case Scenario	$95,000	7.5%	$81,329
7				

Figure 20   Scenario PivotTable report

t. **Save** 💾 your work.

Using Solver

An important item to note is that there is no true or right answer on how to raise prices. The answer relies, in part, on the business person's notion of how much demand he or she believes to be likely at the various prices and what that relationship is for that particular business. It may be risky to raise the price very high because it will lower demand, which means fewer units will be sold at the higher price. If the belief is wrong and the demand stays the same or is higher than expected, the profit potential is also higher. This is when a tool such as Solver can help give a business person enough information to make an educated decision.

Excel's **Solver** is an add-in that helps optimize a problem by manipulating the values for several variables with constraints that you determine. A **constraint** is a rule you establish when formulating your Solver model. You can use Solver to find the highest, lowest, or exact value for a specific outcome by adjusting values for selected variables. Business managers can use Solver to minimize or maximize the output based on the constraints. For example, the golf course manager could use Solver to determine a sales strategy that will help the golf course maximize its profit given a specific mix of services given to clients. In this section, you will learn how to load the Solver add-in; find optimal solutions by setting objectives, changing variable cells, and defining constraints; generate a Solver answer report; and save and restore a Solver model.

Understand the Use of the Solver Add-In

Solver is one of many add-ins installed by default with Excel 2013. However it is not attached to the Ribbon by default. An **add-in** is an application with specific functionality geared toward accomplishing a specific goal. Because companies other than Microsoft develop the add-ins, they are not automatically activated when Excel is installed.

Loading the Solver Add-In

To use the Solver, you need to activate the add-in. This is a one-time setup task as once the Solver add-in is activated it will appear on the Data tab on the Ribbon each time Excel is launched.

E10.12

 To Load the Solver Add-In

a. Click the **FILE** tab.

b. Click **Options**, and then click **Add-Ins**.

c. At the bottom of the View and manage Microsoft Office Add-ins pane, if necessary, click the **Manage** arrow, click **Excel Add-ins**, and then click **Go**.

d. In the Add-Ins dialog box, click the **Solver Add-in** check box, and then click **OK**.

e. To verify the Solver add-in was added properly, click the **DATA** tab, and then check to see that the Solver button is displayed in the Analysis group on the right side of the Ribbon.

SIDE NOTE

The Menu Option Was Already Selected

The default selection in the menu is Excel Add-ins, so it may already be selected for you.

Solve Complex Problems Using Solver

The purpose of using Solver is to perform what-if analysis to solve more complex problems and to optimize the outcome. When you **optimize**, you are finding the best way to do something. For example, the Red Bluff manager may want to find the best product mix of its retail products to maximize profitability. The manager could use Excel's Solver to find the values of certain cells in a spreadsheet that optimize—maximize or minimize—a certain objective. Thus, Solver helps answer this type of optimization problem.

Prior to configuring the Solver constraints, you need to ensure that you create a spreadsheet model that can be used to manipulate the values for your variables. This involves creating a target cell, which defines the goal of your problem. For example, the golf course manager may create a formula that calculates total revenue. Additionally, you need to select one or more variable cells that the Solver can change to reach the goal. You should evaluate your spreadsheet as you define your goal, identify one or more variables that can change when attaining the chosen goal, and then determine the limitations of the spreadsheet model. These variable cells are used to formulate the three Solver parameters—objective cell, changing cells, and constraints.

Your worksheet can also contain other values, formulas, and functions that use the target cell and the variable cells to reach the goal. For the Solver to work properly, the formula in the target cell must reference and depend on the variable cells for part of its calculation. If you do not construct your Solver model in this format, you will get an error message that states, "The Set Target Cell values do not converge."

REAL WORLD ADVICE	Solver Can Be Used for Many Analyses

The Excel Solver add-in can be a powerful tool for analyzing data. In many financial planning problems, an amount such as the unpaid balance on a loan or the amount saved in a retirement fund changes over time. Consider a situation in which a business borrows money. Because only the principal of the monthly payment reduces the unpaid loan balance, the business may want to determine how it can minimize the total interest paid on the loan if it pays more than the minimum payment each month.

Setting the Objective Cell and Variable Cells

The **objective cell** contains the formula that creates a value that you want to optimize—maximize, minimize, or set to a specific value. For example, the golf course manager may want to maximize the gross revenue of golf lessons by analyzing the number of customers per day in relation to the total number of instructors employed. The golf course manager would have to consider many factors; however, deciding the actual goal of using Solver is the first step to creating a Solver analysis.

Solver works with a group of cells, called variable cells, which take part in calculating the formulas in the objective and constraint cells. Solver adjusts the values in the variable cells to satisfy the limits on constraint cells and return the result you want for the objective cell.

The golf course manager wants you to find the number of total number clients, the number of hours of lessons per day, and the number of instructors on duty needed to maximize net income. The worksheet you were given was previously set up with functions to calculate the net income.

E10.13

 To Set the Objective Cell and Variable Cells

a. Click the **GolfLessons** worksheet tab.

b. On the DATA tab, in the Analysis group, click **Solver**.

c. Because Barry Cheney wants to maximize the net income, the cell that holds the net income will become the objective cell. In the Solver Parameters dialog box, in the **Set Objective** box, type $D$20.

d. Because you need to maximize the net income, set the objective to **Max**, which is Excel's default value.

e. Several input variables will be considered in order to maximize the net income. Click the **By Changing Variable Cells** box, and then type $D$4:$D$5.

Defining Constraints

Constraints are the rules or restrictions that your variable cells must follow when the Solver performs its analysis. For example, if Barry Cheney wants to maximize the net income based on how many golf lessons are given per day, he would have to consider how many hours per day the course is open, how many instructors work per day, and how long it takes to give a lesson. In addition, the cost of supplies can vary depending on how many clients the instructors have.

E10.14

 To Define Constraints

a. In the Solver Parameters dialog box, click **Add** to enter the first constraint. The Add Constraint dialog box will open.

b. The golf course can have no more than four instructors scheduled at any given time. In the Add Constraint dialog box, type $D$5 in the Cell Reference box, click the **arrow**, click to select <= in the mathematical operands box, and then type 4 in the Constraint box.

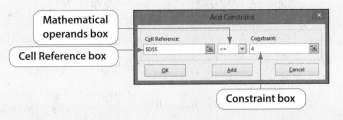

Mathematical operands box

Cell Reference box

Constraint box

Figure 21   Add Constraint dialog box

c. Click **Add** to save the first constraint and add another constraint.

d. Lessons can last from 45 minutes to 90 minutes each, and the golf course is open for 11 hours per day. This means that instructors can give anywhere from 7 to 14 lessons per day. Communicating this requires you to enter two constraints. In the Add Constraint dialog box, type $D$4 in the Cell Reference box, click to select >= in the mathematical operands box, and then type 7 in the Constraint box.

e. Click **Add**, and then in the Add Constraint dialog box, type $D$4 in the Cell Reference box. Select <= in the mathematical operands box if necessary, and then type 14 in the Constraint box.

f. In the Add Constraint dialog box, click **Add**. Because the instructors cannot service part of a client, you have to add a constraint that will ensure the value returned for cell D4 is a whole number. In the Add Constraint dialog box, type $D$4 in the Cell Reference box, and then click to select **int** in the mathematical operands box. Excel will enter the word "integer" in the Constraint box. Click **Add**.

g. Because Red Bluff cannot have part of an instructor working, you have to add a constraint that will ensure the value returned for cell D5 is a whole number. In the Add Constraint dialog box, type $D$5 in the Cell Reference box, and then click to select **int** in the mathematical operands box.

h. Click **OK**. Notice that the six constraints you entered appear under the Subject to the Constraints list of the Solver Parameters dialog box. Leave the Solver Parameters dialog box open for the next step.

SIDE NOTE
You Can Use Either Add Button
Either Add button works—either from within the Solver Parameters dialog box or the Add Constraint dialog box.

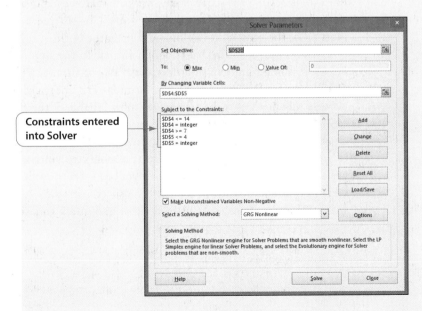

Constraints entered into Solver

Figure 22   Solver Parameters dialog box

The integer constraint—int—mandates that the variable cells remain a whole number. For example, the manufacturers of Red Bluff's retail products—such as golf balls and golf gloves—will not produce partial products. Thus, to guarantee that the variable cell values remain a whole number, you need to create integer constraints for them.

The greater than or equal to zero constraint requires the variable cell values remain greater than or equal to zero when you run Solver. For example, the manufacturers of Red Bluff's retail products will not produce negative amounts of product. However, a negative value in a changing variable cell could possibly produce higher results in the objective cell. By default, the Make Unconstrained Variables Non-Negative check box is selected to guarantee that the variable cells remain greater than or equal to zero. If you want to let a variable cell be negative, you can uncheck the Make Unconstrained Variables Non-Negative check box and create a constraint that allows this to occur—such as D7>=-50.

One item to note: If Solver takes too long to solve, you can press Esc to break Solver and stop running the analysis.

Selecting a Solving Method

Three solving methods are available within the Solver Parameters dialog box— Simplex LP, Evolutionary, and Generalized Reduced Gradient (GRG) Nonlinear. These solving methods relate to **linear programming** (LP), which is a mathematical method for determining how to attain the best outcome, such as the maximum profit or the lowest cost, in a given mathematical model, such as your spreadsheet, for a list of requirements—constraints—represented as linear relationships. Thus, linear programming is a specific case of mathematical programming and compares how the equation is displayed on a chart. When you run Solver, this mathematical programming is occurring behind the scenes.

The **Simplex LP method** is a linear model in which the variables are not raised to any powers and no transcendent functions—such as sine or cosine—are used. To use Simplex LP, your equations must not break the linearity. An in-depth discussion of algebraic linearity is beyond the scope of this workshop. However, in algebra, linear means that the slope-intercept equation for a line—$y = mx + b$—is true. In linear programming, Excel plots all of the constraints as lines and finds the optimal result from the intersections of those lines. So, formulas that function similar to the slope-intercept formula are linear. However, some functions and operators can potentially break linearity—such as MIN, MAX, IF, and DIVISION. If your formulas are linear, select the Simplex LP method because this method is the fastest and most reliable of the three methods. In fact, if you can purposefully design your models as linear, it is better.

For example, perhaps the Red Bluff Golf Course & Pro Shop wants to use Solver to be able to determine what advertisements to purchase to maximize exposures, yet stay under budget. In this case, you take the number of advertising units—the variable—and multiply it by the exposures per unit—a constant—and the cost— another constant—to get the amount of exposures and cost per advertisement type, such as television, Internet, and radio. Then, you add all of those together and constrain it by the maximum amount you can spend—along with any other constraints. Then, you optimize for maximum exposures. Notice, you multiplied the variable cells by a constant and then added them together similar to the slope-intercept formula. Thus, if the constraints were plotted on a chart, the lines would be linear, as illustrated in Figure 23.

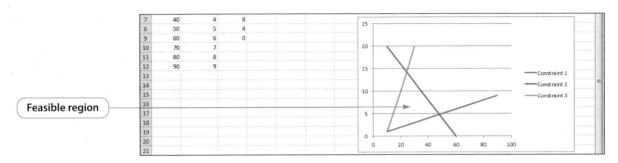

Figure 23   Linear chart with three linear constraints

The **GRG Nonlinear method** is used for more complex models that are nonlinear and smooth. It is also the default method that Excel's Solver uses. Smooth means that when the constraints are graphed, a curve of some kind exists: concave, convex, a wave, and so on. Generally, the model is smooth when it uses trigonometric functions or exponentials, multiplies the variables together, and so on. A nonlinear model is one in which just one of the constraint lines breaks the linearity of the model. You may have several constraints that are linear, but one constraint line that curves breaks the linearity of the model, as shown in Figure 24.

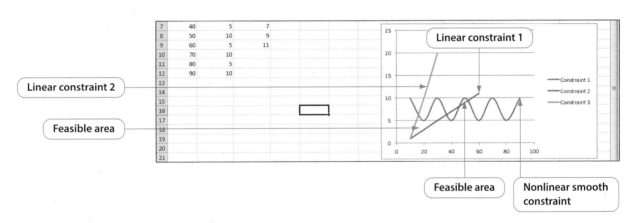

Figure 24   Nonlinear chart with two feasible areas

In the GRG Nonlinear method, Excel uses an iterative process and starting point. You tell Excel where to start, and it starts moving along the constraint lines—linear and nonlinear. The starting point is typically zero, unless specific individualized business knowledge would indicate otherwise. As it moves along the graph lines, Excel is looking for peaks—when maximizing—and valleys—when minimizing. When it finds a significant enough peak or valley, Excel finds an optimal answer. If you give Excel a different starting point, Excel may find a different locally optimal answer, particularly if a higher peak or lower valley exists far away from the starting point used the first time. Thus, GRG Nonlinear is less reliable than the Simplex LP method. However, the Simplex LP method is limited to what can be modeled because linearity must be maintained.

There is a setting in GRG Nonlinear to help resolve this potential issue. You can take advantage of the Multistart method. This allows Excel to have multiple start points to compare all of the locally optimal answers. By way of this comparison, Excel can potentially find a probabilistically global optimal answer.

Finally, integer constraints break the linearity of a model even if you set it to use Simplex LP. Thus, integer constraints force GRG Nonlinear and a special branching method that takes longer. Also, if the model is actually linear, setting the method to GRG Nonlinear will force a linear model to be solved with GRG Nonlinear.

The **Evolutionary method** is used when a worksheet model is nonlinear and nonsmooth and thus the most complex model. Nonsmooth means that the line takes sharp bends or has no slope at all. Typically, these are models that use functions—such as VLOOKUP, PMT, IF, SUMIF, and so on—to derive values based on or derived from the variable cells or changing cells. The Evolutionary method does not make any assumptions about the underlying functions and formulas relationship. Thus, the Evolutionary method uses randomness to pick a population of candidates. Then, it uses the variables—changing cells—and evaluates the result—target cell—for each candidate. It holds the population of candidate answers to help pick the next set of variables to test. The Evolutionary method's name is inspired by nature itself. So, as the method picks random variables, it will use natural selection to reuse certain variables from the population that seem to yield better results. It will also use a crossover effect to combine variables from two known good answers in the population. Further, it will also randomly "mutate" to create new candidates for the population that may or may not be better than the other candidates.

Importantly, this means that the Evolutionary method cannot guarantee the most optimal result, but only the best result it found. Thus, every time you run the Evolutionary method, you might get a different answer. Evolutionary takes more processing power and time than the other methods. The only way the Evolutionary method knows to stop is based on the user-defined setting for length of time, number of iterations, or number of candidates. Therefore, the Evolutionary method is best only in situations that cannot be adequately modeled with an optimal answer method—Simplex LP or GRG Nonlinear. Using the Evolutionary method is beyond the scope of this workshop.

With all three methods, scalability can be an issue. If there is a wide scale for the object or constraint values, then it can cause issues in Solver. If you are dealing with numbers that differ in several magnitudes, consider revising the model to express the values differently. For example, instead of listing the number to purchase as 2,000,000, express the number as 2,000 in units of thousands. While there is an automatic scaling setting, best practice is to uncheck this setting. As of the writing of this book, this setting can cause problems when using the GRG Nonlinear method.

| **Selecting a Solving Method When You Are Not Sure Where to Begin**

Start with Simplex LP. If your model is nonlinear, Solver will notify you. At that point, you can try the GRG Nonlinear model. If Solver still cannot seem to converge—gather or develop—on a solution, then try the Evolutionary model. One of these three models will eventually give you an optimal or good solution.

Generate and Interpret Solver Answer Reports

When you run Solver, an answer report is created in a new worksheet and named "Answer Report." Other items to be considered when producing a Solver Answer Report include the type of report you want to generate—Answer, Sensitivity, Limits, or Population—as well as deciding how you want your worksheet to look after you run the Solver. When the Evolutionary Solving method is used, the Population report is also available. If Solver finds an optimal solution, and there are no integer constraints, two additional reports are available: the sensitivity report and the limits report.

Generating a Solver Answer Report

After you define the objective, variable cells, constraints, and solving method, you are ready to generate a Solver answer report. After you run Solver, you have several options before the report is generated. Once Solver displays a message that states it found a solution, you can choose the type of report that you want—Answer, Sensitivity, Limits, or Population. The **Solver Answer Report** lists the objective cell and the changing cells with their corresponding original and final values for the problem, input variables, and constraints. In addition, the formulas, binding status, and slacks are given for each constraint. The **Solver Sensitivity Report** provides information about how sensitive the solution is to small changes in the formula for the target cell. This report displays the shadow prices for the constraint—the amount the objective function value changes per unit change in the constraint. Because constraints are often determined by resources, a comparison of the shadow prices of each constraint provides valuable information about the most effective place to apply additional resources in order to achieve the best improvement. This report can only be created if your Excel model does not contain integer or Boolean—the values 0 and 1—constraints. The **Solver Limits Report** displays the achieved optimal value and all the input variables of the model with the optimal values. Additionally, the report displays the upper and lower bounds for the optimal value. A variable cell could vary without changing the optimal solution. Finally, the **Solver Population Report** displays various statistical characteristics about the given model, such as how many variables and rows it contains.

You can also choose how you want your Excel model to behave—either restoring it to the original values or keeping the Solver solution. If you restore the original values, the original values that were entered into the variable cells prior to running Solver are restored. This can be helpful in case you have to run Solver again because it keeps you from having to manually change the values back to what they were when you began. If you choose to keep the Solver solution, you will be able to see the final outcome on both the answer report and the Excel model. Regardless of which option you choose, you will still be able to run Solver over and over again as needed.

E10.15

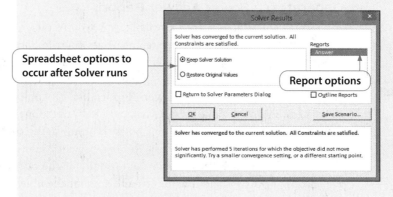

▶ To Generate a Solver Answer Report

a. In the Solver Parameters dialog box, if necessary, click the **Select a Solving Method** arrow, and then click to select **GRG Nonlinear** solving method because the changing cells are being multiplied together.

b. Click **Options**, click the **All Methods** tab, if necessary, and verify the **Use Automatic Scaling** check box is unchecked.

c. Click the **GRG Nonlinear** tab. If necessary, click to check the **Use Multistart** check box, and then click to uncheck the **Require Bounds on Variables** check box. Click **OK**.

d. Click **Solve** at the bottom of the Solver Parameters dialog box.

e. In the Solver Results dialog box, verify the **Keep Solver Solution** option is selected. This will display your optimal results on the spreadsheet as well as your report.

f. Under Reports, on the right side of the Solver Results dialog box, click to select **Answer**, and then click **OK**. Notice that a worksheet tab named Answer Report 1 now exists in the workbook.

Figure 25   Solver Results dialog box

g. Click the **Answer Report 1** worksheet tab, and then **Save** 🖫 your work.

Interpreting a Solver Answer Report

The Solver answer report is divided into four sections—report details, objective cell information, variable cell information, and constraints information. The first three sections of the Answer Report you just created are shown in Figure 26. The report details section displays information about the Solver report—report type, filename, worksheet that contains the Excel model, and the date and time the report was created; Solver Engine details; and Solver Options that you set at the time you created the report.

The second section reports information about the objective cells—cell references; cell names; whether you searched for the minimum, maximum, or a specific value; as well as the original and final objective cell values. For example, in this model you were trying to maximize the net income. Before running Solver, the net income value was "$1,707.50; however, once Solver ran, the net income was maximized. The result indicated that the golf course could make $8,032.90 in profit.

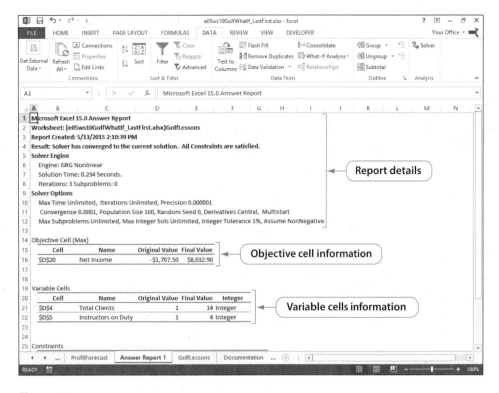

Figure 26 The Solver Answer report

The third section displays information about the variable cells—cell references, variable cell names, original cell values, and final cell values. In your report, you can see that each of the four instructors can see 14 clients per day. This mix will create the profit of $8,032.90 per day.

The fourth section displays information about the constraints you entered—cell references, descriptions, new cell values, formulas, status, and slack—for each constraint. This section of the report can be seen in Figure 27. In your report, notice that the total clients slack is seven, the difference between the lower constraint of 7 and the upper constraint value of 14 for cell D4. A constraint is considered to be a **binding constraint** if changing it also changes the optimal solution. A less severe constraint that does not affect the optimal solution is known as a **nonbinding constraint**.

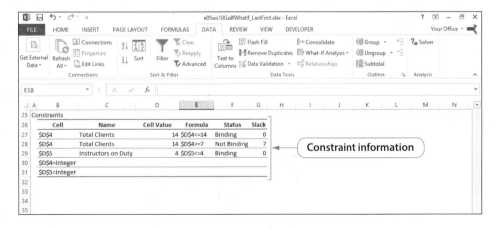

Figure 27 Constraints in the Solver Answer report

One item to note is that if you change your Excel model or Solver parameters, you must run Solver again to create an updated report. The names of new reports will be "Answer Report" followed by consecutive numbering—1, 2, 3, and so on. Simply delete the reports you no longer need.

Saving and Restoring a Solver Model

When you save your workbook, the most recent Solver settings are automatically saved, even if you have multiple worksheets in which you created Solver parameters. For example, if you have made changes to your Solver constraints, the previous ones will not be saved. You can save your Solver settings as you work—that way, you can apply previous settings again in the future. By saving the Solver model, the objective cells, variable cells, and constraints are saved, and Excel places this information in a few cells on the worksheet. Solver models can be easily saved and reloaded by clicking the Load/Save button in the Solver Parameters dialog box.

E10.16

 To Save and Reload a Solver Model

a. Click the **GolfLessons** worksheet tab. You will restore the original values in this worksheet. Click cell **D4**, type **1**, and then repeat typing the same value in cell **D5**. On the **DATA** tab, in the **Analysis** group, click **Solver**.

b. In the Solver Parameters dialog box, click **Load/Save** to open the Load/Save Model dialog box.

c. Excel guides you through the process. Because you are saving this model, Excel prompts you to select a specific number of cells. In this case, Excel needs nine cells to write the objective cell, variable cell, and constraint data. However, you only need to specify the starting cell. Type **$A$23** in the box for the Load/Save Model dialog box, and then click **Save**. Once the Solver model was saved, the Solver Parameters dialog box reopened. Notice how Solver placed data in nine cells beginning with A23.

d. Add a new constraint by clicking **Add**. Barry Cheney is thinking about opening the golf course for more hours during the day—possibly being open for up to 16 hours per day.

e. In the Solver Parameters dialog box, under Subject to the Constraints, click to select **$D$4 <= 14** from the list of constraints, and then click **Change**.

f. In the Change Constraint dialog box, in the Constraint box, change the value of 14 to 25. By adding additional hours and 15-minute lessons, additional clients can be served. Click **OK**.

g. If Barry extends the golf course operating hours, he will need to schedule more instructors each day. He knows that a minimum of four instructors will need to work; however, there could be up to seven scheduled in a given day. In the Solver Parameters dialog box, under Subject to the Constraints, click to select **$D$5 <= 4** from the list of constraints, and then click **Change**.

h. In the Change Constraint dialog box, click the **arrow**, and then click to select >= in the mathematical operands box. Click **OK**.

i. In the Add Constraint dialog box, type $D$5 in the Cell Reference box, click to select <= in the mathematical operands box, and then type 7 in the Constraint box. Click **OK**.

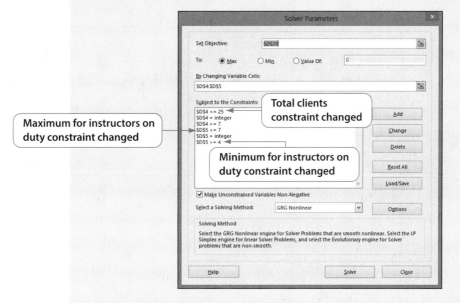

Figure 28   New model loaded into the Solver Parameters dialog box

j. Click **Load/Save** to open the Load/Save Model dialog box, type $B$23 in the box, and then click **Save**.

k. In the Solver Parameters dialog box, click **Solve** to run Solver and open the Solver Results dialog box.

l. Click to select the **Restore Original Values** option, and then under Reports on the right side of the Solver Results dialog box, click to select **Answer**.

m. Click **OK**. Notice that a worksheet tab named Answer Report 2 now exists, and on the GolfLessons worksheet tab, the value of 1 was reset in cells D4 and D5.

n. Click the **Answer Report 2** worksheet tab. Notice that Red Bluff can maximize the instructors' schedule and realize a net income of $29,278.00 per day.

o. **Save** 🖫 your changes and then exit Excel.

p. Complete the Documentation worksheet and submit your file as directed by your instructor.

CONSIDER THIS | **What Does Answer Report 2 Tell You?**

Does it benefit the golf course manager to stay open additional hours? How much more— if any—net income can the golf course generate on a daily basis? How many instructors will need to work each day? What else does the Solver answer report tell you?

QUICK REFERENCE | **Saving Solver Parameters**

You can save the last selections in the Solver Parameters dialog box with a worksheet by saving the workbook. Each worksheet in a workbook may have its own Solver selections, and all of them are saved. You can also define more than one problem for a worksheet by clicking Load/Save to save problems individually.

When you save a model, enter the reference for the first cell of a vertical range of empty cells in which you want to place the problem model. When you load a model, enter the reference for the entire range of cells that contains the problem model.

Concept Check

1. Why do managers use CVP analysis, and what does it help them learn about their business? p. 516

2. Discuss the difference between using a two-variable data table and calculating elasticity when analyzing costs. p. 526–528

3. Give three examples of how you could use Goal Seek. Describe how Goal Seek uses iteration to find the solution. p. 529–530

4. What are scenarios used for, and how can analyzing scenarios assist managers in decision making? p. 532

5. What are the two different types of Scenario reports? List some ways Scenario reports are useful. p. 535–537

6. What is Solver? What can Solver help managers determine? p. 538–539

7. What are the three main parameters needed to use Solver? Briefly define all three. p. 539–541

8. What does a Solver Answer report outline? Why is the option to Restore Original Values helpful? p. 545

Key Terms

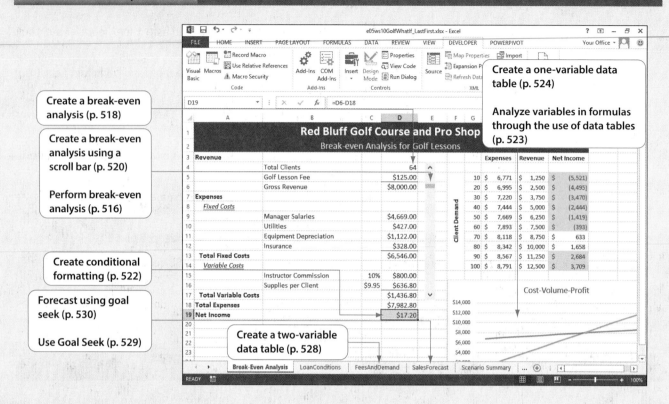

Create a break-even analysis (p. 518)

Create a break-even analysis using a scroll bar (p. 520)

Perform break-even analysis (p. 516)

Create conditional formatting (p. 522)

Forecast using goal seek (p. 530)

Use Goal Seek (p. 529)

Create a two-variable data table (p. 528)

Create a one-variable data table (p. 524)

Analyze variables in formulas through the use of data tables (p. 523)

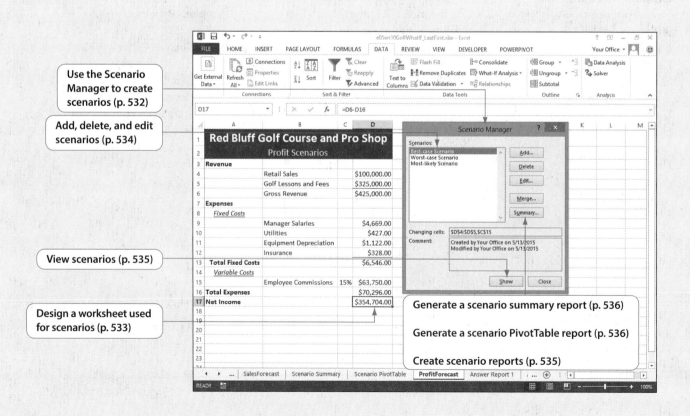

Use the Scenario Manager to create scenarios (p. 532)

Add, delete, and edit scenarios (p. 534)

View scenarios (p. 535)

Design a worksheet used for scenarios (p. 533)

Generate a scenario summary report (p. 536)

Generate a scenario PivotTable report (p. 536)

Create scenario reports (p. 535)

Load the solver add-in (p. 539)

Understand the use of the Solver add-in (p. 538)

Set the objective cell and variable cells (p. 540)

Define constraints (p. 540)

Solve complex problems using Solver (p. 539)

Save and reload a solver model (p. 548)

Generate a solver answer report (p. 546)

Generate and interpret Solver answer reports (p. 545)

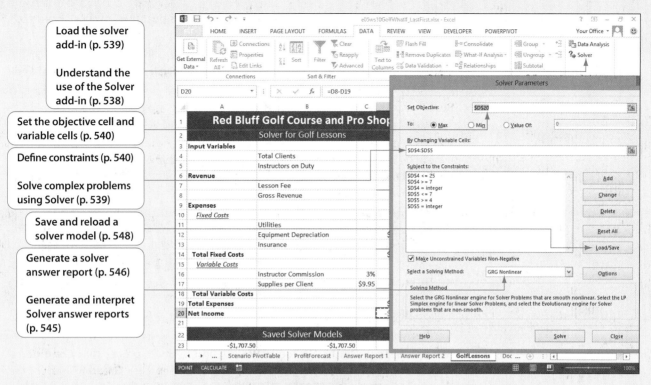

Figure 29 The Red Bluff Golf Course & Pro Shop Business Planning Final Analysis

---

Practice 1

Student data file needed:

 e05ws10Forecast.xlsx

You will save your file as:

e05ws10Forecast_LastFirst.xlsx

Forecasting at the Red Bluff Golf Course & Pro Shop

Sales & Marketing

The Red Bluff Golf Course & Pro Shop needs to analyze current sales trends and forecast prices for the upcoming year to ensure it is maximizing profit. Barry Cheney, the manager, is not certain if the prices he is currently charging are going to help him reach his sales goals. Additionally, he needs some guidance about how many hours a day he should be open for business as well as how many employees he should schedule during operating hours to maximize the pro shop's net income. Mr. Cheney has asked you to perform what-if analyses through the use of a break-even analysis, data tables, Goal Seek, scenarios, and Solver. He has given you templates and data to use to create your analysis. Upon completion, you will need to present your findings to Mr. Cheney.

a. Open **e05ws10Forecast**, and then save the file as e05ws10Forecast_LastFirst using your first and last name. Click **Enable Content** if necessary.

b. If necessary click the **ProductsAndSales** worksheet tab. To insert a filename footer, on the INSERT tab, in the Text group, click **Header & Footer**. On the DESIGN tab, in the Navigation group, click **Go to Footer**. If necessary, click the **left section** of the footer, and then in the Header & Footer Elements group, click **File Name**.

c. Click any cell on the spreadsheet to move out of the footer, press Ctrl+Home, on the VIEW tab, in the Workbook Views group, click **Normal**, and then click the **HOME** tab.

d. Complete the following tasks to forecast prices and sales quantities of specific products using Goal Seek.

- If necessary, click the **ProductsAndSales** worksheet tab, and then click cell **E5**. On the DATA tab, in the Data Tools group, click **What-If Analysis**, and then click **Goal Seek** to open the Goal Seek dialog box.

- Red Bluff wants to set a sales goal of $27,500 for its golf balls. Type 27500 in the **To value** box, and then type $C$5 in the **By changing cell** box. Click **OK** two times, and then open the **Goal Seek** dialog box again.

- Type $E$6 in the **Set cell** box, type 9000 in the **To value** box, and then type $D$6 in the **By changing** cell box. Click **OK** two times, and then open the **Goal Seek** dialog box again.

- Type $E$7 in the **Set cell** box, type 7500 in the **To value** box, and then type $C$7 in the **By changing cell** box. Click **OK** two times, and then open the **Goal Seek** dialog box again.

- Type $E$8 in the **Set cell** box, type 9250 in the **To value** box, and then type $C$8 in the **By changing cell** box. Click **OK** two times, and then open the **Goal Seek** dialog box again.

- Type $E$9 in the **Set cell** box, type 2495 in the **To value** box, and then type $D$9 in the **By changing cell** box. Click **OK** two times.

- Select cell range **D5:D9**. On the HOME tab, in the Styles group, click **Conditional Formatting**, point to **Highlight Cells Rules**, and then click **Greater Than**. In the **Format cells that are GREATER THAN** box, type 100. Click the **with** arrow, and then click **Custom Format**. Under Font style click **Bold**, and then click **OK** two times to apply bold to the font of the product prices, where the price is greater than $100. Press Ctrl + Home.

e. Complete the following tasks to forecast the best-case, worst-case, and most-likely case scenarios using Scenario Manager.

- Click the **MonthlyForecasting** worksheet tab. On the DATA tab, in the Data Tools group, click **What-If Analysis**, and then click **Scenario Manager** to open the Scenario Manager dialog box.

- Click **Add**, type Most Likely Scenario in the Scenario name box, and press Tab. In the Changing cells box, type D4:D5,C15. The values that are currently on the spreadsheet are the values for the Most Likely Scenario. Click **OK** two times.

- Click **Add** to begin creating your second scenario, type Worst-case Scenario in the Scenario name box, and then click **OK**. Type 75000 in row 1, type 125000 in row 2, type 0.09 in row 3, and then click **OK**.

- Click **Add** to begin creating your third scenario, type Best-case Scenario in the Scenario name box, and then click **OK**. Type 200000 in row 1, type 350000 in row 2, type 0.05 in row 3, and then click **OK**.

- In the Scenario Manager dialog box, view each of your scenarios by clicking each **Scenario's name** in the listing box, and then click **Show**. Click **Summary** to create a Scenario summary report, if necessary type D18 in the **Result cells** box, and then click **OK**.

- Click the **Scenario Summary** worksheet tab, if necessary. To add headings to your data, delete the cell reference headings in cells **C6**, **C7**, **C8**, and **C10**. Click cell **B6**, type Retail sales, click cell **B7**, type Equipment sales, click cell **B8**, type Commission, click cell **B10**, and then type Net income. If necessary, format the font as bold.

- Click the **MonthlyForecasting** worksheet tab. On the DATA tab, in the Data Tools group, click **What-If Analysis**, click **Scenario Manager** to open the Scenario Manager dialog box, and then click **Summary**. Select the **Scenario PivotTable report** option. Click the **Result cells** box, if necessary type D18, and then click **OK**.
- Click the **Scenario PivotTable** worksheet tab to format the report to make it easier to read. Click cell **A1**, type Monthly Forecasting Solution, press Ctrl+Enter, and then set the width of column **A** to 27. Click cell **A2**, type Scenario PivotTable Report, press Ctrl+Enter, merge and center the range **A2:B2**, change the font size to **16** point, and then apply **Bold**. Click cell **A3**, and then type Scenarios. Press Tab, in cell B3, type Net Income, press Ctrl+Enter, and then resize the width of column **B** as needed. Select the range **B4:B6**, and then format the cells as **Currency**.

f. Complete the following tasks to create a Solver answer report that determines the maximum net income that can be generated.

- Click the **NetIncomeForecast** worksheet tab, and then on the DATA tab, in the Analysis group, click **Solver**.
- In the Solver Parameters dialog box, click the **Set Objective** box, type D23, and then type $D$4:$D$5 in the **By Changing Variable Cells** box. Click **Add** to begin entering your constraints.
- The pro shop can be open from 12 to 18 hours per day, depending on what Mr. Cheney decides. Using the techniques you have practiced, type $D$4>=12 in the appropriate boxes as your first constraint, click **Add**, and then type $D$4<=18 as your second constraint.
- Click **Add**. The pro shop can have three to seven employees working per day, depending on the day and time of year. Using the techniques you have practiced, type $D$5>=3 as your next constraint, click **Add**, and then type $D$5<=7 as your next constraint.
- Click **Add**. The hours and employees must be integers. Using the techniques you have practiced, type $D$4=integer as your next constraint (*Hint:* Click **int** as the mathematical operand option, and Excel will add the word "integer" for you), click **Add**, and then type $D$5=integer as your last constraint.
- Click **OK**. To save your Solver model, click **Load/Save**, type $A$25 into the box in the Load/Save Model dialog box, click **Save**, and then click **Solve** to run Solver. Click **Restore Original Values**, click **Answer**, and then click **OK** to create a Solver answer report.

g. Complete the following tasks to create a two-variable data table with conditional formatting that will help analyze the break-even point.

- Click the **GolfPricing** worksheet tab, click cell **G5**, type =D19, and then press Ctrl+Enter. To format cell G5 to hide the results of the function, right-click cell **G5**, and then click **Format Cells**.
- Click the **Number** tab, click to select the **Custom** category, and then click the **Type** box. Delete any existing text, and then type ;;;. Click **OK**. Select the range **G5:R21** to select the data for your data table.
- On the DATA tab, in the Data Tools group, click **What-If Analysis**, and then click **Data Table** to open the Data Table dialog box. Type $D$5 in the Row input cell box, type $D$4 in the Column input cell box, and then click **OK**.
- Select the range **H6:R21**, and then format the cells as **Currency**. To view all the data, widen the columns if necessary.

- On the HOME tab, in the Styles group, click **Conditional Formatting**. Point to **Highlight Cells Rules**, click **Less Than** to open the Less Than dialog box, and then type 0 in the **Format cells that are LESS THAN** box. If necessary, click to select the **Light Red Fill with Dark Red Text** option, and then click **OK**.

- Click **Conditional Formatting** again, point to **Highlight Cells Rules**, click **Greater Than** to open the Greater Than dialog box, type 3500 in the **Format cells that are GREATER THAN** box, click to select the **Green Fill with Dark Green Text** option, and then click **OK**. Press Ctrl + Home.

h. Click the **Documentation** worksheet. Click cell **A6**, and then type in today's date. Click cell **B6**, and then type in your first and last name. Complete the remainder of the **Documentation** worksheet according to your instructor's direction.

i. Click **Save**, close Excel, and then submit your file as directed by your instructor.

Problem Solve 1

MyITLab®
Grader
Homework 1

Sales & Marketing

Student data file needed:

 e05ws10Float.xlsx

You will save your file as:

 e05ws10Float_LastFirst.xlsx

Extreme H2O

Extreme H2O is a company that specializes in water sports. It is considering adding some new experiences for its customers. In a nearby community there is a small river that can be used for tubing. The management is trying to figure out how much usage it might receive and where to set the price in order to make a profit. The company seeks to make sure the project would at least break even the first year after development costs. Management has tasked you with developing a worksheet to analyze the situation.

a. Open **e05ws10psFloat**, and then save the file as e05ws10Float_LastFirst using your first and last name. Insert the **filename** in the left section of the footer on the **Break-Even Analysis** worksheet.

b. The company would like a break-even analysis completed. On the **Break-Even Analysis** worksheet, enter the correct formulas to calculate the Gross Revenue, Total Fixed Costs, Total Variable Costs, and Net Income. Place the formulas in the appropriate cells in column **D**.

c. Management thinks an average of 75 guests a day would be a realistic average. Use Goal Seek to find out what the price would need to be to come out exactly even with 75 guests per day.

d. Fill in the Expenses, Revenue, and Net Income columns (range G5:I19) using a data table. Format the range as appropriate for the data.

e. Copy the information in range **A3:D18** from the Break-Even Analysis worksheet and paste it in range **A4:D19** on the worksheet **PriceAndGuest**. Resize the columns to fit the data. Create a data table in the range **F4:N22**. The price needs to start at $3 and increase to $10 in $1 increments, and the number of guest needs to start at 25 and increase in increments of 5.

f. Once the data table has been created, format the data in the data table so any net profit under –$5,000 has a light red background and dark red text, data that is above or equal to –$5,000 and below $5,000 will have a light yellow background and dark yellow text, and anything $5,000 or greater will have a light green background and dark green text. Format cell **F5** to hide the result of the formula in the cell.

g. Copy the information in range **A3:D18** from the sheet Break-Even Analysis to range **A3:D18** on the sheet **DaysAndPrice**. Now add two scroll bars to the sheet to the right of the inserted cells. One scroll bar will change the days of operations per year between the values of 200 and 250 one day at a time. The other scroll bar will change the price between the values of $3 and $10 by $1 increments. Be sure to label the scroll bars as to what the control changes.

h. Complete the **Documentation** worksheet according to your instructor's direction. Insert the **filename** in the left custom footer section of the Header/Footer tab in the Page Setup dialog box on all worksheets in the workbook.

i. Click Save, close Excel, and then submit the file as directed by your instructor.

Perform 1: Perform in Your Team

Student data file needed:

 Blank Excel worksheet

You will save your file as:

e05ws10Charity_LastFirst.xlsx

Charity Shirts

Sales & Marketing

You are raising money for a local charity. To do so, you will be selling t-shirts at your institution. Each shirt will have a logo printed on the front and back. Each t-shirt will initially sell for $10.00. The t-shirts cost $4.99 per shirt to be printed, and you will incur a fixed cost of $150 to place an order for any number of t-shirts. Initially you will consider selling the t-shirts at two different stations at your institution.

a. Open **Excel**, and then create a new workbook. Save it as **e05ws10Charity_LastFirst** using your first and last name. Insert the **filename** in the left section of the footer.

b. Create a break-even analysis for the example described above. Calculate the total amount of donations you will be able to give to charity if the following conditions are met:

- Assume you will sell 10 t-shirts at each station you set up.
- Start with two stations to sell the t-shirts from.
- You will incur a cost of $50 for miscellaneous materials you will need during the course of your fund-raising.
- Calculate your gross revenue, total fixed costs, total variable costs, and the total donation amount.
- Create a two-variable data table that models having between 1 and 4 stations at your institution, each selling between 10 and 50 t-shirts in increments of 5.
- Format the values in the data table appropriately. Use conditional formatting to distinguish values below $0 and values above $200 from the standard formatting.

c. As part of the charity event, your team is considering using a different company from which to order. The new company issues two kinds of shirts, t-shirts and hoodies. Each t-shirt costs $6.99, and each hoodie costs $8.99. There is a $150 fixed cost for ordering any number of shirts from the company. Using the same information from the prior problem, create a new worksheet in your workbook to use Solver to optimize your donations under the following conditions.

- Assume you will sell 20 t-shirts and 10 hoodies per station at your institution.
- Incorporate the revenue gained from sales of the hoodies. Also incorporate the cost of ordering hoodies. Use the same miscellaneous materials cost from the prior worksheet.

- Use your total donations as the Objective cell. You will want to maximize your donations. Use the number of hoodies sold and the price you will charge for each hoodie as the By Changing Variable Cells.
- Assume you have a budget of $700. Add a constraint that keeps your total costs under your budget.
- Add a constraint that keeps the amount you will charge for each hoodie less than or equal to $20. Add another constraint that will make the price of the hoodies greater than the costs of the hoodies.
- Add a constraint that will make the number of hoodies sold an integer value.
- Solve the model with the GRG Nonlinear method and create an answer report.

d. Complete the **Documentation** worksheet according to your instructor's direction. Insert the **filename** in the left custom footer section of the Header/Footer tab in the Page Setup dialog box on all worksheets in the workbook.

e. Click Save, close Excel, and then submit the file as directed by your instructor.

Additional Cases

Additional Workshop Cases are available on the companion website and in the instructor resources.

MODULE CAPSTONE

More Practice 1

Student data file needed:

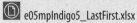 e05mpIndigo5.xlsx

You will save your file as:

e05mpIndigo5_LastFirst.xlsx

Indigo5 Restaurant

Finance & Accounting

Production & Operations

Management at Indigo5, a five-star restaurant that caters to local patrons in addition to clients of the resort and spa, has outsourced its data collection processes to a new firm in town. The data collected is in the e05mpIndigo5 workbook and is not compatible in its current form with the database that Indigo5 currently uses to store this data. You will need to use your knowledge of Excel functions to clean the data so that it can be imported into the database.

Additionally, Indigo5's top chef, Robin Sanchez, is regularly updating data in her database to make certain she has all the ingredients and recipes needed to offer the high-quality food for which the restaurant is known. You have been asked to build a spreadsheet model that will assist managers in answering what-if questions about product pricing when Chef Sanchez wants to add a new menu item. Mr. Dimas, the restaurant manager, gave you an Excel workbook and some data to use while building your spreadsheets. Upon completion, you will present your model to Chef Robin Sanchez and Alberto Dimas.

a. Open **e05mpIndigo5**, and then save the file as e05mpIndigo5_LastFirst using your first and last name.

b. Click the **FoodCategories** worksheet, and then insert the **file name** in the left section of the footer.

c. In cell **B2**, separate the category number from the value in cell **A2**. In cell **B2**, type CAT01 and then press Enter. In cell **B3**, type CAT02 and then press Enter.

d. On the DATA tab, in the **Data Tools** group, click **Flash Fill** to complete the list of categories in column B.

e. Click cell **C2**. Parse out the description of the category from the value in cell **A2**. In cell **C2**, type Appetizer and then press Enter. In cell **C3**, type Fi and notice the suggestion Flash Fill provides. Press Enter to accept the suggestion and complete the list of descriptions in column C.

f. Click the **Reviews** worksheet tab. You will need to convert the text in cell A2 to proper case. In cell **E2** type =PROPER(A2) and then press Ctrl+Enter. Double-click the **AutoFill** handle in cell **E2** to copy the formula down the column. If necessary, use AutoFit on the column so that all contents are viewable.

g. You will need to convert the numbers in B2 into an acceptable date format. Click cell **F2**, type =DATE(LEFT(B2,4),MID(B2,5,2),RIGHT(B2,2)) and then press Ctrl+Enter. Double-click the **AutoFill** handle in cell **F2** to copy the formula down the column. If necessary, use AutoFit on the column so that all contents are viewable.

h. Complete the following tasks to perform a break-even analysis for a new menu item. Fixed expenses have been spread evenly among all menu items.

   • Click the **Break-even Analysis** worksheet tab. Click cell **D6**, type =D4*D5 and then press Enter to calculate the gross revenue—the amount of money generated from selling the new menu item.

- Click cell **D13**, type =SUM(D9:D12) and then press Enter to calculate the total fixed costs. Click cell **D15**, type =D4*C15 and then press Enter to calculate the total food cost based on how many items were sold.

- In cell **D16**, type =D13+D15 and then press Enter to calculate the total expenses. In cell **D17**, type =D6-D16 and then press Enter to calculate the net income—how much profit the restaurant will generate from the new menu item.

- Apply Conditional Formatting to cell **D17** with Custom Format option so numbers that are less than zero are displayed in red text font and numbers that are greater than zero are displayed in green font, and then enter quantities in cell **D4** until you find the break-even point.

- Click cell **F4**, type =D4 and then press Tab. In cell **G4**, type =D16 and then press Tab. In cell **H4**, type =D6 and then press Tab. In cell **I4**, type =D17 and then press Ctrl+Enter. Select cells **F4:I4** to format with the formula results hidden. Right-click any of the cells in the selected range **F4:I4**, and then click **Format Cells**. On the Number tab, click to select the **Custom Category**, click in the **Type box**, remove any existing text, and then type ;;;. Click **OK**.

- Select the range **F4:I18** for your data table. On the **DATA** tab, in the **Data Tools** group, click **What-If Analysis**, and then click **Data Table** to open the Data Table dialog box. Press Tab to move to the Column input cell box, type $D$4 and then click **OK**.

- Select the range **I5:I18**, on the **HOME** tab, in the **Styles** group, click **Conditional Formatting**, point to **Color Scales**, and then click **Green - White - Red Color Scale**.

- Select the range **G3:H3**, press and hold Ctrl, and then select the range **G5:H18**. On the INSERT tab, in the **Charts** group, click **Insert Line Chart**, and then click **Line** in the 2-D Line category. Click the **border edge** of the chart, and then drag to reposition the top-left corner into cell **F20**.

- On the **DESIGN** tab, in the **Data** group, click **Select Data**, and then under Horizontal (Category) Axis Labels, click **Edit**. With the insertion point in the Axis label range box, select the range **F5:F18**. Click **OK** two times.

- Click **Chart Elements**, click the **Axis Titles** arrow, and then select **Primary Horizontal**. Click the **Horizontal (Category) Axis Title** box, and then type Total Ordered. Click the **Chart Title** box, and then type Break-Even Analysis.

- Click an empty cell to deselect the chart, and then press Ctrl+Home.

i. Click the **Documentation** worksheet tab. Click cell **A8**, type today's date, click cell **B8**, and then type your first and last name.

j. Save your work, print or submit your documents as directed by your instructor, and then close Excel.

Problem Solve 1

MyITLab®
Grader
Homework 1

Student data files needed:

 e05ps1Hotel.xlsx

e05ps1Hotel.csv

You will save your file as:

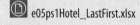 e05ps1Hotel_LastFirst.xlsx

Hotel Reservations and Room Rates at the Painted Paradise Resort and Spa

Research & Development

The hotel area has asked you to develop a spreadsheet model that will assist in determining room rates and the break-even point for specific types of rooms—such as the Grand Villa Suite. As part of this analysis, you will need to import data on reservations made at the hotel. Currently, William Mattingly is not certain whether the pricing helps cover expenses such as housekeeping costs or whether the price even generates a profit for the resort. He would also like you to generate a Scenario summary report that will illustrate the net income based on best-case, worst-case, and most-likely scenarios. Mr. Mattingly gave you an Excel workbook with a partial model already built and some data to use while building your model. Upon completion, you will present your model to Mr. Mattingly before the spreadsheet model is implemented.

a. Open the **e05ps1Hotel** workbook, and then save the file as e05ps1Hotel_LastFirst using your first and last name.

b. On the ReservationData worksheet, insert the **file name** in the left section of the footer.

c. On the ReservationData worksheet, import the text file **e05ps1Hotel.csv** into cell **A1**. The data is delimited by commas and should be imported such that column A contains the ReservationID field and column I contains the RoomType field.

d. The data for CheckInDate and CheckOutDate is formatted as a European date. In cell **J1**, create a heading named GuestCheckIn. Use the Text to Columns wizard to convert the dates in column D from the DMY format into MDY format beginning in cell **J2**. Adjust the width of column J so that the text can be read.

e. In cell **K1**, create a heading named GuestCheckOut. Use the Text to Columns wizard to convert the dates in column E from the DMY format into MDY format beginning in cell **K2**. Adjust the width of column K so that the text can be read.

f. In cell **L1**, create the heading GuestFullName. In column L, use text functions to remove any nonprintable characters and extra spaces from the guest names in column C of the data. Adjust the width of column L so that the text can be read.

g. On the **RatesScenario** worksheet, complete the following tasks to create a Scenario summary report.

- Use the Scenario Manager to add a Most-likely scenario. Use $C$4:$C$7 as the Changing cells. The current values on the worksheet will be your Most Likely scenario values.

- Add a new scenario named Best-case scenario. In the Scenario Values dialog box, in row 1, type 400 and then in row 2, type 200. Click row 3, type 250 and then in row 4, type 125.

- Add a new scenario named Worst-case scenario. In the Scenario Values dialog box, in row 1, type 170 and then in row 2, type 100. Click row 3, type 150 and then in row 4, type 50.

- Create a Scenario summary report using **E17** as your Result cells. Format your report with the appropriate row headings. Resize column B to **23.57**.

h. On the GrandVillaAnalysis worksheet, complete the following tasks to create a weekly break-even analysis for the Grand Villa Suite. If necessary, add the DEVELOPER tab to the Ribbon, as explained in Workshop 12.

- Insert a scroll bar in the area of cells **E4: E14**. In the Format Control dialog box, type the following criteria:
  Current value: 1
  Minimum value: 1
  Maximum value: 20
  Incremental change: Leave as the default value of **1**
  Page change: Leave as the default value of **10**
  Cell link: $D$4

- Click cell **D17**, and apply Conditional Formatting so numbers that are less than zero are displayed in red text, and then use the scroll bar to scroll until you find the break-even point.

- In cells **G4:I4** create cell references for the values that correspond to the headings in G3:I3. Format the range G4:I4 to hide the results of the functions you just referenced by right-clicking any of the selected cells, clicking **Format Cells**, and then using the **;;;** Custom Category format.

- Using the range **F4:I14**, create a one-variable data table. Use **$D$4** as the Column input cell box. Format the cells in columns G:I of the data table as **Currency** with **2** decimal places.
- Use Conditional Formatting to create Data Bars for the range **I5:I14**. Select **Green Data Bar** under **Gradient Fill**.
- Select the range **G5:H14** in the data table, and then create a 2-D line chart. Use the range **F5:F14** as the Horizontal (Category) Axis Labels. Delete the chart title and legend, and add a horizontal axis title that is below the axis. Type Rooms Booked in the **Title** text box, and then move your chart below the one-variable data table.

i. Save your file, and then exit Excel. Submit your work as directed by your instructor.

Problem Solve 2

MyITLab® Grader

Homework 2

Student data files needed:

 e05ps2Vacation.xlsx

e05ps2Guests.xml

e05ps2Stays.xml

You will save your file as:

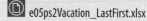 e05ps2Vacation_LastFirst.xlsx

Online Vacation Packages at the Painted Paradise Resort and Spa

Research & Development

The hotel at Painted Paradise Resort and Spa currently offers three types of vacation packages to its customers: a Golf Weekend, a Spa Special, and a Golf and Spa Special. The hotel has recently purchased an online reservation system for booking vacations at Painted Paradise. The new system is currently being tested, and some issues have arisen with how the data is exported from the website. The data has been exported into two XML files that you will need to import and cleanse. As part of the evaluation of this new system, the hotel area has also asked you to generate two worksheet models that analyze the pricing of the vacation packages. The first will be used to determine future pricing of the vacation packages. The second will consist of a Solver answer report that will optimize the price of the vacation packages by modifying the related quantities sold and costs associated with the packages.

a. Open **e05ps2Vacation**, and then save the file as e05ps2Vacation_LastFirst using your first and last name.

b. On the VacationForecast worksheet, insert the **file name** in the left section of the footer.

c. On the VacationForecast worksheet, complete the following tasks to create next year's forecast of vacation packages.

- Management anticipates having a 15% increase over this year's sales. In cell **D5**, type a formula that calculates the forecasted totals for next year. Copy the formula down to cell **D7**.
- In cell **F5**, type a formula for the extended price forecasted for next year's sales. Copy the formula down to cell **F7**.
- Use Goal Seek to determine the price of each vacation package. The resort wants to set a sales goal of $1,000,000 for its Golf Weekend package, a sales goal of $750,000 for its Spa Special package, and a sales goal of $1,250,000 for its Golf and Spa Special package.

d. The three vacation packages offered by the hotel are listed on the **VacationIncome** worksheet along with the current pricing and expenses for each package. Using this data, complete the following tasks to create a Solver Answer report that determines the maximum net income that can be generated next year.

- Open the **Solver Parameters** dialog box, use Net Income as the **Set Objective** cell, and then use the Qty. cells and Misc. overhead per package cell as the **By Changing Variable Cells**.

- Add the following Solver constraints. The resort wants to book at least 100 of each Revenue vacation package. The resort only has the resources to book at most 300 of each vacation package. Each vacation package must be whole numbers—integers—because the resort cannot sell part of a package. The minimum that management wants to spend on Misc. overhead per package is $15, and the maximum that management wants to spend on Misc. overhead per package is $20.

- Create a Saved Solver Models section, and then save your Solver model. Create a Solver **answer report** using the GRG Nonlinear solving method. Be sure to restore original values. (*Hint:* Click **Answer** under Reports. Do not forget to click **Options**, and under GRG Nonlinear, select to **Use Multistart**.)

e. On the Guests worksheet, import the data contained in the **e05ps2Guests.xml** file into cell **A1**. Click **OK** on the message stating the XML source does not refer to a scheme. Complete the following steps to cleanse the data.

- In columns adjacent to the data you just imported, create new headings for FirstName, Initial, LastName and PhoneNumber.

- Use **Flash Fill** to separate the names of the guests into the appropriate columns. (*Hint:* Due to the layout of the data, you may need to invoke Flash Fill on the **DATA** tab.)

- Use **Flash Fill** to change the format of the phone numbers. The number 7025556627 should be formatted as (702) 555-6627.

f. On the **Reservations** worksheet, import the data contained in the **e05ps2Stays.xml** file into cell **A1**. Complete the following steps to cleanse the data.

- The **Date** column in the data imported is the check-in date of the guest making the reservation. The data however is stored as text and cannot be used in date calculations. Create a new column named CheckInDate adjacent to the data you just imported. The new column should contain the data from column D formatted as a date. The value in D2—20150422—should be displayed as 4/22/2015. (Hint: You may want to use several columns of the worksheet to complete this conversion. Label each column you use Step1, Step2, and so on.) Place your final work in the **CheckInDate** column.

- Create a new column named CheckOutDate adjacent to the data you have imported and cleansed. Using the CheckInDate and NumNights data, calculate the date a guest checked out of the hotel. If necessary, format the column of data as **Short Date**.

g. Save your file, and then exit Excel. Submit your work as directed by your instructor.

Perform 1: Perform in Your Life

Student data files needed:

 e05pf1Syllabus.docx

e05pf1GradeScale.txt

Blank Excel workbook

You will save your file as:

e05pf1Grade_LastFirst.xlsx

Using Solver and Goal Seek to Help Calculate Your Grade

Information Technology

This spreadsheet model will help you use Solver to calculate a grade based on a weighted average. The Solver model will allow you to enter multiple grade categories and determine how you can maximize your current grade. This could answer a question such as, "What grades do I need to earn on my research paper and final exam to earn an A in the course?" Additionally, this model will allow you to use Goal Seek to determine the grade you need to earn on an assignment or exam to earn a specific grade in the course. For example, you may currently have a B and want to calculate what grade you need to earn on a final exam in order to earn an A in the course. You need to set up Solver and Goal Seek based on the grading information from your course syllabus.

a. Start **Excel**, and then create a new blank workbook. Save it as e05pf1Grade_LastFirst. Insert the **file name** in the left section of the footer on the first worksheet in the workbook.

b. Build a grading scale to use with grades you import into the model.
   - On a blank worksheet, import the **e05pf1GradeScale** file into your workbook. Use text functions to cleanse the percentage scores and the associated letter grades into separate columns. If the grading scale for your course differs from the imported data, copy and paste the values you just cleansed and make adjustments as needed.
   - Rename the worksheet GradingScale.

c. Open **e05pf1Syllabus** or the syllabus for your course if directed by your instructor. Use the information within the grading section of your syllabus to create your Solver model.

d. Change the name of a blank worksheet to WeightedGrade. Complete the following tasks to build a Solver Answer report.
   - Create a model that lists your grade categories and specific assignments under each one. For example, you may have five assignments. Create a heading for assignments, and then list the specific assignments such as Assignment 1, Assignment 2, and so on.
   - Type a formula that calculates the weighted grade of each category. To do so, you would add what you earned on all items in the category, divide by the total points possible, and multiply by the weighted percent. The result will be a decimal. The sum of the results would then be multiplied by 100 to convert it to a percent—which is your grade. Format your spreadsheet so users can easily read it—such as Number or Percent format.
   - Use the Final Grade Total calculation as your objective cell and the outstanding measurement items—the items that have no grade entered—as your changing cells.
   - Add constraints that set outstanding assignments to specific values. For example, if you want to earn an A in your class, you would add a constraint that limits the result of the objective cell to the lowest and highest values within the grade range—such as 92 percent to 100 percent.

e. Create a Saved Solver Models section, and then save your Solver model. Create a Solver **answer report** using the GRG Nonlinear solving method. Be sure to restore original values.

f. Create a table that will be used for a Goal Seek analysis next to your Solver model. Enter each category, type a formula that calculates the weighted grade of each category, and then enter your grades with the exception of a final grade. Determine what grade you need on the final exam to earn a B in the course by using Goal Seek.

g. Insert a new worksheet and change the name to StraightPercent. Complete the following tasks to create a Solver answer report and Goal Seek model based on a straight percent grading structure.
   - Recreate the Solver model you created on the WeightedGrade worksheet. Modify the formulas on the worksheet as well as the Solver constraints to calculate your grade based on a straight percent calculation. Determine what you will need to earn on outstanding measurement items to earn an A in the course. Create a Solver **answer report** using the GRG Nonlinear solving method. Be sure to restore original values. Format your numbers appropriately.
   - Create a Saved Solver Models section, and then save your Solver model.
   - Recreate the Goal Seek model from the WeightedGrade worksheet on the StraightPercent worksheet. Determine what grade you need to earn on the final exam in order to earn a B+ in the course. Use the same grades that you entered on the WeightedGrade worksheet.

h. Format your spreadsheet so users can easily read it—such as using Number format as appropriate.

i. Save your file, and then exit Excel. Submit your work as directed by your instructor.

Student data files needed:

 e05pf2Charity.xlsx

e05pf2Roster.xml

You will save your file as:

 e05pf2Charity_LastFirst.xlsx

Managing Data for a Charity Fund-Raising Event

Finance & Accounting

This spreadsheet model will help you use the What-If analysis tools to determine how much of the monies raised at a charity event will actually be donated to the charity. When a charity event is held, there are costs associated with setting it up and running it. Jonas Lamar, the event coordinator, has asked you to create a break-even analysis—a one-variable data table to determine the break-even point. Mr. Lamar has given you an Excel workbook and the appropriate information to get started.

The charity uses a website to track those registered for the event. To keep accurate records and maintain communications with the participants, you have been asked to import an XML file of participants so you can cleanse the data.

a. Start **Excel**, open **e05pf2Charity**, and then save it as e05pf2Charity_LastFirst.

b. On the Break-evenAnalysis worksheet, insert the **file name** in the left section of the footer.

c. Click the **Break-evenAnalysis** worksheet, if necessary. Complete the following tasks to build a break-even analysis, a one-variable data table, and build a traditional cost volume profit chart from the one-variable data table that will help analyze the break-even point.

  - Insert the appropriate formulas to cells **D6**, **D11**, **D13**, **D14**, **D15**, **D16**, **D17**, and **D18**.

  - Insert a scroll bar in the area of cells E4 through E16. Type the following criteria in the Format Control dialog box:
    Current value: **10**
    Minimum value: **10**
    Maximum value: **5000**
    Incremental change: **1**
    Page change: **10**
    Cell link: type $D$4

  - Format cell **D18** with conditional formatting so numbers that are less than zero are displayed in red text, and then scroll until you find the break-even point.

  - Click cell **G4**, reference the total expenses cell, click cell **H4**, reference the gross revenue cell, click cell **I4**, and then reference the net income cell. Format the range **G4:I4** to hide the results of the functions you just referenced.

  - Select the range **F4:I19**, and then insert a one-variable data table using Total attendees for the Column input cell. Select the range **G5:I19**, and then format the cells as **Currency** with no decimal places.

  - Select the range **I5:I19**, and then format the cells using the Green - Yellow - Red Color Scale.

  - Select the range **G3:H3**, and then select the range **G5:H19**. Insert a line chart in the 2-D Line category. Use the range **F5:F19** as the Horizontal (Category) Axis Labels. Add a horizontal axis title that is below the axis with Attendees in the title text box. Delete the chart title. Reposition the chart below the one-variable data table.

d. Click the **Participants** worksheet. Import the **e05pf2Roster** file into the worksheet. Complete the following steps to cleanse the data.

  - Create a new column adjacent to the imported data named FirstName. Using the method of your choice, display only the first name from the Name field in the FirstName column.

- Create a new column adjacent to the imported data named LastName. Using the method of your choice, display only the last name from the Name field in the LastName column.

- Create a new column adjacent to the imported data named PhoneNumber. Use Flash Fill to display each number from the Phone field with appropriate formatting. For example, 2145559577 should be displayed as (214) 555-9577.

- Create two new columns adjacent to the imported data. Name the first StreetAddress and the second State. Using the method of your choice, display the portion of the address in the Address field preceding the comma in the StreetAddress column, and the portion of the address in the Address field after the comma in the State column.

- Create a new column adjacent to the imported data named RegistrationDate. Cleanse the date from the DateRegistered field in the proper format using Date and Text functions. For example, 20150517 should be displayed as 5/17/2015.

e. Save your file, and then exit Excel. Submit your work as directed by your instructor.

Perform 3: Perform in Your Team

Student data file needed:
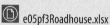 e05pf3Roadhouse.xlsx

You will save your file as:
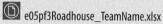 e05pf3Roadhouse_TeamName.xlsx

The Roadhouse Bar and Grill

Production & Operations

You are the bar manager at the Roadhouse Bar and Grill, a local restaurant that specializes in home-cooked meals for breakfast, lunch, and dinner. The general manager has given you an Excel workbook that contains data about the beverages offered and sold. You need to manage the inventory of beverage items to ensure you have enough beverages for each day you are open for business as well as to determine pricing for special drink items.

Additionally, the database used for keeping track of inventory has been corrupted, causing some issues with the inventory data. You will need to use your knowledge of Excel to clean the inventory data.

a. Select one team member to set up the document by completing Steps b–e.

b. Point your browser to either **https://www.skydrive.live.com**, **https://www.drive.google.com**, or any other instructor-assigned tool. Be sure all members of the team have an account on the chosen system—a Microsoft or Google account.

c. Create a spreadsheet, and then rename Sheet1 as Contributors. List the names of each of the team members on the worksheet, and then add a heading above the name to read Team Members. Include any additional information on this worksheet required by your instructor.

d. Open the **e05pf3Roadhouse** workbook, and then save it as e05pf3Roadhouse_TeamName using the name assigned to your team. Insert the **file name** in the left section of the footer.

e. Share the spreadsheet with the other members of your team. Make sure each team member has the appropriate permission to edit the document.

f. On the DrinkForecast worksheet, complete the following tasks to forecast prices for drink specials.

- In range **D5:D9** type a formula that increases this year's quantity sold by 20%. In range **F5:F9** type a formula that calculates the extended price for next year's forecast.

- The current prices are located in range **E5:E9**. Use Goal Seek to determine new prices in **E5:E9**, based on the revenue goals for next year, located in range **G5:G9**.

g. On the DrinkScenarios worksheet, complete the following tasks to create a Scenario summary report.

- In range **E4:E8**, type a formula that calculates the extended price for next year's forecast. In cell **E9** type a formula that calculates the gross revenue.
- In cell **E18** type a formula that calculates the variable cost for all drinks sold.
- Open the **Scenario Manager**. Add a Worst-case scenario, and then use the **Qty** cells as the changing cells. The current values on the worksheet will be your Worst-case scenario values.
- Add a new scenario named Best-case scenario. Use the following values as your Scenario values:
  Mojito: 175
  Fuzzy Navel: 60
  Strawberry Daiquiri: 45
  Pina Colada: 30
  Roadhouse Special: 200
- Add a new scenario named Most-likely scenario. Use the following values as your Scenario values:
  Mojito: 150
  Fuzzy Navel: 45
  Strawberry Daiquiri: 30
  Pina Colada: 20
  Roadhouse Special: 150
- Create a Scenario summary report using the net income cell as your result cell. Format your report with the appropriate row headings, and then resize columns if necessary.

h. On the DrinkScenarios worksheet, complete the following tasks to create a Scenario PivotTable report.

- Modify your result cells to include gross revenue, variable costs, taxes, and net income, and then create a Scenario PivotTable report.
- Format your report with the appropriate row headings and cell formats, and resize columns if necessary.

i. On the Inventory worksheet, complete the following steps to cleanse the data provided.

- Remove any duplicates that exist in the **Inventory** worksheet. Duplicate records occur where two or more rows are identical.
- The stock code should consist of all uppercase letters. Create a new column with the appropriate function to display the stock code correctly.
- Create a new column labeled ItemCode. Construct the item code by combining first the corrected stock code and then the item number.
- The data in the Category/Brand column has been corrupted the most. There are several spaces before and after the data that need to be removed. There are also symbols that need to be removed from the data. Additionally, the category and brand should be in two separate columns. Display the corrected values in their own columns labeled Category and Brand. The category data should be in proper case. Use as many columns to the right of the Inventory data that you need to accomplish these tasks.
- Use functions or Flash Fill to parse the units and measurement into two separate columns.

j. Save the file, and then exit Excel. Once the assignment is complete, share the spreadsheet with your instructor or turn in as your instructor directs. Make sure your instructor has permission to edit the contents of the folder.

Student data files needed:

 e05pf4Online.xlsx

 e05pf4Online.accdb

You will save your file as:

 e05pf4Online_LastFirst.xlsx

Troubleshooting Online Orders

Finance & Accounting

The company you currently work for uses an online system to sell and ship its products to customers. It would like to begin analyzing this data, and management has compiled a subset of the data in an Access database. The company had a prior intern attempt an analysis, but he was not able to work well with the data in its current format. You have been asked to import the data into Excel and cleanse it for further analysis. Additionally, you have been asked to check the what-if analysis that was begun for the Exfoliator product the company sells. The intern attempted to build the what-if analysis, but management believes some mistakes were made in the file.

a. Start **Excel**, open **e05pf4Online**, and then save it as e05pf4Online_LastFirst.

b. On the Transactions worksheet, insert the **file name** in the left section of the footer.

c. On the Transactions worksheet, import the **qryTransactionDetails** table from the **e05pf4Online.accdb** Access database file into cell **A1**. Complete the following steps to cleanse the data.

- The prior intern tried to clean columns B and C using Flash Fill but was unsuccessful. The data in column B represents the transaction date but is stored as text. The data in column C represents the shipping date for the product but is also stored as text. Both columns are in the YYYYMMDD format. Use Text and Date functions to create two new columns and convert the data into date formats that Excel will recognize.

- Using the two date columns created in the prior step, calculate the number of workdays between the date of the transaction and the shipping date. Your calculation should exclude weekends and any holidays. A listing of 2014 and 2015 holidays can be found in the **Holidays** worksheet.

d. On the Customers worksheet, import the **tblCustomers** table from the **e05pf4Online.accdb** database file into cell **A1**. Complete the following steps to cleanse the data.

- The intern you worked with had difficulty using text functions to cleanse the FullName field into a FirstName and LastName field. Use Flash Fill to cleanse the **FullName** field into these two new fields.

- United States zip codes should always be a five-character code. Because some zip codes begin with a zero, upon importing to Excel, the leading zero gets removed. In a new column of data, use the Text function to correctly format the ZipCode field. (Hint: Try using "00000" as the format_text argument of the Text function.)

e. Click the **ExfoliatorAnalysis** worksheet. Complete the following tasks to correct the mistakes. Assume that all payments will be made at the end of the period.

- Apply appropriate formatting to all numbers.

- Check the series data for the chart to ensure they are correct, and then correct them as needed.

- Check all existing formulas to ensure they are correct, and then correct them as needed.

- In column I, ensure the conditional formatting identifies values less than zero with a light red fill and dark red text while values greater than zero have a green fill and dark green text.

- Ensure that the data table is setup correctly, including hiding any references to functions using custom formatting.

f. Save your file, and then exit Excel. Submit your work as directed by your instructor.

WORKSHOP 11 | LOAN AMORTIZATION, INVESTMENT ANALYSIS, AND ASSET DEPRECIATION

OBJECTIVES

1. Construct a loan analysis with PMT, RATE, and NPER   p. 570

2. Calculate cumulative interest and principal using CUMIPMT and CUMPRINC   p. 577

3. Create an amortization schedule using PPMT and IPMT   p. 580

4. Analyze bonds using PV and FV   p. 583

5. Analyze investments using NPV, XNPV, IRR, and XIRR   p. 587

6. Calculate the depreciation of assets using the SLN, DB, and DDB functions   p. 594

Prepare Case

The Turquoise Oasis Spa Financial Analysis

Finance & Accounting

Painted Paradise Golf Resort and Spa CEO William Mattingly recently announced that Genisys Corporation—a large technology company—will soon break ground on their new corporate headquarters about three miles from the resort. In addition, Genisys has proposed a partnership with the resort to provide lodging, recreation conferences, and other services to Genisys Corporation staff, executives, and VIP guests.

Myper / Shutterstock

Turquoise Oasis managers Irene Kai and Meda Rodate believe that the new relationship with Genisys Corporation has the potential to double the Spa revenue. To handle the increased business, they plan several upgrades and improvements. The Spa will have to handle more simultaneous clients while maintaining high-quality service.

The managers would like you to prepare an analysis of several options to finance these improvements and eventual expansion.

REAL WORLD SUCCESS

"As an intern in the accounting department of an electric engineering company, I was asked to transfer some accounting documents to an Excel workbook. During the process I was able to identify an error in how the company calculated the depreciation of one of their assets."

- Emily, recent graduate

Student data file needed for this workshop:

 e06ws11Finance.xlsx

You will save your file as:

 e06ws11Finance_LastFirst.xlsx

Constructing a Financial Analysis on Loans

Businesses need to have cash flow in order to survive. **Cash flow** is the movement of cash in and out of a business. The measurement of cash flow can be used to determine a company's value and financial situation. As an analytical tool, the statement of cash flows is useful in determining the viability and solvency of a company. The statement of cash flows is particularly helpful in assessing a company's short-term viability, which includes its ability to collect cash from customers and to pay bills. The longer a company stays profitable and the better it manages its cash flow, the better its viability. Once a company's value and financial situation are determined, banks can use that information to determine its eligibility for business loans.

From a personal perspective, individuals deal with managing money on a regular basis. People need to understand not only how to successfully invest their money, but also how loans work—such as a car, student, or home loan, known as a mortgage. Personal finance is similar to managing an organization's cash flow, except it relates to the individual's or family's monetary choices. It addresses the ways in which individuals or families obtain, budget, save, and spend money, taking various economic risks and future life events—such as getting married or having a family—into account.

An **economic risk** occurs when there is a concern that a chosen act or activity will not generate sufficient revenues to cover operating costs and repay debt obligations. This notion suggests that a choice has an effect on the outcome. Potential losses themselves may also be called risks. Almost any human endeavor, whether personal or professional, carries some type of risk, but some are more risky than others. For example, the Turquoise Oasis Spa may decide to obtain a bank loan to fund an expansion. Before the bank agrees to finance the loan, they will need to consider many factors, including the spa's cash flow and short-term viability. This will help the bank determine the level of risk—whether the spa will be able to repay the loan on time and in full.

Excel includes financial functions to use for business and personal analysis and financial management. It is important to understand the purpose and features of each function so you can apply them to a specific task or problem. These financial functions are designed to calculate the monthly payment and other components of a loan, determine the future value of an investment, compare and contrast different investment opportunities, and calculate the depreciation of assets over time. In the following section, you will conduct a loan analysis using the PMT, RATE, and NPER functions.

Construct a Loan Analysis with PMT, RATE, and NPER

Many businesses and individuals need to borrow money—it is a fact of life. And if you need to apply for a loan, you will want to know the monthly payment, which is dependent on such factors as the loan terms—the principal amount, the interest rate, and the length of the loan. The type of loan that the Turquoise Oasis Spa is considering is an amortized loan. An amortized loan is a loan with scheduled periodic payments consisting of both principal and interest. This is different from other types of loans with interest-only payment features and balloon payments.

Opening the Starting File

You will be conducting loan analyses on four different loan options to fund the Turquoise Oasis Spa expansion.

E11.00

 To Open the e06ws11Finance Workbook

a. Start **Excel**, and then open the **e06ws11Finance** workbook from your student data files.

b. On the **FILE** tab, click **Save As**, and save the file in the folder or location designated by your instructor with the name e06ws11Finance_LastFirst using your last and first name.

Using the PMT Function

The Payment function, or **PMT function**, can be used to calculate a payment amount based on constant payments and a constant interest rate—payments on business loans, mortgages, car loans, or student loans can be calculated. For example, if the Turquoise Oasis Spa determined that they need to borrow $200,000 to help fund the spa's expansion, and the bank is charging 6.75% interest over a 10-year period, the spa managers could use the PMT function to determine what the monthly payment would be.

> **REAL WORLD ADVICE** | **Additional Costs of a Loan**
>
> The payment amount returned by the PMT function includes principal and interest but no taxes, reserve payments, private mortgage insurance, or fees that may be associated with the loan. Be sure to include other fees and charges when calculating your actual expenses associated with the loan. Additional costs can be quite substantial. If you fail to consider them, you may obtain a loan that you cannot afford!

To use the PMT function for the Turquoise Oasis Spa's loan, you have to understand the structure of the function and what each function argument is determining. The PMT function calculates payments for a loan for a fixed amount with a fixed interest rate and for a fixed period of time. The PMT function syntax uses five arguments, the first three are required, and the last two are optional: (1) interest rate per period (rate), (2) number of periods (nper), (3) present value (pv), (4) future value (fv), and (5) type (type). Notice that the optional arguments are placed in square brackets.

=PMT(rate, nper, pv, [fv], [type])

The **rate** argument is the periodic interest rate—the interest rate of the loan. For example, if the annual percentage rate (APR) is 12% and you make monthly payments, the periodic rate—the rate charged per period and in this case, per month—is 1%. This is calculated by dividing the APR by 12, the number of months in a year.

> **CONSIDER THIS** | **Determining the Per Period Rate of Interest**
>
> The key to determining the rate of interest per period is in the total number of payments and/or how frequently the payments are made each year. If they are monthly payments, then you need to divide the rate argument by 12. What would you divide the rate by if the payments were made quarterly? What if they were made yearly?

The **nper** argument is the total number of payments that will be made in order to pay the loan in full. The term of the loan is generally specified in years; however, payments are made several times a year. If the loan is for five years, and you make 12 monthly payments, you would calculate the nper by multiplying the number of years by the number of payments in one year. Thus, five years times 12 monthly payments equals 60, which is the number to use in the formula.

The **pv** argument is the present value of the loan. Usually the loan amount is used as the present value. The PMT( ) function in Excel returns a negative number by default. This is due to the nature of cash flow when viewed from a business perspective. Incoming cash flows are "positive," whereas outgoing flows are "negative." It pays to keep this in mind when working with financial functions to avoid receiving a wildly incorrect answer. To avoid receiving a negative answer, you can type a minus sign in front of the present value. This will help ensure that your payment result is positive.

The **fv** argument—future value of the loan—is the balance you want to reach after the last payment is made. Consider any type of loan that you may have. The ultimate goal is to pay off the loan, meaning that the future value would be zero. If fv is omitted—because it is an optional argument—Excel assumes that the future value is zero.

CONSIDER THIS | **Using the fv Argument**

A business may lease office equipment and then make regular payments throughout the term of the lease. At the end of the lease, the business may have the option to purchase the equipment for a specific price, determined at the lease signing. The amount would be entered in the fv argument of the PMT function. What are some other uses of the fv argument?

The **type** argument indicates when the payments are due—either at the beginning (1) or the end (0) of a period—such as the end of a month, quarter, or year. If type is omitted (because it is an optional argument), Excel assumes that the value is zero, for an end of the period payment.

The Turquoise Oasis Spa can use the PMT function to calculate the monthly payment on Loan Option 1 for $200,000 at 6.75% annual interest rate over a 10-year period. Thus, the PMT function arguments would be:

- Rate: 6.75% divided by 12 months = .5625%

- Nper: 10 years * 12 months = 120 months

- Pv: −$200,000—Recall that this argument is negative because it represents an outflow of money.

Because the future value and type arguments are not given, you would end the PMT function after entering the present value and calculate the monthly payment as $2,296.48. If you do not have a future value and the payment is made at the end of the period, you can stop at principal—the pv argument—and just type your ending parenthesis.

=PMT(.0675/12,10*12,-200000)

The amount of the payment can change based on when the payment needs to be made—either at the beginning or the end of a period—because of how interest is calculated. If the payments are made at the beginning of a period, the total interest that will be paid on the loan is lower because you are paying down the principal faster. The **principal** is the unpaid balance amount of the loan. Because the future value is not given and you want to enter 1 in the type argument, you would type two commas after the present value argument to indicate that you want to skip the future value argument. The PMT function calculates the monthly payment as $2,283.64 and would be entered as follows:

=PMT(.0675/12,10*12,-200000,,1)

> **CONSIDER THIS** | **What-If Analysis for a Loan**
>
> How could referencing cells with the loan terms allow you to perform what-if-analysis? **What-if analysis** is when you use several different values in one or more formulas to explore all the various results. What if you decided that you could not afford the loan payments? How could you modify the interest rate, loan amount, and terms to find a payment that you can afford?

MyITLab®
Workshop 11 Training

E11.01

 To Calculate Loan Payments Using the PMT Function

a. This workbook includes information for some of the financing options collected by the managers. Click the **LoanAnalysis1-3** worksheet tab. Click cell **B6**, type 200000, and press Ctrl+Enter.

b. On the HOME tab, in the Number group, click the **Number Format** Dialog Box Launcher. In the Format Cells dialog box, on the Number tab, click **Currency**, and then set Decimal places to **0**. Click **OK**. This is the amount that the Turquoise Oasis Spa thinks they may have to borrow from the bank.

c. Click cell **B7**, type .0675 as the rate, and then format the cell as **Percentage** with **2** decimal places.

d. Click cell **B8**, and then type 10 as the term of the loan.

e. Click cell **B9**, and then type 12 because the payments will be made monthly.

f. Click cell **B10**, and then type =PMT(B7/B9,B8*B9,-B6) to calculate a monthly payment that is made at the end of the period. Press Enter.

g. Click cell **B11**, and then type =PMT(B7/B9,B8*B9,-B6,,1) to calculate a monthly payment that is made at the beginning of the period. Press Enter.

   Notice the difference between the periodic payment amounts is dependent upon when the payment is made.

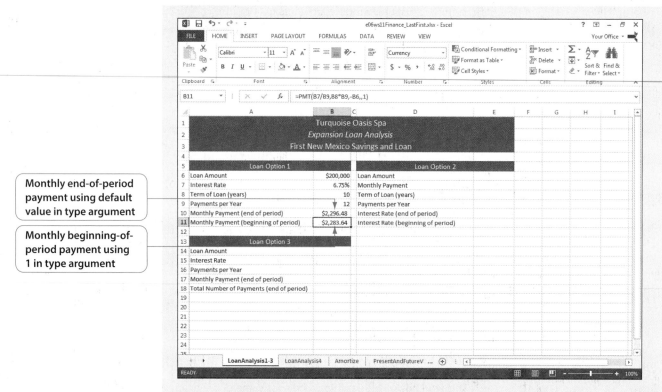

Monthly end-of-period payment using default value in type argument

Monthly beginning-of-period payment using 1 in type argument

Figure 1 Loan analysis using the PMT function

h. Click **Save** 🖫.

<table>
<tr>
<td colspan="2">QUICK REFERENCE</td>
<td>Understanding the PMT Function Syntax</td>
</tr>
</table>

The PMT function syntax has the following arguments:

Argument	Description
rate	The interest rate per period for the loan. Required.
nper	The total number of periods (payments) for the loan. Required.
pv	The present value or the total amount that a series of future payments is worth now; also known as the loan amount. Required.
fv	The future value or a cash balance you want to attain after the last payment is made. If fv is omitted, it is assumed to be 0 (zero), that is, the future value of a loan is 0. Optional.
Type	The number 0 (zero) or 1 and indicates when payments are due. Optional. Set type equal to 0—or omit—if payments are due at the end of the period. Set type equal to 1 if payments are due at the beginning of the period.

Table 1 Description of the PMT function syntax

Using the RATE Function

The **RATE function** calculates the interest rate per period for an investment or loan, given that you know the present value of the loan, payment amount, and number of payment periods. This can be useful if you do not have all the information you need to calculate loan payments with the PMT function or you would like to verify the actual interest rate of the loan.

The RATE function syntax uses six arguments. The first three are required, and the last three are optional: (1) number of periods (nper), (2) payment (pmt), (3) present value (pv), (4) future value (fv), (5) type (type), and (6) interest rate guess (guess).

=RATE(nper, pmt, pv, [fv], [type], [guess])

The **guess** argument is used when you want to guess what the interest rate will be. RATE usually calculates if you enter a guess between zero and one. If nothing is entered, Excel assumes that the guess is 10%. If RATE does not calculate, you can try different values for the guess argument.

The Turquoise Oasis Spa can use the RATE function to calculate the annual interest rate on Loan Option 2 for $200,000 to be paid over 8 years with monthly payments of $2,853. Thus, the RATE function arguments would be:

- Nper: 8 years * 12 months = 96 months
- Pmt: $2,853
- Pv: $200,000

=RATE(8*12, 2853,-200000)

Because the future value, type, and guess arguments are optional, you would end the RATE function after entering the present value and calculate the interest rate as 0.688%. It is important to note that the result in this case is the "monthly" interest rate because you used 12 times the number of loan years. If you were making payments quarterly and used 4 times the number of loan years or annually, the number of loan years only, Excel would calculate the rate as quarterly or annually. If you wanted to calculate the annual interest rate from the monthly result, you could simply multiply the rate by 12. As a result, the bank would be charging the Turquoise Oasis Spa 8.252% annually.

=RATE(8*12,2853,-200000)*12

E11.02

 To Calculate the Interest Rate of a Loan Using the RATE Function

a. Click cell **E6**, type **200000**, and then format the cell as **Currency** with **0** decimal places.

b. Click cell **E7**, type **2853** as the monthly payment, and then format the cell as **Currency**.

c. Click cell **E8**, and then type **8** as the term of the loan.

d. Click cell **E9**, and then type **12** because the payments will be made monthly.

e. Click cell **E10**, and then type =RATE(E8*E9,E7,-E6)*E9 to calculate the annual interest rate for a loan where the payment is made at the end of the period. Format the cell as **Percentage** with **3** decimal places. Notice that the annual interest rate is 8.252% when the payment is made at the end of the period.

f. Click cell **E11**, and then type =RATE(E8*E9,E7,-E6,,1)*E9 to calculate the annual interest rate for a loan where the payment is made at the beginning of the period. Format the cell as **Percentage** with **3** decimal places. Notice that the annual interest rate is 8.448% when the payment is made at the beginning of the period.

> **Troubleshooting**
> If the RATE function returns #NUM! instead of the expected interest rate, then check to make sure there is a negative sign before the pv argument. For the RATE function to work, either the pmt or the pv argument must be negative.

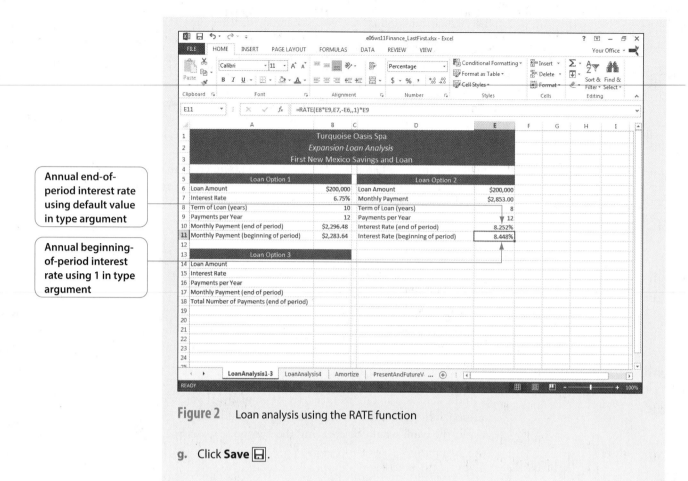

Annotations (left side):

Annual end-of-period interest rate using default value in type argument

Annual beginning-of-period interest rate using 1 in type argument

Formula bar: E11   =RATE(E8*E9,E7,-E6,,1)*E9

	A	B	C	D	E
1				Turquoise Oasis Spa	
2				*Expansion Loan Analysis*	
3				First New Mexico Savings and Loan	
4					
5		Loan Option 1		Loan Option 2	
6	Loan Amount	$200,000	Loan Amount		$200,000
7	Interest Rate	6.75%	Monthly Payment		$2,853.00
8	Term of Loan (years)	10	Term of Loan (years)		8
9	Payments per Year	12	Payments per Year		12
10	Monthly Payment (end of period)	$2,296.48	Interest Rate (end of period)		8.252%
11	Monthly Payment (beginning of period)	$2,283.64	Interest Rate (beginning of period)		8.448%
12					
13		Loan Option 3			
14	Loan Amount				
15	Interest Rate				
16	Payments per Year				
17	Monthly Payment (end of period)				
18	Total Number of Payments (end of period)				

Figure 2   Loan analysis using the RATE function

g. Click **Save**.

Using the NPER Function

The Number of Periods function, or **NPER function**, calculates the number of payment periods for an investment or loan if you know the loan amount, interest rate, and payment amount. The NPER function syntax uses five arguments. The first three are required, and last two are optional: (1) rate (rate), (2) payment (pmt), (3) present value (pv), (4) future value (fv), and (5) type (type).

=NPER(rate, pmt, pv, [fv], [type])

The Turquoise Oasis Spa can use the NPER function to calculate the number of periods on Loan Option 3 for a $200,000 loan with an annual rate of 5.75% if the monthly payment is $3,843.35, and paid at the end of the period. Thus, the NPER function arguments would be as follows:

- Rate: 5.75%
- Pmt: $3,843.35
- Pv: $200,000

=NPER(.0575/12, 3843.35, -200000)

Because the future value and type arguments are optional, you would end the NPER function after entering the present value and calculate the number of periods as 60.

E11.03

 To Calculate the Total Number of Periods Using the NPER Function

a. Click cell **B14**, type **200000**, and then format the cell as **Currency** with **0** decimal places.

b. Click cell **B15**, type **.0575**, and then format the cell as **Percentage** with **2** decimal places.

c. Click cell **B16**, type **12** because the payments will be made monthly.

d. Click cell **B17**, type **3825.02** as the monthly payment amount, and then format the cell as **Currency**.

e. Click cell **B18**, and then type **=NPER(B15/B16,B17,-B14)** to calculate the number of periods for a loan where the payment is made at the end of the period. Format the cell as **Number** with **0** decimal places.

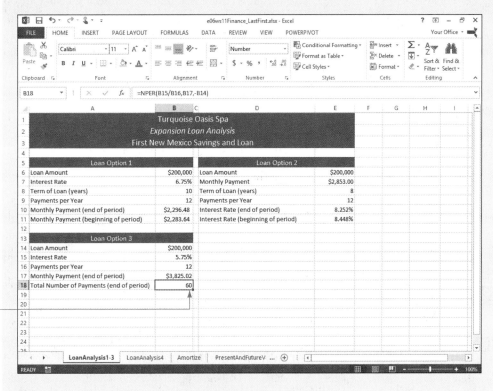

Total number of monthly end-of-period payments using the default value in type argument

Figure 3 Loan analysis using the NPER function

f. Click **Save**.

Calculate Cumulative Interest and Principal Using CUMIPMT and CUMPRINC

Each loan payment in an amortized loan is made up of a principal amount and an interest amount. There are times when you will want to know the total interest or principal amount being paid over a particular time period. Consider a mortgage. If someone is paying on a mortgage, they can use the amount of interest paid throughout the year as a deduction on their federal income taxes. Thus, knowing the amount of cumulative interest paid can make it easier to complete this section on a tax return.

Using the CUMIPMT Function

The Cumulative Interest Payment function, or **CUMIPMT function**, can be used to calculate the amount of interest paid over a specific number of periods, such as quarterly, annually, or for the whole term of the loan. Thus, if you do not want to calculate a running total of the interest paid, you can total the payments between two payment periods. The CUMIPMT function syntax uses six arguments, all of which are required: (1) rate (rate), (2) number of periods (nper), (3) present value (pv), (4) start period (start_period), (5) end period (end_period), and (6) type (type).

=CUMIPMT(rate, nper, pv, start_period, end_period, type)

The two new arguments are start_period and end_period; they indicate the period numbers during the life of the loan. Start_period defines the start of the payment period for the interval you want to sum. The end_period defines the end of the payment period.

The Turquoise Oasis Spa is also considering Loan Option 4 for $200,000 at an 8.25% annual interest rate for 3 years with payments of $18,550.84 made at the end of each quarter. They can use the CUMIPMT function to calculate the cumulative amount of interest payments for all 3 years or for each quarter. Thus, the CUMIPMT function arguments would be as follows:

- Rate: 8.25%
- Nper: 3 years * 4 quarters = 12 quarterly payments
- Pv: $200,000
- Start_period: 1
- End_period: 12
- Type: 0—end of period payments

With this function, Excel does not allow you to place a negative sign in front of the pv argument. Thus, to display numbers as a positive result, you can simply place a negative sign before the function name.

=-CUMIPMT(.0825/4, 3*4, 200000, 1, 12, 0)

E11.04

 To Calculate Cumulative Interest Payments Using the CUMIPMT Function

a. Click the **LoanAnalysis4** worksheet tab.

b. Click cell **B6**, type **200000**, and then format the cell as **Currency** with **0** decimal places.

c. Click cell **B7**, type **.0825**, and then format the cell as **Percentage** with **2** decimal places.

d. Click cell **B8**, and then type **3** as the term of the loan.

e. Click cell **B9**, and then type **4** because the payments will be made quarterly.

f. Click cell **B10**, type **18984.59** as the quarterly payment amount, and then format the cell as **Currency**.

g. Click cell **B13**, type =-CUMIPMT(B7/B9,B8*B9,B6,1,12,0) to calculate the total cumulative interest payments for the life of the loan based on payments being made at the end of the period. Format the cell as **Currency**.

h. Click cell **B17**, type =-CUMIPMT($B$7/$B$9,$B$8*$B$9,$B$6,A17,A17,0) to calculate the cumulative interest paid in the first quarterly payment. Format the cell as **Currency**. Use the **AutoFill** handle to copy the formula down to cell **B28**.

Notice that the amount of the cumulative interest payments decreases with each quarterly payment because the amount of principal is less after each quarterly payment.

SIDE NOTE

Using the ABS Function
An alternative method to using the negative sign to make the result positive is to use the ABS function: ABS(number).

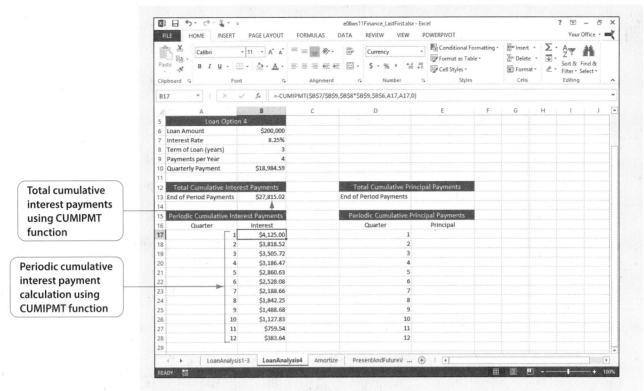

Total cumulative interest payments using CUMIPMT function

Periodic cumulative interest payment calculation using CUMIPMT function

Figure 4 Loan analysis using the CUMIPMT function

i. Click **Save** .

Using the CUMPRINC Function

Similar to the CUMIPMT function, the Cumulative Principal function, or **CUMPRINC function**, can be used to calculate the amount of principal paid over a specific number of periods, such as quarterly or annually. Thus, if you do not want to calculate a running total of the principal paid, you can total the payments between two payment periods. The CUMPRINC function syntax uses the same six arguments that the CUMIPMT uses, all of which are required. Like the CUMIPMT function, you are unable to place a negative sign in front of the pv argument. Thus, to display numbers as a positive result, you can simply place a negative sign before the function name.

=-CUMPRINC(rate, nper, pv, start_period, end_period, type)

E11.05

To Calculate Cumulative Principal Payments Using the CUMPRINC Function

a. Click cell **E13** and type =-CUMPRINC(B7/B9,B8*B9,B6,1,12,0) to calculate the total cumulative principal payments for the life of the loan based on payments being made at the end of the period. Format the cell as **Currency**.

b. Click cell **E17** and type =-CUMPRINC($B$7/$B$9,$B$8*$B$9,$B$6,D17,D17,0) to calculate the cumulative principal paid in the first quarterly payment. Format the cell as **Currency**. Use the **AutoFill** handle to copy the formula down to cell **E28**.

Notice the value of the cumulative principal payments increase with each quarterly payment. This is because with each payment the principal gets smaller and therefore there is less per-period interest accruing on the amount and more of the payment goes toward paying off the principal.

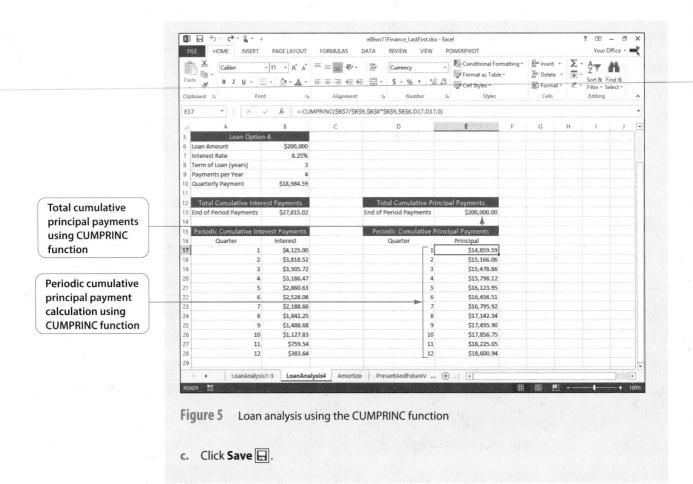

Total cumulative principal payments using CUMPRINC function

Periodic cumulative principal payment calculation using CUMPRINC function

Figure 5 Loan analysis using the CUMPRINC function

c. Click **Save** 💾.

Create an Amortization Schedule Using PPMT and IPMT

With the financial functions you have learned so far you have some effective tools to help you make an informed decision about which loan option is best to finance the expansion project. However, another tool that can help with the decision is an amortization table.

Amortize, with respect to loan balances, refers to repaying the balance of a loan over a period of time in multiple installments—or payments. An **amortization schedule** is a table that calculates the interest and principal payments along with the remaining balance of the loan for each period. Similar to the CUMIPMT and CUMPRINC functions that calculate the cumulative amount of interest and principal paid over a specified period of time, the IPMT and PPMT functions calculate the interest and principal portions that make up each periodic payment.

Using the PPMT Function

The Principal Payment function, or **PPMT function**, calculates how much of a specific periodic payment is going toward the principal amount of a loan. The PPMT function syntax uses six arguments, the first four are required, and the last two are optional: (1) interest rate per period (rate), (2) period (per), (3) number of periods (nper), (4) present value (pv), (5) future value (fv), and (6) type (type).

Its syntax is very similar to the PMT function with the addition of the period (per) argument. The **per** argument is a number that must be between 1 and nper and is the specific period for which a loan payment is being applied. As you make payments on an amortized loan, the amount you pay each period is the same but how much of that payment is being applied toward the principal increases over time. The per argument is needed to keep track of each payment.

Using the IPMT Function

The Interest Payment function, or **IPMT function**, calculates how much of a specific periodic payment is going toward the interest that has accrued on the loan. The IPMT function syntax is the same as the PPMT function. When you begin making payments on an amortized loan, the majority of the amount being paid, in the beginning, goes toward interest that has accrued on the remaining balance and this amount decreases over time as the principal is paid down.

Turquoise Oasis Spa could use an amortization table to analyze the loan options for additional improvements. For example, Irene Kai would like to borrow $25,000 for new equipment and pay this loan off in one year. By creating an amortization table showing the date of each payment, she can see how much will be applied to the interest and principal as well as the balance of the loan. After creating the amortization table, she finds that the payment would be $2,160.29 per month, and the salon would end up paying $923.46 in interest over the life of the loan. In this section, you will create an amortization table that helps Irene Kai analyze the repayment schedule to see if the payments are within the salon's budget.

REAL WORLD ADVICE	Things to Check in an Amortization Table

There are four things that you can check to ensure you have accurately constructed your amortization table:

- The final remaining balance value in your table should be zero.
- A given periodic payment (PMT) will equal the sum of the interest payment (IPMT) and the principal payment (PPMT).
- The sum of the principal payments (PPMT) will always equal the loan amount. If you add interest it will be the total amount paid over the course of the loan term, both in interest and principal.
- All interest and principal paid should equal the sum of all the payments made.

You can check your calculations in one easy step. Highlight a range of cells, such as the IPMT and PPMT calculations for the first period, and Excel displays the Average, Count, and Sum for the selection in the status bar located at the bottom of the Excel window.

Creating an Amortization Schedule

When you create an amortization table, start with the simplest configuration. Initially you should calculate the payment number, payment amount, interest and principal portions, and an ending balance for each payment. You can always add more details and complexity later.

E11.06

 To Create an Amortization Schedule

a. Click the **Amortize** worksheet tab.

b. Click cell **G5**, and then type =C7*C8 to calculate the number of payments that will be made throughout the life of the loan.

c. Click cell **G6**, and then type =PMT(C6/C8,G5,-C5) to calculate the payments that will be made at the end of the period. Notice that the monthly payment will be $2,160.29.

d. Click cell **G7**, and then type =G5*G6 to calculate the total amount that will be paid. Notice that the total amount that will be paid on the loan is $25,923.46.

e. Click cell **G8**, and then type =G7-C5 to calculate the total interest that will be paid on the loan. Notice that the total interest that will be paid on the loan is $923.46.

f. Click cell **C12**, and then type =C5 to begin creating your amortization schedule. This represents the beginning balance of the loan before the first payment is made—the amount borrowed.

g. Click cell **D12**, type =$G$6 to enter your payment, and then copy the formula down to cell **D23** using the **AutoFill** handle.

SIDE NOTE
Interest Payments
Notice how the interest portion of each payment decreases as the loan is paid off, from $140.63 to $12.08 at the end.

h. Click cell **E12**, and then type =IPMT($C$6/$C$8,A12,$G$5,-$C$5) to calculate how much of the monthly payment is being applied to the interest portion of the loan. Copy the formula down to cell **E23** using the **AutoFill** handle.

i. Click cell **F12**, and then type =PPMT($C$6/$C$8,A12,$G$5,-$C$5) to calculate how much of the monthly payment is being applied to the principal portion of the loan. Copy the formula down to cell **F23** using the **AutoFill** handle.

Notice how the principal portion of the payment increases as the loan is paid off, with $2,019.66 total principal being paid in the first payment and $2,148.20 total principal being paid in the last payment.

SIDE NOTE
Remaining Balance
Interest payments are the costs associated with the loan and are never deducted from the beginning balance.

j. Click cell **G12**, and then type =C12-F12 to calculate the remaining balance after each payment by subtracting the principal payment from the beginning balance. Copy the formula down to cell **G23** using the **AutoFill** handle. Note that the calculations will be negative until you fill in the beginning balance.

k. Your beginning balance for the next payment will be the same as the ending balance after the previous payment. Click cell **C13**, and then type =G12 to calculate the beginning balance for the second period. Then copy the formula down to cell **C23** using the **AutoFill** handle to supply the beginning balance for the remaining periods.

l. Click cell **D24**, type =SUM(D12:D23) to verify the total sum of principal payments are equal to the calculation in cell **G7**, and then use the **AutoFill** handle to copy the formula over to cell **F24**.

The results in D24 and E24 should equal your results in cells G7 and G8, respectively, and the total principal in F24 should equal the loan amount in C5.

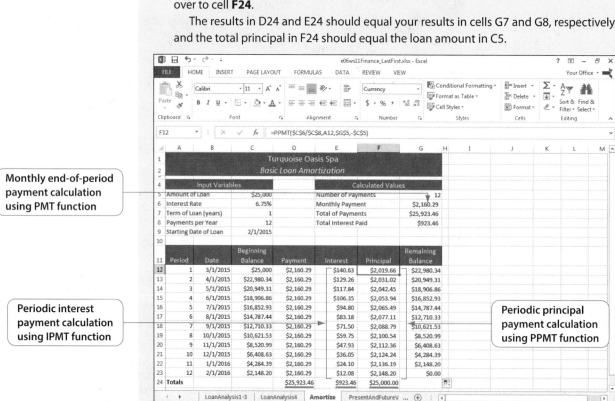

Figure 6 Amortization schedule

m. Click **Save** 🖫.

When deciding between several different loan options with various terms, rates, and payment frequencies, it is important to get the big picture. Time plays an important role in the total cost of a loan. If you are able to afford larger payments, you could save a lot of money by selecting a 15-year loan versus a 30-year loan even if the interest rate is higher. Be sure to use all the tools available to you to thoroughly analyze the options presented to you so that you may make the most informed decision possible.

Constructing a Financial Analysis of Investments

In addition to analyzing possible expansion finance options from a bank, managers at the Turquoise Oasis Spa would like to analyze some possible investment opportunities to help finance the expansion and generate revenue in the long term. Whether you are a business or individual investing money, analyzing how the investments are performing is a critical part of the investment process. There are many methods in which money can be invested. Stocks and bonds are two examples of a category of investment called securities.

A **security** is a legal document that can be bought and sold and holds some financial value. Stocks are categorized as equity securities because the company gives partial ownership of its equity, defined as total assets minus total liabilities, by selling stock in the company. Bonds are categorized as debt securities because the company is indebted to the people who loan the company money through the purchase of bonds.

In terms of economic risk, a bond is typically considered less risky, in part, because if a company fails, the debt owed to the bondholders are top priority and shareholders would lose any money invested in the company. A lower risk investment can also mean a lower return on that investment. A **return on investment**—or ROI—is the ratio of the amount of money gained or lost from an investment relative to the initial amount invested. A stockholder takes on more risk than a bondholder and therefore has the potential for a higher ROI if the company is successful. In this section you will learn how to analyze various investment options from bonds to individual retirement accounts.

Analyze Bonds Using PV and FV

Generally speaking, the way bonds work is that an investor loans a company money for a specified period of time by purchasing a bond certificate. Typically, bonds have a fixed interest rate and the bondholder receives annuity payments either annually or semiannually throughout the life of the bond. An **annuity** is a recurring amount paid or received at specified intervals. Once the specified time period of the bond has been reached, the bondholder is issued the value of the bond.

There are four basic concepts integral to understanding bonds. The first is par value. The **par value**—or face value—is how much the bondholder will receive at maturity. **Maturity** is the second concept and refers to the length of time before par value is returned to the bondholder. Most bond maturities range from 1 to 30 years, but they can have a range anywhere from 1 day to 100 years or more. The third concept is coupon. **Coupon** is the interest rate the bond pays. Typically the coupon payments are made to the bondholder annually or semiannually until the bond reaches maturity. For a majority of bonds, the coupon rate does not vary for the life of the bond. The fourth concept is yield. In its most basic terms, **yield** is the amount of annual interest, expressed as a percentage of the par value and determines how much investors will receive on their investment.

There are several different types of yield when referring to bonds. **Nominal yield** is the same as the coupon or interest rate. It is information provided when the bond is purchased and is considered the least helpful when it comes to analyzing the true value of a bond. **Current yield** considers the current market price of the bond, which may differ from the par value, and gives you a different yield rate on that basis. For example, consider the following: You purchase a bond with the following values on the open market for $800.

Par Value: $1,000
Coupon: 6% annually
Maturity: 1 year

If the bond's purchase price was the same as the par value, the nominal yield would be the same as the coupon of 6%, and you would have $1,060 ($1,000 * .06 = $60) at the end of the year when the bond reaches maturity. However, since it was purchased for $800, a more accurate yield calculation would be the current yield of 7.5% ($60/$800 = 7.5%). **Yield to maturity** or YTM is another yield calculation that takes into account the current market price, and the time to maturity, and assumes that coupon payments are reinvested at the bond's coupon rate. YTM is the most useful calculation in determining the value of a bond investment and also the most difficult to calculate.

Using the PV Function

Regardless of how you decide to invest your money—whether you are saving for a home, college, or retirement—if you understand the basics of analyzing your investment portfolio, you will be able to assess its performance. One of the functions that can help you analyze an investment is the Present Value function, or PV function. The **PV function** is used to calculate the present or current value of a series of future payments on an investment. In other words it calculates what the investment would be worth in today's dollars. It uses the same five arguments seen in other financial functions: (1) rate (rate), (2) number of periods (nper), (3) payment (pmt), (4) future value (fv), and (5) type (type). If you do not know the payment, you must enter the future value.

=PV(rate, nper, pmt, [fv], [type])

For example, if you are given the option of receiving $250,000 today or $300,000 7 years from now, which would you choose? Excel's PV function can help to determine the smarter choice. Assume that if you took the $250,000 today that you could invest that into a guaranteed risk-free bond at 3% yield rate for 7 years. Using the PV function to calculate the present value of $300,000 with a discount rate of 3% for 7 years you see that the $300,000 7 years from now results in a lower present value—$243,927.45—than $250,000 today.

=-PV(0.03,7,0,300000)

Turquoise Oasis Spa managers are considering a different option for financing part of the expansion—investing in a company bond with the following values:

Par value: $50,000
Maturity: 5 years
Coupon: 6%
YTM: 7.75%

The first step in determining whether or not this is a worthy investment is to calculate the present value of the investment.

E11.07

 To Calculate the Present Value of a Bond

a. Click the **PresentAndFutureValue** worksheet tab.

b. Click cell **B5**, type 50000 as the par value of the bond, and then format it as **Currency**.

c. Click cell **B6**, type .06 as the coupon rate, and then format it as **Percentage**.

d. Click cell **B7**, and then type 5 for the years to maturity.

e. Click cell **B8**, and then type =B6*B5 to calculate the coupon payment that will be paid to the bondholder one time a year for five years.

f. Click cell **B9**, type .0775 as the yield to maturity rate, and then format it as **Percentage** with **2** decimals.

g. Click cell **B10**, and then type =-PV(B9,B7,B8,B5) to calculate the present value of the investment as a positive number. Notice the present value of this particular bond is only worth $46,483.24, which is less than $50,000 and therefore not a good investment.

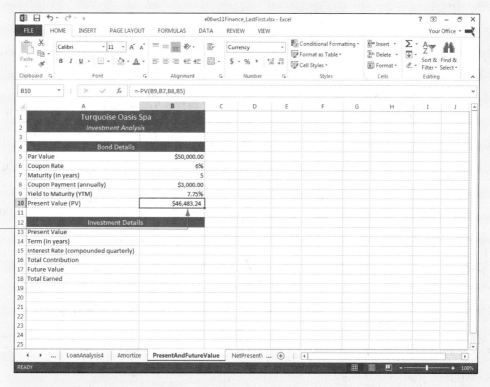

Present value calculation using PV function

Figure 7 Calculating the present value of a bond

h. Click **Save**.

Using the FV Function

The Future Value function, or **FV function**, is used to calculate the value of an investment with a fixed interest rate and term, as well as calculating periodic payments over a specific period of time. The FV function syntax uses five arguments, the first three are required, and the last two are optional: (1) rate (rate), (2) number of periods (nper), (3) payment (pmt), (4) present value (pv), and (5) type (type). If you do not know the payment, you must enter the present value.

=FV (rate, nper, pmt, [pv], [type])

For example, you might decide to start saving for retirement and want to use the FV function to calculate how much you would have by the age of 65. By using the FV function, you can determine how much your Individual Retirement Account (IRA) would be worth when you retire. If you contributed $2,500 per year to your IRA for 40 years—a total of $100,000—with an interest rate of 8% annually, you would have nearly $650,000.

=FV(.08,40, -2500)

Turquoise Oasis Spa managers are considering investing money that would be provided by private investors. This would require them to wait for five years to allow the investment to grow. The managers use the Future Value function to help them make their decision.

E11.08

 To Calculate the Future Value of an Investment

a. Click cell **B13**, type 400000 as the present value of the money that will be invested, and then format the cell as **Currency**.

b. Click cell **B14**, and then type 5 for the number of years the money will be invested.

c. Click cell **B15**, type .06 as the interest rate to be compounded quarterly, and then format your cell as **Percentage**.

d. Click cell **B16**, and then type =B13 because the total investment will be a one time, lump-sum investment.

e. Click cell **B17**, and then type =FV(B15/4,B14*4,0,-B13) to calculate the future value of this investment.

f. Click cell **B18**, and then type =B17-B16 to calculate the total earned.
Notice that the spa would earn $138,742 with this investment option.

SIDE NOTE
Compounded Interest
The interest rate must be divided by 4 and the term multiplied by 4 to account for the quarterly compounded interest.

Future value calculation using FV function

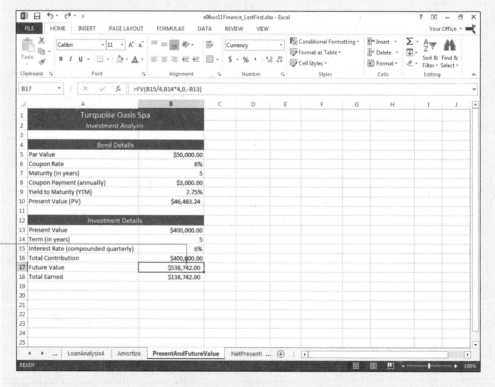

Figure 8   Calculating the future value of an investment

g. Click **Save** 💾.

Analyze Investments Using NPV, XNPV, IRR, and XIRR

Bond investments should be a part of any well-rounded investment portfolio. However, investors must also take into consideration other investment opportunities that may be higher risk but also offer a higher return. One method of analyzing various investment opportunities is to compare the projected future cash flows generated from the investment to a risk-free investment, such as a bond.

Using the NPV Function

The Net Present Value function, or **NPV function**, is used to determine the value of an investment by analyzing a series of future incoming and outgoing cash flows expected to occur over the life of the investment. The function assumes that the cash flows occur at regular intervals, such as weekly, monthly, or quarterly. This function is used for capital budgeting and measures the surplus or deficit of cash flows, in present value terms. **Capital budgeting** is the planning procedure used to evaluate whether an organization's long-term investments—such as acquiring a business or starting a new business, purchasing new machinery and new buildings, or performing the research and development of new products—are worth pursuing.

The NPV function syntax is a little different from other financial functions and includes rate and value arguments. The rate argument is a key variable to the accuracy of the NPV calculation as it is used to discount future cash flows. There are several different approaches a company may take to calculate a discount rate. One approach is to decide the rate that the capital needed for the project could return if invested in a risk-free bond or other low-risk investment. For example, if a risk-free government bond could return 5%, then 5% would be used as the discount rate on the future cash flows to analyze the profitability of the investment based on today's dollars. Another approach would be for the company or investor to establish a required rate of return. A **required rate of return**, or RRR, is the minimum annual percentage that must be earned by an investment before a company chooses to invest.

The value1 argument is required, and subsequent value arguments are optional. The ellipse indicates that additional arguments can be entered, and Excel allows for 1 to 254 values entered—implied by the ellipses. The NPV function uses the order of the value arguments to interpret the order of cash flows. Be sure to enter your values in the correct sequence where the value1 argument is the amount of estimated cash inflow for period 1 and not the initial amount of the investment in year 0. The initial investment amount must be subtracted outside of the NPV function to calculate the true net present value. Note that many times the initial investment amount is recorded as a negative number. If that is the case, then the initial investment would be added outside of the NPV function.

=NPV(rate, value1, [value2],...) + -initial investment

The management at Turquoise Oasis Spa can use the NPV function to see if it benefits them financially to invest in new equipment for the spa. Given an estimate of cash flows that would be generated with the new equipment and a discount rate based on a risk-free bond option, they can calculate whether the purchase of new equipment produces positive financial benefits. If the spa invests $125,000 with a discount rate of 8% and the estimated cash inflows over the next three years were:

Year 1: $56,000.00
Year 2: $45,000.00
Year 3: $33,000.00

The net present value would result in a loss of -$8,371.44. Thus, this would not be a good investment for Turquoise Oasis and could earn more money if they invested in a risk-free bond. If the NPV results in a negative value, then the investment should be rejected, however if the NPV results in a value greater than 0 then the investment should be considered.

=NPV(.08, 56000,45000,33000) + -125000

Turquoise Oasis Spa managers are considering the equipment—such as massage tables, salon chairs, and sinks—that they want to purchase to complete the improvements and expansion. You have been given the estimated cash inflows as a result of the new equipment to use for your net present value analysis.

E11.09

 To Calculate the Net Present Value of an Investment

a. Click the **NetPresentValue** worksheet tab.

b. Click cell **B5**, type **.0256** as the discount rate, and then format it as **Percentage** with **2** decimal places.

c. An investment of $125,000 will be required to purchase the new equipment. Click cell **B6**, type **-125000** as the amount of the outgoing cash flow for the initial investment, and then format it as **Currency**.

d. Click cell **B10**, and then type **=B6** to reference the initial investment amount, which will be the cash outflow for year 0.

e. Click cell **B15**, and then type **=NPV(B5,B11:B13)+B10** to calculate the net present value of the investment.

   Notice that although the estimated cash inflows of the investment had not changed from the example above, the result of the NPV function now yields a positive value of $2,973.76 versus -$8,371.44. This is due to the lower discount rate being a key factor in the calculation.

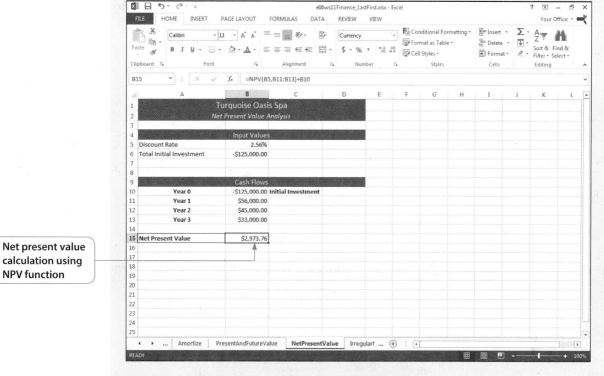

Figure 9 Net present value of an investment

f. Click **Save** 💾.

Using the XNPV Function

Similar to NPV, the Irregular Net Present Value function, or **XNPV function**, determines the value of an investment or business by analyzing an irregular time series of incoming and outgoing cash flows. The XNPV function syntax is a little different from the NPV function and includes rate, values, and dates arguments, all of which are required. The values argument corresponds to payments, and one of these values must be a negative value, which will most likely represent the initial loan disbursement. The dates argument corresponds with when the payments were made, including the date of the initial investment. All subsequent dates must be after the initial investment date, but they may be listed in any order.

=XNPV(rate, values, dates)

Turquoise Oasis Spa managers are considering another investment option that will require an initial investment amount of $125,000 with estimated cash inflows occurring irregularly over the next two years. Use the XNPV function to calculate the net present value of the investment.

E11.10

 To Calculate an Irregular Net Present Value of an Investment

a. Click the **IrregularNPV** worksheet tab.

b. Click cell **B4**, type .10, and then format it as **Percentage** for the company's required rate of return (RRR).

c. Click cell **B7**, type -125000, and then format it as **Currency** as the initial investment amount to be paid on 3/1/2015.

d. Click cell **B20**, and then type =XNPV(B4, B7:B18,A7:A18) to calculate the net present value of the investment based on the irregular cash flows. Format the cell as **Currency** with negative numbers displayed in red with parenthesis.

　　Notice that the npv results in -$371.39; therefore, it does not meet the required rate of return of 10%.

Irregular net present value calculation using XNPV function

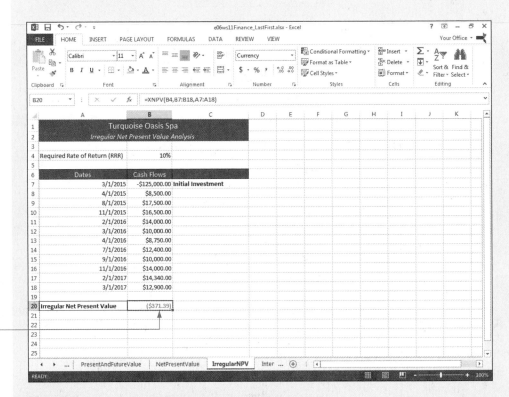

Figure 10　Irregular net present value of an investment

e. Click **Save** 🖫.

Using the IRR Function

The Internal Rate of Return function, or **IRR function**, indicates the profitability of an investment and is commonly used in business when choosing between investments. This function is generally used in capital budgeting to measure and compare how profitable a potential investment is. The IRR of an investment is the rate that makes the net present value of both positive and negative cash flows equal to zero. In other words, the IRR function determines the discount rate at which you would break even on an investment. If an investment's IRR is higher than an interest rate generated by a risk-free investment, such as a government bond, then the investment should be chosen. If you are comparing multiple investment options, the investment with the highest IRR would be considered the best and should be chosen first—assuming all investments have the same amount of initial investment. The IRR function has two arguments, which you have seen in previous financial functions—values and guess—and returns a percentage.

=IRR (values, [guess])

Turquoise Oasis Spa can use the IRR function to see which investment would be the best option. For example: Option 1 requires an initial investment of $125,000 with yearly cash flows of $35,000 totaling $140,000 over a four-year period. Option 2 requires the same initial investment of $125,000 with yearly cash flows also totaling $140,000 but over a six-year period and with a majority of the investment's return occurring in the first two years.

By analyzing the internal rate of return on each of these investments and knowing that the current rate of a risk-free investment is 4.5% management can make a more informed decision on which option is in the best financial interest of the company.

MODULE 6

E11.11

 To Calculate an Internal Rate of Return

a. Click the **InternalRateOfReturn** worksheet tab.

b. Click cell **B13**, type =IRR(B5:B9) to calculate the internal rate of return for investment option 1, and then format it as **Percentage** with **2** decimal places.

c. Click cell **E13**, type =IRR(E5:E11) to calculate the internal rate of return for investment option 2, and then format it as **Percentage** with **2** decimal places.

Notice that both investment options have a higher internal rate of return than the risk-free investment option of 4.5%. However, option 2 has the highest IRR and should be chosen over option 1.

Internal rate of return calculation for investment option 1 using IRR function

Internal rate of return calculation for investment option 2 using IRR function

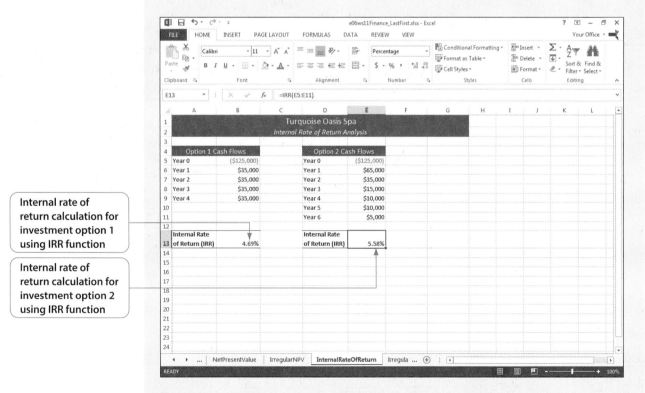

Figure 11   Comparing investments with the internal rate of return

d. Click **Save**.

At first glance, investment option 1 above may have seemed like the better choice since the total return of $140,000 was realized in four years instead of six. However, the IRR function returns a higher rate of return for option 2. What do you think was the primary cause for the higher rate? Why?

Using the XIRR Function

Another way you can analyze the rate of return is to use the Irregular Internal Rate of Return function, or XIRR function. The difference between the IRR function and the XIRR function is that the IRR function assumes that the cash flows are periodic, whereas the **XIRR function** analyzes a series of cash flows that are irregular or not periodic. The syntax of the XIRR function is similar to the IRR function with the addition of the dates argument. Additionally, like the XNPV function, the series of values must contain at least one positive value and one negative value. The dates argument corresponds with when the payments were made, including the date of the initial investment. The first payment date indicates the beginning of the schedule of payments. All subsequent dates must be after the initial investment date, but they may be listed in any order.

=XIRR(values, dates, [guess])

Turquoise Oasis Spa managers are considering another investment option that will require an initial investment amount of $125,000 with estimated cash inflows occurring irregularly over the next two years. Use the XIRR function to calculate the internal rate of return of the investment to determine whether or not it meets the 10% required rate of return.

E11.12

 To Calculate an Irregular Internal Rate of Return

a. Click the **IrregularIRR** worksheet tab.

b. Click cell **B4**, type .1 as the required rate of return, and then format it as **Percentage**.
   Click cell **B17**, type =XIRR(B7:B15,A7:A15) to calculate the irregular internal rate of return, and then format it as **Percentage** with **2** decimal places. Notice that this investment has an internal rate of return of 11.27% and meets the required rate of return of 10%.

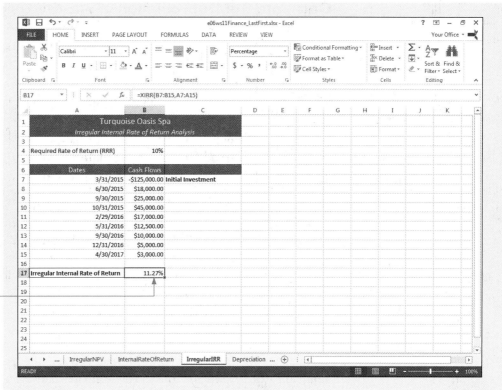

Irregular internal rate of return calculation using XIRR function

Figure 12 Irregular internal rate of return analysis

c. Click **Save** 🖫.

Calculating the Depreciating Value of Business Assets

Businesses are required for tax and reporting purposes to show that the original cost of the property they purchase such as buildings, vehicles, and equipment is reduced—or depreciated—over time as they "use up" these assets. In this section, you will learn how to calculate the depreciation of assets, using three different approved methods.

QUICK REFERENCE	Methods of Depreciation

There are several accounting methods to depreciate an asset, and the IRS allows a business to choose whichever method is most advantageous as long as the same method is used throughout the life of the asset.

1. Straight-line depreciation (SLN)—Simplest and most commonly used method. Assumes that the value of the asset loses the same amount of value each year of its life.

2. Declining-balance depreciation (DB)—Assumes that the value of an asset depreciates more in the first year than in the second year.

3. Double declining-balance depreciation (DDB)—This method requires that the straight-line depreciation method be used first to calculate the total percentage of the asset that is depreciated in the first year and doubles it. Each subsequent year of the asset's life, that same percentage is multiplied by the remaining balance to be depreciated.

Calculate the Depreciation of Assets Using the SLN, DB, and DDB Functions

As you learned, an amortization table can be used to analyze loan balances and repayments. A company can also use amortization tables to show the appropriate accounting or net book value of its tangible assets such as machinery, equipment, buildings, vehicles, or property for tax or reporting purposes. The **net book value** is equal to the original cost of the asset minus depreciation and amortization. To create an amortization table for asset depreciation, you would use functions that allow you to calculate the present value, future value, and depreciation of the asset over its useful life. When you depreciate the original cost of tangible assets, you first need to know the rules for depreciating the particular assets, because there are different rules for different types of assets. Depreciation represents a reduction in the amount of the original cost of a fixed asset that is used to reduce income as an expense for accounting and tax purposes. The idea is that because the item generates income over time, you should be able to deduct from that income the amount of the resource—or asset—used.

To calculate the depreciated value, you need to know the original cost of the asset, the asset's useful life, the asset's salvage value, and the rate at which the asset depreciates over time. The **salvage value** is what the asset is estimated to be worth at the end of its useful life. It is assumed that over time, these assets decline in value because of deterioration and obsolescence and therefore should be depreciated. Depreciation functions provide a method that matches the decline in value with the income that results from using the assets. In addition, you have to know what depreciation method the IRS expects you to apply to particular types of assets. The IRS, Generally Accepted Accounting Principles, and International Financial Reporting Standards all have specific requirements for depreciating assets and reporting depreciation based on the type of asset being depreciated.

To report the net book value of tangible assets, a depreciation schedule must be maintained. A **depreciation schedule** records the date that the asset was placed into service, a calculation for each year's depreciation, and the accumulated depreciation. An asset remains on the depreciation schedule until the asset becomes fully depreciated or is taken out of service—sold or discarded. Finally, the depreciation schedule should be evaluated on an annual basis to ensure accuracy. With a growing business and increased inventory, the Turquoise Oasis Spa must prepare a depreciation schedule for its tangible assets.

REAL WORLD ADVICE | **Have You Thought About Depreciating Your Assets?**

Have you ever run your own business? Maybe you owned a lawn mowing service. Suppose you purchased your own riding lawn mower. Come tax time, one method to reduce your taxes is by using depreciation. Rather than taking the full cost out in one year, you can take out a portion over several years. This is particularly useful for high-priced items.

Using the SLN Function

One way that you can calculate depreciation is using the Straight-Line Depreciation function, or SLN function. The **SLN function** calculates the depreciation of an asset for a specified period using the fixed declining-balance method. This means that the amount of money that is depreciated is the same for each year of the life of the asset. This is the easiest type of depreciation to calculate and is the depreciation method used by the majority of small businesses. The SLN function syntax uses three arguments, all of which are required: (1) initial cost of asset (cost); (2) salvage value (salvage); and (3) useful life (life). The salvage value can be set to zero if that is what the expected salvage value is.

=SLN(cost, salvage, life)

Turquoise Oasis Spa managers need to track the tangible assets—such as massage tables, salon chairs, and sinks—that they previously purchased. You have been given the cost of the asset, salvage value, and useful life to create a straight-line depreciation table.

E11.13

 To Create a Straight-Line Depreciation Schedule

a. Click the **Depreciation** worksheet tab.

b. Click cell **B8**, type =SLN($B$3, $B$4, $B$5), and then use the **AutoFill** handle to copy the function down to **B12**.

c. Click cell **C8**, and then type = B8 to calculate the accumulated depreciation for the first year.

d. Click cell **C9**, type =C8+B9 to calculate the accumulated depreciation for year two, and then use the **AutoFill** handle to copy the formula down to **C12**.

e. Click cell **D8**, type =$B$3-C8 to calculate the book value at the end of the first year, and then use the **AutoFill** handle to copy the function down to **D12**.

   Notice that the book value at the end of year five is $1,750—the same as the estimated salvage value.

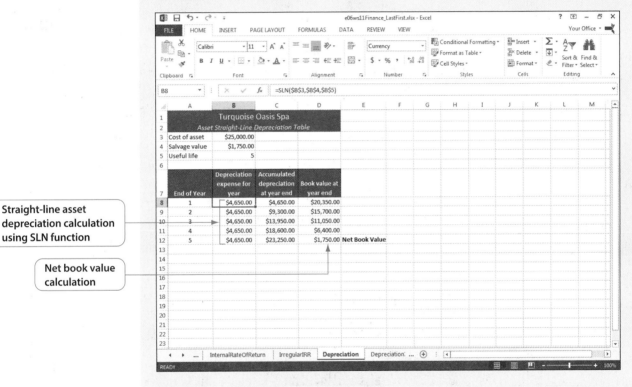

Straight-line asset depreciation calculation using SLN function

Net book value calculation

Figure 13   Straight-line asset depreciation table

f. Click **Save** 🖫.

Using the DB Function

Another way that you can calculate depreciation is using the Declining-Balance function, or DB function. The **DB function** calculates the depreciation of an asset for a specified period using the fixed declining-balance method. The difference between the DB function and SLN function is that when you use the DB function, you can specify the period and month that the asset was placed into service. Thus, instead of spreading the cost of the asset evenly over its life as you did with the SLN function, the DB function calculates the depreciation of the asset at an accelerated rate, which results in higher depreciation in earlier periods and progressively declining depreciation each succeeding period. Because the month argument is optional, Excel assumes the value is 12 if a value is omitted.

=DB(cost, salvage, life, period, [month])

Turquoise Oasis Spa managers have asked you to calculate depreciation using the Declining-Balance function.

▶ To Create a Declining-Balance Depreciation Schedule

a. Click the **Depreciation2** worksheet tab.

b. The equipment was placed into service at the beginning of May of the first year. Therefore, the period for the first year will be eight—May through December is eight months. Click cell **B8**, and then type =DB(B3,B4,B5,A8,8) to begin calculating the declining-balance depreciation of the asset.

c. Click cell **B9**, and then type =DB($B$3,$B$4,$B$5,A9) to continue calculating the declining-balance depreciation. Use the **AutoFill** handle to copy the function down to **B12**. Notice that the depreciation is declining as the periods increase with a depreciation value of $1,231.25 in year five.

d. Click cell **C8**, and then type =B8 to calculate the accumulated depreciation for the first year.

e. Click cell **C9**, and then type =C8+B9 to calculate the accumulated depreciation for year two. Use the **AutoFill** handle to copy the function down to **C12**.

f. Click cell **D8**, and then type =$B$3-C8 to calculate the book value at the end of the first year. Use the **AutoFill** handle to copy the function down to **D12**. Notice that the net book value of the asset at the end of its useful life is $5,190.56.

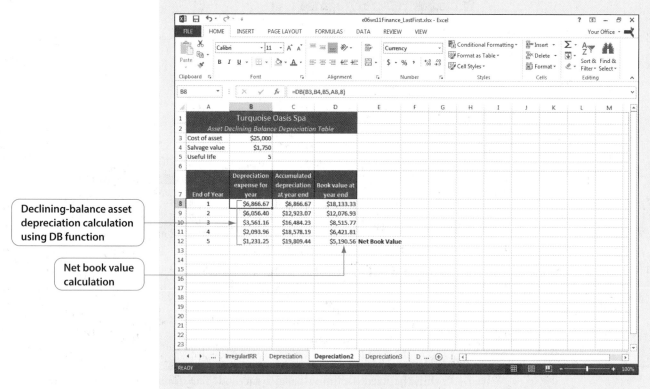

Declining-balance asset depreciation calculation using DB function

Net book value calculation

Figure 14   Declining-balance asset depreciation table

g. Click **Save**.

Using the DDB Function

Still another way that you can calculate depreciation is using the Double Declining-Balance function, or DDB function. The **DDB function** calculates the depreciation of an asset for a specified period using the double declining-balance method. With the straight-line depreciation method, the useful life of the asset is divided into the total cost to arrive at an equal amount per year. The DDB function permits twice the straight-line annual percentage rate to be applied each year. For example, if you have a straight-line depreciation that is depreciating assets over a five-year period, the annual depreciation amount would be 20%. If the initial cost is $1,000, the depreciation would be 20% × $1,000 = $200 each year until the asset reaches a net book value of zero. With the double declining-balance method, the depreciation amount would be 40% each year— 40% × $1,000 = $400 in the first year, 40% × $600 = $240 in the second year, and so on.

The DDB function syntax uses five arguments, four of which are required: (1) initial cost of asset (cost), (2) salvage value (salvage), (3) useful life (life), (4) period for which you want to calculate the depreciation (period), and (5) rate at which the balance declines (factor). The **factor** argument is optional; it is the rate at which the balance declines. If factor is omitted, Excel assumes the value to be 2 (the double declining-balance method). The salvage value can be set to zero if that is what the expected salvage value is.

=DDB(cost, salvage, life, period, [factor])

Turquoise Oasis Spa managers have asked you to calculate depreciation using the Double Declining-Balance function.

E11.15

 To Create a Double Declining-Balance Depreciation Schedule

a. Click the **Depreciation3** worksheet tab.

b. Click cell **B8**, type =DDB($B$3,$B$4,$B$5,A8) to calculate the double declining-balance depreciation of the asset, and then use the **AutoFill** handle to copy the function down to **B12**.

   Notice that you would be able to deduct higher depreciation on your taxes. However, your net book value at the end of the five years would be less than it would be when using the Declining-Balance function.

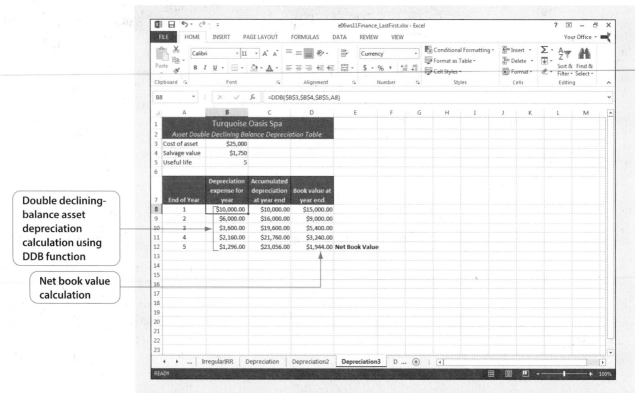

Double declining-balance asset depreciation calculation using DDB function

Net book value calculation

Figure 15 Double declining-balance asset depreciation table

c. Insert the **filename** in the left custom footer section of the Header/Footer tab in the Page Setup dialog box on all worksheets in the workbook.

d. Click **Save** 🖫.

e. Complete the Documentation worksheet and submit your file as directed by your instructor.

REAL WORLD ADVICE | **Choosing a Depreciation Method**

Accountants use depreciation as a method to approximate the value that assets lose over time. As property ages and wears out or becomes obsolete, you can calculate the depreciation and use the depreciation as a potential tax write-off. You learned three different methods to calculate depreciation of assets. All of the depreciation methods are allowed, according to the IRS. You should consult with an accountant before making a final decision as to how you depreciate an asset.

Concept Check

1. What does the PMT function calculate? Describe the required arguments of the PMT function. p. 571–573

2. Explain the CUMIPMT function and its arguments. Why would it be beneficial to know the cumulative interest paid in a particular time period? p. 578–579

3. What is an Amortization Schedule and what is its purpose? p. 580

4. How does estimating the present value of an investment lead to better financial decisions? p. 584

5. Discuss how the IRR and NPV functions can help make informed financial decisions. p. 587, 590–591

6. What are the differences between the three methods of asset depreciation discussed in this workshop? p. 594–598

Key Terms

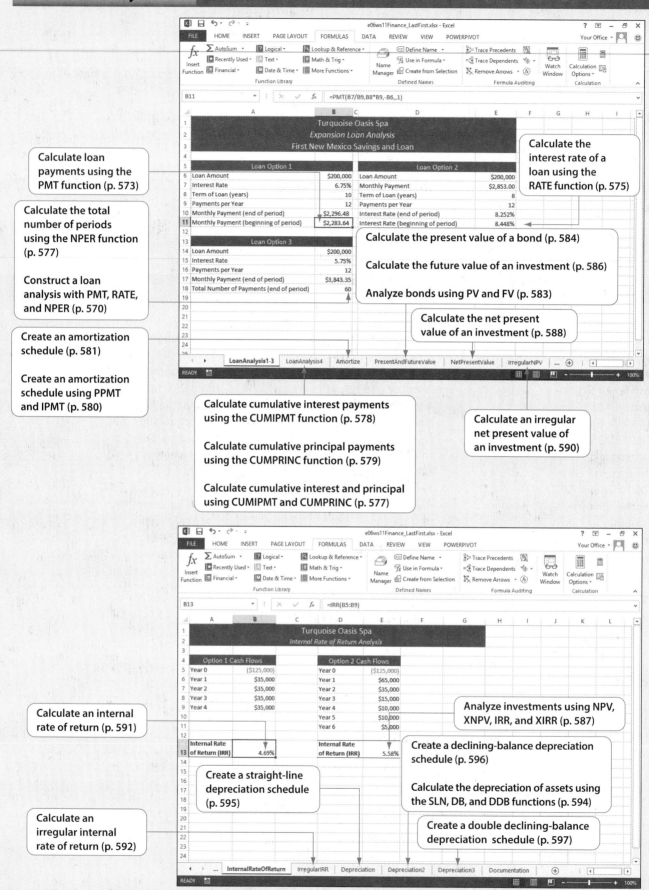

Figure 16 The Turquoise Oasis Spa Final Financial Analysis

Student data file needed:

 e06ws11Equipment.xlsx

You will save your file as:

 e06ws11Equipment_LastFirst.xlsx

Loan Analysis and Depreciating Equipment at the Red Bluff Golf Club

Finance & Accounting

The Red Bluff Golf Club obtained a loan two years ago to purchase new golf carts for its members to use. Unfortunately, the manager, Barry Cheney, has not kept very good records for the loan or for depreciation of the golf carts. You have been asked to create a loan analysis and depreciation schedule. The Red Bluff Golf Club has been making monthly payments, due at the end of the period, but it has not kept track of the actual loan—such as interest and principal. Additionally, depreciation has not been written off on yearly taxes. Mr. Cheney wants to begin writing off a portion of the cost of the golf carts this year, but he is not sure if he should use a straight-line depreciation or declining-balance method. You need to calculate both schedules and report your findings to the manager so he can get them approved by his accountant. Mr. Cheney has given you templates to use to create your analysis.

a. Start **Excel**, and then open the **e06ws11Equipment** workbook from the student data files.

b. On the FILE tab, click **Save As**, and save the file in the folder or location designated by your instructor with the name e06ws11Equipment_LastFirst using your last and first name.

c. On the Analysis worksheet tab, click cell **A10**, and then type =PMT(A6/D6,B6*D6,-C6) to calculate the monthly payment of the loan.

d. Click cell **B10**, and then type =IPMT(A6/D6,1,B6*D6,-C6) to calculate the interest portion of the monthly payment.

e. Click cell **C10**, and then type =PPMT(A6/D6,1,B6*D6,-C6) to calculate the principal portion of the monthly payment.

f. Click cell **D10**, type =-CUMIPMT(A6/D6,B6*D6,C6,1,12,0) to calculate how much interest was paid during the first year of the loan, and then format the cell as **Currency**.

g. Click cell **E10**, type =-CUMPRINC(A6/D6,B6*D6,C6,1,12,0) to calculate how much principal was paid during the first year of the loan, and then format the cell as **Currency**.

h. Click cell **B16**, and then type =IRR(B14:E14) to calculate the internal rate of return of the investment based on the expected cash flows in years 2015-2017. Format the cell as **Percentage** with **2** decimal places.

i. Create a straight-line depreciation schedule by completing the following tasks.

- Click cell **H10**, type =SLN($G$6,$H$6,$I$6), and then use the **AutoFill** handle to copy the function down to **H14**.

- Click cell **I10**, and then type =H10 to calculate the accumulated depreciation for the first year.

- Click cell **I11**, type =I10+H11 to calculate the accumulated depreciation for year two, and then use the **AutoFill** handle to copy the function down to **I14**.

- Click cell **J10**, type =$G$6-I10 to calculate the book value at the end of year one by subtracting the accumulated depreciation at the end of year one from the initial cost, and then use the **AutoFill** handle to copy the function down to **J14**.

- Select cells **H14:J14**, click the **Border** arrow in the Font group, and then click **Bottom Border**.

j. Create a declining-balance depreciation schedule by completing the following tasks.
- Click cell **H17**, type =DB($G$6,$H$6,$I$6,G17), and then use the **AutoFill** handle to copy the function down to **H21**.
- Click cell **I17**, and then type =H17 to calculate the accumulated depreciation for the first year.
- Click cell **I18**, type =I17+H18 to calculate the accumulated depreciation for year two, and then use the **AutoFill** handle to copy the function down to **I21**.
- Click cell **J17**, type =$G$6-I17 to calculate the book value at the end of year one by subtracting the accumulated depreciation at the end of year one from the initial cost, and then use the **AutoFill** handle to copy the function down to **J21**.
- Select cells **H21:J21**, click the **Border** arrow in the Font group, and then click **Bottom Border**.

k. Create a double declining-balance depreciation schedule by completing the following tasks.
- Click cell **H24**, type =DDB($G$6,$H$6,$I$6,G24), and then use the **AutoFill** handle to copy the function down to **H28**.
- Click cell **I24**, and then type =H24 to calculate the accumulated depreciation for the first year.
- Click cell **I25**, type =I24+H25 to calculate the accumulated depreciation for year two, and then use the **AutoFill** handle to copy the formula to **I28**.
- Click cell **J24**, type =$G$6-I24 to calculate the book value at the end of year one by subtracting the accumulated depreciation at the end of year one from the initial cost, and then use the **AutoFill** handle to copy the function down to **J28**.
- Select cells **H28:J28**, click the **Border** arrow in the Font group, and then click **Thick Bottom Border**.

l. Click the **Documentation** worksheet. Click cell **A6**, and then type in today's date. Click cell **B6**, and then type in your first and last name. Complete the remainder of the **Documentation** worksheet according to your instructor's direction.

m. Click **Save**, close Excel, and then submit your file as directed by your instructor.

Problem Solve 1

MyITLab® Grader
Homework 1

Finance & Accounting

Student data file needed:
📄 e06ws11Loans.xlsx

You will save your file as:
📄 e06ws11Loans_LastFirst.xlsx

Loan Analysis

Janette Franklin, owner of Frank Solutions, LLC, is considering borrowing $30,000 to finance the renovation of her office building. She has been given three different loan options with various terms and interest rates. She knows that she can only afford to make payments of $530.00 a month and needs your help to determine which loan option is best.

a. Start **Excel**, open the **e06ws11Loans** workbook, and then save it as e06ws11Loans_LastFirst.

b. On the LoanAnalysis worksheet in cell **C4**, calculate the annual percentage rate for Loan Option 1. Format the cell as **Percentage** with **2** decimal places.

c. In cell **C6**, calculate the total cumulative interest that would be paid throughout the life of the loan if payments were made at the end of the periods. Reference cell **C5** for the **end_period** argument. Be sure that the result of the function is positive, and then format the cell as **Currency**.

d. In cell **C7**, calculate the total cost of the loan by adding the loan amount in cell **C2** to the cumulative interest amount in cell **C6**.

e. In cell **F3**, calculate the end of the period monthly payment for Loan Option 2. Be sure the result of the function is positive, and then format the cell as **Currency**.

f. In cell **F6**, calculate the total cumulative interest that would be paid throughout the life of the loan if payments were made at the end of the periods. Reference cell **F5** for the **end_period** argument. Be sure that the result of the function is positive, and then format the cell as **Currency**.

g. In cell **F7**, calculate the total cost of the loan by adding the loan amount in cell **F2** to the cumulative interest amount in cell **F6**.

h. In cell **I5**, calculate the total number of quarterly payments required to pay off Loan Option 3 if payments are made at the end of the period. Format the cell as **Number** with **0** decimal places.

i. In cell **I6**, calculate the total cumulative interest that would be paid throughout the life of the loan if payments were made at the end of the periods. Reference cell **I5** for the **end_period** argument. Be sure that the result of the function is positive, and then format the cell as **Currency**.

j. In cell **I7**, calculate the total cost of the loan by adding the loan amount in cell **I2** to the cumulative interest amount in cell **I6**.

   Notice that Loan Option 3, although comprised of 24 quarterly payments, breaks down to just under $530.00 a month when the quarterly payment is divided by 3 and the total cost of the loan is about $500 less than Loan Option 1.

k. Create an amortization schedule for Loan Option 3 in cells **C12:F35**. All payments are end-of-the-period payments. Be sure that all formulas and functions result in a positive value. Format all cells as **Currency** with **2** decimal places.

l. Complete the **Documentation** worksheet according to your instructor's direction. Insert the **filename** in the left custom footer section of the Header/Footer tab in the Page Setup dialog box on all worksheets in the workbook.

m. Click Save, close Excel, and then submit the file as directed by your instructor.

Perform 1: Perform in Your Life

Student data file needed:

📄 e06ws11Retirement.xlsx

You will save your file as:

📄 e06ws11Retirement_LastFirst.xlsx

Saving for Retirement

Finance & Accounting

As a college student, retirement may seem like a lifetime away, but it is recommended that you start planning for retirement sooner rather than later. In this exercise you will calculate the amount of monthly payments needed to have enough money to retire at the age of 65 as well as calculate the present value of a bond.

a. Start **Excel**, open the **e06ws11Retirement** workbook, and then save it as **e06ws11Retirement_LastFirst**.

b. On the RetirementPlan worksheet, create a financial model to plan for retirement by completing the following tasks.

- Determine a future value that you would like to have in an account for retirement, enter the value in a cell, and format the value as **Currency**. Add a row label of Future Value.

- You are able to lock in a fixed interest rate of 5.8% from now until you reach the age of 65. Type .058 in a cell, format as **Percentage** with **2** decimal places, and then add a row label of Interest Rate.

- Type the number of years until you reach 65 in a cell, and then add a row label of Years to Retirement.

- Type a formula in a cell to calculate the number of monthly payments you will make between now and when you turn 65, and then add a row label of Total Payments.

- Use the PMT function to calculate the monthly payment amount in order to meet your future value goal. Be sure the monthly payment amount is displayed as a positive value. Add a row label of Monthly Payment.

c. In addition to making monthly deposits into a retirement savings account, you also should consider investing in a risk-free/low-risk bond. Create a financial model to analyze an investment bond by completing the following tasks.

Add the following row labels and values:

Row Label	Value
Par Value	$25,000.00
Coupon Rate	10%
Maturity (years)	20
Yield to Maturity	8%

d. Type a formula in a cell to calculate the annual coupon rate of the investment bond, and then add a row label of Coupon Payment.

e. Use the PV formula to calculate the present value of the bond, being sure the result is a positive value, and then add a row label of Present Value.

f. Complete the **Documentation** worksheet according to your instructor's direction. Insert the **filename** in the left custom footer section of the Header/Footer tab in the Page Setup dialog box on all worksheets in the workbook.

g. Click Save, close Excel, and then submit the file as directed by your instructor.

Additional
Cases

Additional Workshop Cases are available on the companion website and in the instructor resources.

WORKSHOP 12 | BUSINESS STATISTICS AND REGRESSION ANALYSIS

Prepare Case

The Turquoise Oasis Spa: Using Statistics in Decision Making

Sales & Marketing

Just like other businesses, managers at the Turquoise Oasis Spa make decisions about the strategic direction of the company with a lot of uncertainty. Their current decision to fund an expansion of the spa comes with lots of uncertainty with regard to how it will affect their future. Various statistical methods can be applied to business data in order to help make more informed decisions with more certainty about expected outcomes. Business statistics can be applied to many areas of a business, such

rangizzz / Fotolia

as financial analysis, production, operations, and marketing.

The managers would like you to use various statistical methods to analyze their business data in order to understand the data better and so that they may make more informed decisions.

REAL WORLD SUCCESS

"After graduation I got a job at a small e-marketing firm. The managers were looking over some numbers to decide whether or not they should acquire a smaller company. The managers had decided to go with the acquisition until someone used some statistics to analyze the distribution of the data. It turned out that a few outliers were skewing the numbers and it would have been a very bad decision to acquire the company. I never thought statistics had a place in business until I witnessed firsthand how just a few simple statistical methods can prevent bad decisions."

- James, recent graduate

Student data file needed for this workshop:

 e06ws12Statistics.xlsx

You will save your file as:

 e06ws12Statistics_LastFirst.xlsx

Applying Basic Statistical Methods to Business

Businesses today collect large amounts of data about the everyday operations of the company, from prices of raw materials to the number of links clicked on the company website. With so much data so easily available, it is becoming increasingly important that people in business understand how to use that data to make good, strategic decisions. Statistical methods can be used to analyze business data to support good decision making.

Statistics is the practice of collecting, analyzing, and interpreting data. There are two major branches of statistics, descriptive statistics and inferential statistics. **Descriptive statistics** is the process of deriving meaningful information from raw data. An example of descriptive statistics would be to calculate the total revenue that a spa package generates over the course of a year.

Inferential statistics is the process of taking data from a sample of the population and making predictions about the entire population. An example of inferential statistics would be to survey 100 random customers about their opinions on a new service being offered at the spa. Based on the results of that random sample, managers at the spa can make assumptions about whether or not the new spa service would go over well. Inferential statistics rely heavily on laws of probability.

Probability is the likelihood that some event will occur based on what is already known. Statistics typically describe what has already happened and probability describes what is likely to happen in the future. In this section, you learn some of the foundational terminology used in statistics as well as conduct basic statistical analyses using Excel to gain a better understanding of business data.

Understand the Language of Statistics

Businesses can use various statistical methods in many areas to get a better understanding of the organization. Statistics can be used to determine effectiveness of advertising campaigns, to understand what factors contribute to the demand for your products, to spot seasonal trends in the sales of certain products, and much more.

Before you get too far into various statistical methods and how businesses can use them, you must understand some common statistical terms. Statistics constantly refers to data. **Data** are the values that describe an attribute of an object or an event. Almost anything can be considered data, from an employee's salary, to the number of spa packages sold, to the cost of the latest marketing campaign. A **data set** is a collection of related data consisting of observational units and variables. An **observational unit** is a person, object, or event about which data is collected. For example, in a data set consisting of gender, salary, and name of employees, the employees are the observational unit and the variables are the gender, salary, and names.

Statistics often refer to populations and samples. In statistics, a **population** is defined as an "entire" collection of people, animals, plants, or whatever on which you may collect data. For the spa, a population could be the entire population of every guest who ever received spa services. However, by the time you collect the data for the entire population, the spa has likely had more customers. Thus, very rarely are statistics based on populations, as it would be too costly and too time consuming. Instead, statistics focuses on samples. A **sample population** is a subset of a population. More importantly, statistics relies heavily on random samples. A **random sample** is a subset of a population that has been selected using methods where each element of the population has an equal chance of being selected. The more random the sample, the more accurate the statistical analysis will be, in part, because randomness eliminates bias.

Business professionals that use statistical analysis to support their decision making rely heavily on probability distributions. A **probability distribution** describes all the possible values and likelihoods that a given variable can be within a specific range, and they can be in the form of a graph, table, or formula. There are two general classifications of probability distributions: discrete probability distributions and continuous probability distributions. The classifications are determined based on whether they define probabilities associated with discrete variables or continuous variables.

A **discrete variable** is a number that is finite and all possible values are known. Examples of discrete variables in business would be performance classifications of employees, number of soaps in a box, and the number of different services a spa offers its customers. A **continuous variable** can contain an infinite number of different values within a range. Examples of continuous variables in business would be the time between sales transactions, the weight of a package for shipping, and the amount of money a customer spends in any given visit.

Opening the Starting File

You will be using various statistical methods and analysis to better understand the products, revenue, sales volume, and customers of Turquoise Oasis Spa. You will also use various statistical functions to calculate the probability of meeting or exceeding various business goals and discover relationships between variables that may be useful in making predictions.

Understand the Basic Types of Data

Figure 1 illustrates the four basic levels of data used in statistics: nominal data, ordinal data, interval data, and ratio data. Each level adds to the next, thus ordinal data is also nominal data, and so on. Having a strong understanding of these levels will help you to understand how to use various statistical functions and methods as well as how to interpret the results correctly.

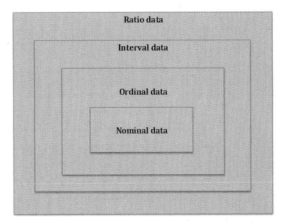

Figure 1 Four levels of data

Nominal data uses numbers for categorical/classification purposes only. Nominal variables are often used to categorize responses in a survey. For example, where respondents answer "Yes" or "No" to a specific question, nominal variables could be used to categorize the responses, such as 1 = Yes and 2 = No. It is also common to use nominal variables to categorize gender, such as, 1 = Female and 2 = Male. It is important to note that some statistical functions such as Average and Sum, would be meaningless to apply to nominal data.

Ordinal data uses numbers to rank data as first, second, third, and so on based on some scale. Ordinal data are useful in situations where it is difficult to obtain accurate measurements. Some statistical analysis can be applied to ordinal data in order to derive additional meaning. For example, if a product is tested 100 times and the rate at which it fails is recorded on a scale of 1 to 10, then the average of all the product's failure rates on the scale could be useful. Ordinal data is more useful than nominal data in terms of what information can be derived, but having the actual time measurements of failure would be better.

Interval data measures the size of the difference between values. For example, with interval data you not only know that one product test succeeded and one product test failed—nominal data, or that one product failed faster than another product—ordinal data), but you also know the difference in time intervals between when a product test failed and when a product test was successful.

Ratio data is similar to interval data except that the differences between the data can be quantified and proportions can be specified. For example, interval data may indicate that product 1 failed after 15 tests and product 2 failed after only 5. Ratio data could state that product 1 passed three times as many tests as product 2.

Conduct Basic Statistical Analyses in Excel

Excel has many built in functions that can be used to conduct basic statistical analysis on data. Knowledge of how to use even the most basic statistical functions can increase your understanding of the data and enable better decision making. In this section you will assist the management of the Turquoise Oasis Spa to better understand their data using basic statistical analysis.

Using the RAND Function to Generate a Random Sample

Randomness in selecting a sample from a population is crucial in conducting effective and accurate statistical analyses. The RAND function in Excel is one method that can help with creating a random sample. The function generates a random number between 0 and 1. The RAND function does not have any arguments.

RAND()

RAND is considered a volatile function because it generates a new number each time the worksheet is calculated. This means that every time any cell is edited or a new formula is created, the value generated by the RAND function will change. It is common practice to use Excel's Copy and Paste Values feature to prevent the values from changing once they have been generated. It is important to note that the values generated by this function are not truly random. Since an algorithm is used to generate the values, it is possible to predict what the next number generated will be; however, it is random enough to work in most situations.

Managers at the Turquoise Oasis Spa would like to select 10 random customers who visited the spa on a given day to take part in a survey about new services that the spa is considering. They plan on using the results of the survey to make decisions on which services to offer. You have been provided with the customer IDs of 34 customers who visited the spa on May 11, 2014. You will use the RAND function to generate 34 random values. You will then use the random values to sort the customer IDs in a random order for selection.

E12.01

 To Create a Random Sample Using RAND()

a. Click the **RandomSample** worksheet tab, click cell **B3**, and then type RAND() to generate a random value between 0 and 1.

b. Use the **AutoFill** handle to copy the function down to **B36**.

c. Press $\boxed{\text{Ctrl}}+\boxed{\text{C}}$ to copy the random values, and then press $\boxed{\text{Ctrl}}+\boxed{\text{V}}$ to paste the random values. Click Paste Options and then in the Paste Values group, click Values to replace the formula with its values.

d. Select the cell range **A2:B36**.

e. Click the **DATA** tab, and in the Sort & Filter group, click **Sort**.

f. Click **My data has headers**, if necessary. Click the **Sort by** arrow, and then select **RAND** as the column to use for the sort.

g. Click **OK**.

h. Select the cell range **A3:A12**.

i. Press $\boxed{\text{Ctrl}}+\boxed{\text{C}}$ to copy.

j. Click cell **E3**, and then press $\boxed{\text{Ctrl}}+\boxed{\text{V}}$ to paste the 10 randomly selected customer IDs.

Random value using the RAND function

Random sample of customers

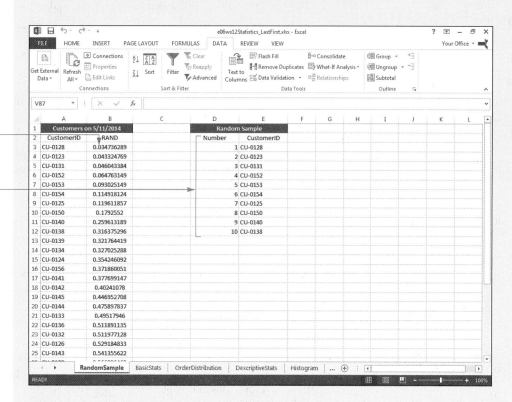

Figure 2 Create a random sample with the RAND function

k. Click **Save** .

Calculating the Mean, Median, and Mode of a Data Set

Three of the most basic descriptive statistics used are mean, median, and mode. Each of these calculations attempts to define the central tendency of a data set. The **central tendency** refers to the way in which data tends to cluster around some value. The **mean** is the average of all the variables in a sample, often referred to as the arithmetic mean. The **median** describes which value falls in the middle when all the values of the sample are sorted in ascending order. For example if there are seven variables, the median value is the 4th variable in the list where there are three variables above and three variables below. If the total number of variables is even, then the median value is the mean of the two middle variables. The **mode** is the value that appears most often in a sample. Modes are only useful with discrete data that is sorted in either ascending or descending order. If there are multiple values in a data set that appear the same number of times, then the mode will be reported in Excel as the value that appears first, either as the lowest value if sorted in ascending order or the highest value if sorted in descending order.

QUICK REFERENCE	Calculating the Central Tendency of a Data Set

Mean, Median, and Mode
- Mean—Sum of all values in a data set divided by the total number of values
- Median—The middle value that separates the higher and lower halves of a data set
- Mode—The value that appears most often in a data set with discrete variables

To calculate the mean in Excel, the AVERAGE function is used. The only arguments inside the AVERAGE function are the values from which an average is to be calculated:

=AVERAGE(number1, [number2],...)

To calculate the median of a data set in Excel, the MEDIAN function is used. Again, the only arguments needed are the values from which the median value is to be calculated:

=MEDIAN(number1, [number2],...)

To calculate the mode of a data set in Excel, one of two functions is used: MODE. SNGL or MODE.MULT. MODE.SNGL returns the value that appears most often in a data set. If more than one variable occurs most frequently, this function returns only the first one. The only arguments used by this function are the values from which a mode is to be calculated:

=MODE.SNGL(number1, [number2],...)

MODE.MULT is an array function that returns a vertical array of the values that occur most often in a data set. If more than one value occurs most frequently, this function returns all of them. The only arguments used by this function are the values from which modes are to be calculated:

=MODE.MULT(number1, [number2],...)

The Turquoise Oasis Spa often sells its house brand of essential oils to other independent massage therapists in the area. Management would like to see if a random sample of orders placed over the past year has a central tendency. Use the data provided to calculate the mean, median, and mode.

E12.02

To Calculate the Mean, Median, and Mode of a Data Set

a. Click the **BasicStats** worksheet tab. On this worksheet, a random sample of 34 orders with the quantity of items sold in each order is provided.

b. Click cell **F2**, and then type =AVERAGE(B2:B35) to calculate the mean of the number of units sold in the sample data set. Format the cell as **Number** with **2** decimal places.

c. Click cell **F3**, and then type =MEDIAN(B2:B35) to calculate the median sales quantity value in the sample data set. Notice that since the number of values is an even number, the MEDIAN function returns the mean of the two middle values 13 and 14.

d. Click cell **F4**, and then type =MODE.SNGL(B2:B35) to calculate the most frequently occurring value in the sample data set.

Mean, median, and mode for finding the central tendency of a data set

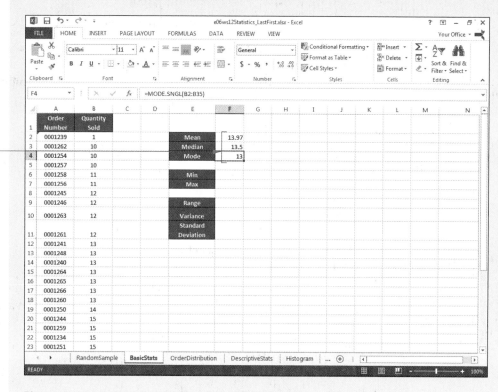

Figure 3   Calculating the mean, median, and mode of a data set

e. Click **Save**.

Calculating the Range, Variance, and Standard Deviation

Calculating the range, variance, and standard deviation of a data set are all methods used to determine the dispersion of a data set. Knowing how a data set is dispersed can provide a better understanding of the data than the mean, median, and mode alone. For example, if a company lists its mean salary as $245,000, one might conclude that all salaries at the company are close to the mean. However, learning more about the dispersion of the salaries by calculating the range, variance, and standard deviation could reveal a much different picture of the salary distribution.

The **range** is the difference between the highest and lowest value in the data set. A range is the simplest method to calculate the dispersion of a data set and can provide a rough idea of how the data set is dispersed. However, a range can be as misleading as a measure of spread if the data set consists of one excessively low value and/or one excessively high value. To calculate the range of a data set, the MIN and MAX functions are used. Subtracting the **minimum** value from the **maximum** value provides the range in a data set.

Variance is a calculation used in statistics to determine how far the data set varies from the mean. The higher the variance calculation the more dispersed the data set. The smaller the variance the more closely the data centers on the mean. Variance provides a more accurate picture of the dispersion of a data set than a range, but due to the way it is calculated, the value is not in the same units as the mean.

To calculate the variance of a data set in Excel, one of two functions is used: VAR.S or VAR.P. VAR.S is used to calculate the variance of a sample data set, and VAR.P is used to calculate the variance of a data set consisting of an entire population. Since most statistical analyses are based on random samples, VAR.S is used most often. The only arguments required are the values from which the variance is to be calculated.

=VAR.S(number1, [number2],…)

The **standard deviation** is the most commonly used method for determining the average spread of a data set from the mean. Mathematically, the standard deviation is calculated by taking the square root of the variance. It is most useful because its value is in the same unit as the median and therefore easier to interpret.

To calculate the standard deviation of a data set in Excel, one of two functions is used: STDEV.S or STDEV.P. STDEV.S is used to calculate the standard deviation of a sample set of data, and STDEV.P is used to calculate the standard deviation of a data set consisting of an entire population. Again, since most statistical analyses are based on random samples, STDEV.S is used most often. The only arguments required are the values from which the standard deviation is to be calculated.

=STDEV.S(number1, [number2],…)

Often, just calculating the central tendency of a data set is not enough. In fact, just finding the central tendency may lead to incorrect assumptions about the data due to possible outliers. **Outliers** are data that are abnormally different from the other values in a random sample. You will calculate the range, variance, and standard deviation of the random sample data set in order to understand how the data is distributed.

E12.03

 To Calculate the Dispersion of a Data Set

a. Click cell **F6**, and then type =MIN(B2:B35) to calculate the minimum value in the sample.

b. Click cell **F7**, and then type =MAX(B2:B35) to calculate the maximum value in the sample.

c. Click cell **F9**, and then type =F7-F6 to calculate the range of values in the sample.

d. Click cell **F10**, and then type =VAR.S(B2:B35) to calculate the variance of the sample. Format the cell as **Number** with **2** decimal places.

e. Click cell **F11**, and then type =STDEV.S(B2:B35) to calculate the standard deviation of the sample. Format the cell as **Number** with **2** decimal places.

   Notice that the standard deviation is quite small at only 3.79, indicating that the sales values stay somewhat close to the mean.

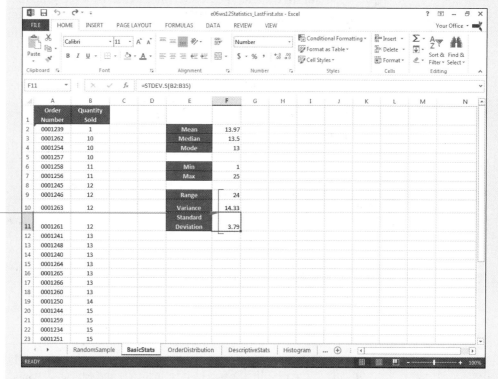

Range, Variance, and Standard Deviation to describe the distribution of a data set

Figure 4 Calculating the dispersion of a data set

f. Click **Save** 🖫.

Creating a Frequency Distribution Using the FREQUENCY Function

Businesses often have to work with data sets that contain thousands of records or more. When working with large data sets, it can be useful to group the data into bins. **Bins** are the intervals you want to group your data into. For example, the Turquoise Oasis Spa places orders for cases of bath salts through a nearby wholesaler. To summarize several orders worth of data, it may prove beneficial to determine how many orders of bath salts were for 1 to 10 cases, between 11 and 20 cases, 21 to 30 cases, 31 to 40 cases, and more than 40 cases.

The FREQUENCY function in Excel is an array function that creates a frequency distribution that calculates how often values occur within a bin. An **array function** is a function that can perform multiple calculations on one or more items in an array. Array functions look different from other functions because curly brackets { } are required for the function to calculate correctly.

The FREQUENCY function uses two arguments: (1) Data_array; and (2) Bins_array.

={FREQUENCY(Data_array, Bins_array)}

The Data_array argument is an array of or a reference to a set of values from which you want to count the number of times a particular range of values occurs. Blank cells and cells containing text are ignored in this argument.

The Bins_array argument is an array or reference to the upper values of the intervals you want to group the values in the Data_array argument into.

The FREQUENCY function always returns one additional value than there are bins referenced in the Bins_array argument. For example, if there are four bins consisting of 10, 20, 30, and 40 the function will return five values including a count of values in the Data_array argument that are equal to more than 40, i.e., counts of $1 \leq 10$, $11 \leq 20$, $21 \leq 30$, $31 \leq 40$, and > 40.

Since the FREQUENCY function is an array function, once it is typed into a cell you must press [Ctrl]+[Shift]+[Enter] instead of just [Enter] in order for it to calculate properly. Array functions are often referred to as "CSE" functions because of the keys pressed to create the function.

You have been given a random sample of 29 orders. You will use the FREQUENCY array function to group the number of cases ordered into the bins provided in column D.

E12.04

 To Summarize Data into Bins Using the FREQUENCY function

a. Click the **OrderDistribution** worksheet tab.

b. Select the range **E2:E6**, type =FREQUENCY(B2:B30, D2:D5), and then press [Ctrl] + [Shift] + [Enter] to make the function an array function.

   When creating a frequency table using the FREQUENCY function, you must select a range of cells that is one more than the cells containing the bin values. Notice the frequency table provides a count of orders that were for 1 to 10 cases, between 11 and 20 cases, between 21 and 30 cases, between 31 and 40 cases, and more than 40 cases.

c. Click cell **D6**, and then type More as the label for the number of orders with more than 40 items.

> **Troubleshooting**
> If the FREQUENCY function is not returning expected results, be sure there are curly brackets surrounding the function. This indicates that it is an array function. {=FREQUENCY(B2:B30, D2:D5)}. If there are no curly brackets then you must delete the functions and start over with Step b.

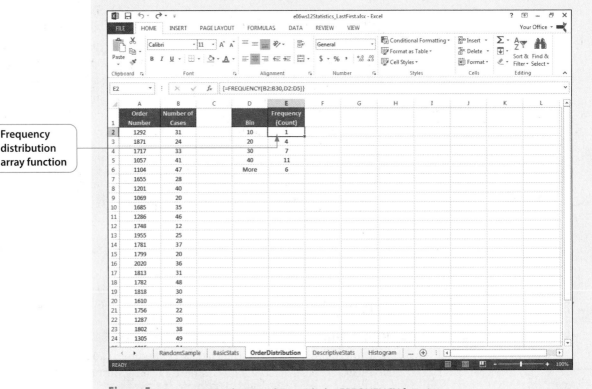

Figure 5 Summarizing data into bins with the FREQUENCY function

d. Click **Save** 🖫.

Generate Descriptive Statistics and Other Analyses Using the Analysis ToolPak

The Analysis ToolPak allows you to conduct a variety of statistical analyses with ease. For example, instead of typing out individual functions to calculate the mean, median, mode, variance, and standard deviation, you can generate all of those and more using the Analysis ToolPak. As of the date of this publication the Analysis ToolPak is not available in Excel 2011 for Macs.

Adding the Analysis ToolPak

Depending on the options that were selected upon the installation of Excel, you may have to manually install the Analysis ToolPak add-in by following the steps below.

E12.05

 To Add the Analysis ToolPak Add-In

a. Click the **FILE** tab, click **Options**, and then click **Add–Ins**.

b. At the bottom of the Excel Options dialog box, ensure that **Excel Add-ins** is selected in the Manage box, and then click **Go**.

c. In the Add-Ins dialog box, click the **Analysis ToolPak** check box, and then click **OK**.

d. Click the **DATA** tab and in the Analysis group, verify that the Data Analysis tool is now available.

Data Analysis ToolPak added

Figure 6   Data Analysis button added to the DATA tab

e. Click **Save**.

Generating Descriptive Statistics

Using the Analysis ToolPak's Descriptive Statistics tool, many of the statistical analyses that you have employed with Excel functions and more can be automatically generated.

Management has provided you with a sample set of data containing monthly revenue amounts for the last year. You have been asked to generate descriptive statistics on the sample data set in order to gain a better understanding of the data.

E12.06

 To Generate Descriptive Statistics Using the Analysis ToolPak

a. Click the **DescriptiveStats** worksheet tab.

b. On the DATA tab, in the Analysis group, click **Data Analysis**.

c. Select **Descriptive Statistics** from the Data Analysis dialog box, and then click **OK**.

d. Inside the Descriptive Statistics dialog box, click the **Input Range** box, and then select the range **B1:B13**.

e. Next to Grouped By, be sure that **Columns** is selected.

f. Click the **Labels in First Row** check box, indicating that the first row contains the Sales Revenue label.

g. Under Output options, click **Output Range**, click the **Output Range** box, and then click cell **E1**.

h. Click the **Summary statistics** check box, and then click **OK**.

Notice many of the basic statistical calculations are generated automatically, including mean, median, mode, range, variance, and standard deviation.

i. Resize columns **E** and **F** to fit the contents by double-clicking the line between column E and column F and the line between column F and G in the heading.

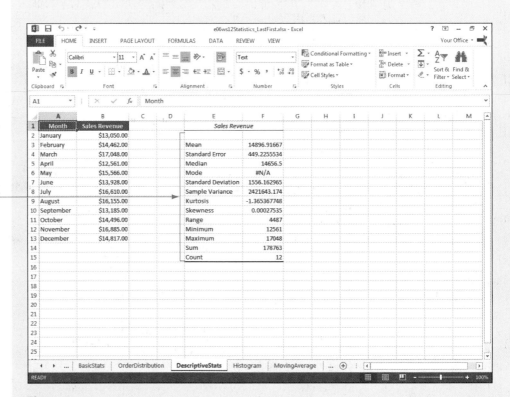

Descriptive Statistics output using the Analysis ToolPak

Figure 7 Descriptive statistics output

j. Click **Save** 💾.

Based on the results of the descriptive statistics output, you can see that the spa's monthly revenues were relatively steady throughout the year with a standard deviation of approximately 1,556.

QUICK REFERENCE	Descriptive Statistics

Below is a list of statistical functions and descriptions that are generated by the Descriptive Statistics tool in the Analysis ToolPak.

Statistical Function	Description
Mean	The average of the variables in the sample
Standard error	Used to determine how accurate the sample mean predicts the population mean by dividing the standard deviation by the square root of the sample size
Median	The middle value(s) when all the values of the sample are sorted in ascending order

(Continued)

QUICK REFERENCE	Descriptive Statistics

Statistical Function	Description
Mode	The value that appears most often in a sample. If there is no Mode, then #N/A will appear
Standard deviation	The most commonly used method for determining the average spread of a data set from the mean
Sample variance	A measure of how far the data in the sample are spread from the mean
Kurtosis	Characterizes the peakedness or flatness of a distribution compared to the normal distribution
Skewness	Characterizes the degree of asymmetry of a distribution around its mean
Range	The difference between the largest and smallest values in the sample
Minimum	The smallest value in the sample
Maximum	The largest value in the sample
Sum	The sum of all values in the sample
Count	The count of all values in the sample

Using a Histogram to Visualize Data in Bins

Earlier you created a frequency distribution using the FREQUENCY array function in Excel. The Analysis ToolPak allows for an alternative and easier method to create a frequency distribution of a data set called a histogram. A **histogram** is a statistical graph that summarizes the distribution of data and how the data fits into defined bins. On the Histogram worksheet tab, sample data from 30 customers is provided along with the number of items each have purchased over the course of one year.

E12.07

 To Create a Histogram

a. Click the **Histogram** worksheet tab.

b. On the DATA tab, click **Data Analysis**.

c. Select **Histogram** from the Data Analysis dialog box, and then click **OK**.

d. Click the **Input Range** box, and then select cells **B2:B31**.

e. Click the **Bin Range** box, and then select cells **D2:D6**.

f. Under Output options, click **Output Range**, click the **Output Range** box, and then click cell **D10**.

g. Click the **Chart Output** check box, and then click **OK**.

h. If necessary, adjust the width of columns **D:E** so that all values are visible.

i. In the histogram chart, select the **Frequency** legend item, and the press Delete.

j. Move the histogram chart so that it is within the range **G10:K19**.

The bin counts and histogram chart illustrate the number of customer orders that were for 20 items or less, between 21 and 30 items, between 31 and 40 items, between 41 and 50 items, between 51 and 60 items, and more than 60 items.

SIDE NOTE

Generating Bin Values

If you leave the Bin Range box blank, Excel will generate bin values automatically.

SIDE NOTE

Selecting Labels

If you ever decide to include column labels in your cell selection, you must click the Labels check box in the Histogram dialog box.

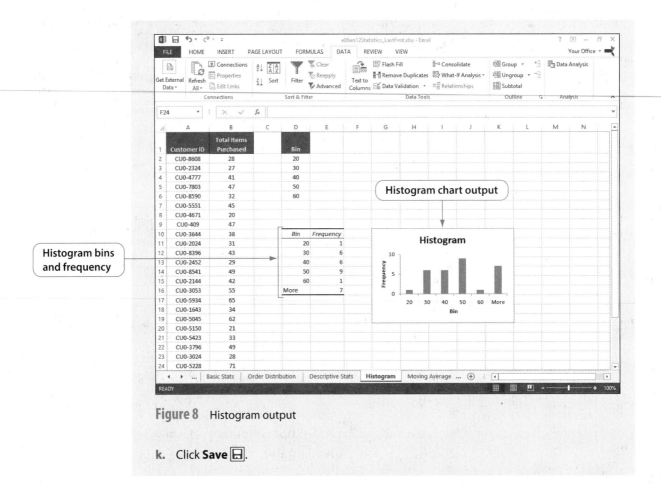

Figure 8 Histogram output

k. Click **Save** 🖫.

REAL WORLD ADVICE | **Creating Bin Values**

Although Excel can automatically generate evenly distributed bin values based on the minimum and maximum values of the input range, it is often better to define your own bins. Here are three steps that you can use to create your own bins:

1. Determine how wide you want your bins to be. In the previous example, each bin represented 10 consecutive values.

2. Calculate the difference between the maximum and minimum values in your data set.

3. Divide the difference in Step 2 by the number from Step 1 to determine how many bin values you need. The example above results in 5 bin values based on $(71-20)/10 = 5.1$.

Calculating a Moving Average

A useful calculation for businesses who wish to track sales over time, for example, is called a moving average. A **moving average** calculates the average of values over time based on specified intervals. For example, a business may wish to see the average sales for every three months in a given year. Moving averages can be useful in spotting trends over a period of time by smoothing out any fluctuations that may occur during each consecutive interval. Moving average data can be used to create charts that show whether the value is trending upward or downward.

You have been provided with monthly sales data for the past year and have been asked to calculate a moving average for every three months in order to determine if there is an upward or downward trend over the course of the year.

E12.08

To Calculate a Moving Average Using the Analysis ToolPak

a. Click the **MovingAverage** worksheet tab.

b. On the DATA tab, click **Data Analysis**.

c. Select **Moving Average** from the Data Analysis dialog box, and then click **OK**.

d. Click the **Input Range** box, and then select cells **B2:B13**.

e. Click the **Interval** box and type **3** to set the interval for every three months.

f. Click the **Output Range** box, and then click cell **C2**.

g. Click the **Chart Output** check box to include a chart, and then click **OK**.

h. Edit the chart title to read Moving Sales Average, edit the horizontal axis label to read Months, and then edit the vertical axis label to read Sales.

Notice the difference between the Actual and Forecast lines included in the chart. This indicates that despite the fluctuations in monthly sales, the overall trend is fairly flat with neither an upward or downward trend.

Moving averages for every 3 months

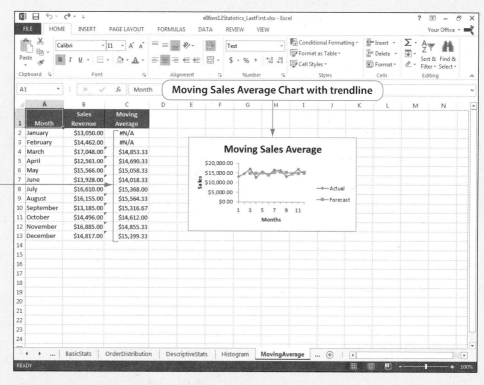

Figure 9 Calculating a 3-month moving average

i. Click **Save**.

CONSIDER THIS | **Selecting Appropriate Intervals**

When calculating a moving average, it is important that the interval chosen is appropriate for the data. What interval would be appropriate for a call center that makes thousands of calls in a day? Or a small business that makes on average 10 outside sales a day?

Applying Probability Distributions to Business

All businesses operate on a large amount of uncertainty. Small businesses like the Turquoise Oasis Spa tend to experience more volatility than large organizations and can therefore benefit greatly from using probability distributions to estimate future outcomes and events. Probability distributions are useful in predicting demand for products and services, successful marketing campaigns, effectiveness of advertising, and much more.

In this section you will use several different probability distributions to predict various aspects of the business. You will use the normal, binomial, exponential, Poisson, and hypergeometric distributions.

Predict Business Outcomes Using Probability Distribution Functions

Excel offers many probability distribution functions with wide applications across many different industries of business, science, engineering, and mathematics. The most commonly used probability distribution functions used in business are NORM.DIST, BINOM.DIST, EXPON.DIST, POISSON.DIST, and HYPGEOM.DIST. In this section you will assist the managers at the Turquoise Oasis Spa in predicting various business outcomes using these probability distribution functions.

Using the NORM.DIST Function

A **normal distribution** is one of the most important distributions in statistics. When charted, as pictured in Figure 10, it takes on the shape of a bell and is often referred to as the "bell-shaped curve" where 68% of all values occur within one standard deviation from the mean, 95.45% of values fall within two standard deviations from the mean, and 99.8% of values fall within three standard deviations. The normal distribution has wide applications in business and can be used to calculate the probability of sales, the number of customers to expect in a given week, employee performance, and operations to name a few.

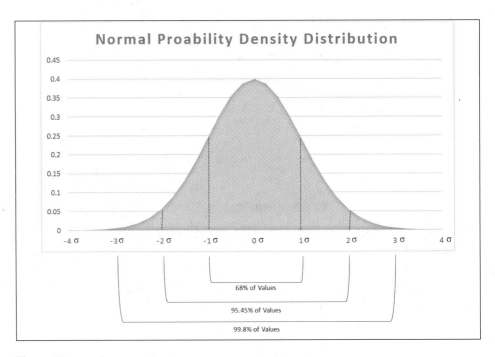

Figure 10   Normal probability density distribution

Many economic, social, and natural events follow the normal distribution:

- 68% of values will fall within one standard deviation.
- 95.45% of values will fall within two standard deviations.
- 99.8% of values will fall within three standard deviations.

The NORM.DIST function can be used to calculate the probability of an event occurring by using the mean and standard deviation of a continuous variable data set, assuming the data follows a normal distribution. The NORM.DIST function uses four arguments: (1) x; (2) mean; (3) standard_dev; and (4) cumulative.

=NORM.DIST(x, mean, standard_dev, cumulative)

- The x argument is the value for which you want to calculate the probability of occurrence.
- The mean argument is the average value in the data set.
- The standard_dev argument is the standard deviation of the data set.
- The cumulative argument accepts either a TRUE or FALSE value. If TRUE, the result will be the probability of a value being less than or equal to the value of the x argument, known as the **cumulative distribution function**. If FALSE, the result will be the probability of a value being equal to the value of the x argument, known as the **probability density function**.

Statistically, the probability of a specific x value for continuous data is 0, but the FALSE argument can be used to create a probability distribution of the data set.

Managers at the spa would like to know how likely it is that they will exceed their goal of selling 30 massages over the course of the next week. You have been given data of weekly massage sales for the past seven weeks to use in your calculation.

E12.09

 To Calculate Probability of Sales Using NORM.DIST

a. Click the **MassageSales** worksheet tab.

b. Click cell **E1**, and then type =AVERAGE(B3:B9) to calculate the mean for the weekly massage sales quantities.

c. Click cell **E2**, and then type =STDEV.S(B3:B9) to calculate the standard deviation of the sample of weekly massage sales volume.

d. Click cell **E4**, and then type 30 as the desired minimum sales goal in week 8.

e. Click cell **E5**, and then type =1-NORM.DIST(E4,E1,E2,TRUE) to calculate the probability of selling more than 30 massages in week 8.

   By default, the NORM.DIST function returns the probability of a value being less than or equal to the x value. Therefore, if the desired probability is for a value greater than the x value, you have to subtract the result from 1.

f. Format the cell as **Percentage** with **2** decimal places.

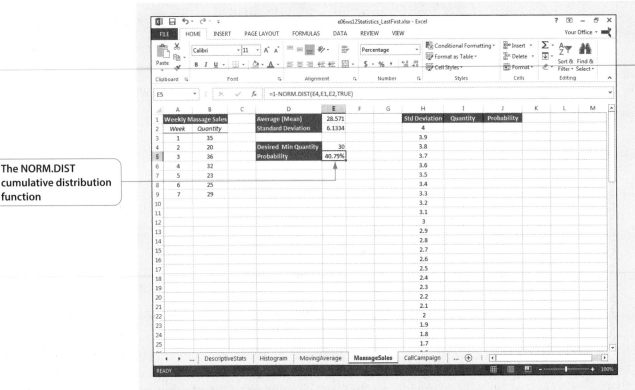

Figure 11 Probability of breaking a sales goal using the NORM.DIST function

g. Click Save .

Charting a Normal Distribution

Visualizing the normal distribution of the weekly massage sales can help to understand what the expectations should be for future weeks. To create a chart that visualizes the normal distribution, one must first calculate the probability of values occurring within four standard deviations of the mean, both positive and negative.

E12.10

To Visualize a Normal Distribution with a Scatter Chart

a. Click the **MassageSales** worksheet tab, click cell **I2**, and then type =H2*$E$2 + $E$1 to calculate what the quantity of massages sold would be if the unit quantity was equal to four standard deviations above the mean. Format the cell as a **Number** with **0** decimal places.

b. Use the **AutoFill** handle to copy the formula down to **I82** (four standard deviations below the mean).

c. Click cell **J2**, and then type =NORM.DIST(I2,$E$1,$E$2,FALSE) to calculate the probability that the spa will sell a number of massages that are exactly four standard deviations above the mean in a given week. Use the **AutoFill** handle to copy the formula down to **J82**.

d. Select cells **I2:J82**, and then click the **INSERT** tab. In the Charts group, click the **Insert Scatter (X, Y) or Bubble Chart** button, and then select the **Scatter with Smooth Lines** chart.

e. Move the chart to within the range **A11:G25**.

f. Click the **Chart Title** text box, and then type Weekly Sales Distribution.

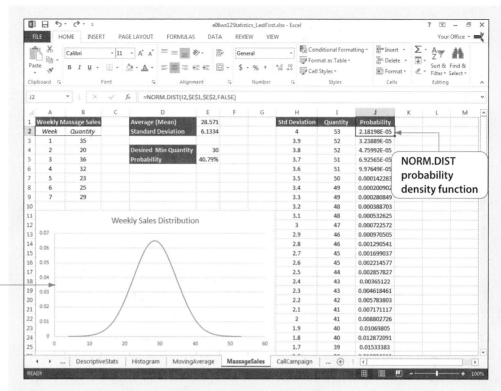

Figure 12 Visualize the normal distribution with a scatter chart

A callout on the left of the figure reads: "Scatter Chart with smooth lines to visualize the Normal distribution"

A callout on the right of the figure reads: "NORM.DIST probability density function"

g. Click **Save** 📇.

Using the BINOM.DIST Function

The spa initiated a phone campaign to get people to subscribe to its health and beauty magazine. After 30 phone calls there was a 35% success rate of converting a prospective customer, or lead, to a paid subscriber. Statistical analysis could be applied to this data to calculate the probability of successfully converting 0 leads, 1 lead, 2 leads, and so on. The binomial distribution can do just that. The binomial distribution is a very common probability distribution that has many applications in business. The **binomial distribution** is a discrete probability distribution that is used to model the number of successful trials based on the total number of trials and the rate of success.

The BINOM.DIST function uses four arguments: (1) number_s; (2) trials; (3) probability_s; and (4) cumulative.

=BINOM.DIST(number_s, trials, probability_s, cumulative)

- The number_s argument is the number of successes for which you want to calculate the probability of occurrence.

- The trials argument is the number of independent trials that have taken place. For the spa, it is the number of subscription phone calls placed.

- The probability_s argument is the probability of success for each trial. This is based on the data previously collected, where 35% of the phone calls placed resulted in the person signing up for the mailing list.

- The cumulative argument accepts either a TRUE or FALSE value. If TRUE, the result will be the probability of a value being less than or equal to the value of the x argument, known as the cumulative distribution function. If FALSE, the result will be the probability of a value being equal to the value of the x argument, known as the probability density function.

Figure 13 shows how a binomial probability density distribution may look when charted.

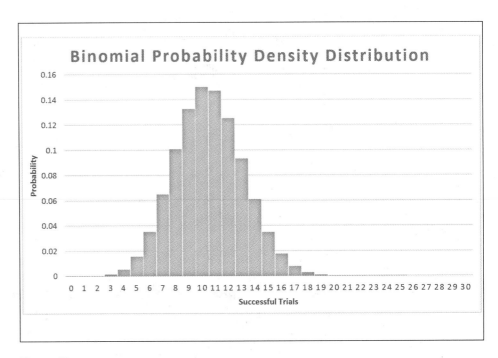

Figure 13   Binomial probability density distribution

E12.11

 To Calculate the Probability of Success Using BINOMIAL.DIST

a. Click the **CallCampaign** worksheet tab.

b. Click cell **B1**, and then type **30** for the number of calls in the sample.

c. Click cell **B2**, and then type **.35** for the percentage of calls resulting in a successful sign-up. Format the cell as **Percentage**.

d. Click cell **B5**, and then type =BINOM.DIST(A5, $B$1,$B$2,FALSE) to calculate the probability that exactly 0 out of 30 calls will result in a successful sign-up. Format the cell as **Percentage** with **2** decimal places.

e. Use the **AutoFill** handle to copy the formula down to **B35**.

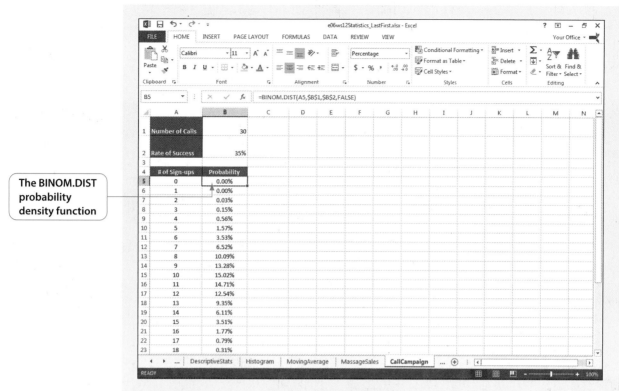

The BINOM.DIST probability density function

Figure 14 Probability of success using the BINOM.DIST function

f. Click Save.

Notice the most likely number of successful sign-ups is 10 out of every 30 phone calls at 15.02%. Managers at the spa can use this information as a way to set expectations for each rep. If a rep is able to consistently outperform the most likely number of sign-ups, then perhaps a best practice can be established to increase the overall rate of success.

Using the EXPON.DIST Function

Managers at the Turquoise Oasis Spa have been tracking how frequently online sales of their spa products have been occurring. They would like to estimate when the next 10 online orders will occur. The exponential distribution can do just that. The **exponential distribution** is a continuous probability function that models the times between events. The EXPON.DIST function uses three arguments: (1) x; (2) lambda; and (3) cumulative.

=EXPON.DIST(x, lambda, cumulative)

- The x argument is the value representing the number of events for which you want to calculate the probability of occurrence.

- The lambda argument is the inverse of the mean and is calculated by dividing 1 by the mean value.

- The cumulative argument accepts either a TRUE or FALSE value. If TRUE, the result will be the probability of a value being less than or equal to the value of the x argument, known as the cumulative distribution function. If FALSE, the result will be the probability of a value being equal to the value of the x argument, known as the probability density function.

Figure 15 shows how an exponential cumulative distribution may look when charted.

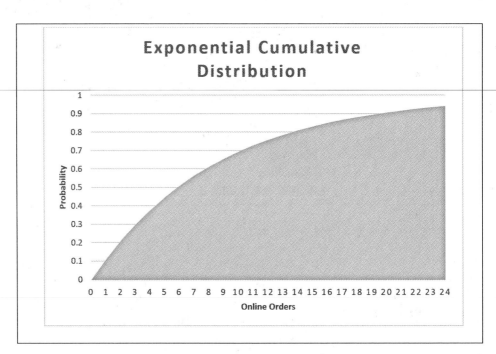

Figure 15 Exponential cumulative distribution

E12.12

 To Calculate the Probability of When a Sale Will Occur Using EXPON.DIST

a. Click the **OnlineOrders** worksheet tab.

b. Click cell **A2**, and then type =EXPON.DIST(B2,1/$D$2,TRUE) to calculate the probability of an online sale taking place in 1 hour or less.

c. Use the **AutoFill** handle to copy the function to **A25**.

Notice the various probabilities for sales taking place within the next 1 to 24 hours. Since TRUE was used for the cumulative argument, each of the probabilities is for less than or equal to the x value.

d. Click cell **F3**, and then type =IFERROR(VLOOKUP(RAND(),$A$2:$B$25,2,TRUE),1).

This formula uses the VLOOKUP function to look up a random probability value generated by the RAND function. Where an approximate match is found it returns the number of hour(s) when a sale will occur from column B. The IFERROR function is necessary because if the random variable generated is less than the probability of a sale occurring in 1 hour or less, the result would be an error, and should be 1.

e. Use the **AutoFill** handle to copy the formula to **F12** to estimate when the next 10 online orders will be placed.

f. Click cell **H2**, and then type =A11-A6 to calculate the probability of an online sale occurring within the next 5 to 10 hours by subtracting the probability of an online sale occurring within 5 hours from the probability of one occurring within 10 hours or less. Format the cell as **Percentage** with **2** decimal places.

SIDE NOTE

Random Probabilities

Due to the volatility of the RAND function, your results will be different the image below.

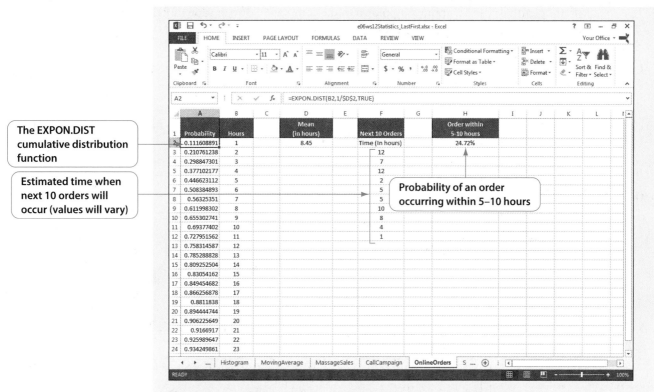

The EXPON.DIST cumulative distribution function

Estimated time when next 10 orders will occur (values will vary)

Probability of an order occurring within 5–10 hours

Figure 16 Predicting the time of online sales using EXPON.DIST

g. Click **Save** 📁.

Managers could use this statistical model to ensure that the IT used to support online sales is able to support the number of online sales expected to occur throughout the day.

REAL WORLD ADVICE **Continually Monitoring Statistics**

These important statistics should be tracked continually and consistently. As the company grows you may find that the average time between orders will decrease and additional employees and/or web and database servers may be required to process the orders.

Using the POISSON.DIST Function

Managers at the Turquoise Oasis Spa have provided three weeks of spa services sales data and are interested in predicting the number of spa services that will be sold over the next seven days. The Poisson distribution can do just that. The **Poisson distribution** is a discrete probability function that has wide business applications. It is used most often to predict demand for a product or service.

The Poisson distribution calculates the probability that a specified number of events will occur based on the mean of the data set. The POISSON.DIST function uses three arguments: (1) x; (2) mean; and (3) cumulative.

=POISSON.DIST(x, mean, cumulative)

- The x argument is the value representing the number of events for which you want to calculate the probability of occurrence.
- The mean argument is the value representing the mean of the data set.
- The cumulative argument accepts either a TRUE or FALSE value. If TRUE, the result will be the probability of a value being less than or equal to the value of the

x argument, known as the cumulative distribution function. If FALSE, the result will be the probability of a value being equal to the value of the x argument, known as the probability density function.

Figure 17 shows how a Poisson cumulative distribution may look when charted.

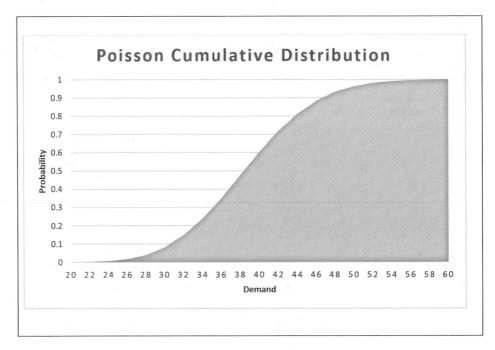

Figure 17 Poisson cumulative distribution

E12.13

▶ To Predict the Number of Orders Placed in the Next Week Using POISSON.DIST

a. Click the **SpaTreatments** worksheet tab.

b. Click cell **B25**, and then type =AVERAGE(B2:B23) to calculate the mean of the number of spa treatments sold.

c. Click cell **D2**, and then type =POISSON.DIST(E2,$B$25,TRUE) to calculate the probability of selling 20 or fewer spa treatments.

d. Use the **AutoFill** handle to copy the function down to **D22 (60 or fewer)**.

e. Click cell **G3**, and then type =RAND() to generate a random decimal between 0 and 1. This will serve as a random probability to aid in estimating the orders for the next week.

f. Use the **AutoFill** handle to copy the function down to **G9**.

SIDE NOTE
Random Probabilities
Due to the volatility of the RAND function, your results will be different from the image below.

g. With cells **G3:G9** selected, on the HOME tab, in the Clipboard group, click **Copy**. Click the **Paste** button arrow, and then under the **Paste Values** heading, click **Values (V)** to replace the volatile RAND function with the values it generated.

h. Click cell **H3**, type =VLOOKUP(G3,$D$2:$E$22,2,TRUE) and then use the **AutoFill** handle to copy the function down to **H9**.

   Notice the VLOOKUP function uses the randomly generated probability value as the lookup value in the function. It then looks for an approximate match in the Poisson Probability column and returns the corresponding number of spa treatment orders in the same row. Managers at the Turquoise Oasis Spa now have an estimated number of spa treatments for the next seven days.

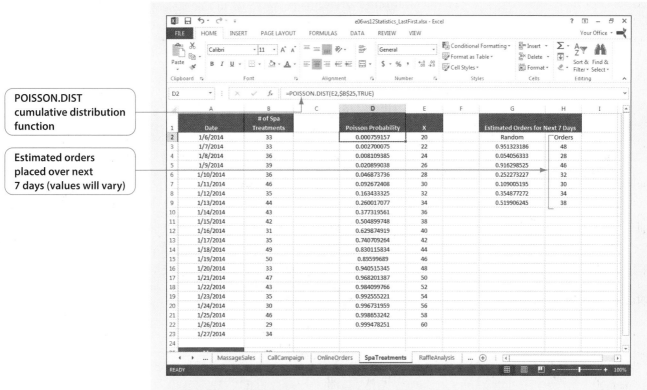

POISSON.DIST cumulative distribution function

Estimated orders placed over next 7 days (values will vary)

Figure 18 Estimate order quantities using the POISSON.DIST function

i. Click **Save** 💾.

Managers at the spa can use this statistical model to assist in scheduling massage therapists for the week to be sure they have enough to meet demand.

Using the HYPGEOM.DIST Function

Managers at the Turquoise Oasis Spa are planning on having a grand reopening once the expansion is complete. To help generate buzz about the event they will be giving away raffle tickets to customers who use the spa services throughout the month of June. The winner will be allowed to draw 10 envelopes from a barrel of 100 envelopes consisting of 80 spa certificates worth $50 each and 20 complete spa packages worth $500 each. The managers would like to know the probability that the winner will draw 1 of the $500 prizes, 2 of the $500 prices, 3, and so on. The hypergeometric distribution can do just that. The **hypergeometric distribution** is a discrete population distribution that calculates the probability of drawing a specific number of target items from a collection without replacement.

The HYPGEOM.DIST function uses five arguments: (1) sample_s; (2) number_sample; (3) population_s; (4) number_pop; and (5) cumulative.

=HYPGEOM.DIST(sample_s, number_sample, population_s, number_pop, cumulative)

- The sample_s is the value representing the number of target items for which you want to calculate the probability of occurrence.
- The number_sample argument is the specific number of items that are to be drawn.
- The population_s argument is the specific number of target items in the collection.
- The number_pop argument is the total number of items in the collection.
- The cumulative argument accepts either a TRUE or FALSE value. If TRUE, the result will be the probability of a value being less than or equal to the value of the x argument, known as the cumulative distribution function. If FALSE, the result will

be the probability of a value being equal to the value of the x argument, known as the probability density function.

Figure 19 shows how a hypergeometric probability density distribution may look when charted.

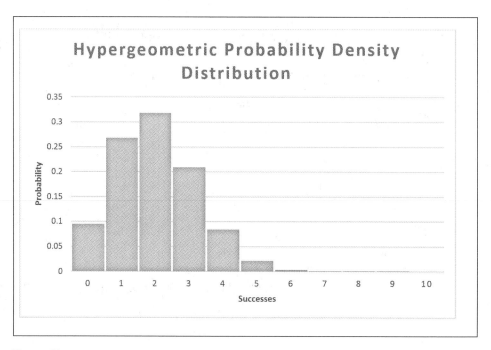

Figure 19   Hypergeometric probability density distribution

E12.14

 To Calculate the Probability of Drawing the Top Prize Using HYPGEOM.DIST

a. Click the **RaffleAnalysis** worksheet tab.

b. Click cell **E2**, and then type =HYPGEOM.DIST(A2,B2,C2,D2,FALSE) to calculate the probability of the winner drawing exactly 0 top prize envelopes. Format the cell as **Percentage** with **2** decimal places. Use the **AutoFill** handle to copy the formula down to **E12** (exactly 10 top prize envelopes).

c. Click cell **F2**, and then type =(A2*500)+(B2-A2)*50 to calculate the total cash value of envelopes drawn if 0 are top prizes. Format the cell as **Currency**, and then use the **AutoFill** handle to copy the formula down to **F12**.

d. Click cell **G2**, and then type =E2*F2 to calculate the expected value of the drawing based on the probability of drawing 0 top prize envelopes and the total cash value of 10 $50 envelopes. Use the **AutoFill** handle to copy the formula to **G12**.

e. Click cell **G13**, and then type =SUM(G2:G12) to calculate the total expected value of the 10 envelopes drawn by the winner, which should equal $1,400.00.

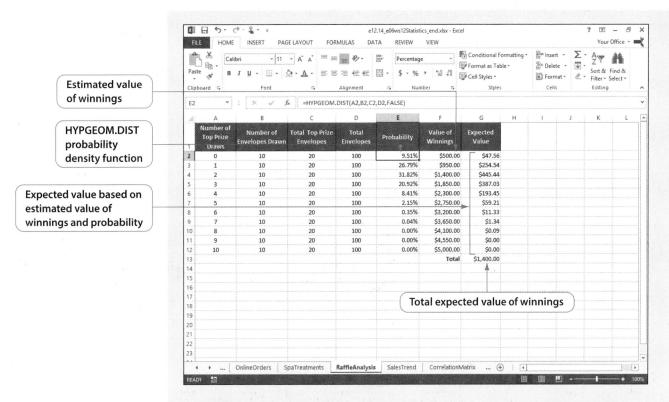

Figure 20 Calculate the probability of drawing the top prize using the HYPGEOM.DIST function

f. Click **Save** 💾.

Raffles and contests like this can raise awareness of a company's existence and services offered, increasing customer traffic. It is important for management to be able to estimate the total costs of the contest winnings in case the winner is extremely lucky and beats the odds.

Finding Relationships in Data

So far, you have learned the benefits of basic statistical analysis in gaining a better understanding of data as well as the benefits of probability distributions in predicting the likelihood that certain events will occur. Identifying relationships in data can help you to answer these questions: Did the most recent marketing campaign increase sales? Does the age and gender of your customers have anything to do with how much money they spend? To understand how to answer these and other similar questions and then move to predicting outcomes you need to understand the concepts of correlation and regression.

In this section, you will learn to identify relationships in your data using covariance and correlation functions as well as regression analysis to identify trends, relationships between variables, and make predictions.

Find Relationships in Data Using COVARIANCE.S and CORREL

Managers at the Turquoise Oasis Spa are interested in knowing whether there is a relationship between the age of their clients and the amount of money they spend. The covariance and correlation formulas are used to describe linear relationships between data. **Covariance** is a formula that can calculate the relationship between two variables, like age and dollars spent as well as the direction of the relationship. If one variable increases and the other variable also increases, then the relationship is considered positive. If one variable increases and the other variable decreases, then the relationship is considered negative.

The correlation formula produces a value between −1 and 1 that is called the correlation coefficient. The **correlation coefficient** is represented by the letter "r" in statistics and is a unitless value that describes the strength and direction of a relationship between two variables. A correlation coefficient of −1 is said to have a perfect negative relationship, a coefficient of 1 is considered to have a perfect positive relationship, and a coefficient of 0 is said to have no linear relationship. The closer the value is to −1 or 1 describes the strength of the relationship. The correlation coefficient is said to have a similar relationship to covariance as standard deviation has to variance, in that both provide a standardized value to allow for easier interpretation of the data.

QUICK REFERENCE	Strength of Relationship

Generally speaking, the following values can be used to determine whether the relationship between the two variables is strong, moderate, weak, or very weak.

Correlation Coefficient	Strength of Relationship
−1.0 to −0.5 or 0.5 to 1.0	Strong
−0.5 to −0.3 or 0.3 to 05.	Moderate
−0.3 to −0.1 or 0.1 to 0.3	Weak
−0.1 to 0.1	Very weak or none

REAL WORLD ADVICE	Correlation Does Not Equal Causation

A correlation coefficient of .889 only tells you that there is a strong positive relationship between the two variables. It does not mean that an increase in one variable actually causes the other variable to increase. Be sure to note that correlation does not imply causation.

Using the COVARIANCE.S Function

To calculate the covariance in Excel, one of two functions are used: COVARIANCE.S or COVARIANCE.P. COVARIANCE.S is used to determine a relationship between two variables in a sample, whereas COVARIANCE.P is used to determine a relationship between two variables in an entire population. You will use COVARIANCE.S since you are dealing with sample sets of data. The only arguments are the arrays of cells that contain the two variables:

=COVARIANCE.S(array1, array2)

The value that the COVARIANCE.S function returns can be difficult to interpret at times because it is not standardized. A covariance of 7, for example, can be interpreted as a positive relationship, but the strength of that positive relationship can only be said to be weaker than if the number had been 10.

Managers at the spa assume that, to a certain extent, the age of a client may be related to how much money they spend at the spa. For example, someone who is 40 years old could spend more money than someone who is 20 years old. You have been given a random sample of sales data along with the age of the customer to use Excel to determine whether or not there is a relationship between age and revenue and the strength of that relationship.

To Determine the Relationship Between Two Variables Using COVARIANCE.S

a. Click the **SalesTrend** worksheet tab.

b. Click cell **D2**, and then type =COVARIANCE.S(A2:A37, B2:B37) to calculate the covariance between age and sales at the Turquoise Oasis Spa. Format the cell as **Number** with **4** decimal places.

Notice the COVARIANCE.S function returns 390.8442 indicating a relationship between age and sales amount. The relationship is positive in that as the age of the customer increases so does the amount of money they spend at the spa.

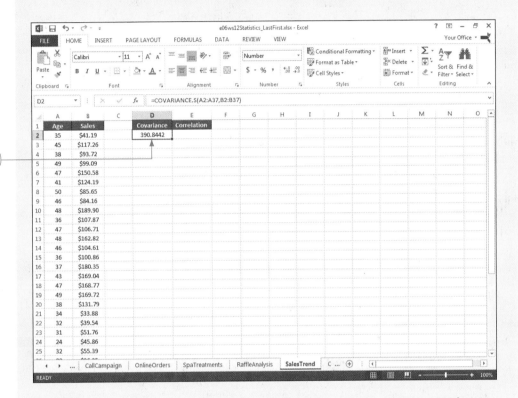

Figure 21 Determine the relationships between two variables using the COVARIANCE.S function

c. Click **Save** 🖫.

Using the CORREL Function

To calculate the correlation coefficient between two variables in Excel, the CORREL function is used. The only arguments are the arrays of cells that contain the two variables.

=CORREL(array1, array2)

To Calculate a Correlation Coefficient Using CORREL

a. Click the **SalesTrend** worksheet tab, and then click cell **E2**.

b. Type =CORREL(A2:A37,B2:B37) to calculate the correlation coefficient between age and sales. Format the cell as **Number** with **4** decimal places.

Notice the correlation coefficient is approximately .65, indicating a strong positive correlation between age and sales.

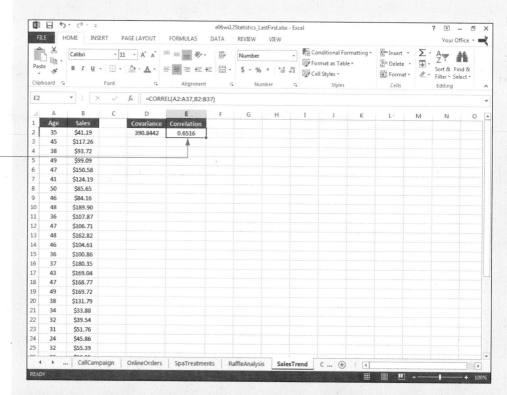

Figure 22 Calculate a correlation coefficient using the CORREL function

c. Click **Save** 🔲.

Visualizing Relationships with a Scatter Chart

Correlation coefficient values are easy to interpret, but it is often more powerful to create a chart that illustrates that relationship visually.

To Visualize Relationships Between Two Variables Using a Scatter Chart

a. Click the **SalesTrend** worksheet tab, and then select **A1:B37**.

b. Click the **Quick Analysis** tool 📊 at the bottom of the range selection, click **CHARTS**, and then click **Scatter**.

c. Click the **Chart Elements** button ➕ next to the chart, and then click the **Axis Titles** and **Trendline** check boxes.

d. Click the **Vertical Axis Title** text box, delete the **Axis Title** text, and then type Sales Revenue.

e. Click the **Horizontal Axis Title** text box, delete the **Axis Title** text, and then type Age.

f. Edit the chart title to read Sales-Age Correlation.

g. Move the scatter chart into the range **D4:J17**.

   Notice the trendline with its upward slope also indicates a strong positive relationship between the age of the clients of the spa and the amount of money spent.

Scatter chart illustrating relationship between age and sales →

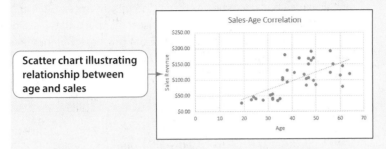

Figure 23   Scatter chart with a trendline

h. Click **Save** .

Determine Relationships Between Multiple Variables Using a Correlation Matrix

Calculating the correlation coefficient using the CORREL function is useful to determine the type and strength of a relationship between two variables. However, in business there may be several independent variables that affect a dependent variable. For example, age of customers may not be the only variable with a relationship to revenue; gender and income could also be factors.

Using the Analysis ToolPak to Create a Correlation Matrix

To calculate the correlation coefficients of several different variables, the Analysis ToolPak offers a method to create a correlation matrix. You have been given a random sample of customer data with age and gender along with the amount of money spent on a given visit to the spa. Since gender is listed as either male or female in the data set provided, you must first convert it to numerical nominal data using an IF function.

E12.18

 To Create a Correlation Matrix Using the Analysis ToolPak

a. Click the **CorrelationMatrix** worksheet tab.

b. Click cell **B2**, and then type =IF(A2="Male",1,2) to create nominal data that can be used in the correlation calculation for gender where male = 1 and female = 2.

c. Use the **AutoFill** handle to copy the formula to **B37**.

d. Click the **DATA** tab, and then click **Data Analysis**.

e. Select **Correlation** from the Data Analysis dialog box, and then click **OK**.

f. Click the **Input Range** box, and then select the range **B1:D37**.

g. Next to Grouped By, be sure that **Columns** is selected.

h. Click the **Labels in First Row** check box, indicating that the first row does contain labels.

i. Under Output options, click **Output Range**, click the **Output Range** box, click cell **F1**, and click **OK**.

j. Adjust the columns to be able to view the contents.

To interpret the results of the correlation matrix, locate the Sales row. Sales is the dependent variable for which you are interested in observing the relationship to other variables. Notice the correlation coefficient in cell G4 is approximately .746, indicating a strong positive correlation between gender and sales. Since you used 1 for male and 2 for female, this means that the spa can expect higher revenues from their female clientele than their male clientele. In fact, it appears that gender is a stronger predictor of sales than age at 0.652.

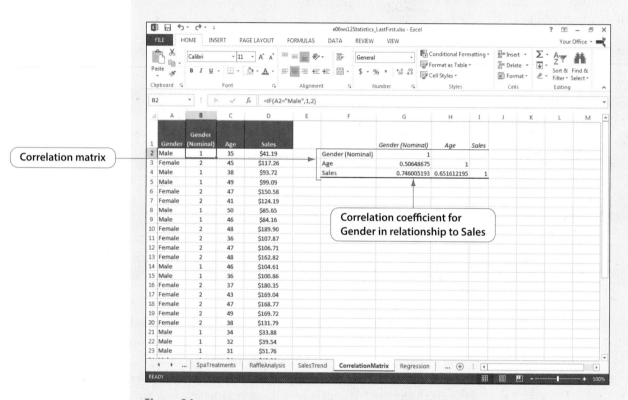

Figure 24 Correlation matrix showing the relationship between multiple variables

k. Click **Save** 🖫.

CONSIDER THIS | **Direction of Relationship**

In the example above you attributed the value of 1 for male and 2 for female. The result of the correlation matrix indicated a strong positive relationship between gender and sales. What would happen to the direction of the relationship between gender and sales if you attributed the value of 1 to female and 2 for male?

Use Regression Analysis to Predict Future Values

The next step in statistical analysis is to put your assumptions to the test and determine if the relationships between the data are strong enough to make predictions about future events. **Regression analysis** is a method used to predict future values by analyzing the relationships between two or more variables. You will examine the relationship between age and gender of your clients with sales a bit further to determine if the combination of age and gender are good predictors of revenue.

Creating a Regression Analysis Using the Analysis ToolPak

Excel's Analysis ToolPak provides an easy way to conduct a regression analysis on two or more variables. One distinction between the variables that must be made up front is which one is the dependent variable and which one is the independent variable. In this scenario, the sales are the dependent variable because sales are what you want to be able to predict. Age and gender become the independent variables, and you want to be able to measure the effectiveness of them as a predictor of sales.

E12.19

 To Conduct a Regression Analysis Using the Analysis ToolPak

a. Click the **Regression** worksheet tab.

b. On the DATA tab, click **Data Analysis**.

c. Select **Regression** from the Data Analysis dialog box, and then click **OK**.

d. Click the **Input Y Range** box, and then select **C1:C37** as the dependent variable of sales.

e. Click the **Input X Range** box, and then select **A1:B37** as the independent variables of age and gender. Note in Excel that the independent variables must be in adjacent columns.

f. Click the **Labels** check box to indicate that the label fields were included in the selection.

g. Under Output options, click **Output Range**.

h. Click the **Output Range** box, click cell **E10**, and then click **OK**.

i. Adjust the columns as necessary so that all values are visible in the SUMMARY OUTPUT.

The summary output produced by the Regression tool includes a lot of information. However, the key to its interpretation is in three values:

- R Square
- Intercept
- Age Coefficient

The **R Square** value, in cell F14 of the SUMMARY OUTPUT, was calculated by squaring the correlation coefficient, labeled as Multiple R in the output. This provides a more conservative estimate of the independent variables' ability to predict the value of the dependent variable.

As you can see, the R Square value is approximately 0.657 or 65.7%. This can be interpreted as age and gender accounting for 65.7% of the sales revenue generated by a customer.

The **Intercept coefficient** value, in cell F26 of the SUMMARY OUTPUT, is the value at which a regression line will cross the y-axis and is used in the slope intercept formula to predict values.

The intercept coefficient value is approximately −46.7.

The regression equation includes the intercept coefficient value (approximately −46.7), along with the age coefficient, and gender coefficient to predict the value of the dependent variable. The age coefficient in cell F27 is approximately 1.59, and the gender coefficient in cell F28 is approximately 56.26.

The resulting regression equation in the context of age, gender, and sales is:

Sales (Y) = (age * 1.59) + (gender * 56.26) + −46.7

 E12.20

To Use the Regression Equation to Predict Values

a. Click cell **G3**, then type =(E3*$F$27)+(F3*$F$28)+$F$26 as the regression equation to predict the sales revenue generated by a client that is 45 years of age and female. Format the cell as **Currency**.

b. Use the **AutoFill** handle to copy the formula to **G6**.

Notice that the sales revenue estimate based on age is closer to some of the actual values near the same age and gender but farther away on others. This is because as the R Square value indicates, age and gender account for only 65.7% of the revenue. Other variables also have an effect on revenue, such as income levels, time of visit, and perhaps even weather.

SIDE NOTE
Residuals

The Regression tool can automatically produce Sales estimates using the regression equation by checking the Residuals check box in the Regression dialog box. These estimates can then be compared to the corresponding actual Sales data.

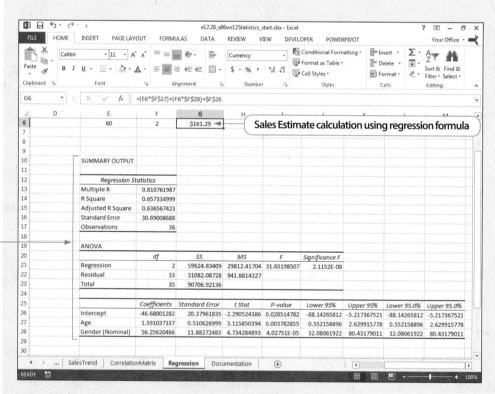

Figure 25 Regression analysis and predicted sales values

c. Click **Save**.

d. Complete the Documentation worksheet and submit your file as directed by your instructor.

You could improve the accuracy of this statistical model by collecting additional customer data and running the regression analysis with other independent variables. Additional or alternative independent variables could increase the R Square value, possibly indicating a more accurate predictor(s) of sales revenue.

Generally, the overall model is considered statistically significant in predicting the dependent variable if the Significance F value (in cell J21) is < 0.05. Each independent variable is considered statistically significant if its p-value (cells I27 and I28) is < 0.05.

Concept Check

1. Discuss the difference between population and sample data. Which one is used most often in statistics and why? p. 606–607

2. Describe the four types of data used in statistics. What is an example of each type? p. 607–608

3. Discuss how calculating the range, variance, and standard deviation of a data set can help to spot differences in two data sets with the same mean. p. 611–612

4. What is a histogram, and how is it beneficial to understanding data? p. 617

5. What are two probability distributions used in business, and what is one practical application for each? p. 620–631

6. What are covariance and correlation, and what can they tell you about data? p. 631–632

7. What can be learned from a correlation matrix? p. 635–636

8. What is the R Square value, and how is it related to the correlation coefficient? p. 637

Key Terms

Array function 613
Binomial distribution 623
Bins 613
Central tendency 610
Continuous variable 607
Count 617
Correlation coefficient 632
Covariance 631
Cumulative distribution
   function 621
Data 606
Data set 606
Descriptive statistics 606
Discrete variable 607
Exponential distribution 625
Histogram 617
Hypergeometric distribution 629

Inferential statistics 606
Intercept coefficient 637
Interval data 608
Kurtosis 617
Maximum 612
Mean 610
Median 610
Minimum 612
Mode 610
Moving average 618
Nominal data 608
Normal distribution 620
Observational unit 606
Ordinal data 608
Outliers 612
Poisson distribution 627
Population 606

Probability 606
Probability density function 621
Probability distribution 606
R Square 637
Random sample 606
Range 611
Ratio data 608
Regression analysis 637
Sample population 606
Skewness 617
Sum 617
Standard deviation 612
Standard error 616
Statistics 606
Variance 612

Add the Analysis ToolPak add-in (p. 615)

Generate descriptive statistics and other analyses using the Analysis ToolPak (p. 615)

Calculate probability of sales using NORM.DIST (p. 621)

Visualize a normal distribution with a scatter chart (p. 622)

Predict business outcomes using probability distribution functions (p. 620)

Create a random sample using RAND() (p. 609)

Calculate the mean, median, and mode of a data set (p. 611)

Calculate the dispersion of a data set (p. 612)

Conduct basic statistical analyses in Excel (p. 608)

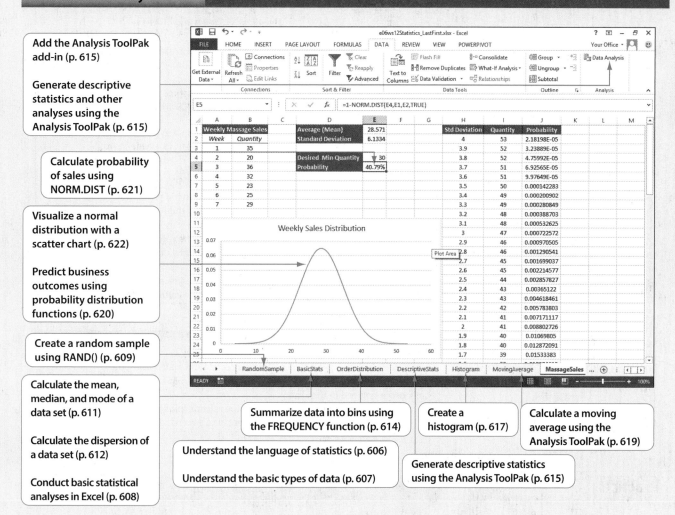

Summarize data into bins using the FREQUENCY function (p. 614)

Create a histogram (p. 617)

Calculate a moving average using the Analysis ToolPak (p. 619)

Understand the language of statistics (p. 606)

Understand the basic types of data (p. 607)

Generate descriptive statistics using the Analysis ToolPak (p. 615)

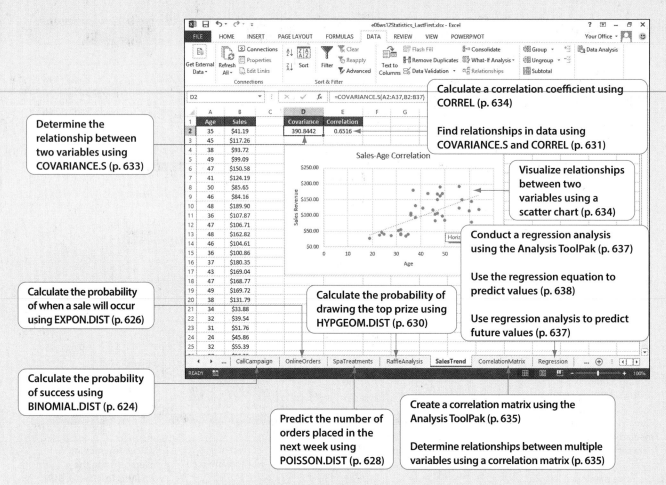

Determine the relationship between two variables using COVARIANCE.S (p. 633)

Calculate a correlation coefficient using CORREL (p. 634)

Find relationships in data using COVARIANCE.S and CORREL (p. 631)

Visualize relationships between two variables using a scatter chart (p. 634)

Conduct a regression analysis using the Analysis ToolPak (p. 637)

Use the regression equation to predict values (p. 638)

Use regression analysis to predict future values (p. 637)

Calculate the probability of when a sale will occur using EXPON.DIST (p. 626)

Calculate the probability of drawing the top prize using HYPGEOM.DIST (p. 630)

Calculate the probability of success using BINOMIAL.DIST (p. 624)

Predict the number of orders placed in the next week using POISSON.DIST (p. 628)

Create a correlation matrix using the Analysis ToolPak (p. 635)

Determine relationships between multiple variables using a correlation matrix (p. 635)

Figure 26 The Turquoise Oasis Spa: Using Statistics in Decision Making Final

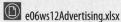

Practice 1

Student data file needed: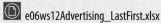
e06ws12Advertising.xlsx

You will save your file as:
e06ws12Advertising_LastFirst.xlsx

Statistical Analysis to Determine Advertising Effectiveness

Sales & Marketing

The Red Bluff Golf Club has started an advertising campaign in an attempt to increase new memberships. They have mailed flyers to a target group of people in the general area. One way to gauge the effectiveness of an advertising campaign is to keep track of new memberships once the flyers have been delivered. You have been asked to conduct some regression analysis on the data to determine if there is a strong relationship between the number of days since the advertising flyers were delivered and the number of new membership sign-ups.

a. Start **Excel**, and then open the **e06ws12Advertising** workbook. Save it as e06ws12Advertising_LastFirst.

b. On the Advertising worksheet tab, click cell **D2**, and then type =COVARIANCE.S(A2:A11,B2:B11) to calculate the covariance between the number of days since the flyer was delivered and the number of new memberships.

c. Click cell **E2**, and then type =CORREL(A2:A11,B2:B11) to calculate the correlation coefficient that describes the type and strength of the relationships between the two variables. Next you create a scatter chart.

d. Select the range **A1:B11**, click the **INSERT** tab, and then in the Charts group, select **Scatter chart**.

e. Reposition the chart to fit within the range **A13:E26**.

f. Click the **Chart Elements** button beside the chart, and then click the **Axis Titles** and **Trendline** check boxes. Modify the chart by adding the following labels:

- Change the Y-Axis Title to read New Memberships.
- Change the X-Axis Title to read Days Since Flyer.
- Change the Chart Title to Advertising Effectiveness.

g. Click outside the chart area, click the **DATA** tab, and then click **Data Analysis**.

h. Select **Regression** from the Data Analysis dialog box, and then click **OK**.

i. Click the **Input Y Range** box, and then select the range **B1:B11**.

j. Click the **Input X Range** box, and then select **A1:A11**.

k. Click the **Labels** check box.

l. Click **Output Range**, click the **Output Range** box, click cell **G1**, and then click **OK**.

m. Adjust the columns as necessary so all the data from the Summary Output can be viewed. Notice that by all measurements, R-square = 0.89, Significance F <0.05, p-value <0.05, the number of days since the advertising flyer was sent out has a strong negative correlation to the number of new memberships. This means that as the days increase since the flyer was sent the rate of new memberships decrease.

n. Click the **Documentation** worksheet. Click cell **A6**, and then type in today's date. Click cell **B6**, and then type in your first and last name. Complete the remainder of the **Documentation** worksheet according to your instructor's direction.

o. Click **Save**, close Excel, and then submit your file as directed by your instructor.

Problem Solve 1

MyITLab®
Grader

Homework 1

Sales & Marketing

Student data file needed:

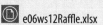 e06ws12Raffle.xlsx

You will save your file as:

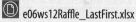 e06ws12Raffle_LastFirst.xlsx

Charity Raffle

A local organization is planning to hold a raffle to raise money for a local animal shelter. Raffle tickets will be sold at various restaurants and businesses in town. The person with the winning raffle ticket will be allowed to choose two out of 15 available mystery bags. Thirteen of the mystery bags contain various gift certificates from local businesses each with a value of $100. Two mystery bags contain gifts that are each valued at $500. You are asked to use the hypergeometric distribution to calculate the probability that the winner will select 0, 1, or 2 grand prize bags. You will also calculate the value of the winnings as well as the expected value.

a. Start **Excel**, and then open the **e06ws12Raffle** workbook. Save it as e06ws12Raffle_LastFirst.

b. On the Raffle worksheet tab, in cell E2, calculate the probability that the raffle winner will select 0 of the grand prize mystery bags using the hypergeometric distribution function. Format the cell as **Percent** with **3** decimal places, and then use the **AutoFill** handle to copy the function to **E4**.

c. In cell **F2**, calculate the estimated costs if the winner selects zero of the $500 mystery bags and two of the $100 mystery bags. Format the cell as **Currency**, and then use the **AutoFill** handle to copy the formula to **F4**.

d. In cell **G2**, calculate the expected value by multiplying the value of the winnings by the probability. Format the cell as **Currency**, and then use the **AutoFill** handle to copy the formula to **G4**.

e. In cell **G5**, calculate the total expected value.

f. Complete the **Documentation** worksheet according to your instructor's direction. Insert the **filename** in the left custom footer section of the Header/Footer tab in the Page Setup dialog box on all worksheets in the workbook.

g. Click Save, close Excel, and then submit the file as directed by your instructor.

Perform 1: Perform in Your Career

Student data file needed:

e06ws12Sales.xlsx

You will save your file as:

e06ws12Sales_LastFirst.xlsx

Analyzing Sales Team's Data

Production & Operations

Buddy's Auto Sales sells new and used cars, trucks, and motorbikes. Throughout the month of September the sales personnel split up into two teams to compete against one another in sales. You have access to each team's daily sales figures throughout the month of September. You have been asked to conduct some statistical analysis on the data.

a. Start **Excel**, and then open the **e06ws12Sales** workbook. Save it as e06ws12Sales_LastFirst.

b. On the Sales worksheet tab, calculate the mean and median value to get an idea of the central tendency of the data.

c. Calculate the standard deviation for each of the team's sales from the sample data, consisting of the September sales.

d. Using the normal distribution function, determine the probability that each sales team will exceed the sales goal of $14,500.

e. Apply appropriate labels and formatting to your calculations so they can be easily read and interpreted.

f. Complete the **Documentation** worksheet according to your instructor's direction. Insert the **filename** in the left custom footer section of the Header/Footer tab in the Page Setup dialog box on all worksheets in the workbook.

g. Click Save, close Excel, and then submit the file as directed by your instructor.

Additional Cases

Additional Workshop Cases are available on the companion website and in the instructor resources.

MODULE CAPSTONE

Student data file needed:

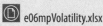 e06mpVolatility.xlsx

You will save your file as:

e06mpVolatility_LastFirst.xlsx

Investment Volatility

Finance &
Accounting

The Painted Paradise Resort and Spa is home to a world-class restaurant, Indigo5, with top chef, Robin Sanchez. Robin is considering some investment options that are expected to increase revenues over the next five years. You have been asked to conduct a net present value analysis on the options and determine the volatility of each investment option using the standard deviation.

a. Start **Excel**, and then open the **e06mpVolatility** workbook from the student data files. Save the file as e06mpVolatility_LastFirst, replacing LastFirst with your actual name.

b. Click the **Investments** worksheet tab, and then complete the following tasks to perform a net present value analysis on Investment Option 1:

- Click cell **B2**, type .051 and then press Enter for the discount rate—the interest rate that can be obtained for a low-risk or risk-free investment. Format the cell as **Percentage** with **2** decimal places.

- Click cell **B3**, type -250000 and then press Enter for the initial investment amount. Format the cell as **Currency** with **0** decimal places.

- Click cell **B7**, type =B3 and press Enter for the expected cash flow of year 0 for the investment.

- Click cell **B14**, type =NPV(B2,B8:B12)+B7 and then press Enter to calculate the net present value of the expected future cash flows from Investment Option 1. Increase the number of decimals to **2**.

c. Complete the following tasks to perform a net present value analysis on Investment Option 2.

- Click cell **E2**, type .051 and then press Enter as the discount rate—the interest rate that can be obtained for a low-risk or risk-free investment. Format the cell as **Percentage** with **2** decimal places.

- Click cell **E3**, type -250000 and then press Enter for the initial investment amount. Format the cell as **Currency** with **0** decimal places.

- Click cell **E7**, type =E3 and then press Enter for the expected cash flow of year 0 for the investment.

- Click cell **E14**, type =NPV(E2,E8:E12)+E7 and press Enter to calculate the net present value of the expected future cash flows from Investment Option 2. Increase the number of decimals to **2**.

    Notice that Investment Option 1 has the higher NPV and appears to be the better investment option. However, volatility also matters when selecting investment options, and Robin Sanchez needs to be able to rely on a steady stream of revenues to be able to operate the restaurant.

d. Complete the following tasks to measure the volatility of each investment.

- Click cell **B15**, type =STDEV.P(B8:B12) and then press Enter to determine the volatility of Investment Option 1 by calculating the standard deviation of all future cash flows. Format the cell as **Comma Style** with **2** decimal places.

- Click cell **E15**, type =STDEV.P(E8:E12) and then press ⌷Enter⌷ to determine the volatility of Investment Option 2 by calculating the standard deviation of all future cash flows. Format the cell as **Comma Style** with **2** decimal places.

  Notice that Investment Option 2 has a much lower volatility with much more consistent expected cash flows, which better suits the needs of Robin Sanchez.

e. Format the page layout to the orientation that works best for each worksheet.

f. Click the **Documentation** worksheet. Click cell **A6**, and then type in today's date. Click cell **B6**, and then type in your first and last name. Complete the remainder of the **Documentation** worksheet according to your instructor's direction.

g. Click **Save**, close Excel, and then submit your file as directed by your instructor.

Problem Solve 1

MyITLab®
Grader
Homework 1

Sales & Marketing

Finance & Accounting

Student data file needed:

e06ps1Rooms.xlsx

You will save your file as:

e06ps1Rooms_LastFirst.xlsx

Hotel Room and Loan Analysis

The hotel is planning for next year and would like to know the probability that they will exceed their room reservation goals for each room type. They have provided you with the mean number of reservations for each room type along with the standard deviations for 2013 and 2014. You will calculate the probability of exceeding each room type's goal using the normal distribution function. The hotel has also secured a loan for some room renovations, and your help is needed to conduct some analysis on the loan.

a. Start **Excel**, and then open the **e06ps1Rooms** workbook from the student data files. Save the file as e06ps1Rooms_LastFirst using your last and first name.

b. On the RoomAnalysis worksheet, click cell **G4**, and then use the NORM.DIST function to calculate the probability that room reservations for the One Double room type will exceed 3,400 in 2015. Format the cell as **Percentage** with **2** decimal places.

c. Use the **AutoFill** handle to copy the function to **G9**.

d. Click the **LoanAnalysis** worksheet tab.

e. Click cell **B5**, and then use the PMT function to calculate the quarterly payment of the loan. Each payment is to be made at the beginning of the period. Be sure that the function returns a positive value.

f. Click cell **B7**, and then use the CUMIPMT function to calculate the total cumulative interest that will be paid over the life of the loan when payments are made at the beginning of each period. Format the cell as **Currency**.

g. Click cell **B8**, and then calculate the total cost of the loan by adding the loan amount to the total interest paid.

h. Create an amortization schedule for the loan in cells **E3:I30** using the PPMT and IPMT functions, along with other necessary formulas. All payments are beginning of the period payments. Be sure that all formulas and functions return a positive value.

i. Format the page layout to the orientation that works best for each worksheet.

j. Complete the **Documentation** worksheet according to your instructor's direction. Insert the **filename** in the left custom footer section of the Header/Footer tab in the Page Setup dialog box on all worksheets in the workbook.

k. Click Save, close Excel, and then submit the file as directed by your instructor.

Homework 2

Sales &
Marketing

Student data file needed:

e06ps2Suites.xlsx

You will save your file as:

e06ps2Suites_LastFirst.xlsx

Grand Villa Suites

There have been some recent improvements made to the Grand Villa Suites at the hotel, and managers are looking to increase the number of reservations. You have been asked to conduct some analysis on the number of Grand Villa Suite reservations made over the last year to determine the central tendency of the data. You will also calculate the probability that the current phone campaign underway will result in successful bookings of a Grand Villa Suite room.

a. Start **Excel**, and then open the **e06ps2Suites** workbook from the student data files. Save the file as e06ps2Suites_LastFirst using your last and first name.

b. If necessary, install the Analysis ToolPak as explained in Workshop 12.

c. On the SuitesAnalysis worksheet, in cells **F2:F8**, type 105 through 165 in increments of 10 for the bin values.

d. Use the Analysis ToolPak to create a Histogram showing the distribution of the number of Grand Villa Suite reservations. Use **D1** as the Output Range, and be sure to include a Chart Output. Adjust the column widths as necessary so that all data can be seen.

e. Edit the histogram chart title to be Suite Distribution and delete the chart legend.

f. Move the histogram chart so that it fits inside the range **F1:K10**.

g. Use the Analysis ToolPak to create descriptive statistics on the number of Grand Villa Suite room reservations.
    - Include the Grand Villa Suite Reservations label in your Input Range, and click the **Labels in first row** check box.
    - Use **D13** as the Output Range.
    - Be sure to include Summary statistics.
    - Adjust the column widths so that all data are visible.

h. Click the **PhoneCampaign** worksheet tab.

i. Click cell **B6**, and then calculate the probability that 0 successful reservations will occur with 30 phone calls using the BINOM.DIST function. Format the cell as **Percentage** with **2** decimal places, and then use the **AutoFill** handle to copy the function to **B36**.

j. Format the page layout to the orientation that works best for each worksheet.

k. Complete the **Documentation** worksheet according to your instructor's direction. Insert the **filename** in the left custom footer section of the Header/Footer tab in the Page Setup dialog box on all worksheets in the workbook.

l. Click Save, close Excel, and then submit the file as directed by your instructor.

Student data file needed:

 Blank Excel workbook

You will save your file as:

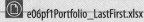 e06pf1Portfolio_LastFirst.xlsx

Personal Investment Analysis

Finance & Accounting

Financial decisions are a part of our lives and knowing how to properly analyze investment options is crucial to making good investment decisions. In this exercise, you will analyze two different investment options.

a. Start **Excel**, create a new blank workbook, and then save it as e06pf1Portfolio_LastFirst.

b. Rename the Sheet1 worksheet to Option1.

c. Set up the worksheet to be able to calculate the irregular net present value of an investment by using the following information.
   - Initial investment amount: $7,500.00
   - Discount rate of 3.5%
   - Expected incoming cash flows are to occur on the following dates:

Dates	Cash Flows
1/1/2015	-$7,500.00
2/15/2015	$1,750.00
4/15/2015	$1,500.00
8/20/2015	$2,350.00
10/20/2015	$1,900.00
12/20/2015	$850.00

   - Format all cash flow values as **Currency** with **2** decimal places.

d. Add a new worksheet to the right of Option1, and then name it Option2.

e. Set up the worksheet to calculate the present value of an investment bond using the following information.
   - Par Value: $7,500.00
   - Coupon Rate: 7%
   - Maturity: 3 years
   - YTM: 5.2%

f. Calculate the annual coupon payment.

g. Calculate the present value of the bond. Be sure the function returns a positive value.

h. Format all cells with appropriate formatting.

i. Add a new worksheet to the right of Option2 and name it Option3.

j. Set up the worksheet to calculate the internal rate of return of an investment using the following expected future cash flows.

Year	Cash Flow
0	-$7,500.00
1	$4,950.00
2	$2,450.00
3	$1,750.00

k. Calculate the internal rate of return based on the series of expected cash flows.

l. Format the page layout to the orientation that works best for each worksheet.

m. Insert the **filename** in the left custom footer section of the Header/Footer tab in the Page Setup dialog box on all worksheets in the workbook.

n. Click Save, close Excel, and then submit the file as directed by your instructor.

Perform 2: Perform in Your Career

Student data file needed:
 e06pf2Predictions.xlsx

You will save your file as:
e06pf2Predictions_LastFirst.xlsx

Predicting Outcomes in Business

Production & Operations

As a business analyst for a small technology manufacturing company, you have been asked to conduct a regression analysis to determine the relationships between several independent variables on costs.

a. Start **Excel**, and then open **e06pf2Predictions**. Save it as e06pf2Predictions_LastFirst, and then insert the file name in the left section of the footer on the Documentation worksheet.

b. On the **CostsModel** worksheet, conduct a multiple regression analysis using costs as the dependent variable and the number of products produced as the independent variables. Click the **Labels** check box. Place the **Summary Output** in cell **H1**, and then adjust the column widths as necessary.

c. Add a column header to the right of **Product 3** to read Costs Estimate. Create the regression equation to estimate the costs for each of the months and format as **Currency**.

d. On the **MaterialsRequests** worksheet, set the worksheet up to predict the next three week's request amounts by doing the following.
   - Calculate the mean value of requests made.
   - Create a column of possible requests values ranging from 640 to 800 in increments of 10, and then add a column label of Requests (x).
   - To the left of the **Requests (x)** column, use the Poisson distribution function to calculate the probability of getting up to 640 requests, and then copy the formula down. Add a column label of Probability.

e. Create a column with three random variables using the RAND function. Copy and Paste Values so that the values produced by the RAND function remain static, and then add a column label of Random.

f. To the right of the random variables, use a VLOOKUP function to predict the number of requests that will take place each week for the next three weeks. Add a column label of Estimated Requests and adjust the column widths as necessary.

g. Format the page layout to the orientation that works best for each worksheet.

h. Complete the **Documentation** worksheet according to your instructor's direction. Insert the **filename** in the left custom footer section of the Header/Footer tab in the Page Setup dialog box on all worksheets in the workbook.

i. Click Save, close Excel, and then submit the file as directed by your instructor.

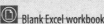
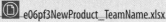
Student data file needed:

 Blank Excel workbook

You will save your file as:

e06pf3NewProduct_TeamName.xlsx

New Product Investment

Finance & Accounting

In this exercise, you will collaborate with a team of three to five students to conduct some statistical analysis on a potential new product investment opportunity. You will use the normal probability distribution to analyze the possible rates of return. You will also use the binomial probability distribution to analyze the number of successful trials one can expect from the product.

a. Select one team member to set up the document by completing Steps b–e.

b. Point your browser to either **https://www.skydrive.live.com**, **https://www.drive.google.com**, or any other instructor-assigned tool. Be sure all members of the team have an account on the chosen system—a Microsoft or Google account.

c. Create a new spreadsheet document, name it e06pf3NewProduct_TeamName using the name assigned to your team.

d. Rename Sheet1 as Contributors. List the names of each of the team members on the worksheet, and then add a heading above the name to read Team Members. Include any additional information on this worksheet as required by your instructor.

e. Share the spreadsheet with the other members of your team. Make sure that each team member has the appropriate permission to edit the document.

f. Create a new worksheet entitled Product Investment. Set up the worksheet to create a normal probability distribution table using the following information.

- Mean rate of return is 12.8%.
- Standard deviation of the rate of return is +/- 3.85%.
- Create column headings for Standard Deviations, ROR, and Probability.
- Under the Standard Deviations heading, create a column of values ranging from 4 to –4 in increments of 0.1.
- Under the ROR heading, calculate the value of ROR if it were to be four standard deviations from the mean, and then use **AutoFill** to copy the formula down the column.
- Under the **Probability** heading, calculate the probability that the ROR is exactly four standard deviations from the mean, and then use **AutoFill** to copy the function down the column.

g. Create a scatter chart with Smooth Lines if using SkyDrive or a regular scatter chart if using GoogleDrive to visualize the normal distribution.

- Give the chart a title of ROR Distribution.
- Adjust the horizontal axis to have a minimum value of -10% and a maximum value of 30%.
- Remove the Legend, and then position the chart near the top of your probability distribution table.

h. Create a new worksheet entitled Product Testing. The manufacturers of the new product claim that the product's battery will last for 12 hours, 90% of the time. Set up the worksheet to calculate the probability of successful trials based on the following information.

- Number of Trials: 130
- Success Rate: 85%

- Calculate the probability of exactly 90 successful trials.
- Calculate the probability of no more than 100 successful trials.
- Calculate the probability of more than 110 successful trials.

i. Insert the **filename** in the left custom footer section of the Header/Footer tab in the Page Setup dialog box on all worksheets in the workbook. In a custom header section, include the **names** of the students in your team—spread the names evenly across each of the three header sections: left section, center section, and right section.

j. Save your work, and then close Excel. Submit the file as directed by your instructor.

Perform 4: How Others Perform

Student data file needed:

 e06pf4Decisions.xlsx

You will save your file as:

e06pf4Decisions_LastFirst.xlsx

Analysis to Support Decision Making

Sales & Marketing

Finance & Accounting

Robert Smith, owner of a small but growing clothing store, is looking for ways to fund an expansion. He had an intern attempt to conduct some analysis on a possible loan and other investments, but Robert suspects the analysis is not accurate and does not want to make any decisions until he is sure he can trust the analysis. The intern also attempted to conduct some statistical analysis on his business. Examine the worksheet, and correct any mistakes in the formulas and functions.

a. Start **Excel**, and then open **e06pf4Decisions**. Save your file as e06pf4Decisions_LastFirst.

b. On the **LoanAnalysis** worksheet you will find a number of visible errors in the loan analysis conducted by an intern.

- Click cell **B6**. The RATE function is returning a #NUM! error message instead of the APR. Correct the formula, and then make sure it returns the correct APR according to the loan information in the cells above. Each loan payment is to be made at the beginning of the period.
- Examine the principal and interest payment formulas in cells C11:D11. The sum of those two calculations does not equal the monthly payment in cell B2. Correct both formulas so they equal the monthly payment, and then use **AutoFill** to copy the formulas down to the end of the amortization schedule.

c. Click the **Investments** worksheet tab. On this worksheet, you will find errors in various formulas and functions causing the investment analysis to lead to bad decisions.

- Click cell **B5**, and examine the formula that is calculating the coupon payment. Make the necessary correction so the coupon payment is calculated correctly.
- Click cell **B7**, and then examine the PV function for errors. Make the necessary corrections.
- Click cell **E13**, and then examine the NPV function for errors. Make the necessary corrections.

d. Click the **Stats** worksheet tab. On this worksheet you will find errors in various statistical functions.

- Click cell **B7**. This function should calculate the probability of earning no more than $13,000 in sales revenue. Examine the function, and then make the appropriate changes.
- Click cell **B8**. This function should calculate the probability of earning more than $12,500 in sales revenue. Examine the function, and then make the appropriate changes.

- Click cell **D6**. This function should calculate the probability of the next customer entering the store within the next five minutes. Examine the function, and then make the appropriate changes. Use **AutoFill** to copy the function down to cell **D17**.

- Click cell **L3**. The function in L3:L9 should calculate the frequency of values based on the data in I3:I17 and the bins in K3:K8. Examine the functions, and then make the appropriate changes.

e. Print or submit your file as directed by your instructor, and then close Excel.

WORKSHOP 13 | DATA MODEL, POWERPIVOT, AND POWER VIEW

OBJECTIVES

1. Understand the basics of dashboard design   p. 654

2. Explore the new data model   p. 658

3. Create advanced data models using PowerPivot   p. 663

4. Create PivotTables and PivotCharts with PowerPivot   p. 676

5. Use Apps for Office for data visualizations   p. 690

6. Prepare a dashboard for production   p. 693

7. Generate visual reports with Power View   p. 696

Prepare Case

The Red Bluff Golf Course & Pro Shop Dashboards, KPIs, and Data Visualizations

Sales & Marketing

Management at the Red Bluff Golf Course & Pro Shop have been collecting data on their business for the past three years. They are looking for ways to create visualizations of their data in order to help make important strategic decisions regarding the future of the company as well as to solicit private investments in Red Bluff. You have been given access to a sample set of sales data from 2012–2014 and have been asked to conduct further analysis, create some useful visualizations of the data, and put together a dashboard of charts and tools for management to easily see the business from multiple perspectives. You will use some new features in Excel 2013 that are scalable for use with millions of records.

bikeriderlondon / Shutterstock

REAL WORLD SUCCESS

"In the summer of 2013 I worked as a consultant for a small clothing store in the Midwest. Management there was just starting to realize the benefits of making data-driven decisions. They used Excel for various accounting tasks but never really thought of it as a way to analyze large amounts of data. I was able to use the PowerPivot feature in Excel 2013 to build a data model that allowed for easy analysis of millions of records from multiple sources and create a simple dashboard to track various metrics. As a result that company is making progress toward its goal of expanding its store locations."

- Lupé, recent graduate

Student data files needed for this workshop:

 e07ws13Sales.accdb    e07ws13Analytics.xlsx

You will save your file as:

 e07ws13Analytics_LastFirst.xlsx

Exploring the Importance of Business Intelligence

Business intelligence is more than just a buzzword. **Business intelligence (BI)** refers to a variety of software applications that are used to analyze an organization's data in order to provide management with the tools necessary to improve decision making, cut costs, and identify new opportunities. The role of BI has increased over the last decade because the amount of data being collected by businesses continues to grow at a rapid rate.

This increasing dependence on BI has manifested itself in many forms in the business community over the past few years. The most recent trend, which shows no signs of slowing, is the desire for digital dashboards. **Digital dashboards** are mechanisms that deliver business intelligence in graphical form. Dashboards provide management with a "big picture" view of the business, usually from multiple perspectives using various charts and other graphical representations. There are many factors that are driving businesses to use the power of dashboards. Figure 1 shows the top pressures that are driving these dashboard initiatives according to Aberdeen Group, Inc., a provider of research helping organizations and individuals make better business decisions. In this section you will learn about the dashboard design concepts, explore Excel's data model, conduct some analysis, and build a dashboard.

BUSINESS DRIVERS FOR DASHBOARD INITIATIVES	
Alignment of strategy and activities	27%
Improved timeliness and accuracy of business decisions	30%
The need for one view of the business date	33%
The need for data-driven decisions	37%
The need to gain visibility into key business processes	43%

Source: Aberdeen Group, 2009

Figure 1   Top pressures driving dashboard initiatives

CONSIDER THIS | **Decisions, Decisions, Decisions...**

A typical manager engages in over 300 different tasks and decisions each day. These often involve interacting with many different people, using a variety of different channels and technologies. The number of channels and technologies a manager must master is growing. Do you think technology increases, decreases, or holds neutral the volume and speed of decision making today?

Understand the Basics of Dashboard Design

Dashboards are becoming more and more important today as a tool for helping managers run their businesses. They are no longer just for executives and are being integrated at all levels of the business and in many different industries. You will likely encounter them in other classes as you discuss management techniques such as Balanced Scorecards and Six Sigma. Both of these management initiatives involve generating key performance indicators and dashboard reports for all levels of the organization. Using dashboards, everyone from the CEO to the delivery truck driver can have a personalized view of information to quickly and easily see how well they are performing.

How a dashboard is designed has just as much of an impact on its effectiveness as the data displayed. Think of the dashboard in a car. The gauges and layout of the dashboard are designed to help the driver make better decisions and interpret important things like relative speed, gas consumption, and critical malfunctions in a very immediate and effective way. The driver of the car has to monitor the situation constantly and make crucial decisions about what to do with the car. An effective dashboard supports effective decision making.

This analogy holds true for the "driver" of a company as well. A manager must be able to quickly review and monitor the current health of the company and make decisions in a timely manner to correct problems. A dashboard can be a huge help to a manager, because it is specifically organized to provide alerts and monitor the business as a whole. Typically, dashboards are also oriented around specific business activities, such as sales analysis, cash flow, employee productivity, and customer service. Some typical features of a dashboard might include the following:

- A single-screen, visually oriented user interface that is intuitive and easy to navigate
- Interactive controls that allow the user to customize the data display
- Integration of multiple types of data from a variety of sources
- Data that is frequently updated so it reflects the current situation
- Information oriented around a specific problem or decision
- A layout that does not require a lot of extra training to use effectively

Dashboard components typically consist of tables, PivotTables, PivotCharts, conditional formatting, and other features available in Excel. There are also some basic design concepts that you need to take into consideration when creating a dashboard.

Keeping It Simple

Adding more and more data and charts is tempting. However, you must always keep in mind the basic principle: When it comes to dashboards, less is more. If users cannot easily interpret your dashboard, then you may have made it too complicated. An overly complicated dashboard is not usable as a management tool. Remember, one of the primary goals is to help the user navigate and interpret a large quantity of data at a glance.

Making Sure It Is Well Defined

Stay focused on a specific business problem. A company can track product sales, employee productivity, customer complaints, revenue, portfolio value, machine defects, and so on. However, doing all of these in the same dashboard is ill advised. As a general rule, the more defined you can make your dashboard theme, the more useful your users will find it.

Knowing Your Users

Not all users are alike. They can have different decision-making styles. You can increase the success of your dashboard by taking personal preferences into account whenever possible. You should interview the main users of the dashboard to see what they would find most useful. The earlier you can let them see your dashboard design, the fewer headaches you will have later in the project. Changes are easier to make early in development rather than when you are almost done.

Defining Crucial KPIs

A **key performance indicator (KPI)** is a quantifiable measure that helps managers define progress toward both short-term and long-term goals. Some KPIs are year-to-date (YTD) sales growth, customer satisfaction, call resolution rates, and percent of market share as shown in the table that follows. In fact, every functional area of business has its own set of commonly used KPIs. Often, many firms in the same industry will all focus on similar KPIs because they are so critical to the nature of their business—for example, profit margin.

Business Area	KPI
Accounting	• Gross profit • Operating margin • Cumulative annual growth rate • ROI (Return on investment) • Cost of goods sold
Finance/Accounting	• Gross yield • Price-to-earnings ratio (P/E) • Earnings before interest, taxes, depreciation, and amortization (EBITDA) • Earnings per share (EPS) • Budget ratio
Marketing/Sales	• Market share by segment • Customer churn rate (rate of growth or decline of customers) • Customer lifetime value • Cost per lead • Productivity by channel
Personnel	• Productivity ratios • Turnover rates • % overtime • Employee satisfaction rates • % absenteeism
Operations	• Out of stock % • Defect rate • Production cycle time • On-time delivery • % downtime
Customer Service	• Customer satisfaction • First call resolution rate • Average wait time • % of dropped calls • Time per call
IT	• Access speed • Site click-through • System availability • Service satisfaction levels • Project success rates

Using Strategic Placement

Successful dashboards should help summarize complex data so users can interpret the information at a glance. The dashboard needs to make it as easy as possible for users to read and understand the data. The layout of the dashboard can have a big impact on its usability. Figure 2 illustrates the particular regions of a screen that a user's eyes tend to pay attention to based on research conducted by the Poynter Institute.

1	1	2	3
1	1	2	2
2	2	2	3
3	3	3	3

Figure 2 Design layout priority zones

Regions with the number 1 appear to have prominence over the other regions. This means that eyes tend to spend more time in that part of the screen than in others. This research can be useful in strategically placing components of a dashboard to maximize its effectiveness.

Designing with White Space

Empty space on the screen that gives eyes a place to rest is called white space. **White space** helps keep a design simple, accessible, and visually pleasing to users. It is not necessarily white, just void of content. There is no rule for how much white space to include in your design. Generally speaking, you should include more white space than you initially think is necessary. However, including too much white space may mean you are wasting valuable real estate. Including the right amount of white space can give an elegant feel to your dashboard and make it easier for the user to read.

Opening the Starting File

You will use various tools, some of which are brand new to Excel 2013, to create data visualizations using apps, create and modify a data model in Excel using PowerPivot, conduct some analysis, and create a dashboard using Excel's Power View.

E13.00

 To Open the e07ws13Analytics Workbook

a. Start **Excel**, and then open the **e07ws13Analytics** workbook from the student data files.

b. Click the **FILE** tab, click **Save As**, and then save the file in the folder or location designated by your instructor with the name e07ws13Analytics_LastFirst, using your last and first name.

There are several commercially available products that exist with the aim of making it easy to create complex dashboards:

- Cognos
- Hyperion
- Dundas
- Corda
- SQL Server Analysis Services
- Oracle Business Intelligence

While these programs may be powerful and effective, they all suffer from two significant drawbacks. First, they require a software purchase; although some tools are nominally "free," the free or trial versions may be limited in functionality and/or may not be legal to use for your company. Second, off-the-shelf software nearly always requires that its users have that particular software installed on their computers.

There are many benefits to using Microsoft Excel to create digital dashboards:

- Minimal costs: Not every business is a multibillion-dollar business that can afford to purchase top-of-the-line BI software. Leveraging the capabilities of Microsoft Excel is a very cost-effective solution without compromising too much on usability and functionality.

- Broad familiarity: From the entry-level sales representative to the CEO, familiarity with Excel is widespread. People will spend less time learning how to use the dashboard and more time getting value from what is displayed.

- Flexibility: With the appropriate know-how, Excel can be much more flexible in the variety of analytics it can provide in a dashboard than many off-the-shelf solutions. Such features as PivotTables, AutoFilters, Form controls, and Power View allow you to create mechanisms that provide the audience multiple perspectives of the data.

- Rapid development: Having the capability of creating your own reporting mechanisms in Excel can reduce your reliance on the IT department's resources. With Excel, not only can you develop reporting mechanisms faster, but you can also have the flexibility to adapt more quickly to changing requirements.

REAL WORLD ADVICE | **Dashboard Design and the SDLC**

Creating dashboards requires far more preparation than a standard Excel model. It requires closer communication with business leaders, stricter data modeling techniques, and following certain best practices. The systems development life cycle (SDLC) provides a structure for managing complex IT projects. One of the SDLC models is broken into six stages: analyze, design, develop, implement, test, and maintain. Following this SDLC model can provide the necessary guidance to creating an effective dashboard.

Explore the New Data Model

There are many different types of models that you can create using Excel. For example, a financial model can be useful in evaluating loans or investments, a statistical model can be useful in predicting demand of a particular product, and a Solver model can be used to determine the optimal number of workers to hire in order to maximize profits. New to Excel 2013 is the ability to create a data model. A **data model** is a collection of tables and their relationships reflecting the real-world relationships between business functions and processes—for example, how products relate to inventory and sales or how customers relate to revenues and sales volume. This new feature allows for your analysis to integrate data from multiple tables, effectively creating a relational data source inside Excel.

Relational data is a topic traditionally reserved for databases like Microsoft Access; however, with this new functionality in Excel you need to have a basic understanding of relational data. **Relational data** are data about a particular person, place, or event that are stored in multiple tables. For example, the employee data are stored in an employee table and the product data that the company sells are stored in a products table. These two tables are related through the transactions that take place when the employee sells the product. Most organizations store their data in a relational database in order to ensure their data are secure, accurate, and consistent. Prior to Excel 2013, it would be very complicated and time consuming to integrate relational data into an analysis.

Data can be added to the data model from a variety of sources. Data from two or more tables imported from an external data source such as an Access database or SQL Server are automatically added to the data model. Data in a text file, in a range of cells, organized into tables, or in a SharePoint list, can also be added to the data model using the PowerPivot COM Add-In.

Building a Data Model Using an Access Database

Many organizations store data inside a relational database such as MySQL, Oracle, or a DBMS like Microsoft Access. Earlier versions of Excel have allowed for data connections from external sources, but new in Excel 2013 is the ability for Excel to maintain the relationships between multiple tables. The e07ws13Sales database contains some sample sales data from Red Bluff Golf Course & Pro Shop that will form the foundation of your analysis. In this exercise you will connect to the database and import all the tables into your workbook.

E13.01

 To Create a Data Connection to an Access Database

a. Click the **DATA** tab, and then in the Get External Data group, click **From Access**.

b. Browse to your student data files, select **e07ws13Sales**, and then click **Open**.

c. In the Select Table dialog box, click **Enable selection of multiple tables**.

d. Click the **Name** check box to select all the tables in the database, and then click **OK**.

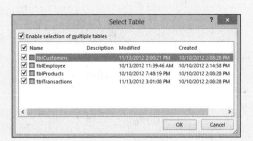

Figure 3   Select Table dialog box

In the Import Data dialog box, click **Only Create Connection**. Notice the **Add this data to the Data Model** check box is selected by default.

e. Click **OK**.

Figure 4   Import Data dialog box

f. Click **Save** 🖫.

Exploring the PowerPivot Window

Now that you have imported relational data into the Excel workbook a data model now exists. As stated previously, this makes it easy to integrate data from multiple tables in your analysis. To view and edit the data model, you must install the PowerPivot COM Add-In. PowerPivot is also available for Excel 2010 but must be downloaded from an external source. Because in Excel 2013 it is part of the Excel COM Add-In, PowerPivot can be added natively and no longer requires an external download. In this exercise, you will install the PowerPivot COM Add-In to view the data model that you created in the previous exercise.

E13.02

To Install the PowerPivot COM Add-In

a. Click the **FILE** tab.

b. Click **Options**, and then click **Add-Ins**.

c. At the bottom of the Excel Options dialog box, select **COM Add-ins** in the **Manage** dropdown box, and then click **Go**.

d. Select the **Microsoft Office PowerPivot for Excel 2013** check box, and then click **OK**.

e. Notice the POWERPIVOT tab that has been added to the Ribbon.

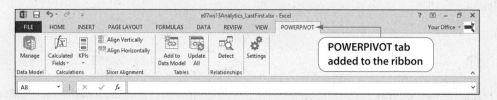

Figure 5   PowerPivot COM Add-In installed

f. Click **Save** 🔲.

Now that you have installed the PowerPivot COM Add-in, you can now explore the PowerPivot window.

E13.03

To Explore the PowerPivot Window

a. Click the **POWERPIVOT** tab on the Ribbon.

b. In the Data Model group, click **Manage** to open the PowerPivot window. If necessary, maximize the PowerPivot window.

   Notice a PowerPivot window opens separately from the workbook. The default view of the data model resembles a traditional Excel workbook with each table appearing on a separate worksheet. The Excel workbook remains open in the background and can easily be viewed by closing the PowerPivot window.

c. The Home tab is where you can perform a variety of tasks including add new data from a variety of data sources; refresh your data model to sync with changes made in the source data; create PivotTables and PivotCharts; format, sort, and filter data; create simple calculations and KPIs; and change views.

Options for additional external data sources

Refresh changes made to the data source

Create PivotTables and PivotCharts from the data model

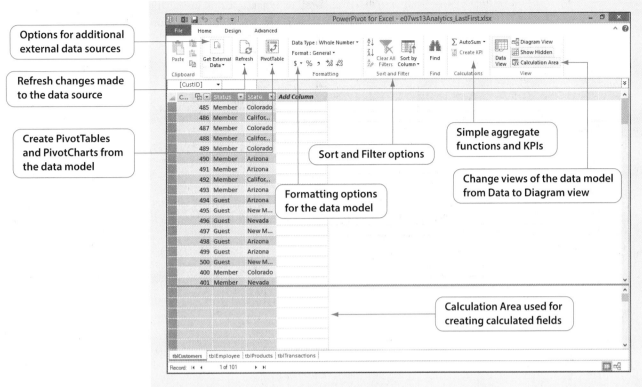

Simple aggregate functions and KPIs

Sort and Filter options

Change views of the data model from Data to Diagram view

Formatting options for the data model

Calculation Area used for creating calculated fields

Figure 6 PowerPivot window Home tab

d. Click the **Design** tab.

The Design tab is where you can modify table properties, create more complex calculated fields, create and edit relationships between worksheets, and more.

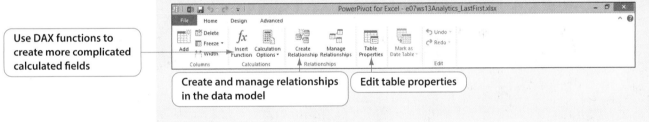

Use DAX functions to create more complicated calculated fields

Create and manage relationships in the data model

Edit table properties

Figure 7 PowerPivot window Design tab

e. Click the **Advanced** tab.

The Advanced tab includes options that go beyond the scope of this book but include changing and managing different data perspectives for a particular user group or business scenario and allowing for easier navigation of very large data sets.

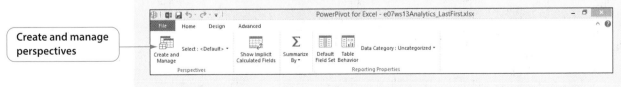

Create and manage perspectives

Figure 8 PowerPivot window Advanced tab

Now that you have an idea of what options are available on each of the tabs on the Ribbon of the PowerPivot window, you will now switch views to see any existing relationships in the data from the database file.

E13.04

 To View Relationships in PowerPivot

a. Click the Home tab.

b. In the View group, click **Diagram View** to see the current relationships in the data model.

c. If necessary, to view all relationships, click **Fit to Screen** ⊞ on the zoom bar. The relationships that are already established were imported from the Access database when the data connection was made.

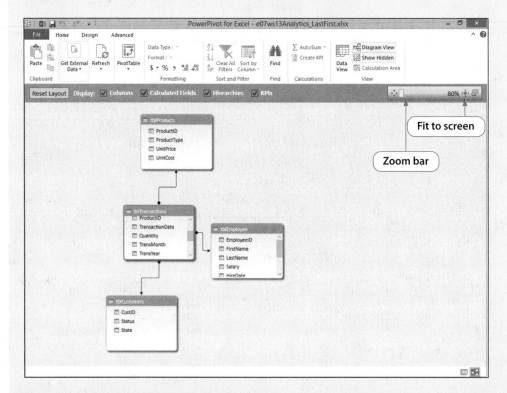

Figure 9   PowerPivot window Diagram view

d. Click **Data View** to switch back to viewing all the data in the data model.
   Click **Save** 🖫. Notice the PowerPivot window minimizes automatically when you click Save and returns you to the workbook.

Adding a Table to the Data Model

Comprehensive data analysis often requires data from different sources. A human resources database may keep track of employees who have attended a required training session, or a separate sales database may keep track of online sales and in-person sales. Often, additional data may need to be incorporated into the data model to make it easier to conduct certain analyses. For example, when month names are part of the data model and used in various analyses the months are automatically sorted in alphabetical order by month name instead of the natural order of how the months occur throughout the year. On the MonthSort worksheet in the e07ws13Analytics workbook, there is an Excel table that has a Month column and an Order column that includes the order sequence that each month occurs. In this exercise you will add this table to the data model and establish a relationship to tblTransactions to be used in future analyses.

 To Add an Excel Table to the Data Model

a. Click the **MonthSort** worksheet tab.

b. Click anywhere in the Excel table.

c. Click the **POWERPIVOT** tab, and in the Tables group click **Add to Data Model**.
   The PowerPivot window opens, and you see the data from the MonthSort table added to a worksheet labeled MonthSort.

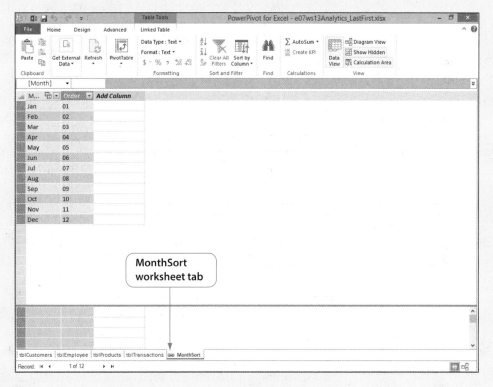

Figure 10   MonthSort added to the data model

d. Click **Save** 🖫.

Create Advanced Data Models Using PowerPivot

PowerPivot and Excel 2013 not only give you the ability to conduct analyses on data from multiple sources, but you can also do more advanced data modeling in PowerPivot. PowerPivot allows you to create calculated columns, calculated fields, and establish KPIs all within Excel, which can then be used in PivotTables, PivotCharts, and other analysis tools. The data provided to you in the e07ws13Sales database did not include

Exploring the Importance of Business Intelligence   663

all the necessary data needed for the various analyses. Management at the Red Bluff Golf Course & Pro Shop would like for you to create additional columns that calculate the revenue, costs, and profit earned from each transaction as well as calculated fields that calculate the total profit earned. You will then use those calculations to create KPIs that will measure each employee's effectiveness in terms of meeting monthly and yearly profit goals.

REAL WORLD ADVICE	Connecting to Large Data Sets Using the Microsoft Azure Marketplace

The Microsoft Azure Marketplace is a cloud computing platform offering a variety of features and services to individuals and businesses. One of the many services it provides is access to very large data sets for use in analysis. There are several data sets available for free, and they can be accessed in the PowerPivot window. Click the HOME tab, in the Get External Data group, click From Data Service, and then click From Windows Azure Marketplace. There are a variety of categories based on type of data and price. Having access to large data sets allows you to explore all the analysis tools available in Excel 2013.

Creating Relationships in the Data Model

When data is imported from a relational database only the data that has predefined relationships in the database are imported into the data model. In a business, data can come from multiple sources. For example, a company may keep important information about employee training programs in a separate human resources database. If that data were needed for analysis it could be imported into the data model, and a relationship could be established to the tblEmployee table.

You added data from the MonthSort table to the data model and, as of now, these data have no relationship with any of the other tables in the data model. In this exercise you will create a relationship between the MonthSort table and the tblTransactions table.

E13.06

 To Create Relationships in the Data Model

a. Click the POWERPIVOT tab, and then in the Data Model group, click **Manage**. In the PowerPivot window, click the **tblTransactions** worksheet tab.

b. Click the **TransMonth** column heading to select the column.

c. Click the **Design** tab, and then in the Relationships group, click **Create Relationship**.

d. Confirm that **tblTransactions** is selected in the first Table list and **TransMonth** is selected in the Column list.

e. Select **MonthSort** from the Related Lookup Table list, and then select **Month** from the Related Lookup Column list.

SIDE NOTE
Creating Relationships
Alternatively you can create relationships between objects in Diagram view by dragging fields from one object to another.

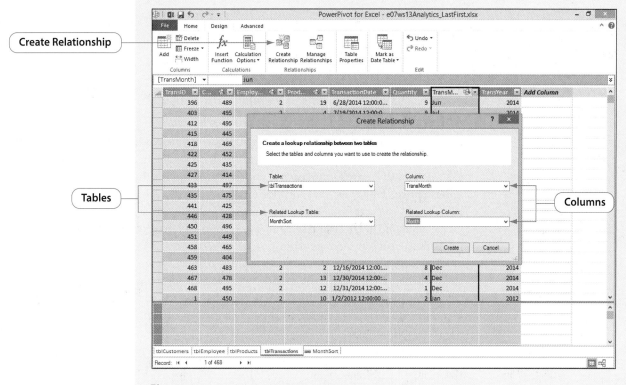

Figure 11 Create Relationship dialog box

f. Click **Create**.

g. Click the **Home** tab, and then in the View group, click **Diagram View** to see the new relationship. Click **Reset Layout**, and then in the Confirm dialog box, click **Reset Layout** again to see all relationships in the data model.

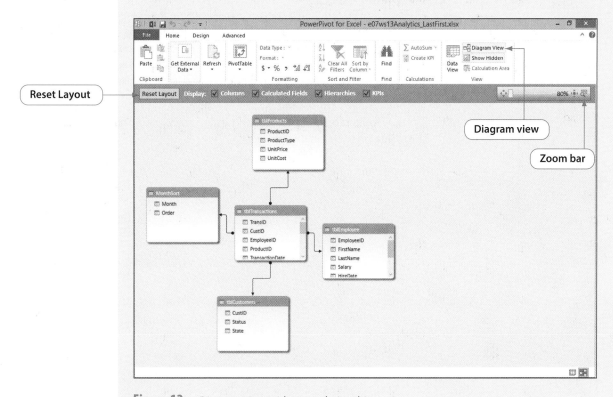

Figure 12 Diagram view with new relationships

h. On the Home tab, in the View group, click **Data View** to return to the Data view of the PowerPivot window.

i. Click **Save** 🖫.

Adding Calculated Columns in PowerPivot

A calculated column is created inside the PowerPivot window and is based on data that are already a part of the data model. The data imported from the Access database included the quantity of items sold in each transaction along with the cost of the product and the selling price. However, these values exist in different tables. Management at the Red Bluff Golf Course & Pro Shop would like for you to include revenue, costs, and profit in future analyses. In this exercise you will create calculated columns for revenue, costs, and profit in the tblTransactions table.

You will also create a calculated column that will concatenate the Order field from the MonthSort table with the month when each transaction took place. The purpose of this calculated column is so that you will be able to sort the months in their order of occurrence instead of alphabetically.

E13.07

 To Create a Calculated Column

a. Click the **POWERPIVOT** tab, and then in the Data Model group, click **Manage**.

b. On the tblTransactions worksheet tab, double-click the **Add Column** column heading, type Revenue as the new column heading, and then press Enter.

c. With the Revenue column selected, type =RELATED(tblProducts[UnitPrice])*[Quantity] and then press Enter.
   The RELATED function is used exclusively inside the PowerPivot window and belongs to a category of functions called Data Analysis eXpressions (DAX) and essentially works the same as a LOOKUP function. It uses the relationships established in the data model to retrieve the UnitPrice value from the tblProducts table for the appropriate item purchased in a particular transaction. The unit price multiplied by the quantity gives you the revenue generated from that transaction.

d. On the Home tab, in the Formatting group, click the **Format : Change Formatting** arrow, and then select **Currency**.

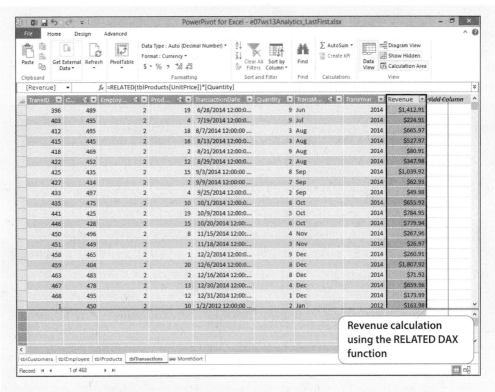

Figure 13   Calculated column of Revenue

e.   Double-click the next **Add Column** column heading, type **Costs** as the name for a second calculated column, and then press Enter.

f.   With the Costs column selected, type **=RELATED(tblProducts[UnitCost])*[Quantity]** and then press Enter to calculate the costs associated with each transaction.

g.   On the Home tab, in the Formatting group, click the **Format : Change Formatting** arrow, and then select **Currency**.

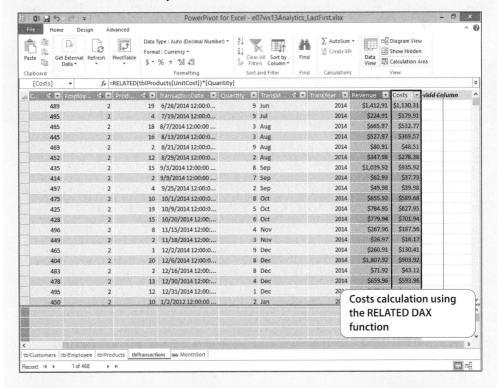

Figure 14   Calculated column of Costs

h. Double-click the next **Add Column** column heading, type Profit as the name for a third calculated column, and then press Enter.

i. With the Profit column selected, type =[Revenue]-[Costs] to calculate the profit generated from each transaction, and then press Enter.

j. On the Home tab, in the Formatting group, click the **Format : Change Formatting** arrow, and then select **Currency**.

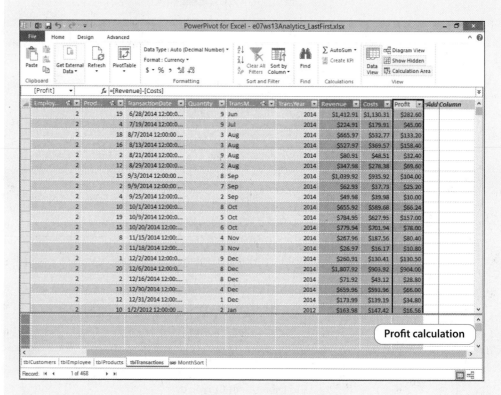

Figure 15   Calculated column for Profit

k. Double-click the next **Add Column** column heading, type Month as the name for a fourth calculated column, and then press Enter.

l. With the Month column selected, type =RELATED(MonthSort[Order])&"-"&[TransMonth] to concatenate the Order field from the MonthSort table with the TransMonth. Press Enter.

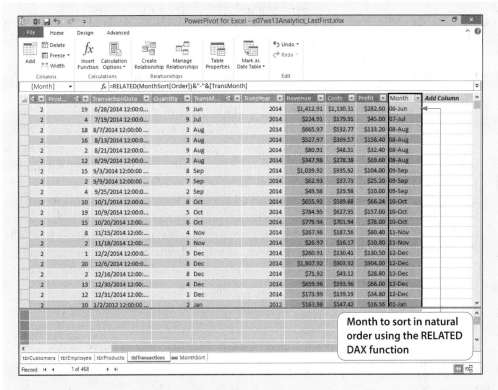

Figure 16 Calculated column for Month

m. Click **Save** 🔲.

There are many DAX functions available for use in PowerPivot. Many of the functions bear the same name and functionality as regular Excel functions you are already familiar with but have been modified to use DAX data types and work with tables and columns. Below are the various categories of DAX functions.

- Date and Time
- Mathematical and Trigonometric
- Statistical
- Text
- Logical
- Filter
- Information
- Parent/Child

Adding Calculated Fields in PowerPivot

A calculated column and a calculated field are similar in that they both are based on a formula or aggregate function; they differ based on how they are used in analysis. In a PivotTable, for example, a calculated column would most likely be placed in a column or row, whereas a calculated field would most likely be placed in the Values area. There are two types of calculated fields, referred to as measures in earlier versions of PowerPivot: implicit and explicit. An **implicit calculated field** is created when you drag a field like Sales or Quantity Sold into the Values area of a PivotTable. The calculation takes place, but a new calculated field is not being created. Implicit calculated fields can only use standard aggregation functions such as AVERAGE, SUM, COUNT, and MAX. An **explicit calculated field** is created when a formula is typed in the Calculation Area of the PowerPivot window. Explicit calculated fields can use a wide variety of functions beyond general aggregation and can be used in any PivotTable, PivotChart, or Power View report. They can also be extended to become a KPI. In this exercise you will create five explicit calculated fields that will calculate 2013 profits and 2014 profits, as well as total costs, total revenue, and total profits for all years in the data set.

E13.08

To Create Calculated Fields in PowerPivot

a. Click the **POWERPIVOT** tab, and then in the Data Model group, click **Manage**.

b. Click the **tblTransactions** worksheet tab, if necessary, scroll left to click the **first cell** in the Calculation Area below EmployeeID, and type
=CALCULATE(SUM(tblTransactions[Profit]),tblTransactions[TransYear]=2013).
Press [Enter] to calculate the total profit for transactions occurring in 2013.

This formula uses the Calculate function from the filter category of DAX functions. The Calculate function works similarly to the SUMIFS function in Excel. It is performing the aggregate function of SUM on the Profit field for records where the TransYear is equal to 2013. The Calculate function can incorporate multiple filters such as year, month, region, and employee ID.

> **Troubleshooting**
> If the Calculation Area is not visible in the PowerPivot window, on the Home tab, in the View group, click Calculation Area.

c. Change the default name of **Calculated Field 1** to 2013 Profit.

d. On the Home tab, in the Formatting group, click the **Format : Change Formatting** arrow, and then select **Currency**.

SIDE NOTE

Calculated Fields in PowerPivot

Calculated Fields can be created in any of the cells in the Calculation Area of the PowerPivot window.

SIDE NOTE

Viewing the Results of the Calculated Field

The results of the calculated field can be viewed by expanding the width of the cell or by hovering your pointer over the calculation.

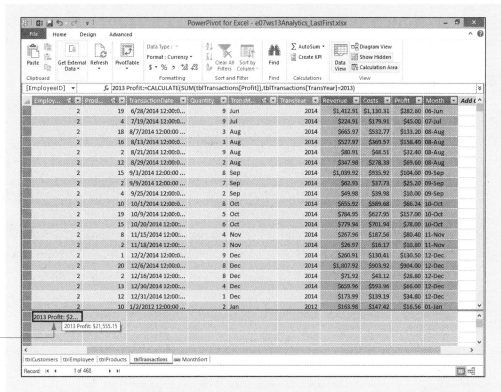

2013 Profit using the CALCULATE DAX function

Figure 17 Calculated field for 2013 Profit using CALCULATE

Click the **cell** to the right in the Calculation Area under the ProductID column to create a second calculated field, type
=CALCULATE(SUM(tblTransactions[Profit]),tblTransactions[TransYear]=2014) and then press Enter. This will calculate the total profit for transactions occurring in 2014.

e. Change the default name of **Calculated Field 1** to 2014 Profit.

f. On the Home tab, in the Formatting group, click the **Format : Change Formatting** arrow, and then select **Currency**.

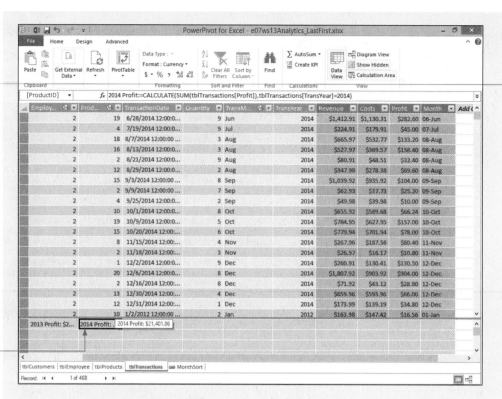

2014 Profit using the CALCULATE DAX function

Figure 18   Calculated field for 2014 Profit using CALCULATE

g. Click the **Revenue** column heading to select the Revenue column. On the Home tab, in the Calculations group, click **AutoSum** to calculate the total revenue for all transactions in the data set. AutoSum uses the Sum function to add up all the values in the column and places a new calculated field in the Calculation Area below the column, titled Sum of Revenue.

h. Click the **Costs** column heading to select the Costs column. Again, click **AutoSum** to calculate total costs for all transactions in the data set.

i. Click the **Profit** column heading to select the Profit column. Again, click **AutoSum** to calculate the total profits for all transactions in the data set.

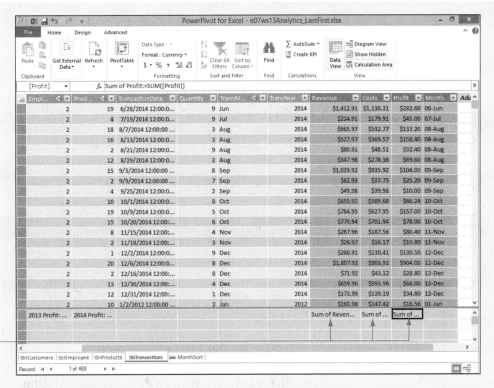

Sum of Revenue, Sum of Costs, and Sum of Profit

Figure 19 Calculated fields: Sum of Revenue, Sum of Costs, and Sum of Profit

j. Click **Save** 🖫.

Defining a Key Performance Indicator

Calculated fields can be extended to become KPIs. Management would like for you to create some KPIs that will measure employee performance. A KPI in PowerPivot includes the following: base value, target value, and status thresholds. A **base value** is a calculated field that resolves to a value. A base value, for example, can be the calculated field created as an aggregate of 2014 Profit. A **target value** can either be another calculated field that resolves to a value or an absolute value. A target value, for example, can be the aggregate of 2013 Profit or a monthly sales goal that every employee should meet. Finally, a **status threshold** is defined by the range between a high and low value. In Excel, the status threshold is displayed with a graphic providing a visual indicator of the status of the base value compared to the target value.

KPIs can either be positive, negative, or bidirectional. A **positive KPI** is when the greater the value the better the KPI, such as a company's profit. A **negative KPI** is when the greater the value the worse the KPI, such as the number of sick days in a specific time period. A **bidirectional KPI** is when the value becomes worse as it deviates too far from the target value in either direction. An example of a bidirectional KPI may be the temperature for storing a particular product; damage could occur if the temperature gets too cold or too hot.

In this exercise you will define two positive KPIs to help management measure employee performance. One KPI will measure each employee's monthly profit earnings to an absolute target value of $4,000, and the other will measure each employee's 2014 profit earnings against his or her 2013 profit earnings.

REAL WORLD ADVICE | **KPIs Without PowerPivot**

KPIs have been a part of business long before PowerPivot became available. If your company is using a previous version of Excel without PowerPivot, you can use Conditional Formatting Icon Sets instead to indicate proximity to various KPI goals.

E13.09

 To Create a KPI with an Absolute Target Value

a. Click the **POWERPIVOT** tab, and then in the Data Model group, click **Manage**.

b. On the tblTransactions worksheet tab, in the Calculation Area, click the **Sum of Profit** calculated field.

c. Click the **Home** tab, and then in the Calculations group, click **Create KPI**.

d. In the Key Performance Indicator (KPI) dialog box, confirm that **Sum of Profit** is selected as the KPI base field (value).

e. Under Define target value, click **Absolute value**, and type 4000.

f. Under Define status thresholds, click and slide the low value threshold to **2800** and the high value to **3800**.

g. Under Select icon style, ensure the first icon style is selected.

When creating KPIs in Excel, only the first icon style can be displayed in PivotTables. The other icon style options are useful when displaying KPI status symbols in a Power View report.

SIDE NOTE
Define Status Thresholds

The low- and high-threshold values can also be typed directly into the boxes attached to the sliders.

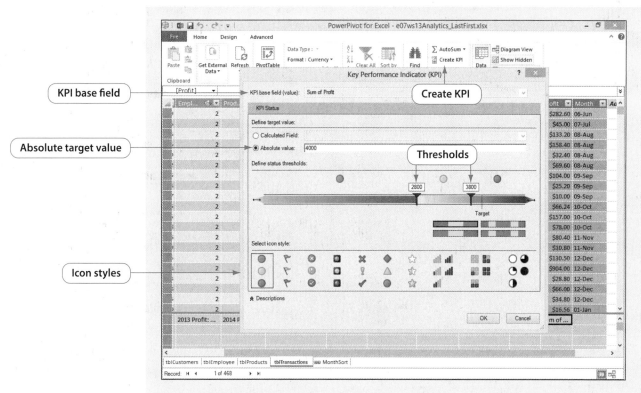

KPI base field

Absolute target value

Icon styles

Create KPI

Thresholds

Figure 20   KPI dialog box; absolute target value

h.   Click **OK**. Notice the ▦ KPI indicator now to the right of the calculated field.

i.   Click **Save** 🖫.

Now that you have created a KPI with an absolute target value, you will next create a KPI with a calculated field as the target value.

E13.10

 To Create a KPI with a Calculated Target Value

a.   Click the **POWERPIVOT** tab, and then in the Data Model group, click **Manage**.

b.   On the tblTransactions worksheet tab, in the Calculation Area, click the **2014 Profit** calculated field.

c.   Click the **Home** tab, and then in the Calculations group, click **Create KPI**.

d.   In the Key Performance Indicator (KPI) dialog box, confirm that **2014 Profit** is selected as the KPI base field (value).

e.   Under Define target value, select **2013 Profit** from the Calculated Field menu.

f.   Under Define status thresholds, click and slide the high threshold value to **105%** and the low value to **80%**.

g.   Under Select icon style, ensure the first icon style is selected.

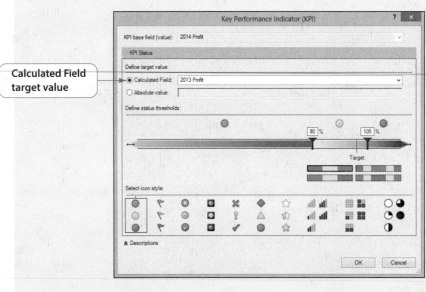

Calculated Field
target value

Figure 21 KPI dialog box; calculated target value

h. Click **OK**.

i. Click **Save** 🖫.

Create PivotTables and PivotCharts with PowerPivot

PivotTables and PivotCharts are a major component in any dashboard, and with Excel 2013 they can be created with data from multiple sources without any additional software or add-ins as long as it is relational data. Having the PowerPivot COM Add-In installed gives you more options than a traditional PivotTable. Not only can you create a single PivotTable or PivotChart on a worksheet with PowerPivot, but you can also create a PivotTable and PivotChart on the same worksheet as well as two PivotCharts arranged vertically or horizontally, or four PivotCharts on the same worksheet. Management of the Red Bluff Golf Course & Pro Shop is interested in getting a better understanding of its sales data over the past three years. You have been asked to create a simple dashboard consisting of four PivotCharts and slicers to be able to easily view different aspects of the sales data. **Slicers** are visual controls that allow you to quickly and easily filter your data in an interactive way. They can be used to replace the filter icons in PivotCharts. Slicers are not compatible with versions of Excel prior to 2010.

Creating a Simple Sales Dashboard with PivotCharts

The PowerPivot window has options to create multiple PivotCharts on the same worksheet using data from all connected data sources. This can be an easy way to create a simple dashboard for management to get a better picture of how things in a particular business area are going.

E13.11

To Use PowerPivot to Create Four PivotCharts

a. Click the **POWERPIVOT** tab, and then in the Data Model group, click **Manage**.

b. In the PowerPivot window, click the **HOME** tab if necessary.

Click the **PivotTable** arrow. Notice the various options for creating combinations of PivotTables and PivotCharts.

c. Select **Four Charts** from the menu.

d. In the Insert Pivot dialog box, click **Existing Worksheet**, click the **Collapse Dialog** button 🔲, and then click the **SalesDashboard** worksheet tab. Click cell **A1**.

e. Click **OK**.

SIDE NOTE
AXIS (CATEGORIES)
Fields placed in the AXIS (CATEGORIES) area make up the horizontal axis (x-axis) of the PivotChart.

Figure 22   Insert Pivot dialog box

f. Click **OK** again to create the layout for four PivotCharts.

g. Complete the following tasks to create a PivotChart comparing the 2012 Costs and the 2012 Revenue by month:

- If necessary, click **Chart 1**. In the PivotChart Fields pane, click **tblTransactions** to view the available fields, and then drag the **Month** field to the **AXIS (CATEGORIES)** area at the bottom of the PivotChart Fields pane.

- Drag the **TransYear** field into the **FILTERS** area.

- Select the **Revenue** field to add it to the **Σ VALUES** area.

- If necessary, expand **tblTransactions** again, and then select the **Costs** field to add it to the **Σ VALUES** area.

- Click the **TransYear** filter on the chart, expand the options, and then select **2012**. Click **OK**.

- Right-click the **chart object** that was just created, and then click **Change Chart Type**.

  In the Change Chart Type dialog box, click **Combo**, and then click **OK**. This combo chart allows you to easily compare the costs and revenue from each month.

- Click the **ANALYZE** tab on the Ribbon, and then in the PivotChart group, in the **Chart Name** box, type Sales-Costs-2012 to name the chart.

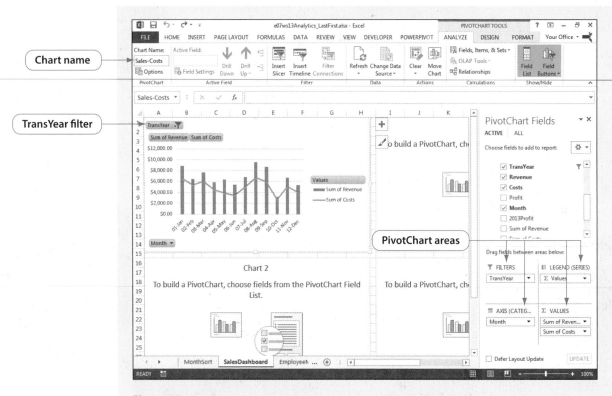

Figure 23 Combo chart for Sales-Costs-2012

h. Click **Chart 2**, and then complete the following tasks to create a PivotChart comparing the 2013 Costs and the 2013 Revenue by month:

- If necessary, in the PivotChart Fields pane, click **ALL** under the PivotChart Fields heading to view all available tables in the data model. Click **tblTransactions** to view available fields, and then drag the **Month** field to the **AXIS (CATEGORIES)** area.
- Drag the **TransYear** field into the **FILTERS** area.
- Check the **Revenue** box, and then check the **Costs** box to add them to the **Σ VALUES** area.
- Click the **TransYear** filter on the chart, expand the options, and then select **2013**. Click **OK**.
- Right-click the **chart**, and then click **Change Chart Type**.
- In the Change Chart Type dialog box, click **Combo**, and then click **OK**.
- On the ANALYZE tab, in the PivotChart group, click the **Chart Name** box, and then type Sales-Costs-2013 to name the chart.

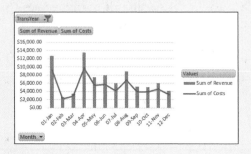

Figure 24 Combo chart for Sales-Costs-2013

i. Click **Chart 3**, and then complete the following tasks to create a PivotChart comparing the 2014 Costs and the 2014 Revenue by month:

-   If necessary, in the PivotChart Fields pane, click **ALL** under the PivotChart Fields heading to view all available tables in the data model. Click **tblTransactions** to view the available fields, and then drag the **Month** field to the **AXIS (CATEGORIES)** area.
-   Drag the **TransYear** field into the **FILTERS** area.
-   Check the **Revenue** box, and then check the **Costs** box to add them to the **Σ VALUES** area.
-   Click the **TransYear** filter on the chart, expand the options, and then select **2014**. Click **OK**.
-   Right-click the **chart**, and then click **Change Chart Type**.
-   In the Change Chart Type dialog box, click **Combo**, and then click **OK**.
-   On the ANALYZE tab, in the PivotChart group, click the **Chart Name** box, and then type Sales-Costs-2014 to name the chart.

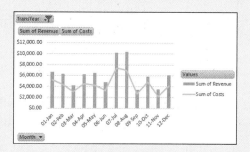

Figure 25   Combo chart for Sales-Costs-2014

j. Click **Chart 4**, and then complete the following tasks to create a PivotChart based on all sales from 2012–2014 by employee:

-   In the PivotChart Fields pane, click **ALL** under the PivotChart Fields heading to view all available tables in the data model. Click **tblEmployee** to view the available fields, and then drag the **LastName** field to the **AXIS (CATEGORIES)** area.
-   Scroll down, click **tblTransactions** to view the available fields, and then check the **Revenue** box to add it to the **Σ VALUES** area.
-   Right-click the **chart object** that was just created, click **Change Chart Type**, and then in the Change Chart Type dialog box, click **Bar**. Click **OK**.
-   On the ANALYZE tab, in the PivotChart group, click the **Chart Name** box, and then type Employee-Sales-2012-2014 to name the chart.

Troubleshooting

Some of the axis values on the charts may be out of place or overlapping. You will improve upon the formatting of the charts in the next exercise.

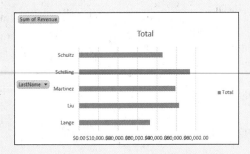

Figure 26   Bar chart for Employee-Sales-2012–2014

k. Click **Save** .

Improving Design with Chart Elements and Styles

Dashboards should be visually appealing without being distracting. Some simple and modest modifications to the charts can increase the readability and create a better user experience.

E13.12
To Improve Dashboard Design

a. Click the **Sales-Costs-2012** chart, and then complete the following tasks:

- Click **Chart Elements** ⊞, and then click **Chart Title** to add a chart title above the chart.
- Edit **Chart Title** to read 2012 Sales and Costs.
- Click the **FORMAT** tab, and then in the Current Selection group, select **Series "Sum of Revenue"** from the Chart Elements menu.
- Click **Format Selection**, in the Format Data Series pane, adjust the Gap Width to be 100% and then close the pane.
- Click **Chart Styles** ✐ next to the chart, and then select **Style 3** from the Style list.
- Click the **ANALYZE** tab, and then in the Show/Hide group, click **Field Buttons** to hide the filters on the PivotChart.

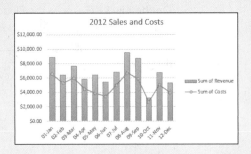

Figure 27   2012 Sales and Costs combo chart formatted

b. Click the **Sales-Costs-2013** chart, and then complete the following tasks:

- Click **Chart Elements** ⊞, and then click **Chart Title** to add a chart title above the chart.
- Edit **Chart Title** to read 2013 Sales and Costs.
- Click the **FORMAT** tab, and then in the Current Selection group, select **Series "Sum of Revenue"** from the Chart Elements menu.
- Click **Format Selection**, in the Format Data Series pane, adjust the Gap Width to be 100% and then close the pane.
- Click **Chart Styles** ✐, and then select **Style 3** from the Style list.
- Click the **ANALYZE** tab, and then in the Show/Hide group, click **Field Buttons** to hide the filters on the PivotChart.

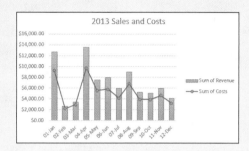

Figure 28   2013 Sales and Costs combo chart formatted

c. Click the **Sales-Costs-2014** chart, and complete the following tasks:

- Click **Chart Elements** ⊞, and then click **Chart Title** to add a chart title above the chart.
- Edit **Chart Title** to read 2014 Sales and Costs.
- Click the **FORMAT** tab, and then in the Current Selection group, select **Series "Sum of Revenue"** from the Chart Elements menu.
- Click **Format Selection**, in the Format Data Series pane adjust the Gap Width to be 100% and then close the pane.
- Click **Chart Styles** ✐, and then select **Style 3** from the Style list.
- Click the **ANALYZE** tab, and then in the Show/Hide group click **Field Buttons** to hide the filters on the PivotChart.

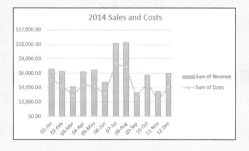

Figure 29   2014 Sales and Costs combo chart formatted

d. Click the **Employee-Sales-2012-2014** chart, and then complete the following tasks:
- Edit **Chart Title** to read 2012-2014 Sales by Employee.
- Click the **FORMAT** tab, and then in the Current Selection group, select **Horizontal (Value) Axis** from the Chart Elements menu. Click **Format Selection**.
- Expand the **Number** section, select **Currency** from the Category menu, change the **Decimal places** to 0 and close the pane.
- Click **Chart Styles** , and then select **Style 3** from the Style list.
- Click the **ANALYZE** tab, and then in the Show/Hide group, click **Field Buttons** to hide the filters on the PivotChart.
- Click the **chart legend** to select it, and then press Delete.

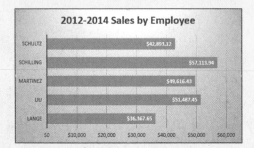

Figure 30   2012–2014 Sales by Employee bar chart formatted

e. Click **Save** 🖫.

Enhancing a Dashboard with Slicers

The current dashboard with four pivot charts is lacking an easy and efficient way to filter the sales data in order to see the data from different perspectives. For example, management at the Red Bluff Golf Course & Pro Shop would like to be able to see the sales and costs for particular product categories, type of guest, or even by employee. In this exercise you will be adding slicers to the dashboard.

E13.13

▶ To Add Slicers

a. Click the **SalesDashboard** worksheet tab, and then click the **2012 Sales and Costs** chart.

b. Click the **ANALYZE** tab, and then in the Filter group, click **Insert Slicer**.

c. In the Insert Slicers dialog box, click the **All** tab.

d. Scroll to the **tblCustomers** table and, if necessary, expand to view the table fields. Click the **Status** box.

e. Scroll to the **tblEmployee** table and, if necessary, expand to view the table fields. Click the **LastName** box.

f. Scroll to the **tblProducts** table and, if necessary, expand to view the table fields. Click the **ProductType** box.

g. Click **OK** to create a slicer for each of the boxes checked.

h. If necessary, click the **ProductType** slicer to select it. On the OPTIONS tab in the Slicer group, click **Report Connections**.

i. In the Report Connections dialog box, confirm that **Sales-Costs-2012** is checked, and then click **Sales-Costs-2013**, **Sales-Costs-2014**, and **Employee-Sales-2012-2014** to connect the ProductType slicer to all the charts.

Report Connections

Report Connections dialog box

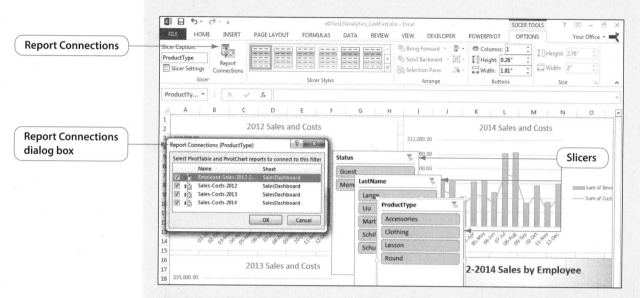

Figure 31 Report Connections (ProductType) dialog box

j. Click **OK**.

k. Repeat Steps **h–j** for the **LastName** and **Status** slicers.

l. Reposition the **2014 Sales and Costs** and **2012-2014 Sales by Employee** charts at the far edge of column **R** to make room for the slicers.

m. Reposition and resize the **slicers** to fit between the charts within columns H:J.

Slicers repositioned

Figure 32 SalesDashboard with Status, LastName, and ProductType slicers

n. Click the **2012-2014 Sales by Employee** chart, click the **ANALYZE** tab, and then in the Filter group, click **Insert Slicer**.

o. Locate the tblTransactions fields, click **Month** and **TransYear**, and then click **OK** to add the two slicers to the dashboard.

p. Resize and reposition the two **slicers** to the right of the 2012-2014 Sales by Employee bar chart.

Notice the Sales Dashboard now has easy and effective ways to filter the data displayed in the charts. Multiple fields can be used simultaneously to filter the data by holding Ctrl while clicking each field.

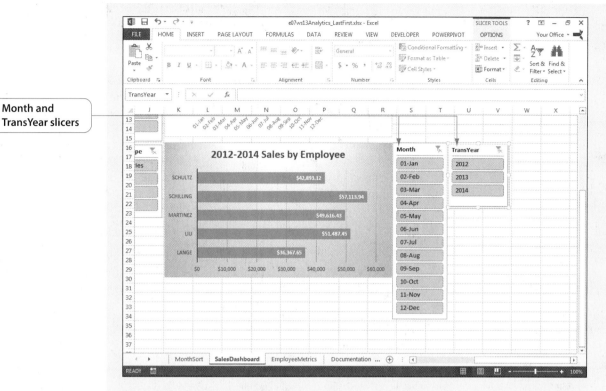

Month and TransYear slicers

Figure 33 SalesDashboard with Month and TransYear slicers

q. Click **Save** .

Incorporating KPIs into a Dashboard

In an earlier exercise you created two KPIs. One KPI measures profit earnings to an absolute target value of $4,000, and the other compares 2014 profit earnings against 2013 profit earnings. These KPIs can be incorporated into PivotTables with additional values and/or filters.

Management would like you to create another dashboard displaying the KPIs and additional analysis.

E13.14

To Incorporate the Yearly Profit Goal KPI into a Dashboard

a. Click the **EmployeeMetrics** worksheet tab, and then click cell **A1**. Click the **INSERT** tab, and then in the Tables group, click **PivotTable** to create a PivotTable.

b. In the Create PivotTable dialog box, click **Use an external data source**, and then click **Choose Connection**.

c. In the Existing Connections dialog box, confirm that **e07ws13Sales** is selected under Connections in this Workbook, and then click **Open**.

d. In the Existing Worksheet field, confirm that **EmployeeMetrics!$A$1** is the Location, and then click **OK**.

e. In the PivotTable Fields pane, scroll down to **tblEmployee**, and then drag the **LastName** field to the **ROWS** area.

f. Scroll down to **tblTransactions**, and then drag the **TransYear** field to the **ROWS** area, below **LastName**.

g. Click **Profit** to add the field to the **Σ VALUES** area.
   Click the **Sum of Profit** KPI to expand it, and then click **Status** to add the KPI status threshold symbols to the PivotTable. Notice that both Lange and Schilling fell below the bottom threshold value of $2,800 in one of the years.

h. Make the following changes to the PivotTable.
   - Click cell **A1**, and then edit **Row Labels** to read Employee by Year.
   - Click cell **A1** again, if necessary. Click the **HOME** tab, and then in the Alignment group, click **Wrap Text** to wrap the new label in cell A1.
   - Click cell **B1**, and then edit **Sum of Profit** to read Yearly Profit.
   - Click cell **C1**, and then edit **Sum of Profit Status** to read $4,000 Goal Status.
   - Adjust the width of columns **A**, **B**, and **C** to automatically fit to their contents.
   - Click the **ANALYZE** tab, and then in the PivotTable group, change the PivotTable Name to Profits-2012-2014.

i. **Close** the PivotTable Fields pane.

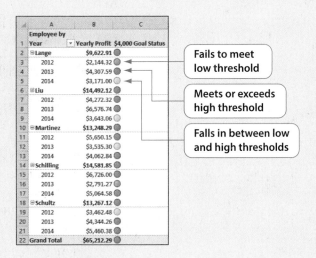

Figure 34   Yearly Profit KPI

Now that you have incorporated the yearly profit goal KPI to the dashboard, you will now incorporate the 2014 profit KPI.

E13.15

 To Incorporate the 2014 Profit KPI into a Dashboard

a. Click the **EmployeeMetrics** worksheet tab, and then click cell **A24**.

b. Click the **INSERT** tab, and then in the Tables group, click **PivotTable**.

c. In the Create PivotTable dialog box, click **Use an external data source**, and then click **Choose Connection**.

d. In the Existing Connections dialog box, confirm that **e07ws13Sales** is selected under Connections in this Workbook, and then click **Open**.

e. In the Existing Worksheet field confirm that **EmployeeMetrics!$A$24** is the Location, and then click **OK**.

f. In the PivotTable Fields pane, scroll down to **tblEmployee**, and then drag the **LastName** field to the **ROWS** area.

g. Scroll down to **tblTransactions**, expand the **2014 Profit KPI**, and then click **Value (2014Profit)** to add the calculated field to the **Σ VALUES** area.

h. Click **Status** to add the KPI status threshold symbols to the PivotTable.

Notice Employees Lang and Liu fell below the lowest threshold of 80% of 2013 profits and the remaining three employees met or exceeded the highest threshold value of 105% of 2013 profits. The total profits for 2014 fell within 80% and 105% of the 2013 profits.

i. Make the following changes to the PivotTable.

- Click cell **A24**, and then edit **Row Labels** to read Employees.
- Click cell **C24**, and then edit **2014 Profit Status** to read % of 2013 Goal.
- Adjust the width of columns **A**, **B**, and **C** to automatically fit to their contents.
- Click the **ANALYZE** tab, and then in the PivotTable group, change the PivotTable Name to Profits-2014.

j. **Close** the PivotTable Fields pane.

Employees ▾	2014 Profit	% of 2013 Goal
Lange	$3,171.00 ◯
Liu	$3,643.06 ◯
Martinez	$4,062.84 ◯
Schilling	$5,064.58 ◯
Schultz	$5,460.38 ◯
Grand Total	$21,401.86 ◯

Figure 35 2014 Profit KPI

k. Click **Save** .

In this next exercise you will incorporate the Sum of Profit KPI into a chart to add a visualization that shows how each employee's yearly profits compare to the goal.

E13.16

▶ To Incorporate the KPI Goal into a Combo Chart

a. Click the **EmployeeMetrics** worksheet tab, and then click cell **D1**. Click the **INSERT** tab, and then in the Charts group, click **PivotChart**.

b. In the Create PivotChart dialog box, click **Use an external data source**, and then click **Choose Connection**.

c. In the Existing Connections dialog box, confirm that **e07ws13Sales** is selected under Connections in this Workbook, and then click **Open**.

d. In the Existing Worksheet field, confirm that **EmployeeSalesMetrics!$D$1** is the Location, and then click **OK**.

e. Click the **ANALYZE** tab, and then in the Show/Hide group, click **Field List** to display the PivotCharts Fields pane. In the PivotChart Fields pane, scroll down to **tblEmployee**, and then drag the **LastName** field to the **AXIS (CATEGORIES)** area.

f. Scroll down to **tblTransactions**, and then drag the **TransYear** field to the **AXIS (CATEGORIES)** area, below **LastName**.

g. Click **Profit** to add the calculated field to the **Σ VALUES** area.

h. Click the **Sum of Profit** KPI to expand it, and then click **Goal** to add the KPI target value to the **Σ VALUES** area.

i. Right-click the **chart object** that was just created, and then click **Change Chart Type**.

j. In the Change Chart Type dialog box, click **Combo**, and then click **OK**. Notice the line chart where the yearly profit goal of $4,000 appears as a line across the chart.

k. Make the following changes to the chart:
   • Click **Chart Elements** ⊞, and then click **Chart Title** to add a chart title above the chart.
   • Edit **Chart Title** to read 2012-2014 Profit Goals.
   • Click the **FORMAT** tab, and then in the Current Selection group, select **Series "Sum of Profit"** from the Chart Elements menu.
   • Click **Format Selection**, in the Format Data Series pane adjust the Gap Width to 100% and then close the pane.
   • Click the **Chart Styles** ⟋ next to the chart, and then select **Style 8** from the Style list.
   • Click the **ANALYZE** tab, and then in the PivotChart group, edit **Chart Title** to read ProfitGoals-2012-2014.
   • On the ANALYZE tab, in the Show/Hide group, click **Field Buttons** to hide all filters.
   • Reposition the chart to fit within the range **D4:K18**.

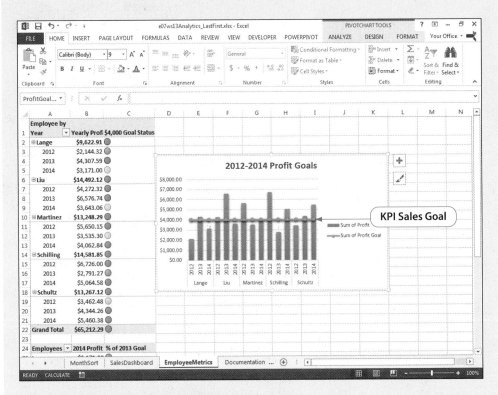

Figure 36   KPI Goal added to combo chart

l. Click **Save** 🖫.

Creating PivotTables with Sparklines

Another common method of representing data graphically for dashboards created in Excel is to use sparklines. **Sparklines**, or miniature charts, provide a way to graphically summarize a row or column of data in a single cell. There are three different types of sparklines: line, column, and win/loss. Management at the Red Bluff Golf Course & Pro Shop feels that it would benefit from comparing trends in sales revenue from each sales representative. In this exercise you will create a PivotTable adding sparklines that illustrate the trend over each month of 2014 for each sales representative.

E13.17

 To Add Sparklines to a PivotTable

a. Click the **EmployeeMetrics** worksheet tab, and then click cell **A34**. Click the **INSERT** tab, and then in the Tables group, click **PivotTable** to insert another PivotTable into the Dashboard.

b. In the Create PivotTable dialog box, click **Use an external data source**, and then click **Choose Connection**.

c. In the Existing Connections dialog box, confirm that **e07ws13Sales** is selected under Connections in this Workbook, and then click **Open**.

d. In the Existing Worksheet field confirm that **EmployeeMetrics!$A$34** is the Location, and then click **OK**.

e. In the PivotTable Fields pane, scroll down to the **tblEmployee**, and then drag the **LastName** field to the **ROWS** area.

f. Scroll down to **tblTransactions**, drag **TransYear** to the **FILTERS** area, and then drag the **Month** field to the **COLUMNS** area.

g. Click **Revenue** to add the calculated field to the **Σ VALUES** area.

h. Make the following changes to the PivotTable:

- Select **2014** from the TransYear report filter.
- Click cell **A34**, and then edit **Sum of Revenue** to read 2014 Monthly Revenue. Click the **HOME** tab, and in the Alignment group, click **Wrap Text** to wrap the text within the cell.
- Click cell **B34**, and then edit **Column Labels** to read Months.
- Click cell **A35**, and then edit **Row Labels** to read Employees.
- Click the **DESIGN** tab, and then in the Layout group, click **Grand Totals**. Click **On for Columns Only**.
- Adjust the width of columns **A:M** to automatically fit to their contents.
- On the ANALYZE tab in the PivotTable group, edit **PivotTable Name** to Revenues-2014Trends.

i. Click cell **N35**, type 2014 Trends as a column heading for the sparklines, and then press Enter.

j. Click cell **N36**. Click the **INSERT** tab, and then in the Sparklines group, click **Line**.

k. In the Create Sparklines dialog box, select cells **B36:M40** for the Data Range, select cells **N36:N40** for the Location Range, and then click **OK**.

l. Click the **DESIGN** tab, and then in the Show group, click the boxes for **High Point** and **Low Point** to highlight the lowest and highest monthly profits for each employee.

m. Select cells **M34:M35**. Click the **HOME** tab, and then in the Clipboard group, click **Format Painter** to copy the formatting of the selected cells. Select cells **N34:N35** to paste the formatting to the selected cells.

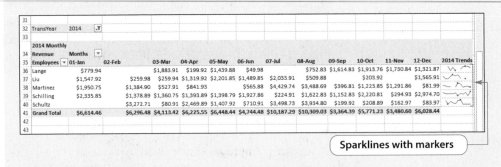

Figure 37 EmployeeMetrics dashboard with PivotTable and sparklines

n. Click **Save** 🖫.

Use Apps for Office for Data Visualizations

New to Office 2013, Microsoft introduced apps for Office. The apps for Office platform allows app developers to create new and engaging consumer and enterprise experiences within the Office applications, such as Word, Excel, and Outlook. An **app for Office** is essentially a web page that is hosted inside an Office application. These apps can be used to extend the functionality of the application. For example, Bing Maps has an app for Office that displays demographic data on a map to create stunning data visualizations. Other apps for Excel provide advanced analytic capabilities or data visualizations.

Locating and Installing an App from the Office Store

The first step to using an app for Office is to locate and install the app for use. In this exercise you will locate the Bing Maps app in the Office Store and install it.

E13.18

▶ **To Install the Bing Maps App for Office**

a. Click the **INSERT** tab, and then in the Apps group, click **Apps for Office**.

b. In the Apps for Office dialog box you see a list of current Apps installed. Click **Find more apps at the Office Store** at the bottom to locate new apps.

c. Type Bing Maps in the search box, and then press ⌐Enter¬.

d. Click **Bing Maps**, and then on the next page, click **Add**.

> **Troubleshooting**
> If you are not already logged in to your Microsoft account then you will be prompted to sign in before the app can be installed.

e. Click **Continue** to confirm that you wish to add the app and close the browser window.

f. Return to the Excel workbook. On the INSERT tab, in the Apps group, click the **Apps for Office** button, and then confirm that **Bing Maps** is now added to your list of installed apps.

> **Troubleshooting**
> If the Bing Maps app is not displaying on the MY APPS page, click Refresh.

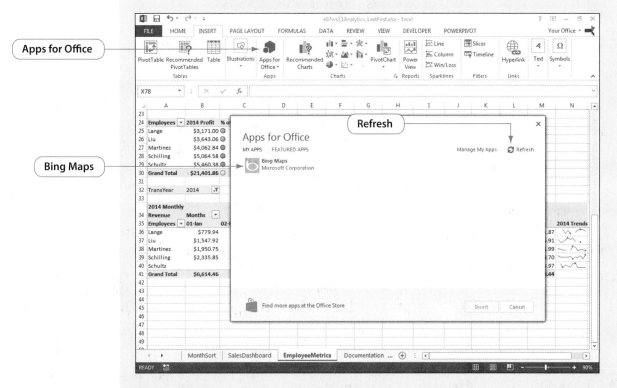

Figure 38 Bing Maps app added

g. **Close** the Apps for Office dialog box, and then click **Save** 🔲.

Incorporating Bing Maps Visualization

Red Bluff Golf Course & Pro Shop tracks some demographic information about its customers, including their home state. In this exercise you will incorporate state and revenue data from the data model and chart it using the Bing Maps app from the Office Store.

E13.19

▶️ **To Use the Bing Maps App**

a. Click the **EmployeeMetrics** worksheet tab, and then click cell **L1**. Click the **INSERT** tab, and then in the Tables group, click **PivotTable** to insert another PivotTable into the Dashboard.

b. In the Create PivotTable dialog box, click **Use an external data source**, and then click **Choose Connection**.

c. In the **Existing Connections** dialog box, confirm that **e07ws13Sales** is selected under Connections in this Workbook, and then click **Open**.

d. In the Existing Worksheet field, confirm that **EmployeeMetrics!$L$1** is the Location, and then click **OK**.

e. In the PivotTable Fields list, scroll down to **tblCustomers**, and then drag the **LastName** field to the **ROWS** area.

f. Scroll down to **tblTransctions**, drag **TransYear** to the **COLUMNS** area, and then click **Revenue** to add it to the **Σ VALUES** area.

g. Make the following changes to the PivotTable:

- Click cell **L1**, and then edit **Sum of Revenue** to read Total Revenue.
- Click cell **L2**, and then edit **Row Labels** to read State.
- Click cell **M1**, and then edit **Column Labels** to read Year.
- Click the **DESIGN** tab, and then in the Layout group, click **Grand Totals**. Click **Off for Rows and Columns**.
- Click the **ANALYZE** tab, and then in the PivotTable group, change the PivotTable Name to YearlyRevenuesByState.

h. Click the **INSERT** tab, and then in the Apps group, click **Apps for Office**.

i. Click **Bing Maps**, and then click **Insert**.

j. Resize the **map**, and then reposition it so that it fits below the YearlyRevenuesByState PivotTable. The map should fit within the range **L8:O27**.

k. Select the data in the range **L3:O7**, and then on the Bing Map click the **Plot Locations** icon.

Notice the Zoom in, Zoom out, and pan navigation buttons at the top of the map. Explore the controls. Also explore the Filter ▼ and Settings ⚙ features.

SIDE NOTE

Bing Maps and State Abbreviations

The Bing Maps app is more accurate if the name of the state is used as opposed to state abbreviations.

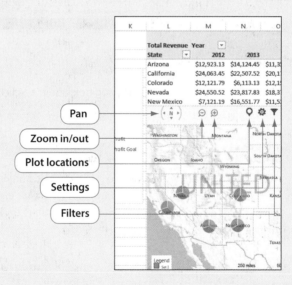

Figure 39   Revenues by State added to Bing Map

l. Click **Save** 🔲.

Prepare a Dashboard for Production

Once a dashboard has been designed to meet the business requirements, there are several steps you need to take to get it ready for use. This process may include protecting various worksheets and cells from accidental mistakes, hiding various elements from the user that are not necessary for the dashboard, and making some simple design modifications to enhance the user experience.

Protecting Excel Worksheets

Because dashboards are designed for the specific needs of an end user, it is important to ensure once the dashboard contains all the required data that certain protections are in place to avoid accidental deletion of various objects or incorrect modifications. Managers at the Red Bluff Golf Course & Pro Shop who will be benefiting from these dashboards are not as comfortable in Excel as you are and do not want to accidentally delete data or otherwise compromise the data. In this exercise you will work to protect the important elements of the workbook.

E13.20

To Protect a Worksheet

a. Click the **SalesDashboard** worksheet tab.

b. Click the **REVIEW** tab, and then in the Changes group, click **Protect Sheet**.

   Notice in the Protect Sheet dialog box there is an option to set a required password to unprotect the worksheet. This may be necessary to prevent intentional attempts to destroy the data.

c. Scroll through options of actions that users can still perform if the worksheet is protected, and then click **Select locked cells** and **Select unlocked cells** to clear the check boxes. Click **Use PivotTable & PivotChart** and **Edit objects** to allow the PivotCharts and slicers to be used.

Figure 40   Protect Sheet dialog box

   Click **OK**. With the sheet protected, no cells can be selected, no additional data can be added to the worksheet, nor can columns or rows be inserted or deleted.

d. Click the **EmployeeMetrics** worksheet tab.

e. Before protecting the worksheet make sure that all columns have been adjusted to automatically fit to their contents.

SIDE NOTE
Protect Sheet and Edit Objects

To be able to manipulate Slicers, you must allow users to Edit Objects, which does allow changes to the PivotCharts.

f. Click the **REVIEW** tab, and then in the Changes group, click **Protect Sheet**.

g. Scroll through the options of actions that users can still perform if the worksheet is protected, and then click **Select locked cells** and **Select unlocked cells** to clear the check boxes. Click **Use PivotTable & PivotChart** to allow for the PivotTable filters to be used.

h. Click **OK**.

i. Click **Save** 🖫.

CONSIDER THIS │ **Using Excel Web Apps**

Excel Web Apps are a great option that encourages sharing and collaboration. However, the Excel Web App does not support all the features available in the full desktop version of Excel, such as Protected Sheets. What other things should you take into consideration based on how people are expected to access your Excel workbook?

Hiding Unnecessary Screen Elements

Many of the interactive elements of Microsoft Excel can be hidden from users. Normally controls such as the Ribbon and scroll bars are useful and necessary parts of working with Excel. However, when a dashboard is presented to a user, it is preferable to hide any unnecessary objects that may distract the user from the dashboard's content.

E13.21

 To Hide Screen Elements

a. Click the **FILE** tab, and then click **Options**.

b. In the Excel Options dialog box, click **Advanced**.

c. Under Display options for this worksheet, if necessary, select **EmployeeMetrics** from the menu, and then click **Show row and column headers** and **Show gridlines** to deselect them.

d. Select **SalesDashboard** from the menu, click **Show row and column headers**, and then click **Show gridlines** to deselect them.

e. Click **OK**.

SIDE NOTE
Toggle the Ribbon
You can expand and collapse the ribbon by pressing Ctrl + F1 .

f. Right-click the **MonthSort** worksheet tab, and then click **Hide** to hide the worksheet from view.

g. Press Ctrl + F1 to minimize the Ribbon and maximize dashboard space.

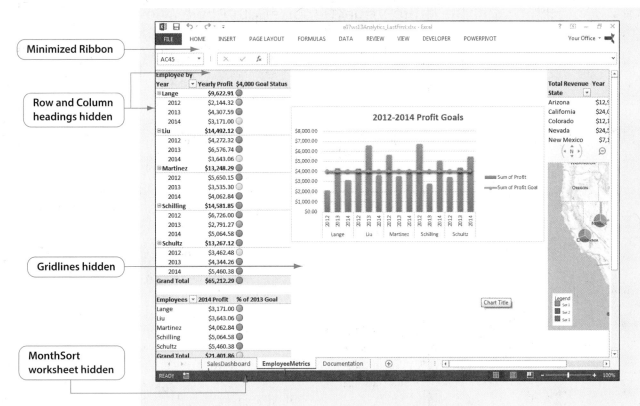

Minimized Ribbon

Row and Column headings hidden

Gridlines hidden

MonthSort worksheet hidden

Figure 41 EmployeeMetrics dashboard with elements hidden

h. Click **Save** 🔲.

Exploring the Benefits of Personalized Business Intelligence

Dashboards are great for people who know exactly what questions they have and what answers they want to derive from the data. However, it is often necessary to view data from multiple perspectives first, in order to gain a better understanding of the data, before those questions can be known. Microsoft knows that being able to quickly analyze large amounts of data is extremely important for business intelligence. This is why PowerPivot was integrated in Excel 2013. Microsoft also understands the benefits of being able to quickly analyze that data visually, which is where Power View comes in.

Power View, combined with PowerPivot in Excel 2013, provides all the BI tools necessary to lead to better decision making. In this section you will explore the Power View tool and create a report for the managers of the Red Bluff Golf Course & Pro Shop that demonstrates some of the key features.

Generate Visual Reports with Power View

Power View is now fully integrated into Excel 2013, offering powerful data visualization tools that were once only available in third-party business intelligence applications. **Power View** is an interactive data visualization, exploration, and presentation experience that encourages the creation of ad-hoc reports.

Power View reports are created from data that have been added to the data model. A Power View report can be created without the use of PowerPivot by using data from separate tables or ranges. However, by creating relationships using PowerPivot, you can create a much more robust Power View report. If the data model is connected to an external data source and that source contains updated information, any Power View reports will be refreshed to accommodate the updated data. In Power View you can quickly create a variety of data visualizations, from tables to pie, bar, column, and bubble charts, to maps and more.

Beyond quick and easy visualizations, Power View allows for several ways to filter the data. Power View uses metadata in the data model to understand the relationships between the different tables and fields used in the report. Because of this, one visualization can be used to filter and highlight all of the visualizations in the report. You can also take advantage of a filter area to filter data on a single visualization or to all of them.

Slicers can also be added to a Power View report. Slicers allow you to easily filter the data in multiple visualizations, similar to how slicers work in Excel. In addition to slicers, Power View also allows for easy sorting of data and switching to full-screen mode for some visualizations.

Installing the Silverlight Plug-in

Excel's Power View requires that Microsoft's Silverlight be installed. **Silverlight** is a powerful tool that creates engaging, interactive user experiences. It is a free plug-in, powered by the .NET framework and compatible with multiple browsers, devices, applications, and operating systems.

E13.22

 To Install Microsoft Silverlight

a. Point your browser to **http://www.microsoft.com/silverlight/**.

b. Click **DOWNLOAD NOW** to begin the download and installation process of the latest version of Silverlight.

c. Follow the prompts to download and install Silverlight, and then close your browser.

Inserting a Power View Report Sheet

The Power View report sheet has a fixed size, unlike other worksheets in Excel. There are no scroll bars, and the report sheet may remind you of a PowerPoint slide. When you first insert a Power View report sheet, three panes are visible: the Design pane, Filters pane, and the Power View Fields pane. Before any data is added to the Power View report, the options available on the Power View tab on the Ribbon are limited to only a few options, such as Undo and Redo, setting a theme, adding a picture or image, refreshing the data, and creating and editing relationships in the data model. Additional contextual tabs will become available once you begin creating the report. In this exercise you will insert a new Power View report sheet into the workbook and explore the layout.

E13.23

 To Insert a Power View Report Sheet

a. Press Ctrl+F1 to expand the Ribbon, if necessary. Click the **EmployeeMetrics** worksheet tab. Click the **INSERT** tab, and then in the Reports group, click **Power View**.

b. If prompted, click **Enable** to enable the Power View COM Add-In.

> **Troubleshooting**
> If you do not have Silverlight installed you will be prompted to install it before you can continue. If necessary, click Install Silverlight and follow the prompts. Once installed, click Reload.

c. Right-click the **Power View1** worksheet tab, and then click **Rename**.

d. Type InteractiveReport as the worksheet name, and then press Enter.

e. Examine the various components that make up the Power View report builder.

f. Click the **Click here to add a title** text, and type Red Bluff Golf Course & Pro Shop Sales Report.

g. Click the **POWER VIEW** tab, and then in the Themes group, click **Themes**. Select **Hardcover** in the seventh row of the fourth column to add a theme to the Power View Report.

h. In the Themes group, click **Background**, and then select **Dark1 Vertical Gradient**.

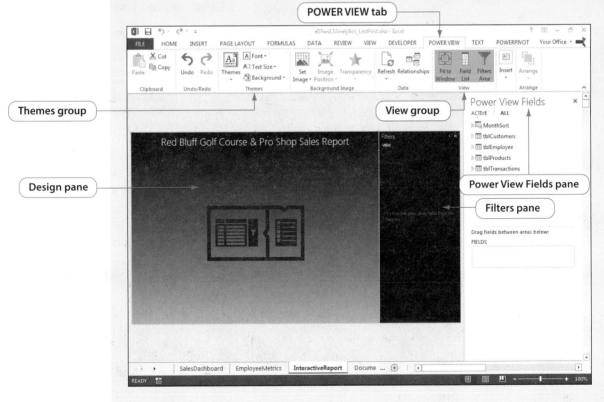

Figure 42 Power View report builder

i. Click **Save**.

Creating a Visualization with Multiples

Power View allows for you to create visualizations called "multiples." **Multiples** are a series of identical charts with the same x- and y-axes but that contain different values. These repeating charts make it easier to compare many different values at the same time. When you create multiples, Power View creates a container with one chart for each of the values. For example, if you have a column chart of monthly sales you could add a year field to the multiples field and have one column chart for each year. There are two different types of multiples: vertical multiples and horizontal multiples. **Vertical multiples** will expand across the width of the container and wrap down the container in the available space. If all multiples do not fit in the available space, a vertical scroll bar is also added. **Horizontal multiples** expand across the available space in the container, and if additional space is needed a horizontal scroll bar is added.

In this exercise you will create a Clustered Column chart with horizontal multiples to display the monthly sales from year to year.

E13.24

▶ To Create Multiples

a. Click the **InteractiveReport** worksheet tab, scroll through the Power View Fields pane, and then expand **tblTransactions** to view available fields.

b. Select **Month** and **Σ Revenue**. Notice that once data has been added to the Design pane, the DESIGN tab appears on the Ribbon.

c. On the DESIGN tab, in the Switch Visualization group, click **Column Chart**, and then click **Clustered Column**. Notice in the Power View Fields pane the choices have changed to accommodate the options for a Clustered Column chart.

d. In the Power View Fields pane, drag **Σ TransYear** to the **HORIZONTAL MULTIPLES** area.

e. In the Design pane, drag the **edge** of the Clustered Column chart to the right so that all three charts are visible.

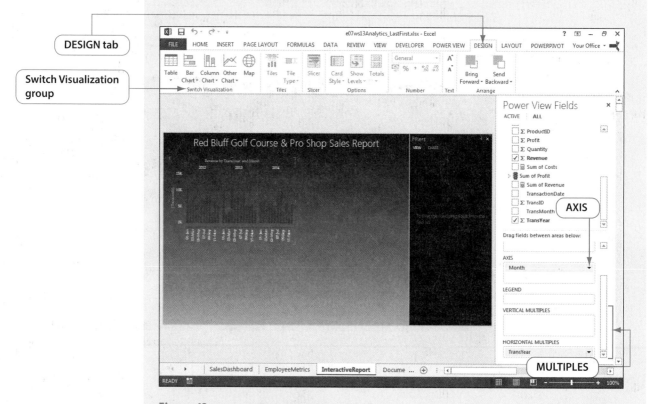

Figure 43 Horizontal Multiples visualization

f. Point to the chart and click the **Pop out** ⌐ icon in the top-right corner of the chart to see the chart in full-screen view.

g. Click the **Pop in** ⌐ icon to return the chart to its previous size.

h. Click **Save** ⊟.

Creating a Visualization with Tiles

Multiples are a great way to see all the charts at one time. However, that may not always be the most effective way to analyze data. Power View offers a visualization feature called "tiles." **Tiles** provide a dynamic navigation strip allowing you to navigate through a series of charts based on a particular value, such as a chart visualizing sales by employee with tiles for each product category. This allows for the user to quickly see data from a specific product category with the click of a tile.

In this exercise you will create a bar chart visualization that will compare total sales for each employee with tiles based on product type.

E13.25

To Create a Bar Chart with Tiles

a. Click the **POWER VIEW** tab, and then in the View group, click **Field List**, if necessary, to display the Power View Fields pane. Click an empty area of the Design pane to deselect the chart.

b. In the Power View Fields pane, expand **tblEmployee**, and then select **LastName**. Notice a new table is being created to the right of the chart.

c. In the Power View Fields pane, scroll down to **tblTransactions**, and then select **Σ Revenue**.

d. Click the **DESIGN** tab, and then in the Switch Visualization group, click **Bar Chart**. Click **Clustered Bar**.

e. In the Design pane, expand the size of the Clustered Bar chart so all values are visible.

f. In the Power View Fields pane, scroll up and expand **tblProducts**, and then drag **ProductType** to the **TILE BY** area.

g. Drag to expand both the **tile container** and the **clustered bar chart** to be the same height as the Clustered Column chart. Notice that with a tile container there is no longer an option to **Pop out** ⌐ on the chart.

h. **Close** the Filters pane and the Power View Fields pane.

i. Click on the various tiles to see how the employee sales compare for other product types.

j. Explore the ability to filter all visualizations by clicking the bar for the last name **Lange** on the Revenue by LastName bar chart.

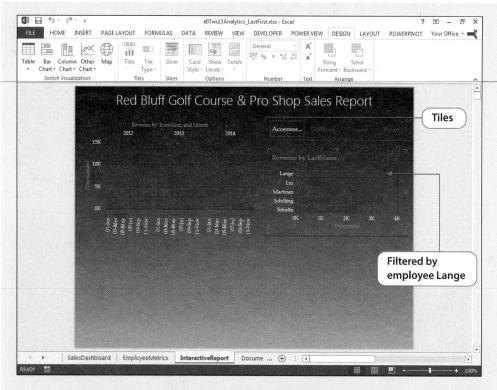

Figure 44   Power View report filtered by employee Lange

k. Click anywhere inside the chart container but not on a bar to remove the filter.

l. Click **Save** .

Creating a Map Visualization in Power View

The Bing Maps app is one way to create data visualizations that illustrate data with a geographic element. However, the Bing Maps app is limited in its interactive capabilities. Beyond zoom and panning around there is no interaction. Excel's Power View report includes a map visualization that can be used with filters or slicers, or even used to filter other charts in the report. In this exercise you will create a map visualization to add to the Power View report.

E13.26

To Create a Map Visualization in Power View

a. Click an empty area below the **Revenue by TransYear** and **Month** column chart.

b. Click the **POWER VIEW** tab, and then in the View group, click **Field List** to display the Power View Fields pane. In the Power View Fields pane, expand the **tblCustomers**, if necessary, and then click **State**. Expand **tblTransactions**, if necessary, select **Σ TransYear**, and then select **Σ Revenue**. Under the Fields section, click the **Σ TransYear** arrow, and then click **Do Not Summarize**.

c. Click the **DESIGN** tab, and then in the Switch Visualization group, click **Map**.

d. Drag the **right-middle sizing handle** to the right to expand the width of the Map visualization. Click **Zoom Out** ⊖ so that the following states are visible: California, Nevada, Arizona, Colorado, and New Mexico. If necessary, click **Enable Content** in the Privacy Warning bar.

e. On the Map visualization, on the legend, click **2012** to filter all other visualizations to only show 2012 Revenue.

f. **Close** the Power View Fields pane.

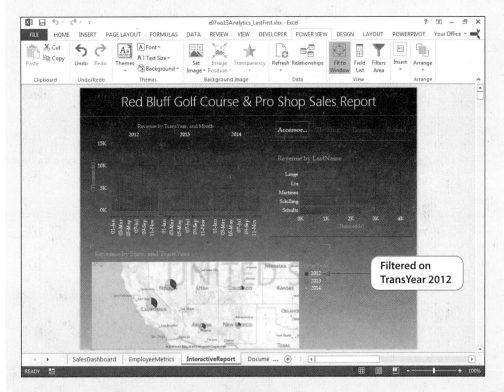

Figure 45 Power View report filtered on TransYear 2012

g. Click just below the **TransYear** legend to clear the 2012 filter.

h. Click **Save** 🖫.

Adding Slicers to a Power View Report

Slicers in a Power View report work just like they do in an Excel worksheet, allowing for an easy way to filter data and charts with the click of the button. As you have already seen, the Power View report makes it easy to filter data from other data visualizations; however, it is often useful to add slicers for data that are not necessarily a part of any of the visualizations. In this exercise you will add Status and ProductType slicers to the report that will allow managers to see the revenue for members and guests as well as any particular product type.

▶ To Add Slicers to a Power View Report

a. Click the **POWER VIEW** tab, in the View group, click **Field List** to view the Power View Fields pane. Click an empty area of the Design pane to the right of the map.

b. Expand **tblCustomers**, if necessary, and then click **Status**.

c. Click the **DESIGN** tab, and then in the Slicer group, click **Slicer** to create a slicer from the Status field.

d. Adjust the height of the Status slicer by dragging the **bottom-middle sizing handle** up to just below **Member**.

e. Click an empty area below the **Status** slicer. Expand **tblProducts**, if necessary, and then click **ProductType**.

f. On the DESIGN tab, in the Slicer group, click **Slicer** to create a slicer from the ProductType field.

g. Drag the **ProductType** slicer below the Status slicer. Adjust the size appropriately.

h. Use the slicers to filter the report to show only revenue from **Members** and **Clothing**.

i. **Close** the Power View Fields pane.

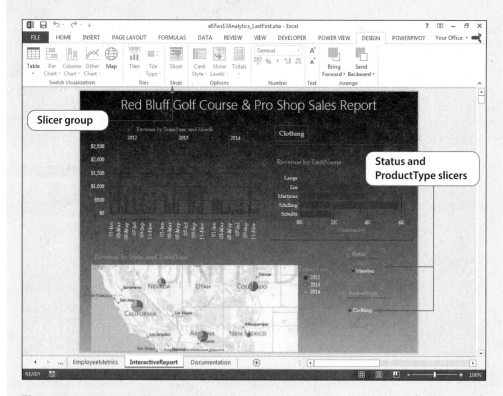

Figure 46 Slicers added to Power View report

j. Click **Clear Filter** 🔣 on the Status and ProductType slicers.

k. Click **Save** 🖫.

l. Complete the **Documentation** worksheet, and submit your file as directed by your instructor.

Concept Check

1. What are some basic design concepts to consider when creating a digital dashboard? p. 654–658

2. Describe the data model, and explain how it may improve data analysis. p. 658–663

3. Discuss some of the advanced data modeling techniques made possible with the PowerPivot COM Add-In. p. 663–676

4. Describe how PowerPivot can be used to create a simple dashboard, and discuss a few simple ways to enhance the value of a dashboard. p. 676–690

5. What are apps for Office, and what are some benefits of using them? p. 690–691

6. What are some things needed to prepare a dashboard for production and why? p. 693–694

7. What are the benefits of a Power View report, and how is it different from a dashboard? p. 696

Key Terms

App for Office   690
Base value   673
Bidirectional KPI   674
Business intelligence (BI)   654
Data model   658
Digital dashboards   654
Explicit calculated field   670
Horizontal multiples   698

Implicit calculated field   670
Key performance indicator (KPI)   655
Multiples   698
Negative KPI   674
Positive KPI   674
Power View   696
Relational data   658
Silverlight   696

Slicers   676
Sparklines   689
Status threshold   673
Target value   673
Tiles   699
Vertical multiples   698
White space   657

Visual Summary

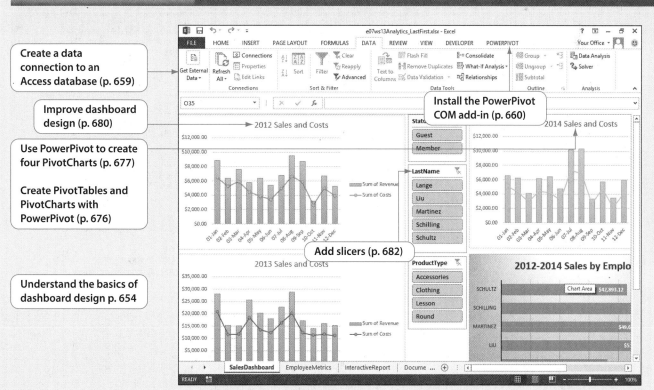

Create a data connection to an Access database (p. 659)

Improve dashboard design (p. 680)

Use PowerPivot to create four PivotCharts (p. 677)

Create PivotTables and PivotCharts with PowerPivot (p. 676)

Understand the basics of dashboard design p. 654

Install the PowerPivot COM add-in (p. 660)

Add slicers (p. 682)

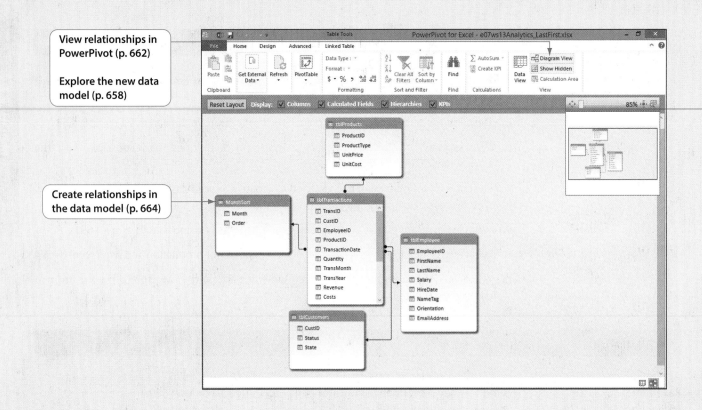

View relationships in PowerPivot (p. 662)

Explore the new data model (p. 658)

Create relationships in the data model (p. 664)

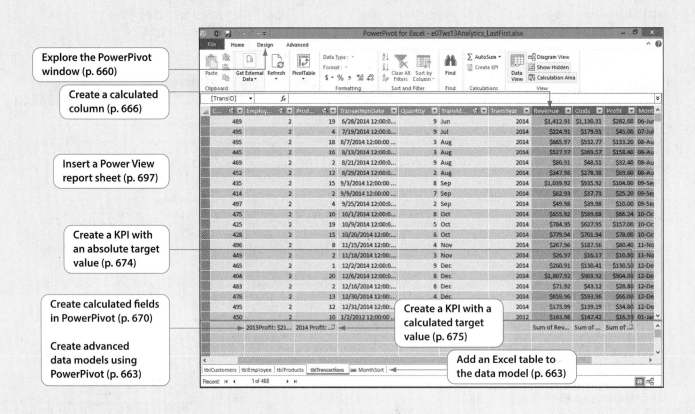

Explore the PowerPivot window (p. 660)

Create a calculated column (p. 666)

Insert a Power View report sheet (p. 697)

Create a KPI with an absolute target value (p. 674)

Create calculated fields in PowerPivot (p. 670)

Create advanced data models using PowerPivot (p. 663)

Create a KPI with a calculated target value (p. 675)

Add an Excel table to the data model (p. 663)

Install the Bing maps app for Office (p. 690)

Incorporate the yearly profit goal KPI into a dashboard (p. 685)

Hide screen elements (p. 694)

Incorporate the KPI goal into a combo chart (p. 687)

Protect a worksheet (p. 693)

Prepare a dashboard for production (p. 693)

Incorporate the 2014 profit KPI into a dashboard (p. 686)

Use the Bing maps app (p. 691)

Use Apps for Office for data visualizations (p. 690)

Add Sparklines to a PivotTable (p. 689)

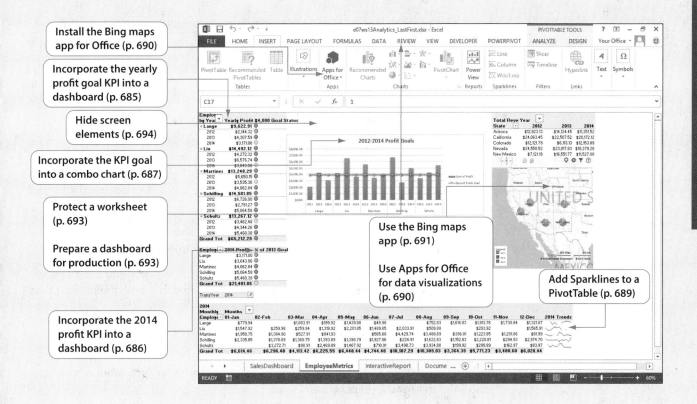

Create multiples (p. 698)

Create a map visualization in Power View (p. 700)

Use Apps for Office for data visualizations (p. 690)

Add Sparklines to a PivotTable (p. 689)

Install Microsoft Silverlight (p. 696)

Create a bar chart with tiles (p. 699)

Generate visual reports with Power View (p. 696)

Add slicers to a Power View report (p. 702)

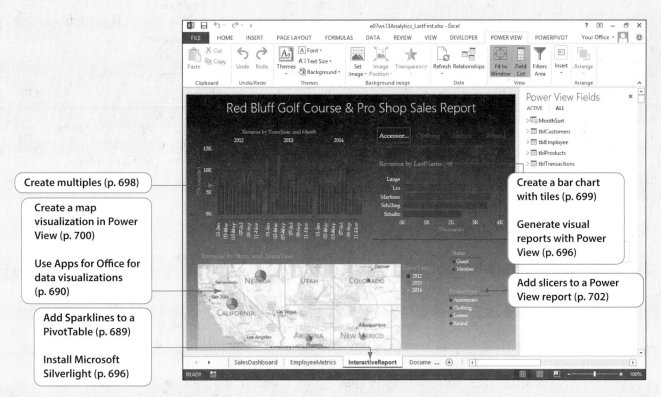

Figure 47 The Red Bluff Golf Course & Pro Shop Dashboards, KPIs, and Data Visualizations Final

Student data file needed:
e07ws13SpaRevenue.xlsx

You will save your file as:
e07ws13SpaRevenue_LastFirst.xlsx

Advanced Analysis at the Turquoise Oasis Spa

Sales &
Marketing

Managers at the Turquoise Oasis Spa have read about the benefits of Power View to explore their data. They have provided you with some sample data and need you to create a data model that they can use to build their Power View report. In this exercise you will create a data model with the data provided, create calculated fields, calculated columns, KPIs, and relationships.

a. Start **Excel**, and then open the **e07ws13SpaRevenue** workbook. Save it as e07ws13SpaRevenue_LastFirst using your last and first name.

b. Click the **SalesData** worksheet tab, and then click any cell in the Turquoise Oasis Spa Sample Sales 2011–2013 table. Click the **POWERPIVOT** tab, and then in the Tables group, click **Add to Data Model**.

c. Minimize or close the PowerPivot window, and then click the **Goals** worksheet tab.

d. Click any cell in the 2013 Monthly Revenue table. On the POWERPIVOT tab, in the Tables group, click **Add to Data Model**. Minimize or close the PowerPivot window, and then repeat for the **Total Orders by Rep** table.

e. On the POWERPIVOT tab, in the Data Model group, click **Manage**, and make the following changes to the **SpaSales** sheet in the data model:

   - Double-click the **Add Column** column heading, type Revenue and then press [Enter]. Type =[UnitPrice]*[QuantitySold] and then press [Enter]. Click the **HOME** tab, and then in the Formatting group, click **Format: Change Formatting** arrow, and then select **Currency**.

   - Double-click the **Add Column** column heading, type Costs and then press [Enter]. Type =[UnitCost]*[QuantitySold] and then press [Enter]. On the HOME tab, in the Formatting group, click **Format: Change Formatting** arrow, and then select **Currency**.

   - Double-click the **Add Column** column heading, type Profit and then press [Enter]. Type =[Revenue]-[Costs] and then press [Enter]. On the HOME tab, in the Formatting group, click **Format: Change Formatting** arrow, and then select **Currency**.

f. Click the **RevGoals2013** worksheet, and then make the following changes to the RevGoals2013 worksheet in the data model:

   - Select the **MonthlySalesActual** column. On the HOME tab, in the Formatting group, click **Format: Change Formatting** arrow, and then select **Currency**.

   - Select the **MonthlySalesGoal** column. On the HOME tab, in the Formatting group, click **Format: Change Formatting** arrow, and then select **Currency**.

   - Select both the **MonthlySalesActual** and **MonthlySalesGoal** columns, and then in the Calculations group, click **AutoSum** to create two calculated fields in the Calculation Area: Sum of MonthlySalesActual and Sum of MonthlySalesGoal.

   - Click the **Sum of MonthlySalesActual** calculated field in the Calculation Area, and then in the Calculations group, click **Create KPI**.

   - Under Define target value, in the Calculated Field box, select **Sum of MonthlySalesGoal**.

   - Under **Define status thresholds**, click and slide the low value threshold to **75%** and the high value threshold to **100%**.

   - Under **Select icon style**, select the flags icon set (the second option from the left).

   - Click **OK**.

g. Create a relationship in the data model between the SpaSales table and the OrdersByRep table by completing the following tasks:
- Click the **OrdersByRep** worksheet tab in the PowerPivot window, and then select the **SalesRep** column.
- Click the **DESIGN** tab, and then in the Relationships group, click **Create Relationship**.
- In the Related Lookup Table box, select **SpaSales**.
- Verify that **SalesRep** is selected in the Related Lookup Column field, and then click **Create**.

h. Click the **Documentation** worksheet. Click cell **A6**, and then type in today's date. Click cell **B6**, and then type your first and last name. Complete the remainder of the **Documentation** worksheet according to your instructor's direction.

i. Click **Save**, **close** Excel, and then submit your file as directed by your instructor.

Problem Solve 1

MyITLab® Grader
Homework 1

Sales & Marketing

Student data file needed:

 e07ws13PaperSales.xlsx

You will save your file as:

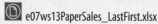 e07ws13PaperSales_LastFirst.xlsx

Visualizing the Paper Mill's Data

The Paper Mill is a mid-sized business that specializes in selling printer paper to small U.S. businesses at a discount. You have been asked to create a Power View report that uses visualizations to illustrate how the business is doing from a few different perspectives. You will use the Power View tools to create a column chart, line chart, and a map visualization based on the sales data provided.

a. Start **Excel**, and then open the **e07ws13PaperSales** workbook. Save it as e07ws13PaperSales_LastFirst using your last and first name.

b. Click the **Sales** worksheet tab, and then select any cell in the **PaperSales** table. Click the **POWERPIVOT** tab, and then in the Tables group, click **Add to Data Model**.

c. Close the PowerPivot window. Click the **INSERT** tab, and then in the Reports group, click **Power View**.

d. Rename the Power View1 worksheet tab to SalesReport and add a title to the Power View Report of Paper Mill Sales Report.

e. Click the **POWER VIEW** tab, and then in the Themes group, select the **Slipstream** theme to apply to the report.

f. Apply a **Dark1 Vertical Gradient** background to the report.

g. Create a **Clustered Column** chart that shows the 2014 Sales by Month Order.

h. To the right of the 2014 Sales by Month Order chart, create a **Line chart** showing 2014 Sales with Month Order on the Axis and Region as the Legend.

i. Add a visualization using the **Map** tool that shows the 2014 Sales by State.

j. Drag the **Region** field into the **COLOR** area to create different colored markers for each of the four regions.

k. Create a **slicer** for the Power View Report that will allow the easy filtering of the data based on State.

l. **Close** the Filter Area and Power View Fields pane.

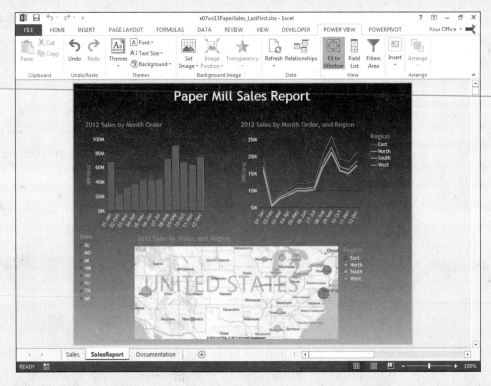

Figure 48 Paper Mills Sales Report

m. Complete the **Documentation** worksheet according to your instructor's direction. Insert the **filename** in the left custom footer section of the Header/Footer tab in the Page Setup dialog box on all worksheets in the workbook.

n. Click **Save**, **close** Excel, and then submit the file as directed by your instructor.

Perform 1: Perform in Your Career

Student data files needed:

e07ws13StockData.txt

e07ws13Stocks.xlsx

You will save your file as:

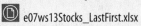

e07ws13Stocks_LastFirst.xlsx

Stock Trader Dashboard

Information
Technology

A local firm that specializes in trading stocks has hired you. Management would like to easily monitor specific stocks of interest and has asked you to create a simple dashboard for that purpose. In this exercise you will create a data connection to a tab-delimited text file, add the data to the data model, and create a simple dashboard consisting of various charts and slicers.

a. Start **Excel**, and then open the **e07ws13Stocks** workbook. Save it as e07ws13Stocks_LastFirst using your last and first name.

b. Click the **StocksDashboard** worksheet tab, and then import the data from the tab-delimited text file named **e07ws13StockData** located in your student files.

• Be sure to indicate that your data contains headers in Step 1 of the Text Import Wizard.

• Add this data to the data model and only create a connection to the data file.

c. Make the following changes to the data model in the PowerPivot window:
- Format the **Date** field as ***3/14/2001**.
- Format the Open, High, Low, and Closing fields as **Currency**.
- Format the Volume field with a thousands separator and 0 decimal places.
- Create a calculated column titled Change that will subtract the Open value from the Closing value.
- Format the Change field as **Decimal Number**.

d. Use the PowerPivot window to generate a dashboard with four charts in cell **A1** of the StocksDashboard worksheet.

e. Use the following guidelines for chart type, style, formatting, and placement.
- Chart 1 should be a Clustered Column chart showing the average opening value each month for all stocks.
- Chart 2 should be a Clustered Column chart showing the average change value each month for all stocks.
- Chart 3 should be a Clustered Column chart showing the average closing value each month for all stocks.
- Chart 4 should be a Line with Markers chart showing the average volume each month for all stocks.

f. Make the following formatting changes to the charts:
- Apply **Chart Style 5** to Chart 1, edit **Chart Title** to be Average at Open, and then delete the chart legend. Sort the **month** values in ascending "natural" order, and then hide the filter buttons.
- Apply **Chart Style 5** to Chart 2, edit **Chart Title** to be Average Change, and then delete the chart legend. Sort the **month** values in ascending "natural" order, and then hide the filter buttons.
- Apply **Chart Style 5** to Chart 3, edit **Chart Title** to be Average at Close, and then delete the chart legend. Sort the **month** values in ascending "natural" order, and then hide the filter buttons.
- Apply **Chart Style 12** to Chart 4, edit **Chart Title** to be Average Volume, and then delete the chart legend. Sort the **month** values in ascending "natural" order, and then hide the filter buttons.

g. Add a slicer for the **Ticker**, and then connect it to all four charts. Apply **Slicer Style Dark 5** to the Ticker slicer, and then place it to the right of the charts.

h. Modify the options for the Stocks Dashboard worksheet to hide column and row headings as well as gridlines.

i. Protect the worksheet allowing only the options to Use PivotTable & PivotChart and to Edit objects.

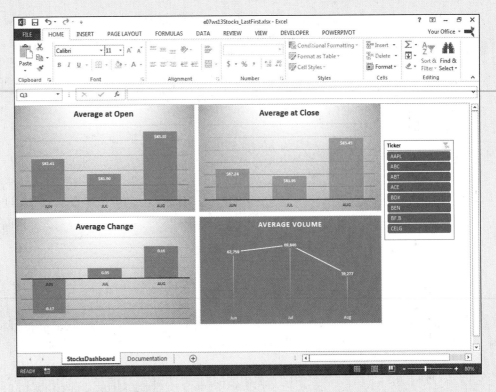

Figure 49 Stocks dashboard

j. Complete the **Documentation** worksheet according to your instructor's direction. Insert the **filename** in the left custom footer section of the Header/Footer tab in the Page Setup dialog box on all worksheets in the workbook.

k. Click **Save**, **close** Excel, and then submit the file as directed by your instructor.

Additional Cases

Additional Workshop Cases are available on the companion website and in the instructor resources.

WORKSHOP 14 | VISUAL BASIC FOR APPLICATIONS

Prepare Case

The Red Bluff Golf Course & Pro Shop Spreadsheet Enhancement with Form Controls and VBA

Sales & Marketing

Managers at the Red Bluff Golf Course & Pro Shop have been using dashboards to keep track of sales from golf lessons, clothing, accessories, and so on. You have been given access to a workbook with a sample dashboard and Power View report based on the sales from 2010 to 2012. You have been asked to use some of the developer tools— including form controls and VBA—

bikeriderlondon / Shutterstock

to enhance the dashboard and Power View report, provide more security, and add new functionality.

REAL WORLD SUCCESS

"I interned for an auto parts manufacturing plant last summer and was asked to assist with a data cleansing project. The person working on the project had spent hours cleaning the data and was not getting very far. I was able to use a little bit of VBA to loop through thousands of rows in a matter of minutes."

- Francis, former student

Student data file needed for this workshop:

 e07ws14Dashboards.xlsx

You will save your files as:

 e07ws14Dashboards_LastFirst.xlsm

 e07ws14Module1_LastFirst.txt

 e07ws14DebugVBA_LastFirst.txt

Enhancing the Readability and Interactivity of Dashboards

Digital dashboards are mechanisms that deliver business intelligence in graphical form. Dashboards provide management with a "big picture" view of the business, usually from multiple perspectives using various charts and other graphical representations. Simple dashboards may consist of a few charts that represent sales data over a particular period of time or from various perspectives such as product category or department. Dashboards are typically designed to encourage interaction with the user. Slicers are one way to encourage interaction. **Slicers** are visual controls that allow you to quickly and easily filter your data in an interactive way. If you are interested in knowing how to create dashboards in Excel, please refer to Workshop 13 of the Excel Comprehensive book . In this section, you will use form controls to encourage more interaction with dashboards and create dynamic labels to increase the readability of a dashboard.

Enhance Spreadsheets with Form Controls

Form controls have many uses in Excel. **Form controls** are objects that can be placed into an Excel worksheet, providing the functionality to interact with your models. Form controls can be used to help users select data by providing menus, lists, spinners, and scroll bars. In the context of dashboards, form controls can provide a simple way to interact with your analysis in a way that is backwards compatible with earlier versions of Excel.

Opening the Starting File

You have been given access to a workbook that is connected to the Red Bluff Golf Course & Pro Shop sales database with an existing dashboard and Power View report. Throughout this workshop you will use a variety of developer tools to enhance the functionality of the dashboard and Power View report. Some of the changes you will make to the workbook require it to be saved as a macro-enabled workbook.

E14.00

 To Open the Starting File

a. Start **Excel**, and then open the **e07ws14Dashboards** workbook from the student data files.

b. Click the **FILE** tab, and then click **Save As**. Click **Browse**, click the **Save as type** arrow, and then select **Excel Macro-Enabled Workbook (*.xlsm)**. Navigate to the folder or location designated by your instructor, and then save the file with the name e07ws14Dashboards_LastFirst using your last and first name. Click **Enable Content**, if necessary.

Adding the Developer Tab

To access the form controls in Excel, you must first add the Developer tab to the Ribbon.

E14.01

 To Add the Developer Tab

a. Click the **FILE** tab, and then click **Options**.

b. In the Excel Options dialog box, in the left pane, click **Customize Ribbon**.

c. In the Main Tabs list, click the **Developer** check box.

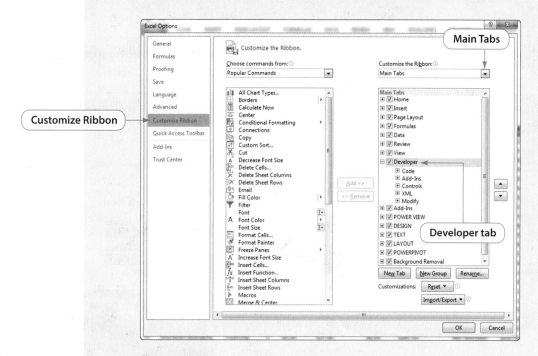

Figure 1   Excel Options dialog box

d. Click **OK**.

Adding a Spin Button

Spin buttons and scroll bars can also enhance a user's experience with a dashboard. A **spin button**, also referred to as a spinner, is a form control that is linked to a specific cell. As the up and down arrows on the button are clicked, the value in the linked cell increases and decreases accordingly. In this exercise, you will create a simple spin button to provide the user with an easy way of increasing and decreasing the year of the sales data.

E14.02

 To Add a Spin Button

a. Click the **RevenueDashboard** worksheet tab. This worksheet consists of a simple dashboard with charts, tables, slicers, and sparklines.

b. Click cell **A19**. Click the **DEVELOPER** tab, and then in the Controls group, click the **Insert** arrow.

c. Under Form Controls, click **Spin Button (Form Control)**.

d. Drag a **vertical rectangle** in cell **A19** to the right of the year value.

e. Right-click the **spin** button, and then click **Format Control**.

f. In the Format Control dialog box, select the value in the **Current value** box, and then type 2010.

g. Select the value in the **Minimum value** box, and then type 2010.

h. Select the value in the **Maximum value** box, and then type 2012.

i. Confirm that the Incremental change box contains a **1**. Click the **Cell link** box, click **A19**, and then click **OK**.

j. Click cell **A19** to deselect the spin button, and then test the added functionality by clicking the up and down arrows to increase and decrease the year and observe the changes in the table below and the chart to the right.

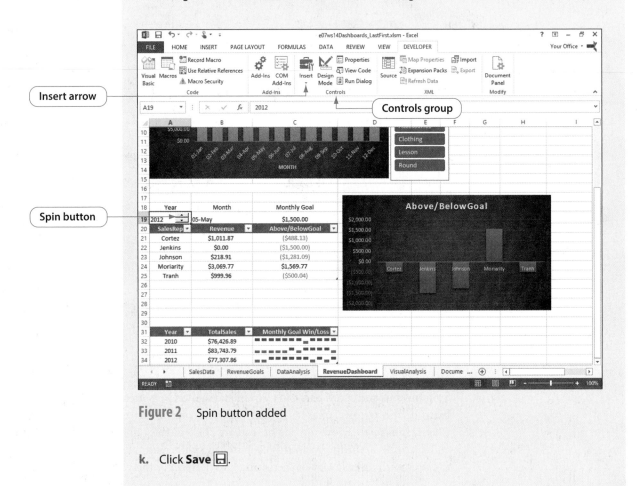

Figure 2   Spin button added

k. Click **Save** 🖫.

Creating a Lookup Table to Use with Form Controls

Some form controls, like the scroll bar, require some additional work to create the values that will be used by the object. Creating a lookup table and using the VLOOKUP function is a common approach to linking values to various form controls. In this exercise, you will create a lookup table for months to use with a scroll bar control.

To Create a Lookup Table

a. Click the **DataAnalysis** worksheet tab.

b. Click cell **E1**, type 1 and then click cell **F1**. Type '01-Jan. The apostrophe is required so that Excel does not interpret this as a date.

> **Troubleshooting**
> If Excel interprets the value in E1 as a date, be sure to include the apostrophe ' as the first character so that the value is formatted as text.

c. Click cell **E2**, type 2 and then click cell **F2**. Type '02-Feb.

d. Continue creating the lookup table with the following values in cells **E3:F12**.

3	'03-Mar
4	'04-Apr
5	'05-May
6	'06-Jun
7	'07-Jul
8	'08-Aug
9	'09-Sep
10	'10-Oct
11	'11-Nov
12	'12-Dec

e. Select the range **E1:F12**. Click inside the **Name** box, type Month_Range, and then press Enter to create a named range for the lookup table.

f. Click the **RevenueDashboard** worksheet tab, click cell **B17**, and then type 1. This value will be used as the lookup value in the VLOOKUP function to retrieve the appropriate month from the Month_Range named range.

g. Click cell **B19**, select the text, and then type the following function:
=VLOOKUP(B17, Month_Range, 2, False).

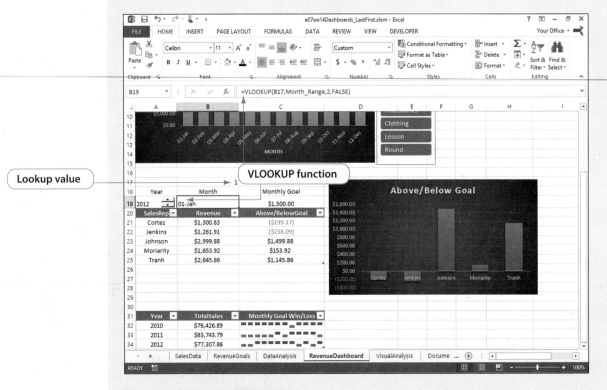

Figure 3 VLOOKUP function added

h. Click **Save** 🖫.

Adding a Scroll Bar

Now that you have created a lookup table with the appropriate values and have added the VLOOKUP function to cell B19, you will now add the scroll bar form control. A **scroll bar** has a very similar function as the spin button. However, with a scroll bar, the value of the linked cell is increased or decreased by sliding the scroll bar to the left or right. In this exercise, you will create a scroll bar so that the user can easily scroll through different months.

E14.04

▶ To Add a Scroll Bar

a. Click the **DEVELOPER** tab, and then in the Controls group, click the **Insert** arrow. Under Form Controls, click **Scroll Bar (Form Control)** ▤.

b. Drag a **horizontal rectangle** inside cell **B19** to the right of the value.

c. Right-click the **scroll bar**, and then click **Format Control**.

d. In the Format Control dialog box, on the Control tab, select the value in the **Current value** box, and then type 1.

e. Select the value in the **Minimum value** box, and then type 1.

f. Select the value in the **Maximum value** box, and then type 12. Leave the existing values in the Incremental change and Page change boxes.

g. Click the **Cell link** box, click cell **B17**, and then click **OK**.

h. Click cell **B17**, and then change the font color to white so that it is not visible in the model.

i. Test the added functionality by sliding the **scroll bar** to the right and left.

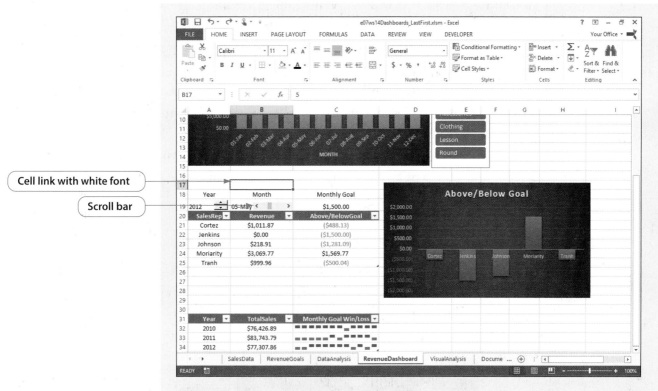

Cell link with white font

Scroll bar

Figure 4 Scroll bar added

j. Click **Save** .

Creating Dynamic Labels

Labels are critical to dashboard design and can add clarity to the graphics being displayed. Dynamic labels offer additional clarity in PivotCharts by displaying the year and/or month that is being displayed when filtered.

E14.05

> **To Create Dynamic Labels**
>
> a. Click the **INSERT** tab, and then in the Text group, click **Text Box**.
>
> b. Drag to create a box in the top-left corner of the **Sales Revenue Column** chart.
>
> c. Click the **formula bar**. Type =, click the **DataAnalysis** worksheet tab, and then click cell **B1**. Press Enter.
>
> > **Troubleshooting**
> > If you did not click the formula bar before typing =, then the cell reference will not work. Just delete the typed =, click the formula bar, and type = again.
>
> d. On the HOME tab, in the Font group, increase the font size to 14. Click the **Fill Color** arrow, and then select **No Fill** to remove the default white fill.
>
> e. Click the **Font Color** arrow, and then select **White, Background 1**.
>
> f. Click the **DRAWING TOOLS FORMAT** tab, and then in the Shape Styles group, click the **Shape Outline** arrow. Select **No Outline**.
>
> g. Test the functionality of the dynamic label by clicking on different years in the **Year** slicer. You will now add another dynamic label for the SaleType.

Enhancing the Readability and Interactivity of Dashboards   717

h. Click the **INSERT** tab, and then in the Text group, click **Text Box**.

i. Drag to create a box in the top-right corner of the **Sales Revenue Column** chart.

j. Click the **formula bar**. Type =, click the **DataAnalysis** worksheet tab, and then click cell **B2**. Press Enter.

k. On the HOME tab, in the Font group, increase the font size to 14. Click the **Fill Color** arrow, and then select **No Fill** to remove the default white fill.

l. Click the **Font Color** arrow, and then select **White, Background 1**.

m. Click the **DRAWING TOOLS FORMAT** tab, and then in the Shape Styles group, click the **Shape Outline** arrow. Select **No Outline**.

n. Click **Accessories** in the SaleType slicer, and then adjust the size of the box to accommodate the value.

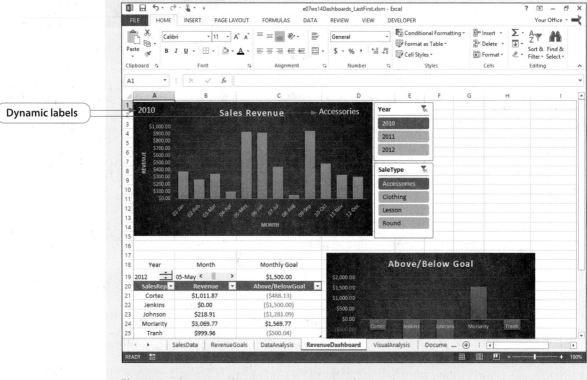

Figure 5 Dynamic labels added

o. Click **Save**.

Leveraging the Power of Visual Basic for Applications (VBA)

VBA (Visual Basic for Applications) is a powerful programming language that is part of most Microsoft Office applications—Word, Access, Excel, and PowerPoint. VBA allows a user to implement a wide variety of enhancements to any of these Microsoft Office applications. VBA is particularly valuable in automating repetitive tasks similar to macros, but it also provides additional tools that can enhance functionality and usability of an Excel application. VBA is considered a very basic form of object-oriented programming. **Object-oriented programming (OOP)** uses a hierarchy of objects—also called classes—as the focus of the programming. VBA manipulates objects by using the methods and properties associated with them. In this section you will explore the various components of VBA and create simple procedures that will enhance the workbook and provide additional security to protect the data.

Understand the Components of VBA

The key to effectively using VBA to enhance your dashboard or any other Excel application is to understand Excel's object model. An **object model** consists of a hierarchical collection of objects, consisting of properties, methods, and events that can be manipulated using VBA. Excel is made up of several dozen objects. **Objects** are combinations of data and code that are treated as a single unit including workbooks, worksheets, charts, PivotTables—and even Excel itself is an object. Objects can also serve as containers for other objects. For example, Excel is an object called an application. This application object contains workbook objects, workbook objects contain worksheet objects, and worksheet objects contain cell range objects. Figure 6 shows a partial object model for Excel.

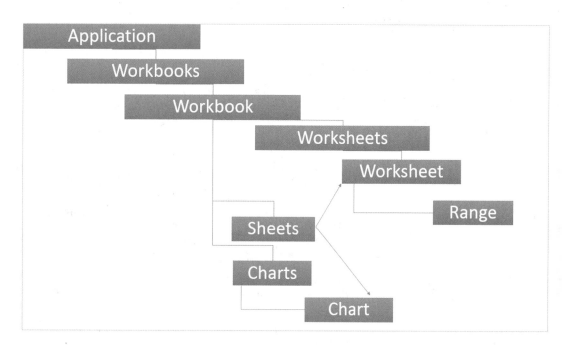

Figure 6 Partial hierarchical object model

Objects are often grouped together into what are called **object collections**, which are also objects. For example, a worksheet is an object in a workbook, and all worksheets in a workbook are also an object. A particular object can be referenced inside a collection by referring to the object collection and then the name or number that represents that specific member of that collection. For example Sheets("Sheet2") is a reference to a worksheet with the name Sheet2 that is a member of the Sheets object collection.

QUICK REFERENCE — Object Collections

Object Collection	Description
Workbooks("Book1")	Refers to a workbook named Book1
Sheets("Sheet1")	Refers to a worksheet named Sheet1
Range("A2:C23")	Refers to a range of cells A2:C23
Charts(2)	Refers to the second chart in a workbook
ChartObjects(3)	Refers to the third embedded chart in a worksheet
Windows(3)	Refers to the third open Excel workbook window

To refer to a particular object using VBA, the objects need to be referred to in their hierarchical structure. For example, to refer to cell A1 in a specific worksheet, the following code would be necessary:

Application.Workbook (workbookname.xlsx).Sheets("Sheet1").Range("A1")

The periods in between each object are referred to as separators. **Separators** indicate the distinction between the object container and the member of that container. Having to type the entire hierarchy each time a particular object is used can be tedious. Because of this, VBA provides special object names that can be used to refer to specific objects. For example, ActiveCell refers to the specific cell that is currently selected in the workbook.

QUICK REFERENCE — VBA Special Object Names

Property	Description
ActiveCell	The currently selected cell in the workbook
ActiveChart	The active chart sheet or chart contained in a ChartObject on a worksheet. This property is Nothing if a chart is not active.
ActiveSheet	The active worksheet
ActiveWindow	The active window
Selection	The selected object. It could refer to a range object, shape, chart, and so on.
ThisWorkbook	The workbook object that contains the VBA procedure being executed. This object may or may not be the same as the ActiveWorkbook object.

Every Excel object has properties. **Properties** are attributes of an object that can be referred to or manipulated using VBA. For example, the cell range object has properties such as value and address.

QUICK REFERENCE	Properties of Common Objects	
Object	**Properties**	**Description**
Workbooks	Name	The name of the workbook
	Path	The directory in which the workbook resides
	Saved	Whether or not the workbook has been saved
	HasPassword	Whether or not the workbook has a password
Worksheets	Name	The name of the worksheet
	Visible	Whether or not the worksheet is visible
Range	Address	The cell reference of the range
	Comment	A comment attached to the cell
	Formula	The formula entered in the cell
	Value	The value entered in the cell
Chart	ChartTitle	The text of the chart's title
	ChartType	The type of chart—bar, column, line
	HasLegend	Whether or not the chart has a legend

An object's properties can be easily modified with a simple expression: Object. Property = expression. For example, to rename a worksheet that is currently selected, using VBA you would type the following expression: ActiveSheet.Name = "NewSheetName".

Excel objects also have methods. A **method** is an action Excel performs with an object. For example, one of the methods for a Range object is ClearContents. When this method is called, values would be cleared from the range. The basic syntax required to call an object's method is

ObjectName.Method

For example, to clear the values in the cell range A1:A5, you would type

Range("A1:A5").ClearContents

QUICK REFERENCE	Common Methods and Descriptions	
Object	**Methods**	**Descriptions**
Workbook	Close	Closes the workbook
	Protect	Protects the workbook
	SaveAs	Saves the workbook with a specified file name
Worksheet	Delete	Deletes the worksheet
	Select	Selects and displays the worksheet
Range	Clear	Clears all content in the range
	Copy	Copies the values in the range to the Clipboard
	Merge	Merges the cells in the range
Chart	Copy	Copies the chart to the Clipboard
	Select	Selects the chart
	Delete	Deletes the chart
Worksheets	Select	Selects all the worksheets in the workbook
Charts	Select	Selects all chart sheets in the workbook

Methods often have parameters that must be included to use the method on the object. A **parameter** is a special kind of variable used to refer to one of the pieces of data provided in a method. For example, the Workbook object has a SaveAs method that requires the file name as a parameter. Most methods contain required and optional parameters. The basic syntax for providing parameters in a method is

object.method parameter1: = value, parameter2:= value2

For example,

ActiveWorkbook.SaveAs Filename:="NewWorkbookName", FileFormat:=52 saves the active workbook as NewWorkbookName.xlsm.

QUICK REFERENCE	Common FileFormat Values
FileFormat Value	**File Extension**
51	.xlsx
52	.xlsm
6	.csv
−4158	.txt

Exploring the Visual Basic Editor

The **Visual Basic Editor (VBE)** is the tool built into Microsoft Office that is used for creating and editing VBA. At the top of the VBE screen is the title of the workbook that is currently open and being edited. Directly under the application title are the File menu and Standard toolbars, which are visible by default. On the left side of the Visual Basic Editor is the Project Explorer. The **Project Explorer window** contains a hierarchical list of all the objects in open workbooks, including macros, modules, and worksheets. VBA in an Excel workbook can be contained either in a specific worksheet, the specific workbook, or within a module. Below the Project Explorer window is the Properties window. The **Properties window** contains a list of all the properties of a selected object such as name, size, and color. Depending on your system settings, the Property window may not be displayed by default when the VBE is opened. The larger window on the right of the Visual Basic Editor is the Code window. The **Code window** is where all the VBA code is typed and also where VBA generated by a recorded macro can be viewed and edited.

E14.06

 To Explore the VBE

SIDE NOTE
Displaying the VBE
You can press [Alt]+[F11] to access the VBE and toggle back and forth between the VBE and the Excel workbook.

a. Click the **DEVELOPER** tab, and in the Code group, click **Visual Basic**.

b. If the AnalysisToolPak Add-in is installed in Excel, you will see an open Code window with FUNCRES.XLAM in the title bar. **Close** this window, if necessary.

c. Click **Insert**, and then click **Module**.

d. Notice the Project Explorer window, Properties window, and Code window.

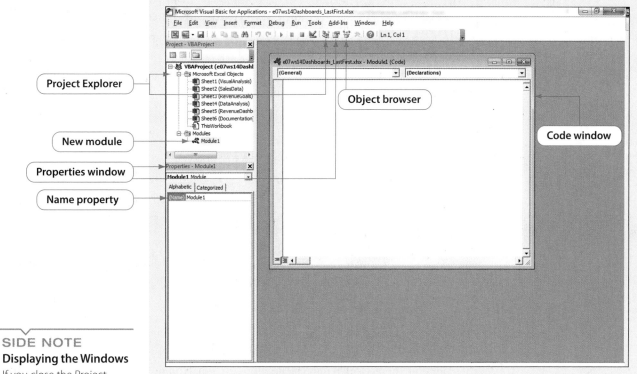

Figure 7 The Visual Basic Editor

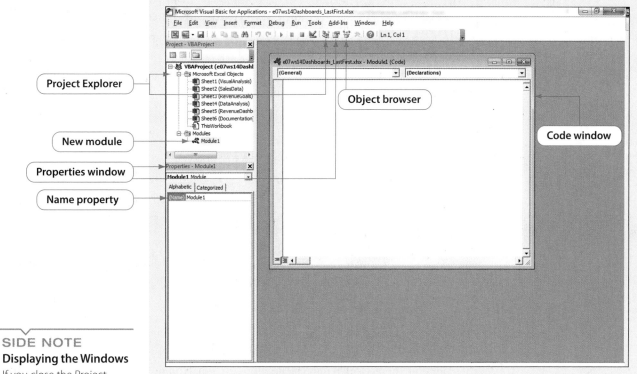

Labels on figure: Project Explorer, New module, Properties window, Name property, Object browser, Code window

SIDE NOTE
Displaying the Windows
If you close the Project Explorer you can press [Ctrl] and type **r** to display it. Pressing [F4] will display the Properties Window if it is closed.

e. In the Properties window, click inside the **Name** box, and then type **e07ws14Module1_LastFirst** using your last and first name.

A **module** is simply a container for code. The two primary types of procedures that are supported by VBA are Sub procedures and function procedures. A **Sub procedure** performs an action on your project or workbook, such as renaming a worksheet or clearing filtered values from PivotTables. A **function procedure** is a group of VBA statements that perform a calculation and return a single value. Function procedures are often used to create custom functions that can be entered in worksheet cells. You can have zero or hundreds of Sub procedures and functions written within a single module. Modules are most often used to store any public procedures that are not event driven. If a Sub procedure is to run when a workbook opens or a worksheet becomes active, then it is typically stored in the workbook or worksheet object to take advantage of the Procedure menu at the top of the Code window.

REAL WORLD ADVICE   Organizing VBA Code by Type

If you have several Sub procedures within a workbook, it can easily become challenging to keep track of where a specific Sub procedure is within a module. It is best to group your Sub procedures together by what they do into separate modules, renaming the module appropriately to describe the kind of procedures it contains. For example, Sub procedures that format a workbook can all be grouped into one module, and Sub procedures that are used to manipulate data can be stored in another.

Create Custom Functions with VBA

Function procedures can provide custom calculations that are used frequently in a business and are not part of the extensive functions available in Excel. These custom functions do not have to be complicated, but instead they can be created to ensure consistency in calculations.

To create a function procedure you must first declare it is a function, and then provide the function with a name and an opening parenthesis. After the opening parenthesis you must provide a name for the value or values that the function needs to perform its calculation and declare the data type(s) that Excel should expect from the value(s). Lastly a closing parenthesis is required to end the function.

Function Commission (totalSales As Currency)

The next line of code is where the calculation of the function is defined. Simply type the FunctionName, declared in the first line, an equals sign, followed by the ValueName, defined in the first line, and then the calculation you would like the function to perform.

Commission = totalSales * 0.15

Creating a Function Procedure

In this exercise, you will create a custom function that will take the total sales value and multiply it by 15% to calculate the total commission paid.

E14.07

 To Create a Function Procedure

a. Click inside the **Code window**, declare a function procedure by typing Function COMMISSION(salesTotal As Currency) and then press Enter. The Function key word is what tells Excel that you are creating a function procedure. COMMISSION is the name given to the function. The value that the function will use in its calculation is named salesTotal and will be a Currency data type.

b. Type the comment 'This function will multiply the total sales amount by 15% and then press Enter.

c. On the next line type COMMISSION = salesTotal * 0.15 and then press Enter.

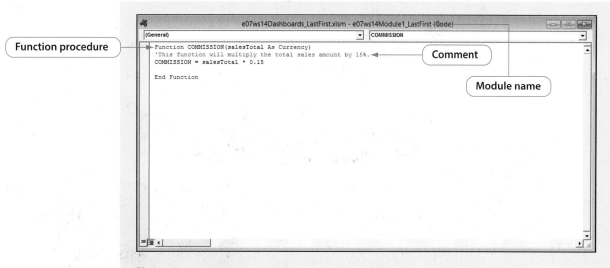

Function procedure

Comment

Module name

Figure 8　COMMISSION function procedure

d. Click **Save** 🖫.

Using a Custom Function

Now that you have created a new function that will require a currency value and then multiply it by 0.15, you will use the function on the RevenueDashboard worksheet.

E14.08

 To Use a Custom Function

a. Press ⌐Alt⌐+⌐F11⌐ to switch to the workbook.

b. On the RevenueDashboard worksheet click cell **A27**, and then type Total Sales.

c. Click cell **B27**, and then type =SUM(RevenueGoals[Revenue]) to sum the values of the Revenue column in the RevenueGoals table. Format B27 as **Currency**.

d. Click cell **A28**, and then type Commission.

e. Click cell **B28**, and then type =COMMISSION(B27) to use the COMMISSION function. Format cell B28 as **Currency**.

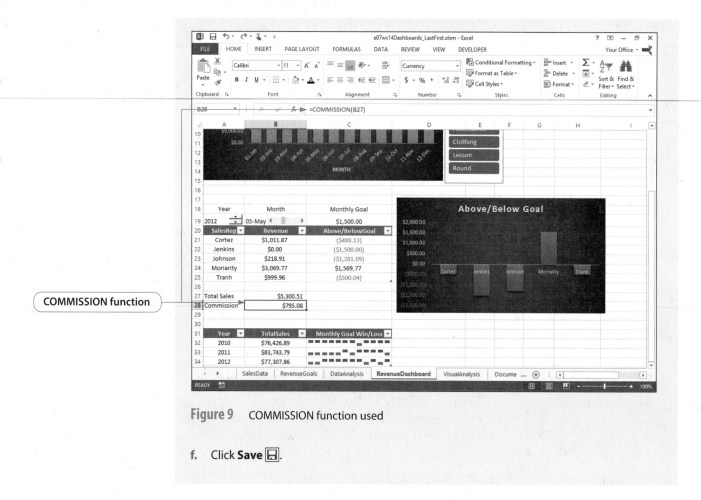

Figure 9 COMMISSION function used

f.   Click **Save** 🖫.

Improve Readability of VBA with Formatting and Structure

An important aspect of writing VBA is making sure the code is easy to read so that you and others can interpret what is happening. This means frequently using indentation, comments, and line breaks. This is especially true when working with more complex code.

You need to take extra steps to keep the code legible and to document what steps you are taking and why. This will make it easier on you and others who may need to edit, analyze, or troubleshoot the code. One of these extra steps will be using ⎡Tab⎤ to create indentations in the code.

Commenting code in VBA is an excellent way of explaining the purpose and the intention of a procedure. This way, you can add straightforward documentation as to what the procedure is doing and what steps to take next. If you are developing more complicated procedures you might want to leave yourself notes about what still needs to be completed or what statements are not working as expected. Adding comments in the Code window is as simple as typing an apostrophe. The (') symbol tells the VBE to ignore any text following the apostrophe on a line of the code.

Also, the VBE interprets code on a line-by-line basis, which means that if you type part of a statement on a line and press ⎡Enter⎤ before the end of the statement, it will create a syntax error. This means that lengthy statements become difficult to read, because without pressing ⎡Enter⎤, the lines of code will extend continuously to the right. To break a line of code across two lines, a space followed by an underscore character can be used. This tells the VBE that the two lines of code should be treated as one.

Using the Macro Recorder to Learn VBA

An easy way to gain a better understanding of how VBA works is to use the Macro Recorder to generate VBA code for actions you want to complete. See Workshop 8 for information about recording macros. The code generated can be useful in identifying the key elements of the language and how the objects, properties, methods, and events work together to accomplish specific tasks.

Using VBA to Clear Slicer Filters

The RevenueDashboard worksheet contains two slicers used for filtering on Year and SaleType. You have been asked to write VBA code that will clear the filters on the slicers. You will be calling the ClearManualFilter method for the SlicerCaches collection that is part of the ThisWorkbook object.

E14.09

To Clear Slicer Filters Using VBA

a. Click Alt + F11 to switch back to the VBE. Click inside the Code window just below the **End Function** statement, type Sub clearSlicers() and then press Enter to create a new Sub procedure.

b. To add a comment to the Sub procedure type 'This code clears all slicer filters specified. Press Enter. The (') symbol at the beginning of the line indicates that it is a comment and not a line of code that Excel needs to execute.

c. Type ThisWorkbook.SlicerCaches("Slicer_Year").ClearManualFilter and then press Enter.

d. Type ThisWorkbook.SlicerCaches("Slicer_SaleType").ClearManualFilter and then press Enter.

SIDE NOTE
Naming Sub Procedures
Names for Sub procedures must begin with a letter and cannot contain any spaces.

SIDE NOTE
View the Object Browser
Press F2 in the VBE to display the Object Browser, which shows properties, methods, and events for an object.

clearSlicers Sub procedure

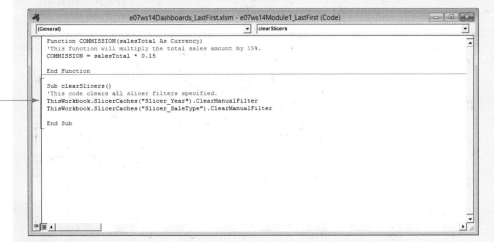

Figure 10 clearSlicers Sub procedure

e. Click **Save** 💾.

f. To test the VBA code, press Alt + F11 to toggle back to the workbook. Click **2011** on the Year slicer and **Accessories** on the SaleType slicer.

g. Press Alt + F11 again to toggle back to the editor. Press F5 to run the clearSlicers Sub procedure.

h. Press Alt + F11 again to toggle back to the workbook and observe all the slicer filters have now been cleared.

i. Click **Save** 💾.

Assigning VBA Code to a Button Control

The clearSlicers Sub procedure is not very useful without giving the end user a way of running the code from the dashboard. Sub procedures can be added to command buttons for easy access.

E14.10

 To Assign a Sub Procedure to a Button Control

a. Click the **DEVELOPER** tab, and then in the Controls group, click the **Insert** arrow. Under Form Controls, select **Button (Form Control)** 🔲.

b. Drag to create a **rectangular button** to the right of the **Year** slicer, within the range **H1:I2**.

c. In the Assign Macro dialog box, select **clearSlicers**, and then click **OK**.

d. Right-click the **button form** control, and then click **Edit Text**. Delete the existing button text, and then type Clear Slicers. Click outside the button to confirm the change.

e. To test the functionality of the new button, apply some filters using the slicers, and then click the **Clear Slicers** button to clear them.

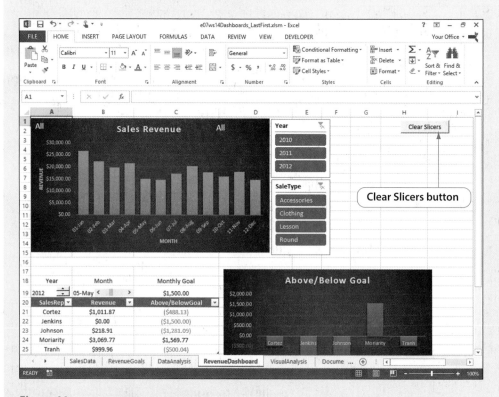

Figure 11 Clear Slicers macro button

f. Click **Save** 💾.

Troubleshoot VBA

You may have encountered some errors when attempting to write VBA code. Some of the errors may have been caused by pressing [Enter] to break up a line of code without inserting a "_" or some other syntax error. With those types of errors, the VBA code cannot be executed until the problem is corrected. The other common VBA error is called a run-time error. A **run-time error** occurs when the code is executed, displaying a description of the error. The VBE includes a tool called the debugger to help troubleshoot run-time errors. When using the debugger, the code is executed one line at a time to make it easier to identify the exact point that the run-time error occurs.

In this exercise, you will create a new module and enter a simple Sub procedure with a fairly obvious error in order to learn how to use the VBE debugger.

E14.11

▶ To Debug VBA

a. Press [Alt]+[F11] to switch to the VBE. Click **Insert**, and then select **Module**.

b. In the Properties window, select the text in the **Name** property, type **e07ws14DebugVBA_LastFirst** using your Last and First name, and then press [Enter].

c. Any spelling errors in this code are intentional for the purposes of this exercise. Please type this code exactly as follows:
   - Private Sub troubleShoot () and then press [Enter].
   - Sheets("RevenuDashboard").Range("A16"). Valu = "Red Bluff Monthly Revenue" and then press [Enter].

d. Press [F8] to enter debug mode. Notice the first line of code is highlighted in yellow.

SIDE NOTE
Debug Mode
You can also enter debugging mode by clicking the Debug command and then clicking Step Into.

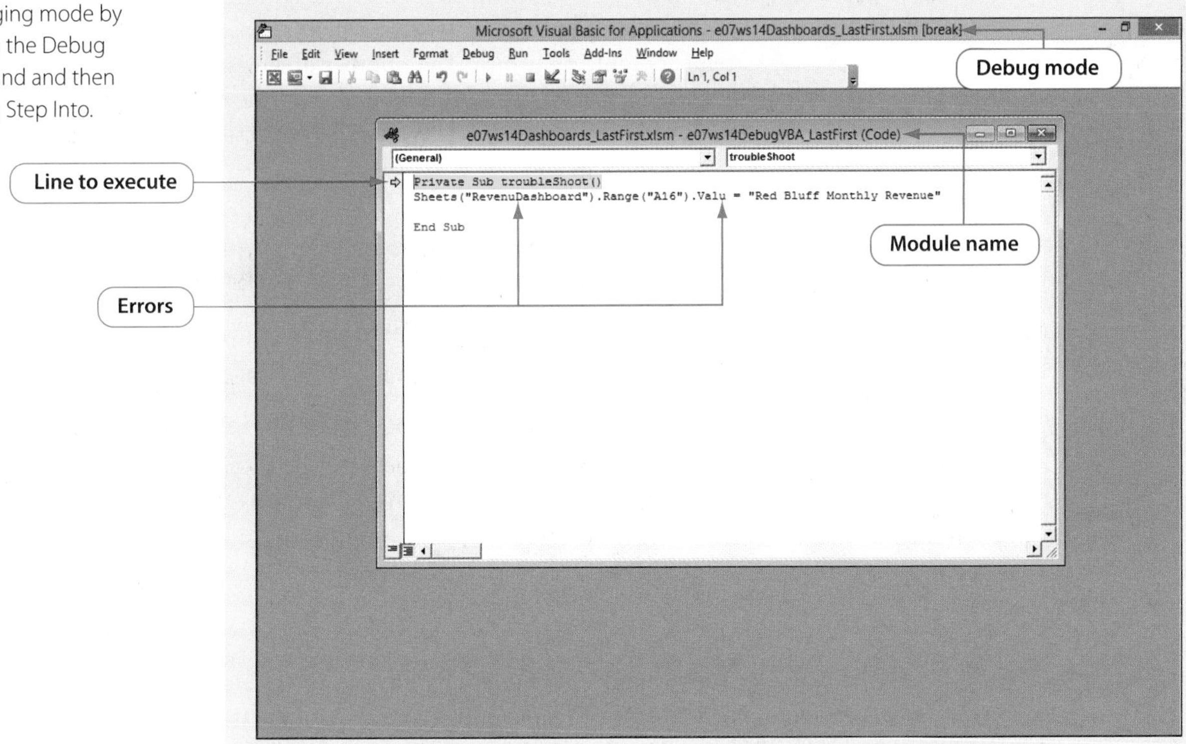

Figure 12   VBA debug mode

e. Press `F8` again to execute that line of code. No warnings or errors are displayed, and the next line of code is now highlighted.

f. Press `F8` again to execute the second line of code. A run-time error is displayed, stating Subscript out of range.

 This error can occur due to a variety of reasons, but a very common one is when the code refers to an object that does not exist in the workbook. In this case the name of the sheet is misspelled.

g. Click **Debug**, and then correct the spelling of the sheet name to RevenueDashboard. Press `F8` to execute the second line again.

h. Another error message is displayed, indicating that the object does not support this property or method. Click **Debug**, and then notice the Value property is misspelled as **Valu**. Correct the spelling of the Valu property to Value. Press `F8` to execute the second line again.

i. The second line of code executes without any additional errors, and the first line of code in e07ws14Module1_LastFirst is highlighted. Press `F5` to exit debugging mode.

j. Press `Alt`+`F11` to switch back to the workbook. Notice the text has been added to cell A16.

k. Click **Save** 💾.

Create and Use Loops in VBA

The clearSlicers Sub procedure created earlier to automatically clear the filters from the Years and SaleType slicers was effective, but if more slicers are added to the dashboard the procedure would have to be modified to include the additional slicers. A more effective use of the VBA code would be to use what is called a loop. **Loops** are used to execute a series of statements multiple times. The number of times the code is executed can be determined by a specified number, until a condition is true or false, or the code can continue to execute however many objects there are in a collection. There are essentially two categories of loops: Do loops and For…Next loops.

QUICK REFERENCE		Types of Loops in VBA
Loop Type		**Description**
Do loop	Do…While loop	Loops while a specified condition is true
	Do…Until loop	Loops until a specified condition is true
For…Next loop	For loop	Loops until a specified number of loops have been completed
	For…Each loop	Loops through an object collection or an array

 The appropriate loop needed to be able to clear the filters for all slicers in a workbook is the For…Next loop. The syntax of the For…Next loop is

For Each element In group

code to execute

Next element

In the context of using the For…Each loop to loop through a collection of objects, the element is the object and the group is the collection of those objects. In the syntax of the For…Each loop, the data type of the element and group must be the same. This often requires that in the VBA code before the loop begins that variables are declared with a data type specified.

Declaring a Variable

A **variable** is space in a computer's memory that is given a name and is used to store a value of a specified data type. To create a variable, the space needs to be allocated in the computer's memory. This is known as dimensioning a variable. VBA abbreviates this as Dim, and it is a required command before a variable can be created.

The syntax for declaring a variable and assigning a data type to it is

Sub procedureName ()

Dim variableName As DataType

End Sub

QUICK REFERENCE	Restrictions to Naming Variables

Similar to names for procedures, there are specific requirements that must be taken into consideration when naming variables.

1. Variable names must start with a letter and not a number.
2. Variable names cannot have more than 250 characters.
3. Variable names cannot be the same as any one of Excel's key words. For example, a variable cannot be named "Sheet" or "Workbook".
4. Spaces are not allowed in variable names. You can separate words by either capitalizing the first letter of each word or by using the underscore character.

You can also declare multiple variables and assign them all a data type at one time by using the following syntax:

Sub procedureName ()

Dim variable1 As DataType1, variable2 As DataType2, variable3 As DataType3

End Sub

There are several data types in VBA to use, the most common ones being Currency, String, Single, Double, Boolean, and Variant.

Name	Description	Example
Boolean	Used in true or false variables	True or False
Integer	Numeric data type for whole numbers	125
Long	Numeric data type for large integer numbers	9,000,000,000
Currency	Numeric data type that allows for four digits to the right of the decimal and 15 to the left	1234.67
Single	Numeric data type used for numbers that can contain fractions	125.25
Double	Numeric data type used for large numbers that can contain fractions	9,000,000,000.25
Date	Stores date and time data	7/1/2015 8:35:56 AM
String	A variable length of text characters	"A message to the user"
Variant	The default data type if none is specified; can store numeric, string, date/time, empty, or null data	125, "Hello," 7/1/2014, etc.

In this exercise, you will be working toward creating a For…Each loop that will clear the filters on any number of slicers that may be added to the RevenueDashboard worksheet.

E14.12

To Declare a Variable

a. Press Alt+F11 to switch to the VBE.

b. Click the **e07ws14Module1_LastFirst** Code window, just below the End Sub statement of the clearSlicers procedure, and then press Enter.

c. Create a new Sub procedure by typing Sub slicerLoop () and then press Enter.

d. Type the following comment: 'This code will loop through all slicers in the workbook and clear the filters. Press Enter.

e. Declare a variable of the SlicerCache type by typing Dim slicers As SlicerCache and then press Enter twice to make the code easier to read. Now that you have created a variable of the type SlicerCache you are now ready to begin the For…Each loop.

Creating a For...Each Loop

You will now create the VBA code to loop through all of the SlicerCache objects in the collection of SlicerCaches in the ThisWorkbook object.

E14.13

To Create a For...Each Loop

a. Begin the loop by typing For Each slicers In ThisWorkbook.SlicerCaches and then press Enter twice.

   This line of code is what begins the loop. Excel will go through each of the slicerCache objects in the collection of SlicerCaches and perform the next line of code.

b. Create the code to execute by typing slicers.ClearManualFilter and then press Enter twice.

c. End the loop by typing Next slicers and then press Enter.

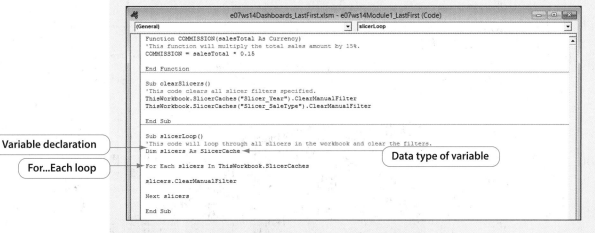

Variable declaration

For...Each loop

Data type of variable

Figure 13   slicerLoop Sub procedure

d. Click **Save** 🖫.

Adding Slicers to Test Loop Effectiveness

Now that you have created a For...Each loop to accommodate the addition of more slicers on the RevenueDashboard worksheet, you will add two additional slicers, filter the chart using all four slicers, and run the loop by clicking the Clear Slicers button.

E14.14

To Test Effectiveness of the For...Each Loop

a. Press Alt+F11 to switch to the RevenueDashboard worksheet, and then click the **Sales Revenue** column chart.

b. Click the **ANALYZE** tab, and then in the Filter group, click **Insert Slicer**.

c. Check the boxes for **SalesRep** and **Status**, and then click **OK**.

d. If necessary, click the **Status** slicer, and then resize it to be 1" in height and 1.5" in width. Click the **OPTIONS** tab, and then in the Slicer Styles group, select **Slicer Style Dark 3** from the Dark category.

e. Click the **SalesRep** slicer, and then resize it to be **2"** in height and **1.5"** in width. Click the **OPTIONS** tab, and then in the Slicer Styles group, select **Slicer Style Dark 3** from the Dark category.

f. Reposition the **Status** and **SalesRep** slicers to the right of the Year and SaleType slicers. If necessary, right-click the **Clear Slicers** button, and then drag to the right to make room for the slicers.

g. Use each of the four slicers to filter the Sales Revenue column chart, and then click the **Clear Slicers** button. Notice that since the Clear Slicers button is still assigned to the clearSlicers procedure, the additional slicers are not affected by the code.

h. Right-click the **Clear Slicers** form control button, and then click **Assign Macro**.

i. Click **slicerLoop** to change the macro assigned to the button, and then click **OK**.

j. Click any cell to deselect the Clear Slicers button.

k. Click the **Clear Slicers** button to confirm that the code now affects all slicers and that there are no errors.

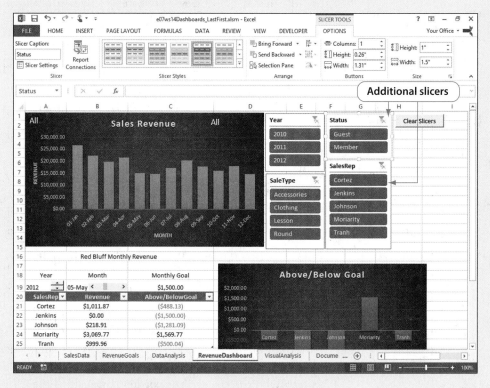

Figure 14 Additional slicers added

l. Click **Save** 🖫.

Assign VBA Procedures to Events

VBA code can be executed by a variety of methods, most commonly by assigning the code to a button or by setting up the code to execute when an event occurs. An **event** is an action initiated either by a user or by VBA code. An example of an event at the application level would be when a user creates a new workbook; an event at the workbook level would be when a user opens or closes a workbook.

Object	Event	Description
QUICK REFERENCE		**Common Events**
Application	SheetCalculate	Detects when formulas in any worksheet have been recalculated
	NewWorkbook	Detects when a user creates a new workbook
	WorkbookBeforeClose	Occurs after a user closes a workbook but before Excel actually closes it
Workbook	Open	Detects when a workbook is opened
	BeforeClose	Runs specified code before a workbook closes
	BeforeSave	Occurs after a user has clicked Save but before Excel actually saves the file
Worksheet	Activate	Detects when a specified worksheet is activated
	Deactivate	Detects when a specified worksheet is no longer the active sheet
	Change	Detects when any cell in a specified worksheet is changed

If the managers like the enhancements you make to the workbook they will connect the data in the workbook to their database so that the most recent data available is always part of the analysis. In this exercise, you will create code that will execute when the workbook is opened and that will display a message asking if the user wants to refresh the data connection in the workbook. If the user clicks Yes, then the data connection will be refreshed and a confirmation message will be displayed. If the user clicks No, then a message will be displayed informing the user that the data connection has not been refreshed.

Incorporating Conditional Statements into VBA

The most basic method of running VBA commands in response to a specific condition is the If statement. A VBA IF statement is very similar to the Excel IF function. The main difference is that with the Excel IF function you are limited to only one outcome if the condition is true and one outcome if the condition is false. With the VBA If-Then-Else control structure there is virtually no limit to the commands and logic that can be applied. The basic syntax of the If-Then-Else structure is

If Condition Then

Command if condition is true

Else

Commands if condition is false

End If

The condition portion of the structure is an expression that is resolved to either true or false. If it is true, then the first set of commands is run; otherwise, the second set of commands is run. In this next exercise, you will create an If-Then-Else statement in which the condition is to check how the user responds to a message box asking whether or not to refresh the data connection. The commands will make use of message boxes.

A **message box** is a dialog box object that is created using the MsgBox command. The message box is used to display an informative message to the user and includes buttons the user can interact with. The MsgBox syntax is as follows:

MsgBox("Message Text", Buttons, "Message Title")

The only required argument in the MsgBox is the Message text or Prompt argument. This exercise requires a more complicated procedure, and therefore you will also be including comments and adding indentations to make the code easier to read and understand.

E14.15

To Incorporate Conditional Statements

a. Press Alt + F11 to switch to the VBE.

b. Click the **Code window** just below the End Sub statement of the slicerLoop procedure, and then press Enter.

c. Create a new procedure by typing Sub refreshData() and then press Enter.

d. Type the following comment: 'This line of code will display a message box to the user. Press Enter twice.

e. To create a message box, type dataConnection = MsgBox("Would you like to refresh the data connection?", vbQuestion + vbYesNo, "Data Connection"). Press Enter twice.
    This line of code creates a message box with the message text, a question style with Yes and No buttons, and a title of Data Connection. The user's response of Yes or No will be stored in the dataConnection variable.

f. Type the following comment, using multiple lines.
    'This If statement will refresh the data connection and display a confirmation message 'if the user clicks Yes to the message box. If the user clicks no, another message box 'will be displayed informing the user that the data connection was not refreshed.

g. Press Enter twice, and then begin the If statement by typing If dataConnection = vbYes Then. Press Enter twice. This line of code will check the value of the message box, and if the user clicks the Yes button, it will execute the next block of code.

h. Type ThisWorkbook.Connections("ThisWorkbookDataModel").Refresh and then press Enter twice. This line of code, when executed, will refresh the dashboard with any changes made to the data model. This will be useful once the dashboard is connected to the sales database.

i. To create a confirmation message box, type MsgBox ("The data connection has been refreshed."). Press Enter twice, type Else to begin the Else statement, and then press Enter twice.

j. To create a message box if the user clicks No, type MsgBox ("The data connection has not been refreshed."). Press Enter twice.

k. To end the If statement, type End If and then press Enter.

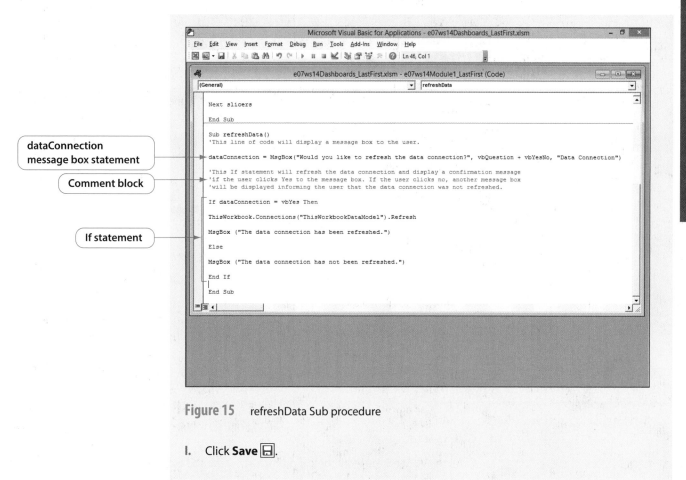

dataConnection message box statement

Comment block

If statement

Figure 15 refreshData Sub procedure

l. Click **Save** 💾.

Assigning a VBA Procedure to the Open Event

The refreshData Sub procedure is not complete. You will now call the procedure to execute when the workbook opens using the Open event in the ThisWorkbook object.

E14.16

 To Assign a VBA Procedure to the Open Event

a. If necessary, press Alt + F11 to switch to the VBE and in the Project Explorer window, double-click the **ThisWorkbook** object to open the Code window for ThisWorkbook.

b. To create a new private Sub procedure for the Open event, type **Private Sub Workbook_Open()** and then press Enter.

c. To call the refreshData procedure, type **Call refreshData** and then press Enter.

SIDE NOTE
Using the Object and Procedure Lists
Alternatively, you can select Workbook from the Object list at the top of the Code window and select Open from the Procedure list.

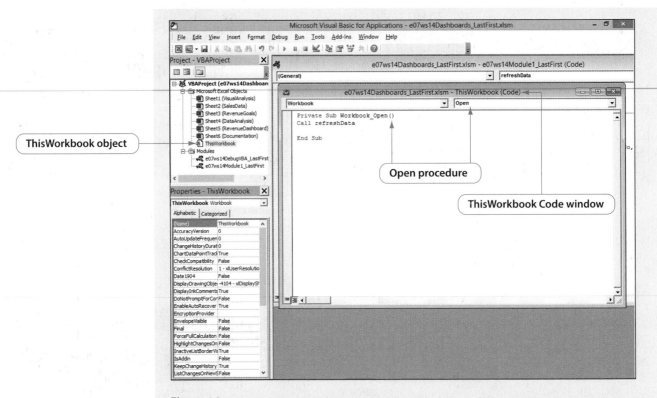

Figure 16 Call procedure from Open event

d. Click **Save** 🔲.

e. Close the VBE and the workbook; if prompted to save the workbook, click **Save**.

f. Test the **procedure** by opening the workbook again.

g. Take note of the Data Connection message box, and then click **Yes**.

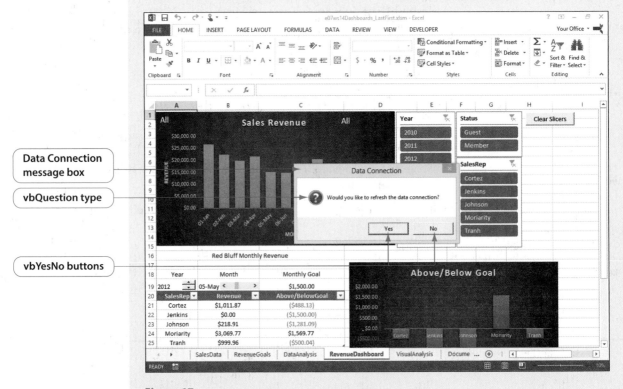

Figure 17 Data Connection message box

Assigning a VBA Procedure to the Activate Event

The e07ws14Dashboards_LastFirst workbook contains a Power View report located on the VisualAnalysis worksheet. **Power View** is an interactive data visualization, exploration, and presentation experience that encourages the creation of beautiful ad-hoc reports. Power View is new to Excel 2013, and therefore the managers at the Red Bluff Golf Course & Pro Shop may not be familiar with the tool. In this exercise, you will create a procedure that will display a message box providing the user with some definitions of the data used in the report. This message box will include line breaks to make its content easier to read and concatenation symbols to allow the code to be broken up into multiple lines. You will use the character code Chr(13) to indicate a carriage return and an ampersand (&) to concatenate text in the prompt argument. The message box will open automatically when the VisualAnalysis worksheet is activated.

E14.17

 To Assign a VBA Procedure to the Activate Event

a. Press [Alt]+[F11] to switch to the VBE. Click the **e07ws14Module1_LastFirst** code window just below the End Sub statement of the refreshData procedure, and then press [Enter].

b. To create a new Sub procedure, type Sub powerView () and then press [Enter].

c. Type the following comment block:

   'This procedure displays a message box providing definitions for data used in the report. 'It will be assigned to the Activate event of the VisualAnalysis worksheet. Press [Enter] twice.

d. To create the message box, type Description = MsgBox("This report is designed to provide you with an interactive visual summary of the sales data. " & _

   "Some of the data is described below." & Chr(13) & Chr(13) & _

   "TotalSales: Total sales revenue of items sold." & Chr(13) & _

   "TotalCosts: Total costs of items sold." & Chr(13) & _

   "Profit: Total sales revenue - total unit costs. " & _

   "This does not account for any non-unit based costs." & Chr(13) & Chr(13) & _

   "Feel free to explore the visualizations.", vbInformation, "Power View")

e. In the Project Explorer window, double-click **Sheet1(VisualAnalysis)** to view the Code window.

f. To create a new private Sub routine, type Private Sub Worksheet_Activate() and then press [Enter].

g. To call the powerView routine, type Call powerView and then press [Enter].

h. Click **Save** 📇.

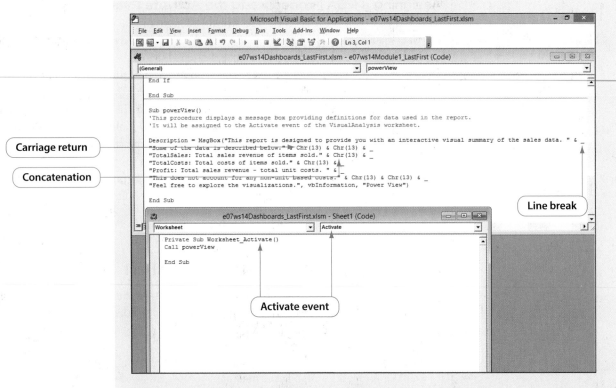

Carriage return

Concatenation

Line break

Activate event

Figure 18 powerView Sub procedure on Activate event

i. Press [Alt]+[F11] to switch back to the workbook, and then click the **VisualAnalysis** worksheet tab to see the message. Click **OK** to close the message box.

Protect and Secure a Workbook

The managers at the Red Bluff Golf Course & Pro Shop who will benefit from Excel dashboards and Power View reports have varying competencies when it comes to using Excel. You do not want to risk giving an Excel novice access to the worksheets containing the raw data where he or she could potentially damage or delete the data.

Protecting worksheets from intentional or unintentional modification can be done by simply hiding the worksheets in the Excel workbook. However, those worksheets can easily be made visible with a right-click or through the Options menu under the File tab. VBA provides a more secure method of hiding worksheets by using the xlVeryHidden property. In this exercise, you will make the worksheets containing the raw data invisible with VBA and protect the data on the visible worksheets from being deleted.

Using the xlVeryHidden Property

In this exercise, you will use the xlVeryHidden property of the Sheet object to hide specific worksheets in the workbook. The sheets hidden by this property cannot be made visible without altering the VBA code. Therefore, this method is more secure.

E14.18

 To Make Sheets Very Hidden

a. Press Alt+F11 to switch to the VBE.

b. Click the **e07ws14Module1_LastFirst** code window just below the End Sub statement of the powerView procedure, and then press Enter.

c. To create a Sub procedure, type Sub hideSheets () and then press Enter.

d. To add the following comment, type 'This procedure will make the SalesData, RevenueGoals, and DataAnalysis worksheets hidden. Press Enter twice.

e. To hide the SalesData worksheet, type Sheets("SalesData").Visible = xlVeryHidden and then press Enter.

f. To hide the RevenueGoals worksheet, type Sheets("RevenueGoals").Visible = xlVeryHidden and then press Enter.

g. To hide the DataAnalysis worksheet, type Sheets("DataAnalysis").Visible = xlVeryHidden and then press Enter.

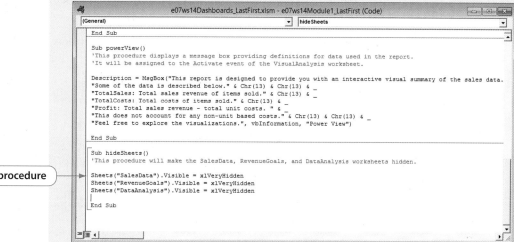

hideSheets procedure

Figure 19 hideSheets Sub procedure

h. Click **Save** 💾.

i. Press F5 to run the procedure. Press Alt+F11 to switch back to the workbook, and then observe that the three worksheets are no longer visible.

Providing Access to Hidden Worksheets

Some managers may need to access the raw data in a workbook and should not be required to know VBA to be able to unhide those worksheets. In this exercise, you will create a procedure that upon execution will prompt the user for a password to make the hidden sheets visible. This will require the use of an input box. An **input box** is an effective way of using VBA code to increase the interactivity of a dashboard by prompting the user for information and storing that information in a variable to be used later.

E14.19

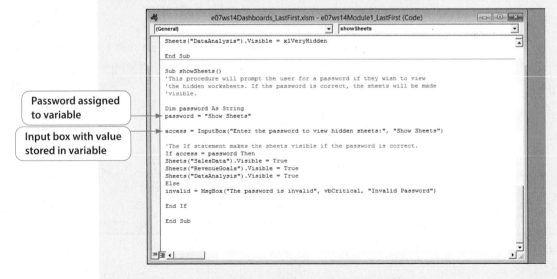

To Provide Access to Hidden Sheets

a. Press [Alt]+[F11] to switch back to the VBE.

b. Click the **e07ws14Module1_LastFirst** code window just below the End Sub statement of the hideSheets procedure, and then press [Enter].

c. To create a new Sub procedure, type Sub showSheets () and then press [Enter].

d. Type the following comment block:
   'This procedure will prompt the user for a password if they wish to view 'the hidden worksheets. If the password is correct, the sheets will be made 'visible. Press [Enter] twice.

e. To declare a new variable to store the password, type Dim password as String and then press [Enter].

f. To provide the password variable with the password, type password = "Show Sheets" and then press [Enter].

g. To create a variable to store the password response of the user, type access = InputBox("Enter the password to view hidden sheets:", "Show Sheets") and then press [Enter] twice.

h. Type the following comment: 'The If statement makes the sheets visible if the password is correct. Press [Enter].

i. To begin the If statement to compare the value stored in the access variable from the Input Box to the password variable, type If access = password Then and then press [Enter].

j. Make the sheets visible if the condition is true by typing
   • Sheets("SalesData").Visible = True and then press [Enter].
   • Sheets("RevenueGoals").Visible = True and then press [Enter].
   • Sheets("DataAnalysis").Visible = True and then press [Enter].

k. Type Else to begin the code if the condition is false, and then press [Enter].

l. To create a message box that informs the user of an invalid password, type invalid = MsgBox("The password is invalid", vbCritical, "Invalid Password") and then press [Enter].

m. End the If statement by typing End If and then press [Enter].

Password assigned to variable

Input box with value stored in variable

Figure 20 showSheets Sub procedure

n. Click **Save** 🔲.

o. Click the **RevenueDashboard** worksheet tab. Assign the showSheets macro to a button on the RevenueDashboard worksheet by completing the following tasks:

- Press Alt+F11 to switch back to the workbook. Click the **DEVELOPER** tab, and then in the Controls group, click the **Insert** arrow. Under Form Controls, select **Button (Form Control)** 🔳.

- Drag a **rectangular button** within the range **I6:I8**.

- In the Assign Macro dialog box, select **showSheets**, and then click **OK**.

- Select the **button text**, type View Hidden Sheets and then click any cell to deselect the button.

- Click the **View Hidden Sheets** button, type Show Sheets as the password, and then click **OK**. Confirm that the three sheets are now visible.

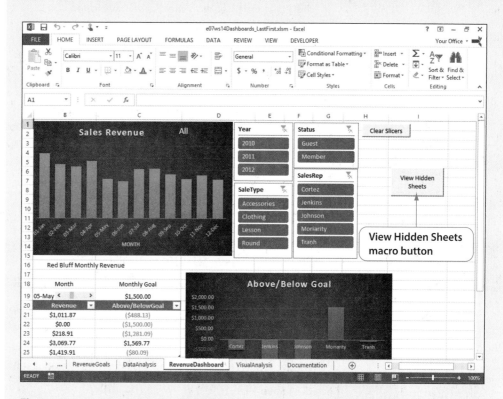

Figure 21 View Hidden Sheets button

p. Click **Save** 🔲.

Assigning a Procedure to the BeforeClose Event

Now that the hidden sheets are visible, you will need to run the hideSheets procedure again so that no unauthorized person can access the sheets. In this exercise, you will call the hideSheets procedure to execute when the BeforeClose event occurs.

To Call a Procedure on the BeforeClose Event

a. Press [Alt]+[F11] to switch to the VBE.

b. In the Project Explorer window, double-click **ThisWorkbook** to open the Code window.

c. Click the **Procedures** arrow, scroll up, and then select **BeforeClose**. A new Private Sub procedure is created on the BeforeClose event that will execute before Excel closes the workbook but after the user has clicked Close.

d. To call the hideSheets procedure, type Call hideSheets and then press [Enter].

e. Click **Save** 🖫. Close the VBE, and then close the workbook.

f. Open the **e07ws14Dashboards_LastFirst** workbook, and if necessary, click **Enable Content**. Click **No** when prompted to refresh the data connection, click **OK**, and then verify that the three worksheets are now hidden.

Protecting a Worksheet

The RevenueDashboard worksheet is now in its final state and needs to be protected to prevent unintentional changes. Before the worksheet is protected, you need to ensure that cells that need to be allowed to be changed to use the dashboard are not locked. Cells A19 and B17 need to be allowed to change as they are linked cells to the spin button and slider.

 To Protect a Worksheet

a. Right-click cell **A19**, and then select **Format Cells**. In the Format Cells dialog box, click the **Protection** tab, and then click the **Locked** check box to unlock the cell. Click **OK**.

b. Repeat Step a for cell **B17**.

c. On the RevenueDashboard worksheet, click the **REVIEW** tab, and then in the Changes group, click **Protect Sheet**.

d. In the Protect Sheet dialog box, scroll down, select the check box next to **Edit objects**, and then click **OK**. The worksheet is now protected but still fully functional.

e. Click **Save** 🖫.

Protecting the VBA Code with a Password

Protecting the VBA code with a password ensures that no unauthorized person will access the code. It is considered best practice to export any VBA modules as text files before protecting them with a password. This way if the password is lost or the workbook becomes corrupt, you will have a copy of the VBA code. In this exercise, you will export the VBA modules and then protect the VBA with a password.

E14.22

▶ To Protect the VBA Code with a Password

a. Press `Alt`+`F11` to switch to the VBE.

b. In the Project Explorer window, right-click **e07ws14Module1_LastFirst**, and then click **Export File**. Navigate to where you are saving your student files, click the **Save as type** arrow, and then select **All Files**. Click inside the **File name** box, edit the .bas extension to **.txt** and then click **Save**.

c. Right-click **e07ws14DebugVBA_LastFirst**, and then click **Export File**. Click the **Save as type** arrow, and then select **All Files**. Click inside the **File name** box, edit the .bas extension to **.txt** and then click **Save**.

d. Click **Tools**, and then click **VBAProject Properties**.

e. Click the **Protection** tab, and then in the Lock project area, select the **Lock project for viewing** check box.

f. Click the **Password** field, and then type Password.

g. Click the **Confirm password** field, and then type Password again.

h. Click **OK**.

i. Close the VBE, and then click **Save** 🖫. The password will not take effect until the workbook is closed. Close the workbook.

j. Open the **e07ws14Dashboards_LastFirst** workbook. Click **No** to the Data Connection prompt, and then click **OK**. Press `Alt`+`F11` to switch to the VBE.

k. If necessary, press `Ctrl` and then type r to view the Project Explorer window; then double-click **VBA Project (e07ws14Dashboards_LastFirst.xlsm)**. Type Password in the VBAProject Password dialog box, and then click **OK**.

l. Complete the **Documentation** worksheet, and then submit your file as directed by your instructor.

Concept Check

1. What are form controls, and how can they be used to enhance interactivity with a dashboard? p. 712–718

2. Describe the object model in Excel. p. 719–722

3. What are function procedures and how can organizations use them? p. 724–726

4. What are some common practices that can help improve the readability and understanding of VBA code? p. 726

5. Describe the purpose of debug mode in the VBE and why it is useful. p. 729

6. List the categories of loops used in VBA, and describe each type of loop. p. 730

7. Describe three scenarios where assigning a VBA procedure to an event would enhance the workbook. p. 734–740

8. What can be done to ensure unauthorized changes are not made to a workbook? p. 740–745

Key Terms

Code window   722
Digital dashboards   712
Do Until loop   730
Do While loop   730
Event   734
For…Each loop   730
For loop   730
Form controls   712
Function procedure   723
Input box   741
Loops   730

Message box   736
Method   721
Module   723
Object collection   719
Object model   719
Object-oriented programming
   (OOP)   718
Objects   719
Parameter   722
Power View   739
Project Explorer window   722

Properties   720
Properties window   722
Run-time error   729
Scroll bar   716
Separators   720
Slicers   712
Spin button   713
Sub procedure   723
Variable   731
VBA (Visual Basic for Applications)   718
Visual Basic Editor (VBE)   722

Add the Developer tab (p. 713)

Protect a worksheet (p. 744)

Create dynamic labels (p. 717)

Add a scroll bar (p. 716)

Enhance spreadsheets with form controls (p. 712)

Create a lookup table (p. 715)

Add a spin button (p. 713)

Use a custom function (p. 725)

Assign a sub procedure to a button control (p. 728)

Test effectiveness of the For...Each loop (p. 733)

Provide access to hidden sheets (p. 742)

Protect and secure a workbook (p. 740)

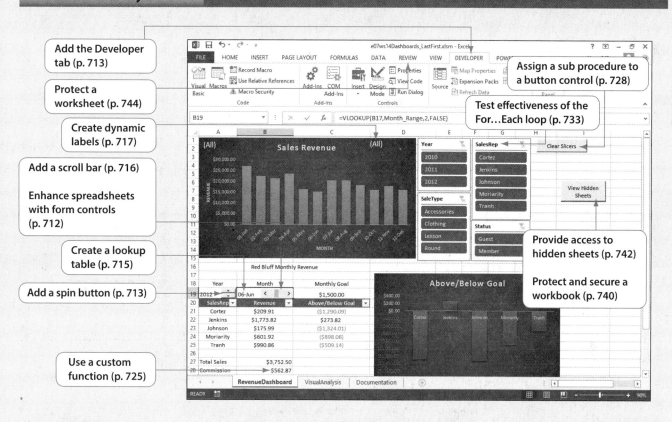

Create a function procedure (p. 724)

Create custom functions with VBA (p. 724)

Assign a VBA procedure to the Open event (p. 737)

Assign VBA procedures to events (p. 734)

Debug VBA (p. 729)

Troubleshoot VBA (p. 729)

Explore the VBE (p. 722)

Understand the components of VBA (p. 719)

Declare a variable (p. 732)

Clear slicer filters using VBA (p. 727)

Improve readability of VBA with formatting and structure (p. 726)

Create a For...Each loop (p. 733)

Create and use loops in VBA (p. 730)

Incorporate conditional statements (p. 736)

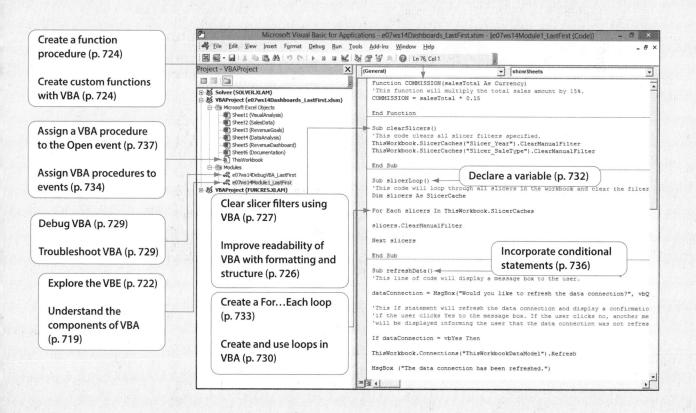

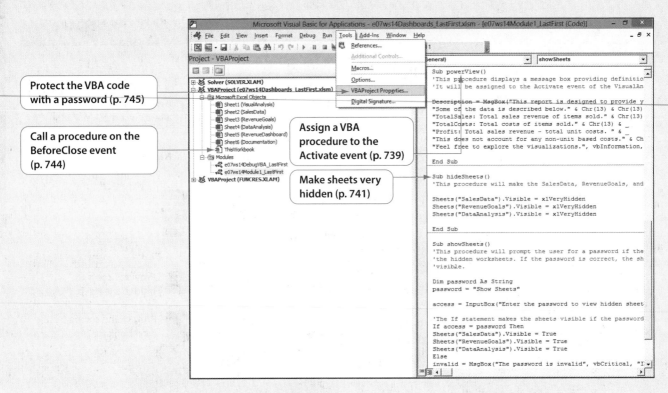

Protect the VBA code with a password (p. 745)

Call a procedure on the BeforeClose event (p. 744)

Assign a VBA procedure to the Activate event (p. 739)

Make sheets very hidden (p. 741)

Figure 22 The Red Bluff Golf Course & Pro Shop Spreadsheet Enhancement with Form Controls and VBA Final

Practice 1

Student data file needed:

 e07ws14Reviews.xlsx

You will save your file as:

e07ws14Reviews_LastFirst.xlsm

Enhancing the Performance Review Dashboard

Sales & Marketing

Managers at the Red Bluff Golf Course & Pro Shop have realized how form controls and VBA can enhance their dashboards. You have been provided with another dashboard used to aid managers in employee performance reviews. In this exercise, you will enhance the dashboard by adding some form controls, dynamic labels, and VBA.

a. Start **Excel**, and then open the **e07ws14Reviews** workbook. Save it as a Macro-Enabled workbook named e07ws14Reviews_LastFirst.

b. Click the **Dashboard** worksheet tab. On the Quarterly Revenue line chart create a dynamic label based on the **Year** slicer by completing the following tasks:

   • Click the **INSERT** tab, and then in the Text group, click **Text Box**.

   • Drag a **rectangle** in the top-left corner of the Quarterly Revenue line chart.

   • Click the **Formula bar**. Type =, click the **Analysis** worksheet, and then click cell **B1**. Press [Enter].

   • With the box selected, click the **DRAWING TOOLS FORMAT** tab. In the Shape Styles group, click the **Shape Outline** arrow, and then select **No Outline**.

   • Click the **HOME** tab, and then in the Font group, increase the font size to 16.

   • Adjust the size of the box as necessary to accommodate the font size.

c. Repeat Step b to add a **dynamic label** in the top-left corner of the Revenue and Costs combo column chart and the Total Revenue pie chart.

d. Add a **spin button** form control to cell **I23** by completing the following tasks:

- Click the **DEVELOPER** tab, and then in the Controls group, click the **Insert** arrow. Select **Spin Button (Form Control)**.
- Drag the small square **Spin** button in cell **I23** to the right of the year.
- Right-click the **Spin** button, and then click **Format Control**.
- Type 2010 in the Current and Minimum value fields.
- Type 2012 in the Maximum value field.
- Click the **Cell link** field, click cell **I23**, and then click **OK**.

e. Create a lookup table to be used with a scroll bar form control by completing the following tasks.

- Click the **Analysis** worksheet. Click cell **I1**, type Value and then in cells **I2:I5** type the values 1, 2, 3, and 4.
- Click cell **J1**, type Quarter and then in cells **J2:J5** type the values Q1, Q2, Q3, and Q4.
- Select **I1:J5**, click the **Name** box, and then type Quarters to give the range of cells a name.

f. Add a scroll bar to the right of Q1 in cell **J23** on the Dashboard worksheet by completing the following tasks.

- Click the **Dashboard** worksheet, click cell **J21**, and then type the number 1 to be used as the lookup value.
- Click cell **J23**, and then type =VLOOKUP(J21,Quarters,2,FALSE).
- On the DEVELOPER tab, in the Controls group, click the **Insert** arrow, and then select the **Scroll Bar (Form Control)**.
- Drag a **horizontal rectangle** in cell **J23** to the right of the Q1 text.
- Right-click the **scroll bar**, and then click **Format Control**.
- Type 1 in the Current value and Minimum value fields.
- Type 4 in the Maximum value field.
- Click the **Cell link** field, click cell **J23**, and then click **OK**.
- Click cell **J21**, click the **HOME** tab, and then in the Font group, change the font color to **White**.

g. Create a VBA Sub procedure that will clear filters in all slicers in the workbook, even if more slicers are added, by completing the following tasks.

- Press [Alt]+[F11] to switch to the VBE, click **Insert**, and then select **Module**.
- In the Properties window, click the **Name** field, and then type ReviewModule_LastFirst using your last and first name.
- Click the **Code window**, type Sub clearSlicers () and then press [Enter].
- Type the following comment: 'This code will loop through all the slicers in the workbook and clear all filters. Press [Enter] twice.
- Type Dim allSlicers As SlicerCache to declare a variable with a data type of Slicer Cache, and then press [Enter] twice.
- Type For Each allSlicers In ThisWorkbook.SlicerCaches and then press [Enter] twice.
- Type allSlicers.ClearManualFilter and then press [Enter] twice.
- Type Next allSlicers and then press [Enter].

h. Assign the Sub procedure to a Button form control on the Dashboard worksheet by competing the following tasks.

- Press [Alt]+[F11] to switch to the workbook.
- On the DEVELOPER tab, in the Controls group, click the **Insert** arrow, and then select **Button (Form Control)**.

- Drag a **button** within the range **J1:J3**. In the Assign Macro dialog box, select **clearSlicers**, and then click **OK**.
- Edit the button text to Clear Slicers and then, if necessary, adjust the size of the button so that all text is visible.

i. Add the **SalesRep** slicer to the dashboard by completing the following tasks.
   - Click the **Quarterly Revenue** line chart.
   - Click the **ANALYZE** tab, and then in the Filter group, click **Insert Slicer**.
   - Click the **SalesRep** check box, and then click **OK**.
   - Resize the **SalesRep** slicer to be 1.2" in width and 2" in height.
   - Reposition the **SalesRep** slicer to fit within the range **J5:K14**, in between the Year and SaleType slicers and the pie chart.
   - Click the **OPTIONS** tab, and then in the Slicer Styles group, select **Slicer Style Dark 6**.
   - On the OPTIONS tab, click **Report Connections**, click the **PivotTable2** check box, and then click **OK**.

j. Click the **Documentation** worksheet. Click cell **A6**, and then type in today's date. Click cell **B6**, and then type your first and last name. Complete the remainder of the **Documentation** worksheet according to your instructor's direction.

k. Click **Save**, close Excel, and then submit your file as directed by your instructor.

Problem Solve 1

Student data file needed:

 e07ws14Blarneys.xlsx

You will save your files as:

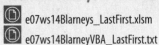 e07ws14Blarneys_LastFirst.xlsm
e07ws14BlarneyVBA_LastFirst.txt

Blarney's Clothing Store

Sales & Marketing

Blarney's is a small boutique clothing store located in Arizona. The owner has developed a simple dashboard to help the managers keep track of their top customers, sales, and employee performance. The managers would like to share this information with other employees, but they are concerned about the data slipping into a competitor's hands. You have been asked to use VBA to make the workbook more secure and require a password to be able to view any of the worksheets.

a. Start **Excel**, and then open the **e07ws14Blarneys** workbook. Save it as a Macro-Enabled workbook named e07ws14Blarneys_LastFirst.

b. Create a new VBA module with the name e07ws14BlarneyVBA_LastFirst using your last and first name.

c. Create a new Sub procedure that will hide all worksheets in the workbook. To ensure that all worksheets are hidden even if new worksheets are added, you will use a For…Each loop.
   - Name the Sub procedure hideSheets.
   - To add a comment that describes the procedure, type 'This procedure hides the data and dashboard worksheets.
   - Press [Enter] twice before writing the next line of code.
   - On the next line type Sheets("Data").Visible = xlVeryHidden.
   - On the next line type Sheets("Dashboard").Visible = xlVeryHidden. Press [Enter] twice.

d. Assign the **hideSheets** Sub procedure to the BeforeClose event in the This Workbook Code window.

e. Create a new Sub procedure in the e07ws14BlarneysVBA_LastFirst Code window. This procedure will declare a password variable, and then prompt the user to provide the password in order to show the hidden worksheets in the workbook.

- Name the new Sub procedure showSheets.
- Declare a variable named psw as a String data type.
- Set the psw variable to be Password1234.
- Create an input box and a variable to store the response. The variable to store the response should be auth, the input box message should be Enter the password to view the hidden sheets, and it should have a title of Authorized Personnel Only.

f. Create an If statement that compares the auth variable to the psw variable, and if they are the same, unhide the Data and Dashboard worksheets and make the Dashboard worksheet active.

- To make the Dashboards worksheet activate use Sheets("Dashboard").Activate.

g. Create the Else statement to display a message box.

- Name the variable invalid for the message box.
- The message box text should be The password is invalid!
- Use **vbCritical** as the message box style and Invalid Password as the title.

h. Assign the **showSheets** Sub procedure to the Open event in the This Workbook Code window.

i. Export the **e07ws14BlarneyVBA_LastFirst** module as a .txt file.

j. Lock the VBA project from viewing, and then require a password of VBAPassword to be able to view the contents of the VBE.

k. Complete the **Documentation** worksheet according to your instructor's direction. Insert the **filename** in the left custom footer section of the Header/Footer tab in the Page Setup dialog box on all worksheets in the workbook.

l. Click **Save**, close Excel, and then submit the file as directed by your instructor.

Perform 1: Perform in Your Life

Student data file needed:
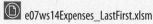 Blank Excel workbook

You will save your file as:
e07ws14Expenses_LastFirst.xlsm

Personal Expenses Dashboard

Finance & Accounting

Keeping track of personal expenses is the first step to becoming financially independent. If you are able to keep track of what you spend your money on then you may be able to find areas where you can save money to afford a car payment or start paying back any student loans. In this exercise, you will create a few simple charts on a dashboard based on data that you will provide. You will then enhance the dashboard by adding form controls and VBA.

a. Start **Excel**, create a new blank workbook, and then save it as a Macro-Enabled workbook with the name e07ws14Expenses_LastFirst using your last and first name.

b. Rename Sheet1 to be ExpenseData. Use this worksheet to make a table of expenses. Be sure to make a note of the date, a description of the expense, amount of the expense, and the category to which the expense belongs. Some examples of categories may be Food, School, Entertainment, Rent, ATM withdrawal, and so on. If you have a bank account, you may be able to export a file of expenses from the bank's website.

c. Create two additional worksheets in the workbook, and then rename one Analysis and the other Dashboard.

d. You will use the Analysis worksheet to create any lookup tables necessary for use with form controls such as scroll bars or spin buttons or PivotTables.

e. Create two charts and one table on the Dashboard worksheet based on the data on the ExpenseData and/or Analysis worksheets. One of the charts should be created from the data in the Excel table.

f. Add two slicers to the Dashboard worksheet that will allow you to filter the data in the chart.

g. Add one form control, either a spin button or scroll bar, to the Dashboard worksheet that will allow you to easily see expense data from different days or months.

h. Create a VBA module named ExpenseModule_LastFirst using your last and first name.

i. Create a VBA Sub procedure that will loop through all slicers and clear the filters, and then assign that Sub procedure to a form control button on the Dashboard worksheet.

j. Insert the **filename** in the left custom footer section of the Header/Footer tab in the Page Setup dialog box on all worksheets in the workbook.

k. Click **Save**, close Excel, and then submit the file as directed by your instructor.

Additional
Cases

Additional Workshop Cases are available on the companion website and in the instructor resources.

More Practice 1

Student data files needed:
- e07mpIndigo5.accdb
- e07mpMetrics.xlsx

You will save your file as:
- e07mpMetrics_LastFirst.xlsm

Restaurant Metrics

Sales & Marketing

Robin Sanchez, owner and chef of the Indigo5 restaurant, would like to start paying closer attention to the sales data in order to make strategic decisions about the future of the restaurant. Robin has provided you with a small sample of sales data from 2012–2013 in an Access database. You have been asked to import the data into the Excel data model, conduct some analysis, create a simple dashboard, and then enhance it with some simple VBA.

a. Start **Excel**, and then open the **e07mpMetrics** workbook from the student data files. Save the file as a Macro-Enabled workbook with the name e07mpMetrics_LastFirst using your last and first name.

b. On the **SalesDashboard** worksheet, import the data from the e07mpIndigo5 database into the Excel data model by completing the following.
   - Click the **DATA** tab, and then in the Get External Data group, click **From Access**.
   - Browse to your student data files, select **e07mpIndigo5**, and then click **Open**.
   - In the Select Table dialog box, click **Enable selection of multiple tables**.
   - Click the **Name** check box to select all the tables in the database, and then click **OK**.
   - In the Import Data dialog box, click the **Only Create Connection** option, and then click **OK**.

c. Click the **MonthSort** worksheet tab, click the **POWERPIVOT** tab, and then in the Tables group, click **Add to Data Model**. If the POWERPIVOT tab is not visible, you will need to install the COM Add-in as explained in Workshop 13.

d. Enhance the data model by completing the following.
   - In the PowerPivot window, click the **Design** tab, and then in the Relationships group, click **Create Relationship**.
   - In the Create Relationship dialog box, **MonthSort** should be selected as the Table value and **Month** as the Column value. Select **Transactions** from the Related Lookup Table list, select **MonthName** from the Related Lookup Column list, and then click **Create**.
   - Click the **ProductCategories** worksheet tab, and then click the **AvgPrice** column heading. Click the **Home** tab, and then in the Formatting group, click the **Format** arrow. Select **Currency**.
   - Click the **Transactions** worksheet tab, and then click the **TransDate** column heading. Click the **Home** tab, and then in the Formatting group, click the **Format** arrow. Select ***3/14/2001**.
   - Double-click the **Add Column** column heading, and then type MonthOrder. Press Enter, and then type =RELATED(MonthSort[Order])&"-"&[MonthName].
   - Double-click the next **Add Column** column heading, and then type TransYear. Press Enter, and then type =YEAR([TransDate]).

- Double-click the next **Add Column** column heading, and then type EstimatedRevenue. Press Enter, and then type =RELATED(ProductCategories[AvgPrice])*[Qty].
- On the Home tab, in the Formatting group, click the **Format** arrow, and then select **Currency**.

e. To create a calculated field in the Calculation Area just below the ServerID column, type 2013Revenue:=CALCULATE(sum(Transactions[EstimatedRevenue]),Transactions[TransYear]=2013). On the Home tab, in the Formatting group, click the **Format** arrow, and then select **Currency**.

f. To create another calculated field in the Calculation Area just below the CategoryCode column, type 2014Revenue:=CALCULATE(sum(Transactions[EstimatedRevenue]), Transactions[TransYear]=2014). On the Home tab, in the Formatting group, click the **Format** arrow, and then select **Currency**.

g. Create a new KPI for Sales Revenue by completing the following.
- Click the **2014Revenue** calculation. Click the **Home** tab, and then in the Calculation group, click **Create KPI**.
- In the Create KPI dialog box, under Define target value, select **2013Revenue** from the Calculated Field list.
- Adjust the status thresholds to be a low of 90% and a high of 105%.
- Click **OK**.

h. Create a simple dashboard by completing the following.
- Click the **Home** tab, and then click the **PivotTable** arrow. Select **Chart and Table (Horizontal)**.
- In the Insert Pivot dialog box, click **Existing Worksheet**, click the **Range Selection** button, and then click the **SalesDashboard** worksheet tab. Click cell **A1**.
- Click **OK**, and then click **OK** again.

i. Create a PivotChart by completing the following.
- In the PivotChart Fields pane, expand **Transactions**, and then drag **TransYear** into the FILTERS area.
- Drag **EstimatedRevenue** into the Σ VALUES.
- Expand **ProductCategories**, and then drag **CategoryDescr** into the LEGEND (SERIES) area.

j. Improve the design of the PivotChart by completing the following.
- Click the **Chart Styles** icon to the right of the PivotChart, and then select **Style 13**.
- Click the **Chart Elements** icon to the right of the PivotChart, and then click **Chart Title**.
- Edit the Chart Title text to be Indigo5 Revenue.
- On the Ribbon, click the **ANALYZE** tab, and then in the Show/Hide group, click the **Field Buttons** icon to remove the filter buttons from the PivotChart.

k. Add slicers to the PivotChart by completing the following.
- On the ANALYZE tab, in the Filter group, click **Insert Slicer**.
- Click the check box for **CategoryDescr** and **TransYear**, and then click **OK**.
- With the CategoryDescr slicer still selected, on the OPTIONS tab, in the Slicer group, click **Report Connections**.
- Click the check box for **PivotTable1**, and then click **OK**.

l. Modify the slicers by completing the following.
- On the OPTIONS tab, in the Slicer Styles group, select **Slicer Style Dark 3**.
- Right-click the **CategoryDescr** slicer, and then select **Size and Properties**.
- In the Format Slicer pane, expand **POSITION AND LAYOUT**. In the Number of columns field, increase the number to 2 and then close the Format Slicer pane.

- Adjust the size of the **CategoryDescr** slicer to be 2.75" in height and 2.2" in width. Reposition the slicer to fit within the range **J9:K22**.
- Click the **TransYear** slicer, and then select **Slicer Style Dark 1**.
- Adjust the size of the TransYear slicer to be 1.3" in height and 1.4" in width. Reposition the slicer to fit within the range **H16:I22**.

m. Create a PivotTable by completing the following.

- Click the **PivotTable1** placeholder, and then in the PivotTable Fields pane, expand **Employees**. Drag **LastName** into the ROWS area.
- Expand **Transactions**, expand **2014Revenue**, and then drag **Value (2014Revenue)** into the Σ VALUES area. Drag **Status** into the Σ VALUES area.

n. Create a VBA Sub procedure using a For...Each loop to clear all slicers by completing the following.

- Press [Alt]+[F11] to switch to the VBE.
- Click **Insert**, and then select **Module**.
- In the Properties Window, select the text in the **Name** property, and then type Indigo5VBA_LastFirst using your last and first name.
- Click the **Code Window**, type Sub clearSlicers () and then press [Enter].
- To add a comment to the procedure, type 'Procedure clears all slicers in workbook using a For Each loop. Press [Enter] twice.
- To declare a variable with a data type of SlicerCache, type Dim slicers as SlicerCache and then press [Enter].
- To create a For...Each loop, type For Each slicers in ThisWorkbook.SlicerCaches and then press [Enter]. Type slicers.ClearManualFilter and then press [Enter]. Type Next slicers and then press [Enter] twice.

o. Click the **Documentation** worksheet. Click cell **A6**, and then type in today's date. Click cell **B6**, and then type in your first and last name. Complete the remainder of the **Documentation** worksheet according to your instructor's direction.

p. Click **Save**, close Excel, and then submit your file as directed by your instructor.

Problem Solve 1

Student data file needed:

 e07ps1Hotel.xlsx

You will save your file as:

 e07ps1Hotel_LastFirst.xlsx

Hotel Analysis with Power View

Sales & Marketing

The hotel managers at the Painted Paradise Resort have read about other businesses benefiting from using Power View in Excel 2013 to get a different perspective on their data. You have been asked to create a Power View report based on some room reservation data provided to you by the hotel management.

a. Start **Excel**, and then open the **e07ps1Hotel** workbook from the student data files. Save the file as e07ps1Hotel_LastFirst using your last and first name.

b. Insert a new **Power View** report using the data on the RoomsData worksheet.

c. Rename the Power View 1 worksheet tab as RoomsReport.

d. Type Painted Paradise Rooms Report as the Power View report title.

e. Apply the **Equity** theme and **Dark2 Vertical Gradient** background to the Power View report.

f. Add a **map** visualization to the Power View report. Use **GuestState** for the LOCATIONS, **NightsStay** for the Σ SIZE, and **DiscountType** for the COLOR.

g. Adjust the size of the map visualization using the figure below.

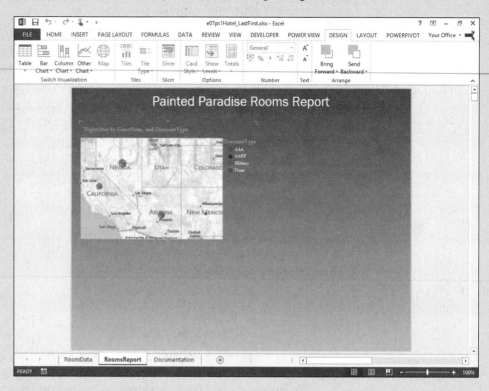

Figure 1 Map visualization

h. Create a **pie chart** illustrating total room charges by year and room type with horizontal multiples to the right of the map visualization. Use **Σ TotalRoomCharge** as the Σ SIZE, **RoomType** as the SLICES, and **Year** as the HORIZONTAL MULTIPLES.

i. Adjust the size of the pie chart using the figure below.

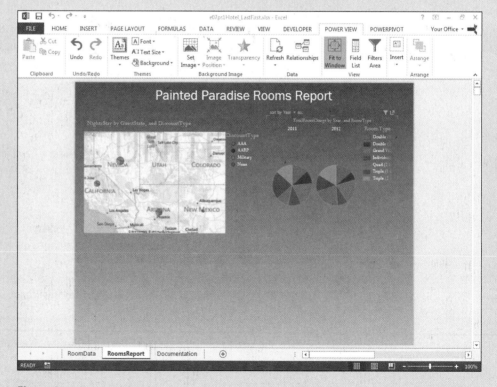

Figure 2 Pie chart

j. Create a **line chart** illustrating the total room charge by month at the bottom of the report. Use **Σ TotalRoomCharge** as the Σ VALUES and **Month** as the AXIS.

k. Adjust the size of the line chart using the figure below.

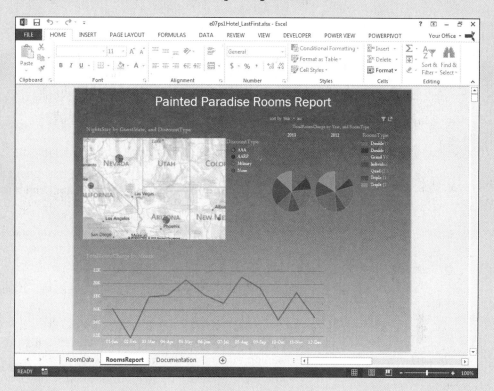

Figure 3 Line chart

l. Add a **Year** slicer to the Power View report in the space to the right of the line chart. You will need to modify the field options to not summarize the year data.

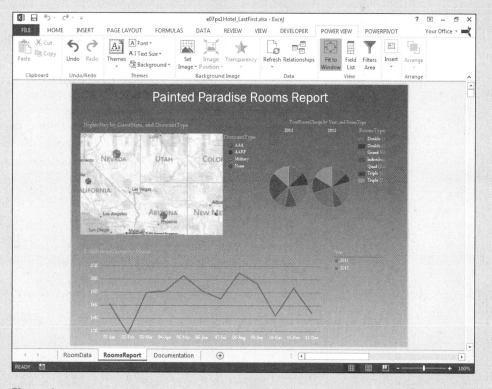

Figure 4 Power View report

m. Complete the **Documentation** worksheet according to your instructor's direction. Insert the **filename** footer in the left custom footer section of the Header/Footer tab in the Page Setup dialog box on all worksheets in the workbook.

n. Click **Save**, close Excel, and then submit the file as directed by your instructor.

Problem Solve 2

MyITLab®
Grader
Homework 2

Sales & Marketing

Student data file needed:

e07ps2Dashboard.xlsx

You will save your file as:

e07ps2Dashboard_LastFirst.xlsm

Enhancing the Hotel Dashboard

Managers at the hotel have been using a simple dashboard to keep track of revenues and room reservations. You have been asked to enhance the dashboard by adding some form controls, a Bing map, and VBA.

a. Start **Excel**, and then open the **e07ps2Dashboard** workbook from the student data files. Save the file as a Macro-Enabled workbook with the name e07ps2Dashboard_LastFirst using your last and first name.

b. Add a **scroll bar** to the Dashboard worksheet to allow users to easily change the month in cell F18 by completing the following.

- On the **Analysis** worksheet, create a **lookup table** that will be used on the Dashboard worksheet to select various months. In cell D1, type Lookup Value as the column heading, and then in cell E1, type Month.
- Type the numbers 1 through 12 down column D, and then type '01-Jan through '12-Dec down column E. Name the range D1:E13 MonthData.
- On the **Dashboard** worksheet type 1 in cell F16, and then in cell F18 type =VLOOKUP(F16,MonthData,2,False).
- Insert a **Scroll Bar** (Form Control) in cell F18 to the right of the text.
- Set the current and minimum values to 1, the maximum value to 12, and the cell link to **F16**.
- Change the font color in cell F16 to **White, Background 1**.

c. Add a **Spin Button** (Form Control) to cell E18 to the right of 2011.

- Set the current and minimum value to 2011, the maximum value to 2012, and the cell link to **E18**.

d. Insert the **Bing Maps** app into the Dashboard worksheet.

- Use the data in **A2:C5** to plot the locations onto the map.
- Reposition and resize the **Bing map** to fit inside the range A6:D23.

e. Add a **Year** and **RoomType** slicer connected to the Total Revenue Line chart.

- Apply the **Slicer Style Dark 1** to both slicers.
- Resize the **Year** slicer to be 1" height and 1" width.
- Reposition the **Year** slicer to fit within the range K1:K5.
- Resize the **RoomType** slicer to be 2.5" height and 2.5" width.
- Reposition the **RoomType** slicer to fit within the range L1:N12.

f. Create dynamic labels for the Total Room Revenue line chart for Year and RoomType using cells B1 and B2 on the Analysis worksheet.

- Position the dynamic label for **Year** in the top-left corner of the chart with a font color of **White, Background 1**, no fill color, and no outline.
- Position the dynamic label for **RoomType** in the top-right corner of the chart with a font color of **White, Background 1**, no fill color, and no outline. Adjust the width and height of the box to accommodate the text of the various room types.

g. Create a new **VBA Module** with the name HotelVBA_LastFirst using your last and first name.

h. Create a new **hideSheets** Sub procedure in the HotelVBA_LastFirst module.

- Hide the RoomData and Analysis worksheets using the xlVeryHidden property.

i. Assign the **hideSheets** Sub procedure to the BeforeClose event in the ThisWorkbook Code Window.

j. Create a new **showSheets** Sub procedure in the HotelVBA_LastFirst module.

- Declare a new variable with the name psw and a data type of string.
- Assign the password value of Password1234 to the psw variable.
- Create a new input box with the message Enter Password to Show All Sheets: and then assign it to the variable userPassword.
- Create an **If** statement that checks to see if "psw" is equal to "userPassword". If true, set the visible property for the RoomData and Analysis worksheets to **true**. If false, display a message box assigned to the variable "invalid" with the message Invalid Password and a VbMsgBox Style of vbCritical.

k. Assign the **showSheets** code to a Button (Form Control). Position the button on the Dashboard worksheet within **K7:K9** with the name Show Sheets (Admin Only).

l. Using the Excel Options menu, hide the gridlines as well as the row and column headings on the Dashboard worksheet.

m. Complete the **Documentation** worksheet according to your instructor's direction. Insert the **filename** footer in the left custom footer section of the Header/Footer tab in the Page Setup dialog box on all worksheets in the workbook.

n. Click **Save**, close Excel, and then submit the file as directed by your instructor.

Perform 1: Perform in Your Life

Student data file needed:

 Blank Excel worksheet

You will save your file as:

 e07pf1Grades_LastFirst.xlsx

Visualizing Course Grades

Information & Technology

Looking at your grades from a different perspective may provide you with some additional insight into the areas you tend to thrive in and the areas you tend to struggle in. In this exercise, you will collect some data on courses, assignments, exams, and grades earned. You will then create a Power View report to visualize that data.

a. Start **Excel**, create a new blank workbook, and save it as e07pf1Grades_LastFirst using your last and first name.

b. Rename the **Sheet1** worksheet to GradesData. On the GradesData worksheet you will create an Excel table for each course that you have taken or that you are currently enrolled in.

c. Each table should include column headings for Assignment, PointsPossible, and PointsEarned. Above each table, merge and center three cells, and then type the course name. You may format the tables in any way you see fit. Be sure to name each table appropriately based on the course name and include a total row that calculates the sum of PointsPossible and PointsEarned.

d. You may generalize your assignments into Homework, Quiz, and Exam if you do not want to include the specific item names.

e. Create a **Power View** report, and then rename the worksheet GradesReport.

f. Apply your choice of **theme** and **background** to the report, add a **title**, and create at least three visualizations using the data from the Excel tables.

g. Use the **LAYOUT** tab to remove titles, modify legends, and add or remove data labels as you see fit.

h. Insert the **filename** in the left custom footer section of the Header/Footer tab in the Page Setup dialog box on all worksheets in the workbook.

i. Click **Save**, close Excel, and then submit the file as directed by your instructor.

Perform 2: Perform in Your Career

Student data file needed:
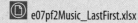 e07pf2Music.xlsx

You will save your file as:
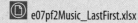 e07pf2Music_LastFirst.xlsx

Independent Music

Sales & Marketing

You are the owner of Independent Music, a small record store that specializes in promoting and selling music from local independent musicians. You have recently launched an online music store where people from all over the country can purchase music. In this exercise you will create a data model with the sample data provided, conduct some analyses, and create a simple dashboard.

a. Start **Excel**, and then open the **e07pf2Music** workbook from the student data files. Save the file as e07pf2Music_LastFirst using your last and first name.

b. Add each of the tables on the SalesData worksheet to the Data Model using the **POWERPIVOT** tab.

c. Create a relationship between **SalesData2013** and **MonthOrder** using the Month field.

d. Create a relationship between **SalesData2013** and **VolumebyEmp** using the EmployeeID field.

e. Create a calculated column to the SalesData2013 data named MonthOrder. Use the RELATED DAX function to concatenate the Order value from the MonthOrder data with a "-" and the Month value from the SalesData2013 data.

f. Create another calculated column to the SalesData2013 data named Revenue that takes Price * Quantity, and then format it as Currency.

g. Create a calculated field named Total Revenue that calculates the sum of all revenue, and then format it as Currency.

h. Create a **KPI** with Total Revenue as the base field and an absolute value of $450 as the target value. Adjust the thresholds to be 250 and 400.

i. Create a simple dashboard, starting on the **Dashboard** worksheet in cell A1.

j. Add at least two **PivotCharts** and one **PivotTable** to the Dashboard worksheet.

k. Insert at least one **slicer** in the dashboard. Format and resize appropriately.

l. Add appropriate **titles** to any chart, and then format the charts.

m. Incorporate the **KPI** into the dashboard either in a PivotTable or a PivotChart.

n. Add at least one visualization from an app in the Apps for Office store.

o. Complete the **Documentation** worksheet according to your instructor's direction. Insert the **filename** in the left custom footer section of the Header/Footer tab in the Page Setup dialog box on all worksheets in the workbook.

p. Click **Save**, close Excel, and then submit the file as directed by your instructor.

Perform 3: Perform in Your Team

Student data file needed:

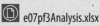 e07pf3Analysis.xlsx

You will save your file as:

e07pf3Analysis_TeamName.xlsx

Team Analysis

Sales & Marketing

A local department store would like to reap the benefits of using data analysis to make strategic decisions about the future of the business. In this exercise you will collaborate with a team of three to five students to develop a data model in Excel and use it to create a simple dashboard. Owing to the complex nature of this assignment you will be limited to the use of Microsoft's SkyDrive as your collaboration tool as Google Drive does not support PowerPivot in its spreadsheet application.

a. Select one team member to complete Steps b through e.

b. Start **Excel**, and then open the **e07pf3Analysis** workbook located with your student files.

c. Save the workbook as e07pf3Analysis_TeamName using the team name assigned to your team by your instructor.

d. Open your browser, and then navigate to **https://skydrive.live.com**. Be sure all members of the team have a Microsoft account.

e. Upload the e07pf3Analysis_TeamName workbook to your SkyDrive account, and then share it with each of your team members, ensuring that each of them has permission to edit the document.

f. Examine the steps below and meet with your team members to discuss who should take on which tasks. Some steps will need to be done before others can be completed.

g. Create a new table on the Data worksheet named MonthSort with the following data:

Order	Month
'01	Jan
'02	Feb
'03	Mar
'04	Apr
'05	May
'06	Jun
'07	Jul
'08	Aug
'09	Sep
'10	Oct
'11	Nov
'12	Dec

h. Add each of the **tables** on the Data worksheet to the data model.

i. Establish the appropriate **relationships** between the tables based on common fields.

j. Format the **fields** in the PowerPivot window appropriately.

k. Create a calculated column for **Revenue** using the Transactions and Products data, and then format it as **Currency**.

l. Create a calculated column for **MonthOrder** using the appropriate DAX function and the MonthSort data to concatenate the Order a "-" and the Month.

m. Create a calculated field for **2012 Total Revenue** using the appropriate DAX function, and then format it as **Currency**.

n. Create a calculated field for **2013 Total Revenue** using the appropriate DAX function, and then format it as **Currency**.

o. Create one more **calculated field** of your choosing, and then format it appropriately.

p. Create two **KPIs** of your choosing, one with an absolute value as the target value and one with a calculated field as the target value.

q. Create a **dashboard** on the Dashboard worksheet using data from the data model. At a minimum the dashboard must include the following items.
   - Add two **PivotCharts**, one of which displays the KPI goal in a combo chart.
   - Add one **PivotTable** that displays the other KPI status value.
   - Add two **slicers** that are connected to either both PivotCharts or one PivotChart and the PivotTable.
   - Format all of the items to create a nice-looking dashboard.

r. Complete the **Documentation** worksheet according to your instructor's direction. Minimally, include enough detail to identify which parts of the worksheets or workbook each team member completed.

s. Insert the **filename** in the left custom footer section of the Header/Footer tab in the Page Setup dialog box on all worksheets in the workbook. In a custom header section, include the **names** of the students in your team—spread the names evenly across each of the three header sections: left section, center section, and right section.

t. Save your work, and then close Excel. Submit the file as directed by your instructor.

Perform 4: How Others Perform

Student data file needed:
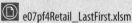 e07pf4Retail.xlsm

You will save your file as:
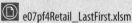 e07pf4Retail_LastFirst.xlsm

Dashboard Errors

Sales & Marketing

Peter Shaw, a manager at Goods & Stuff, a small retail store in the Midwest, attempted to create a dashboard to keep track of sales. The dashboard is not working as expected, and he is getting error messages when trying to run some VBA code. In this exercise, you will examine the dashboard, and then make the changes necessary.

a. Start **Excel**, and then open the **e07pf4Retail** workbook. Save the file as e07pf4Retail_LastFirst using your last and first name.

b. Explore the elements on the Dashboard worksheet. Notice the slicer is not operable and that when you use the spin button and scroll bar an error message appears.

c. Unprotect the worksheet, and then unlock the cells linked to the form controls.

d. Use the **Month** slicer and notice that the label on the Revenue by Category Pie chart does not change.

e. Modify the value in the box on the Pie chart to be a dynamic label for Month using the appropriate field on the Analysis worksheet.

f. Protect the worksheet, ensuring the slicer object can still be used.

g. Click the **Show All Sheets** button, and then use the Debug mode to locate and fix the error in the showSheets Sub procedure.

h. Save and close the workbook, and you will notice another VBA error message. Enter Debug mode, and then locate and fix the method causing the error.

i. Save and close the workbook.

j. Open the workbook again, click the **Show All Sheets** button, and then type Password as the password to show all sheets.

k. Insert the **filename** in the left custom footer section of the Header/Footer tab in the Page Setup dialog box on all worksheets in the workbook.

l. Click **Save**, close Excel, and then submit the file as directed by your instructor.

EFFICIENT INTERACTION WITH A TOUCH SCREEN

OBJECTIVES

1. Understand variations in tablets   p. 766

2. Understand methods for interacting with a tablet PC   p. 768

3. Use flick, touch, and bezel gestures   p. 772

4. Use Office 2013, and other, touch features p. 777, 778

Prepare Case

Painted Paradise Resort and Spa Works with Touch Features

Information Technology

In his position as the CIO of Painted Paradise Resort and Spa, Aidan Matthews travels frequently. Traditionally, Aidan would take four devices with him—a laptop to work on Microsoft Office files, a Kindle to read, a Google tablet to watch videos, and an iPhone to make phone calls. He recently acquired a Windows 8 tablet PC and Windows 8 phone with Office 2013. This will allow him to only carry two devices and still complete all the same tasks. Aidan has asked you to teach him the most efficient ways to interact with his new Windows 8 tablet PC, a Surface Pro.

NAN / Fotolia

REAL WORLD SUCCESS

"As a business analyst for a large technology consulting company, I travel four days a week. Most of my colleagues carry four or more devices while traveling. I only carry my Windows 8 tablet PC and phone. I can do everything my colleagues can and more—with less hassle in the security line and more room in my luggage! My colleagues and clients have been quite impressed with the efficiency of the touch and pen integration."

- Dana, recent graduate

Interacting with a Windows 8 Tablet PC

Microsoft Windows 8 is the latest version of the Windows operating system. The **operating system** is system software, which controls and coordinates computer hardware operations so other programs can run efficiently. The operating system acts as an intermediary between **application software**—programs that help you perform specific tasks, such as word processing—and the computer hardware.

Like previous versions of Windows, Windows 8 uses a **graphical user interface (GUI)**, an interface that uses icons, which are small pictures representing commands, programs, and documents. However, Windows 8 introduces a number of new features that will leave even an experienced user in need of some retraining.

Windows 8 has moved away from the Start button and moved towards a touch-screen interface. Windows 8 also supports gesture recognition, which allows you to control the computer with gestures instead of mouse clicks, if you have a touch-screen device. Gestures allow you to perform actions like zooming and switching programs by performing certain movements. In this section, you will learn about the various ways to efficiently interact in the Windows 8 environment.

Understand Variations in Tablets

People use different devices for different purposes. You may use your tablet for information consumption and entertainment. Likewise, you may prefer your desktop computer to write a paper. These preferences account for the vast market diversity in devices. You may even know someone who regularly uses five or more devices. The capabilities of these devices can be quite divergent and cause consumer confusion. Further, some consumers— particularly cost-conscious consumers—seek to minimize the number of devices.

There are many types of tablet computers in terms of hardware, software, and size. Further, the types are constantly changing as new versions come out. Some of the most popular currently available devices are the Microsoft Surface, Apple iPad, and the Android tablet computer. Each device runs a different operating system and has different features and capabilities. Which tablet is the best for you depends on many questions.

- How much are you willing to spend?
- Do you need to use it for business production?
- Do you need to connect to specific hardware such as a camera or microphone?
- Do you want a high-quality display?
- How does the device feel when you hold it?
- Do you find the device easy to use?
- Do you need it to connect to a cellular network?

One major discriminator when answering these questions is the operating system it runs. Table 1 describes the capabilities of the various operating systems and the devices they are found on. Since technology is constantly changing, you should research any potential changes to the table that follows.

Operating System	Software It Runs	Types of Devices	Hardware Manufacturers	Office Capabilities
Mac OS X	Runs software written for the Mac OS X operating system	Laptops and desktops	Apple only	Mac Office versions such as Office 2011 and PC versions via dual boot or parallels
Windows 8	Runs software written for Windows 7 and above. Also, runs apps from the Windows store	Laptops, desktops, and some newer Intel chip-based tablets	Various: Microsoft, Lenovo, Dell, ASUS, and others	Full Office 2013
Windows 8 RT	Runs apps from the Windows store only	ARM chip-based tablets	Various: Microsoft, Lenovo, Dell, ASUS, and others	Office 2013 RT: Visually, the same as the full Office 2013 but lacks some sophisticated Office features
Android	Runs apps from the Google Play Store only	Smartphones and tablets	Various: Google, Samsung, ASUS, HTC, LG, and others	Some limited native capability to work with Office files
iOS	Runs apps from the iTunes Store only	iPads and iPhones	Apple only	Very limited ability to work with Office files. Some capability with purchased third-party apps
Windows Phone	Runs apps from the Windows store only, including Office 2013 for Windows Phone	Smartphones	Various: Nokia, HTC, Samsung, and others	Office 2013 for Windows Phone: Visually different than the full Office 2013 but similar functionality to Office 2013 RT
Blackberry	Runs apps from BlackBerry App World only	Smartphones and tablets	Blackberry only	Very limited ability to work with Office files. Some capability with purchased third-party apps

Table 1 Operating system capabilities

Tablets can run one of two kinds of chips: an Intel-based or ARM-based chip. An **Advanced RISC Machine chip (ARM chip)** is designed for low-energy embedded systems, such as in an iPad. An **Intel chip** is a series of microprocessors made by the manufacturer Intel, for example the chip used in most traditional laptops or desktops.

In October 2012, Microsoft released the Surface tablet. This tablet comes in two versions, the Surface and Surface Pro—as seen in Figure 1. The Surface RT runs on an ARM chip device and contains substantively similar functionality for Word, PowerPoint, Excel, and OneNote as the Windows version of Office 2013. Visually, Windows RT even looks the same as the full Office 2013 for Windows. However, applications that run on Windows Phone and RT do not support some of the more sophisticated Office features or back-end Visual Basic programming.

The Surface Pro tablet runs Windows 8 Pro and is built with a more traditional Intel chip hardware that lets it perform like a traditional PC. Tablets capable of performing like a traditional PC are typically referred to as a **tablet PC**.

Aidan Matthews purchased a Surface Pro tablet PC because he can use it for personal, business, and mobile tasks. Thus, you need to learn about the touch interface for the full Windows 8 specifically—the same touch interface for any PC with any kind of touch screen.

Figure 1   Microsoft Surface

Understand Methods for Interacting with a Tablet PC

Users can interact with the tablet PC via several built-in ways: speech, keyboard, track-pad, digitizer pen, or touch screen. Windows 8 is smart enough to detect the method of input you are using and adapts the menus and options accordingly. To maximize your efficiency, you need to understand when to use which method of input.

Inputting Text with Speech Recognition

Speech recognition in Windows 8 is better than any prior version of Windows. Typically, whether speech recognition is desirable or efficient is highly dependent on voice, accent, and personal preference. Windows 8 has a built-in speech recognition app. By default, the app is not pinned to the Start screen. However, you can easily find it by doing a search as shown in Figure 2. While the Surface Pro includes a microphone, most users prefer and have better accuracy with a headset or desktop microphone—purchased separately.

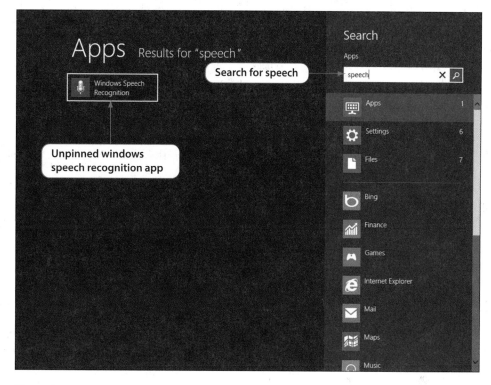

Figure 2   Search for speech recognition app

Using the Keyboard and Trackpad

The Surface comes with two types of covers: the touch cover and type cover as seen in Figure 3. The type cover provides a depression keyboard similar to traditional keyboards. Both keyboards have the same functionality except that only the type cover has the traditional F1–F12 keys. Thus, personal preference is the most important determinant on which is best. Even though Windows 8 has a touch keyboard, most users still find an actual keyboard preferable when needing more than a few words entered.

Figure 3   Microsoft Surface covers

The covers come with a built-in **trackpad**—a pad that works like a traditional mouse but uses touch. Trackpads are typically found on laptops and tablet PCs. Many users find a trackpad awkward when needing to drag. Thus, a user that drags a lot may want to consider purchasing a USB wireless mouse.

The touch interface can replace the need for a mouse in many situations. In fact, keyboard shortcuts can also cut down dramatically on the need for a mouse. Thus, keyboard shortcuts improve efficiency in Windows 8 more than any prior version of Windows.

REAL WORLD ADVICE	Using Keyboard Shortcuts and KeyTips

Keyboard shortcuts are extremely useful because they allow you to keep your hands on the keyboard instead of reaching for the mouse to make Ribbon selections. This can dramatically increase your efficiency and save you time.

Pressing the Alt key will display KeyTips—or keyboard shortcuts—for items on the Ribbon and Quick Access Toolbar. After displaying the KeyTips, you can press the letter or number corresponding to Ribbon items to request the action from the keyboard. Pressing Alt again will remove the KeyTips.

Many keyboard shortcuts are universal to all Windows programs. Keyboard shortcuts usually involve two or more keys, in which case you hold down the first key listed, and press the second key once.

QUICK REFERENCE	Common Keyboard Shortcuts
Press Ctrl and type C	Copy the selected item
Press Ctrl and type V	Paste a copied item
Press Ctrl and type A	Select all the items in a document or window
Press Ctrl and type B	Bold selected text
Press Ctrl and type Z	Undo an action
Press Ctrl + Home	Move to the top of the document
Press Ctrl + End	Move to the end of the document
Press F1	Microsoft Help
Press Ctrl and type S	Save a file

Using the Digitizer Pen

The Surface Pro tablet PC also comes with a **digitizer pen**—a device that allows you to write on a touch screen like a pen does on paper as shown in Figure 4. Windows 8 can recognize whether you use a mouse, finger, or digitizer pen. Apps may react differently based on your input method.

Figure 4   Surface digitizer pen

If you use the pen in Word, the Pens contextual Ribbon tab automatically appears for drawing options: Highlighter, Eraser, or Selection as seen in Figure 5. Word accepts only drawing input from the pen and cannot recognize handwritten text. Thus, best practice is to use the pen in Word to replace a mouse or to draw a picture.

If you want to take handwritten notes—for example in a meeting—best practice is to use OneNote. OneNote has excellent handwriting-to-text conversion capabilities using the Ink to Text button as shown in Figure 6. Thus, you gain efficiency by using the pen in situations where handwriting is most natural.

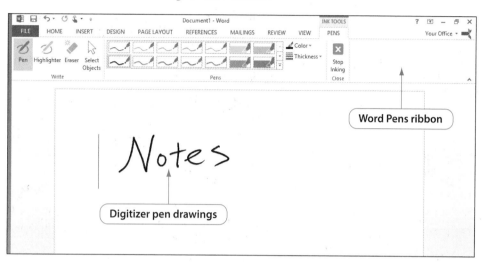

Figure 5   Pens Ribbon in Word

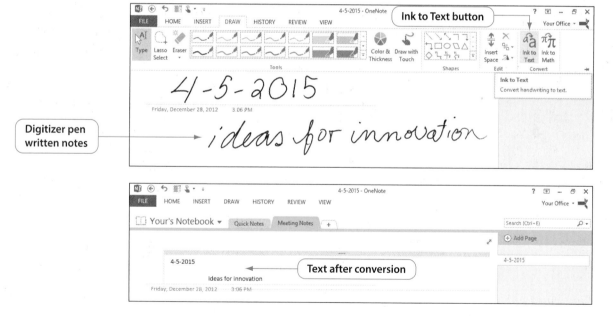

Figure 6   Handwriting in OneNote

Understanding When the Touch Interface Is Effective

Windows 8 and Office 2013 have fully integrated the touch environment. If you have a touch screen, you can manipulate Windows, Office, and other apps by just touching the screen. Fingers are larger than a mouse point. Thus, the app must be designed to be easy to use with a simple touch. One of Microsoft's main goals with the latest release of Windows and Office was to make it easier to use with touch. Touch increases efficiency and productivity when used while mobile, to replace traditional mouse movements, and to use apps specifically designed for touch.

Using the Touch-Screen Interface

One of the key features that sets Windows 8 apart from previous versions is the built-in touch-screen recognition. A **gesture** is a movement of the user's finger, fingers, or pen on a touch screen resulting in a particular action. Many gestures are available, and several factors determine the result.

- Are you using one or two fingers?
- Where did your finger start on the screen?
- Where did your finger end on the screen?
- At what speed did you move your finger?
- Did you make one or several movements together?
- On the screen, was the Start screen showing, an app running, or an app that runs on the desktop—such as Word?

Touching a screen and not understanding why the resulting action occurred is frustrating. In this section, you will learn about the types of touch and other touch-friendly features.

Use Flick, Touch, and Bezel Gestures

Intuitively, you may think of a "touch" as a simple finger tap. However, Windows 8 distinguishes between several different types of touch gestures—flicks, touch, and bezel. Knowing these different touch features will help decrease frustration, increase efficiency, and increase productivity.

Using Flick Gestures

Flick gestures (flicks), as shown in Table 2, are quick short gestures that can be made with a finger or a pen. Flicks cannot start at the edge of the screen—the **bezel**. There are two types of flicks, navigational and editing. **Navigational flicks** are enabled by default and are quick short gestures either in a vertical or horizontal direction that either scroll up and down or move forward or backward a page. **Editing flicks** are not enabled by default and are quick short gestures in a diagonal direction that either delete, copy, paste, or undo.

Flick Gesture	Result Action	Image
Up	Scroll up	
Down	Scroll down	
Right	Turn page to the right	
Left	Turn page to the left	
Diagonally to upper left	Delete	
Diagonally to upper right	Copy	
Diagonally to lower left	Undo	
Diagonally to lower right	Paste	

Table 2   Flick gestures

You can adjust settings, modify sensitivity, enable editing flicks, turn flicks off, and practice flicks from the Pen and Touch dialog box. To modify these settings, search Windows settings for flicks as seen in Figures 7 and 8 shown here. In the same dialog box, you can also change settings and customize the pen and other touch actions.

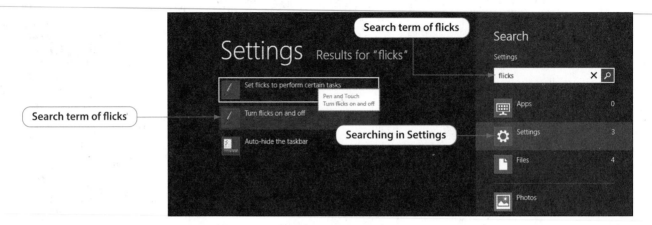

Figure 7   Search settings for flicks

Figure 8   Pen and Tools dialog box

Using Touch Gestures

Touch gestures are gestures made with a finger. Generally, these gestures cannot be completed with a pen—except pen actions set by default for tap, double-tap, and tap and hold. Touches can bring up additional menus and mimic traditional mouse actions such as double-clicking. Table 3 shows the available touch gestures.

Touch Gesture	Result Action	Image
Tap	Same action as a single mouse click	
Double-tap	Same action as a double-click on a mouse	
Tap and hold	Same action as a right-click on a mouse	
Slide	Pans or scrolls	
Pinch and stretch	Zoom in or out	
Rotate	Rotates the item that is selected	
Tap and swipe in the opposite direction as any scroll bars, not starting at a bezel	Selects the item and brings up additional menus	

Table 3 Touch gestures

Using Bezel Gestures

A **bezel gesture** is a gesture that starts and/or ends at the edge of the screen, as shown in Table 4. For example, a left bezel starts with your finger on the left edge—middle of the screen is the easiest—and swipes to the center of the screen. Some tablet cases can make these gestures difficult. These gestures are easiest when they start completely off screen.

Bezel Gesture	Result Action	Image
Left bezel	Switches to the last app that was used	
Right bezel	Opens the charms menu	
Top bezel	Brings up additional menus dependent on the currently open app. On the Start screen, it brings up menu to go to all apps. In Internet Explorer, it brings up a menu of all tabs.	
Bottom bezel	Brings up additional menus dependent on the currently open app; usually, a menu similar to the options given from a right-click on a mouse	
Left bezel and then back to left bezel again	Brings up a menu of all open apps	
Slow left bezel*	When multiple apps are open, snaps the current app to a docked position to view more than one app at the same time on the same screen	
Top bezel ending at the bottom bezel	Shows the app window shrinking and then closes the app when the bottom bezel is reached	
From title bar of a program window to the left or right bezel*	Snaps app to left or right portion of the screen docking it to view multiple apps on the same screen	

*Must have a screen resolution of at least 1366 * 768 to snap.

Table 4   Bezel gestures

Use Office 2013 Touch Gestures

Gestures can be combined or have different effects within different apps, including Office 2013. For example, the Mini toolbar is particularly helpful with the touch interface. When Office recognizes that you are using touch instead of a mouse or digitizer pen, it creates Mini toolbars that are larger and designed to work with fingers easier. To get the Mini toolbar in Excel, a combination of several gestures are needed.

1. Tap a cell.
2. Use the touch handles to select the desired cells.
3. Tap again anywhere but on the handle.

Figure 9 is an example of a touch Mini toolbar in Excel when using touch input.

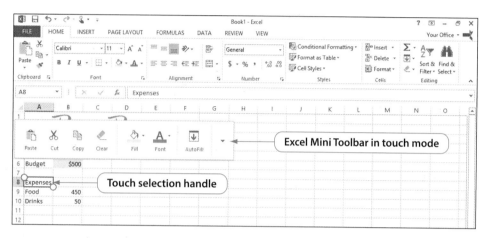

Figure 9 Excel Mini toolbar when using touch input

If you need to use Office by touch for an extended period of time, you can also use touch mode. **Touch mode** switches Office into a version that makes a touch screen easy to use, as shown in Table 5. Click the Touch Mode button 👆▾ on the Quick Access Toolbar, and the Ribbon spreads its icons further apart for easier access to fingers. When you toggle this display mode, the on-screen controls space out a bit from each other to make them more accessible to users via touch. Figure 10 displays the normal Word 2013 Ribbon. Figure 11 displays the Ribbon in touch mode.

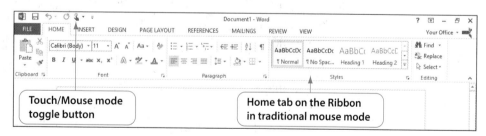

Figure 10 Normal Ribbon

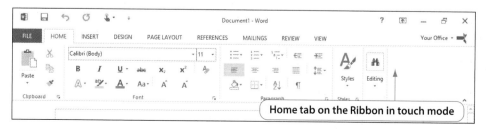

Figure 11 Touch mode Ribbon

To	Gestures Steps
Place the cursor insertion point	Tap the location for the cursor.
Select and format text	Tap the text, drag the selection handle to the desired selection, and tap the selection to show and use the Mini toolbar.
Edit an Excel cell	Double-tap.
Change PowerPoint slides in Normal view	A quick vertical flick
Customize the Quick Access Toolbar	Tab and hold any button on the Quick Access Toolbar.

Table 5 Common Office 2013 gestures

Use Other Touch Features

To make the touch experience as versatile and robust as possible, a few last touch-friendly features exist. When a keyboard is not available, a touch-screen keyboard can be used. Conversely, when a touch screen is not available, several options exist for accessing the same items achieved with touch.

Using the Touch Keyboard

If a keyboard is not available, Windows 8 provides an on-screen touch keyboard. You can access this keyboard by tapping Touch Keyboard ▦ in the taskbar. Tapping Dock ▭ will make the keyboard stay open. Tapping Undock ▭ will make the keyboard float allowing you to move it to various parts of the screen. Tapping Keyboard Mode ▦ allows you to switch between a full, thumbs, or pen handwriting mode as seen in Figures 12, 13, and 14.

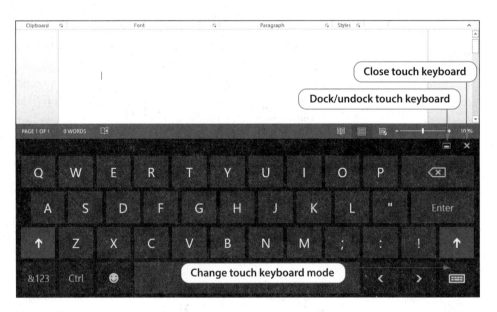

Figure 12 Docked touch keyboard in full mode

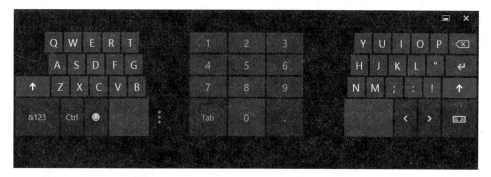

Figure 13   Docked touch keyboard in thumbs mode

Figure 14   Docked touch keyboard in pen handwriting mode

Using Alternatives to a Touch Screen

If a touch screen is not available, you have three choices. You can use a traditional mouse and point it in particular places to access the Start screen and charms menu as shown in Table 6. You can use gestures on your trackpad or Windows 8 mouse. Not all gestures work on the trackpad and may be slightly different than on a touch screen. However, device makers can add custom gestures accessible via the trackpad only. You should consult your touchpad or Windows 8 mouse manufacturer for specifics. Lastly, you can use keyboard shortcuts to access the most common bezel gestures as shown in Table 7.

Result Action	Mouse Equivalent
Start screen	Point mouse to edge of lower-left corner.
Charms menu	Point mouse to edge of lower-right or upper-right corner.

Table 6   Mouse alternatives for Windows 8

Result Action	Touch Gesture	Keyboard Shortcut
Charms menu	Right bezel	Press [Windows] and type C
Additional menus, similar to the right-click menus, when additional options exist	Bottom bezel	Press [Windows] and type Z
Switch between open apps	Left bezel swipe and then back to bezel	Press [Windows] + [Tab] or press [Alt] + [Tab]
Shrinks and then closes program	Top bezel to bottom bezel	[Alt] + [F4]

Table 7   Keyboard shortcut alternatives for bezel gestures

Concept Check

1. What is the difference between a tablet and a tablet PC? Provide an example of each. p. 767

2. What is a digitizer pen, and when is it the most effective to use? p. 770

3. What is the difference between a flick, touch, and bezel gesture? Provide an example of each. p. 772–776

4. Does touch differ at all inside of Office 2013? Explain. How could you use a tablet PC without a keyboard? How could you use a tablet PC without a touch screen? p. 779

Key Terms

Advanced RISC Machine chip (ARM chip)   767
Application software   766
Bezel   772
Bezel gesture   776
Digitizer pen   770

Editing flicks   772
Flick gestures (flicks)   772
Gesture   772
Graphical user interface (GUI)   766
Intel chip   767
Navigational flicks   772

Operating system   766
Tablet PC   767
Touch gestures   775
Touch mode   777
Trackpad   770

Glossary

3-D formula—A formula that references the same cell, or range of cells, across multiple worksheets in a workbook.

3-D named range—A named range that references the same cell, or range of cells, across multiple worksheets in a workbook.

3-D reference—Allows formulas and functions to use data from cells and cell ranges across worksheets.

A

A1 reference method—This refers to the way cell references are written. If letters appear for the column headings, the reference style for Excel is currently A1. In this mode, cells are referenced using a letter for the column and a number for the row.

ABS function—A function that returns the absolute value of a number—the number without its negative sign.

Absolute cell reference—The exact address of a cell, when both the column and row need to remain a constant regardless of the position of the cell when the formula is copied to other cells.

Absolute macro reference—A macro that affects the same cells every time it is run.

Active cell—Identifiable as the cell with the thick green border. Only the active cell can have data entered into it.

Active worksheet—The worksheet that is visible in the Excel application window. The active worksheet tab has a white background.

Add-in—An application with specific functionality geared toward accomplishing a specific goal.

Advanced filter—A way to filter data where the filtering criteria are set up on the spreadsheet; the filtering criteria must be set up as rows above the data table with field headings that are identical to the data set; criteria can be set up in one or more cells below the field names.

Advanced RISC Machine Chip (ARM chip)—This microprocessor chip is designed for low-energy embedded systems and used in devices such as an iPad.

Aggregate—To consolidate or summarize data with functions like SUM, COUNT, or AVERAGEIF.

Amortization schedule—A table that calculates the interest and principal payments along with the remaining balance of the loan for each period.

Amortize—Refers to repaying the balance of a loan over a period of time in multiple installments.

AND function—Returns TRUE if all logical tests supplied are true; otherwise, it returns FALSE.

Annuity—A recurring amount paid or received at specified intervals.

Any value validation—A type of data validation that utilizes the input message as a means to communicate rules for entering data in a cell.

Application software—Programs that help you perform specific tasks, such as word processing.

Application Start screen—The first screen seen when an existing program file is not open but when the program is launched. On the screen you can select a blank document, workbook, presentation, database, or one of many application specific templates.

Apps for Office—Essentially a web page that is hosted inside an Office application. These apps can be used to extend the functionality of the application. These third-party applications run in the side pane to provide extra features like web search, dictionary, maps, and so on.

Area chart—Emphasizes magnitude of change over time and depicts trends.

Argument—Variables or values the function requires in order to calculate a solution. A value passed to a function, either as a constant or a variable.

Argumentation objective—A position you want supported visually in a chart.

Array function—A function that can perform multiple calculations on one or more items in an array.

AutoFill—Copies information from one cell, or a series of adjacent cells, into adjacent cells in the direction the fill handle is dragged.

AutoRecovery—A feature that attempts to recover any changes made since the prior save to a document if something goes wrong; for example, automatically saving a backup version at specified time intervals.

AVERAGE function—A function that returns a weighted average from a specified range of cells.

AVERAGEIF function—Averages the number of cells that meet the specified criteria.

AVERAGEIFS function—Averages a range of data, selecting data to average based on the criteria specified.

B

Banding—Alternating the background color of rows and/or columns to assist in tracking information.

Bar chart—Displays data horizontally and is used for comparisons among individual items.

Base value—A calculated field that resolves to a value as part of a KPI.

Bezel—The edge of the screen.

Bezel gesture—A gesture that starts and/or ends at the edge of the screen. For example, a left bezel gesture starts with your finger on the left edge and swipes horizontally towards the center of the screen.

Bezel swipe gesture—A touch gesture that starts on the physical touch insensitive frame that surrounds the display. The user swipes a finger from a part of the display edge into the display.

Bidirectional KPI—When the value becomes worse as it deviates too far from the target value in either direction. An example of a bidirectional KPI may be the temperature for storing a particular product; damage could occur if the temperature gets too cold or too hot.

Binding constraint—A constraint is binding if changing it also changes the optimal solution.

Binomial distribution—A discrete probability distribution that is used to model the number of successful trials based on the total number of trials and the rate of success.

Bins—Intervals in which you want to group your data.

Bootcamp—Mac software that allows the user to decide which operating system to launch on Intel chip-based Macs.

Break-even analysis—Used to calculate the break-even point in sales volume or dollars, estimate profit or loss at any level of sales volume, and help in setting prices.

Break-even point—The sales level at which revenue equals total costs; there is neither a profit nor a loss.

Built-in cell style—Predefined and named combination of cell and content formatting properties.

Built-in function—A function included in Excel that can be categorized as financial, statistical, mathematical, date and time, text, or so on.

Business intelligence (BI)—Refers to a variety of software applications that are used to analyze an organization's data in order to provide management with the tools necessary to improve decision making, cut costs, and identify new opportunities.

C

Capital budgeting—The planning procedure used to evaluate whether an organization's long-term investments are worth pursuing.

Cash flow—The movement of cash in and out of a business.

Cell—The intersection of a row and a column in a worksheet.

Cell alignment—Allows cell content to be left-aligned, centered, and right-aligned on the horizontal axis, as well as top-aligned, middle-aligned, and bottom-aligned on the vertical axis.

Cell reference—Refers to a particular cell or range of cells within a formula or function instead of a value.

Central tendency—Refers to the way in which data tends to cluster around some value.

Change history—Information that is maintained about all changes made in past editing sessions to a shared workbook.

Changing cell—The cell or cells used to identify the various data cells whose values can differ in each scenario.

Charms—A specific and consistent set of Windows buttons available to every application: Search, Share, Connect, Settings, and Start.

Chart sheet—A tabbed sheet that only holds a chart.

Circular reference—An error in a worksheet indicating a single formula that references itself or multiple formulas that reference each other.

Clean—Remove any nonprinting characters from a text string.

Close—The command to close an Office file without exiting the associated program.

Cloud computing—Computing resources—either hardware or software—being used by another computer over a network.

Code window—Where VBA code is typed and also where VBA that is generated by a recorded macro can be viewed and edited.

Codification scheme—Rules that combine data values in specific formats and locations to generate a new data value.

Codified data value—A value created by following a system of rules where the position of information is tied to its content.

Collaboration—Allows workbooks to be shared among different users and then merged together for a final product.

Column—A vertical set of cells that encompasses all the rows in a worksheet and only one cell horizontally.

Column chart—Used to compare data across categories and show change, sometimes over time.

Combination chart—A chart that displays two different types of data by using multiple chart types in a single chart object.

Compare and Merge Workbooks—The command that will compare the changes made in each shared workbook and then provide you with the option to update the workbook with those changes.

Competitive advantage—A strategic advantage that a business has over its competition. Attaining a competitive advantage strengthens and positions a business better within the business environment.

Complex function—A function that combines multiple functions within a formula.

CONCATENATE—A text function used to join up to 255 text strings into one text string.

Conditional aggregate function—A function that aggregates a subset of data that has been filtered based upon one or more criteria.

Conditional formatting—Allows the specification of rules that apply formatting to cells, appointments, contacts, or tasks as determined by the rule outcome. Also, applies custom formatting to highlight or emphasize values that meet specific criteria and is called "conditional" because the formatting occurs when a particular condition is met.

Conditional math function—A function that works in a similar fashion as statistical functions and include the SUMIF and SUMIFS functions.

Consolidate by category—Aggregates data in cells with matching row and/or column labels. Data does not need to be in the same relative position to create a summary sheet.

Consolidate by position—Aggregates data in the same position in multiple worksheets. A summary sheet can be created but only when the source worksheets have an identical structure.

Constant—A value that does not change.

Constraint—A rule that you establish when formulating your Solver model.

Contextual tab—A Ribbon tab that contains commands related to selected objects so you can manipulate, edit, and format the objects. This Ribbon tab does not appear unless the object is selected.

Contextual tools—Tools that only appear when needed for specific tasks.

Contiguous cell range—A range consisting of multiple selected cells, all of which are directly adjacent to at least one other cell in the selected range.

Continuous variable—Can contain an infinite number of different values within a range.

Convert Text to Columns Wizard—A step-by-step guide used to separate simple data cell content such as dates or first and last names into separate columns.

Convert to range—An option used to convert a data table back to a range of data; the formatting remains, but the functionality of tables, such as adding new columns or rows, will no longer automatically be added or updated to the named ranges, and formulas and would need to be manually copied down a column.

Correlation coefficient—A unitless value that describes the strength and direction of a relationship between two variables. A correlation coefficient of -1 is said to have a perfect negative relationship; a coefficient of 1 is considered to have a perfect positive relationship; a coefficient of 0 is said to have no relationship. The closer the value is to –1 or 1 describes the strength of the relationship.

Cost-volume-profit (CVP) analysis—The study of how cost and volume are related and the effect their relationship has on profit.

Count—The count of all values in a sample.

COUNT function—A function that returns the number of cells in a range of cells that contain numbers.

COUNTA function—A function that returns the number of cells within a range that contain any type of data.

COUNTIF function—Counts the number of cells that meet the specified criteria.

COUNTIFS function—Allows for multiple criteria in multiple ranges to be evaluated and counted.

Coupon—The interest rate a bond pays the bondholder.

Covariance—A formula that can calculate the relationship between two variables, like age and dollars spent, as well as the direction of the relationship. If one variable increases and the other variable also increases, then the relationship is considered positive. If one variable increases and the other variable decreases, then the relationship is considered negative.

CUMIPMT function—Used to calculate the amount of interest paid over a specific number of periods, such as quarterly, annually, or for the whole term of the loan.

CUMPRINC function—Used to calculate the amount of principal paid over a specific number of periods, such as quarterly or annually.

Cumulative distribution function—The probability of a value being less than or equal to the value of x.

Current yield—Considers the current market price of the bond, which may differ from the par value, and gives you a different yield rate on that basis.

Custom validation—A more complex type of data validation that allows the user to apply multiple criteria simultaneously by using formulas.

D

Data—The values that describe an attribute of an object or an event.

Data bars—Graphical display of data that is overlaid on the data in the cells of the worksheet.

Data cleansing—The process of fixing obvious errors in the data and converting the data into a useful format.

Data exploration objective—Manipulating data to evaluate and prioritize the interpretations or messages.

Data model—A collection of tables and their relationships reflecting the real-world relationships between business functions and processes.

Data point—An individual piece of data being charted.

Data series—A set or subset of data that is charted.

Data set—A collection of related data consisting of observational units and variables. Also, organized data; includes fields and data that have context and meaning.

Data table—A what-if analysis tool that takes sets of input values, determines possible results, and displays all the results in one table on one worksheet.

Data validation—Rules that determine what can and cannot be entered in specific cells.

Data verification—The process of validating that the data is correct and accurate.

Data visualization—The graphical presentation of data with a focus upon qualitative understanding.

DATE—A function that returns the sequential serial number that represents a particular date.

Date and time functions—Functions that are used for entering the current day and time into a worksheet as well as calculating the intervals between dates.

Date data—Data recognized by Excel as a date. Date data takes the form of a serial number, with the number 1 representing January 1, 1900.

Date validation—A type of data validation that specifies only a date can be entered into a cell.

DATEDIF function—A function that enables you to calculate the time between two dates.

DATEVALUE—A function that converts a date in a text format into a serial number.

DB function—Calculates the depreciation of an asset for a specified period using the fixed declining-balance method.

DDB function—Calculates the depreciation of an asset for a specified period using the double declining-balance method.

Decimal validation—A type of data validation that restricts users to enter only data that contains digits and a decimal place.

Decision tree—A diagramming tool that allows you to break down potential decisions in a logical, structured format.

Default—A setting that is automatically in place unless you specify otherwise.

Delimiter—A way of separating text data segments or elements in text files.

Dependent cell—A cell whose value depends on the value in the active cell for its result.

Depreciation schedule—Records the date that the asset was placed into service, a calculation for each year's depreciation, and the accumulated depreciation.

Descriptive statistics—The process of deriving meaningful information from raw data.

Destination cell—The cell that received the result of an operation, such as Paste or an AutoSum function. Also, the cell to be modified by a copy, move, or paste operation.

Destination worksheet—The worksheet to be modified by a copy, move, or paste operation.

Developer tab—A tab that is not visible by default on the Ribbon that contains the buttons needed to create, edit, and run macros.

Dialog box—A window that provides more options or settings beyond those provided on the Ribbon.

Dialog box launcher—An icon on the Ribbon that opens a corresponding dialog box or task pane.

Digital dashboards—Mechanisms that deliver business intelligence in graphical form. Dashboards provide management with a "big picture" view of the business, usually from multiple perspectives using various charts and other graphical representations.

Digitizer pen—A device that allows you to write on a touch screen like a pen does on paper.

Discrete variable—A number that is finite; all possible values are known.

Do…Until loop—Loops through code until a specified condition is true.

Do…While loop—Loops through code while a specified condition is true.

Document—Depending on the application, a document can be a letter, memo, report, brochure, resume, or flyer.

Double prime symbol—Quotation marks that are used in functions and formulas to let Excel know that the element is a text string and not a numeric value, cell reference, or named range.

Drilling down—A method for accessing the detailed records used in a PivotTable to get some aggregated data.

DSUM function—A database function that is ideal for setting up a criteria range and then calculating the sum based on the filters within that criteria range.

E

Economic risk—Occurs when there is a concern that a chosen act or activity will not generate sufficient revenues to cover operating costs and repay debt obligations.

Editing flicks—These are quick short gestures in a diagonal direction that either delete, copy, paste, or undo, and are not enabled by default.

Elastic—A product or service is elastic—or responsive to change—if a small change in price is accompanied by a large change in the quantity demanded.

Encryption—A method of protecting a workbook by assigning a password that unscrambles the code once it has been opened.

Error message—A message that informs a user when entered data violates validation constraints.

Evaluate formula—A tool that breaks down a formula into its individual pieces and evaluates each part separately so you can see how the formula works.

Event—An action initiated either by a user or by VBA code.

Evolutionary method—The method used when a worksheet model is nonlinear and nonsmooth and uses functions—such as VLOOKUP, PMT, IF, and so on—to calculate the values of the variable cells or constraint cells.

Excel database—A way of storing data in Excel that is made up of records and fields.

Exit—The command to close all of the program's files and close the program itself.

Explicit calculated field—Created when a formula is typed in the Calculation Area of the PowerPivot window. Explicit calculated fields can use a wide variety of functions beyond general aggregation and can be used in any PivotTable, PivotChart, or Power View report. They can also be extended to become a KPI.

Exponential distribution—A continuous probability distribution that is used to model the time in between events.

External data—Any data that is not stored locally or not in an Excel format (.xls or .xlsx).

F

Factor—An optional argument in the DDB function; the rate at which the balance declines.

Field—A column in an Excel database. Also, an item of information in a worksheet column that is associated with something of interest.

File extension—Letters that follow the name of a file that indicates the file type. These are assigned by the Office program.

Fill Across Worksheets—A command that can be used to copy cell contents, formats, or both contents and formats to worksheets in a group.

Fill color—The background color of a cell.

Filtering—A process of hiding records that do not meet specified criteria in a data set.

Financial functions—Functions that are used for common financial calculations such as interest rates, payments, and analyzing loans.

FIND function—Locates one text string within a second text string, and returns the number of the starting position of the first text string from the starting character of the second text string.

Fixed cost—An expense that never changes regardless of how much product is sold or how many services are rendered.

Flash Fill—A new feature in Excel that recognizes patterns in data as you type and automatically fills in values for text and numeric data.

Flick gestures (flicks)—Quick short gestures that can be made with a finger or a digitizer pen.

For loop—Loops through code until a specified number of loops have been completed.

For…Each loop—Loops through an object collection or an array.

Foreign key—A shared field that is not a primary key but serves as a link to a table in which the same field is a primary key of the other table.

Form controls—Objects that can be placed into an Excel worksheet, providing the functionality to interact with your models.

Format Painter—A tool that enables you to copy the format of objects, such as text or pictures, to paste on other objects.

Formula—Performs a mathematical calculation (or calculations) using information in the worksheet to calculate new values; can contain cell references, constants, functions, and mathematical operators.

Function—A built-in program that performs operations against data based on a set of inputs and returns a value such as SUM or AVERAGE. Some functions, called null functions, do not require arguments.

Function Arguments—A dialog box that provides additional information and previews the results of a function being constructed.

Function procedures—A group of VBA statements that perform calculations and return a single value.

FV function—Used to calculate the value of an investment with a fixed interest rate and term, and periodic payments over a specific period of time.

Fv—The future value of the loan; the balance you want to reach after the last payment is made.

G

Gallery—A set of menu options that appear when you click the arrow next to a button which, in some cases, may be referred to as a More arrow.

Gantt chart—A type of bar chart showing a project schedule where each bar represents a component or task within the project.

Gesture—Movement of the user's finger, fingers, or digitizer pen on a touch screen resulting in a particular action.

Goal Seek—A scenario tool that maximizes Excel's cell-referencing capabilities and enables you to find the input values needed to achieve a goal or objective.

Graphical format—The presentation of information in charts, graphs, and pictures.

Graphical user interface (GUI)—An interface that uses icons.

Graphics—Pictures, online pictures, SmartArt, shapes, and charts.

GRG nonlinear method—A method used when the worksheet model is nonlinear and smooth; it is the default method that Excel's Solver uses. A nonlinear and smooth model is one in which a graph of the equation used would not show sharp edges or breaks if you were to plot the equation on a graph.

Gridlines—The vertical and horizontal lines on a worksheet that help define a cell's boundaries.

Grouping—Selecting multiple worksheets at a time.

Grouping variable—A field that could be used to categorize or group for the purpose of comparison.

Guess—An optional argument used in the RATE function and others. It is used when you want to guess what the interest rate will be. RATE usually calculates if you enter a guess between zero and one. If nothing is entered, Excel assumes that the guess is 10%.

H

Help—Microsoft Help is a window opened via the Help button or the F1 key.

Histogram—A statistical graph that summarizes the distribution of data and how the data fits into defined bins.

HLOOKUP function—Helps retrieve values located in another location and is used when your comparison values are located in a row—horizontally—above the data that you want to find.

Horizontal multiples—Expand across the available space in the container, and if additional space is needed a horizontal scroll bar is added.

HTML—Short for Hypertext Markup Language, this language defines how web page content is displayed in a browser.

Hypergeometric distribution—A discrete population distribution that calculates the probability of drawing a specific number of target items from a collection.

Hyperlink—A link that opens another page or file when you click on it.

Hypothesis testing objective—Using charts to visually support or refute a hypothesis.

I

IF function—A function that returns one of two values depending upon whether the supplied logical test being evaluated is true or false.

IFERROR function—A function used for detecting an error and displaying something more user-friendly than the error message.

Implicit calculated field—Created when you drag a field like Sales or Quantity Sold into the Values area of a PivotTable. The calculation takes place but a new calculated field is not being created. Implicit calculated fields can only use standard aggregation functions such as AVERAGE, SUM, COUNT, MAX, etc.

INDEX function—Works in conjunction with the MATCH function; returns the value of an element in a table or array selected by the row and column number indexes and has two argument lists to select.

INDIRECT function—A function that can change a text string within a cell to a cell reference.

Inelastic—A product is inelastic—or not responsive to change—if a large change in price is accompanied by a small amount of change in demand.

Inferential statistics—The process of taking data from a sample of the population and making predictions about the entire population.

Information—Data that has context, meaning, and relevance and thus value to the user.

Information management program—Provides the ability to print schedules, task lists, phone directories, and other documents.

Input box—An effective way of using VBA code to increase the interactivity of a dashboard by prompting the user for information and storing that information in a variable to be used later.

Input message—The message that appears when a user makes a validated cell active and prompts a user before data is entered with information about data constraints.

INT function—Rounds a value down to the nearest whole integer.

Intel chip—A series of microprocessors made by the manufacturer Intel and used in devices such as a tablet PC, laptop, or desktop.

Intercept coefficient—Part of a regression analysis; the value at which a regression line will cross the y-axis which is used in the slope intercept formula to predict values.

Interval data—Measures the size of the difference between values.

IPMT function—Calculates how much of a specific periodic payment is going toward the interest that has accrued on the loan.

IRR function—Indicates the profitability of an investment and is commonly used in business when choosing between investments.

Iteration—A process that repeatedly enters new values in the variable cell or cells to find a solution to the problem.

K

Key performance indicator (KPI)—A quantifiable measure that helps managers define progress toward both short-term and long-term goals.

Key tip—A form of keyboard shortcut. Pressing [Alt] will display key tips (or keyboard shortcuts) for items on the Ribbon and Quick Access Toolbar.

Keyboard shortcut—Keyboard equivalents for software commands that allow you to keep your hands on the keyboard instead of reaching for the mouse to make Ribbon selections.

Kurtosis—Characterizes the peakedness or flatness of a distribution compared to the normal distribution.

L

Landscape—For page layout and printing purposes, landscape orientation indicates the longer dimension of the page is on the horizontal axis.

LEFT function—Returns the characters in a text string based on the number of characters you specify starting with the far-left character in the string.

LEN—This function returns the number of characters in a text string.

Line chart—Used to show continuous data over time; great for showing trends.

Linear programming—A mathematical method for determining how to attain the best outcome in a given mathematical model.

List validation—A type of data validation that presents the user with a list of data values that the user can choose from.

Live Preview—Shows the results that would occur in your file if you were to click that particular option.

Local templates—Templates stored in the default Templates folder on your hard drive.

Logical function—A function that returns a result, or output, based upon evaluating whether a logical test is true or false.

Logical operator—Used to create logical tests and includes <, >, <=, >=, and <>.

Logical test—Also known as a logical expression, an equation with comparison operators that can be evaluated as either true or false.

Lookup and reference functions—Functions that look up matching values in a table of data.

Loops—Used in VBA to execute a series of statements multiple times.

LOWER—This function converts all uppercase characters in a text string to lowercase.

M

Macro—A program using VBA that records keystrokes and plays them back when the macro is run.

Markup language—Uses special sequences of characters or "markup" indicators called "tags" inserted in the document to indicate how the document should look when it is displayed or printed.

MATCH function—Looks for a value within a range and returns the position of that value within the range.

Mathematical operator—Parentheses ( ), exponentiation ^, division /, multiplication *, addition +, and subtraction.

Maturity—Refers to the length of time before par value is returned to the bondholder.

MAX function—A function that examines all numeric values in a specified range and returns the maximum value.

Maximize—The button is located in the top-right corner of the title bar. This option offers the largest workspace.

Maximum—The largest value in the sample.

Mean—The average of all the variables in a sample, often referred to as the arithmetic mean.

Median—Describes which value falls in the middle when all the values of the sample are sorted in ascending order.

MEDIAN function—A function used to measure the central tendency or the location of the middle of a set of data.

Message box—A dialog box object created in VBA and used to display informative messages to the user that includes buttons the user can interact with.

Metadata—Data about data. It describes the content and context of the data.

Method—An action that Excel performs with an object that can be called using VBA.

Microsoft Query—A query wizard used to connect to external data sources, select data from those external sources, import that data into a worksheet, and refresh the data as needed to keep the worksheet data synchronized with the data in the external sources.

MID—This function returns a specific number of characters from the middle of a text string, starting at the position you specify, based on the number of characters you specify.

MIN function—A function that examines all numeric values in a specified range and returns the minimum value.

Mini toolbar—A menu that appears after text is selected and contains buttons for the most commonly used formatting commands, such as font, font size, font color, center alignment, indents, bold, italic, and underline.

Minimize—Used to reduce a window to a taskbar button.

Minimum—The smallest value in the sample.

Mixed cell reference—Using a combination of absolute cell referencing and relative cell referencing for a cell address within a formula by preceding either the column letter or the row value with a dollar sign to "lock" as absolute while leaving the other portion of the cell address as a relative reference.

Mixed cost—A cost that contains a variable component and a fixed component.

Mode—The value that appears most often in a sample.

MODE function—A function that returns the most frequently occurring value in a range of data.

MODE.MULT function—A function that returns the most frequently occurring values in a range of data.

MODE.SNGL function—A function that returns the most frequently occurring value in a range of data.

Module—A container for VBA code.

Most Recently Used list—A list maintained by Office of your most recently modified files: documents, spreadsheets, databases, and presentations.

Moving average—Calculates the average of values over time, based on specified intervals.

Multiples—A series of identical charts with the same x- and y-axes but that contains different values.

N

Name Manager—Used to create, edit, delete, or troubleshoot named ranges in a workbook.

Named range—A set of cells that has been given a name, other than the default column and row cell address name, that can then be used within a formula or function.

Navigational flicks—Quick short gestures either in a vertical or horizontal direction that either scroll up and down or move forward or backward a page and are enabled by default.

Negative KPI—When the greater the value the worse the KPI, such as the number of sick days in a specific time period.

Nested IF function—A function that uses IF functions as arguments within another IF function and increases the number of logical outcomes that can be expressed.

Net book value—Equal to the original cost of the asset minus depreciation and amortization.

NETWORKDAYS—This function calculates the number of available work days between two given dates and will omit holidays, if supplied.

Nominal data—Uses numbers for categorical/classification purposes only.

Nominal yield—The same as the coupon or interest rate.

Nonbinding constraint—A less severe constraint that does not affect the optimum solution.

Noncontiguous cell range—A range consisting of multiple selected cells, at least one of which is not directly adjacent to at least one other cell in the selected range.

Normal distribution—One of the most important distributions in statistics. When charted, it takes on the shape of a bell and is often referred to as the "bell-shaped curve," where 98% of all values occur within three standard deviations from the mean.

NOT function—A function that is used when there are many options that fit the desired criteria and only one option that does not fit the criteria.

NOW function—A function used to display the current date and time in a cell.

Nper—The total number of payments that will be made in order to pay the loan in full.

NPER function—Calculates the number of payment periods for an investment or loan if you know the loan amount, interest rate, and payment amount.

NPV function—Used to determine the value of an investment by analyzing a series of future incoming and outgoing cash flows, expected to occur over the life of the investment.

Numeric data—Data that contains only the digits 0–9 and possibly a period (.) for a decimal place.

O

Object collections—Groups of objects that are also considered objects themselves, such as sheets and workbooks.

Object model—Consists of a hierarchical collection of objects that can be manipulated using VBA.

Objective cell—A cell that contains the formula that creates a value that you want to optimize—maximize, minimize, or set to a specific value.

Object-oriented programming (OOP)—Uses a hierarchy of objects, also called classes, as the focus of the programming.

Objects—Combinations of data and code that are treated as a single unit including workbooks, worksheets, charts, PivotTables, and even Excel itself.

Observational unit—A person, object, or event about which data is collected.

Office 365—A cloud-based version of Office offered on a subscription basis.

Office Backstage—Provides access to the file-level features, such as saving a file, creating a new file, opening an existing file, printing a file, and closing a file, as well as program options and account settings.

One-variable data table—A data table that can help you analyze how different values of one variable in one or more formulas will change the results of those formulas.

Online templates—Templates that can be found online and downloaded to your hard drive.

Operating system—System software that controls and coordinates computer hardware operations so other programs can run efficiently.

Optimize—To obtain a solution and find the best way to do something.

OR function—A function that returns TRUE if any one logical test supplied is true; otherwise, it returns FALSE.

Order of operations—The order in which Excel processes calculations in a formula that contains more than one operator.

Ordinal data—Uses numbers to rank data as first, second, third, and so on based on some scale.

Outliers—Data that are abnormally different from the other values in a random sample.

P

Par value—Is how much the bondholder will receive at maturity, also referred to as the face value.

Parameter—A term generally used to describe a value included for calculation or comparison purposes that is stored in a single location (a worksheet cell, for example) so that it can be used many times but be edited in a single location. Also, a special kind of variable used in VBA to refer to one of the pieces of data provided in a method.

PDF—Portable Document Format, an open document representation standard developed by Adobe Systems.

Per—A number that must be between 1 and nper and is the specific period for which a loan payment is being applied.

Pie chart—Displays a comparison of each value to a total.

PivotChart—A built-in analysis tool that allows for graphical representations of a PivotTable.

PivotTable—Interactive tables that extract, organize, and summarize source data.

PMT function—A function used to calculate a payment amount based on constant payments and a constant interest rate.

Poisson distribution—A discrete probability function that has wide business applications. It is used most often to predict demand for a product or service.

Population—Any entire collection of people, animals, plants, or whatever on which you may collect data.

Portable Document Format (PDF)—A file type that preserves most formatting attributes of a source document regardless of the software the document was created in.

Portrait—For page layout and printing purposes, portrait orientation indicates the longer dimension of the page is on the vertical axis.

Positive KPI—When the greater the value the better the KPI, such as a company's profit.

Power View—An interactive data visualization, exploration, and presentation experience that encourages the creation of ad-hoc reports.

PPMT function—Calculates how much of a specific periodic payment is going toward the principal amount of a loan.

Precedent cell—A cell that supplies a value to the formula in the active cell.

Primary key—A unique field that functions as an identifier for each row or record.

Principal—The unpaid balance amount of the loan.

Print Preview—Backstage view of how a worksheet or workbook will appear when printed.

Probability—The likelihood that some event will occur based on what is already known.

Probability density function—The probability of a value being equal to the value of x.

Probability distribution—Describes all the possible values and likelihoods that a given variable can be within a specific range; can be in the form of a graph, table, or formula.

Project Explorer window—Contains a hierarchical list of all the objects available in open workbooks including macros, modules, and worksheets.

PROPER—This function capitalizes the first letter in each word of a text string with remaining characters for each word in lowercase.

Properties—Attributes of an object that can be referred to or manipulated using VBA.

Properties window—Contains a list of all the properties of a selected object such as name, size, and color.

Protected view—The file contents can be seen and read, but you are not able to edit, save, or print the contents until you enable editing. By default, Office will open files from e-mail or a web browser in this view.

Pseudo code—The rough draft of a formula or code. It is intended to help you understand the logic and determine the structure of a problem before you develop the actual formula.

Pv—The present value of the loan.

PV function—Used to calculate the present or current value of a series of future payments on an investment.

Q

Query—A way of structuring a question so that the computer can retrieve data.

Quick Access Toolbar—Located in the top-left corner of the Office window, it can be customized to offer commonly used buttons.

Quick Analysis—A contextual tool that appears when you select data in a worksheet that offers single-click access to formatting, charts, pivot tables, and sparklines.

R

R Square—Part of a regression analysis; calculated by squaring the correlation coefficient. This provides a more conservative estimate of the independent variables' ability to predict the value of the dependent variable.

R1C1 reference style—This refers to the way cell references are written. If numbers appear for the column headings, the reference style for Excel is currently R1C1.

Random sample—A subset of a population that has been selected using unpredictable methods where each element of the population has an equal chance of being selected.

Range—A group of cells in a worksheet that have been selected or highlighted; performed commands will affect the entire range. Also, the difference between the highest and lowest value in the data set.

Rate—An argument in several financial functions that refers to the interest rate per period.

RATE function—Calculates the interest rate per period for an investment or loan, given that you know the present value of the loan, payment amount, and number of payment periods.

Ratio data—Similar to interval data except that the differences between the data can be quantified and proportions can be specified.

Raw data—Elements or raw facts—numeric or text—that may or may not have meaning or relevance.

Read Mode—A view of the document that hides the writing tools and menus to leave more room for the pages themselves. This is optimized for touch screens.

Recommended Charts—A feature that quickly analyzes a selection in a worksheet and recommends chart types that best fit your data.

Record—All of the categories of data pertaining to one person, place, thing, event, or idea, and that is formatted as a row in a worksheet, or database table.

Regression analysis—A method used to predict future values by analyzing the relationships between two or more variables.

Relational data—Data about a particular person, place, or event that are stored in multiple tables.

Relational database—A 3-dimensional database able to connect data in separate tables to form a relationship when common fields exist—to offer reassembled information from multiple tables.

Relative cell reference—Default cell reference in a formula to a cell reference position that will automatically adjust when the formula is copied or extended to other cells; the cell being referenced changes relative to the placement of the formula.

Relative macro reference—A macro that identifies cells relative to the location of the active cell when the macro was recorded.

Remove Duplicates—A tool in Excel for removing duplicate entries in data.

REPLACE—This function replaces part of a text string, based on a starting position and the number of characters you specify, with a different text string.

Required rate of return (RRR)—The minimum annual percentage that must be earned by an investment before a company chooses to invest.

Restore down—Allows you to arrange and view several windows so they all can be viewed at the same time.

Return on investment (ROI)—The ratio of the amount of money gained or lost from an investment relative to the initial amount invested.

Ribbon—Where you will find most of the commands for the application. The Ribbon differs from program to program, but each program has two tabs in common, the FILE tab and the HOME tab.

Ribbon display options—Three options—Auto-Hide Ribbon, Display Tabs, and Display Tabs and Command—that are located next to the Help button in the top-right corner.

RIGHT—This function returns the characters in a text string based on the number of characters you specify starting from the far-right character position.

Roaming settings—A group of settings that offer easy remotely synced user-specific data that affects the Office experience.

ROUND function—A function that is used to round a number to a specific number of digits.

Row—a horizontal set of cells that encompasses all the columns in a worksheet and only one cell vertically.

Run-time error—Occurs when VBA code is executed, displaying a description of the error.

S

Salvage value—What the asset is estimated to be worth at the end of its useful life.

Sample population—A subset of a population.

Scatter chart—Shows the relationship between numeric variables.

Scenario—Allows you to build a what-if analysis model that includes variable cells linked by one or more formulas or functions.

Scenario Manager—Allows you to manage scenarios by adding, deleting, editing, and viewing scenarios and to create scenario reports.

Scenario PivotTable report—The report you can create that includes the summary results of the scenarios in PivotTable format.

Scenario Summary report—The report you can create that includes subtotals and the results of the scenarios.

Scenario tool—A tool that enables a user to calculate numerous outputs in other cells by referencing the target cell in formulas and functions.

ScreenTip—Provides a name or other information about the object to which you are pointing.

Scroll bar—A form control that is linked to a specific cell. As the scroll bar slides left to right or up and down the value in the linked cell increases or decreases accordingly. Also, a form control used in what-if analyses that allows you to change a number in a target cell location in single-unit increments.

Security—A legal document that can be bought and sold and holds some financial value.

Separators—Indicate the distinction between the object container and the member of that container in VBA.

Shortcut menu—A group or list of context-sensitive commands related to a selection that appears when you right-click.

Silverlight—A powerful tool that creates engaging, interactive user experiences. It is a free plug-in, powered by the .NET framework, and compatible with multiple browsers, devices, applications, and operating systems.

Simplex LP method—A linear model in which the variables are not raised to any powers and no transcendent functions—such as sine or cosine—are used. A linear model can be charted as straight lines.

Skewness—Characterizes the degree of asymmetry of a distribution around its mean.

SkyDrive—An online cloud computing technology that offers a certain amount of collaborative storage space free that is integrated with Office 2013.

Slicer—A window used for quickly filtering data in a PivotTable or data table. Also, a visual control that allows you to quickly and easily filter your data in an interactive way to replace filter icons in PivotCharts or data tables.

SLN function—Calculates the depreciation of an asset for a specified period using the straight-line depreciation method.

Solver—An add-in that helps you optimize a problem by manipulating the values for several variables with rules that you determine.

Solver answer report—This report lists the target cell and the changing cells with their corresponding original and final values for the problem, input variables, and constraints. In addition, the formulas, binding status, and slacks are given for each constraint.

Solver limits report—This report displays the achieved optimal value and all the input variables of the model with the optimal values. Additionally, the report displays the upper and lower bounds for the optimal value.

Solver population report—This report displays various statistical characteristics about the given model, such as how many variables and rows it contains.

Solver sensitivity report—This report provides information about how sensitive the solution is to small changes in the formula for the target cell. This report displays the shadow prices for the constraint—the amount that the objective function value changes per unit change in the constraint. This report can only be created if your Excel model does not contain integer or Boolean—the values 0 and 1—constraints.

Source cells—The cells that are to be the source of data for the AutoSum function.

Sparkline—Small charts embedded into cells on a spreadsheet, they provide for a way to graphically summarize a row or column of data in a single cell with a miniature chart.

Spin button—A form control that is linked to a specific cell. As the up and down arrows on the button are clicked, the value in the linked cell increases and decreases accordingly.

Spreadsheet—A software application that organizes data in a row and column format and supports manipulation of data to facilitate decision making.

Standard deviation—The most commonly used method for determining the average spread of a data set from the mean. Mathematically, the standard deviation is calculated by taking the square root of the variance.

Standard error—Used to determine how accurate the sample mean predicts the population mean by dividing the standard deviation by the square root of the sample size.

Standard filter—Displays the values in the field that can be toggled on and off through the use of check boxes.

Static data—Data that has been manually calculated and then typed into a worksheet.

Statistics—The practice of collecting, analyzing, and interpreting data.

Status threshold—Defined by the range between a high and low value as part of a KPI.

Sub procedure—VBA procedure that performs an action on your project or workbook.

SUBSTITUTE—This function substitutes new_text for old_text in a text string.

SUBTOTAL function—A function specific to the filtering mechanism that will only run calculations on the data that is in the subset when a filter is applied. Also, a function that can return any of 11 different values including all of the AutoSum functions, the product, standard deviation, and variance.

Sum—The sum of all values in the sample.

SUMIF function—Sums the number of cells that meets the specified criteria.

SUMIFS function—Sums a range of data, selecting data to total based on the criteria specified.

Summary variable—Data that is not categorical in nature and would likely be used for summarization.

Syntax—The structure and order of the function and the arguments needed for Excel to run a function.

T

Table—An organized grid of information, arranged in rows and columns.

Table style—A predefined set of formatting properties that determine the appearance of a table.

Tablet PC—Tablets that perform like a traditional PC.

Tabular format—The presentation of information such as text and numbers in tables.

Target value—Can either be another calculated field that resolves to a value or an absolute value as part of a KPI.

Task pane—A smaller window pane that often appears to the side of the program window that offers options or helps you to navigate through completing a task or feature.

Template—A workbook that provides a starting point for building other similar workbooks.

TEXT—This function allows you to display numeric data as text in addition to using special formatting strings to display the text.

Text data—Can contain any representable character, often generically described as letters of the alphabet, the digits 0–9, and special characters such as punctuation.

Text file—A file structured as a simple container of text data and sometimes structured by the use of delimiters to separate text.

Text functions—Functions that manage, manipulate, and format text data.

Text length validation—A type of data validation used to limit the number of characters that can be entered into a cell.

Text-to-speech—A feature that reads the values of text back to you. Headphone or speakers are required for this feature to work properly.

Thumbnail—A small picture of the open application file.

Tiles—Provide a dynamic navigation strip allowing you to navigate through a series of charts based on a particular value in a Power View report.

Time data—Data recognized by Excel as representing time. Time data is represented as a decimal value where .1 is 144 minutes, .01 is 14.4 minutes, etc.

Time validation—A type of data validation that restricts only time values to be entered into a cell.

TODAY function—A function that is used to return the current date into a cell.

Toggle button—A type of button that one click turns the feature on and a second click turns the feature off.

Touch gestures—Movements that allow a user to use fingers with specific gestures to emulate a mouse click or drag. Generally, these gestures cannot be completed with a pen, except pen actions set by default for tap, double-tap, and tap and hold.

Touch mode—Applies to touchscreen devices—the Ribbon and shortcut menus are enlarged to make selecting commands with your fingertip easier. Also, switches Office into a version that makes a touch screen easy to use.

Trace dependents—A tool that automatically draws arrows from the active cell to its dependent cells.

Trace precedents—A tool that automatically draws arrows from the precedent cells to the active cell.

Trackpad—A pad that works like a traditional mouse but uses touch. A trackpad is typically found on a laptop or a tablet PC.

Trendline—Graphing the trend in the data with the intent of helping predict the future.

TRIM—This function removes all spaces from text except for single spaces between words. Use TRIM on text that you have received from another application that may have irregular spacing.

Trusted location—A folder that has been identified in the Microsoft Office Trust Center as a safe location from which to open files that contain active code, including macros.

Two-variable data table—A data table that can help you analyze how different values of two variables in one or more formulas will change the results of those formulas.

Type—Indicates when the payments are due—either at the beginning (1) or the end (0) of a period.

U

UPPER—This function converts text in a text string to uppercase.

USB drive—A small and portable storage device popular for moving files back and forth between a lab, office, or home computer.

V

Validation criteria—Constraints that limit what users are allowed to enter into a particular cell.

Variable—A value stored in a cell and used in a formula or function. The value can be changed to see how the change affects other values. Also, space in a computer's memory that is given a name and is used to store a value of a specified data type.

Variable cost—A cost that changes based on how many products are sold or services rendered.

Variance—A calculation used in statistics to determine how far the data set varies from the mean.

VBA (Visual Basic for Applications)—A powerful programming language that is part of most Microsoft Office products that users can use to implement a wide variety of enhancements to Microsoft Office applications.

Vertical multiples—Expand across the width of the container and wrap down the container in the available space. If all multiples do not fit in the available space, a vertical scroll bar is also added.

Visual Basic Editor (VBE)—The tool built into Microsoft Office that is used for creating and editing VBA.

Visual Basic for Applications—A computer language used to create macros in Excel.

VLOOKUP function—A function that matches a provided value in a table of data and returns a value from a subsequent column. Also, helps retrieve values located in another location and is used when your comparison values are located in a column—vertically—to the left of the data you want to find.

W

Watch Window—A feature that makes it possible to monitor cells the user considers important in a separate window.

Web query—A tool for importing data into a spreadsheet directly from a web page.

What-if analysis—Changes values in spreadsheet cells to investigate the effects on calculated values of interest, and allows you to examine the outcome of the changes to values in a worksheet.

White space—Empty space that helps keep a design simple, accessible, and visually pleasing to users. It is not necessarily white, just void of content.

Whole number validation—A type of data validation that requires only integers, or whole numbers, be entered in a cell.

Windows Phone—A version of Windows that runs on phone devices that has some of the same functionality as full Windows 8 but not all.

Windows Run Time—A version of Windows that runs on devices with an ARM chip that has many of the same functionality as full Windows 8 but not all.

Windows Start screen—The main interface to launch applications; it replaces the Windows 7 Start button.

Workbook—An Excel file that contains one or more worksheets.

Workbook theme—A collection of built-in cell styles associated with a workbook theme name.

Worksheet—Traditionally referred to as a spreadsheet.

Worksheet navigation—Moving the location of the active cell.

Workspace—A special file type that identifies multiple workbooks and remembers the manner in which you want them arranged.

X

XIRR function—Indicates the profitability of an investment by analyzing a series of cash flows that are irregular or not periodic.

XML—Short for Extensible Markup Language, XML allows users to define their own tags in order to define the content of the document. Used for web documents and transmitting data between systems.

XML element—Includes the start and stop tags and everything in between them.

XML map—The same as an XML schema in that it describes the structure of an XML document. Excel creates an XML map either based on an existing schema or creates a default map.

XML schema—Describes the structure of an XML document in terms of what XML elements it will contain and their sequence.

XNPV function—Determines the value of an investment or business by analyzing an irregular time series of incoming and outgoing cash flows.

Y

Yield to maturity (YTM)—Another yield calculation that takes into account the current market price, and the time to maturity, and assumes that coupon payments are reinvested at the bond's coupon rate.

Yield—The amount of annual interest, expressed as a percentage of the par value and determines how much investors will receive on their investment.

Index